The Blue Guides

W9-BXW-003

China

Frances Wood, with Neil Taylor

A&C Black • London
WW Norton • New York

BLUE GUIDE

Second edition 2001
First edition 1992
Published by A & C Black (Publishers) Limited
37 Soho Square, London W1D 3QZ

ISBN 0-7136-4247-5

Published in the United States of America by
W W Norton & Company, Incorporated
500 Fifth Avenue, New York, NY 10110

Published simultaneously in Canada by
Penguin Books Canada Limited
10 Alcorn Avenue, Toronto
Ontario M4V 3BE

ISBN 0-393-32204-1 USA

The author and the pulbishers have done their best to ensure the accuracy of all the information in Blue Guide China; however, they can accept no responsibility for any loss, injury or inconvenience sustained by any traveller as a result of information or advice contained in the guide.

Frances Wood studied Chinese at Cambridge (1967–72); joined a worker-peasant-soldier class in Chinese history at Peking University (1976), and obtained a PhD in Chinese architecture from London University. She first visited China in 1972 and began to lead tours there in 1977, later accompanying three Parliamentary delegations, and from 1980 began to travel more extensively. She has translated Chinese fiction (Dai Houying, *Stones of the Wall*, 1985), written children's and general books (*Companion to China*, 1988), and on Chinese illustration, gardens and architecture. Her most recent books are *Did Marco Polo go to China?*, 1995, *No Dogs and Not many Chinese: Treaty Port life in China 1843–1943*, 1998 and *Hand Grenade Practice in Peking: my part in the Cultural Revolution*, 2000. She is Curator of the Chinese section of the British Library.

Neil Taylor has been Director of a specialist British tour operator to China since 1976 and also writes frequently on travel to China in the consumer and trade press. His first visit there was in 1971 and he has returned almost every year since then. Hs particular interest is China's relationship with all its neighbours and the effects these have on travel.

Cover picture: Boating on the river watched by a man on the bank with two tigers in the foreground, from Keepsake from the Cloud Gallery, Yun tai xian rui, 1750?, now in the British Library. Reproduced here courtesy of the Art Archive.
Title page illustration: woodblock print of a bronze vessel for playing a game where you have to toss sticks into the three cylinders at the top.

Printed and bound in Great Britain by Butler & Tanner Ltd, Frome and London.

Introduction

This Blue Guide is the result of trips to China made over a period of nearly 20 years, wearing, as the Chinese would say, a variety of different hats. I visited a very different China for the first time in 1971 but really got to know Peking in 1975–6 when I was a student there. Travel then was difficult and the rules and regulations off-putting but after Mao Zedong died in 1976, China began to open up. In gathering information, I have relied upon some 30 visits made between 1977 and 2001 as guide or guide-lecturer accompanying groups and delegations, and many trips made with friends. Dates have been included occasionally in the text to indicate the current state of affairs, particularly where things appear likely to change. The size of the country and the slow pace of travel there have made it impossible to dash back and check everything.

Putting China into a single volume presents problems: places have been omitted and maps are necessarily very small-scale. However, as the vast majority of travellers visit China on tours which cover many towns across the country, division by region, for example, would mean carrying several volumes. As few visitors spend more than a few days in any place, extravagant detail would add pounds to their luggage.

I have tried to include enough detail to be of use to long-stay visitors and, particularly, to try and encourage them to visit surrounding sites (Chengde and Tianjin from Peking, for instance, and the wealth of towns in the Yangtse delta that are easily accessible from Shanghai). I hope, too, that those on package tours will find accessible sites they might prefer to an afternoon officially designated 'shopping' or 'free' and dare to take a bus or taxi. Extending a package tour is now very easy and much to be recommended for it can allow more time in places of personal interest.

I have not included the wealth of material on police stations, very cheap dormitory hotels and travel details included in the *Lonely Planet* or *Rough Guide* series which are ideal for the back-packer. The slightly less-adventurous traveller should find that resorting to the services of the local Chinese travel offices (for booking and buying train or air tickets) will involve a modest fee but saves much time and trouble trying to comprehend the railway timetable, hanging about in stations or re-visiting airports.

Moving about in China is not easy: buying train tickets in a station (bellowing through a knee-high pigeon-hole) is a difficult business (see Getting around, p 16) complicated by the absence of return tickets and locally varying regulations about not buying tickets more than a fixed number of hours before departure, but it can be resolved as suggested above by using local agencies. I often think travel is easier for those who do not speak Chinese. They can get away with being in the wrong place, with buying tickets at the wrong time (for the regulations are in Chinese) and, as the entire nation is trying to improve its English, there is always someone longing to help.

Getting around towns can also be difficult. Though Peking has all its major streets labelled in pinyin romanisation, while in places like Kunming, only the major central streets are named in pinyin which makes it difficult for me to plan and describe the classic Blue Guide itineraries through major towns. I have tried to do so, as far as possible, but owing to the size of many cities and their widely dispersed temples, taxis or the new underground lines in Peking and Shanghai, in particular, are often the best solution, especially if time is short.

I am grateful to everyone involved in the production of the guide: Gemma Davies for enduring the wait, Tom Neville for his editorial work on the first edition, and Lisa Adams and Kim Teo for their work on the second. For this edition edition, I have been greatly helped by Neil Taylor whose long experience of organising China travel for others and meticulous attention to practical detail make up for my failings. Helen Espir helped enormously with the first editions by generously sharing what she knows and has seen, and by explaining the railway timetable, and K who likes to take his time in temples has been galloped round more cities than I can count. All the mistakes are mine.

Acknowledgements

Every effort has been made to contact the copyright owners of the extracts reproduced in this Guide. We should be delighted to hear from any copyright owners that we have not been able to reach.

For permission to reproduce extracts of text in Blue Guide China the publishers gratefully acknowledge the following:

page 222, *The Ford of Heaven* by Brian Power, Peter Owen Ltd, London, 1984.

pages 258, 261, *A Journey to War* by W.H. Auden and Christopher Isherwood, Faber & Faber Ltd, London, 1973.

page 358, poem by Song Zhiwen, translated by Edward H. Schafer in *Vermilion Bird: T'ang Images of the South*, © Copyright 1967, The Regents of the University of California.

page 677, *South of the Clouds* by Gerald Reitlinger, Faber and Faber Ltd, London, 1939.

Contents

Maps and plans

PRACTICAL INFORMATION

 Planning your trip

When to go

The vast area of China means that there is a variety of climates. The subtropical south and southwest are subject to heavy rain in the summer months, which are also uncomfortably hot (over 30°C). Air-conditioning is now common but by no means universal. Even the northern cities like Xi'an and Peking have temperatures in the 30s and some quite heavy rain and humid weather in July and August. Winters are equally extreme in the north, with temperatures descending to -5°C on average in Peking and -20°C in Harbin. A compensating factor in the northern winter is the lack of rain and bright blue sunny skies. The appalling growth in air pollution in cities like Peking and Xi'an (which can make asthmatics quite ill) means that the skies there are no longer bright and clear in the winter.

Buildings in the north are well-heated from mid November to March, at least in places where foreign tourists are likely to find themselves, such as hotels, restaurants and trains. Places on or just south of the Yangtse, like Shanghai and even Guangzhou, where the temperature can occasionally hover around freezing, have little or no central heating. It is generally true that late September to early November is the ideal time to visit most of China: rainfall should be light and temperatures warm but comfortable.

Spring (late March–early May) is also often recommended although the weather is more changeable. The changeover periods in early November and March, when central heating is abruptly switched on or off regardless of actual weather conditions, can be cold in the north. Certain areas like Tibet and the Silk Road virtually close down for the winter from November to April. The popularity of October means that hotels and sites tend to be crowded. It is also true that the world's weather is getting less predictable, so it may pour with rain throughout October, when it should not.

What to take

As most trips to China involve a lot of walking and travelling (many itineraries rush groups from one place to the next every two days or so), clothing should be comfortable and practical. All hotels offer a laundry service but it is not always very quick: if your schedule is tight, you should check before handing your clothes over. Business travellers who are likely to attend formal banquets should take a suit. Women can wear skirts, dresses or smart trousers at such occasions although it is interesting to note that at the grand banquet celebrating the 50th anniversary of the founding of the People's Republic of China (1949–1999) in London, at least, although 'Lounge suit' was indicated on the invitation, the Chinese women present wore floor-length velvet or silk *cheong-sams* (long, tight-fitting gowns with split side seams), so more formal banquets in China may involve more dressing up.

In changeable seasons like spring, it is best to take clothing that can be worn in layers for warmth if necessary. A light mackintosh and a change of footwear are recommended in case of rain. In the coldest months of winter, warm outdoor clothing is most important—bring a thick outdoor coat, warm footwear, a hat and gloves.

The formalities

For China, a visa is required. If you are only visiting Hong Kong, most nationals, other than UK citizens, do not require a visa. The same is true of Macau. Most nationals of European countries, with the exception of the UK, can obtain a Chinese visa cheaply and conveniently on arrival at the airport as long as they have a visa authorisation provided by their travel operator.

Visitors on official business should receive an invitation from their host organisation and take this to their nearest Chinese consulate. Tourists travelling in a group will usually be included in a group visa arranged by their travel agent; individuals can also get a travel agent to obtain a visa for them. You may find this useful for although Chinese consulates will accept applications by post, completed visas must be collected in person. If you do not live near a Chinese consulate, it is easier to pay a small sum for the travel agent to do this for you. Those travelling on group visas must enter and leave together.

Visas for journalists and those in media organisations are difficult to obtain; such travellers should consult their tour operator before paying for any flights or tours. The standard visa is good for one entry and exit; those planning to enter China twice will need to apply for a double-entry visa. Those planning to travel by train across Siberia or Vietnam will need a series of visas which can take up to five weeks to collect unless very high express fees are paid.

In theory, once you have a visa, you can travel to any open area in China. Tibet requires special permission and this is often, although not always, also required for Xinjiang province (and the Silk Road). If you list such destinations on your visa application, this may result in considerable delay. Be guided by your travel agent.

Chinese consulates (for visas)

UK
31 Portland Place, London W1N 3AG, ☎ 020 7631 1430, fax 020 7588 2500; www.chinese-embassy.org.uk

Denison House, 49 Denison Road, Rusholme, Manchester M14 5RX, ☎ 0161 224 8672, fax 0161 257 2672

43 Station Road, Edinburgh EH12 7AF, ☎ 0131 316 4789, fax 0131 334 6954

USA
2300 Connecticut Avenue NW, Washington DC 20008, ☎ 202 328 2500, fax 202 588 0032; visa section ☎ 202 338 6688, fax 202 588 9760; www.Chinese-embassy.org

100 W. Erie Street, Chicago, Il. 60610, ☎ 312 573 3070, fax 312 803 0122

3417 Montrose Boulevard, Houston Tx 77006, ☎ 713 524 0778, fax 713 524 7656; visa@chinahouston.org

443 Shatto Place, Los Angeles CA 90020, ☎ 213 807 8018, fax 213 265 9809

520 12th Avenue, New York NY 10036, ☎ 212 868 7752, fax 212 502 0245; www.nyconsulate.prchina.org

1450 Laguna Street, San Francisco CA 94115, ☎ 415 928 6931, fax 415 563 4861

Canada
515 St Patrick Street, Ottawa, Ontario K1N 5H3, ☎ 613 789 3434, fax 613 789 1911; www.chinaembassy-canada.org

1011 6th Avenue SW, suite 100, Calgary AB T2P OW1, ☎ 403 264 3322, fax 403 264 6656

240 St George Street, Toronto, ON M5R 2P4, ☎ 416 964 7260, fax 416 324 6468

3380 Granville Street, Vancouver BC V6H 3K3, ☎ 604 734 7492, fax 604 737 0154

Australia
15 Coronation Drive, Yarralumla, Canberra ACT 2600, ☎ 6273 4783, fax 6373 4987; www.chinaembassy.org.au

75–79 Irving Road, Melbourne, Victoria 3142, ☎ 9822 0604, fax 9822 0320

15–17 William Street 3rd fl., Australia Place, Perth WA 6000, ☎ 9481 3278, fax 9321 8457

539 Elizabeth Street, Surrey Hills, Sydney NSW 2010, ☎ 9319 0678, fax 9319 2430

Tourist information
UK 4 Glentworth Street, London NW1 5PG ☎ 020 7935 9787, fax 020 7487 4842

USA 350 5th Avenue suite 6413, New York NY 10118, ☎ 212 760 8218, fax 212 760 8809; www.cnto.org

333 West Broadway suite 201, Glendale CA 9120, ☎ 818 545 7507, fax 818 545 7506

Canada 480 University Avenue suite 806, Toronto, Ontario M5G 1V2 ☎ 416 599 6636, fax 416 599 6382

Australia 44 Market Street/19th floor, Sydney NSW 2000, ☎ 612 9290 4057, fax 9290 1958; chinainfo@cnto.org.au or www.cnto.org.au

Disabled travellers
Unfortunately, China and, to a slightly lesser extent, Hong Kong are not easy destinations for the disabled. It is possible to get around in a wheelchair if you can manage stairs and steps on foot but it would be very difficult indeed for those who are completely wheelchair bound. Steps abound, pavement or other ramps are virtually non-existent. There are steps down to the underground in both China and Hong Kong and in Hong Kong, many walkways above street level are mainly accessed by flights of steps. Taxis are not designed to take wheelchairs and whilst, in China in particular, you may be lucky to find many pairs of helping hands, this cannot be relied on. Chinese trains stations are full of stairs or ridged ramps and the trains themselves have massive steps which are quite difficult for anyone, especially with luggage. New double-decker trains used on short inter-city lines have steps to both upper and lower decks. Many Chinese airports still lack lifts so travellers need to climb steps, within the airport and up to the planes. The *Hong Kong Tourist Association* produces a free guide: Hong Kong Access Guide for Disabled Visitors and many associations for the disabled world-wide offer advice. There are a couple of web-sites that may be of use: www.acces-able.com and www.disabilitytravel.com.

Women travelling alone

China is a fairly good and safe place for lone women travellers for it is unusual to suffer much unwanted harassment. Dress sensibly and take normal precautions, perhaps covering yourself more in the Muslim areas in Xinjiang, for example. Take sanitary protection with you as it may be difficult to find in China.

Getting there

By air

Most major airlines have direct flights from major cities to China, mainly to Peking, but a growing number also fly direct to Hong Kong, Guangzhou and Shanghai and an increasing number of other destinations. Useful new ports of entry include Almaty (Kazakh visa required) to Urumqi in the northwest and Bangkok to Kunming in the southwest.

Travel from Britain

Air China and *British Airways* both operate non-stop flights from Heathrow to Peking three to four times a week. Air China offers discounted domestic flights within China to passengers booked on their international service, and BA does the same within the UK. *Virgin* fly non-stop from Heathrow to Shanghai, again three-four times a week. Fares are at their lowest in November and February, at their highest in July and August. All three offer reductions through their specialist agents if hotel accommodation is booked in conjunction with the flights. It is possible to 'open-jaw' using say one airline to Peking and another back from Shanghai or Hong Kong. British Airways can also open-jaw between St Petersburg or Moscow and Peking or Hong Kong for travellers taking the Trans-Siberian Railway from Russia to China.

Air France, *Austrian Airlines*, *Lufthansa*, *KLM* and *SAS* all offer connections from the UK to Peking, Shanghai and Hong Kong. For travellers who do not wish to travel via London, they can often provide convenient routings through Europe from provincial and Scottish airports. They too usually offer lower fares if booked in conjunction with hotels in China. Most airlines offer a discounted business class to China through their specialist agents, charging about £1200 extra above their economy fare. With Air China, the supplement is usually lower than this, around £600. All airlines to China are now non-smoking.

On domestic flights within China, it is well worth paying what is often a very low supplement for travel in business class. An extra £30 or so can often mean instant check-in, a lounge, wide seating and enhanced catering.

Airlines

Air China, ☎ 020 7630 0919, www.air-china.co.uk
British Airways, ☎ 0990 444 000/0345 222 111, www.british-airways.com
Virgin Atlantic, ☎ 01293 747 747, www.virgin-atlantic.com
Air France, ☎ 0845 8545 111/444, www.airfrance.fr
Austrian Airlines, ☎ 020 8750 3300, www.aua.com
Lufthansa, ☎ 0345 737 747, www.lufthansa.com
KLM, ☎ 01279 660 400, 08705 074 074, www.klmuk.com

SAS, ☎ 01426 931 301, www.scandinavian.net

Tour Operators

About 40 operators now include China in their programmes. Some cater for individuals, some for specific specialisations such as wild-life and others offer general interest tours. The following have all been active in China for at least ten years.

Bales Tours, Bales House Junction Road, Dorking RH4 3HB, ☎ 01306 885991 fax 01306 740048. General interest group tours.

Explore Worldwide, 1 Frederick Street, Aldershot, Hants GU11 1LQ, ☎ 01252 760 000, fax 01252 760 001. Walking and light adventure.

Kuoni Travel, Kuoni House, Dorking RH5 4AY, ☎ 01306 740 888, fax 01306 744 484. General interest group tours.

Regent Holidays,15 John St, Bristol, BS1 2HR, ☎ 0117 9212 1711, fax 0117 927 2120. Individual tours.

Travel from the USA and Canada

For travellers from the West and mid-West, *Air China*, *American Airlines*, *Northwest Airlines*, and *United Airlines* offer direct flights several times a week from San Francisco and Los Angeles to Beijing, Shanghai and Hong Kong, with *Air Canada* offering similar services from Vancouver. It is however often cheaper to use flights via Japan and Korea and these have a wider range of entry points into China for visitors wanting to include cities such as Harbin, Shenyang and Dalian in their tours. Most carriers offer open-jaw facilities allowing travel into say Peking and then out from Shanghai or Hong Kong. From the East Coast, it is often cheaper to travel via Europe, particularly through London given the very low fares often available between New York and London.

Airlines

Air China, www.airchina.com.cn
American Airlines, ☎ 1 800 223 5436, www.aa.com
Northwest Airlines, ☎ 1 800 447 4747, 1 800 441 1818, www.nwa.com
United Airlines, ☎ 1 800 538 2929, www.ual.com
Air Canada, www.aircanada.com

Tour Operators

The following have all been active in the China field for over ten years.

Abercrombie and Kent, 2635 West Washington Boulevard 2/F, Dock 7 Bellwood, Il 60104, ☎ 708 544 0015, fax 708 544 0160. Individual tours.

Travcoa, 2350 S.E. Bristol St, Newport Beach CA 92660, ☎ 949 476 2800, fax 949 476 2538. Individual and group tours.

Victoria Cruises, 5708 39th Avenue, Woodside, New York NY 11377, ☎ 212 818 1680, fax 212 818 9889. Yangtse cruises.

By train

It is also possible to travel to China from Europe by rail, taking the Trans-Siberian train from Moscow. There are two through departures per week, one by the Chinese train (leaves Moscow on Tuesdays, Peking on Wednesdays), one by the Russian train (leaves Moscow on Mondays, Peking on Saturdays). The former takes six days via Mongolia (Outer and Inner; Mongolian and Russian visas required), the latter ten days via Dongbei (Manchuria) and Siberia (Russian visa required). The routes split after Irkutsk, where a stopover can be made. On the

Mongolia route, stopovers can also be recommended in Ulan Bator, and on the Manchuria route, at Harbin and Shenyang. Other international trains operate from Kunming to Hanoi in Vietnam, from Peking to Pyongyang in North Korea and from Urumqi to Almati in Kazakhstan. There is a weekly train from Ulan Bator on Thursday, which is useful for those in transit through Mongolia. It is generally advisable to travel on the Chinese train as it is better staffed and cared for.

The mealtimes on the Trans-Siberian are a bit changeable and timings very difficult to work out, as stations in Russia run on Moscow time despite the intervention of several time-zones in Siberia, while the train tends to run on its own time. There is a Russian dining car in Russia (with a vast menu, most of which is 'off' and was probably never really on), a Mongolian one in Mongolia, and a Chinese one attached at Erlian on the Chinese border, where the bogies (the pivoted undercarriage of a train) are also changed owing to differing gauges. It is advisable to take emergency snacks with you, although beware of fruit which may be confiscated at borders.

You will need to obtain transit visas in advance and, if travelling on the Chinese train through Mongolia, obtain a Russian one before the Mongolian one when leaving China and vice versa on leaving Europe, as the Mongolian authorities appear keen to know you can leave.

Group travel

Most tourists visit China in groups and group travel is most commonly arranged by tour operators with a Chinese counterpart. In the 1970s this was only possible through *Zhongguo guiji luxingshe* (Chinese International Travel Service) but there is a growing number of Chinese travel companies. It is well worth looking for China tours arranged by or for specialist societies as travelling with fellow enthusiasts can be rewarding and the tours themselves are more likely to reflect the specialist interest of the group and include more specific sites. The *British Museum Society* (☎ 020 7636 1555), the *Oriental Ceramic Society* (☎ 020 7636 7985) and the *Garden History Society* (☎ 020 7608 2409) are amongst many organisations which occasionally run tours to China for their members. Travel companies can arrange a variety of itineraries, most for general tourists, some with specialist interests (bird-watching or railway enthusiast tours, for example). For all such groups, the Chinese bureau will provide all the in-China service: booking trains, planes and boats, arranging hotels and buses and (usually) a 'national guide' to accompany the group throughout the tour with a 'local guide' in each place visited. Variations in the price of otherwise similar tours reflect differing overheads and charges, as well as extras such as a Chinese-speaker or specialist accompanying the group or more expensive catering or hotel accommodation (for example, a Chinese five-star hotel rather than a three-star one).

Individual travel

A growing number of people visit China as individual tourists. This can be arranged quite independently or with varying degrees of pre-arrangement. Those intending to make all their own arrangements are advised to consult guidebooks written specially for individual travellers. Those who cannot face the mobs at railways station booking offices and the uncertainty of finding hotel rooms or air flights, or whose time is limited, can opt for an individual package tour (for any number), arranged in advance, through a specialist tour operator. The tour operator can pre-book hotels, make travel arrangements and arrange for a supply of guides (usually a new guide in each place, with no 'national guide'). This method can be useful for those who want to extend a business trip or a group tour.

From my experience not just as a traveller but as a tour leader, I would highly recommend at least an element of individual travel. For 2–4 people, it should not cost more than about 25 per cent above the cost of a 'group tour'. It is unlikely that any tour will completely satisfy each individual; specialist interest can be covered by adding a few days on at either end of a tour (remembering that a separate visa will be necessary). A group of like-minded friends can band together and create their own tour. Those who have already 'done' Peking and Shanghai but never seen the Buried Army at Xi'an might do this, with a longer stay in Xi'an visiting the more distant tombs and temples; garden enthusiasts could elect to stay five days in Suzhou (rather than the average two) and thus see all the gardens rather than the usual three. A longer stay, especially in a small town, can be very rewarding after a group tour, which involves endless getting on and off buses and rushing to the next place.

Travel agents

A list of travel agents specialising in China travel can be obtained from Chinese embassies or consulates and tourist offices. You can find a number of web sites through searching for www.china_travel/china_tourism.

Getting around

By air

Air travel is expanding fast in China. Until recently there was only one (state-owned) airline, *CAAC* (Civil Air Administration of China) but deregulation means that a number of independent airlines have sprung up. Air travel is slightly more expensive than soft-class train travel (see below). Airline booking offices are sometimes some distance from airports, so the principle of using the *China Travel Service* or business travel offices in major hotels applies as with rail tickets. On the major routes, such as Peking–Shanghai, there are now three classes and on most other routes, two. The difference in price between economy and business class is not great and well worth paying. Separate check-in desks are provided and separate lounges, which are much more spacious and comfortable.

In the early 1990s China led the world in airline accidents but major carriers all now use recently acquired western aircraft on major routes and safety standards have greatly improved. It is still advisable to travel with the major airlines (consult your tour operator when booking from home).

By train

Considering the size of the country, China's rail network is not very extensive but, where convenient, train travel can be quite a relaxing way of seeing the country. As more and more Chinese fly, the trains are sometimes less spick and span than they used to be and are used by a rougher group of travellers. It is wise to be careful of belongings when you leave a compartment at any time; call an attendant to lock an unoccupied compartment. It is also common for group passengers and their luggage to be separated on train journeys, so it is prudent to have a suitcase that locks (sometimes the railway authorities insist on this) and to have an overnight bag with ALL essentials in it as the luggage will become truly inaccessible. We once had a narrow escape with contact lens equipment which entailed a dash down the train to the luggage compartment before departure.

There are three to four classes on trains: **hard seat** (narrow wooden benches crammed with passengers), **hard sleeper** (triple-tiered wooden slat bunks filling an entire carriage with no separate compartments; cool in summer but noisy); **soft sleeper** (four soft bunks to a compartment, rather questionable bedding provided as well as vacuum flask and tea-cups).

For short journeys there are now **double-decker trains** with long carriages filled with two levels of soft seats and video screens.

There are also different sorts of train: **te kuai**/very fast; **zhi kuai**/direct and fast and **kuai ke**/'fairly fast' are the main categories (with others like 'mixed' or 'local' which are probably largely irrelevant to all but the most impoverished back-packer). All trains have numbers: the smaller the number the faster the train, and the fewer stops. All long-distance trains have dining cars which provide sit-down meals in shifts (book your time with the carriage attendant) and lunch-boxes, once of returnable, re-usable tin but now white expanded polystyrene which litter the rail-lines like a covering of snow.

It is useful to carry a small towel which you can also use to cover the pillow, sleeping pills and a small cup of your own (teeth-cleaning, whisky-drinking) for overnight train travel, as well as cheering items like drinks or snacks. Tea-bags will be provided for a small charge and very hot water should be available from boilers at the end of the carriage. The lavatories may not be very inviting and will also be locked a surprisingly long time before stations are reached.

Individuals may encounter difficulties using trains as the timetable is immensely complicated (and only in Chinese) and there is no such thing as a return ticket yet. Tickets are supposed to be purchased no more than eight hours before departure. In order to avoid spending all your time at the station, it is often possible to get *China Travel Service* (which usually has a desk in most hotels) to buy rail tickets for you on payment of a small extra charge.

By boat

Owing to the scarcity of railway lines, especially along the Yangtse River and the coastal areas of Fujian and Guangdong provinces, boat travel can be fairly convenient, if slow. Booking offices are usually close to the docks. There are various classes on most passenger boats which make overnight journeys. On most Chinese boats (except the luxury liners on the Yangtse), 'second' class is the most luxurious, with two beds and a washbasin, then there are various sizes of dormitory cabins and, finally, the equivalent of 'hard' class on trains.

By car

More and more roads are being built in China, including a number of toll-paying motoways. The pace of road-widening and improvement is, however, slow, and travel on the older roads, although picturesque, is still subject to problems of excessive traffic of a varied nature. Buffalo carts, overloaded bicycles, tourist coaches and army trucks do not mix well on the narrow roads of the countryside.

In the Yangtse Delta, quite a few motorways have been constructed and may be used for coach travel between Nanjing, Hangzhou, Zhenjiang, Yangzhou and Suzhou, for example. They are still relatively empty and quite fun, in a strange way. Great pride is taken in the construction of junctions, which are lovingly described as 'a double-peony overpass' or 'a triple knot flyover'; roundabouts are planted or embellished with whitewashed concrete sculptures; there are motorway pull-ins for drinks and snacks and the whole experience is an interesting introduction to the changing China.

It is, apparently, possible to hire cars to drive yourself within Peking, Shanghai, Hong Kong and Hainan Island. You need an international driving licence and a credit card. I would not recommend it as the traffic is simply appalling in most of China's cities: there are rivers of cyclists who weave around you taking no notice of traffic lights or regulations and there is nowhere very safe to park.

By taxi

In most towns there are now an enormous number of metered taxis, so that it is possible to go to a temple, look round it, and come out to hail another taxi. If you are far from the city centre, however, it may be best to ask the driver to wait for you in order to avoid being stranded. Always watch the meter to make sure it is on; it may be better to get out and find another if it is obviously faulty, to avoid incomprehensible arguments.

On some intercity routes (Jingdezhen–Nanchang, for example) you may have to pay the return fare if the driver cannot arrange to pick someone else up. If taxis are hired for overnight journeys (Taiyuan–Wutaishan, for example), you will have to pay for the driver's accommodation and meals.

By bus

As well as separate buses for tour groups, there is a considerable network of local and long-distance buses which, because they are the cheapest form of travel, are the most popular. City buses are usually jammed with passengers, as are the long-distance buses where luggage has to be piled on the roof. Buses are economical but very uncomfortable. Take chopsticks, a mug and a bowl if you are planning to eat at stops on long-distance bus routes—the food will be freshly-prepared and cooked but the washing-up facilities less fresh. There are new buses on routes in Fujian, for example, but they are fitted with videos showing ancient episodes of 'Dynasty' dubbed into Cantonese.

By bicycle

Bicycles can be hired in most places (enquire at the hotel desk) although they are not always hired out in a very road-worthy condition and may require a first stop at a roadside repair shop. If you do hire a bike: the Chinese drive on the right and everyone has priority over bicycles. Buses pull in to bus stops through the bicycle traffic. At traffic lights the usual rules apply, although no one pays much notice: the green and yellow lights shining together mean that you can, in theory, turn left across the traffic. Although everyone does, it is forbidden to carry passengers or an umbrella while cycling and fines can be imposed on the spot by the traffic police.

By underground train

In Peking, Shanghai and Guangzhou the newly constructed underground lines are the most convenient means of travel, although the networks are not very complex as yet. Underground travel avoids the appalling congestion of the roads above. The stations are well signposted (in pinyin).

Health

Upon arrival in China, you must fill in a form guaranteeing that you do not have TB, AIDS or any other infectious disease. No inoculations or vaccinations are required but those against typhoid, cholera, polio and hepatitis are recommended, as are malaria precautions for the Yangtse area and the extreme south and southwest (Guangdong and Yunnan): consult your doctor.

It is important to take any medicines you require with you, although Chinese hospitals in major cities are generally of a high standard and many Chinese physicians speak some English.

Medical insurance is essential, as you will be expected to pay for any treatment. As Chinese food is generally prepared on the spot, few tourist suffer from stomach upsets, although it is wise to be prepared; also, avoid shellfish, particularly if you are a long way from the sea. Many tourists suffer from colds in China so it is a good idea to take cold relief preparations, or else try Chinese cold cures (read the counter-indications).

Water is treated in the major cities but in the countryside, smaller towns and on trains, unboiled water must be avoided. This is not difficult as the Chinese themselves always boil water before drinking, a sensible precaution which dates back to before the days of sewage treatment. They do not like to drink cold water themselves but acknowledge that visitors do. Hotel rooms should be provided with a vaccum flask full of hot, boiled water or a water-heater and, increasingly, a carafe of cool boiled water (usually the remains of what was in the flask).

If you are ill

Many of the large hotels in the major cities have clinics for their guests and it is probably best to go to one of these, or ask at a hotel reception desk for a doctor since they will know of English-speaking doctors or dentists. The Chinese attend hospital clinics for all ailments, from colds upwards and you may be directed to the nearest hospital where, again in the major cities, it is quite likely that there will be a doctor who speaks medical English. Treatment will almost invariably be with 'western' medicine (antibiotics, etc) and traditional Chinese treatments should only be embarked upon in cases of non-acute problems.

Money and banks

The Chinese have a non-convertible currency known as **renminbi** ('people's currency') of which the major unit is the **yuan** (c 10 yuan to £1). This is subdivided into 100 **fen**. There are coins of 1,2 and 5 *fen*. There is a subdivision of the *yuan* into 10 *fen* (known as a **jiao** on banknotes but popularly referred to as a **mao**) and there are small notes of 1 *jiao* (10 *fen*), 2 *jiao* (20 *fen*) and 5 *jiao* (50 *fen*). Banknotes for the *yuan* come in denominations of 1, 2, 5, 10 and 100 (there may be higher denominations but I have not seen them).

Renminbi are now obtainable from **Bank of China** branches outside the country and, in theory, upon arrival at branches in airports and railway stations. Unfortunately, such branches open at 09.00 and close firmly at 17.00 so travellers on late flights (or Sundays) may find it difficult to obtain cash. When tourists leave China, their remaining *renminbi* can be changed back into foreign currency against production of an exchange slip from a bank; *renminbi* below 1 *yuan* will not be changed.

Most travellers will find it convenient to change their money at the **Bank of China** branches in virtually all hotels. Friendship Stores (run for foreigners, offering a wide range of goods and souvenirs) also have Bank of China exchange counters and there is no variation in the rate of exchange between the bank, hotel, or Friendship Store counters, although exchange rates for travellers' cheques are much more favourable than for cash.

Major **credit cards** are increasingly widely accepted in shops, restaurants and hotels and are, indeed, expected, at major hotels. There are some cash machines which take these in hotel foyers and at airports, although I have yet to find one that worked for me.

Where to stay

There are various grades of hotel, although most tourists will normally only see the luxury and semi-luxurious categories. There is a Chinese grading system by stars and most foreign tourists will be accommodated in five-, four- or three-star hotels, although some of the three-star hotels may also offer dormitory accommodation for the back-packer.

Most of the luxury hotels are recent constructions, built since 1980, often with a certain proportion of foreign investment and many are run as joint ventures. Major chains, such as **Holiday Inn** and **Sheraton**, are widely represented in the larger cities. Rooms in these hotels, which are bookable from abroad, may cost several hundred US$ a night, although those travelling with groups will benefit from discounted rates offered to the tour operator. The rooms are of international standard, with western or Japanese bathroom fittings, and the hotels have bars, several restaurants (usually with one serving non-Chinese food) and business centres as well as bank counters, souvenir shops and hairdressers.

Some of the semi-luxurious hotels are new, some are old hotels built during the 1950s to accommodate Soviet advisers and technicians. Most of the latter type have been modernised in the last decade so that much of their interior is quite comfortable (with western bathroom fittings) and prices have risen in consequence. As fewer are foreign-managed, bars may close early and western food is more basic. Even after modernisation, rooms are invariably twin-bedded and for members of tourist groups, prices are calculated on room-sharing, so a supplement must be paid if a room is to be occupied by a single person, unless there are uneven numbers of males and females who are not compelled to share.

Rooms all have their own bathroom, desk, armchairs, telephone, vacuum flask and cups and almost invariably a television. Many hotel televisions carry western channels including CNN and the BBC overseas channel.

Group travellers eat together and the usual pattern is a western-style breakfast of toast and jam, eggs and coffee, with Chinese lunch and dinner, unless guests have made special requests in advance. Strict vegetarians and those on special diets will find Chinese food difficult as mainly vegetable dishes often include a little pork or a few prawns and may not have been cooked in vegetable oil. They should express their needs well in advance through their guide and perhaps bring some emergency rations.

Virtually all hotels have a bank counter and post office, some have hairdressers as well as shops which sell basic toiletries and some imported goods: photographic film, not in a very wide range and rarely slide film, alcohol and cigarettes.

We have recommended hotels that are well-situated in centres to facilitate walking, or others with special features. Longer lists may be obtained through your travel agent or the national tourist offices.

 Food and drink

Restaurants

The national hobby of the Chinese is eating. Each region has its specialities which can be found in restaurants in most major cities. Tourist groups will frequently be taken to restaurants, although their food there will be ordered in advance. Being taken out for every meal except breakfast is an irritating new feature of group travel and has more to do with pay-offs for guide and driver than convenience. For the tourist it means that extra film and other essentials have to be carried all day and the exhaustion of the trip is increased by not getting back to the comforts of the hotel room and bed until quite late in the evening. In Peking and Shanghai, in particular, where sites and hotels are spread out over a considerable area and traffic jams can be appalling, tour guides and individual tourists are advised to get the full itinerary from the Chinese guide and go through it, preferably with a map, to ensure that time is not wasted trying to get to a distant restaurant through solid traffic.

If you wish to eat out, it is best to arrange this through the guide; meals are usually booked at a fixed price per head, often with some local dishes specified if desired. We have not included many restaurant names as quality goes up and down alarmingly, although I would highly recommend Peking's oldest vegetarian restaurant, **Gongdelin**, at 158 Qianmen nan da jie. Although the food is given all the usual meaty names (*Shizitou*, or 'Lion's head' meatballs, *Gongbao rouding*, 'Palace pork', etc) all the dishes are made from vegetarian ingredients with much use of *doufu* (tofu) or bean-curd and aubergine instead of duck. There is also a branch of **Gongdelin** in Shanghai on Huihai lu, just north of Nanjing xi lu. Restaurant recommendations are very welcome.

In the Chinese tradition, a cold plate appears first at a formal meal: lightly pickled vegetables, sliced beancurd, liver, beef and chicken. These are often arranged in the form of a phoenix, butterfly or goldfish, with dyed and carved radishes and turnips for decoration. There then follows a series of dishes of pork, chicken, duck, fish, a little rice and, finally, a soup. Soup is regarded as a digestif, so traditionally it comes at the end of a meal. Sometimes there are slices of fresh orange or watermelon to round off the meal. There is no final sweet course; such sweet northern dishes as 'toffee apples' (apple and banana chunks in batter covered with toffee) may arrive at any point in the meal and everything has to stop while the toffee apples are dipped into cold water to make them set.

Drink

Traditionally, the Chinese do not drink with meals as the soup provides enough liquid and alcohol is drunk on separate occasions with a few accompanying dishes of peanuts or pickles. The western habit, however, of drinking with meals has now become common practice at banquets, although not for ordinary dinners (where beer or soft drinks are usually offered to foreign diners). At banquets, guests are provided with three glasses: a tumbler for beer, mineral water, orangeade or, increasingly, Coca Cola; a small wine-glass for 'ladies wine', usually a sweet red grape wine; and a tiny wineglass for 'white spirit', *Maotai*. Recently it has become more common to avoid the expensive and highly intoxicating *Maotai* and the sweet red wine in favour of a somewhat drier white grape wine. There are several of these, mainly made in China with foreign advice. Toasts can be sipped from any of these but the white spirit glass should be drained and held upside down. The traditional toast is *gan bei*, which means 'dry glass'.

The 'white spirits' vary as each region distills its own from various grains, usually sorghum or millet, and they are all extremely strong. I find them pleasantly fragrant. The most famous, *Maotai*, comes from Guizhou, where it is made from spring water and sorghum. It is sold in an opaque white glass bottle, which some have rudely suggested makes it look like a lavatory cleaner.

Etiquette

This matters most at banquets but in general the Chinese are fairly relaxed and informal. On informal occasions, when dishes are placed on the table, diners help themselves directly with their own chopsticks. Many western visitors feel that this is unhygienic (and it is probably more unhygienic with clumsy chopstick users poking about and dropping things) and serving spoons are usually provided for them. The late Party Secretary Hu Yaobang (d. 1989) agreed with this view and suggested that knives and forks were perhaps to be preferred. He also personally abandoned the Mao suit (Sun Yatsen suit in Chinese) in favour of western suits before he fell from power in 1988.

At banquets, serving chopsticks are placed in front of the host (and the host on each table if there are more than one). The most important thing to remember at a banquet is that if you are a guest, you must not start eating until your host has served you. If you are the host, you must serve your most important guest, at least, with the serving chopsticks. If you are not very good at using chopsticks, it is enough to touch the serving chopsticks, then everyone can begin eating. The same is true of drinks. No-one should drink until the host has proposed a welcoming toast and the chief guest has replied. After that, people can drink and propose more toasts at will. Guests at a banquet should take care to arrive after their hosts and leave before them (soon after the arrival of the fresh fruit announcing the end of the meal). If you are the host, you must arrive before your guests and depart after them.

Chinese people are fairly relaxed about westerners' hopelessness with chopsticks but you could bear in mind that while it is not considered impolite to hold your bowl close to your mouth (and thus avoid accidents), it is considered bad manners to put your fingers in your mouth to extract bones etc. This should be done with chopsticks and you can forget everything your mother said about sitting up straight for it is quite easy discreetly to extract a fishbone with chopsticks if you have your face practically on the table. As river fish are full of bones, crayfish are served in their shells and Chinese poultry is served chopped up into small pieces, bones and all, getting rid of bits can be quite a problem in polite society.

Some typical dishes

There is a saying that the Cantonese will eat everything with four legs except the table and everything that flies except aeroplanes and this is broadly true of the other culinary regions, although it fails to acknowledge the delicate flavourings used to produce splendid dishes from a very wide source of raw materials. For those who enjoy food but are squeamish, it is better not to ask what you eating unless you are sure you can stomach answers like sea slug, terrapin, beef sinews or worse.

Ordinary Chinese families eat simple meals most days: a breakfast of plain rice porridge with salted and pickled vegetables, lunch of soup noodles and dinner of rice with some pork, eggs and vegetables in one or two dishes. On feast days and in restaurants they will eat a variety of dishes, just as tourist groups do at lunch and dinner.

Food is divided into two broad categories: rice or wheat (the latter in the form of pancakes, noodles or the casing for ravioli and dumplings), both of which are sometimes rather misleadingly listed in English language menus as 'food', and 'dishes' of meat, eggs, fish and other seafood cooked in various ways with varying seasonings.

It is important to remember that, for the Chinese, food is not only a matter of survival and enjoyment but is also closely connected to traditional views on health. Chinese medicine lays great stress on the importance of balancing the two principles of *yin* and *yang* (crudely translated as the dark, cold, feminine, negative aspect and the light, strong, hot, masculine aspect respectively).

Foods are divided into *yin* and *yang* types. *Yin* or cooling foods (often pale and light in colour) include cucumber, crab, beancurd, green tea and oranges. *Yang* or warming foods include meat, apricots, sugar, black tea, chilli, ginger and wine, all of which are regarded as stimulating, almost irritant. To maintain the balance, most dishes will include both types and people with certain ailments will be recommended by traditional medical practitioners to eat or avoid certain foods.

The aesthetic aspect of food is also important: without necessarily resorting to excessive decoration, colours should be varied and attractive, a few slivers of carrot or green peppers improving the appearance of a dish.

Culinary regions

Although four major culinary regions are usually described, the greatest distinction is between north and south China and is based on the 'food' divisions. North of the Yangtse, the traditional staples are wheat, maize and millet, used for porridges or in the form of flour as the basis for noodles and pancakes. South of the Yangtse, rice has long been the staple food and the variety of crops (and year-round growing season) means that the southern cuisine is more varied than that of the north.

The north Northern food is more robust: more dishes are slow-cooked, braised and stewed and many are flavoured quite strongly with spring onion and garlic. Mongolian and Muslim influences mean that mutton is quite common, used in spicy kebabs (*kao yang rou*), in 'hamburgers' eaten in sesame buns and in *shuai yang rou* or 'Mongolian hotpot'. This, a convivial winter dish popular throughout the north, is a kind of fondue: water is boiled in a special copper vessel with a central chimney and paper-thin slices of mutton, spring onions, noodles and cabbage are held in the boiling water with chopsticks, then dipped in small dishes of spicy sauces. Many solid steamed bread rolls (*mantou*) are eaten as a staple and although most people eat large *mantou*, stuffed with pork, cabbage, onion and garlic and then steamed (*baozi*), there are more delicate, open-topped steamed ravioli in Peking, called *shaomai*. The most famous northern dish is Peking duck, a force-fed meaty fowl carefully roasted so that the skin is crisp and the flesh moist. It is eaten in slices, wrapped up in thin pancakes with sliced spring onion, cucumber and a sweetish sauce, and is also best in winter.

The east The food of eastern China (roughly Jiangsu, Zhejiang, Anhui, Fujian, Hubei and Jiangxi provinces, all of which are largely south of the Yangtse) is more delicate, with much use of fish and shellfish (both freshwater and marine) and more sugar in sauces than elsewhere. This is one of the most subdivided areas, with each town boasting special dishes. 'Sweet and sour' dishes, flavoured with sugar (*tang*) and vinegar (*su*)—thus *tangsu rou* is sweet and sour pork, *tangsu yu*, sweet and sour fish, originate here—but, by contrast, there are also simple steamed fish, crabs and tiny elvers (in season). As Shanghai is and was a city of very rich inhabitants, food had to be of the best and the tradition is continued. Shanghainese are sweet-toothed and, apart from the sweet flavour of local dishes, also enjoy western puddings and cakes from the French tea rooms on the Huaihai road.

The west By contrast, western Chinese food is strongly spiced and often very peppery. Hunan and Sichuan are the major provinces (also Guizhou and Yunnan) and the Hunanese Mao Zedong was so fond of hot food that he had peppers baked into his bread on the Long March. Although chilli is used, one of the major flavouring agents is Sichuan pepper, small red peppercorns that provide a crunchy texture and an almost lemony flavour. Some of the best Sichuanese dishes have very odd names: *mapo doufu*, or 'pock-marked granny's bean curd', is a beancurd and minced pork dish with a chilli and crunchy pepper sauce and *mayi shang shu*, or 'ants climbing trees', is a hot dish of minced pork and rice noodles. Other notable dishes include tea-smoked and camphor-smoked duck and beef with ground rice.

The south Southern food is very delicate in flavour and immensely rich in ingredients. Fish and seafood are popular and fish-farming is a major industry in the south. Food is cooked quickly (stir-fried and blanched) so that vegetables remain crisp and flavours distinct. As in the eastern area, simple steamed fish is popular, cooked with only a little ginger and spring onion and basted with a light stock. A major Cantonese speciality is *dianxin*/dimsum/'dot hearts', a huge range of steamed and fried lunch-time snacks, including spring rolls and tiny stuffed dumplings of all sorts, usually served in bamboo steamers. Dimsum restaurants are noisy lunch-time meeting places. Waiters rush around with trolleys piled with steamers, shouting their wares, and guests are charged by the number of steamers they collect on their table.

Local delicacies

Some are listed by place, others by province as the boundaries vary.

Peking Peking duck, Mongolian hotpot, kebabs, *shaomai* (small dumplings) and *jiaozi* or *shuijiao* (boiled pork dumplings).

Xi'an *Yangrou shuijiao*, a mutton version of the *shuijiao* or *jiaozi* dumplings filled with pork, cabbage and onion that are eaten all over northern China. One of the most famous Xi'an dishes, *yangrou paomo*, is a mutton, vegetable and noodle soup poured over broken flatbread and has been described as 'haggis stew, noodles and digestive biscuits'. There is a very good crunchy pepper sauce to be found in Xi'an (similar to that of Sichuan).

Xinjiang, Gansu (the Silk Road) Mutton kebabs and *kao baozi* (bun stuffed with mutton and onions) and pilau rice with apricots and sultanas, also noodle soup with mutton and peppers (*la tiaozi* with *la zirou*) and, in summer, fresh grapes and Hami melon.

Sichuan In tourist hotels the food is underspiced. Those who like spiced or hot food are recommended to order separate dishes: *huiguo rou* (spiced stewed pork), *mapo doufu* (hot beancurd with pork) and *mayi shang shu* (hot pork with rice noodles). Specialities include smoked duck (*Xiangsu ya*), *gongbao rouding* or *gongbao jiding* ('palace treasure' pork or chicken, cubed and fried with chillies and peanuts), sizzling rice with pork where a pork and vegetable sauce is poured over crispy rice and the noise of sizzling should be deafening.

Kunming in Yunnan *Yunnan huotui* (Yunnan ham), *rubing* (a mild cheese often fried and an unusual dish in China where milk is not much liked) and *qiguo ji*, boiled chicken with 'medicinal' ingredients. These include the little brown rubbery caterpillar-like stalks of *Cordyceps fungus*. The life cycle of this parasitic fungus is appalling (involving taking up residence in a caterpillar and eating it up from the inside out) but it is an important ingredient in Chinese medicine, apparently producing a natural antibiotic. As part of the delicately boiled chicken and soup, it is interesting, if chewy.

Another famous dish from Kunming is *guoqiao mian*, 'crossing the bridge noodles', a boiling meat broth with side dishes of finely sliced chicken, duck and pork, scallions, rice noodles and seasonal vegetables, which are all dropped into the soup to cook. The dish was supposed to have been invented by the wife of a poor scholar who locked himself away in order to prepare for the imperial examinations. Anxious to maintain his strength, his wife prepared meals for him but they all got cold as she walked across the bridge to the island where he had his study. She finally discovered that if she made a soup, poured a fine layer of oil on it and kept the other ingredients aside, the broth stayed hot until she had crossed the bridge.

Shanghai 'Drunken' chicken cooked in Shaoxing wine, *shizi tou*, 'lion's head meatballs' (large pork and cabbage meatballs), smoked fish, braised sea slugs and shrimps fried in egg white (*furong xia*). The freshwater crab season is from

October to December. The crabs are dipped in a vinegar, ginger and scallion sauce. In spring there are elvers.

Yangzhou   Yangzhou fried rice.
Hangzhou   West Lake fish with vinegar.
Guangzhou   Dimsum.

Public holidays and festivals

The major public holidays are:1 January; the Spring Festival which, because it is a moveable feast marking the beginning of the Lunar Year varies from late January to early February; 1 May (International Labour Day) and 1 October (National Day). For Spring Festival, most Chinese have up to a week off (time to visit their families) and they have about three days off around 1 May and 1 October. There are other holidays for sections of the public: Women's Day on 8 March, Children's Day on 1 June and Army Day on 1 August. On these days, parades or large meetings may be held.

1 May and 1 October see public parks decorated with pot plants, red lanterns and fairground attractions, such as stalls where you can shoot at tin ducks, and giant chessboards to follow the course of exhibition games. These are usually the two traditional forms of Chinese 'chess'. *Xiangqi* closely resembles western chess but it is more closely associated with battle formations. Known certainly since the Tang dynasty, *xiangqi* is not as ancient as *weiqi* ('Go' in Japanese, 'Othello' in the UK), a game played with black and white counters. *Weiqi* was listed, along with playing the lute, calligraphy and painting as one of the pastimes of the traditional gentleman.

Spring Festival   The traditional festivals of the lunar calendar begin with the Spring Festival. Preparations begin some days in advance when the house is thoroughly cleaned and New Year pictures (*nianhua*, traditionally coloured woodblock prints of auspicious scenes and guardians for the doors) pasted up. The stove is smeared with honey, for the God of the Stove/Kitchen God is supposed to make an annual trip to heaven to report on household activities and the honey is varyingly interpreted as intended to sweeten his tongue or to stick his lips together. Traditionally, debts had to be paid by Spring Festival as part of the 'clean sweep' and fire-crackers are let off to scare away evil spirits. The day itself was, and is, one of visiting friends and relations, eating sweets, peanuts and melon seeds.

Lantern Festival   This follows soon after the Spring Festival (15th day of the first Lunar Month) when more fire-crackers were let off and children taken to buy lanterns (in Peking, the Lantern market, or *deng shi*, ran across Wangfujing: the northernmost crossroads is called Dengshikou, or Lantern market crossroads). These lanterns, fashioned out of paper or silk, in the form of animals, boats, insects or just great round red balls, were lit by a candle inside and small children can still be seen carrying their great red globes through the night.

Qingming Festival The Qingming ('pure and bright') Festival follows on about 5 April. This is a festival of the dead, when people go out to sweep, weed and tidy up their ancestral graves and to make offerings of food and paper money there. The festival is officially a remembrance of the revolutionary dead, when school children are taken to martyrs' memorials and instructed in their heroism, but in recent years the traditional grave-tidying has undergone a revival and streamers of yellow paper can be seen over many graves in the countryside.

Dragon Boat Festival The fifth day of the fifth month (usually late May or early June) is the Dragon Boat Festival, celebrated in different ways throughout China. It was more of a southern festival and in south China, and especially Hong Kong, it is marked by races between decorated dragon-prowed boats. In the north it is mainly marked by the sale of *zongzi*, sweet sticky rice and dates wrapped in triangles of dried leaves. The origin of the festival was said to be the suicide of the upright official (and major poet) Qu Yuan c 288 BC. Having warned his ruler of the appalling state of national affairs, when his warning went unheeded and he was criticised, he threw himself into a river. He was greatly admired by the local people who did not want the fish to eat his body (for that would have distressed his soul) so they threw bundles of sticky rice into the river for the fish to eat instead.

Mid Autumn Festival This falls on the 15th day of the eighth lunar month (the autumn equinox, usually late September), when people gather, often on hills, to admire the full moon, to eat and make presents of moon cakes, which are stuffed with bean paste and sometimes eggs and stamped on the outside with auspicious characters.

A great number of old festivals of great charm have vanished now: the third month when winter fur hats and gold hairpins were exchanged for cool summer hats and jade hairpins; the tying of tiny silk tigers, mulberries and gourds onto the little tufts that children's hair was dressed in 'to prolong life' at the Dragon Boat Festival; the 'laying down of needles' (seventh day of the seventh month) when needles were floated on a bowl of water and the clarity of the shadow cast indicated whether a small girl would be good at embroidery or not. This coincided with the 'bridge of magpies', said to be formed on the same day so that two stars, representing separated lovers (the herd boy and the spinning girl), could cross the Milky Way that divided them. Some seasonal traditions still persist, such as the viewing of seasonal flowers in the parks and kite-flying on windy spring days (Tiananmen Square in Peking has often been a good place to see enormously long, articulated dragon kites).

Additional information

Crime and personal security

There has been a considerable increase in theft, with pick-pocketing, sometimes including bag-slitting, becoming more common. Take the obvious precautions: concealing a money belt, not hanging a bag over the back of a chair in restaurants and keeping handbags in sight. Hotel rooms are generally secure though it is a good idea to lock cases containing valuables. Suitcases are often locked into special luggage vans on trains but it is still important to have a suitcase that locks.

Losses of important items must be reported to the Public Security Bureau whose lengthy forms will help you to make a claim against your insurance company on return. They charge fees for the forms and for issuing new exit permits in replacement passports (about 20–50 yuan) so it is a good idea to keep money for such emergencies separately in case you lose a wallet or purse.

If you need a new passport (this has happened to me), you will have to go to the nearest Embassy or Consulate after reporting the loss to the PSB, taking the PSB report with you.

Peking

British Embassy, 11 Guanghua lu ☎ 6532 1961, fax 6523 1937
US Embassy 3 Xiushui bei jie ☎ 6532 3831, fax 6532 6057
Irish Embassy 3 Ritan dong lu ☎ 6532 2691, fax 6532 2168
Netherlands Embassy: 4 Liangmahe nan lu ☎ 6532 1131, fax 6532 4689
There are US Consulates in Shanghai, Guangzhou and Shenyang, and British and Netherlands Consulates in Shanghai.

Cultural organisations

Asia House (UK), 105 Piccadilly, London W1 7NJ, ☎ 020 7499 1287, email: enquiries@asiahouse.org, www.asiahouse.org. Asia House is a non-profit organisation 'dedicated to deepening understanding of the cultures, societies and economies of Asia'. It arranges exhibitions and events.
Asia Society (USA), 725 Park Avenue and 70th Street, New York, NY 10021, ☎ 212 288 6400, www.asiasociety.org.

Customs and etiquette

The Chinese are fairly relaxed in everyday situations, though they do not often shake hands with each other. Indeed, the Rev. Arthur Smith, writing in the 19th century, noted that in the past, it was common for gentlemen to greet each other by raising their own hands, clasped together in the long sleeves of their gown. Today, a smile and the simple greeting '*Ni Hao*' (How do you do) is enough when you meet someone. The answer to '*Ni Hao*' is another '*Ni Hao*'. Obviously, formal meetings are more formal and it is easiest simply to follow since in most situations, you will be the guest, so the host leads in greeting and initiating conversation. If the conversation is being interpreted, speak simply and in short sentences, leaving a clear break for the interpreter. Interpreting is difficult and it is important to help the interpreter gently if it becomes apparent that messages are not getting through. Be very sensitive about this and avoid any possibility of public humiliation. It is better to repeat yourself or talk privately to the interpreter if you feel that held is needed.

For eating see the etiquette section in Food and Drink, p 22.

If you are going to meet Chinese friends, by all means take presents for them. They may not open them in front of you as it is not the Chinese custom. It is not worth taking presents for interpreters, etc, on group tours as they will expect money (see Tipping). You can try passing on discarded English-language books or magazines, as long as they are suitable, but they may not be welcomed with much interest.

Some group tours visit Chinese homes. If you like, you could take small gifts such as calendars or key-rings, but this is not necessary as the home-owners will have been paid a small sum to receive you.

Drugs

There is a considerable drug problem in the southwestern provinces (Yunnan, Guangxi) owing to their proximity to Burma and Laos and heroin. Marijuana grows wild in parts of China. The Chinese government has a very hard line on drug use and drug-trafficking which is punishable by death. Drug-users have been blamed for the spread of HIV in China, a growing problem of uncertain extent. Blood products appear to have been quite widely contaminated in many parts of China where blood-donors are paid and equipment not always satisfactorily sterilised.

Electricity

Voltage: 220/240 volts, 50 cycles AC.

Entertainment

Peking opera and other local operas can be experienced in a variety of ways. In major cities there is usually a dedicated theatre troupe offering evening performances (check the *China Daily* or local listings magazines, ask at the hotel or through **China Travel Service**). Unless you have a guide with you, the experience may be somewhat mystifying. There is a large modern Peking Opera theatre on Chang'an jie (7 Jianguomen nei dajie, tickets 80–800 yuan) and the old Zhengyici theatre at 220 Xiheyuan da jie offers more atmosphere at a higher price of c 150 yuan.

In some tea houses, for example at the Gongwang fu in Peking and the Huxinting in Shanghai, opera performers and instrumentalists give solo or duet performances for groups of elderly Chinese and sometimes for tourists, too, continuing a long tradition.

In Shanghai there are occasional concerts in the newly-built concert hall in Renmin Square but tickets are extremely difficult to obtain (check listings magazines and with larger hotels), whilst in Peking, before the completion of the glass egg opera house (2004), there are occasional gala performances like the Zefirelli-Mehta *Madame Butterfly* in the Forbidden City (1999). The tickets for this, advertised in advance, were so expensive that, in the end, it was possible for people who found themselves in Peking at the right time, to get in quite cheaply.

Many tourist groups are offered evening entertainment in the form of acrobatics. These have a very long history in China with clay models of acrobats and jugglers appearing amongst the tomb models of the Han dynasty.

Maps

If you are intending to explore, it is worthwhile looking for good city maps. Good local maps can usually be bought in hotels or in branches of the Xinhua bookshop.

Newspapers

The *China Daily*, a locally produced English-language newspaper (every day except Sunday) is widely available in hotels. It covers national and international news (with quite a lot of international sport). It also lists exhibitions and events (mainly in Peking) and has a Shanghai counterpart (not, unlike the China Daily, available outside Shanghai), the *Shanghai Star*. In the larger hotels, you may also find Hong Kong English-language newspapers and the *Asian Wall Street Journal* on sale in lobby shops, together with English-language magazines like *Time*, *Newsweek*, the *Far Eastern Economic Review*, the *Economist*, *Der Spiegel* and *l'Expres*.

'Local' free papers, listing cafés, restaurants and local events, particularly designed for the increasing expatriate population, can be found in the lobbies of larger hotels in cities like Peking, Shanghai, Tianjin, Kunming and Guangzhou.

Opening times

Museums are often closed on Mondays, otherwise they are normally open from about 08.30 to 17.00. Quite a number of small museums (the residences of famous persons, for example) close at midday from about 11.30–14.00. It should also be noted that many sites have a 'last ticket' time. In the case of the Ming tombs and Forbidden City, this is at 16.00. Many larger sites (Bishushanzhuang in Chengde, the Buried Army and Lama temple) require separate tickets for separate halls or areas.

Mosques sometimes require female visitors to wear trousers and long sleeves—be more sensitive in strongly Muslim areas like the Silk Road. Shoes are always removed outside prayer halls in mosques.

Photography

Colour print film, increasingly manufactured in China by firms like Fuji and Kodak, is very widely available in hotels, shops and roadside stalls at tourist attractions but usually only as 100 ASA. Slide, Polaroid or video film or variant ASA types are very difficult to find, as is black and white film and these should be brought with you. You may be able to find replacement lithium batteries in large hotels or specialist camera shops in the big cities but it is best to bring plenty with you.

Some people, especially in the countryside, may not wish to be photographed: be discreet. Photography is forbidden in aeroplanes, railways stations, airports and harbours. If caught taking pictures in such places, you will probably be required to hand over the entire film on the spot. It is also often prohibited in museums and at some tourist sites where the management prefer you to either pay an enormous fee for permission or buy locally produced slides and guide-books.

It is probably wiser to carry film with you through airport check-in areas although the X-ray machines are invariably labelled 'film-safe'.

Postal services and telecommunications

Most hotels have post office counters which sell stamps and postcards (but hotel email services can be expensive, so it better to visit one of the increasing number of Internet cafés that can be found in even the smallest places). From Peking and the major cities, postcards and letters sent by airmail take about one week or less to reach their destinations but from distant parts this may be considerably longer. If you wish to mail parcels, this may be possible in your hotel, although you may have to go to a post office. You will need to provide (or purchase at the post office) all the wrapping materials. Do not wrap a parcel before going to the post office as the officer will need to examine the contents. Chinese postal authorities are fairly tough about regulations (no letters inside parcels).

The major hotels offer telephone and, increasingly, fax and email facilities. Local call charges vary from hotel to hotel. Direct dial to Chinese numbers and abroad is normally available from hotel rooms. Charging starts from when the line connects, not when it is answered, so a charge will be made even if no-one picks up the call and there is usually a minimum charge of one minute, irrespective of whether the call is answered or not. Faxes and emails can be sent to visitors in Chinese hotels but may not reach their destination if the room number is not included.

Sport and leisure

Group travellers will find they have little time to spare and such a full programme, including Sunday, that they will not be able to avail themselves of the increasing number of leisure facilities now offered.

There is an artificial ski slope on the outskirts of Peking, should you happen to have your skis with you (although they can be hired) and there are a number of golf courses, which are as expensive as anywhere else in the world: for details look in the free glossy 'what's on' magazines supplied to hotels and for expatriates. It is possible (by arrangement with the China Tourist Office) to visit the Olympic training village outside Peking, though not to join in.

Walking is possible in many of the mountain areas, for example around Chengde or on Wutai shan, Jiuhua shan, Putuo shan and Emei shan. You may be joined by many others in popular walking areas such as Emei; and the paths are often stepped. Despite the temptation, it is unwise to stray far off main paths for there is no organised mountain rescue.

Participation in some of China's martial arts is possible in and around the Shaolin temple, although few will spend enough time there to get very far.

Time difference

China is seven hours ahead of London (GMT), 13 hours ahead of New York and summer times alter these figures slightly. China adopts a summer time in June (one hour ahead of standard time) and, despite a number of time zones, Peking time is standard throughout the country. In the far west, in Gansu and Xinjiang, in order to accommodate the different hours of sunlight, tourists may find that they are served breakfast at 09.00 (instead of the 07.00 or 08.00 starts in eastern China). The Chinese generally adopt fairly early hours, frequently with a long lunch break (c 11.30–14.00), sometimes with a siesta. Chinese restaurants usually close by about 21.00 and banquets start between 17.00 and 18.00, finishing before 21.00. Restaurants catering for foreigners stay open much later and bars within hotels keep similarly long hours. There are now many cafés, bars and nightclubs in all parts of China, often with foreign names and themes, that stay open very late; China has changed greatly in this respect over the last decade.

Tipping

The Chinese do not tip, so it is not necessary to tip taxi-drivers or restaurant staff although they will not back away, offended, if you do, as they did in the Maoist past. If you are travelling with a group, your tour operator should have specified that all tips for guides, bus-drivers and bell-boys in hotels are covered in the quoted price of the tour. Tour leaders will dispense these tips. They are calculated roughly as follows: the main guide, the bus-driver and the local guide receive £1/$1.50 per tourist per day (rounded down rather than up). This can obviously be adjusted according to the work done: sometimes a local guide does nothing other than meet a group at a railway station and point out the local driver and his bus and thus does not qualify for a tip; sometimes bus-drivers or guides go out of their way to be helpful and perhaps deserve recognition.

For individuals or small groups, tips should amount to about £10/$16 a day, half for the guide, half for the driver.

Unfortunately, guides and drivers assume they are entitled to such tips and may complain that they cannot survive without them: I met one guide who insisted on sitting down and demanding a fixed daily fee before I had even managed to get a group into their hotel rooms after an overnight flight. Guides and drivers also rely on various kick-backs or bribes offered by restaurants and, particularly, commission shops. For every foreign tourist they get in through the door of a jade 'factory' or silk shop, they receive commission, which rises with purchases. Sadly, this can lead to visits to museums and sights being cut short in order to visit a distant commission shop: tour leaders need to be alert to such dangers. It is sometimes possible to compromise and agree to visit such shops for a few minutes only.

Useful telephone numbers

See p 28 for the telephone numbers of the embassies in Peking.

Emergency numbers

The emergency number for fire/police/ambulance in Hong Kong and Macau is 999, in China you dial 110 for the police; 119 for fire and 120 for the ambulance service. As whoever picks up the phone is highly unlikely to know foreign languages, such emergencies are best dealt with by your hotel, your guide or almost anyone else.

Lost credit cards

For lost American Express cards issued anywhere in Europe, the Near East and Africa, ☎ 00 44 1273 576 360. For lost American Express cards issued in the US ☎ 00 1 800 440 519

As Visa cards, for example, are issued by a wide number of institutions, the best way to protect your cards against illegal use after theft is to use a card protection service and keep the number in a variety of places: a single call should secure all the cards listed.

BACKGROUND INFORMATION

History

Recent western views of Chinese history have emphasised the agrarian nature of Chinese society, borrowing from Mao's stress on the peasantry. Indeed, the breakdown of the highly organised, centrally controlled society is a relatively recent phenomenon, dating back to the mid 19C when Qing rule began to crumble. For much of China's history, the civilisation is better viewed as one which was highly organised and technological, with a well-maintained system of roads, staging posts, canals and government granaries. Technologically, China's superiority begins in the Shang dynasty with the sophisticated bronze industry and later saw the development of cast iron (by the 4C BC), porcelain (6C AD), papermaking (c 2C BC), printing (by the 7C AD), as well as gunpowder and firearms (10C AD) and textile technology which played an important part in exports of silk (to Rome in the 3C BC).

Another view of Chinese history is that of the traditional historians of China. The first great historian was Sima Qian (died c 90 BC) whose *Shi ji* (often translated as *Records of the Grand Historian*) recounted the history of China from the earliest times to the Han. In works such as this, events and stories are mixed to the point that Professor David Hawkes (formerly of the University of Oxford), discussing some of the Shang legends, has said that the method could either be characterised as the 'historicisation of myth' or the 'mythicisation of history'.

If Chinese historiography begins in the Han, it was to continue throughout the succeeding millennia with ever greater significance. Each dynasty compiled the official history of its predecessor, which it had overthrown, based on the massive imperial archives. Someone recently described peasant China as a 'vegetable civilisation' but a better description of medieval China would be a 'paper civilisation' with a passion for documentation. Although it antedated the invention of paper, the first documented ruling house of the **Bronze Age** already possessed a script used to record events on bones which were then carefully stored as an official archive.

Neolithic period The earliest inhabitants of China so far unearthed lived at Lantian (Shaanxi province) 600,000 years ago. China's civilisation, however, begins with the **Neolithic** era in which there were two major cultures with strong local variations. The **Yangshao** culture, characterised by the use of a red earthenware, sometimes decorated with swirling black designs, was mainly concentrated in the northwest of China, while the **Longshan** culture, characterised by the use of fine, wheel-made, burnished black pottery, was more eastern. In the central Chinese province of Henan, Longshan cultural layers overlie those of the Yangshao and the Longshan exhibits more characteristics that were to be developed in the subsequent Bronze Age. Longshan settlements were surrounded by walls of tamped (pounded in layers) earth, a technique also used in architecture.

Their ceramic forms included tripods and tall libation cups, forms that were to continue in Shang bronzes. Late in the Longshan culture there is evidence of the use of divination.

First dynasties Chinese historiography begins with the gods, legendary figures who invented all the techniques and implements useful to man, but the first 'dynasty' recorded is the **Xia**. As yet no cultural remains have been unearthed that are definitively of the Xia, although some suggest that a late Longshan group may have been the Xia. Archaeology and history unite in the **Shang** (c 16C BC–c 1066) which is divided into three phases exemplified by three major sites: early Shang at Erlitou (c 2000–1500 BC), middle Shang at Zhengzhou and late Shang at Anyang (all in Henan province). Sometimes known as the *Yin* in Chinese (the remains of one of the Shang capitals at Anyang are called 'The Wastes of Yin'), the Shang rulers inhabited palaces in considerable walled settlements which included suburbs where specialised industries (bone, bronze, pottery) were concentrated. The Shang palaces were apparently constructed using similar techniques to those seen in the Neolithic Longshan, with hard, well-prepared tamped earth floors, but there were also stone pillar-bases, sometimes with bronze plates on them as a protection against damp. The Shang aristocracy used fast horse-drawn chariots with bronze fittings for hunting and warfare, which were both amongst the activities listed in their oracle bone divination records.

The rulers appear to have been shamans of a sort, consulting the gods on the outcome of military campaigns, hunts, illnesses and other natural events. In this oracular consultation they used prepared bones (scapulae of oxen, ventral shells of turtles). Shallow grooves were carved on the bones and heat applied to produce a t-shaped crack which was 'read'. The questions and answers were later inscribed on the bones in the first written language of any complexity to have been seen in China. The script comprises some 5000 characters, which include simple graphs, more complex signs for abstract ideas and phonetic symbols, of which only 1500 have been deciphered with certainty, partly with the aid of the *Shuo wen* dictionary of c AD 100. Characters also appear cast on Shang bronzes, although it was during the succeeding Zhou dynasty that bronzes were widely inscribed. The excavated Shang bronzes that survive are almost all from tombs and formed part of sets of 'ritual' bronzes, presumed to have been used for food and wine sacrifices to heaven and then buried with nobles whose spirits were assumed to continue with the same sort of rituals after death.

The Shang aristocracy constructed enormous underground graves in which the coffin of the deceased was accompanied by sets of ritual bronzes wrapped in silk and filled with offerings of food and wine, chariots, complete with horses and drivers, and in some cases dozens of human sacrifices. The human victims may have been prisoners of war, captured in some of the Shang campaigns against their neighbours. Major sacrifices were held on fixed dates when dead kings were commemorated and records of these enable archaeologists to construct a genealogy of the Shang kings, as well as providing evidence of a form of ancestor worship which was to survive as a major form of family worship throughout the rest of China's history. Other aspects of Shang worship which were to continue were the cult of a supreme god, controller of natural forces and the political fate of rulers, and of gods of the compass points and mountains.

Zhou dynasty The Shang rulers were eventually overthrown by the **Zhou**, a warlike group with effective chariots and harnesses who came from the west (Shaanxi province) of the Shang kingdom. The Zhou continued many of the Shang practices, such as the ritual use of bronze and jade, the same sort of burials, although not on quite the same barbaric scale, but they discontinued the use of oracle bones. At first, most Zhou texts were inscribed on bronzes, later on silk and strips of bamboo and wood.

The chronology of the Zhou is complicated: a fundamental break occurred in 771 BC when the Zhou were forced to move their capital east from the Wei Valley to Luoyang. Nomadic tribes were pressing forward in the west, threatening the old capital. Throughout succeeding centuries dynasties attempted to establish their capitals reasonably, but not dangerously, near the significant frontiers. Being near was important, to ensure that frontier garrisons were adequately supplied and supported; being too near meant that the capital might have to be evacuated, as the Han discovered when they had to move their capital several times.

The move of the capital, the survival of historical records and the gradual breakdown of centralised rule are reflected in the traditional divisions of Zhou rule which appear in the chronological tables:

Western Zhou 1066–771 BC ⎫ these two deriving their names
Eastern Zhou 770–256 BC ⎭ from the move of the capital

Subdivisions of the Eastern Zhou
Spring and Autumn Period 722–481 BC
Warring States Period 403–21 BC

The **Spring and Autumn Period** takes its name from an historical record of the same name which describes events in the state of Lu (modern Shandong), for which the last entry is in 481 BC. A text of commentary on these annals is called the *Zuo zhuan* and Chinese historians sometimes use the two names together as a name for the period.

The **Warring States Period** also derives its name from a document, the *Zhan guo ce* or *Records of the Warring States*. The name reflects the breakdown of Zhou power as separate states, derived from fiefs, grew in power and began to fight each other for supremacy. The Shang had ruled a smaller area without delegation but as the Zhou expanded their territory (northeast to Peking and the northeastern province of Shandong, south to the Yangtse plains), it became the practice to enfeoff noble families with cites, towns or regions. The gift was commemorated by the presentation of inscribed bronzes, cowrie shells, chariots, weapons and animal sacrifices. Within the earthen banks that demarcated their lands, the ruling house performed the major sacrifices but held power through the size of its chariot army.

The separation into states is reflected in distinct regional art forms: bronzes of the northern and 'metropolitan' areas are cast with strong, plain interlaced dragons, while those of the south are covered in more complex, smaller scrolling decoration. Jades, too, show regional variations similar to those of the bronzes, with dragon heads in the north and spiralling forms based on dragons in the south.

Cast-iron production It was during the 6C BC that iron began to be worked in China, cast into mass-produced agricultural implements which were improved during the Qin and Han. Europe was not to see cast iron until the late Middle Ages but, owing to long experience in the bronze industry, metallurgical progress was rapid in China: steel was made in the 1C AD, thanks to the perfection of a double-action piston bellows. Agricultural improvements led to the growth of cities and trade between the states which did not, however, bring them closer together for each state had a different form of currency (bronze coins cast sometimes in the shape of knives or ploughs reflecting the agricultural economic base), slightly different writing styles and different systems of weights and measures.

The development of the literary official Administering these and the other affairs of each ruling house was a growing official class of ministers, scribes, officers and specialists. The growth of the literary official as distinct from the military officer is reflected in a change in use of the term *shi* which originally meant a knight (or 'gentleman at arms') but later came to mean an educated gentleman. **Confucius** was a representative of this class, having served as an officer in the State of Lu (in present-day Shandong province) and although his expressed views on political morality and public ethics were to dominate Chinese thought from the Han, he was not widely known during and immediately after his lifetime. Another philosophical theory, **Legalism**, was to play an important, although short-lived, part in the unification of the separate states.

Unification of China under the Qin

The rule of Emperor Shi The **Legalists**, one of whose major writers was Han Fei (or Han Fei zi, died 234 BC), saw law as order rather than as arising out of custom or common practice in the settlement of disputes. Their aim was to substitute the customary rights and privileges of the old society by an all-embracing legal system including collective responsibility, impartial rewards and punishments and uniformity of weights and measures. The system was adopted by the ruler of the Qin state, **Shi huangdi** (Emperor Shi), who is best known for the 'buried' army that protected his tomb. By 221 BC he had conquered all the other states, thus unifying China for the first time. This was not a purely military process: he also unified weights and measures, introduced a copper coin (round with a square hole in the middle), which remained the standard until the 20C, and imposed the Qin writing style and a standard cartwheel gauge. The Qin emperor began the development of a road and canal system and pulled down the walls of the separate states, while building the **Great Wall** on his northern frontier. In 213, in order to 'unify' thought, he ordered the destruction of all works except those on medicine, agriculture and divination (the 'burning of the books') and the execution of some 400 opponents of his regime. The human expense of the construction of the roads, canals and Great Wall by workers on 'corvée labour' (a form of government service similar to military conscription by which able-bodied men had to work on government projects for a specified period each

A string of coins

The burning of the books and the burial of Confucian scholars by the First Emperor of the Qin

year), as well as his expensive military campaigns in Central Asia and Vietnam, took their toll.

Liu Bang forms the Han Dynasty Uprisings began and the dynasty did not long survive his death in 210 BC. In 206 BC **Liu Bang**, leader of one of the insurgent rebel bands, managed to defeat the Qin army, overcome his rivals and proclaim himself emperor of the **Han** dynasty. The Han was one of the most significant and long-lasting dynasties in China and the pattern it established of a ruthless unification followed by a stable 'golden age' was to recur throughout Chinese history. It illustrates the danger of fragmentation which haunted all of China's rulers, for the size of China and the strength of local loyalty made centralised government difficult.

Han Dynasty: 206 BC–AD 220

The 'golden age' of the Han is subdivided into two major periods: **Western Han** (206 BC–AD 23) and **Eastern Han** (AD 25–220). The two major periods represent the different sites of the capital, first in Chang'an (modern Xi'an) in the west and later in the eastern city of Luoyang. The brief intervening period is known as the **Wang Mang interregnum**, for Wang Mang attempted to set up a new dynasty and to improve economic and social conditions by returning to theories of a past 'golden age' mostly based on myth. Wang Mang is characterised as a 'reformist' rather than a 'modernist' and struggles between reformists and modernists persisted during the Han and, to some extent, throughout Chinese history. The relative positions were taken on the basis of texts and reflect the supreme importance that the Chinese have always given to the written word and its interpretation. The possibilities of interpretation and varying positions taken up on the basis of such interpretations reflect an aspect of the nature of the written language, which the French sinologist Jacques Gernet called 'the first shorthand in history'.

The Han reformists based their position on texts written in the old script that had survived the Qin emperor's burning of the books, while the modernists used texts copied out in the modern script. Arguments over variant characters and passages have raged ever since. The desire to set down the approved text of the Confucian classics that no-one could dispute provoked a Han emperor to have them carved in stone in AD 175. Despite the Wang Mang interregnum, the Han dynasty established the basis of the Chinese system of bureaucratic government and bureaucrats' education which persisted until 1911.

Also important was the Han expansion into the western desert and the establishment of trade routes across the deserts of Central Asia. Along these routes, silk was exported to Rome and fine horses for the imperial cavalry were brought to China from Ferghana, as well as luxury foods such as grapes, pomegranates, walnuts, sesame, onions, coriander and cucumber. China's expansion south of the Yangtse also began in the Han when expeditions were sent to the Kingdom of Dian (around Kunming in the southwestern province of Yunnan), to Vietnam, Burma and the Nanyue kingdoms of the Guangdong area where commanderies were set up.

The establishment of a centralised bureaucratic government was based on the Confucian ideology of paternalistic rule by superior, educated and moral men. An imperial university was set up in 124 BC. Within a hundred years it had 3000 students. The curriculum consisted entirely of the Confucian classics with forms of examination being held at court based on the Confucian texts to select 'men of talent' to govern. The Han bureaucracy was smaller than that of later dynasties; local officials did not penetrate below the level of towns of a reasonable size from where they collected the agricultural taxes, on products as varied as raw lacquer and silk as well as grain, that supported the imperial government.

The government also controlled by monopoly important products such as salt mined in Sichuan province and iron. As under the Qin, apart from producing agricultural goods as tax, men were compelled to do military and corvée labour service to maintain roads and mines and construct grand imperial buildings. This control of taxation and labour was based on an efficient system of data collection and the Han censuses are still considered to be remarkably accurate.

The extent of the Chinese bureaucracy can be seen in the surviving records of the administration. Many of these have survived in the dry desert of Gansu province, at the western extremity of the Great Wall. The Han, particularly under Wu Di (the 'Martial Emperor'; 14–47 BC), waged a series of campaigns against their northwestern neighbours, the **Xiongnu** tribes, sometimes identified as Huns, and gained control of much of Central Asia, extending the Great Wall west. Having established control of Gansu, it was necessary to garrison the Wall. Surviving garrison records consist of documents written on thin strips of wood and bamboo. Inscribed with ink and brush, top to bottom, these were then tied together and rolled up for storage. They describe the daily tasks of these distant garrisons: inspecting the woodpiles kept to fire the signal beacons, clearing stray dogs and reporting on local conditions to superior officers.

Technical progress and population growth Despite the economic strains of maintaining the garrisons in the west and launching military campaigns which included an occupation of much of Korea, China's population flourished during much of the Han and the census of AD 2 revealed a population of nearly 60 million with cities of up to a million inhabitants. Technological progress continued with the use of the breast-strap harness (first seen in the Warring States) and the improvement of iron tools so that an ox-drawn iron plough became commonplace, the introduction of the donkey from the West and the invention of the wheelbarrow (the Chinese wheelbarrow places the load directly above the wheel so that, although the barrow is difficult to balance, it is a most effective means of transport). Ceramic tomb models of the Han illustrate both town and country life: rural farmhouses with tiled roofs contrast with grand watchtowers constructed with wooden brackets to support the tiled roofs; fish ponds full of fish, ducks and geese; figures play boardgames, oxen pull carts.

Houses (also depicted on the tomb bricks lining underground burial chambers) had a series of courtyards with the main hall raised on a stone platform and an open verandah in front. Despite the wealth that was being created by the merchant class, the Han saw the first laws controlling merchant activities. The introduction of the government monopoly on salt and iron was one (for these were most profitable). In succeeding dynasties the attempt to control these commodities was balanced by the wealth of the merchants who dealt in them, like the Ming salt merchants of the central province of Anhui. Merchants were also forbidden to wear silk, to ride horses or to carry arms and these restrictions were extended in later dynasties, effectively preventing the merchant class from rising in society except by educating its sons to become bureaucrats, rather than merchants.

Popular philosophies Although Confucianism triumphed as the state philosophy in the Han, it was not unchanged, nor was its supremacy unchallenged by Taoist and other cults which were taken up at court. A major aspect of Han thought was interpretation by means of the Five Elements (wood, metal, fire, water and earth) and *yin* and *yang* (dark, female, weak versus bright, male, strong) by which all living things could be classified. **Dong Zhongshu** (1C BC), a leading figure in the establishment of the imperial university to train future government officials, linked historic events in the Confucian classics to the Five Elements. Critics, such as the rationalist Wang Chong, attacked this as a superstitious approach and deplored the reliance on portents and omens that had crept into Confucianism.

The Han empire crumbles In the Eastern Han, as under the Western Han, initial stability gave way to the growth of huge estates, with the consequence that many peasants became landless, and expensive military campaigns which led in turn to higher taxes, turning more impoverished peasants off the land. This pattern is another that was to be repeated throughout China's history as dynasties gradually lost control of the economy through corruption or incompetence. When large numbers of peasants became landless, they easily grouped into antidynastic armies and, although it was rare for peasant leaders to establish a dynasty themselves, they often paved the way for others.

As the Eastern Han lost control, picturesquely named millenarian peasant bands rose up throughout China, notably the Yellow Turbans, the Red Eyebrows and the Five Pecks of Rice Band (inspired by magical Taoism), and the Han fell.

In this case, no single leader emerged to reunite China and a period of disunion followed, rather like the earlier Warring States.

Period of Disunion: 220–581

Fourteen different short-lived dynasties and sixteen 'kingdoms' were established in this period when China was divided, with different rulers in different parts, and there was almost constant warfare. According to one view, the population dropped by 30 million between AD 156 and 280 BC but it is likely that the drop was not entirely due to the casualties of war but also to the not-unrelated fact that thousands or millions were forced to leave their land and were no longer registered. Between the 3C and the mid 5C a migration south to the Yangtse by dispossessed northerners and the development of this fertile area led to a subsequent increase in population in the Yangtse delta.

Buddhism In this period when Confucianism with its view of the moral ruler, governing by grace of heaven and maintaining the welfare of his subjects, was clearly somewhat irrelevant, Buddhism with its path to salvation and sense of abstract continuity in the endless cycle of rebirths made great progress. It was brought to China by foreign missionaries such as the Parthian known in China as An Shigao (late 2C) and the prolific translator Kumarajiva (late 4C) who had an Indian father and a Kuchean mother.

In the late 4C Chinese Buddhists began to make lengthy journeys to the Indian homeland of Buddhism to collect sutras, bringing them back to China for translation. The first of these was Fa xian, who returned to Nanjing in 414 after a 15 year journey which he later described in detail. The work of translating the sutras was monumental, for there are 1662 works in the Chinese Buddhist canon, most of them translated by the early Tang dynasty. It was frequently a bi- or tri-partite interpretation with a Central Asian monk who knew Sanskrit, giving a verbal translation which then had to be translated into Chinese. There were varying approaches to translation, some favouring literalness, others trying to achieve a more polished style which would appeal to the literary Chinese. Although he devoted much of his life to translation, Kumarajiva is supposed to have said that reading sutras in translation was like eating rice that someone else had already chewed.

There was also a renewed interest in **Taoism**, both philosophical and alchemical. Groups of intellectuals gathered to drink wine, write poetry, play the lute and discuss Taoist philosophy in what were called 'pure debates'. One of the most famous of these groups was the Seven Sages of the Bamboo Studio who met in the late 3C. One was always accompanied by a small boy carrying a jug of wine and a spade so that he could bury his master should he suddenly drop dead. There was a growing interest in Taoist immortality through bodily means: by diet, abstinence, sexual practices and breathing exercises and through the often explosive or poisonous alchemical search for an elixir of life. Recipes for such an elixir appeared in Ge Hong's *Bao pu zi*, compiled in the early 4C.

The period, with its military heroes and wily strategists, has also provided rich material for later folklore and literature. The **Three Kingdoms** (220–265) was later depicted in the *San guo yan yi* (*Romance of the Three Kingdoms*) by Xia Naian in the 14C. The ruler of the state of Wei, Cao Cao, figures as a grand strategist from the north but the most exciting characters (in fiction and folklore at least) came from Shu, in present-day Sichuan province. Liu Bei ruled with his generals Zhang Fei and Guan Yu (the latter was eventually deified as the God of War in another example of the mythicisation of history), and his prime minister, Zhuge Liang, a strategist of inventive genius. Much of Sichuan is associated with grand battles involving these god-like figures.

The Northern Wei Another ruling house to leave a lasting impression, at least on the landscape, was the **Northern Wei** (386–534). A non-Chinese people, the Wei, thought to be of Turkic or Tungusic origin, first established their capital at Datong in the northern province of Shanxi where they financed the carving of the huge cave-temple complex at Yungang (460–494), with massive Buddha fig-ures and highly-decorated caves based on the carved rock temples of India and the giant Buddha at Bamiyan. When the Wei moved their capital southeast to Luoyang, near the Yellow River in Henan province, they started work on another great cave-temple complex in the cliffs of Longmen in 494.

Reunification under the Sui Dynasty: 581–618

Just as the first Qin emperor united the separate states in 221 BC into a short-lived empire characterised in folklore as ruthless and tyrannical, the **first emperor of the Sui** reunited the country and gained a similar position in folklore as a brutal tyrant. In both cases it is partly the 'golden age' that followed their necessarily rigorous regimes that colours the traditional view.

The Sui emperor in his dragon boat being pulled to Yangzhou

The father of the first emperor of the Sui was forced to change allegiance from one small ruling house to another and his father-in-law was forced to commit suicide. Born in 541, the first emperor was brought up for the first 12 years of his life by a Buddhist nun, in separate quarters from his parents. He remained committed to Buddhism all his life, making huge donations to Buddhist monasteries after some of his murderous rages. Consciously or unconsciously, he followed the Qin pattern of setting up a complex legal system, enforced with draconian severity, and he ordered major works on the existing canal system, bringing grain to his capital at Yangzhou and his armies (the beginnings of the Grand Canal). Five and a half million conscripted labourers worked on this and the extension of the Great Wall, while over a million men were sent to subdue the ruler of Korea, who inflicted an ignominious defeat on this vast army. The first Sui emperor was succeeded in 604 by his son, who may well have ordered his father's death and who in turn was murdered in his bathhouse in 618 by the descendants of the Wei ruling house which had been almost wiped out by his father.

Although chronologies list the Tang dynasty as following immediately upon the Sui (618–907), it took ten years for the Li family to establish control after the murder of the second Sui emperor.

The Tang Dynasty: 618–907

The Tang dynasty is viewed as another 'golden age' in which Chinese culture flourished with a solid economic base for the prosperity of the country, based on an early enforcement of the 'equal field' system by which all eligible able-bodied males were supposed to receive almost 5.7 hectares (14 acres) of land. Only one-fifth of this could be permanently held; this was known as 'mulberry land' for long-lasting investment crops, like mulberries to feed silkworms, could be planted there as opposed to annual tax crops such as grains. At the beginning of the Tang the reimposition of the system was essential to re-establish cultivation on abandoned land and to provide the tax income required by the government.

A giant bureaucracy A vast revenue was needed to support the growing bureaucracy, for the Tang restored the old Han system and refined it into an enormous pyramid with the emperor at the top, served by his imperial Chancellery, imperial Secretariat and Department of State Affairs. The last supervised six ministries (of officials, finance, rites, army, justice and public works). There were also nine 'offices' and five 'bureaux' as well as the Board of Censors who reported on the officials. These ministries and boards were grouped around the imperial palace in the centre of the capital. The rest of the country was divided for administrative purposes into 15 circuits, 350 prefectures and 1500 counties, the last administered by local magistrates at the lowest level of the imperial civil service. As the system was based on that of the Han, so were the newly-revived civil service exams, which still meant, in theory, that a career in the bureaucracy was open to all. In actual fact the long years of schooling required eliminated the poor and positions could still be bought.

Nevertheless, from the Tang onwards, upward mobility in China was via the civil service exams and a civil service career. Merchants, whose wealth could not improve their low social status, were forbidden by law from taking the exams. They first invested in land (to change their status) and on that basis they could educate their sons to become officials. Towards the end of the Tang the merchants' investment in land, together with the increasing wealth of the aristocracy, who were exempt from taxes, meant that there was ever less land for distribution and, in consequence, ever fewer tax-paying peasants.

For the first 200 years the Tang saw expansion. The agricultural centre shifted south as wet rice cultivation developed with new planting techniques producing greater yields and new tools suited for use in paddy fields. Rice, transported along the expanding canal network, was stored in massive imperial granaries at canal junctions to alleviate famine. Through military campaigns and diplomacy, Chinese influence was extended into the northwest, along the **Silk Route**, and good relations were established with the Tibetans. The Koreans and Japanese, acknowledging the cultural domination of China—with its complex government system, elegant architecture, flourishing literature and marvellous handicrafts combining in an extremely elegant lifestyle—borrowed all these institutions and techniques.

The capital of the Tang, **Chang'an** (today's Xi'an) covered an area far greater than that delineated by the surviving Ming (1368–1644) city wall. The markets of the capital were strictly controlled and the citizens lived in walled districts which were closed at night. Apart from the local population, a considerable number of foreign traders from the Middle East also lived in the city and had their own mosques, Zoroastrian and Manichean temples and Nestorian Christian churches. They came to trade in silks, porcelain and other luxury goods and in turn they brought luxuries: pearls, Arabian horses for the emperor's games of polo, grapes and melons, precious stones, silver and gold vessels.

One woman rose to power during the Tang, the **Empress Wu** (reigned 660–705), traditionally characterised as a despot, like the later Dowager Empress Cixi of the Qing (1835–1908). Both seem to have ruthlessly eliminated potential rivals, even poisoning many of their close relatives, although both were patrons of Buddhism. Despite her popular reputation, the Empress Wu promoted the examination system (decreasing the possibility of purchase of office) in order to recruit independent administrators and break the power of the aristocracy. Her reign also saw an episode of peony-mania, similar to the tulipomania that struck 17C Holland.

An Lushan and the fat concubine By the middle of the 8C imperial power was declining; Tang armies were defeated by the Arabs in Central Asia, losing control of the westernmost end of the Silk Road in 751. In 755 the dynasty was almost overthrown by the An Lushan rebellion. An Lushan (of Central Asian origin) was a general, favoured by the fat concubine Yang Guifei. He led an army to take the capital city and proclaimed himself the new emperor. The Xuanzong emperor (reigned 712–756) fled the city, taking Yang Guifei with him but, on the way to exile in Sichuan, his bodyguards insisted on strangling her. The rebellion was put down but the emperor never recovered, abdicating in favour of one of his sons. The flight to Sichuan with its tragic finale and the romantic misery of the bereaved emperor have been favourite subjects for poets and painters ever since.

Economic decline and the persecution of Buddhists Towards the end of the Tang, when the economy was in crisis, a great persecution of Buddhism took place (841–846), following the eradication of the Manichean Church. The persecution, which returned 260,000 monks and nuns to secular life, was fundamentally an attack on the great wealth of the Buddhist Church which owned vast estates and was exempt from taxes. Although the Buddhist Church never regained its position as a powerful landlord, it remained an important popular faith.

As the economy began to founder and more and more peasants became landless, the Tang began to collapse in a series of rebellions and, in the endlessly repeated pattern, China was again divided. The great legacy of the Tang was both governmental and cultural. The pattern of imperial government was established, to change little in succeeding centuries, and the poetry of the dynasty is still considered China's greatest.

Art and literature under the Tang The two best-known poets of the period are **Li Bai** (c 705–762; Li Po in Wade-Giles) and **Du Fu** (712–770; Tu Fu). The former is known as a great drinker and his best-known poem describes drinking with the moon and his shadow for company. Du Fu is currently regarded as a more profound observer for his poems reflect the misery of exile (he fled to Sichuan during the An Lushan rebellion and was sometimes out of favour with his bureaucratic superiors) and, importantly for Communist literary historians, one of his poems described the sufferings of the poor at the gates of rich men's mansions.

The wealth of individual aristocrats of the Tang has survived as hoards buried during the An Lushan rebellion when the court fled from the capital. Many have been unearthed with sets of silver and gold chased tableware and pots of expensive medicaments. The recent discovery of imperial donations to the Fa men Temple outside Xi'an includes fine porcelain tea implements of silver and robes of silk gauze. Although few paintings which can definitively be ascribed to the period have survived, the beginnings of the great landscape style can be seen in the wall-paintings of the Dunhuang caves (Gansu province, extreme west on the Silk Road) and tomb frescoes and their furnishings of ceramic models have supplied illustrations of the court dress of the time (including the new mid 8C fashion for loose dress based on Central Asian styles and said to have been popularised by Yang Guifei, fat concubine of the Xuanzong emperor), gentlemen playing polo and court entertainments.

Feng Dao (881–954). Although credited with the invention of woodblock printing, he is a bit too late (from the Wushang pu, *1743)*

Wood block printing Perhaps the greatest contribution of Tang China was the invention of woodblock printing some time before the mid 9C. Paper, an essential prerequisite for the technique, had been discovered in the early Han and was apparently in quite widespread use by the 5C as the mass of Buddhist manuscripts on paper discovered at Dunhuang testifies. During the height of the Tang, government departments used millions of sheets of paper every year.

One of the documents discovered at Dunhuang was a printed copy of the Diamond sutra with a colophon that dated its printing to AD 868. The work, printed on separate sheets of paper pasted together to form a scroll approximately 7.5m long, is preceded by a beautifully cut frontispiece of the Buddha preaching. Although it is clearly the product of a mature industry, few other dated examples have been found to illustrate the development of the technique. It is probable that some of the small Buddha figures printed in long series on paper scrolls, also found at Dunhuang, may have helped to furnish the inspiration for the repetition of texts which was an act of merit for Buddhists.

Whatever the source, printing quickly spread from Buddhist centres to the outside world and examples of printed calendars of the early 10C have been found at Dunhuang, privately printed in defiance of a government regulation which stipulated that calendars should be official publications. By the Song a whole range of works were printed for wider circulation: histories, poetical works, technical and medical books, although great religious printing enterprises also continued.

Period of Division: Five Dynasties and Ten Kingdoms: 907–960

The period of division following the collapse of the Tang is known as the **Five Dynasties** and **Ten Kingdoms**. The Five Dynasties were short-lived military dictatorships in the north of China, while the Ten Kingdoms coexisted more peacefully in the south.

The Song Dynasty: 960–1279

The Song dynasty was founded by the leader of the Imperial Guard of one of the Five Dynasties, **Zhao Kuangyin**. One of his first actions was to concentrate the best troops in the imperial capital of Kaifeng rather than on the periphery. This was done in order to abolish the 'warlordism' (seizure of local control by military commanders) that had helped to destroy the Tang and kept China divided into the Five Dynasties. He also gathered more bureaucratic power into his own hands rather than trust powerful and potentially threatening ministers. The examination system continued to be the method of entry into the civil service but during the Song the exams were held more regularly and high standards were established by regulations controlling possible corruption.

Confucianism re-examined In contrast to the expansionist Tang when the capital was filled with foreign traders and artisans, the Song was a period characterised more by productive introspection. As it involved both philosophical and artistic retrospection, with ceramics and jades made in the form of Shang and Zhou bronzes, it was a true 'revival'. Confucianism was re-evaluated in the light of social change and of Buddhist influence. Ouyang Xiu (mid 11C) continued the work begun by the great Tang thinker Han Yu. He re-examined Confucian concepts and deplored the divorce between political function and culture: politics without culture was corrupt, culture without politics, meaningless. More philosophers sought to identify the natural order and find man's place in the cosmos, basing themselves on the Confucian classics and Buddhist metaphysics and finding a dualism between order and spirit.

Zhu Xi (1130–1200) used a metaphysical approach in his re-examination of Confucianism. He ascribed to all things their own pattern (*li*) and their own 'matter' or 'essence' (*qi*). In a complex scheme, he fitted the varying theories of *yin* and *yang* (femaleness, darkness, submissiveness versus maleness, light and strength), and the five elements (essences of manifested nature: metal, air, fire, water, wood) to the *li* and *qi*, incorporating a cyclical theory of chaos and order, which owes something to Buddhism, into a comprehensive view of the nature of things. This was combined with the adoption of the view, held by Confucius' disciple **Mencius**, of human nature as essentially good, dropping the opposite view of Xun zi, the 3C BC philosopher whose tough legalist philosophy had been adopted by the Qin emperor. Zhu Xi's belief that man's essential goodness could be cultivated, his essential *li* developed from his rather chaotic *qi*, also owes something to Zen Buddhist ideas of self-cultivation towards enlightenment. Despite the metaphysical input, Zhu Xi's neo-Confucianism was essentially conservative, preserving the family as the basis of society and the paternal figure of the emperor as the father of his people. Geography, map-making, archaeology, mathematics, astronomy and historiography all made great strides during the Song, while the expansion of overseas trade (in well-made boats with nautical compasses) and major agricultural innovations in the form of new, faster-growing rice strains, all served to assist the development of an advanced economy and an urban society.

The new bureaucracy A major figure reflecting the new idealism of the bureaucracy was **Wang Anshi** (1021–86), who attempted drastically to reform the economy in the face of changes. The population of China increased steadily during the Song and began to concentrate in growing towns, leaving a smaller number of registered payers of the agricultural tax to support the government. Wang Anshi abolished the corvée labour system, replacing it by further taxation which, in conjunction with his graduated tax system based on the productivity of the soil and a system of government loans to peasants, meant that the tax burden fell more heavily on the rich. He brought the government further into the economy by setting up government pawnshops and establishing a system by which the government purchased local goods for redistribution elsewhere, thus stabilising commodity prices. He also expanded the number of government schools to prepare students for the civil service exams, widening the possibilities of a bureaucratic career. He was bitterly opposed by the more conservative bureaucrats in government, as well as by the rich, and was forced to resign in 1076 when conservatives managed to reverse many of his policies.

Trade within the empire grew and merchant trade guilds expanded into a country-wide network, with provincial merchants eventually building their own inns or hostels throughout China. The growth of local trade was accompanied by the increasing use of proto-banknotes, promissory notes on paper. These were issued both by the government and by large merchant houses because both faced the problem of moving large sums of bulky copper cash coins about the country. The government, which in previous periods had received virtually all its taxes in the form of grain, cloth, lacquer and other raw materials, was beginning to take more taxes in the form of money.

Foreign trade overland was difficult but the sea trade from southern coastal ports (most notably Quanzhou and Ningbo) flourished. Silks and porcelain were shipped in long, narrow boats to Southeast Asia, Korea and Japan and the boats returned loaded with spices, ivory, luxury timbers and medicinal herbs.

Some idea of the activity of the capital is gathered from Zhang Zeduan's narrative scroll *Going Up the River on the Eve of the Qing Ming Festival* (late 11C–early 12C), a portrait of the capital, Kaifeng. It depicts the bustling streets with their open-fronted shops and the variety of road traffic: officials with 'eared hats' on horses, the characteristic Chinese wheelbarrow (with the weight over the central wheel), carts packed with merchandise, ladies in sedan-chairs with brightly-patterned curtains, pedlars with loaded baskets on carrying poles. Many of the buildings have a verandahed upper storey and the internal courtyards behind the shops can be seen.

The way that the women are concealed within the sedan chairs is an indication of the increasing enclosure of women which was reinforced by the then-new practice of foot-binding. Originally an upper-class fashion, it gradually spread to all but the very poor who depended upon the work of women as well as men. When girls were between 4 and 7, their feet were tightly wrapped in wet strips of cloth, bending all but the big toe underneath the sole of the foot. A small block of wood was included in the bandages under the heel to enable the victim to walk.

The division of the Song The division of the Song into the **Northern Song** (960–1127) and **Southern Song** (1127–1279) reflects the forced move of the capital from Kaifeng on the Yellow River, south to Hangzhou. The move was forced by increasing military power and threat from northern peoples, most notably the Khitan, Jurched and Tanguts and, later, the Mongols. The Khitan, who were also of Mongolian origin, founded the **Liao** dynasty in northern China (947–1125) but were later driven west by the Jurched and set up the **Western Liao** dynasty (1124–1211) in eastern Turkestan. The Jurched, of the Tungusic language group, founded the **Jin** dynasty in northern China (1122–1234), coexisting with the Tanguts, who spoke a language of the Tibetan group and whose **Xi Xia** kingdom dominated northwest China from 1038 to 1227. Continuing the threat from the north, the Mongols swept all aside, including the Khitan, Jurcheds and Tanguts, and finally overthrew the Song in 1279, establishing the **Yuan** dynasty.

The Mongol Yuan Dynasty: 1279–1368

Although non-Chinese dynasties had been ruling the north of China for some time, the rise of the Mongols swept them and the Song rulers aside. The sudden rise of the Mongols in the 12C and their conquests of Central Asia, China and eastern Europe remains a matter of debate. It has been suggested that Central Asia suddenly became drier and less hospitable to these nomads but this theory has not stood close examination. Others suggest that a purely nomadic society such as that of the Mongols suffered from economic instability for nomadism without pastoralism could not provide the grains needed to supplement the milk and meat diet, nor could nomads produce the iron that was essential to their horsemanship for both stirrups and arrows had to be purchased from sedentary mining communities. The need for these commodities, it is suggested, forced the Mongols into conquest.

Genghis and Khubilai Khan The sudden change in Mongol history was probably a combination of such factors, together with the divided and unstable nature of the neighbouring countries and the rise of a charismatic leader in **Chinggis** (or Genghis) **Khan** (c 1167–1227). Orphaned as a child, he later subdued all the other Mongol clans and groups and began the apparently inexorable expansion. His army of 130,000 was far smaller than that of the Chinese but his troops were extremely well-disciplined. The Mongol army was said to practise 'hunting' techniques, groups of cavalry encircling enemy forces like herds of deer, and sudden manoeuvres, drawing the enemy into pursuit and then suddenly wheeling to confront them with their longbows.

Chinggis divided his ever-growing empire between his sons but relied on local advisers to assist in day-to-day local government, using the Uighur Turks in Turfan and borrowing the alphabetic Uighur script to write Mongolian for the first time, and Chinese advisers in northern China. It was **Khubilai Khan** (1215–94), a grandson of Chinggis, who supervised the conquest of southern China, overthrowing the Song dynasty and establishing the Yuan dynasty. The name means 'first', 'beginning' or 'fundamental principle', and it was the first time that a dynastic name was chosen for its meaning; all previous ones were either surnames or place names of significance. As Chinggis Khan had realised, 'the empire is conquered on horseback but it cannot be governed on horseback' and the Chinese system of government through the imperial offices and their subordinate ministries down to the local magistrate was continued.

The description of Mongol China contained in *Marco Polo's Travels* is detailed, including mention of the regular grid-pattern of the street layout of Peking, the markets, craftsmen's guilds and pleasure boats on the lake at Hangzhou, the silks and myriad bridges of Suzhou, the use of paper money, the collection of customs tariffs during transport of goods, systems of household registration and the posting of names of inhabitants at the door of every residence. Significant omissions in the text include the Great Wall, footbinding, tea and tea-drinking, printing and the peculiarities of Chinese language and script. As all place names are rendered in Persian, rather than in Chinese or Mongol forms, it has been suggested that this vivid account was possibly based on a contemporary Persian guidebook compiled for the numerous Persian travellers and merchants journeying to China, rather than personal observation.

The Mongol capital was established in the north, in **Peking**. Although previous small capitals had existed in the area, an entirely new city was built to the Chinese city planning ideal with walls enclosing a central palace surrounded by a grid system of streets. The tamped earth walls enclosing the city had one Mongol aspect in the enclosure of pasture land to the north of the city proper. By making use of the Yellow River, the Grand Canal was extended north to reach Peking and supply the capital with grain from rice-producing south China.

The Mongols kept themselves separate from the Chinese, with the barrier of their non-Chinese advisers between them. Khubilai promoted the state cult of Confucius and eventually re-established the examination system, but the Mongols at this time adopted the Tibetan form of Lamaist Buddhism and patronised Buddhist monasteries and temples.

The first papal envoys came to China during the Mongol era when travel across Europe and Central Asia was relatively free. One of the reasons for papal interest was the relative strength of Nestorian Christianity amongst the Uighur Turks and Mongols, Khubilai's own mother being amongst the believers. Papal envoys who reached China included: John of Montecorvino, who died in Peking c 1328, having spent some 30 years in the city whence his successor took a letter from the Khan to Pope Benedict XII; Odoric of Pordenone (c 1286–1331), the first European to mention Lhasa; and John of Marignolli, who arrived in China c 1342. In the light of Marco Polo's text, it is interesting that Odoric of Pordenone wrote an account of China, borrowed and embroidered by Sir John Mandeville, that did include mention of footbinding and the long fingernails of the scholar-class as well as details such as the use of cormorants for fishing. The veracity of Odoric's account, however, has also been questioned, leaving us with a variety of texts all purporting to be first-hand accounts but which may simply reflect the state of knowledge of China in 13C and 14C century Europe.

Two cultural developments which took place during the Yuan, reflecting how little Chinese culture was affected by alien rule, were the rise of Chinese drama and the first appearance of novels, a published form probably based on the narrative style of travelling story-tellers.

After the death of Khubilai's successor, Temur, no Mongol ruler managed to control warring factions within the Mongol nobility and, as old family rivalries were multiplied by new ones, the Mongol hold on China weakened. As with other dynasties in decay, there were other symptoms. Paper currency was over-issued, causing serious inflation. A disastrous change in course of the silted Yellow River, flooding an area of more than 7000 hectares (17,296 acres), was seen as a significant omen of the withdrawal of the heaven-given 'mandate to rule'. Armed uprisings of landless peasants began in the 1320s; civil war between Mongol nobles broke out in 1328 and the secret society of the **White Lotus**, a millenarian Buddhist sect, led a peasant rebellion in central China as did another 'restore the Song' peasant secret society, the **Red Turbans**. In the past, peasant uprisings had helped to bring dynasties down or served as decisive indicators of decay, only to be followed by the victorious establishment of a new aristocratic ruling house rising out of the chaos. The rebellions at the end of the Yuan were different, for the founder of the Ming dynasty was actually an impoverished member of just such a peasant army who rose to supreme power.

Ming Dynasty: 1368–1644

Zhu Yuangzhang Zhu Yuanzhang, founder of the Ming ('Bright') dynasty, was born into a poor tenant family in Fengyang, Anhui province in 1328. When he was 17 his entire family succumbed to the effects of famine and disease and he entered a Buddhist monastery as a novice. He joined the Red Turbans where he quickly distinguished himself and, despite his poor background and lack of formal education, soon became the leader of a disciplined army which attracted wide such support that he managed to drive the Mongols back to the Gobi Desert. Although a formidable and capable leader in his early years, in later life, he is said to have became increasingly cruel. Chinese historians have compared him to Liu Bang, the founder of the Han, who also rose from obscurity to establish a grand dynasty.

Zhu Yuanzhang and his supporters, having overthrown an alien dynasty, looked back to the great Chinese dynasties of Han, Tang and Song as models. In the first years of his administration, Zhu Yuanzhang allowed peasants to return to the land, as in the 'equal field' system, and recover it for agriculture without paying taxes. When taxes were imposed, they were collected twice yearly; the 'summer tax', mainly of winter wheat, was collected in the eighth month and the 'autumn grain' was collected after the main rice crop of the centre and south. Taxes were also collected in the form of silver and bolts of silk and the government maintained its monopoly taxes on tea and salt. Corvée labour service was required from adult males. Like the Yuan government, the Ming began by issuing paper money but soon reverted to metal coinage to prevent inflation.

In the early Ming, the government system of the Song was revived but in the later years of his reign Zhu Yuanzhang abolished the post of Prime Minister, assuming a more autocratic role than previous emperors, a practice which was to continue throughout the dynasty. In his direct handling of the many memorials to the throne and issuing of edicts, he was assisted by Grand Secretaries, and the Grand Secretariat came to serve as a kind of imperial cabinet, above the Six Ministries. Although there had been eunuchs at court from the Tang, in the Ming and Qing they assumed far more power in the Inner Court than they had had before and were often in conflict with the bureaucrats of the Outer Court.

The civil servants were still selected by examination according to a system that was continued to the end of the Qing. There were first district exams to qualify candidates to enter for the prefectural examinations which offered the lowest degree level, *xiu cai* ('flowering talent'). *Xiu cai* degree-holders were exempt from corvée labour and certain forms of legal punishment. The next level of exams was held at the provincial capital where exam candidates were locked into individual cells in examination compounds. One in a hundred (or less) would pass and become eligible to take the highest level exams in Peking. Success there (after

---

Naming emperors

The system of naming emperors was changed in the Ming. Zhu Yuanzhang is known by his posthumous title as the **Hongwu** ('Vast Martial Power') emperor, a term which was originally used as the name of a reign period. From the Han it had been customary for emperors to assume an imperial name but their reigns were frequently divided into several reign periods, with equally auspicious names which were changed to avert disaster or to try and improve events. For example, the ninth ruler of the Tang dynasty is known as the **Xuanzong** emperor. Xuanzong is a posthumously awarded dynastic title meaning 'Powerful Ancestor'. His surname, that of all the Tang ruling house, was Li, which is not reflected in any of the names by which he is now commonly known. His reign is divided into two reign periods: **Kai yuan** or 'Opening and Beginning', 713–742, and **Tian bao**, 'Favoured of Heaven', 742–756.

The reign periods were not of any ordained length. Sometimes a reign name would be changed suddenly after a natural disaster in the hope that heaven would be placated; the Xuanzong emperor's successor changed his reign name every two years for no particular reason. From the reign of Zhu Yuanzhang, in the Ming, it became the practice to have a single reign name for each reign, although emperors still had a variety of other names ranging from their real name to their posthumous title.

being locked into a similar complex of cells, formerly located to the west of the Friendship Store in Peking) meant achieving the title *jin shi* ('presented scholar'), being presented to the emperor and appointed to a post.

In 1369 Zhu Yuanzhang decided to establish his capital in **Fengyang**, Anhui, his home town and the place where he had begun his rebellion against the Yuan. For six years work was carried out on the palace and city walls, and the tiny plot where his parents had been buried was enlarged into an imperial mausoleum, larger than any succeeding imperial mausoleum of the Ming or Qing and severely damaged at the fall of the Ming. It was soon decided that Nanjing was a more suitable site for a capital and work began there on the construction of his palace and his own tomb.

The Yongle emperor Zhu Yuanzhang may have had good reason for his paranoia in later life; having set up his sons as princes in different parts of China, he appointed his grandson as his successor. One of Zhu Yuanzhang's sons, Prince of Yan, who controlled the north from his base in Peking, led an army against his nephew on the death of the dynastic founder, captured Nanjing and proclaimed himself emperor (his posthumous title is **Yongle** or 'Eternal Joy'). He proceeded to remove the capital to his own power-base in **Peking**, for it was strategically more sensible to have the capital nearer the Great Wall, source of the greatest external threats from the non-Chinese tribes in Mongolia and Manchuria. There were some who felt that the *feng shui* or 'good luck' of the site of Peking had been exhausted with the conquest of the Mongols and the razing of their capital but the Yongle emperor found *feng shui* experts who thought otherwise, and constructed the grand capital with its central 'forbidden city' or palace. The layout of today's streets and lanes in Peking is the same as it was in the early 15C (except for the ring roads) and the city, constructed on a flat plain, surrounded by fine walls and filled with a checkerboard of streets surrounding the imperial palace and government buildings, with imperial altars on all four sides, was considered to represent the ideal of the Chinese city plan according to principles which dated back to the Zhou period.

Technological progress Technological progress during the Ming included the perfection of blue and white porcelain, which was to play an important role in China's export trade, and improvements in both silk and cotton looms, which also produced valuable export commodities. Agricultural machinery was improved and new crops like peanuts, maize, sorghum and the sweet potato, introduced by the Portuguese and the Spaniards, improved peasant livelihood.

For intellectuals, knowledge was spread widely through a massive increase in the printing industry where the perfection of multi-coloured woodblock printing led to the production of fine illustrated albums and painting manuals. The output was enormous and included a great number of works on agricultural techniques, military science and medicine. One of the finest is the *Tian gong kai wu* (*Creations of Nature and Man*) which illustrates ceramic, textile and paper production, smelting and forging and the production of carved jades from the search for the raw material (by diving women). Geography, philology and hydrology made great progress: the geographer Xu Xiake spent much of his life travelling throughout China, tracing the source of the Yangtse and the Xi jiang and publishing the results, while others produced works about foreign countries (Korea, Japan, Vietnam, Central Asia and Tibet).

Philosophy and literature Philosophically, the Ming was a period of 'rein-forcement' of Song neo-Confucianism, although there was a move away from the reading and interpretation of texts (as advocated by Zhu Xi, 1130–1200) and a stress on personal conduct. The most famous thinker of the period is **Wang Yangming** (1472–1528) who developed Mencius' idea of 'innate goodness' which had to be rediscovered by stripping away egotistical thoughts and desires.

The expanding urban class was provided with a new wealth of popular litera-ture in the printed editions of Fujian. The two most famous examples are *Xi yu ji* (*Journey to the West*; c 1570), a fantastic and amusing version of the pilgrimage to India of the Tang monk Xuan zang who, in the novel, is accompanied by a pig (representing human failings and desires) and a magical monkey; and the *Jin ping mei* (*Plum Blossom in a Golden Vase*; 1619), a novel of manners, describing the life and loves of a Shandong merchant.

A maritime power It was during the Ming that much of the Great Wall, which was regarded as a crucial defensive barrier against northern barbarians, was faced with brick. At the outset, the Ming was not, however, an inward-looking dynasty for during the reign of the Yongle emperor a series of grand maritime expeditions were launched under the command of admiral **Zheng He**, a Muslim eunuch from Yunnan. Between 1405 and 1433 seven expeditions set out to the Persian Gulf, Southeast Asia and the east coast of Africa. The expense of the expeditions was one reason for their cancellation and the Chinese never regained the same status as a maritime power.

The decline of the Ming empire Towards the end of the Ming, considerable damage to the economy was inflicted by Japanese pirates and by official inactiv-ity in the face of a huge rise in smuggling and dealing in contraband by both Chinese and Japanese (brought about by unenforceably rigid official policies on trade and the intense demand for Chinese products such as silk in Japan). The government still profited from the trade with Japan, Korea and the Dutch: a 17C writer, Gu Yanwu, stated that tax levied on only 20–30 per cent of goods shipped by sea paid for half of the state's expenditure at the end of the 16C. On the seas, however, piracy was almost uncontrollable and the Ming government was also forced into a very expensive war against Japan which invaded Korea in the last years of the 16C.

External threats (also from the Mongols) and ethnic uprisings in Guizhou were matched by chaos within the palace, largely as a result of feeble emperors sur-rounded by rapacious eunuchs; there were said to be 100,000 eunuchs, effec-tively controlling the ministries, by the end of the Ming period. In 1620 the **Taichang** ('Exalted and Glorious') emperor was poisoned by the eunuchs who controlled his weak heir and when scholars of the ancient Donglin academy, call-ing for a return to strict Confucian ethics, attempted to curb the eunuchs, many were killed.

As peasants were driven from their land in the last decades of the Ming when, with the government coffers empty, and disastrous famines notwithstanding, taxes were exacted with increasing ferocity, they once again banded together in anti-dynastic armies. Led by a peasant from the northern province of Shaanxi, Li Zicheng (1606–45), the peasant army entered Peking. Abandoned in his palace, the last Ming emperor fled to Coal Hill (just behind the palace) and hanged him-self from a tree. Li Zicheng's peasant army did not manage to gain control of the whole of China for the Manchus, a non-Chinese group from the northeast who had been progressively absorbing the Chinese system of government in preparation, swept down upon them, capturing Peking in 1644.

The Qing Dynasty: 1644–1911

The Manchus take control The Manchus, who established the **Qing** ('Pure') dynasty, were descendants of the Jurched who had established the Jin dynasty in northern China (1122–1234). **Nurhaci** (1529–1626), effectively the founder of the Qing, first proclaimed a 'later Jin' dynasty in 1616. He was chief of the Aisin Gioro clan and one of his major contributions to the success of the Manchu conquest was the organisation of the scattered tribes into a proto-state, and the formation of the 'Eight Banners' or companies of warriors, each with a distinctive banner. All Manchus were registered under their local banner and taxed, conscripted and mobilised according to the needs of the new state. Breaking tribal divisions and establishing his own clan as the leading family, Nurhaci built up a strong basis for a disciplined army. He also used captured Chinese civil servants to help him set up a bureaucracy in his capital in Shenyang.

Although Nurhaci died in 1626 during a campaign against the Ming, his son, Abahai, continued his efforts and it was he who proclaimed the new Qing dynasty in 1636 (before the total subjugation of China). Abahai's son, although young and in the control of his uncle as regent, finally presided over the seizure of power in China. The Manchus' adoption of Chinese methods of rule through their Chinese advisers was significant: they had no desire to be seen as mere 'policemen' as the great sinologist and translator Arthur Waley described the earlier Mongol rulers of China. The conquest of China took decades, for groups of Ming loyalists held out in Yunnan and Taiwan. The north fell fast but the last Ming stronghold, the island of Taiwan, was not captured until 1683, owing to the fierce resistance of Zheng Chenggong (Koxinga) and his family. The Qing also pursued a policy of conquest in Turkestan, Mongolia and Tibet, areas which had fallen out of Chinese control.

Despite their tactical adoption of Chinese methods, the Manchus were keen to remain separate: Manchus were forbidden to marry Chinese women and various occupations (such as trade) were forbidden to them. All Bannermen were allocated land and a stipend for life. They remained different in appearance for they wore their own costume and their women never bound their feet. Chinese men had to follow the Manchu male custom of shaving the front of the head and braiding the rest of the hair into a long plait, instead of the Ming hairstyle of a topknot, which, if assumed, was seen as a sign of resistance.

In government the tiny minority of Manchus managed to retain control for 400 years. Military power underlaid the successful maintenance of internal peace for much of the period. As under the Ming, the emperor retained ultimate control over all details of government, while the lower levels of government (from the Six Ministries downwards) were jointly staffed by Chinese and Manchus, just as there were three Chinese Grand Secretaries and three Manchu. The provincial administrations were similarly mixed, with the Manchus also working with a number of Mongols. The dual administration meant complexities of translation in the early years when Manchu was the official Court language.

It was eventually superseded by Chinese, which became the sole language of the administration, but to the end of the dynasty all court documents relating to the imperial house were produced in both Manchu and Chinese.

Qing expansionism The first 150 years of the Qing saw a huge expansion of Manchu power throughout Central Asia and Siberia as far as Lake Baikal and the borders of Nepal. Great care was taken to obtain and retain the loyalty of major Mongol and Tibetan leaders who were entertained in specially-built Lamaist temples in Chengde and Peking. One of the major campaigns of the Qianlong emperor was that of 1791, carried out against the Gurkha tribes of Nepal to punish their incursions into Tibet. After military campaigns, areas such as Yunnan and Xinjiang province (the 'New Border') were colonised by Chinese settlers and by the military. Towards the end of the 18C revolts of the colonised ethnic peoples became more and more frequent as Chinese officials in the distant areas grew increasingly corrupt. Campaigns to quash the rebellions drained government finances.

Under the early Qing rulers, however, China prospered and expanded. The most prominent of these were the **Kangxi** ('Vigorous and Splendid') emperor (1654–1722) and his grandson, the **Qianlong** ('Lasting Eminence') emperor (1711–99). It was the Kangxi emperor who in his youth had directed the capture of south China from the last Ming loyalists. Soon after that he was involved in the settlement of border disputes with the Russians, signing a treaty of peace in 1689, before personally leading an army into Outer Mongolia and Turkestan. He made six tours of inspection to south China, particularly to examine water conservancy projects, and was concerned with improving communications via the Grand Canal and with making the Yellow River safe.

The Kangxi emperor supervised the construction of the Summer Palace at Chengde, about 150km northeast of Peking, the Bishu shanzhuang or 'Mountain Village Where You Can Escape the Heat', a hunting park dotted with pavilions and pools, surrounded by the eight 'outer temples' in the Tibetan style. Here he entertained Mongolian and Tibetan leaders. It was the Kangxi emperor who appointed Jesuit missionaries to run the imperial Board of Astronomy and he made use of Jesuit missionaries like Gerbillon as interpreters during negotiations with Russia. Jesuits and Chinese made maps for the Kangxi emperor, showing the areas of his new conquests, and Matteo Ricci made copper engravings of maps, drawings of military scenes and illustrated editions of the emperor's poems. Viewed popularly in China as something of a polymath, the Jesuit Matteo Ripa (1628–1745) in his *Memoirs* voiced a more jaundiced view:

> *The emperor supposed himself to be an excellent musician and a still better mathematician, but although he had a taste for the sciences, he knew nothing of music and scarcely understood the first elements of mathematics.*

Kangxi's successors Although he had 28 children who survived infancy, the only son born to the empress (rather than a concubine) was apparently mentally unstable and was incarcerated on his father's order, leaving the succession a matter to be fought over after the emperor's death. **Yin zhen**, fourth son of the emperor by a palace maid, cultivated the friendship and support of influential courtiers, including the head of the Peking garrison, the Bannerman Lungkodo. Although it is thought that Kangxi named **Yin ti** (his fourteenth son, whose mother was the same palace maid) as his successor, Yin ti was commanding border armies in the northwest so Lungkodo and Yin zhen seized power and Yin zhen ruled under the reign name of **Yongzheng** (1678–1736). He was reasonably successful in controlling official corruption (by offering financial rewards), thereby improving the state's financial position. He named his fourth son as heir, although the nomination was kept secret until after his death to prevent quarrels.

The **Qianlong emperor** (reigned 1736–96) personally led many military campaigns, particularly in Central Asia, Burma and Vietnam, which, with the exception of the Central Asian campaigns, were not very successful and enormously expensive. They virtually wiped out the government reserves, leaving China quite unable to withstand foreign encroachments in the succeeding century. Another intimation of the impending problems of foreign relations was the attitude of the emperor and his court to the embassy of Lord Macartney sent to open China to foreign (or at least British) trade (1792–94). The emperor was not completely unaware of the possible consequences of his refusal to grant a single concession for he instructed his officials in Canton to try and prevent other European merchants from allying themselves with the British.

Like his grandfather, the Qianlong emperor made use of the special talents of the **Jesuit missionaries**, who seem to have spent more time ingratiating themselves with the Court and teaching European sciences and arts rather than gathering converts, a fact which contributed to the dissolution of the order in 1773. He particularly favoured the painter Castiglione, and Father Benoît who contributed the 'European' palaces and Italianate gardens to the emperor's summer palace (the 'Old' Summer Palace), the Garden of Perfect Brightness on the outskirts of Peking.

One of the Qianlong emperor's greatest projects, the compilation of a vast collectanea in 36,000 manuscript volumes, the *Si ku quan shu* (*Complete Collection of the Four Treasuries*), intended to preserve rare works from oblivion, involved a vast literary inquisition on a scale not to be repeated until the Cultural Revolution of the 1960s. Provincial officials were required to collect rare works for inclusion but all works submitted were also scrutinised for anti-Manchu sentiments. Hundreds of volumes were destroyed and the authors and their families killed or subjected to posthumous disgrace.

Towards the end of his reign, corruption amongst officials rose unchecked, the economy was drained by military campaigns and the traditional cycle of peasant uprisings heralding the end of a dynasty began.

The Taiping uprising Local officials' embezzlement of funds intended for flood prevention work led to the calamitous change in course of the Yellow River (1855) when it broke its banks and moved from the north to the south of the Shandong peninsula, a distance described by Jacques Gernet as that from London to Newcastle. This occurred during the disastrous **Taiping** ('Great Peace') **uprising** of 1850–64. The Taiping rebels were led by **Hong Xiuquan** who mixed idealistic Confucianism with Christianity which he had learnt from an American missionary in Canton. Hong Xiuquan looked back to a golden age of equal land distribution and forward to greater equality between the sexes. Calling himself Jesus' younger brother, he wanted to create a 'Heavenly Kingdom of Great Peace' in China where all would be brothers. Some of the early practices of the Taipings were indeed 'egalitarian' for captured spoils were shared equally.

The vague Christianity of some of the Taiping ideas was supported at first by missionaries and foreigners but they eventually decided, as the Taipings established themselves in Nanjing and moved to threaten the Qing, that their trading interests were better served by the dynasty that they knew. In the end, the Taipings were crushed by a combination of imperial forces and the foreign-led 'Ever-victorious Army', commanded at first by an American, Frederick Ward, and subsequently by General Gordon (later of Khartoum). There was also a long and damaging rebellion in northern China in the mid 1800s (the Nian rebellion), and a Muslim uprising in the northwest (1862–73), which was savagely crushed.

Dowager Empress Cixi These took place during the period in which control of imperial power had passed into the hands of the Dowager Empress Cixi ('Motherly and Auspicious'). Born in 1835 into a Manchu family of the Bordered Blue Banner, she entered the palace in 1851 as a concubine to the emperor whose only son she bore, thereby raising her status. The emperor died in 1861 and Cixi, together with the senior consort, acted on her son's behalf. There were eight official regents but Cixi personally held the imperial seal required for all edicts and, using the pretext of their weakness over the British and French invasion of 1860, Cixi managed to get one regent executed and the rest punished.

When her son died of smallpox in 1875, she chose her younger sister's son as the heir-apparent in a flagrant breach of protocol (the decision was not hers to make) and practice (new emperors were supposed to be chosen from the generation after that of the late emperor to avoid confusion of relative positions within the imperial clan). Even when the new **Tongzhi emperor** reached his majority, she continued to manoeuvre her associates into positions close to the emperor. In 1898, when the young emperor began to associate with reformers who pledged to modernise and reinvigorate China in the face of foreign incursion and the country's evident incapacity to face the 20C, she had him imprisoned in the 'New' Summer Palace which she had been improving, apparently with money designated for, and badly needed by, the Navy.

Weakened by the endless series of rebellions and by an increase in population which food production was not matching, the mid Qing also saw a series of disastrous wars with foreign powers anxious to open China to foreign trade: the first Opium War with Great Britain (1840–42), the Arrow War (or Second Opium War) with Britain and France (1856), the Sino-Japanese War (1894–95) and skirmishes with Russia.

Cixi seems to have been, at best, contemptuous of foreigners, and, at worst, is thought to have given support to the **Boxers**, which may originally have been an anti-dynastic movement but which concentrated its later efforts on the massacre of foreign missionaries. When the Boxers reached Peking in 1900, a Japanese diplomat was murdered by Chinese troops and the foreign diplomats requested military protection from their governments. As an eight-nation army assembled on the coast, the empress asked all foreign diplomats to leave and the German ambassador was killed by imperial troops. It became clear that the Court was actively supporting the Boxers and the siege of the foreign legations in Peking was laid both by Boxers and imperial troops. When the Allied army finally arrived, the empress dowager fled to Xi'an, issuing edicts in the emperor's name taking the blame for everything. A protocol was signed by which the Chinese government paid reparation for the loss of life and Cixi eventually returned to

Peking and began to give a series of receptions for foreigners who were charmed by the 'old Buddha'.

The Qing dynasty did not long survive the death of Cixi in 1908. Its downfall was finally achieved by an uprising which declared a Republican government in 1911. This western-influenced movement was the result of more than 50 years' search for a new pattern of society which had been forced on China by western encroachment. During the late Qing this had had a profound and disastrous effect, although it had begun several centuries before.

Modern China

Foreign relations From the end of the 18C it was clear that China, closed, conservative and uninterested in trade, was bound to clash with the brash, expansive and mercantile West. China had not always been closed to the outside world yet even during the cosmopolitan Tang dynasty foreign policy was conducted on the basis of 'tribute'. Missions came from the rulers of surrounding countries, such as Burma, as well as from the Japanese and Korean courts, and all acknowledged China's superiority by presenting their 'tribute' on a regular basis.

The earliest western visitors to China were papal envoys during the Yuan, followed by the Jesuit missionaries to the early Qing. The latter were anxious not to upset the Chinese for they felt that pleasing the emperor was the best way into China. Their success, achieved through astronomic, mathematical, architectural and painterly skills, was such that they provoked considerable jealousy amongst those like the Franciscans, who accused them of succumbing to idolatry, and their attitude was diametrically opposed to that of the European traders who arrived in the 17C.

Both the Dutch and the British first traded through their East India Companies, behind which lay government power. From 1757 the Chinese authorities restricted all foreign trade to the city of Canton. Foreign traders were not even allowed to reside in Canton throughout the year; they had to retreat to the Portuguese colony of Macau outside the trading season. They were not permitted to bring their wives or any foreign women into Canton; they were only permitted to live on a narrow strip of river shore and compelled to trade with a limited number of licensed traders.

Frustration with restrictions led to the embassies of Lord Macartney (1792–94) and Lord Amherst (1816) which sought to open the rest of China to trade and diplomacy. Both missions foundered for the Chinese insisted that European envoys should behave in the same way as envoys from surrounding states bringing tribute, and to *kowtow* (to knock one's head on the ground three times) which British dignitaries refused to do.

The role of opium The 19C saw continuous pressure, often enforced by gunboats, to concede opening the whole of China to foreign traders, missionaries and diplomats. A triangular trade between Britain, China and India (in Chinese tea and porcelain and Indian cottons) was costing Britain silver but a solution to the drain of silver was found in the form of opium, specially grown in India for (illegal) shipment to China. There had previously been no addiction problem in China where opium was used medically as a painkiller. The silver drain was reversed when the British also started tea plantations in their colony of India, supplying the demand for tea which had previously been met by imports from China. The two **Opium Wars** (1842, 1856) were waged mainly by the British in defence of their illegal opium traders and forcibly opened China to trade and foreign residents. The European powers subsequently divided China into 'spheres of influence', with the French strongest in the areas bordering on Vietnam, the Germans effectively controlling Shandong and the British strongest along the Yangtse and in Shanghai.

Modernism One of the effects of this foreign invasion was to demonstrate to intellectuals the need to modernise, although there was profound disagreement throughout the late 19C and early 20C on the best methods. Supporters of the **Reform Movement** of 1898 sought Confucian 'self-strengthening', combined with the adoption of western technology and educational methods. Many of their proposals: the adoption of foreign arms-manufacturing and boat-building techniques, foreign language study and study abroad, were implemented in the first years of the 20C after the Boxer uprising. One of the students who went abroad to study, supported by his brother who had emigrated to Hawaii, was **Sun Yatsen** (1866–1925), who studied medicine in Hong Kong and, being to some extent influenced by foreign ideas, developed his Three People's Principles. These were Nationalism (aimed both against western imperialists in China and the Qing government), Democracy (not a Chinese concept) and 'People's Livelihood', a policy of economic reform involving the redistribution of land, which could be said to have its roots in traditional Chinese reforms, and control of capital. He founded a 'Revive China Society' in 1894 but was forced to flee China after an unsuccessful rising against the Manchus in Canton in 1894.

A stronger anti-Qing organisation was the **Tongmenghui** ('United League'), which was behind the finally successful rising against the Qing in 1911. Sun was in America raising funds at the time, but returned to China to be elected provisional President of the Republic of China in 1911. He was forced to resign in favour of Yuan Shikai, a general who had betrayed the 1898 reformers to the Dowager Empress. Yuan was in command of one of the regional armies established at the end of the Qing. Yuan died in 1916, just after declaring himself emperor, and, although Sun Yatsen held power in Canton (his ancestral base), the rest of China came under the control of other regional army generals, like the late Yuan Shikai. From 1916 until 1949, in effect, China was divided between these 'warlords'.

The Kuo-min-tang and the Communist Party The **Nationalist Party** (*Kuo-min-tang* in the Wade-Giles romanisation, KMT for short, *Guomindang* in pinyin) was led by Sun until his death in 1925, when he was succeeded by a young general, **Chiang Kai-shek** (1887–1975). Chiang had divorced his first wife and converted to Christianity in order to marry Song Meiling, daughter of a Christian Chinese who had spent years in the USA and whose son and sons-in-law were amongst the richest and most powerful people in early 20C Shanghai. Chiang had studied at a military school in Japan and become commandant of the KMT's crucial Whampoa Military Academy in Canton. Chiang Kai-shek used his military position to seize power in the KMT through the Canton coup in 1926, after the death of Sun Yatsen.

The **Chinese Communist Party** was founded in 1921. At its third congress in 1923 it was decided to unite with the KMT in the struggle against the war-lords, a decision upheld by Moscow. The 'united front' did not survive long for in 1926 Chiang expelled the Communists from the KMT. During the 1927 'Northern Expedition', when Chiang Kai-shek led his army north against the warlords to establish a Nationalist capital in Nanjing, the Communist-led workers of Shanghai, who had seized the city for the army, were turned on and massacred by underworld gangsters at Chiang's instigation. The Communist Party was driven underground; **Mao Zedong** retreated to the countryside to work amongst the peasants, while others, faithful to Moscow's instructions, continued to organise uprisings in the cities, where they were doomed to failure.

By cultivating the peasants, particularly in remote areas, seizing and redistributing land and running educational programmes, Mao became convinced that a movement based amongst the peasantry was possible. It took him many years to convince other members of the Communist Party and Mao's rise to the chairmanship was an intense struggle in which he displayed considerable ruthlessness in the elimination of opposition, a trait which was to persist after 1949.

Mao becomes leader In 1930 Mao and the military specialist Zhu De founded the Jiangxi soviet. On the borders of several provinces, in high mountains, both administratively and physically remote, the Jiangxi soviet was supported by local peasants after land redistribution and new marriage laws were enacted. In his determination to get rid of the Communists, whom he saw as a greater threat than the warlords, Chiang Kai-shek launched five massive encirclement campaigns and finally drove the Communists out of the soviet area in 1934. Turning defeat into a moral victory, Mao led his troops off and away on the **Long March**.

Starting out with some 100,000 soldiers, after a journey of 9500km (6000 miles) on foot, the Red Army reached an equally inaccessible mountain fastness in Yan'an (north Shaanxi province) with only about 8000 survivors, a year after they had set out. There were serious factional struggles during the March, against Zhang Guotao and, at Zunyi, against the 'Twenty-eight Bolsheviks', Communist Party members who had studied in Moscow and still adhered to the anti-guerrilla warfare line of the Comintern. It was at Zunyi in 1935 that Mao emerged as the unchallenged leader of the Chinese Communist Party and his policy of guerrilla warfare was upheld.

From 1936 to 1945, Yan'an was the headquarters of the Chinese Communist Party and the base both for guerrilla warfare and for the land reform, social reform and educational programmes that were to form the basis of Communist Party policy after 1949. Mao's army, although ill-equipped, was strongly disciplined, an almost unprecedented thing in China where most soldiers were regarded as little better than bandits. The army was used to help peasants in educational programmes, agriculture and building works.

War with Japan A further blow came with the Japanese occupation of Manchuria in 1931—where the last Qing emperor, Henry Aisin Gioro Pu yi, who had been deposed by the Republic, was enthroned as puppet ruler—and the full-scale Japanese invasion of China in 1937. By the end of the year, much of the north of China, Shanghai and the Yangtse valley and Nanjing had fallen to the Japanese, who treated the inhabitants of Nanjing in particular with unbelievable savagery, soldiers indulging in an orgy of rape and murder, with the tacit approval of their officers, that left more than 300,000 civilians dead. Chiang

Kai-shek's government fled, first to Wuhan where the order was made to breach the Yellow River dykes to stop the Japanese advance, a measure which achieved its tactical end but killed hundreds of thousands of Chinese peasants. The Nationalists continued their flight west to Sichuan where they established a new capital in Chongqing.

By its failure to resist the Japanese advance and by its secret agreement with the Japanese to withdraw Chinese troops from the province of Hebei, the Nationalist government began to lose the support of the intelligentsia. By contrast the smaller Red Army, mobilising peasants for support in information-gathering and back-up to guerrilla attacks in the northwest, was offering a stronger resistance to the Japanese. Intellectuals began to leave the cities, making their way to the tiny mountain town of Yan'an. Even the warlords were disappointed in Chiang Kai-shek: as early as 1936, Chiang was seized and held prisoner in Xi'an by two of them, Zhang Xueliang and Yang Hucheng, who demanded that he stop the civil war against the Communists and mobilise instead against Japan. Negotiations involved Communist leaders, including Zhou Enlai, and Chiang was finally released, promising to purge the KMT of pro-Japanese members, release political prisoners and prepare to resist Japan.

A KMT leader, **Wang Jingwei**, conducted secret negotiations with the Japanese and left Chongqing for Nanjing to proclaim a rival, Japanese supported, puppet 'Nationalist Government' in 1940. In the following year, the second 'united front' between the Communists and the KMT, set up after the Xi'an incident, collapsed when the KMT army which had been skirmishing with the Communist forces, turned on the Communist New Fourth Army of 10,000 men, of whom 1000 managed to escape, 2000 were killed and the rest were taken prisoner and held in KMT concentration camps.

With the entry of the USA into the Second World War, the KMT was supplied with American advisers and arms and financial support. Despite this, Chiang Kai-shek's regime failed to lead resistance against Japan and nearly 60 of the KMT generals joined the Wang Jingwei regime where they were instructed by the Japanese to fight the Communist guerrillas. General Stilwell was sent by Roosevelt to be Chiang Kaishek's chief of staff but reported that the KMT army was 'underfed, unpaid, untrained, neglected and rotten with corruption'. Despite a successful publicity campaign, masterminded by his beautiful wife, which painted Chiang as a clean-living simple man without a single vice, a devout and moral Christian, there was appalling corruption in the KMT and an economic crisis with consequences recalling the downfall of many a previous dynasty.

Uncontrolled inflation meant hardship for all and failure to provide any relief after a drought in Henan (1942–43) led to the deaths of between two and three million people. A group of American observers travelled to Yan'an to look at the Communist resistance to Japan where the enthusiasm and organisation provided a telling contrast with Chongqing, although for this positive report many were later to fall foul of Senator Macarthy.

The Communist victory After Japan's defeat in 1945, despite efforts at mediation by the Americans and continued pressure from Stalin on the Communists to lay down their arms and join the Nationalists, civil war finally broke out in 1946. In 1947 the Communist armies, which had been actively carrying out land reform to ensure the support of the people in the countryside, turned from guerrilla tactics to strategic offence. The separate armies attacked KMT troops in pincer movements and, as they went, captured an enormous number of weapons from the KMT army, which was being supplied both by the USA and the Soviet Union. Between 1948 and 1949 they gained decisive victories and on 1 October 1949 Mao stood on the great Gate of Heavenly Peace in Peking and proclaimed the Communist victory: 'The Chinese people have stood up...'.

Chiang Kai-shek and his followers had made preparations, removing treasures from the Palace Museum, which are now exhibited in Taipei, and gold to the island of Taiwan where they set up a Nationalist government.

The task faced by the Communists in 1949 was a daunting one. For a hundred years China had been torn by wars with foreign countries and finally the Japanese invasion and civil war had devastated agriculture and industry. Many of the factory-owners and managers, who at least had industrial experience, had fled to Hong Kong or Taiwan and foreign industrialists all left by the early 1950s.

Most experts agree that the Communists defeated the KMT for a combination of reasons: the skilful enlistment of the peasants through land reform and the involvement of the intellectual class which threw itself behind the war against Japan and the war against corruption in a 'nationalist' or patriotic movement; the powerful and visionary leadership of Mao Zedong, the effective collapse of the KMT, internally corrupt and unable to control inflation.

In the first years after 1949 there was unity in the task of national reconstruction. Among the first laws to be passed were the **Land Law**, giving men and women equal rights to hold land and involving the seizure of land from landlords which, in some parts of China was carried out with savagery, and the **Marriage Law**, outlawing arranged marriage. The central government presided over the remnants of a military organisation, for local government in the early years was organised on the basis of military regions. In government and in the take-over of industrial enterprises a triple alliance was instituted, consisting of trustworthy survivors of the previous administration (in factories this could include the factory owner if he had stayed behind), army representatives and party members.

Between 1951 and 1952, while China felt itself severely threatened by the Korean War, mass movements were organised throughout the country, to bring the entire population into the struggle against KMT supporters, to wipe out corruption in the Communist Party and bring its members into line and to clean up 'undesirable' elements.

In agriculture, land reform cut the land into small pieces which were individually worked by peasants who were encouraged to form 'mutual aid teams', pooling resources such as animals and ploughs. By the early 1950s these small teams had been largely reorganised into rural co-operatives which were larger than the teams. In 1956 the co-operatives were regularised by household, when it was stipulated that they should consist of 300 households in flat areas, 200 in hilly areas and 100 in true mountains where households were few and far between. They were subdivided into brigades of between 20 and 40 households, often reflecting the size of the previous 'mutual-aid teams'. In effect, most collectives were old villages.

In industry, the Soviet model and Soviet aid was of early significance. The Soviet Union had not been quick to recognise Mao's victory. Nevertheless, Soviet loans and expertise were essential, particularly in redeveloping heavy industry. The Soviet management model was followed, as was the Soviet system of five-year plans, and a large number of Soviet technical experts came to China to set up plant.

Mao's reforms The major movements of the 1950s and 1960s, the **Great Leap Forward** (1958) and the **Cultural Revolution** (1966–76), were launched with the aim of transforming the economy and purifying the Party, in the context of Soviet models which Mao increasingly felt to be inefficient and corrupt. Not all Chinese Party leaders agreed with him; some resisted, only to be dismissed; examples include Minister of Defence Peng Dehuai in 1959 for opposing the Great Leap and for continuing to advocate close ties with the USSR, as Mao took the opposite direction, and Liu Shaoqi, Chairman of the People's Republic, 1959–69, for opposing the Cultural Revolution.

The **Hundred Flowers Movement** of 1957 was a prelude to the Great Leap:

> *It is correct to let a hundred flowers blossom and a hundred schools of thought contend. Truth develops in the struggle with falsehood ... Good things and good men develop in comparison with and in struggle against bad men ... We people in the Communist Party know too little of our opponents...*

In response, intellectuals called for a loosening of Party control, academic freedom and a return to the work of legal reform, until in June, appalled at the flood of criticism it had unleashed, the Party turned on them in an 'anti-rightist movement'. Nearly ten per cent of the students at Peking University (the nation's most prestigious university) were denounced as 'rightists' and, together with many other critics, sent to the countryside for years of manual labour as a corrective.

Mao then turned to rural and industrial reforms, proclaiming in 1958 the foundation of the People's Communes, far larger collective units of local government than the previous collectives. It was envisaged that the commune would replace the family, providing communal meals and childcare to release more women for manual work. A further plan was for all communes to set up some form of industry, most commonly smelting plants to produce iron for farm tools. Mao called this ruralisation of industry 'walking on two legs', joking that Stalin only had one leg, which was heavy industry. In retrospect, although some aspects of the commune, such as widespread medical provision and the ability to organise a greater number of people to carry out irrigation and road-building, were positive, there were also many disasters. Apart from serious accidents in the smelting plants, the success of the Great Leap was compromised by the falsification of production figures. Local officials concealed problems with impossibly high figures causing the central authorities to set next year's projections even higher. These factors combined with natural disasters in the 'three disastrous years' of the early 1960s when harvests failed and tens of millions starved to death.

This new and unorthodox pattern of development together with Chinese attacks on Soviet foreign policy threatened Russia's traditional leadership of the Communist world. In 1960 all Soviet loans were frozen, projects abandoned and technicians withdrawn. Forced to readjust in the context of the disastrous harvests and Soviet withdrawal, the communes were reduced in size and centralised control of industrial enterprises was lessened. In 1961 private plots were reintroduced as an incentive to peasants to produce more for free sale.

While **Liu Shaoqi**, who had succeeded Mao as State Chairman in 1959, and **Deng Xiaoping** attempted to correct the worst excesses of the Great Leap and to improve the food supply, Mao went into semi-retirement. In 1965 he returned to the task of purifying the Communist Party which he saw as thoroughly corrupt, launching the **Cultural Revolution** against 'revisionists' and 'capitalists'. The campaign was so-named, taking the Marxist term 'culture' to cover all aspects of social organisation that were not part of the economic base, for Mao felt that after the industrial and agricultural base had been socialised, it was necessary to transform culture. It was wrong to study anything that did not have a direct connection with socialist transformation, it was wrong to read old novels or to watch Peking opera; the new culture should reflect nothing but the new society.

In launching the Cultural Revolution, Mao made great use of four people (later caricatured as the **Gang of Four**): Yao Wenyuan, editor-in-chief of the *Shanghai Liberation Army Daily*; Zhang Chunqiao, a propagandist and critic; Wang Hongwen, a young worker who rose to prominence during the Cultural Revolution in Shanghai; and Mao's third wife, an ex-film star called Jiang Qing.

Mao's first wife, Yang Kaihui, had been executed by the KMT in 1930, leaving two small sons: he then married He Zizhen who accompanied him on the Long March when their two children, left behind with peasants, disappeared forever. He was still married when Jiang Qing arrived in Yan'an from Shanghai but he soon divorced He Zizhen to marry Jiang Qing. As became quite clear during the televised trial of the Gang of Four (1980–81), Jiang Qing used the terror of the Cultural Revolution to eliminate those who knew about her past or who had offended her.

Mao called on the young to 'bombard the Headquarters' and for some years, the Cultural Revolution was an attack by the young on the old; students virtually seized power in many parts of China and were able to ransack houses and torture elderly writers, professors and intellectuals. Specialisation and expertise were regarded with suspicion and virtually all office workers and administrators, ballet-dancers, musicians, surgeons, specialists from museums and teachers had to spend years in backward parts of the countryside doing heavy manual work in order to understand the struggles of the peasants and the dignity of labour.

School children were sent off to the countryside in the same way, while many cities were 'ruled' by armies of young Red Guards who quarrelled amongst themselves and fought pitched battles in the city streets. The army was brought in to end street violence in 1968 and by 1971, the year which saw the mysterious death in a plane crash over Siberia of Mao's 'heir-apparent', Lin Biao, and the extraordinary announcement of President Nixon's impending visit, such irrational violence was over, although the country was still firmly controlled and directed. All institutions, whether factory, office or school, were run by 'revolutionary committees' consisting of representatives of army, party and 'masses' seeking to achieve the goals of the Cultural Revolution: the elimination of corruption and favoured positions and the establishment of absolute egalitarianism in the age of the 'new socialist man'. There were no more private plots in the countryside, no free markets, all was for the community, not the individual. There were no bonuses in the factories, only moral incentives. In education, the universities were reopened to 'worker-peasant-soldier' students, while the children of intellectuals were positively discriminated against. The goal of education was to produce socialists, not specialists.

Post Mao On 9 September 1976 Mao died. Just under a month later the Gang of Four was arrested on 6 October by the army guard unit appointed to the State Council, the highest administrative body of the state, which co-ordinates the work of the ministries. Within months the policies of the Cultural Revolution were abandoned, to great popular relief. Within a year, Mao's long-time opponent, Deng Xiaoping, emerged as the *de facto* leader of the state and put into practice the economic reforms that were pioneered in his native province of Sichuan by Hu Yaobang and Zhao Ziyang. The major priority was the development of the economy and to this end financial incentives (bonuses) were introduced in factories; land was once more allocated to peasant families and the family was made the basic agricultural production unit. Throughout the early 1980s the economy made great progress, particularly in agriculture where bustling free markets improved the quality of city life and made many peasants comparatively rich.

By the end of the 1980s, however, the economy was increasingly troubled by rising inflation and a general lack of control. There were serious shortages of power and fuel and a threatened shortage of grain, which peasants were abandoning in favour of cash crops. Deng Xiaoping's economic liberalism was not matched by political or cultural relaxation and intellectuals as well as city workers, the latter more strongly affected by rising inflation than the peasants, joined students in their call for democracy and an end to corruption. The movement for greater democracy was bloodily suppressed in Peking's Tiananmen Square on 4 June 1989.

Although many student leaders and intellectuals fled abroad, many others were arrested and their continuing detention, together with that of other political opponents of the regime, contrasted with China's desire to attract more international business and meant that Human Rights became an increasingly important aspect in international relations.

The 1990s saw the greatest physical change in China since the building of the treaty ports. Peasant families in the richer agricultural areas all built new houses, breaking with traditional designs and constructing multi-storeyed villas with moon gates, coloured tile decorations and blue glass windows. Rural architecture had previously demonstrated strong local traditions, from the black and white half-timbered farm-houses of Sichuan to the black painted doors outlined in red of the Xi'an area and the white-washed houses of Anhui with their black and white painted decoration at the top of the gables. It was thus possible to tell where you were from the form of the local houses but now they are internationalised and all similar.

In the towns of the richer eastern seaboard, massive high-rise buildings began to dominate city centres which, like the rural areas, lost their distinctiveness in a sea of mirrored glass. Motorways now link many cities, replacing the narrow old roads that passed through villages with carved wooden shop-fronts.

City centre shops are now filled with imported cosmetics and foodstuffs or their Chinese-made equivalents. Clothing and hair styles, jewellery and make-up are now international and the television, once a vehicle for propaganda and serious information, now shows game shows and imported soap operas. Many Chinese have become rich through commercial enterprise; there are now stock exchanges in the major centres, and many services devoted to the new rich, such as private schools for their children.

The gap between rich and poor is widening fast; with the poorer areas of the interior and northwest lagging far behind the eastern seaboard. Many parts of the old infrastructure are now crumbling: roads and ditches, once maintained by peasants organised through the People's Communes during the slack season, are no longer maintained by peasant families who prefer to concentrate on amassing family wealth. Poorer peasants from the interior flock to the cities to sell produce in the markets or seek work on the innumerable and rather dangerous building sites. Rural migrants can be found crowding station forecourts waiting for work and beggars are more widely seen although both groups are constantly harassed and moved on by the police. Such rural migration to the cities marks a 20th century version of the landless peasants forced off their land as dynasties declined and they are seen as a real threat to stability.

The death of Deng Xiaoping in 1997 caused no great upheaval; it had long been expected. In 1997 Hong Kong was handed back to China, an event that had been anticipated in the count-down clock that was put up in Tiananmen Square which was then re-wound for the count-down to the return of Macau to China in December 1999.

Chronological Table

Shang	c 1600–1066 BC	
Zhou	Western Zhou 1066–771 BC	
	Eastern Zhou 770–256 BC	
		Spring and Autumn Period 722–481 BC
		Warring States Period 403–221 BC
Qin	221–206 BC	
Han	Western Han 206 BC–AD 23	
	Eastern Han 25–220	
Three Kingdoms	Wei 220–265	
	Shu 221–263	
	Wu 222–280	
Western Jin	265–316	
Eastern Jin/ Sixteen Kingdoms	Eastern Jin 317–420	
	Sixteen Kingdoms 304–439	
Northern and Southern States	**Southern States**	Song 420–479
		Qi 479–502
		Liang 502–557
		Chen 557–589
	Northern States	Northern Wei 386–534
		Eastern Wei 534–550 Northern Qi 550–577

	Western Wei 535–557
	Northern Zhou 557–581
Sui	581–618
Tang	618–907
	Later Liang 907–923
	Later Tang 923–936
	Later Jin 936–946
Five Dynasties	Later Han 947–950
	Later Zhou 951–960
	Ten Kingdoms 902–979
Song	Northern Song 960–1127
	Southern Song 1127–1279
Liao	907–1125
Western Xia	1032–1227
Jin	1115–1234
Yuan	1279–1368
Ming	1368–1644
Qing	1644–1911
Republic	1912–1949
People's Republic	1949–

Emperors of the Qing dynasty (1644–1911)

Emperors	reigned
Shunzi	1644–1662
Kangxi	1662–1722
Yongzheng	1723–1735
Qianlong	1736–1795
Jiaqing	1796–1820
Daoguang	1821–1850
Xianfeng	1851–1861
Tongzhi	1862–1874
Guangxu	1875–1908
Xuantong	1909–1911

Religion and Beliefs

The two major indigenous systems of thought in China, **Confucianism** and **Taoism**, arose at about the same time in the 5C BC. Neither was originally a 'religion', Confucianism being a reiteration of current moral values which became the basis of the imperial cult and Taoism a system of belief based upon a harmonisation of man with the natural order. Taoism, in particular, saw a split between the original philosophy and a developing popular religion closely associated with alchemy which sought to find an elixir of long life. Both added to the gradual growth of a mixed 'popular religion' which came to dominate popular belief after the Tang dynasty.

Two non-indigenous religions came to play an important part in Chinese life. **Buddhism**, which entered China during the Han dynasty (206 BC–AD 220) permeated Chinese life to a great extent, achieving its greatest power during the Tang dynasty when it was ruthlessly suppressed by Tang emperors concerned about the wealth and power of the great monasteries and temples. It survived the suppression although it never reached the same heights and many of its deities and tenets were incorporated into popular religion. **Islam**, which entered China soon after its inception (in the 7C), was largely concentrated in the far northwest (Xinjiang province) but uprisings, uncertainties and persecutions in that area led to massive migrations so that Chinese Muslims can now be found scattered throughout China, although they are still most numerous in Xinjiang and the northwest.

Confucius Confucius is a Latinised version of *Kong fu zi* ('Master Kong') a term used by the Jesuit missionaries to China in the 17C. Confucius was born in Qu Fu in the State of Lu in 551 BC and what little is known about his life is mainly gleamed from the *Lun yu* (usually translated as the *Analects*), a collection of his statements made by his disciples, probably after his death. He is thought to have become Chief of Police in the state of Lu but to have left suddenly in 497. Explanations for his precipitate departure vary; some suggest it was because he disapproved of the arrival of singing girls, whilst his most famous disciple Mencius (c 372–288 BC) suggests that it was because the State of Lu failed to observe the proper rites (or ritual). He travelled, attempting to influence other rulers but, unsuccessful, eventually returned to Qu Fu where he died in 479 BC. The *Analects* are full of detail about the Master, how he avoided dark purple and maroon silk for collars and cuffs and did not wear red or violet informal robes, how he lifted his gown and held his breath when he entered his master's hall and ate sparingly, although the only rule he set himself with regard to alcohol was to stop drinking before he became confused. The impression is that of a rather pedantic and extremely fussy person, who could not sit if his mat was not straight and would not talk in bed, although D.C. Lau (who has translated the *Analects*), describes him as 'a man whose life was full of joy'. The 'joys' he lists: eating coarse rice and drinking water, eschewing wealth immorally gained and going swimming in spring 'with five or six adults and six or seven boys ... and then to go home chanting poetry' are the joys of a scout master.

Confucius is associated with a group of texts, the *Five Classics* (*Shi jing* or 'Book of Songs', *Shu jing* or 'Book of Documents', *Yi jing* or 'Book of Changes', *Chun Qiu* or 'Spring and Autumn Annals' and the *Li ji* or 'Record of Rituals') and the *Four Books*: the *Analects*, the *Mencius* and two chapters from the *Li ji*: 'Great Learning' and the 'Doctrine of the Mean'. A later classification of relevant texts lists 13 'classics': the *Five Classics* (with the *Chun qiu* counting as three when accompanied by three major commentaries on it, including the *Zuo zhuan*), the *Analects*, the *Mencius*, the *Xiao jing* (or 'Classic of Filial Piety', a 3C or 2C BC reworking of elements in the *Li ji*), the *Er ya* (a 3C BC collection of glosses on the texts, forerunner of later Chinese dictionaries), the *Yi li* ('Ceremonials and Rituals') and the *Zhou li* ('Rituals of Zhou', a Confucian reconstruction of the supposed governmental system of the early Zhou dynasty of almost 1000 years before). The inclusion of texts relating to the early Zhou (11C–8C BC) is important for Confucius used to insist that he was not an innovator but simply that he wished to return to the great era of the Duke of Zhou (Zhou gong). The duke was the brother of the king who overthrew the Shang dynasty (in either 1122 or 1027 BC) and who effectively consolidated Zhou rule.

The ideas which Confucius expressed were those current during his lifetime, with his own stress on the duty of rulers to set an ethical example. Although he acknowledged the existence of heaven and the spirits, he did not often discuss the after-life or the spiritual side of human experience. In order to return to the order of the golden age of the past, he believed it was important for all to recognise their place in society and to act accordingly. One of his most famous tenets is: 'Let the ruler be a ruler and the subject a subject; the father a father and the son a son'. This idea of making a concept into reality, with the ruler acting in accordance with the theory of rule, was later greatly expanded in 'the rectification of names'.

Order in society did not stop with the relationships between ruler and subject, father and son, for his concepts of subordination (common at the time) included the absolute subordination of women, not only to their husbands but also to their sons. Correct relationships between men and women were not only dependent on acceptance of subordination but also governed by contemporary rules of propriety. These rules were elaborated over the centuries, to the point that a Ming work on the correct running of a household contained a map with marked paths through the maze of courtyards to be used either by men or by women. If they adhered to these paths, they would not meet, which was proper, for in extended family groups there were people in different kinship relations who should not enjoy encounters. A Confucian dilemma was that of whether it was proper for a man to rescue his sister-in-law (whom he should not touch) from drowning by holding out his hand to her.

The concept of government by ethical example and of the 'gentleman', versed in literature, music and the rites, were the most important ideas developed by Confucius. These were set in the context of two ideas: those of 'the Way' and of virtue. D.C. Lau suggests that for Confucius, 'the Way' is virtually synonymous with 'Truth' in western religion and philosophy and that virtue is conferred by heaven but must be cultivated in order to govern properly. Neither of these were original ideas but were current at the time. As he laid little stress on rewards after death, for Confucius the pursuit of morality was a duty to be undertaken for its own sake. Men who did so were *jun zi* or 'gentlemen', the rest were 'small men', effectively synonymous with rulers and subjects. The major attribute of the gentleman was *ren* or 'benevolence', a word stretched infinitely to encompass 'do as you would be done by', loving others and not exploiting small men inappropriately. Loving others was set against the background of the family system and one's first duty of love and loyalty was to the immediate family. An interesting passage in the *Analects* occurs where someone criticised a man known as 'Straight' because he reported his father to the authorities for stealing a sheep. Confucius retorted that in his village it was 'straight' to stand up for your relatives.

A further stretching of 'benevolence' took it to include rites (rituals, including sacrifices, which expressed ancient views of morality). Other aspects of the gentleman include his attention to the study of literature and music and other gentlemanly skills such as archery, charioteering, writing and mathematics. But it is above all the gentleman who has cultivated *ren*, courage, reliability, reverence and respectfulness and righteousness, who is fit to rule. The two major relevant passages in the *Analects* state: 'Guide them by edicts, keep them in line with punishments and the common people will stay out of trouble but will have no sense of shame' but 'Guide them by virtue, keep them in line with the rites and they will, besides having a sense of shame, reform themselves' (D.C. Lau, *The Analects*, Penguin, 1979).

The success of Confucianism in China lay in its theoretical stimulus to 'good government' and its usefulness as a philosophy for the bureaucracy which was growing as China moved from fragmentation to centralised government. It provided a theoretical basis for the traditional idea of the 'mandate of heaven' by which a ruler governed and which could be withdrawn if he failed to set a fine moral example. The collapse of enfeebled dynasties in natural disasters and peasant uprisings, both either exacerbated or directly inspired by the failure of central government to protect the livelihood of its subjects, were explained in terms of the withdrawal of heaven's mandate from an unfit ruler.

The subjects that a Confucian gentleman was expected to master became the basis for the examinations for entry into the imperial bureaucracy first established during the Han dynasty. Candidates memorised vast tracts of the Confucian classic texts and practised writing essays of commentary on these works; their education was liberal but not necessarily very practical as a preparation for government. Although the basic texts (the foundation of the examination 'syllabus') remained unchanged for 2000 years, commentaries grew. During the Song (960–1279) there was a massive renewal of interest in the Confucian texts, a revival of interest in the past, which extended to archaeology and the decorative arts, and a re-examination of the Confucian texts in the light of a new era. This movement to re-examine the Confucian texts and theories is known as **Neo-Confucianism**.

Interestingly, there is no term for 'Confucianism' in China; what we would call 'Confucian scholars' are simply known as *ju* or 'scholars'. The dominance of the literati in traditional China was such that the physical attributes of the scholar (paleness, weakness to the point of anaemia and long fingernails) were those of all the heroes of novels and dramas, whilst tall, strong robust men were generally villainous or 'small' in heroic terms. Aside from cultural heroes, some of the ideas associated with Confucianism (while not in fact innovations of the Master) that have survived longest in China include filial piety, which is not only a moral but also a legal duty in contemporary China where it is an offence for people to fail to take care of their elderly parents, and veneration for education. The importance of family loyalty, mentioned by Confucius in connection with informing on a sheep-stealing parent; see above) was also written into the traditional legal system; families were also held responsible for errant members and disgrace could affect an entire group. The same principle persists in China; in 1949, people were given class labels on the basis of parental status. These were hard to shake off and families are still communally disgraced by a single offender. One of the grimmest reminders of family responsibility is the fact that today families are expected to pay a tiny sum for the bullet used to kill a condemned family member.

Legalism The severity of punishments in contemporary China perhaps owes something to another strand of thought that flourished briefly during the reign of the First Emperor of the Qin, Shi huangdi (reigned 221–210 BC). Legalism disparaged Confucian thought with its assumption of the basic goodness of man. Rather than lead men through precept and example, the Legalists considered that human beings could only be controlled through the application of a strictly enforced series of rules and regulations. Their prescriptions, which covered all aspects of life, led to another long-surviving principle, the concept of the 'height' of legal responsibility. In 20C China, a metre-high mark beside ticket offices and on the doors of buses was used to determine when a child should pay full fare.

Taoism Taoism, whose major philosophers lived at about the same time as Confucius, can be seen as the antithesis of his views, although some of the terms used are the same, for the historical background was identical. The first figure is **Lao zi** (c 570–490 BC) said to have been an archivist and 'keeper of the lacquer grove' (lacquer, the sap of an indigenous tree, was an important, taxable product, protecting the timber of buildings and used as a water-, heat- and acid-proof covering for food vessels). He is traditionally viewed as the author of the *Dao de jing* (*Classic of the Way and of Virtue*; *Tao te ching* in Wade-Giles), a somewhat mystic collection of passages (probably a composite text dating from the 3C BC and which, according to a recent discovery, should probably be renamed the *De dao jing*). Part of the mysterious quality of the work derives from the fact that it attempts to describe the indescribable, the *dao*. Many of the descriptions are essentially non-descriptions in the form of 'without it, X would not be X'; 'without what makes it full, a valley might run dry'; 'without what makes it settled, the earth might sink' and so on.

The *dao* is the source of all life, the hidden principle. An ideal human state exemplifying the *dao* is that of a baby, soft and supple, attributes that are borne out by mention of the contrast between a living person, 'supple and weak' and a 'hard and stiff' corpse.

A more accessible text is that of the *Zhuang zi*, also probably 3C BC but attributed to **Zhuang zi** (c 369–286 BC). A wonderful collection of parables, metaphors and poetry, the *Zhuang zi* conveys more of the Taoist ideal of suppleness in fitting in with natural patterns. For example, Zhuang zi was found cheerfully singing and drumming on an upturned bowl (a baby-like state) after the death of his wife. He explained to a shocked visitor that:

> *Man's being has its seasons, its sequence of spring and autumn, summer and winter. If someone is tired and gone to lie down, we do not pursue him with shouting and bawling. She whom I have lost has lain down to sleep for a while in the Great Inner Room. To break in upon her rest with noise of lamentation would but show that I know nothing of nature's sovereign law... .*

(Arthur Waley, *Three Ways of Thought in Ancient China*, London 1939)

Another major concept in Taoism was that of *wu wei*, 'non-action' or 'inaction', the opposite of Confucian 'activity' in the form of organisation and government.

Later Taoism was divided into various schools, some more contemplative, seeking to learn from nature by retirement from the world into mountain retreats, some more active in the pursuit of an elixir of life. The former contemplatives are considered by Joseph Needham, author and 'overseer' of the fascinating and encyclopaedic *Science and Civilisation in China* (Cambridge University Press) to have practically reached Darwinian ideas of natural selection through their earnest contemplation of nature in the search for its essential 'pattern' to which they sought to cleave. He has also found much of interest and amusement in the alchemical searches for the elixir of life, which involved some unfortunately explosive accidents.

The search for eternal life had its roots in an earlier Chinese belief that physical immortality, or the preservation of the body after death, conferred longer life on the soul. Chinese burial practices included the use of jade (in the Han, jade 'bodysuits' of hundreds of tiny plaques joined by gold and silver wire), which was believed to preserve the body, as well as various forms of preservation and occasional deliberate mummification. The Taoists took the matter further, eating gold and poisons like cinnabar and setting off on sea voyages to Penglai, the islands of the immortals.

In simple terms, the two major ways of thought can be seen as contributing to the traditional concept of the scholar. In his early life he devoted himself to study in preparation for the exams which led to a place in the imperial bureaucracy and government service; in his leisure and when he retired, he would ideally retreat to a mountain cottage to drink wine, write poetry (full of natural imagery), paint and practise calligraphy. A popular saying in China which sums up the different ways of thought and their relevance to stages in life refers to the gentleman as 'Confucian in office, Taoist in retirement and Buddhist as death approaches'.

Buddhism in China Confucianism was very much to do with life and although Taoism dealt with the fact of death, its matter-of-fact approach did not allow for the consolation of ceremonial, which **Chinese Buddhism** provided. I use the term Chinese Buddhism for the philosophy of the North Indian founder of the faith, Sakyamuni (c 566–486 BC), was a rather bleak, distinctly unceremonial and reclusive search for enlightenment through abstention from desire.

Buddhism was transformed gradually in China. It seems to have arrived, via Central Asia, before or during the Later Han (AD 25–220) but its influence grew after the period of disunion that followed the fall of the Han, when the official 'Confucian' ideology of the guiding centralised state had clearly failed. After the re-establishment of central power under the Sui (581–618) tension between the state and the growing Buddhist monasteries was accompanied by tension between family worship (ancestor worship, antedating but sanctioned by Confucius) and the seclusion of the monastic system, integral to Buddhism. For the state, the wealth and consequent economic power of the tax-free monasteries was an economic threat; similarly, seclusion in a monastery, which meant that an individual could not carry out the essential duty of feeding and caring for the ghosts of his ancestors, was a real threat to the social order.

Several major persecutions of Buddhism, particularly under the Tang (618–907), meant that China never became a Buddhist state, although Buddhism entered and contributed to popular beliefs, especially those concerning death and the after-life. When Buddhist texts were first translated into Chinese (in large numbers from the mid 2C AD), translators borrowed from existing Taoist ideas of eremitism, meditation (Taoist contemplation of nature) and Taoist magic ritual, associated with Buddhist Tantrism, all of which have been discussed at length by Erik Zurcher in his *Buddhist Conquest of China* (Leiden, 1959).

The greatest contribution of Chinese thought to Buddhism was the development of the **Chan** (Japanese Zen) **school** which, in simple terms, provided the possibility of sudden enlightenment to the lay person, against the prevailing theory that enlightenment was only available to those who withdrew from family life into a monastery. Popular religion made most use of the power of the Amitabha Buddha who presided over the 'pure land' or western Paradise, where pure souls might find a haven after death. The Buddhist holy mountain of Jiuhua shan in Anhui, dedicated to Ksitigarbha, the Boddhisattva who led souls to the western Paradise, sees many two-part funerary services in which the Boddhisattva Ksitigarbha first 'judges' the soul of the dead and then the Boddhisattva Amitabha receives the soul into paradise.

Feng shui, Yi jing, and the Chinese horoscope Other aspects of popular belief drew upon a variety of sources: Taoist priests presided over the choice of a site for buildings and tombs and an auspicious date for works to commence according to the *feng shui* system. *Feng shui* (literally 'wind and water') texts date back to the Han but the system certainly antedates the texts. It prescribes the siting of buildings, oriented southward, with hills to the north and water nearby, all eminently practical aspects overlaid by post-facto textual justification, and the use of the geomancer's compass, marked with the hexagrams and trigrams also used in the classic of divination, the *Yi jing*. Geomancy, whilst practised all over China, seems to have been strongest in the south, probably because of the practice there of secondary burial. In the north bodies were buried once, under rounded mounds, which can still be seen in the fields. Graves in the south were more elaborate affairs, with horseshoe-shaped walls protecting the mound. It was common practice to bury bodies for a period of a year or two in temporary graves then they were dug up, the bones scraped clean and sometimes crushed by relatives performing a filial duty, placed in small ceramic urns with elaborately decorated lids and buried in a second, permanent grave. Geomancers were also often responsible for the erection of pagodas on hilltops to avert local disasters and they are still used widely in Hong Kong, not only in the siting of new buildings but in the periodic rearrangement of office furniture to improve a company's fortune.

The eight trigrams (providing all possible combinations of a series of three broken and unbroken lines) used in divination, consulting the *Yi jing* and a handful of yarrow (or milfoil) sticks, are not the only numerical group of significance in China. The somewhat mysterious Ten Heavenly Stems are combined with the Twelve Earthly Branches to form the 60-year cycle, the Chinese equivalent of our century. Traditional dates were always written in the form of a stem and a branch, indicating where they came in the 60-year cycle, although not in which cycle the date fell. Personal horoscopes were cast in the form of stems and branches, as well as the 12-year cycle represented by 12 animals, and were used to judge the suitability of marriage partners. The 12 animals are the rat, ox, tiger, hare, dragon, snake, horse, sheep, monkey, cockerel, dog and pig (2001 is a snake year, 2002 will be a horse year, etc).

Taoist priests also carried out exorcisms and provided spells for all sorts of events, most notably in the case of disease. Magical formulae were written on pieces of paper which were burnt and the ashes made into a sort of tea to be drunk by the patient: another example of the view of the power of words in China.

Christianity Christianity, whose 19C and 20C missionaries made valiant attempts to wipe out such superstitions, was said by one expert to have arrived too late in China, when the popular pantheon was already overcrowded with a deity for every occasion and every social group. The **Jesuits**, the first major group of missionaries to arrive in China (in the last years of the 16C), sought to influence the emperor and the court, believing that the whole of China would then follow. Other groups of Catholic missionaries followed, jealous of the Jesuits' success at court, which was mainly won by skilful calendrical and math-ematical calculation, cannon casting and artistic and architectural skills.

The **Rites Controversy** which raged in the 18C over whether or not ancestral rituals could be performed by Christian converts (Pope Clement XI in 1715 and Pope Benedict XIV in 1742 were against this) was largely responsible for the decline of Jesuit influence, followed by the suppression of the order in 1774. They achieved a degree of popular success in that Matteo Ripa did join the Chinese popular pantheon as the patron saint of watchmakers. The Jesuits were succeeded by the **Lazarists** but the greatest influx of Christian missionaries, now including non-Catholics, came after the enforced opening of China to the outside world after the Opium Wars in 1843. Converts were made, although the faith has only survived in any strength in the coastal treaty ports, and medical missionaries opened the first western-style hospitals in China, most notably the Rockefeller-funded Peking Union Hospital (which, until it reassumed its original name in the 1980s, was previously the Peking No. 1 Hospital). Some strange small sects survive, notably a group of ranters in Fujian who are subject to pub-lic order complaints as they shout loudly during services.

Religion today In contemporary China religion is not outlawed by the consti-tution, but preaching is. There are sizable Christian communities in the old treaty ports and Christianity is currently enjoying something of a vogue amongst the young. The Catholic Church has been split: the Protestant groups banded together soon after 1949 and formed a 'patriotic' organisation with a first loyalty to the state; whilst some Catholics did the same, others insisted on the primacy of the Pope and have suffered imprisonment in consequence.

Islam is still strong, mainly in the northwest, but it is Buddhism in its popular form that remains the most widely followed religion. Even during the Cultural Revolution both Islam and Buddhism gained some strength from the support of overseas co-religionists, whilst Taoism, a uniquely Chinese system of belief, suf-fered, especially because of superstitious practices such as making spells and talismans. Today there is a growth in the study of philosophical, if not religious, Taoism. Similarly, Confucianism declined with the end of the traditional state but many of its tenets persist, particularly those relating to family observances and respect for authority and education.

Art, Craft, and Architecture

Painting

Although wall paintings have survived in tombs and cave temples, the fragility of most Chinese painting, together with the painters' training, which consisted largely of making exact copies of great works of the past, make the attribution and dating of paintings in China extremely difficult. Chinese painting is usually done on paper or silk, using a brush and, frequently, black ink alone. The ink was made from soot or lampblack, mixed with animal glue and scents such as musk or camphor to hide the smell of the glue. The ink was then pressed into moulds, often impressed with delicate designs and good inksticks could be extremely expensive and valued as heirlooms. Brushes were made of animal hairs glued into bamboo (occasionally enamel or porcelain) tubes. The hard inkstone was ground and mixed with water on an inkslab, made of slate or jade, carved with a shallow depression at one end. Depending on the amount of water mixed, the ink would be solid and black or a thin grey wash; shades of black and grey are found in traditional paintings.

From the Zhu Pu *(Primer of Bamboo)*

Painting manuals contained examples of mountains, huts, bamboos, pines, figures and other essential elements of the classic painting. The amateur would copy these endlessly until he had mastered every detail and only then would he feel confident that he could combine such elements into his own painting. Innovators who developed the possibilities of the ink and wash include: **Ni Zan** (1301–74) with his 'dry brush' style, **Liang Kai**'s impressionistic portraits (13C), his near-contemporary, **Mu Qi**'s *Six Persimmons*, similarly simple and impressionistic, **Shi Tao** (1630–1707), whose *Ten-thousand Ugly Ink-blots* starts with splashes which are combined into a long landscape scroll (Suzhou Museum), and **Zhu Da** (or Ba da shan ren; 1626–1705), whose solidly blocked fish and brooding birds form dark abstract forms on the white paper.

Very few paintings which can be attributed with certainty survive from before the Song. Exceptions include the **silk scroll** from the Han dynasty (206 BC–AD 220) **Mawangdui Tomb** (Changsha) and the **wall paintings** at **Dunhuang**, dating from the Tang, which show the beginnings of a great landscape style in the background to paintings of the life of the Buddha. Literary reference provides more information on the development of traditional ink and wash painting: Xie He's *Gu hua pin lu* (*Classification of Ancient Paintings*) of the 6C AD described the principles, which included composition and placing of elements, transmission by copying ancient models, accurate use of colour and accurate depiction and the first and most important principle of 'spirit resonance' by which the painter had to 'become' the subject before he could paint it.

There were various groups of painters in China: those who were paid for their paintings (craftsmen), amateurs and educated gentlemen like the Tang painter, **Yan Liben**, who devoted himself to painting while holding a variety of official positions, Senior Secretary of the Peerage Bureau, President of the Board of Works and Minister of State.

Two major schools During the Song two major 'schools' of Chinese painting emerged, one based upon the **Imperial Painting Academy** set up (on the basis of previous academies) by the Hui zong emperor (reigned 1101–26). The favoured style in the Academy was delicately naturalistic, depicting birds and flowers on silk album leaves. Every feather of the bird, every petal and leaf of each flowering branch was painted with minute attention to detail of appearance and, in the pursuit of accuracy, jewel-like coloured pigments were used. This '**academic**' style continued in favour throughout succeeding centuries, co-existing with the very different '**literati**' style. The latter was more scholarly in theory, basing itself on such essays as Xie He's. It was both style and subject matter which distinguished the academic and literati painters; the former concentrating on natural detail in birds and flowers, the latter expressing the grandeur of nature in lofty monochrome mountain scenes.

Landscapes Guo Xi (c 1020–90), himself a major landscape painter, described the painter's methods for depicting depth and distance which help in the reading of a landscape with its various viewpoints, a technique quite distinct from that of the western landscape, viewed from a fixed spot. First is *jin yuan* ('near distance') where the viewer looks across a flat ground into the distance; next, *shen yuan* ('deep distance') where the viewer appears to be standing on a raised area in the foreground; and, finally, *gao yuan* ('high distance') where the viewer looks up from the foreground to towering mountains. These principles are best expressed in hanging scrolls, although they are also used to provide a series of landscape foci in handscrolls. To aid the viewer to take the appropriate viewpoint, a tiny figure is often included in the foreground and landscapes often include small huts with scholarly recluses enjoying wine or music, attended by small boy servants or figures approaching these rustic retreats on donkey-back, again with a small boy carrying a *qin* ('zither') or rolls of paper for painting.

Because of their fragility and the fugitive nature of the colours, Chinese paintings were never intended for permanent display. Handscrolls and albums were kept closed in damp-proof camphorwood boxes until friends came round and then they would be unrolled and enjoyed in company, the landscapes of handscrolls gradually unfolding as they were unrolled. Even hanging scrolls would be put up only when visitors arrived or on special occasions. Great care would be taken to choose the right painting for the occasion, with huge calligraphic scrolls of auspicious characters reserved for birthdays and paintings reflecting the seasons hung as appropriate.

The ancestral portrait and genre painting Other types of painting include the decorative ancestral portrait. Often produced in pairs (husband and wife), these were usually posthumous paintings of the deceased dressed in wonderfully lavish silken clothing with, in the case of men, all their official regalia. Another type, scorned by the literati, less colourful than the academic paintings but just as detailed, is the 'genre' painting, depicting bustling street scenes and events. The best known example is the 11C–12C handscroll by **Zhang Zeduan**, *Going Up the River on the Eve of the Qing Ming Festival*, depicting the busy streets of Kaifeng in ink and wash.

In the Ming there was a fashion for a sort of combination 'genre' and academic painting of children at play, showing every detail of the children's faces, clothing and top-knotted hairstyles as well as their games, but using colour (unlike Zhang Zeduan). In the Qing imperial events were often depicted in this colourful, detailed style and there are many examples in the collections in the Gu gong (Forbidden City Museum in Peking, where the original of the Zhang Zeduan painting is also held). The oldest paintings in the imperial collection (pre-Ming) are only displayed in October when the weather conditions are best, being neither too hot nor too damp.

Painting in the 20C Painting is still immensely popular in China and remains an amateur enthusiasm as well as an art-school speciality. Two major painters of the 20C helped to bring a new vitality to brush painting: **Qi Baishi** (1863–1957), whose strong black brush-strokes are combined with equally strong splashes of colour, and **Xu Beihong** (1896–1953). Xu studied in Paris in the 1930s and was a master of both western oils and traditional Chinese brush painting, painting the galloping horses (1944) that were popular in the West in the 1950s. Like Qi Baishi, he combines colour with his strong brush strokes in many of his paintings. There are a number of Xu Beihong's paintings in the Shanghai Museum and a special museum devoted to his work, with models of his studio, in the north of Peking.

Ceramics

There were two major ceramic types during the Neolithic period, a fine-grained reddish earthenware associated with the Yangshao culture (5–3 millennium BC), sometimes decorated with mainly black pigments in geometric and animal designs (seen in the Neolithic village of Banpo, outside Xi'an), and a fine black burnished ware made on the wheel produced by the Longshan culture. Particularly in the Longshan, the forms of ceramic vessels, including a high-footed cup and many forms of tripod, appear to anticipate the succeeding Bronze Age forms.

Bronze Age During the Bronze Age (c 1500 BC–4C BC) ceramics were used in daily life although they were subordinate in ritual (and therefore in burial) to bronzes. Even so, during this period there was a technical breakthrough in the manufacture of **stonewares**. The clays used for stoneware can be fired to a higher temperature than earthenware and at these higher temperatures they fuse to form a relatively impermeable (waterproof) body which is harder and more resilient than earthenware. The stonewares were often partially glazed with a transparent glaze on the shoulder of vessels. Green lead glazes appeared in the Han when ceramics were very widely used in burial. Models of houses, granaries, farmyards with pigs in their sties and watchdogs curled up inside the gate, human figures playing board games, all made in low-fired earthenware covered with a green lead glaze, were placed in tombs to accompany the spirit to the next world.

Yue ware and porcelain In the period after the fall of the Han such models were still made, although often in the olive-glazed stoneware characteristic of southern China and known as **Yue ware** after the southern kingdom of Yue (southeast China). Water-droppers, for use with inksticks and brushes in calligraphy or painting, chicken-headed ewers and shallow dishes, sometimes carved with a simple lotus flower design symbolising Buddhism, which had just entered China, were also common Yue ware products.

The same period saw the gradual development of **porcelain**, which first appeared in Sui tombs. Made from special clays, which vary slightly from north to south China, although they are always feldspathic, porcelains are high-fired, with the glaze fused completely with the body, translucent, if the body is thin enough, and make a musical note when struck. During the Tang, plain white porcelains were used as practical, durable and non-porous containers for food and drink. They were also exported in great quantities and have been found at contemporary sites in Egypt and along the African coast. Porcelain remained a mystery, first to Arab travellers and later to westerners, until the early 18C when Böttger managed to make true porcelain at Meissen.

Funerary ceramics during the Tang Tang funerary ceramics were very different from the elegant monochrome porcelain. Following the Han tradition, models were still placed in tombs to accompany the spirit but while the Han stressed ordinary life, with an accent on agricultural production in the farmyard and fishfarm models, the Tang, the great age of overseas trade, elegance and wealth, stressed these even in burial models. Made of earthenware, splashed with blue, green, yellow, brown and cream glazes, Tang funerary models are of all-female orchestras, fat fashionable court ladies (reflecting changes in current fashions and the devastating effect of the concubine Yang Guifei on the female form), officials in high hats and camels and horses, representing the trade with Central Asia. Some of the horses had real horsehair tails and manes. These funerary models were mass-produced in piece-moulds, and produced as matching sets. There were sumptuary regulations, just as there had been during the Han, forbidding excessive consumption at funerals and restricting both the number of figures and their maximum height (about 30cm), but these regulations were frequently broken, as museum exhibits testify.

Most ceramics dating from these early periods and now to be seen in museums, were funerary wares, produced specifically for the grave. Although they may reflect styles and forms used in daily life, they must be primarily considered in terms of their funerary function. During the Han, for example, the rich did not use pottery vessels at table, but ate and drank from lacquer vessels and, during the Tang, gold and silver dishes were similarly used, although the invention of more durable porcelain meant that vessels of porcelain began to be used in daily life.

Liao dynasty In the period between the Tang and Song, the most notable ceramics were those produced by the northern dynasty of the Liao (947–1125; founded by a Mongolian group). Surviving Liao ceramics are funerary earthenwares using the same palette as the Tang but in rather eccentric shapes of a particular elegance. They include elongated ceramic versions of the leather water-bottles used by nomadic horsemen.

Song dynasty The Song was one of the great periods of ceramic production with a multitude of kilns, north and south, producing a variety of ceramics from stonewares to porcelain in distinct types of kiln: most notably coal-fired *mantou* (or 'steamed bread bun') kilns in the north, and long 'dragon kilns' in the south, built up hillsides and invariably wood-fired. Porcelain production was beginning to concentrate in the south where the best clays were to be found and translucent vessels with a glassy glaze with a blueish tinge (*qingbai* or 'blue-white') are characteristic of the south while northern porcelain, often known by its kiln name of Ding, was a creamy colour, frequently with moulded designs. Ding bowls were fired upside down on bare rims which were later bound with dark brown copper bands, providing an elegant contrast with the cream coloured body. Another major northern ware used the same techniques of production: wheel-thrown plates and bowls were pressed onto moulds carved with floral designs and then covered with an olive green glaze. Known to the Chinese as 'green ware', sometimes further distinguished by its kilnname, the European name of **'celadon'** was first applied by the French, borrowing the name from a character who wore green-grey clothing in *Astrée*, an 18C French play by D'Urfé.

Southern green wares (or celadons) of the Song were also covered with an iron-oxide glaze but their blue-green colour reflects the different physical conditions in the kilns. Other northern wares whose glaze colour was also based on iron oxide, were the grey blue Ru ware, crackled Guan and the grey-blue suffused with purple known as Jun. Ru is extremely rare, produced at the northern imperial kilns (in Kaifeng) where manufacture was interrupted after only a few years when the north of China was invaded and the court fled south to Hangzhou (1127). Only some 30-odd examples are known and most are in collections outside China.

Before widespread excavation of kiln sites (mainly after 1949), it was thought that ceramic kilns specialised in one particular ware and, indeed, traditional Chinese connoisseurs often referred to ceramics by the name of the kiln as an indicator of type. Excavation has revealed a more complex picture: although kilns did tend to produce more of one kind of ware, in northern kilns specialising in white wares, for example, numbers of black and green shards have also been found. Thus, although black-glazed wares are often known as **Jian wares** (after a kiln in Fujian province), black glazed shards have been found in a large number of other kiln sites. Jian wares were very popular in Japan where they are known as *temmoku*. The majority of those that found their way to Japan were probably produced in Fujian whose ports saw a vast volume of trade with Japan (and Korea and Southeast Asia) during the Song. Dark-toned Jian wares were predominantly large tea bowls, used in the Japanese tea ceremony, with a glaze that was subtly spotted with silver ('oil spot') or streaked with dark brown ('hare's fur'). These effects were also produced by manipulating iron oxide in the glaze. The way that the thick glaze gathered in drips near the foot was also much appreciated by the Japanese who like the combination of haphazard unevenness of surface with the perfection of body form.

With one major exception, most Song ceramics relied for their dramatic effect on their elegant form and monochrome glaze. The moulded designs on some northern vessels remains a subtle, underglaze effect. The exception is known as **Cizhou ware** (after the Cizhou kilns in Hebei), a stoneware covered with a cream glaze and surface-decorated either by carving down through the slip to the greyer body beneath or by painting, usually in dark brown, sometimes red and green, floral designs or scenes from novels and folk stories.

The overall decoration of Cizhou wares may have been one inspiration for a major development in ceramic taste which occurred during the Yuan, the development of 'underglaze blue' or 'blue and white' wares. Other Yuan ceramics continued Song styles, although the vessels tended to be rather more massive, compared with their slim and elegant predecessors. The technique of blue and white underglaze painting, using cobalt on the body of the vessel (over a white slip) before covering with a translucent glaze and firing the vessel, was a complicated one, particularly because porcelain is fired at such high temperatures that many colouring materials behave unpredictably. Previously, coloured glazes had been applied to earthenwares or stonewares which were fired at lower temperatures. During the Yuan, at the same time as they experimented with cobalt blue, the Chinese potters also tried to use copper to produce an underglaze red effect but the results, which can be seen in many museums, were unsuccessful for the red is often greyish; copper did not behave as predictably as cobalt.

The origins of **blue and white ware** are complex for the cobalt was imported from the Near East; Chinese native cobalt contained a lot of manganese, which was difficult to control and was not used until methods of purification were perfected in the 15C. Many of the designs, too, painted on vessels were taken directly from the incised floral scrolls on Near Eastern metalwork. This has led some to assume that the technique itself originated in Persia. The major feature, however, was the use of porcelain; while other nations could use cobalt on earthenware, none but the Chinese could make porcelain at this time, and there are also the experiments in underglaze red which were conducted in China. It must be concluded that this was a Chinese invention based on imported cobalt and imported metalwork designs, facilitated by the *pax mongolica* which reigned from China across the Gobi into the Near East, allowing free trade through the Mongol dominions. Almost as soon as the technique was perfected, huge blue and white vessels began to make their way back across Central Asia to Turkey and Persia where there are impressive collections of early 14C Chinese blue and white ware in the Topkapi Museum in Istanbul and at the Ardebil shrine (in Iran).

Throughout the Yuan and the Ming blue and white ware was improved. The achievements can be seen in the contrast between the thick, heavy vessels of the Yuan with their uneven spotted blue decoration and the tiny, light and translucent bowls of the Chenghua period (mid 15C) with their pure sky-blue floral scrolls.

Ming dynasty Although blue and white porcelain dominates Ming ceramics, the same period also saw the deliberate revival of Tang dynasty **'three-colour' earthenware**, imitating Tang funerary wares. The Ming palette was different from the yellow, browns and greens of the Tang, preferring purple and blue with some yellow and green, but the style of glazing earthenware was the same. This type of ware was used for pots as well as in roof tiles, and the last of the funerary models, for paper substitutes were being used in increasing numbers.

Towards the end of the Ming, when ceramic control was very good and some fine blood-red pieces were being made, in contrast with the Yuan failure to produce red at high temperatures, the beginnings of the last great innovation in Chinese ceramics can be seen. This was the use of **overglaze enamel colours**. Unlike underglaze colours which, because they had to endure the high temperatures of firing porcelain, were restricted to a few minerals, overglaze decoration was done on finished porcelain. After painting, the vessel was fired a second time at a very low temperature, sufficient to soften the glaze surface and allow the colours to adhere but not hot enough to affect the pigments used, making a much wider range of colours possible. In late Ming examples blue and white underglaze designs were often further embellished with overglaze enamels. This made ceramic production complicated for porcelain, with or without underglaze blue designs, was made in Jiangxi province at the small town of **Jingdezhen**, the porcelain capital of China for hundreds of years. Jingdezhen was well inland and porcelain was brought to the coast by water. Enamelling was often done in **Guangzhou**, on the coast, hundreds of kilometres away. As the export trade developed in the 17C and 18C, plain porcelain vessels were shipped to Guangzhou for enamelling according to European orders but the early blue and white export wares had to be made inland, in Jingdezhen.

The colours of enamels allowed for all sorts of landscape scenes, interiors, portraits, animals, birds and flowers to be painted in a variety of colours on pieces of porcelain. In the early period, at the end of the Ming, the enamels were translucent, the white of the body showing through, but in the early years of the 18C new colours were employed, a pink (made from gold) and a solid white, which meant that enamel painting could achieve a new, non-translucent solidity. During the Qing, monochromes were also popular with numerous reds, turquoise, coffee and cream, 'peach bloom' (pink shading to green), 'tea-dust' (a sort of olive green-brown) and ceramics imitating lacquer, jade and wood. Forms were equally varied: from tall teapots in the form of auspicious characters to duck-shaped tureens and imitations of Meissen openwork baskets.

Bronze and Metalwork

Song and Zhou dynasties During the Shang and the Zhou (16C BC–221 BC) elaborately cast bronze vessels were used in ritual worship and burial. No substantial evidence has yet been unearthed of a period of development which scholars assume must include a phase of wrought-metal work. In the earliest Shang site (Erlitou near Luoyang), bronze vessels cast in pottery piecemoulds have been found and it is this technique that is characteristic of all subsequent Bronze Age production. Multi-part moulds inscribed with designs that were to cover the body of the bronze were luted together and filled with molten bronze, a different alloy from that used in western Asia. The inevitable breaks in pattern where the mould parts joined were exploited in decorative projecting flanges. Lost wax (*cire-perdue*) does not appear to have been used until about the 5C BC.

Some of the vessels produced reflect late Longshan ceramic forms: tripods, jugs, tall libation cups. The vessels are all food and wine containers and during the Shang there was complex animal decoration: sometimes the whole vessel is in the form of an animal (or animals), the surface is decorated with small animals in low relief and covered in an overall scrolling pattern between them. Thus a vessel in the form of two rams may have pairs of birds on the neck, wings on the shoulders and curly dragons lower down with serpent-like scales between them. Most Shang bronzes bear several *taotie* 'monster' masks, with a pair of high relief eyes, beneath curling horns and sometimes pointed, elfin ears, with a snarling upper jaw beneath the eyes. Sometimes a raised flange forms a sort of nose between the eyes. The significance of the *taotie* is not known, although in bronzes used in burial it may have acted as a protection against evil spirits.

Bronzes were frequently produced in matching sets, rarely found in western museums where they appear as individual items; the display in the treasury in the Xi'an Provincial Museum emphasises this aspect. It appears that they were used in life to offer food sacrifices to the gods and that they were later buried with their owner who could continue his offerings in the other world.

In the succeeding Zhou period, inscriptions appear quite frequently on bronzes, sometimes commemorating the gift of land or a victory. Later Zhou bronzes were sometimes inlaid with copper or gold in the increasingly linear decorative style that was to continue into the Han.

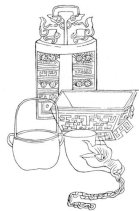

Bronze vessels for food

Han and Tang dynasties Bronzes were still produced in the Han but their forms were simpler and the use of ritual bronzes appears to have been dying out as the Confucian state came into being. Bronze was used into the Tang period for mirrors with one highly polished surface and a decorated back. With the taste for archaic, archaeological forms in the Song, Ming and Qing, more bronzes were made, imitating the Shang and Zhou forms but now used as flower vases rather than significant objects of ritual.

Gold and silver were used most notably during the Tang, for chased vessels, often of silver inlaid with gold are common, but gold and silver never occupied the position of opulence that they do in the West. They were used in jewellery and in filigree hair-ornaments worn by women, but it is thought that the Tang vogue for chased silver was due to the presence of Near Eastern silversmiths in the Tang capital of Chang'an.

Yuan and Ming dynasties A later metalware form, developed during the Yuan and perfected in the Ming, was *cloisonné* enamelling. A plain bronze vessel was covered in tiny wire shapes (outlines of lotuses and other flowers and leaves) glued on with rice paste. Thick enamel colours were painted in between the wires, which served to separate the colours, and the vessel was fired at a low temperature, after which the surface was polished to make the colours and the fine golden wires shine. The vessels are richly coloured in a sort of stained-glass effect.

Sculpture and Carving

Much sculpture in China is associated with religion and ritual. The Qin emperor's tomb outside Xi'an is known for its three armies of larger-than-life earthenware soldiers and other ceramic and bronze sculpture. From the Han dynasty, tombs were fronted by stone sculptures: carved stone columns with leonine figures around the base and supporting a square inscription at the top and great figures of elephants, horses and lions which were developed into the major spirit roads of the Tang-Qing, including numbers of human figures. The interiors of Han tombs were either painted, lined with bricks or stones, stamped or carved with figures and animals or constructed of stone imitations of timber constructions. The great Buddhist cave temples are filled with life-sized or larger stucco statues, as are Buddhist, Taoist and Confucian temples. Wooden or lacquer figures, often of the Buddha and his disciples, and smaller bronze figures used as altarpieces fill the temples of China.

In contrast, the carving of semi-precious materials, including jade, ivory and wood, is frequently not religious. Tiny carved figures were carried in the sleeve, larger pieces placed in the home, on wooden stands or in specially constructed pieces of furniture with multiple shelves intended to display bibelots. Scholars used jade brush-rests in the form of pointed rows of mountains, carved ivory or bamboo wrist-rests when writing, and they set small carvings of mountains with trees, tiny figures and pavilions in jade or other hardstones on their painting tables for inspiration.

Many Neolithic cultures used **jade** but only in China did it survive the Stone Age to become significant as a material believed to have the magical property of preserving the body after death and as symbolic of Confucian virtues: unbending, translucent (honest) and musical (when struck). Jade is a name given to two hardstones, jadeite and nephrite, similar in appearance but chemically distinct. Neither was found in traditional China, and jadeite was only imported from Burma in the 18C AD. The nearest source of nephrite was Central Asia and the use of nephrite from the Neolithic period is surprising, suggesting that there must have been trade routes as early as the third millennium BC, bringing nephrite thousands of kilometres to China. Jade is a hard material (nephrite is 6.5 on Moh's scale) and cannot be cut by a steel knife without an abrasive so it must have been extremely hard to work in the Stone Age. From well before the Han, it was used for adornment, carved into decorative plaques for belts or sewn onto the clothing or suspended from a silken girdle. Later pieces were often 'pocket pieces', in the form of small animals. In the Qing, jade-carvers, producing decorative pieces for display, made use of the different colours in a single stone to carve a floral spray in green with a tiny brown grasshopper or used a piece that shaded from green to white to carve a tiny Chinese cabbage.

Lacquer

Produced from the sap of the *Rhus verniciflua*, a tree native to China (and later introduced to Korea and Japan), lacquer was first used well before the Han as a timber preservative for it has the unusual property of hardening in the damp. During the Han, before the invention of porcelain, lacquer was widely used on a fine wooden base to make practical food vessels: plates and double-lugged cups. At that time lacquer was one of the materials (like silk and rice) used for tax purposes. Coloured with various substances—mercury sulphide, iron oxide and cadmium, producing red, black and yellow—Han artists used it as a paint on lacquered vessels, tracing sinuous cat-like animals, mist-shrouded mountains and swirling scrolls of cloud.

Carved lacquer was a comparatively late discovery, emerging in the Yuan, after lacquer had fallen behind porcelain as a major material for eating utensils. Again using a wooden base, many layers of lacquer were painted on, mainly in red, sometimes with interspersed yellow or black layers used as markers or to provide contrast. The lacquer was then carved, to some depth, when it was of a rubbery consistency. As the colour red is associated with good fortune in China, red lacquer pieces of the Ming and Qing were auspicious presents, frequently associated with marriage.

Textiles

Silk was known to the Shang, although a cut cocoon has been found at a Neolithic site, perhaps suggesting earlier use, and has survived in traces in burial when silk fabrics were used to wrap bronzes. While little survives from the early period, literary accounts mention the use of linen and hemp for clothing and fur pelts, with silk reserved for ceremonial garments. Most garments were made from plain twill, satin or gauze weave silk but there was one type of tapestry weaving, called *ke si*, which was traditionally done by men and used for imperial clothing.

As little has survived, evidence for changes in dress style has to be drawn from wall-paintings in tombs and ceramic tomb figures although some examples of Tang silks and articles of clothing have recently been unearthed in the Gobi desert. Major changes in styles of dress can be seen in the Tang and the Qing. In the Tang there was a development from the high-waisted, light-bodiced female dress to the looser robe, combined with large turban-like hats and padded-toed shoes almost upholstered at the toe end. Loose, V-necked, crossover gowns belted at the waist and worn over under-trousers (for both men and women) were worn in the Song, Yuan and Ming, while it was in the Qing that the Manchu style of high-necked crossover garments, sometimes with a high collar, was introduced. As before, clothing was multi-layered, with perhaps several gauze undergowns beneath a thicker embroidered outer gown. It was common, both in the Qing and earlier periods, for women of the higher classes to wear wraparound pleated skirts under their gowns, while working women commonly wore a shortish jacket and trousers for convenience of movement.

Architecture

As Chinese builders have always relied on timber as the primary structural material, their buildings have been relatively short-lived. The earliest surviving timber building is the small hall of the **Nan chan Temple** on **Wu tai shan** (618–782); other pre-Ming examples are extremely rare. Material for the history of Chinese architecture has to be gathered elsewhere: from excavated foundations (from the Neolithic period onwards) and architectural items such as tiles and pillar bases (Warring States onwards), and most usefully Han tomb models, stone tomb components in architectural forms and tomb bricks with carved pictures of courtyard houses and city gates.

From the late Neolithic, house floors were carefully prepared from tamped earth with postholes for the timber columns supporting the roof. From the Warring States, at the latest, roofs were covered with ceramic tiles and circular end tiles at the eaves bore stamped decorations.

Eaves bracketing at the Jin ci, near Taiyuan

Han and Tang dynasties By the Han, a characteristic timber-frame, post-and-beam construction was used. Upright timber columns supported cross-beams which were placed one on top of the other, in diminishing size, to create a pitched roof in a series of steps. On top of the crossbeams, eave purlins were laid and rooftiles placed on these. From the Han, if not earlier, Chinese eaves projected quite a way beyond the front row of timber columns, presumably to protect them from rain. The projecting eaves with their heavy load of tiles (the roof was made heavier in the north by an insulating couch of mud laid on the roof below the tiles) required support in the form of brackets projecting beyond the columns, taking the load of the eaves. In the Han these were quite simple, with a W-shaped bracket on a block above the column, but by the Tang the eave brackets had developed into complex pieces of joinery, strong structural members under the eaves. The eaves of Tang buildings already seem to show a slight uplift at the corners, anticipating the fancifully curved eaves still seen in southern China. On the tiled roof, decorative circular end-tiles finish the eaves and the ridge of the roof was built up and finished with an incurving 'owl's tail' at each end of the ridge. As the folklore relating to buildings developed, these owls' tails were transformed into water-bearing dragon heads, apparently eating each end of the ridge and performing the dual function of frightening evil spirits and protecting the building from fire. The circular end tiles often bore auspicious designs, sometimes lions' heads with bared teeth, or dragons (associated with water) or auspicious characters. On grand buildings the four corners of the roof were protected near the eaves by a little series of ceramic animals: lions, dragons and frightening mythical beasts, best seen on the roofs of the Forbidden City in Peking.

Design and orientation Even in the Neolithic buildings at Banpo near Xi'an, the characteristic orientation of houses to the south is seen. Although some variations are found in the Neolithic period, the practice of orienting major buildings towards the south soon became universal. Orientation, siting and plan are all affected by the theory of **feng shui** ('wind and water') or geomancy, whose texts claim an ancient history but do not seem to antedate the Han. Geomancy has its roots in practicality: major halls and buildings are always oriented towards the south to make the most of the sun and closed to the cold winds of the north. Ideally, a building, or a city, should be protected to the north by hills and should have a water-supply to the south.

The universality of the **courtyard plan** in Chinese architecture (whether domestic, religious or imperial) has no such scriptural justification and must presumably arise from a desire to enclose possessions and, in the case of domestic architecture, women. Buildings generally consist of a series of courtyards, the main halls oriented to the south, with a strict balance on either side of the central axis and with the more 'public' areas inside the gate and the private apartments (whether of a family or monks) to the rear. It is common for writers on Chinese architecture to stress the similarity between the enclosed rectangle of the courtyard plan and the ideal walled city.

Chinese settlements were surrounded by a wall from the late Neolithic period (at Banpo there is no wall but a defensive ditch). In subsequent periods they were as subject to geomantic considerations as were houses. The ideal rectangular plan was only possible in the north and northwest (Peking and Xi'an are good examples); the hillier topography of the south made rectangular city walls difficult, as is clear from the plan of Nanjing. Imperial or administrative buildings were ideally sited in the centre of the city, with a drum tower and bell tower to announce the hours of the day and the time when the city gates were opened and closed. During the Tang market areas were strictly controlled and the city divided into walled 'wards' which were locked up at night. By the Song these inner walls had almost all disappeared and markets were deregulated to a large extent.

Although it is a very late example of a system which dates back in theory to the Zhou, **Peking** is (or was, until recently) the best example of the town-planners' ideal: protected to the north by mountains, open to the south, with a river drawn in from the northwest to make a moat and provide water, the city was surrounded by a regular rectangular wall pierced by huge gates and had, at its heart, the imperial palace, surrounded by government buildings. The most prominent road, until the widening of Tiananmen Square and the construction of Chang'an jie, was that leading south from the imperial palace (today's Qianmen wai dajie) on the central axis. Peking's streets were a perfect grid, with neat, south-oriented courtyard houses set between them.

The buildings in a courtyard complex, whether domestic or religious, have an uneven number of *jian* or bays (defined by the upright columns) and division into rooms is usually made on the basis of the bay, although a three *jian* building may be undivided, divided into three rooms or two. The uneven number of bays gives a natural prominence to the central bay which, in the main wing of a domestic building, is used as a reception room and ancestral shrine for family worship. The disposition of the limited amount of furniture reflects the balance of rooms: a centrally placed table is flanked by a chair on either side. Domestic buildings in north China almost invariably had a built-in *kang* or brick platform which was used as a seating platform by day and a bed by night. The hollow *kang* could be heated from underneath by a small stove, or sometimes the flue from the cooking stove was led underneath it. It was covered with straw matting and, in Shanxi province, a brightly-painted black oilcloth. *Kang* furniture, ideally of a dark hard-wood, consisted of small, very low tables and silk cushions arranged to form a couch; in poor houses, the folded bed-quilts served the same purpose. *Kang* are fast disappearing as western furnishing styles have become more popular and they take up too much space, which is now being filled with wardrobes, armchairs, couches and coffee-tables. Possessions were traditionally stored in wooden chests.

Much is made of the similarity in plan, orientation and construction between grand and minor buildings. To some extent, the difference is, indeed, a matter of degree, although a vital element of construction, the *dou geng* or bracket, was forbidden in domestic architecture according to the sumptuary laws of the Qing and perhaps even previous dynasties.

Regional variations Another major distinction, more marked in domestic that in grander buildings, was that of regional variation. Temples vary less in plan and construction but houses used to be very different. In **Anhui province** and much of the south, houses appeared to be solid rather than open courtyards, although they were built around an internal courtyard with only a small opening in the roof for ventilation and shade. In **central** and **southern China**, gable-ended walls were built up and stepped or curved (an elaborate curve with two uptilted ends was called 'arched cat's back') and perhaps painted with black and grey landscape scenes in cartouches along the edge of the gable. In **Sichuan**, farmhouses were often thatched, whitewashed and dark-timbered with strong L-shaped brackets supporting the overhanging eaves. In the **northwest** loess areas around Xi'an and Yan'an troglodyte courtyard houses were carved out of the loess and their window and doorframes painted black with a thin red outline. In the **north**, eaves were less up-turned, buildings are stronger and plainer, although there was a greater use of colour (green roofs, red painted timber), perhaps to compensate for the lack of natural colour during the long winters. In the **south**, roofs were up-tilted and colours restricted to dark browns and greys and white. In the ideal house-garden complexes of Suzhou and other small towns of the Yangtse delta, these colours provided a perfect background for plants and the up-tilted roofs seemed to echo the curving forms of nature. The curve of southern roofs compared with the relative straightness of the north remains a mystery; early 19C western writers, whose knowledge of Chinese history stopped with the nomadic Mongols, suggested that it was because the Chinese used to live in tents from which they had inherited curved roof-ridges.

As so much new building has been carried out in the 1980s and 1990s, traditional domestic architecture is now best seen in the houses of famous people opened as museums.

Temple Layout

The characteristic **Buddhist temple plan** involves elements from Indian architecture that have been sinicised such as the pagoda and the *pailou*. Temples generally have a 'spirit wall' outside the main gate (in domestic buildings, this was found inside the main gate) to prevent the ingress of evil spirits which can only travel in straight lines. Beyond, there may be a *pailou* (a free-standing decorative archway of timber with extensive bracketing supporting a tiled roof) and a gate house in front of the first courtyard. This first gate may hold the figures of temple guardians: in Buddhist temples there are four guardians, two on either side of the gateway or hall. The guardian of the east has a white face and carries a spear; the guardian of the west has a blue face and carries a lute, at the sound of which all the world listens; the guardian of the south has a red face and carries an umbrella 'of chaos'. If he raises it, universal darkness ensues; if he points it downwards, it produces earthquakes and thunderstorms. The guardian of the north has a black face, two whips and a panther-skin bag in which he keeps a white man-eating rat, which turns into a white, winged elephant when released from the bag. One sometimes carries a pagoda. There is an equivalent Taoist quartet, found near the entrance gate to Taoist temples: generals who assisted Tang and Song emperors and who hold a pagoda, a sword, two swords and a spiked club.

The first courtyard normally contains a pair of small tower-like buildings, the

bell and **drum towers**, equivalent to those found centrally in walled towns, used to mark special events and the hours of the day. In the first hall of the temple there is usually a figure of the fat 'laughing' Buddha, one of the manifestations of **Maitreya**, the Buddha of the Future, who is elsewhere depicted sitting in a more solemn style, always with both legs pendant. Behind the Maitreya figure, facing the main hall, is another guardian figure, **Wei tuo**, dressed as a general. In the main hall or halls there is frequently a trinity of three: the historic Buddha, **Sakyamuni**, flanked by **Amitabha** of the western Paradise and the **Buddha of Medicine**, with **Guan yin** (Avalokitesvara) behind the screen at the rear of the trinity, often depicted on a rock above the sea holding a small flask. The major trinity can vary somewhat: it can consist of the past, present and future Buddhas, while the attendant Bodhisattvas vary: Samantabhadra may appear, on his white elephant, or Manjusri with a lion. Side or subsidiary halls contain figures of different Bodhisattvas and deities.

Towards the rear of the temple, the hall that is used for worship usually has mats or circular patchwork cushions laid out on the floor. If there is a library building, it is often two-storeyed and found at the rear of the temple, with the monks' living quarters, dining rooms and kitchens.

Taoist temples are very similar to Buddhist establishments, although the groups of deities found in the series of halls are, of course, quite different.

Drama

Chinese drama, known popularly in the West as 'Peking Opera', is a relatively recent development. The combination of spoken monologue, singing, formalised gesture and stunning acrobatics appeared in its mature form during the Mongol Yuan dynasty. There are a great variety of regional operas, each subtly different from the next, and regional pride is considerable. The characteristically high-pitched tone of the singing voices makes it sometimes difficult for western visitors to appreciate and the repertoire of gestures needs explanation. A leg raised high may indicate departure on horseback, fingers run rippling, riverlike, down a long beard to indicate worry, and so on. Not all gestures are so obscure: I remember a Sichuan opera in which a doll 'baby' was vigorously beaten to death but a large number of women were 'murdered' by a mere pointing finger which caused them to leave the stage. The stories are frequently based on heroic 'historic' characters or Confucian love affairs, where pursuit of examination success and devotion to elderly parents rank higher than simple love. Until quite recently, all women's roles were taken by male singers such as Mei Lanfang (see p 146), who took Peking opera abroad on numerous trips during the 1950s.

Language and Script

The Chinese script presents an immediate barrier to the western traveller for it is non-alphabetic. While it is quite possible to learn the different symbols of the Greek or Cyrillic systems in order to be able to read street names in Greece or Russia, the Chinese script requires a mastery of several hundred characters before you can begin to 'get by'. Even then, the characters used in place names, temple names and street names are frequently recondite or archaic and would involve a knowledge of several thousand characters at least.

In many places, street names are written up in roman script in the romanisation system known as **pinyin** which has been taught in all Chinese schools since 1958. This will enable travellers to read simple maps, at least in city centres. Station names are similarly rendered, which is useful, although it should be remembered that these, often involving ancient characters, are romanised for the benefit of a not-tremendously-literate population, unfamiliar with the nearly 40,000 characters contained in the 18C *Kangxi* dictionary, rather than for the less numerous foreign visitors.

The Chinese script developed out of a form of picture writing (possible examples can be seen on some of the pottery vessels from Banpo near Xi'an, c 5000 BC) but by the second millennium BC, writings on shell and bone, recording oracular divination, illustrate a development towards a genuine script which reflected the complexities of language. One of the major methods of expanding the script was the *rebus* (or pun), borrowing a similarly pronounced 'picture' character to write words whose meanings were not easy to represent graphically. Thus the verb 'to come, to arrive', pronounced 'lai', was rendered by the use of the character (a graphic representation) for a stalk of wheat which was also pronounced 'lai'; the number 10,000 (pronounced 'wan') was indicated by a drawing of a sort of scorpion which was also pronounced 'wan'.

Although the oracle bone script was very much a beginning, it has been largely deciphered thanks to the existence of a dictionary, the *Shuo wen* (*Explanation of Writing*), compiled in about AD 100 when the script was still comprehensible. When the *Shuo wen* was compiled, during the Han, the form of script commonly used was basically similar to that used today so that contemporary Chinese can read a Han text aloud quite easily, although they might not be able to understand the classical language.

The *Shuo wen* also revealed a further development of the script through its classification by 540 'radicals' (214 of which are still in current use). Radicals were parts of characters, particularly those which had been developed through the rebus system, that signified an element of meaning. Thus characters which incorporate radical 61, 'heart', usually mean something to do with emotions, feelings or thoughts, and those with the 'water' radical usually have watery meanings. The remaining part is often referred to as the phonetic although, again, it only offers a hint of how to pronounce the word.

The question of pronunciation is linked to that of the relationship between the script and the spoken language and the development of dialects or languages in different parts of China. The fact that it was largely meaning that was conveyed in the script, rather than pronunciation, meant that the written word could be commonly used to communicate throughout the vast land mass where people spoke dialects or languages that were mutually unintelligible. Thus, while a local official in south China might need a couple of interpreters to speak to local people, he could write a letter to them and to his superiors in Peking that, as long as it wasn't read aloud, could be understood in both places.

Some have argued that this loose relationship between script and speech 'allowed' dialects to develop; others feel that the gradual spread of Chinese culture throughout the land mass and its incorporation of local cultures meant that these, and their different languages, influenced local developments. Linguistic maps of China show a strong north–south divide, the south (the provinces of Hunan, Jiangxi, Zhejiang, Fujian, Guangdong and Guangxi) being further subdivided by six language regions. In the north, **Mandarin** (as the Portuguese translated the Chinese term *guan ha* or 'official language', using their own verb *mandar*, 'to rule') is supposed to be spoken everywhere but the Mandarin of rural Sichuan and Shaanxi, for example, is pretty hard for a native of Peking to understand. The difficulties are insurmountable, however, for a northerner in a Cantonese area: it has been said that the languages are as different as English and Dutch; only the odd word is mutually comprehensible. The question of the origin of such divergence is discussed particularly in reference to **Cantonese**. The far south was one of the last areas to be colonised by the Chinese, in the Tang dynasty, when parts such as Hainan Island were used as places of banishment for political exiles, and Cantonese, which has more tones than Mandarin and more varied endings to words, is often regarded as closely preserving Tang dynasty pronunciation and has been used in the reconstruction of the rhyme scheme of Tang poems, which, when read in today's Mandarin, no longer rhyme. Its relative archaism has been explained by some scholars as preservation through isolation (rather like Pennsylvania Dutch) and by others as the result of its use by non-Chinese peoples of the south who preserved what they learnt, rather than letting the language develop naturally as in the north.

Whatever the reasons for divergent developments, the spoken language of the north, in particular, is relatively poor in sounds, which can lead to confusion, even for the Chinese. For example, the pocket dictionary *Xin hua zi dian* lists 27 characters pronounced 'chang'. These are subdivided by four different 'tones' (even, rising, falling and rising, falling), but even so the chances of misunderstanding, for non-standard speakers especially, are quite high. This is particularly the case when monosyllables are used: I have been given sugar (*tang*, rising tone) instead of soup (*tang*, even tone); a friend was dragged to the fish (*yu*, rising tone) market when he wanted to buy jade (*yu*, falling tone), and even Chinese children, used to calling their mother *ma* (even tone) are surprised at their first sight of a horse (*ma*, falling and rising). Many words are, however, bisyllabic now, which reduces the problem to some extent, and, of course, they are all distinguished in the written language by different characters.

The grammar of Chinese is simple as the language is uninflected. One of the problems that I have encountered in writing temple and street names has been that of word division, which remains a rather fluid notion. In the modern spoken language, referred to as *putong hua* ('common speech') rather than Mandarin or *guan ha* these days, words are constructed of a number of elements. In the written language, each character is separately written so that word division is not reflected, except grammatically, but when writing in romanisation the problem arises. One answer is to separate every part of compound words: thus *Tian an men*

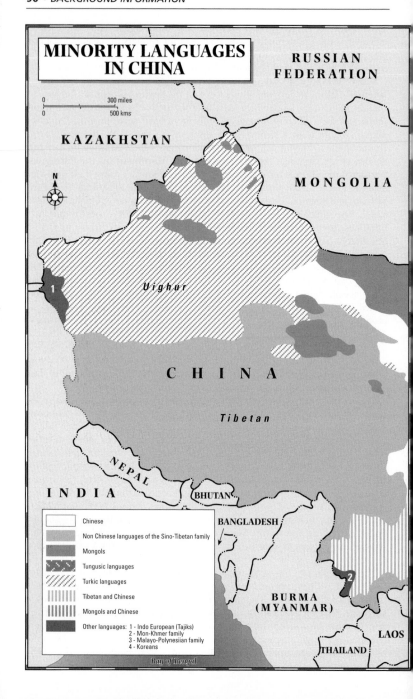

MINORITY LANGUAGES IN CHINA

RUSSIAN FEDERATION

KAZAKHSTAN

MONGOLIA

Uighur

1

CHINA

Tibetan

NEPAL

INDIA

BHUTAN

BANGLADESH

BURMA (MYANMAR)

2

LAOS

THAILAND

Bay of Bengal

0 — 300 miles
0 — 500 kms

	Chinese
	Non Chinese languages of the Sino-Tibetan family
	Mongols
	Tungusic languages
	Turkic languages
	Tibetan and Chinese
	Mongols and Chinese
	Other languages: 1 - Indo European (Tajiks)
	2 - Mon-Khmer family
	3 - Malayo-Polynesiian family
	4 - Koreans

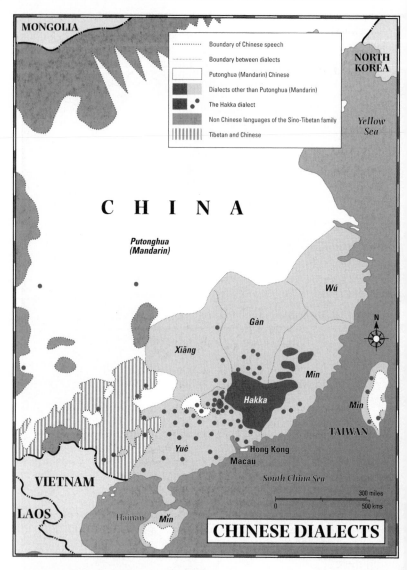

Boundary of Chinese speech
Boundary between dialects
Putonghua (Mandarin) Chinese
Dialects other than Putonghua (Mandarin)
The Hakka dialect
Non Chinese languages of the Sino-Tibetan family
Tibetan and Chinese

MONGOLIA

NORTH KOREA

Yellow Sea

C H I N A

Putonghua (Mandarin)

Wú

Gàn

Xiāng

Min

Hakka

Min

TAIWAN

Yuè

Hong Kong
Macau

South China Sea

VIETNAM

LAOS

Hainan

Min

300 miles
0   500 kms

CHINESE DIALECTS

guang chang (Tiananmen Square). Another is to join them all up: *Tiananmenguangchang*, creating something of a mouthful. I have tried to separate elements in a sensible manner. Thus temples, where the full name is given in romanisation, are separated into the name of the temple and then the word for temple (usually *si*, sometimes *miao*). I have separated words for village (*cun*), town (*zhen*), and county (*xian*). Street names have been divided by name and the word for street: *Renmin lu* ('People's Road'), *Zhongshan lu* ('Sun Yatsen Road'),

Chang'an jie ('Avenue of Eternal Peace'). Some long streets are divided into sections, usually into northern, central, southern, or west, central and eastern sections (*bei, zhong, nan, xi, zhong, dong*) and I have separated these elements.

The pinyin system

I have used the pinyin system of romanisation, developed in China in 1958, rather than the Wade-Giles, developed by two English scholars in the 19C, since it is used throughout China to render station names or street names. Owing to the uncertainty about word division I cannot guarantee that the word division or juncture will tally with mine.

As with Wade-Giles, pronunciation rules need to be learnt and a rough guide follows:

a   as in 'bar'
b   (Wade-Giles p) as in 'bar'
c   (Wade-Giles ts), initial consonant, 'ts' as in 'its'
d   (Wade-Giles t) as in 'dog'
e   as in 'her'
f   as in 'far'
g   (Wade-Giles k) as in 'go'
h   as in 'her'
i   varies according to the preceding consonants: pronounced 'ee' unless preceded by c, ch, r, s, sh, z, zh, when it is pronounced 'er' as in 'her'
j   (Wade-Giles ch) as in 'jingle'
k   (Wade-Giles k') as in 'kill'
l   as in 'lad'
m   as in 'man'
n   as in 'man'
o   as in 'or' in 'lord'
p   (Wade-Giles p) as in 'pick'
q   (Wade-Giles ch) as 'ch' in 'chick'
r   (Wade-Giles j), an unrolled 'r'
s   (Wade-Giles s, ss, sz) as in 'Sunday'
sh   as in 'shift'
t   (Wade-Giles t) as in 'tuck'
u   either 'oo' as in 'fool' or, with an umlaut, as the German 'u'
(no v)
w   as in 'wall'
x   (Wade-Giles hs) between 'ss' and 'sh'
y   as in 'yellow'
z   (Wade-Giles ts, tz), 'ts' as in 'its'
zh   (Wade-Giles ch), 'j' as in 'jingle'

There is a slight complication to the pinyin system: vowel combinations like 'i' and 'a' (as in *tian*, 'heaven'), are not pronounced quite as the individual vowels but sound more like 'yeh' in combination. Thus *tian* is pronounced 'tien'. Similarly, 'o' in *guo* ('country') is pronounced in the standard manner but when followed by 'ng', as in *zhong* ('middle'), is rather longer thus *Zhongguo* ('the middle country' or China) is pronounced 'joonguohr'.

Further reading

History

Jacques Gernet, *A History of Chinese Civilisation*, Cambridge, Cambridge University Press, 1972.

Witold Rodzinski, *The Walled Kingdom: a History of China from 2000 BC to the Present*, London, Fontana, 1984. Two elegantly written, highly readable chronological histories.

Jessica Rawson, *Ancient China*, London, British Museum, 1980. A comprehensive description from the Stone Age to the Han; useful for archaeological sites and ancient capitals.

Ann Paludan, *Chronical of the Chinese Emperors*, London, Thames and Hudson, 1998. A well-illustrated reign-by-reign account of the emperors: a traditionalist view which helps to understand how the Chinese see their emperors.

Gina L. Barnes, *The Rise of Civilisation in East Asia: the Archaeology of China, Korea and Japan*, London, 1999.

Jacques Gernet, *Daily Life in China on the Eve of the Mongol Invasion 1250–1276*, Stanford, Stanford University Press, 1970. Describes Hangzhou and Kaifeng in particular.

Jonathan Spence, *The Search for Modern China*, London, Hutchinson, 1990. From the Ming to the present day.

F.W. Mote, *Imperial China 900–1800*, Cambridge Mass., Harvard University Press, 1999.

Valerie Hansen, *The Open Empire: a history of China to 1600*, New York, Norton, 2000.

Jonathan Spence, *God's Chinese Son: the Taiping Heavenly Kingdom of Hong Xiuquan*, London, Harper Collins, 1990. Biography of the leader of the Taiping rebellion (finally put down with the help of foreign troops and General Gordon) which almost ended the Qing dynasty in the mid 19C.

Frank Ching, *Ancestors: 900 Years in the Life of a Chinese Family*, London, Pan, 1989. A Chinese-American journalist described his ancestors, officials from the Wuxi area.

Cesar Guillen-Nunez, *Macau, Macau*, Hong Kong, Oxford University Press, 1984. A history of the Portuguese colony (returned to China in December 1999) which, unlike Hong Kong, preserves many elegant colonial monuments.

Frances Wood, *No Dogs and Not Many Chinese: Treaty Port Life in China, 1843–1943*, London, John Murray, 1998. Describes the life of foreigners in major ports like Tianjin and Shanghai as well as smaller places like Ningbo and along the Yangtse.

Kong Demao and Kong Delan, *The House of Confucius*, London, Hodder and Stoughton, 1988. Autobiography of the last descendant of Confucius to inhabit the family mansion in Qufu.

Lettres edifiantes et curieuses par des missionaires Jesuites 1702–1776, Paris, Garnier-Flammanon, 1979. The first detailed accounts of China seen through western eyes.

L.C. Goodrich, *The Literary Inquisition of Ch'en-lung*, New York, Paragon reprints, 1966 [1935]. The dramatic and murderous 18C inquisition which recalled the Burning of the Books (2C BC) and anticipated the paranoia of the Cultural

Revolution, raising the question of the possibilities for change in a long-lived culture.

Jonathan D. Spence, *The Death of Woman Wang*, Harmondsworth, Penguin, 1979. Drawn from 17C sources which reveal peasant life.

Jonathan D. Spence, *Emperor of China: Self-portrait of K'ang-hsi*, Harmondsworth, Penguin, 1974. Based on contemporary letters and court memorials.

Marina Warner, *The Dragon Empress*, London, Cardinal, 1974. Well-illustrated account of the life and times of the Dowager Empress Cixi (1835–1908).

Modern History

Edgar Snow, *Red Star over China*, Harmondsworth, Penguin, 1978. First published in the late 1930s, this was the first book to describe the (then) young Communist leaders such as Mao.

Jonathan D. Spence, *The Gate of Heavenly Peace, the Chinese and their Revolution 1899–1980*, Harmondsworth, Penguin, 1982. Uses individuals—poets, writers, thinkers—to illustrate the introduction of reformist ideas.

Sterling Seagrave, *The Soong Dynasty*, London, Sidgwick and Jackson, 1985. The family of a poor Chinese convert to Methodism. His daughters married Sun Yat-sen, Chiang Kai-shek, and his Minister of Finance. Useful background for the Republican period.

Zhang Xinxin and Sang Ye, *Chinese Lives: an Oral History of Contemporary China*, London, Macmillan, 1986. Depressing but varied introduction to the citizens of post-Mao China and their values.

Lynn Pan, *The New Chinese Revolution*, London, Hamish Hamilton, 1987. The immediate post-Mao era described in detail.

Barbara Tuchman, *Sand against the Wind: Stilwell and the American Experience in China*, London, Futura, 1981. The American General, sent to assist Chiang Kai-shek, wrote his own account of Chinese corruption.

W.H. Auden and Christopher Isherwood, *Journey to a War*, London, Faber, 1973. The civil war through literary eyes.

John Gittings, *Real China: from Cannibalism to Karaoke*, London, Simon and Schuster, 1996.

Flora and Fauna

E.H.M. Cox, *Plant-hunting in China*, Hong Kong, Oxford University Press, 1986 [1845]. Reprint of a history of botanical adventure.

Zhai Ji, Zheng Guangmei, Wang Huadong and Xu Jialin, *The Natural History of China*, London, Collins, 1990.

Rodolphe Meyer de Schauensee, *The Birds of China*, Oxford, Oxford University Press, 1984.

Roy Lancaster, *Travels in China*, London, Antique Collector's Club, 1988.

Peter Vayder, *The Garden Plants of China*, London, Weidenfeld and Nicolson, 1999. Stunning photographs of plants *in situ* in temple courtyards and gardens throughout China. It is exceptionally useful if you are looking for particular specimens.

E.H. Wilson, *A Naturalist in Western China: With Vasculum, Camera and Gun*, London, Cadogan Books, 1986 [1913]. Wilson flung himself into all three activities, at some personal risk.

Literature

Any of Arthur Waley's translations of Chinese poems, his *Ballads and Stories from Tunhuang* [Dunhuang], *Monkey* and his biographies of Bai Juyi, Po Chu-I and Yuan Mei. Out of print but obtainable through libraries.

Arthur Cooper, *Li Po and Tu Fu*, Harmondsworth, Penguin, 1973. Translations of the two great Tang poets in the Penguin Classics series which contains other Chinese volumes.

Lao Tzu, *Tao Te Ching*, translated by D.C. Lau, Harmondsworth, Penguin, 1963. The major Daoist classic.

Mencius (1970) and *The Analects of Confucius* (1979) translated by D.C. Lau, published by Penguin. The major Confucian classics.

Ezra Pound, *The Classic Anthology Defined by Confucius*, London, Faber, 1984.

Pound's translations of the *Shi jing, Book of Songs* eccentrically convey ther-rhythms of monosyllabic classical Chinese.

Cao Xueqin, *The Story of the Stone*, translated by David Hawkes and John Minford, Harmondsworth, Penguin, 1973–84.

The Dream of the Red Chamber in a multi-volume translation of great elegance and accuracy.

A.C. Grayling and Susan Whitfield, *China: a Literary Companion*, London, John Murray, 1994. A useful selection of mainly western writers.

Occasionally recent novels from China are published in translation; most notably the works of Zhang Xianliang and Zhang Jie, Dai Houying and Wang Meng are to be recommended. Mo Yan is good but not easy reading. There is also a whole new genre of agonised female 'reminiscence' (*Wild Swans, Falling Leaves*, etc.), which describes the horrors of life from bound feet and concubinage to Red Guard atrocities, by way of unhappy home life and unfairness to daughters. Much of this I would class as largely fiction, which may account for its popularity.

Travel

Barry Till, *In Search of Old Peking*, Hong Kong, Joint Publications, 1982.

Pan Ling, *In Search of Old Shanghai*, Hong Kong, Joint Publications 1982.

L.C. Arlington and W. Lewisohn, *In Search of Old Peking*, Hong Kong, Oxford University Press, 1991 [1935]. In this case, much has been lost since 1935.

Marco Polo, *The Travels*, Harmondsworth, Penguin, 1958. For the 13C armchair traveller.

Frances Wood, *Did Marco Polo Go To China?*, London, 1993. I attempted to set out the considerable doubts which have been raised since the 18C about Polo's veracity.

Judy Bonavia, *A Guide to the Yangzi River*, Hong Kong, China Guides Series, 1985. One of a series, each covering a small area in considerable detail; useful for travellers to a single destination.

Judy Bonavia, *The Silk Road: from Xi'an to Kashgar*, Hong Kong, Odyssey, 1992.

Kathleen Hopkirk, *Central Asia: a Traveller's Companion*, London, John Murray, 1993. A literary companion with much useful historical material.

All About Shanghai, introduction by H.J. Lethbridge, Hong Kong, Oxford University Press, 1983 [1935]. Detail for travellers and residents in the mid 1930s.

Peter Hopkirk, *Foreign Devils on the Silk Road*, Oxford, London, 1980. The gripping story of the race for buried treasure on the old Silk Roads at the turn of the century.

Peter Fleming, *News from Tartary*, London, Futura, 1983 [1936]. Across the Gobi desert.

Ella Maillart, *Forbidden Journey*, London, Century, 1983 [1937]. The author travelled with Peter Fleming; their accounts are complementary.

Mildred Cable and Francesca French, *The Gobi Desert*, London, Virago 1984 [1942]. An account by intrepid lady missionaries.

Art

Jessica Rawson (ed.) *The British Museum Book of Chinese Art*, London, British Museum, 1992.

Margaret Medley, *The Chinese Potter*, Oxford, Phaidon, 1978.

Mary Tregear, *Chinese Art*, London, Thames and Hudson, 1980.

Ann Paludan, *The Imperial Ming Tombs*, New Haven and London, Yale University Press, 1981. Particularly recommended to those with time in Peking to visit the lesser-known tombs, with a supplement for bird-watchers.

Ann Paludan, *The Chinese Spirit Road: the Classical Tradition of Stone Tomb Statuary*, New Haven and London, Yale University Press, 1991. Indispensable guide to tombs and sculpture.

S.J. Vainker, *Chinese Pottery and Porcelain from Prehistory to the Present*, London, British Museum, 1991.

Roderick Whitfield and Ann Farrer, *Caves of the Thousand Buddhas: Chinese Art from the Silk Route*, London, British Museum, 1990. The British Museum's collection of paintings and banners from Dunhuang.

Frances Wood, *Chinese Illustration*, London, British Library, 1985. The history of printing and book production as seen in the British Library collections.

Yu Zhuoyan, *The Palaces of the Forbidden City*, New York, Viking, and London, Allen Lane, 1984. Beautifully illustrated and very detailed account of the most important buildings of late traditional China.

Ronald G. Knapp, *China's Traditional Rural Architecture: A Cultural Geography of the Common House*, Honolulu, University of Hawaii, 1986. The author has written a series of books on traditional housing.

Maggie Keswick, *The Chinese Garden*, London, Academy, 1978.

Ji Cheng, *The Craft of Gardens*, New Haven and London, Yale University Press, 1988. Early 17C work on garden design.

Norah Titley and Frances Wood, *Oriental Gardens*, London, British Library, 1991. The Chinese section contains illustrations of the desired effects achieved in gentlemen's gardens.

Nancy Schatzman Steinhardt (ed), *Chinese Traditional Architecture*, New York, China Institute in America, 1984. Descriptions of major buildings.

Along the Ancient Silk Routes: Central Asian Art from the West Berlin State Museums, New York, Metropolitan Museum, 1982. For the western-most sites on the Silk Routes: artefacts removed by German archaeologists.

Susan Whitfield, *Life on the Silk Road*, London, John Murray, 1999. Uses contemporary sources to describe daily life in Dunhuang and China's Central Asian outposts in the 7C–10C.

Rose Kerr (ed.), *The T.T. Tsui Gallery of Chinese Art: Chinese Art and Design*, London, Victoria and Albert Museum, 1982. Sets Chinese art in its social context.

Craig Clunas, *Chinese Furniture*, London, Bamboo, 1988.

Craig Clunas, *Superficial Things: Material Culture and Social Status in Early Modern*

China, Cambridge, Polity Press, 1991. Linking textual sources and artefacts, demonstrates how people viewed and used their possessions.

Rose Kerr, *Later Chinese Bronzes*, London, Victoria and Albert Museum, 1990.

Rose Kerr, *Chinese Ceramics: Porcelain of the Qing Dynasty*, London, Victoria and Albert Museum, 1986.

Craig Clunas, *Chinese Carving*, Singapore, 1996. An introduction to a variety of bamboo, ivory, rhino-horn and soft-stone carvings in the Victoria and Albert Museum.

Jean-Francois Billeter, *The Chinese Art of Writing*, Geneva, 1990. An introduction to calligraphy, the highest form of Chinese visual art.

Carl Crossman, *The Decorative Arts of the China Trade: Paintings, Furnishings and Exotic Curiosities*, Woodbridge, 1991.

Thought

Fung Yu-lan, *A Short History of Chinese Philosophy*, New York, Free Press, 1966.

Bob Whyte, *Unfinished Encounter: China and Christianity*, London, Collins, 1988. Particularly strong on (fairly) recent events.

Jacques Gernet, *China and the Christian Impact*, Cambridge, Cambridge University Press, 1985. The early history of missionary activity.

Kenneth Ch'en, *Buddhism in China*, Princeton, Princeton University Press, 1973. Lucid account of the faith and its Chinese transformations.

J. Prip-Moller, *Chinese Buddhist Monasteries: Their Plan and its Functions as a Setting for Buddhist Monastic Life*, Hong Kong, Hong Kong University Press, 1967 [1937]. Useful guide to the layout and history of many well-known temples.

C.K. Yang, *Religion in Chinese Society*, Berkeley and London, University of California Press, 1977. Covers popular religion.

Michael Pollak, *Mandarins, Jews and Missionaries: the Jewish Experience in the Chinese Empire*, New York, Weatherhill, 1998. Fascinating detail of the old communities, most notably of Kaifeng.

General

Joseph Needham, *Science and Civilisation in China*, Cambridge, Cambridge University Press, 1954– (in progress). Dr Needham's monumental work is accurately titled: the section on architecture and engineering is particularly useful but those interested in any aspect of Chinese scientific history will find all the information they need.

Endymion Wilkinson, *Chinese History: A Manual*, Harvard University Asia Centre, 1998. Essential academic reference for the Chinese view of Chinese history.

Michael Dillon (ed) *China: A Cultural And Historical Dictionary*, London, Curzon, 1998. Useful reference.

Philip Snow, *The Star Raft: the Chinese Encounter with Africa*, London, Weidenfeld and Nicolson, 1988. Scholarly work with much information on traditional Chinese geographical knowledge, attitudes to the outside world and the great early 15C navigator, the eunuch admiral Zheng He.

Edward H. Schafer, *The Golden Peaches of Samarkand: A Study of T'ang Exotica*, Berkeley and London, University of California Press, 1963. Extravagant imports into Tang China, from ermine to lychees; one of Professor Schafer's fascinating books on the period.

K.C. Chang (ed.), *Food in Chinese Culture*, New Haven and London, Yale University

Press, 1977. A scholarly history of the most important aspect of life in China.

S. Robert Ramsay, *The Languages of China*, Princeton, Princeton University Press, 1987. The language and its many dialects.

Oliver Moore, *Chinese: Reading the Past*, London, British Museum, 1999.
One of a new British Museum series on ancient writing systems.

Samuel Couling, *The Encyclopaedia Sinica*, Hong Kong, Oxford University Press, 1983 [1917]. A good source of biography and descriptions of cities and institutions, up to 1917.

Denis Twitchett, *Printing and Publishing in Medieval China*, London, Wynken de Worde Society, 1983. The invention of paper and printing in China and the rapid growth of the industry. (A reprint is being prepared by the British Library.)

Jonathan Spence, *The Chan's Great Continent: China in Western Minds*, Harmondsworth, Penguin, 1999. From Marco Polo to Communist advisers to Mao.

Lynn Pan, *Sons of the Yellow Emperor: The Story of the Overseas Chinese*, London, Secker and Warburg, 1990. The Chinese diaspora; of interest to visitors to Guangdong and Fujian.

Barbara Baker (ed.) *Shanghai: Electric and Lurid City*, Oxford, 1998. A collection of writings about and illustrations of Shanghai, from the late 19C to the present.

Martin Palmer, *Travels through Sacred China*, London, 1996.

Useful web-sites

That may be something of a contradiction in terms. Some of the tourist offices have quite useful web-sites, notably the Hong Kong and Macau Tourist Authorities (**www.hkta.org** and **www.macautourism.gov.mo**), although visa information for Hong Kong (**www.info.gov.hk**) is pretty grimly presented.

There are a number of sites which offer bits of tourist information, pictures of major sites such as **www.china.org.cn/English** and **www.china.org.cn/Pictorial** and **www.chinapage.com**. This begins with a business page at www.china-pages.com.cn but if you add a backslash, it subdivides into such unlikely features as 'China the Beautiful: Portraits of Emperors', **www.chinapages.com.cn/emperor/html** or **www.chinapages.com.cn/chinese_culture**; for brief introductions to architecture at **/architecture/architecture html** or opera at **www.china-pages.com.cn/chinese_culture/opera/opera.html**.

Some specific sites are **www.kashrus.org/asian/china.html**, which has an interesting essay on the Jewish community of Kaifeng, **www.sh.com/oldshhai/oldsshai.htm** and **www.accesschina.com/city/shanghai.htm** for aspects of old Shanghai.

Good background to current events and debates as well as book reviews can be found at the American **www.virtualchina.com**.

Asian-related art events, books and some useful links can be found through the New York Asia Society's web-site **www.asiasource.org** and a fine source for Chinese art and archaeology, news of exhibitions and publications is **www.chinese-art.com**.

An important UK site for anyone proposing to visit Dunhuang and the Silk Road is the online database: **http://idp.bl.uk**.

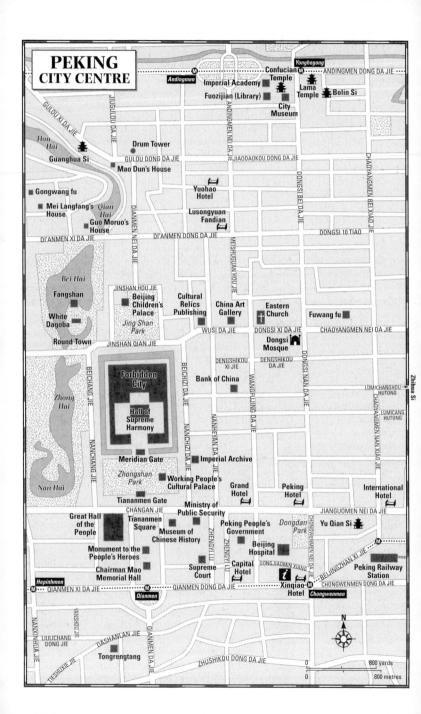

PEKING CITY CENTRE

Andingmen

Yonghegong

ANDINGMEN DONG DA JIE

Confucian Temple

Imperial Academy

Fuozijian (Library)

Lama Temple

Bolin Si

City Museum

GULOU XI DA JIE

JIUGULOU DA JIE

ANDINGMEN NEI DA JIE

DONGSI BEI DA JIE

CHAOYANGMEN BEI XIAO JIE

Hou Hai

Guanghua Si

Drum Tower

GULOU DONG DA JIE

JIAODAOKOU DONG DA JIE

Mao Dun's House

Yuohao Hotel

Gongwang fu

Mei Langfang's House

Qian Hai

Guo Moruo's House

DIANMEN NEI DA JIE

Lusongyuan Fandian

DI'AMMEN XI DA JIE

DI'ANMEN DONG DA JIE

DONGSI 10 TIAO

MEISHUGUAN HOU LU

Bei Hai

Fangshan

JINSHAN HOU JIE

Beijing Children's Palace

Cultural Relics Publishing

China Art Gallery

Eastern Church

Fuwang fu

White Dagoba

Jing Shan Park

WUSI DA JIE

DONGSI XI DA JIE

CHAOYANGMEN NEI DA JIE

Round Town

JINSHAN QIAN JIE

Dongsi Mosque

DENGSHIKOU XI DA JIE

DENGSHIKOU DA JIE

DONGSI NAN DA JIE

Zhong Hai

BEICHANG JIE

NANCHANG JIE

Forbidden City

Hall of Supreme Harmony

BEICHIZI DA JIE

NANCHIZI DA JIE

NANHEYAN DA JIE

Bank of China

WANGFUJING DA JIE

LUMICHANGHOU HUTONG

Zhihua Si

LUMICANG HUTONG

CHAOYANGMEN NAN XIAO JIE

Meridian Gate

Imperial Archive

Zhongshan Park

Working People's Cultural Palace

Nan Hai

Tiananmen Gate

CHANGAN JIE

Grand Hotel

Peking Hotel

International Hotel

JIANGUOMEN NEI DA JIE

Ministry of Public Security

Great Hall of the People

Tiananmen Square

Museum of Chinese History

Peking People's Government

Dongdan Park

Yu Qian Si

Monument to the People's Heroes

ZHENGYI LU

ZHENGYI LU

Beijing Hospital

Chairman Mao Memorial Hall

Supreme Court

Capital Hotel

DONGJIAOMIN XIANG

CHONGWENMEN NEI DA JIE

Peking Railway Station

BEIJINGZHAN XI JIE

Hepinhmen

QIANMEN XI DA JIE

Qianmen

QIANMEN DONG DA JIE

Xinqiao Hotel

Chongwenmen

CHONGWENMEN DONG DA JIE

NANXINHUA JIE

YANSHOU JIE

QIANMEN DA JIE

LIULICHANG DONG JIE

DASHANLAN JIE

Tongrengtang

TIESHUXIE JIE

ZHUSHIKOU DONG DA JIE

N

0   800 yards

0   800 metres

THE GUIDE

Peking

Peking, China's capital, lies at the edge of a plain which stretches hundreds of miles south to comprise much of Hebei, Henan, Shandong and Anhui provinces. Peking itself is close to a semi-circle of mountains, the foothills of the Mongolian plateau, which surround the plain to the west, northwest and north, where the Great Wall was built to protect the open plain. Although smaller states established their capitals in the Peking area (whose earliest inhabitants include 'Peking Man' of c 500,000 BC), the city has only been a dynastic capital since the early 15C. It was then that the name *Beijing* (Northern Capital) was first applied to the city and it has been used ever since, with the exception of the brief period of Chiang Kai-shek's Nanjing government (1928–49) when it was renamed Beiping (Northern Peace).

> ### *Peking versus Beijing*
> The spelling Peking reflects a peculiar early Jesuit romanisation which assigned a 'k' to the sound value 'j' (Nanjing-Nanking, Beijing-Peking) but I continue to use it for to non-Chinese (and even to some literary Chinese) it is a name with resonance and historical associations. The venerable Peking University recently announced that it wanted to continue to be known as such, not as Beijing University.

Considerably ravaged by city-planners, who tore down the city walls and continue to flatten the traditional low grey-roofed courtyard houses in favour of blocks of flats or high-rise office blocks, and spoiled by careless industrial development to the west and east in particular the city nevertheless contains a multiplicity of monuments.

Group tourists are not often allowed much time in Peking, just the couple of days needed to see the Forbidden City, Great Wall and Ming tombs and perhaps the Temple of Heaven and Summer Palace. Longer stays in the city can provide a wealth of temples and sites, with an increasing number of 'houses of the famous' being opened to allow a view into the otherwise enclosed courtyard houses.

Practical information

Getting there
By air

The city's airport is to the northeast, some 30km from the city centre. It is China's major airport, with many international flights daily and departures to all other airports in China. A new terminal was built for the fiftieth anniversary of the founding of the People's Republic (October 1999).

Some hotels have courtesy buses, otherwise the taxi trip to the town centre takes just under an hour, depending upon the traffic, and costs about 100 yuan.

It is wise to arrive two hours before departure for international flights (including those to Hong Kong which are no longer 'international') and an hour before departure on domestic flights. Systems change but recently it has been the practice to x-ray all baggage before you even get to the check-in desk; the queue for the x-ray machines stretches to the outer door. Airport taxes are 90 rmb for international flights (including Hong Kong) and 60 rmb for domestic flights which have to be paid in cash on departure: they are not included in airline ticket prices.

There are several hotels near the airport which can help transit passengers or those with early or late flights. The *Movenpick hotel* (Guodu da fandian; ☎ 6456 5588, fax 6456 5678), near the airport, supplies free airport transfers and is situated in a small village which is pleasant to walk in before or after flights and offers an interesting contrast with the city centre.

By train

There are now two stations in the city. The old station (one of the Ten Great Buildings put up in 1958) with its twin towers is in the southeast part of the city centre. This is mainly for trains for the north and east. The new West Station in the southwest of the city is a strange, Chinese style, twin-towered fairy palace for trains from the south and west, although these divisions are a bit arbitrary and by no means mutually exclusive. Trains to Nanjing (south) which travel along the eastern seaboard depart from the old station, while trains from the south which run along the new central route arrive at the West Station.

The Trans-Siberian (from the old station) is in fact two trains: the Chinese one departs on Wednesdays and takes the shorter route via Mongolia (five days to Moscow) while the Russian train leaves on Saturdays and goes via Manchuria.

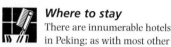 ### Where to stay

There are innumerable hotels in Peking; as with most other centres, many of the newer hotels have been built in somewhat inaccessible high-rise suburbs. It is worthwhile checking the location of your hotel as reduced hotel rates over the last two years reflect the availibity of central hotel rooms. Notable hotels include the old *Peking Hotel*, 33 Dong Chang'an jie, ☎ 6513 7766, fax 6513 7703, just next-door to the Forbidden City (the best site). It is composed of three parts, based on the old Wagons-lits Hotel, with additions built in the early 1950s and mid-1970s. The hotel is not the most efficient but its location makes up for any deficiencies. The bars and coffee-shops on the ground floor are useful meeting places. The western end of the old Peking Hotel has now been oddly incorporated into a new luxury hotel, the *Grand Hotel*, 35 Dong Chang'an jie, ☎ 6513 0057, fax 6513 0050, email: sales@mail.grandhotelbeijing.com.cn. The atrium of the Grand Hotel is well worth visiting. Its western wall is the former end of the Peking Hotel whose rooms look into the atrium. There is also a fascinating fountain with the twelve animals of the Chinese zodiacal cycle carved in white marble and spouting water in turn. This fountain is a replica of one built by the Jesuit Benoît for the Qianlong emperor at the Yuan ming yuan (Garden of Perfect Brightness or 'Old' Summer Palace) to the north of the city. Razed by a combined British and French force in 1860, the original fountain can only be distinguished by its vast shell-shaped base.

The first 'joint-venture' hotel in Peking was the *Jianguo* (5 Jianguomen wai da jie, ☎ 6500 2233, fax 6500 2871, Sales@hoteljianguo.com.cn), on Chang'an jie, some blocks east of the Friendship Store in the diplomatic quarter of Jianguomen wai. Reasonably conveniently situated, the Jianguo set the pace for Chinese hotels and later joint-ventures. It is an ugly building but service is generally good. The *Xiangshan Hotel* (*xiangshan* means 'fragrant hills'; see below, p 203), designed by I.M. Pei, is by far the most interesting hotel architecturally and is set in a tranquil area with many opportunities for walks but it is distant from anything except the Fragrant Hills (although there is a free bus service to the Peking Zoo). The new white block of the *Beijing International Hotel* (Guoji Fandian), 9 Jianguomen nei da jie, ☎ 6460 6688, well-situated not far from the railway station, was said to be managed by Zhao Ziyang's daughter. The *Capital Hotel*, 3 East Qianmen Ave, 10006, ☎ 6512 9988, fax 6512 0309, is nicely placed in the centre of the old Legation quarter and the *Xinqiao Hotel*, 2 Dongjaiominxiang, 100004, ☎ 6513 3366, fax 6512 5126, just at the eastern end of the Legation quarter. Just north of the Forbidden City is a courtyard house hotel, *Lusongyuan Fandian*, 22 Banchang hutong, ☎ 6401 1116, fax 6403 0418; another is the *Youhao Binguan*, 7 Houyuansi, ☎ 6403 1114, fax 6403 4603, once inhabited by Chiang Kai-shek.

Getting around
By bus

Peking is large and its monuments are unfortunately rather scattered. The enterprising could use buses (cheap, somewhat infrequent and incredibly crowded—it is difficult to get both feet on the floor at once and since the conductors sometimes have to use force to get people in and the doors shut, you can end up with dusty footprints up your back). Many maps include bus routes and mark the stops clearly.

By underground

The underground is useful for visitors and easier than buses. There are announcements in English and plenty of signs in English, too. A ticket costs 2 rmb and for a circuit of the city (like a mole following the old city walls) or east–west travel below Chang'an jie, it is far more reliable than any other form of transport since Peking's roads are perpetually blocked with traffic.

By taxi

It is probably easiest to use taxis for the far-flung sites. There are several grades of taxi, all of which can now be flagged down on the streets. The price varies according to the size of the vehicle and some hotels refuse to allow the smaller, cheaper, red taxis into their precincts so you will have to go out onto the street to find one and expect to be dropped at the hotel gates. There are also little **yellow minibuses** for short distances, which take a number of passengers like a Turkish *dolmus*, but these are being phased out with no new licences issued.

It is important to check that the taxi meter is on and operative. Tipping is not customary, although a few extra yuan are always welcomed. I have arranged groups of monuments on the assumption that taxis are taken from hotels.

On foot

One particular area is good for exploring on foot, that around the Back Lakes, north of the Forbidden City, taking in the Drum Tower and the Bell Tower. Many of the few remaining *hutong* (lanes) reminiscent of old Peking can be found there, with small street markets and a number of restored residences of famous writers and politicians.

History

In the hills to the west of Peking is Zhoukoudian where the first relic of **Peking Man** (a wisdom tooth), who lived some 300,000–500,00 years ago, was discovered in 1921 by Otto Zdansky. In 1927 Birger Bohlin unearthed another tooth and, ten years later, further excavations by Teilhard de Chardin, Franz Weidenreich and W.C. Pei unearthed the remains of some 40 individuals, including the famous crania which were lost in 1941 in transit to the United States. The first major settlement in the area was probably near the Zhoukoudian site, southwest Peking, but at some time during the **Zhou** period (1066 BC–221 BC; see p 35), the major settlement, referred to in literature as *Ji* (Reeds), was sited in the southeast suburbs of present-day Peking.

Western Zhou tombs with elaborate ritual bronzes have been unearthed at Liulihe, south of Peking. During the Warring States Period, Ji was the capital of one of the northern states, Yan, which means 'swallow'. The name *Yanjing* (Capital of Swallows)—appropriate as swallows nest under the eaves of tall buildings, including the halls of the Forbidden City and the surviving gates, and fly around at dusk—is still often applied to Peking.

According to the great Han historian Sima Qian, the city of Yan under the **Qin dynasty** (221–206 BC) was a thriving market with goods traded from Shandong and Hebei and as far away as Korea. Its northern site meant that Peking, known in the **Tang dynasty** (AD 618–907) as *Yuzhou*, was used as a base for expeditions against Korea. With the end of the Tang, the gradual encroachment of northern, non-Chinese people (which was to culminate in the Mongol Yuan dynasty some 300 years later) was reflected in Peking's history. The **Khitan**, a semi-nomadic, Mongolian-speaking people from the area around Chengde, northeast of Peking, who adopted the dynastic name of Liao (and ruled the north of China from 907 to 1125), established their capital in Peking in 936, calling it instead *Nanjing* (Southern Capital) as it was south of their ancestral home.

In 1125 Peking was taken by yet another of the northern tribes, the **Jurched**, also an Altaic people but whose linguistic affiliations were Tungusic, rather than Mongolian. They had lived a more settled life than the Khitan, fishing, hunting and cultivating the river valleys of north and east Dongbei (Manchuria). The Jurched assumed the dynastic name of **Jin** (Golden) and ruled the north from 1125 to 1234, pushing the Song dynasty further south by their capture of the capital of Kaifeng in 1126. This move followed the unsuccessful Song policy of trying to regain power by pitting 'barbarian against barbarian' which had involved a treaty with the Jurched to expel the Khitan. Nothing now remains visible of the Jin city, in the southwest of today's Peking.

The Jin were in their turn driven out by the **Mongols**, who took Peking in 1215 and built a new capital, known to them as *Khanbalik* (City of the Khan) and to the Chinese as *Dadu* (Great Capital). The **Yuan** (Mongol) city had high earth walls, parts of which can still be seen along Xueyuan lu in the northwest of the city and also along the road to the Great Wall to the northeast. In keeping with their nomadic origins, the Mongols enclosed a huge area within their city walls in order to give space for their horses to graze. The southern wall of the Yuan city ran roughly along the same line as that of the Ming and Qing 'Tartar City' (from Xuanwumen xi da jie to Qianmen dong da jie with

Qianmen in the centre) but the northern wall was far to the north of the later city wall.

During the Yuan the checkerboard arrangement of city streets was laid out which survives to this day, although the city was pretty much destroyed in the battles at the end of the Yuan. The description of the capital in Marco Polo's *Travels* probably reflects something of its appearance and grandeur, even if Marco Polo cribbed his material from a Persian guidebook:

Built in the form of a square ... enclosed by earth ramparts ... the whole interior of the city is laid out in squares like a chessboard with such masterly precision ... All the way down the sides of every main street there are booths and shops of all sorts. All the building sites throughout the city are square ... and on every site stand large and spacious mansions with ample courtyard and gardens ... In the centre of the city stands a huge palace in which is a great bell; in the evening this peals three times as a signal that no one may go about the town ....

His description could well have stood for Peking some 500–600 years later although the spacious mansions were crowded in by little low grey houses, still built to the courtyard plan on small square sites determined by the checkerboard of the streets. Chinese guidebooks to Peking in the 19C refer to the tiny lanes—known as *hutong* or 'barbarian alleys', a name which no one has successfully explained, although some suggest it refers to the Mongol (non-Chinese) foundation of the city—as being as fine and numerous as hairs on a cow.

The first **Ming** emperor established his capital in Nanjing (after a first tentative attempt to set it up in his home village in Anhui), centred on his own power base. His successor (not his appointed heir but another of his sons who seized control) had been enfeoffed in Peking, however, and so decided to move the capital there in 1402. Not only had it been his personal power base but a major factor in the transfer of the capital was its relative proximity to the major threats to Ming control (which still came, like the Khitan and Jurched, from the north and northeast). It was military strategy which determined these shifts of capital: during the Han and Tang the greatest threat came from the northwest, hence the maintenance of their capital in Xi'an. Peking was close enough to the Great Wall to be able to maintain its garrisons and morale of the border guards; Nanjing was too distant.

The site of Peking is geomantically 'good', with its open plain to the south and east (well supplied with water led from the Yongding River) and its almost encircling mountains to the north, protecting the site from evil, northern influences. There was, however, some doubt that the 'good luck' of the site might be exhausted with the downfall of its previous occupants and the bloody, destructive battles that had nearly destroyed it. The Yongle emperor (reigned 1402–24) consulted geomancers and even the major philosophers of the day about his decision and they felt able to reassure him.

The **Ming city walls**, which were most unfortunately demolished during the Great Leap Forward (1958) but whose form can be traced through streetnames referring to the ancient gates, were set to the south of the Yuan walls. The street-names with the suffixes *-men nei* or *-men wai* indicate 'inside X gate' or 'outside X gate' respectively. With the exception of those in the Forbidden City, the only gates left standing are the **Desheng men** (Gate of the Victory of

Virtue) in the northwest, **Dongbian men** (Eastern side Gate) in the southeast (seen from the railway) and **Qian men** (Front Gate) just south of the Forbidden City. The high city walls faced with grey brick were similar to those that still surround the Forbidden City, broader at the base but still wide enough for several horsemen to ride abreast along the top, between the battlements.

This part of Peking was known as the **Inner City** (and, later, by foreigners, as the Tartar City or Manchu City) in contrast with the southern part of the city (a broader, west–east rectangle which enclosed the main shopping areas and the Temple of Heaven) which was walled (in earth ramparts in 1524 and faced with brick in 1543) and known as the **Outer** or **Chinese City**. The Inner City, with the Forbidden City in its centre, contained all the government buildings and imperial granaries as well as housing areas, while the southern, outer city, was the commercial, theatrical and entertainment sector, although also containing several major buildings of imperial significance, such as the Temples of Heaven and Agriculture. Although the Forbidden City, in particular, saw constant additions as required as well as constant rebuilding of its halls as a result of fire through the Ming and Qing dynasties, with 22 major fires between 1421 and 1891 (some caused by lightning, others by fireworks and other accidents), the palace remained basically the same throughout the two dynasties, as did the layout of the city of Peking.

The old walled 'inner' city of the Ming and Qing, despite being a relatively recent construction, was held up as the classic example of **Chinese town-planning theory**, traditionally ascribed to such classic works as the *Kao gong ji* (or *Record of Trades*) of the Warring States Period. The city should be rectangular in plan, surrounded by a wall, with its palace in the centre, close to government buildings; its geomantic situation was also important and Peking's site, according to Father De Groot, is 'perfectly in accord with the principles of geomancy', although the flatness of the northern plain made such siting easier than in the case of, say, Nanjing.

The nine gates in the city's outer walls were explained in terms of the significance of the number nine, the number 'with greater prestige than any other' in north China (Hong Kong and the south favour eight for its pronunciation in Cantonese rhymes with the word for 'wealth'). All sorts of legends grew up around the perfect city and its construction. The major theme concerns a strange, eight-armed small boy called *Ne zha* (who could ride dragons and 'stir up' the sea) who passed the town planners puzzling over their designs (apparently unable to get the city right). Flapping his arms in his oddly-shaped red coat, he suggested that they copy him for a solution. Thus the central southern gate is Ne zha's head, the two wells at the gate, his eyes, its subsidiary flanking gates, his ears. The two northern gates are his legs and his eight arms the other gates, east and north. The 'imperial way' from the southern gate to the palace is his alimentary canal and the Imperial (Forbidden) City contains his viscera while the streets which cross Peking with such regularity are his ribs.

Although Peking is not perfectly aligned on a north–south axis (due to the westwards declination of the magnetic compass needle after AD 1050), its basic orientation and the regularity of the street-grid is such that its inhabitants still commonly eschew the use of 'right' and 'left' in giving directions or descriptions, preferring to use the points of the compass.

The greatest changes to the city came after 1949, when **Tiananmen**, the Gate of Heavenly Peace, the national emblem, was rebuilt for parades and the great square in front of it, Tiananmen Square, opened up for the same purpose. With the clearance of the square and the construction of the major avenue running east–west through Peking traversing the square, the pivot of the city was altered. The main **'imperial way'** had run south to the southernmost gate of the Chinese or Outer City (today's Qianmen da jie), in the traditional manner but the major axial route in today's Peking is the east–west Chang'an jie.

During the Qing, whenever the emperor processed south from his palace to the Temples of Heaven and Agriculture, along the 'imperial way', shops were closed and shuttered for no commoner was allowed to see him. All the major streets were lined (as they are today) with shops but the old shops had richly carved wooden frontages, horizontal boards carved with plum blossom, lotuses, meander and other patterns, a few of which can still be seen. The shops faced outwards onto the street but behind the shopfronts were courtyards just like those of ordinary dwellings.

One further loss, with the disappearance of the city walls and the gradual demolition of vast tracts of the low, grey-roofed courtyard houses that filled in Marco Polo's checkerboard of streets, is the view of the city which to 19C and early 20C visitors was a *rus in urbe*, the trees planted or shade in every courtyard affording a view to Pierre Loti in 1901 of 'Peking at my feet, like a forest'. A British 'student-interpreter' (trainee diplomat) in 1885 wrote of looking down onto the city from the wall in summer when:

… very little was to be seen of the houses, so thickly are trees planted about them. Indeed, Peking might seem to be a green wood, surrounded by a high wall … nothing can be seen of the squalor and dirt of the streets and houses.

To most visitors, Peking is a modern city filled with concrete blocks of flats and anonymous administrative buildings; an impression that grows by the day. Even ten years ago the area between the Zoo and the University was still rural, with low peasant courtyard houses standing in green cabbage fields, but now the road out to the Summer Palace is lined with the same concrete blocks of flats that fill the city proper and the university area, Peking's 'silicon valley' is filled with brightly-lit business premises and shops with neon signs. There are a few islands of traditional houses and shops left (from Qian men to Liulichang and around the Back Lakes just south of Gulou Xi da jie) but much of the city's historic architecture, ancient sites and its grand city plan survive only in the street names.

Around the Forbidden City

Tourist groups are usually taken through from south to north, along the main axis then to the east through the 'treasury' to the garden at the rear. They rarely have time to see the private apartments open on the west side of the main axis, nor to pause in the museum display areas—these latter routes could take several visits.

At the heart of the inner city, the 72-hectare enclosure of the Forbidden City, filled with red-walled, yellow-roofed halls, served both as the centre of the imperial administration and as a home for the imperial family and retinue.

Its name in Chinese, *Zi jin cheng*, is slightly complicated. *Jin cheng* means 'forbidden city' and entry was indeed forbidden to all except members of the imperial family and those on official business (who were only admitted to the front halls). The character *zi* refers to the pole star (*ziwei* means star) at the apex of the heavens where the supreme deity lived in his palace; the emperor, son of heaven, therefore lived in the earthly equivalent. The usual contemporary name for the Forbidden City is the Gu gong or Ancient Palace.

The front half of the palace, the more public area, consists of three broad axes with wide open courtyards and large halls. The rear part, the imperial dwelling area, is more tightly packed with smaller courtyards surrounded by lower buildings, a garden and a maze of open corridors. The palace was inhabited by the last Emperor of the Qing, the Xuantong (Proclaiming Unity) emperor, Henry Aisin Gioro Pu Yi, until 1924, although some of the southern parts of the Forbidden City (the great halls connected with imperial ritual and government) were opened to the public in 1914, three years after the overthrow of the Qing dynasty and the establishment of the Republic.

The palace is surrounded by a moat 52m wide, built in the Ming; the excavated earth was piled up to the north of the moated palace to form *Mei shan*, called Coal Hill by 19C foreigners, probably mistaking the character *mei* ('beautiful') for that which means 'coal'. Vital things, such as the palace's water-supply, had already been laid out by the planners of the Yuan palace, conducting water from a pool in the northwest through the western part of the palace, across the wide front courtyard inside the Wu men (Meridian Gate) where it is called the Jin shui (Golden Waters) and is crossed by five white marble bridges.

On either side of the front part of the palace are two parks, both interesting for their venerable trees in particular. On the left is **Zhongshan Park** (Sun Yatsen Park), once the site of the Ming dynasty altar to the earth and harvests.

The altar is a square white marble terrace filled with different coloured earths (white–west, green–east, black–north, red–south and yellow–centre) and symbolising the imperial control of China's earths from all quarters with their colour associations, part of the major system of the 'five elements'. The emperor made twice-yearly sacrifices in spring and autumn to pray for and give thanks for the harvest.

North of the altar is the **Hall of Prayer** which was later (1928) dedicated to Sun Yatsen. North of the Hall of Prayer is the **Hall of Halberds** where sacrificial implements were kept, including 72 halberds used in the protection of the altar. Just inside the entrance to the park is a white marble *pailou* (ceremonial gateway) with blue tiled roofs, the **Ketteler Memorial** which used to stand in Chongwenmen da jie (known as Hatamen Street by foreign residents).

Baron Clement August von Kettler

Baron Clement August von Kettler (1853–1900), the German Ambassador to China, was on his way to the Zongli yamen (Tsungli yamen in Wade-Giles), the imperial foreign ministry, to protest about the growing menace to the foreign legations of the Boxer Movement when he was murdered by Boxers on 20 June 1900. His memorial bears inscriptions in Chinese, German and Latin expressing the emperor's regret. It used to stand on the spot where he was killed but was moved to its present location in 1918.

Peking: the Forbidden City

The park to the right of the entrance to the Forbidden City is now known as the **Workers' Cultural Palace** (Gongren wenhuagong) but was previously the Temple of the Imperial Ancestors. Yongle established it here in 1420 and it was rebuilt in 1544. Ceremonies in honour of ancestors were held here by both Ming and Qing emperors on New Year's Day and other important occasions, such as weddings and coronations. Although it is now a public park, it is interesting to note that the ashes of celebrated leaders (Zhou Enlai, Zhu De, etc) are laid out here for the masses to file past (the equivalent of lying-in-state but it happens after cremation), thus its connections with the souls of the dead are retained.

Tiananmen and the Square

Tiananmen (Gate of Heavenly Peace) lies well south of the moat and the truly 'forbidden' city yet it once marked the outer limit of the imperial domain and the emperor would only on rare occasions sally forth through the gate. Before the widening of the square, the ministries of the imperial government lay on either side of the 'imperial way' that led south through the Qianmen (Front Gate), still visible on the far side of the square. To the east were the Ministries of Rites, Works and War and the Astronomical Office; to the west, the Ministry of Justice, the Office of Sacrifices and the Court of Censors.

In front of Tiananmen stands the **Monument to the People's Heroes** (1958), a granite obelisk on a double terrace. The inscription to the north is in Chairman Mao's calligraphy and reads: 'The peoples' heroes are invincible'. To the south is a longer inscription in the neater, more clerical hand of Zhou Enlai.

The low relief carvings depict: (east) Lin Zexu destroying chests of opium in Canton, 1842, and the Taiping Uprising of 1851; (west) the guerrilla war against Japan, 1937–45, and the Nanchang Uprising of 1927; (north) Communist troops cross the Yangtse,1949, and (right) provision of grain for the troops and (left) 'Long Live the Liberation Army'; (south) the Qing Uprising of 1911, the 4 May demonstration against the terms of the Treaty of Versailles, 1919, and the 30 May demonstration in Shanghai against the British and Japanese, 1925.

The monument is appropriately sited for the square has seen many of the early 20C demonstrations, such as that of 4 May 1919. As I was writing the first edition of the *Blue Guide*, it had just seen its bloodiest suppression, that of the students and citizens supporting a movement for greater press freedom and democracy on 4 June 1989. After the Tiananmen incident, the square was heavily policed in order to prevent any further protests: two men were arrested there for leafleting on the tenth anniversary of the massacre. The square was closed for many months before the celebration of the fiftieth anniversary of the founding of the People's Republic of China (1 October 1999), partly to maintain public order, although ostensibly to replace the paving stones before the celebratory tanks and missiles were driven through.

Beyond the monument is the **Mausoleum for Chairman Mao** built by 70,000 volunteers in ten months (October 1976–August 1977). It is built in the 'national style' (related to the 1958 Great Hall of the People to the west and the Historical Museum to the east), flat-roofed with rather Egyptian columns and a narrow line of yellow tiles along the roofline. The 13 pine trees from Yan'an recall Mao's 13 years there (1936–49) and the interior is lavishly decorated with a huge tapestry of hills and rivers based on a design by the contemporary painter Huang Yongyu. There are marble floors and a crystal coffin containing the embalmed body (visitable but with changing opening times).

Just south of the Mausoleum, or Maosoleum, is the barbican gate, the **Qianmen** (Front Gate), which used to stand in the wall separating the inner and outer cities. Like other fine gate structures in Peking and elsewhere (Xi'an for example), its grey brick base is topped with a tiled roof and timber-framed gatehouse.

The west of the square is largely occupied by the **Great Hall of the People** where large government assemblies meet. This can be visited by tour groups. It is a fine example of high Fifties design, Chinese style, filled with interminable red-carpeted corridors and massive rooms. Each province of China has its own room which is decorated with local materials. Fujian province is famous for its lacquer, for example, so lacquer dominates the Fujian room. There are massive screens and huge heroic wall-hangings or paintings and giant examples of acceptable art forms like cork carving or filigree iron-work. Behind (west) is the building site where the French architect Andreau's 'glass egg' theatre and concert hall is being constructed, amid much controversy.

On the east of the square is the **Historical Museum**, one of the most important displays (arranged chronologically) in China. Its official name is the Museum of Chinese Revolutionary History but the exhibits cover a far longer period than the name suggests, from Peking Man up to 1949. The fact that the display does not cover the period after 1949 reflects the problem of the continuous reasessment of history which has gone on in China, particularly during the Cultural Revolution (1966–76) and after. Western experts continue to argue over the validity of the displays: are the objects real or clever facsimiles? As this is rarely made clear by labels, it remains a question of the pull of Peking versus the non-metropolitan authorities (although the best exhibits are, for reasons of conservation, almost all facsimiles, with the originals stored in better conditions). English language labels are being gradually installed and there are frequent temporary exhibitions. The English language newspaper, *China Daily*, lists the temporary exhibitions held here and in other galleries throughout the city.

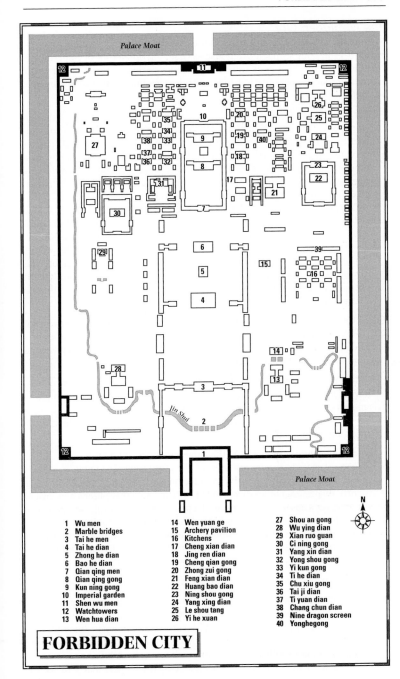

1 Wu men	14 Wen yuan ge	27 Shou an gong
2 Marble bridges	15 Archery pavilion	28 Wu ying dian
3 Tai he men	16 Kitchens	29 Xian ruo guan
4 Tai he dian	17 Cheng xian dian	30 Ci ning gong
5 Zhong he dian	18 Jing ren dian	31 Yang xin dian
6 Bao he dian	19 Cheng qian gong	32 Yong shou gong
7 Qian qing men	20 Zhong zui gong	33 Yi kun gong
8 Qian qing gong	21 Feng xian dian	34 Ti he dian
9 Kun ning gong	22 Huang bao dian	35 Chu xiu gong
10 Imperial garden	23 Ning shou gong	36 Tai ji dian
11 Shen wu men	24 Yang xing dian	37 Ti yuan dian
12 Watchtowers	25 Le shou tang	38 Chang chun dian
13 Wen hua dian	26 Yi he xuan	39 Nine dragon screen
		40 Yonghegong

FORBIDDEN CITY

The Forbidden City

Tiananmen Gate, the entrance to the Forbidden City, is another massive gate with the same wooden gatehouse as Qianmen and a roof of imperial yellow tiles. In front of it runs the moat that flows around the palace, and the gate is approached over five low marble bridges leading to the five openings in the gate.

The central opening was previously reserved for the emperor, although empresses could pass through it on their wedding days and the three top candidates in the highest civil service exams left the palace through it after accepting their honours. Princes and members of the imperial family used the gates to either side while those furthest to the left and right were only opened when the emperor held court and then civil officials used the east gateway, and military officials the west.

The gate is now decorated with one of the rare surviving portraits of Mao Zedong (whose image, whether graven or painted, has disappeared from most other public buildings) and two signboards reading (west) 'Long live the People's Republic of China' and (east) 'Long live the great unity of the peoples of the world'. Since 1949 the gate has been used as a stand for high officials to view occasional parades in Tiananmen Square and it has recently been opened to visitors. It offers a fine prospect of the square below although 'Visitors who are not clean and tidy in dress cannot be [let] in'.

Inside the Tianan Gate there is a longish walk, through a courtyard lined with low office buildings, to the **Wumen** (**Meridian Gate**) in the walls of the Forbidden City proper, just inside the moat. The walls are nearly 8m high, 8.6m broad at the base and 6.6m broad at the top.

With a core of rammed earth, the walls were unusually solid in construction, having a triple layer of bricks on either side, finished with mortar to give a smooth surface. The bricks used on the outer surface were made in Linqing in Shandong province and are 48 x 24 x 12cm, each (of the 12 million used) weighing 24kg.

During the Qing (1644–1911) the emperor would stand on the wall in the gatehouse above to receive prisoners of war after military campaigns, to issue proclamations or to present the almanac on the first day of the tenth lunar month. Inspection parades were held before the gate three times a month in the emperor's absence (if he was in the palace, his tri-monthly acceptance of memorials from his officials was held in the Hall of Supreme Harmony to the north). During the Ming, punishment of officials by beating was carried out on the eastern side of the 'imperial way' in front of the Meridian Gate.

The Meridian Gate was built in 1420 and substantially restored in 1647 and 1801. It is unusual in that it is constructed with two wings stretching south on either side.

- **Tickets** It is at the Meridian Gate that visitors buy their entrance tickets to the Palace complex. It is worth arriving early (it opens at 08.30) to avoid crowds. Ticketing systems for the Forbidden City vary. At the moment there are two forms of ticket: 30 yuan 'basic' and 50 yuan 'all-in' and the latter is recommended as it allows entrance into extra gardens and exhibits. For those who have time in Peking it is worth paying several visits, particularly to see the western axis and the exhibition halls. Visitors may only enter the Forbidden City through the Meridian Gate, although they may leave by the same gate, or by the northernmost gate, the Shenwumen, or by the southern of the two eastern gates, the Donghuamen (a rather pleasant walk).

Inside the Meridian Gate is a vast paved courtyard through which the Jin shui flows in a balustraded channel spanned by five marble bridges. At the far end of the courtyard the **Gate of Supreme Harmony** (Taihemen, rebuilt in 1890) leads to the courtyard in front of the **Hall of Supreme Harmony** (Taihedian, one of the three great halls). The courtyard is the largest in the palace and was very much part of the ceremonial significance of the Hall of Supreme Harmony. The central

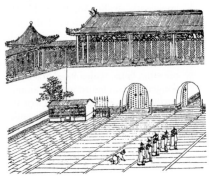

The Wumen (Meridian Gate)

'imperial way' leading across the courtyard is of marble, the rest of the courtyard paved with grey bricks, similar to those of the surrounding walls. The soft bricks require frequent replacement.

As court paintings of the Qing show, the emperor sat on his throne, high up in the hall (which is raised on a three-tiered platform). The front of the hall is made up of folding panels, with solid bottoms and lattice windows above. These could be folded back to allow the emperor a view of his officials lined up in the vast courtyard below. White stone slabs laid in the grey bricks of the courtyard indicated where the imperial guard should stand and foot-high bronze markers in the shape of mountains (inscribed with degrees of rank in Chinese and Manchu) indicated where officials of each rank should be.

The hall stands on a white marble platform which supports the other two major halls behind. It is known as the Sumeru Terrace after the multi-tiered mythical mountain of Buddhism and, while most major buildings are raised on stone platforms, triple tiers are rare except in imperial buildings (including the Temple of Heaven). The balustrades of the terraces are lavishly carved, in this case with cloud scrolls on the post capitals (elsewhere in the Forbidden City, variant decorations are found on balustrades and post capitals) and the drainage channels end in elaborate gargoyles in the form of *chi* (hornless dragons). There are two rows of steps leading up to the hall and a central stair slab, an elaborately carved ramp of white marble over which the imperial sedan chair was carried. This one is carved with dragons chasing pearls amongst clouds over mountains.

The dragon is the symbol of the emperor (as well as an auspicious, rain-bearing beast) and the pearl is variously explained as a symbol of purity or of rain-heralding thunder. In other parts of the Forbidden City there are differently decorated stair slabs: the phoenix, symbol of the empress, is found on that before the Palace of Inheriting Heaven in the northeast corner of the inner court, where women lived, and is also used as a ceiling decoration in the same area.

The vast hall (2730 square metres) is a nine-bay construction (11 bays if you include the narrower side verandas) with a double-eaved, hipped roof covered in yellow tiles.

At either end of the main ridge is the open-mouthed dragon (*chi wen*) apparently swallowing the end of the ridge; the *chi wen* is supposed to be a particularly watery child of the dragon whose damp presence would protect a building from fire. This gives the ridge the characteristic form of the Ming-Qing. Along the ridge at the eaves end is the equally characteristic row of tiny animals in the same yellow glazed tile: they comprise dragons, phoenix, lions, scaled lions, sea horses, fire-eating beasts, scaled oxen and a winged human figure with an animal face leaning on a sword, and are often enclosed between another *chi wen* and, at the eaves end, a human figure riding a chicken (possibly the legendary tyrant Prince Min of Qi who was hanged from the eaves as a lesson to others). Below, the brackets supporting the painted tie-beams are reduced in size but increased in number, when compared with the magisterial bracketing of earlier Tang and even Song buildings, forming a decorative frieze above the tie-beams. The internal and external timbers are painted, here in the multi-coloured *he xi* style used in the grandest halls. A similar style, also found in grand halls, is the *xuan xi* (which is less angular, incorporating more rounded forms); the Suzhou style, found predominantly in garden pavilions and women's living quarters, incorporates realistic flowers and genre scenes in cartouches.

Inside the hall, the floor is paved with hard dark tiles known as 'metal bricks' (as they make a metallic sound when struck), produced for the palaces in the Suzhou area and ferried up the Grand Canal. To protect these tiles, visitors are no longer allowed to wander freely within the halls. The timbers are of *nan mu* (*Phoebe nanmu*) from Sichuan province, the huge logs destined to form single columns in the great halls floated by river to the Grand Canal, taking three to four years en route.

The columns and external timbers were, and still are, coated in a thick protective mixture of hemp, clay, tong oil and pigs' blood, then painted red in the traditional manner, using a bunch of paint-soaked rags rather than a brush. The layers can be seen during repairs, and where the coating is damaged it is still possible to see the half-inch-thick hemp and clay mixture.

Above the red columns, the ceiling is painted mainly in green and gold in the *he xi* style with angular cartouches enclosing golden imperial dragons in different forms. There is a fine coffered ceiling. The columns surrounding the raised throne are painted gold with dragons in relief and the same dragon motif is seen on the golden screen behind the throne and on the carved and gilded throne itself.

The hall was relatively rarely used: the emperor would proceed southwards from his apartments in the inner court on New Year's Day when all his officials would wait below with the court orchestra as the emperor cracked his 10m-long red silk whip. He would also attend ceremonies here at the winter solstice, on his birthday, when the list of successful candidates in the imperial examinations was published, and at the beginning of a major military campaign.

Behind is the **Hall of Perfect Harmony** (Zhonghedian), a charming and elegant square building with a hipped pavilion roof topped by a roof pommel. It was restored in 1627 and 1765 and now contains various of the imperial sedan chairs.

In both the Ming and Qing it was a place of preparation before major ceremonies: the emperor would read the scripts of memorials to be presented to him and inspect the grain and agricultural implements he was to use in ceremonies in which he inaugurated the agricultural year by ploughing a ceremonial furrow and planting seed in the Temple of Agriculture in the south of the town. During the Qing it was decided that the imperial genealogies, known as the *yu pu* or jade lists, should be revised every ten years and the emperor read the revised versions here.

Behind is the **Hall of Preserving Harmony** (Baohedian), rectangular in plan, with a double-eaved hip and gablet (mini gabled) roof. Its previous names were Hall of Respectful Care and Contentment in the early Ming, and Hall of Establishing Supremacy during the late Ming. It was given its present name in the early Qing. Its interior appears lighter than that of the Hall of Supreme Harmony for, using a Song and Yuan technique called 'without pillars', several of the interior columns were 'missed out', creating a wider, more open effect.

The emperor sometimes assumed his imperial robes here before proceeding by sedan chair to the Hall of Supreme Harmony. He also held banquets here and the examinations for the title of *jin shi* (presented scholar), the highest level of the three-tiered exam system.

Behind the hall there is a fine view of the rear garden of the palace area and the external gardens around the **Bei Hai Lake** (North Sea Lake) with the white stupa. The stair slab behind the Hall of Preserving Harmony is the largest in the entire palace.

Carved from a single slab of marble, it is decorated with a classic scroll border enclosing dragons in clouds above mountains and waves (representing the earth). The great slab of marble came from Fang shan (also known as Shijing shan) some 48km away and, weighing over 200 tons, took some 20,000 men 28 days to drag it to its present position. Some said that it was moved in the depths of winter when water was thrown on the roads to form slippery ice to facilitate the task.

The galleries that surround the courtyards beside the Three Great Halls were used as stores for such items as ceramics, winter and summer garments, furs and weaponry.

Behind the Hall of Preserving Harmony is a wide courtyard whose walls mark the boundary between the inner and outer courts. Beyond is the truly 'forbidden' city where only the thousands of eunuchs (nearly 1500 were dismissed in 1922 when the last emperor's tutor, Sir Reginald Johnston, discovered that some were secretly selling off palace treasures for their own profit), maids and members of the imperial family were allowed. Most tourist groups are led eastwards to the treasury but I will complete the central axis and then describe the western and eastern ones.

Immediately north of the Hall of Preserving Harmony is the **Palace of Heavenly Purity** (Qianqinggong), first built in 1420 but three times destroyed by fire (last reconstructed, apparently using many of the original timbers, in 1797). This, together with the Hall of Union (Jiaotaidian) and the Palace of

Earthly Tranquillity (Kunninggong), forms the **Three Palaces** (paired with the Three Great Halls) and was, in the Ming, the living area for the emperor and empress, hence their position on the central axis.

The side wings of the courtyard before the Palace of Heavenly Purity contained the emperor's clothing (east in the Hall of Accomplishing Uprightness), his office and study (west in the Hall of Industrious Energy), a secretariat staffed by scholars from the Hanlin Academy ready to answer queries on the emperor's behalf (east end of the southern gallery) and the classroom of the heir to the throne (west end of the southern gallery). To the north were the imperial apothecary, the chief eunuch's office and the treasury office.

The emperors slept here until Yongzheng (reigned 1723–36) moved to the Hall of Mental Cultivation (Yangxindian) in the courtyard immediately to the west. The palace was henceforth used for greeting foreign emissaries. The emperor also received congratulations from his own officials on his birthday in this palace and gave banquets, notably the 'thousand old men banquets' held in 1722 (the sixty-first year of the reign of Kangxi) and 1785 (the fiftieth year of Qianlong) when 3000 men of all ranks over the age of 60 were invited and presented with walking sticks.

There is still a throne in the centre of the hall, and huge mirrors and carved cupboards.

Until the mid 19C, a custom inaugurated by the Yongzheng emperor to avoid unseemly factional struggles over a death-bed was to make a second copy of the name of the designated heir and place it in a box behind the horizontal board, inscribed with the characters for 'upright and pure in mind'. The emperor carried the other copy on his person.

Beside the throne, similar in design although somewhat more ornate than those in the Three Great Halls, apart from the cloisonné incense burners, are two cranes (symbols of longevity) bearing lotus leaves in their long beaks with spikes to hold candles. It was the practice for dead emperors to be laid out temporarily in this palace before being moved to Coal Hill and thence to the two Qing tomb enclosures outside Peking.

Outside, tubs of dwarf pomegranate trees have been placed along the 'imperial way' approaching the palace whose name-board (blue with gold characters and frame, hung under the upper eaves) is inscribed in both Manchu and Chinese, unlike those of the Three Great Halls where only Chinese is used.

Behind the Palace of Heavenly Purity is the smaller **Hall of Union** (Jiaotaidian), built in 1420 and restored in 1655. In design and position (between the two grander halls) it echoes the Hall of Perfect Harmony (Zhonghedian) in the outer court. It also has a pyramid pavilion roof culminating in a golden roof pommel but lacks the verandah of the former.

This used to be the throne room of the empresses, where they received homage on the main festivals of the year, until the 18C when the imperial family moved their living quarters to halls on the west and east (the latter axis favoured by women). During the reign of the Qianlong emperor it became the practice to store the imperial seals here in caskets. These, the equivalent of the imperial signature, were of great value and importance. They can still be seen, their caskets covered with yellow silk damask covers.

The hall contains much calligraphy by the Qianlong emperor and two clocks, a chiming clock produced in the palace (late 18C) and a clepsydra of c 1800. Above the throne is a tablet inscribed with the two characters *wu wei* (refrain from action), one of the Taoist ideals.

Behind is the **Palace of Earthly Tranquillity** (Kunninggong) with its relatively simply decorated interior. This was the official residence of the empress, although during the Qing she no longer actually lived here.

It was, however, used as a bridal chamber for most emperors who would spend the first three nights after the wedding in the eastern 'warm' chamber of the palace where the bed, surrounded by a carved wooden frame, was hung with silken curtains embroidered with the traditional theme of the 'hundred children at play' (often seen in Ming paintings and in New Year prints).

The palace is said to be decorated in the Manchu style: with long wooden *kang* lining the walls, some with yellow silk cushion-seats.

> ### Kang
> The *kang* or brick bed (a hollow brick platform which could be heated by braziers from underneath) was a standard fixture against the southern or outer walls of traditional houses throughout north China but the Manchu, coming from the extremely cold northeast, often had *kang* platforms all round the room, not just under the windows. In both the Forbidden City and the Summer Palace low wooden platforms (*yi he yuan*) are used instead of the crude brick platforms of ordinary homes and their disposition reflects Manchu taste.

Manchu taste can also be seen in the filigree corner decorations of the plain ceiling panels (not unlike the cut-work decoration found on Tibetan tents) which stand out in marked contrast to the overall painting of the Chinese-style rooms on the eastern axis.

The 'Last Emperor', Henry Aisin-Gioro Pu Yi (1906–67), was meant to spend his wedding night here in 1922 in what he described as 'rather a peculiar room: it was unfurnished except for the bed-platform which filled a quarter of it and everything about it except the floor, was red' (the Chinese colour for good luck, always used at weddings). There were 'red bed-curtains, red pillows, a red dress, a red skirt, red flowers and a red face ...' since the bride was clad entirely in the auspicious colour. Pu Yi, said to be keener on ants than women, 'decided that [he] preferred the Mind Nurture Palace Hall of Mental Cultivation, and went back there'.

The western part of the palace, once the empresses had moved out, was used for sacrifices to Chinese and Manchu gods and has a sort of kitchen where sacrifices were made and food for offerings prepared, including 1300 pigs for the kitchen god annually. Once the food offerings had been made to the spirits, they were eaten by the participating human beings, including the emperor and empress.

Behind the Palace of Earthly Tranquillity are the northernmost galleries (with the imperial apothecary and pharmacy, eunuchs and treasury offices), the right-hand one now housing a display of the Last Emperor's possessions, including his toys.

Pu Yi was declared heir to the throne on the death of the Guangxu emperor in 1908. He was only two (and not the correct heir; his nomination was one of the Empress Dowager Cixi's last attempts to retain power) so he was brought up in the palace.

Between the galleries is the **Gate of Earthly Tranquillity** which leads straight in to the **Imperial Garden** (Yu huayuan). The major (but not the only) garden in the Forbidden City, it was laid out in the Ming and remains little changed (quite a number of the trees are thought to be original). It is 80m by 140m and sparsely provided with the water that is an integral part of the traditional Chinese garden. Although there are two lily pools beneath the balanced pair of the Pavilion of Auspicious Clarity in the northwest corner and the Jade Green Floating Pavilion in the northeast corner, the garden focuses on buildings, rockeries, trees and *pen jing* (or 'pot scenes').

On the central axis is a long path leading to a gate, the **Tian yi men** (First Gate of Heaven, a name commonly found in temples) which cuts the vista, offering a glimpse of two pines twisted together. Beyond is the major building of the garden, the **Hall of Imperial Peace** (Jin'an dian). The simple grey First Gate of Heaven, made of finely ground grey bricks, is flanked by two bronze *qilin*: mythical beasts, often identified with unicorns, they have the bodies of deer, horses' hooves, ox tails and single horns; these are variant beasts with flaming manes. *Qilin* are said to be only visible when a wise ruler is on the throne. Behind the *qilin* are two meteorite-like rock clusters mounted on carved stone pedestals, some of the many interesting rocks, including fossil tree-trunks, a cluster of fossilised seaslugs and more common lake rocks from near Wuxi, which are mounted as *pen jing* on finely-carved stone bases throughout the garden.

Apart from the central axis, the buildings are arranged in pairs, east and west, like the two pavilions over pools. Their names are frequently paired, too: just south of the two pool-pavilions are a pair of pavilions that are cross-shaped in plan, to the west the **Pavilion of a Thousand Autumns** and to the east the **Pavilion of Ten Thousand Springs**.

The major rockery (there are several) is set against the back wall, just to the east of the gate. It is high enough for the **Pavilion of Imperial Prospect** on top of it to afford a view of the outside world.

For the women of the imperial family, this was probably their only view of the outside and the rockery's position, against the wall, is typical. Chinese fiction and legends are full of lovers' meetings amid rockeries, the woman, forbidden to leave the house, climbing up to speak to her lover who is outside on the road. At festivals, where it was traditional practice to ascend hills, as in the Mid-Autumn Festival in the eighth lunar month when the full moon was viewed from high places, the imperial family would climb up this artificial mountain (the Hill of Piled Excellence).

A notable feature of the garden is the widespread use of pebble-patterned pavements with many-coloured stones laid in different patterns or forming horses, pots of flowers, figures from opera and even a depiction of the bridge and bronze oxen at the Summer Palace.

A double gate leads to the outer part of the palace, just inside the northernmost gate, the **Gate of Martial Spirit** (Shenwu men). It is composed of the **Gate of Inherited Light**, which is flanked by two gilt bronze elephants on carved stone pedestals, the elephants' legs, like those in the Potala at Chengde, uncomfortably bent the wrong way at the knee, on the basis of which they may be assumed to be 18C. In the outer wall is the **Gate of the Pursuit of Truth**, the inner rear gate of the Forbidden City, leading out to the broad road that runs between the inner and outer walls. At either corner of the outer walls, the complex corner towers can be clearly seen at this point. In the Shenwu men, there is a dark exhibition hall at the top of the gate which sets out some of the aspects of the construction of the Forbidden City, with some of the small wooden models made by the architects and other relics like ceramic drain pipes and roof tiles.

The incredibly complex arrangements of double-hipped roofs and gablets of the corner watchtowers create the effect of 'floating eaves'. One Peking legend has it that when the builders of the Forbidden City were absolutely stumped by the corner towers, they were assisted by the sudden appearance of an old man carrying a beautiful birdcage made of straw with an incredibly complicated roof. The old man who provided the model for the solution of the problem was Lu Ban, the legendary patron saint of carpenters and builders, who arrived in the nick of time.

Returning to the division between the inner and outer courts, behind the **Hall of the Preservation of Harmony** (Bao he dian), the small building in the northwest corner of the courtyard was the office of the Grand Council. Beside it a small gate leads to a long corridor which runs between the Three Rear Palaces (on the right) and the living quarters of the Qing emperors (on the left).

The **Hall of Mental Cultivation**, built in the Ming, became the living quarters of the emperor from the Yongzheng period (1723–36) when the Yongzheng emperor decided not to live in the Palace of Heavenly Purity where his father had resided for more than 60 years. The hall is H-shaped in plan (with the H on its side); the emperors used the front part as an office and the rear part as a bedroom. South of the hall, the long gallery was the dining room of the inner court. There were no fixed times for meals for emperors, whose food was brought to them as required, wherever they were. As they spent much time here (after Yongzheng), the dining room was most conveniently situated. The side halls to east and west housed Buddhist shrines. The galleries outside the courtyard were the duty rooms of the eunuchs.

In front of the gate leading to the hall is a large jade tablet, the centre of which is in the form of a *bi disc*, pierced and surrounded by carved five-clawed dragons (five-clawed dragons were 'imperial' symbols, 'ordinary' dragons were three-clawed). Inside the gate is a screen, hiding the interior from view and preventing the ingress of malevolent spirits, who were believed only to be able to fly in straight lines. Such screens, known as 'spirit walls', are commonly found in domestic architecture.

The hall itself has a variant roof, the front part covered with a 'rolled pitched roof', curving smoothly over the ridge, without the raised line of upstanding roof tiles found on other roof ridges in the palace. The three-bay front hall has a central throne room which is, however, more businesslike in arrangement than other throne halls in the palace for bookcases curtained in black and blue silk line the walls on either side of the throne.

The western bay, called the **Room of the Three Rarities**, was where the emperors summoned their grand councillors. The front part of the bay has an unusual floor of blue and white ceramic tiles and a huge painting opposite the door (by the Jesuit Giuseppe Castiglione and Jin Tingbao, 1756) involves a *trompe l'oeil* depiction of the floor tiles and window lattices, apparently extending the room. The Qianlong emperor used to keep three extremely rare pieces of calligraphy by Wang Xizhi (see p 125), Wang Xianzhi and Wang Xun in the room, hence its name.

The Qianlong emperor was a great connoisseur of the arts, although some now find it hard to forgive his habit of inscribing his extremely rare and valuable paintings himself. While this was a common practice and could enhance the value and interest of a painting, showing who had owned it and what they thought of it, the Qianlong emperor's inscriptions, in a large, bold hand, were often placed centrally (most connoisseurs would inscribe the margins only), tending to spoil the overall design.

The room is light and pleasant and a fine example of imperial interior design.

The room to the east of the main throne room with a rare carpet on the floor (carpets were more often placed on *kang* platforms) was the one in which the Dowager Empress Cixi used to control the infant emperors she placed on the throne (Tongzhi, reigned 1862–75, and Guangxu, reigned 1875–1908). Even when they grew up, these emperors could never quite escape her despite a brave attempt by Guangxu in 1898, prompted by a series of memorials addressed to him (but frequently intercepted) by the reformer Kang Youwei (1858–1927).

Kang's ideas on a constitutional monarchy and 'national self-strengthening' based on Confucian ideals were advanced, given China's evident weakness in the face of western and more humiliating Japanese threats, and the emperor was keen to support them. For 100 days plans were made to create modern armament factories in China, to found modern universities (including Peking University) and to begin teaching science and politics and abandon the traditional examination system based on literary classics. The Dowager Empress intervened, however, to imprison those reformers she could catch (Kang Youwei fled abroad) and the emperor, whom she kept under house arrest until his somewhat suspicious death in 1908.

The throne in the western room shows how she controlled affairs: behind it hangs a yellow silk curtain concealing another chair behind, where the Dowager Empress sat listening while affairs of state were discussed. The large, rather horrible piece of calligraphy to the right is by her.

A corridor links the front and back parts of the hall. The rear rooms are all provided with *kang* (hollow platforms to be heated from underneath) and the furnishings are largely as they were during the Guangxu period (1875–1908). Pu Yi, the last emperor, also lived here but, despite his interest in Charlie Chaplin and his frequent assumption of western-style dress, including pink spats, probably had little lasting effect on the decoration. On the far west of the rear hall is the **Hall of Festive Joy** where concubines and palace maids 'waited' and to the east is the **Hall of Manifest Compliance** used as a bedchamber by the manifestly uncompliant Dowager Empress Cixi whenever she stayed with the emperor.

Behind the Yangxin dian are the **Six Western Palaces**, reached from an alleyway that runs from the northwest corner of the Yangxin dian.

They were fundamentally used as residences by the empresses, secondary wives, widows and children from the mid 17C. Like the Yangxin dian, they are furnished much as they were in the late 19C when the last empresses, concubines and children of the imperial family lived here.

First, on the left, immediately northwest of the Yangxin dian is the **Hall of the Ultimate Principle** (Taiji dian), originally named the Palace of Infirmity; later, because the Zhengde emperor of the Ming (reigned 1506–22) was born there, his son renamed it Palace of Initiating Auspiciousness in 1535 and it was given its present name during the Qing. It has a pleasant shady courtyard full of trees and a large spirit wall (screen) of glazed tiles.

Immediately behind it is the **Hall of Manifest Origin**, built in the late Qing, with an extension at the back to form a stage visible from the Palace of Eternal Spring, which lies to the north. The **Palace of Eternal Spring**, without a stage, was originally the residence of Concubine Li of the Tianqi emperor of the Ming (reigned 1621–28) and later used by the Dowager Empress when she was acting as Regent for the infant Tongzhi emperor in the mid 19C. It was she who had the stage installed so that plays could be performed for her. The concubines of the Guangxu emperor and Pu Yi also lived here. The dark hardwood throne with its yellow and blue embroidered cushions stands in front of a screen painted with bamboo and birds, lightening the somewhat oppressive gloom of the furniture.

The walls of the corridors surrounding the palace building have an unusual series of paintings illustrating scenes from the great novel *Hong lou meng* (*Dream of the Red Chamber/Story of the Stone* by Cao Xueqin, c 1760). As the book contains many episodes relating to the life of women inside a grand but declining household, the subject is most appropriate to the setting. Probably executed towards the end of the 19C, the works make considerable use of western painting styles (perspectives, *trompe l'oeil*).

Immediately east of the Palace of Eternal Spring, on the other side of the alley, is the **Palace of the Emperor's Assistance** which has the most lavish 'hanging curtain partitions' of openwork carved hardwood. These partitions, like great swags of flowers and foliage, are found in various interiors in the Forbidden City, usually placed between columns. The palace also has very lavish door plates and handles decorated with bat motifs (a *rebus* for wealth) and stylised characters meaning longevity. North of the Palace of the Emperor's Assistance is the **Hall of Manifest Harmony**, which has a particularly fine ceiling painted in the Suzhou style, with landscapes, floral and genre scenes amongst gilt dragons and enclosing geometric and curvilinear forms.

The northernmost of the Six Western Palaces is the **Palace of Gathering Excellence** and it is perhaps the most lavishly

Illustration to the Dream of the Red Chamber *by Cao Xueqin*

decorated. Built in 1420, it was last refurbished in 1884 for the fiftieth birthday of the Dowager Empress Cixi, who lived in it for the next ten years. It is a five-bay hall with a single-eaved hip and gablet roof and stands in a broad courtyard with two old cypresses. The bronze dragons and deer in front of the terrace date from 1884. The ceiling inside is painted in the Suzhou style. In the central bay is a wooden platform with a carpet (this arrangement was more common than placing a carpet on the floor) in front of a mirrored screen behind the throne which is surrounded by the usual impedimenta of incense burners, ceremonial fans and high tables with pots of jewelled flowers. The partition doors on either side are of rosewood, the lower panels carved with bamboo and magnolia, the upper panels containing silk paintings made by senior officials enclosed within glass.

To the west was the Dowager Empress's sitting room and beyond that, separated by a large mirror carved with the characters for good luck and longevity, her bedroom. The bed, with its double curtains and marvellously variegated quilts, is splendid. The upper parts of the lattice windows incorporate the Buddhist swastika, which goes the other way from that of the Nazis and is a symbol of good fortune, and circular motifs made up of bats and, again, the character for long life. In the eastern side rooms are asymmetrical open display cabinets and a gaudy ivory model of a dragon boat.

Leaving the Palace of Gathering Excellence, immediately to the east are the Imperial Garden and the northern gate of the Forbidden City. In the parallel series of **Six Eastern Palaces**, most of the halls are now filled with displays of *objets d'art*, many, but not all, from the old imperial collections, such as remain after Chiang Kai-shek had many of the treasures moved with him to Taiwan in 1949.

These and the major display of historical relics in the side halls to the east and west of the Three Great Halls could be visited together. Starting from the south, on either side of the raised Sumeru platform on which stand the Three Great Halls (Supreme Harmony, Perfect Harmony and Preservation of Harmony), in the galleries which were once imperial storehouses is a display of 'historical art', a chronologically arranged display which goes from early man to the late 19C. Not particularly linked to the imperial buildings, imperial family or their collections, it is, in effect, another historical museum of a high standard.

Behind the Hall of Preservation of Harmony, to the east of the gate that leads into the Palace of Heavenly Purity, is a small side gate. This leads to an alleyway that runs north and gives access to the Six Eastern Palaces. The first (southernmost) buildings to the right (east) of the alley, not strictly part of the Six Eastern Palaces, are the **Hall of Abstinence** (Zhai Gong) where the early Qing emperors would come to fast for a day before proceeding to the **Temple of Heaven** or Altar of the Earth (in the northeast suburbs) and the associated **Hall of Sincere Respect**. Fasting apparently meant 'total abstention from wine, music, hot and spicy foods, as well as onions and garlic'.

In these and the next building, the **Palace of Great Benevolence** (Jing ren gong), are displays of bronze vessels arranged in chronological order and including items from the old imperial collections.

> The Palace of Great Benevolence was where the Kangxi emperor was born to the 15-year-old empress Xiaokang in 1654. Both the Qianlong and Daoguang emperors lived here as heirs-apparent and Zhen Fei, the beloved Pearl Concubine of the Tongzhi emperor (said to have been killed at the Dowager Empress Cixi's order), also lived here for a time.

The next building to the north is the **Palace of Inheriting Heaven**, a residence for concubines. It has a fine ceiling decorated with paired phoenixes (symbols of women, as opposed to the male dragon). It used to contain Buddhist shrines for the concubines to worship. In the winter, bird-cages with songbirds and aquaria were stored here. It now houses a display of ceramics, which is continued in the **Palace of Eternal Peace** (Yonghe gong) immediately to the east. The Yonghe gong was once the residence of the imperial concubine Jin Fei (1874–1924), older sister of the Pearl Concubine.

North of the Jing ren Gong is the **Palace of Gathering Essence** (Zhongcui gong) used as the residence of the heirs-apparent in the early Ming. It has fine bamboo carving on the partition doors and unusually early *xuan zi* style painted decoration on the inner eaves. Most of the surviving *xuan zi* painting is Qing, whereas this is Ming in date.

Immediately east of the Zhongcui gong is the **Palace of the Great Yang** (Jingyang gong) with a single-eaved hip roof, similar to that of the Tang dynasty Foguang si on Wutai shan, and a wonderful ceiling painted in the Suzhou style with a paired crane motif.

The next hall to the south of the Palace of the Great Yang is the **Yong he gong** and south of that is the **Palace of Prolonged Happiness** (Yanfu gong).

If you then return to the courtyard behind the Hall of the Preservation of Harmony and take the gate to the east, opposite is a gateway that leads to the **Hall for Worshipping Ancestors** (Juxian dian) in which there is now a large display of clocks and watches.

Originally a Ming construction, the large H-shaped hall was renovated in 1676, 1679, 1681 and 1737. The crossbeams are painted in a particularly decorative version of the *xuan zi* style and the interior columns are gilded. During the Qing the hall was used to hold ancestral tablets (small painted wooden tablets on which the names of the deceased were inscribed and which 'represented' them). The tablet of Nurhaci (1559–1626), founder of the dynasty, was placed in the front part of the hall, those of his ancestors behind. The lower panels of the outer doors have a curly gold outline pattern known as the *ruyi* pattern. As with the curled jade 'sceptres', S-shaped carved jades about 30cm long known as *ruyi* sceptres, the term is somewhat baffling. The characters used mean 'as you wish' or 'according to your wishes', so the intention when presenting jade *ruyi* or decorating a door with the *ruyi* pattern is to hope that wishes will come true.

The clocks displayed include a massive Chinese clepsydra of great complexity: bronze buckets slowly drain downwards, raising a tiny gilt tongue-shaped baton (representing ivory aide-memoires held by officials during imperial audience) held in the hand of a tiny figure near the bottom—a massive construction although the actual part telling the time requires binoculars. There are inscriptions in English which reveal that many of the enormously elaborate 18C and 19C timepieces were made abroad—in France, England, Switzerland and elsewhere—and were presented by foreign envoys (shades of the mechanical toys brought by the Macartney mission of 1793). They grow increasingly elaborate: birds in gilded cages, elephants, pheasants, vases of flowers, some (like the Chinese clepsydra) with a tiny wristwatch somewhere in the composition.

South of the Hall for Worshipping Ancestors was a vast empty space stretching southwards to the front wall of the Palace. It is now planted with pines. The **Arrow Pavilion** was the only building to break the view. Not strictly a pavilion, it is really a hall with a grand hipped and gabled roof and a large number of columns supporting the eave-boards of the surrounding verandah (thus reducing the number of intercolumnar brackets and reversing the normal Qing style). In this huge open space, the once-nomadic Manchu emperors rode their horses and practised archery and, in the Arrow Pavilion, tested the martial skills of examination candidates.

In the northeast corner of the great open space is a small gate leading to a courtyard with a fine nine-dragon screen of coloured ceramic tiles on the right. This and the series of buildings on the left, known as the **Palace of Tranquil Longevity** (Ningshou gong), were built by the Qianlong emperor in 1722–26 as he intended to retire and spend his declining years here.

There were buildings on the site dating from 1689 but the emperor constructed his garden and the associated buildings and screen in order to cut himself off from the outside world. He retired there in 1795 and spent the last four years of his life in the palace. In 1889 the deserted buildings were reoccupied by the Dowager Empress Cixi and it was from here that she fled to Xi'an in 1900 when European troops entered Peking to relieve the siege of the foreign legions that had been laid by Boxer rebels (with at least tacit support, if not more, from the court).

The **Gate of Imperial Supremacy** on the right leads to the courtyard in which stands the **Hall of Imperial Supremacy** (Huangji dian), approached by a raised stone walkway. This now contains a painting exhibition.

Ming and Qing paintings from the imperial collections are displayed in the hall, except during the month of October when some of the very early paintings are displayed. This only happens in October when the weather conditions (dry and fine, neither too hot nor too cold nor too damp) are appropriate.

The early paintings include a wonderful scroll of oxen, said to be Tang in date, the famous scroll by Zhang Zeduan (late 11C–early 12C), *Going up the River on the Eve of the Qingming Festival* (*Qing ming shang he tu*), a lively depiction of daily life in the bustling capital of Kaifeng at the time, and many other significant works. After the death of the Dowager Empress in 1908, her coffin lay in state here for over a year, awaiting an auspicious day for burial.

Behind the Hall of Imperial Supremacy is the **Palace of Tranquil Longevity** (Ningshou gong) on the same stone platform. The painting exhibition is continued in here and in the galleries to the west and east that run around the courtyard. Behind, the **Gate of Spiritual Cultivation** (Yangxing men) leads to a small area with three axes, built as the private living quarters of the Qianlong emperor.

To the west (left) is the entrance to the charming **Garden of the Palace of Tranquil Longevity**, built by the emperor. It is long and narrow, but perfectly designed to provide a series of pavilions and views in a restricted space (a clever example of the sort of garden that was associated with grander domestic buildings of the north). Its northernness is seen in the use of colour: the pavilions are painted red and green with Suzhou style painting under the eaves, whereas southern garden architecture is monochrome in order not to compete with the plants, which, in the north, are absent in winter.

Inside the **Gate of Spreading Happiness**, on the right is the **Pavilion of the Carpenters' Square** (a name redolent of simplicity and unworldliness) and on the right is the most notable pavilion, the **Pavilion of the Ceremony of Purification** with the maze-shaped channel in the floor, a 'cup-floating stream', other examples of which can be seen in the Tanzhe Temple outside Peking and at Shaoxing.

Cup-floating stream

That at Shaoxing is the 'original' version, where the famous calligrapher Wang Xizhi (321–379) is supposed to have originated the 'party game' of floating a wine cup along a meandering stream on whose banks his friends sat. When the cup floated in front of one, he would have to compose a poem or, as a forfeit, drink the cup of wine, thus creating an atmosphere of 'literati' conviviality. Here, given the lack of running water, huge vats were used to store well-water which was poured along the channel.

Rockeries with hidden steps and paths complete the first courtyard of the garden, which stretches back through four more with intervening halls. The central part has not been open recently but if it is possible to walk right through the garden, the rear building, the **Study of Peaceful Old Age**, has a very interesting interior with a small stage and the most extraordinary *trompe-l'oeil* wall and ceiling paintings, with a grape arbour on the ceiling and bamboo fencing concealing further buildings on the walls.

The central axis of this northeast corner of the Forbidden City is occupied by a series of charming low halls of a domestic character which now house some of the palace treasures. As it is normal to exit through these halls, first go to the far end of the courtyard where you will find the **Pavilion of Pleasant Sounds** (Changyin ge), the largest of the theatrical stages in the Forbidden City. It houses an exhibition of photographs of palace actors in opera costume, props and costumes and some unusual manuscript playscripts.

The stage was built by Qianlong, although he rarely visited it. It was used far more frequently by the Dowager Empress Cixi when she lived in the adjoining halls. Although a troupe was maintained within the palace, in the late 19C famous actors from outside, such as Mei Lanfang (1894–1961) who made many performing visits outside China, were also invited to perform here. In China theatrical performances were associated with festivals, whether popular or restricted, such as guild celebrations, and this was also true in the Forbidden City.

Performances were given on birthdays, at ceremonies of granting titles or the accession to the throne as well as at the annual festivals of the Beginnning of Spring, Mid-Autumn, New Year and many others. For the sixtieth birthday of the Dowager Empress, performances lasting six to seven hours were given over two periods of a week each.

The pavilion is a three-storey building, with the stage on the central floor as the upper and lower floors were used for special effects (people or backdrops ascending and descending). Opposite is the two-storey **Imperial Viewing Building** (Yueshi lou).

On the way back to the central axis, note the unusual pillar in the corner of the courtyard with a little grey 'palace building' with arched openings on top of it. Its position suggests to me that it is a chimney although others have suggested that it is a dovecote.

The treasury is housed in two charming halls on the central axis of this corner of the Forbidden City: the **Hall of Spiritual Cultivation** (Yangxing dian) and the **Hall of Pleasurable Old Age** (Leshou tang), both of which are built on a small scale and decorated in a way very different from the grand halls of the outer court.

They contain palace treasures, many of which are self-explanatory: gold ingots, golden bells (cast in 1715 using 422kg of gold), 18C jade musical stones imitating those of the Shang dynasty), gold and silver vessels from the imperial table and a wonderful collection of translucent 'spinach' green jade bowls of great elegance (which look like vichyssoise). The stupa-shaped reliquary of cloisonné was made in 1777 to contain the hair of Qianlong's mother on her death. There is armour with gilded and silver links, there are silken robes, countless necklaces of interestingly mixed stones in subtle colours (and great use of baroque pearls), head-dresses of kingfisher feathers, mats made from plaited strands of ivory (cool to sleep on in hot summers, used by the Yongzheng emperor in the 'Old' Summer Palace (Yuan ming yuan) and a lot of *pen jing* (pot scenes) of jade, amethyst, rose quartz and other semi-precious stones carved into flowers and leaves. There is a huge block of jade weighing some 5 tons, carved in the Qianlong reign with scenes of the Great Yu 'taming the floods' and controlling China's rivers. New displays of furniture and other items are gradually being installed.

The buildings themselves are very much domestic; the rear hall has a screen made of irregular openwork display panels (Qianlong intended it as a library) and a low upper storey. The ceilings are painted in the Suzhou style.

As you leave the Hall of Pleasurable Old Age, you pass a small well-cover (a 30cm high ring of stone with a metal bar through it). This is known as the **Well of the Pearl Concubine** (Zhen Fei jing) for she was supposed to have been drowned in it in 1900, when the Dowager Empress fled the palace as the western troops entered the city. The concubine, who was only 25 when she was unceremoniously bundled down the well (supposedly for trying to encourage the Emperor to stay in Peking and face the consequences of Cixi's support of the Boxers), must have been remarkably slender.

Just beyond the well is a gate that leads out of the inner wall of the Forbidden City. As you walk west towards the northern gate, notice the wonderful long corridors that run down between great red walls.

The southeast corner of the Forbidden City, from which the **Eastern Flowery Gate** (Donghua men) exit gate leads out to Nanchizi Street, is the library and cultural section of the palace. From the north, a small back gate leads into the enclosure and the first hall (to the north) is the **Hall of the Literary Abyss** (Wenyuan ge) built in 1774–76 by the Qianlong emperor to house one of the copies of the vast imperial collectanea, the *Si ku quan shu* (*Complete Treasury of the Four Storehouses*), a huge manuscript encyclopaedic work in 36,000 volumes containing copies of some 3450 works.

A similar building is to be found in the Bi shu shan zhuang in Chengde, and in Shenyang (Wensu ge) and all are said to be modelled on the Tianyi ge Library in Ningbo (see p 321) although, as the latter is a southern construction with uplifted eaves and the imperial versions are all rather solid northern constructions, the similarity is spiritual rather than demonstrable. All have pools and rockeries around them to help prevent fire, however, and are two or more storeys high.

Just south of the library building is the H-shaped **Hall of Literary Glory** (Wenhua dian) where the emperors would come once a year for a reading from the Confucian classics. A wall, with a main gate in the south, surrounds the whole.

On the other side of the palace, west of the Gate of Supreme Harmony, is a parallel series of buildings, including the **Hall of Military Eminence** (Wuying dian).

During the Ming this was a place where the emperor could 'purify' himself by fasting and separating himself from his concubines; during the period when the peasant leader Li Zicheng briefly took Peking at the very end of the Ming (1644), he directed his affairs of state from this hall.

Its name is well-known to bibliographers for, during the Qing, it housed the palace printing establishment (known by the name of the hall) where imperial editions were prepared and printed. Unusually, for virtually all of China's publishing up to the mid 19C was by the woodblock technique, a font of copper moveable type was prepared in the Wuying dian in order to print another massive collectanea (this time more of an encyclopaedia for it was composed of extracts from former works arranged by topic), the *Gu jin tu shu ji cheng* (*Synthesis of Books and Illustrations of Ancient and Modern Times*), printed in an edition of 64 in 1728. The work consisted of 10,000 volumes covering all sorts of subjects, thus the font was massive, comprising over a quarter of a million pieces of copper type. As traditional printers might have guessed, the use of moveable type proved unwieldy and the method was not repeated in the Wuying dian; such was the value of the copper that the font was soon melted down and used for coinage.

Central Peking

The Forbidden City used to be surrounded by another larger rectangular enclosure some six times the size of the palace proper, which contained granaries, parks for rearing sheep and cows, storehouses, residences of princes and high officials and the numerous craftsmen who worked both on the upkeep of the city itself (carpenters, masons, painters, brick-makers) or in the imperial workshops producing such goods as clocks and watches, clothing, glasswares, metalwares, jewellery and ceramics. The ceramics were usually porcelains made in Jingdezhen in Jiangxi province and shipped, undecorated, to the palace where overglaze enamel decoration was applied.

The outer walls of the 'imperial city' have largely disappeared except to the south where a high red wall with a yellow ceramic tile top extends from beside the Peking Hotel (east) to the western end of the Nan hai (Southern Sea) Lake. To the west, the whole area around the Zhong hai (Middle Sea—also the name applied to the Mediterranean) and the Nan hai, known collectively as **Zhongnanhai**, is

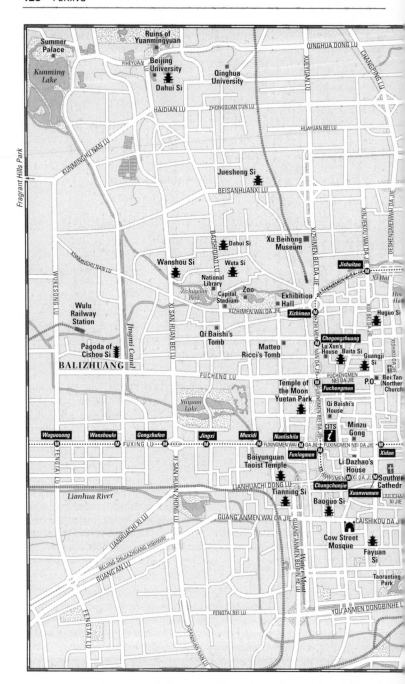

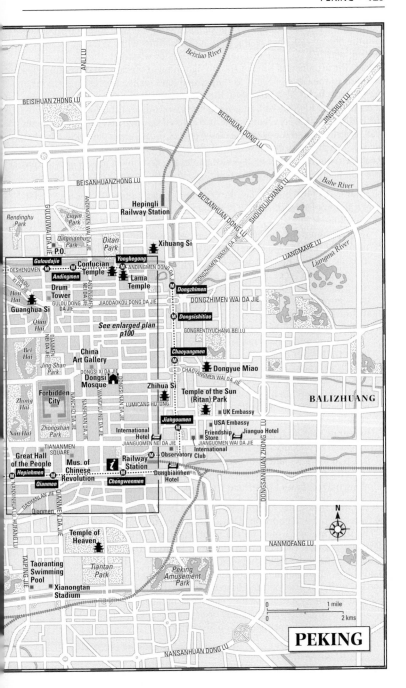

PEKING

closed to the public and, as in the past, houses the supreme government organs and the official residence of the Head of State. Thus when protesters gather in Peking, whether they are peasants or students or whatever, they frequently sit outside the ornamental gates of the Zhongnanhai in the hope of presenting their petitions to the Head of State, as they would have waited to present petitions to the emperor or his high officials in the past.

A narrow road, Nanchizi, runs along the eastern side of the Forbidden City. At the end where it meets Chang'an jie, it is entered through an archway in the red wall, indicating that it was once a closed part of the extended 'imperial city'. Not far up Nanchizi, on the east side of the road is the yellow-roofed **Imperial Archive** (Huang shi cheng). It now includes the Wan fu art gallery, presumably as a side-line money-earner.

Built in 1534, rebuilt under the Qing and recently restored, it is an interesting fireproofed brick-vaulted building with a roof of imperial yellow tiles. As the Chinese had always set such store by documents and history (and the Qing, although originally non-Chinese, adopted Chinese methods of government and traditions), it was essential to guard imperial archives against fire. The *Shi lu* (*True Records*), used in compiling dynastic histories and therefore not necessarily 'true' but rather reflections of the official view, were kept in the archive, as were imperial edicts. Official biographies were compiled for each emperor. During the Qing paperwork proliferated as all official records of this sort were written out both in Chinese and Manchu, although towards the end of the dynasty, Manchu was increasingly abandoned.

The Ming and Qing imperial archives have, unfortunately, been separated between Taiwan and Peking and the vast majority of those that remain in Peking are now housed in a separate archive building. The imperial archive still contains some of the copper-covered chests in which the archives were originally stored on a long stone platform and there is an exhibition of various types of archive material, including examples of imperial annotations in vermilion ink. Other documents displayed in the enclosure include charming paintings, half-architectural, half-decorative, of buildings visited and used as temporary residences by the emperors on their tours of inspection of the south in the 18C, and of imperial parks.

A little further up Nanchizi, also on the eastern side but further off the road along narrow lanes, is the Pudu si (Temple of Universal Rescue; closed, 1988).

On the west side of the road, at no. 15, is the house where the Reuter's journalist Antony Grey was imprisoned for a year during the Cultural Revolution.

The third major turning on the right (east) up Nanchizi, Dengshikou xi jie (Western Lantern Market Street) leads to **Wangfujing** (Well of the Princely Mansion), one of the main shopping streets in Peking. In Dengshikou xi jie there is a Bank of China building on the left (north) and just beside a narrow lane runs north. The first house (on the left, west) was the home of Lao She (1899–1966), one of the great writers of the 20C. The house, inhabited until very recently by his painter widow and daughter, is now open to the public (19 Fengfu hutong). The persimmon trees were planted by Lao She himself for he was a great plant-lover.

Lao She

Lao She was the son of an impoverished Manchu bannerman. Under Nurhaci (1559–1626), the Manchus organised themselves into 'banners', military groupings into which all villagers and tribes were recruited. The 'banners' were effectively garrisons but they carried with them their wives and families. Some of the former village settlements in the northern suburbs of Peking preserve the banner names, such as Lanqi ying (Blue Banner Barracks). A member of the imperial guard, Lao She's father was killed in 1900 during the siege of the foreign legations by the Boxers.

Lao She, who later worked as a Chinese-language tutor in London University's School of Oriental and African Studies, is very much a Peking novelist. His most famous work, *Luo tuo xiang zi* (*Rickshaw Boy*, 1936) is about a rickshaw puller in the city, gradually worn out and forced into poverty. Yet some of his most charming work is autobiographical and describes life in old Peking in wonderful detail.

Continue east to the crossroads with Wangfujing and turn north into Wangfujing. The Jesuits' **Eastern Church** (Dong tang) is a little way up on the east side of the road at no. 74 . For a long time it was a primary school, but services are now held there on Sundays.

The present building dates from the early 20C but it stands on the site of Adam Schall von Bell's house, where he died in 1666. Verbiest, his successor as Director of the Board of Astronomy and Mathematics, took it over on behalf of the Portuguese Jesuits and built St Joseph's Church on part of the site. Destroyed in the early 19C, this was said to have been built in the Ionic style and to be the most beautiful church in Peking. After the suppression of the Jesuits, Portuguese Lazarists took over the church but they were expelled in 1811, only to return in 1860. They then built another church on the site with an altar of Neapolitan inlaid marble and red sandstone pillars with gilt capitals but this was destroyed by the Boxers in 1900.

In Dongsi nan da jie, the road that runs parallel to Wangfujing to the east, just south of the crossroads with Dongsi xi dajie is the **Dong si Mosque** on the west side of the road. Also known as the Faming si (Temple of the Propagation of Brightness), it was first constructed in 1356 and restored in 1447, when the costs were borne by Chen You, a Muslim military commander.

Covering an area of 10,000 square metres, its main constructions include the prayer hall, a pair of subsidiary teaching halls, a library and a pool for purification. It is said to preserve a mixture of Ming and Islamic building styles. The rear part of the main hall is brick-vaulted, a form found commonly in northern mosques (in Peking's Niu jie Mosque for example), creating a characteristically low-ceilinged, broad hall; the interior is richly caned and gilded, with Koranic texts.

The mosque contains many relics, including a Yuan manuscript Koran, the 1468 bronze finial of the minaret and an inscribed stele in both Chinese and Arabic dated to 1579, recording the 1447 restoration.

Old Foreign Legation Quarter

The entire block south of the Peking Hotel—stretching westwards to include the area now covered in the northern part by the Historical Museum and bounded to the south by Qianmen dong da jie, to the east by Dong dan gongyuan (Dong dan park) and to the north by Chang'an jie—used to be the **Foreign Legation Quarter**, besieged by Boxer rebels in 1900. As you walk through it, you can still see plenty of older western style buildings.

The first foreigners to occupy a building in the area were the Russians in 1727, when they were permitted to maintain a permanent ecclesiastical mission according to the terms of the Treaty of Kiachta (or Kiakhta). This was negotiated by Savva Lukitch Vladislavich, the 'Illyrican Count', who went as ambassador to China in 1725 to announce the death of Peter the Great and the accession of Catherine. In Peking he accomplished little but his treaty, signed on the border, regularised trade contacts, fixed borders and opened the ecclesiastical mission which occupied the area subsequently used for the Russian Legation (on the north side of Dongjiaomin xiang, west of Zhengyi lu). The area had formerly contained the internal customs house and Dongjiaomin xiang means Lane of Contact with Eastern Peoples, some say because traders from outside Peking came here to do business. During the Cultural Revolution, when some embassies were still housed in the area, the streetname was changed to Anti-imperialist Street.

After the Russians, the French and British opened their legations in the area (the British immediately to the north of the Russians and the French further east, on the corner of Dongjiaomin xiang and Taijichang da jie). It is said that they chose the area, not because the Russians were there but because of its proximity to the Six Boards (ministries) of the Qing government, lining what is now Tiananmen Square. They naturally assumed that the Chinese 'foreign office' would be conveniently close but the Chinese, incensed that the foreigners had not accepted their offers of land well outside the city, in 1860 created a new office to deal with foreigners, the Zongli yamen (its full name being *Zongli geguo shiwu yamen* or 'Office in Charge of the Affairs of All Countries') and set it well to the northeast of the expanding Legation Quarter, off Dongdan da jie.

Until 1900 the area included many Chinese houses between the embassies but after the Boxer siege destruction of the Legations (and at the insistence of the victorious foreign powers), all Chinese dwellings were cleared and the spaces fitted with more legations, banks, hotels, Kierulf's stores, much favoured by the Manchu nobility and their trains of concubines, and other essential offices.

The area used to be surrounded by a glacis and Dongdan Park was once the polo ground, bounded on the east side by Hatamen Street (Chongwenmen nei da jie) and on the west by Avenue Yamato. The slightly curving **Dongjiaomin xiang**, running just north of and roughly parallel to Qianmen dong da jie, was once called Legation Street.

Along it were, from the east: the **German compound** and German barracks and the Belgian Legation to the south with the Post Office next to the Catholic church of St Michael on the corner of Rue Marco Polo (now Taijichang da jie). St Michael's Church (11 Dongjiaomin xiang), with its twin towers, was built in

1902, probably to replace the old Catholic cathedral in the northeast of the town which was burnt down by the Boxer rebels in 1900, when hundreds of Chinese Catholic converts were massacred and the priests forced to flee into the Legation Quarter. It is now the **Dongjiaomin xiang Church**, run by the Chinese Patriotic Catholic Church. On the opposite side of the junction with **Taijichang da jie** was the **French Legation**, now the Peking residence of the Cambodian King Sihanouk; it has a fine mixed entrance with a brutalist concrete top, a pair of marble pillars and great stone lions, as well as 'magnolia' lamps. Turning up (north) Taijichang da jie, on the right was the French Barracks and the Peking Club (still used as the International Club in the early 1970s) and, on the left, the **Italian Legation** and the Imperial Maritime Customs compound, which have now been taken over by the Chinese People's Association for Friendship with Foreign Countries.

Along **Chang'an jie**, but set back beyond the glacis, were the **Austrian Legation**, the Italian Legation and the huge area of the British Legation (which was built from 1860 in the grounds of a princely mansion belonging to Prince Liang, who could no longer afford to maintain it). If you return to Dongjiaomin xiang and walk westwards, you will soon notice, on your right, a tree-lined, double street, **Zhengyi lu**. In the 1860s this was a rather smelly 'imperial canal'. After decades of complaint about the smell, in the 1920s it was filled in, planted with trees and set with flower-beds and benches, rather as it is today. There is a modern sculpture of a girl reading at the southern end of the central path. The west side of the street used to be known as British Road, the east side, **Rue Meiji**. There is a pedestrian path up the centre of the street where very smart dogs (tiny white pomeranians, genuine Pekinese Pekinese) are walked. At the bottom corner with Dongjiamin xiang, on the Rue Meiji side, was the Yokohama Specie Bank. Further up Zhengyi lu, on the same side, were the Japanese barracks and the **Japanese Legation**. This now houses the **Peking Municipal People's Government**. On the opposite side of the road was the **British Legation**. It is now occupied by the **Ministry of Public Security** and only the (firmly closed) gate can be seen, a classical facade with mounting blocks. South of the British Legation, on the north side of Legation Street at its westernmost end, was the **Russian Legation**, reasonably acceptable in 1860 but considered uncomfortably close by the British after 1917. All but the gates have been demolished and the ground is now occupied by the **Supreme People's Court** and Procuracy. On the southern section of Zhengyi lu (south of Dongjiaomin xiang) was the Wagons-lits Hotel.

Continuing westwards along Dongjiaomin xiang, there are two fine bank buildings on the south side. The **Banque de l'Indochine et de Suez** with its two tiered facade and the imposing colonnade of the **First National City Bank** next door are now the headquarters of the **Peking Fire Department**. The **United States Barracks and Legation** were on the south side of Legation Street at the western end, near Qian men, where, until 1992, there was the bizarre Black Forest castle building of the Deustche-Asiatische Bank; until its demolition, it was used as a film set for Chinese horror films. By 1976, with the exception of the large Soviet Embassy, all embassies and their personnel were moved to two new settlements at Jianguomen wai, near the International Club and Friendship Store, and Sanlitun in the northeast, near the Changcheng (Great Wall) Hotel.

Jing shan Park and Bei hai Lake

Behind the Forbidden City is the separate entrance to **Jing shan Park**. Jing shan, or Scenic Mountain, is the contemporary name for the artificial hill built with the earth excavated from the moat of the Forbidden City and formerly known as Mei shan, Coal Hill, to early western visitors.

It stands on the site of an imperial garden of the Yuan dynasty but was made into a hillock, or a series of five ascending hillocks, under the Ming. In the mid 18C the Qianlong emperor had pavilions built on the hillocks and fruit trees planted on the slopes, giving rise to an alternative name, the Garden of One Hundred Fruit Trees. The small enclosure was also said to have been stocked with hares, rabbits and singing birds. In 1993, the entire area was re-stocked with giant dinosaur figures which boomed and moaned and groaned in Jurassic style. They seem to have moved away but beware similar visitations. The park is used for occasional seasonal flower displays, most notably peonies in May.

Opposite the southern gate is the **Qiwang lou** (Tower of the Beautiful View), dedicated to Confucius. The central pavilion on top of the hill is called the **Wanchun ting** (Pavilion of Ten-thousand Springs—spring as a season); the Buddha figure is recent. From here, to the south you get a useful overview of the Forbidden City with its long axes of main halls in the centre and the tightly-packed rear private buildings.

On the west side of Jing shan, at the base, is the **Dagaoxuan dian** (Great Tall Dark Hall) built by the Ming Jiajing emperor (reigned 1522–67) and containing a Taoist temple, as its name implies. The emperors used to come here to pray to the Yellow Emperor (a legendary ruler of China, 2698–2598 BC, whose benevolence was recognised by the appearance of *qilin*, Chinese unicorns, and phoenix) for rain. The temple is closed to the public.

At the foot of the hill, on the east side, is the tree from which the last Ming emperor (Chongzhen) is said to have hanged himself in 1644. As the troops of the rebel leader Li Zicheng entered the palace, the emperor is said to have fled to the hill behind and bidden farewell to his family before taking off his boots and hanging himself.

North of the hill is the Qianlong period **Shouhuang dian** (Hall of Imperial Longevity), where the portraits of previous emperors used to be kept; it is now part of the Peking Children's Palace.

Northwards, up Di'anmen dajie, there are two major monuments, essential features of the traditional city plan. The area between them remains one of the few areas of narrow lanes (*hutong*), courtyard houses, tiny shops and street markets in Peking. The first is the broad **Drum Tower** (Gu lou), built in 1420 in a similar style to the major gates in the city walls with a broad brick base and a wide hall, its columns beautifully painted, above. It marks the centre of the Yuan capital of Dadu and stands on the site of the first drum tower built in 1272. Drum towers, once found in all major towns, housed huge drums to beat the hours through the day and night (traditional Chinese hours were two hours long). It is still worth fighting your way past the antique sellers and climbing to the top of the tower for a good view of the surrounding streets and some remaining courtyard houses. There are temporary exhibitions held in the hall on the top of the Drum Tower, usually with strong Peking associations.

Behind it, slightly to the northeast, is the **Bell Tower** (Zhong lou). First built in the early Ming, it was burned down and the present building is mid 18C. Its great bell, used to mark the closing of the city gates in the evening, is no longer in place. It is narrower with a taller base than the Drum Tower and is made of grey brick. The area between the two, particularly near the Bell Tower, is one of the few parts of Peking with surviving narrow *hutong*, courtyard houses and street markets and is well worth wandering in. Some enterprising young people have set up a rickshaw tour of this and the corner of the Back Lake area. The tours, organised by the ***Beijing Hutong Tour Company*** (☎ 6615 9097), last three hours, with frequent stops for the young bicycle-rickshaw pullers (mostly recruited from Shanxi province) and shopping opportunities for their passengers.

Immediately to the west of Jing shan, the road (Wenjin jie) crosses a lake, called Zhongnanhai to the south (and closed to all but government employees) and Beihai to the north. The broad bridge looks a place of good omen now but, according to Peking legend, there used to be a ghostly donkey-driver who offered lifts here and then tipped his victims into the lake to drown. Tucked into a corner on the northern side of the street, just beside the bridge is the main entrance to the **Bei hai Park**.

The northernmost of the three lakes that formed part of the gardens associated with the Forbidden City (until the end of the Qing, these were, of course, well inside the imperial city so not easily accessible to the masses), the Beihai Lake is the focus of a public park which includes the Round Town Peninsula, the ancient site of the Altar of Silkworms (now a children's park) and a group of garden buildings constructed during the reign of Qianlong in the north-west corner.

The park occupies a site that was used as a garden by the Liao emperors (907–1125) although the lakes were not dug out until the succeeding Jin dynasty (1115–1234) occupied Peking. Khubilai Khan chose this area as the site for his palace, which he built in the small enclosure on the south bank of the lake now known as the Round Town. At the beginning of the 15C the Ming divided the lakes, separating Beihai from the double Zhongnanhai and, when the old Yuan palace was in ruins, the White Dagoba was built in 1651 on the circular island of Qiong hua (Hortensia Island). Qianlong made many improvements to the garden in the mid 18C, although the area was damaged in 1900 when Western Allied troops sacked the palace area during the suppression of the Boxers.

The present bridge (presumably no longer haunted) crosses the southern end of the Bei hai where it joins the southern lakes was built in 1956.

Immediately inside the gate is the entrance to the **Round Town** (separate entrance ticket) which encloses a courtyard with fine white pines and cypresses (said to be Liao or Jin in date) and a small blue-tiled pavilion (1745). This houses a huge black jade wine bowl carved with mountain streams, dragons and fish.

The bowl is said to have been presented to Khubilai Khan in 1265 and inscriptions in its praise are housed in the pavilion. According to one account, it was lost at the end of the Yuan and rediscovered in the early years of the Qing in a small temple where it was used for pickling vegetables.

Behind is the **Chengguang dian** (Hall of Inherited Lustre) which houses a white jade Buddha brought from Burma in the last years of the 19C.

> The British Minister, O'Connor, was received in the Round Town when he pre-sented his credentials to the Guangxu emperor in 1893 (instead of the more usual hall in the Zhongnanhai) and it was used as a prison for Cao Kun, last President of the Chinese Republic in 1924–26. Imprisoned by one warlord, Feng Yuxiang (the 'Christian General', said to have baptised his troops with a hosepipe), who occupied Peking in 1924, he was released by another, Zhang Zuolin, the 'Old Marshall', ruler of Manchuria from 1911 until he was blown up in a train in 1928 by the Japanese Kwantung Army which was taking over his area of command.

North of the Round Town is a bridge leading to the circular **Hortensia Island**, so-called because eating hortensia was supposed to confer immortality, dominated by the White Dagoba (Tibetan-style stupa). A pair of *pailou* stand at the end of this bridge and the other which leads to the eastern shore of the lake. The inscriptions on the *pailou* read 'accumulated moisture of heaven' and 'piled clouds'.

The **White Dagoba** towers over the major lower buildings: those immediately at the end of the bridge form the **Yongan si** (Temple of Everlasting Peace), also built in 1651 to celebrate, together with the dagoba, the first visit by a Dalai Lama to Peking. Pavilions inside the temple *pailou* contain stone-carved inscriptions written by the Shunzhi and Yongzheng emperors recording the construction of the temple and other buildings. Behind the eastern pavilion is a large rock inscribed with the characters *kun lun* (Chinese for Sumeru, the Buddhist holy mountain).

Over to the west is the two-storey **Qingxiao lou** (Pavilion of Felicitous Skies) where the Qianlong emperor used to come with his mother on the eighth day of the twelfth month (January) to watch skating parties on the lake (the ice smoothed with flat-irons so as not to trip the imperial guards as they performed). Above is the White Dagoba, a Tibetan inscription meaning 'the all-powerful ten' on its south side, opposite a small square building covered with multi-coloured glazed tile Buddha figures. Inside is Yamantaka, one of the 10 'irate protectors', Lamaist guardians of the faith.

On the northern side of the island, the **Yilan tang** (Hall of Rippling Waves) and associated buildings are now occupied by a restaurant (Fangshan or 'Imitation Delicacies' fandian) which is famous for its 'imperial' cuisine, especially the *petits fours* faintly resembling miniature *wowotou*, the great indigestible lumps of maize flour eaten by peasants.

> It is said that on the Dowager Empress's flight to Xi'an in 1900, when she was terribly hungry on her hurried journey a peasant served her *wowotou*, the only food he had. As she was famished, she enjoyed them greatly and, when reinstated in the palace, ordered her cook to make them. Knowing the she would be unlikely to enjoy them quite as much in her more comfortable sur-roundings, he made tiny *wowotou* using light water-chestnut flour instead of heavy maize.

Round to the west of the island, one of the major buildings is the **Yuegu lou** (Tower for the Inspection of Ancient Scripts), a crescent-shaped hall where 400 stone tablets inscribed with the calligraphy of great masters of the past (including the 'Three Wangs', Wang Xizhi, Wang Xianzhi and Wang Xun of the 2C AD) are set into the walls. These, the best possible selection made by the scholars of the imperial academy (the Hanlin or 'Forest of Brushes Academy'), were chosen for the Qianlong emperor.

The eastern shore of the Bei hai leads past the site of the imperial boat house to where the Hall of Imperial Silkworms and the Altar of Silkworms used to stand (now a children's park).

Altar of silkworms

Two stone terraces (altars) were used for examining mulberry leaves before giving them to the silkworms (which were kept in houses along the outer walls) and where offerings were made to the God of Mulberries. During the third lunar month empresses (or their deputies) used to come and make offerings to the Goddess of Silkworms, for sericulture was supposed to have been invented by Xi ling, wife of the Yellow Emperor (in 2602 BC). In fact, a silk cocoon, apparently partly cut in half, presumably by human agency, was discovered in 1927 in a Neolithic Yangshao site of c 5000–4000 BC; thus the actuality of sericulture may even antedate the legend.

If you walk on, past the northern gate, the group of buildings clustered in the northwest corner of the park were mainly built in the mid 18C by the Qianlong emperor, although they were later favoured by the Dowager Empress Cixi in the later 19C. The easternmost is a walled enclosure, a tiny garden filled with pools, bridges and pavilions with names such as Playing the Lute Studio and House of Rare Paintings, which indicate Qianlong's hand and interests. The garden, a very fine example of a northern garden, built in a small space and filled with brightly coloured pavilions and piled rocks, is called the **Qingxin zhai** (Studio of the Restful Mind). It was restored a few years ago, although it has sometimes been closed since.

Many of the other buildings are now used as exhibition halls and places of popular entertainment but they were previously: immediately west of the garden, the Pavilion of 10,000 Buddhas (behind) and Small Western Sky (Xiaoxi dian), a temple group with a three-storeyed building behind covered with green and yellow glazed tile Buddha figures, and the Nine-dragon Screen, similar to that in the Forbidden City, a huge screen wall covered with glazed tile dragons and built in 1417 in front of a temple. Next to the west is the walled enclosure of the **Songpo tushuguan** (Pine Hill Library) containing three halls: the Hall of Crystal Waters, Porch Where Orchids are Washed (on the fifth of the fifth lunar month at the Dragon Boat Festival) and the Hall of Joyful Snow, a name taken from one of Wang Xizhi's poems. The poet and calligrapher was apparently describing a snowstorm in verse when snowflakes began to fall, hence his joy.

On the lake shore, in front of what is now a children's science museum, are the **Wulong ting** (Five Dragon Pavilions), five little pavilions built out in the lake in the form of a curved dragon's spine. Against the western wall is an **open-air cinema**, once the Great Western Heaven Temple, with glazed tiles inscribed with Buddhist texts. The building is unusual in construction with four *pailou*, one on either side, and a massive roof frame supported by four rows of columns.

Returning to the main gate by the western side of the lake, the buildings just outside the southwest corner of the park used to be the National Library, founded in 1910.

The library has now been largely rehoused in a new, air-conditioned tower block beside the Zizhu yuan (Purple Bamboo Park) in the northwest of the city, not far from the major university campuses. Some of the collections are still in the old library building, mainly the late traditional thread-bound books (1989). Behind the library there was until 1900 a famous temple which used to contain a 1.5m red sandalwood Buddha figure and where Peking's Lamaists used to come and worship every year on the eighth day of the first lunar month; all that now remains of the temple is in the name of the small street north of the Library, Zhantansi jie (Red Sandalwood Temple Street).

Bei Tang

Immediately west of the southern entrance to the Beihai Park are the Bei Tang (Jesuit, or Northern Church), Guangji si (Temple of Universal Rescue), the White Pagoda Temple (Miaoying or Baita si) and the residence of Lu Xun.

The **Bei Tang** or Northern Church is at Xishikou, just to the north of Xi'anmen da jie, west of the old National Library building, up a narrow lane leading north from the main road. Its twin spires and grey and white-painted wedding-cake facade are clearly visible.

This is the third 'Northern Church'. The first was built after a grant of land within the imperial city from the Kangxi emperor in 1693 and consecrated in 1703. The group of French Jesuits sent to China by Louis XIV (including Fathers Gerbillon and Bouvet) gained favour with the Kangxi emperor by acting as interpreters during the negotiations with Russia over the Treaty of Nertchinsk in 1689 (allowing the Russians to build a fort there and fixing a river boundary) and by making astronomical calculations. They persuaded him to sign an 'edict of tolerance'. The gift of land for a church was made, however, after they had cured him of a serious illness by using the newly discovered quinine (sent from Pondicherry by a fellow Jesuit).

During the reign of Yongzheng the Jesuits fell from imperial favour and, following the suppression of the order (1773), despite Louis XVI's Lazarist mission (intended to take over the Bei tang), the church land was sold to a mandarin in 1827 and the building demolished. The Convention of Peking (1860) included a stipulation that Catholic mission property should be returned, so a new building was erected on the old site in 1867, including the stone steps of the former cathedral and a wrought-iron grille of the period of Louis XV.

This second cathedral was the subject of fierce arguments with the Chinese who objected to the height of the spire. The Chinese believed that good spirits flew at a height of 30m and therefore no towers should be built that might impede their passage. This second church was therefore built with an impressive triple arched facade but nothing much in the way of a spire. No sooner was the church finished, however, than it had to be abandoned because the Dowager Empress Cixi had decided to live on the shore of the Zhong hai (she had to leave her apartments in the Forbidden City on the marriage of the Guangxu emperor) and she did not want the church nearby. Li Hongzhang (1823–1901) one of the 'modernising' officials (associated with modern arsenal, steamship and naval projects and the establishment of modern naval and military academies) negotiated with Monsignor Favier and the site, on which today's Bei tang still stands (within the imperial city but in an area near stores) was selected. The third building was consecrated in 1889.

The old Bei tang had been used as a store for Cixi's possessions and Pierre Loti described a visit during the plunder of the city by the allied armies after their defeat of the Boxers in 1900:

...imperial robes of heavy silk brocaded with gold dragons lie on the ground ... we walk over them, we walk over carved ivories, over pearls and embroideries galore ... This church, so full of pagan riches has kept its organ intact, although it has been silent for thirty years. My comrade mounts with me to the gallery to try the effect of some hymns of Bach and Handel, while the African chasseurs, up to their knees in ivories, silks and court costumes, continue their task of clearing things out below. (*The Last Days of Peking*, translated from the French, Boston, Little Brown, 1902)

The building was destroyed in 1911. Meanwhile, the third Bei tang had been besieged by the Boxers at the same time as the Foreign Legation Quarter to the southeast and 400 Chinese Christians were killed assisting Italian and French soldiers to defend the church, which was subsequently relieved by Japanese soldiers.

Although it was made into a school during the Cultural Revolution, the Bei tang has now once again been restored to the Peking Catholic Patriotic Association (Beijing shi tianzhujiao aiguo hui) and during 1985 it was extensively restored and reopened on 24 December 1985; the Bishop is Fu Tieshan.

The Gothic facade (its twin towers were increased in height after 1900) is cheerfully painted and the interlaced columns of the vaulted interior are striped red and black, creating a Strawberry Hill gothic effect. Much of the stained glass has survived intact. Outside, the gardens and the Grotto of Our Lady (a wonderful mixture of Lourdes and Chinese garden rockeries) have been restored and the twin Chinese pavilions have been rebuilt to house imperial stelae. Some of the pieces of imperial calligraphy (such as the red board inscribed in gold by the Kangxi emperor with the words 'Profoundly true origin') are replicas. The church is now open to visitors and worshippers.

West of the Bei tang is one of the major temples in Peking, the **Guangji si** (Temple of Universal Rescue). Take Xi'anmen da jie west until you reach Xida bei da jie and turn right (north). The next crossroads is Xi si (West Four), paired with Dong si, where once four *pailou* stood across the roads. Take the turning on the left (west), Fuchengmen nei da jie. The temple, behind green arched gates in a grey brick wall, is on the north side of the street.

The site has been occupied by a temple since the 12C, when it was the temple of West Liu village in the northern outskirts of Zhongdu, the 'Middle Capital'. It was rebuilt in the Yuan and again in 1457 and expanded in 1466, 1584 and 1694. It has seen three disastrous fires, the last in 1934 when the main and rear halls were largely destroyed and the Ming edition of the Tripitaka (Buddhist scriptures) and a white sandalwood Buddha figure (a gift from abroad) were also destroyed. Major restorations were undertaken in 1952 and 1972.

The facade of the temple, aside from its great doors, has an inscription in yellow lozenges reading 'the wheel of the law turns eternally'. The gates open onto a very spacious courtyard. On the main axis are a gatehouse, the Hall of Heavenly Kings, a main hall, Guanyin Hall and library. Inside a courtyard on the western

axis is a triple-tiered white marble ordination platform where ordination ceremonies were performed, which include the shaving of monks' and nuns' heads
and the burning of little piles of incense on the scalp: these scars persist for some
time and a triple or double row of tiny burn marks on a shaved head can indicate
that the person is no longer a novice but has been ordained.

Inside the **main hall** the most important element is the very rare painting on
the back of the screen behind the altar. This monochrome of the *Buddha
expounding the Law* is by the 18C artist Chuan Wen and is a 'finger painting' (or
a finger and fingernail painting).

> Eccentric painting implements have a considerable history in China and are
> particularly associated with Chan (Zen) Buddhist painters. Some of the earli-
> est Tang Chan painters used to paint with the end of their long hair, as well
> as fingers. Chuan Wen's large painting is wonderfully vigorous, crowded with
> lively figures.

In the **Guanyin Hall** behind there is a Qing 'thousand-eyed, thousand-armed'
(omnipotent) Guanyin; a smaller copper figure of the deity on a lotus flower
(Ming), and a great number of gifts from Buddhists abroad.

> The temple is the headquarters of the Buddhist Association of China and is
> therefore visited by an enormous number of Buddhist pilgrims (mainly from
> Japan and Southeast Asia).

A little further west along the same street (also on the north side), a middle
school now occupies the remains of the **Lidai diwang miao** (Temple of
Generations of Rulers). The temple was used by both the Ming and Qing emperors to house the ancestral tablets of long-dead rulers; those of their personal
ancestors were kept in the imperial palace.

> The temple was built in 1530 and restored in 1729. A white marble
> balustrade in front of the main hall is said to be a fairly rare example but the
> school is not open to visitors.
>
> This secondary temple echoes traditional practice: families usually kept the
> tablets of the last three generations in their home, to include these recent
> ancestors in family worship. If the family were rich enough to possess an
> ancestral hall in the village they stored the tablets of long-dead, long-forgot-
> ten ancestors there. There were sometimes differing viewpoints and tablets
> were removed and replaced according to the prevailing view: Khubilai Khan's
> tablet moved a couple of times during the Qing.

Baita si

Further east, just past the next crossroads (with Taipingqiao da jie to the south),
on the north side of the road, is the huge white dagoba of the Miaoying si (Temple
of the Miraculous Response), familiarly known as the Baita si (White Pagoda
Temple). It is reached by a narrow lane off the main road, usually impenetrable to
motor traffic.

> The temple was first built in 1271; a Nepalese temple designer, Arniger,
> assisted in the construction. A large temple, which stood in front of the
> dagoba, was one of the major constructions of the reign of Khubilai Khan
> (1264–95) and the dagoba itself remains the largest standing Yuan con-

struction in Peking. Its consecration was an occasion of considerable celebration and the fact that it is not recorded in Marco Polo's book, although it took place during his supposed stay, is another of the questionable aspects of his account.

The dagoba, which dominates the temple, is 50.9m high, standing on a lotus-petal base, which (to quote the official guide) 'is surrounded by five "king kong" hoops that make the square base grow into the round pagoda body much naturally. The body of the pagoda is like a huge upside-down almsbowl ...' and is made of brick faced with white stucco. At the top, beneath the copper finial, a wooden canopy covered with copper has a sort of copper-link fringe from which hang 36 aeolian bells.

The great pagoda was built to house relics, which must have been added to during later repairs for when the dagoba was being restored in 1978, some scriptures and other items, including coins of Han to Qing date, were found in the umbrella-shaped crown, placed there in 1754. In 1457 and 1465 the dagoba was restored; during the 1465 restoration brick niches were built round the gallery to hold lanterns at festivals.

The sculpture of two deer supporting a wheel of the law at the top of the steps to the gallery symbolically represents the Buddha's sermon given at Benares (and is commonly found in Lamaist art). The dagoba courtyard is at the end of the axial line of low halls forming the temple, in which is a collection of Buddhist (Lamaist) sculpture, scriptures and robes.

These include a fine series of cast-iron lohan figures (Ming), some small gilt-bronze lamaist deities on lotus-petal bases (Ming), a thousand-eyed, thousand-armed Guanyin in bronze (Qing), Qing tangkas (Buddhist paintings of Lamaist deities), embroidered silk boxes, 'Five-Buddha hats' in velvet and 'patchwork' robes of silk damask (the patchwork effect symbolised the poverty and lack of possessions of a monk; in rich silks it is somewhat incongruous).

Lu Xun's House

A little further west along the main road (Fuchengmen nei da jie) is Lu Xun's House (Lu Xun guju; open 09.00–16.00, closed Mondays), at 21 Xisantiao hutong, just north of the main road (but the approach is visible from it).

Lu Xun occupied this small house between 1924 and 1926, although his mother stayed on here into the early 1930s. It is a good example of a simple courtyard house. Entered by a gate in the southeast corner of the courtyard (most courtyard houses in Peking had their entrance at this point, although grand houses and houses in other places were entered on the central axis; this variation represents a Peking version of *feng shui*), the courtyard is surrounded by buildings (not all houses have a southern wing, sometimes the southern part of the courtyard is simply enclosed by a wall).

The southern wing was the reception area, with the kitchen in the southwest corner. This is characteristic of the smaller courtyard houses. Tradesmen would be seen at the door; visitors might be ushered into the reception area and only close family friends or relatives would be entertained in the northern wing, furthest from the gate. The two side wings (east and west) are both two *jian* or two-bay constructions, while the southern and northern wings are three bays wide.

Lu Xun

Lu Xun (1881–1936; see Shaoxing, his birthplace) is still celebrated as the greatest Chinese writer of his time. He was born into a declining family of landlords and officials and, after a classical education, went to Japan to study medicine. There, faced with (tiny) Japan's triumph over Russia in 1905 (following her earlier humiliation of the enfeebled giant of China in the Sino-Japanese War, 1894–95), he decided to abandon medicine (which could only cure individuals) in favour of literature which could rouse thousands. He was a major participant in the New Culture Movement which followed the 4 May uprising of 1919 and which advocated writing in *baihua* or 'plain language', the language of the masses rather than the extremely restricted classical language of the official class which had hitherto dominated.

His satirical short stories, some based on his childhood reminiscences, and his equally pointed essays are still justifiably popular. His greatest stories are, perhaps, the *Diary of a Madman*, whose persecution mania illustrates the violent and unsympathetic nature of late imperial China, and the *True Story of Ah Q*, a hopeless labourer, symbolic of China's self-inflicted hopelessness.

Most Chinese buildings are of uneven bays: three or five being common in domestic architecture. Side wings, however, in small houses, were not uncommonly only two bays. The two lilacs in the front courtyard are said to have been planted by Lu Xun himself. The northern wing is unusual in that it has an extra room built on at the back, on Lu Xun's order: this was his bedroom and study where he wrote the collections of essays entitled *Wild Grass* (*Ye cao*) and *Wandering* (*Pang huang*). Known as 'the tiger's tail', Lu Xun himself called it 'the green study' for it looks out onto the back courtyard with its well and plum trees. The dark wood furniture and simple possessions in the house (washbasin, vases, brushes, alarmclock) are said to be just as they were when he lived there and they give a good idea of interior decoration in the 1920s.

East of the house is a new building housing a **Lu Xun Museum**, filled with photographs (and paintings where these are lacking) illustrating Lu Xun's life and career: translations of his works, copies of the Jules Verne novels (*Voyage au centre de la terre* and *Autour de la lune*) that he translated into Chinese and some of his possessions including Han bronze mirrors.

The Back Lake area

The Back Lake area includes Song Qingling's house, Mei Lanfang's house, Guo Moruo's house, Mao Dun's house, the Gongwang Fu, Huguo si, Desheng Gate, Guanghua si and the bell and drum towers.

The long strip of three joined lakes (Xi hai, Hou hai and Qian hai: West Sea, Back Sea and Front Sea) lying northwest of the Forbidden City formed an area that was favoured by high officials for their residences.

Just east of the top northwest corner of the old city walls stood the **Desheng men** (Gate of the Victory of Virtue), now rather isolated by wide motorways and roundabouts. Built in 1439, it was rebuilt under the Qing.

A double gate (a third part was lost in 1969 during the construction of the underground railway beneath it), it is similar to others in that it appears somewhat grey, blank and fortified to the north but open and pavilion-like to the south. It is known as the Arrow Tower because of the 82 small square openings for defensive archers that pierce the outer wall; it was the only 'arrow tower' of the nine old gates of Peking. There is an exhibition of ancient coins in the gate tower (open 09.00–16.00, closed Mondays).

Despite the endless destruction of small courtyard houses, the **Gulou xi da jie**, which leads diagonally southeast from the Desheng men, remains a rather good example of an old street lined with low houses and shops. It leads to the **Drum Tower**, with the **Bell Tower** visible just behind to the northeast.

North of the Drum Tower, the second turning on the left off Gulou bei da jie leads to the *Zhuyuan Bingguan* (Bamboo Garden Hotel), which also has a fine Cantonese restaurant. The garden with its piled rocks and somewhat westernised buildings was once the residence of Kang Sheng (d. 1975), head of the Secret Police for many years and not everyone's favourite person.

Song Qingling's House (open daily 09.00–16.30) lies on the northern shore of the Hou hai (Back Lake), best approached by turning east along Houhai bei yan from Deshengmen nei da jie. The great red gates announce that it was once a princely mansion (*fu*), said by some to be the birthplace of the last emperor Pu Yi, and some of the outline of the garden can still be seen in the heaped and piled rocks and pools but Song Qingling built herself a modern house in the grounds. There is a fine grouping with a wisteria trained through a pierced rock and there are fine tree peonies, one of the palest pink with both single and double flowers.

Song Qingling

Song Qingling (1892–1981) was the middle daughter of Charlie Soong, a Shanghai comprador who had been converted to Methodism when he went to the United States in his youth. His eldest daughter married into China's richest banking family, while Song Qingling married Sun Yatsen, his youngest daughter married Chiang Kai-shek and his son, T.V. Soong, was Minister of Finance, Premier and Minister of Foreign Affairs in his brother-in-law Chiang Kai-shek's government as well as being governor of the Central Bank of China. In this wealthy group, Song Qingling was the idealistic exception, marrying the 'Father of New China' when he was nearly 50 and she 30 years younger. Despite the involvement of the rest of her family in the Nationalist Government (and various money-making schemes), she sided more closely with the Communist Party and remained in China after 1949, taking an interest in welfare work and childcare, founding, amongst others, a major children's hospital in Shanghai and the China Welfare Institute.

The **museum** commemorating her life is in a small traditional building behind handsome *Cedrus deodara* and pots of *Cycas revoluta*. There is a display of her possessions (fascinating dresses and shoes), photographs of her life from the delicate, rosebud-lipped bride of Sun Yatsen to the handsome dowager with her hair scraped back into a bun, photographs of her Persian cats with one blue and one brown eye (a prized feature often portrayed in Suzhou embroidery) and the rather ghoulish scene of her final admission into the Communist Party on her deathbed. As with Lu Xun, who never joined the Communist Party during his lifetime (claims were made during the Cultural Revolution that his application had been lost in the post), looking at the prone woman with unseeing eyes and a drip, one wonders whether she actually wanted to join.

Continuing southeast along the lake, along Houhai beiyan, take the first turning to the left and on Ya'er hutong (running parallel to the lakeside Houhai beiyan) is the entrance to the **Guanghua si** (Temple of Great Transformation). This is the only one of the several temples once situated in the area to survive. It has recently been restored but I have not managed to get in yet.

The Guanghua Temple was repaired in 1634 by a eunuch, whose work is commemorated in a stele in the main courtyard. The temple takes its name from a legend about a wandering monk who finally took up residence on the wasteland here in the Yuan dynasty. For 20 years he meditated and lived on rice supplied by local people. He only ate half the rice he was given, saving the rest to build a temple, His frugality impressed people, who started to make donations and since the rice he did not eat was 'transformed' into a temple, it gained its present name.

More famous was the **Longhua si** (Temple of Civilising Influences) with a pagoda that once stood at the western end of the lake. The lakes at the time were known as the Shicha hai (Ten Temples of the Sea) and were supposed to have been dug out during the Ming in the hope of recreating a scene reminiscent of the south with its rice paddies and lotus pools. The Longhua Temple is supposed to have owned a small paddy field where homesick southerners would come to smell the flowering rice. This and other temples, together with the lakes, were said to have been constructed in the Wanli reign period (1573–1620) by an official from Shaanxi province.

Festivals were held on the lakes, including the annual 'washing of the horses' from the imperial stables, which took place on the sixth day of the sixth month. At the Zhonghua festival on the 15th day of the seventh lunar month (when ancestral graves were swept), lanterns made from lotus leaves (candles glowing through the green leaves), Artemisia lanterns and paper lanterns in the form of lotuses were floated on the lake.

South of the lake on Qianhai xi jie is the Gongwang fu. Continue along the Houhai beiyan until you reach the little bridge and cross to the other side. Walk back (northwards) along Houhai nanyan until you reach the first turning on your left, Liuyin jie. Turn down Liuyin jie and you will soon find the high wall of the Gongwang fu on your left. The entrance to the garden section is along a narrow lane to your left.

A little further on, on the right hand side of the road, is a monument to a soldier who died saving a child from the frozen lake quite recently.

The **Gongwang fu** (Mansion of Prince Gong) runs from Qianhaixi where the main entrance to the mansion part of the large enclosure stands. As is evident from the number of signs on either side of the gate, it is inhabited by various institutes, most notably part of the Beijing Conservatoire. The residential part of the mansion is therefore not open to visitors, which is a great pity as it is a classic *fu* and has the most magnificent north wing, two stories high and nearly 20 bays wide. If it is ever opened it should be well worth visiting as it is reputed to be the mansion on which Cao Xueqin based his *Dream of the Red Chamber* of c 1760 (see also p 121; the best translation is by David Hawkes and John Minford, *The Story of the Stone*, Penguin).

The mansion once belonged to the Manchu bannerman, Heshen (1750–99), who rose to become the favourite and confidant of the Qianlong emperor. He rose to power through his military career (putting down various Muslim rebellions in Yunan and Gansu) and was rewarded with such privileges as being allowed to ride on horseback through the Forbidden City (all others except elderly high statesmen were required to dismount) and the gift of the mansion. He was also in charge of arrangements for the Macartney mission to the emperor in 1793 and was treated by Dr Gillan, the mission's doctor, when he fell ill with rheumatism. He is also said to have served as the model for a truss which Dr Gillan provided for the emperor himself as it was not proper for the emperor to submit himself to the hands of a foreigner. Heshen owed his position to his closeness to the emperor and when his protector died in 1799, he was arrested, his property confiscated and he was allowed to commit suicide. The mansion was later owned by Prince Gong (1833–98), sixth son of the Guangxu emperor, who was largely responsible for the establishment, in 1861, of the Zongli yamen, which dealt with the newly arrived foreign ambassadors.

There is no suggestion that Cao Xueqin, the impoverished author of the *Dream of the Red Chamber*, actually lived in the mansion; it is thought that he may have lodged with relatives not far away, near the Bei hai. Yet as a member of an aristocratic family—his grandfather had been an imperial salt commissioner and had entertained the Kangxi emperor on his trips to the south in the Cao family's ancestral home in Nanjing—he was likely to have been familiar with some of the other Manchu nobility.

The Gongwang fu garden has various pavilions that bear the same names as those used by Cao for his fictional family mansion. The plan of the imaginary mansion and garden are remarkably similar to that of the Gongwang fu. The mansion and its garden occupy an area of about 300 hectares. Only the garden is open to the public.

The garden, separated from the mansion by a narrow alley that runs along the back of the massive north wing (notice the elaborate windows in the form of fans, pomegranates, leaves, etc.) is approached through a small stone gateway in the 'Jesuit barock' style. It is interesting that Heshen copied his emperor's taste, imitating on a small scale the Jesuit buildings of the Yuanmingyuan or 'Old' Summer Palace.

The garden is crammed with interest. To the west is an open area around a pool, to the north a rising hill with walkway and pavilions and to the east an extraordinary tea house with a stage, where Peking opera performances take place all day long for local pensioners and tourists. The tea house and stage are painted all over with vines and flowering plants on a pale green ground, reminiscent of the Chinese wallpaper that found favour in 18C Europe.

The Gongwang fu is an interesting example of contemporary horticulture in an older site. The edges of the garden are crammed with potted plants ready to be placed on ornamental rocks, often still in their pots, when their flowers are at their best. The Australian botanist Peter Valder notes that the recon-struction of the garden has been done with its history in mind. One of the more recent inhabitants, the Manchu prince Puru (one of Puyi's brothers) used to hold parties in the garden when the crab apples (semi-double *Malus spectabilis*) were in flower. Osbert Sitwell attended a crab apple party there in 1934 and another Peking resident of the period described how the trees were planted at the north end of the lake. Peter Valder found no sign of them in 1994 but 'on returning in 1996, I found they had been replanted'. (Peter Valder, *The Garden Plants of China*, London, 1999.)

Just southwest of the Gongwang fu is the **House of Guo Moruo** (1892–1978). Follow Liuyin jie round to the front of the Gongwang fu mansion, where it is called Qianhai xijie. On the right hand side of the second turning on the right (also Qianhai xijie) is the impressive gate and plaque.

Guo Moruo (see Leshan, Sichuan, p 572) was a poet, self-confessed pantheist, novelist, archaeologist, epigrapher, historian, playwright, literary critic, cul-tural administrator and tireless apologist for whatever seemed safest to defend.

The residence is rather messed about, with old walkways glassed-in and new buildings, but the collection of his possessions is as fascinating as always.

Now walk back to the Gongwang fu and carry on westwards along Dingfu jie, at the major crossroads with Deshengmen nei da jie turn right (north) and take the first turning on the left (west), Huguosi jie. Not far along on the right (north), No. 9 is the old **House of Mei Lanfang** (open 09.00–11.00 and 13.00–16.00, closed Mondays), the greatest 20C exponent of Peking Opera, a specialist in female roles, which were traditionally performed by men, although this is now changing. On a recent map of Peking this has been marked as the 'Pantheon' of Mei Lanfang.

> ### Mei Lanfang
> Born into a theatrical family, Mei Lanfang (1894–1961) saw the develop-ment of a more modern style of Peking Opera, in a sort of equivalent of the *bai hua* or 'plain speech' movement in literature. He popularised new stories and frequently gave virtuoso performances of the most striking extracts from longer operas. He travelled abroad, meeting many fellow performers and impressing Bertolt Brecht with his miming and ability to convey a wealth of information through simple gesture.

His house, a fine courtyard house of some elegance (note that the main hall and side wings have verandas in front and are raised on low stone platforms) is a good example of the better class of courtyard house and contains a small exhibition about his life. The house is entered from the southeast, which accords with the Peking variant on *feng shui*, probably out of deference to the emperor whose palace had its main entrance in the centre so local residents stood to one side, and two small side courtyards are entered through moon gates. The main wing (northern wing of the first courtyard) has some painting on the beams which indicates that it was once a house of someone of high status.

A little further along the street is the crumbling hall of the **Huguo si** (Temple to Protect the Country). Once a Mongol prince's palace under the Yuan, the mansion was transformed into a temple in his honour, after he had been disgraced, committed suicide and been rehabilitated—shades of contemporary China.

The temple used to be famous for its fairs (on the seventh, eighth, 17th, 18th, 27th and 28th days of every month) where curios, calligraphy, paintings, food, flowers, birds, insects and fish, entertainers and fortunetellers were to be found. It operated in parallel with the Longfu Temple where fairs were held on alternate days and which lay just north of Dongsi xi da jie; the next street to the north is called Longfusi jie but the temple is now covered by the Renmin shichang, a huge department store. In both, the seasonal flowers were most spectacular (when I went to look for the Huguo si, it was almost hidden under piles of seasonal cabbage in November).

On the far side of the lakes, over to the east, is the residence of the great novelist Mao Dun. From the Drum Tower (Gu lou), take the road running due east, Gulou dong da jie, and at the second crossroads take the road running due south, Nanluogu xiang. **Mao Dun's House** is on the north side of the second turning on the left (east) at no. 13 Houyuanensi hutong. This is a simpler courtyard dwelling than that of Mei Lanfang, without the red painted columns and beam painting, but it is a very characteristic Peking dwelling. Entered from the south-east, the main courtyard has a southern building with sofas, used as a reception room. The rooms to the north and in the next courtyard were those used by Mao Dun and his family until his death in 1981.

Mao Dun

Born in 1896 Mao Dun was an active participant in the 'Fourth of May New Culture Movement' and also served as secretary to Mao Zedong for a time during the 1920s. His most famous work is *Midnight*, a long, Zolaesque novel about the shadowy business world of Shanghai in the 1930s, which first appeared in 1933. After 1949 he served as Chairman of the Writers' Union and, for a time, Minister of Culture.

The main hall of the first courtyard is raised on a stone platform and is a three bay building with *er fang* (literally 'ear rooms' or small subsidiary rooms added to either end of a building) on either side. There is some fine cut-brick decoration to the main wing in the courtyard, which also has a verandah, but the side wings are plain. Inside the main hall are photographs of the author (looking sinister in a tie and dark glasses in the Fourth of May period) and stills from films of his works. To the left of the building is a tree and beside that a great waterpot: many houses in Peking did not have their own well, so water had to be purchased daily from the watercarriers, most of whom were from Shandong province.

In the reception rooms of the front court are his eyewash cups, a tin coffee pot, a magnifying glass and an English-Chinese dictionary. One of the rooms, presumably used as a reception room at the time, has a carpet on the stone flagged floor, sofa and armchairs and a lacquer smoking set. The carpet is a western touch for traditionally carpets were placed on *kang* brick beds but not on the floor. Early western visitors to China used to complain about cold feet when they visited Chinese dignitaries. The little red plastic-covered books are his membership cards for the Communist Party and credentials as a delegate to various congresses of the National People's Party. Fountain pens which he used to write his manuscripts in the 1950s are on display, as are the seals ('chops') he used and a National tape-recorder he used when writing his memoirs late in life.

In the courtyard behind is the five bay wing where Mao Dun lived after his wife died in 1970. He suffered from arthritis and other ailments of the elderly, as is obvious from the 12 bottles of medicine and teaspoons laid out ready for use. His old man's padded waistcoat is visible, as is a Snowflake brand fridge (which in the 1970s would only have been accessible to the rich and famous). There is also a rather terrible old towelling vest which, I presume, falls into the well-known Chinese archaeological category of 'revolutionary relics'. These are the ex-possessions of great revolutionaries which are often worn and old to demonstrate the simplicity and frugality of the true revolutionary.

East of the Forbidden City

Due east of the Forbidden City are the China Art Gallery, Fuwang fu and the Zhihua si. They are rather far apart, too far for all but the most enthusiastic walker, and involve a lot of main roads, probably best done by bus or taxi.

If you are travelling along Wusi da jie from Coal Hill and the north gate of the Forbidden City, the road bends slightly to the north and a large, oldish red brick building is on the left (north) just after the bend. Today the centre of the *Cultural Relics Publishing House* (Wenwu chubanshe), this was the original home of Peking University.

Built on the site of the Temple of Horses in 1898, the Imperial University (as it was known at its founding) was renamed Peking University in 1911. Its students played a major part in the demonstrations of the Fourth of May Movement in 1919, inspired by the treachery of the Versailles Treaty which, instead of allowing China to recover the old German Concession areas in Shandong, gave Japan a 'special interest' in them. Japan had been an ally of the western powers in the First World War, hence the concession.

Yet the students were not only enraged by the western powers, they were also appalled that the Chinese warlord government had accepted the terms in return for a massive loan. The Chinese had not officially participated in the World War, although a considerable number of 'coolie labourers' had served close to the front lines carrying munitions and many hundreds had died.

It was in this building that Mao Zedong worked as a junior library assistant in 1918, when his mentor Li Dazhao was librarian. In 1953 the university moved from the cramped building to the spacious campus of the American Missionary Foundation, Yenching University, out to the northwest of the city near the Summer Palace. Peking University, which has chosen to remain known in English as such, rather than Beijing University, still occupies the site.

The **China Art Gallery** is on Wusi da jie, where it meets Wangfujing. A massive yellow-roofed building, it has no permanent exhibition but houses temporary exhibitions of modern Chinese art and artefacts. See the *China Daily* or other free magazines available in grand hotels for listings.

Continue along Wusi da jie, which then becomes Dongsi xi da jie, past two major crossroads. At the third, turn left, up Chaoyangmen bei xiao jie and left again to find the **Fuwang fu**, once the mansion of the 13th son of the Kangxi emperor, Yinxiang (1686–1730), later that of the ninth son of the Daoguang emperor, Prince Fu (1845–77). Not yet open to the public, it is said to be the best preserved of Peking's princely mansions.

Returning to the main road, Chaoyangmen nei da jie, at the crossroads turn south down Chaoyangmen nan xiao jie and take the third turning on the left (east), Wenfangjia hutong. At the end of the lane, turn right into Xiaobeifang hutong and then take the first right, Lumicang hutong; the name means 'Storehouse of Glutinous Rice' and between 1644 and 1654–81 granaries were constructed here to store rice used to pay government officials.

On the right (no. 5 Lumicang, north side of the lane) is the **Zhihua si** (Temple of the Transformation of the Intellect), built in 1443 by a eunuch, Wang Zhen. It first served as a family temple and used to house a statue of Wang Zhen placed there in 1457. He purchased a copy of a Ming printing of the Tripitaka together with all of its notes, which were housed in the main hall. In 1742 a Qing official removed Wang's statue but the printed volumes still remain in the temple. The dark blue, almost black tiled roofs of the temple halls have been frequently restored but are said to retain a Ming style.

Inside the Rulai (Buddha of the Future) Hall are some fine carved wooden Buddha figures and there is also a revolving library in a side hall to store the Buddhist sutras. The ceiling of the Rulai Hall was removed by the monks in the 1930s and is now in the Nelson Atkins Museum in America. There is a display of ceramics in the temple (open 09.00–16.00).

East central Peking

South of the main west–east avenue, Jianguomen nei da jie (Chang'an jie in the centre of the city), between Dong dan crossroads and the road that leads south to the old railway station, is the **Yu Qian si** (Temple to Yu Qian) on Xibiaohou hutong, which runs parallel with the main street, just to the south. The temple appears to have vanished under modern buildings.

> ### Yu Qian
> Yu Qian (1398–1457) was a native of Hangzhou. In 1449, when a Mongolian group attacked northern China, the Zhengtong emperor (1436–50) personally led the campaign against him but was defeated and taken prisoner. Officials in the capital, Peking, panicked but Yu Qian, who was Minister of War, personally took charge and led the local people to defend themselves. When the emperor was freed to return to Peking, Yu Qian was branded a traitor and executed in 1457. He was posthumously reinstated in 1466 and his residence was made into a temple.

Proceeding east along the main road (Jianguomen nei da jie), after the right-hand turning to Peking Railway Station (south), the **Peking Observatory** comes into view on the south side of the road, a square grey brick platform with strange bronze implements on the roof. This is the old Jesuit observatory (Guanxiang tai). Opposite, on the north side of the road, was the site of the examination halls (Gong yuan), now covered by the buildings of the **Chinese Academy of Social Sciences**, the highest scholarly body in the humanities—not an inappropriate replacement. One of the lanes leading north used to be called Gongyuan xi hutong, Lane West of the Examination Halls.

The huge area of 8500 individual brick cells was built at the beginning of the Ming occupation of Peking (1420s) on the site of the Yuan dynasty Ministry of Rites. Every three years, during the third lunar month, graduates of the first stage of the imperial exams would arrive in Peking to take the next degree. They had to change into fresh clothes and were then locked into their personal cells for three days (and the intermediate two nights). Despite such precautions, some candidates appear to have found ways of cheating: in the Forbidden City collection there is an entire gown completely covered with the texts of the Confucian Classics for reference purposes and in the British Library there are two very fine silk gauze squares, similarly inscribed. The traditional examinations in the Classics were no longer held after 1900 and the cells were demolished in 1913.

The observatory terrace stands on the site of earlier observatories.

The Jin brought astronomical instruments that they had captured in Kaifeng, the Northern Song capital, but it was Khubilai Khan who first established the observatory in this place. He appointed two astronomers to recalculate the calendar, which was faulty (perhaps because the lunar calendar needs intercalary periods to be inserted every so often). Muslims were later put in charge of the observatory, to be supplanted by the Jesuits in the 17C. Notable Jesuit astronomers such as Matteo Ricci (1553–1610), Schall von Bell (1591–1666), Director of the Board of Astronomy, and Verbiest (1623–88), made Director of the Observatory in 1669, impressed the Kangxi emperor with the accuracy of their calculations, particularly in their prediction of an eclipse, whose accuracy surpassed that of the Muslims.

Verbiest published a couple of Manchu-Chinese-Latin accounts of eclipses witnessed during his stay in Peking (of which there are copies in the British Library). In 1674, after he had already cast a number of cannon, Verbiest was commanded to produce a new set of five astronomical instruments for the terrace; a sixth was said to have been presented by Louis XIV. Their subsequent history and that of the Ming pieces previously in use is somewhat confused. Some were removed to Potsdam in 1900 (but some were returned in 1919), while others were moved to the observatory in Nanjing in 1933.

The observatory was restored in 1983 and the instruments now in place are said by some to be the originals, although which originals is uncertain. The *Zhong guo ming sheng ci dian* says that they include two-thirds of the original Ming pieces (the remaining third being replicas) but, unless it is a misprint, this fails to explain what happened to Verbiest's Qing pieces.

The layout in 1935, for those who can distinguish an armilla from an altazimuth, was as follows: northwest corner, quadrant (1674; an instrument for taking angular measurements of altitude) with dragons; then moving south along the western wall, celestial globe (1674), in the southwest corner was an ecliptic armilla (1674; an armilla was used to show the recurrence of equinoxes and solstices). Moving east along the southern wall, west to east after the ecliptic armilla were an altazimuth (1674; a surveying instrument for measuring vertical and horizontal angles), a theodolite (1715; a surveying instrument with a rotating telescope for measuring angles), a sextant (1674; instrument used for measuring the angular distances between objects) and a zodiacal armilla (1674). On the northern wall between the quadrant (dragons) and the steps was a new armilla (1744); none of these was Ming in date. There are exhibitions about astronomy on the two interior floors; the captions are all in Chinese and astronomy is not my strongest subject but knowledgeable visitors will find the illustrations helpful.

From the top of the observatory (assuming that the high rise mania has slowed a little) to the south you should be able to see the grey brick tower of the fortified corner tower of the old city walls standing on the southeast corner. The Tonghui River flows beneath it. To the northeast, outside the point where the Jianguo (Establish the Country) Gate once stood, beyond the motorway are the tower blocks of one of the two diplomatic quarters of Peking. Behind them are the lower embassy buildings stretching east from the motorway.

On the far side of the motorway, on the north side of the main west–east road, Jianguomen wai da jie, are the *International Club* (provided for diplomats but the restaurants are open to all foreigners; I'm not sure about Chinese) and, beyond that, the *Friendship Store*. This is larger than most other Friendship Stores and sells items for tourists (clothing, embroideries, silks, jade, lacquer, jewellery, carpets, antiques, ceramics, etc.) as well as foodstuffs for the diplomatic corps. There is a small flower, bird and goldfish shop inside, too.

North of the Friendship Store, in the diplomatic quarter, is the Ritan (Temple to the Sun) Park and, further north, the Dongyue miao (Temple of the Eastern Peak).

Ritan Park, formerly called the Chaori tan (Altar for Worship of the Sun), was built in 1530 on a piece of land formerly owned by Xiao Ying of the Ming imperial guard, who was 'Protector of the Brocade Robes'. Court astrologers are said to have recommended the purchase of the land as its area was appropriate. The form of the enclosure is interesting: the walls encompass a horseshoe-shaped area with a straight side to the west. It is entered from the northwest corner by a triumphal arch inscribed 'Gateway to the worship of the sun spirit'. The small courtyard enclosing low buildings immediately inside the archway was the disrobing pavilion where the emperor changed robes for ceremonies. To the east were a bell tower, a repository for musical instruments, sacrificial vessels and carpets, while in the northeast corner was another enclosed courtyard with the Hall for Spirit Tablets, a kitchen and a smaller walled enclosure to the rear where the sacrificial animals were slaughtered. In the centre of the whole is a red circular wall encompassing a low square altar platform of white marble. The wall is pierced by small gates to the north, south and east and a triple gateway to the west.

Ceremonies of homage to the sun were carried out before sunrise on the 15th day of the second lunar month at the spring equinox, when the emperor came on alternate years (with official deputies in the intervening year) to worship the Spirit Tablet of the Sun placed on the altar and offer up the animal sacrifices.

The park now houses restaurants much favoured by diplomatic families.

Dongyue miao

Almost due north of the Ritan Park on the north side of Chaoyangmen wai da jie (the major road reached by taking the road leading north from the park: turn left at the junction with the main road) is the Dongyue miao (Temple of the Eastern Peak) with its ornate green and yellow tiled *pailou*. The *pailou* was all that remained in a sea of rubble in 1998 but in May 2000 the temple was reopened to the public. Rebuilding has always been part of China's architectural history. As readers of this guide will soon see, temples described as being founded in the 3C AD have invariably been rebuilt, more or less totally, up to a dozen or more times in their history. It is, generally, the site that is sacred, not the structure.

The Dongyue miao was the largest temple of the alchemical sect of Taoism in North China, which may well account for its tardy reopening as philosophical Taoism is acceptable in contemporary China but superstitions and alchemy are not. The founder of the sect, **Zhang Daoling** (AD 34–156), used to charge five measures of rice for every case of sickness successfully treated by his spells and the practice gave its name to the Five Pecks of Rice band of Sichuanese Taoist rebels who, together with the Yellow Turbans (another Taoist rebel group from eastern China) virtually brought the Han dynasty down in the early 3C.

The temple named after Tai shan (the Taoist holy mountain in Shandong) was founded in 1312 but burnt down in 1698 and re-established in 1761. Although the temple buildings were Qing in date, the central axis is said to preserve the Yuan style and the new buildings do, indeed, reflect the 'gong character' plan (like an H on its side) characteristic of the Yuan. Another description of the temple (*In Search of Old Peking*, Arlington and Lewisohn, Peking, 1935) says that it is dedicated to the legendary Huang Fei Hu, deified for his rebellion against Zhou Xin, the tyrannical last emperor of the Shang dynasty; elsewhere, however, Huang Fei Hu is identified with the Buddhist God of Hell. Confusions over the origins of the temple probably result from the fact that it was effectively a multi-deity temple. Buddhist temples have different halls dedicated to different deities, although they retain a basic unity.

The Dongyue miao was a Taoist department store with different halls dedicated to immensely different deities and sects, each with separate feast days. In the second courtyard of the main axis were the 72 'Chiefs of Department', each responsible for some human activity or force of nature (deities of seas, rivers, mountains, thunder, various animals, those that supervised official rank, riches, literature or various sins). Other deities, whose effigies stood in company with others or in separate halls in the temple, include the Fangsheng si, 'a kind of Inspector of the Cruelty of Animals Society from whom one can obtain good marks by setting free caged birds, or even fish', the Spirit of Plagues and Boils (suitably afflicted), the Goddess of Birth (surrounded by small plaster dolls) and the Xianbao si, 'a kind of Lost and Stolen Property Office' where lost or stolen articles could be retrieved by drawing lots of thin numbered slips of bamboo. A chest of drawers nearby contained printed slips with numbers corresponding to those on the bamboo slips, which bore rough directions on how to find the missing article. There was a deity worshipped by actors, the God of Literature, the Goddess of Smallpox and another who looked after children's eyesight (she was depicted holding a spare set of eyes), shrines for travellers, where the fox, weasel, snake, hedgehog and rat were worshipped for their ability to exorcise evil spirits and protect travellers, and there were various kings of hell.

A separate shrine was that of **Lu Ban**, patron saint of carpenters and builders (also masons, bricklayers, house-painters and paper-hangers) and members of the trade guild named after Lu Ban would hold annual ceremonies here on Lu Ban's birthday, as would other guild members whose patron deities were enshrined in the temple.

In June 2000 rebuilding was complete but the clay effigies in the little separate halls of the 'departments' were still being constructed. First, a wooden armature was made and then covered with clay and straw to form an attentuated, Giacometti-style figure. These were then covered with a finer clay and eventually painted. The figures include the accused, looking suitably chastened, the central judge and various attendants, many fierce, animal-headed figures. Go soon and you can enjoy the sight of the posthumous work of Giacometti and the very funny labels to each little shrine in slightly odd English (the underlying concepts are equally odd). Shrines with particular relevance to life today (those that bring riches or sons) are decorated with sheafs of red ribbons and votive plaques.

On the eastern outskirts of town, just south of the towering new Great Wall Hotel (Changcheng fandian), is the green tile roofed **Agricultural Exhibition Hall** (Quanguo nongye zhanlanguan). This is one of the Ten Great Buildings (which include Peking's Railway Station, the Great Hall of the People and the Historical Museum) constructed during the Great Leap Forward (1958).

These were mostly built in a new 'national style'. Exemplified by the Railway Station and the Agricultural Exhibition Hall, this involved the use of western concrete below and 'Chinese' tiled roofs above. The major theorist of this new style was **Liang Sicheng**, son of the great reformer Liang Qichao, who had studied architecture at the University of Pennsylvania and pioneered architectural history in China, rediscovering the Tang dynasty Fo guang Temple on Wutai shan. Liang Sicheng was later strongly criticised for the 'wastefulness' of the Chinese roofs. He found himself in a political and aesthetic no-win situation, for not only was it difficult to solve the problem of transition from timber frame to concrete frame but the rising slogan of post-Great Leap architecture was 'utility, economy and, if possible, beauty'.

Northeast Peking

The northeast corner of town includes the Imperial Academy (Guozijian), Confucian temple and City Museum (Shoudu bowuguan), the Lama temple (Yonghe gong) and Bolin si.

A small street running west off Yonghegong da jie in the northwest corner of the old walled town is called Guozijian jie. On it lie the old **Imperial Academy** (Guozijian or College for the Sons of the Nation) and the Confucian temple. It is the only street in Peking which still has a number of *pailou* (triumphal arches) standing across the road. Great timber constructions painted in blue, green, red and gold with high stone bases, such arches stood in many places in China's towns and cities; in Peking there were groups at Xi si, Dong si, Dong dan and Xi dan. They were sometimes erected in commemoration of 'virtuous widows', women who had committed suicide on the deaths of their husbands, sometimes merely as decoration. Here they mark the importance of this narrow, tree-lined lane with its collection of major educational establishments.

At the western end of the road is the **Guozijian**, now housing the capital's main library (as distinct from the National Library), which was the most prestigious school in the land from the Yuan to the Qing. It is open daily 09.00–17.00.

Founded in 1306 under the Yuan (some of the cypresses are said to date from that period), in the first years of the Ming it was known as the School of the Beiping Commandery but it was renamed the College for the Sons of the Nation in 1404.

The present buildings date from different periods. The pavilion behind the Yilun tang, used as the office of the director, was built in 1528 and the Great Hall in the centre, the Bi yong (Hall of Sovereign Harmony), which stands in the middle of a circular pool once filled with carp and lotuses, was built in 1784 under the Qianlong emperor. It is approached through a triple arch covered in yellow tiles, which bears an inscription from the Confucian *Analects*: 'All under heaven benefit from instruction'.

Here the emperors used to come in the second month every year, cross the marble bridges, sit in the hall in front of the Five Mountain Screen and expound upon the Confucian Classics. The courtyard walls were set with 190 stones engraved in 1794 with the texts of the Confucian Classics (comprising over 630,000 characters); these have now been moved into halls specially built in 1956. The Guozijian is not now normally open to foreigners unless they have a library ticket.

Confucian temple ~ City Museum

East of the Guozijian is the **Confucian temple**, Kong miao or Wen (Literary) miao, which also houses the **Peking City Museum**. This is an ideal temple to visit for it seems to be off the usual beaten track and is therefore very tranquil (open 09.00–16.00, closed Mondays).

Founded in 1302 under the Yuan, it was first rebuilt in 1411 and frequently restored during the Ming; under Wanli (1567–73) the halls were tiled in green. During the subsequent Qing dynasty the same process of restoration and improvement continued; under the Qianlong emperor most of the halls were retiled in yellow. The main hall was expanded in 1904, although its bracketing is still in the heavy and simple Yuan style.

The temple's spirit wall is on the far side of the street. In the first courtyard, amongst the old trees, are numerous stelae engraved with the names of successful examination candidates throughout the centuries from the Yuan to the late Qing. On either side of the first great gate, some of the 'stone drums' (or replicas of them) are exhibited.

These are problematic stones, with rather illegible inscriptions said to date from the Zhou (770–221 BC) and to have been lost and rediscovered in the Tang. Despite their weight, they were carted about by fugitive emperors (the

Song), dragged back to Peking in 1192 and placed in the Confucian temple in 1307. It is said that the originals were removed by the Nationalist Government in 1933 but that facsimiles had been carved in the 18C at the order of Qianlong to preserve the fading inscriptions. These are in *da zhuan* or 'great seal script' (the second major style in the development of the Chinese script after that found on oracle bones of the Shang) and record episodes in a hunting expedition along a riverbank led by the Duke of Qin (who may have lived c 375 BC). The ancient trees in the courtyards are home to a large number of birds. Some of the trees are so ancient that they have died but one dead juniper still stands as a support for a wisteria.

Inside the gate the main courtyard has ten yellow tiled stelae pavilions (closed), whose stelae record famous victories and conquests of the Kangxi, Yongzheng and Qianlong emperors. They are in pretty worrying condition. The main hall (Dacheng dian or Hall of Great Perfection) is huge, nine bays broad, five deep, raised high on a 'moon platform' of white marble with white marble railings. It may be closed but contains (or contained) the spirit tablet of Confucius and his major followers, beams of teak from Burma and Indochina and special straw matting presented from southern China.

On either side of the courtyard, the side wings house exhibitions. On the west is a very interesting permanent display relating to the history of Peking, from Peking Man to recent times (all explanatory material is in Chinese). It includes a number of architectural relics (drainage tiles, roof tiles, etc.). The east wings house temporary exhibitions. One of the most fascinating related to the work of a Peking antiquarian who had rescued the most extraordinary collection of ancient and not so ancient bronzes from scrap-metal collection points. There have also been displays, such as one on 'women revolutionary martyrs' which contained touching blurred photographs and some sad little garments amongst artists' impressions of often terrible fates.

Worship in the temple took place in the spring and autumn, with the 27th day of the eighth lunar month (Confucius' birthday) seeing the greatest festivities. After 1911 under the Republic the worship of Confucius declined for a while but was officially reinstated in 1934, only to be abandoned again in 1949.

Lama temple

At its east end, the lane runs into Yonghegong da jie and the entrance to the Lama temple (Yonghe gong or Palace of Harmony) is virtually opposite.

Built in 1694, it originally served as the palace (or mansion) of the Kangxi emperor's son who became the Yongzheng emperor. In 1725 it was converted into a temple, since according to custom the palace of a prince who ascended the throne could not be inhabited by his descendants, hence the movement around the Forbidden City too. Stelae in the front courtyard, with inscriptions by the Qianlong emperor, refer to this custom. The Yongzheng emperor was not the heir-apparent, so he could not have known that his palace would have to be abandoned, as he was the fourth son of the Kangxi emperor. The heir-apparent showed signs of mental instability, which led to an unseemly scramble for power amongst his brothers, which the Yongzheng emperor won.

The temple was first used by the imperial family to house ancestral portraits and the roofs of major halls were therefore tiled in imperial yellow. In 1744 it was made into a Lamaist temple.

It covers a considerable area and has five major courtyards. Partly because of the impropriety of some of the Tantric statues, which are now usually covered with white and yellow silk scarves arranged rather like nappies (diapers), and partly because of the rather wild behaviour of some of the Tibetan lamas, as late as 1935 visitors were warned never to allow themselves to be alone with a lama. Arlington and Lewisohn warned:

In former days the Yonghe gong had a very bad reputation for assaults on foreigners and sometimes the complete disappearance of solitary sightseers. Even in quite recent times there have been numerous authentic cases where single foreign visitors have undergone very unpleasant experiences there. As recently as 1927, one of the authors was enticed into one of the buildings on the pretence of being shown some rare ornaments and nearly had the door closed on him. When he pulled out his revolver ... the lama at once let go of the door explaining that he had only closed it because he did not want the Head Lama to see him showing visitors around. He was, however, not content with this explanation and reported the man's action to the Head Lama and had the pleasure of seeing him give the rascal a good thrashing until he shouted for mercy.

In the 1930s 'devil dances' were still performed in the temple at the end of the first lunar month (the Tibetan New Year) but even then, apparently, the police had ordered the omission of 'the more exciting and horrible parts' (where a doll made of dough and filled with a red liquid was torn up and chewed in a representation of human sacrifice).

The long approach to the temple used to be lined with the dwellings of the lamas. Beyond the spirit wall and *pailou*, the temple proper is entered through the Chaotian men (Gate of Shining Glory) which leads to a courtyard with bell and drum towers on either side, then a pair of Qianlong period bronze lions standing between two open stelae pavilions. These contain inscriptions in Chinese, Manchu (left), Tibetan and Mongolian (right) with Qianlong's account of the foundation of the temple. Throughout the temple there are examples of the curious great pine poles found in Lamaist temples.

The first hall is not very different from that in any Chinese Buddhist temple: it contains the Four Heavenly Guardians, ranged on either side, a 'fat' Maitreya (Buddha of the Future) facing south with Wei tuo, defender of the faith, standing behind looking north. Although the temple is generally Chinese in architectural style, it may be noted that this hall's facade is reminiscent of some of the Eight Outer Temples at Chengde and the mosque in Cow Street. With three arched doorways, the rest of the facade is filled in with planking and painted deep red. This style appears to be associated with 'non-Chineseness'.

In the second court is a fine incense burner (they are all very good in this imperially favoured temple) with flattened lions floating in a brocade sea (dated 1746), which stands in front of a double-roofed pavilion over a stele inscribed with the history of Lamaist Buddhism, again in the four languages: Chinese, Manchu, Tibetan and Mongolian. Another bronze incense burner in the form of the Buddhist holy mountain, Sumeru, stands in front of the Hall of Eternal Harmony with its three Buddhas (past, present and future) and 18 lohan figures.

The Lama Temple is the best place I have found for hearing the aeolian bells which hang from the eaves of halls and pavilions: the wind seems frequently to rustle through the bamboos and move the little bronze bells.

At the south end of the third courtyard is the Yongyou dian (Hall of Eternal Protection) with the Buddha of Medicine (favoured by Lamaists) on the left of the Buddha of Longevity. Opposite is the cruciform Falun dian (Hall of the Wheel of the Law) with Tibetan stupa (dagoba) shaped roof decorations. This was the centre of religious devotion in the temple. It contains a 6m bronze statue of Tsongkhapa, 15C founder of the Yellow Hat sect of Tibetan Buddhism. Paintings of his life cover the walls.

Tsongkhapa's sect gradually achieved supremacy over the older Red Hat sect in Tibet and this ascendancy continued after the establishment in 1578 of the title of Dalai Lama (head of the Yellow Sect, based in Lhasa, as opposed to the Panchen Lama, who was head of the Red Hats and whose base was Shigatse or Rikaze).

Behind, on the main axis, is the three storey **Wanfu ge** (Tower of Ten Thousand Happinesses). There are numerous side buildings beside and behind the Hall of the Wheel of the Law, to which we will return.

The Wan fu ge was built in 1750 (and thoroughly rebuilt in 1988) and is linked to two side pavilions by 'flying corridors' (bridges at the second storey level). The height of the building was determined by the massive (18m) Maitreya figure inside. Said to have been carved out of a single trunk of either cedar or white sandalwood, when I last saw it, it was black with dust and visible only from below, as the upper galleries were unsafe. Black and cobwebbed, it was an awesome sight, in keeping with the rather terrifying nature of Tibetan Buddhism.

The only form of banditry currently practised in the Lama temple is the occasional proliferation of entrance tickets, as many of the rear side halls containing treasures require separate tickets. On either side of the Falun dian are two dark-roofed halls: to the left the Jietai (Ordination Platform) building and to the right the Panchen building, constructed to house the sixth Panchen Lama when he came to pay his respects on the occasion of Qianlong's 60th birthday in 1780. This contains a silver and gilded statue of the Panchen himself and a variety of gifts and objects used in Tibetan daily life. These range from cups, bowls, inlaid chopsticks, butter churns (tall, very narrow, cylindrical churns), snuff bottles, silver altarpieces, Qianlong's throne, robes, Tibetan musical instruments, including conch shells and long trumpets, sculpted and padded hats, bird and flower paintings and a collection of modern Japanese offerings of little flags and fountain pens.

Against the wall just northeast of the Panchen building is the Zhaofo building which contains a beautifully carved *Phoebe nanmu* niche with dragon columns, all over floral scrolling and hanging lotus bud bosses.

South of the Panchen building, in the eastern side hall, the images include those of some of the fiercer defenders of the Lamaist faith, including Yama, the bull-headed 'god of death' and Lha mo, the 'terrible goddess', the Tibetan equivalent of Kali.

Leaving the Lama temple, turn south (left) down the main road and take the first lane on the left, which leads around the southern end of the temple and then turns up north, taking you to the nearby Bailin or **Bolin si** (Temple of the Cypress Grove).

Founded in 1347, it was enlarged during the Ming and Qing and an inscription was written for it by the Kangxi emperor: 'Forest of ten thousand ancient cypresses'. The temple houses the woodblocks used to print an edition of the Buddhist *Tripitaka* (canon), called the *Dragon Tripitaka* published in a woodblock edition between 1733 and 1738 in 7240 fascicules (booklets). They were printed from 79,036 woodblocks of which 78,230 survive. This is the earliest surviving set of woodblocks for the *Tripitaka* to survive in China.

Apparently the temple was used as a 'summer retreat' by lamas from the Lama temple. As it is only next door it is difficult to imagine what they managed to retreat from at such proximity.

Immediately north of the Yonghe gong, on the far side of the Andingmen dong da jie motorway, is the **Ditan gongyuan** (Park of the Altar to the Earth), of which little remains except the enclosure of the altar, since much of the site has been occupied by the Beijing Hospital for Infectious Diseases; it is hardly worth the trip.

Originally, the Ming emperors had worshipped at the Altar to Heaven and Earth in the Temple of Heaven enclosure in the south of the town but in 1530 the Jiajing emperor was persuaded by his court astrologers to build a separate Altar to the Earth on the site of an old temple in the northeast suburbs just outside the city walls. It apparently remained a modest affair until the Jiaqing emperor (reigned 1796–1821) decided to completely remodel the altar. The entire area was squared, for the earth was believed to be square while heaven was round, as is clearly expressed in the Temple of Heaven. Otherwise, the layout was not dissimilar to that of the Ri tan (Temple of the Sun).

Approached from the west through a *pailou*, the double-walled square enclosure contained a hall of abstinence where the emperor fasted and changed his robes before participating in the annual ceremonies, a bell tower, storehouses and a slaughterhouse for animal sacrifices, a hall of the imperial gods where imperial spirit tablets were housed (until used for firewood by soldiers in the 1930s). The altar itself was a two-tiered square structure of white marble, surrounded by a moat. The emperor came annually to perform ceremonies very similar to those performed in the Temple of Heaven except that here they were performed at the summer solstice.

Northern suburbs: Xihuang si, Dazhong si

Not far to the west of the Ditan (Temple of the Earth Park), on the far side of the Anding men wai da jie (the main road leading north from the Anding men or Gate of Peaceful Pacification), about 800m west of the site of the gate was the **Russian Cemetery** (not found by the author but probably part within the Russian Embassy and part destroyed by the new road).

This used to belong to the old Russian Mission which occupied the site now covered by the large Soviet Embassy, filling the angle of the extreme northwest corner of the old city wall. The area was first occupied by Albazin prisoners brought back to China in 1685 after Kangxi had been out to suppress border incursions on the Amur River. They remained in this area, although they gradually intermarried with the Manchus and in 1858 the Russian Ecclesiastical Mission was moved here from the old Legation area. The mission buildings were destroyed in 1900 when the Boxers murdered hundreds of Chinese Christians who had taken refuge there.

Aside from Russians, including some Romanovs, in the cemetery, there was a memorial to eight Sikhs, one British attaché, three soldiers, including Captain Brabazon, and *The Times* correspondent, T.W. Bowlby, who died as prisoners 'treacherously seized in violation of a flag of truce on the 18 September 1860', although apparently Captain Brabazon's body was never found.

The **Xihuang si** (Western Yellow Temple) is off Huang si lu, northwest of An ding men.

There was a temple on the site from the Liao but it was destroyed in 1643 when the rebel leader Li Zicheng and his troops arrived to attack Ming Peking. The history of the present structure dates back to 1652 when the Shunzhi emperor had it restored for the fifth Panchen Lama on his official visit. There were two parts to the temple: the temple proper was called the East Yellow Temple (Dong huang si) and the residential quarters were called the Xi huang si (West Yellow Temple). Under Kangxi, the temple was further restored and used as a residence for Tibetan and Mongolian Lamaist dignitaries on official visits.

In 1708 the sixth Panchen died of smallpox and, although his ashes were returned to Peking two years later, the Qianlong emperor ordered the construction of a white stupa in his memory in one of the temple courtyards. The temple continued in use, serving as a stopping place for Mongol merchants en route for Peking and the 13th Dalai Lama stayed here in 1908.

The Hall of Guardians, with four fierce figures, still stands and the remains of the Eastern Temple can be seen in the pillar bases but the major surviving construction is the white stupa. Raised high on a platform, the central dagoba in the Tibetan style is surrounded by four lesser stupas in the Chinese style and the whole is surrounded by a white stone railing. The Chinese style stupas are covered with carved Buddhist texts. The central dagoba has a fine gilded crown and the base is finely carved with lotus flowers, Buddha figures, lohans and landscapes with scenes from the life of the Buddha. The carvings were badly damaged by foreign troops in 1900.

If you are in a car (or on a bicycle), between the two temples you could make a small detour northwards to see the **Jimen stele**. This stands on a small remaining portion of the old Yuan earthen wall to the west of Xueyuan lu, which runs north from the North Circular Road at the major intersection west of Beitaipingzhuang. The stele has inscriptions in the hand of the Qianlong emperor with the four-character phrase 'A haze of trees at the gate of Jin' on one side and a seven-line poem on the reverse commemorating the site of Jin, a town of the Warring States period said to have stood here.

The Yuan wall, an earthen rampart stretching far north of the Ming and Qing city walls, runs for some way along the west side of Xueyuan lu, which leads to many of the educational institutes built in the northwest suburbs (the name means 'Academy Road').

Northwest of the Yellow Temple, on the western part of the North Circular Road (Beisanhuanxi lu), just east of the junction with Haidian lu, is the **Juesheng si** (Temple of the Enlightened Life), better known as the Dazhong si or Great Bell Temple (now housing the Guzhong bowuguan or Museum of Ancient Bells).

The temple was built in 1733. A famous bell cast in 1406 was brought here in 1743 from the Wanshou si just to the west and the temple gained its present name. The temple is of considerable size and emperors came here to pray for rain and carry out other Buddhist observances.

Its great bell was cast in the Hanjing foundry, just inside the Desheng Gate. It is almost 7m high, 22cm thick at the lip with a circumference of 3.3m and it weighs 46.5 tons. There are 17 Buddhist texts cast on the surface of the bell, including sutras and dharani (incantations) with over 227,000 characters. When struck (like most Chinese bells, it has no clapper but was struck on the outside) it resonates for more than two minutes. Underneath is a small seated figure in bronze.

A common legend related to bell casting is applied to this bell (and others): the craftsman failed to produce a perfectly resonant bell until his daughter threw herself into the molten metal, sacrificing herself for her father's work.

The temple, which crouches under one of the flyovers of 'West Bei huan Three Road' or Third Northern Ring-road West, now houses a small museum of bells with examples from the Song onwards displayed in its halls and courtyards (open 08.30–17.30, closed Mondays).

Northwest suburbs

Peking's northwest suburbs include the Zoo, Exhibition Hall, Xu Beihong Museum, Dahui si, Qi Baishi's Tomb, Wanshou si, Wuta si, Yuan ming yuan, the Summer Palace and Xi shan.

Baishiqiao lu leads north from the **Peking Zoo** (on Xizhimen wai da jie), not too horrible a zoo and often visited for its pandas.

It occupies an area which was a Qing imperial park, renovated by the Qianlong emperor for his mother's 60th birthday (175l) and again by the Dowager Empress Cixi. In 1902, when the Viceroy of Shanxi returned from a trip to 17 different countries, he brought back a collection of animals from Germany as a present for Cixi. They were housed here and the park was renamed the 'Park of Ten Thousand Animals'. In 1908 the zoo was opened to the public, although it was badly neglected during the civil war period (leaving only a one-eyed ostrich, 12 monkeys and a few old parrots). Since 1949 the zoo has, however, been restocked with native fauna and some animals acquired from abroad through exchanges.

The zoo is next door to the Russian style **Exhibition Hall** (Zhanlanguan) with its star-topped spire (similar to the Shanghai Exhibition Hall) and Russian and Qiaozhou restaurants.

Due east of the Exhibition Hall, just north of the junction called Xinjiekou (where Xizhimen nei da jie meets Xinjiekou bei da jie) is the **museum** devoted to the life and works of the painter **Xu Beihong** (1895–1953). There used to be a museum in his old house near the railway station but this was demolished in 1957 and the new museum at Xinjiekou was opened a few years ago.

The museum's display begins with Xu Beihong's birthplace, Yixing, famous for its little brick-red teapots. It includes replicas of two rooms in his old house, one of which is the painter's studio. Xu Beihong studied painting in France in 1918 and became one of the first Chinese successfully to master oil-painting techniques. His oil-covered easel contrasts with his desk covered with Chinese brushes. The curtains are of Chinese *lan bu*, or blue cotton, indigo-dyed cloth with wax-resist patterns, here restricted to a border.

There are some fine oil paintings and numerous sketches in the western style, many of which were done in Paris. His most famous paintings, however, are the galloping horses in monochrome ink wash (in the Chinese style) first painted in 1941 and which became extremely popular in the west in the 1950s. The works exhibited demonstrate his mastery of both Chinese and western techniques with some very charming sketches, particularly of his small son asleep.

A major intellectual figure of the 1930s, he painted portraits of distinguished visitors to China, such as the Bengali poet and philosopher, Tagore. As a result of his stay in France, he romanised his name himself, often signing his works 'Peon' (for Beihong). The museum is open 09.00–11.00, 13.00–16.00, closed Mondays.

Returning to the Zoo and Exhibition Hall area, on the corner of Xi zhi men wai da jie and Baishiqiao lu is the **Capital Stadium**, built in 1968. At the southern end of Baishiqiao lu, on the west side of the road, is the double-towered new **National Library** building and the **Purple Bamboo Park** (Zizhuyuan gongyuan).

The park was the site of lakes and a canal built in the Yuan dynasty by the engineer Guo Shou in order to regulate the flow of water from the Jade Fountain and the Bai River into the city of Peking. During the Qing, 'travelling palaces' were built here so that members of the imperial family travelling back to the city from the Summer Palace by boat could stop and rest. The lakes remain but the only old building in the park is the nine storey Ming pagoda.

The main road crosses a small stream. Just beyond the stream, on the east side of the road, is a small lane which leads behind the stadium and the zoo to the **Wuta si** (Five Pagoda Temple).

During the reign of the Yongle emperor of the Ming (1403–25), an Indian monk called Pandida presented the emperor with five golden Buddha images and a model of the Diamond Temple at Boddhgaya. The Zhenjue si (the formal name of the Five Pagoda Temple), or Temple of the True Enlightenment, was built on this site to house the precious relics. In 1473 a five pagoda building, modelled on the Diamond Temple, was constructed in the middle of the temple. Apart from this five pagoda structure which still stands, the rest of the temple suffered damage inflicted by foreign troops in both 1860 and 1900.

The building has a square base covered with bas-relief carvings. There are five stepped, tapering Indian style pagodas on the top with a rather incongruous

Chinese style glazed tile pavilion in the centre with images of the Buddha's foot-prints. The interior of the square base has a stone staircase leading up to the top. The bas-relief carvings on the exterior are divided into seven bands: the upper five have multiple images of the Buddha in different positions (particularly vary-ing the positions of the hands, in the set of gestures known as *mudra*); below are bands of lotus petals, Sanskrit characters and Buddhist symbols: celestial guardians, the wheel of the law, vases of flowers and various animals such as a lion, *garuda* (human-headed bird), peacock, elephant and horse. In the court-yards are stelae from the tombs of notable Jesuits who served in the Chinese court in the 17C and 18C.

Due west of the Five Pagoda Temple is the **Wanshou si** (Temple of Ten Thousand Longevities). It is on the northern bank of the same small canal that runs past the Five Pagoda Temple, just outside the northwest wall of the Purple Bamboo Park. It is most easily reached by going all round the outside of the Purple Bamboo Park. The Zizhuyuan lu runs along the south wall; take the first turning on the right (north) and the temple is visible to the east.

It is said to have been built in 1577 by Feng Bao, a favourite eunuch of the Ming Wanli emperor, and once housed the bell that is now in the Great Bell Temple. This temple was also used as a resting place by the Dowager Empress Cixi as she made her stately way to the Summer Palace.

A 1935 description of the temple notes a piled stone rockery in the eastern courtyard from which the Dowager Empress used to survey the scenery. There was also a stele with an inscription by the Qianlong emperor (in Chinese, Manchu, Mongolian and Tibetan) recording the history of the temple. It seems that, although Feng Bao was favoured by the Wanli emperor, he fell from grace in 1584 when he was stripped of his titles and had his property confiscated on the grounds of arrogance and excessive power.

Returning to Baishiqiao lu and heading north, the road is lined with great edu-cational institutes, for this area of Peking is the academic centre, with Peking University and Qinghua University to the north. The **Minzu xueyuan** (Minorities Institute) is on the left, the medical and agricultural institutes on the right. About half way up the road, blocks of flats now stand where there was once a village called **Weigongcun** (Duke Wei's Village) which, as late as 1976, was surrounded by fields.

Just south of Weigongcun, a road to the right (east) leads to the great hall of the **Dahui si** (Temple of Great Wisdom), commonly known as the Dafo si (Great Buddha Temple).

Founded in 1513 by Zhang Xiong (another powerful eunuch), the temple's great hall with its double roof is the only surviving building and, despite repairs in 1757, still retains its Ming style timber construction. There was a huge bronze Buddha in the hall which was taken away by the Japanese dur-ing their occupation of Peking in 1937 and replaced by a wooden figure. The wall paintings and stucco figures of the 18 lohans are Ming. The wall paint-ings illustrate stories of the potential achievements of ordinary people who devote their entire lives to good (Buddhist) works.

At the northern end of Weigong cun, a road to the left (west), Weigongcun lu, leads past a housing estate close to the main road. There, amongst the blocks of flats and visible from the road, is the concrete tump of the **Tomb of Qi Baishi** (1863–1957) and his wife.

Qi Baishi

Born into a very poor family, Qi Baishi learnt the craft of seal carving as a child and only in later life managed to survive as a painter, becoming, along with Xu Beihong, one of the most famous of China's 20C painters. Working in the traditional style with ink and brush, he added bright splashes of colour. His paintings frequently include groupings of objects (books, candles and jugs of wine, chrysanthemums and small wine-cups) in the *literati* tradition, recalling Li Bai's poems on drinking, or unusual animal and vegetable groupings with a great fondness for shrimps and minnows. Immediately attractive, they are enhanced by his characteristic calligraphy and a variety of simple seals which he cut for himself.

Qi Baishi's old house at 13 Lipingche hutong, just north of the Minzu gong (Palace of the Minorities) on the western part of Chang'an jie, is shown on maps but is not yet open formally; the courtyard will require considerable renovation before it becomes an attractive site.

After crossing the (third or inner) North Circular Road (Bei san huan xi lu), Baishiqiao lu is renamed Haidian lu and leads through the eastern edge of the old village of **Haidian** (Sea of Lakes). It was previously an important stage on the road to the Summer Palaces and also served as a provisioning point. It was surrounded not only by the palaces to the north but also by many great country seats of high officials.

The centre of the village can be reached by turning left at the fork in the road just beyond the Haidian Hospital (on the left). There used to be some rather well-carved facades to the shops and houses lining the main street, particularly north of the main department store and on the narrow street to the right near the new supermarket, but Haidian is not what it once was, as the area is now Peking's 'Silicon Valley' filled with tower blocks housing the businesses that have sprung up in proximity to the university with its computer specialists.

Continue along Haidian lu to the next large intersection, Zhongguancun. Haidian lu turns sharp left and runs along past the southern wall of **Peking University**. This part of the university is fairly new, with grey brick dormitory blocks built in the 1950s, but at the bottom of the hill, Haidian lu turns right (north) again and runs past the main gates of the university which are more impressive, with fine stone lions.

The university stands on the site of two mansions, one of which was owned by Heshen (1750–99), who also owned the Gongwang fu (see p 144) near the Back Lakes just north of the Bei hai Park. The other was the Shao yuan (Ladle Garden) which belonged to the painter Mi Wanzhong (late 16C–early 17C). A poet and calligrapher as well as a painter, he used to paint scenes of his garden on lanterns, a practice which became extremely fashionable at the time. The rather luxurious new dormitory block for overseas students is called Shao yuan in commemoration of Mi's garden.

> ### Heshen
> A Manchu soldier of relatively poor origins, Heshen's sudden acquisition of the ear and favour of the Qianlong emperor in 1775 is still somewhat inexplicable (and scurrilous stories are generally discounted). He was instantly granted various important military positions and led some successful campaigns, although he had to be recalled from the mission to suppress a Muslim uprising in Gansu as he was doing so badly. His power was paramount, especially as the emperor became increasingly senile, even after Qianlong's 'retirement' in 1796, when he did not in fact relinquish the reigns of power but left them in Heshen's hands. Heshen amassed a fortune and a vast collection of treasures, some of which were kept in his 'villa' at Haidian.

The gardens surrounding the villa still stand (although nothing much remains of any 18C building), with pools, hills and tiny lodges for porters; a 'stone boat', a version of that in the Summer Palace (a simple carved stone platform without the Mississippi riverboat superstructure), still stands by the main lake, known as 'No Name Lake'.

As he was in charge of the arrangements for the visit, Heshen welcomed Lord Macartney to his country villa in 1792. Early in the 1920s Yenching University, set up by American missionaries to provide an education in English to Chinese students, built its campus on the site of the two gardens, adding a 'pagoda' (actually a watertower) and the earliest group of dormitory buildings (grey brick with green roof tiles) near the lake designed by an American architect, Killam Murphy. In 1953, when the missionary university had removed itself to Harvard, Peking University (founded in 1898) was moved from the cramped 'red house' at the back of the Forbidden City out to this spacious site and building work continued, although the lake area remains as a pleasant rustic garden.

This is where half of Edgar Snow's ashes were scattered in 1972, at a spot beside No Name Lake marked by a marble slab with an inscription. Snow (born in Kansas in 1905) was an American journalist who first came to China in 1928 when he began work as a reporter in Shanghai on the *Shanghai Weekly Review*. Moving to Peking in 1933 and finding journalistic work hard to come by, he taught at Yenching University for a year in 1934 before making his famous trip to Yan'an in 1936 where he interviewed Mao and the other Communist leaders. His most famous book, *Red Star Over China*, based on the trip, was first published in 1938 (see S. Bernard Thomas, *Season of High Adventure: Edgar Snow in China*, Berkeley, 1996).

Opposite the main gate of Peking University, on the other side of the road, are the remains of another gate which used to lead to the Qinghua yuan of Li Wei, a distant relative of the Wanli emperor of the Ming who was the first to build a villa and garden in the Haidian area.

At the northern end of Haidian lu there is a T-junction. To the west the **Yiheyuan lu** leads to the 'New' Summer Palace, while to the east it leads to the Yuanming yuan or 'Old' Summer Palace beyond **Qinghua University**. Now paired with Peking University but slightly stronger in technical and scientific subjects, whereas Peking University is famous for the humanities, the university was started in 1911 as a preparatory institution for students about to go abroad to study. It was financed by some of the American part of the Boxer indemnity, paid in reparation for the damage and loss of life sustained by Americans during the Boxer uprising.

Yuanming yuan ~ 'Old Summer Palace'

The Yuanming yuan (Garden of Perfect Brightness) is sometimes known as the 'Old' Summer Palace. Not strictly older than the series of imperial gardens to the west, now known as the 'New' Summer Palace, the garden seems older today, for after its destruction by British and French troops in 1860, it was never rebuilt, while the Dowager Empress Cixi continued to spend vast sums on the 'New' Summer Palace every time it was damaged by foreign troops (1860 and 1900). There are ambitious and expensive plans to rebuild the Yuanming yuan, which to the western eye would be a terrible pity as the area is now one of romantic ruins. Reconstruction would run the risk of creating a Qianlong 'theme park'.

The Yuanming yuan was made up of three gardens in an enclosure about 10km in circumference. All were established by Qing emperors (beginning in 1709) and were traditional Chinese gardens with lotus pools, piled rocks and over 140 pavilions. There were considerable apartments, banqueting halls and a library building, the Wenyuan ge (Pavilion of the Source of Literature), built like its pairs in the Forbidden City and the Summer Resort at Chengde to house a copy of the imperial collectanea, *Si ku quan shu* (*Complete Treasury of the Four Storehouses*).

Nothing now remains of the major Chinese part of the garden: what was not burnt down by looting French and British troops in 1860 was probably carried away for building materials by local peasants. There are traces of rockeries, the remains of pools and, in what was the northern part of the Garden of Everlasting Spring, the remains of the **Xiyang lou** ('Western Buildings', often described as the 'European Palaces').

Constructed between 1747 and 1759, these stone buildings were all made to the designs of Jesuit fathers and laymen (Sichelbarth, Benoît and the painter Castiglione), who also acted as foremen during the building operations. Although only a few pieces remain, the Jesuits themselves recorded the fruits of their labours (which 'could stand comparison with Versailles and St Cloud' they said) in a series of engraved 'views' (an almost complete copy of which is held in the British Museum, while the Bibliothèque Nationale de France in Paris has a complete set and reproductions have been published).

The 'European Palaces' included a pavilion with music rooms, a labyrinth, an aviary, a gazebo, five kiosks and the major 'Palace of the Calm Sea' with fountains, as well as a theatrical representation of the scenery near Aksu (Xinjiang) with moving stage scenery made for Xiang fei, a favourite Uighur concubine of the emperor who suffered from homesickness.

The stone animals that spouted the 'pyramid of water' forming the fountains in front of the Palace of the Calm Sea are gone (they can be seen in replica in the atrium of the Grand Hotel at 35 Dongchangan jie) but a huge open seashell in stone, which was the centre of a tiered group of fountains, remains. Father

Benoît, who designed the fountains, spent much effort on the production of a water clock, using the 12 animals which represent the 12 two hour long 'hours' of the traditional Chinese day as well as representing the 12 year cycle. The rest of the stone remains: columns encircled by flower swags and arches with acanthus leaf bases, which almost look as if they have been turned upside-down, are in what one Chinese guidebook calls the 'barock style' and which is elsewhere described as 'Jesuit colonial architecture' (of the type found in Argentina and Paraguay).

Considerable efforts have been made in recent years to gather up the remaining stones and attempt to group them. The labyrinth has been completely rebuilt in shining white marble and is quite fun: a maze, not of box or of any other plants but of stone. There is also a new long, shiny marble wall carved with the entire text in Chinese of the Treaty of Nanking (1842), the first of the 'unequal treaties' which established foreign treaty ports in China after the First Opium War. A modern tripod urn near the entrance to the site was presented to commemorate the return of Hong Kong to Chinese rule in 1997 after it had been ceded 'in perpetuity' to Great Britain in 1842.

In the southeast corner of the old garden area is a small **museum** relating the history of the gardens and including a model reconstruction. The exhibits include a letter from Victor Hugo expressing his horror at the destruction of the Yuanming yuan, which is ironic since Hugo's father had served with the French troops that had looted Spain in 1811–12.

There also used to be a collection of carved stones gathered from other sites. Some of the most curious included depictions of Darwin, Erasmus and Democritus; these were originally carved for the old National Library of Peking and, since the library has largely vacated its original site, were brought to this small 'stone-carving museum'. They may have been relocated in the Wuta si.

The history of the destruction of the Yuanming yuan in 1860 (when British and French troops were sent to Peking to force ratification of the Convention of Peking, opening China to diplomatic representation) still creates conflict. Some French writers blame the British entirely, to the point of accusing them of misleading the French troops about the route to the Summer Palace. It would seem, however, that blame must be equally apportioned: in the British Library, as well as a tiny jade-covered Buddhist work said to have been found 'in the Emperor's bedroom' and volumes of fine illustrations of imperial costume and ritual items generally assumed to have been removed from the 'Old' Summer Palace, there is also a lacquer-bound volume of Qianlong's own calligraphy which the Library purchased from General de Montaubon who had led the French troops to the site in 1860. During the sack of the palaces, certain of the better items were kept aside for Queen Victoria and Napoleon III, an auction of the remaining items was held amongst the officers and a resulting sum distributed amongst the ordinary soldiers, after which the area was set on fire.

Yiheyuan ~ 'New Summer Palace'

To the west, the 'New' Summer Palace, better distinguished by its Chinese name Yihe yuan (Garden of the Preservation of Harmony), suffered the same fate but was rebuilt in 1888 by the Dowager Empress Cixi, allegedly with money that should have been spent building up the Chinese Navy. The Yihe yuan covers an area of 290 hectares, with the vast Kunming Lake to the south and the Wanshou (Ten Thousand Longevities) Hill to the north.

Before the Yuan dynasty the hill was known as Weng shan (Jar Hill) and a small lake beneath it, fed by a number of springs on the hill, was also known as Weng shan Lake. One of the Jin emperors constructed a 'travelling palace' (or temporary residence) here in 1153.

In the Yuan the lake was dredged by the engineer Guo Shoujing and the spring waters diverted to the Tonghui River. During the Ming the area was cultivated, springs filling paddy fields and lotus and water-chestnut pools; the aquatic scenery that resulted was compared in poems to the West Lake at Hangzhou. During the Ming the imperial residence here was rebuilt and the area named the Garden of Wonderful Hills (Haoshan yuan). Great men wrote poems about it: Wen Zhengming (1470–1559), a famous painter, pupil of Shen Zhou, wrote: 'A spring lake in the setting sun, orchids moving with the gentle flow; buildings within the shadow of heaven tower above and below'; a contemporary poet, Yuan Zhongdao, in his 'Ten Notes on the Western Hills', described the area thus: 'When summer is at its height, the hibiscus blooms for miles like a tapestry, its fragrance wafted afar by the breeze. Men and women gather by the flowing water, filling their wine cups to the brim. What can be more delightful?' (Liu Zuohui, a horticulturalist of the Peking Municipal Bureau of Parks and Gardens notes that by hibiscus, he means lotus and there are still plentiful lotus flowers in the lake.)

As the area had been compared to the West Lake at Hangzhou, it is not surprising that the Qianlong emperor, who loved to travel to the south, making six southern trips during his reign and sending his gardeners south to study landscape gardening, should choose to build himself a garden here. In 1749 work began on his **Qingyi yuan** (Garden of Clear Ripples), enlarging the lake and building up mountains. The lake was renamed Kunming hu (Vast Bright Lake), a name derived from a legendary lake of that name supposedly created near Xi'an under the reign of the legendary emperor Yao, 2357–2258 BC, and Jar Hill was renamed Wan Shou shan (Longevity Hill). The buildings constructed at his orders totalled 3000 jian (bays, sometimes 'rooms'). Construction was completed in 1764.

The name of the hills and many of the buildings on it—the Hall of Benevolence and Longevity (where the emperor held court), the Hall of Happiness in Longevity (residential)—were given in honour of the emperor's mother's 60th birthday (60 was considered a major achievement, the marker of venerable old age).

Unfortunately, the many pavilions and their treasures were ransacked and destroyed in 1860 by British and French troops at the same time as the destruction of the Yuanming yuan, leaving standing only the Bronze Pavilion (to the right of the central group of buildings on Longevity Hill) and the Sea of Wisdom Temple of brick and tile (behind the major group on Longevity Hill). A poet of the period, Wang Kaiyun, wrote of the desolate garden: 'Jade fountain laments and Kunming mourns; alone, the bronze ox guards the thistles and thorns; in the hills of blue iris the fox calls in the night; beneath the bridge of soft ripples fish weep at the sight'.

In 1886 the **Dowager Empress Cixi** rebuilt the imperial garden and called it **Yihe yuan** (Garden of the Preservation of Harmony). After its second destruction by foreign troops in 1900, she had it rebuilt in 1902, personally visiting the site with great frequency and demanding progress reports every five days. She spent the summers there, from the flowering of the magnolia to the withering of the chrysanthemums, rather than in the more distant Bishushan zhuang at Chengde, dragging the Guangxu emperor with her in case, left to himself, he made a further attempt at reform after the failure of the 1898 Reform Movement.

Cixi either travelled by road (with a retinue of over 1000), which meant instant road repairs and restoration of all possible 'resting places', or by boat, which meant a total eradication of all duckweed for the water surface had to be 'mirror-smooth' for her. When she arrived in 1905, 458 eunuchs were lined up to greet her. Every day 100 separate dishes were served at the two main meals of the day (with 20–50 dishes for light refreshment in between). The dining table in the Hall of Happiness in Longevity (on the northeast corner of the lake, where Cixi usually stayed) was designed to hold 100 dishes in set patterns. The wardrobe she kept in the Summer Palace (in 3000 chests) contained robes reflecting the change of the seasons, embroidered with wintersweet, peonies or wisteria for spring, lotuses for the summer and chrysanthemums for autumn, with every accessory embroidered to match. A 348 member opera troupe was permanently installed to perform for her in the theatre in the Dehe yuan (Palace of Virtue and Harmony), just east of her residence. On her birthdays, extravagance was unbridled: theatrical performances lasted for days, banners, garlands, lanterns, flowers, flags and ribbons decorated the buildings and trees, while chrysanthemum flowers were strewn underfoot (chrysanthemums are the flowers of longevity).

The unfortunate Guangxu emperor died here mysteriously on 14 November 1908 and Cixi died the next day. When the Qing dynasty was overthrown in 1911, the garden remained the property of the last emperor Pu Yi but the grounds were opened to the public for a small fee. In 1924 it was declared a public park, although the ensuing decades of warfare and invasion left it in a somewhat dilapidated state until its restoration after 1949. As before, people come in crowds to view seasonal flowers: the fine almond, cherry and plum blossom on the northern slopes of the hill in late winter, wisteria and peonies in spring, lotuses on the lake in August and chrysanthemums in autumn.

On major public holidays the park is decorated much as it might have been for Cixi's birthdays: with lanterns, flags and special displays of pot plants and one 1 May, when the spring blossoms had already fallen, tiny flowers made of pink lavatory tissue twisted into every tree.

- Most tourist groups appear to be very restricted by their guides, who put them in a boat to cross the lake to the Stone Boat whence they walk to the northwest gate along a path which merely provides shopping opportunities. This is a waste of time: much of the northern side of the lake can be seen easily in a half day and those with extra time could walk around to the Back Lake area (quieter and more restrained) or else walk the entire circumference of the lake in order to be able to look back at Longevity Hill.

The architecture and decoration of the Summer Palace is much as it was after its last major restoration in 1902, although the timberwork is constantly repainted. Despite its being a UNESCO world heritage site, the kitchen areas were demolished in 1999 to make way for a hotel, underground carpark and entertainment centre.

A grand *pailou* (ornamental arch) stands across the approach road (the two-character inscriptions on either side mean 'water and hills') with lesser versions inside the entrance (the East Palace Gate).

This eastern gate, opposite which stands a protecting screen wall, was formerly restricted and used only by members of the imperial family (lesser mortals used the North Gate). The low buildings on either side of the gate were for the duty officers. The pair of bronze lions sitting on stone pedestals on either side of the gate date from the Qianlong's Garden of Clear Ripples (mid 18C). They are virtually identical to pairs in the Forbidden City and are usually described as male (with embroidered and tasselled ball under one paw) and female (with a cub under one paw).

> I have heard guides explaining that the cub is suckled through the mother's claws but can find no authority for this statement and the representation simply looks to me like well-observed cat behaviour. I have yet to hear a guide mention the fact that the phrase 'the lion plays with the embroidered ball' is said by Professor Wolfram Eberhard of Berkeley to be a metaphor for sexual intercourse.

The stone stair slab leading up to the gate, carved with a dragon and cloud design, is also mid 18C and was brought here from the ruins of the Yuanming yuan.

At the far end of a courtyard filled with cypresses and a *pailou* is the single-storeyed, grey tile-roofed **Hall of Benevolence and Longevity** where the Dowager Empress used to conduct state affairs, at first from 'behind the screen', although after the abortive 1898 reform she held the Guangxu emperor a virtual prisoner and sat on the yellow-silk cushions of the throne herself.

The hall was built on the site of the Hall of Diligent Government, which was also used as an audience hall in the 18C. In the middle of the courtyard is a bronze *qilin* (sometimes translated as a Chinese unicorn, even though this and many, but not all, examples have two horns) with cloven hooves, scaly skin, the head of a dragon, the tail of a lion and deer's antlers. Bronze dragons and incense burners stand on the terrace in front of the hall. The furnishings are as they were when Cixi sat

A qilin

on the throne: rows of enamelled cranes with lotus leaf candle-holders, cloisonné enamel incense burners and heavily carved dark Victorian furniture.

Behind the hall is a rockery through which a path winds to the next building, the **Hall of Jade Billows**. Like all the other buildings in the 'eastern palaces', this had a simple unglazed grey tile roof, although the tie beams are painted in the Suzhou style, also found in the Forbidden City. The relative simplicity of these single-storeyed buildings imparts a sort of 'Petit Trianon' rusticity to the imperial summer retreat (also to be seen at Chengde).

> The Hall of Jade Billows was the residence of the Guangxu emperor and, from 1898 until his death, effectively his prison. The interior furnishings, including the carved red sandalwood table and chair, the dais, screens and ornamental

fans, are all of the period. Behind the main hall were (left) the bedroom with the original bed-hangings and quilts, (centre) the wardrobe and (right) a dressing room. In the western and eastern side buildings in the courtyard it is possible to see a brick wall built right through the buildings to prevent the emperor from escaping, for these side wings had front and rear entrances.

From the Hall of Jade Billows, go to the lakeside and turn north (right) when you will pass the Xijia lou, the two storey Pavilion of Beautiful Sunsets, which looks west and offers an uninterrupted view of sunsets over the lake.

The next courtyard to the right (north) is that of the **Lodge of the Propriety of Weeding** (another rustic note) used as a residence by empresses from the 18C. The southern gate to the courtyard is a fine example of an interior gate of the *chuihua* ('hanging flower') type with elaborately carved pendant bosses. On either side of the gate are stone-carved calligraphic slabs, moved from the ruined Huishan Garden (destroyed in 1860). Behind the lodge, connecting the rear part of the Hall of Happiness in Longevity (see below) with the Garden of Virtue and Harmony (its stage), is a covered gallery with lattice windows in the southern wall and quaintly shaped glazed windows (teapot, persimmon, diamond and peach) in the north wall. The Dowager Empress would sit on her gold lacquered throne in the Hall of Health and Happiness watching the performances on the three level stage. On either side of her throne, decorated with a scene of a hundred birds paying homage to a phoenix, is a pair of gilded cages with clockwork birds inside, 'presents from a foreign power' as a Chinese descriptive work notes. The stage closely resembles those in the Forbidden City and Chengde but is larger than either. The principle is the same: action took place at the central level and while angels and good spirits could descend from above, devils could rise from below.

Due north of the stage courtyard, a little way up the hill, on the way to the Garden of Harmonious Interest, is the **Pavilion of Blessed Scenery**, a large building with an interesting roof made from three *juanpeng* ('rolled-up mat') ridges.

Here, where there is an open view of the lake, the Dowager Empress used to come and watch the moon and the rain and sometimes entertain the families of foreign ambassadors. In 1948, when the People's Liberation Army had encircled Peking, negotiations with the KMT on the peaceful hand-over of the city were conducted here.

Beyond, to the northeast, is the 'garden within a garden', the **Xiequ yuan (Garden of Harmonious Interest)**, built in 1751 as a fairly faithful representation of the Jichang yuan at Wuxi (originally called the Huishan Garden). In his preface to the poems on the eight scenes of the Huishan Garden, the Qianlong emperor wrote:

> The garden is the oldest villa garden in south China. My imperial forebears renamed it the Garden of Ease. In 1751, when I was on a tour of inspection in the south, I was much attracted by its quiet beauty, so brought back a detailed drawing and had a likeness of it produced at the eastern foot of Longevity Hill.

In 1811 the garden was rebuilt and renamed the Garden of Harmonious Interest.

Centred on a lotus pool, surrounded by covered walls and low, open greyroofed buildings, there is a low white stone bridge at the eastern end of the pond copied from the bridge in the Wuxi garden. The white stone arch at the end of the bridge bears the characters for 'know your fish' in the calligraphy of the Qianlong emperor.

The lowness of the bridge enables passers-by to see the fish below clearly but the inscription refers to a famous story about the philosopher Zhuangzi (4C BC) and the logician Huizi, who often appears to serve as the straight man for Zhuangzi's playful wordplay. Walking over a bridge, Zhuangzi remarked on the happiness of the minnows darting below. Huizi asked, since Zhuangzi was not a fish, how could he know what made a fish happy? Zhuangzi replied: 'You are not me, so how can you know that I do not know what makes a fish happy?' Huizi insisted that his argument still stood: if he could not know because he was not Zhuangzi then because Zhuangzi was not a fish he could not know what a fish felt. Zhuangzi returned to the beginning of the conversation: 'You asked me how I knew what made fish happy so you already knew that I knew it. And I knew it just by standing here on this bridge.'

In the northwest corner of the garden is a 'gorge' of rough rockery stones through which water from the Back Lake outside the little garden tumbles into the lotus pond; it is called the **Jade Zither Gorge** as the sound of the water is said to resemble zither music. The Dowager Empress favoured this little garden and there is a strange surviving photograph of her, elaborately dressed and coifed, sitting in a boat amongst the lotus leaves in the middle of the pool; the photograph was used as the basis for a scene in Bertolucci's 1988 film, *The Last Emperor*.

Returning to the lakeside, the **Lodge of the Propriety of Weeding** (see above) is just at the northeast angle of the lake. Immediately to the west of the lodge is the **Hall of Happiness in Longevity**, a large complex of two courtyards and various side wings. This was the residence of the Dowager Empress Cixi from spring to autumn during most of her last years. The courtyards used to be full of magnolias and so especially lovely in March and April when they flowered but almost all were destroyed in 1900, except for one white and one purple magnolia, the latter standing just behind the hall.

On the lake south of the hall is the jetty (an open hall called the Hall of Affinity between Wood and Water) where the Dowager Empress would disembark if she had arrived by boat; on either side the lakeside is lined by a whitewashed walkway, its walls pierced with fanciful double-glazed windows in which candles would be set at night. The eastern courtyard of the Hall of Happiness in Longevity is planted with peonies; in the northern wall, a moon gate shaded by wisteria led to the apartments of the chief eunuch, Li Lianying (d. 1911).

The hall itself was lavishly furnished with dark, carved wooden tables and stands supporting giant double-peach incense burners that look like gilded cottage loaves. The coloured glass chandeliers were installed in 1903 and are said to be 'the first electric lamps in China'. The west 'inner' chamber was Cixi's bedroom and the saffron satin bed-curtains and multi-coloured quilts are original, as are most of the heavily carved pieces of furniture. The east inner chamber with its *kang*-like wooden benches and low *kang* tables (short-legged tables made specially for use on *kang* beds) is a good example of Manchu interior design and was used as a breakfast room by the Dowager Empress.

In the main courtyard there is a huge boulder standing on a marble pedestal carved with waves. It is called 'Blue Iris Hill' and is said to have been found in

Fangshan (not far from Peking, where the marble used in the construction of the Forbidden City came from) by a stone-loving official called Mi Wanzhong. He wanted to move it to his garden in Peking but the effort was too costly and the stone was abandoned halfway. Years later, the Qianlong emperor heard of it and ordered it to be dragged along frozen waterways to his garden.

An adjoining courtyard northwest of the Hall of Happiness in Longevity, reached through a moon gate, beyond a square pool, is the Fan Pavilion, built high up above a rockery on the mountainside. Constructed in 1888, it is a small, simple building in the shape of a fan, with fan-shaped windows and a terrace in front made of radiating marble slabs resembling the ribs of a fan. It is a charming little building, occupying a site where the 18C imperial family kept their pet fish and birds. Just below the hall, tumbling over the rockery, are two wonderfully architectural bushes of a white, single *Rosa banksiae* with a marvellous scent in May.

From the Hall of Happiness in Longevity, the long promenade runs all the way along the north shore of the lake. It was first built in 1750 and late reconstructed. Four pavilions break up the long covered walk: Retain the Good, Living with the Ripples, Autumn Water, and Clear and Far Pavilion. All the beams and lintels of the covered walk are painted in the Suzhou style, with elaborate cartouches enclosing flower paintings, genre scenes, landscapes and scenes from mythology and literature (keeping its paintings fresh is an unending Fourth-Bridge task). Some of the 14,000 paintings are quite odd: I once discovered a scene of tattooing.

Halfway along the promenade, in the centre of the southern slope of **Longevity Hill**, a group of buildings rises against the hill, quite distinct from the eastern palaces for all their roofs are tiled in yellow, some with a green border. The timber frame halls were built in 1886 and restored in 1902, while the solid, tiled buildings are those put up by the Qianlong emperor in honour of his mother's 60th birthday in 1750.

At the lakeside is an elaborate *pailou*, the **Arch of Gorgeous Clouds and Jade Eaves**, beside which is a row of 12 lake stones in fantastic shapes, each supposed to resemble an animal, either real or mythical. Behind this is the **Gate that Dispels the Clouds**, named after a phrase in a poem by Guo Pu (3C): 'The immortals emerge from between parting clouds; a terrace of silver and gold appears'. Beside it stand two 18C bronze lions cast in the Qianlong reign and considered the finest in Peking. Beyond the gate is a courtyard with a square pool, over which is the Golden Water Bridge (echoing the layout of the Forbidden City); beyond that is the second Palace Gate which opens onto the courtyard in front of the Hall that Dispels the Clouds (closed: peer through the windows). In the hall the Dowager Empress sat on the Nine Dragon Throne to receive congratulations on her birthday.

The innumerable presents offered to her are displayed in the rear rooms, still with their yellow paper slips, 'Respectfully presented by your lackey'. The rear chambers are divided by fine lattice work. The hall contains a portrait of Cixi by the Dutch artist, Hubert Vos, painted in 1905 when she was 71. Richly dressed, holding a silk-embroidered fan in her long claw-like nail-protectors of gold, the Dowager Empress looks exceedingly young for her years. It was Sarah Pike Conger, wife of the American Ambassador (who met the Dowager Empress a number of times) who found the artist.

Behind, on a massive 21m stone platform, reached by stepped side walkways and a final double staircase on the platform itself, is the **Foxiang ge (Tower of the Fragrance of Buddha)**. The three storey octagonal structure with four tiers of eaves dominates the group but there are important buildings on either side. To the east is the Zhuanlun cang (Revolving Archive), now no longer open. In its courtyard is an elaborately carved stele inscribed in the Qianlong emperor's hand, 'Kunming Lake, Longevity Hill' (with an account of the building of the garden on the reverse). Twin pavilions with green tiled roofs flank the stele. Behind is the main hall which, unusually for northern China, has three little glazed tile figures on the roof-ridge (representing, left to right: happiness, emolument and longevity). The pavilions contain revolving sutra libraries, architectural in form, which once held books: classical works and Buddhist sutras. The main hall was used for prayers.

Images of the lion dog can be seen at the Summer Palace

To the west is a courtyard surrounded by green tiled pavilions. A bronze pavilion is raised on a high, balustraded platform of carved white marble in the centre.

Similar to the bronze pavilions on Wutai shan and in Kunming, this is a miniature version of a timber frame building but made entirely of cast bronze. It was cast in 1750 (some say under Jesuit supervision), is 7.55m high and weighs 207 tons. All the details of carved timber doors and end-tiles, roof-ridge monsters and bracketing are perfect imitations of normal timber construction, although the lattice windows are missing. In the past Lamaist monks were summoned to the tiny pavilion to recite scriptures and pray for the emperor and empress on the first and 15th of every month when huge Buddhist banners would be hung on the wall behind.

The pavilion survived the destructions of the surrounding palaces, although nothing remained of its contents except the bronze offerings table (again modelled on wooden prototypes). In 1945 the Japanese were preparing to take this and a bronze jar, which stood in the courtyard, to Japan but they were abandoned in Tianjin and later restored to the Summer Palace.

Behind the Tower of Fragrance, on the central axis of the hill, is a strangely stepped, rockery path leading to an archway of glazed tiles that leads to the brick and stone **Sea of Wisdom Temple** (Zhihuihai). This is an 18C construction which survived, with its arch, the fires that destroyed most of the buildings of the Summer Palace, although many of the small glazed tile Buddha figures that cover the temple have had their heads smashed by foreign troops. The temple building is yet another example of a 'beamless' brick-vaulted hall, like those in Nanjing, Taiyuan and Wutai shan. Entirely covered with mainly green and yellow tiles, mostly in the form of small niches containing a seated Buddha, the roof is also elaborately decorated with tile dragons and dagobas. On the roof are blue and purple tiles amongst the green and yellow; the elaborate ridge is more like that of a southern Chinese temple.

Down beside the lake, almost at the end of the long gallery, is a small pavilion (**Building Where the Colours of Lake and Hill Merge**) which stands just before the group of buildings known as the **Pavilion for Listening to Orioles** (Tingli guan). In front of it, jutting out into the lake, is the small **Fish Amongst the Pondweed Pavilion** (Yucao xuan) from where the Dean of Peking University, Wang Guowei, drowned himself somewhat prematurely in 1928 'in despair at the state of the country, then on the verge of going "red" ...' (as was reported in 1935). The **Pavilion for Listening to Orioles** is reached by a flight of steps beyond a garden of bamboo and begonia.

> First built in the 18C and rebuilt in 1892, the pavilion group includes a small stage, which fell into second place when the far larger stage in the Garden of Virtue and Harmony (Eastern Palace) was built. The pavilion is now used as a restaurant and sales area mainly for foreign tourists.

On the hillside above the Pavilion for Listening to Orioles is the **Strolling amidst Paintings Complex (Huazhong you)**, centred on a two storey, open octagonal pavilion with rockeries and a serpentine covered walk behind. Smaller octagonal pavilions stand at either end of the walkways and from them further covered walks lead down to the base of the main pavilion. The whole complex is a very interesting one, making use of the varied topography of the hillside to create an effect of studied irregularity. Qianlong and his courtiers used to drink wine and compose poems here, looking over the lake, although according to an official guide, Cixi, 'turned these pavilions into a place of debauchery and merry-making'. A flight of steps leads to a white stone archway with a stele; beyond is a Buddhist 'Hall of Fasting' with galleries leading up and down the hill. The courtyard behind, surrounded by a whitewashed wall, has a 'hanging flower' gate at the eastern end which leads to the western summit of Longevity Hill and the Pavilion of the True Concept of Lake and Hill.

At the far western end of the long gallery is the 'marble boat', officially known as the **Boat of Purity and Ease**. The marble base was built in 1755 and had a Chinese style timber superstructure. This was destroyed in 1860 and rebuilt in 1893 when the Dowager Empress, with her usual exquisite taste, ordered a west-ern style superstructure and waterwheels, so that Qianlong's marble boat became a Mississippi paddle-steamer with stained glass windows. Mirrors are positioned on each floor to reflect scenes of the lake and there are Minton floor tiles.

Immediately north of the marble boat is a small creek, crossed by a stone bridge with an open pavilion above it, known as the Bridge of Floating Hearts. In the creek below, a miniature metal paddleboat was found, the Yonghe (Eternal Peace), a gift from the Japanese to the Dowager Empress, who used to cruise on the lake in it. Behind can be seen the imperial boathouses, which are restfully simple.

The Back Lakes and the northern slopes of Longevity Hill were badly damaged and have been less restored than the rest of the Summer Palace. They are also less popular with visitors and rather attractive in a very different, less decorated manner. Of the Hall of Pines, Xumi Temple, Pavilion of Fragrant Rocks and Ancestral Seals, 'Four Great Regions', Temple of the Emergence of Virtue, Hall of Painted Fragrance and Temple Where Clouds Gather, only the main hall of the latter, the glazed tile pagoda and the Pavilion of Fragrant Rocks and Ancestral Seals (built in 1890) remain. The slopes are planted with early-flowering prunus.

The **Temple Where Clouds Gather** is not far below the Sea of Wisdom Temple. Only one of the three great bronze Buddhas in sculpted niches now remains (mid 18C) but the temple courtyard is quiet and filled with pines and cypresses. Over to the east is a gate, reminiscent of a city gate, with a pavilion-like building above a castellated grey brick wall; this is the Gate of Exuding Pleasure. Further east, rising above the trees, many of which are early flowering fruit trees, is the glazed tile pagoda (Pagoda of Many Treasures), a seven storey octagonal pagoda more than 16m high.

Along the north side of the bottom of the hill runs the **Back Lake**, also known as the **Suzhou Creek**. Crossed by fine bridges, lined with angular brick walls and stone embankments, this was once an extraordinary model marketplace: shops were built along both sides of the creek in imitation of a canal-side market in Suzhou (Jiangsu province). When the Qianlong emperor and his retinue arrived, eunuchs would dress up as shopkeepers and merchants and play at buying and selling to entertain the imperial passers-by. A fine three-arched stone bridge crosses the canal or lake at the point where the toy shops were in the 18C. North of the bridge is a mock mountain of rock stones from Lake Tai (Wuxi) and north of that is the Northern Gate of the Summer Palace, built as a two-storeyed structure by Qianlong, whose mother used to watch the cavalry practice of the guard outside the palace from this gate.

The lake itself has dykes and a long bridge leading to the small round island near the east bank. The dykes—the major one being the West Dyke, which almost cuts the lake area in two—were built in imitation of the dykes on the West Lake at Hangzhou at the order of the Qianlong emperor. They serve to enhance the sense of space by breaking up the expanse of water. This is also done decoratively: the dyke is planted with willows and mountain peach and pierced by high, arching stone bridges (the elegant Jade Belt Bridge) and small, pavilion-topped bridges (the White Silk Bridge and Mirror Bridge). The Jade Belt Bridge on the West Dyke and the similar Bridge of Embroidered Ripples in the far southeast corner of the lake, where the emperors arrived by boat, are amongst the best examples of Qing stone carving, very elegant, with fine, high arches (which, when reflected in the still water, form a 'full moon' circle) and carved balustrades.

The other major bridge is the 17 arch bridge from the eastern shore to South Lake Island. Near the east end of the bridge, close to the main east entrance to the Summer Palace, a fine, **life-sized bronze ox** looks out over the water.

A long inscription on its side refers to the Great Yu's taming of the floods, for the ox was cast in 1755, after the Qianlong emperor had ordered the expansion of the lake. The inscription includes the lines: 'The Great Yu harnessed the rivers, the iron ox spread his fame ... the broad-backed ox, broad as the universe, keeps the river-dragons at bay and crocodiles and turtles ... the divine ox shall keep the floods of the Kunming lake under rein.'

Somewhere on the east side of the lake, all guidebooks (except Nagel) state that the Tomb of Yelu Chucai (1190–1244) can be seen, although I have yet to find it. He was a descendant of the Khitan royal family and became Ghengis Khan's adviser on Chinese style administration, industry and taxation, teaching the Mongols how to utilise the Chinese economy (a foreign thing to semi-nomadic horsemen).

Just beyond the ox is an unusually large, open, octagonal double-roofed pavilion, called either the **Spacious Pavilion** or the **Eight-sided Pavilion**. When Cixi went to the island for banquets, the sedan chairs would wait here, with imperial officials. The pavilion holds some stelae with poems by the Qianlong emperor and responses by scholars. The bridge, paved with stone slabs, has 500 stone lions, 'no two alike', on the balusters, each sitting on a little brocade mat.

The island, which is surrounded by white marble balustrades, is called the **Dragon King's Island** and the temple, reached through a fine small *pailou*, contains an image of the Dragon King (who, like the Great Yu, is always associated with the control of water; an alternative name for the temple is the Temple of Beneficial and Blessed Rain). On the northern side of the island, built on a high, heaped stone rockery, is the Hall of Forbearance and Humbleness. During Qianlong's reign there was a three storey building modelled on the Yellow Crane Tower in Wuchang (Wuhan), where it is said that the imperial family watched naval exercises on the lake.

The lake is extremely shallow (the navy must have used flat-bottomed boats) with a swimming area and many row-boats for hire, as well as larger boats used to tow tourist groups about. In winter it is a popular area for skating (and the hill with its pavilions looks magical when covered in snow), in summer, for swimming. The anniversary of the day in 1969 when the elderly Mao Zedong swam in the Yangtse with assembled bodyguards (26 August) often sees the entire lake filled with schoolchildren, swimming in convoys and attempting to wave clenched fists (when they usually sink).

Balizhuang

At Balizhuang, due east of the Forbidden City, is the pagoda of the **Cishou si** (Temple of Benevolence and Longevity), all that now remains of the temple.

The temple was founded in 1576 in honour of the mother of the Wanli emperor, on land formerly belonging to one of the Zhengde emperor's eunuchs. The temple fell down in the late Qing, leaving only the pagoda; and in the 1970s a record factory was built around it. A 13 storey, octagonal construction with a 'close eaves' top, it is 50m high. The carved brickwork of the base and body of the pagoda is particularly fine and there are marvellous celestial guardian figures beside the doors on the central part of the body.

On the North Circular Road (here called Xi san huan bei lu), which runs parallel to the Indigo Factory Road, nearly due east of the pagoda, is one of the few interesting modern buildings in Peking: the dormitory blocks of the **Peking Art School**. Clustered around a small pagoda (about which I can find no information), they are built of dark grey brick with window and roof details recalling traditional domestic architecture in an economical but elegant manner.

West of the city

One of the routes to the Summer Palace, Lanqingchang nan lu (South Indigo Factory Road), runs alongside the **Jingmi Canal**, which takes water from the Kunming Lake to the old moat running around the southern city.

Yuetan Park

Due west of the Altar to the Sun Park (Ritan gongyuan) is the parallel **Altar to the Moon Park** (Yuetan gongyuan) on the west side of Nanlishi lu, which runs north–south between Fuchengmen wai da jie and Fuxingmen nei da jie.

The Altar was built in 1530, oriented towards the east (the triple gateway is on the eastern side), with a square white marble altar in a circular enclosure. To the north is a Bell Tower, to the northeast is the Jufu dian, or Robing Hall. The major sacrifices took place in the autumn between 18.00 and 20.00. The moon tablet was apparently yellow and offerings of white jade and yellow silk were laid before it and then white sheep, oxen and a white pig were sacrificed.

The park was used in 1979 as a home for da zi bao or 'big character posters' of protest. These were plastered along the walls on Chang'an jie near the Xi dan crossroads (west of the Forbidden City) during what proved to be the first of many movements calling for democracy following the end of the Cultural Revolution and the downfall of the Gang of Four in 1976. This was the 'Democracy Movement' which flared up in 1978–79, when students and young artists and poets called for a 'fifth modernisation', that of political reform and greater democracy, following Deng Xiaoping's reform and 'liberalisation' of the economy through his 'four modernisations' of agriculture, industry, science and technology and national defence.

One of the first to put up a political poster in 1978, Wei Jingshen, was arrested on a charge of treason and served decades in prison before being released in 1999 and exiled. His arrest, with that of other young protesters, coincided with Deng Xiaoping's decision that all posters be moved from the centre of town to the rather hidden Altar of the Moon Park. Although that first Democracy Movement was suppressed, student movements continued to erupt throughout the 1980s, leading to the downfall of Hu Yaobang (1988) and the massive protests of Tiananmen in May 1989, which resulted in the downfall of Zhao Ziyang, Hu Qili and the arrest of some 40 professors, academics and workers. The number of demonstrators killed when army tanks rolled into the Square on 4 June 1989 and continued shooting as they moved along Chang'an Avenue is still unknown.

Temple of the White Clouds ~ the Baiyunguan

Almost due south of the Altar to the Moon Park is the Boyunguan or Baiyunguan (the second, more modern pronunciation is better known to the younger generation, which includes all taxi-drivers), the Temple of the White Clouds, the major Taoist temple in Peking. It stands on Binhe lu, north of Baiyunguan jie, just west of Xibian men and just south of the main east–west road, Chang an jie (here called Fuxingmen wai da jie).

It was the centre of one of the major Taoist sects, the Quan zhen pai (Total Truth sect), founded in 1167 in Shandong by Wang Chongyang. He is said to have died here in 1227 at the age of 80 and under one of his various sobriquets, Chu Ji (Control of Means), is the patron saint of the temple. His sect stressed purity of action and thought rather than recourse to alchemy and potions. It also required that its monks remain celibate, which was by no means the case in other sects.

The temple is said to have been founded in 739, well before the birth of its founder, and to have changed its name three times before 1394, when it acquired its present name.

The temple is of considerable size and the surviving buildings are late Qing or later (and, sadly, not very distinguished). The temple is the headquarters of the **Taoist Association** and is inhabited by Taoist monks who still wear their hair in the style that was normal for Chinese men before the Qing (and the imposition of the queue or plait), in a bun fixed on top of the head by a silver or jade hairpin.

Just after the spring festival, a huge street fair has recently been revived, filling the side streets on the approach to the temple. This is the only surviving example of the major temple festivals and is held on the 19th of the first lunar month, when the eight Taoist Immortals were supposed to descend from heaven at midnight. Horseraces of various sorts used to be held on a nearby piece of land when, as one guidebook of 1935 noted: 'a veritable orgy of gambling succeeded a few days of religious worship'. Today there are stalls of all sorts as well as entertainments and extra activities within the temple to raise funds.

Inside the first courtyard the similarity of all temple plans becomes apparent: there are bell and drum towers just as in a Buddhist temple and temple guardian figures in the hall at the far end of the courtyard. In the second courtyard is the **Yuhuang dian** (Hall of the Jade Emperor). The incense burner in front of it is said to be late 16C. Inside the hall is an image of the Jade Emperor and paintings of Taoist sages (paralleling the Buddhist saints or *lohans*). Peaches and cranes, symbols of longevity (also common to Chinese folklore), a particular goal of Taoists, abound. Other Taoist decorations, which, together with the sculptures of Taoist deities, are all that mark this as a Taoist rather than a Buddhist temple, include the lingzhi, or magic fungus, and the eight trigrams used in divination.

In the third courtyard are a bronze bell and bronze horse, which were moved from the Dongyue miao in east Peking. The hall is the Laolu tang, containing a Ming drum painted with a dragon. The next courtyard houses the hall dedicated to the founder of the sect, who is buried beneath it, and the figures are said to be mid 18C. The great offering bowl was a gift from the Qianlong emperor and comes from Xinjiang. Behind is a courtyard with the two storey **Siyu dian** (Four Great Men Hall), dedicated to the four major protectors of Taoism, who hold a pagoda, sword, two swords and a spiked club and are said to have assisted the Tang and Song emperors. In the hall above are the 'Three Pure Ones', the Jade Emperor, Dao Jun, controller of *yin* and *yang*, and Lao zi, one of the major Taoist philosophers. This hall also contains a mid 15C Ming woodblock edition of the *Dao zang* (the complete Taoist scriptures).

In a garden behind is the ordination platform, again similar to that found in some Buddhist temples, such as the Jie tai si (Ordination Platform Temple) outside Peking. This example has niches around it in which ascetics would fast and meditate.

Tianning and Baoguo Temples

The pagoda of the **Tianning si** (Temple of Heaven's Will) is south of the Boyunguan, just outside Dong an men, to the west of Binhe lu. The temple, which has disappeared, was an old foundation, dating back to the Northern Wei (5C). The pagoda was built during the Liao (907–1125) and is similar in style to that of the Cishou Temple, an octagonal, 13 storey, 'close eaves' brick construction,

57.8m high. It has very fine carvings of guardian figures and Bodhisattvas on the central part of the body.

The **Baoguo si** (Protect the Nation Temple) is east of the Tianning si Pagoda, just south of Xuanwu yiyuan (a park), reached by taking the small turning north of Guangan men nei da jie beside the Xiaoxing luguan (Small Star Hotel).

> The temple was founded under the Liao and was in poor condition by the Ming. But because the younger brother of the Chenghua emperor's mother became a monk there, the temple was rebuilt in 1466. The western part of the temple contains a hall dedicated to Gu Yanwu (1613–82), a leading scholar of the early Qing, who frequently stayed in the temple and who spent his life trying to demonstrate the emptiness of Song Neo-Confucianism and to revitalise Confucianism.

North of the Baoguo si, in a narrow lane to the west off Tonglinge lu, which runs south from Chang'an jie immediately opposite the Minzu gong (see below), is the **House of Li Dazhao** (1888–1927).

> The 'Father' of Chinese Communism, Li was Director of the Peking University Library when the young Mao Zedong worked there as a library assistant (1918) and Professor of History in the same university. With Chen Duxiu (Dean of the Faculty of Letters) he founded and contributed to various journals (New Tide, Weekly Critic and New Youth) that spread Marxist ideas amongst students and intellectuals. He was captured in 1927 in the garden of the Soviet Embassy in the Legation Quarter by the secret police of the warlord, Zhang Zuolin, and executed. The house is marked by a plaque.

The **Minzu gong** (Palace of the Minorities) is a giant white and green tiled building; it used to house an exhibit on the national minorities of China and a shop where minority costumes and handicrafts could be purchased but recently seems to be given over to exhibitions of refrigerators and electric fans; this may change.

In the next lane to the north of that in which Li Dazhao's house stands is the old **Women's Teacher Training College** whose students were particularly active in the Fourth of May Movement in 1919, a very unusual role for young women at the time.

Cow Street Mosque ~ Niu jie

South of Li Dazhao's house is Peking's major mosque, the Cow Street Mosque. To reach it continue south down Tonglinge lu until it reaches a T-junction with Xuanwumen xi da jie; turn right (west) and take the first major turning left (south), which is Changchun jie. This runs into Niu jie at a T-junction. Turn right (still south) and cross the major road, Guang'anmen nei da jie, and soon you will see the grey carved brick spirit wall of the mosque on the right and the minaret and green trees of the mosque enclosure on the left.

> The name of the street, Niu jie, means 'Cow Street', in deference to the Muslim avoidance of pork, and the whole area around the mosque is full of Muslim shops of all sorts, Muslim primary schools and men wearing little white crocheted skull caps, not to be confused with the white cotton caps worn by almost all who handle food.

The mosque is the largest and oldest in Peking; founded in 996, it was restored in

1442 and 1696. It is constructed in the Chinese timber style but the arrangement of the buildings and some of the decoration reflect Islamic influence. The main prayer hall—like the mosque in Dong si in northeast Peking—is covered by three linked double-pitched roofs and a hexagonal pavilion style roof. It is oriented west–east and the interior is broad but with a low ceiling and filled with columns and carpets. There are five 'naves' with differently treated ceilings, some coffered, some with open beams. The columns and the coffered ceilings are decorated in the 'Arabic' style with Chinese flowers mixed in with Arabic inscriptions. The mihrab is beautifully carved and thought to be Ming. The tower beside the entrance is a Chinese style 'Moon Watching Tower', hexagonal in plan, used for making the astronomical calculations for which the Arabs were famous in China until supplanted by the Jesuits in the 17C.

The minaret is in the centre of the courtyard in front of the prayer hall; it is a square, double-eaved pavilion and before it is the Hall of Veneration of the Scriptures, where two Arabs came to preach during the early Mongol period and where the holy books are stored. On either side of the minaret stand stelae pavilions housing stelae with funerary inscriptions in Arabic dated to 1280 and 1283, commemorating the two Arabs who were buried here, and an inscription in Chinese and Arabic of 1496 on the history of the mosque. The mosque is open to visitors but it is also an active centre of worship.

Fayuan si

Not far east is the Fayuan si (Temple of the Source of the Law), one of Peking's pleasantest and quietest temples. It is famous for the lilacs that grow in the courtyards.

In my inherited copy of Arlington and Lewisohn's *In Search of Old Peking* (published in 1935 by Henri Vetch of the French Bookstore in Peking) is an old newspaper cutting from the English language *Peiping Chronicle* of Tuesday, 27 April 1937 which reads: 'The Fa Yuan Su in Hsi Chuan Hutung, outside the Hsuan Wu Men, is noted for its lilacs, which are in full bloom at this time of the year. The abbot of the temple has issued invitations for a reception to be held at 6 o'clock this afternoon to view the lilacs.' The bushes of Syringa oblata, the north China purple lilac, still flower and fill the courtyards with scent in mid to late April.

To reach the temple from the mosque, continue south down Niu Jie and take the first turning on the left (east). Go straight across the main road, where on your left you will see the strange pale green five-domed building of the **Islamic Association of China**; the lane will lead you straight to the Fayuan si on your left, with its spirit wall on your right.

Historically, the oldest temple in Peking, it now houses a museum of Buddhist relics of the area, which is being expanded to cover the whole of China, and the Buddhist 'college' where young novices are taught the rudiments of the faith; they can sometimes be heard chanting in their classrooms, which line the rear courtyards.

In 645, when the Tang Taizong emperor returned from his unsuccessful campaign in Korea, he founded the temple to placate the souls of his soldiers who had died far away. Completed in 696, it was then called Minzhong si (Temple of Grief for the Loyal). Its name was changed many times, the first during the mid 8C An Lushan rebellion, when it was renamed 'Temple of

Heaven's Will'. As it was dedicated to the memory of long dead soldiers, it was not really maintained after the end of the Tang. The Huizong emperor of the Song was imprisoned here when he was captured by the Jin in the 12C and in 1173 it was used as an examination hall, not for the Chinese bureaucratic exams but for those who were to take the examinations in the Tungusic language of the Jin themselves. Unlike their Mongol conquerors and successors, the Jin maintained a dual administration with dual languages and scripts. In 1734 the temple was given its present name and established as a Buddhist college.

The present buildings are not very old, few probably even dating back to the 18C, but the layout reflects the original plan. In the first courtyard are drum and bell towers. In front of the drum tower is a tree which was of a considerable size when the Qianlong emperor visited the temple in 1780 and which was frequently visited by one of the eight eccentric painters of Yangzhou (a group that included Gao Qipei of the early 18C), Luo Pin. The tree is called Wenguan guo (Fruit of Literature and Officials).

At the end of the courtyard is the **Hall of the Heavenly Kings**, a solidly built hall with two arched windows framed in white carved stone and an arched door in the centre of the solid facade. In front of the hall is an iron incense burner (probably 1730) with the eight trigrams on its body, which are more usually associated with Taoist fortune-telling. The pair of bronze lions are similar to those found in the Yihe yuan (Summer Palace) and are mid 18C. The bronzes in the hall are all Ming.

The gilded fat Maitreya, the Buddha of the Future, faces you as you enter the hall. Behind him are fine figures of the four Heavenly Kings and behind them, facing the main hall, is Wei tuo, defender of the faith; the latter all bear traces of gilding and are very beautifully cast. Behind is a courtyard with a number of elaborate Ming and Qing stelae on stone turtles giving accounts of the restorations and history of the temple.

The **Daxiongbao dian** (main hall) stands on a high stone platform and is a five-bay construction, now with glass where its lattice windows would have been. In front of it is a tall iron incense burner with a pavilion-shaped cover and a date of 1575. Inside the hall is a plaque suspended from the beams with an inscription in the hand of the Qianlong emperor reading 'The true source of the vast ocean of Buddha truth' (in four characters); to the left is a bell and to the right a drum. The bell was cast in the Forbidden City in 1531. The three figures, the 'Three Sages' of the Huayan or Garland sect, are the historic Buddha in the centre with the Bodhisattvas Manjusri on his right and Samantabhadra on his left. The gilded stucco figures (with a wooden skeleton) are Ming in date and rare in Peking temples, while the wooden lohan figures along the side walls are slightly later (Qing). In the centre of the hall two stone pillar bases carved with flowers are preserved. These are Tang (726) in date, relics of the original foundation, and appear not to have been carved from local stone; the imperial interest in the temple probably meant that excellent materials were brought from distant parts.

Behind this main hall is a **pavilion**, said to resemble in construction the Pavilion of Ten Thousand Springs in the rear garden of the Forbidden City, standing on what is popularly known as the Minzhong Platform. In it are displayed some of the treasures of the temple: stone carved records and scriptures from 757 to 1909 and some Tang sculptures only recently discovered during restoration work. Into the outside walls are set stone carvings from the Tang to Qing. In the courtyard is a stone incense burner (1793), with a double pavilion roof, a rare form amongst stone incense burners. Behind is a stone 'alms bowl' on a stone base, carved with dragons and other fabulous beasts amongst waves. According to a local history of the Qing, this was once in a nunnery near Xihua men but was removed by the Qianlong emperor to the Beihai 'Round Fort' and only recently moved here. Two stelae bear images of Guanyin (1589) and the Chan Damo, or Bodihidharma (1591), which were in the nearby Shangan Temple that collapsed.

Behind is the **Great Pilu Hall** with a 4.6m high bronze Vairocana Buddha (the Buddha of All-pervasiveness or Light) sitting on a double round lotus base with tiny Buddhas in each petal and the Buddhas of the Four Directions below. The group was cast in the Ming.

Behind this is the **Dabei tang** (Hall of Great Compassion), now housing an exhibition of gifts from Buddhists overseas, while behind that is the Cangjing ge (Sutra Store Hall or Library) in front of which stands a gingko tree over 100 years old and two flowering crab-apples planted in the 18C, about which many poems have been written. The three Buddha figures in the upper hall are Ming in date, made of lacquer on a wooden frame. In the hall, examples of Ming and Qing woodcut editions of the Buddhist canon (Tripitaka) are displayed. On the lower floor is an exhibition relating to the famous Buddhist monk and doctor of the Tang, Jian Zhen (688–753), who travelled to Japan during the Tang dynasty (see Yangzhou, p 350) and settled in Nara to teach. Of the four central lotus petal carved pillar bases in this hall, two are fairly recent (and made of 'green stone') but the other two are differently carved and are thought to date from the 1031 rebuilding.

Small halls to either side of the main axis are now being developed as a **museum** of Buddhist art and history. A major section is devoted to the stone carved sutras of Fang shan, not far southwest of Peking, the source of most of the marble in the Forbidden City. The museum is still being built up so its displays may well change.

Amongst the other items on display is a cloisonné reliquary of the Qianlong period (mid 18C), which houses a piece of Xuan zang's skull. When the famous Buddhist pilgrim died in Xi'an, he was eventually buried in the Xingjiao si but his tomb was apparently violated in the 9C during the rebellions that marked the downfall of the Tang and a piece of skull was taken to Nanjing. It was buried beneath the Baoen Temple, which was in turn destroyed during the Taiping uprising in the mid 19C. Japanese excavators rediscovered the relic in 1943 and broke it up; one piece eventually reached the Fayuan si in 1950 from a temple near the Beihai Park.

There are Buddhist paintings of the Ming and Qing, a variety of northern and southern editions of the Tripitaka, musical instruments, ritual implements (including those used in Lamaist worship) and a variety of figures.

The Southern Cathedral and Matteo Ricci's Tomb

Almost due north of the Fayuan si is the **Nan Tang**, the Southern Cathedral. It stands on Xuanwumen dong da jie, not far east of the junction with Xuanwumen wai da jie. To reach it from the Fayuan si, return north up Niu jie to Guanganmen nei da jie and turn right (east) along that. The second major turning on the left (north) is Xuanwumen wai da jie. Turn left (north) and continue to the next major intersection with Xuanwumen xi da jie (left) and Xuanwumen dong da jie (right). Turn right and the Nan Tang with its grey baroque facade is visible, set back from the north side of the road.

The cathedral was built on the site of the house in which Matteo Ricci lived from 1601 to 1610. The German Jesuit Adam Schall von Bell took over from Ricci as head of the mission and inherited his residence. In 1650, having impressed the new Qing Kangxi emperor with his astronomical skills, Schall obtained permission and even a financial contribution to build a church on the site. Finished in 1703, the church burnt down in 1775 and, although the Qianlong emperor offered money for repairs, the coincidental suppression of the Jesuits made rebuilding complicated.

During the Jiaqing emperor's suppression of foreign missionaries, Portuguese Lazarists were sheltered here, after being driven out of the Eastern Church, but their last missionary Pires (tolerated for his astronomical skills) died here in 1853. In 1861, when all church property was returned to foreigners, French Lazarists under Monsignor Mouly had the church rebuilt within a year and dedicated to the newly proclaimed dogma of the Immaculate Conception. The Nan Tang was destroyed in 1900 during the Boxer uprising when hundreds of Chinese Christians were killed or burnt alive.

The present building dates from 1904. It is the major Catholic church in Peking, with a baroque-ish facade of plain grey brick. The interior has pillars, with Corinthian capitals, painted to look like marble. Outside is a Chinese garden style rockery grotto filled with plastic flowers and lanterns and a statue of the Virgin.

Permission to visit the **Tomb of Matteo Ricci**—in the north of the city, unfortunately sited within the Peking Communist Party School, which does not welcome casual foreign visitors—must be obtained here in writing. The tomb is inside the school at Erligou dong kou on Chegongzhuang da jie, just east of the intersection with Zhanlanguan lu.

Until recently, it was merely a concrete-covered mound, all that remained of the old ecclesiastical burial ground known as Cha la. The cemetery has now be restored and the graves are marked by elaborate white marble stelae topped with twisted dragons. The Wanli emperor of the Ming gave the Jesuits this piece of ground when Ricci died in 1610, although it was covered by a Buddhist temple built by a palace eunuch, who had recently been condemned to death and his property confiscated. It was used until 1704 to house the bodies of other Jesuits, including Schall, the painter Castiglione and Verbiest, at whose funeral the Kangxi emperor's father-in-law and five high officials represented the emperor. It was later transferred to the care of the Russian Mission but in 1861 was handed over to the French Lazarists. It was looted by the Boxers in 1900, who destroyed the great statue of St Francis Xavier and the imperial marble stelae on turtles' backs.

Just west of the Nan Tang, on the west side of the crossroads, beside the Xuan wu Gate, which used to stand at the intersection of the two main roads, the **imperial elephants' stables** were once to be found.

Elephants were sent as tribute gifts from neighbouring small states, such as Burma and Vietnam, as early as the Tang dynasty. The imperial elephants of the Tang were used in one of Bai Juyi's poems in which he compared the wise and noble rule of the previous emperor, when the elephants had enjoyed good health, with the terrible conditions currently prevailing, which were reflected in the elephants' poor condition. The Ming emperors built the elephant stables in 1495 to house yet more gifts from Burma and Vietnam.

There were said to be six rows of eight large stables, surrounded by a trench; a small temple to the 'tutelary deity of elephants' was also provided The elephants took part in ceremonial processions and used to pull the emperor's carriage when he went annually to the Temple of Heaven. Their keepers used to charge the public admission to see the beasts and the annual washing of the elephants in the nearby moat (on the sixth day of the sixth lunar month) was a popular sight. The keepers made a little extra money by selling the dung, which was supposed to make hair glossy and to soothe cuts on the shaven heads of men who had the front of the head shaved, with the long queue behind.

The last elephants were presented in 1873. One escaped in 1884, causing absolute chaos in the neighbourhood until it was recaptured in an alley, and it was decided to stop using them in imperial processions. The rest are thought to have died slowly of starvation as so little money was allocated for their upkeep; a fate which the Tang poet would have seen as clearly illustrating the decline of the Qing imperial house. The buildings that housed China's first Parliament (1912–24) were put up on or near the site of the old elephant houses.

The **Xuanwu Gate** (Gate of the Proclamation of Military Strength), also known as the Shunzhi men (Gate of Direct Rule)—the westernmost gate in the south wall of the northern, Manchu city—was always considered unlucky, for it stands in the 'cutting off of life' quarter according to geomantic belief.

For the same reason, the main door to houses in Peking was always sited in the southeast corner of the courtyard and unimportant buildings, like storehouses and kitchens, were sited in this dangerous quarter.

The unluckiness of the gate was reinforced by the fact that condemned criminals were led through it to the old execution ground due south of the gate at the next major crossroads, known as Caishikou (Vegetable Market Corner). As the execution ground was near the Vegetable Market, a common curse in late traditional Peking was to suggest that someone should go to the vegetable market, in other words, 'go hang'.

South of the city

This route takes in Liulichang, the Temple of Heaven (Tian tan), the remains of the Altar of Agriculture, Taoranting Park and China's first 'theme park', the Daguanyuan.

Liulichang, or **Glazed Tile Factory Street**, is a narrow road which runs west–east across Nanxinhua jie, which runs north–south from Xuanwumen dong da jie and Qianmen xi da jie. For hundreds of years it was the centre of the antiquarian book trade and antique shops in general. In the last few years it has been rebuilt as a 'Qing dynasty shopping street' with brightly painted facades concealing the antique shops behind. A possible walk through some of the smaller lanes of Peking, lined with courtyard houses, takes you from the Qianmen shopping area to Liulichang.

Starting from Tiananmen Square, head south for the great double **Qian men** (Front Gate) at the southern end of the square. The road that leads due south is **Qianmen da jie**, one of the busiest shopping centres in Peking. To the right (west), running parallel to the main street, is a narrower lane, also lined with shops but here and in the lanes running west many of the shopfronts are of brightly coloured tiles or beautifully carved wood. The third lane on the right is called **Dashanlan** and is lined with shops.

Peking shopfronts, Qianmen district

The lane takes its name from the wooden gates (*lan*) which used to stand at the end of the street so that it could be closed at night against thieves and looters. This whole area was a rather louche place in the late Qing, the centre of the theatre world (and no respectable ladies were allowed into theatres) as well as being full of restaurants, teahouses and shops.

Take this turning and note the wrought iron work and carved headboards of the old shopfronts. On the left there is a famous old pharmacy, the **Tongren tang**, founded in 1669. The coloured and carved stucco shopfronts in a sort of western style date from after 1900, for parts of the area were burnt after the Boxer uprising. As the lane leads into a residential area, the high grey walls of courtyard houses, pierced by gates with little tiled roofs, succeed the shops.

Although little can be seen of the houses behind the walls, some have handsome stone bases for the doorposts, circular and carved like drums or square and carved with flowers. Some gates have cut brick work on the pilasters and some of the roof ridges bear decoration.

This area is one of the best in Peking for hearing flocks of pigeons with pigeon whistles ('aeolian flutes') attached to their tails, which hum as the wind rushes through them. The wheeling flocks of pet pigeons produce an almost electrical humming as they fly. You can often see 'pigeon lofts' built out of old packing cases suspended beneath the eaves of the houses.

If you continue to follow Dashanlan, it will bring you to **Nanxinhua jie**, a little to the south of the point where **Liulichang** crosses the street, so turn right (north) until you reach the crossroads, marked by the gaily painted carved *pailou*-like structures in front of the restored shops. It is possible to wiggle through the *hutongs* (the local names for small lanes; its literal meaning 'together with barbarians' is mysterious) to reach Liulichang precisely, although directions are difficult as the *hutongs*, unlike the main streets, do not have pinyin street names. Not far beyond the point where the shops give way to houses, turn right and then left and this lane should bring you to **Yanshou je** (Street of Extended Longevity), a name reminiscent of the Peking novels by Daniele Vare written in the 1920s, which runs at an angle of 90 degrees to Liulichang. Turn left (south) into Yanshou jie and Liulichang is the first main turning on the right (west).

During the Ming, Liulichang was the site of a workshop producing coloured glazed tiles for the Forbidden City. Before that the area was a suburban village called Haiwangcun (village of the King of the Sea), for in the late 10C, when the area was crisscrossed by creeks, a local entrepreneur set up a business involving boats ferrying grain around on the creeks. His extortions were such that he became known as the 'King of the Sea'. In 1770 a Liao tomb (10C) was found in the area, testifying to the village name.

When the Ming Yongle emperor decided to make Peking the capital, the work begun on the imperial city required a second glazed tile factory—there was only one, in the eastern suburbs, managed by a native of Shanxi, the province famous for its tiles—and so one was established at Liulichang, hence its present name. The glazed tile works were abandoned and destroyed at the end of the Qing but in the meantime the area had become a popular market which, by the beginning of the Qing, began to specialise in books, antiques, articles sought out by scholars, men of taste and would-be men of taste, those who followed 'style manuals' when decorating their studies with fashionable paintings, *objets d'art* and the appropriate books. Peking's booksellers congregated in Liulichang and printers also set up shop in the area. Perhaps the most notable printing enterprise in Liulichang was the production in 1792 of the major trilingual (Manchu–Mongolian–Chinese) dictionary.

A major fair used to be held in the first two weeks of the lunar New Year, when curios could be picked up at very reasonable prices. As Arlington and Lewisohn describe it: 'Here Manchu princes and high Chinese officials used to stroll up and down looking into the shops and inspecting the old books and pictures and the art shops still sell fine papers, brushes, ink-stones and other "articles of the scholar's table" to calligraphers and painters'.

The **Rongbao zhai** (Studio of Glorious Treasures), on the west side of the street, still produces fine woodblock prints of paintings by famous contemporary masters, most notably Qi Baishi, which are a reasonably priced substitute for a real painting. Visits to the workshop, where the woodblock prints are produced from multiple pearwood blocks, can be arranged through travel agents such as CITS.

The street used to be charming, if rather run-down, with carved wooden shopfronts and courteous elderly gentlemen who served customers with great discretion. The area has now been 'restored', the shops rebuilt in the Qing style, their newly carved and painted wooden boards hung in front of traditional style buildings made of concrete instead of timber.

The effect is rather that of a film set yet it closely resembles 19C paintings of Peking shops—examples can be seen in the Museum of Peking History in the Confucian temple, Wen miao, in the northwest of the city—so that, while not a real reconstruction of Liulichang, it is an accurate representation of an imaginary 19C Peking shopping area.

Due south of Liulichang, on **Taiping jie**, beside the southern city moat, is the **Taoranting gongyuan** (Carefree Park). During the Yuan it was an area of temples but in the Ming more ceramic kilns were set up here.

The Carefree Pavilion against the northern wall of the park was built in 1695 by the Minister of Works, Jiang Zao, and the two characters tao ran inscribed in gold on the board hanging from the eaves are in his calligraphy. They are taken from a verse by the Tang poet Bai Juyi: 'Let us wait until the chrysanthemums are golden and the home-brewed wine is ready, then together we will be drunk and carefree.' The same characters are carved in stone on the southern wall of the pavilion.

The area was made into a public park in 1952 with two wooden structures moved from the Zhongnanhai area west of the Forbidden City (the new 'forbidden' area inhabited by China's leaders): the Yunhui lou (Cloud Painting Tower) and the Qingyin ge (Pavilion of Clear Sounds). It is also said that the great wooden arches (*pailou*), which used to stand at the crossroads of Dong dan and Xi dan in the north of the city, were moved here but, if they were, they have long since disappeared.

The **Cibei an** (Hermitage of Benevolence and Pity), in the park to the east of the Carefree Pavilion, is a Yuan dynasty foundation, one of the many temples that stood here at the time. It houses two stone pillars (chuang) dated to 1099 and 1131 and inscribed with Buddhist texts.

During the years before and after the Fourth of May Movement (1919), Li Dazhao (1888–1927), Professor of History at Peking University, who was one of the first to propagate Marxism in China, hired a temple building for meetings, which were attended by Mao Zedong and Zhou Enlai, amongst others.

West of the Taoranting Park, on the north side of Baizhifang dong jie, is **Wanshou Park**, notable for its pet market. Aside from animals like the white angora kittens with one blue and one brown eye, much favoured by Song Qingling and Suzhou embroiderers, you can also buy traditional glass or ceramic and modern plastic items for fish tanks and bird cages.

Further west, on the edge of the southern city moat, in the southwest corner of the southern city, between Zuoan men and Nancaiyuan jie, is Peking's first 'theme park', the **Da guan yuan** (Garden of the Great View) built in the mid 1980s according to the description of the mansion and garden in Cao Xueqin's *Hong lou meng* (*Dream of the Red Chamber/Story of the Stone*).

It is ironic that it should have been constructed in this southwest corner of the city, when the probable real model for the garden, the Gongwang fu, is now partly open in the Back Lakes (Hou hai) area to the north of the Forbidden City. It is quite a pleasant garden in the traditional style but not an essential sight.

Tian tan ~ the Temple of Heaven

One of Peking's greatest temples, Tian tan (the Temple of Heaven), is also in the south of the city, immediately east of Qianmen da jie, which leads south to the Yongding (Eternally Stable) Gate. The enclosure is square to the south with a rounded wall to the north—the earth is said to be square, the heavens round in traditional Chinese cosmology—and is almost 6.5km from north to south. A smaller inner wall in the same form encloses the temple buildings and the whole enclosure is planted with fine cypresses, unusually, in straight lines, like ranks of soldiers. The ground used to be bare, stripped of all grass and weeds in the traditional style, but in the last few years, anachronistic western style grass has been planted. The sight of a lawn-mower in the Temple of Heaven is quite extraordinary.

The major entrance is to the north and it leads to a series of buildings: the Qinian dian (Hall of Prayer for Good Harvests), the smaller Huangqiong yu (Imperial Heavenly Vault) and the circular white marble Altar of Heaven, all linked by a high stone causeway.

The two halls are exceptional in that they are circular in plan with cone-shaped roofs covered in wonderful dark blue tiles topped with a golden ball. The plan derives from the traditional view that the heavens were circular; the roof colour, echoing the blue of the sky, is also symbolic.

First built in 1420, the enclosure was then known as the Temple of Earth and Heaven but in 1534 it was renamed the Temple of Heaven for the Jiaqing emperor had built the three other altars (of the earth, sun and moon: Ditan, Ritan, Yuetan).

As its relative size might suggest, the sacrifice at the Temple of Heaven saw the most important of the imperial observances, during both Ming and Qing. On the day before the winter solstice the emperor proceeded to the temple in his elephant-drawn chariot with a retinue of some 2000. Entering by the northernmost of the two west gates, he went straight to the smaller of the two circular halls (Huangqiong yu) to burn incense and prostrate himself before the ancestral tablets there. He then returned in his chariot to the Hall of Abstinence (a blue-roofed hall, rectangular in plan), which stands against the inner wall of the enclosure to the west, between the two circular halls. He spent the night '… in fasting and meditation, his eyes fixed on a life-size brass image, said to be that of a certain eunuch of the Ming dynasty who had changed his earthly for an ethereal form and implored his spirit to intercede with Heaven …' (Arlington and Lewisohn, In Search of Old Peking, 1935).

The next day, the emperor, dressed in plum silk robes with a black hat and blue silk boots, went to a yellow silk tent erected in the grounds and to the circular, triple-tiered white marble altar where animal sacrifices were offered, together with bundles of silk and jade. The tablets of the imperial ancestors were brought to the altar to 'participate' in the sacrifice. In this ceremony, the emperor spoke directly to the heavens of all the events of the previous year. In the first month he returned to the Temple of Heaven and, in the larger of the two circular halls, prayed for heaven's favour in the coming year and for a good harvest.

The northernmost of the two circular halls, the Qinian dian, was built In 1420; it was restored in 1751 and again in 1889 after it had been struck by lightning. It stands on a circular triple-tiered platform, identical to the Altar of Heaven, with eight flights of steps.

The hall is 30m in diameter and 37.5m high; 28 columns of *Phoebe nanmu* from Yunnan support the roof, in which no nails were used. The four central columns (18m high) symbolise the four seasons, while the other 24 represent the 12 months and the 12 hours into which the Chinese divided the day. The red columns are decorated with dragons and the roof timbers are brightly painted with, amongst other things, the imperial dragon and empress phoenix. In the centre of the floor is a circular stone with interesting veining; this is known as the dragon and phoenix stone. The thrones in the hall were used for the imperial ancestral tablets, which were brought here when the emperor came in the first lunar month, before being returned to the Huangqiong yu where they were normally stored. A small, black-draped altar to the Qing emperors has recently been set up behind the hall (1998).

A door on the east side of the Qinian dian enclosure leads to a covered way to the sacrificial kitchens, slaughter-houses and other essential offices. Just southwest of this covered walkway is a pile of rough stones known as the Seven Meteorites (which they are not); prayers for rain were said to have been made to them.

Red gates pierce the walls that enclose each of the halls. The next hall to the south is the smaller Huangqiong yu, 15.5m in diameter and 19m high, with a cone-shaped blue tiled roof with a gilded ball on top; the roof is supported on eight columns.

Peking: a ceiling in the Temple of Heaven

The vault was built in 1530 and restored in 1752. The blue-topped wall surrounding it is said to produce an acoustic phenomenon: people on either side of the enclosure standing close to the wall can apparently speak to each other without raising their voices, although there are so many people trying to do so that I have never experienced the phenomenon.

Through the gates to the south is the **Altar of Heaven**, a triple-tiered circular platform with white marble balustrades. It is approached through four white stone triple gates with stone 'clouds' piercing the upright columns.

The stones of the terrace are carefully organised to add up to multiples of nine and eighty-one, lucky numbers for the Chinese. The top terrace, for example, has a circular stone in the centre, surrounded by nine stones which are, in turn, surrounded by twenty-seven stones and so on, until the magic number of eighty-one is reached in the outermost circle. There is also said to be an echo effect if noises are produced in the centre of the terrace but, again, the cumulative effect of many tourists trying to achieve this tends to reduce the chances of success.

Built in 1530, when the outer walls of the altar were covered with blue tiles, the altar was enlarged in 1749, when the white marble balustrades replaced the blue tiles. It was here that the sacrificial animals and bundles of silk were burnt, to send them up to heaven.

Immediately west of the Temple of Heaven was the **Altar of Agriculture** (Xiannong tan), a slightly smaller enclosure which has not survived intact. Now set off Xiannong tan jie which runs parallel to Qianmen da jie, between a sports stadium and the Taoranting swimming pool, all that survive are the small Altar of Agriculture, the Terrace for Watching the Ploughing, where the emperor watched everyone else after he had ploughed his eight furrows, and two halls: the Qingcheng gong (Palace of Celebration of Achievement), where the empress awaited the emperor in order to congratulate him on his achievements, and the Dasui dian (Hall of the Year God).

The enclosure actually contained a number of halls devoted to different deities, so Xiannong tan or Altar of Agriculture is a rather restricted name. For example, sacrifices to the Year God, represented by the planet Jupiter, were carried out in a special courtyard and hall on the last day of the year and the two southernmost altars (Altar to the Spirits of the Earth and Altar to the Spirits of Heaven) were surrounded by separate shrines to wind, cloud, rain, thunder, mountains, rivers and seas. The small square altar, which gave the complex its name, was dedicated not just to agriculture but also to the 'first agriculturist'.

The southern part of the enclosure (Altars to Earthly and Heavenly Spirits) was built in 1420 and the rest added in 1530. The emperor would come every spring to plough a small plot in order to inspire his subjects and to initiate the agricultural year. The emperor then sowed rice, while other officials who came with him to plough their own plots sowed four varieties of millet. All the emperor's implements—plough, harness, trowels and even the oxen that pulled his plough—were yellow, the imperial colour but also the colour that represented the earth. The emperor would plough eight furrows, the official in charge of the Board of Finance followed on his right wielding a whip, while the Viceroy of the Metropolitan Province on his right bore the box of seed. Lesser persons ploughed 18 furrows and 'finally some aged peasants completed the work'.

It is ironic that Arlington and Lewisohn, writing in 1935, should comment gloomily about the Temple of Heaven: 'It is doubtless only a matter of time before the whole place will be razed to the ground and converted into a municipal swimming-bath or a stadium, or some other equally utilarian structure' for such has been the fate of the next door temple instead.

Excursions outside Peking

Excursions outside Peking include the Great Wall, the Ming Tombs, the Qing Tombs, Tanzhe and Jietai Temples, Fragrant Hills, Wanping, Zhou kou dian and the Yunju Temple at Fang shan.

The Great Wall

China's greatest monument can be seen in many places, most notably at Shanhaiguan, on the coast north of Peking and at the Jiayuguan fortress in the

The Great Wall at Badaling

distant northwest province of Gansu, but most people probably visit the Wall from Peking. The most popular spot is at **Badaling**, some 70km northwest of Peking (and it can be reached by car, taxi, several public buses, tourist bus or train). There are, however, a number of alternatives which are often less crowded. They can be reached by a series of public buses, by minibus tours and, probably most conveniently, by taxi (300–400 yuan for a round trip and it takes 2–3 hours to get to most of the more distant sites). **Mutianyu** (90km northeast of Peking) is a dramatic site with the Wall running along a ridge. There is a cable car. **Simatai** (110km northeast) is less restored than other parts and very dramatic indeed with steep climbs and dizzying drops; though there is now a cable car there, too. **Jinshanling**, 10km west of Simatai is one of the least developed area of the Wall; **Huanghua** (70km north of Peking) or **Jiugulou** (40km north of Huairou) are other wild, quiet areas.

Advantages of Badaling are that the gateway and fort stand amongst impressive hills, the view of the Wall there is wonderful and it is easier to combine that particular stretch of the Wall with a visit to the Ming Tombs and the Juyongguan Gate.

History

Known for some centuries to foreigners, the Wall received some recent publicity when it was said (inaccurately) to be the only man-made structure distinguishable from the moon. It is too narrow to be easily visible from that distance. Dr Johnson commented on it in 1778:

He talked with an uncommon animation of travelling into distant countries; that the mind was enlarged by it, and that an acquisition of dignity of character was derived from it. He expressed a particular enthusiasm with respect to visiting the wall of China. I catched it for the moment and said I really believed I should go and see the wall of China, had I not children of whom it was my duty to take care. 'Sir, (said he) by doing so, you would do what would be of importance in raising your children to eminence. There would be a lustre reflected upon them from your spirit and curiosity. They would be at all times regarded as the children of a man who had gone to visit the wall of China. I am serious, Sir.'

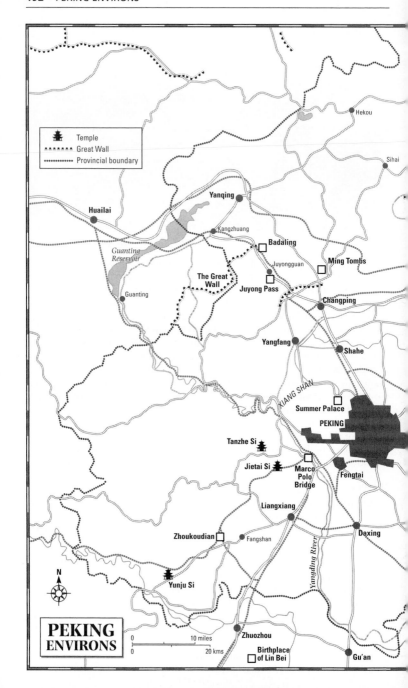

Temple
Great Wall
Provincial boundary

Hekou

Sihai

Yanqing

Huailai

Kangzhuang

Guanting Reservoir

Badaling

Juyongguan

Ming Tombs

The Great Wall

Juyong Pass

Guanting

Changping

Yangfang

Shahe

XIANG SHAN

Summer Palace

PEKING

Tanzhe Si

Jietai Si

Marco Polo Bridge

Fengtai

Liangxiang

Zhoukoudian

Fangshan

Yongding River

Daxing

Yunju Si

PEKING ENVIRONS

N

0   10 miles
0   20 kms

Zhuozhou

Birthplace of Lin Bei

Gu'an

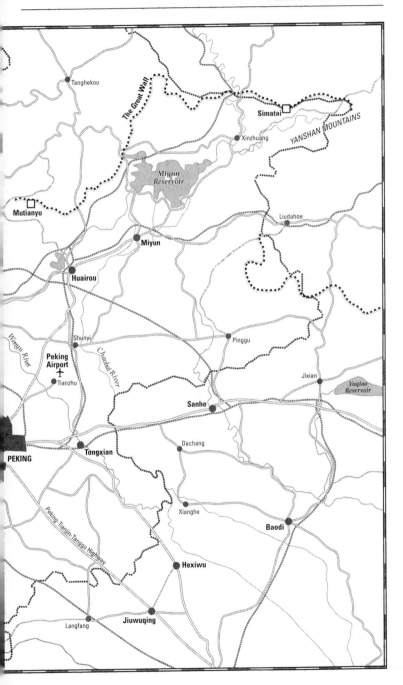

There is also a Chinese saying (sometimes attributed to Mao Zedong), to the effect that there is no great man who has not been to the Great Wall.

Known to the Chinese as *wanli changcheng*, 'the 10,000 *li fortification*' (a *li* or Chinese mile is about 530m), it is in fact considerably longer than that. Including a secondary 'outer' wall, built during the Han dynasty, it is some 20,000 *li* or about 10,000km long although it has been estimated that if all the bits were added to the original Qin Wall, it would be 50,000km long.

The history of the Wall begins in the 7C BC when the State of Chu built a defensive wall and this fortification was copied by others of the Warring States (Qi, Zhongshan, Wei, Zheng, Han, Qin, Yan and Zhao), some of whose walls were several thousand *li* long. The first emperor of the Qin, who unified China in 221 BC, had a great deal of work done on the present Wall, extending it to some 10,000 *li* (and that was when it acquired its present name). The Han, an expansionist dynasty, extended the Wall right out into the Gobi Desert to protect its far-reaching territory but above all to provide a means of military communication. All the way along the Wall small fortresses were constructed and their garrisons maintained a constant supply of brushwood to fire signal beacons which could instantly transmit the news of military emergencies through fire and smoke signals. A quantity of wood and bamboo slips used by Chinese garrison commanders to record events in and around their fortresses have been unearthed in the dry sands of the Gobi Desert to provide a picture of frontier life (with much checking of brushwood piles and counting of logs).

The greatest periods of construction of the Wall were the Qin, Han, Jin and Ming, for various reasons. During the Jin and Ming dynasties (1115–1234 and 1368–1644 respectively), the Wall was strengthened and extended because of a real threat from the north, beyond the Wall. The Jin was eventually overthrown by the Mongol Yuan dynasty (from beyond the Wall) and the Ming empire was overrun by the Manchu, again, from north of the Wall. Thus it was not particularly effective, partly because its enormous length made it impractical to garrison effectively. The fact that the Tang, for example, did not do much to maintain the Great Wall reflects on the contemporary perception of threat which, to the Tang, came from the west, not the north.

Most of what we see today reflects Ming improvements to the Wall. Originally made of tamped earth, much of it was faced with brick in the Ming. Those who worked on the Wall included soldiers, men on corvée duty (corvée labour being a form of taxation paid through the performance of public works by all able-bodied men) and criminals (the latter especially in the 'exile' area of Gansu province). They built a Wall that was some 6.7–7.9m high, 6.4m wide at the base and 5.5m wide at the top. Its width meant that up to five horsemen could ride abreast along it and it served as a military road through difficult terrain. 10,000 small beacon towers were built along the Wall, and 12 military garrisons controlled its total length from the watch-towers and secondary fortresses (like that at Badaling near Peking or Jiayuguan in Gansu).

On the way to Badaling the road passes beside a fine stone gateway, the **Guojie ta** (Tower that Straddles the Road) at Juyongguan (pass). Built in 1345, the square gate has a flat roof which may once have had a stupa on it.

Inside are very fine bas-relief stone carvings of Buddhist figures and inscriptions of Buddhist *dharani* or incantations in Chinese, Sanskrit, Tibetan, Uighur, Mongolian (in the *Phags-pa* script of 42 alphabetic symbols invented by a young Tibetan lama for Khubilai Khan in an unsuccessful attempt to supplant the modified Uighur alphabet for writing Mongolian) and Tangut (or *Xi Xia*, the language of a Tibetan people who set up an independent kingdom in Gansu in the 11C and whose script, which is not fully deciphered, was based on Chinese characters).

Near the Juyonggan Gate and Badaling is Qinglongqiao Station on the Peking–Kalgan (Zhanjiakou) railway. This was the first to be built entirely with Chinese funds and was completed in 1909 by Zhang Tianyun who had studied engineering at Yale. A statue on the station platform commemorates the chief engineer and there is a railway museum nearby (not seen; open 08.30–16.30).

The Ming Tombs

The Ming Tombs, known to the Chinese as the **Shisan ling** (Thirteen Tombs) lie c 48km north of Peking, on a road which branches off from the one leading to the Great Wall (hence a brief visit to the tombs is usually combined with the Great Wall for tourist groups).

The founder of the Ming dynasty is buried near his capital of Nanjing but of the total of 16 Ming emperors 13 are buried in what was once a huge enclosed area north of Peking. The Jingtai emperor who ruled from 1449 to 1457 (during the time that his brother, the Zhengtong emperor, had been taken prisoner by the Mongols) was regarded as a usurper and buried in the Western Hills (see p 202) and it is not known where the second Emperor of the Ming, who was quickly dethroned by his uncle (the Yongle emperor), was buried.

As soon as Yongle decided to move the capital to Peking he had geomancers decide upon a suitable site for the imperial tombs. These 'mountain cockroaches', as some called them, chose a valley some 5km long north–south and 3km wide, bounded to the north by hills. The entire site is very beautiful and when you stand high on the ramparts of a tomb, you can see the yellow-tiled roofs and red walls of the stele towers of other tombs amongst the tall trees, arranged in a semi-circle against the hills.

The size of the area and its quiet beauty make the Ming Tombs one of the most pleasant outings from Peking. Two of the tombs have been officially opened to the public, one has been extensively excavated (Ding ling) and the other has been restored above ground level (Chang ling). The other tombs have been recently closed to the public, but in the hope that this situation changes, I have left the descriptions as they were.

General layout of the tombs

The general layout of all the tombs is similar and has its roots in previous tomb design; it was also continued in the two groups of Qing tombs in Hebei province.

They consist of two major, linked parts. The front courtyard is square in plan (representing the earth) and contains buildings above the ground where ritual implements were stored and rituals took place (on the birthdays of the deceased and traditional days of tribute to ancestors). Behind, enclosed by a high rampart, is the circular tomb mound (representing heaven) with a high stele tower in front of it. The tombs grouped together in the valley, which was itself enclosed (the remains of the wall could still be seen in 1920) and whose approach was indicated by a series of stone monuments.

As you approach the tomb area, the first sight is of the great stone pailou (1540). Built entirely of white marble, with a superstructure which perfectly reproduces the details of a timber and tile roof construction, it has extremely fine carved column bases with three-dimensional lions and *makara* (serpent gods of Indian origin, later associated with Buddhist mythology), above bas-relief carvings of more lions, dragons and *makara*. Even the background to the bas-relief panels is carved with damask-like patterns.

Beyond the *pailou* is the **Great Red Gate** which stands at the proper entrance to the valley and its tombs, and which was once set in the enclosing walls. In design and colour similar to buildings in the Forbidden City, the gate was probably built in 1425. Its central opening was for the defunct emperor in his coffin, living emperors used the doorway on the left. It was at this point that all attendants had to dismount and make the rest of the journey on foot.

500m further along the road is the double-roofed, four-doored **stele pavilion**, flanked by four highly carved stone columns. The pavilion houses the largest memorial stele in China, standing on a stone turtle.

Apparently stone turtle as stele bearers were first used during the 6C AD although their use was restricted to the three highest grades of officials and the imperial family. The turtle was a symbol of longevity. It was also common from the end of the Han to decorate the tops of stele with some intertwined, bottle-horned dragons that were considered to bring benefit.

The giant stele bears the names of the Ming emperors buried in the necropolis and, although dated 1425, it was not put in place until 1435. The carved columns with clouds piercing the top (beneath the lion or *qilin* seated on a canopy) are similar to the pair (also Ming) which stand beside the Gate of Heavenly Peace (Tiananmen) at the south end of the Forbidden City (see p 112). The columns are thought to be based on Han dynasty pillars which were used to signal staging posts in the imperial postal system but by the Ming they were certainly more decorative than indicative.

Beyond the stele pavilion is the famous 'spirit road' lined with carved stone figures. The road is curved, apparently to confuse evil spirits who could only fly in straight lines. The whole series of figures is now somewhat hidden by the orchards that line the road (photographs taken early in the 20C show the stone figures in a completely barren landscape).

First are a pair of carved stone columns with dragons all over them and rather stubby tops—these are symbolic beacons; they are followed by pairs of animals (in double pairs, one standing, one sitting): lions (Buddhist guardians), *xiezhai* (with leonine heads, horses' bodies and symbolising justice), camels, horses, elephants and *qilin* (augurs of wise rule). These are followed by human figures: four warriors, four civil officials and four imperial councillors. The officials wear the uniform of a President of one of the Six Boards (effectively a Minister), with badges of office embroidered on the front and back of their robes. They hold carved stone versions of the ivory boards which were used to write notes on matters to be raised in audience with the emperor. The last four figures are also officials but higher in rank, members of the imperial Grand Secretariat and they have flat-topped embroidered hats.

In the 1970s, they were open to the public to crawl all over them but they have since been surrounded by protective railings.

At the end of the avenue is a Dragon and Phoenix Gate with stone lintels topped with what look like versions of the Buddhist Wheel of the Law.

The tombs all have different names, which have no connection with the several names of their inhabitants. I shall first describe the two tombs which are generally open to the public and visited by tour groups, then the others in chronological order. The first tomb is some 4km beyond the last gate.

Chang ling (Long-lasting Tomb) is the burial place of the Yongle emperor, 1424, and his empress, who had died in 1407. Chang ling is not always on the tourist itinerary, if time is short, but it is very much to be recommended for its above-ground architecture. The tomb is approached through a yellow-roofed triple gate which leads to a courtyard, in the middle of which stands the Gate of Heavenly Favours, with a stele pavilion on the right housing a stele with inscriptions dated 1659, 1786 and 1804 recording penalties for felling timber in the area and dates of repairs.

Although the tomb was built for the Yongle emperor (reigned 1403–24) during his lifetime, the succeeding Qing dynasty made attempts to maintain the necropolis of their forerunners, probably for superstitious reasons: it was believed that the disturbed souls of the deceased could influence events negatively.

Beyond the gate is the main courtyard of the Hall of Heavenly Favours. On either side of the path are small green and yellow tiled 'buildings', actually ovens in which paper offerings were burnt. The great hall is one of the largest traditional buildings in China (only very slightly smaller than the Hall of Supreme Harmony in the Forbidden City). The triple-tiered marble terrace on which it stands is the earliest example of the type. Similar to the later versions in the Forbidden City (where construction began some years after the Yongle emperor had begun his tomb), this has dragon-topped pillars, bottle-horned dragon gargoyles and a fine carved slab in the centre of the staircase with dragons writhing above waves.

The interior of the hall is exceptionally grand with huge columns of cedar (brought from Sichuan province on a journey that probably took some three years and thousands of unlucky labourers to drag them here). 10m high and 1m in diameter, these great columns are now unpainted (they may well have been painted red in the past) although the ceiling panels are painted in green, gold and blue. Their sombre colour adds to the grandeur of the hall (which is now unfortunately guarded by attendants in bright 'Ming costumes' and filled with a small exhibition of Ming artefacts).

Sir Reginald Johnston, tutor to the last Qing emperor, records how a descendant of the Ming royal house carried out his last ancestral sacrifices in the hall in 1924 before following Puyi into exile.

Behind the hall a triple doorway leads to another courtyard. A narrow screen door of wooden panels set between high white marble columns with *qilin* sitting on top (these columns, without the doors, can be seen in many of the ruined Ming tombs), stands in front of the great white marble 'altar' table with five marble versions of ritual bronze vessels, symbolic of those used in the rituals carried out in the Great Hall. Behind the marble 'altar' is the stele tower. Built above the battlemented circular brick wall that surrounds the tomb mound, it resembles a city gate with solid red walls and yellow tiled roof. At its base is a tunnel which leads up to the paved walk that runs around the battlements. Above, in the tower, is the stele simply engraved with an inscription that states whose tomb it is. The tomb mound, which gives no indication of where the body actually lies (to confuse robbers), is thickly planted with pines and thujas. Walking round the ramparts, above the persimmon trees and fields below, you can see the yellow tiled roofs of other stele towers in the distance.

Ding ling (Stable Tomb) is that of the Wanli emperor (d. 1620) and two empresses, both called Wang. One was a concubine who bore the heir to the throne so that she was raised to the status of empress.

The tomb was excavated in 1956–58. The underground chamber is open to visitors and there are halls of exhibits in the front courtyards. The discovery of the underground chamber was fortuitous (and the amount of luck required helps to explain why none of the other tombs has yet been excavated). When archaeologists were examining a weak spot in the encircling wall they found a tunnel. This was not the entrance to the underground chamber for it led to a dead end but, fortunately, the builders' instruction on how to find the burial chamber (inscribed on a small stele) had been left in the tunnel. Such instructions were apparently left by the original builders for those who would have to open the tomb when the emperor actually died and was to be buried in it. The stele should have been removed after the funeral. The tomb chamber was bricked up and beyond the brick wall was a pair of marble doors. These were extraordinarily difficult to open as they had been closed by a special buttress which fell against the doors as they were closed.

Like the Chang ling, Ding ling has three front courtyards forming its rectangular 'earth-shaped' section. Beyond the triple entrance gate are the remains of the Gate of Heavenly Favours and the Hall of Heavenly Favours. In the third courtyard, on either side of the marble altar, are exhibition halls.

The west hall contains mainly the effects of the emperor and that on the east those of the empresses. The emperor's several hats include one of black velvet studded with gems and pierced Munster-like with a great jade pin (for use when travelling), with rows of curtain-like tassels and beads for audiences, a plumed black iron helmet and a gold gauze hat with dragons. There are wooden models of furniture, gold, jade and miniature pewter vessels and wooden figurines, rolls of brocade, silver and gold ingots cast in Wanli's reign, a jade belt and a number of *meiping* blue and white porcelain jars. The empresses' possessions in the tomb include hairpins and jewellery, silken shirts and jackets, jade belt pendants, copies of the phoenix crowns decorated with kingfisher feathers stuck on paper and more jade and gold vessels.

The tumulus can be entered from the front or rear of the mound behind the stele tower (traffic problems sometimes dictate a one-way flow from either entrance). Beyond the antechamber are the great marble doors with the hole in the floor behind them where the heavy stone prop fell into place as the tomb was sealed. The chamber is beautifully constructed with carefully worked stones that fit neatly together without any cement. The main corridor leads to a major coffin chamber (with crude copies of three coffins on a raised stone dais) and there are side corridors leading to parallel side chambers (also with stone coffin platforms but which were empty). The main corridor has three stone thrones and huge blue and white porcelain vats which were filled with sesame oil to serve as 'everlasting' lamps (which had gone out as the oxygen was depleted). The side chambers had entrances with the same self-locking doors, leading to the outside; it is assumed they were there for any wives of the emperor who survived him and had to be buried here later. Paintings on the walls depict the construction of the tomb (which took six years and cost more than half a million pounds, using a corvée workforce of 600,000 men). The grave mound, like the front courtyards, planted with pines and thujas, has been tidied up considerably.

The other tombs are (west to east): Si ling, Zhao ling, Kang ling (behind Ding ling), Tai ling, Mao ling, Yu ling, Qing ling, Xian ling (just west of Chang ling), Jing ling (east of Chang ling) and Yong ling. In chronological order they were built as follows:

Xian ling (Offering Tomb) is the burial place of the Yongle emperor's sickly son, the Hongxi emperor (who died having reigned for barely a year), and his empress. The unlucky emperor's tomb (some 700m northwest of Chang ling) is also geomantically rather odd for a small hill (Jade Table Mountain) intrudes on the axis of the tomb, splitting the entrance gate and sacrificial hall from the altar table courtyard and the mound. Little remains of the first courtyard, although the stele tower is in good condition. The mound is unusually elongated (hog's back shape) with thujas on top and Chinese oaks on the lower slope. These are extraordinary trees with huge leaves that seem to grow straight from the trunk creating the impression that they were drawn by a child (they can be found in many of the overgrown tombs).

Jing ling (Scenic Tomb) is the tomb of the Xuande emperor (d. 1435) and his empress. It lies to the east of Chang ling and, like the Xian ling, is one of the smaller tombs. The tortoise stele that stands in front of the tomb has been surrounded by village buildings but behind, the double courtyard and long mound (also similar in shape to that of the Xian ling) are in quite good condition. Although the sacrificial hall is now only visible through its pillar bases, it was still intact in 1931. The stele tower is built on a terrace with a steep approach ramp and side ramps running up to the battlements on either side.

Yu ling (Lucky Tomb) is the burial place of the Zhengtong emperor (d. 1464) and two empresses. It lies west of Xian ling and is reached by a small cobbled road which runs north from a bus stop. It is rather isolated (with no nearby village) and very quiet. The Zhengtong emperor's reign was interrupted in 1449 when he was taken prisoner by the Mongols after a military defeat and only managed to regain the throne from his brother in 1457. His tomb houses two empresses' bodies, in defiance of tradition for one of the empresses had not borne a son (and should therefore have been excluded). Beyond the tortoise stele are three arched bridges crossing a stream. The two courtyards are in ruins although there is a fine marble slab carved with mountains and clouds (the lack of dragons is quite restful) leading to the platform of the sacrificial hall.

Mao ling (Flourishing Tomb) is that of the Chenghua emperor (d. 1487) and three empresses, who also represent the major break in tradition for one was son-less and two were buried in the tomb after the emperor, which in previous periods of Chinese history was extremely unusual as it was considered unlucky to re-open a tomb; only tough characters like the Tang empress Wu were prepared to overrule the geomancers. It lies quite close to the main road, just west of the Yu ling and is not in terribly good condition.

Tai ling (Peaceful Tomb) is the burial place of Hongzhi (d. 1505) and one empress. It lies just west of Mao ling and is in poor condition with the first court-yard open to a village, although the small offering oven is still in place.

Kang ling (Healthy Tomb) is the burial place of the Zhengde emperor (d. 1521) and one empress (d. 1535). It is one of the prettiest tombs, situated just south-west of Tai ling (it was common for sons to site their tombs as near as possible to those of their fathers). Just beyond Mao ling a small path on the left leads through a persimmon orchard and across a river to the tomb which is rather tucked away. There is a wonderful view from the front of the tomb to distant mountains through the orchards. The tomb mound (whose ramparts also offer spectacular views) has a smaller group of mounds on top, said by some to represent children surrounding their father.

Swallow, from Illustrations of the things mentioned in the Book of Songs, 1771

Yong ling (Eternal Tomb) is the burial place of Jiajing (d. 1567) and three empresses who prede-ceased him. It is the easternmost of the tombs, reached by a road to the right of the main tomb road which branches off some time before the Chang ling is visible. One of the best preserved of the 'ruined' tombs, it is also rich in wild flowers, handsome trees and birds. The marble slab leading to the platform on which the Gateway of Heavenly Favours once stood has a phoenix and dragon carved on it; this is the first appearance of the empress's symbol along-side that of the emperor in the Ming tombs. The proportions of the tomb are generous: there are wide steps and a broad ramp beside the equally broad stele tower whose workmanship is far more careful than that found elsewhere.

Zhao ling (Shining Tomb) is that of Longjing (d. 1572) and three empresses and it is reached only by foot, through the fields southwest of Ding ling from the lower part of the parking area there. Here there is also a triple bridge over a stream behind the tortoise stele, which is surrounded by parts of a finely carved wall, and a once impressively raised gateway. The triple doorway of the second courtyard is still largely intact and although the stele tower was said to have been burned down by Li Zicheng's troops in 1644, it was restored.

Qing ling (Celebration Tomb) is that of the Taichang emperor (d. 1620) and three empresses who predeceased him.

> Taichang died a month after ascending to the throne. As he had not had time to prepare his own tomb he is buried in someone else's. Conveniently, when the Zhengtong emperor was taken prisoner by the Mongols in 1449, his brother, the Jingtai emperor, who was placed on the throne instead, prepared a tomb for himself. When the Zhengtong emperor was restored to the throne in 1465 Jingtai was denounced as an usurper and his imperial tomb was destroyed above ground. Thus the Qing ling's substructure dates from about 1450 and the superstructure was added in 1620–21.

Like the Xian ling, there are two parts to the tomb, divided by a small hill. The Qing ling lies west of the Chang ling (second tomb on the right). The tortoise stele is to the left of the main road, the entrance gate and sacrificial hall and mound to the right. The stele tower is slightly unusual in that it has two small side ramps and a staircase up to the terrace and the walkway round the grave mound is also slightly different in arrangement and has stone 'gates' which led to the mound. These have recently fallen over but were in place in 1971. The mound also has a 'very well developed' drainage system.

Ann Paludan, whose loving and detailed guide to the area is indispensable to the serious Ming tomb visitor (*The Imperial Ming Tombs*, Yale, 1981) is a keen student of tomb drainage and reports that 'this is the 'first tomb to show a complete system of drainage in both mound and courtyards' and she illustrates some of the drain covers.

De ling (Virtuous Tomb—although Piet Van der Loon, former Professor of Chinese at the University of Oxford, would massacre me for that translation: he prefers the Latin term *virtus* which includes an element of masculinity and strength quite lacking in 'virtuous') is the burial place of the Tianqi emperor (d. 1627) and his empress who strangled herself at the orders of the last Ming emperor as Li Zicheng's rebel troops entered Peking marking the downfall of

Turtle, also from Illustrations..., 1771

the dynasty. At the very farthest point east in the necropolis east of Chang ling (beyond Yong ling), this is a very beautiful tomb. Set quite high, with a marvellous view of the valley below from the gate and turtle stele, its small size is belied by the spacious courtyards. The turtle stele on its stone platform is in good condition, beautifully carved with turtle, prawn, fish and crab on the corners of the base. The tomb is built on rising ground, the second courtyard higher than the first and the crumbling stele tower set in front of an oval mound. As Ann Paludan says: 'Although it has no particular architectural interest, De ling is beautiful ... a place of utter peace and many birds.'

Si ling (Meaningful Tomb) lies far to the west, strictly outside the imperial necropolis. It was originally a concubine's tomb, part of a complex of concubines' and imperial children's cemeteries in the area, and it was opened up to receive the bodies of the last Ming emperor, Chongzhen, and his empress in

1644. The tomb and the concubine cemeteries are not easy to find: take the road west off the main road just beyond the dragon and phoenix gate (at the north end of the spirit way of animals). At a T-junction within sight of the hills, turn left and follow the road along the hills west past the remains of concubine cemeteries and round to the Si ling. Originally it had no tumulus but one was added, with a surrounding Wall. All that survives today is the tumulus, the marble altar and its altar objects and a stele standing on a charmingly carved square base (instead of the usual imperial turtle).

The Western Hills

The **Xiang shan** (Western or Fragrant Hills) are 20km northwest of Peking, beyond the Summer Palace. On the way to the Xiang shan are the Wofo si (Temple of the Sleeping Buddha) and the tomb of the Ming Jingtai emperor.

The **Tomb of the Jingtai Emperor** is 4km from the Summer Palace, off the main road at the point where the Jade Fountain Pagoda (standing on a hill in a military area which was once an imperial palace for the Jin and a garden for the Kangxi and Qianlong emperors of the Qing) is to the left and a village (Niangniangfu) and an army camp on the right. A ditch between these two leads to the stele pavilion of Jingtai's tomb.

> The Jingtai emperor usurped the throne in 1449, when his elder half-brother, the Zhengtong emperor, had been captured by the Mongols. On Zhengtong's restoration he was disgraced and possibly murdered (he died suspiciously soon after). Denied a place in the Ming necropolis (Shisan ling; see p 195), the Jingtai emperor was reinstated in 1475: thus his stele is inscribed with the characters for the name of the dynasty and he himself described as 'reverent and peaceful'.

His turtle stele stands in a small square pavilion with a painted beam and glazed tile roof (the only Ming stele pavilion to survive in Peking). Inside the simple three-bay gatehouse is an enclosure which is rectangular to the south and curved to the north, thus incorporating both the square earth and circular heaven symbols. No buildings remain inside the enclosure, no hall or stele tower, just a simple grave mound with the characteristic earth cone on top.

The **Wofo si** (Sleeping Buddha Temple) is not far beyond. At a crossroads a road leads north to the temple. The road to the south leads to one of the Eight Great Sites (Bada chu), that to the southwest leads to the Xiang shan/Fragrant Hills Park.

> The temple was founded during the Tang and expanded in 1320–31. Owing to its proximity to the imperial parks and gardens, various Ming and Qing emperors presented sutras and built halls and pagodas in the temple. The last major rebuilding was in 1734.

The temple is entered through a glazed tile *pailou* gateway at the end of an avenue of fine old cypresses. Beyond is a bridge over a pool with the bell and drum towers on either side and in the first hall are statues of the Heavenly Kings. In the second courtyard are two old Bodhi trees, *Shorea robusta*, said to have come from India: in front of the hall are a Qianlong-period incense burner, inside the Maitreya (Future) Buddha with guardian figures, and a Wei tuo (Protector) behind. In the next hall are the Historic Buddha with Amitabha and the Buddha of Medicine and Guan yin behind (with luohans on either side). The great sleeping Buddha in the fourth hall is of lacquered bronze (over 5m long) and was cast in 1321.

> That, at least, is the literary account, but many believe that the present figure is a later copy. The image is that of the dying Buddha, about to enter nirvana (rather than simply sleeping: the name of the temple should be more accurately translated as the Reclining Buddha Temple) and it is surrounded by smaller figures of Bodhisattvas and giant shoes presented as offerings to the Buddha.
>
> From the earliest period, the Buddha's feet or footprints have been used as symbolic representations of his presence. The soles of his feet were traditionally believed to have been different from those of ordinary mortals, imprinted with 108 symbols of good fortune (including conch shells under each toe).

There are east and west axes to the temple: the buildings to the west were used by the Ming and Qing emperors as 'travelling palaces'; those on the east were the monks' dwellings, kitchens and refectory.

Just northwest of the temple is the **Yingtaogou yuan** (Garden of the Cherry Valley) where there was once a Taoist hermitage (founded in 1442, enlarged in 1486), of which nothing now remains. In the park are the Bailu yan (Cliff of the White Deer) where a sage was said to have landed during the 10C, flying in on a white deer. A cave where Taoist hermits meditated can be seen along with several pavilions.

South of the Temple of the Sleeping Buddha, on the road that eventually leads south to the Eight Great Sites, is the round fort, **Tuan Cheng**, built in the mid 18C by the Qianlong emperor. It was built to help prepare troops for military manoeuvres during uprisings in the southwest: all that now remains is a small watchtower.

The **Fragrant Hills Park** lies beyond. It has long been a park, used as a hunting ground by emperors ever since the 12C.

> In the 18C it was walled for, as game was scarce, 'horse deer' (*Cephus elaphurus*) were brought from Manchuria. The many temples and pavilions built here were damaged by the French and British armies in 1860 and by the Allied army at the end of the Boxer uprising (1900).

Just outside the walls on the left of the path is the new *Xiang shan Hotel*, designed by the American Overseas Chinese architect I.M. Pei in 1983.

> Certainly one of the most striking modern buildings in China, it is an interesting if slightly antiseptic mixture of the southern (Suzhou) garden-house complex and the grandeur of Chengde. Great flat white walls (Chengde without the red) surround a group of buildings linked by moon-gates and with other garden-like window-openings, most grouped around gardens and pools. The management has no doubt changed since I visited it soon after opening when the administration was the usual friendly, lethargic shambles at odds with the pristine elegance of the polished white halls. The hotel's distance from the centre of town makes it inconvenient for tourists but it would be an ideal conference centre.

Beyond is the entrance to the hilly park. Inside, along a path which leads first west then north, is the **Zhao Miao** (Luminous Temple), built by the Qianlong emperor in 1780 in the Tibetan style (recalling Chengde's outer temples, in particular the Xumifushou Temple).

It was constructed, like the latter, for visiting Tibetans, in particular the Panchen Lama, for him to use whenever he visited Peking (and its distance from the centre makes his use of the Huang si or Yellow Temple as a stopping place more explicable).

Like the temples in Chengde, it has a 'false' facade, with blind windows in the Tibetan style, breaking the monotony of the wall. The nearby seven-storey Glazed Tile Pagoda also resembles that at the Xumifushou Temple. Octagonal in plan, it has 56 bronze bells suspended from the eaves.

The **Jianxin zhai** (Pavilion of Introspection) is north of the Luminous Temple. Built in the reign of the Ming Jiaqing emperor (reigned 1522–1567), it was enlarged later. This is a courtyard residence built in the 'southern style'. In the centre of the courtyard is a semi-circular pool in which spring water spouts from a stone dragon head. The pool is surrounded by a covered walk.

Due south of the Pavilion of Introspection and the Zhao miao is the **Xiangshan si** (Fragrant Hills Temple), founded in 1186 and rebuilt in 1312. The Kangxi emperor of the Qing used it as a 'travelling' or temporary palace and it was again enlarged in 1745. Little remains but the stone terraces of what was once a huge temple for it was burnt down in 1900.

South of the temple are the remains of the **Shuangqing bieshu** (Two Springs Villa) where the two springs are named in the Qianlong emperor's calligraphy. The villa was used by Mao Zedong and others in March 1949 to plan the Red Army's crossing of the Yangtze River to liberate south China. He moved directly from this spot to Zhongnanhai (immediately west of the Forbidden City, still the residence and official centre of government) in November of the same year.

The highest peak in the park, the **Xianghu feng** (Incense Burner Peak) is in its western corner, 557m above sea level and crowded with visitors in the autumn when the leaves (of the Huanglu smoke tree) are red.

Outside the north gate of the Xiang shan Park is the **Biyun si** (Temple of the Azure Clouds), built against rising ground with the Diamond Throne Pagoda (a white marble version of the Wuta si (see p 161), an Indian-style building with five tapering, stepped pagodas on top) visible above the trees.

There was apparently a Buddhist convent on the site in 1330. In the early 16C a group of eunuchs had the temple enlarged, planning to be buried there, but the work was later abandoned. The Diamond Throne Pagoda and Luohan Hall were built in 1748. Sun Yatsen's body lay in the pagoda from 1925–29, when it was transferred to his grave outside Nanjing, and a small commemorative museum is housed in the back halls of the temple.

The **Gate of Heavenly Guardians**, which stands beyond a bridge over a ravine and two Ming stone lions, contains fine figures of 1513, some 5m high. In the first courtyard are the bell and drum towers and a hall with a Ming figure of Maitreya (the Buddha of the Future). There is a pool in the centre of the second courtyard and two octagonal pillars carved with sutras: behind is a hall with a Buddha image and plaster figures (the upper register depicts Xuan zang's pilgrimage to India during the Tang dynasty).

On the south side of the third courtyard is the **Luohan Hall** (modelled on that at the Lingyin Temple at Hangzhou) with 500 lacquered carved wooden figures, a group of seven saints and a tiny figure of the monk Jian gong carved on a roof beam (making 508 figures in all). In the same courtyard is the **Puming juemiao Hall** where Sun Yatsen's body lay. Behind is the **Diamond Throne Pagoda**, nearly 35m high with an interior staircase.

Inside are buried Sun Yatsen's clothes and hat, repeating the old tradition that if bodies could not be found clothing would be buried. In this case, Sun Yatsen was not lost but, as the Father of the Nation, Peking wanted to keep a little of him, symbolically.

On the roof are two small dagobas with five square 13-storey close-eaved pagodas. The whole is covered with fine carvings of Buddhas, heavenly guardians, dragons, phoenix, lions, elephants, etc. Behind are hills, woods and a spring.

The Eight Great Sites

The Eight Great Sites, or **Bada chu**, are eight temples situated on three hills, south of the Western Hills. They were closed for years as they were in a military area also peppered with villas, to which the Politburo retired in times of crisis (as in June 1989 after the Tiananmen massacre). The site has now been opened and enhanced by a fairground. It is easily reached by taxi or a 347 bus from the Zoo in Peking.

Changan si (Temple of Everlasting Peace) was founded in 1604; described by Arlington and Lewisohn in 1935 as 'completely in ruins' but by Nagel's *Guide* (1979) as housing a fine gilded Guan Yu (God of War) figure of the Ming and a Niangniang Hall dedicated to a version of the Bodhisattva Guanyin, here as a giver of children to the childless. The figure was flanked by minor female deities who protected children from illness. There are two Yuan dynasty trees in the first courtyard, white-barked dragon-claw pines.

Lingguang si (Temple of Divine Light) was founded in the 7C; destroyed by the Allied armies in 1900, when a box was found in the ruins of the pagoda which contained a Buddha tooth, for which a new pagoda was built in 1959. There is also a pond with enormous goldfish said to be over 100 years old.

Sanshan an (Three Hills Nunnery) was founded in 1442; reconstructed in 1697 and 1786. It is popularly known as the Ma Family Nunnery (presumably because some nuns of the Ma family resided there. A great 'jade stone' in the doorway of the main hall is called the Water and Cloud Stone because of its veining.

Dabei si (Temple of Great Compassion) was founded during the Song, with an interesting stone entrance gate carved with animals, both real and mythological. The luohan figures in the first hall are said to be the work of a famous Yuan dynasty (1279–1368) sculptor, Liu Yuan. Behind the main hall are two gingko trees said to be 800 years old.

Longwang tang (Dragon King's Temple) was founded in 916, restored in 1180 and frequently during subsequent dynasties. Its name comes from a spring which pours out of the mouth of a carved stone dragon's head. There is a charming illustration of the pool with its many and varied pierced openings in the surrounding wall and a single giant black carp floating in the water in

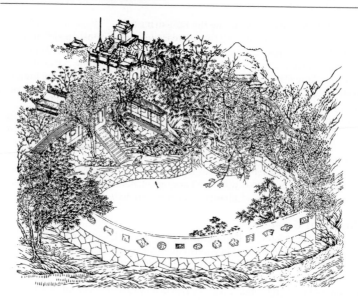

Longwang tang, from Hong xue yin yuan, The illustrated autobiography of Linqing, *1847–50*

Linqing's 19C memoir, *The Tracks of a Wild Goose in the Snow* (translated in part by T.C. Lai). Linqing included accounts of his visits to many famous temples which he admired particularly for their plants and garden features.

Xiangjie si (Temple of the Fragrant World), the major temple of the group, was founded in 619 and restored in 1426, 1678 and 1749, the last restoration under Qianlong who built himself a garden and a 'travelling palace' here, gave the temple its present name and wrote an inscription on the temple's history which has been carved on a stele.

Baozhu dong (Precious Pearl Cave), a temple which existed before 1326. Nagel says it is approached through a fine wooden *pailou*; in 1935 Arlington and Lewisohn recorded that there had once been a *pailou* which had since disappeared.

Zhengguo si (Temple of Buddhahood), founded in 620, destroyed in 1900. Traditionally believed to be the home of a hermit of the Tang dynasty, Lu Shi, who came from the south and lived in a cave here.

Arlington and Lewisohn also describe the **Tiantai si** (Monastery of Exalted Heaven), 'about one and a half hour's walk' from site no. 7, which contains a mummified figure.

South of the Bada chu, near the village of Moshikou is the **Fahai si** (Temple of the Sea of the Law), founded in 1439 and paid for by the eunuch Li Tong. Despite later repairs it is said to preserve the early Ming style of building. The internal ceiling beams of the gate were painted in the early Ming and there are Ming frescoes of Buddhist deities on the walls of the main hall (not seen).

In the eastern suburbs of Peking, along the road that runs south from the Zoo (Sanlihe lu), to the west is the **Diaoyutai guo binguan** (State Guesthouse of the Angler's Terrace). Here state visitors stay in villas in the extensive grounds; the Queen of England, George Bush and Mikhail Gorbachev have been among them. Some groups of tourists may get to stay in the complex.

According to tradition, the Zhangzong emperor of the Jin (reigned 1190–1209) used to fish here where the Jin poetWang Yu had 'built a terrace and lowered his fishing line'. During the Yuan the area was a park; during the Qing, the Qianlong emperor had one of his innumerable 'travelling palaces' here. The gardens are laid out as they were in the Qing and many of the trees date back to that period.

At the bottom of the road, where it joins Changan jie (here called Fuxingmen wai da jie), are the great grey buildings of the Academia Sinica, the **Chinese Academy of Science** (on the east side of the road). Some kilometres along Fuxingmen wai da jie, out beyond the built-up area, is the cemetery of **Babao Shan** where the ashes of prominent citizens are placed.

Southwest of Peking

Southwest of Peking are the Marco Polo Bridge, or Lugouqiao, the site of the finds of Peking Man at Zhoukoudian, the two temples—Tanzhe si (Temple of the Pool and the Mulberry) and the Jietai si (Temple of the Ordination platform). Further on are the Yunju si (Temple of the Habitation in the Clouds) and nearby Shijing shan/Fang shan (Stone Sutra Mountain).

Marco Polo Bridge, Wanping and 'Peking Man'

The **Marco Polo Bridge**, known to the Chinese as *Lugouqiao* (Bridge over the Lugou River) is 16km west of the Guang'an men in the southwest of the city.

The main road out of the city through the site of the Guang'an men is called Guang'an men wai da jie, then Lugouqiao lu. It crosses the river once known as Lugou, now as the Yongding. The stone bridge (replacing previous pontoon bridges which were always being washed away) was built between 1189 and 1192.

There is a description of the bridge in Marco Polo's *Travels*: '... it is quite 300 paces long and quite eight paces wide ... all of grey marble very well worked and well founded'. Although he mentions stone lions, he fails to mention the 140 balusters each with a little stone lion on top or the stone elephants at either end of the bridge (nudging the parapets with their foreheads).

Marco Polo is supposed to have seen the bridge in 1276, hence the name used for it from the late 19C by foreign residents and visitors, but his description which, as usual, misses the most striking of the bridge's decorative features, could well have been copied from elsewhere. One of the arguments against Polo's having seen things personally (and the likelihood that he copied his account from Persian travel books) is his use of Persian names, never Chinese or Mongol: he calls this bridge *Pulisangin*, from the Persian *pul* for bridge and *sang* for stone.

At either end of the bridge are stele pavilions housing a stele describing restoration work of 1698 and one describing the morning moon on the bridge as one of the 'eight views of Peking'.

The bridge gained a 20C notoriety as the site of the 'Marco Polo Bridge Incident' of 7 July 1937, which provided the Japanese with a pretext for the invasion of north China. The Boxer Protocol of 1901 had allowed the establishment of a Japanese garrison in the area which had been holding manoeuvres by the bridge. Claiming that a soldier was missing, the troops attempted to search the small walled town of Wanping at the east end of the bridge. The Chinese garrison commander refused to let them in so they bombarded the town, occupied it, and commenced their total invasion of China from the north.

There is a small museum, **The Chinese People's Anti-Japanese War Memorial Hall** at 10 Chengnei Street, Wanping (closed Mondays; open 08.00–11.00, 13.00–16.30), commemorating the incident. There is also a **Museum of the History of the Marco Polo Bridge** beside the bridge.

It is possible to climb up onto the walls of **Wanping** from where you can look down into the courtyard houses below. Houses in the town (and throughout these western suburbs out to the Ordination Platform Temple, Jietai si) often have rather wonderful lattice windows, some with auspicious characters and symbols worked into them, some with the five pointed star of the army.

Beyond the bridge (48km from Peking) is **Zhoukoudian**, where Teilhard de Chardin found relics of **Peking Man** (of 300,000–500,000 years ago) in 1929. The first cranium excavated disappeared mysteriously during the Sino-Japanese War; some say it was taken by the Japanese for shipment to Japan, others that the Americans took it. Further fragments were found by Chinese archaeologists in the early 1950s.

Animal bones were associated with the early-man remains; it is also clear that fire was used in the caves. Teeth marks and breaks on some of the bones have led some to suggest the practice of cannibalism but it is also likely that animals were responsible.

Peking Man, otherwise known as *Sinanthropus pekinensis*, *Pithecanthropus pekinensis* and *Homo erectus pekinensis*, walked upright, had a considerable cranial capacity and used stone tools, lived mainly by hunting and cooking meat but also ate nuts. Some of the limestone caves on Longgu shan (Dragon Bone Hill) where the excavations were carried out can be visited.

A second group of early inhabitants have been distinguished: Upper Cave Man (of some 50,000 years ago). Upper Cave Man also worked bone and antlers into needles and necklaces and seems to have had a reasonably complex burial ritual (the Upper Cave remains seem to be those of a burial).

There is a museum at the site, illustrating both the finds of the site and the life of its earlier inhabitants and the development of man in general.

Yunju si

120km (75 miles) southwest of Peking are the remains of the Yunju si (Temple of the Habitation in the Clouds) and the stone sutras of **Fang shan**. The temple was founded during the Sui (6C) and almost completely destroyed by the Japanese during the War (1937–45). All that remains in this beautiful mountain site is a group of stupa pagodas. These include a group of four beautifully carved stone 'relic' pagodas or stupas with fine figures on each of its facets, dating from the Tang, surrounding a 30m Liao dynasty (907–1125) pagoda. There are also six Liao brick pagodas.

When I visited the site in 1984 with some of the first foreign visitors, apart from the modern buildings housing stone slabs and offices, there was nothing remaining of the temple save the pagodas and stupas. An article in the *China Daily* of 7 November 1987 states, however, that a 'restoration' of the temple is under way, which has so far included 'work on the Vairocana, Mahakaruna and Devajara Halls totalling 1500 square metres.' It may have been very sensitively undertaken but to the English eye, at least, the ruined stones, grass, wild flowers and surrounding mountains were extremely lovely and in no need of further restoration.

The founder of the temple, a monk called Jingyuan, began the work of carving the Buddhist sutras on stone, in imitation of the imperial carving of the Confucian classics on stone, a practice which began in the Han and was intended both to allow rubbings of the text to be taken before the development of woodblock printing and to lay down the 'authorised' version of the text. Carving of the sutras continued after his death, up to the Ming, and 4915 slabs were carved. Rubbings of the texts are still taken in the traditional manner, by inking the slab, spreading a sheet of fine paper over it and pounding it with a soft cloth pommel.

Although many of the sutra stones are now in the modern buildings beside the pagodas, they were originally housed in caves on top of the nearby Shi jing shan (Stone Sutra Mountain), across the railway line. It is possible to climb the picturesque mountain and see the caves where the slabs were stored.

Jietai si

Due west of Peking, beyond the enormous cement and steel works of Shijing shan, are two marvellous temples in the southern part of the Western Hills. The lower one, 35km from Peking, is the Jietai si (Temple of the Ordination Platform). It is on the slopes of Ma'an shan in the Mentougou area and was founded in 622. Its famous ordination platform was constructed during the Liao (907–1125) by a monk called Fa Jun. With the exception of the platform (which in its present form dates from the Ming) and some funerary stupas, the surviving buildings are Qing in date (and have been extensively restored in the early 1980s). Below and beside the temple is a 'cemetery', a group of finely carved funerary stupas in stone and brick (most imitating timber construction), dating from the Liao, Yuan and Ming, standing amongst **white-barked pines** against the red walls of the temple.

The present buildings are not intrinsically very interesting (and their sculptures are all modern), although the courtyard layout is very pleasing, as is the surrounding scenery. The trees in the courtyards are famous and they include 'pagoda pines, sleeping dragon pines, living pines and nine dragon pines'. A poem states: 'The Tanzhe Temple is famous for its spring, the Jietai for its pines'. One of the most famous of the pines has died and its original site is marked by a stone tablet on the left of the hall behind the main hall. It was known as the 'moving' pine because it was said that if one of its branches was touched, the entire tree would shake.

The Ordination Platform is some 3m high and must have been reached by temporary timber or bamboo structures when used (as it was annually). It is made of white marble in three tiers and carved with hundreds of figures, some c 1m high. It was used both for an annual gathering of local monks who came to hear their superiors preach from the terrace and also for ordination ceremonies of novices. Young monks and nuns who had served their noviciate would gather together, their heads freshly shaved. Part of the ceremony included the placing of rows of little piles of incense on their bald heads. These were burnt, leaving the classic marks of the true monk in the row of dotted scars on the shaved scalp.

Tanzhe si

The Tanzhe si (Temple of the Pool and the Mulberry) is 45km from the centre of Peking, beyond the Ordination platform Temple, on the Tanzhe shan (Pool and Mulberry Mountain) from which it takes its name, near Mentougou. The *tan* means 'pool' and the *zhe* stands for *Maclura tricuspidata* or *Cudrania tricuspidata*, a relative of the mulberry. The original *zhe* trees of the temple had apparently been cut down with only only stumps remaining in the 1930s but there is a small clump of new trees by the entrance now and they are, in the words of the Australian botanist Peter Valder, 'From an ornamental point of view ... nothing to write home about.' (*The Garden Plants of China*, 1999). As they were used to feed silkworms, their significance may have resided in their use rather than their appearance.

> The temple foundation is immensely old, dating back to the Jin (265–316); a popular saying describes its antiquity as being greater than that of Peking itself. The present buildings date from the Ming and Qing.

The forest of stupas below the temple includes funerary stupas from the Jin to the Qing and forms a marvellous approach to a temple which offers some wonderful views and venerable trees. It is built against a steep mountain slope, each court-yard towering over the next. On the central axis is a *pailou* archway, the gate-house (or 'mountain gate'), the Hall of Heavenly Kings, and the main hall, behind which was the Hall of the Three Sages, which no longer survives. Beside it stands the 'imperial tree', a gingko some 30m high with a span of 6–7m. It is said to date from the Yuan and its 'imperial title' was conferred by the Qianlong emperor of the Qing in the mid 18C. On the other side of the site of the hall is another tree, 'the emperor's wife', said to put forth a new branch every time a new emperor was born.

The highest point on the central axis is reached in the **Vairocana Hall**. The main hall is tiled with imperial yellow tiles with yellow ridge acroteria for the temple enjoyed especial imperial favour under Khubilai Khan (whose daughter was buried here) and Qianlong who built a 'travelling palace' in the eastern axis of the temple (in which visitors can still stay overnight).

On the western axis is a modest ordination platform and **Guanyin Hall** (amongst others), while the western axis is composed of more domestic court-yards. Amongst them is a 'cup-floating pavilion' (similar to that in the Forbidden City, see p 125), called the **Yilan ting** (Pavilion of Ripples). The floor has a curl-ing groove where water from the Dragon Spring was led in and imperial guests would float winecups and play a forfeit game which involved composing a line of poetry if a cup floated towards them.

There is a marvellous view of mountains from the high terrace of the temple which is one of the most beautifully sited in China.

> This was the temple that the novelist Ann Bridge (the pen-name of Lady O'Malley, whose husband served in the British Embassy in Peking during the 1920s and 1930s) used as the major setting for *Peking Picnic* (1932). It was

common practice at the time for Peking residents to take themselves off to the temples of the Western Hills during the hot, humid summer:

Nothing is stranger to the new-comer to China than this custom of temple author-ities of throwing open their sacred precincts to European visitors. A courtyard or two, or three, according to their needs, is let off to each party, and there with their beds, food, chairs and servants they establish themselves for a day or two.

Some famous Peking residents, such as Sir Reginald Johnston, tutor to the last emperor, hired temples on a long-term basis (Johnston re-named his tem-ple 'Cherry Glen') and spent much time there; temporary visitors in the 1930s were recommended to 'take bedding and provisions'. Ann Bridge's characters first spend a night in the Jietai si which at the time was, like the Tanzhe si, still a practising religious centre. She describes how the visitors moved on to the Tanzhe si to view the 'imperial' gingko and its 'wife', how 'the whole temple was full of the gentle voice of water', the hillsides planted with thujas, and the cemetery below the temple where Khubilai's daughter the nun was buried. The story continues, involving a bandit attack in this idyllic setting, and an escape up the mountainside which you can re-run if you take the novel with you.

Tanzhe si, southwest of Peking, from Hong xue yin yuan, The illustrated autobiography of Linqing, *1847–50*

Tombs of the Qing Emperors

The two groups of Tombs of the Qing Emperors, the Dong ling (Eastern Tombs) and Xi ling (Western Tombs) are c 125km and 135km from Peking (in opposite directions as their names suggest). Their distance makes a day trip something of an ordeal: the Eastern Tombs can be seen by making (quite) a detour on the road to Tianjin. It is best to see the Ming tombs first for the Qing tombs, although beautifully sited, are almost parodies of those of the Ming.

The Eastern Tombs were the first to be used (by the first and second Qing emperors) and the first tomb in the western group is that of the (third) Yongzheng emperor who died in 1735. Thus the Ming practice of sons building their tombs adjacent, or close, to those of their fathers, was broken in the Qing. The tombs themselves are much smaller than those of the Ming, with funny little stumps of mounds, although some of the preceding halls are extremely grand, and the bridges and streams of the Eastern Tombs are relatively elaborate. The carving of the spirit way figures is far cruder than seen in the Ming tombs.

Eastern Tombs

The Eastern Tombs (Xi ling) are in Zunhua xian (county), north of the road that runs between Ji xian and Zunhua, set against the foothills of the Changrui Mountains.

The journey now takes some three to four hours depending on traffic problems; it is extraordinary to think that in 1924 the *Japanese Railway Guide* stated that it took nearly a week to reach them from Peking, 'on four days of which crude native means of transport or horses have to be used'.

Five emperors are buried here: Shunzhi (the first Qing emperor, d. 1661), Kangxi (the second Qing emperor, d. 1722), Qianlong (the fourth emperor, d. 1799), Xianfeng (the seventh emperor, d. 1881) and Tongzhi (the eighth emperor, d. 1875) as well as 14 empresses (including the Dowager Empress Cixi (d. 1908) and 136 concubines. The whole cemetery area which was previously enclosed as a forbidden area, covers 48 square km and is ideally sited to accord with *feng shui* beliefs with hills behind to the north and a flat plain with a river (the Xida he), from which a canal was led, in front.

Three tombs have been restored and opened to the public: those of the Qianlong emperor (the Yu ling or Fortunate Tomb), his empress and concubine Rong (the Yufei or Fortunate Concubine's Tomb) and the pair of tombs in which the Empress Dowager Cixi and the senior consort Ci'an were buried (known as the Ci'an and Cixi Tombs).

Ci'an was the empress of the Xianfeng emperor (d. 1862), although Cixi, originally a lowly concubine, was raised in rank when she bore the emperor's only heir, the Tongzhi emperor (d. 1875). As he was a child when he succeeded his father, the two women acted as his regents (having got rid of the official regents), although the less ambitious Ci'an was seen as being under the thumb of the ruthless Cixi and was widely believed to have been poisoned by her when she died in 1881.

The enclosure is entered through a stone archway, beside which is the **Zhaoxi Tomb** (of a concubine) and behind which is a great red gate and a robing hall. Behind that is a stele pavilion and the spirit road then leads to the row of stone statues and the dragon and phoenix gate. This spirit road leads directly to the tomb of the Shunzhi emperor, **Xiao ling** or Filial Tomb. Off to the right (east) are the **Hui ling Tombs**, those of the Tongzhi emperor and a concubine, illustrating the common Qing practice, at variance with that of the Ming emperors, of constructing paired but separate tombs for emperors and their concubines. To the left of the main spirit road, a subsidiary line of stone animals sandwiched between another stele pavilion and stone gateway leads to the **Yu ling Tomb** of the Qianlong emperor and (further to the left) the **Cixi** and **Ci'an Tombs**, with the **Ding ling** (Secure Tomb) of the Xian feng emperor at the far left (west) end approached by yet another small spirit way.

> In plan, the tombs are similar to those of the Ming emperors—rectangular in front (representing the earth), circular behind (representing heaven). Each is preceded by a turtle stele in a pavilion, the base surrounded by a fish, crab, prawn and turtle emerging from the waves and a smaller stele or stone horse instructing officials to dismount for, as in the Forbidden City and the Ming tombs, they had to proceed on foot. The arrangement of water, which had to lie in front of the tomb according to the *feng shui* belief, is very elegant, with flattish triple bridges of white marble crossing broad expanses of water.

In the long rectangular courtyard in front, the **Sheng'en dian** (Hall of Great Compassion) stands in the centre with (unlike the Ming tombs) side wings for the display and inspection of grave goods, for Lamaist prayers and kitchens (described as 'pastry and food halls') on either side of the courtyard. A gateway leads to the rear courtyard where, behind the gate with its *qilin* topped pillars, a stone altar with stone 'ritual vessels' stands before the stele tower in front of the burial mound itself.

Although the Qianlong emperor's tomb has a grassy mound, the later mounds are rounded, asphalted tumps (not the rustic, tree-covered hills of the Ming emperors) and below, the underground palaces are also treated in a different manner. Far less effort was expended in concealing the entrance to the burial chamber, but far more on decorating its stone walls and doors with very fine low relief carvings of Buddhist figures and Buddhist inscriptions. This Buddhist theme is even carried over into the official figures of the spirit ways who wear Buddhist rosaries instead of carrying the ivory tablets used by officials at court and depicted in the figures at the Ming tombs. The attention paid to the decoration of the inner chamber (contrasted with the simple brick vault of the Ming tombs) recalls earlier burial traditions as can be seen, for example, in the Tang royal tombs near Xi'an.

> The tombs of Qianlong and Cixi were robbed by soldiers of a minor warlord, Sun Tianying, in 1928, when it is said that the body of Cixi was frighteningly well-preserved. Manchu nobles went to the scene of desecration and reburied the bodies but it was too late to recover much of the jewellery.
>
> The last emperor, Pu Yi, who was then in nearby Tianjin, is said to have been enraged by the news that some of the pearls from Cixi's phoenix crown had found their way onto the toes of Mme Chiang Kai-shek's shoes. Cixi's jewellery was legendary. Sir Edmund Backhouse (1873–1944), a peculiar

adventurer who purchased some fine palace editions for his alma mater, Oxford University, attempted to sell guns that he did not have and claimed to have slept with every notable of the late 19C from Lord Roseberry, Verlaine and Oscar Wilde to Cixi herself, also claimed to possess a jacket made entirely of huge pearls that had belonged to Cixi.

There are, however, a very wide range of items on exhibit in the hall of Cixi's tomb and other halls: fine robes, some of which display a slightly European influence, most notably a spring robe embroidered with wisteria and decorated with imported butterfly lace panels. Some of the garments, worn by the deceased, are very tattered. There are small gilt-bronze Buddhist images (in the Tibetan or Lamaist style), altar sets, food-serving dishes and compartmented trays for sweetmeats, a great collection of unguents and medicines including bear fat (for the hair) and tigerbone ointment in a porcelain jar decorated with birds amongst roses. Dominoes, playing cards and theatrical robes are displayed with a stern notice describing Cixi's luxurious and spendthrift habits, as is a stuffed Pekinese dog wearing a blue and purple damask jacket. Cixi had many dogs, mostly small Pekinese or Lhasa terriers, all with their own wardrobes and all of whom had their portrait painted.

There is also a fascinating collection of turn-of-the-century western cigarette packets, and cigarette cards, Muratti's after-lunch cigarettes (London and Manchester), Duke's Cameo cigarettes (with cards) and a tin of King Whiff extra-length high-grade Virginia cigarettes. Clocks in glass domes were made in France and imported by Allman and Co. of Shanghai and Hong Kong or Kieruff's of Peking. There are tattered garments of the Qianlong emperor and some dirty old *hada* (white scarves traditionally presented by and to Lamas), earrings, hairpieces, strings of pearls, jade *ruyi* sceptres, a 'good-luck hat' which looks like an army cap that has seen better times, sedan chairs, military uniforms and weapons and many locks and hinges from the boxes that held the grave goods.

Western Tombs

The Western Tombs are 120km southwest of Peking, 15km west of Yixian below the Yongning Mountains.

There used to be a railway line to Lianggezhuang (until 1906 forbidden to the public) to enable the court to get to the tombs in five hours (followed by an hour's donkey ride). The site was chosen at the order of the Yongzheng emperor in 1730, despite the existence of the earlier Eastern Tombs complex. Yongzheng's successor, the Qianlong emperor, decided to be buried next to his grandfather at the Eastern Tombs. Qianlong suggested that emperors should henceforth alternate between the two sites but this practice was not followed.

Interred at the Western Tombs are the Yongzheng (d. 1736, buried in the Tai ling or Peaceful Tomb), Jiaqing (d. 1821, buried in the Chang ling or Flourishing Tomb), Dao guang (d. 1851 and buried in the Mu ling or Admiration Tomb) and Guangxu (d. 1908 and buried in the Chong ling or Lofty Tomb), emperors, as well as their consorts and a number of concubines, in 14 tombs altogether. The area covers some 100 square km and was surrounded by a wall 21km long.

The tombs and the associated Lama temple have red walls and yellow tiled roofs, while those of the wives, princes and concubines have red walls and green tiled roofs (reflecting a distinction that can also be seen in Peking's architecture). The main tomb is that of the Yongzheng emperor, to which the spirit road with its animal figures and stele gate leads. With the exception of the tomb of the Daoguang emperor, the other tombs are all similar in construction.

The major tomb, the **Tai ling**, is approached through a great red gate, with a robing hall inside and a 30m high stele pavilion with a yellow tiled roof. Beyond is the row of carved stone animals and a small hill which serves as a spirit wall. The dragon and phoenix gate lies behind the hill, embellished with dragons and clouds in carved glazed tilework. Inside the tomb enclosure, the main hall, with brightly painted ceilings and gilded pillars, is flanked by side halls and small stoves for burning offerings. In the mound behind the stele tower, the Yongzheng emperor was, unusually, buried with his empress and concubines.

The **Mu ling**, the westernmost of the tombs, also holds the bodies of the Daoguang emperor and his three empresses. His grave had originally been constructed in the Eastern Tomb Cemetery but, after one empress had been buried there, the tomb was flooded (apparently construction had been skimped) so another tomb was started in the Western Tombs Cemetery. It is rather small, lacking a stele pavilion, row of stone animals and stele tower. The main hall is built of unpainted *nanmu* cedar with carved windows, beams and ceiling. The wood is fragrant so it is said of this hall, filled with carved dragons, that 'ten-thousand dragons are gathered, puffing out incense from their mouths'.

The most recent tomb, that of the Guangxu emperor who died in 1908, was not begun until 1909 and he was buried there with his empress in 1915, well into the Republican period. The tomb is small, lacking a stele pavilion and avenue of animals, and the workmanship is poor, with nails used on the timber structure of the hall. The setting, however, with silver and lohan pines and a surrounding orchard, is very pretty.

Also in **Yixian** (the nearest town) is a temple, the **Kaiyuan si**, founded during the twenty-sixth year of the Kai yuan reign period of the Tang (738).

Shijiazhuang, c 230km southwest of Peking, is the capital of Hebei province. The town grew with the railways from the late 19C to become the Crewe of China, standing at the junction of three main lines. It has major textile factories and is also the current site of Norman Bethune's grave.

Norman Bethune

Born in 1880, Bethune was a Canadian surgeon who made significant contributions to thoracic surgery and volunteered as a doctor, first in Spain during the Civil War. There he realised the importance of quick treatment and mobile blood-transfusion units, to prevent wounded soldiers dying unnecessarily from shock and blood loss. He continued these methods, as far as possible, in China where he arrived in 1938. Unfortunately, he died in the same year of septicaemia, after cutting himself during an operation, illustrating the pressures under which front-line surgeons worked. He was first buried elsewhere, but his body, together with that of the Indian Dr Kotnis, who had also volunteered to work with the Red Army, was moved to Shijiazhuang for the convenience of visitors.

12km north of Shijiazhuang, in **Zhengding**, is the **Longxing Temple**, famous for its colossal bronze Guanyin figure (more than 22m tall, cast in the late 10C), and its revolving library, similar to that on Wutai shan.

Tianjin

Tianjin is one of the major maritime ports of China, c 120km southeast of Peking. It lies on the Hai River, at the junction with the Grand Canal, some 30km from the coast (at Tanggu).

Opened to foreign trade in 1860 by the Convention of Peking, separate foreign concessions were quickly opened in the city, Austrian, Italian and Russian and Belgian running west to east along the north bank of the Hai River, Japanese, French, British and German running west to east along the south bank. After the First World War the German and Austro-Hungarian Concessions were renamed 'Special Districts' and reverted to Chinese control. The closeness of the concessions and their retention of separate control (as opposed to the mixed 'International Settlement' of Shanghai) has meant that the separate areas are still architecturally distinct. The British Concession had its solid bank buildings and the Scottish baronial of Gordon Hall, château-like roofs and towers characterise the French Concession and strange modernistic buildings were to be found in the ex-German Concession.

Tianjin, now a sprawling industrial centre whose size (with over nine million inhabitants in the entire municipal territory) has been acknowledged in its status which is equivalent to that of a province, suffered greatly in the 1976 Tangshan earthquake. Its recovery was dramatic, largely owing to the efforts of the then mayor, Li Ruihuan, an ex-carpenter.

Li Ruihuan

Dangerous as it is in days of political ups and downs to single out personalities, Li Ruihuan had a considerable effect on the city. He was locally born in 1934 and worked as a construction worker in Peking from 1951 to 1965, joining the Communist Party in 1959. His bureaucratic career started in 1965 but took off after 1971. He was then based in Peking (where he was concurrently secretary of the Party Committee of the Peking Construction Timber Plant, deputy secretary of the Party Committee of the Peking Bureau of Building Materials, Vice-chairman of the Peking Capital Construction Commission, Director of the headquarters of the Peking Capital Construction Commission, Vice-chairman of the Peking Trades Union Federation, a permanent member of the All-China Federation of Trades Unions and a member of the Standing Committee of the Fifth National People's Congress). In 1981 he moved to Tianjin where he became a member of the Standing Committee of the Communist Party of Tianjin, Deputy Mayor, Party Secretary, Acting Mayor and Mayor of Tianjin (this list, which I assume should be understood to represent a sequence of posts, was taken from the *China Daily*).

Since the Tiananmen massacre of 1989, Li has been moved away from Tianjin, to higher office in Peking, in control of censorship. Recently leaked papers recording the reactions of senior officials during the Tiananmen demonstrations (and subsequent massacre) in 1989 reveal Li Ruihuan to have been part of a conciliatory and liberal minority.

Practical information

Getting there
By air

There are flights to and from Tianjin to most major cities except Peking which is too close. The airport is some 15km east of the city. Airport buses deliver passengers to the *CAAC* office at 242 Heping lu in the centre of town. Taxis from the airport cost about 50 yuan. Tianjin is probably best visited from Peking by bus or train. It can be used as a transit stop for those going southwards by train to Shanghai or northwards to Beidaihe.

By train

There are three railways stations in Tianjin but the most convenient (a stop for most of the trains to and from Peking) is the main station, on the north bank of the Hai River, just opposite the iron bridge that leads to the French Concession on the south side. Tianjin is very conveniently reached from Peking by double-decker trains which leave every hour from 07.00 and take up to 90 minutes.

By bus

The opening of the Peking–Tianjin expressway has meant that the bus trip (from the west side of the car park in front of Peking Railway Station to the main railway station in Tianjin) takes 2½ to 3 hours. Although longer than the train trip, it is much cheaper. There are also direct buses from Tianjin to Peking airport.

Getting around

There is a subway in Tianjin but it has only one line, running from the West Station to Yingkou dao (following Nanjing lu) so it is only really useful if you want to do the length of Nanjing lu.

Where to stay

The best old hotel is the *Astor House Hotel* in the British Concession, 199 Jiefang bei lu, ☎ 23311688, fax: 23316282. Its timbered halls and dining rooms dark wood double staircase and original entrance have been left intact whilst the back entrance (33 Taierzhuang lu now the main reception area) has been internationalised, as have the rooms. Its Chinese name is (and always has been) *Lishun Fandian* or Profit and Success Hotel. Just down the road are the twin towers of the odd-looking *Tianjin Hyatt* (complete with presidential suite), the first new high-rise building to despoil the city. It is at 219 Jeifang bei lu, ☎ 23301234, fax: 23311234. There is now a wide range of foreign hotels (*Sheraton*, *Hilton*, etc) in Tianjin though some are inconveniently located. They are provided with copies of little English-language papers produced for local ex-patriates which list special events, 'night-clubs' and local places of interest.

History

Tianjin's history is surprisingly short for it stands on an area that was originally under water and only gradually silted up to become inhabitable. It was first mentioned as a trading port during the Song dynasty, growing during the Ming (and being surrounded by a wall in 1404) when it was apparently colonised by people from Anhui (presumably because opportunities were lacking in that province which has been described as the Appalachians of China) and the Tianjin dialect is said to reflect this migration. In the 18C the river-port town was extremely prosperous as was noted by members of the first Dutch embassy in 1655: '... surrounded by sturdy walls over 25 feet high with watchtowers ... the town has many temples: it is thickly populated and trade is very brisk ... because all the boats which go to Peking, whatever their port of origin, call here ...'.

The first **European settlers** were Anglo-French troops in 1860 (after the Treaty of Tianjin, 1858, was ratified in Peking, 1860) and the concession areas soon sprang up south of the Chinese town on both sides of the Hai River. In 1870 Tianjin was, in the eyes of Europeans, 'disgraced by the Tianjin massacre' when ten Sisters of Charity (mostly French with one Irish and one Italian sister), two Lazarist priests and an entire congregation mainly of Chinese orphans were killed by a mob which also claimed a Russian merchant (Protopopoff) and his wife, a French merchant (M. Chalmaison) and his wife, and the French consul. It was said that the riot started as a result of the belief that the Sisters of Charity kidnapped Chinese orphans for sinister purposes (there was a Chinese belief that railway lines required a human sacrifice under each sleeper) though in fact the mob first attacked the French Consulate so it may be considered as generally anti-foreign. Twenty or more Chinese were beheaded as a result, a considerable amount of money was awarded in recompense and the Prefect and Sub-prefect of Tianjin were 'banished to the Amur province, with hard labour'.

Life for foreigners in pre-Liberation (or pre-Japanese invasion) Tianjin was luxurious, with pastries and hot chocolate served in *Kiessling and Bader's Restaurant* (see p 226) as violinists played Strauss amongst the palms, bands playing in Victoria Park, Gordon Hall illuminated like Harrods for the coronation of George VI, the Empire Cinema (where the violinist from Kiessling's also performed), shops like those of Shanghai—Whiteway, Laidlow and Co., Aux Nouveautes in the French settlement—and the whole governed (in the British settlement at least) by regulations. Chinese nursemaids (*amahs*) required non-transferable passes before being allowed into Victoria Park with their small white charges and were to note 'That the cenotaph being a memorial to the dead, Amahs must exercise the greatest vigilance to prevent the children under their care from playing on the Cenotaph steps, or from touching any flowers or wreaths that may be deposited thereupon.' No dogs or bicycles were allowed although 'this Rule does not preclude wheeled toys for children such as bicycles, wooden horses, etc'. Regulations covered everything from the running of Aerated Water Factories (first in the long list of licensed premises' regulations in the 1920 'Municipal Handbook') to 'the maximum quantity of loose straw which may be stored in a Chinese house or shop at one time is TWO piculs' (their capitals) and, in re bicycles, brakes, bells and lights were required and 'Furious riding' was forbidden on the roads of the Concession.

Tianjin was a centre for traditionalist Chinese secret societies and anti-foreign movements in the 19C (whilst Shanghai tended to conceal more of the modern anti-colonialists); the **White Lotus Society** (Bailian hui), a secret society of long-standing which dated back to well before the Ming, was, and some say still is, strong in the area. The Ming founder, Zhu Yuanzhong, was associated with the White Lotus, a millenarian popular society influenced both by Buddhism and Manicheanism, although once he became emperor he turned on secret societies for they were almost invariably anti-imperial. The Manichean influence on the White Lotus is clear in its vocabulary and stress on 'light' and the name of the Ming dynasty (*ming* means 'bright' or 'shining') and the Buddhist influence is clear in the name of the society and its enthusiasm for a non-canonical Buddhist work, the *Mu niu* (*Taming the Ox*) classic where the illustrations depict a black ox slowly turning white as it is tamed by a small boy, implying the possibility of the taming of the self or self-cultivation. The White Lotus were active throughout the late 19C and early 20C, capturing rice-laden junks on the Grand Canal and setting fire to the Standard Oil Company's storage tanks in 1929 and, under cover of the confusion, seizing grain from the old imperial granary. The shorter-lived but more terrifying **Boxers**, who rose against the imperial dynasty in 1900 but quickly (with imperial assistance) turned their murderous attention to the foreign community in the north of China were also active and perhaps connected with the White Lotus movement in Tianjin and the surrounding countryside.

The *Japanese Railway Guide* for 1924 noted that: 'situated on a large sandy plain, without hills or mountains to retrieve the view [Tianjin] has scarcely any place in its neighbourhood noted for the beauty of natural scenery, nor has it many temples or other works of ancient art as its importance only began with the opening to foreign trade in 1860'. It was, until recently, a neat and compact treaty port with the most varied foreign architecture to be seen (and many treasures perhaps to be found: I have spent days searching for the expressionist factory of A. Faust and Co., but so far have failed to track it down).

Sites to visit in Tianjin include the Mosque, the Museum, the Dabeiyuan Monastery and the Wenhua jie area with the Tianhou gong Temple and Folk Art Museum. These completed, Tianjin is small enough for walks through the British, German and French Concessions. These are fast being replaced by high-rise buildings: remnants of colonial architecture can be seen but the Italian concession on the east side of the Hai river is relatively untouched.

North Tianjin

The Mosque, the Dabei yuan, Wenhua jie, the Luzu tang, Wanghai lou and Santiaoshi Museum are all in the north of the city and could be seen in a rather full morning's taxi ride.

The Mosque, **Qingzhen da si**, is in the northwest corner of the old Chinese city, just off Dafeng lu, near Xiaohuo xiang. The streets are incredibly narrow, so if you are travelling by car you may have to park some 100m away from the wrought-iron entrance to the mosque. Founded in 1703, it is a well-preserved example of a Chinese mosque, with minaret, entrance hall, prayer hall, study hall, side rooms and washing pool. The prayer hall is oriented east–west and its

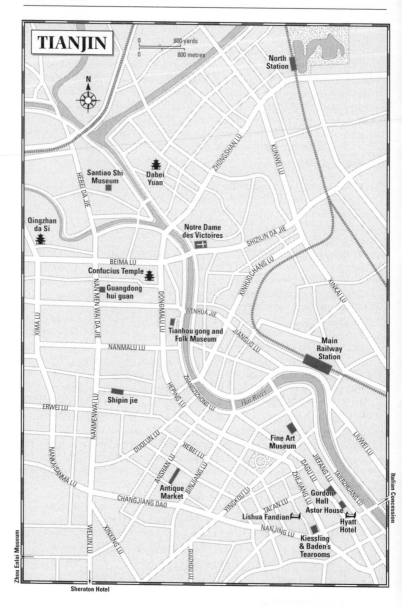

size is achieved through a four-roof construction with a complex pavilion-like roof at the rear, all with unusually upturned eaves for a northern building. Inside the two little pavilions are boards bearing the characters for 'looking at the moon' and 'time for sound' indicating the importance of time (for prayers) and the noisy call to prayer for Muslims.

The windows and much of the timber of the mosque is very beautifully carved with floral designs (following the tradition of not depicting the human form), combining this Islamic tradition with a Chinese woodcarving tradition.

As the mosque is an active centre of worship, visitors are no longer allowed inside the halls. A new mosque is being built near **Shenyang jie** (the antique market street, see p 222, which opens early and closes down by about 3.30 pm).

The **Dabei yuan Temple** is on the far side of the narrow Ziya he (Ziya River). Between the mosque and the temple is the **Santiaoshi bowuguan** (Santiaoshi Museum) in the centre of the old industrial quarter of Tianjin where, in the 17C and 18C, before the arrival of foreigners, metalwork and machinery of all kinds was produced, contributing to the trading and industrial reputation of Tianjin.

In 1926 the Fujuxing factory was set up in the area, producing watercarts (important in those pre-sewer days: the *Japanese Railway Guide* noted in 1924 that 'the lower-class natives depend mostly on the river for their drinking water ... almost any day there may be seen along the river many wheelbarrows, each loaded with a water barrel ...), 'ox-headed' planing machines, oil-presses and other pieces of machinery that 'were exported to other provinces. Apprenticeships were encouraged. The original equipment and workshops have been preserved as part of the museum.

Beyond the Industrial Museum is the **Dabei yuan** (Temple of Great Compassion) at no. 26 Tianwei lu, the largest and best-preserved Buddhist temple in Tianjin. It consists of two parts, the old temple (founded not long before 1669; since Tianjin is a relatively new city, its temples do not trace their foundation back to the 3C as so many others do) and the new temple, founded in 1940. The 1940 extensions (including the 'Hall of Heavenly Doorkeepers', Mahavira or Great Hall and the Dabei Hall) were made after Tan Zu, a monk and noted calligrapher, had collected contributions. Despite severe damage during the 1976 earthquake, the temple was restored in 1980 and many of the old pine trees survived.

The temple used to contain a holy relic, part of Xuan zang's cranium (see Xi'an, Big Goose Pagoda and Fayuan si, Peking) which was apparently presented to the Nalanda Temple in India in 1956 (though there is still a Hall of Xuan zang's cranium in the Dabei yuan). The western courtyard houses the head-quarters of the Buddhist Association of Tianjin and a **Cultural Relics Hall** which displays the best Buddhist relics found in the Tianjin area. Made of bronze, iron, wood and stone, they date back to the Nan bei chao (420–581).

Also on the north side of the Ziya River, just south of the major bridge which crosses it just south of the point where the Grand Canal joins the river, is the **Wanghai lou** (Sea-watching Tower) or **Notre Dame des Victoires** (Shengmu desheng tang). It stands just to the north of a smaller bridge across the Hai River, the Shizi lin qiao (Bridge of the Forest of Stone Lions).

The cathedral was built by the French Lazarists in 1869 and burnt down during the Tianjin massacre (known more delicately in Chinese as the 'Religious incident at Tianjin') in the following year. In 1897 it was rebuilt with money from the Qing government demanded in recompense by the foreign settlers, only to be burnt down again in 1900 during the Boxer Uprising. The current building is the third, built in 1904 and is said to be very similar to the earlier constructions with stained glass and very pretty floor tiles inside. The interior is only open to the public on Sundays when services are held.

Wenhua jie

One of the most spectacular rebuilding efforts of the post-earthquake administration under Mayor Li Ruihuan is the **Wenhua jie** or **'Ancient Culture Street'** which is on the west side of the Hai River, just south of the Sea-watching Tower. The area is similar to (but larger than) the Liulichang area of Peking, an old shopping centre with traditional Chinese shops (rather than the grand foreign department stores of Heping lu, previously Asahi gai/Rue du Chaylard). It is quite prettily restored and, as a pedestrian area, pleasant to wander in. Shops on the Wenhua jie offer an enormous range of the locally-produced '*niren*/mud figures', now brightly-painted and frequently sold in pairs. There are also antique shops selling all sorts of things from paintings to bronzes and stalls with fridge magnets and other trinkets.

Tianhou gong and the Folk Museum

Wenhua jie lies to the side of one of the major temples of Tianjin, reflecting its maritime and riverine situation, the **Tianhou gong** (Hall of the Heavenly Empress).

> According to legend, the Heavenly Empress (sometimes known as Niangniang, the Good Mother) was a local sailor's daughter who saved her father from a shipwreck. A temple was built in her honour where sailors would bring a model of their ship to pray for her protection. It is interesting to note that Nagel's guide (very extensive and impressive and compiled in the late 1960s) states that 'the temple still existed in 1936 but has now disappeared' for it was rebuilt (on the original site) in 1985.

The temple, apparently founded in 1326, now houses an interesting **Folk Museum** (open 09.00–17.30). The main hall has a statue of Tianhou with Buddhist figures and there are the usual temple guardians in the first gate hall (thus the mixing of established and popular religions). Surrounding the inner courtyard are a number of small exhibition halls. The first hall contained gongs and bowls (also to be struck) and other implements once used in the temple and a mud sculpture of a construction worker apparently trying to extract a dragon from a stone. There are a number of other smaller brown 'mud people' (*ni ren*), tiny figures which used to be made on the streets by local pedlars and were an acclaimed speciality of the Tianjin streets. Brian Power, brought up in Tianjin, describes in his haunting book about a Tianjin childhood (*The Ford of Heaven*, London, Peter Owen, 1984) how the pedlars made the figures:

> The high back wall of the granary formed one side of the marketplace. Against this wall the acrobats story-tellers, magicians and conjurors performed ... Next to the conjurors sat a row of men making little figures about 6 inches high out of different coloured clay mixed with water. The figures were called ni ren in Chinese which meant 'mud men'. You could ask for anything you wished, an opera singer, dancer, mandarin or warrior. Some of the ni ren makers were especially good at making soldiers. They would watch the foreign soldiers parading in the streets and within minutes they could make a lifelike figure of the commanding officer. Sometimes they got into trouble with the police over their caricatures and were banned.

The *ni ren* were apparently the invention of a man named Zhang in the 19C (they are also mentioned favourably by Pierre Loti in *Les Derniers Jours de Peking*, 1901) and his descendants still make them and sell them on Wenhua jie, though they are now less political and covered in bright paint.

In the museum are mud figures showing the dramas and entertainments (acrobats, stilt dancers) performed on the day sacred to the Heavenly Empress (23rd day of the 3rd month of the lunar calendar). There are also examples of the woodblocks of Yangliuqing, one of the major centres of popular colour printing in China.

Yangliuqing

From the 16C this village near Tianjin (now in the western suburbs and worth visiting for its domestic architecture, see below) became one of the major centres producing brightly coloured 'New Year Pictures' (*nianhua*) which had their origin in the pictures of door gods and seasonal calendars that people pasted up on their walls at the New Year (following a great spring cleaning). By the early 17C Yangliuqing was producing some 20 million pictures a year (in two editions in spring and autumn, with particular care being devoted to the spring or New Year pictures). The pictures were produced from multiple woodblocks in bright colours (and production in the traditional manner has now been moved to Changchun jie in Tianjin itself; the workshop can be visited by arrangement through tourist agencies). Smaller items of folk art on display in the museum include hair ornaments (of a sort of felt), kites (a known Tianjin speciality), papercuts, spinning tops and other toys, and in the second hall there is a lovely collection of the model boats presented to the Heavenly Empress, all painted with big eyes on the prow (to ward off evil spirits). There are high-backed seagoing junks like those that can still be seen on the coast. There is a nice fire engine and a large display of items relating to traditional shops: big blue jars in which soy sauce was sold, biscuit moulds, toffee (crab) apples, a pedlar's portable stove and models of the *goubuli baozi* that are the most famous delicacy of Tianjin.

The name of these meat-stuffed dumplings means 'dogs wouldn't touch them' and is sometimes said to refer to the dumplings themselves (food for the poor) and sometimes to the hideousness of the man who is said to have invented them. The major outlet for them today is the *Goubuli restaurant* near the corner of Binjiang lu and Xinhua bei lu in the '**Food street**' shopping centre. Other attractions in Food street include deep-fried dough twists in a wide variety of sizes. As Tianjin is famous for these dough twists, they are the sort of gift that Chinese visitors carry away from Tianjin.

The shop signs on display used to hang down from carved wooden shopfronts and are sometimes self-explanatory: shoes and pipes, but sometimes mysterious: a wooden fish or a child and fishes means a medicine shop, a string of coins and silver ingots means a sort of primitive bank (money shop), a double gourd indicates a doctor's establishment.

There is a model of a marriage procession and examples of all sorts of items associated with marriage from the red bridal-gown with red scarf to cover the face, and children's clothing including tiger shoes, pig shoes and patchwork 'hundred family' jackets where different family members donate different bits of cloth and the garment is supposed to convey a hundred years of life on the child. The little metal lockets children wore around their necks were also called 'hundred family' for the same reason but they were often shaped like Chinese locks to 'lock' the child to life. There is a child's tiny abacus and a copy of the 'San zi jing' (Three

Character Classic, by which children learned to read through memorising a series of three-character phrases about Chinese history and folklore) and some examples of the funny backless aprons that tiny children wore in hot summers.

There is a small household temple to hold the household gods, equipment used by geomancers in siting houses (compasses and textbooks), garments of all sorts and a huge variety of cricket-cages in which prized fighting crickets were kept (especially during winter). Cricket-cages were, and are, often made of gourds with finely carved lids. Birdcages, also displayed, are of equal importance to bird-lovers and often highly decorated and provided with tiny porcelain water and seed pots. There are teapots and tea-nests, locks and keys and a fine hand-warmer—a small metal container with a handle and an openwork top, to be filled with charcoal and slipped carefully into long sleeves on cold days.

The **Luzu tang** is closed and surrounded by one of the largest areas of urban clearance I have ever seen. The temple is visible, however, and in quite good condition so it is likely to re-open (and it is listed in the Tianjin Municipal Government's Tianjin Guide (1998). The address is 18 Hejia hutong, Ruyian Street, Hongqiao district and it is described as the 'Tianjin Boxers Memorial Hall' so it was strange to find it closed in the centenary year. The temple was originially a Daoist foundation, dedicated to the worship of Lu Dongbin, one of the 'Eight immortals' of Daoism. Supposedly a real person who lived from 755–805, 'He was 5 feet 2 inches in height and at twenty was still unmarried' (E.T.C. Werner, *Dictionary of Chinese Mythology* 1932, 1961, p 348), he met a fire dragon who presented him with a magic sword. Using his sword rather like a skate-board, he zipped through the clouds, 'slaying dragons and ridding the earth of divers kinds of evils, during a period of upward of four hundred years' which is a bit difficult to reconcile with the traditional date of his death. The temple was taken over by Cao Futian, a Boxer leader, in 1900, to 'guide the Boxer fight against invading imperialists'. It was rebuilt in 1985 and made into the Boxer Memorial Hall.

The **antique market** (open early in the morning and largely finished by 15.30), is at the crossroads of Shenyang lu and Shandong lu in Heping district. Bargaining is important, as is the need to retain a certain cynicism about the antiquity of many of the items offered for sale. If you like an object and the price is acceptable then it is worth buying even if it does not turn out to be a museum piece.

West Tianjin

In the west of the city, though not far from Wehuajie, on Nanmen nei da jie is the **Guangdong hui guan** (Guangdong Guildhall). To reach it from Nankai, turn left along Nankai er wei lu and take the second major turning on the left. The Guildhall is a little way up the road, on your right. It is the largest and best-preserved guildhall and 'locality' temple in Tianjin (in the 1920s, the Zhejiang, Fujian, Jiangsu and Shanxi merchants also had fine guildhalls). Serving as a trade centre for locals of Guangdong province, the guildhall was very beautifully constructed, in the southern style. It has a gate, main hall and a particularly well-preserved stage (for guild dramas and local operas to be performed). The ceiling is in the 'chicken coop' style and the four characters Tian guan ci fu (May the heavenly officials bestow good fortune) are painted on the back wall. The hall now houses an opera museum.

Just east of the Theatre Museum/Guangdong guild hall is the **Confucian Temple**: a group of largely empty buildings with a fine half-moon pool in the first courtyard, a stone-lined pool crossed by a stone bridge. There is little that recalls the worship and cult of Confucius and unlike the Confucian temple in Beijing, there are no stone stelae listing local examination candidates names.

The **Fine Art Museum** (Yishu bowuguan; open 08.30–12.00, 13.30–17.00) is at 77 Jiefang bei lu in the old French quarter. The street used to be called Rue de France until it crossed Bristow Road (today's Yingkou dao) the border of the British Concession, when it turned into Victoria Road. The museum (founded in 1928) is in a grand old building which is not entirely suited to its present function. The permanent collections on display include a great number of *ni ren* or mud men figures, many by the Zhang family, and a considerable display of Yangliuqing woodblock new year prints. There is also a major display of silhouette shadow puppets made from coloured donkey skin.

Some of the other collections of the museum which are shown in special or temporary exhibitions include Tianjin carved bricks (used to decorate doorways), woodcarvings, contemporary paintings and seal carvings, ancient bronzes, ceramics, jades, seals, calligraphy and painting.

Old European concessions

A walk that takes in the French, British and German Concessions with their varying architecture, passing by the Fine Art Museum, can start from the railway station. Visiting Tianjin in August 2000, I was struck by the size of the areas of demolition and very little that remained from the past can be relied upon for any length of time ....

Leave the railway station by the main entrance and walk straight down the approach road which takes you to the river. Diagonally opposite is a bridge with huge curved iron girders, **Liberation Bridge (Jiefang qiao)**, built, according to the French authors of the Nagel guide, by French engineers in 1903 (others suggest the Austrians built it). Cross the bridge and carry on straight ahead, away from the river. This is **Jiefang lu** (formerly the Rue de France in the **French Concession**) and the first building, on the right-hand corner of the road, facing the river, was the Imperial Hotel.

On the northwest side of the next crossroads (the northwest corner with Binjiang dao) was the French Club. On the southwest corner of the next crossroads (Haerbin dao) were the French Municipal Council Offices and on the southeast corner of the next crossroads (Chifeng dao) is the Fine Art Museum (see above). On the northwest corner of the next-but-one crossroads (Yingkou dao) was the Tianjin General Post Office and, opposite it (southwest corner), the Yokohama Specie Bank.

Yingkou dao, formerly Bristow Road, marked the beginning of the British Concession. On the east side of the road, a yellow and red brick building with bulging balconies was the Russo-Asiatic Bank.

Continuing down Jiefang lu, on the east side of the road (on the corner of the second lane on the E side) was the Chartered Bank of India, Australia and China, next, Jardine & Matheson, with Butterfield & Swire a tiny bit further down on the same side and the US Consulate opposite Swire on the west side of the road. Just before the *Astor House Hotel* (with a modern, plastic-fronted branch of the Hong Kong and Shanghai Bank in front of it), were the Tientsin Press (east) and the British Municipal Council in the bizarre Gordon Hall, a dark, battlemented castle-like building, put up in 1887 (in the year of Queen Victoria's jubilee). **Gordon Hall** has, alas, disappeared.

This was not only the British Municipal Council Office (where the regulations against furious bicycle riding were promulgated) but also the police station, law court and concert hall and assembly room. It was described by its clergyman designer as 'Victorian Tientsin' in style though others said it recalled a prison hospital on the outskirts of Edinburgh. It took its name from General Charles George 'Chinese' Gordon who, although later to serve in the imperial forces against the Taiping rebels (see Shanghai), had served as a captain in the Royal Engineers in 1860 and had surveyed and fixed the boundaries of the British Concession. In 1900, when the Boxer rebellion threatened, the British community took refuge in Gordon Hall.

The Astor House Hotel Ltd.
(Incorporated in Hongkong)
TIENTSIN.

In the centre of the British Concession within easy walking distance of the leading shops, offices and banks.

Cables :—ASTOR-TIENTSIN   Paul Weingart, *Manager.*

An old advertisement for the Astor House Hotel

Next to Gordon Hall (opposite the Astor House), was the tiny **Victoria Park** where there used to be a Chinese pavilion which served as a bandstand and which was the social centre for British children, their wooden horses and their *amahs*. It was opened for Victoria's jubilee, like Gordon Hall. It has now vanished but the trees in the forecourt of the massive modern skyscraper opposite the Astor House Hotel are probably survivors. Just south of the Astor House Hotel, also on the east side of the road, was the **Tientsin Club** (which could not bring itself to admit the deposed emperor Henry Aisin Gioro Pu Yi even as a 'special member' during his stay in Tianjin (1925–30), although he was invited to guest nights.

You could consider returning to the river along the Bund at this point where you would pass the old British Consulate (on the corner of the fourth turning on the left), the old Hong Kong and Shanghai Bank building (on the south corner of the fifth turning on the left, Yingkou dao), with the old Customs House on the north corner and the French Consulate on the north corner of the next turning on the left.

Alternatively, from the Astor House Hotel, turn right (west) along the next main road (Tai'an dao) and diagonally opposite, on the south corner of Tai'an dao and Zhejiang lu is the old Protestant Church of All Saints, now some sort of storehouse (its back entrance is no. 11 Tai'an lu). Behind you is the immensely long facade of the huge Kailan Mining Administration Building (controlling the British-owned coalmines near Tianjin) and next to it the British Consul's Residence, a peculiarly stepped building with a colonnaded verandah and strange octagonal tower.

Continue south down **Zhejiang lu** (this is two streets to the west of Jiefang lu/Victoria Road). It ends on a wide open space with a roundabout. On your left, facing the roundabout is all that remains of the old *Kiessling and Bader's*

Tearooms (known prosaically in the Cultural Revolution as the Tianjin Canteen although it still served chicken Kiev and ice-cream with chocolate sauce), *Qisilin canting*, in Chinese. If you haven't already eaten, you could take coffee (and perhaps a beef stroganoff) here. But most of the building is now devoted to Kentucky Fried Chicken.

The road diagonally opposite Zhejiang lu on the far side of the roundabout is **Machang dao** (previously known as Racecourse Road, which is what *machang dao* means) which used to mark the border between the British and the German Concessions. It is lined with grand buildings of all sorts. You could follow Machang dao as it twists southwest, heading back north perhaps along the fifth turning on the right (north), Yunnan lu. Yunnan lu crosses two roads and then reaches a crossroads where three roads meet. Turn left here up Guizhou lu and you should see the twin onion domes of another **Roman Catholic church**, open on Sundays when services take place, at the top of Guizhou lu. On the far side of the church, the main road running west–east is Shengli lu and was Elgin Avenue. Take the road running northeasst (in front of the church), Binjiang dao, which will take you to the major shopping street (ex Asahi Road/Rue du Chaylard), Heping lu. You could look at the huge old shop buildings along Heping lu and the Zhang Garden (now the offices of the Tianjin Daily) where the last emperor Henry Aisin Gioro Pu Yi lived (from 1925), enjoying 'flush lavatories and central heating'. Or continue straight up Binjiang lu (north) which will take you to Jiefang lu (second on the left after Heping lu) and the bridge leading to the railway station.

There is more walking that can be done in the **German Concession**, and indeed, all the concession areas. For those with a good sense of direction or an ability to retrace their steps, the old Chinese town is north, bordered by the Bei ma lu, Nan ma lu, Dong ma lu and Xi ma lu. The Japanese settlement was bordered by Duolun dao. Shengli lu, Jiangzhou dao and the river. The French settlement was bordered by Jianzhou dao and Yingkou dao; the British settlement by Yingkou dao and Machang dao; south of Machang dao was the German Concession. The buildings in some parts offer clues: Scottish baronial, French château and German expressionist, although there are traces of southern colonial and international bank styles that cross boundaries.

The **Italian concession** is now the best preserved 'concession area' in Tianjin. On the opposite side of the river from the British and French concessions, it is best reached across the bridge from Fuma dao and can be found on either side of Minzu Road in Hebei district. Houses with grand iron-work gates can be seen surrounding a small circus where it is planned that a new statue of Marco Polo (an old one once stood there) should be erected. Walking away from the river along Minzu dao, **Liang Qichao**'s old home can be found at no. 46. A dilapidated foreign-style building with a strange stone shell on the lower balcony, this was the home of one of China's greatest modernisers during the 1920s.

Liang Qichao

Liang Qichao (1873–1929) had a traditional Chinese education and passed the first two imperial exams (to enter the government bureaucracy) but failed the top (metropolitan) exam in 1890. He was influenced by translations of modern western literature acquired in Shanghai and came under the influence of Kang Youwei (1858–1927), the leader of the 1898 'Hundred Days Reform' when the enfeebled Guangxu emperor made a last attempt to modernise China through reform of the education, legal, administrative and military systems along western lines. The Dowager Empress Cixi quashed the revolt and imprisoned the emperor, forcing Kang Youwei, Liang Qichao and their followers to flee to Japan. Towards the end of his life, Liang Qichao travelled to Europe but found it depressed and depressing in the aftermath of the First World War.

The **Zhou Enlai-Deng Yingchao Memorial Hall** is in the southwest of the city, adjoining the Water park/Shuishang gongyuan and entered from Shuishang gongyuan xilu. It was opened in 1985, the 100th anniversary of Zhou Enlai's birth.

Zhou Enlai

Zhou Enlai (1895–1976) was one of the most successful politicians of 20C China. His early revolutionary activities began when he studied at Nankai University in Tianjin and he rose through the Communist ranks to the position of Premier: never directly in line of succession to Mao (who was notoriously jealous), he showed the same skill in his handling of China's foreign relations when he charmed every world leader he met. He married Deng Yingchao, a round-faced young Communist activist of considerable bravery. They were present on the Long March and the risks they ran in the Communist underground, together with the hardships of the March and Deng Yingchao's subsequent illness meant that they never had children of their own. Though she survived him for a decade, Deng Yingchao's evident distress in the years after his death, as well as Zhou Enlai's powerful charm which worked its magic on the entire population of China, mean that they have been commemorated here as a couple. Outside the hall is a large white stone sculpture of their heads (when young) and it is evident that the romantic myth of the dashing young couple is being used to try and interest the young (bussed in droves to the museum, wearing jeans and tee-shirts, with reddish dyed hair and sunglasses) in the exciting history of the Communist Party.

For a pair who lived through dangerous times, they seem to have managed to preserve an inordinate number of photographs, many of which show interesting glimpses of the early 20C in China, a period when fashions were including western dress or modernised versions of traditional Chinese dress (favoured by Deng Yingchao). There are photographs of Zhou Enlai when he studied abroad in France and Germany, wearing a tight western suit with rather short trousers; there are videos of him meeting many world leaders and, outside, under an awning is a plane that he used frequently.

Outside Tianjin ~ Yangliuqing

A very rewarding trip for those interested in China's traditional domestic architecture is to Yangliuqing. This village in the western suburbs (Xiqing district) is still very much a traditional settlement with tiny lanes where two people cannot pass in the narrow passages between low grey courtyard houses. Some of the doorways still retain the traditional cut-brick work characteristic of northern houses, and fine stone drums in which the outer doors are set. Many inhabitants keep pretty little 'Pekinese' dogs.

In the centre of the village is the **Shi jia dayuan**/Great courtyard of the Shi family, open to the public 09.00–17.00. It is a multi-courtyard dwelling with its own theatre on the central axis. There are exhibitions in some of the halls of fine cut-brick work panels (for doorways); a model of the old village main street with all the varying little shops, peddlars and entertainers; a model of a wedding procession with a real red-silk covered bridal sedan chair and the characteristic red embroidered garments worn by bride, groom and attendants; a room full of the calligraphic greetings of local worthies (made to celebrate the opening of the house in 1998), the family altar and an exhibition on the manufacture of Yangliuqing New Year Prints (nianhua). The designs for the prints, the tools for cutting and printing the multiple colour blocks, as well as finished prints which are characterised by added hand-colouring of flesh-tones, for example, are all displayed (the captions are only in Chinese but the exhibits are fairly self-explanatory).

Some miles southeast of Yangliuqing is the small **house of Huo Yuanjia** (in Xiaonanhe village, Xiqing district). It is easily included in a morning's taxi ride from Tianjin (approximate cost 100 yuan). Huo Yuanjia was a local peasant's son who became a famous martial arts practitioner in the early 20C: there are photographs of martial arts tours of Overseas Chinese communities in Southeast Asia. His house, which has clearly been rebuilt, is a charming peasant building with *kang* (brick beds) under the windows in the side rooms and cooking stoves in the central room, whose flues travel under the brick beds for after-dinner heating. The furnishings have been well-chosen and reflect traditional peasant taste with dark wood storage units and printed cottons. It is a very attractive reconstruction of a typical north Chinese peasant house.

Chengde

Chengde, previously known to the Chinese as *Rehe* (Warm River) and to western visitors as *Jehol*, is a small town about 200km northeast of central Peking. Very early in the Qing dynasty the emperors established first a small lodge, then the great Summer Mountain Retreat in a vast walled enclosure surrounded by eight 'outer temples'.

Chengde is an ideal weekend trip from Peking, a minimal weekend visit involving an early Saturday morning departure, and leaving Chengde just after lunch on Sunday. For those who drive, perhaps hiring a car or taxi from Peking, it is possible to stop at some of the parts of the Great Wall passed en route; and to take copies of Lord Macartney's account of his long road trip (made on horseback, accompanied by a ramshackle troupe of attendants and soldiers).

Practical information

Getting there
By train

Although it is now possible to drive to Chengde, a good way to travel is by train from Peking, a journey of some 5 hours. The train passes through marvellous mountain scenery, passing dramatic sections of the Great Wall.

By minibus

If you hire a minibus for the journey from Peking, you can stop and visit the Wall en route.

Where to stay

The best place to stay is the *Shanzhuang Hotel*, 127 Xiaonanmen lu, ☎ 202 3501, fax 202 2457, opposite the main entrance to the Imperial Summer Resort. Inside the resort, to the west, is the traditional-style *Yiwanglou Binguan*, ☎ 202 4385. These hotels can be reached by taxi from the station.

History

The Imperial Summer Resort was begun in 1703 by the Kangxi emperor, following a tradition linking the now-established Manchus with their past life of mounted hunting expeditions. Early in his reign Kangxi had built small lodges (including one near Chengde in 1677) in the north where the court established itself for hunting expeditions and archery competitions. These annual northern trips were more than merely sporting for they were also used to forge links with other northern groups such as the Mongols who inhabited border regions of great strategic importance. The use of the Summer Resort as a diplomatic centre was continued in the reign of the Qianlong emperor who constructed the extraordinary 'outer temples', some in the Tibetan architectural style, deliberately chosen to impress visiting Tibetan and Mongolian Lamaist dignitaries.

To the northwest of the town, a great walled enclosure, its peripheral wall 10km long—with a lake area surrounded by palace buildings and pavilions, the rest wild hills for hunting—was constructed over an 80-year period, with further later additions in succeeding reigns, and named *Bi shu shan zhuang*, or the 'mountain village where you can escape the heat'. Sometimes confusingly known as the 'Summer Palace'—confusing since there are two 'summer palaces', old and new, in Peking—the Imperial Summer Resort at Chengde was the home of the court for virtually six months of every year during the reigns of the Kangxi and all succeeding emperors until 1820. In that year the Jiaqing emperor died in the resort, probably of an apoplexy although legend had it that he was struck by lightning. The death, by whatever means, was regarded as a portent of bad things and the resort was avoided for some decades afterwards.

The belief that bad luck was associated with the resort was reinforced when the Xianfeng emperor fled Peking as French and British troops approached in 1860. He stayed at Chengde even after peace was restored, refusing to grant an audience to foreign envoys (one of the conditions of the peace treaty) which would have involved the humiliation of their not performing the humble *kowtow* (kneeling, forehead on the ground in front of the emperor). Devoting himself, instead, to 'excesses', he, too, died in the Resort in 1861.

The relationship of Chengde to the Peking summer palaces is interesting.

The 'Old' Summer Palace, Yuan ming yuan (Garden of Perfect Brightness) was built, with the help of Jesuits, by the Qianlong emperor in the mid 18C on the foundations of garden palaces built by the Kangxi and Yongzheng emperors and sacked in 1860 by British and French troops. The 'New' Summer Palace, Yi he yuan (Garden of the Cultivation of Harmony), was laid out mainly by Qianlong on the basis of earlier (12C Yuan and Ming) gardens, sacked in 1860 and then rebuilt in 1888 by the Dowager Empress Cixi who favoured it above all others. All were used by the Emperors during the hot summer months but the longest periods were spent at Chengde during the 17C and 18C, when the whole court decamped.

The resort almost fills a valley in the hills of southern Manchuria through which the Warm River flows to the west and a smaller stream to the east of the enclosure. The surrounding hills with their strangely-shaped rocks (most prominently the phallic Club or Anvil Rock to the east) form part of the whole of the garden enclosure. It is here, where an entire valley has been taken over for imperial pleasure, just as in the vast imperial palace in the centre of Peking with its endless series of halls and dazzling white courtyards, that you sense the amazing scale of the grandeur of imperial China at its height in the early Qing.

The Jesuit Matteo Ripa (1682–1745), who lived in Peking from 1711–23, described the surroundings:

It is situated in a plain surrounded by mountains, whence flows a torrent ... A hill rises gently from the plain, its side studded with buildings destined for the Emperor's followers and a copious spring of water forms a noble lake ... the plain, the slopes and the hill are thickly covered with foliage; and the filberts, corianders, pears and apples, although growing wild, have so delicious a flavour that they are served on the Emperor's table. The plain, the slopes and the hill are so extensive that it took me an hour to make the tour of the inclosure on horseback ...

The Kangxi emperor himself (his words 'reassembled' by Jonathan Spence) described the coolness and freedom of the Chengde area:

... it is when one is beyond the Great Wall that the air and soil refresh the spirit: one leaves the beaten road and strikes out into untamed country; the mountains are densely packed with woods 'green and thick as the standing corn'. As one moves further north the views open up, one's eyes travel hundreds of miles; instead of feeling hemmed in, there is a sense of freedom. It may be the height of summer but there is dew on the trees, and some of the leaves are turning yellow already, as if it were late autumn; you have to wear a fur jacket in the mornings, even although in Peking it is so hot that you hesitate about having the eunuchs lead the consorts out of the palaces to greet you on your return.

In the great imperial valley even the emperor could recapture the outdoor freedom of his hunting ancestors:

There is tea, made from fresh snow on the little brazier slung between two horses. There is the perfect flavour of bream and carp from the mountain streams, caught by oneself in the early morning ... There is venison, roasted over an open fire by a tent pitched on the sunny slope of a mountain; or the liver of a newly killed stag, cooked with one's own hands (even if the rain is falling), and eaten with salt and vinegar ...

The Imperial Enclosure

The Imperial Enclosure covers an area of over 5.5 square km, and is surrounded by a battlemented wall 10km long. Most of the buildings (constructed between 1703 and 1790) are concentrated in the east of the enclosure, near the lakes, and they fall into two major categories: palace or domestic and garden buildings. To the west, the hilly area to the left of the main gate was allowed to remain wild for hunting.

The **Palace Enclosure**: situated in the southeast of the whole enclosure, this originally consisted of three virtually parallel 'palaces'. The Eastern Palace (to the east) has since disappeared. It lay within the small Dehui men or Gate of Assembled Virtues and led to the long dyke of the triple Lake Heart Pavilion at the southern end of the lake. Beyond this is a children's playground; it had a temporary exhibition of animated model dinosaurs in it in 1998, which accounted for the mournful hooting sounds that echoed over the lake. The main surviving palace building is the **Zheng gong** (Main Palace). The outer gate, **Lizheng men** (Gate of Beauty and Uprightness), serves as the main entrance to the whole enclosure now. There are three openings in the gate: the central one, which is paved with white stones, was reserved for the emperor and close family members, just as in the Forbidden City in Peking. Where the two stone lions stand outside the gate there were once stone notices requiring officials to dismount (just as at the Qing imperial tombs) or descend from their sedan chairs.

Inscriptions throughout the palace are either in Chinese or the four other languages (Manchu, Mongolian, Tibetan and Uighur) used out of politeness to the envoys from border areas who were frequently entertained here. A further gate lies inside the Gate of Beauty and Uprightness and beyond is a courtyard where officials and envoys from the borders awaited their audience with the Emperor. All of the courtyards in the palace are relatively small, surrounded by simple, low, buildings, almost domestic in appearance. The simple plan and careful axial balance, with matching side-wings and main halls oriented to the south, are characteristic of domestic architecture in north China, although the floors and materials of this 'simple' complex are luxurious and frequently expensive. Nevertheless, the whole retains a feeling of an imperial country retreat, if compared with the pomp of Peking.

Beyond is another major gate, the **Bi shu shan zhuang men** (Gate of the Mountain Village Where You Can Escape the Heat, the humble name for a summer palace echoing the relative simplicity of the architecture) whence the emperors, seated on soft cushions, watched archery contests and saw officials. The major activities at this gate are described in four lines of poetry by the Qianlong emperor: 'On return from the hunt, officials kowtow on the steps; In the autumn with bows lightly held, the noblemen's arrows hit the target; As the moon grows to a circle.'

Behind is a courtyard planted with 42 old pines, the **Courtyard of the Tranquil Heart and Honour to Sincerity** (Tanpo jingcheng dian). The Main Hall (on the north side of the court), the most important in the palace, is deceptively simple, single-eaved with seven bays. It is raised on a stone platform and the timber used in construction (including the carved ceilings) is cedar, brought thousands of kilometres from western China (the hall is sometimes called the Cedar Hall). The floors are paved with polished, patterned, marble-like rock but the simple grey eaves tiles are in contrast to the imperial yellow glazed tiles of the Forbidden City. Side rooms are lined with bookcases originally constructed to hold a copy of the 10,000-volume *Gu jin tu shu ji cheng* (*Synthesis of Books and Illustrations from Ancient to Modern Times*), printed, at imperial order, using copper movable type in 1728.

This work was an encyclopaedic collection of quotation and reference, most interesting for its technical features. Movable type was experimentally used in China in about 1040 but was (given the nature of the Chinese script) not an economical advance on the system of carving whole pages onto woodblocks. The experimental imperial printing of the *Tu shu ji cheng* involved a font of over 250,000 pieces of types, of such value as metal that it was never reused but melted down for coinage.

In the smaller courtyard behind, the small **main hall** was named 'Compliance with Clarity and Freedom from Worries' by the Kangxi emperor but renamed 'Study of the Four Branches of Knowledge' by the Qianlong emperor. The sixth Panchen Lama was received here in 1779. The main building in the courtyard behind is a long, **19-bay hall** (A Thousand Years of Brightness), which divides the public, front part of the palace from the private imperial living-quarters behind (the same layout is found in the Confucian Family Mansion in Qu Fu, Shandong). In this hall banners and weapons were laid out before the emperors went out on hunting expeditions in the nearby hills, progressing from the private quarters at the rear to the front gate.

In the courtyard behind (Refreshed by Mist-covered Waters) were the **living quarters**. In the main hall were thrones and Buddhist shrines and the room to the far left was the emperors' bedroom where the Jiaqing and Xianfeng emperors died. The concubines' and wives' apartments are connected to the bedroom. Behind is a **two-storey hall** (Landscape amid Clouds and Mountains) with a mock mountain in front of it in which a series of steps allows you to reach the upper storey. Inside all the halls are unlit displays of porcelain, jade and other vessels once used by the imperial inhabitants. Behind the two-storey hall is a decorative 'hanging flower' gate which leads to the park.

If you leave from this gate just to your left is the **Tame Deer Slope** where the Père David deer that used to roam the park came to be fed.

Tame Deer

These peculiar animals, *Elaphurus davidianus*, named by Père Armand David (1826–1900), a Lazarist missionary and naturalist, were extinct in China by about 1900. Manchu accounts of the 18C say that they lived in the Kokonor area and also in Manchuria and they were first described in French by David. He saw a herd of some 120 in the imperial hunting park, Nan yuan, south of Peking, but they certainly also existed in Chengde. They had disappeared from the Nan yuan by 1900, killed and eaten by park-keepers and by the local poor whenever they could, and the same fate must have overtaken those at Chengde. The Dukes of Bedford had a herd and in the mid 1980s presented some 20 of them to the Chinese government for reinstatement in the Imperial Resort. They are large, peculiar-looking animals with reindeer-like horns and a donkey's tail and the popular Chinese name for them, 'four dissimilarities', is appropriate. They say that the horns are like deer horns but it is not a deer, the head is like a horse's head but it is not a horse, the body is like a donkey's but it is not a donkey and the hooves are like a cow's but it is not a cow. I looked for them in 1999 but failed to find any.

There are exhibits of imperial possessions—bronzes, ceramics and jades—in some of the halls of the main palace.

To the east (right) is a smaller, parallel palace enclosure of low, grey-tiled courtyards called the **Pine and Crane Study** (Songhe zhai) which was inhabited by Qianlong's mother. To the east of that, the eastern palace, which has since disappeared, was where the Qianlong emperor received Lord Macartney in September 1793.

There, the English aristocrat shared a display of 'tightrope walking and wrestling' with six ambassadors from Outer Mongolia and was shown the lake area of the park. His description serves to introduce it:

> We rode about three miles through a very beautiful park, kept in the highest order, and much resembling the approach to Luton in Bedfordshire; the grounds gently undulated and chequered with various groups of well-contrasted trees ... an extensive lake appeared before us, the extremities of which seemed to lose themselves in distance and obscurity ... The shores of the lake have all the varieties of shape which the fancy of a painter can delineate ... one marked by a pagoda, or other building, one quite destitute of ornament, some smooth and level, some steep and uneven and others frowning with wood or smiling with culture ... One thing I was particularly struck with, I mean the happy choice of situation for ornamental buildings. From attention to this circumstance they have not the air of being crowded or disproportioned; they never intrude upon the eye but wherever they appear always show themselves to advantage, and aid, improve and enliven the prospect ...

The Lake Park Macartney's description is a sensitive one of an ideal Chinese garden (combining water, buildings and plants with interest) and as the David Deer have returned from Woburn, they, too, may have felt a similarity noted by Macartney to 'the soft beauties of Woburn' (*An Embassy to China ... the Journal Kept by Lord Macartney*, edited and with an introduction by J.L. Cranmer-Byng, Longman, 1962).

Although Lord Macartney retained a favourable impression of the palace and its landscape, his meeting with the Qianlong emperor was not a success. Instructed, indeed begged, to *kowtow* to the emperor by the two Chinese officials who accompanied him and his retinue, he refused to do more than sink to one knee, as he would have done before his own sovereign. Even if he had kowtowed, it would probably not have made any difference since an imperial letter refusing Britain's demand for free trade in the interior of China and a permanent resident ambassador in Peking had been written before Macartney even reached China.

Entering the park from the rear of the palace, walk along the western (left-hand) shore of the lake, past the major islands, to the far end of the lake where a small stream continues north. As you walk alongside the stream, soon, on your left, you will find the **Wenjin ge** (Pavilion of Literary Delights), one of the imperial libraries. This is not included in the general ticket: a separate entrance ticket has to be purchased here. Built to house one of the four original sets of the vast imperial manuscript collectanea, *Si ku quan shu* (*Complete Treasury of the Four Storehouses*), which was completed in 1785 (this copy is now in the National Library, Peking), the two-storey library building was once surrounded by other buildings whose foundations can still be seen.

Like all the other buildings constructed to hold the imperial collectanea (which comprised 3470 titles copied out in some 36,300 slim volumes), the building was based on the privately owned Tianyi ge library in Ningbo (see p 321) although a comparison of the two reveals the fundamental differences between northern and southern styles of building. The Tianyi ge has dark-tiled roofs with upswept eaves, while the Wen jin ge is a solid little northern building with straight eaves. For fire protection, however, it is set on a high stone platform, originally surrounded by water, with a stone rockery in front of it, just like the setting of the Tianyi ge. The Qianlong emperor wrote a poem about the Wenjin ge which begins: 'The Tianyi ge had a pool in front of it and piled rocks to the south; the Wenjin ge was modelled on it and stones were piled up into a mountain; there are peaks and a gully and the sound of the qin floats over the water.'

The building appears from the outside to consist of two storeys although inside there are three. It was originally roofed with black glazed tiles, which would have looked closer to the dark tiles of the Tianyi ge, but when part of the roof fell down in 1866 it was reroofed with grey unglazed tiles in the northern domestic style. The painted eaves are particularly interesting for they are decorated with pictures of traditional Chinese books in their blue cloth wrappers. In 1980 it was handed over to the town and it was intended that a reprint of the original collectanea (published in late 1987) would be housed in the building.

Beyond the library, further north, almost at the northern wall of the enclosure, is the **Liuhe ta** (Pagoda of Six Harmonies), all that remains of the grandest of the Buddhist temples constructed within the park in 1751. Its name recalls the pagoda at Hangzhou and southern inspiration is widely found throughout the park.

Returning to the lake, it is possible to cross a bridge to the central island where the **Yanyu lou** (Misty Rain Tower) is based on a southern building on the South Lake near Shanghai. On the far side of the lake, the three-storey tower rising above lower buildings (called **Jinshan si** or Gold Mountain Temple) is also modelled on the Shangdi ge (Gods' Pavilion) at Zhenjiang on the Yangtse. Both of these are no doubt the result of the Qing emperors' many tours of inspection of the luxurious south where they frequently stayed in beauty spots which they had recreated in the drier, colder north.

A copper-engraved volume produced by the Jesuit Matteo Ripa (1711–12) contains illustrations of all the major sites at Chengde with accompanying poems in Chinese and Manchu by the Kangxi emperor. Of the Jinshan si, he says:

A mountain suddenly rises from the lake, flat-topped with a three-roofed pavilion; To the north is the hall of the supreme god, above are layers of cloud, below is azure water; To ascend it is like climbing a magical peak, the north is enclosed in banks of cloud, to the open south, scenes merge into a view.

The Eight Outer Temples

These are best visited by taxi (half a day if you hurry) as they are some distance apart.

The eastern temples are, in general, earlier than the western, so it is convenient to start with the Puren si. In the past there were 12 temples, but these eight are all that remain today. Built between 1713 and 1779, their religious significance to the emperors was, as noted, subordinate to their political usefulness in wooing the adherents of Lamaist Buddhism in the border regions of Mongolia and Tibet.

Puren si (Temple of Universal Love). Built in 1713, for Kangxi's 60th birthday (the only one of the outer temples to date from his reign), the Puren si was said to have been built for the Mongol princes who had expressed a wish to attend the celebrations. Building temples for them meant that they could continue their Lamaist devotions while in Chengde. Built in the Chinese style, to a Chinese plan, typically expressed as 'temple guardians and seven halls', nothing remains of any Tibetan elements, said to have been present in the past, in painted ceilings and Buddha images.

Pushan si (Temple of Universal Goodness). Little remains of the temple, built at the same time and for the same reasons at the Puren si. The ruins and old photographs suggest that it was a Chinese style temple of several courtyards.

Pule si (Temple of Universal Joy). Sometimes called the Temple of the Round Pavilion, after the form of its Pavilion of the Rising Sun, the Pule si was built in 1766–67 for the western Mongols who came each year to pay homage to the emperor. Standing high on the hillside, surrounded by vegetable fields and with wind-bells ringing in the breeze, it is a wonderfully peaceful place. A Tibetan advisor was employed in the construction of the temple. Oriented east–west (which is almost unheard of in Chinese temple architecture), the front part of the temple is, nevertheless, reasonably Chinese in design. The gateway, however, has arched doors with carved stone lintels, in a form which is widely seen in the outer temples at Chengde and also in 'minority' buildings in Peking, like the Lama Temple (see p 155) and also the Cow Street Mosque (see p 179). Owing nothing obvious to Tibetan architecture, the form may be Islamic in inspiration, although the lotus carvings are Buddhist. Before the gate, on either side of the stone lions, are the tall pine poles or 'banner masts' which are a feature of Lamaist architecture. In the Hall of Heavenly Guardians (behind the gateway), the facade of wood with its arched doorways repeats the form of the stone gateway in timber.

The most striking features of the temple are to be found in the third courtyard which is filled with a circular, double-roofed Pavilion (of the Rising Sun), reminiscent of those in the Temple of Heaven in Peking. The circular pavilion with its spectacularly carved, gilded ceiling is still a Chinese form but it encloses a strange columnar construction in the form of a cross, a three-dimensional representation of the mandala of Samvara, a protective Tantric deity. The circular enclosure is part of the scheme, as is, apparently, the orientation of the temple, all recommended by the Tibetan advisor. It is interesting to note that some of the great incense burners in the temple echo the form of the circular Pavilion of the Rising Sun. From the back of the temple it may be noticed that it is oriented in a direct line with the peculiar Anvil Rock ahead.

Anyuan miao (Temple of Distant Peace). This temple was constructed in 1764 by the Qianlong emperor for the tens of thousands of western Mongols that he had brought to Chengde as part of the complex manoeuvres of control in the desert area of Xinjiang.

In Yili (near Yining), Turkic princes had ruled until Mongol tribes established themselves in the 17C. They became converts to Lamaist Buddhism through the neighbouring Tibetans. Qianlong was, like Kangxi before him, worried about this alliance and began to re-establish Islam in the area, moving groups of people and destroying major Lamaist temples.

The Anyuan miao was modelled on one of the temples in Yili which had been destroyed, apparently a Tibetan-inspired building of three storeys surrounded by a high wall, These two elements are virtually all that survive of the original temple. In plan, it consists of two square enclosures separated by a wall, the whole forming a great rectangular enclosure. The first enclosure, through the gate, is filled with trees; behind, in the second court, is the main hall. Apparently, the second court also enclosed numerous low buildings which have since disappeared. The hall is supported on 60 columns, the lower part of the exterior columns hidden in an apparently solid but actually non-load-bearing red painted wall. A narrow roof above the red wall is surmounted by a double roof covered with yellow and black glazed tiles, with a tiny ceramic stupa in the centre of the ridge. Inside, galleries surround the hall, which has a gilded figure of Ksitigarbha (Bodhisattva who presides over the underworld); the *caisson* (coffered) ceilings are richly carved with phoenix and dragons.

Guangyuan si (Temple of Extended Causation). Nothing remains of this small temple built in 1780, just to the east of the Puyou si, although it was apparently constructed in the Chinese style.

Puyou si (Temple of Universal Help). The temple was built in 1760 inside the walls of the Puning temple. Nothing remains now but the surrounding wall, a terrace with a square pavilion and small side buildings all with green and yellow tiled roofs.

Puning si (Temple of Universal Peace). One of the grandest of the outer temples, this was the first to be built by the Qianlong emperor in Chengde in 1755.

Although it anticipated the event by some four years, it was built to celebrate the pacification of the Yili area and the bloody suppression of the Jungar Mongols, who were already destroying themselves in fratricidal struggles. Fearful of Russian intervention, the emperor ordered forced resettlement of the area and its occupation by penal colonies. Much of the temple design was based on that of the oldest Tibetan temple, the Sam-yas, although apparently the Panchen Lama, who visited the temple, failed to recognise its inspiration.

Built against a hill, to the northeast of the palace enclosure, the temple rises towards the back. It consists of two parts, the front in the Chinese style, the back in a parody of the Tibetan. In the first part, the most impressive building is the **Da xiong bao dian** (Precious Hall of the Great Hero, referring to the Buddha's demon-conquering powers) in the centre of the second courtyard of the 'Chinese' style front part. The walls are covered with paintings in the Tibetan style. Steps lead up to the rear, Tibetan part of the enclosure where a major hall, the **Mahayana Hall**, stands on a high platform, five storeys high with a complex roof formed of four lower square gold tiled roofs topped by a larger central square roof. It contains a massive wooden figure of the thousand-armed Guanyin, 28m high with two 12m attendants. The walls of the hall are covered with niches where pilgrims used to place tiny Buddha figures.

In front and beside the Mahayana Hall are numerous smaller buildings in the Tibetan style: solid, whitewashed constructions with blind windows in the form of tapering rectangles. The solidity of many of these subsidiary buildings and the fact that their windows are simply decorative give the feeling of a stage set. Although the Chinese emperors adopted the Tibetan style of building to make their Mongol and Tibetan visitors feel at home, the theatrical effect of the false facades suggests that there was a slightly hollow ring to the Chinese desire to please.

Xumifushou miao (Temple of Happiness and Longevity in Mount Sumeru). The temple was built for the sixth Panchen Lama when he came to visit the Qianlong emperor who was celebrating his 70th birthday in 1780; it is said to have been inspired by the Panchen's residence, Tashilumpo, at Shigatse in Tibet. One of the most lavish of the outer temples, rendered quickly obsolete as the

Panchen died soon afterwards in Peking, it is also built against a hill, the enclosure terminating near the summit with a glazed turquoise and yellow pagoda. Inside the gate is an almost garden-like area, containing the stele describing its construction in a pavilion, and a rustic path of uneven stones leading to a stone and tile *pailou* (decorative gateway) flanked by two stone elephants with uncomfortably bent forelegs. These recall the gilded elephants at the rear of the Forbidden City in Peking which are also anatomically

Chengde: one of the elephants at the Xumifushou miao

incorrect in the forelegs. Behind is a great square enclosure surrounded by a high red wall pierced with Tibetan style windows. The enclosure is almost entirely filled with a four-storey (17m high) square building with a gilt roof, its four ridges embellished with sinuous crawling dragons. The red wall is lined with wooden galleries and the central hall is galleried within and without. There is a grand central gilded ceiling with dragons but the *caisson* ceilings elsewhere bear Sanskrit characters. Immediately behind is a small pavilion with a roof ridge decorated with a pair of ceramic deer and a central sun, in imitation of the gilt figures on many temple roofs in Tibet.

To the right, behind the main hall, is a three-storey building with a decorative wooden façade, the **Jixiang faxi dian** (Hall of the Law and Good Fortune), built as a dwelling for the Panchen Lama. The surrounding buildings (now in disrepair) were for his attendant monks. At the rear of the enclosure is the pagoda, the tile-clad tower rising from an open, octagonal base. The pagoda is not unlike the tiled pagoda at Xiangshan (see p 204), just outside Peking.

Putuozongcheng miao (Temple of the Putuo Sect). Otherwise known as the Potala Temple for its most striking feature is the great red wall at the back, based on the Potala Palace of the Dalai Lamas in Lhasa; the temple was actually built for Mongols from the Kokonor area and Eleuths who came to pay their respects to the Qianlong emperor on his 60th birthday (1770) and his Dowager Empress on her 80th birthday (1771). Construction began in 1767 and was finished in 1771.

A further reason for celebration through temple construction was the return of many exiled Central Asian Torguts from Astrakhan and Russian influence.

Chengde: the Putuozongcheng miao

The Qianlong emperor was worried about Russian influence in Central Asia (just as he was beginning to be concerned about the East India Company's activities in North India) and any anti-Russian feeling was seized upon. The temple, which covers a greater area (220,000 square metres) than any other at Chengde, consists of an open front area dotted with trees and irregularly disposed Tibetan-style buildings (many solid and unusable), dominated by the massive red walled enclosure at the back, further up the hill. The stele describing its foundation states that it was based on the Potala palace but, although the great red wall at the back does recall the Potala, the latter is a more solid building while the Chengde version encloses a Chinese style pavilion; and the open area in front owes little to the Tibetan original. The irregular placement of buildings is, however, very un-Chinese so the whole is perhaps best considered as a 'rendering' of the Potala. As in the Xumifushou Temple, many of the small whitewashed buildings with Tibetan-style windows, sometimes topped with pepper-pot *dagoba* (Tibetan stupas), are solid and unusable, presenting, once again, a theatrical effect.

From the gate a path leads through the stele pavilion and a second gate, through a glazed tile *pailou* into the wooded, rocky area dotted with whitewashed buildings. Above looms the great red wall of the mock Potala, whose Tibetan form windows are mostly blank and purely decorative. From its terrace there is a fine view of the wide enclosure below and the back wall of the imperial palace enclosure. As in the Xumifushou Temple, the red wall encloses a double-roofed square building in the Chinese style. Inside, a central gilded ceiling is surrounded by a *caisson* ceiling and the main columns are painted red. No central Buddha figure survives but a series of smaller figures and pieces of altar furniture stand in the centre.

Shuxiang si (Temple of the Statue of Manjusri). Built in the purely Chinese style, the Shuxiang si was constructed between 1774 and 1776, based on the temple of the same name at Wutai shan (in Shanxi province).

Wutai shan, the northern Buddhist holy mountain, was dedicated to Manjusri, the Boddhisattva favoured by Lamaist Buddhists, and was a major centre of pilgrimage for Mongolian Buddhists, thus its cult was important to Chengde where temples were built for Lamaist dignitaries. The mother of the Qianlong emperor, a devout Buddhist, had made a pilgrimage to Wutai shan.

The **gate-building** (Shan men or Mountain Gate) is interesting for its stone carving. On either side of the entrance are two stone 'windows', arched and with stone-carved lattice. While other examples of such carving over doorways and windows in Chengde usually involve the Buddhist lotus emblem, the carvings here are more geometric (and reminiscent of furniture decoration). Many of the original buildings in the enclosure are now in ruins but the seven-bay main hall with its double roof covered in imperial yellow tiles still stands. Inside are three gilded Manjusri figures with flame mandorlas. The Bodhisattva is characteristically depicted riding a lion. Behind the hall is a mountain garden with rocks and pines.

Guang'an si (Temple of Great Peace). Nothing remains of this temple. It was constructed to the west of the Shuxiang si in 1772 in honour of the 80th birthday of Qianlong's mother (when the Ten-thousand Buddha Pavilion in Peking's Beihai Park was also built). It was apparently built in the Tibetan style with none of the ideal Chinese axial balance.

Luohan tang (Hall of the Lohans). Nothing remains of this hall, built 1774, although some of the gilded statues of the 500 lohans may still be seen in the Puning si.

Shenyang

Shenyang, capital city of Liaoning province, has recently seen considerable industrial investment from Japan and South Korea; most tourists come from these countries and the high standard of the hotels reflects their demands.

Practical information

Getting there
By air

Shenyang can be reached by international flights from Irkutsk, Osaka, Seoul and Tokyo. There are three to four flights a day to major Chinese cities.

By train

It is on the trans-Russian (rather than trans-Mongolian) branch of the Trans-Siberian Railway and also on the route to North Korea.

Getting around
The sights of Shenyang are scattered in and around the sprawling city and so are best reached by taxi.

 Where to stay
Meisan Binguan, 48 Xiaoxi lu, ☎ 2273 5538, near the Imperial Palace, or the **Gloria Plaza Hotel** (one of a luxury chain), 32 Yingbin jie, near the north train station, ☎ 2252 8855, fax 252 8533.

History

Shenyang was formerly known as Mukden (in a western variant of its Manchu name). In 1625 it was declared the first capital of the Manchus, who were to conquer all of China and establish the Qing dynasty in 1644. And, as the *Japanese Railway Guide* noted, like all the major centres in northeastern China, it 'occupied a most advantageous position in regard to railway facilities'. It was also, like Changchun, economically involved with beans, its chief products being bean-cakes and bean oil. The guide contains a long section on the organisation and management of *you fang* or 'oil-manufactories' which used horses or donkeys to power the bean-cracking machines.

Nurhaci (1559–1626), founder of the Qing dynasty, was born into the Aisin Gioro clan which held the hereditary chieftainship of one of the Juchen tribes. The Juchen or Jurched were of Tungusic stock: the Tungus were tribes inhabiting eastern Manchuria (or *Dongbei* as the Chinese call it, a name meaning the 'Northeast') and lived by a combination of hunting and agriculture (which included pig-raising). Although the Chinese built palisades (ditches with embankments planted with willows) to divide Manchuria into the region controlled by China and that beyond, the whole area was naturally an undivided plain, inhabited by various settled tribes. Nurhaci was later to forbid the use of the term *Nuzhen* (Juchen or Jurched in western usage) because it smacked of Chinese suzerainty (the first character in Chinese means 'slave'), which he spent his life overcoming, preferring *Man zhou* (Manchu), a term whose origins are obscure.

Through a combination of marriages (to the daughter and granddaughter of two of his rival chiefs) and warfare, through which he united the major Jurched tribes against the Chinese (who had killed his father and grandfather in battle), Nurhaci rose to prominence in the Liaodong peninsula. He extended his control by developing trade with the Chinese in the highly prized medicinal root ginseng, which grew locally, and in horses, thereby establishing a sound local economy. He also set up the beginnings of a state bureaucracy which used a new system of writing, the Manchu language based on the Mongol alphabet. Classic Confucian works were translated into Manchu and a captured Chinese official, Fan Wencheng, advised Nurhaci on the establishment of his administration. He regrouped the Manchus into companies of warriors called 'banners' into which all warriors and their dependants were registered, taxed, conscripted and mobilised as necessary. He moved his capital to Shenyang in 1625, when the building of his palace began. On his death in 1626 he was succeeded by his eighth son, Abahai (1592–1643), who began the preparations for the conquest of northern China. This was finally achieved in 1644 under Dorgon (1612–50, the 14th son of Nurhaci), who officially only acted as regent for Abahai's small son.

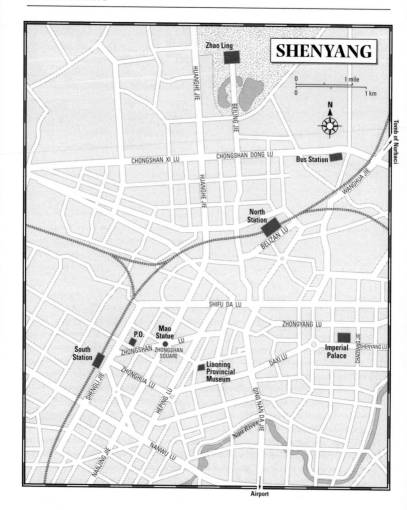

Monuments relating to Nurhaci's capital are the most important sites in Shenyang today.

Imperial Palace

The old Imperial Palace, originally named Shengjing gong (Palace of the Prosperous Capital), was renamed Travelling Palace of Upholding Heaven in 1644 when the Manchu capital was moved to Peking. The term *xing gong* or 'travelling palace' is more commonly used to refer to buildings used occasionally by the Qing emperors on their regular 'tours of inspection'. These were mostly made to the prettier parts of the Jiangnan or Yangtse delta area so the Shenyang travelling palace is an unusual northern example. It stands in the centre of the old city of Shenyang. Covering an area of 60,000 square metres, it was begun in

1625 and basically completed in 1636, although additions were made in the 18C. It consists of a walled enclosure surrounding over 300 'rooms' in ten court-yards grouped in three axes. The central axis, entered through the Daqing (Great Purity) Gate, leads through the main hall, the Chongzheng (Esteem Government) Hall to the rear palace (from the Fenghuang or Phoenix Tower) where Nurhaci and his family had apartments.

The eastern axis is most typically Manchu in architectural disposition for a long courtyard is filled with ten regularly spaced pavilions, the Shi wang or Ten Kings' Pavilions where the heads of the Eight Banners and the Two Kings of the Left and Right Wings (in other words the highest placed officials and chiefs of the Manchu administration) had their own offices. At the northernmost end of the enclosure is the octagonal, double-roofed, ceremonial Dazheng dian (Hall of Great Government). The Chongzheng Hall, on the central axis, was built in 1632. The roof is tiled in yellow with a green border and decorated ridge while the ceiling is painted with 'flying clouds and pouring water'. Between two dragon pillars is a gold dragon screen and throne where the emperor was to discuss mil-itary or governmental affairs and receive foreign ambassadors and the envoys of minorities such as Tibetans and Mongolians. It was here that the name of the dynasty (*qing* meaning 'pure and bright') was proclaimed in 1636. Whenever emperors stayed in Shenyang on trips to the north, government matters were dis-cussed in this hall.

The tallest structure in the palace is the three storey **Fenghuang Tower**, which acts as a gate marking the entrance to the 'inner' Qingning Palace where the emperor and his family had their private apartments; it was also the place where imperial banquets were held and military campaigns were planned. When the court was moved to Peking in 1644, and the Manchus 'entered the passes' (the term used to mean entering China proper from outside the Chinese pale), palace archives and seals relating to the beginnings of Qing rule were kept here. Behind the Fenghuang Tower, on the same axis, is the Qingning Hall, standing on a stone platform 3.8m high at the northern end of the courtyard. The empresses used the eastern side of the hall (in Chinese practice they would prob-ably have been on the west) and ancestral and other ceremonies were held in the western side under the supervision of shamans at dawn, midday and dusk and on festival days. In the southeast corner of the courtyard is a pole topped by a tin measure where grain used to be set out to feed the sparrows and other birds.

The most important building on the western axis of the palace is the **Wensu ge** (Hall of the Source of Culture), built in 1782 to house one of the first four sets of the *Si ku quan shu* (the imperial collectanea, *Complete Collection of the Four Treasuries*, a manuscript edition of some 3450 works; see Peking, Hangzhou and Chengde where other copies were housed). This library building is somewhat dif-ferent from the others in that it has a stage in front, although, like the others, it is said to be modelled on the private library, Tianyi ge, in Ningbo. Inside the hall is a plaque with an inscription by the Qianlong emperor: 'The flavours of the ancient and modern are contained within; plucking from it is to explore the ten thousand phenomena and the deep blue sea. With rites and music, respect for fundamentals is celebrated from the Three Rivers to the Milky Way and the vast oceans.' There is also a stele in a pavilion to the east of the hall with a Chinese-Manchu inscription commemorating the establishment of the Hall.

In the suburbs of Shenyang are two imperial tombs and a temple. In Heping qu on Huangsi lu is the **Shisheng** (True Victory) **Temple**, also known as the Huang si, Imperial Temple, and the Huang si, Yellow Temple, both *huang* being second tone but written with different characters. It was the most important Lamaist temple in Shenyang before 1644. Built in 1638 and substantially restored in 1726, it covers an area of over 5500 square metres and contains some imposing buildings.

The **Tomb of Nurhaci**, true founder of the Qing, is c 11km northeast of the city and is known as the Fu ling (Fortunate Tomb) or Dong ling (Eastern Tomb). Built against the Tianzhu mountains with a river in front, in an area thick with conifers, it was started in 1629 and finished in 1651, although later embellishments were added in the 18C. The area enclosed by its surrounding wall is 194,800 square metres. In front of the gate is the usual notice to dismount (also found at the other Qing tomb enclosures), while inside is an avenue of paired animals: camels, lions and horses. On either side of the stele tower are buildings originally intended to serve as stores for ceremonial vessels and materials used in sacrifices. There is a 'lacquer vessel' store, a 'sacrificial animal' store, a 'document' store and so on.

The tomb itself lies beyond, within a fortified-looking wall which encloses a three storey tower. This 'Square City' with its corner towers stands in front of the 'Jade City', the circular enclosure with the tree-covered mound beneath which the emperor, empresses and concubines are actually buried. Like the other Qing tombs, it was forbidden for anyone to enter the tomb enclosure during the life of the dynasty, unless they came officially to make sacrifices and offerings on birthdays and festivals.

The similar **Zhao ling** (Clear Tomb), also known as the Bei ling (Northern Tomb), is in the northern suburbs of Shenyang and contains the bodies of Abahai and his wife. It is the largest and best-preserved of the Qing tombs that lie 'beyond the passes'. It was built between 1643 and 1651 with additions and alterations by the Qianlong and Kangxi emperors, who were incapable of leaving anything alone. Before the gate are stone lions, stone bridges (crossing the waterway required by *feng shui* beliefs), mounting stones (where visitors were required to dismount), two pavilions (one for robing and one for sacrifices) and a finely carved *pailou* (archway) in black Liaoyang stone. In the avenue of paired animals beyond, the horses are said to have been modelled on Abahai's favourite mounts. In the Square City is the Long'en Hall with a curtained bed in one alcove and another containing the spirit tablets of the emperor and his wife, as well as various items of furniture: incense burners, palace lanterns and candle-holders.

In the centre of Shenyang, a **statue of Chairman Mao** (one of the few surviving) presides over Zhongshan Square. Dating from 1969, the base is decorated with peasants, workers from the nearby Daqing oilfield and students waving copies of the *Little Red Book*. Above them, Mao, dressed in a white concrete overcoat, waves.

Harbin

Harbin (properly rendered in pinyin as Haerbin), on the banks of the Songhua or Songan River, capital of Heilongjiang, China's northernmost province.

Practical information

Getting there
It can be reached by many of the same means as Shenyang with international flights to Korea, Siberia and Japan and the Trans-Siberian railway.

Where to stay
The oldest hotel in Harbin (1906) is the **Modern Hotel** (Madieer Binguan), 89 Zhongyang da jie, ☎ 461 5846, fax 461 4997. At the corner of Zhongyang da jie and Jingwei jie is the **Holiday Inn** (Wanda jiari jiudian), 90 Jingwie jie, ☎ 422 6666, fax 422 1661. Both are well-situated for walks to the river.

History

Harbin is a city that grew with the railways. For the *Japanese Railway Guide* to Manchuria (1913) it was 'a child, bred, reared and supported by the Chinese Eastern Railway'.

By 1933 the child had grown and, according to Carl Crow, in his *Handbook to China*: 'It now has a population of about 200,000, half Chinese and half Russian, thus having the largest European population of any city in Asia.' The Russian population of Harbin was enormously swelled by the influx of White Russian refugees from the 1917 Revolution. Yet even before the expansion of 1917, the *Japanese Railway Guide* states that 'every visitor who does not already know Russian will soon wish he did'. There is still a tiny, but rapidly aging, White Russian population left in Harbin, although most Russians there nowadays are transient, younger businessmen crossing the border to buy cheap Chinese goods.

The continuing attraction of Harbin is its Russian-ness, with stucco buildings perfectly resembling those of St Petersburg lining the streets and the onion domes of Orthodox churches visible above. One of the best areas for wandering is the old South Riparian Quarter on the south bank of the river, around Youyi lu, Shangzhi and Zhongyang da jie. The riverside park is Stalin Park, a popular place for walking, with street vendors and entertainers. Back from the riverside, on the corner of Zhaolin jie (east of Zhongynag da jie) is the Church of St Sophia (1907).

Another aspect of Harbin's history is seen in Pingfang qu, in the **Japanese Germ Warfare Experimental Base** where quite horrific experiments were secretly carried out on Chinese people during the Second World War. Bubonic plague was injected into some victims, while others contributed to knowledge of how the body behaves at extreme temperatures by being frozen (the results were eventually useful in early open-heart surgery) or by being roasted alive, which has not advanced the cause of science at all. The establishment was not dissimilar to those in some German concentration camps and, as with various German scientists, some of the 'scientists' were protected after the end of the Second World War by the US government, which was interested in some of their results.

Today Harbin is famous for its **Ice Festival**, held annually from 1 January till early March. Ice sculptures of stunning technical achievement but doubtful aesthetic value (Mickey Mouse is tending to replace Chinese dragons) are created; some with lanterns inside them and some that can be climbed by children and slid down are set up in the Zhaolin Park. The Sungari also freezes over and can become a road, bearing the load of lorries when it is 1m thick.

It is said that a Father Christmas grotto is planned to supplement the winter tourist attractions (watch out Lapland). For adults, however, Harbin is quite often visited by bird-watchers looking for cranes and by railway enthusiasts drawn by the steam engines which are still extensively used.

Beidaihe

Beidaihe, on the Hebei coast, is a seaside resort favoured by foreign diplomats since the last years of the 19C. In those days foreign missionaries also came to Beidaihe for their summer holidays; nowadays, although foreign diplomats still come, they are vastly outnumbered by Chinese visitors. In the summer, when sea-bathing is most popular, it is virtually impossible for a Chinese person without 'connections' to find a place to stay and the beaches are completely covered with people.

Practical information

 Getting there
Five or six hours by train (north on the line to Shenyang) from Peking and also accessible by air from Peking or Qinhuangdao, it is a pleasant place, preferably out of season, unless you are very keen on crowds. The railway station is 15km north of the town: a no. 5 bus or a taxi will take you to the centre.

 Where to stay
The best place to stay is the *Diplomatic Guesthouse* (Waijiao renyuan binguan), 1 Baosan lu, ☎ 404 1287, which has a private beach, barbecues and tennis courts.

Apart from new hotels and shops, the older buildings still retain something of the flavour of the past. In Ann Bridge's novel *Four-part Setting* (1939), Beidaihe is the setting for a tale of restrained romance, with bungalows 'half-hidden in the native growth of bushes and small trees, mimosas and thorns', convenient cover for kisses 'amongst the polygonums'. After shopping for 'such articles as cannot well be left to the discretion of their Number One Boy' in the shopping centre, 'an untidy row of shacks, a sort of tumble-down tin-town, in which the big shops from Tientsin and Shanghai open ephemeral branches for the summer season', holidaying foreigners would return to their bungalows where the verandah 'ran the whole length of the bungalow; a dining table stood at one end; rush chairs with cushions, a bridge table and gramophone occupied the centre—the further end was littered with tennis racquets, a fishing rod and other sporting gear.' The writer continues: 'It was the custom in Beidaihe to lunch in negligees in one's own house', so one donned a kimono and espadrilles after a sitz bath and recuperated from shopping over cocktails on the verandah.

A rather less ephemeral branch of the famous Tientsin/Tianjin restaurant, *Kiesslings*, originally run by Austrians, still exists in Beidaihe, serving coffee, bread and cakes. The accommodation available includes some of the old bungalow buildings: the *Diplomatic Guesthouse* (see above) and the *Xishan Guesthouse*.

From Beidaihe it is possible to visit **Shanhaiguan**, 50km north, the point where the Great Wall tumbles into the sea. Nearby is the **temple** dedicated to Meng Qiang nu, the legendary wife of a man who was conscripted during the Qin (221–206 BC) to build the Great Wall.

> Her husband was away for many years and her family threatened to marry her again so she set off to try and find him. At Shanhaiguan she finally discovered that he had died during his corvée service. On hearing the news, her tears made the wall fall down. Her devoted search for her husband is the subject of many popular stories and operas.

In the temple are paired inscriptions outside the main hall: 'the waves of the sea break break break break break break'; 'the floating clouds drift drift drift drift drift drift'. The rear hall is devoted to the Bodhisattva Guanyin.

Shanghai

Shanghai, China's largest city with a population of 16 million (there were 10.8 million in 1982) living in an area of 6100 square kilometres, lies on the Huangpu River in the Yangtse delta. The small seaport, surrounded by a circular defensive wall built in 1553 to prevent raids by Japanese pirates, was recognised as a port with trade potential and forcibly opened to foreign trade at the end of the First Opium War in 1842. It quickly attracted entrepreneurs and a poor reputation, of which the term 'to shanghai' (first used in 1871), meaning 'to drug or otherwise render insensible and ship on board a vessel wanting hands' is an illustration. Its early growth as a treaty port was steady but saw a dramatic increase during the First World War when European trade was disrupted. Its prosperity in the 1920s and 1930s is demonstrated in the grand office buildings that line the riverfront and its reputation as 'the wickedest city in the world'.

The Japanese invasion and occupation of Shanghai in 1942–45, during which foreign residents were interned, marked the beginning of the end of Shanghai as a treaty port. Most foreign firms left after 1949, although the last foreign factory, a Swiss-owned aluminium mill, was not taken over until 1960.

Shanghai is one of China's three 'municipalities', with the equivalent status to a province, and is still a major port and industrial area. Traces of its 'foreign' history are rapidly disappearing as the most extraordinary variety of skyscrapers rise above the squat forms of old rusticated stone banks and offices. The 'lane houses' in which most of the Shanghainese lived can still be seen in some areas, from the triple-decker motorways that now swarm over the city, but they are being demolished steadily and their inhabitants moved out to vast new high-rise housing estates on the Pudong side of the river.

Practical information

Getting there
By air

There are both domestic and international departures from the old airport (Hongqiao or Rainbow Bridge Airport, named after the suburb immediately to the south) which is 15km west of the city centre. A new airport was opened on the Pudong side of the river on 1 October 1999, to celebrate the 50th anniversary of the founding of the People's Republic of China, with a motorway and underground connections to the centre of the city. The division of flights between the old and new airports is not yet clear, although all foreign airlines are expected to fly to and from Pudong airport from 2001; as they are on opposite sides of the vast city, you are advised to check carefully before setting off for a flight. Taxis to and from Hongqiao Airport take about 1½ hours (70–80 yuan). There is a shuttle bus between the two airports (every 20 minutes; journey time c 1 hour, 30 yuan). Taxis from Pudong to the Bund area take about 1½ hours and cost c 150 yuan. There may be supplementary charges on taxis from both airports for the elevated roadways (15 yuan). Once the metro line is completed this will be a convenient way to get to Pudong Airport.

Getting around
By underground

Shanghai's new and quite extensive underground system makes it easy to get around the city, particularly as road traffic is frequently at a standstill.

By boat

Passenger boats depart from the numbered quays on the Bund (Zhongshan lu, near the junction with Dongmen lu leading east from the old Chinese city) and the advance booking office is at 1 Jinling Donglu.

By train

The Railway Station is in the north of the city, near the junction of Henan bei lu and Tianmu lu and is now more accessible if you haven't too much luggage since it is on the end of the underground line which leads southwestwards across the city to Renmin Square in the centre and the old Jesuit settlement of Xujiahui in the southwest.

Where to stay

Shanghai now bursts with hotels and most of the major international chains are represented but the older hotels in Shanghai are of greater interest. On the Bund (Zhongshan lu), overlooking the Huangpu, is the *Peace (Heping) Hotel*, 170 Nanjing xilu, ☎ 6321 6888, fax 6329 0300, which has two buildings: that on the south side of the road was formerly the Palace Hotel while the taller building on the north side was Sassoon House, comprising office buildings of the Sassoon family and the old Cathay Hotel, built in 1930. Noel Coward stayed there soon after the opening in 1930 and, suffering from influenza, is said to have completed the draft of *Private Lives* using an Eversharp pencil. Although the rooms have been refurbished, which involved the removal of much of the British bathroom porcelain and the chaise-longues in curtained alcoves which used to grace the rooms, the corridors are unchanged, with dim '30s' light-fittings, the originals by Tiffany. The hotel is still famous for its bar and the pre-war swing played every night by an increasingly elderly group of gentlemen. For decades, this was the only jazz combo surviving in China. Such was the popularity of the Peace's band that there are now several others.

Just to the north of the Peace, on the north side of the Suzhou Creek which joins the Huangpu, is the **Shanghai Mansions** (Shanghai daxia), formerly Broadway Mansions, 20 Bei Suzhou lu, ☎ 6324 6200, fax 6306 5147, which was built in 1934 as an apartment hotel with small suites for long-term residents. A tall, block-like '30s building, it affords a fine view of the Bund area from the top floor and in the 1930s used to have a band playing in the evening led by Howard 'Zing' Wu with 'Shorty' on the piano. This hotel has also been refurbished and little of the original interior remains.

In the centre of the city is the **Overseas Chinese Hotel** (Huaqiao fandian), dwarfed by its next-door neighbour, the 24-storey **Park Hotel** (Guoji fandian), 170 Nanjing xilu, ☎ 6327 5225, fax 6327 6958, which was advertised as 'ready for occupancy September 1934'. Then it boasted that it was the tallest building in the Far East, with 205 luxury furnished rooms,

apartments and unfurnished flats, and it still has an amazing art deco dining room high above the Nanjing Road.

West of the central district is the **Jing'an Guesthouse** (formerly Haig Mansions), 370 Huashan lu, ☎ 6248 1888, fax 6248 2657, near the old 'Bubbling Well' which gave the name to the road that is now known as Nanjing xilu. Set behind a large and beautifully-kept lawn with pretty gardens, it stands in what used to be a smart residential area.

In the old French district is the **Jinjiang Hotel**, 57 Maoming lu, ☎ 6258 2582, fax 6472 5588, a huge complex of castellated towers originally constructed, like the Shanghai Mansions, as an apartment hotel. A flight of steps sweeps up to the entrance of the main building, and the lifts, with their clock-dials, used to figure in Chinese films of the 1950s when pre-liberation luxury was depicted. The Jinjiang has been refurbished; much of the lobby has been buried. south of the Jinjiang Hotel is the **Ruijin Guesthouse**, 118 Ruijin erlu, ☎ 6472 5222 x 1000, www.shedi.net.cn/OUTEDI/Ruijin, once a private house, said to have been owned by Chiang Kai-shek's brother-in-law. It has dark wooden panelling, 1930s furniture and black tiled bathrooms as well as a garden.

Other hotels

Luxury

Huating, 1200 Caoxi bei lu, ☎ 6439 1000, fax 6255 0830

Xijiao Binguan, 1921 Hongqiao lu, ☎ 6219 8800, fax 6433 6641

Shanghai Hilton, 250 Huashan lu, ☎ 6248 0000, fax 6248 3848, email: shhilton@public.sta.net.cn

First class

Longbai (Cypress) **Fandian**, 2419 Hongqiao lu, ☎ 6268 8868, fax 6242 3739.

Donghu Guesthouse (Du Yuesheng's old

residence), 70 Donghu lu, ☎ 6415 8158, fax 6433 1275

Standard

Hengshan Hotel (previously Picardie Mansions), 534 Hengshan lu, ☎ 6437

7050, fax 6433 5732

Shanghai Hotel, 505 Wulumuqi bei li, ☎ 6248 0088, fax 6248 1056

Xingguo Guesthouse, 72 Xinggua lu, ☎ 6212 9998, fax 6251 2154

History

It was Shanghai's position in the **Yangtse delta** that first attracted Europeans looking for a trade port. The Yangtse flows through much of China's richest and most fertile territory, from Sichuan province in the west, through the silk, tea and rice-producing delta to the sea. The river brings much silt with it, as the early western port engineers discovered in the latter part of the 19C, and this has shaped Shanghai's history. The name *Shanghai* means 'on the sea' or 'beside the sea' and although this name has only been used from the Song dynasty (before that it was probably almost non-existent, described as 'part of Hua ting county'), it may well be that Shanghai used to be nearer the sea. Literary accounts describe how the Suzhou River (originally known as the Wusong River) was much wider in the Tang but had shrunk to less than half its width by the Song and continued to narrow as more silt was brought down through succeeding centuries until it became the narrow flow that the European inhabitants of Shanghai knew as the Suzhou Creek. Another, older name for the Suzhou or Wusong River was the Hudu, and the first character *hu* became the literary name for Shanghai, which is still used in, for example, railway timetables.

By the Song dynasty Shanghai had acquired the name *Shanghai zhen*, or 'Market Town by the Sea', and in 1292, under the Yuan, it was elevated to the status of county town. As trade, notably with Japan, in silks and tea grew during the succeeding centuries, Shanghai's key position, situated at the head of the Yangtse which, with its tributaries, flowed past all the most important silk- and tea-producing towns of the delta, meant that it became one of China's major ports. Coastal traffic was officially controlled and boats from the north were allowed no further south than Shanghai (and vice versa) so that it became an interprovincial entrepot. Incursions by Japanese pirates in the early 16C led to the walling of the town for protection. Although the city walls were demolished in 1912, the ring road circling the 'Chinese' town in the southeast of the city still indicates the form of the enclosure and the roads that led out from the gates are named for them. Shanghai's steady growth as a local port with a volume of trade probably equal to that of London in the 19C was, however, interrupted by western trading interests which eventually came to shape the modern city.

Although trade was dramatically to affect the city, the first foreign 'influence' came from the Jesuit missionaries of the 16C. One of Ricci's converts was **Xu Guangqi** (1562–1633), a native of Xujiahui (which means Xu Family Village), now part of metropolitan Shanghai but then a village within Shanghai county. Xu, who was baptised Paul in 1603, had left his native village to become an official in Peking, working first in the Board of Rites, later in the Imperial Library. He was the highest-ranking Chinese official to convert and family land was later given to the Catholic Church which established an observatory and cathedral in Xujiahui.

A century later, when foreign traders had established themselves in some discomfort in Canton and Macau, confined to a narrow strip of coast, compelled to deal with imperially-appointed merchants, they began to cast about for more favourable sites. An **East India Company** report of 1756 noted that Shanghai was a desirable place for trade, owing to its protected site away from the typhoons of the coast and its pivotal point of access to the tea and silks of the hinterland. An East India Company vessel, the *Lord Amherst*, made an exploratory trip up the Huangpu in 1832 and although Mr Lindsay, who headed the commercial mission, managed to see the local official in charge, there was no question at the time of opening Shanghai to trade. Lindsay was very enthusiastic about Shanghai's potential, despite his frosty reception, counting the junks in the river whose numbers suggested that Shanghai was, even then, one of the world's busiest ports, hoping for a market for British woollens in the colder western provinces of the upper Yangtse and concluding that '... considering the extraordinary advantages which this place possesses for foreign trade it is wonderful that it has not attracted more observation.'

Under Chinese restrictions of foreign traders even observation was difficult but the **Treaty of Nanking**, imposed upon the Chinese after defeat in the **First Opium War** (1842), negotiated after British warships had sailed up the Yangtse, past the point near Shanghai where the Huangpu joined the great river, succeeded where more peaceful commercial missions had failed. Shanghai, Canton, Amoy (Xiamen), Fuzhou and Ningbo were not only opened to trade but British consuls and the families of both merchants and consuls were to be admitted (women had not previously been allowed into the 'factories' in Canton and Macau). According to land regulations negotiated with the senior Chinese official, the Daotai, after the treaty, foreigners were still not allowed into the walled city but were allocated a plot of land immediately north of the city, reaching up to the Suzhou river, with anchorage extending some 300m across the Huangpu. The area allocated was bounded by ditches which, with the exception of the Suzhou River, have since been filled in. Amongst the earliest works initiated by Captain George Balfour, the first consul, were drainage works, which were to continue for as one of Shanghai's historians remarked:

Within the memory of the present writer the positions now occupied by the Russian and German consulates were under water, and the Bund foreshore was unfilled, the tides coming up to the footpath.

Embankments were constructed on the tidal foreshore, a process known by the Anglo-Indian term 'bunding' which gave the waterfront road its name. Struggles with water marked much of Shanghai's early foreign history. Not only did the foreshore need strengthening, but the drinking water supply required urgent attention. At first, local water was taken out by ship and settled with alum, then boiled before consumption, until a water company working under contract to the Shanghai Municipal Council began to supply piped and chlorinated water in 1883. This had the further advantage of wiping out 'Shanghai itch' a skin rash caused by wearing clothes that had been washed in the filthy local water. Some residents had resorted to sending their washing to Japan on a fortnight's round trip to avoid 'the itch' but were now able to have their laundry done at home.

Struggles with the silt of the delta were another problem. As the estuary is tidal, silt not only flows downstream but is also sucked upstream with the tide. From the 13C various forms of flood gates had been set up at the mouth of the Suzhou Creek to prevent the inflow of silt, and the main channel, the Huangpu, was endlessly scoured to prevent it silting up and inhibiting the passage of deep-draught ships which often had to wait for the tide before they could enter the channel. Between 1905 and 1930 Dutch and Swedish hydraulic engineers supervised the dredging of nearly 26 million cubic metres (34 million cubic yards) of mud from the Huangpu shipping channel. The subsoil of the riverbank gave cause for considerable worry, as Lanning described in 1920:

What Shanghai is built on we now know with some degree of certainty and detail. When our first iron bridge was in course of construction in 1871 on the site of the present Garden Bridge (over the Suzhou Creek on the Bund), visitors to the Public Garden were astounded one afternoon to see it bodily sinking before their eyes. Its collapse and disappearance gave the first serious object lesson regarding the foundational value of Shanghai subsoil.

Perhaps because of the problematic subsoil, the first British buildings in Shanghai were based on those of Canton: bungalows and offices of no more than two storeys with open verandahs, mostly built by workmen brought up from Canton. A major priority with the early British settlers was sport; a racecourse was built at the western end of Park Lane (later the Nanjing Road) and excursions were made into the flat surrounding countryside of the delta, to shoot snipe. Later, the racecourse was moved west, along the Nanjing Road, to the area now occupied by the Renmin Park and the square, despite the fact that the area had been occupied by Chinese graveyards and much local opposition was encountered. The 1904 map of Shanghai shows the racecourse with swimming baths and cricket ground within its circular enclosure.

Balfour's major tasks were to open Shanghai to foreign trade and to establish the rules by which foreign traders could lease land, providing they allowed former owners to visit their ancestral graves. Foreign representatives had long been trying to establish a right of 'extraterritoriality' in China which, in the words of an early colonial legal expert, Sir Francis Piggott, once Chief Justice of Hong Kong, meant that: '... the foreign sovereign enforces the duties of his subjects, representing the oriental sovereign *pro haec vice*, but does not protect their rights, except in the single instance of disputes amongst themselves.' In other words, foreign residents had to observe local laws but did not need to attend local courts. Consular courts were set up in 1842, and in 1863 the British Consul established the Mixed Court, a 'tribunal for the decision of cases in which foreigners were either directly or indirectly interested ... in which due attention to foreigners' interests might be secured by the presence of their representatives, while the jurisdiction of the native authorities was left untouched.' It acted as a police court when a Chinese officer tried cases involving Chinese in the Settlement that had been brought by the police, while in criminal cases brought by foreigners against Chinese, a Chinese magistrate delivered judgement in the presence of a Consular Assessor.

By the end of 1843 there were 11 foreign firms operating in Shanghai—mainly British and American businesses formerly based in **Canton**—and by

1849 there were 175 foreigners resident in Shanghai. The position of the Americans was different: never directly associated with the unpleasant business of Opium Wars and subsequent treaties, they established themselves in **Hongkou** on the north bank of the Suzhou Creek, although in 1863 their settlement was merged with that of the British to form the new 'international settlement' under the control of the Shanghai Municipal Government which had formerly only controlled the British Settlement. Japanese had also begun to settle in Hongkou, where rents were lower than in the British Settlement on the south side of the Suzhou Creek, and the French, who had arrived in 1846, (although according to one supercilious English writer, their trading interests consisted of only one shopkeeper) negotiated the lease of a separate plot of land south of the British concession between the British and the Chinese city.

In the early days, up to 1890, foreign firms traded mainly in **tea**, **silk** and (illegal) **opium**. While these were the major commodities of interest to foreign traders, Shanghai's importance as a port of transhipment is evident in the fact that overseas imports in the first 100 years almost always exceeded exports by about 10 per cent per year. Until 1900 Shanghai had a virtual monopoly of world trade in tea and silk but, as with other agricultural goods like rubber and sugar, the monopoly declined and a more varied trade pattern emerged in the 20C. An early visitor to Shanghai was Robert Fortune, a well-known plant-hunter. In the early 1850s he travelled in China on behalf of the British East India Company collecting tea cuttings and information on tea-growing in order to set up rival plantations in India, precisely in order to break China's monopoly of tea production. Silk exports declined partly because of changes in fashion and partly because the Japanese began to make determined efforts to overtake China as a silk producer and introduced mechanisation to the detriment of the handicraft methods of the Chinese.

The import of opium, whose consumption had long been known in China but whose spread was promoted by the early foreign traders, was officially banned by the Chinese but it continued to be brought into Shanghai illegally on foreign ships. This posed a problem for the British Consuls who were caught between Chinese law which prohibited it and British law which did not. The first British Consul, Balfour, acted decisively against those ships whose manifests (lists of ship's cargo) showed chests of opium but, nevertheless, it was well known that there were often as many as six ships loaded with opium anchored at Shanghai.

In the first decade of foreign residence in Shanghai the life of the trader varied between the frenzied activity of the early summer silk-buying season, complicated by the slowness of communications with the home markets (seven weeks by sea until the telegraph line through Siberia was set up in 1871), and the relative quiet of the rest of the year. A visitor in the late 1850s stated that it was:

... the most rowdy and disreputable place imaginable ... the bulk of the population is composed of a number of lively spirits who drive about in pony traps the whole day and call themselves brokers, but whose occupation, like Othello's, is apparently gone ... California in its worst days could not have been worse than Shanghai today.

The entry 'Sink of Iniquity' in Couling's *Encyclopaedia Sinica* (1917) refers to

'... an expression used by the Duke of Somerset in Parliament in 1869 ... the accusation was against the commercial morality of the place'.

Residents took exercise by shooting pheasant, teal and woodcock on the mud-flats, and riding, although there were complaints about the condition of the ponies which was such that in 1852, a 'man and horse race, 50 yards there and back, was won by the man.' Class distinctions were already apparent for the regatta featured 'mainly ... merchant crews'.

A source of material on the early social life of Shanghai is the *North China Herald* which commenced publication on 3 August 1850, its 'northernness' being relative to Canton, the first foreign base in China, reflecting the inward-looking attitude of the foreign residents. Serving less than 150 residents, the *North China Herald* describes performances of amateur dramatics in the New and Imperial theatres, which included an operatic burlesque extravaganza entitled *Roofscrambler* and something else called *Bombastes Furioso*. The **Northern Lodge of Freemasons** held its first meeting in 1849 and the first bachelor's ball was held in 1850, although dancing was difficult due to the lack of female partners.

The original Catholic settlement at Xujiahui, established in the 17C, had suffered from persecution and the church became a temple to the god of war. It was later returned to the French but meanwhile, in 1848, the foundation stone of a new cathedral was laid. In the same year a wooden Protestant Episcopalian church was built, although its roof fell in within two years and it was decided that it must be replaced with something more substantial, which was to be one of Gilbert Scott's earliest commissions in 1862. Missionaries arrived with the first traders: Dr Medhurst of the London Missionary Society conducted a service in the British Consulate in 1843, Dr West J. Boone of the Protestant Episcopal Mission arrived in 1845, bringing Miss Fay, the first unmarried American lady to come to China; the Church Missionary Society arrived in 1849 as did Dr M.T. Yates of the Southern Baptist Convention, and others came from the Northern Presbyterian Church and the Southern Methodist Episcopal Mission.

In 1853 **Taiping rebels** took nearby Nanjing and the foreign community in Shanghai had to consider its defence. Opinion amongst the foreign community was divided for the leader of the Taiping rebels, Hong Xiuquan, had learnt something about Christianity, apparently from the Rev. Issachar J. Roberts of the American Baptist Missionary Union in Canton, and believed that he was Christ's brother. The editor of the *North China Herald* supported the Taiping rebels against the imperial forces, as did many missionaries. But when Nanjing fell and an army of the **Small Sword Society** (Xiao dao hui), a branch of the Triad secret society from Guangdong province, took advantage of the turmoil caused by the Taiping and seized the Chinese city of Shanghai in September 1853, the foreign community felt forced to take action. An international group, the Shanghai Volunteer Corps, was formed and its first action, the Battle of Muddy Flat, was to clear an encampment of imperial troops which had been made within the boundaries of the International Settlement. The Small Sword Society was finally driven out of the Chinese city in 1855 and the Taiping rebels never managed to enter the city but the incidents had a considerable effect on Shanghai's development.

The **Shanghai Municipal Council**, comprising British, French and American representatives, was inaugurated on 11 July 1854. It immediately formed new committees such as that of 'Roads, Jetties and Police' and adopted a set of 'Land Regulations'. These recognised Chinese sovereignty over the land of the settlement and that all land leases should be conducted with the Chinese through the renter's own consul. One of the effects of civil disorder had been a huge number of Chinese refugees arriving in the settlement, seeking safety. It was therefore agreed that Chinese should be allowed to lease buildings in the International and French settlements, thus completely altering the nature of the settlements and laying a new pattern for Shanghai's development.

As a result of the disruption caused by the Small Swords' occupation of the Chinese city and the powerlessness of the Chinese Daotai who, like thousands of other Chinese, had been forced to seek refuge in the British Settlement, the regulation of customs and collection of customs duties had lapsed completely and the Daotai agreed with the foreign Consuls that they should appoint customs inspectors henceforth to collect customs duties due to the Chinese government. Thus the basis of the Chinese Maritime Customs, staffed by foreigners answerable to the Chinese government, was set in 1854. Many famous figures served in the Chinese customs, including **Sir Thomas Wade**, co-inventor of the Wade-Giles romanisation system and a considerable sinologist, and **Sir Robert Hart**, whose name is virtually synonymous with the Chinese Customs Service for which he worked from 1863 until his death in 1911. In 1864 the Customs Service employed some 1000 Chinese and 400 foreigners. By 1916 the numbers had swelled to 6325 and 1321 respectively, the foreigners by then representing some 20 nationalities.

The **Second Opium War**, or Arrow War, of 1856 was ostensibly the result of an insult to the British flag on a Chinese-owned ship, the *Arrow*, in Canton, but it offered the British, French, Americans and Russians an excuse to press the Chinese imperial government for further opening of the country. The *Arrow* was boarded by a Chinese patrol looking for pirates; they lowered the British flag and arrested 12 Chinese sailors. The Consul's request for an apology was refused; British forces from Hong Kong seized the forts outside Canton; the Chinese set fire to the British 'factories'; an Anglo-French force attacked Canton, while another Anglo-French force set out from Shanghai, making for Peking but settling instead in Tianjin where the **Treaty of Tianjin** was signed in 1858, which considerably expanded the provisions of the Treaty of Nanjing (1842). Another 'unequal' treaty, forced upon the Chinese on a fairly flimsy pretext, this finally 'opened' the interior of China, with ten new treaty ports (mostly on the Yangtse), better conditions of travel and residence in the interior for missionaries and traders, and permanent diplomatic representation in Peking for Britain, France, Russia and the United States. Opening more ports along the Yangtse to foreign trade led to an increase in Shanghai's importance as the starting point and headquarters of up-river ventures.

Oddly, against this background of deliberately-applied pressure, there was considerable co-operation between imperial forces and foreign volunteer forces in the final campaigns against the Taiping rebels (1860–64) in the towns of the Yangtse delta. The Ever-Victorious Army, led first by Ward, an

American who was killed in 1861, later by the British **General Charles Gordon**, who was to die in Khartoum, was paid for by worried Chinese merchants resident in Shanghai. Many thousands of foreign troops, British, Indian and French, released from 'operations in the north' (or sacking the Summer Palace in an effort to enforce the Treaty of Tianjin), also joined the imperial forces against the Taiping rebels.

The Chinese refugee population which had arrived in the foreign settlements as a result of the Taiping upheavals numbered nearly half a million, as against approximately 570 foreigners including 300 British, 60 Indians and about 120 Americans (and 74 women). This ratio of Chinese to foreigners was maintained as Shanghai's population gradually increased, most dramatically between 1910 and 1940 when the foreign population rose from some 10,000 to 60,000, many of the new arrivals consisting of Japanese (who arrived in large numbers after the defeat of China in the Sino-Japanese War of 1894–95 and numbered 20,000 in 1936), White Russians fleeing the Bolsheviks (15,000 in 1936) and some 5000 Germans and Austrians, many of them refugees from Hitler.

The latter half of the 19C saw the physical development of Shanghai with road improvements, the advent of gas street-lights, attempts to establish a railway in 1865–77, which met with hostility from the Chinese, who were unwilling to give up land and in any case regarded railways as interfering with local spirits, the introduction of modern cotton mills, the extension of the settlement, to allow for industrial development up the Huangpu beyond Hongkou, and the construction (on underground rafts of timber from the Puget Sound) of the grand edifices, office blocks in the commercial centre and mansions along Bubbling Well Road, that dominated the Shanghai skyline until the late 1980s.

Many of the names associated with the early trade and later industrial development of Shanghai are still significant in the Far East. *Jardine & Matheson* and *Butterfield & Swire*, Scottish trading companies, were typical, trading in tea and silk (and, in the case of Jardine's, opium) as well as a variety of other goods like bristles and leather, horsehair and cotton piece-goods, as well as dealing in insurance, shipping and land and house agencies. The varied nature of their dealings and their stress on intelligence made them able to cope with the changes in trade patterns. Other major names were those of the Sassoons and, later Hardoon.

Sassoon and Hardoon

Both of these were Jewish families from Baghdad but while the Sassoons had been trading in cotton (and opium) in India and first arrived in Shanghai in 1844, Silas Hardoon was originally employed by the Sassoons and later made his own fortune. **Sassoon House** and the **Cathay** (now Peace) **Hotel** still stand, as does the old Sassoon home, 2409 Hongqiao Road (next to the zoo), a half-timbered, mock-Tudor mansion set in extensive grounds which the Gang of Four (including Jiang Qing, a connoisseur of luxury) used for meetings during the Cultural Revolution. In the late 1970s it became the Shanghai office and residence of the British Petroleum representative. It has since been incorporated as a guest house in the grounds of the *Cypress*

Hotel (and is worth trying to see). Hardoon House was a 26-acre (10.5 hectare) complex including a Buddhist temple (now demolished; the site is occupied by the Shanghai Exhibition Hall). Rising through rent collection to make a fortune in opium and property, Hardoon had married an Eurasian who was a devout Buddhist and paid for the printing of the massive Buddhist canon, while her husband paid for the construction of the Beth Aharon synagogue in the 1920s (now demolished). His funeral consisted of both Chinese and Jewish obsequies. Another grand mansion that still stands, although nowadays occupied by the Number One Children's Palace, is that of the Kadoorie family, a pink and white classical structure of considerable size, which once included a billiard room with several full-size tables.

On the Bund, the **Customs House** and the **Hong Kong and Shanghai Bank** building (now occupied by the Municipal Government), the **Bank of China** building and the pointed peak of the **Peace Hotel** express in stone the wealth of Shanghai in the 1920s and 1930s. It was during this period that the separate existence of the Chinese majority was most strongly felt. The small park on the Bund, laid out beside the bridge over the Suzhou Creek by a Scottish gardener, was infamous to the Chinese who claimed that it had a notice on the gate saying 'No dogs and no Chinese'. This was only partly true for, like any other British municipal park, it was governed by a long list of regulations which did include a prohibition against dogs and, originally, Chinese, except for those accompanied by their foreign employers (this was a let-out clause for the Chinese *amah* or nanny). Owing to confusion over the status of Japanese, the regulation was later amended to allow in 'well-dressed' Chinese but the privacy of the park was strictly guarded by the foreign minority. To a great extent, foreigners and Chinese led separate lives, although they lived in close proximity.

For foreigners, as for Chinese, Shanghai was a luxury shopping paradise, the finest ladies' silk underwear could be found in **Yates Road (Shanxi lu)**, entire trousseaux of the finest hand embroidery from the Door of Hope Mission on **Nanjing Road**, which took in child prostitutes, antiques and silks in Nanjing Road, the best tailors on Avenue Joffre (Huaihai lu) in the French Concession, rugs and carpets in Bubbling Well Road, furniture from such emporia as the Charming Artistic Furniture Co. on the Route des Soeurs, and Parker pens in the middle section of **Fuzhou Road**, without straying into the red-light district, also on the Fuzhou Road, full of young girls, all described as natives of Suzhou, where traditionally the prettiest women with the most seductive voices originate.

Residents, keen to maintain a European life-style, were supplied with aerated water from *Watson's Mineral Water Company* (327 Jiangxi lu), canned goods from *Sun Sun Co.* (470 Nanjing Road) and *Tai Kong Canned Provisions* (377 Nanjing Road), milk from dairies like the *Model Dairy Farm*, *Steys Dairy Farm* and *Ice Factory* and the *Yah Shing Dairy* on the western outskirts of the city. *Moutrie's* supplied pianos proofed against the ravages of the tropics and kept them tuned, while cars were supplied and maintained by the *Central Auto Supply Co.* (411 Avenue Foch) or the *Foo Lai Tyre* and *Rubber Repair Co.* on Park Road. Madame Soloha, a clairvoyant, maintained two consulting rooms on Bubbling Well Road and Wah Kee Avenue and a number of dentists (Dr John Hoh, Dr K.L. Kormilitzina and Dr T.P. Lews, amongst others) advertised their services. Many of the names of pre-war Shanghai—the department store *Lane Crawford*, the bookseller and publisher *Kelly and Walsh*, as well as Watson's Mineral Water—are still well-known in Hong Kong, whence they decamped after the Anti-Japanese War and the Communist takeover. The Sikh guards employed by many Hong Kong jewellers also recall the turbaned Sikh policemen of pre-liberation Shanghai.

The dual nature of Shanghai in 1931, a year in which over 20,000 corpses were collected from the pavements of the International Settlement alone, was described by Christopher Isherwood:

Seen from the river, towering above their couchant guardian warships, the semi-sky-scrapers of the Bund present, impressively, the façade of a great city. But it is only a façade. The spirit which dumped them upon this unhealthy mud-bank, thousands of miles from their kind, has been too purely and brutally competitive. The biggest animals have pushed their way down to the brink of the water; behind them is a sordid and shabby mob of smaller buildings ... Nevertheless the tired or lustful businessman will find here everything to gratify his desires. You can buy an electric razor, or a French dinner, or a well-cut suit. You can dance at the Tower Restaurant on the roof of the Cathay Hotel, and gossip with Teddy Kaufman, its charming manager, about the European aristocracy or pre-Hitler Berlin. You can attend race meetings, baseball games, football matches. You can see the latest American films. If you want girls, or boys, you can have them, at all prices, in the bath-houses and the brothels. If you want opium you can smoke it in the best company, served on a tray, like afternoon tea. Good wine is difficult to obtain in this climate but there is enough whisky and gin to float a fleet of battleships. The jeweller and the antique dealer await your orders, and their charges will make you imagine yourself back on Fifth Avenue or in Bond Street. Finally, if you ever repent, there are churches and chapels of all denominations.

After the Japanese had bombed Shanghai, destroying much of the poorer, Chinese quarter of the city, exacerbating the appalling conditions in which many Chinese were living, their numbers swelled by refugees from Japanese invasion, Auden and Isherwood were taken to some of the factories in Hongkou:

In the accumulator factories, half the children have already the blue line in their gums which is a symptom of lead poisoning. Few of them will survive longer than a year or eighteen months. In scissors factories you can see arms and legs developing chromium-holes. There are silk-winding mills so full of steam that the fingers of the mill-girls are white with fungus. If the children slacken in their work the overseers often plunge their elbows into the boiling water as a punishment. There is a cotton mill where the dust in the air makes T.B. almost a certainty. In this city the gulf between society's two halves is too grossly wide for any bridge. There can be no compromise here. And we ourselves, although we wear out our shoes walking the slums, although we take notes, although we are genuinely shocked and indignant, belong, inescapably, to the other world, we return, always, to Number One House [the British Ambassador's private residence] for lunch.

In the early days of foreign trade the Chinese *comprador*, the middle-man who straddled the gap between the western merchant and his Chinese suppliers, was an essential member of any trading house. Many *compradors* became rich in their own right and as Shanghai prospered in the period during and after the First World War, when European manufacturers presented little competition, many set themselves up as independent entrepreneurs. Some of today's 'national bourgeoisie', such as Rong Yiren, whose family fortunes were based on Shanghai cotton mills, are the descendants of Chinese breakaway *compradors* although others, who made their money from opium, gambling, prostitution and extortion, also made fortunes in the 1920s and 1930s. **Du Yuesheng**, who controlled much of the vice in the French Concession, was described in the Shanghai *Who's Who* as the '... most influential resident, French Concession, Shanghai. Well-known public welfare worker. 1932, councillor, French Municipal Council ...', with a string of respectable directorships. While serving as a board director of the Red Cross, Du Yuesheng was also a leader of a Shanghai secret society, the Green Gang, which in 1927 he unleashed upon workers and communists in Shanghai, securing the city for Chiang Kai-shek and the Kuomintang.

The protective nature of foreign concessions meant that underground political movements could thrive, partly because of the possibilities of escape across boundaries, for there were separate police forces in the International and French settlements, and partly because they could exploit the ignorance of the foreign policemen who knew little or no Chinese. The acute problems of workers in the Shanghai factories and the natural antipathy to the contrasting luxury of the life of Shanghai's foreign residents also made Shanghai an obvious site for the secret founding meeting of the Chinese Communist Party in July 1921. The meetings were held in 106 Rue Wantz (now 76 Xingye Road) in the French Concession, the home of one of the 12 delegates, who are said to have stayed in the empty girls' school in Rue Auguste Boppe (127 Taicang lu). The meeting was not without incident; the French police interrupted it and the delegates scattered, to re-group in a houseboat on the Nan hu, 100km southwest of Shanghai. From this small and inauspicious beginning Communist influence grew in Shanghai, as students and intellectuals began to oppose the foreign domination of their city.

In 1925, when a Communist labour representative was killed in a Japanese-owned cotton mill, thousands of students demonstrated against Japan in the International Settlement on 30 May and many were arrested by the police. Thousands of sympathisers gathered outside the police station and a British police officer ordered his men to fire on the crowd, killing ten. Communist-organised reaction included a strike, although the most successful strike was in Hong Kong (it lasted 16 months), and was combined with a boycott of all British goods from Hong Kong in Canton.

Protected, to some extent, from events in the rest of China by extraterritoriality, the Shanghai Volunteer Corps and police were, however, mobilised in 1913, 1924, 1925 and 1927 as warlord armies fought battles near the city. In 1926 Chiang Kai-shek launched the **Northern Expedition**, taking the Kuomintang army from its base in Canton to seize territory from the Northern warlords. At the beginning the Kuomintang and the Chinese Communist Party were nominally united and Communist Party activists did much preparatory work, organising strikes and mobilising peasants and workers in support of the troops. In Shanghai, as elsewhere, armed volunteer workers led by Zhou Enlai, amongst others, took control of the Chinese city in anticipation of the arrival of the Kuomintang troops. On 12 April 1927 the Kuomintang army arrived but it disarmed the workers and, with help from Du Yuesheng who mobilised the underground Green Gang in return for obtaining the government opium monopoly, arrested and executed all known Communists who could be found, driving the rest underground and effectively beginning the civil war that was to last over 20 years. The Shanghai Volunteer Corps was fully mobilised to defend the International Settlement but all the fighting took place in the Chinese city and suburbs.

The arrival of **Chiang Kai-shek** brought changes to Shanghai: the Mixed Court was abolished in favour of entirely Chinese courts which could try Chinese and 'non-treaty' foreigners like Germans and Russians. Chinese were finally admitted to the public parks although, as Davidson-Houston notes, 'The problem of admitting Chinese to public parks was solved in 1928 by making a small charge, which limited the numbers to a tolerable level. Most of the clubs, however, were still closed to them, as foreigners felt strongly that some refuge must be left where they could retain something of the atmosphere of home.' This also meant that few clubs admitted any women, foreign or otherwise.

The Japanese invasion of Manchuria in 1931 had repercussions in Shanghai where progressive Chinese were quick to react. A boycott of Japanese goods was organised and a mob attacked a group of Japanese monks in January 1932. This led to a battle between Japanese and Chinese troops in the Zhabei (Chapei) district to the west of Hongkou where most Japanese were resident. Japanese planes dropped incendiary bombs on the crowded quarter of Zhabei and the Shanghai Volunteer Corps was mustered to protect the International Settlement until May when an 'armistice' was signed. Throughout the succeeding years there were anti-Japanese incidents but Shanghai flourished as never before. Visitors from all over the world came to shop and stare at such sights as the **Great World Amusement Centre**, described by Joseph von Sternberg in the mid 1930s:

On the first floor there were gambling tables, singsong girls, magicians, pickpockets, slot machines, fireworks, bird cages, fans, stick incense, acrobats and ginger. One flight up were the restaurants, a dozen different groups of actors, crickets in cages, pimps, midwives, barbers and ear wax extractors. The third floor had jugglers, herb medicines, ice-cream parlours, photographers, a new bevy of girls, their high-collared gowns slit to reveal their hips, in case one had passed up the more modest ones below who merely flashed their thighs; and, under the heading of novelty, several rows of exposed toilets, their impresarios instructing the amused patrons not to squat but to assume a position more in keeping with the imported plumbing. The fourth floor was crowded with shooting galleries, fan-tan tables, revolving wheels, massage benches, acupuncture and moxa cabinets, hot-towel counters, dried fish and intestines, and dance platforms serviced by a horde of music makers competing with each other to see who could drown out the others. The fifth floor featured girls whose dresses were slit up to the armpits, a stuffed whale, story tellers, balloons, peep shows, masks, a mirror maze, two love-letter booths with scribes who guaranteed results, 'rubber goods' and a temple filled with ferocious gods and josssticks. On the top floor and roof of that house of multiple joys, a jumble of tightrope walkers slithered back and forth, and there were see-saws, Chinese checkers, mahjong, strings of fire-crackers going off, lottery tickets and marriage brokers.

The Great World Amusement Centre was one of the scenes of bloodshed early on in the **Anti-Japanese War** (1937–45) in Shanghai. The Japanese had provoked various incidents—by trying to enter the Chinese military airfield at Hongqiao, demanding the withdrawal of all Chinese troops from Shanghai, arranging acts of 'sabotage' and shooting the British Ambassador—and the Chinese began a clumsy retaliation by air on 14 August 1937, first dropping a huge bomb on the Bund end of the Nanjing Road and then dropping two on the Great World. In the two incidents 1740 were killed and 1873 wounded. These accidents confused the flow of refugees, first fleeing into the city from the skirmishes outside, now fleeing out of the city away from bombing.

Throughout the next five years the Japanese increasingly insisted on control in Shanghai, in 1938 demanding that senior administrative posts, including that of Deputy Police Commissioner, should be given to Japanese, and they took control of the Customs. In 1941 the chairman of the Japanese Ratepayer's Association inexplicably tried to shoot J.H. Keswick, British chairman of the Shanghai Municipal Council, at a special General Meeting of Ratepayers, and on 8 December 1941, just after Pearl Harbour, the Japanese shelled the British riverboat *HMS Peterel*, killing seven and wounding seven. The attack on the *Peterel* provides an early hint of the threat to Shanghai in J.G. Ballard's novel *Empire of the Sun*.

Life for most foreigners, however, continued much as usual until 1943 and is neatly described by Christopher Isherwood (1937):

It is the Ambassador's turn to give an official garden-party. The preparations are elaborate. They require the co-operation of the ladies of the British colony, the Seaforth Highlanders, the Embassy staff. Invitations are sent out. The drinks and cold buffet are organised ... Next morning, the local newspaper will carry photographs of the most distinguished guests. Out on the lawn, the Scottish pipers play their airs.

Everything goes off like clockwork. It is a beautifully contrived charade, the perfect image of another kind of life—projected, at considerable expense, from its source on the opposite side of the earth ... But gaily as the charade-players laugh, and loudly as they chatter, they cannot altogether ignore those other, most undiplomatic sounds which reach us, at intervals, from beyond the garden trees. Somewhere, out in the suburbs, machine-guns are rattling.

The Chinese were subject to persistent humiliation and terror. The refugee situation grew increasingly acute, with currency devaluation adding to the misery of those compelled to live in refugee camps on 'family bunks', or those who had to pay rent to live on a mere landing or in a room subdivided by sheets. Many of the 20,000 corpses picked up in 1937 were those of the homeless who had simply frozen to death in the streets.

In January 1943 all enemy nationals were interned by the Japanese in seven enclosures in Japanese-controlled China. Ironically, the same month saw the signing of a treaty between the British and American governments and that of Chiang Kai-shek in the temporary capital of Chongqing, far up the Yangtse in the western province of Sichuan, ending all extra-territorial rights and giving up the concessions. 8000 were interned, while life outside the camps continued with murders and brutality as the order of the day. Collaborators were murdered, there were reports of human flesh being sold as food became scarce and Japanese bombers flattened parts of the Settlement and the French Concession. Yet such was the resilience of the Shanghainese, both foreign and Chinese, that within a year after the defeat of the Japanese (1945), despite civil war raging across China, the proportion of China's foreign trade passing through the city was almost double the pre-war figure.

On 25 May 1949 Communist troops peacefully entered the city and established a new, military government. In the first months foreign governments were keen to recognise and accept Mao's new regime for British commercial investments alone were thought to be worth £300 million.

The **Korean War** of 1950, however, marked the beginning of the end, although the Communists themselves were keen to maintain Shanghai's flourishing economy. The new Chinese government preferred to deal direct with governments rather than commercial intermediaries and so one by one the foreign trading houses shifted their bases away from Shanghai, often to Hong Kong. The government embarked upon an ambitious retraining programme for the thousands of prostitutes suddenly abandoned by their clientele, turning them into respectable cottonmill workers and eradicating venereal disease.

Shanghai did not visibly change much at first: the European buildings were reallocated and occupied by offices of the municipal government and, although Shanghai's port has recently been overtaken by Ningbo which is being developed as a deeper draught container port, Shanghai has remained a major manufacturing centre, a centre recognised throughout China as producing high-quality, well-designed goods. Shanghai enjoyed a brief further fling of leadership during the Cultural Revolution when a series of strikes in 1967 led to the formation of the **Shanghai People's Commune** under the leadership of Zhang Chunqiao and Yao Wenyuan, later to be vilified as members of the Gang of Four, and a young worker, Wang Hongwen, later also classified as a member of the Gang, rose to sudden prominence.

In the mid 1980s, the famous skyline began to change. Japanese hotel chains and businesses, in particular, embarked on a massive building programme. Shanghai's proximity to Japan and the relaxation of Communist controls made it an attractive centre for trade and tourism. This spate of construction was as destructive of 'old Shanghai' as the earlier Japanese bombing raids. A new, Japanese-built road to the airport cut through the Tudorbethan suburbs and a massive hotel tower was put up in the garden of the old International Club. In 1993, I was informed that the world's 16 largest cranes were all active in Shanghai, building skycrapers, as a triple decker road was put up to circle the city centre, high above the old 'lane houses'. By now, although many projects have had disastrous effects for Shanghai's residents, forced out of the city centre into forests of high-rise blocks of flats on the Pudong (eastern) side of the river, the city has become a thrilling supermodern metropolis. The huge Pearl television tower on Pudong has laser lights playing up and down it and the varied sky-scrapers and bizarre new buildings that crowd the old city centre make the city seem excitingly modern. Although one might regret the old treaty port skyline, Shanghai has always been a modern city, set apart from traditional Chinese urban centres by its history and architecture, and today it is simply continuing and moving forward, more successfully than many other Chinese cities whose new architecture is less accomplished or appropriate.

The Bund

The *Shanghai Mansions* (Shanghai daxia), formerly Broadway Mansions, a 22-storey red-brick building (a hotel, see p 249) with art deco detailing, faces south down the Bund, standing on the northern bank of the Suzhou Creek opposite the Waibaidu Bridge, known to foreign residents as 'Garden Bridge', an iron structure built in 1906 to replace the wooden one, infamous during the Japanese occupation for all Chinese crossing it had to bow low to the Japanese soldiers on duty there.

On the other side of Changzhi lu, towards the Huangpu River, a series of consular buildings used to stand. Only the blue **Russian Consulate** remains (occupied for years by the Seamen's Club); beside it, the American and Japanese consulates have disappeared under a new hotel. Opposite the Russian Consulate is the *Pujiang Hotel*, once the prestigious Astor House Hotel (palm garden, cuisine under French chef, Trocadero tearoom at back).

Crossing the iron bridge, the river side of the Bund (Zhongshan lu) is still a garden, the riverside promenade that was once forbidden to dogs and Chinese, except those accompanying Europeans. Its entrance (for which, as with all gardens in China, there is a small fee) is in the bus station to the south.

Pleasure steamers

Near the entrance to the garden is the pier from which the Huangpu pleasure steamers leave at 14.00 for a 2½ hour trip up the Huangpu to its confluence with the Yangtse and back. Tickets can be purchased at the pier (28 Zhongshan dong lu); prices vary between 100 and 55 rmb. The extraordinarily rapid development of the Pudong side of the river now provides additional interest. The trip passes the international passenger terminal, the container port and the site of the Wusong fort, before reaching the confluence of the muddy brown Huangpu and the clearer, salty water of the Yangtse estuary. The best part of the trip is the view of the grand buildings of the Bund on the return.

Immediately opposite the Shanghai Mansions, on the south side of the bridge, is the old enclosure of the **British Consulate**, with trees and lawns and flower beds as well as low stone buildings (replacing the original building that was burnt down in 1870), the windows hung with tattered blue-and-white awnings. There was a church in the northwest corner and until a few years ago the Shanghai Friendship Store was housed in the old consulate so it was possible to enter. The *Friendship Store* is now in a huge new building just around the corner (40 Beijing dong lu). According to old maps, the building on the north side of Beijing lu and the Bund was the Masonic Club.

Going south along the Bund, between Beijing lu and Zhenchi lu stood the Yokohama Specie Bank, the **Bank of China**, a square skyscraper which once housed the German Club and stands next to the green tiled pyramid-tower of the *Peace Hotel* (formerly Sassoon House and the Cathay Hotel), which is on the corner

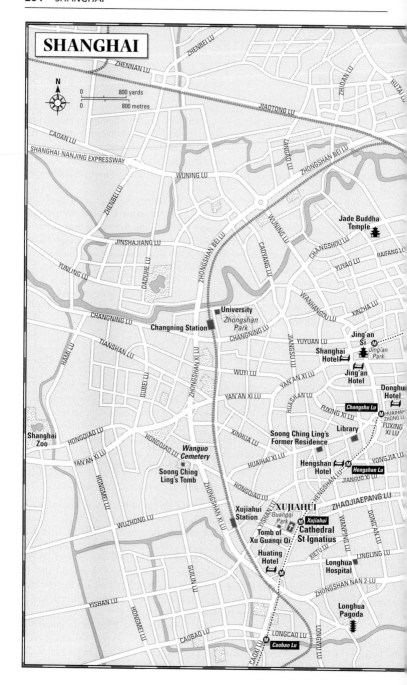

SHANGHAI

N

| 0 | 800 yards |
| 0 | 800 metres |

ZHENBEI LU

ZHENNAN LU

ZHIDAN LU

HUTAI LU

JIAOTONG LU

CAOAN LU

SHANGHAI-NANJING EXPRESSWAY

ZHENBEI LU

WUNING LU

ZANGAO LU

ZHONGSHAN BEI LU

JINSHAJIANG LU

DADUHE LU

WUNING LU

CAOYANG LU

CHANGSHOU LU

Jade Buddha
Temple

YUYAO LU

HAIFANG LU

YUNLING LU

ZHONGSHAN BEI LU

WANHANGDU LU

XINZHA LU

CHANGNING LU

University
Zhongshan
Park

Changning Station

CHANGNING LU

JIANGSU LU

YUYUAN LU

Jing'an
Si M

Jing'an
Park

HAMI LU

TIANSHAN LU

GUBEI LU

ZHONGSHAN XI LU

WUYI LU

YAN'AN XI LU

HUASHAN LU

Shanghai
Hotel

Jing'an
Hotel

Donghu
Hotel

FUXING XI LU

Changshu Lu M

HUAIHAI
ZHONG LU

FUXING
XI LU

Shanghai
Zoo

HONGQIAO LU

YAN'AN XI LU

XINHUA LU

Library

Soong Ching Ling's
Former Residence

YONGJIA LU

HONGMEI LU

Wanguo
Cemetery

Soong Ching
Ling's Tomb

HONGQIAO LU

HUAIHAI XI LU

ZHONGSHAN XI LU

HONGQIAO LU

Hengshan
Hotel

M Hengshan Lu

JIANGUO XI LU

WUZHONG LU

GUILIN LU

Xujiahui
Station

XUJIAHUI

Guangqi
Park

M Xujiahui

Cathedral
St Ignatius

ZHAOJIAEPANG LU

WANPING LU

DONGAN LU

LINGLING LU

YISHAN LU

Tomb of
Xu Guanqi

Huating
Hotel

M

XIETU LU

Longhua
Hospital

HONGMEI LU

ZHONGSHAN NAN 2-LU

WUZHONG LU

CAOBAO LU

LONGCAO LU

CAOXI LU

M Caobao Lu

LONGWU LU

Longhua
Pagoda

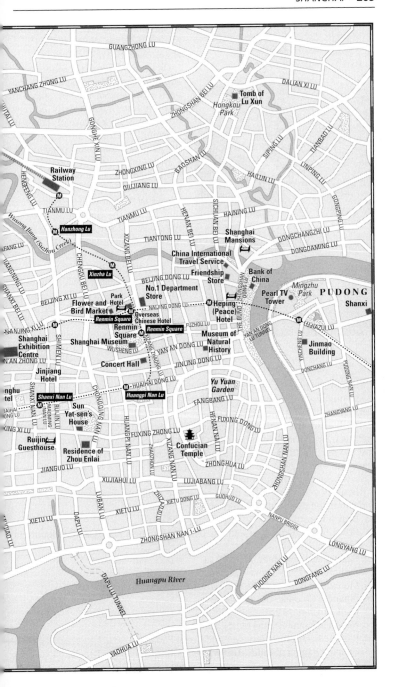

Shanghai: the Bank of China

of the Bund and Nanjing lu. Across Nanjing lu is the annexe to the Peace Hotel, once the Palace Hotel.

On the river side of the Bund, opposite the Peace Hotel, there is a wide open space, one of the best places in Shanghai to watch elderly citizens performing their graceful *taijiquan* morning exercises (from around 06.30) or practising ballroom dancing.

Here once stood the Parkes Monument commemorating **Sir Harry Parkes** (1828–85), British consul at Canton who 'distinguished himself' in the Second Opium, or Arrow, War (1856) and became commissioner at Canton after the capture of the city. Between 1862 and 1865 he was consul in Shanghai. Parkes has been replaced by a white statue of **Chen Yi** (1901–72), a distinguished military commander of the Red Army and the New Fourth Army in the 1930s who had previously studied in France (in 1921). In 1949 he was made Mayor of Shanghai and in 1958 he became Foreign Minister.

The next turning off the Bund (south of Nanjing lu) is Jiujiang lu. Some 500m along Jiujiang lu, standing back from the road, next door to a solid mansion-block now housing the Huangpu district government, is the small, red-brick **Cathedral of the Holy Trinity**, built to designs of the distinguished British architect, Sir Gilbert Scott, in 1866. It is said that his original designs would have cost too much so they were pared down in Shanghai. A mixture of Gothic windows and almost Romanesque patterning in grey and red brick, the cathedral has not been used for worship for years.

Retracing your steps to the Bund, the major buildings, mainly housing banks and commercial institutions, were as follows:

33. British Consulate
27. China Textiles Export Corporation, once the Jardine & Mathieson headquarters (1922)
29. Banque de l'Indochine, built 1914
27. Benjamin & Potts (brokerage house)
26. Mercantile Bank of India and Danish Consulate
24. Japanese Chamber of Commerce
23. Bank of China, 1936
21. Nederlandische Handel Mastschappij
20. Banque Belge pour l'Etranger and Credit Foncier
18. Chartered Bank of India, Australia and China and Credit Foncier d'Extreme-Orient

17. North China Daily News, also the Canadian Trade Commissioner and the British Chamber of Commerce

15. the pinkish-yellow Russo-Chinese Bank

14. Bank of Communications

13. the rusticated stonework of the Customs House, 1927, whose chime, originally relaying Big Ben's tones at 06.00 and 18.00, has been altered to play a rather odd version of 'The East is Red'

12. the classical facade and dome of the Hong Kong and Shanghai Bank, for many decades the seat of the Shanghai Municipal Government but now housing the Pudong Development Corporation

7. Commercial Bank of China

6. P & O Banking Corporation

3. Shanghai Club, 1911, which used to boast the longest bar in the world (over 30m long), now the Dongfeng Hotel

1. Philippine National Bank in the McBain building, 1915

Shanghai Club

The Shanghai Club was not only closed to women but fairly difficult of access to all but the higher *taipans* ('big bosses'), as western businessmen in Shanghai called themselves. Drinking was a major pastime in Shanghai from the earliest days, and young 'griffins' fresh from home were surprised to be offered jugs of cocktails shortly after breakfast. Carl Crow, an American journalist long resident in China, contrasted the strict (unwritten) rules of the Shanghai Club where:

the end of the bar facing the Whangpoo was reserved for the taipans of the big hongs [firms] ... down to the end of the bar which was waggishly referred to as being reserved for the unemployed with the more democratic bar ... of Lane, Crawford and Co., general storekeepers. Every morning at 10.30 the venerable Mr Crawford, who had been doing the same thing for more than twenty years, would empty a bottle of gin in a pitcher of ice, add other ingredients and serve a drink which was known as a 'Crawford Special'.

(Carl Crow, *Foreign Devils in the Flowery Kingdom*, New York and London, c 1937)

The famous long mahogany bar is no longer in the Dongfeng Hotel but has been resurrected in the Shanghai Centre on Nanjing Xilu, in a complex of hotels and apartments, near the Jing'an temple.

The Shanghai Museum (see p 274) used to be housed in a handsome striped bank building, easily reached from the Bund, at 16 **Henan zhong lu**, near the junction with Yan'an dong lu (which ends at the Bund). The high, pointed redbrick building was originally the headquarters of the **Zhong Hui Bank**, set up in 1929 by Du Yuesheng and others. Du Yuesheng, associate of Chiang Kai-shek and the Green Gang of underworld thugs, chief of the illegal opium trade, was president. The characters *zhong hui* can still be seen engraved in the glass windows on the ground floor and the building, with its open hall and galleries, retains the feeling of a grand banking hall. The contents of the museum were moved to the central Renmin Square in 1995.

At the corner of Sichuan lu and Guangdong lu is the *Golden Cage Hotel* (93 Guangdong lu). This was the house where Yu Aqing's concubines lived and was subsequently a bank, now a hotel with much stained glass and ceiling mosaics.

On the corner of Jiangxi Zhonglu and Fuzhou lu (180 Jiangxi Zhonglu) is the *Metropole Hotel*, once such a smart place that Chiang Kai-shek and Soong Mei-ling's wedding reception was held here in 1927.

The Chinese city

Although the walls encircling the Chinese city were torn down in the first year of the Republic (1911), the circular form of the city is still indicated by the roads Zhonghua lu and Renmin lu.

Take Sichuan lu, cross Renmin lu (the road then changes its name to Lishui lu) and ahead are the multi-storey 'Chinese style' buildings that surround the **Yu yuan** (Mandarin Garden) and the Huxinting Teahouse. In the centre is an open square beside the pool across which a zig-zag bridge (now in pink concrete) leads past the teahouse. On the far side of the pool is the Yu yuan, behind it (approached from the back exit to the garden across Anren jie) is the **Chenghuang miao** (Temple of the City God); the whole area used to be part of the City God Temple Enclosure. The Chenghuang miao is a fascinating place, like a long dark corridor lined with gilded figures of different deities, all bringers of different sorts of good fortune. All Chinese cities used to have such a local temple, distinct from the more sober Buddhist or Taoist institutions and packed with local gods and spirits. As Shanghai residents are traditionally supposed to be pre-occupied with making money, the temple is thronged with worshippers waving bundles of lighted incense sticks in front of their favourite god. Although the *Lonely Planet Guide* describes it as overrated, it is a rare piece of reality in an area that has been largely re-built and recreated as a 'traditional market' overhung by multi-storey restaurants, offering endless shopping and eating opportunities. It was built on the foundations of the 15C Jinshan miao, a temple constructed to commemorate the legendary general **Huo Guang**. The ceremonial archway, stage and main hall of the temple have been restored, although the temple is a shadow of what it was when it was a centre of fairs and markets and seasonal flower shows: plum-blossom in early spring, followed by orchid displays and chrysanthemums in autumn. There is a small entrance fee and the staff of bad-tempered monks are clearly more interested in collecting money from local people willing to pay to have the gods solve their problems than entertain foreign visitors.

The **Huxinting Teahouse** (Pavilion in the Heart of the Lake), a five-sided building of two storeys with exaggeratedly upturned eaves to the grey tiled double roof, was constructed in 1784 using money donated by a group of blue-cotton-cloth merchants. Originally used for cotton broking (the original regulations forbade the practice of medicine and fortune-telling as well as selling tea on the premises), the pavilion became a teahouse in the reign of the Guangxu emperor (1879–1908) and remains a popular teahouse today. The bridge was built in its zig-zag form because of the Chinese belief that evil spirits could only travel in straight lines.

Opposite the teahouse is the entrance to the **Yu yuan** (Garden of Content), originally built by Pan Yunduan, an official who, although a native of Shanghai, had held high office in Sichuan province. Construction lasted from 1559 to 1577 and the garden was built for his father. It is a very characteristic southern garden, combining pools, rockeries, winding walkways and pavilions, creating an illusion of space and depth within a small area. A rather exaggerated feature is the dragon walls: grey overlapping tiles, reminiscent of the scales of a dragon, on top of the white-washed dividing walls, are finished off with dragon heads. The huge pock-marked rock standing in front of the **Yuhuatang** (Hall of Jade Magnificence)—considered by connoisseurs to fulfil all the desired qualities of a garden rock, being *zhou*, *shou* and *tou* (rough, craggy and holey)—is said to have been destined for the imperial gardens. The Huizong emperor of the Northern Song (reigned 1100–26) sent 'notorious' rock-collectors to south China in search of treasures but this particular prize was shipwrecked in the Huangpu and was dredged up by Pan Yunduan for his garden.

Shanghai: the Yu yuan

The Yu yuan has a particular place in Shanghai's history, recalled in the **Dianchun tang** (Hall of Heralding Spring), for the Small Sword Society, a branch of the Triad secret society from the south, used the hall as their head-quarters (1853–54), during the unrest of the Taiping uprising. Led by a Cantonese, Liu Lichuan (ostensibly a sugar-broker but suspected of opium trafficking), the Small Swords captured the Chinese city during the Taiping uprising, forcing the Chinese Daotai to flee into the British concession. Relics of the unsuccessful attempt to overthrow the dynasty in the shadow of the Taipings are displayed in the hall.

The detailed woodcarving of the timber doors and lattice windows, seen at its best in the **Sansui tang** (Three Ears of Corn Hall), which is carved with rice, millet, wheat and fruit, is exceptional but other details are also beautifully observed; note the curved fish carved on stone drain covers. Opposite the Sansui tang is a stone-carved essay on the garden by its builder; calligraphy and literary reference being essential features of the traditional Chinese garden. The south part of the garden, called the **Nei yuan** (Inner Garden), was a later (1709) addition to the Yu yuan.

Just to the west of the garden, at 29 Chenxiangge lu, is the **Chenxiangge Temple**, once part of Pan Yunduan's estate, which included the Yu yuan. During the Cultural Revolution, it suffered considerable depredations and was restored and re-opened in 1994.

In the southwestern corner of the old Chinese city, on Wenmiao lu is the old **Confucian Temple** (*wen miao* means 'cultural temple' in other words Confucian temple).

Shopping

The area around the Yu yuan, as will be immediately apparent, is one giant 'shopping opportunity' for arts and crafts and souvenirs. It is a place, too, where beggars congregate and besiege tourist buses. Not all the shopping opportunities are bad: this is probably the best place in Shanghai to find the attractive little Yixing teapots which come in all sorts of differently coloured clays and are, at their finest, plain and elegant. Here you may also find the indigo resist-dyed cloth, *lanbu*. There is a daily 'antiques' market not far away, in Dongtai lu, which runs parallel with Xizang Nanlu, and a Sunday market at Fangbang jie, off Renmin lu on the west side of the Chinese city. With antiques, as with anything else, it is best to buy what you like, at a price which seems acceptable to you and not cherish too many illusions about authenticity. Frequent visitors to China can grow cynical at the sight of new waves of 'antiques' which suddenly appear in all the shops and markets. About ten years ago, there was a vogue for lacquered tiered baskets; in 1996, the street markets were filled with amusing little ceramic boxes in the shape of peanuts and all with Qianlong marks (these are now available in the UK through mail order) and in 1998 Peking's antique shops were suddenly filled with wooden buckets with handles which were (or were modelled upon) grain measures. Red Guard memorabilia is everywhere.

To the north of the Chinese city, in the block bounded by Sichuan nan lu (old Rue Montauban), Jiangxi lu, Renmin lu and Jinling dong lu, rises the spire of **St Joseph's Catholic Church**. To the northwest, at the crossroads of Xizang lu and Yan'an lu, stands the restored wedding cake tower of the old **Great World Amusement Centre**, in the 1980s still labelled the Shanghai Youth Palace but now with its old name restored and four floors of entertainment including distorting mirrors although not much of the exotica described by Joseph von Sternberg (see p 260).

Frenchtown

Stretching west from a narrow strip of waterfront, bounded on the east by Avenue Edouard Vll (**Yan'an lu**) and the Avenue des Deux Republiques (**Renmin lu**) which runs along the northern edge of the Chinese city, the French Concession is at its most distinctively 'French' further west, the roads lined by plane trees (still associated in the Chinese language with the French), the windows of many buildings shuttered, in contrast with the tattered awnings of the old International Concession.

While the commercial and banking sectors were concentrated in the International Settlement, apart from the smart shopping streets like Huaihai lu (Avenue Joffre), the French Settlement was largely residential. The streets were lined with narrow 'terraced' lanes interspersed with solid bourgeois houses with mansard roofs and shutters similar to those on the outskirts of any French town.

The central section of Avenue Joffre (**Huaihai lu**) used to be known as 'Little Russia' for it was here that most of the White Russian refugees congregated, including the bar hostesses (almost a White Russian monopoly) and such famous figures as the singer Alexander Vertinsky (whose great recorded hits included 'Magnolia' and 'The Mad Organ-grinder'). The section of **Huaihai zhong lu** just south of the Jinjiang Hotel still has cake shops, like the famous *Laodachang* on the corner of Maoming lu which advertises 'cake a la française' [sic] and sells wedding cakes, lemon-meringue pie, apple pie and ice cream and coffee. On the opposite corner is the Cathay Theatre (a cinema).

North, up **Maoming lu**, is the *Jinjiang Hotel*, a towering complex with herringbone brickwork and inset stone panels. The north wing is the oldest part of the hotel which started out in 1929 as an apartment hotel called Cathay Mansions. Until recently, the lifts in the north wing featured a clock-like indicator showing which floor the lift had reached. These have gone, which is sad because they figured prominently in a 1950s Chinese film about the underground Communist movement in Shanghai before 1949 which was depicted as being run from a private lunatic asylum on the fourth floor of the Jinjiang. Early visitors after the Cultural Revolution sometimes got the impression that nothing had changed. Richard Nixon stayed here in 1972. But there used to be wonderful waiters there on the top floor dining room. When I struggled to ask in Chinese for some mineral water (*laoshan shui*, 'very sulphurous'), a charming man aged about 80 asked me, 'Madame would like some Vichy water?'

Opposite the Jinjiang Hotel was the *Jinjiang Club*, formerly the Cercle Sportif Française, with ballroom, bars and huge swimming pool surrounded by wicker basket chairs. This has, unfortunately, been taken over by a Japanese concern and a modern tower-block hotel has been built in the beautiful, once extensive, garden.

Further north along Maoming lu is the **Shanghai Art Theatre**, formerly the Lyceum Theatre, opened in 1931 by the British Consul for the Amateur Dramatic Society. Along Changle lu (which crosses Maoming lu beside the Shanghai Art Theatre), on the corner with Shaanxi nan lu, is the *Hong fangzi* (Red House Restaurant, 37 Shaanxi nan lu), formerly Chez Louis, a restaurant specialising in western food—minestrone, chicken Kiev, stroganoff and soufflé—Grand Marnier (during the Cultural Revolution you had to bring your own Grand Marnier).

Turn left down **Shaanxi nan lu** and take the first turning on the right, Xinle lu, with the green onion domes of one of the two Russian Orthodox churches, on the corner with Xiangyang bei lu. Turn left down Xiangyang beilu (which runs beside Xiangyang Park, on the left), to Huaihai zhong lu.

South of Huaihai lu down Shaanxi nan lu, at the point where it intersects with Yongjia lu, on the left is the **Wenhua gongchang** (Culture Square), formerly the greyhound racing centre or 'Canidrome', opened in 1928. Northwest of the Canidrome, at 7 Xiangshan lu (formerly Rue Molière), just beyond the giant north–south fly-over road, is the old **home of Sun Yatsen** (he moved in in 1920 and his wife, Soong Ch'ing-ling/ Song Qingling stayed on for 12 years after his death in 1925) with a garden behind with a fine 'British' lawn on which he met delegates from the Communist Party. The two-storey house is said to be preserved as it was during his life, with the addition of interesting photographs, and 'most' of the items on display are original including his gramophone. Open daily 09.00–16.30; entrance fee.

The **Library** (once in the Racecourse Club building, see p 276) has now been installed on a site once occupied by one of the dairy farms that were so important to the survival of the treaty port inhabitants and their families (on Huaihai zhonglu and Gaoan lu just east of Soong Ch'ing-ling/Song Qingling's former residence). Serving as a municipal library, the collections range from the general to a notable collection of *shan ben* (rare or antiquarian volumes) that is second only to that in the National Library in Beijing. Opening hours for readers are 08.30–20.30.

Just south of Sun Yatsen's house, at 73 **Sinan lu** (Rue Massenet) (cross Fuxing lu) is one of Zhou Enlai's many residences. Although he did not often stay here, it is another fine example of Shanghai domestic architecture and furnishing, open on Monday and Thursday afternoons and on Tuesday, Wednesday, Friday to Sunday from 08.30–11.00, 13.30–16.00.

Northwest of Sun Yatsen's house, at 76 **Xingye lu**, is the grey brick building where the first congress of the Chinese Communist Party was held in June 1921. The building is an interesting 'lane house' with a forbidding, windowless facade embellished with fine red, almost armorial tile work over the dark red door. Inside are the 12 chairs, teacups and ashtrays supposedly used by the delegates until the police raid forced them to move outside Shanghai. A small exhibition commemorates the history of the Communist Party and the fate of the 12 delegates (two later collaborated with Japan and almost all later clashed with Mao). Open Tuesday to Sunday 08.00–12.30 and 13.00–16.00, closed Thursday mornings.

Three hotels

Three hotels in the Frenchtown area are worth trying to see. There is the *Hengshan Hotel*, 534 Hengshan lu, not far from the Hengshan lu underground station (walk down Hengshan lu towards the southwest) which was once the Picardie Mansions; the *Donghu Hotel* (70 Donghu lu), not far from Shaanxi nan lu underground station (walk westwards along Huaihai Zhonglu and Donghu lu is a couple of blocks along on the right). One of the buildings (Number One) was originally owned by Shanghai's most famous gangster, Du Yuesheng, and many still retain the dark wood panelling that was such a feature of Shanghai interiors of the 1920s and 1930s.

The *Ruijin Hotel* (118 Ruijin lu) can also be reached from Shaanxi nan lu underground station. Walk eastwards along Huaihai Zhonglu until you reach the (major) crossroads with Ruijin lu. Turn right down Ruijin lu and the hotel is in the third block on the right. Like the Donghu, it was formed from a group of villas, previously known as Morriss Villas. The main building was once inhabited by the proprietor of the *North China Daily News*, China's foremost English language treaty port newspaper, but others say that rather sinister off-shoots of the Kuomintang Party used to meet here. There is much dark timber panelling, Tudor style fireplaces and the sort of bath (with glass sides carved with fish) satirised as typical of the kept woman in Nancy Mitford's *The Pursuit of Love*.

At the east end of **Yan'an dong lu**, near the Jing'an Guesthouse, 64 Yan'an dong lu, is the main **Children's Palace**, once the Kadoorie family residence, viewed by appointment only. Although there are 12 other 'children's palaces', places where children of working parents can go after school and where their special talents can be developed, this one is run by the Municipality and the children selected because of their abilities. Music, painting and sports activities predominate, with special classes in academic subjects to promote talent, all in the grand rooms and fine garden of the pink, classical Kadoorie mansion which used to have a billiard room with half a dozen tables.

Further east along Yan'an dong lu (1000 Yan'an zhong lu) is the **Shanghai Exhibition Centre**, built to Russian designs in 1955 (and virtually identical with the Beijing Exhibition Centre). The steel spire is topped by a red star and the huge enclosure of over 8360 square metres is built in the garden of what was once the Hardoon House. The exhibition halls contain displays of Chinese modern technology and light industrial products with a special display of locally produced arts and crafts which are sold at counters in the display area.

At the far end of Huaihai Xi lu (northwest of the Hengshan lu underground station: best reached by taxi or a stiff 20 minute walk) is **Soong Ch'ing-ling's former residence**; used from 1948 until her death in 1981 when she was not in Peking. This is a rather grander suburban mansion surrounded by camphor trees, befitting one of the daughters of the rich and entrepreneurial Charlie Soong who sent his daughters to Wellesley. Soong Ch'ing-ling married Sun Yatsen; her younger sister Mei-ling (surviving as a centenarian in America) married Chiang Kai-shek, another sister married a descendant of Confucius and her brother 'T.V.' was Minister of Finance under Chiang Kai-shek. Their marriages disunited the family: all but Soong Ch'ing-ling left for Taiwan or the USA in 1949. She stayed on, founding Shanghai's Children's Hospital and promoting charitable work.

The **Shanghai Historical Museum** is at 1286 Hongqiao lu; open daily 09.00–16.00. It contains a multitude of photographs of Shanghai, at its most prosperous and wicked, and maps and relics of the city's past.

The city centre

Opposite the Jing'an Park, off Nanjing xi lu is the **Jing'an Buddhist Temple**, known to foreign residents of the past as Bubbling Well Temple, although its name, which dates from 1008, means Tranquil Peace Temple. According to literary records, its history goes back to the Warring States Period (238–251) but the original temple was situated on the north bank of the Wusong (or Suzhou Creek) and was moved to its present site in 1216 because the original site was flooded. The new site was near the 'Bubbling Well'. This spring, also called 'the eye of the sea' and 'the sixth spring in the world', was surrounded by a stone railing in the Qing but covered over after Liberation in 1949 because it impeded traffic flow. The temple fell into ruins and the present buildings date from the Guangxu period of the Qing (1875–1909); they have been thoroughly restored recently.

Three main halls, with side buildings enclosing three courtyards, are constructed in the characteristic southern style: yellow-washed walls pierced with decorative circular openwork tile windows, and facade s of dark-painted wood are topped with grey tiled roofs. The ends of the eaves are curved and topped with openwork tile decoration while large fish acroteria curl on the straight ridges.

Shanghai Museum

Before Liberation the temple was famous for its abbot, 2m (6ft 7in) tall, with a very wealthy wife, 'seven concubines and his own White Russian bodyguard'. There is a piece of stone-carved calligraphy in the temple, dating from 1183, written by the Guangzong emperor (reigned 1190–95) before he ascended the throne, as a celebration of the library of the scholar Qian Liangchen; the stone was moved to the temple when the library building was destroyed.

Shanghai Museum

Further east along Nanjing xi lu is the great open space of **Renmin Guanchang** (People's Square) and **Renmin Park**, the roughly circular form of the whole indicating that this was once the racecourse. On the south side of the square is a strange light grey building with semi-circular 'handles' on the roof. This is the new Shanghai Museum whose external architecture is based upon the form of an ancient bronze with its lug handles. It was designed by a local architect Xing Tonghe and opened in 1995.

- Opening times are Sun–Fri 09.00–17.00, Sat 09.00–20.00. Entrance fee 20 rmb. There is a café and a very good shop.

The museum was originally established in 1952 in a former bank building near the Bund and is unusual in that it reflects the history of collecting in China. Apart from the Gu gong in Peking whose 'founding collection' was that of the emperors (although it also includes later purchases and excavated items), the Shanghai Museum is the only museum in China to be based firmly on collection rather than excavation. The museum still obtains items from notable collections, as Nien Cheng describes in *Life and Death in Shanghai* when, after her porcelains had been returned to her in 1979 (after confiscation in the Cultural Revolution and processing by the 'Bureau for Sorting Looted Goods'), the Shanghai Museum approached her asking to buy 15 pieces. Its displays are also the best-designed in China, the work of a staff-member of great talent, who began his work of transformation in the old bank building soon after the Cultural Revolution when materials and inspiration were hard to find in China.

Arranged on four floors, with a central atrium, the galleries are entered from the landings. On the ground floor is a very good shop which sells a wide range of reproductions, very good postcards and a substantial selection of books on Shanghai, the museum's collections and Chinese art. Just beside the shop is a stone carved wall inscribed with the names of donors who supported the building of the new museum, detailing the exact amount they gave! On the ground floor is a gallery used for temporary exhibitions which have included displays from abroad and interesting displays of newly excavated materials from Xinjiang, for example.

Bronze Gallery The Bronze Gallery contains one of the great collections of bronzes in China; formerly grouped in strict chronological order, the exhibits are now arranged in a rough chronological order but grouped by type. The display includes a rare **'transparent mirror'** of the Western Han which can both reflect an image and also display the designs cast on the reverse when a strong light is beamed on the reflecting surface. There is a notable set of **bronze bells** from the tomb of Marquess Su of Jin (late 9C BC, a fine inlaid axe head dated to the 'late Xia' dynasty (18C–16C BC) whose existence is still shady and a brilliant group of **animal style vessels** from the Spring and Autumn period (6C BC–476 BC), some with animals crawling all over them and dragon spouts, others in the form of animals like an ox with a snake on its nose.

Ceramic section The ceramic section is fundamentally chronological but includes a section on kiln construction. There are Neolithic pots, an interesting glazed cup from the Shang dynasty (16C–11C BC) with an impressed string decoration and a fine range of later ceramics. There is a fine little white-glazed funerary pillow in the form of a small building with a figure at the door (907–1127) and some interesting Tang funerary figures, the most striking one of a woman wearing a tall witches hat sitting on a white horse. In a special gallery (the **Zande lou room**) are 130 pieces donated by Hu Huichun and his wife Wang Huayun. Their collection is especially strong in paired imperial pieces but there is another charming funerary pillow in the form of a child holding up a lotus leaf (1115–1234).

Painting gallery The painting gallery reflects the wealth of the collection as well as the newest technology with a protective lighting system that comes into operation as the viewer approaches a painting. The displays are changed frequently to protect the fragile paintings which were never intended to be permanently hung like a western oil painting but were brought out by the painter or collector on special occasions like family celebrations or visits from appreciative friends. All the exhibits have English captions so changes in display will not affect visitors.

The collection of paintings by **Zhu Da** (1626–1705), brooding birds captured in long brush-strokes, is very fine. There are a number of early paintings from the Tang and Song in the collection, notably the long handscroll of hermits by **Sun Wei** (618–907), a marvellous bird on a snowy tree by **Li Di** of the Southern Song (1127–1279) and **Xu Xi**'s painting of bamboo in the snow (907–979). The collection also includes later work such as a wonderful long scroll of a pine tree by **Xu Beihong** (1896–1953).

Sculpture gallery The Sculpture gallery has been designed to reflect a temple setting, with niche-like wall-cases, and includes sculptures in stone, wood and ceramics, from Han tomb figures, through the great age of Buddhist carving (4C–10C).

Calligraphy gallery The Calligraphy gallery offers the best chance you will have to see calligraphic works on paper in considerable quantity. Eighty pieces dating from the Tang to the Qing are shown in a display that changes often. Even without understanding the content, the vigour and excitement of cursive scripts in particular is very well depicted. Calligraphy was traditionally valued above painting as an art form, calligraphy fetching higher prices than paintings in the Ming, for example.

Coin gallery In the Coin gallery, over 7000 different coins are displayed, including a special donation of coins from the Silk Road from the collection of Roger and Linda Doo. The Chinese exhibits include the funny spade-shaped currency of the Spring and Autumn period and continue through to bank-notes of the Qing and silver coins of the same period which show a distinct western influence.

Joseph Hotung, who has been a generous benefactor to the British Museum (in the Hotung gallery of Oriental Art and the exhibition space in the new central court) sponsored the **Jade gallery**, reflecting a personal interest in jade. The lighting has been specially designed to highlight delicate carving. The earlier work is mostly flat but there are some 3D later pieces in spectacular colours.

Gallery of seals Calligraphy and carving are united in the objects in display in the Lincoln and Lillian Chin gallery of seals, the first of its type in the world. Seals or 'chops' were not only used in place of a signature to validate documents or 'sign' paintings in vermillion ink, they were prized objects in their own right, produced in a wide variety of precious materials and often decorated with fine carving. The names on the base were usually carved in one of the two archaic forms of 'greater' or 'lesser' seal script, in relief or intaglio, and form a significant part of the calligraphic history of China. The seals are all tiny, most carved in a variety of stones, although there are some charming metal cast seals, and they often have delightful tiny animals or figures on the top of the seal.

Furniture gallery Though there are now some fine pieces of furniture displayed in the Forbidden City in Peking, a much wider variety of pieces can be seen in the Ming and Qing furniture gallery. Many of the objects displayed were collected by Wang Shixiang, China's foremost historian of furniture and lacquer. Confiscated during the Cultural Revolution, he found only one piece missing when he was rehabilitated and it was returned. He used to live in a Peking courtyard house, surrounded by his collection, terrifying visitors when he informed them that they had just sat down heavily on a Ming *huanghuali* chair. The furniture is grouped in domestic settings.

National Minorities art gallery The Kadoorie Gallery of National Minorities Art was sponsored by the family that had such a long connection with Shanghai (and whose marvellous home is now the Shanghai No. 1 Children's palace). The display includes costumes, textiles, embroideries, metal and wood-work, sculpture, pottery, masks and bamboo and cane.

On the east side of the square is a long dark building with a clock tower, once the **Racecourse Club** building; until 1997 it housed the Shanghai Library, with one of the finest collections in China (see p 272). The Race Club building is now the home of the **Shanghai Art Museum**, which mainly shows temporary exhibitions of modern Chinese painting; open 09.00–11.00, 13.00–16.00, closed Mondays.

Renmin Square is on the site of Shanghai's third racecourse, the first, between Henan zhong lu and Jiangxi zhong lu and Nanjing dong lu, opened in 1851 and abandoned in 1853 when land prices in the area rose after the Small Swords uprising. The second was immediately to the east of the third, the curve of Hubei lu indicating its form. The grandstand was immediately next door to the present Number One Department Store.

Because of rising land prices, the racecourse was moved in the early 1860s, the acquisition involving a dispute over graves on the site which lasted more than 30 years. A memorial archway to Xu Yuanlai's wife (recorded in the local annals of 'chaste widows and virtuous women') stood inside the racecourse until Liberation, as the family refused to move it. When it was damaged, a director of the Race Club Board called Moller paid for its repair. Moller and his brother are described in a recent Chinese publication as 'out and out adventurers' whose house (now housing the Shanghai Municipal Committee of the Communist Youth League, 30 Shaanxi nan lu), was 'a building in a convex and concave shape with a spired roof and said to be in the Norwegian style', its garden filled with the graves of horses and greyhounds, 'benefactors who helped the Moller brothers to become millionaires' through racing. It is very well worth going to peer at the 'Norwegian style' which is more like nightmare fairytale.

Huangpi bei lu runs beside the Shanghai Library and running between Huangpi bei lu and Chengdu bei lu is Jiangyin lu (parallel with Nanjing lu) where you can find the **Flower and Bird Market**. On the other side of the park, at 328 Xizang zhong lu, near the junction with Jiujiang lu is the old American Baptist Church, built in 1929 and still functioning.

Opposite Renmin Park on Nanjing lu are the two fine 1930s hotels, the *Guoji Fandian* (Park Hotel) and, next door to it (no. 170), the *Huaqiao Fandian* (Overseas Chinese Hotel) with a dining room which has a view over the park.

Nanjing lu, particularly eastwards from the square, was one of the major shopping streets in old Shanghai and retained that position after 1949. The pressure of shoppers, both local and from all over China, was such that raised crossings had to be built in the 1970s to prevent pedestrians straying into the traffic and the bottom of the road is now closed to traffic. I used to think that shopping on Nanjing lu made Christmas shopping in Oxford Street seem like solitary confinement.

The next block east along Nanjing xi lu from the square is the *Number One Department Store*, formerly the Sun Department Store; further along, on the corner of Zhejiang lu, is the Number Ten Department Store, formerly the Wing On Department Store and further down, again, the Shanghai Number One Clothing Store which used to be the Sincere Department Store.

The surviving cosmopolitanism of Shanghai is as evident on the Nanjing lu as on Huaihai lu; opposite the junction with Jiangning lu and Nanjing xi lu is a reminder of the pre-war White Russian community in the *Number One Xibiliya Fur Shop* (*xibiliya* means 'siberian') and on the junction with Tongren lu is the Shanghai Kafei ('coffee') House.

Outer Shanghai

Xujiahui

The old Jesuit centre of Xujiahui, the Xu family village, as its name implies, was once a village some distance from the old walled town of Shanghai. Now a suburb in the southwest of the city, it is quite conveniently reached by underground from the centre of town (Renmin Square to Xujiahui). One of the members of the Xu family, Xu Guangqi (1562–1633), convert and pupil of the Jesuit Matteo

Ricci, left land for the Jesuits to establish a seminary, observatory and church in Xujiahui, where the *Sheraton Hotel* has been built, together with comfortable blocks of flats for 'returned Overseas Chinese'.

The Jesuit settlement, known to foreigners as Siccawei or Zikawei, was founded in 1848 and the **Cathedral of St Ignatius** was built in 1906 with its twin 50m spires and space for 2500 worshippers. The observatory is still in use.

The cathedral is on Caoxi lu, just south of the Xujiahui roundabout (the terminus of the no. 15 bus from Nanjing lu and the no. 26 from Huaihai lu). As with other religious buildings, there is no official entrance fee or opening times but the doorkeeper will admit visitors, and crucifixes and religious tracts can be purchased in lieu. The newly restored cathedral includes 'stained-glass' windows made from plastic by the pastors who worked in a plastics factory manufacturing umbrella handles during the Cultural Revolution (1966–76).

Just close to the cathedral (walk along towards the back of the cathedral along Ziyang lu, take the first left, Wending lu, where the back of the park will soon appear on your left, then turn left into Nandan lu), in a park which is known both as Guangqi Park and Nandan Park, on Nandan lu, is the **Tomb of Xu Guangqi**, a mound with a modern bust of Xu Guangqi in front of it.

The **Longhua Pagoda and Temple**, south of Xujiahui, lie in an area that was used as a prison and execution ground, mainly for Communists in the pre-Liberation period, by the Kuomindang and which is commemorated by a memorial on the west side of Caoxi lu. The pagoda is said to have been first built in the Three Dynasties (238–251, contemporary with the Jing'an Temple). It is an octagonal, seven-storey structure of wood and brick, with up-turned 'flying' eaves of grey tiles. The brick foundations date from the Song (977).

According to literary records, the temple buildings were founded in 687 and have been rebuilt many times since. Those that stand today date mainly from the Guangxu period of the Qing (1875–1909). Similar to those of the Jing'an Temple, they include a Maitreya Hall, Hall of the Heavenly King, Grand Hall, Three Sage Hall and Abbot Chamber.

The area, and the temple in particular, has long been famous for its peaches, described in a couplet: 'a riverside village surrounded by willows, ten *li* [Chinese miles] of red peaches'. Visitors come especially to see the peach-blossom in spring.

Just west of Xujiahui is the **Wanguo Cemetery** where Soong Ch'ing-ling and her faithful maid Li Yan'e, who worked for her for more than 50 years, are buried. Soong Ch'ing-ling is not difficult to find as she is buried in a mausoleum with a white marble statue of herself inside.

Northwest Shanghai

On Anyuan lu, in northwest Shanghai, the **Jade Buddha Temple** (Yu fo si) is a very late establishment (1882), set up by a monk from Putuo shan to receive a gift of white jade Buddhas from Burma, which were originally housed in the Jiangwan Temple. The temple was abandoned after the 1911 revolution but restored between 1918 and 1928. Of little architectural interest, except as a late version of the other southern-style temples in Shanghai, the major features are the two Buddha figures: that on the lower floor is a reclining figure less than 1m long, while upstairs is a seated Sakyamuni image, almost 2m tall, embellished with semi-precious stones. The temple is now fairly active with a number of monks in attendance, partly to cope with the tourist trade, partly for the faithful.

Northeast Shanghai

Hongkou Park, known to previous residents as Hongkew Park (laid out in 1905 in the Japanese quarter of the city), now, apart from rowing boats on the lake and the occasional autumn chrysanthemum display, houses the **Tomb of Lu Xun** (1881–1936) which was moved here in 1956, and a **Lu Xun Exhibition Hall**.

Lu Xun

One of China's great modern writers of short stories and satirical essays, Lu Xun was a pioneer of the *baihua* or 'plain speech' movement of the early 20C, attempting to break away from the stilted and incomprehensible prose of the ruling class and write in the language of ordinary people. A reformer, determined to change China for the better, Lu Xun spent some years in Shanghai (1933–36), living in a small three-storey red-brick house on Shanyin lu (no. 9 Luxincun, just south of the park), now open to the public. On the ground floor are the reception room and dining room; on the first floor, his study with writing desk and rattan chair by the window, and bedroom. On the third floor was his small son's room and a guestroom where Qu Qiubai often stayed. This was the house in which Lu Xun died.

In Hongkou Park his grave is marked by a seated statue, two trees planted by Zhou Enlai and Lu Xun's young widow (she had been one of his students) and a calligraphic inscription by Mao Zedong. There is also an exhibition hall detailing his life and work which, apart from his own writing, included active promotion of woodcuts as an art form and the revival of the dying woodblock fine-art printing craft.

Western Shanghai

In the western suburbs, bordering the Wusong River (Suzhou Creek) is **Zhongshan (Sun Yatsen) Park**. Laid out in 1914, it was known to the foreign residents of Shanghai as Jessfield Park. It contains impressive flower beds, notably of roses and peonies, and borders the campus of the old (missionary-founded, English-language) St John's University, now the Huadong zhengfa xueyuan (East China Politics and Law Institute). Many of Shanghai's progressive entrepreneurs, including Rong Yiren, graduated from St John's before 1949.

Shanghai Zoo

Situated near the airport on Hongqiao lu, the site used to be that of the golf course but was converted into a zoo in 1954. Covering over 80 hectares, this is one of the most pleasant zoos in China as the animals have a considerable amount of space to themselves. Species include giant panda, golden monkey, red-crowned crane, northeastern tiger, Asian elephant, Chinese alligator and red pandas, which are particularly recommended as they make the most of the space available.

Not far from the zoo, on the airport road, is the *Cypress Hotel*, 2419 Hongqiao lu. One of the guest houses in the grounds is the Sassoon Villa.

The skyline of Pudong

Pudong

In a fine guidebook to Shanghai published in 1987 (*A Guide to Shanghai* with a foreword by Lynn Pan, Collins, London) there is no mention of Pudong at all. There was no need for there was nothing there except docks. In 1990 it was decided that the area should be developed and within a decade many of Shanghai's residents have been moved to Pudong, to vast areas of new apartment blocks. There is a tunnel to Pudong from Yan'an dong lu in central Shanghai; and two of the largest cable bridges in the world cross the Huangpu.

For 50 rmb, those with no fear of heights can ascend the 457m **Pearl Television Tower** (08.00–21.30; 50 rmb), with its prominent globes. Pudong also boasts a theme park, the **Shanghai Ancient Customs Entertaining Village** in the Lujiazi Financial and Trade Zone.

Suzhou

Suzhou lies in the south of Jiangsu province, on the Grand Canal, and is most famous for its silk and its gardens. Lying in the low, flat Jiangnan ('South of the Yangtse') area, the city, like Shaoxing, was compared to Venice for it was crisscrossed with canals. The comparison is not particularly helpful for both Shaoxing and Suzhou, although important cultural centres, were more reminiscent of small country towns than Italian city states; their narrow canals are lined with low, grey tiled and whitewashed houses with steps leading down to the water where women wash clothes and vegetables. The town is much less full of canals than it was in the past as many have been filled in, partly to improve road communications and partly for reasons of hygiene; thus, in more ways than one, the town has lost some of its atmosphere. Despite its nomination by UNESCO as a 'World Heritage' site, Suzhou was one of the first cities in China to suffer from major destruction in the post Cultural Revolution drive to modernise. To one side of Suzhou is an industrial zone and Singapore kindly offered to build a modern enterprise zone on the other side, to create a sort of silicon valley. In order to improve communications between the two zones, a motorway was driven right through the centre of the historic city. Local planners explained that it would have been more expensive to build a ring road around the historic area.

Silk is produced in the neighbouring countryside and brought to the town for spinning and weaving and Suzhou houses the national *Embroidery Research Institute*. Although the famous gardens date back to the 10C, the most significant periods of garden building were the Ming and Qing, when rich officials retired to the picturesque town, a centre of cultural activity and of the publishing trade, and built themselves house-garden complexes for their old age.

The prettiness of the old town was reflected in folklore, in the saying that 'there is heaven above, on earth, Suzhou and Hangzhou'. Hangzhou's beauty is primarily scenic, Suzhou's man-made: the old whitewashed, grey tiled houses of the town lay amid green rice-paddies and sparkling water, the green and peaceful gardens hidden behind white walls. Traditionally, too, China's prettiest women come from Suzhou and the local dialect is regarded as particularly charming when spoken by women.

Practical information

Getting there
By train
Suzhou is an hour away from Shanghai on the Shanghai–Nanjing line. The station is in the north of the town on Chezhan lu. The frequent trains to Shanghai and Nanjing make this the simplest means of access (and there is no airport, the nearest being Shanghai).

By bus
The long-distance bus station is in the north of the town of the town, near the railway station.

By boat
It is also possible to travel by boat from Hangzhou along the Grand (not quite so grand these days) Canal.

Where to stay
Convenient hotels are the *Nanlin Hotel*, 21 Gunxiu fang (just north of Youyi lu), ☎ 519 6333, fax 519 1028, and the *Suzhou Hotel*, at 115 Shiquan jie in the southeast corner of the town (some 20 minutes from the railway station by taxi), ☎ 520 4646, fax 520 4015 (the hotel also houses the Suzhou branch of the *China Travel Service*). Both hotels are close to the most perfect garden, the Wang shi yuan, and another, less frequently visited, the Cang lang ting, and the Twin Pagodas.

History

The town of Suzhou was first laid out by **He Lu**, king of the state of Wu, which controlled the area in the 6C BC during the period of division (the Warring States). He is credited with digging canals to control the low water-table and floods of the Yangtse delta and digging a moat to surround the walled town. As late as the 1920s the walls, pierced with water gates, still stood (4km east to west and 5.5km north to south) and the city was often approached by boat from Hangzhou, Yangzhou and Shanghai, the piers being located outside the Panmen gate in the southwest corner of the wall. Boats are still used as a major form of transport between villages in the area. When He Lu died in 496 BC, according to tradition, his son Fu Chai buried him on Tiger Hill, west of the town. The great historian of the Han, Sima Qian (d. c 90 BC), visited the town and was impressed by the beauty of its buildings.

Throughout the succeeding centuries Suzhou attracted many of the refugees who fled fighting in the north and its economic importance was enhanced by the construction of the Grand Canal which made use of He Lu's Hangou canal (from Yangzhou to Huaiyin, linking the Yangtse and the Huai rivers) but extended water links from the Sui capital of Luoyang to Hangzhou (passing by Suzhou) in the south and Zhuoxian (near Beijing) in the north. This great burst of canal construction, which brought the rice and silk of the south to the north and to the Sui capital, took place between AD 605 and 611 and involved several million labourers.

Suzhou silk, made from silk cocoons raised in farms in the surrounding districts and fed on the low mulberry bushes that you will see lining paddy fields, was always highly prized. A 13C dandy of Hangzhou who would call his tailor instantly if there was anything wrong with the hang of his gown, wore shoes and stockings 'of fine satin and Suzhou silk'. The unreliable Marco Polo described the inhabitants of 13C Suzhou: 'They live by trade and industry, have silk in great quantity and make much silken cloth for their clothing.' He also described the canals and bridges that filled the town: 'There are fully 6000 stone bridges, such that one or two galleys could readily pass under them', and, despite the exaggeration in the number of grand bridges, it is clear from this and from other accounts that the shape and form of the city has not changed since.

During the Ming, when Suzhou became a fashionable cultural centre, a Mecca for retired officials, the silk industry adopted very intensive production methods. Workers were hired by large contractors as they could not afford their own machinery for spinning and weaving and, at the mercy of the contractors, they would queue up in their hundreds at dawn, hoping for a day's work. A rebellion in 1626, known as the 'Rebellion of the Five' as it was led by five workers, did little to improve their lot and stone-carved stelae from 1715, 1734 and 1822 have been found with edicts forbidding silk-workers to strike. In contrast to the Dickensian conditions of the silk-workers, one of the members of Lord Macartney's embassy to China (1792–94) described the town as:

... the school of the greatest artists, the most well-known scholars, the richest merchants, the best actors, the most nimble acrobats, is also the home of delicately-made women with tiny feet. It rules Chinese taste in matters of fashion and speech, and is the meeting-place of the richest pleasure-seekers and gentlemen of leisure in China.

In 1860 the Taiping rebels captured Suzhou with ease and established themselves there. Their leader, Li Xiucheng, lived in a grand house (now the Historical Museum) and a nearby fan factory was once a grand mansion taken over by the Taipings.

Chinese gardens

The city was filled with famous gardens, built from the 10C to the late 19C (12 are now open to the public). The greatest concentration of private gardens is in Suzhou, built by retired generals, officials, scholars and painters, adjoining houses. The aesthetic of the Chinese garden, so influential in Japan (and in Europe, particularly in the late 18C), is different from that of the West. For the Chinese it is an integration of dwelling, other buildings (built to admire aspects of the scene), water (freely available in watery Suzhou), rocks piled up into 'mock mountains' and, finally, plants. A garden must contain all of these and, since they were constructed within a crowded city, there is an element of miniaturisation in what is essentially intended as a microcosm of nature. The contrast with the great landscaped parks of the 18C English is complete. Although the Chinese sought to imitate nature, they did so in a tiny, confined space, by means of controlled views, rather than the great expanses of the English parklands. They sought the opposite in architecture, as in gardens: rather than a single great vista, they created a series of views and scenes, like a series of handscrolls being opened one after another. Another vital ingredient in the Chinese garden is poetry and calligraphy.

Poetry and quotation were the final touch to a garden; for a full account of how pavilions were named see Chapter 17 of the famous 18C novel by Cao Xueqin, *The Story of the Stone* (translated by David Hawkes, Penguin Books, 1973). Although the names of garden buildings seem simply charming—Pavilion of the Pagoda's Shadow, Retreat among the Bamboos, Kiosk Where One Awaits the Hoarfrost, Pavilion of Distant Perfume—they are almost invariably literary in origin, quotations from famous poems which are appropriate to the building and its surroundings. The names were inscribed over the doors, while names for rocks or appropriate quotations were carved into the rocks themselves. Some gardens (like the Cang lang ting) make a special feature of calligraphy carved in stone and set into the garden walls so that the whole, with its allusive names and beautiful calligraphy, becomes a sort of literary quiz-game where visitors must guess the origin and significance of a name.

Suzhou's gardens

Wang shi ~ Master of the Nets Garden

The Wang shi (Master of the Nets Garden) is at 10 Shijin jie, virtually opposite the Suzhou Hotel. It is the best garden to visit first for its tiny size makes it easiest to grasp and it contains all the essential garden features. Like most of the gardens it is open daily 07.30–17.30.

It was originally the home of Shi Zhengzhi, an official of the Southern Song, when it was known as 'Fish Shade'. It later fell into disrepair. Its current name was adopted in the late Qing (1875–1908) and is obviously related to the former since the 'master of the nets' is a fisherman.

Yan Guang, a friend of the Han emperor Guangwu, who preferred fishing to court life

Suzhou: the Wang shi Garden

The garden lies to the west of the house and the entrance from Shijin jie is actually a back entrance to the whole enclosure which covers eight *mou* (1 *mou* is 2.7 hectares or 6.6 acres). The garden, with its surrounding halls, is centred on a small pool surrounded by buildings, rocks, pines and a very old wisteria. Entering from the back, through a small courtyard which leads to the Staircase to the Clouds Hall, you are led to the right and approach the pool through one of two halls, the **Hall of Gathered Emptiness** and the **Verandah for Looking at the Pines** and **Studying Paintings**; the latter has a wonderfully carved wooden facade which can be fully opened to the view or closed so that the greenery and water is glimpsed through decorative lattice. As you approach the central scene through these elegant halls, the principle of 'framing a view' is apparent. The halls and buildings have carved and pierced dark wood windows and doors and hanging screens carved with sinuous vegetation which frame the view beyond.

The pool is clear: lotuses and waterlilies were restricted in garden pools for the surface of the water was best left clear so that its varying moods, reflecting clouds and overhanging plants or stirred by wind, could be appreciated. On the right is a small six-sided pavilion with exaggeratedly up-turned eaves, perched on rocks and with an elegant 'goose-neck' railing to sit against. The pavilion is called 'The Moon Sinks and the Wind Gets Up', suggesting that you can sit there and admire the reflection of the moon and the ripples of the wind on the water. In the back of the pavilion a mirror is set, to provide the illusion of a further view beyond.

The little pavilion sits against a whitewashed wall which is pierced with windows affording a view of the courtyard on the other side, full of plants, rocks and more buildings. The window openings are themselves decorative, made of plaster-covered wire, so that the view beyond is seen through a decorative lattice, another aspect of 'framing a view', creating the desired effect of walking past a series of paintings.

The Master of the Nets is an ideal garden to begin with, both because of its small size and because it still contains the ideal combination of house (including a library near the Shijin jie entrance) and garden, the latter including a vegetable plot to the west. Notice the paved stone floors, sometimes prettily made out of pebbles forming patterns and pictures, and the raised stone beds for seasonal flowers like roses and peonies; also the pot plants (including some fine cacti) and *pen jing* or 'pot scenes' where tiny plants are combined with volcanic rocks to create a truly miniature landscape. These can be moved around the garden and its buildings, stored when dormant and brought out when at their best.

Canglang ting ~ Pavilion of Dark Blue Waves

The Canglang ting (Pavilion of Dark Blue Waves) is not far from the Master of the Nets. Turn left onto Shiquan jie and take the first left (Wuqueqiao long); the entrance to the garden is across a bridge over a broad stream. This is one of the oldest of Suzhou's gardens.

In the late Five Dynasties (907–960) one of the military officials of the state of Wu Yue, Sun Chengyou, had a villa on the site, which later fell into ruins. In the middle of the Northern Song, Su Wuqin built a garden which was famous for its natural scenery and it was later inhabited by Han Shizhong (1089–1151), a noted military commander whose wife helped him in his military career by caring for his soldiers and even beating drums in battle. He led many successful campaigns against the northern invaders who were threatening the court and also suppressed banditry in south central China. Nevertheless, he was a supporter of Buddhism and Taoism and gave himself the name of 'the gentleman who lives in cool purity' although he had many honorific titles conferred on him by the grateful ruling house. He asked to be relieved of the post of Military Commissioner and retired in 1140 to a life of unpolitical peace. He greatly enlarged the garden which later came to be owned by a Buddhist temple.

The garden was rebuilt in 1697 and the entrance and the bridge over the stream date from that time. Further major renovations were carried out in 1874.

The name of the garden was suggested by Su Wuqin (or Su Zimei), who had owned it in the Northern Song. Himself a poet, he took the name from a passage in the *Chu ce* (*Songs of the South*, by the 3C BC poet, Qu Yuan) where an old fisherman says that if the dark blue waters are clean, he washes his hat ribbons, if they are dirty, he washes his feet. The phrase came to stand for necessary adaptation to circumstances and a relaxed attitude, and the name recurs in other gardens.

The garden makes use of the water outside, in another favourite garden technique, 'borrowing a view'. This means making use of an external feature (a technique which can be seen in the Summer Palace at Peking where external pagodas set on hills form a focal point seen from within the garden). A number of pavilions and walkways offer views of the water outside, like the tiny **Watching Fish Pavilion** on the southwest corner and the larger **Water Verandah** just to the west of the entrance. Within the garden the central focus is a 'mountainous area' of lake rocks, bamboos and trees, with the **Dark Blue Waves Pavilion** perched on high. Inside the main entrance are several inscribed stelae with poems by Su Zimei and a bird's-eye view of the garden carved in stone. Stone carvings of calligraphy are a great feature of this garden, set in the walls of covered walkways around the central hillock and in other buildings, emphasising the importance of poetry and calligraphy in a Chinese garden. The calligraphic stones cover several centuries in date and the most recent addition is political. Lin Zexu (the Opium Commissioner at the time of the Opium Wars) was previously Circuit Intendant of Jiangsu province, whose capital is Suzhou; there is a new notice, near an engraved map of the garden, reminding us of the significance of the handover of Hong Kong.

At the back of the garden, in the north, is the **Mountain View Tower**, from which the hills southwest of the town can be seen. Between this and the central

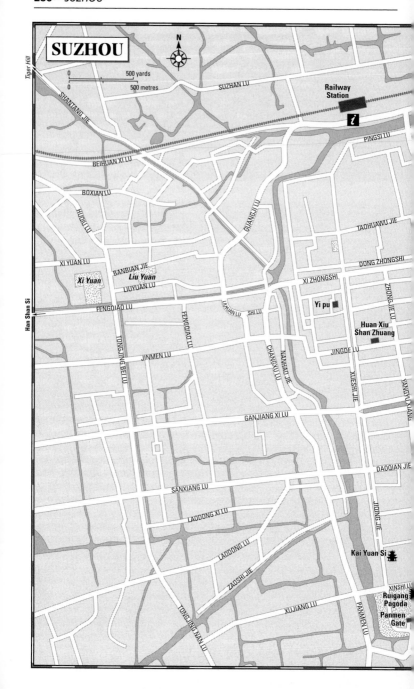

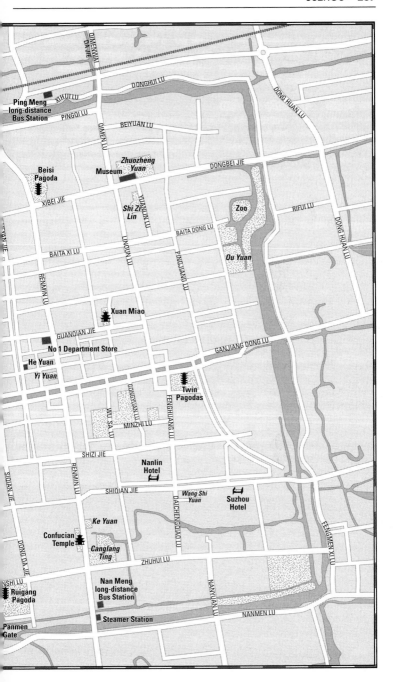

mountain are a number of buildings including the **Five Hundred Sages Hall** with portraits of eminent men. As with the richly carved front entrance of the Master of the Nets Garden, there are a number of carved bricks (grey bricks carved in high relief, a speciality of architectural decoration in Suzhou, also to be seen in Guangzhou and, in lower relief, in Peking).

Ke yuan ~ Suitable Garden

Just north of the Canglang ting, near the Suzhou Medical School, is the Ke yuan (Suitable Garden, also known as the Le yuan or Garden of Joy). This was part of the larger Cang lang ting Garden in the Song dynasty and was rebuilt as a separate garden in 1767. It used to house the Suzhou Library and now contains a pool surrounded by pavilions and dark groves and a winding walkway.

Returning to Shiquan jie, turn left and, at the junction with Renmin lu, turn left and go south down the main road. Not far down on the right is the **Confucian Temple**, almost totally rebuilt in 1864 after destruction during the Taiping uprising. It was originally a Song building (1034) and the only surviving early hall is the Ming (1506) main hall, seven bays wide, with fine brackets under the eaves and a moon terrace in front. In the temple several very important stone carvings are preserved. One is the map of the town (then called *Pingjiang*) dating to 1229, the earliest city map in China; the other is a star map of 1247, not the earliest star map from China (there is a 10C example on paper from Dunhuang now in the British Library) but one of the earliest to survive.

Continuing down Renmin lu, take the second major turning on the right, Xi er lu, and at the T-junction at the end of the road you are opposite the **Ruiguang Pagoda**. Although founded in AD 241, the present building dates from the Song (1119–25) and is seven storeys, 43m, high, octagonal in plan, with a brick core and wooden verandahs. Although the top finial and the eaves decorations are missing, the fine Buddhist carvings at the base remain. The pagoda was popularly believed to be associated with the well-being of the imperial family and in the 18C the mother-loving Qianlong emperor covered it with lanterns to provide light for his mother's soul after her death. When the pagoda was restored after the Cultural Revolution a Buddhist column in silver decorated with pearls, presented by the wife of an official in 1013, was found.

North of the Ruiguang Pagoda is the 'beamless hall' of the **Kaiyuan Temple**, all that remains of the original temple complex.

> Built in 1618, this is one of several examples of the type; others are on Wutai shan, near Nanjing, in Taiyuan. A practical solution to the increasing deforestation of China in the Ming and consequent shortage of building timber, the beamless or brick-vaulted hall does not seem to have survived the Ming or enjoyed widespread acceptance. This was originally the temple library (and as a fireproof building was most suitable for the purpose; the only later example I know is the Qing Archive Building associated with the Forbidden City in Peking). It is in two-storeys, like the Wutai shan example, with five doors. The brickwork is decorative.

Turning right down Dong da jie, the road curves round to the west. The **Panmen Gate** stands at the southwest corner of the city, the only surviving part of the old city wall. The gate in its present form (restored in 1978) dates from 1351, standing over the moat that surrounds the town. Over the moat is one of the handsome hump-backed bridges that use to be legion in the town.

To return to the hotel area retrace your steps to the Ruiguang pagoda, take Xi er lu (leading east from the pagoda) to Renmin lu, turn left and take the second major turning on the right, Shijin jie.

Twin Pagodas and Yi yuan ~ the Garden of Happiness

Another itinerary that can be made on foot from the hotel area of Youyi lu includes the Twin Pagodas, the Yi Garden, the centre of town and the Xuanmiao Taoist Temple.

From Shijin jie, go north up Fenghuang jie. After the second crossroads the next turning on the right is Dinghuisi xiang and the **Twin Pagodas**, all that remains of the original twin-pagoda temple which, from the name of the street (Street of the Temple of Certain Wisdom), was presumably originally named the Dinghui Temple.

Indeed there is a reference in the late 19C Suzhou Gazetteer: '... in the Yongxi period of the Song (984–988), Wang Wenhan built two identical brick pagodas and that was how it got its popular name'. They were in fact built by Wang and his brother apparently in honour of their teacher (for both were successful in the bureaucratic exams) and are identical in every detail. Octagonal, seven-storeyed, they stand over 30m high and are relatively rare as identical twin pagodas are not often found in China, although in the Indian temples that provided the distant model for Buddhist temples there were always twin towers. In Chinese temples these have gradually become the twin bell towers that stand in the first court of most temples, while pagodas have generally developed into 'single' structures. They are careful copies of timber constructions, with upturned eaves and supporting brackets all in brick.

There are doors on four of the eight faces, with brick lattice 'windows' on the other four. Both are topped with iron *ksatriya* spires (said to be based on monastery flagpoles surmounted by gilt pearls, symbolising Buddhism itself), nearly 8m high. During restoration after Liberation, on the second storey, an inscription was found recording repairs in 1135 and stating that they were built in 982, a date which conflicts slightly with the 19C account and therefore baffles the literary-minded compilers of the *Zhong guo ming sheng ci dian*, but I would have thought the near-contemporary account would be more reliable.

Turn back to Fenghuang jie and, at the junction with Ganjiang lu, turn left and follow the road. Cross Renmin lu (the major north–south artery) and one of Suzhou's pleasantest gardens, the **Yi yuan**, which used to lie back from the main road but, owing to its widening, now opens onto the road.

The Yi yuan (Garden of Happiness) is a very late construction, built in the late 19C on the site of the house of one of the ministers of the Ming period, Wu Kuan (1436–1504), also a noted poet and calligrapher. The garden is part of a major complex, separated by a narrow lane (called Minister's Lane) from the dwelling area to the south and with a large ancestral hall originally lying to the west. The official who rebuilt the garden in the late 19C is said to have spent 200,000 ounces of silver on it and, apart from gaining inspiration from other gardens, used famous and much admired rocks from three gardens that had been abandoned.

The garden itself is built around a pool surrounded by rocks and broken into three parts by a crooked bridge virtually across the centre and a narrow bridge of rocks to the west.

The garden is entered from Renmin lu through a broad, empty courtyard with a pebble-patterned floor. Then the path winds westwards through courts and buildings until the crooked walkway that runs along the east bank of the pool, pierced with stucco openwork windows, is reached. The major viewing point for the central pool is the **Lotus-root Fragrance Hall** with its dark lattice facade which can be folded back to reveal the whole scene, On the far west side of the garden is a 'dry boat' (an open, rectangular pavilion built out into water) which provides a view back across the rocks that narrow the main pool.

Return to Renmin lu, go left and take the first turning on the left. At the junction turn right and the **He yuan** (Crane Garden) is at 4 Hanjia xiang. This is a late Qing official's private garden. With a small central pool surrounded by rocks and a crooked covered walk, an entrance hall, the Four-sided Hall overlooking the pool, a library and main hall at the back, it is less full than many other gardens, the halls standing relatively clear of the rocks and water.

Return to Renmin lu, turn left (north) and take the third turning on the right, a pedestrian road called Guanqian jie which leads to the **Xuanmiao Taoist Temple**, which lies on your left, behind the Friendship Store and Antique Store. First constructed in the 4C AD, it once covered a far larger area than it does today. The main Hall of Three Pure Ones dates to the Song (1179) when it was designed by the younger brother of the famous painter Zhao Boju. This hall and the great entrance gate which leads to it are all that survive of the early temple. The hall is the largest early Taoist building in China: it is 45m by 25m, nine bays wide and six deep and has a double roof with strong brackets supporting the up-turned eaves. The internal roof structure has curved 'moon' beams. There is a finely carved platform for the three deities in gilt stucco which are also thought to be Song. Outside the hall the carved stone railings with their human and animal figures have been much restored but the carvings on the southwest corner are thought to be Song in date.

Although the temple was wrongly identified as Buddhist in the 1924 *Japanese Railway Guide*, the market function of this central temple was still apparent at the time:

> *The temple is a favourite resort of the people of the city and in its compound, besides tea-houses, variety shows, photographers, etc., are open-air stalls where various articles are sold. The street in front of the temple is one of the busiest...*

Three more gardens

If time allows, three further gardens can be reached on foot: the Huan xiu shan zhuang and Yi pu to the west and the Ou yuan to the east.

The **Huan xiu shan zhuang** (Village Encircled by Splendid Mountains) is at 280 Jingde lu, which is the west continuation of Guanqian jie (on the other side of Renmin lu). It is now part of the *Embroidery Research Institute* (usually included in tourist itineraries) where the most extraordinary, almost painfully fine, double-sided embroideries are produced, with different pictures on either side of a piece of translucent silk gauze (sometimes the back and front of a kitten or a puppy). It is also possible to see the production of *kesi* woven silk tapestry, once widely used in imperial clothing and previously always done by men, while the embroidery is generally a women's craft. Still highly prized in Japan and used to mount Tibetan *tankas*, the last time I visited the Institute the *kesi* loom was still being used by a man.

The Huan xiu shan zhuang was built as an official's private residence in the Qianlong period (1736–96), on the site of a Five Dynasties garden and a Ming villa: with the exception of the Autumn Mountain Residence, most of the other buildings had disappeared before 1949. This small garden is one of the most 'mountainous' and is a complex maze of mountain and water. The piled rock mountains are said to have been constructed by the famous mountain-maker, Ge Yuhang, in the Qianlong period. Constructed in a tiny space (about 2.4 hectares), mountains of white tufa are the major feature, with a twisted figure-of-eight water channel as the secondary feature, sometimes appearing in deep gullies beneath the piled rocks which are ascended by steps. There is a zig-zag bridge in the southwest corner, low over the water. The garden is not well maintained: creepers are damaging the mountains and weeds are rampant.

Just to the northwest of the Huan xiu shan zhuang, across a small canal, off Wuqu fang (which runs along the west side of the canal) at Wenwu nong is the **Yi pu** (Garden of Skill) built in the Ming and later owned by Wen Zhenmeng, great-grandson of Wen Zhengming (1470–1559), a local painter, one of the most prominent figures responsible for the growth of Suzhou as an artistic and cultural centre.

> Significantly for art historians, Wen Zhengming is one of the first Chinese painters and calligraphers whose work has survived in reasonable quantity. When his great-grandson owned the garden, it was known as the Physick Plot, presumably because it was planted with medicinal herbs. Consisting of an almost equal area dedicated to house and garden, the garden contains a pond (the focal point) with a rockery beyond, best viewed from the house. Although the garden is thought to preserve most of its late Ming early Qing features, a painting by the Kangxi period (1662–1723) artist Wang Hui reveals that the Waterside Pavilion was a simple platform at the time with a pavilion to the west which had, apparently, disappeared before 1949.

The major water surface is broken by waterlilies and also by two low bridges, one low on the water, zig-zagging across a corner, the other very slightly arched but still low. Although the pool, with its built-up rockery, provides the main focus of the garden, a moon gate (circular opening in a wall) leads to a further courtyard in the southwest corner so that the whole of the garden is not visible all at once, a major feature in Chinese garden planning.

To reach the **Ou yuan** (Paired Garden) near the Zoo in the northeast corner of the city, continue east along Guanqian jie to the junction with Lindun lu. Turn left along Lindun lu and take the fourth turning on the right, Liuzhi xiang. When you reach the outer moat, the Ou yuan is on your right, at 6 Xiaoxinqiao xiang. The space is mainly occupied by fine buildings, and the garden gets its name from the fact that there are two separate garden areas to the east and west of the dwellings.

The proportion of building to garden, particularly in the west, where the garden area is very small, is more reminiscent of the north of China where small garden plots were often associated with grand houses. The domestic buildings are characteristic of Suzhou, with whitewashed walls and façades consisting almost entirely of dark wooden lattice backed with white window paper. The rockeries in the western garden are very varied, not only consisting of the characteristic pitted pale-grey lake rock but also the more solid chunks of 'yellow rock'. In the centre of the pool in the western garden is a charming open pavilion called, appropriately, the **Pavilion between Mountains and Water**. The long pool surface is broken again to the north by a low zig-zag bridge. The entire complex is set between water to the north and south.

The museum and gardens in north Suzhou

In the north of the city, reached by a no. 2 bus (going north up Fenghuang jie) from the east side of the Nanlin Hotel, getting off at the sixth stop on the corner of Xibei jie and Lindun lu, are the Suzhou Museum, the Beisi Pagoda, and two major gardens, the Zhuo zheng yuan and Shi zi lin.

Shi zi lin ~ Forest of Stone Lions

The Shi zi lin (Forest of Stone Lions) is on Yuanlin lu, which runs north–south off Shilinsi xiang, a turning off Lindun lu, just south of its junction with Xibei jie. It is 'one of the four great gardens' of Suzhou and the one that is perhaps most in the Chinese taste, more inaccessible to Europeans unless they are very fond of the pitted, oddly shaped lake rocks that are the major feature of the garden.

It was originally constructed in 1342 as a back garden of a temple built by a monk to commemorate his master. Four famous garden designers were involved and the garden's name is taken partly from the Lion Cliff where the Zen master had lived, partly from the significance of lions as guardians of the Buddhist faith and partly from the fact that the stones are considered to resemble lions. There is a picture of the garden by one of the best-known of all China's painters, Ni Zan (c 1301–74), obviously made soon after it was completed. While some appreciated the garden greatly, the later writer Shen Fu in his *Six Records of a Floating Life* (1809) said that the 'most famous place in Suzhou itself' reminded him of a heap of clinker 'covered with moss and ant hills, without the least suggestion of the atmosphere of mountains and forests', and added, 'In my humble opinion there is nothing particularly wonderful about it.'

One of the larger gardens, despite its name, it also contains a considerable central pool, crossed by a zig-zag bridge, which passes through the pavilion in the heart of the lake, and also features a stone boat. The buildings lying north–south along the side of the garden (and through which it is entered) are particularly fine, with delicate lattice tracery set under the eaves of walkways and pavilions and a multitude of differently shaped doors cut through the whitewashed walls. It is said that the last private owners of the garden were relatives of I.M. Pei, the Chinese American architect who built the Xiangshan Hotel (Peking) and the new Bank of China building (Hong Kong) as well as sections of the Louvre in Paris and many buildings in the USA.

Suzhou Museum

Just north of the Shi zi lin, on Xibei lu, is the **grand mansion** once inhabited by Li Xiucheng, leader of the Taiping rebellion, when Suzhou was the Taiping headquarters in 1860.

> It was originally the residence of the adjoining Zhuo zheng yuan, taken over and converted for the Taiping 'King' and, with the defeat of the rebellion, used as his headquarters by Li Hongzhang, who was in charge of suppressing the Taipings.

Parts of the original have been destroyed, although the main axis remains impressive with double gate, main hall and back hall. The courtyards on either side of the main axis were those built by the Taipings. Behind is a garden on which noted craftsmen worked and which still includes a Mountain-viewing Tower and Magnolia Pavilion. The stone lions in front of the main gate, the lattice windows of the double hall and the painted beams all date from the Taiping era.

The building now houses the **Suzhou Museum**. Exhibits are arranged chronologically and refer to local excavations and finds. They stress the canal-building and related technology and, later, silk technology. Three of the stelae forbidding strikes are displayed in the museum, as well as rubbings of the early town and star maps.

Zhuozheng yuan ~ the Humble Administrator's Garden

Immediately east of the museum is the Zhuozheng yuan (translated as either the Humble Administrator's Garden or the Plain Man's Politics Garden). This is considered the greatest of all the Suzhou gardens and it is certainly the largest. It is therefore better to see the smaller gardens first to enable you to see how the simple can be expanded into the complex.

> It was laid out in the mid 16C by a retired censor Wang Xianchen and the name, appropriate to a retired official, was taken from an earlier writer who said that in cultivating a garden one met one's daily needs and that is what is meant by 'the politics of the plain man'. Wang's son later gambled away the family fortune and the garden was sold many times in the succeeding centuries.

The garden is laid out in two major parts, east and west, separated by a wall, and water is a major feature in both. The major water area is broken up by islands. The central part contains a large hall, the **Hall of Distant Fragrance** (named for lotuses planted nearby whose fragrance is supposed to waft towards the hall), which faces an island on which stands the **Hall of the Scent of Snow and Rosy Clouds**. The island is linked by zig-zag bridges to a central dyke to the west, which is viewed from the Magnolia Hall on the south side of the garden. On the far side of the dividing dyke, which is crossed by a covered walk, a smaller, more irregular pool is created by a triangular island, linked by low bridges to the north bank. The dividing wall between east and west is pierced with openings and the eastern part of the garden is less full of rocks and buildings, almost bare in comparison with the rest.

> A painting of the garden by Wen Zhengming (1470–1559) shows that more of the banks beside the water were left as natural earth than is apparent today where most are rock-covered. There are also fewer water plants in Wen Zhengming's depiction.

To the right, along Xibei jie, is the **Beisi** (North Temple) **Pagoda**, all that remains of a former temple complex, traditionally said to date back to the Three Kingdoms (220–280), although the present structure is fundamentally Song (of the Shaoxing reign period, 1131–63). It is a nine-storey, octagonal pagoda, 76m high, with a brick base and external structure of brick and wood with a wooden staircase which can still be ascended. The grey tiled roofs of each storey are sharply up-tilted in the southern style and climbing the pagoda to get close to the eaves is a good way of seeing southern architectural structure close to.

Liu yuan ~ Garden to Linger In

Just outside the town, to the west are two more gardens, the Liu yuan and the Xi yuan. These can be reached by taxi or a no. 2 bus going west from just beside the Nanlin Hotel (alighting at the seventh stop). A road leads north from Fengqiao lu and the Liu Yuan Garden is to the right (east), the Xi yuan to the left (west) on the first crossroads (Liuyuan lu).

The Liu yuan (Garden to Linger In) is one of the largest in Suzhou, comparable with the Zhuozheng yuan.

It was originally one of a pair of gardens, east and west, laid out by a Ming official, Xu Shitai. In 1800 a new garden was built on the ruins of the old east garden and, since the owner at the time was surnamed Liu, it was called the Liu Garden. As the surname and the character meaning 'to linger' are pronounced in the same way, the garden gradually acquired its present name as a pun.

The centre of the garden has a pool surrounded by rocks, with a further rocky area to the west and a mixture of building, courtyard and rocks to the northeast. The garden is entered through the substantial ancestral hall (the domestic buildings were to the east of this but no longer exist) which ends in a stone platform looking out over the pool. Characteristically, the water is broken up: to the right is a tiny island, **Xiao penglai** (Miniature Island of the Immortals), reached from a rocky promontory by a crooked bridge. In the far left-hand corner a channel, crossed by several small bridges, leads off towards the covered walkway that runs along the west and north sides of the pool.

To the east of the central pool is an area that is as naturalistic as is possible in the man-made world of the Chinese garden, while the more complex eastern side of the garden includes the **Hall of the Spirits of the Five Peaks**, surrounded by rocks, the **Place Where I Read Books** overlooking a rockery and close to the **Hall of Tall Trees and Springs** with the small **Pool for Washing Clouds**. There are several small courtyards in this part of the garden, with calligraphic inscriptions over the door, decoratively paved floors and raised beds of bamboo or single massive lake rocks in the centre of the small enclosure, providing a rich series of small spaces. Opposite the **Hall of Mandarin Ducks** in the far northwest corner of the garden is the **Cloud Cap Peak**, a huge, single lake rock, pitted with holes, remarkable for its size (for many of the rockeries are skilful concoctions of much smaller stones).

West Suzhou

Xi yuan ~ West Garden

The Xi yuan (West Garden) was originally the pair of the Liu yuan, built as part of his private garden by Xi Shitai in the Ming. This part of the garden was later given by his son (an official of the Board of Works) to a Buddhist temple. During the Taiping uprising (1860), which destroyed so many buildings in Suzhou, the temple was burnt down and subsequently rebuilt in the late 19C. The **Jiechuang** (Vinaya Pillar) **Temple**, although obviously late, is considered a fine example of southern temple building with its grand halls with upturned eaves, and the Hall of Five Hundred Lohans, built as a copy of the Lohan Hall of the Lingyin Temple at Hangzhou, is important as the model was subsequently destroyed. The garden area is now to the west of the temple. It consists mainly of a large pool with a small six-sided pavilion in the centre, reached by zig-zag bridges.

Further outside the town to the west are the Hanshan Temple and Tiger Hill, best reached by taxi or tourist bus. For the intrepid: take a no. 4 bus from beside the *Nanlin Hotel* (heading north) to its terminus inside the Changmen Gate. Outside the gate on the other side of the moat is a bus station. From there you can take a no. 6 to the Hanshan Temple (alight at the fourth stop) or a no. 5 to Tiger Hill which is the terminus.

Hanshan Temple

The Hanshan Temple stands opposite a fine hump-backed bridge on a canal, the **Maple Bridge** (Feng qiao).

The temple itself was founded under the Liang (502–557) but takes its present name from one of two famous monks of the Tang dynasty who are said to have lived here. Hanshan (Cold Mountain) was an early 7C Chan (Zen) Buddhist monk and poet, 300 of whose poems survive. He was very friendly with another monk, Shide, and stone-carved depictions of the two in the temple show a couple of tubby and jolly men with slightly wild hair and dishevelled robes. The temple was, like the Jiechuang Temple and so many others, destroyed in the Taiping uprising and subsequently rebuilt, mainly in the late 19C.

Recent rebuilding, particularly of the entrance, is evident for the photograph in the 1924 *Japanese Railway Guide* shows a western influence to the contemporary gateway, which was curved with a sort of Dutch gable effect and decorated with lozenge designs in different coloured bricks, rather different from the yellow-washed walls of today. One of the most famous aspects of the temple was its bell, which has been returned to the bell tower. A Tang poem by Zhang Ji (inscribed in Wen Zhengming's calligraphy on a stone preserved in the temple) entitled *Anchored at Night by the Maple Bridge*, includes the lines: 'The moon sinks, the crow calls and the night is filled with frost; under the Maple Bridge, the glare of lanterns prevents sleep. Outside Suzhou is the Hanshan Temple, in the middle of the night I can hear its bell from my boat.' The original bell was lost and the Ming copy was taken away by the Japanese; the writer and reformer Kang Youwei (1858–1927) wrote a poem in reply, some 1000 years later (also inscribed on stone in the temple): 'The sound of the bell is over the eastern sea; cold silence fills the Hanshan temple.' The bronze bell now hanging in the bell tower was cast in 1905 by a Japanese as a gift to the temple.

Tiger Hill

Northwest of Suzhou is Tiger Hill, a multiple scenic spot.

It is variously described as having been the the site of the 'travelling palace' (or alternative palace) of the kings of Wu during the Spring and Autumn period, or the imperial mausoleum of He Lu, founder of Suzhou and King of Wu. The hill derives its name from the legend that a protective tiger appeared on the hill three days after He Lu was buried. Others say that the hill is in the shape of a crouching tiger, hence the name. In the Eastern Jin (317–420) villas were built here, later a temple, called Tiger Hill Temple. In the Tang the temple had to change its name for 'tiger' (*hu*) appeared in one of the names of the founder of the Tang dynasty and the character was therefore declared taboo.

This practice of outlawing characters that occurred in imperial names was common in the Tang and later dynasties; it made life difficult for writers and could even bring a sentence of death if ignored, even inadvertently. It also became a forger's weapon: documents would be prepared using the common 'substitute' characters used to avoid the taboo characters in the hope of providing a false date. The temple regained its name in the mid Qing.

A path starts at the bottom of the hill with the first gateway, crosses a bridge and leads up to the second gateway known as the Broken Beam Hall because of the oddly shaped, 'moon' beams used inside; it was originally constructed in the Tang and rebuilt in 1338. Beyond it, to the right of the path is a huge boulder split in two—according to legend this was when He Lu tried one of his swords on it (the swords of the period made in Suzhou were famous).

Passing a restaurant on your left, and the 'pillow rock' where the monk Shengong is said to have rested, a path to the right leads to the **Zhenniang Tomb**, said to be that of an honourable widow of the Tang dynasty who was to be sold as a concubine after her husband's death but committed suicide to avoid the disgrace. Ahead, slightly to the right, is a plateau covered with stones, called the **Thousand Men Stones**; according to one legend they are the followers of He Lu, incarcerated with him when he was buried (as had been the custom). To the right is a lotus pool, to the left, the Pool of Swords is a deep cleft in the rock, surrounded with rocks covered with calligraphy (the largest inscription beside the cleft reads 'Tiger Hill Pool of Swords'). This is said to be the **Tomb of He Lu**, buried with his huge collection of swords, hidden beneath the water.

Crossing a bridge, the path winds up to the leaning **Pagoda of Tiger Hill**. Built between 959 and 961, it is the earliest Song pagoda surviving but preserves many Tang features (especially in the interior which is painted). Built of brick in imitation of a wooden construction, it is octagonal, seven-storeyed and stands 47.5m high with an incline of some 3m. In 1957, when repairs were carried out to strengthen the pagoda and prevent further inclination, workmen found sutra caskets and a record of the date of construction (now housed in the Suzhou Museum). A tapering cone in form, the pagoda is valued for the particular closeness of the brick construction to wooden architecture, both internal and external.

Surrounding temple halls on the hill are all late 19C, dating from after the Taiping destruction.

Beyond the Hanshan Temple, c 7km outside the town is the **Lingyan Hill** and **Temple**. The hill is covered with springs and oddly-shaped stones, the larger ones identified as resembling 'drums' or animals, the smaller, fine-grained stones used as inkstones (for grinding ink for painting and calligraphy). These were (according to Mi Fei, the famous 11C painter) slowly roasted after being cut to shape, which coloured them purple. The hill is still a very popular burial place; hundreds of tombs can be seen on the slopes.

The existing Lingyan (Cliff of Spirits) Temple was built on the ruins of one of the Qianlong emperor's 'travelling palaces', specially built or converted for one of his six, immensely expensive tours of inspection of the Yangtse Valley (1751–84). The fact that the emperor (and his grandfather before him) stayed here underlines the Chinese appreciation of the site with its strange stones and pretty springs.

Suzhou: pagoda of Tiger Hill

The old temple and 'travelling palace' were destroyed in the destructive Taiping uprising in 1860 and rebuilt after 1927.

The temple, perched on top of the hill, contains a Hall of Heavenly Guardians, a bridged courtyard with a pool and a large central hall with lohan figures. The temple and its pagoda were said to be originally Song in foundation, rebuilt in the Ming and heavily restored in 1980. The pagoda's wooden interior was destroyed by lightning in 1600, although the brick exterior was unharmed. It is a tapering, pointed, almost rocket-like structure.

Hangzhou

Hangzhou is the capital of **Zhejiang province**. With its numerous waterways and rice-fields, the province contains most of the features which gave rise to the appellation 'land of rice and fish' applied to the region 'south of the Yangtse' (Jiangnan). Fish were caught in rivers and streams and reared in special pools set amongst the irrigated paddy fields. The towns and villages of the Jiangnan area were criss-crossed by waterways and filled with riverine streets and hump-backed bridges of great charm.

Hangzhou lies on the bank of the Qiantang River, which winds its way to the sea (the Bay of Hangzhou), c 100km to the east. To the west of the city is the West Lake and the city marks the southern end of the Grand Canal (a section built in the Sui dynasty). Set in the fertile Yangtse delta area, the surrounding farmlands produce rice, hemp, silk cocoons and fish, although an awful lot of agricultural land is now occupied by the bizarre, Disney-style houses with little pointed turrets and blue glass windows, favoured by the local agriculturalists. The local tea, Longjing or 'Dragon Well', is one of the most famous in China. The waist-high bushes, picked into bun-shapes, can be seen in road-side plantations. Long famous as a beauty spot, the West Lake of Hangzhou has been painted and praised in poetry for centuries.

Practical information

Getting there
By air
The airport some 16km outside the town, was completed in 1972 for President Nixon's first visit to China. As Hangzhou is, perhaps, the pre-eminent beauty spot in China, frequent flights connect with all major cities. A shuttle bus from the *CAAC* office, 390 Tiyuchang lu, in the north of the town, connects with the airport.

By train
The station is in the east of the town on Jiangcheng lu, within walking distance of the centre if you are not carrying luggage; Hangzhou is some 2 hours by train from Shanghai. It lies on the Ningbo–Shanghai line and is a major terminus on the eastern route south from Shanghai, with frequent trains.

By boat
It is not uncommon now for tourist groups to arrive in Hangzhou from Suzhou by steamer, a method of travel also possible for individuals. The boats arrive on the Grand Canal, in the northwest of the city, by Huancheng bei lu, near the long-distance bus station.

Where to stay
The major hotels are grouped around the lake. The most prominent is the *Shangrila Hotel*, 78 Beishan lu, ☎ 707 7951, fax 707 3545 on the northwest corner of the lake. The local office of the *China Travel Service* is in the Shangrila Hotel. Others include the *Huaqiao* (*Overseas Chinese*) *Hotel*, 15 Hubin lu, ☎ 707 4401, fax 707 4978 on the east side of the lake, the nearby *Dahua Hotel* (favoured by Mao Zedong and Zhou Enlai), 171 Nanshan lu, ☎ 701 1901, fax 706 1770, and a number of guesthouses around the shores. The Shangrila Hotel is taken as a starting point for excursions.

History

Hangzhou does not have a very long history for it took time for the river to silt up and enclose the **West Lake**, once an inlet off the estuary. By the 6C AD, when the south part of the Grand Canal was built (to reach the plentiful supplies of rice from the Hangzhou area), the city was walled, although it was still frequently threatened by flood as the lake waters flowed out into the river. The latter is itself raised every month by the famous 'Hangzhou bore' when strong tides force the river water back inland. At the autumn equinox, usually around 23 September, the Hangzhou bore is most spectacular, with a wall of water, at its highest some 7m high, 75km downriver from Hangzhou.

It is said to roar as thunderously as the Niagara Falls.

From this early period, the lake was divided by a sandbank linking the small Gu shan Island (opposite the Shangrila Hotel) with the northern shore. During the Tang the first dyke (the Bai Causeway) was built with bridges with locks to control the flow of water. The dyke was strengthened by a famous poet, **Bai Juyi**, who was an official serving as governor of Hangzhou in the early 9C, and it is still called after him. A later dyke, creating the 'western inner lake' running north to south, was built by another famous poet, **Su Dongpo**, when he, in turn, served as Governor between 1089 and 1091. This second dyke is named, for him, Su Dyke. Just prior to Su Dongpo's period of service, during the Five Dynasties period (907–978) when Hangzhou was ruled by the independent kings of Wu Yue, pagodas and temples were built around the lake and one, the Liu he ta (Pagoda of Six Harmonies), still stands (much restored) on the banks of the Qiantang river; this was constructed in the hope of subduing the threatening bore. Hangzhou's development was vastly encouraged when it was chosen as the capital of the **Southern Song**, after the court had been driven from the capital, Kaifeng, by the invasion of the north in 1126.

Although Hangzhou was reduced to ruins by the Taiping rebellion in 1860–62 and all its major temples and buildings were destroyed, there are numerous accounts both in Chinese and western languages testifying to its magnificence in previous centuries. Odoric of Pordenone (1286–1331), who visited the city in the early years of the 14C, had never seen 'so great a city'. He described how it was crammed with buildings: 'houses of ten or twelve storeys high, one above the other' and 'eleven thousand bridges'. A surviving plan of the city from 1274 shows that the ramparts surrounding the town were c 16km long and were doubled on the river side to protect the town from naval attack. A central 'imperial way' ran from the imperial palace in the north to the altars to heaven and earth in the south. The population at the time was over one million and some of the Marco Polo manuscripts include notes on the Mongols' imposition of household registration by which all the inhabitants had to list at the door those who lived within, scratching out the names of the dead and adding those of the newborn.

The multi-storeyed houses (extremely rare elsewhere in China and during later periods), crammed into the walled city, were very vulnerable to fire. Fires broke out almost every other month in the early years of the 12C until a fire-prevention system was established with watch-towers provided with scythes, hatchets and buckets. There was plenty of water for fighting fires for the city was criss-crossed with canals which, in the early years of the Southern Song, were lined with stone balustrades to prevent drastic numbers of drunken revellers from falling in. Ten great markets supplied the huge population with food: cereals, fish and pork were the staples but the rich could enjoy lotus seeds, 11 varieties of apricots, pears, paw-paw, shellfish, venison and other luxuries.

Such was the sybaritic life of the rich in Hangzhou that there were pet shops selling fish for pet cats and items for cricket cages and it seems that some people even used to dye the coats of their pet dogs and cats with pink balsam leaves crushed with alum (a preparation normally used by women to tint their fingernails). One man was said to have covered the floor of his house with tiles inlaid with silver. The tender jasmine flower was brought in from

Fujian province to scent the houses of the rich. There were restaurants and teahouses near the imperial way but the lake itself was a major pleasure area, its surface covered with boats for hire, boats full of sing-song girls, jugglers, operatic performers and musicians, restaurant and teahouse boats, with tiny boats paddled by peasants selling snacks amongst the grander barges. There was a special area for male prostitutes outside the New Gate.

Despite the conspicuous consumption of Southern Song Hangzhou, a 13C account summarises Hangzhou's enduring attraction for the Chinese (the reason why it attracted so many famous poets as Governor):

Green mountains surround on all sides the still waters of the lake. Pavilions and towers in hues of gold and azure rise here and there. One would say a landscape composed by a painter. Only towards the east, where there are no hills, does the land open out, and there sparkle, like fishes' scales, the bright coloured tiles of a thousand roofs.
(Jacques Gernet, *Daily Life in China on the Eve of the Mongol Invasion*, Stanford University Press, 1970)

During the Ming Hangzhou remained a trading centre, visited by many foreigners, and it was then that the silk industry began to flourish in the town. In the Qing it was a popular place for Chinese tourists who used simple woodblock guidebooks with illustrations of the temples and pagodas in the lakeside hills.

It was during this period that the major sights of the area were classified according to traditional practice: tourist sites were supposed ideally to have ten 'prospects' and this love of numbers persists in Chinese in, for example, the Ten Great Buildings of the Great Leap Forward in Peking. As with so many other place names in gardens, the view is associated with an activity or a season at which the prospect is at its best. One of the ten is some distance from the lake: this is the Twin Peaks Piercing the Clouds, two hills by the side of the road to the Lingyin Temple. The others surround the lake: Lotuses Stirred by the Breeze from the Distillery (just south of the Yue Fei Temple), Spring Dawn at the Su Causeway (in the centre of the causeway crossing the lake from north to south), Observing the Fish at the Flower Harbour (in the Huagang Park at the southwest corner of the lake), Reflection of the Moon above Three Deep Pools (the three stone pagodas rising from the lake near the Island of Little Oceans), Setting Sun by Thunder Peak Pagoda (south tip of the lake shore), Sound of the Evening Bell below Southern Screen Hill (by the Jingci Temple, whose bell has since disappeared, near the southeast corner of the lake), Listening to the Orioles in the Willows (in the Children's Park on the east side of the lake where the orioles would be silenced by today's children), Snow on the Bridge (by the Brocade Belt Bridge on the Bai Causeway at the northeast corner of the lake) and Autumn Moon on the Lake (on Gushall Island).

Hangzhou was favoured by the Kangxi and Qianlong emperors (much of whose clothing was made from Hangzhou silk brocades). The Qianlong emperor built a palace on the Gushan Island in the lake. It included the Wenlan ge Library housing one of the second series of manuscript collectanea, *Si ku quan shu* (*Complete Library of the Four Storehouses*). There were four sets of the collectanea made for library buildings in Peking (one for the Forbidden City, one for the Old Summer Palace), Chengde and Shenyang, while a subsequent three sets were copied for Hangzhou, Yangzhou and Jinjiang. The Wenlan ge on the island in the lake was looted during the

Taiping occupation of Hangzhou (1860–62), when a local man, Ding Bing (1832–99), whose family library had been destroyed in 1860, realised that volumes from the imperial library were appearing on the open market. He bought as many as he could and persuaded a Shanghai bookseller to enter Hangzhou, which was still in the hands of the Taipings. The bookseller pretended that he was piously 'rescuing' paper with characters on it to prevent it being used for unsuitable purposes and managed to acquire many more volumes of the *Si ku quan shu*. This custom, known as 'respectfully cherishing paper with characters on it', like the use of 'taboo characters' (usually those in the names of the reigning emperor) illustrates the traditional Chinese preoccupation with words and their elevation to an almost sanctified position. Ding Bing eventually built a library on the site of the old one, although the Hangzhou copy of the *Si ku quan shu* remains incomplete, with odd volumes scattered throughout the world.

Like the library, many of Hangzhou's famous temples were rebuilt in the late 19C and early 20C; little ancient architecture remains. Yet the lakeside parts of Hangzhou have escaped the worst effects of the massive skyscraper building craze of the last two decades and, although the trees are hung with fairy lights, the area remains quite elegant. Many rich Chinese have built themselves villas in Hangzhou but these are mostly concealed from view by the trees that surround the lake.

Circuit of the lake

Turning right out of the Shangrila Hotel, past the small bridge that links the west tip of Gushan Island to the shore, the red-walled **Temple to Yue Fei** appears on your right.

Yue Fei

Yue Fei (1103–42) was a general of the Southern Song, a character whose extreme loyalty to an effete ruling house has elevated him to an almost godlike status. Countless stories are told about him and, as a popular hero, he is commemorated in opera, popular fiction and iconography. As the north of China was invaded Yue Fei led a peasant army to defeat the Jin (the Jurched, ancestors of the Manchus, who established the Jin dynasty in north China, 1122–1234) in 1140 at Yancheng. He was keen to proceed with the recapture of the whole of north China for the Song but he was ordered to withdraw. It is thought that his army was seen as even more of a threat to the enfeebled Song than the invaders. The prime minister, Qin Hui, had Yue Fei imprisoned and later executed with his adopted son, while the court concluded a treaty of vasselage with the Jin. Yue Fei was later buried by the lake and in 1221 a temple to his memory was built by the grave.

The present buildings, rebuilt after the Taiping destruction, date from the last years of the 19C and were thoroughly restored in 1979. In front of the temple is a three-arched stone gateway with four characters—jade, blood, cinnabar, heart—and behind is a huge double-eaved gate building which leads to the large courtyard, at the far end of which is the main hall. This contains a recent statue of Yue Fei made in the local art school, above which is the inscription 'return our mountains and rivers'. On either side are four stone carved characters (written by Hong Zhu of the Ming), 'ultimate loyalty to the country', which Yue Fei's mother is supposed to have tattooed on his back before he went off to battle (a scene which can be found in popular cartoon strip woodblocks of his life). The wooden ceiling of the hall is painted with white cranes, symbols of eternal life. Subsidiary halls on either side of the courtyard commemorate two faithful followers of Yue Fei, Niu Gao and Zhang Xian, and members of his family.

To the left of the temple, **Yue Fei's Tomb** is approached by a small avenue of stone statues: lions, rams, horses and officials. There are also over 100 stone stelae, including Hong Zhu's four characters ('ultimate loyalty to the country') whose inscriptions relate to Yue Fei, some, in extravagant characters, based on his own hand. The most famous is Yue Fei's own poem, written in prison, in the calligraphy of Wen Zhengming (1470–1559). The central tumulus is that of Yue Fei; on the left is that of his adopted son, Yue Yun. They are surrounded by a stone railing and planted with pines. There are four kneeling figures in iron, their hands bound behind their backs, facing the tomb. They represent Yue Fei's persecutors: Prime Minister Qin Hui, his wife, Zhang Jun (a general jealous of Yue Fei's success) and Wan Qixie (said to be the prison governor). An inscription reads: 'loyal bones are gloriously buried in a green mound, the sycophants are cast in iron'. The figures were cast in the first years of the 19C.

An earlier group was cast in 1503 but they were lost by 1731 when a new set was cast. Because of their deteriorating condition, they were replaced by the present group. In the past it was customary for visitors to the temple to spit on the figures, which may have caused the rapid deterioration; a notice requests today's visitors to refrain for reasons of conservation and hygiene. The use of iron for the statues of villains is significant. Stone, a permanent material, was restricted to statues of 'good' people. Iron figures were often recast, the melting-down process indicating that these 'bad' images, and therefore the souls of those they represented, were impermanent.

The road past the temple leads west to the **Hangzhou Botanic Gardens**, built in 1956 on the site of a 5C temple (whose buildings were only removed in 1964). There is a spring, the Jade Spring, rising in a square, stone-railed pool, long famous for its large red and black goldfish, still raised there. Goldfish of all sorts form one of the sights of the gardens which are also famous for their many varieties of bamboo, the herb garden and extensive collection of trees and plants.

Returning to the lake, you pass the site where lotuses are best viewed (one of the Ten Prospects) on your right, then the Su Causeway leads across the lake from opposite the Yue Fei Temple. Walking along the Su Causeway, in the centre of the lake, on your right is the **Island of Small Seas** with its four pools. Just south of the island the three stone pagodas rise from the lake (one of the Ten Prospects: Reflection of the Moon above Three Deep Pools). This is the point on the Su Causeway at which you should be viewing the spring dawn (another of the Ten Prospects) which might conflict with reflections of the moon. Just before you reach the end of the causeway, on your left is the **Huagang Garden** (Flower Harbour Garden) where, according to the rules of prospect, you should observe fish and, indeed, the park is full of goldfish pools. The garden is said to have been built originally by a eunuch of the Song dynasty.

At the end of the causeway turn left. On your right you will find the **Jingci** (Pure Compassion) **Monastery** at the foot of the Nanping Hill. Founded in 954,

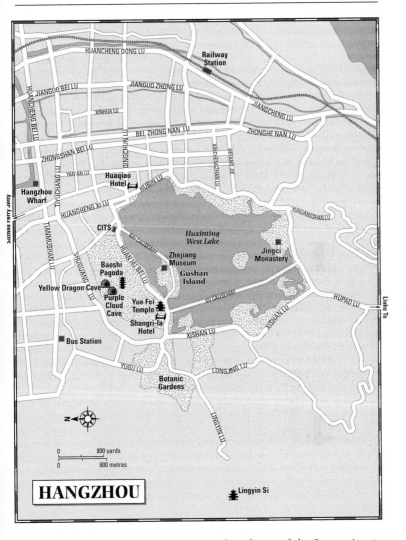

it was originally called the Hall of the Eternal Brightness of the Compassionate Sun but acquired its current name in 1139. The main hall was restored in 1960. The sound of the Jingci Monastery's bell at evening was one of the ten 'prospects', heard no more. Poets praised the sonorous quality of the bell but the *Japanese Railway Guide* says: 'being struck at dawn it was supposed to wake up everything within hearing'. A famous monk of the Song, Daoji, was commemorated in one of the halls and there used to be a well called the Timber Transporting Well because when timber was short during reconstruction, Daoji got drunk and slept for three days, waking to find the required timbers had appeared in the well.

Opposite the Jingci Monastery is a promontory, **Diezhao shan** (Sunset Hill), and on the lakeside is a column which marks the site of the **Lei feng** (Thunder Peak Pagoda) which collapsed in 1924.

Built in 975 by Prince Qian of Wu Yue, constructed from brick and timber, it was a major landmark, even after being burnt down by Japanese pirates in the 16C in case it was used as a watchtower to warn of their approach. The brickwork of the seven storey pagoda survived for hundreds of years despite the depredations of superstitious peasants and trophy-hunting tourists who removed bricks. The peasants scattered brick dust on their fields, believing that it would bring the good fortune of a fine crop through the benevolence of the Buddha or else they sprinkled it in drinks for their health.

Suddenly, on 25 September 1924, 'on a still afternoon the pagoda sank into a shapeless mound of bricks'. When it collapsed, it was discovered that many of the bricks were hollow and contained small rolled-up pieces of paper printed by woodblock with an illustration and the Chinese translation of a Sanskrit Buddhist text, *Sarvatathargatadhishthana – hrdaya – karandamudra – dharani – sutra* (a short text, despite the promise of the title), believed by early Chinese Buddhists to act as a protective charm. These tiny scrolls are amongst the earliest examples of printing in the world. It is not known how many scrolls were walled up in the pagoda; legend states that the pagoda was constructed from 84,000 bricks (a symbolic number in Buddhist legend) and that there must, in consequence, have been 84,000 scrolls. There were certainly a considerable number (one is displayed in the Zhejiang Provincial Museum on Gushan Island) but there is also an incredible number of fakes which still circulate. The British Library acquired a genuine copy in the year of its discovery and the Library of Congress and the National Library of China also have genuine examples. It is interesting to note the description of the pagoda in the *Japanese Railway Guide* published a year before the collapse, accompanied by a photograph of an indistinct, stubby tower: 'the pagoda is so thoroughly ivy-mantled that no trace of the material of the original building is visible'.

One of Hangzhou's most famous stories (often performed as an opera) is the White Snake. A white snake which could turn itself into a beautiful woman to ensnare young men was eventually trapped in the foundations of the pagoda. At the end of the story is the warning that when the pagoda falls, the river bore fails to appear and the West Lake dries up, the snake will be released. So far only one of these conditions has been met.

Following the road around the lake, towards the west side, a park with drooping willows is the Listening to the Orioles in the Willows prospect and north of that is the Children's Park. In the top northeast corner of the lake is the **Bai Causeway**, creating a small inner lake and leading to Gushan (Lonely Hill) Island. There are two bridges on the causeway. The first, near the lake shore, is the Interrupted Bridge (Duan qiao), where the white snake first entrapped her young lover (before being buried under the Thunder Peak Pagoda). Walk across the Bai Causeway to **Gushan Island**.

The first building on the eastern tip of the island is one of the Ten Prospects, Autumn Moon on the Lake. During the Tang dynasty there was a 'lake-watching pavilion' here which was extended in 1699 during the reign of the Kangxi emperor. An Imperial Books Pavilion anticipated the later arrival of the Wenlan ge Library in the reign of the Qianlong emperor. In front of this a stone platform was constructed for viewing the autumn moon over the tranquil lake. The area was expanded in 1959 when, according to one account, 'garden workers knocked down the high wall of the Hardoon Garden, occupied by the imperialist'. This is presumably Silas Aaron Hardoon (1847–1931), the industrialist and financier of Shanghai, who might well have come here from nearby Shanghai, although Nagel's guide mentions 'a European house, which was to be the palace of Prince Henry of Prussia' and which was built on the ruins of the imperial residence constructed here by the Qianlong emperor in the 18C.

On the building by the stone platform are the words: 'through the lattice comes the fresh breeze of summer and the rays of winter sun; rolling up the blinds, the bright moon appears before the mountains, behind are mountains and mountains'. Nearby among the piled rocks are cassia trees and wisteria and the area is one of which poets of the past wrote: 'The vast lake is like a mirror; the moon is at its best in autumn.'

Turn right onto the path along the inner lake, towards the north of the island. On the far side of a small Nine-bend (crooked) Bridge is the Pavilion where the cranes were released and the tomb of the bird-loving poet Lin Hejing (967–1028).

> The pavilion was first built in the Yuan, in memory of Lin, a native of Hangzhou who lived on Gushan Island for 20 years, planting plum trees and rearing cranes (both symbolic of long life), to the point that he was said to 'have married a plum and had a crane for a son'. It is said that if he was out when friends called, his servant would send a crane out to fetch him.

On the wall of the pavilion is the calligraphy of the Kangxi emperor (modelling his style on the Ming calligrapher Dong Qichang) and the stone carved poem, 'Dancing Cranes', by the 5C writer Bao Zhao. Plum trees are planted nearby for this is the place in Hangzhou where plum blossoms are to be appreciated.

Further along the northern shore of the island is a small pavilion marking the Cloud Spring, then a monumental archway in memory of Sun Yatsen and, at a bend in the path, a memorial to the messengers of the People's Liberation Army during the Liberation War, called the 'Chicken-feather Letter Memorial'.

> In the past, messages sent by post horse were marked 'urgent' by attaching a chicken feather to them. During the guerrilla war against first the Japanese, then the Nationalists, the Communist armies' messengers were often young boys and, since their work was dangerous, all messages were effectively 'chicken-feather letters', after which they were named.

Close to the Xiling Bridge, which leads from the western tip of the island to the shore, on the shore side is a pavilion marking the **Tomb of Su Xiaoxiao**, a beauty of the 5C who met her lover, he on a black horse, she in a painted lacquer sedan chair, here by the pines of Xiling.

Turning back to the west and south shore of the island, on the north side of the slope is a small stone pagoda, alternatively called the **Huayan jing ta** (Garland Sutra Pagoda) or the Pagoda of the Xiling Seal-engraving Society for it lies in the garden behind the headquarters of the Seal-engravers' Society of Zhejiang (Xiling she) on the island. It was built in 1903 when the society, which encourages research into and the practice of seal-carving, was founded and is just over 10m high. It is carved with the text of the Buddhist *Garland Sutra* but because of its situation amongst trees, engraved rocks and plants, is viewed as a 'scenery enhancing' rather than a strictly religious pagoda. Beyond the Seal-engravers' headquarters, amongst the ruins of the 18C imperial gardens are, from west to east, a restaurant, the antiquarian section of the **Zhejiang Provincial Library** (modern works are kept elsewhere), much of which was built in the 1940s, and the **Sun Yatsen Park**. The park is formed of part of the old imperial garden with ancient cypress trees, considerably antedating Sun Yatsen.

Slightly set back, between the park and the Zhejiang Provincial Museum, is the **Pavilion of Literary Waves**, built by Ding Bing in the last decades of the 19C to house the 9000 or so volumes of the copy of the *Si ku quan shu*, deposited in the old Wenlan ge by the Qianlong emperor in 1782–87, that he had rescued after the library's destruction during the Taiping uprising. Ding's 9000 volumes represent about a quarter of the original.

Next to the Pavilion of Literary Waves is the **Zhejiang Provincial Museum**. Apart from important exhibits relating to the history of Hangzhou (including the brick from the Leifeng Pagoda with its tiny paper scroll, copies of early stone-engraved maps of the town and woodblock illustrations of the Ten Prospects, as well as much information on the history of silk technology in Hangzhou), the museum contains important exhibits from elsewhere in the province. Notable are the finds from Hemudu which include 7000-year-old cultivated rice (the earliest so far discovered in China) and fascinating remains of early wooden construc-tions. There is also the skeleton of a whale, beached in Zhejiang, interesting because from the Song dynasty, if not before, such events were often associated with disaster. When a whale was beached in 1282, a terrible fire in the town which ensued was blamed on people who, rather than try to rescue the whale, had cut it up for meat.

Next to the museum are the remains of the Shengyin Temple constructed by the Qianlong emperor.

The Hill behind the Hangzhou Hotel

Turn right out of the *Shangrila Hotel*, taking the lakeside road towards the Yue Fei Temple. Before you reach the temple, on your right, is the **Tomb of Qiu Jin** (1879–1907), the woman martyr from Shaoxing, whose remains were eventually moved here after 1911. An early member of Sun Yatsen's anti-Manchu Republican movement, she had abandoned her husband and children to help organise an uprising in Zhejiang when she was executed by the Qing government forces.

Behind the Yue Fei Temple a path leads up towards the hills behind. Up on the hill are a number of caves. First on the left is the **Yanxia dong** (Cave of Twilight Mists), full of small Buddhist figures, including icons of the Bodhisattva Guanyin and 16 lohans dating from the 10C and later. Just beyond, on the right of the path, is the **Tomb of Niu Gao** (1087–1147), another Song general who fol-lowed Yue Fei in his campaigns against the Jin and who died of poisoning. Up to the left, beyond, is the **Ziyun Cave** (Purple Cloud Cave), surrounded by trees and offering a fine view of the lake. Up to the left, near the summit, is the **Huanglong Cave** (Yellow Dragon Cave) where a spring gushes from a stone dragon's head into a pool. Pavilions have been constructed nearby and a stele beside the pool bears the inscription: 'where there is a dragon, there are spirits'; nearby the famous 'square' bamboo grows. There was a Taoist temple here and the buildings have recently been restored.

Returning to the main path, at the eastern end of the hill is the **Bao Chu Pagoda** (Protect Chu Pagoda), sometimes known as the Needle Pagoda because of its sharply tapering form. First built between 968 and 975, the pagoda is said to have been constructed when Prince Qian Sichu was held prisoner by the Song court at Kaifeng; it was erected by his mother and brothers in the hope of divine intercession for his return. Restored in 998–1003, 1789 and 1933, it was a mixed timber and brick construction, although none of the timber has survived, hexagonal in plan, seven storeys and approximately 30m high. It once formed a sort of pair with the Lei feng Pagoda on the opposite, south bank of the lake but it alone remains as one of the major focal points around the West Lake. To return to the hotel, either retrace your steps or take the lakeside road beneath you (to the right).

The Pavilions at the Heart of the Lake

The only way to reach the lake centre is, naturally, by boat. Boats depart from Gushan Island (opposite the hotel), or from the Flower Harbour (Huagang) Park in the southwest corner of the lake or from just north of the Children's Park on the east side of the lake. Between Gushan Island and the larger Small Seas Island are two small islets. The western one is an earth mound, formed by dredged mud (dredged on the instructions of an official called Ruan and now known as Ruan's Island); the eastern one, which can be visited, is called the **Huxin ting** (Pavilion at the Heart of the Lake; previous names included Pavilion of Pure Joy and Pavilion Where the Herons Flap their Wings) and was first constructed in 1552. The present building, with its double-eaved and yellow tiled roof, was built in 1953. It was described by a poet: 'Returning after long travels, the solitary pavilion sits between water and clouds; open on all sides, to one side the city, the rest is mountain.'

The **Island of Small Seas** (Xiaoyang zhou), beyond, consists of four pools enclosed by dredged mud in 1607, with the first pavilions put up in 1611 and the Nine Bend Bridge in 1727. Just south are the three small stone stupa-like 'pagodas', facing the **Wo xin xiang yin** (Reflections of My Heart Pavilion) on the island. They are said to have been first set up by the Song poet Su Dongbo, when he was Governor, to warn against the planting of water-chestnuts and gorgon fruit here in order to avoid clogging up the lake. The original pagodas were lost and those that still stand date from 1621. They stand about 2m high with hollow, bulbous bodies. When the moon is full they have a candle placed inside and the openings are covered with paper so that they seem like three small moons joining the reflection of the full moon in the lake. A poetic description of the scene runs: 'The moon floats on the water, the three pools are bright; on the boats at night, there is singing and dancing as people cross the mirror.'

One of the members of Lord Macartney's embassy (1793) described an excursion on the lake, full of pleasure-boats:

> We had a splendid yacht, and another made fast to it to serve as a kitchen: the dinner ... consisted of at least a hundred dishes in succession ... the water was as clear as crystal. Vast numbers of barges were sailing to and fro, all gaily decorated with paint and gilding and streaming colours; the parties within them apparently all in pursuit of pleasure ...

Marco Polo's account of Hangzhou noted that 13C weddings were held on the islands of the lake which were specially equipped for such events. Today, Hangzhou's newly-weds in their (western-style) bridal clothing, pose for photographs on the lakeside beneath the willows.

The Lingyin Temple

In the hills to the west, beyond the Botanic Gardens, is the **Lingyin** (Spirit Retreat) **Temple**, one of the most famous Chan (Zen) temples in China, founded by an Indian monk, known in Chinese as Huili, in 326. Huili was particularly impressed by the rocky formation to the left of the path that leads to the temple and which is known as the Fei lai feng, the 'Peak that Flew'.

> Huili said: 'This is a small peak of the Grdhrakuta (Vulture Peak) Mountain in India; when did it fly here? When the Buddha was alive there were many miracles.' In the 10C the temple was twice enlarged and had 72 halls and 3000 monks. It was destroyed in the Taiping rebellion, rebuilt in the early 20C, although the main beams of the main hall collapsed again in 1924 and a disastrous fire in 1936 further reduced it. The present buildings were reconstructed in 1956 and again in 1970, after the Cultural Revolution.

Inside the gate a path leads to a small covered bridge, the Chun cong ting (Pavilion of the Gurgling Stream in Spring), beside which, on the left, is a small stupa, called **Sir Li's Pagoda**, said to contain the remains of Huili, the Indian founder of the temple. A path beside the stream to the left leads to three caves: Dragon Depths Cave, Jade Milk Cave and Green Forest Cave. You can either take the path straight to the temple (on the right-hand side of the stream) or, better, walk on the left side of the stream, along the cliff of the 'Peak that Flew' where there are over 380 Buddhist images carved in the rock, dating from the Five Dynasties, Song and Yuan periods (10C–14C). The largest is a very fat Maitreya (in his 'Laughing Buddha' form) of the Song but the majority of figures date from the Yuan. The whole forms the most important group of Buddhist rock carvings in southern China.

The temple, which faces the stream, consists of an entrance hall with guardian figures and a Great Buddha Hall behind. The entrance hall has a double-eaved roof and contains the standard icons: the four protective guardians, two on either side, a fat, laughing Maitreya welcoming visitors and, behind him, the Weituo guardian figure. The Maitreya is said to be 18C; the Weituo figure is said to be Song in date and carved in camphor wood. On either side of the entrance hall are two stone sutra pagodas, dated 969. Across a broad courtyard is the triple-roofed **Great Buddha Hall** which, although fundamentally dating back only to 1956, is an impressive building and is flanked by two early multi-storeyed stone pagodas. The central gilded wooden Buddha figure inside the hall was made in 1956. The temple is a very active one, visited by enthusiastic pilgrims and local worshippers.

Outside the temple, on the cliff opposite, is the **Cuiwei Pavilion** (*cuiwei* is a poetic word for the iridescent green of hillsides), first built in the Southern Song in memory of Yue Fei. The whole area is a pleasant, if crowded, place in which to wander. A cable-car (one of the first in China) can take visitors to the summit of the Northern Peak; the Taoguang Hermitage (the name is taken from that of a Tang period hermit) to the northwest was celebrated by the poet Wei Fangtai in 1724:

> *A stone-paved pathway hidden deep in myriad bamboos*
> *Tempts me to climb with an old friend to meditation's home,*
> *Suddenly, as we unbar the gate, our eyes delighted see*
> *Beyond the lake, the city's smoking hearths; beyond the river, hill.*
> (Translated by A.C. Moule, *Quinsai, with other notes on Marco Polo*, CUP, 1957)

Dragon Well Tea and the Tiger Spring

South of the Lingyin Temple, west of the lake, is the area in which Hangzhou's most famous tea, Longjing or Dragon Well, is grown and dried. The tea-producing areas can be visited by appointment, arranged through the **China Travel Service** (the office is in the **Shangrila Hotel**). The scenery is wonderful, with green hills, pickers dressed in bright blue and pink bending over the dark-green bushes, while the simple process of drying the tea-leaves is interesting. The processing is brief and the leaves remain intact, to open out like privet leaves in hot water and produce a refreshing, fresh-tasting, leafy green tea.

The best spring water for making Dragon Well Tea (the combination is described as the 'two superlatives') is found in the Tiger Spring to the southeast of the tea-growing area, midway between the lake and the Pagoda of Six Harmonies on the Qiantang River. In the teahouses there you will see people floating light Chinese coins on bowls of spring water for it has a strong surface tension and notable meniscus (curving up from the edge of the bowl). The spring is said to have arisen in 819 when a monk lived here, suffering from a lack of water. One day two tigers leapt from the earth and a spring bubbled up. The spring is called the 'Third Spring Under Heaven'.

Pagoda of Six Harmonies (Liuhe ta)

The pagoda stands beside the railway bridge across the Qiantang River, high on a hill. It was first built in 970 in an effort to subdue the river bore and has long served as a landmark, with a lantern on its tip to help sailors. It was built beside the Liuhe (Six Harmonies) Temple, which has long since disappeared, leaving its name to the pagoda. It has been constantly rebuilt throughout its history, in 1121, 1153, 1163, 1524, 1735 and 1900.

Octagonal in plan, it is almost 60m high and although from the outside it appears to have 13 storeys, internally it has only seven. The core is of brick, the exterior wooden. A spiral staircase inside enables visitors to climb to the top. The internal brickwork is decorated with birds, flowers and animals.

To the east of the pagoda, the hill between the river and the lake, the **Yuhuang (Jade Emperor) Hill**, used to be covered with temples. On the lake side was the Song Altar of Heaven and Field of Eight Trigrams where the Southern Song emperors ploughed their ceremonial furrow to inaugurate the agricultural year. The form of the fields can still just be seen and, like the Lingyin Temple area, this is a pleasant area for walking (and is less crowded).

The mosque, called the **Fenghuang si** (Phoenix Temple), is in the south-central area of the town itself, at no. 325 in the central section of Zhongshan lu. It is easily reached on foot from the Children's Park on the east side of the lake. Take the road leading east, away from the lake, opposite the park (Kaiyuan lu) which, with a slight wiggle at the end, arrives at the major north–south road, Zhongshan lu. Turn right and not far down on your right is the mosque. Founded in the Tang, it is one of the 'four great' mosques in China and has been much restored. The surviving great hall is a Yuan brick structure with vaulted roof and carved brick decoration.

The Grand Canal can be seen to the north of Huancheng bei lu (to the right of the junction with Zhongshan bei lu), in the north of the city. It leads north.

Wuxi

Wuxi, which stands on the edge of Lake Tai (Tai hu), some 48km west of Suzhou in Jiangsu province, is an old city whose origins as a small country town go back to the Han. Its name, which means 'no tin', is said to derive from the fact that during the Zhou and Qin periods tin (*xi*) was extensively mined on Xi shan (Tin Hill) in the western suburbs but the supplies became exhausted during the Han (*wu xi shan shan wu xi*: 'there is no tin on "no tin" town's Tin Hill' is a local tongue-twister) when the town grew up. As with many of the towns in the area, the Grand Canal passes through the centre and one of its gardens, in particular, excited imperial interest in the 18C. In the early 20C it became a centre for silk production using modern machinery, with 45 filature factories. It is also known for the production of clay figurines.

Practical information

Getting there
By train
Wuxi is on the main Peking–Shanghai line with frequent express trains. The station is in the northeast of the city on Tonghui dong lu, some distance from the town centre.
By boat
There is a daily service (13 hours) on the Grand Canal between Wuxi and Hangzhou.

Where to stay
It is most peaceful to stay in hotels beside Lake Tai, some 20 or more minutes from the town. The *Taihu Hotel* on Xiehui lu, ☎ 551 7888, is the oldest (although a luxury building has been added); the *Hubin Hotel*, Li yuan garden, ☎ 510 1888, fax 275 2781, was built in 1978 (Li yuan garden), ☎ 510 1888, fax 275 2781.

Lake Tai
One of the largest freshwater lakes in China, Lake Tai is best known for the curiously-shaped rocks it produces; limestone boulders scoured and holed by the action of the water. The Huizong emperor of the Song dynasty (reigned 1101–26) was an enthusiastic petromane (stone collector) who almost brought the country to bankruptcy with his extravagant expenditure on stones. The celebrated painter Mi Fei (12C) had a huge stone that he bowed to deeply every morning and addressed as his elder brother.

Although not all garden stones came from Lake Tai (for volcanic and ore-bearing stones were also appreciated for their varying textures and colours), many of the best did and they can be seen in all the gardens of Suzhou, especially the Shizi lin (Grove of Stone Lions). Lake stones were supposed to be 'holey, slim and leaky', pierced through with holes and, ideally, balanced on a narrow base, flaring outwards, the heavier top on its slim foot apparently defying gravity. Connoisseurs spent hours scraping the stones, scouring their hollows and, occasionally, resorting to chisels to improve a little on nature. The 12C *Yun lin shi pu* (*Stone Catalogue of the Cloud Forest*) describes

Lake Tai stones hauled up from the lake as 'huge specimens, up to 50 feet high, with a colour range from white through pale blue to blue-black ... the most desirable have tortuous, rugged contours, and abundant hollows.' According to the translation of the Swedish sinologist, Osvald Siren, small surface cavities 'are called arbalest pellet nests', by which he may mean the type of swallows' nests used for bird's nest soup.

Opposite the Taihu Hotel is a promontory called **Guitou zhu** (Turtle's Head Peninsula), because it apparently looks like a turtle's head. Reached by pleasure boat from below the Taihu Hotel, it is a favourite spot for Chinese tourists. Beside the Hubin and Shuixiu Hotels is the bridge linking the promontory with the lakeside road (Huanhu lu) and next to this is the **Li** (Worm-eaten) **Garden**, which some guidebooks ('hideous circus', 'tatty affair', 'concrete labyrinth') would consider an appropriate name, although they never seem to translate it. It is not enormously to be recommended except for a view of the lake, if the crowds permit.

The garden was made between 1927 and 1930 out of two gardens, the original Worm-eaten Garden and the Yu zhuang (Fishing Village) Garden. The 'worm-eaten' bit takes its name from a part of the lake which was originally known as Li hu (Worm-eaten Lake) but is now known as Wuli hu (Five-mile Lake). Li hu, in turn, is said to derive its name from Fan Li, the great statesman of the state of Yue at the end of the Spring and Autumn Period who retired here to relax on a boat.

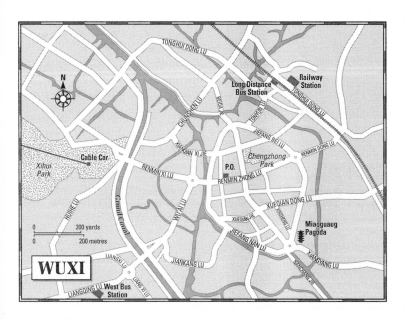

San shan (Three Hills) **Island** in the lake, a former haunt of bandits, can be reached by boat.

On the road towards town from the Taihu Hotel is the **Mei Yuan** (Plum Garden), named for the plum trees in it, although in the late Qing it was known as the Xiaotao yuan (Small Peach Garden). Originally belonging to a scholar called Xu Dian, in 1912 it became the private garden of a family called Song who planted the plum trees, which are particularly beautiful in flower in the early spring. Autumn visitors need not despair for wonderfully scented cassia (*Osmanthus fragrans*) bushes are another feature of the garden. Amongst the many pavilions, the **Songbin tang** (Hall Where the Praises of the State of Bin are Chanted) was built from *nanmu* (a cedar) wood and the three-storey brick **Nianqu** (Contemplation of Effort) **Pagoda** was built by Song Zongjing and Song Desheng, two major industrialists, to commemorate their mother's 80th birthday. It affords a view of the distant lake.

To the west of Wuxi city is **Xihui Park**, constructed in 1958 by linking the Xi shan (Tin Hill) and the famous Hui shan (Generosity, or sometimes, using another *hui*, Wisdom Hill). On the small (74.8m) Xi shan is the 16C **Longguang** (Dragon Brilliance) **Pagoda** and **Temple**; on the much more lofty (328.9m) **Hui shan** are nine peaks, sometimes known as nine dragons, as well as the 'second spring' in the world.

So named by Lu Yu of the Tang who, in his *Cha jing* or *Classic of Tea*, paid as much attention to the ceramics in which tea was served—did the colours enhance the colour of the tea or not?—and the water from which tea was brewed, as the primary raw material itself. The spring produces water that is sweet and 'thick' with the same sort of meniscus as found in the spring at Hangzhou (see p 309). The Huizong emperor of the Song gave the spring water a form of 'royal warrant' declaring it a 'palace product'.

Peony and rock

Also on Hui shan are a Song dynasty bridge, the **Jinlian** (or Golden Lotus) **Bridge**, the seal-script inscription *ting song* or 'listening to the pines' by the Tang calligrapher Li Yangbing and the beautifully carved Tang and Song 'sutra pillars' outside the gate of the Hui shan Temple. That to the north side of the gate dates from the Tang (876) and has the *Dharani Sutra* carved on it; the Song pillar is to the south of the gate and, like the Tang one, is just over 5m high with *dharani* carved on it.

One of the most famous gardens in China now forms part of the Xihui Park. This is the **Jichang yuan** (Attachment to Freedom Garden) which so impressed the Qianlong emperor on one of his visits to the south that he commissioned a copy of it for the Yihe yuan (Summer Palace) in Peking, the Xiequ yuan (Garden of Harmonious Interest), built in 1750. It is interesting to compare the two, if you can, for they provide the best possible example of the difference between northern and southern garden styles. The plans are fairly similar, centred on water surrounded by covered walks and verandahs, but the narrow columns and lightly up-turned eaves of the south give way to more solid construction with thicker columns and heavier roofs with little upturn to the eaves in the northern Xiequ yuan.

The Jichang yuan stands on the site of a Yuan dynasty monastery which became a garden in the Zhengde period (1506–22) of the Ming. It was originally called Fenggu xingwo (Temporary Nest in Phoenix Gully). The garden is fundamentally divided into two parts: east and west. Water and surrounding walkways are the focus of the eastern part; piled rocks and 'mock mountains' dominate the west. The higher parts of the garden afford views over the hills of the surrounding park in a garden design technique called 'borrowing a view', commonly used in the small gardens of the Yangtse delta towns.

Yixing

Yixing is a small town on the west side of Lake Tai in Jiangsu province, on the opposite side of the lake from Wuxi. It is best known for the production of small pottery teapots and other items made most commonly from a dark brick-red clay. The pottery is still made in Dingshu zhen, some 20km southwest of Yixing town. Also southwest of the town are a number of curiously-shaped karst caves which are frequently visited.

Practical information

Getting there
Yixing is not on a railway line and is best reached by bus (c two hours) or car from Wuxi which is on the railway, intermediate between Zhenjiang and Suzhou. Dingshu zhen and its potteries, as well as the karst caves, may be reached by public bus or car from Yixing.

Where to stay
The *Yixing Guoji Fandian* is at 52 Tongzhenguan lu, ☎ 791 8888, fax 790 0767.

History

Set in beautiful scenery of lakes, canals, rivers and paddy-fields, the Yixing area has long been famous for its beauty. During the Warring States period (403–221 BC), the ex-minister of the State of Yue, Fan Li, came to live in Yixing, then known as Jingqi, a name which was changed during the Qin dynasty (221–206 BC) to Yang xian. The name Yixing dates from the Song (960–1279). Fan Li is supposed to have produced ceramics at Yixing and is therefore worshipped as the patron deity of potters.

Another legend credits the beginnings of the local ceramic industry to the arrival of a monk who offered 'riches or honours'. Ridiculed by the townspeople, he led them to a cave where clay of brilliant colours was found. This account first appeared in print in the late 16C in the *Yang xian ming hu xi*

(*Account of the Famous Teapots of Yang County*) by Zhou Gaoji. At the time of its publication, Yixing was already known for its production of utilitarian objects such as flowerpots for the local tea bushes and drainpipes.

It was during the 16C that local kilns began to produce the characteristic small teapots, water-droppers and decorative objects that are now known as **Yixing ware**. Another Chinese name for the ware is 'purple sand' in reference to the dominant colour, which is a dark red (produced by a high level of iron in the clay), although green, grey, buff and black clays are also used. All the clays are locally found and the wares were fired in multi-chambered dragon kilns built up the local hills and fuelled with local timber. In the past, the multitude of waterways meant that transport of the wares to nearby centres like Shanghai, Nanjing and Suzhou was easy and cheap.

It is not only the colours that distinguish Yixing wares; they are also very amusingly shaped. Tiny teapots may look like teapots, often further embellished with incised calligraphy or drawings, or they may be made in the form of melons, pumpkins, peaches, gnarled tree-stumps or bundles of books wrapped in cloth. In other small pieces, the varying colours of local clays are used to produce three-dimensional 'still-lifes', baskets with yellow peanuts, grey crabs and green leaves in them, or life-like walnuts, sweet chestnuts and snail-shells. Some of the plain teapots have speckled finishes or tiny gilt spots on their surface. Although virtually all other Chinese ceramics are anonymous products, many Yixing pieces were signed with the seal of the potter, a tradition which continues today.

There is a Confucian Temple in Yixing, said to contain fine statuary (closed for renovation). It stands behind a fine white stone *pailou*, or arch, dated to 1627. The temple is also said to be 17C.

On Heping jie is an old house, used as a residence by the Taiping 'king' Yang Fuqing after the capture of Yixing in the mid 19C. It still contains painted decoration of the Taiping period, including murals depicting agricultural scenes, discovered in 1958.

Dingshu zhen

Reached by bus or car from Yixing (some 20km away), Dingshu zhen is the centre of contemporary ceramic production, with some 25 factories, many of which still make domestic articles, such as drainpipes and flowerpots, while the Zisha (Purple Sand) factory continues to produce the highly-prized tiny teapots. Stalls selling flowerpots, teapots and teasets, as well as some of the small decorative pieces, line the streets of the town and the **Pottery Exhibition Hall** may be visited. To visit a ceramic factory, it is necessary to make arrangements through the *China Travel Service* (ask at your hotel).

Tourist buses leave from Dingshu zhen for the various karst caves in the locality. These include the **Zhang Gong Cave**, 22km southwest of Yixing, reputedly a place where various eminent Taoists lived and cultivated 'the way', notably Zhang Daoling of the Han dynasty and Zhang Guolao of the Tang, hence its name, 'Duke Zhang's Cave'. It consists of an inner and outer chamber, covering 3000 square metres. There are over 72 caves in all, including smaller chambers.

The main inner chamber is said to hold 5000 visitors and on holidays it may appear to do so.

The **Linggu dong** or Spirit Cave is 6km beyond the Zhang Gong Cave, near a major tea plantation. This contains, amongst many varied stone formations, a large white stone 'screen', 17m high and 5m wide, which was discovered and praised by the Tang dynasty poet Lu Guimeng when he came to Yixing to buy tea.

The **Shanjuan Cave**, also 25km southwest of Yixing, is divided into three levels and, as it is partly water-filled, can be visited by boat. Some of its scenic highlights have been embellished with stone-carved calligraphy, including one piece dated AD 850 and another by the noted calligrapher of the Liang (502–557), Tao Hongjing.

Putuo shan

Putuo shan, Potala Mountain, is one of the islands in the Zhou shan archipelago, off the coast just south of Shanghai. Since the 10C it has been celebrated as one of the four Buddhist mountains (the others are Wutai shan in Shanxi, Jiuhua shan in Anhui and Emei shan in Sichuan). These sacred mountains are places where Bodhisattvas appeared; Putuo is the abode of the Bodhisattva Avalokitesvara or Guanyin in Chinese. The mountain home of Avalokitesvara was named Potalaka in Sanksrit, translated by sound into Putuo in Chinese. The palace in Lhasa, Tibet, historically the home of the Dalai Lama, is called the Potala for the same reason, as the Dalai Lama is believed to be a reincarnation of the Bodhisattva Avalokitesvara.

The Zhou shan archipelago is very beautiful; small green islands with beaches of clean, pale sand rise from a clear blue sea if you travel in the spring to autumn period; Gutzlaff in February 1831 found the weather 'generally dark and stormy'. The first view of Putuo Island from the jetty is of a low, yellow-painted temple building ahead, a naval settlement with elderly submarines and sailors playing basketball to the left and the green island behind. For the missionary Gutzlaff, whose 'zeal never failed' and who arrived in late winter, the island first appeared:

> ... barren and scarcely habitable, but as we approached it, we observed very prominent buildings, and large glittering domes. A temple built on a projecting rock, beneath which the foaming sea dashed, gave us some idea of the genius of its inhabitants, in thus selecting the most attractive spot to celebrate the orgies of idolatry.

The spot was also attractive to the East India Company, which set up a factory on Zhou shan, the major island of the archipelago, in 1700, from where Cunningham, the company doctor, visited Putuo and acquired a couple of woodblock printed guidebooks from the monks which he sent to the collector, Sir Hans Sloane, in 1703; they are now in the British Library. Attempts to enter China proper from the archipelago failed and the Company had to retreat to Canton. The British continued, however, to seize Zhou shan occasionally (1840, 1842 and 1860).

Practical information

Getting there

Putuo is reached by boat from Shanghai (two overnight boats and one day boat) or a four hour trip from Ningbo.

Getting around

The island is small and there is little motor trafflc. It is wise to bring as little luggage as possible as there is no certainty of finding any motor transport at the jetty and you may have to walk (c 20 minutes) along the stepped path to the hotel. There are tourist minibus trips starting from the west side of the Pu ji Temple to the Foding (Universal Wise Sovereign)

Mountain, Fayuchan (Rain of Buddha Truth) Temple, Fanyin (Sanskrit Sound) Cave, Zizhulin, and other temples en route.

Where to stay

The *Xilin Fandian*, ☎ 609 1303, fax 609 1199, is beside the Puji Temple. The new *Huanguang shanzhuang Hotel*, ☎ 609 2667, fax 609 2537, is near the Fayu temple.

Information

The **Tourist Office** is on the west side of the Puji Temple; information may also be obtained in the hotel.

History

Putuo's significance is said to date from 847 when a vision of the Bodhisattva appeared to an Indian monk meditating in the Chaoyin cave. In 916 a Japanese monk, who had taken a figure of Guanyin from the sacred mountain of Wutai in Shanxi, passed the island en route for Japan. A sudden typhoon blew up and he was unable to continue. He retired to a rustic hut in the Purple Bamboo Grove and the episode of divine intervention is commemorated in the temple called Bukenqu guanyin yuan (Hall of the Stopping of Guanyin). From the Song dynasty, the monks adhered to the Chan (Zen) sect and many of the temples are named *chan si* (meditation temple).

The Bodhisattva Avalokitesvara was associated with compassion in early Indian belief and the full Chinese name, Guan shi yin, is a translation of one of Avalokitesvara's epithets, 'the one who hears the cries of the world'. The Indian deity was, if anything, masculine, but in China Guanyin was gradually transformed into a sort of female icon (although ambiguous, for sculptures never reveal bound feet), as the association with compassion was conceived of as a female virtue. The childless and the sick still pray to Guanyin and miracles of healing were soon reported from Putuo island. It is still quite common to find very sick people on the boat from Shanghai, amongst the tightly packed crowds of ordinary tourists.

Among the tourists, many of whom come on organised tours from Shanghai and are led by a whistle-blowing guide across the island, wearing identical peaked caps, are a number of pilgrims, some monks and nuns from other Buddhist centres but often groups of middle-aged and elderly ladies carrying yellow cotton bags. The pilgrim bags, decorated with woodblock prints of lotuses (symbols of Guanyin) and Guanyin images, are stamped with the seal of the temple in each temple the pilgrims visit. In order to get a monk or nun to stamp the bag a payment must be made. The patron saint of the island has recently been commemorated in a 30m high statue.

The buildings on the island, of which there were said to be 218 occupied by over 2000 monks and nuns in 1949, have suffered throughout the centuries from pirate attacks and the island is thought to have suffered badly during the Cultural Revolution, presumably because it was such a charming place to visit, even for Red Guards on a rampage. It is therefore not of any great architectural significance but it is a very pretty island and a great place to walk, particularly if you avoid the main paths, which can get crowded. For that reason, and since the island is only 8.6km north–south and 3.5km west–east, after describing the route from the jetty to the hotel, I will simply list places to see and suggest that you make

Putuo shan: temple interior

your own itinerary, avoiding the worst of the crowds.

From the jetty, the path to the village at the centre of the island, where the Puji (Universal Succour) Temple and the hotel are situated, leads off to the right (away from the naval base). Passing the Haiyan *pailou* (Monumental Arch on the Edge of the Sea), a modern construction, the path, lined with stalls selling religious and secular souvenirs, breaks away from the road, to the left, leading up over a hill in a series of shallow steps. The slopes are planted with small tea bushes and certain old trees appear to have achieved some sort of sanctity for joss-sticks are placed beneath them—the trees on Putuo are wonderful; it is a mercy that Red Guards did not include tree-felling in their acts of desecration. As the path descends through the trees, buildings appear on either side, dormitory hotels with washing hung in the windows. Ahead is an open area with a large pool crossed by a stone bridge and embellished by an octagonal pavilion with upturned eaves, the whole dominated by the main temple on the island, the **Puji Temple**, surrounded and filled with magnificent trees. Like most of the temples on the island and throughout Zhejiang province, it is yellow-walled with grey tiled roofs. First mentioned in 1699, it contains nine main halls and 36 other buildings. On the main axis are the Hall of the Heavenly Kings, the Hall of the Universal Penetration of Wisdom, the Library and the Abbot's Hall. The hotel lies behind the temple.

Across the bridge is a small pagoda and beyond that, the sea. A major group of buildings lies on a promontory to the right: the Zizhulin (Purple Bamboo Grove), the Chaoyin (Wave Sound) Cave, where the presiding Bodhisattva first appeared, and the Hall of the Stopping of Guanyin.

The **Purple Bamboo Grove** is named after the purplish colour of the rock formation and the bamboo leaf patterns that are said to be visible in the rocks; it was here that the Japanese monk lived after he failed to transport his Guanyin figure to Japan.

The **Chaoyin Cave** is famous for the thunderous sound of breaking waves. During the Song and Yuan it was a common place for suicide so in an attempt to prevent people throwing themselves into the sea a pavilion called the No-suicide Pavilion was constructed here. It has since been destroyed.

Around the promontory, heading west towards the jetty, is the **Nantian men** (Gate to the Southern Heavens), on another rocky promontory.

North from the Puji Temple, at the far left of the beach is the **Chaoyang** (Facing the Sun) **Cave**, in the past surmounted by a three-storey building. Beyond, to the north, is another long beach, the Thousand-pace Beach, with a concrete tank, presumably for defensive purposes, parked in the dunes and, on the right-hand side of the road, first the **Cultural Hall**, which contains a small exhibition of very few local relics and, further on, set back from the road on the left, the **Dacheng** (Mahayana) **Nunnery**, which no longer seems to be restricted to the female sex.

At the far end of the beach is another of the major temples, the **Fayu Temple**, founded in 1580 as the Sea Wave Nunnery. Destroyed by fire, it was rebuilt in 1699 and much restored in succeeding centuries. It stands high on a stone platform. On the main axis are the gate (from whence you climb), the Bell Tower, the Jade Buddha Hall, the Guanyin Hall, the Jade Tablet Hall, the Mahavira Hall, the Library and the Abbot's Hall. The Guanyin Hall is also called the Nine Dragon Brackets Hall because of the complexity of the roof construction. In front of the temple is a pool fed by streams from the hills behind. On a large promontory projecting to the east from the temple is the **Fanyin Cave**.

From the Fayu Temple a stepped path leads to the summit of the **Foding Mountain**, 291m above sea level, affording a marvellous view of sea and islands. The major temple at the summit is the **Huiji** (Favour and Succour) **Temple**, originally merely a stone pavilion gradually built up from 1793 to 1907 into a complex of four main halls with painted beams, seven smaller halls and six pavilions. To the left of the temple is a famous 'goose-ear oak' tree of some rarity. There is a beacon on the summit to aid navigation at sea. The tea grown on the mountain slopes is called 'Buddha's tea'.

The **village**, to the north of the Puji Temple, with its public washing place (like the *lavoir* in a French village), surrounding walls and narrow streets lined with small restaurants serving delicious fresh fish and marvellous shrimps (better than the food in the hotel) is well worth visiting.

Ningbo

Ningbo, c 20km up the Yong River from the coast, was China's greatest port from the Song to the end of the Ming, trading mainly with Japan and Korea. The position of the port was ideal, close to the ceramic producing areas of Jiangxi and Zhejiang and the tea and silk producing southern provinces, whose products were transported to Ningbo by sea or river. Its natives were, and still are, known for their trading abilities and the city is has been developed as a major container port with help from one of its best-known native sons, the shipping magnate Sir Y.K. Pao (d. 1991).

Practical information

Getting there
By air

Although there is an airport, Ningbo is best reached by rail, boat or high-speed motorway bus.

By train

The Shanghai–Ningbo line was one of China's earlier railways, rights to build being granted to a British firm in 1898, although the construction was transferred to two Chinese firms in 1905. The *Japanese Railway Guide* (1924) says of the Shanghai–Hangzhou–Ningbo line: 'This railway now connects Shanghai and Hangzhou.' The Hangzhou–Ningbo link still appears incomplete in the map drawn for Carl Crow's 1933 *Handbook for China*. Today there are five trains a day via Hangzhou and Shaoxing to Shanghai. The station is in the south of the city, just to the west of Changchun lu, five minutes by car from the two hotels.

By bus

Buses to the Baoguo Temple leave from the Northern Bus Station (Daqing nanlu, near the passenger boat dock). Buses to the Tiantong si leave from the Eastern Bus Station, on the eastern side of the river, Shuguang lu. Fast, long-distance buses (to Hangzhou and Shanghai) leave from the southern bus station beside the railway station.

By boat

The passenger ferry piers are on the west side of the Yong river near the Northern Bus Station. Tickets may be obtained from the general office on the north side of Xinjiang qiao (Xinjiang Bridge). There are boats every day to Putuo shan (four to five hours) and to Shanghai (overnight).

Where to stay

The *Overseas Chinese Hotel* (Huaqiao Fandian) is close to the Tianyige at 130 Liuting jie, ☎ 729 33175, fax 729 4790. Further south is the *Nanyuan Fandian*, 2 Lingqiao lu, ☎ 729 5678, fax 729 7788.

History

Although a small town was built in the hills to the south, capital of the Kingdom of Yue during the Warring States period (435–221 BC), Ningbo's period of glory was from the **Song** to the end of the **Ming**. During the 9C the local governor built a series of locks and canals to drain the area and in the 12C a protective breakwater was constructed on the coast. During the succeeding centuries, when China's foreign trade emphasis shifted from the overland silk routes to the coast, ships plied between Japan, Korea and Ningbo, loaded with celadon wares from Zhejiang and, later, blue-and-white ceramics from Jingdezhen in Jiangxi, silks from the Yangtse delta and locally produced salt, for which the Japanese paid in gold and silver. Coastal fisheries have flourished for hundreds of years. Traditional products of continuing importance include bamboo shoots (which can be seen in the markets in spring, great fat shoots, the size of a large loaf of bread) and dark wood furniture inlaid with coloured pieces of shell.

In the Tang and Song the town was named Mingzhou and renamed Ningbo

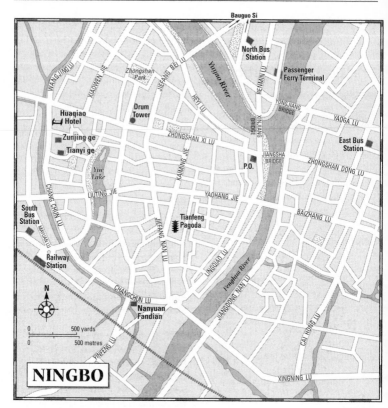

NINGBO

Baugua Si

North Bus Station

Passenger Ferry Terminal

Yuyao River

Zhongshan Park

Huaqiao Hotel

Drum Tower

Zunjing ge

Tianyi ge

Yue Lake

ZHONGSHAN XI LU

KAIMING JIE

LIUTING JIE

YAOHANG JIE

South Bus Station

Railway Station

Tianfeng Pagoda

Nanyuan Fandian

CHANGCHUN LU

JIEFANG NAN LU

LINGQIAO LU

Fenghua River

JIANGDONG NAN LU

YAOGA LU

East Bus Station

ZHONGSHAN DONG LU

BAIZHANG LU

CAI HONG LU

XINGNING LU

N

0   500 yards

0   500 metres

(Calmed Waves) at the beginning of the Ming. The town was subject to frequent attacks from pirates and as late as 1924 was still surrounded by 'strong walls' encircling the old town to the southwest, now replaced by Yongfeng lu, Lingqiao lu, Changchun lu and Wangjing lu. One of the best-known defenders of the nearby coast from pirates was **Qi Jiguang** (1528–88) a famous military strategist and author of *Ji xiao xin shu* (*A New Treatise on Tactics*), a work in which he recommended that soldiers drill in the traditional martial arts as part of their training. Even the idea of training soldiers was a new one, for the Chinese traditionally believed that, just as you did not waste good iron by making it into nails, good men did not become soldiers, who were regarded as little better than brigands. Despite his high military position, Qi Jiguang is said to have been dominated by his wife, who is supposed to have taken command of a coastal fort besieged by pirates.

Outside the walled town, on the north side of the Yao River (across Xinjiang Bridge), was the foreign concession area, for Ningbo is known as the first area in which foreign traders settled. The Portuguese Fernando de Andrade and George Mascarenhas reached Ningbo c 1517 and by 1533 a Portuguese trading colony was flourishing there until Ferdinand Mendez Pinto landed. **Mendez Pinto** (c 1509–c 1581) travelled widely in the Far East, visiting

Japan in the uplifting company of St Francis Xavier but arriving, by contrast, in Ningbo in 1545 with 'a troop of other desperadoes', according to the *Encyclopaedia Sinica*. They plundered tombs on a nearby island and, after a shipwreck, were taken prisoner by the Chinese, 'thrown into a pond and almost devoured by leeches' and were eventually sentenced to a year of corvée labour on the Great Wall. Saved by the arrival of the conquering Manchus, Mendez Pinto was said to have made a subsequent trip to China which was 'less full of excitement'. The behaviour of the desperadoes, together with the 'insolence and licentiousness of the colonists', provoked an attack by imperial orders in which over 1000 Christians, nearly half of them Portuguese, were killed and many ships burnt.

During the 18C and early 19C the British East India Company made several attempts (1701, 1736, 1755, 1832), to settle in Ningbo, only to be prevented by imperial edicts restricting all but the Russians (who maintained a small establishment—a priest, three curates and five or six language students—in Peking from 1727, as well as trading posts on the Russo-Chinese frontier) to seasonal trade at Canton. In 1840 British warships blockaded Ningbo and the British entered the city in 1841. It was one of the ports opened to foreign trade by the Treaty of Nanking in 1842 after the Opium War. A British consulate, post office and other port buildings were constructed in the northern part of the city, outside the walls, and in the early years of the 20C the non-missionary foreign population was about 60. Ningbo was not a very important centre of foreign trade after 1842, for Shanghai's growth eclipsed it, but in the mid-1980s the Chinese began to develop a computerised cargo port along the river when Shanghai's silted channels provided insufficient draught for huge container ships.

Ningbo's most famous monument is the **Tianyi ge**, a private library constructed between 1561 and 1566. Its name means 'Pavilion of Heaven's First Creation', a name deriving from a traditional saying that 'heaven first created water', which was intended to protect its contents from fire, as was the brick and tile involved in its construction. The library is easily reached from the *Huaqiao Hotel*: turn right out of the hotel and take the first major turning on the right, Changchun lu, which runs alongside a long, river-like pool. The two-storey building is visible at the end of the next turning on the right, effectively behind the hotel.

Despite fire dangers, it is fundamentally a two-storeyed, six-bay timber structure with the dark tiled, upturned eaves characteristic of southern architecture. Within the gate is a small courtyard; the library is behind, with a pool and rockery (complete with tiny garden pavilion) in front of the library. The pool and rockery were constructed during the Kangxi period (1622–1723) by descendants of the original owner, Fan Qin.

Fan Qin

Fan Qin (1506–85) passed the third-degree exams in the capital in 1532 and later became Vice President of the Ministry of War. He retired to Ningbo with a library of Ming editions, both woodblock printed and manuscript, which included items purchased from other famous collectors, such as Feng Daosheng, heir to the Wanjuan lou (Ten-thousand Fascicle Pavilion) Library and Fan Dazhe.

The Tianyi ge is the oldest surviving private library building in China—private as opposed to temple library, for Buddhist temples have sutra halls—and said to have inspired the Qianlong emperor (reigned 1736–96) to construct the Wenyuan ge (Pavilion of the Deep Pool of Learning) in the Forbidden City in Peking to house the new manuscript imperial collectanea, for he sent an official to inspect the Tianyi ge in 1774. The Wenyuan ge, a building in the northern style, perfectly harmonising with surrounding buildings in the Forbidden City, bears no resemblance to the Tian yi ge, except that it has two storeys and a rockery in front of it; it was presumably a mainly spiritual inspiration. The emperor knew of the Tianyi ge through the collection of material for his great collectanea, *Si ku quan shu* (*Complete Library of the Four Storehouses or Branches of Literature*), which was begun in 1772 when an imperial edict went out ordering provincial authorities and private book collectors to supply rare books for copying into the collectanea. In 638 Fan Mouzhu (1721–90) sent items of which 473 were described in the imperial catalogue and 96 were actually copied in the collectanea. The emperor was so impressed with the collection that he wrote two poems celebrating rare items and also presented to the library two sets of paintings commemorating Qing military conquests and a set of the printed imperial encyclopaedia *Gu jin tu shu ji cheng* (*Synthesis of Books and Illustrations of Ancient and Modern Times*).

In keeping with Fan Qin's fear of fire, his descendants maintained strict rules forbidding the use of fire and artificial lighting in the library; they also guarded against theft. No books could be removed from the library and the doors were locked with a series of keys held by different branches of the family (all of whom needed to be present to open the door). Unfortunately, considerable losses were incurred during the Taiping rebellion (1853–64) and it is said that in 1840 British forces removed some of the gazetteers for which the library is most famous. A catalogue of 1808 lists 4094 items in 53,799 fascicles (excluding the 10,000 fascicles of the *Imperial Synthesis*), whereas a catalogue of 1889 lists only 2065 items, of which a mere 1270 were complete. By 1930 only 310 items were complete, out of a total of 962 titles in 7991 fascicles (Chinese books, consisting of a series of flimsy paper-bound 'fascicles'). Most of the surviving works, as well as others subsequently recovered, are now held in the **Zhejiang Provincial Library** in Hangzhou, although a few items are displayed in the Tianyi ge now.

All southern book collectors had problems other than fire to worry about, most notably damp and bookworms. In the library, a piece of limestone was placed beneath each book case to prevent damp, camphor wood box-cases were made for precious items for they absorbed damp and were insect resistant. In the Tianyi ge a special herb was also placed in the book cases to prevent worm attacks. It was also traditional to 'air' books in the early spring (before the atmosphere became humid).

Beside the library building, in the north of the compound, is the **Zunjing ge** (Pavilion of Respect for the Classics), moved from the Ningbo Confucian Temple in 1933 with a number of Song and Yuan stelae from the temple. The enclosure is quiet and shady with bamboos growing by the rockery and pool; the whole enclosed by whitewashed walls.

Surrounding the Tianyi ge, between Chanchun lu and Jiefang nan lu, with the Yue hu (Moon Lake) in the centre, is the oldest quarter of Ningbo, well worth wandering in. The large houses, enclosed by whitewashed walls topped with grey unglazed tiles, are the crumbling remnants of its former commercial glory, built for the rich burghers of the Ming and Qing dynasties. They are characteristic of the southeast: their gable-end walls are either curved into what the Chinese call 'arched cat's back' gables or else 'stepped'. Where you can see into the courtyard, two-

Ningbo: a lion in the garden of the Tianyi ge

storeyed buildings with wooden verandahs surround the court, the woodwork often carved.

Through the lanes, work your way north to Zhongshan xi lu, a main road crossing the old town, where the **Drum Tower**, now incongruously furnished with a modern electric clock, stands back from the road, up Gongyuan lu, which leads to a park. Returning to Zhongshan lu, turn left and take the second major turning on your right (Kaiming jie), lined with shops and small restaurants. At the bottom of the road, near the bent T-junction where the right turn leads to Jiefang lu, the **Tianfeng Pagoda** used to stand. It was mentioned in all guidebooks but had been knocked down in 1986. It has now miraculously reappeared, so a description of its history and former appearance is included here.

First built during the Tang dynasty, the most recent interior brick structure was fundamentally of the Yuan (1330), although the outer wooden galleries were destroyed by fire during the Qing (1798). During a complete restoration in 1957 relics were found at the very top of the pagoda. The pagoda was octagonal and seven-storeyed, c 30m high.

From the site of the pagoda, return to Kaiming jie, turn left then take the right turning that leads back to Jiefang lu and follow the narrow streets westward until you reach the **Moon Lake** (Yue hu), which is crossed by Liuding jie, on which the Huaqiao Hotel stands.

Another area in which to wander is the old Foreign Concession, north of the Xinjiang bridge, close to the waterfront and quays, where the crumbling western style buildings contrast with the crumbling Chinese mansions of the old city.

From Ningbo it is possible to visit two temple complexes, Baoguo si to the northwest, and the Ayuwang si, Wufo ta and Tiantong si to the southeast. They can be reached by taxi or bus.

The no. 11 bus (from the Northern Bus Station) takes approximately 45 minutes to reach the **Baoguo si** (Temple to Protect the Nation), 15km outside Ningbo in the Lingshan Hills. A waterfall on the tree-covered hill, against which the temple is built, descends from a dragon's head spout. The temple itself is laid out in the standard pattern with the Heavenly King Hall, the Mahavira Hall (the Hall of the Great Hero, one of the titles of the Buddha), the Guanyin Chamber and the Library on the main north–south axis, with the monks' accommodation, reception rooms and the bell and drum towers on either side. The Mahavira Hall, although restored, is the earliest surviving wooden building, not only in Zhejiang province but in the whole of the Yangtse delta area, dating from the Song (1013). Despite restoration, the interior in particular preserves early features in the chunky *dougeng* brackets and the crescent-moon shaped beams. There are three caisson (coffered) ceilings, also solidly constructed in the Song style (consider, in comparison, the Qing dynasty coffered ceilings in the halls of the Forbidden City, Peking, where the structural parts have been miniaturised and multiplied into a filigree decoration). The external appearance of the halls is typically southern, with strongly up-turned double eaves and decorated ridge.

The **Ayuwang**, or Asoka, **Temple**, some 20km east of Ningbo and reached from the Eastern Bus Station, is not itself architecturally distinguished but is famous for its tiny carved wooden relic pagoda, of uncertain date. Only some 15cm high, it is said to contain a relic of Sakyamuni. Legend has it that it was dug up in the late 3C and was believed to be one of the 84,000 reliquaries made by King Asoka (the Indian King, first major patron of Buddhism, who ruled c 274–237 BC). The reliquary is square, carved with Buddhist scenes in high relief and surmounted by four flaring tips with a central spire. Its date is uncertain but literary records recount pilgrimages made to see the relic by famous monks, such as Jian Zhen of the Tang, who travelled to Japan, as recounted in the *Zhong guo gu ta* by Luo Zhewen, 1985.

Not far from the Asoka Temple is the **Wu fo ta** (Five Buddhas Pagoda) and 100m further east is the **Tian tong si** (Temple of the Heavenly Child), founded in the late 3C, famous as a Chan (Japanese Zen) centre in the Tang and Song, attracting such famous Japanese monks as Eisai (1141–1215) and his disciple Dogen (1200–53), who introduced the Rinzai teachings, based on those of the Chinese Chan master Lin Ji, and Soto Zen respectively. Eisai also introduced tea drinking to Japan on his return from China. The buildings that survive today are not architecturally remarkable.

Shaoxing

Shaoxing, a small town some 100km west of Ningbo, was until recently one of the prettiest and most unspoilt towns in China. Criss-crossed with canals, filled with whitewashed houses, quite a number of which are now open as museums commemorating the lives of their famous inhabitants, its narrow streets and hump-backed bridges often impassable to motor traffic, it was quiet and relatively unmodernised, its tranquillity belying its traditional reputation for producing more corrupt government servants than anywhere else in China. The strength of the belief that all natives of the town were scheming shysters was such that one of its most famous recent inhabitants, the writer Lu Xun (1881–1936), would often only admit to coming from Zhejiang province without specifying his home town.

Shaoxing's industrial areas have grown considerably and dominate the approach to the town by road. The town centre is also now filled with tall office buildings and new shops, leaving only a few areas of stagnant canal as a reminder of its past prettiness.

The town is well-known for its rice-wine, *Shaoxing jiu*, which, like Japanese *sake*, is drunk warm and tastes pleasantly of glue. Since it improves with age, local people are said to bury sufficient jars at the birth of a daughter to celebrate her wedding.

Practical information

Getting there
By train

Shaoxing is on the Ningbo–Shanghai line, just over half-way from Ningbo to Hangzhou. There are five fast trains a day. As motorways have been built in Zhejiang, motorway buses are now fast and convenient. The Shanghai–Ningbo buses stop in Shaoxing at the bus station on Jiefang lu, just south of the railway station.

Where to stay

Shaoxing Fandian, 9 Huanshan lu, ☎ 515 5888, fax 515 5565, in the west of the town is one of the most attractive hotels in China. It uses old buildings (formerly a merchants' guild headquarters) set around paved courtyards full of plants. A fish-pool lies at the back of the hotel and the dining room, in what must have been the rear hall, is reached by a raised walkway which passes over a pool with fountains. The hotel has been restored and expanded with some care.

History

The legendary founder of the **Xia dynasty**, Yu the Great, is supposed to have been buried south of the town. He is supposed to have ascended the throne as first emperor of the Xia in 2205 BC, after taming the dragons who lived underground and caused floods, hence his sobriquet, 'tamer of the floods'. The Xia dynasty, recorded in China's literature, remains a puzzle to archaeologists for no sites which can be definitely ascribed to it have yet been discovered. During the Warring States period the capital of the state of Yue was in Shaoxing. Gou Jian, ruler of Yue, fought long battles against the neighbouring state of Wu throughout the 5C BC, only overcoming the ruler of Wu by the stratagem of sending a beautiful woman to him so that his energies were dissipated; in 473 BC Yue annexed Wu.

The town grew rapidly during the **Southern Song** (1127–1276) when the imperial capital was moved to nearby Hangzhou, and very scanty remains of six imperial tombs of the Song have been found southeast of the town in Zangong shan. In succeeding centuries Shaoxing's reputation for sharp practice grew: in Ming dramas clerks were usually from Shaoxing and there was a popular saying that Shaoxing had 'hills but no wood, water but no fish and men but no righteousness'. It may have been pressure of population that drove Shaoxing's inhabitants out into the empire to buy magistracies and make money elsewhere, for in 1820 it was the fourth most densely populated prefecture in China. Together with natives of Ningbo, men of Shaoxing dominated the native banks or 'money shops' of 18C and 19C Shanghai. Indeed, the first money shop had been opened by a Shaoxing charcoal merchant in the 18C. All of Suzhou's cloth-dyers and most of the soy-sauce merchants were from Shaoxing and, in 1892, 15 per cent of all county jail wardens in China were from Shaoxing. The position of jail warden was one of great possibilities with prisoners' families only too willing to pay for privileges.

The charm of the town belied its unsavoury reputation: E.H. Parker, a visiting British Consul, wrote in 1884:

The country realises to the full the 'willow pattern' ideal of China. Stone bridges of elegant shape are seen or passed every few minutes ... there seems to be little means of inter-communication except by boat ... many of the small ones are worked with the feet.

The bridges and boats can still be seen, although they are fast being filled up or dying through filling up with plastic and other rubbish. Small boats were worked by an oar from the back, lazily moved with one foot by boatmen who wore the distinctive Shaoxing hat of squashed black felt, strongly reminiscent of Chico Marx's hat. These wonderful, waterproof items can still be bought in the hotel shop.

Starting from the *Shaoxing Fandian*, turn left into the road that passes below the hilly park in front of the hotel, turn left, right and left again into Guangming lu. Soon, the **Dashan** (Great Good) **Pagoda** will be visible on the left. It is a six-sided, seven-storey pagoda, 40m high, and was first built in 504 when it was part of the Da shan Temple, whose ruins are now covered by the largest department store in the town. The present structure dates from the Ming (1403) and a major restoration was carried out after 1949.

At the T-junction with Jiefang bei lu turn left and then right along Laodong lu where **Zhou Enlai's Residence** can be found on the left.

> ### Zhou Enlai
> Zhou Enlai (1898–1976) was a long-time revolutionary who finally became China's Premier. His ancestral home was in Shaoxing, where his family was thought to have arrived during the Ming. As one of his Qing dynasty forebears lived for 91 years and his wife for 100, their home was afterwards called Baisui tang (Hundred-year Hall). Zhou Enlai studied at Nankai University in Tianjin and in Paris, where he joined the China Socialist Youth League. A pragmatic man, with great diplomatic skills, he worked both underground and above from the 1920s to the 1940s. He was one of the most important negotiators over the Second United Front against the Japanese (1937) and negotiated the release of Chiang Kai-shek after the Xi'an incident (1936). His personal contact with Shaoxing seems to have been minimal: one guidebook describes at length a visit he made in 1939, concluding that 'although he only spent four or five days in Shaoxing, he did a great deal of revolutionary work.' Thus the house must viewed as a place where Zhou Enlai may have slept.

The original building was a Ming construction but its dilapidation was such that an entirely new building was constructed on the site after 1949. Entered by

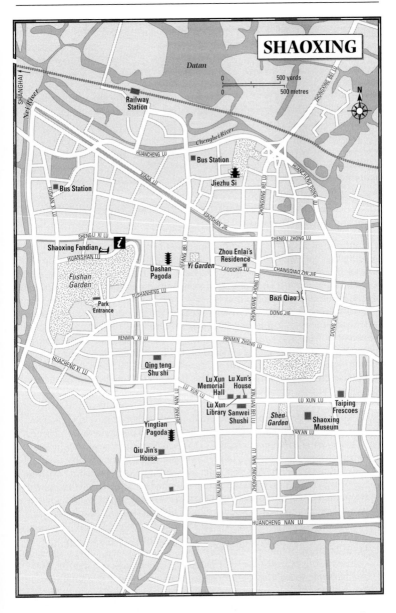

a lacquered black door in the centre of a three-bay entrance building, with its narrow 'heaven-well' courtyard inside leading to other halls separated by paved courtyards, it is a typical Shaoxing structure. The halls now house a **museum** commemorating Zhou Enlai's life.

Shaoxing: canal-side houses

Continue east (the road's name changes to Changqiao zhi jie) until you reach a T-junction with Guangningqiao zhi jie. Turn right here and you will soon reach one of Shaoxing's oldest bridges, the **Bazi qiao** (Bridge in the Shape of the Character for 'Eight'). The flat-topped stone bridge was built between 1201 and 1204. Beside it is a Catholic church.

Walk west back along the house-lined canal. You may still see local people outside their houses, starting their little clay stoves with a tall stovepipe to get the charcoal glowing and washing vegetables in the canal as small boats of all sorts pass. Continue west along the canal until you reach Xinjian bei lu and turn right (south) until you reach Lu Xun lu and turn left into it. The new buildings on your left house the **Lu Xun Museum**, and his House lies behind.

> ### Lu Xun
>
> Lu Xun (whose real name was Zhou Shuren) was born into a landlord family in Shaoxing in 1881 and some of his childhood memories are recounted in his short stories, most notably *Gu xiang* (*Ancestral Home*) in which his playmate is an agricultural labourer's child of great charm and imagination called Run Tu. Run Tu's son later ran the Lu Xun Museum. True to Shaoxing's traditions, Lu Xun's grandfather had been sentenced to death for attempting large-scale bribery in the provincial examinations and his father was an opium addict, who frequently sent his small son out to collect expensive and useless medical concoctions which failed to cure his T.B. Watching his father die, Lu Xun determined to become a modern doctor and went to Japan to study. While he was there his class was shown lantern slides of Chinese being executed for their part in the Russo-Japanese War of 1905 and he began to feel that China's ills were not to be cured by a single doctor but, perhaps, by literature.
>
> Returning to China, Lu Xun was a major participant in the movement to simplify the written language, a movement which gained momentum and political significance after China's post World War One humiliation at Versailles, when Japan was granted control over the German Concession in Shandong province. The May Fourth Movement (as it was called, after a

patriotic demonstration) tried to transform China through simplifying literature and making it more accessible to a greater public. Lu Xun's own short stories are characteristic of May Fourth literature and his sharp, bitter and satirical essays indicate his firm political commitment to reform. He saw much interfactional struggle in his life as well as the tragic sacrifice of many of his young students. Although sympathetic to the Communists in their anti-Japanese stance and lack of the corruption which was increasingly obvious in Chiang Kai-shek's regime, he never actually joined the Party. Many observers consider that he would eventually have fallen out with the Communists over literary policy but he died of T.B. in 1936 before he had a chance to do so. He is perhaps the most respected literary figure in modern China.

The museum contains a large display of photographs, editions of works by and about Lu Xun and some relics, including his tiny gown and shoes. The lovely family house, in which Lu Xun was born, is a large series of dark buildings grouped around courtyards, characteristic of grander buildings of the region. It has a vegetable garden at the back and quite a lot of typical furniture.

On the other side of the road is the **Sanwei shushi** (Three Flavour Study), the traditional private school which Lu Xun attended as a small boy until his grandfather's disgrace in 1893 and his father's death in 1897 made schooling too expensive. Although the canal which runs beside it is now very smelly, it is a charming example of traditional architecture.

A little further along **Lu Xun lu** (c 400m) on the right is one of the several houses in Shaoxing with fragmentary remains of murals of the Taiping Kingdom (1850–64), which raged in the south of China, threatening the Qing dynasty. The houses are not formally open to the passing public but the gate-keepers will sometimes let curious visitors in for a moment. Back on Lu Xun lu, almost opposite the museum is a small turning on the right, Chunpo long, which leads southwards to Yan'an lu.

At the T-junction with Yan'an lu turn left and take the next turning on the left, Yanghe long, where you will find the **Shen Garden**. This was a famous garden of the Shen family during the Southern Song (1127–79), of which only a corner still survives. It is particularly the garden buildings that have disappeared for the small gourd-shaped pool in the centre is original, as is the stone slab bridge and 'mock mountain'. The poet **Lu You** (1125–1210), another of Shaoxing's famous sons, wrote a poem about the garden where he used to meet his wife; there is a small exhibition on his life and work in a new building beside the garden. Although a considerable amount of reconstruction has taken place since 1986, when I first visited it, with strange pavilions covered with hairy coconut matting, the paved paths, the (modern) bamboo fencing and the flowering trees of the small, peaceful garden are not without charm.

Returning to Yan'an lu, turn right and walk back west until you reach the junction with Shaoxing's busy main street, **Jiefang nan lu**. Ahead is the second famous pagoda of Shaoxing, the **Yingtian** (Heaven-answering) **Pagoda**. This was originally part of a temple founded under the Song. The whole was destroyed during the Taiping uprising (1850–64) and rebuilt afterwards.

Xu Wei's house

Turning right up Jiefang nan lu, heading north, past the crossing with Lu Xun lu, a small lane on the left, Qianguan xiang, leads to Dacheng long, where the **Qing teng shu shi** (Green Vine Study) lies. Perhaps the most perfect example of domestic architecture surviving in China, this was the home of the extraordinary poet, painter, calligrapher and dramatist Xu Wei (1521–93), who also murdered his wife. (Open daily 08.00–16.30.)

> ### Xu Wei
> Xu Wei's paintings are remarkably modern and free, while his calligraphy has been described as 'turbulent'. Some of his dramas are still performed and 'strike a very modern note' for his heroines attain military and academic distinction, which was hardly common at the time. The murder of his third wife was extraordinary: his protector, a general whom he served as secretary, was thrown into prison in 1565 and Xu Wei seems to have suffered a nervous breakdown or period of dramatic insecurity approaching paranoia, for he became suspicious of his wife and beat her to death. His biography contains the mysterious information that he had previously 'destroyed his own testicles'. Condemned to death, his sentence was commuted to seven years imprisonment. The tiny house is, by contrast, exceedingly tranquil.

Approached through a garden with a rockery, full of bamboos, the building's whitewashed facade is pierced with two doors, one a circular moon gate, the other almost Islamic in feel with its pointed top. The house consists of two main rooms, the southern one with a pool beneath the window, overhung with creepers. In the other room is a small **exhibition** of Xu Wei's work and that of the late Ming painter Chen Hongshou, who later lived here. The second room opens onto a small walled courtyard with *pen jing* and *pen cai* (pot scenes and bonsai).

Returning to Jiefang lu, turn left and head north. The third major turning on the left is Guangming lu which leads back to the Shaoxing hotel.

Qiu Jin's house and the Yu ling

It would be possible to include a visit to Qiu Jin's house, which lies behind the Yingtian Pagoda, before Xu Wei's studio. Otherwise, it is well combined with the Yu ling (Tomb of the mythical Emperor Yu), either by car or by bus. If the latter, take the no. 2 bus from the corner of Fuheng jie and Jiefang lu (heading south) and get off at the Ying tian Pagoda, continuing on foot down Jiefang lu and turning right into Hechang tang; Qiu Jin's House is on the right. To get to the Yu ling, return to the bus stop and take a no. 2 in the same direction to the Yu ling, outside town.

Qiu Jin's House, another example of local domestic architecture with whitewashed walls, dark wood and narrow, stone-paved courtyards, was once the home of a famous woman martyr, born here in 1875, who was executed in 1907. The house was formerly the 'villa' of the Ming scholar, Zhu Xu.

Inside the house, which is set against a hill on the outskirts of the town, is an exhibition commemorating Qiu Jin's life.

Qiu Jin

Qiu Jin reacted violently against the contemporary subjection of women, unbinding her feet and abandoning her children and husband, to whom her marriage had been arranged by her family, in order to go to Japan and study in 1904. There she met other Chinese students, anti-Manchu radicals determined to overthrow the decaying Qing government and establish a progressive government.

Qiu Jin seems to have been almost overwhelmed by possibilities, working with activists who made bombs and practising martial arts. A photograph survives of her, taken in Japan, where she wears a man's suit and flat cap, a costume she continued to wear on her return to China where, in 1907, she became director of a progressive girls' school near Shaoxing. She continued her revolutionary, anti-Manchu activities, for which she was beheaded.

The **Tomb of the Emperor Yu** (Yu ling), mythical subduer of floods, lies 4km to the southeast of the city and while there have been buildings on the site since the 6C, those that stand today are modern: many buildings are said to be of the Qing, the great hall was rebuilt in 1934 and there was extensive rebuilding in 1986.

The 'tomb', if a mythical subduer of floods can be said to have a tomb, consists of a stone tablet, engraved with the three characters, 'Great Yu's Tomb', written by Nan Daji of the Ming, standing under a very new pavilion with upturned eaves. Nearby is the temple complex with a meridian gate, sacrificial hall and great hall on the main axis, built against a hill so that the buildings to the back on their high stone platforms tower over those at the front. The temple is not of great architectural interest but the area, with its canals, streams and pools where fish and freshwater pearls are farmed, is typical of the 'land of rice and fish', as the area is named.

The **East Lake**, 3km east of the town (at the end of the no. 1 bus route, which also passes down Jiefang lu before heading east along Renmin lu), is a well-known scenic area, with the lake lying beneath a towering cliff. Dykes and humpbacked bridges cross the lake and boat-trips take you through natural openings in the cliff. It is also possible to climb up the cliff for a view over the lake and surrounding countryside.

14km southwest of Shaoxing (at the end of the no. 3 bus route, which starts from the corner of Jiefang bei lu and Shengli lu, just northeast of the hotel) is the **Lan ting** (Orchid or, more technically, Epidendrum Pavilion), a place of pilgrimage for Chinese calligraphers, for on the site (or somewhere nearby, the exact site is now unknown) China's greatest calligrapher, **Wang Xizhi** (321–379), held a party with 40 friends in 353.

Visiting the Lan ting, the complexities of China's view of her own past are made concrete. The exact site of the original pavilion is unknown, but people are quite happy to visit an approximation. At the party sacrifices were made to dispel bad luck and the gentlemen then sat, floating small cups of wine on the pool's surface. Whenever a cup of wine floated in front of a guest, he had to compose a poem on the spot or pay the forfeit of drinking the wine. At this gathering, 26 people wrote 37 poems and Wang Xizhi wrote a preface to the collection. The collection was carved in stone and thus his calligraphy has been preserved and prized for hundreds of years. The event itself inspired the construction of garden pavilions with stone floors carved with maze-like runnels which were filled with water so that groups of friends could play the same drinking and writing game. Examples can be seen in the Tanzhe Temple outside Peking and in the Forbidden City (the 'cup-floating stream' in the garden of the Palace of Tranquil Longevity). The resonance of the Orchid Pavilion for the Chinese is enormous.

Inside the entrance, on the left, is a pavilion covering a stele with the two characters for 'swan pool' carved on it. They are said to have been written by Wang Xizhi and his son. Wang Xizhi had just written 'swan' when he was told that a message from the emperor had arrived so he rushed off, leaving his son to write 'pool'. The eponymous pool lies behind the pavilion.

The Orchid Pavilion outside Shaoxing

Crossing the pool, the **Orchid Pavilion** is to the left (the building is modern). The inscription was badly damaged in the Cultural Revolution but was originally by the Kangxi emperor. Straight ahead is the **Liushang tang** (Floating Cup Pavilion) and behind it is a stele inscribed with the Kangxi emperor's preface to the Lan ting poems. To the right, surrounded by the Ink Pool, said to have been the place where Wang Xizhi washed his brushes, is the **Zuojun ci** (General's Temple, for Wang held military office), plastered with stones carved with calligraphy by the famous.

Nanjing

Nanjing, capital city of Jiangsu province, situated on the lower reaches of the Yangtse, has been a city of major importance for 2000 years, serving as the capital of the Southern Kingdom of Wu (229–280), the Eastern Jin (317–420), the Southern States of the Nan bei chao era (420–589), the early period of the Ming dynasty (1368–1420), the Taiping Heavenly Kingdom (1851–64) and the Chinese Republic (1911–49). As wars were fought around and over Nanjing, the city has suffered considerable devastation throughout the centuries but many relics remain, including substantial portions of the massive city wall.

Practical information

Getting there
By air

The airport is 40km south of the city. *CAAC* buses run frquent services to the town centre (25 yuan). As a major centre, there are flights to many Chinese cities throughout the week.

By train

The station is in the north of the city and is on the main Peking–Shanghai line, as well as the branch line to Tongling in Anhui province. Beware of the station taxi drivers, some of whom are bandits; make sure the meter is on.

Where to stay

One of Nanjing's older hotels is the *Nanjing Fandian*, 259 Zhongshan bei lu, ☎ 341 1888, fax 342 2261. The *Jinling Fandian*, towering over the central roundabout at Xinjiekou, is a luxury hotel, ☎ 471 1888, fax 470 4141, email: hotel@jinlinghotel-nanjing.com.

History

Nanjing has long been viewed as strategically well-placed: surrounded by hills, it is situated on the south bank of the Yangtse at a point where the river narrows, now marked by the huge Nanjing River Bridge built in the 1960s, beginning with Soviet aid which was suddenly withdrawn in 1960. The first settlements of c 7000 BC were those of the Beiyinyang neolithic culture, characterised by reddish pottery, stone tools and evidence of cloth weaving. In 1955 a large number of Beiyinyang burials were discovered near the Drum Tower in the centre of the city. Subsequent bronze age settlements of the Shang and Zhou have been found on both sides of the Yangtze. During the Warring States period (770–221 BC), an early arms factory, using raw materials from the surrounding hills, made swords during the late 5C BC for the three 'warring' states whose borders lay near Nanjing. The site of the sword factory is now occupied by the Chaotian gong Temple-museum. A walled town was built in 333 BC when the leader of the state of Chu overthrew the Yue Kingdom.

The town, built to the west of Nanjing just beside the communications tower, was first known as *Jinling* (Golden Hill), a name preserved in Jinling Hotel, amongst other contemporary institutions, later as *Shitou cheng* (Stone City) and centred on Qingliang Hill (now the Qingliang Park). It is said that Qin shi huang, Emperor of the Qin, the 'Great Unifier', came to Nanjing in 210 BC and was told by a geomancer that a new emperor would arise in Nanjing. Paranoid, the Qin emperor saw this as a threat to himself and ordered earthworks to be dug to alter the *feng shui* of the area. Despite his precautions, many future rulers, albeit short-lived and usually regional, later arose in Nanjing.

Sun Quan (AD 185–252) established the **state of Wu** (one of the Three Kingdoms, 220–280), moving his capital to Nanjing in 229 and constructing a new walled city on the site of the previous 'stone city'. Part of his sandstone wall can still be seen in the west of the city, overlaid by the 14C Ming city wall. It was during Sun Quan's reign that Kang Senghui, or Samghavarman, a Sogdian Buddhist missionary and translator of Sanskrit sutras into Chinese, arrived in Nanjing bearing a Buddha relic, for which Sun Quan built a temple. Sun Quan's successors as rulers of Wu were less effective than he and the state was overthrown in 280 by the Western Jin rulers based in Luoyang, to the north.

In succeeding centuries the confusing rapidity of the rise and fall of local dynasties was evident in the Nanjing area. The Western Jin were overrun by western barbarians in their capital, whereupon a member of the Jin ruling house, who had been governing the Nanjing area, proclaimed the Eastern Jin with Nanjing as capital. The Eastern Jin failed to regain control of the occupied northern territory and failed to deal successfully with the influx of distressed refugees from the north, yet Nanjing became a cultural centre, graced by the presence of the painter **Gu Kaizhi**, c 344–406 (whose work survives in rare, later copies, including examples in the British Museum and the Freer Gallery in Washington), the wonderful but rarely translated poet **Xie Lingyun** and the calligrapher **Wang Xizhi**, associated with the Lan ting Pavilion near Shaoxing. Buddhism continued to flourish in this period of disunion with the arrival of the great translator, **Fa Xian**. One of the reasons for the attraction of Buddhism was that it filled a spiritual vacuum, as Confucian orthodoxy appeared to have failed to effect governmental cohesion.

In 420 one of the Eastern Jin's generals, Liu Yu, seized power and established the **Liu Song dynasty**, which lasted 60 years. With the exception of its founder, this dynasty was characterised by brutal and extravagant rulers and savage wars with the Northern Wei which ruled China north of the Yangtse. It was overthrown by a general who established the **Southern Qi dynasty** (479–502) which, like the Liu Song, was nasty, brutish and short-lived. The material remains of the Southern Qi include a beautiful series of tombs at Danyang, 70km east of Nanjing. Avenues of large carved stone animals stand in the fields; the chimera, in particular, beautifully curved and feline, in great contrast with the stubby, solid animals of the later Ming tombs in the outskirts of Nanjing.

At **Qixia shan**, 20km east of Nanjing, there is a series of Buddhist caves filled with substantial stone figures, the walls carved with smaller figures in niches. Although the caves were added to during succeeding periods, as late as the Ming, 1000 years later, they were founded by a hermit called Ming Sengshao in the late 5C, under the Southern Qi.

Once again (and the pattern is characteristic of disturbance when military power is all) the ruling house of the Southern Qi was overthrown by a general who established the **Liang dynasty** (502–577), retaining Nanjing as his capital. As was often the case in Chinese history, the first emperor of the Liang was a man of vision and accomplishment, setting up state-funded colleges for free education, promoting trade links to obtain exotic products from the south and building avenues, canals and palaces in Nanjing. Towards the end of his life the first emperor of the Liang became a fanatical Buddhist, apparently withdrawing to the contemplative life in one of the many temples he had constructed and from which he had to be ransomed to return, reluctantly, to government. He funded the first publication of the complete collection of Buddhist scriptures (the *Tripitaka*), wrote on Buddhist ritual and is frequently depicted in the frontispieces to southern Buddhist works, in earnest discussion with Buddhist monks. Towards the end of the Liang, a rebellion led by a general called Hou Jing caused incredible destruction and, with a population already pressed by the arrival of refugees from the equally turbulent north of China fleeing to the grain-rich south, led to a famine in which up to half the population died of starvation.

The Liang dynasty staggered on for a few years until, in its turn, it was overthrown by yet another general who founded the **Chen dynasty** (557–589). Although the Chen dynasty managed to regain a small amount of territory from the Northern Qi, it was defeated in further attempts by the Northern Zhou, soon to be overthrown in turn by the founder of the **Sui dynasty** (581–618), which finally reunited China; the discrepancy in dates between the founding of the Sui and the downfall of the Chen indicates that the process was a lengthy and bloody one. As Nanjing had been the capital city of southern China virtually throughout the period of division (since the end of the Han dynasty in 220), the first Sui emperor presumably regarded the city and its inhabitants as potentially threatening and he ordered the city to be razed. No longer a capital, Nanjing managed to retain its position as a cultural centre and a major southern city. At the end of the Tang, when China was once again fragmented, it was made the capital of the Southern Tang dynasty (937–975), overthrown in turn by the Song dynasty, which once again reunited China.

Nanjing's next great period of importance came with the establishment of the **Ming dynasty** (1368–1644). The first emperor of the Ming, Zhu Yuanzhang, came from a very poor family in Anhui, although he later said that his family had moved there from the Nanjing area. Typically faithful to his native place, he first established his capital at Fengyang in Anhui. After six years of palace building and the construction of a tomb complex for his parents, which still stands, he was advised to move his capital to Nanjing, which he did in 1356, where, after capturing the south and proclaiming the Ming (Bright) dynasty, he built a second palace and surrounded the city with a huge wall. On his death he was officially succeeded by his grandson but one of Zhu Yuanzhang's own sons, who had been appointed to rule the Peking area, seized power and moved the capital to Peking in 1420, leaving much of Nanjing, including his father's palace, in ruins. During the late Ming the Jesuit missionary Matteo Ricci finally obtained permission to reside in Nanjing in 1599.

Nanjing was to be a capital twice more: first when the Ming dynasty fell to the invading Manchus and a Ming prince proclaimed the **Southern Ming** dynasty with Nanjing as its capital, partly in an attempt to revive the creative spirit of Zhu Yuanzhang, partly because the north was in the hands of the Manchus. The Southern Ming only lasted from 1644 to 1645. The last episode (leaving out the anti-Manchu Taiping leaders whose major base was Nanjing) came in 1912, during another period of division, when the Republic of China was proclaimed, with Nanjing as its capital, while those in favour of a constitutional monarchy, led at first by General Yuan Shikai, held on to power in Peking until 1928. Nanjing then became the capital of China but the external threat of the Japanese and the internal threat of the growing Communist Party meant that little power was actually concentrated in Nanjing. Nevertheless, the city today, its streets lined with plane trees and solid western-style government buildings, with the great monument to Sun Yatsen in the hills, retains an architectural flavour of the 1920s and 1930s. The contemporary municipal government offices occupy the old government buildings of the Republic and Beijing lu (west of Xinjiekou) is the old diplomatic quarter. Although Nanjing's buildings did not suffer drastically during the Japanese invasion, the occupation of Nanjing was one of the bloodiest episodes of the Japanese invasion. It is estimated that 400,000 civilians died between 1938 and 1945, many raped and butchered in a horrifying manner. When Chiang Kai-shek's Nationalist Government fled west to Chongqing, the Japanese set up a puppet government under Wang Jingwei, who died in Tokyo in 1944, although his collaborationist colleagues, including Zhou Fuhai and Chen Gongbo, both founding members of the Communist Party in 1921, were executed.

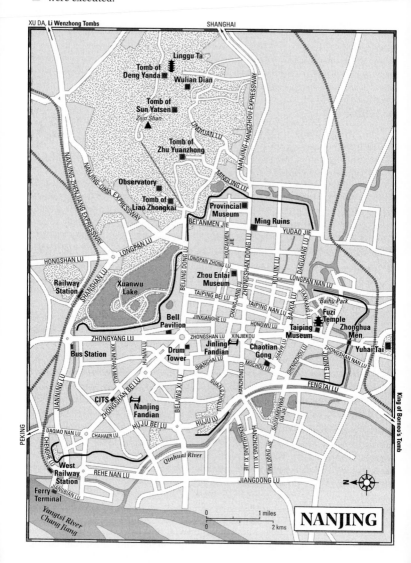

NANJING

From the Zhonghua Gate to Xinjiekou

The **city wall** of Nanjing is not the regular rectangle required by traditional Chinese town-planning theory. As the terrain is hilly and also surrounded by areas of water, like many southern city walls, that of Nanjing, built over a 20 year period by the first Ming emperor in the mid 14C, follows the contours of hill and pool in an irregular manner. Its full length was over 33km and it was the longest city wall in the world. The average height from the ground is 12m and the wall is roughly 7m broad at the top. A number of sections survive: along the Xuanwu Lake in the north, on the southern edge of the Zijin hills and in the south of the city. There, the most impressive gate, the **Zhonghua men**, still stands and has been restored.

The original name of the gate was Jubao (Massed Treasure) and the name Zhonghua, one of the words for 'China', was first used for the gate in 1912. This is a well-fortified gate constructed from stone and grey clay bricks with three inner gates, covering an area of over 15,000 square metres. There are several narrow tunnel-like openings in the solid defensive walls and smaller side tunnels in which soldiers could be hidden. As with the bricks that form the floors of the Forbidden City in Peking, many of the grey bricks used in the Nanjing wall and gates are stamped with the name of the kiln where they were made and they come from several surrounding provinces. It is possible to climb up onto the grassy wall on the east side of the Zhonghua Gate and walk quite a way.

Back on the main road (Zhonghua lu) inside the gate, head north towards the city centre. Take the first major turning on the right (Changle lu) and then the second turning on the left (a lane called Dong pailou) which leads up to an open stretch of water. On the far side of the water is Zhanyuan lu.

Turn left and at no. 128 is the **Taiping Museum** (open 07.00–17.00). The museum, which commemorates the anti-dynastic uprising of 1851–64, is located in a residence used by one of the Taiping 'Heavenly Princes', as the leaders were known. This was the headquarters of the 'Eastern Prince', Yang Xiuqing, and it incorporated an old garden, the Zhan (Enthusiasm) Garden, which had formerly belonged to the first Ming emperor and later to his general Xu Da. Centring on a pool surrounded by piled rocks, pavilions and walkways, the garden also contains two notable pieces of calligraphy, a single vigorous character 'tiger' (*hu*) and the name of the garden in the calligraphy of the Qianlong emperor.

The museum itself is laid out in three parts, the last two rooms being part of the same hall. Exhibits include copies of many documents, maps of the progress of the Taiping armies, which from their stronghold in Nanjing even threatened Peking, as well as seals and coins cast with the name of the Heavenly Kingdom of Great Peace (Taiping tianguo), used as currency during the period. There are Taiping soldiers' and officers' uniforms and, in the second room, weapons. Many of the texts displayed outline the Taiping ideology, which included attempts to redistribute land and establish equality in marriage and the abandonment of the Confucian classics as the basis of education. In the last room there are accounts of contemporary rebellions, like that of the Small Swords who attacked Shanghai, and references to the internal divisions amongst the Taiping leaders and to the foreign army that helped the Qing armies finally to destroy the Taipings. The display is updated as new discoveries are made; the recent restoration of the tomb of Lindley (an adventurer who helped the Taipings) in a London cemetery is marked by a photograph.

Due north of the Taiping Museum (on the east side of Changjiang lu, behind no. 30 Meiyuancun) is a **museum** commemorating Zhou Enlai who stayed in Meiyuancun (1946–47) as a leader of the Communist Party delegation that attempted to negotiate a peace settlement with the KMT government after the defeat of Japan. The new museum building of brick, to harmonise with surrounding 1940s western style buildings, and window details faintly reminiscent of the Shanghai house where the Communist Party first met in 1921, won a national architectural prize in 1991.

Back on Zhan yuan lu, turn left, bear left (the road running alongside the canal is called Gongyuan lu). Soon the entrance to the **Fuzi** (Confucian) **Temple** can be seen to the left.

Founded in 1034, the temple was destroyed by fire not long after but rebuilt and the huge examination hall complex was built nearby. The present buildings are said to date from 1869 although there has been considerable recent rebuilding. The halls contain a small exhibition of local folk arts: paper cuts and various embroidered articles like children's tiger hats and openwork 'cloud collars' (shawl-like collars with decorative lappets) for women.

The area around the Confucian Temple is being thoroughly rebuilt in the traditional southern style (and is interesting to compare with the northern style of shopfronts found in restored areas such as Liulichang in Peking and Qu Fu in Shandong). Whitewashed walls with stepped gables, dark painted woodwork and dark grey tiles, upturned eaves and decorated edges are all characteristic of southern building and the restoration of a popular shopping area is not without sensitivity.

Opposite the Confucian Temple at the end of Baishiba jie, against the city wall, is the **Bailu** (White Heron) **Park**, originally owned by the Ming general Xu Da. The pavilions were all destroyed during the Taiping occupation but the park was restored in 1951.

Retracing your steps from the Confucian Temple, past the Taiping Museum and back to **Zhonghua lu**, turn right up Zhonghua lu and walk until you reach the junction with Jianye lu (west) and Baixia lu (east). This is a major junction where most buses turn left and then right, heading for Xinjiekou. Turn left along Jianye lu and take the fourth major turning on the left (Mochou lu) where you will find the **Chaotian gong** (Heaven-facing Palace), a Confucian temple with a fine entrance.

Temples had been built on the site since AD 390 but the present buildings were built in 1860s as a government school and centre for Confucian worship. Covering a considerable area, the Chaotian gong includes many gateways (with different names), bell and drum towers, covered walks and halls. It is now used as a municipal museum, with a display of artefacts locally unearthed, from Shang bronzes to Qing calligraphy (by the ever-active Qianlong emperor).

Perhaps the most notable relics are those of the famous **Porcelain Pagoda**. Built in the early 15C by the Ming Yongle emperor in a moment of filial piety to honour his mother, the Baoen (Debt of Gratitude) Pagoda stood in a temple of the same name which was an earlier foundation.

The pagoda was clad in white glazed brick, each of the eaves covered in green tiles and the whole surmounted by a golden dome. Destroyed in the Taiping period, the pagoda was a marvel to foreign visitors such as Nieuhoff (1623):

In the middle of the plain stands a high steeple or tower made of porcelain which far exceed all other workmanship of the Chineses in cost and skill; by which the Chineses have declared to the world the rare ingenuity of their artists in former ages. The tower has nine rounds and a hundred eighty four steps to the top; each round is adorn'd with a gallery ... The outside is all glaz'd over and painted with several colours, as green, red and yellow ... Round about all the corners of the galleries hang little bells, which make a very pretty noise when the wind jangles them: the top of the tower was crowned with a pineapple, which (as they say) was made of gold ... This wonderful pile (as they inform us) the Chineses built at their own charges ...

The pagoda was also included in Longfellow's *Keramos*:

And yonder by Nanking, behold
The Tower of porcelain, strange and old,
Uplifting to the astonished skies
Its ninefold painted balconies,
With balustrade of twining leaves,
And roofs of tile beneath whose eaves
Hang porcelain bells that all the time
Ring with a soft melodious chime...

Leaving the Chaotian gong and its relics (the Porcelain Pagoda was seen as the symbol of Nanjing by early foreign visitors), turn left into Mochou lu and then right into Chaotiangong xi lu (lined with small shops and stalls). The street soon changes its name to **Tangzi jie**. At no. 74, on the right wall, paintings of the Taiping Kingdom survive (they were rediscovered in 1952). The house was taken over by one of the members of the entourage of the 'Eastern Prince' Yang Xiuqing and pictures of animals (deer, horses and peacocks), flowers and the magical *lingzhi* fungus, as well as the famous watchtower used by the Taipings, were painted on the walls (not by an amazingly skilled artist).

Turn right out of the house and follow Tangzi jie until it reaches a T-junction with the busy Hanzhong lu; turn right and walk (or take a no. 5 or a no. 18 bus in the same direction) to Xinjiekou, the main roundabout dominated by the Jinling Hotel tower.

Drum Tower and Xuanwu Lake

The next major roundabout north of Xinjiekou (reached by foot from Xinjiekou or by a no. 35 bus going north up Zhongshan lu) is that of the **Drum Tower** (Gu lou), which dominates the open space. First constructed in 1382 by the first Ming emperor, it has been much restored since. Built on a brick and stone platform, once pierced by three tunnels, the upper part of the tower is a double-roofed, grey tiled wooden structure which once housed a number of sets of drums, mainly used to mark the watches of the night but also to sound the alarm or welcome visiting dignitaries. There is a fine view of the city from the top of the tower.

Northeast of the Drum Tower (approached from Dazhongting jie, the first turning on the right north of the roundabout) is the **Bell Pavilion**, first built in the Ming but destroyed in the early part of the reign of Kangxi (1622–1723) and rebuilt in 1889. It contains a massive bronze bell (estimates of its weight vary from one ton upwards), cast in 1388.

One of the largest bells in China, the folktale attached to it is the same as that associated with all large bells: the bellsmith, failing to achieve the appropriately musical tone, or distressed by cracks during casting, was in despair until his daughter threw herself into the molten metal; the resulting cast was perfect.

From the Bell Tower, continue east towards the city walls, behind which lie the **Xuanwu Park** and **Lake**. The area, bounded by the lake to the north, Beijing lu to the south and Zhongyang lu to the west, was the old diplomatic quarter of the Republican period (1912–49) and contains some solid buildings. Xuanwu Park consists mostly of a 15km long lake.

The lake was important as a water source to the many dynasties occupying the area and it was known by a variety of names until the Song period (960–1279, during which time it was used for naval exercises) when a black monster was seen to emerge from the water and the lake was renamed Xuanwu (Dark Warrior), after the turtle that presides over the north (for the lake is also in the north of the city). In the centre of the lake, linked by dykes, is a series of small islands which, under the Republic, were named after the continents; the state archives were housed on 'Australia' for a while.

Provincial Museum and the Ming Palace

Take a no. 5 or a no. 9 bus east along **Zhongshan dong lu** to the **Provincial Museum** (321 Zhong shan dong lu; open 09.00–11.00, 14.00–17.00). The museum was founded in 1933 at the instigation of Cai Yuanpei (a major scholar, friend of Qiu Jin of Shaoxing and Dean of Peking University during the May Fourth period) amongst others, and was built in 1950 in the traditional style. It houses the major provincial collection and includes a wonderful Han dynasty 'money tree' and a jade body suit of the early Han amongst other exhibits arranged in chronological order.

In the early 1980s the museum was mysteriously closed (it is still closed on Mondays) because the director, who had fallen out with his colleagues and provincial superiors, committed suicide inside the museum. His family, resenting his treatment, refused to allow the body to be moved for some time. His action, committing suicide in the place where his problems had occurred, was utterly traditional. During the Qing a whole section of the legal code was devoted to the act of 'pressing a person into suicide'. It was not uncommon for people who felt that they had been wronged and who could find no redress to commit suicide in the home of the wrongdoer, who was then held responsible by the courts. The end of the museum director's case is not known but it is a fascinating insight into the persistence of traditional views in modern China.

If you walk from Xinjiekou to the museum, at the large junction with Taiping lu turn left into Taiping bei lu and then take the first on the right, Changjiang lu (which, further east, becomes Hanfu jie). On your left you will soon find the old **Kuomintang Government Buildings** (at no. 292, seat of the Republican government). The garden in which the buildings are situated was once the headquarters of the leader of the Taiping uprising (1853). All that survives of the extensive house-garden complex is a 'stone boat' (or pavilion built out over water) in the western garden, in this case very closely modelled on a boat.

At the end of Hanfu jie turn right along Xihua gai, back to Zhongshan dong lu and east to the museum.

Just before you reach the Provincial Museum a park which crosses the main road indicates the site of the old **Ming Palace**. To the left it is simply an expanse of grass but to the right there are finely carved marble pillar bases indicating the sites of previous buildings, five small marble bridges crossing a pool, the remains of an impressive gate (the Wu men or Meridian Gate) and, beyond, five more marble bridges. The park has been planted with trees which now cover the area once dominated by buildings. When Zhu Yuanzhang first built his palace in Nanjing in the early 14C it consisted of three major courtyards with massive buildings raised on platforms and, on either side of the axis, an altar to the earth and a temple to his ancestors, with ministries in the first courtyard.

Zijin shan

This itinerary is best covered by car or bicycle.

Beyond the museum, outside the city walls, the east of Nanjing is dominated by the **Zijin shan Hills**. This huge area of tree-filled park is full of sites of interest. In the west is the modern **Tomb of Liao Zhongkai** and He Xiangning, his wife. Built in 1935, the tomb has lion-topped columns echoing the Liang dynasty tomb columns in the vicinity, although the tomb itself is a bun-shaped stone mound with a stone tablet in front of it.

Liao Zhongkai was a Cantonese closely associated with Sun Yatsen; he was assassinated not long after Sun's death (in 1925). His body was brought to Nanjing for burial in 1935 and his wife, a well-known calligrapher and painter, was buried with him in 1972.

North of the tomb, on top of a hill, is the **Zijin shan Observatory**, still the largest in China. Founded in 1934, it still displays copies of the bronze Ming and Qing astronomical instruments cast for the early Jesuit astronomers who worked from the observatory in Peking for the Qing emperors in the early 18C.

Southeast of the observatory are the remains of the **Tomb of Zhu Yuanzhang**, founder of the Ming dynasty and the only Ming emperor to be buried in the vicinity of Nanjing; the tombs of the others are outside Peking (see p 195).

Zhu Yuanzhang began the construction of the tomb in 1381, 18 years before he died. In the following year the Empress Ma, known as the 'filial empress', died and was buried in the tomb, which was thereafter known as Xiao ling (Filial Tomb). Construction of the tomb, surrounded by a wall over 22km long, was completed in 1383. The tomb has been badly damaged and now consists of two main parts, the approach and the tomb proper.

The tomb is approached from the southeast; the indirect line of approach partly forced by the terrain, partly due to the traditional belief that evil spirits could only travel in straight lines and therefore an angle in the approach road would throw them off course. The great walls surrounding the enclosure have vanished, leaving only the entrance, the stone archway called **Xiamafang** (Place where Officials Dismount from their Horses); the **Dajin men** (Great Golden Gate) with its three arches is some 700m behind it and close behind is the **Sifang cheng** (Square City), a brick structure with a huge stone turtle stele inside, erected by his son, the Yongle Emperor, and inscribed with a long description of Zhu Yuanzhang's accomplishments.

From the Square City the path turns west and is lined with a magnificent series of stone **animal sculptures**, just like the spirit way to the Ming tombs outside Peking.

Each animal type occurs in two pairs: two sitting lions are followed by two standing lions, two 'couchant' camels are followed by two standing camels, and so on. The animal figures are between 1.5m and almost 4m high and they include lions, rather doggy *xiezhi* (described in a guidebook as 'fabulous sheep said to be able to gore wicked men during fights between the good and the evil'), camels, elephants, *qilin* (often translated as 'unicorn', scaled and hoofed quadrupeds) and horses.

Beyond the horses the path turns north, past two carved columns, through the **avenue of figures of military and civil officials** (over 3m tall), before twisting again until the tree-lined approach to the tomb itself leads north.

This originally consisted of a walled enclosure containing a major hall, with an enclosed walk behind leading to the tower in front of the vast mound in which the emperor was buried. Today little remains of the structures, save the stone floors and pillar bases and small stone bridges over dry waterways. Even the huge tower fronting the mound has lost its wooden superstructure, although the enclosure has recently gained a herd of spotted deer to the east. In front of the mound, the original great hall was destroyed in 1853 and replaced by a much smaller building (built in 1865, restored in 1873) which stands incongruously amongst the broadly-spaced stone pillar bases of the original floor. The carved stone ramps are still very fine and much planting of ornamental flowering trees enhances the rather desolate enclosure.

East of Zhu Yuanzhang's tomb is the **Sun Yatsen Mausoleum**.

Sun died in 1925 and his body was laid out in the Biyun Temple in Peking's Western Hills. A competition was held to construct a grand tomb and it was won by Lu Yanzhi (Y.C. Lu), a graduate of Cornell University School of Architecture whose 'untimely death robbed the Renaissance of its most promising Chinese exponent'. It was originally intended to display Sun's embalmed body in a crystal coffin but mortuary technology was not up to the task and a recumbent sculpture lies over Sun's remains.

Borrowing from the Ming tomb nearby, the tomb, whose white marble and blue tiled roofs symbolise the white sun and blue ground of the Kuomintang flag, is approached through a series of walks, steps and archways—the first of which bears the characters *bo ai* ('universal love'), while the next bears the phrase 'the world belongs to all'—and a stele pavilion. Beyond this is a huge flight of white marble steps leading to the tomb itself, which is carved inside with the Republican constitution in Sun's own hand. The seated figure was carved by a Polish sculptor resident in Paris, Landowski, and a Japanese artist also contributed to the construction of the huge tomb, which took some three years to complete.

To the east of Sun Yatsen's Tomb is the Linggu (Spirit Valley) Pagoda, constructed in 1929 at Chiang Kai-shek's suggestion and designed by an American architect, Henry Killam Murphy, architectural adviser to the Chinese government in the 1930s, architect of Peking University and teacher of Lu Yanzhi, who designed Sun Yatsen's Tomb.

It seems that the pagoda was intended to be part of a Revolutionist's Memorial, commemorating the 1911 Republican Revolution, in which 'purely Chinese architectural features were carried out in [a] reinforced concrete construction'. Only the pagoda still stands today, with its blue and green glazed tiles and 'full Chinese colour scheme, red columns with polychrome entablatures ... in permanent cement colours built in without the use of paint' (H.K. Murphy, in *China*, ed. H. Farnsworth Macnair, Berkeley, University of California Press, 1946).

Just south of the concrete pagoda is the **Wuliang dian**, or Beamless Hall, a Ming structure built entirely of brick, which was incorporated into the Revolutionist's Memorial area by a restoration in the 1930s.

This hall is relatively unusual in China where timber remained the fundamental structural material. During the Ming timber shortages were acute and several of these brick-vaulted halls were built (another fine example is on Wutai shan and there is one in Taiyuan) but the practical solution to the timber shortage did not catch on. The hall was part of a temple that originally stood in the tomb area of Zhu Yuanzhang. When the first Ming emperor began the construction of his tomb he had the temple pulled down and rebuilt to the east. The hall was originally named the Wuliang shou fo dian (Hall of the Buddha of Eternal Longevity) and its present name, Wuliang dian, involves two entirely different characters pronounced in the same way as *wuliang*, meaning 'eternal' or 'boundless'.

Just northwest of the hall is the small (now concrete) *tumulus* of the 6C monk Bao zhi. The tomb is called **Zhigong ling** or Duke Zhi's Tomb. To the northeast is the **Tomb of Deng Yanda** (1895–1931), a close supporter of Sun Yatsen who opposed Chiang Kai-shek and was therefore executed.

There is a completely reconstructed Ling gu Temple now standing south of the pagoda, with monks and some precious relics of the Tang dynasty Buddhist pilgrim, Xuan zang.

More tombs

There are a large number of tombs, particularly of the Ming period, scattered around Nanjing, some inaccessibly tucked away in factories and housing estates—listed in Barry Till, *In Search of Old Nanking* (Hong Kong, Joint Publishing, 1982)—but two are reasonably accessible by car or by no. 11 bus from the Drum Tower, descending at the terminus, Yingtuo cun, and walking back towards Nanjing, where they can be found on the right. They stand on the Ningqi lu, between Bancang cun and Yingtuo cun.

The first that you encounter if you head northeast along the Ningqi lu is the **Tomb of Xu Da** (1332–85). His tomb is characteristic of the non-imperial tombs of the Ming: a tumulus at the back with a stone in front of it simply saying that it is Xu Da and his wife's tomb, preceded by a small spirit way of carved stone figures and a tortoise stele. In the non-imperial Ming tombs, the first figures are usually a pair of horses with attendants, the solid little figures enlivened by the carving of the animals' saddles. These are followed by a pair of sheep, a pair of tigers, military officials and civil officials.

> ### Xu Da
> Xu Da was a famous general, a native of Fengyang in Anhui, close to Zhu Yuanzhang's home, a factor which must have brought them closer for trust in traditional China was often established on the basis of kinship or 'native place' ties. He fought alongside Zhu Yuanzhang from 1353, taking Peking with considerable restraint (allowing no pillage) and leading armies out across the Gobi Desert to pursue the Mongols.

The **Tomb of Li Wenzhong** is a few hundred metres further along the road. He was a virtual contemporary of Xu Da, also a general in the Ming army but noted for his scholarly tastes. His funerary stele was inscribed by the first Ming emperor himself and stands out of line with the spirit road. One of the first figures (the horse and attendant) is missing from the spirit way but a large slab of stone to the right appears to be the half-finished raw material for the missing figures. The presence of this block has led to the suggestion that figures for such tombs were perhaps carved in situ.

Excursions outside Nanjing

The King of Borneo's Tomb

The tomb of the visiting King of Borneo, who died in Nanjing in 1408, was discovered in 1958. It lies off the Ning dan gong lu, outside the city walls to the south (beyond Ande men). From the Zhonghua Gate it is only a couple of kilometres and is marked by an almost invisible sign on the main road. It is some distance off the main road, to the west, beyond a hamlet. The first glimpse of the tomb, which is set against a small hill, is the tortoise stele. The figures of the spirit way are almost hidden by trees and undergrowth and are almost identical with those in other non-imperial Ming tombs.

> The King of Borneo was only 28 when he died, after arriving in Nanjing with his wife, brothers and sisters and children in 1408 on a tribute mission. Apparently, Borneo had been sending tribute to China since 977 and when the first Ming emperor assumed power, he sent envoys out to foreign countries, including Borneo, in order to re-establish the old tribute system. The then king was apparently not very willing to acknowledge Chinese superiority but by 1371 was persuaded.

On the way to the King of Borneo's Tomb, outside the Zhonghua Gate, the road passes **Yuhua tai** (Terrace of the Rain of Flowers) where, according to legend, during the reign of the pious Buddhist ruler, Wu Di of the Liang (502–557), a monk preached on the hill to such effect that a rain of flowers fell upon his audience. The flowers then turned into little coloured pebbles (which are still offered for sale there in saucers of water). Under the Kuomintang the area was used for executions and possibly 100,000 Communists died on Yuhua tai, now commemorated in a great stone monument.

> The brutal murder by Japanese troops of more than 300,000 Chinese civilians in 1937–38 is also commemorated at **Jiangdongmen**, to the west of the city. There, a field of pebbles represents the innumerable pieces of bone dis-

covered at the site, one of many Japanese killing fields in Nanjing. It was after the Japanese army seized Nanjing on 13 December 1937 that Japanese soldiers began a six week orgy of rape and murder. Accounts of murderous rape and killing fill the pages of Iris Chang's *The Rape of Nanking, the Forgotten Holocaust of World War Two*, 1997, and one of the most disturbing aspects is the Japanese soldiers' pride in their bestiality. They posed for photographs standing over their victims' bodies, or even in the act of rape and murder, and sent the films off to be developed in Shanghai, where they were copied by a horrified chemist, so the news of the massacre began to get out.

Within Nanjing, some foreign residents made determined efforts to save as many as they could. Led by the local Siemens' representative, Johan Rabe, a stout, uxorious bourgeois and an unlikely hero, a group of American missionaries, including Minnie Vautrin, Dean of Studies at Ginling Women's College, did their best to protect women and children, escorting them to hospital and sheltering them in their own compounds. Minnie Vautrin, whose college was besieged by Japanese soldiers, never recovered from the horrors of the experience and committed suicide shortly after she returned home.

It is a deeply upsetting place, best visited only in the spirit of remembrance. It remains a bitter problem in Sino-Japanese relations for the Japanese continue to refuse more than the occasional verbal apology and still publish school histories of the war which contain no mention of Chinese suffering at the hands of the invading Japanese army.

Qixia Temple and the Liang Tombs

About 15km northeast of Nanjing is the **Qixia Temple**, founded in 483, although the surviving buildings are basically of the very late Qing (1908), apart from some stone carvings. Carved into the hill are almost 300 caves and niches, the earliest dating back to the mid 5C.

A monk was said to have been reading the *Wu bang shou jing* (*Sutra of Eternal Longevity*) when a Buddha appeared against the hill and the character for 'hall' also appeared. Although the monk in question (Ming Sengshao) died soon after, his son began the carving of the Buddhist caves, most notably the Three Saints Hall, or San sheng dian, which is also, confusingly, known as the Wuliang (Eternal) dian with its 10m figures of the Buddha and attendant Bodhisattvas. Unfortunately, many of the figures in the niches, which were still being carved as late as the Ming, were damaged during the Taiping rebellion and late 19C restoration was almost as harmful.

To the east of the Great Buddha Hall of the temple itself is a small stone pagoda, **Sheli ta**, said to date from 601 but restored during the Southern Tang (937–975). Octagonal, 15m high, with five storeys, the carving is in the lively Tang style, with scenes of the life of the Buddha near the base, then a series of small figures supporting the pagoda, above them a circle of lotus petals surmounted by architectural details interspersed with carvings of the guardians of the four quarters and a pagoda-like top with stone-carved eave details.

Beside the road to Qixia si there are a number of **tombs** of the Liang dynasty (502–557) only a few kilometres outside the city. Standing in green fields, these tombs are recognisable from the tall, sometimes fluted columns and the solid but curvy winged lions carved with cloud patterns, their mouths open in a snarl. The tombs are those of Xiao Jing, a cousin of the Emperor Wu Di, who served as an official and died in 528, and the Emperor's younger brother, Xiao Dan, who died in 522 and whose tortoise stele bears characters carved from the calligraphy of the great master Wang Xizhi. Further on there are two more tombs of brothers of the Wu Di emperor, with similar assemblages of winged lions, tortoise stelae and lion-topped columns. The sinuousness of some of the lions and the scrolling lines of the patterns that cover them stand in marked contrast to the other great group of funerary figures to be found in Nanjing, the stolid, almost naive non-imperial Ming figures.

Yangzhou

Yangzhou, in Jiangsu province, situated near the junction of the Grand Canal, some 80km northeast of Nanjing, is one of the historic towns of the Yangtse delta area. It was a charming city with many canals and bridges and spectacular domestic architecture, although it is particularly famous for its gardens and cultural connections, both intellectual and popular. Unfortunately the city centre is now filled with towering blocks of mirror glass and looks like downtown Atlanta (or so I was informed; I haven't seen Atlanta). A major new local product is fresh-water pearls, grown on ugly lumps of polystyrene in all the ponds.

Practical information

 ### Getting there
Yangzhou is not on the rail network, nor does it have an airport. It is most easily reached by bus from Nanjing (about two hours on one of China's first dual carriageway motorways) or Zhenjiang (usually less than one hour including the crossing of the Yangtse). The motorway is rather wonderful. Relatively empty of traffic, it nevertheless boasts motorway filling stations and diners and offers a depressing view of the Yangtse delta towns today. Like Japan, China's countryside is filling up fast with three-storeyed houses with blue mirror glass windows, from which the inhabitants must reel out into the sunlight, and most of the towns with their high-rise centres look a

bit like Birmingham from the M1–M6 interchange, although Birmingham is pleasantly filled with trees while these are not.

 ### Where to stay
The *Xiyuan Fandian* (West Garden Guesthouse) at 1 Fengleshang jie, ☎ 734 4888, fax 723 3870, is said to have been constructed on the site of one of the villas laid out for the Qianlong emperor's visits to Yangzhou. The emperor's boat was said to have been moored on the section of moat that runs through the garden. Next door is the multi-storeyed *Yangzhou Binguan* (Yangzhou Hotel), 5 Fengleshang jie, ☎ 734 2611, fax 734 3599.

History

Yangzhou's recorded history begins with construction of the town of Hanjiang and canal construction in 486 BC. For many hundreds of years, particularly after the construction of the Grand Canal linking Yangzhou with the Sui capital at Luoyang in the 7C, Yangzhou was extremely prosperous and, as the *Japanese Railway Guide* (1924) has it: 'The place has always been known as one of pleasure and gaiety ... In the palmy days of Yangzhou, it was said that a man having once entered the city in search of pleasure would find himself unable to leave it until he had squandered his all'. When the Sui Emperor linked Yangzhou by canal to his capital in Luoyang he celebrated the link by arriving in a flotilla of gloriously decorated dragon boats which were pulled along the canal by teams of beautiful girls. The dragon boats have largely been replaced by flocks of swan-shaped pedalos.

At the fall of the Song in the 13C the Grand Canal was in disrepair; Yangzhou's fortunes declined and with them the gardens that had been famous from the Tang dynasty. It has been claimed that Marco Polo served for three years as governor of Yangzhou which he described as 'great and prosperous', with a population of 'idolators' but his further account of the city where 'accoutrements for horses and men-at-arms are produced ... in great quantities' hardly tallies with Yangzhou's fame as a **cultural centre** whose handicrafts included lacquered pottery, carved jade, embroidery and painting. If he had, indeed, been governor, he was remarkably out of touch since he concluded that, beyond the men-at-arms and their accoutrements, there was 'nothing else here worthy of note'. China's foremost Polo scholar, however, the octogenarian Yang Zhijiu (writing in 1983) demonstrated that the myth was due to a misreading of *sejourna* ('stay') for *gouverna* ('govern') in one Polo manuscript.

At the beginning of the Ming the **Grand Canal** was restored and with it, Yangzhou's prosperity, based not only on silk and rice but also on salt. Salt was a major item of taxation in traditional China and much of the salt trade was controlled by merchants from Anhui province, who lived in Yangzhou in large numbers, constructing elegant houses and gardens for themselves. Yangzhou was one of the major stopping points for the imperial tours of inspection of the south in the mid to late 18C; whenever these occurred the salt merchants vied with each other to build lavish gardens and villas to accommodate the imperial visitors.

The **gardens** of Yangzhou are, in general, smaller in scale than some of those in Suzhou and more invariably associated with houses or temple buildings. In some, the garden area is far smaller than the residential part. Chen Congzhou has written of the mixture of influences in Yangzhou's architecture and garden design, combining forms from Anhui with aspects of northern design. He states that some of the garden areas of the Yuanming yuan ('Old' Summer Palace) in Peking used a Yangzhou design method and the smallness of the garden areas also recalls the private gardens of the north. The rockeries and rather solid pavilions are also reminiscent of the north while the domestic architecture, with its stepped and curved gable end walls, is firmly of the south.

Aside from its domestic architecture, much of which is well-preserved despite destruction over the centuries—during the fall of the Ming and the

Taiping uprising in particular—Yangzhou is also famous for a group of painters, the 'Eccentrics of Yangzhou' whose work was said to have been excluded from the imperial collection on the grounds of its unconventionality. The 'Eccentrics' are often numbered as eight but the actual number must be taken as more flexible, representing a group of painters associated with the cultural centre of Yangzhou and characteristically bold in their approach. **Gao Qipei** (1672–1734) grew a fingernail and specialised in 'finger painting' which we normally associate with pre-school children. His incredibly sparse paintings include a wonderful series of album leaves now in the Nanjing Museum. A water buffalo in a pool is depicted, the top of its head and horns sketched lightly, a single splash of paint to indicate its rump. In another leaf, duckweed (a series of dark splodges of paint laid on with the finger tip) serves as an attraction for three prawns and a shoal of tiny minnows, scratched in with his fingernail. **Hua Yan** (1682–1786) used brushes in his *Wutong Tree and Squirrels* (in the Palace Museum Collection in Peking) rather contradicting the traditional new of imperial disapproval, although the painting may have been acquired later. Charmingly lively squirrels painted with tiny furry strokes dash about in branches which have been painted with a softer, wetter brush.

Another, earlier master who lived in Yangzhou, was **Shi Tao** (also known as Dao Ji), 1642–c 1717. A very distant relative of the Ming imperial family, Shi Tao became a Buddhist monk with the fall of the Ming, adopting the Buddhist name Dao Ji. He was one of the most innovative of all China's painters, perhaps his best-known painting being the long landscape scroll, now in the Suzhou Museum, sometimes known as the *Ten-thousand Ugly Ink-dots*. Shi Tao himself describes in a colophon how he 'splashed the ink' and how the spots would annoy the great masters. Beginning with splashes of ink thrown across the paper, he built up a landscape, straggling lines linking the blots to form mountains and trees. Shi Tao also painted marvellous album leaves (there are examples in the Shanghai Museum) with funny little figures dwarfed by mountains. The association of these major masters with Yangzhou serves to emphasise its position as a centre of culture in the area.

In popular culture, Yangzhou gives a name to a form of recitation or story-telling, *ping hua*. In the 18C, platforms were set up along the streets near the town gates and performers would re-enact entire novels in narrative form; each performer specialising in a specific genre of story. Performances of this type still take place in Yangzhou. There is also a form of local opera, *yang ju*.

Some of the major sites of Yangzhou lie just outside the town, to the northwest and are best visited by car, such as the **Tomb of the Sui Emperor Yangdi** (reigned 605–617).

The emperor visited Yangzhou three times—in 605, 606 and 612—celebrating the construction of the Grand Canal. He died 'of excesses' in Yangzhou and was first buried elsewhere. The tumulus was constructed in 622 but soon fell into disrepair. In 1807 a local scholar had it tidied up and a new stone bearing the emperor's name was carved by a contemporary calligrapher, Yi Bingshou.

Returning to Yangzhou, 3km outside the town, to the northwest, are the ruins of

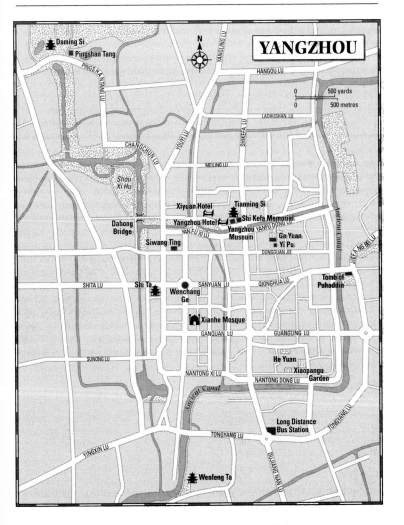

the Tang **city wall**. During the Tang the town was divided into two parts, one containing the administrative offices (*yamen*) and one enclosing dwellings. The site is that of the former, administrative enclosure; the other is buried under today's buildings to the southeast. Excavations of the site have yielded many burials, ceramics, building materials (tiles and bricks), as well as sites of carved bone and smelting workshops.

In the southwest corner of the Tang ruins is the **Guanyin Hill** (Guanyin shan) with stone steps leading to the top where all the buildings are late Qing or later, although there was a tower here during the Sui on whose ruins a temple was built during the Song.

Just west of the Guanyin shan is the **Daming si** (Great Brightness Temple). It was founded during the Great Brightness reign period of the Liu Song dynasty (457–465), hence its name. It is also sometimes known as the Qiling si (Temple of the Home of the Spirits) after the Qiling Pagoda constructed here in 601. When the Qing Qianlong emperor visited the temple in 1765 he wrote, in his own hand, the name Fajing si (Silence of the Law Temple). The surviving buildings all date from the late Qing, after the Taiping rebellion, so it must be assumed that the temple was damaged or destroyed at the time. In the main hall are three Buddhas; behind them is Guanyin on his island in the sea and there are 18 lohans on the side walls, all 'finely carved in clay'. One of the side buildings contains an exhibition of the life of the Tang dynasty monk, Jian Zhen.

A notable feature of the temple is the **Jian Zhen Hall**, built by the Japanese in 1973. The hall is modelled on the main hall of the Toshodai Temple in Nara (Japan) built by Jian Zhen after his arrival in Japan in 753. Jian Zhen (688–763) was a monk of the Daming si who went back to Japan with two monks who had come to seek a master required to impose discipline on the lax Japanese Buddhist community. It took five attempts at the sea voyage before he succeeded on the sixth voyage and he is commemorated by a dry lacquer statue which still stands in the Toshodai Temple. He is credited with introducing not only Chinese Buddhist discipline but also medicine, language, architecture, sculptural techniques and printing to Japan. Memorial activities were held in Yangzhou, jointly sponsored by the Chinese and the Japanese in 1963 for the 1200th anniversary of his arrival in Japan. The clean lines of the hall, reminiscent of the Tang buildings on Wutai shan in distant Shanxi, are characteristic of the Tang and there is an elegant cedarwood sculpture of Jian Zhen in the hall, as well as murals commemorating his life and work.

Shou xi hu

Just east of the Daming Temple is the Shou xi hu or 'Narrow West Lake', an area of park and garden with a long, thin stretch of water in it which is, indeed, narrower than Hangzhou's West Lake. It has been, as Chinese guidebooks have it, a favourite 'scenic spot' since the Six Dynasties (AD 222–589). The area contains many of the sights of Yangzhou.

The **Bai ta** or White Dagoba (a dagoba is a Tibetan style stupa) is modelled on that in the Beihai in Peking and it is said to have been constructed by a rich salt merchant, anxious for imperial favour, after the Qianlong emperor had remarked that a dagoba, like that in the Beihai, would improve the scenery of the Narrow West Lake area.

The **Five-pavilion Bridge** (Wuting qiao) in the Narrow West Lake Garden was built in 1757 over a lotus pool, also at the expense of a local salt merchant in anticipation of one of the Qianlong emperor's visits. It is not unlike a three-pavilion bridge in the imperial park at Chengde (Hebei) but it is more complex in construction. The willow-shaded dyke on the west side of the lake is called the 'Long Dyke' and the pavilion in the middle bears the inscription 'Spring willows over the dyke'.

The **Xu yuan** (Xu Garden), with its Listening to Orioles Pavilion, with marvellously carved woodwork in the interior, is at the north end of the dyke. In front of the pavilion are two iron cauldrons, supposedly used to control the flow of canal water during the Liu-Song era. The **Pingshan tang** (Mountain-flattening Hall), on a hill in the garden, very near the Daming Temple, was first built in 1048 by Ouyang Xiu (1007–72), a famous man of letters who was governor of Yangzhou and who often came to the hall to drink and write poetry. He looked out over the scenery from his vantage point where he was on the same level as the surrounding hills, hence the name of the hall. The present building dates from the late Qing (post Taiping period).

There is a temple to Ouyang Xiu nearby containing a stone-carved, painted statue of the writer. To the southeast of the Pingshan Hall is the **Pingyuan lou**, a three-storey, late Qing structure; views from each floor are said to demonstrate the theories of perspective advanced by the Song painter Guo Xi. The flowers on the ancient trees in the courtyard are said to be the legendary red jade flowers which first attracted the Sui emperor to Yangzhou.

The **Xiao Jin shan** (Small Golden Hill) is an island in the lake, dotted with Qing period pavilions and rockeries (although there were said to be garden buildings on it as early as the Liu-Song period). It is named after the Golden Hill at nearby Zhenjiang which it is said to resemble. At the western extremity of the hill is the flat Diaoyu tai (Anglers' Terrace) where the Qianlong emperor is supposed to have fished, and at the south end of the lake is the Rainbow Bridge, a stone structure dating from the Qing (restored after Liberation) which replaces an original wooden bridge of Ming date.

On the moat which leads to the east off the Narrow West Lake are three gardens and the **imperial jetty** (where Qianlong's barge was moored) beside the *Xiyuan Guesthouse*. The jetty consists of a charmingly rustic group of whitewashed, thatch-roofed buildings (recently restored) set amongst trees. Instead of imperial barges, there is now a fleet of swan-shaped pedalos moored there. Immediately east of the Rainbow Bridge is the **Xi yuan** (West Garden), built in

The imperial library, Wen hui ge, *Yangzhou, from* Hong xue yin yuan, *The illustrated autobiography of Linqing, 1847–50*

1751 which, apart from rockeries and old trees, includes the Imperial Inscription Pavilion (Qianlong) and a spring, the 'Fifth Spring Under Heaven'. The **Hong yuan** (Red Garden) is to the east of the West Garden and is thick with *pen cai* (bonsai) plants in marvellous pots; this, in turn, leads to the **Yechun yuan** (Beauty of Spring Garden).

Immediately south of the moat is a group of buildings: the Shi ta, Siwang ting and the Wenchang ge. The **Shi ta** (Stone Pagoda) on Shita lu (which intersects with Huaihai lu, leading south from the Hong Garden; take the second turning on the right) was built within a temple in 840. It was originally outside the city walls and was moved to its present position in the Southern Song period (1127–1279). Many of the small Buddha figures on the pagoda were recut in the Qing. It is a five-storey, six-sided construction with a stone platform inside and finely carved railings on the upper register carved with animals including dragons, phoenix, oxen and horses. The stone-carved architectural detail includes upturned eaves and tiles.

Walking due east, along Shita lu, you pass a Tang dynasty gingko tree and arrive at the **Wenchang ge** (Promoting Literature Pavilion) at the intersection with Wenhe lu.

> This used to stand in front of the Confucian Academy of Yangzhou (and was one of a pair), dating from the Ming (1585). The academy, or college, was established at the order of the first Ming emperor who, being of very low birth, was a great egalitarian and believed in educational opportunities for all, hence his promotion of educational establishments. The present structure, all that remains of the Confucian Academy, is late Qing. It is a three-storeyed, octagonal wooden pavilion, the lower storey faced with brick.

Walking north up Wenhe lu, the first turning on the left (Xianxue jie) leads to the **Siwang ting** (Pavilion of the Four Views). This was also part of an educational establishment, the Provincial College.

> The college was also established at the order of the first Ming emperor. The pavilion was said to have been used for astronomical observation. Built in the Ming (1559), restored in the Qing, it is a three-storey, octagonal tower of complex timber construction (the four pillars of the lower storey lead right up to the top). It was used as a lookout by the Taiping army that took Yangzhou, hence its present name.

From the Xiyuan Guesthouse, the Tianning Temple, Museum and Shi Kefa Memorial are easily reached. Turn right along Yanfu xi lu and the **Yangzhou Museum** (open 08.30–17.30) is on the left. It is housed in the temple complex dedicated to Shi Kefa (1601–45), a loyal official in Yangzhou when the Qing seized power. He refused to surrender Yangzhou, attempted to commit suicide and was arrested and executed. His body was never found but his belt of 20 pieces of jade was buried (and rediscovered in 1979 when the tomb was restored) and the temple in his memory (Shi Kefa ci) built in 1772. Two fine gingkos grow in front of the main hall; his tomb is behind on Plum Blossom Hill. The buildings now house the museum with exhibits referring to the 'Eight Eccentric Painters' and their followers. There are some fine exhibits of locally excavated artefacts and the temple halls are still very impressive. There is also a small Marco Polo hall to the left, filled with photographs and evidence of Sino-Italian co-operation.

Behind is the **Tianning si** (Temple of Heaven's Will). This was built on the site of a villa and in 418 a famous Nepalese monk came here to translate Buddhist sutras. It was destroyed in the Song, rebuilt in the Ming. When the Qianlong emperor came on his southern tours, Cao Yin, a high official and grandfather of the famous novelist, Cao Xueqin (1716–64), ordered the block printing of presentation volumes of the *Complete Tang Poetry* (amongst others) to be undertaken in the temple. The emperor stayed in the temple on his trips south, when his barge was moored on the moat nearby. The gate, three halls and some side buildings are all that remain.

Southwest of Yangzhou is the **Wenfeng ta** (Pagoda of the Literary Peak), best reached by car. It stands by the old Grand Canal and was built in 1582. Constructed of a mixture of timber, mud and brick, it is octagonal in plan and six storeys high, marking the point where Jian Zhen set off for Japan.

The famous **salt merchants' houses** of Yangzhou are mostly to be found in the east of the town around Dongguan jie. One of Yangzhou's most famous 'gardens', the **Ge yuan** (also on Dongguan jie) is an example, for these gardens were essentially part of a dwelling. Dongguan jie runs parallel to Yanfu dong lu (the eastwards continuation of Yanfu xi lu) immediately to the south. The Ge yuan is traditionally supposed to have been the home of the famous painter Shi Tao but in the mid-19C it was remodelled by a rich salt merchant, Huang Yingtai. The bamboos of the garden have leaves that are supposed to resemble the three simple strokes of the character *ge* (which means single, self), hence the name. There is an almost equal area of building to that of garden and to those who are not fond of oddly shaped stones and rockeries, this, like the other Yangzhou gardens, will be something of a trial. The buildings are beautifully carved and detailed, the garden lovingly designed, full of rockeries and winding paths. There are moon gates, flat stone zigzag bridges in corners of the pool and high piled groups of curiously shaped stones from nearby lakes.

Not far from the Ge yuan is the **Tomb of Puhading**. Go east along Dongguan jie until you reach the main road, Taizhou lu, which runs alongside the eastern moat. Turn right (south) and just beyond the next crossroads, on the right (across the moat, immediately south of Jiefang qiao or Liberation Bridge) is the Hufhul tang (Muslim Hall). Here there is a mid Qing mosque and the Tomb of Puhading (Behao Alding), a Muslim teacher who died in Yangzhou in 1275. According to an inscription, he was a 16th generation descendant of the Prophet and he was buried here (according to a Chinese source) in an 'Arab style' rectangular building with a vaulted ceiling, the actual grave in the centre of the floor, the walls carved with Koranic inscriptions between floral scrolling. Nearby are other graves of noted Muslims of the Song and Ming periods. There is also an historical exhibition on the friendly relations between China and Arab countries.

Near the southeast corner of the city is the **He Yuan**, named after a later owner, a late (19C) Qing official called He Zhengdao who enlarged and rebuilt it. An alternate, possibly earlier, name is Jixiao shanzhuang (Mountain Village of Sighs). It is entered from a small lane, Xuning men jie (opposite Xuning men Bridge, close to the southeast corner of the city and moat). The garden is divided into two parts and buildings occupy more of the ground than open, garden spaces. There is much light, southern lattice in the buildings, many two-storeyed with open verandahs, although some of the smaller pavilions are slightly heavy and northern in feel, such as the Chi xin ting (Pavilion in the Heart of the Pool).

> Rocks and grand old trees are important features and the smallness of the garden courtyards, combined with the rather bare garden areas, combine to hint at northern influence which is said to have resulted from northerners coming to Yangzhou to work in gardens as well as the Yangzhou workers influencing northern gardens.

If you follow the Xuning men jie round to the north and west, you will find the tiny **Xiaopangu Garden** on Dashu gai. This is a late 18C construction and once belonged to a governor general of the city. The small area is cunningly divided into two in order to provide more separate 'views' on either side of the tile covered walk that divides the space. There are fine details, stone tables and seats beside a whitewashed wall against which a small prunus grows and a wonderful peach-shaped moon door, framing a view.

If time allows, other small gardens that can be seen in Yangzhou include the **Yi Pu** (Pleasure Garden), the garden-house of the Li family at the western end of the Ge garden on Dongguan jie; the **Yi Lu** (House of Joy), once the home of the silver merchant Huang Yizhi in Jijiawan; the garden and house of another salt merchant (19C), the **Yu yuan** (Remaining Garden); and Ube Chen family's **Wei pu** (Luxuriant Garden) on Fengxiang gai. These are similar in style and detail to the more famous gardens and well worth visiting for their architecture, as well as the gardens.

Zhenjiang

Zhenjiang, on the south bank of the Yangtse, where a ferry crosses the massive river, is a convenient point from which to visit Yangzhou. Zhenjiang itself, like Yangzhou, owes its past prosperity to the opening of the Grand Canal in the 6C under the Sui. This connected it (and its silk and rice production) to the capital in Luoyang, further north.

Practical information

 ### Getting there
Zhenjiang is an hour by train or bus from Nanjing, 3 hours from Shanghai.

 ### Where to stay
The *Dahuangjia Jiudian* (Royal Hotel) is in the centre of the old town at 35 Boxian lu, ☎ 527 1438.

Marco Polo praised Zhenjiang's silk, especially the golden fabrics sold by rich merchants. It was a foreign concession town, with French and British consulates established. The latter can still be visited (it stands at the corner of Bo xian Park) as it now houses the local **museum** (open daily 08.00–11.30 and 13.30–17.00). The most interesting exhibits are the preserved body of a local scholar, buried holding his examination certificate in his hands, and the anchor of the *Amethyst*.

This was a British gunboat sent up the Yangtse in April 1949 with supplies for the British Embassy in Nanjing. It was an unfortunate moment to choose for the Communist forces launched their attack across the Yangtse at the very same time and the *Amethyst* was caught in the battle. Attempts to rescue the ship, by sending other gunboats and a third secretary (later to become a distinguished ambassador) from the Nanjing Embassy to negotiate with the Communist forces failed and it was months before the *Amethyst*, which had suffered some losses, managed to sail back to the coast.

The American novelist, Pearl Buck (1892–1973), who brought Chinese rural life to millions in the West through *The Good Earth* (1931), grew up in Zhenjiang. Her childhood home is now part of the Zhenjiang Semi-conductor Factory and the school she attended, and where she subsequently taught, is now the Zhenjiang Middle School.

Although Zhenjiang is now a busy commercial centre, its setting on a rocky outcrop is attractive and there are temples and other sites of interest in the surrounding hills. It was at the centre of the massive Yangtse floods in the summer of 1998; when I saw it in May 1998, the river was already frighteningly high.

The **Ganlu si** (Sweet Dew Temple) is in the northeast of the town. There has been a temple on the site since the 5C, although successive structures seem to have suffered from constant destruction and the surviving buildings are Qing in date.

On top of the hill is a pavilion, the **Lingyun ting** (Soaring Clouds Pavilion), considered to be one of the finest anywhere by such diverse figures as the outstanding Song painter Mi Fei (1051–1107) and the Qing reformer Kang Youwei (1858–1927). Not far away is the 'First Scenic Stele under Heaven' in the east wall of the temple, said to have been carved to commemorate the fact that the 6C Liang emperor considered this spot to be the first (or best) scenic place under heaven. The stele has suffered multiple destruction, like the temple; the current one dates from the 18C.

Nearby is the **Iron Pagoda** (Tie ta) erected to commemorate a noble of the Tang dynasty in the Tianbao era (825–826). Iron was used in its construction: hence its name. The original was destroyed at the end of the Tang; a replacement erected during the Southern Song was blown over in 1582. Its successor has also suffered from wind and lightning and only the base and first two storeys date from the Song; the top was added later.

The tomb of the famous artist of the Song (1051–1107), noted for his use of flat blobs of ink to delineate mountains, is on Huanghe shan. Mi Fei's (or Mi Fu's) *zi* or 'style' (the name taken at the age of about 20) was Mi Yuanzhang and his tomb is known as **Mi Yuanzhang mu**. He had always loved the Helin si (Goose Grove Temple) at Zhen jiang and was buried near it. In front of the tree covered mound is a stone altar and a stele.

Jin shan, or Golden Mountain, in the northwest suburbs was originally an island in the Yangtse. 'Golden Mountain' refers to the fact that gold was mined on the hill during the Tang dynasty. By the end of the Qing silting had joined the island to the shore. The **Helin si** on the ex-island was built against the hillside, pavilions and halls rising above one another; it was locally described as the 'mountain within a temple'.

Founded in the Eastern Jin (317–420), the temple has had various names throughout its history. The Qianlong emperor named it Jiangbanchan si (Meditation Temple by Hills and River) on one of his southern journeys. The Song poet and official Wang Anshi wrote: 'Many halls rise in serried stone ranks, windows open on all sides to the winds; suddenly I see a bird rise in flight and feel frightened by the void.'

On the west of the hill is the **First Spring Under Heaven**. It was first graded as no. 7 by Lu Yuping of the Tang but shortly afterwards Liu Bochu awarded it first place (on the basis of the taste of the water boiled for tea). A stone railing surrounds the spring, there are pavilions around it and the calligraphy describing it as the 'First Spring' is by the Qing calligrapher Wang Renkan.

Also on Jin shan is the **Cishou** (Benevolence and Longevity) **Pagoda**. Originally one of a pair known as the Zunci (Amassing of Benevolence), traditionally supposed to have been built in the 6C, although archaeological and literary evidence places them in the Tang dynasty (618–907). This one, built on the ruins of the northern one of the pair, was last rebuilt in 1900, some say to celebrate the 65th birthday of the Dowager Empress Cixi, hence the addition of *shou*, or 'longevity', to the name.

Jiao shan (Scorched Hill) is northeast of Zhenjiang, on the banks of the Yangtse. It is famous for its scenery, views from pavilions overlooking the river and its ancient trees, which reputedly include a Six dynasties (222–589) pine, a Song dynasty cassia and a Ming gingko. The **Dinghui Temple** (Settling of Wisdom, a name given by the Qianlong emperor) was founded during the Eastern Han (AD 25–220), destroyed and rebuilt through the centuries, the last major rebuilding occurring after the Taiping uprising (1850). Repairs since Liberation have 'preserved the Ming style' and it is a major Buddhist centre of the Yangtse delta area.

On the eastern slope of the hill are the remains of the fortifications against the English, built during the Opium War (1842) and reinforced in 1845 and 1874. The fortifications were severely damaged by the Taiping rebels in 1853 and, after rebuilding, were used from 1880 as an astronomical observatory.

Guangzhou

Guangzhou, known in English as Canton, the capital of Guangdong province, is a major river port situated at the northern end of the Zhu jiang (Pearl River) delta, close to the South China Sea, but protected from coastal typhoons by its inland position. Its riverine communications with the hinterland are good, for three tributaries of the Pearl River—the Dong Jiang, Xi Jiang and Bei Jiang— converge at Guangzhou. The city is vast and sprawling and yet has an incredible population density of over 420 people per square km, not counting the influx of jobless peasants and migrants.

Although fast losing most traces of its past, as the double-decker motorways built in the 1980s now groan under an excess of largely stationary traffic, such remnants as survive reflect Guangzhou's history as a southern Chinese centre— the temple at Fo Shan and the Chen Family Ancestral Hall are southern buildings at their most flamboyant—and a foreign settlement, with overgrown mansions on Shamian Island and arcaded shopping streets right out of Northern Italy via Portugal and its empire.

Practical information

Getting there
By air

Baiyun airport is 12km from the centre of town and one of the busiest in China, with four or more daily flights to Hong Kong and many others to major Chinese cities, as well as direct flights to Bangkok, Hanoi, Jakarta, Singapore, Penang, Kuala Lumpur, Manila, Sydney and Melbourne. Beware of the appalling cross-city traffic and leave plenty of time to get to the airport. Taxis cost about 40–50 yuan and there are airport buses (8 yuan) to and from the *CAAC* office on Huanshi dong lu.

By train

The station is in the north of the town at the north end of Renmin bei lu. The main line north from Guangzhou connects with lines to Fujian, the west, northwest and northeast. Hong Kong and Shenzhen are easily reached by express train (Hong Kong in two and a half hours).

By bus

The long distance bus station is just west of the railway station.

By boat

The terminal for boats to Fujian and Shanghai is on the riverfront to the east of Yangjiang lu and further down is the hydrofoil station for Hong Kong (daily departure 13.00 for a three to four hour ride). There are slower overnight ferries to Hong Kong and Macao and steamers to Wuzhou (for Guilin and Yangshuo). **River trips** depart from Xiti wharf, opposite the Customs House on Yanjiang lu.

By underground

The underground is a useful new way of getting around.

Where to stay

The best places to stay are in the Pearl River area near Shamian: the *Furama* (Fulihua dajiudan), ☎ 8186 3288, fax 8186 3388, at 316 Changdi lu, the *Hotel Landmark Guangzhou*, Yanjiang lu, ☎ 8335 5988, fax 8333 6197 and the *White Swan Hotel* at no. 1 Shamian nan jie (despite the fact that its erection ruined the waterfront of Shamian), ☎ 8188 6968, fax 8186 1188.

History

Guangzhou has had many histories. An independent Neolithic culture—whose artefacts are characterised by earthenware pots with all over stamped designs, some of which are intriguingly close to later bronze designs—was overlaid by a distinctive southern version of the Longshan ('black pottery') culture. As yet there is no evidence of a continuous bronze-producing culture in southeast China. Lack of evidence is no basis on which to hypothesise but traditionally the province of Guangdong and the neighbouring southeast were regarded by northern Chinese from the cultural heartland of the Yellow River as non-Chinese. An American scholar has described southeast China, Hainan and adjacent Vietnam as 'a linguistic Balkans in which relatively recent arrivals are intermingled with very ancient groups'. The distinctive language of Guangdong province, **Cantonese**, which appears to preserve many archaic forms now lost in northern dialects (such as more tones and endings), has also been used to explain the gradual colonisation of the south. Xia Nai, the foremost archaeologist of modern China (d. 1986), believed that the archaism of the language was preserved because it was learnt by local people whose fundamental cultural affinities lay more with the people of Vietnam than with the northern Chinese. Imported as a 'foreign' language in the Tang dynasty, it did not evolve as in the north but preserved Tang dynasty endings, which had been used to recreate the rhymes of Tang poetry, lost in northern speech. Another theory about the archaism of Cantonese is that it was preserved by frontiersmen, far from their cultural heartlands, rather like Pennsylvania Dutch.

The south was colonised by the Qin emperor in the 3C BC and the Han Chinese proclaimed nine provinces in the area, sending colonists and magistrates to enforce Chinese rule. Their hold on the south was, however, precarious and with the end of the Han, Chinese sovereignty retreated, although it was more firmly established during the **Tang**. For the Tang, the south was both a source of exotica—glossy purple stone for ink-stones (from west of Guangzhou), cinnabar, coral, pearls, cinnamon, cardamon, rosewood, oranges, tangerines, limes, bananas, lychees, camellia, hibiscus, francolins and parrots—and also a place of exile. Although the major posts (Office of the Legate at Guangzhou) were granted to favoured officials, many lesser posts were filled by exiles who had offended the court. Although they hoped to return north, many died prematurely of tropical disease and left behind despairing poems which, while sometimes acknowledging the beauty of the sub-tropics, were filled with nostalgia for home. Song Zhiwen, banished by the Tang empress Wu, wrote:

Climbing figs sway in the blue air
Arenga palms veil the cyan moss ...
Hugging the leaves, the dusky langurs whistle
Biting on blossoms, the kingfishers come ...
Yet my glossy black hair will shortly become white
My loyal vermilion heart has already turned to ashes.
Then how shall I ever head out on the homeward road
To work the shears on my old garden's weeds?
(from E.H. Schafer, *The Vermilion Bird: Tang Images of the South*, Berkeley, University of California Press, 1967)

During the Tang, Guangzhou developed as a major south coast port, attracting overseas traders from Southeast Asia and India and, like Quanzhou in Fujian, acquiring a sizeable Muslim population. Communications with the interior were improved during the Song, as roads were built and Guangzhou became less a place of exile and more a trade centre.

During the **Qing**, as westerners began to arrive in China, many approached through Guangzhou (including the British Macartney mission in 1793, which first requested permission to enter China from the coast of Guangdong). The **British East India Company**, granted royal permission to trade with China in 1609, established a factory in Guangzhou in 1684, although the Portuguese had arrived in 1516 and the Dutch about 100 years later. Foreign traders were restricted to the shoreline of the city and at first were not allowed to reside in Guangzhou throughout the year, being compelled to retreat to Macau, which was also the only place in which the families of merchants and missionaries were allowed to live before the Opium Wars. Without any civilising influences, the young Englishmen who went out as 'supercargoes' (a name given to those in charge of East India Company affairs abroad) tended to behave rather like schoolboys on the loose. William Hickey (1749–c 1830), the diarist, called in at Guangzhou on his return from India. He described his friend Bob Pott's approach to washing the dishes in Guangzhou: 'I never suffer the servants to have the trouble of removing a tea equipage, always throwing the whole apparatus out of the window or downstairs. They easily procure another batch from the steward's warehouse.'

The waterfront at Guangzhou in the late 18C and early 19C was dominated by the fine 'factories' of the various East India Companies: two storey European style buildings flying national flags and at first built of timber, although this was soon superseded by rusticated stonework, colonnades and open verandahs. Here the supercargoes lived and worked, trading with Chinese-appointed traders in tea, any porcelain to survive Bob Pott, silk and luxury goods, paying for these first in silver bullion and increasingly with Indian opium. William Hickey described the waterfront in 1796:

The view of the city, as you approach it, is strikingly grand and at the same time must always suprise strangers. The scene upon the water is as busy a one as the Thames below London Bridge, with this difference that instead of our square-rigged vessels of different dimensions, you there have junks .... About half a mile above the city suburbs ... is a wharf, or embankment, regularly built of brick and mortar, extending more than half a mile in length, upon which wharf stands the different factory or place of residence of the supercargoes, each factory having the flag of its nation on a lofty ensign staff before it. At the time I was in China, they stood in the following order: first, the Dutch, then, the French, the English, the Swedes and last, the Danes. Each of these factories, beyond admirable banqueting, or public rooms for eating etc., having attached to them sets of chambers varying in size according to the establishment. The English being far more numerous than any other nation trading with China, their range of buildings is much the most extensive ... with a small garden and every sort of convenience. Besides the factories which belong to the East India Company, there are others, the property of Chinese, who let them to Europe and Country Captains of ships, merchants and strangers whom business brings to Canton. For several years there has been an Imperial flag flying before a

factory occupied by the Germans. The Americans (whom the Chinese distinguish by the expressive title of Second Chop Englishmen) have also a flag.
(from the *Memoirs of William Hickey*, edited by Peter Quennell, London, Century, 1975)

Relations with the Chinese deteriorated as western traders chafed at their restriction and confinement (both physical and economic). Couling defines **'Opium War'** in his *Encyclopaedia Sinica* thus: 'a question-begging epithet ... The seizure of the opium by Commissioner Lin was the occasion of the war, but the causes were the insults, indignities, oppressions and injustices of all the years during which the British and others had sought legitimate trade with China ...' and he reflects the view of the expansionist West of the 19C. The Chinese could well define the Opium War in similar terms but stressing instead the continuous provocation of expansionist westerners who did not understand the traditional Chinese control of foreigners and trade, the frequent, sometimes murderous, brawls of western sailors and the determination of western traders (the British in particular) to pay for their purchases with addictive and illegal opium. The East India Company held the monopoloy of opium cultivation in Bengal and the opium was shipped to China and traded illegally. In 1839, Lin Zexu (see Fuzhou, pp 360 and 364) was appointed Opium Commissioner in Guangzhou and destroyed 20,000 chests of the drug there, provoking the despath of a British expeditionary fleet in 1840. The fleet blockaded ports, besieged Guangzhou and occupied much of the southern coast, forcing the Chinese to open more ports to trade through the Treaty of Nanjing (1842).

The **Second Opium War**, or Arrow War (Second Opium War, (1856) also took place in Guangzhou. When the Chinese authorities, in search of pirates, boarded a Chinese owned ship, the *Arrow*, which was flying a British flag (to enable it to sail into all Chinese coastal ports) the insult was described as an insult to the flag. The British Consul in Guangzhou, Sir Harry Parkes, ordered the occupation of the city by 1000 British troops. The incident was a useful pretext for revising and expanding the Treaty of Nanjing by means of the **Treaty of Tianjin** (1858) which gave foreigners the right to a permanent minister in Peking and further freedom to travel, trade and settle in the interior.

Parkes acquired the sandbank or mudflat known as Shamian (Sandbank) Island in the Pearl River in 1859. This was to become the major foreign settlement in Guangzhou and the best surviving collection of colonial buildings is now there, as the factories have disappeared.

Although the city was much marked by foreign influences and retains some of the arcaded shopping streets that are found in so many ex-colonial towns, after the 1911 Revolution it became an important nationalist centre, particularly since Sun Yatsen returned to the city to found the KMT in 1923, after the 1911 Revolution failed really to establish democratic government. The prestigious **Whampoa Military Academy** was founded in the suburbs in 1924 (with Chiang Kai-shek as head, Zhou Enlai as political commissar and the Russian General Galen as adviser) to improve the quality of leadership in the Nationalist Army. In 1923 the **Peasant Movement Institute** was set up by the Communist Party in the former Confucian temple in the east of the town and in 1925 the workers of the city went on strike in support of the Hong Kong workers, who were themselves on strike against the British.

Chiang Kai-shek, who had his base in Guangzhou, whence he set out on the Northern Expedition in an attempt to take the rest of China (in 1927), had some 5000 workers killed in the city in 1927.

In the late 1970s and 1980s, through its proximity to Hong Kong and the establishment of a 'special economic zone' based on nearby Shenzhen, Guangzhou saw a vast increase in sweat-shop work to boost the production of goods 'made in Hong Kong'. Its streets filled with traffic well before those of Shanghai and Peking, mainly because of the number of trade vehicles supplied from Hong Kong.

Shamian Island and the Market

The *White Swan Hotel* is on the waterfront of Shamian. Behind it is the old island where a few surviving colonial buildings crumble slowly in the damp. Under the vast banyan trees were the French Consulate (east tip), a British Consulate, whose bricked up Gothic windows now conceal a workshop, Protestant and Catholic churches. The French Catholic church has now been restored. There was a masonic lodge and there were several banks. In the past the gates beside the

Guangzhou: bicycle-/footbridge

bridges of the tiny island were closed every night at 22.00. On the quay, on the far side of the bridge at the east end of the island, a stone stele used to stand, commemorating Chinese workers killed by foreign bullets on the very spot in 1925.

Take the northern bridge from Shamian to the mainland (to Liuer san lu). A little to your right you will find the entrance to the **Qingling street market** which fills all the small streets north of Liuer san lu to Heping lu.

For those with strong stomachs, indifference to animal suffering and a total lack of enthusiasm for ecology and the protection of endangered species, it is possible to pass through the food section of the market and reach the *bonsai* and antiques sections to the north. I have never made it much beyond the first (medicine) section, as the sight of edible kittens is too much, but I understand that there are some handsome pots for sale and reasonable prices can be achieved by bargaining.

Retreating to Liuer san lu, turn left, heading towards Renmin lu. The **Wenhua gongyuan** (Cultural Park), opened in 1956, is on the left. In the evenings this is packed with people watching open-air entertainment, which includes some traditional forms like puppet shows, Cantonese opera and acrobats, as well as space-invader machines.

As the streets and all forms of public transport in Guangzhou are impossibly

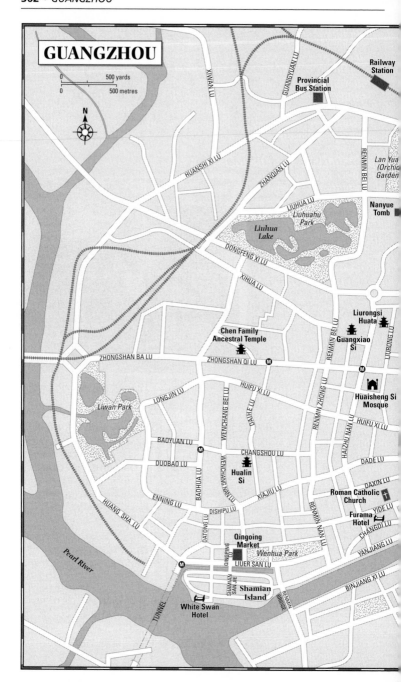

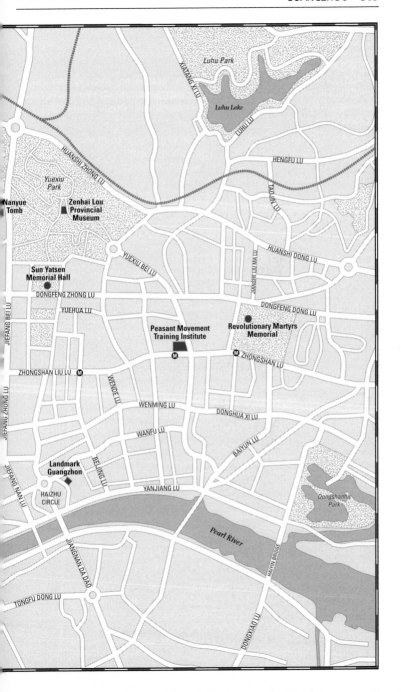

packed and distances are considerable, especially in the humid heat, it is better to visit other sites in groups by taxi.

Roman Catholic Cathedral

The Roman Catholic Cathedral (known locally as Shi shi or Stone Room) is at 56 Yide zhong lu. It stands on the ground once occupied by the old Chinese Viceroy's palace destroyed in an attack by French and British troops in the Arrow or Second Opium War.

Building started in 1860 to designs in the Gothic style by the French architect Guillemin and finished in 1880, although the cathedral was consecrated in 1863. The land was granted to the French in recompense for 'losses in the interior' incurred during the Arrow War and the resulting cathedral was described by J.A.Turner in his *Kwang Tung, or Five Years in South China* as: 'a fine Gothic building, which, with its magnificent granite spires, towers nobly above the dead level of the native houses, a grand example of "music in stone".' The bells in the adjacent tower were cast in France.

Peasant Movement Training Institute

The Peasant Movement Training Institute, where Mao Zedong was a tutor in 1925–26, is at Zhongshan lu Section 4.

This was founded in 1924 and its first head was Peng Pai (1896–1929), who came from a local landlord family but was one of the first Chinese Communists to work with the peasants rather than industrial workers, who were more politically correct in Marxist-Leninist terms. Peng Pai was betrayed and executed in 1929. The Peasant Institute was housed in the former Confucian temple of the Ming period, portions of which still remain; the rest of the dormitories and schoolrooms were those used by many of the great figures of the Communist Party—Mao Zedong, who became head of the Institute in 1926, Zhou Enlai, Qu Qiubai, Guo Moruo and Peng Pai—until the school was closed when Chiang Kai-shek turned on the Guangdong workers in 1927.

There is a rather wonderful display of revolutionary relics of peasant students and blurred photographs of associated events, with English captions.

South of the Peasant Training Institute on Yuexiu lu is the **Provincial Museum** (open 09.30–16.30), which has a variety of rather dusty displays. The ground floor is devoted to Guangzhou's industry and there is a surprising natural history section which stresses conservation (in contradiction to the sales in the Qingping market). There is a fine art section displaying porcelain, furniture and jade.

A little further along Zhongshan lu (Section 3) is the **memorial** to the 5000 workers killed at Chiang Kai-shek's orders on 13 December 1927.

Local workers, led by local Communist leaders, had set up the Canton Commune only two days before in outraged response to the massacre of the Shanghai workers, who had seized Shanghai in order to welcome Chiang Kai-shek and his Northern Expedition in the spring of the same year but had been mown down in their thousands in April. The monument was built in 1957 and consists of a grand gate and paved way which leads to a huge tumulus surrounded by a marble wall.

On Qingquan lu, opposite Yuexiu Park, set in the middle of a vast green lawn is an auditorium in the form of Peking's Temple of Heaven. This is the **Sun Yatsen Memorial Hall** built in 1931 on the site where in 1923 Sun was proclaimed head of the new government in Guangzhou, while the rest of the country was in the hands of others. There is a photographic exhibition commemmorating Sun Yatsen's life (no English captions).

On the northern side of Qingquan lu, in Yuexiu Park, is the **Memorial Tower to Sun Yatsen**, a granite obelisk with his last testament carved on the front. This was built in 1929.

Yuexiu Park

Yuexiu Park contains the Municipal Museum in the Zhenhai lou, the Five Rams statue and a theme park based on the *Journey to the West* (*Xiyuji*), the popular novel about Xuan zang's pilgrimage to India accompanied by a pig and a monkey (partially translated into English by Arthur Waley as *Monkey*) and it is in the throes of the construction of an 'American style water theme park' with water slides and a wave pool. Until such new attractions arrived, it was quite spacious and was a convenient place to re-site the tombs of local notables which had been displaced by building work. These include the tomb of one of the last members of the Ming imperial house who held out against the Qing in Guangzhou for 40 days in 1646 (his tomb was moved here in 1955) and Wang Xing (1615–59), a local Ming loyalist who defied the Qing until 1659 but committed suicide 'when his food ran out' (after 15 years).

The **Five Rams statue** (1959) commemorates the myth of Guangdong's foundation by five immortals who arrived riding on five rams and symbolically planted five sheaves of grain to ensure that famine would never strike in the area.

The 28m high **Zhenhai lou** (Pavilion Guarding the Sea; open 09.00–16.00, closed Mondays) was built in 1390 on a high point behind the town. It was intended as a watchtower, for during the early Ming, 'dwarf pirates' (as the Japanese were known) were a tremendous nuisance to China's coastal towns. According to one account, it was burnt down and rebuilt in 1686 and it was certainly restored in 1928 when much of the five storey timber structure was replaced by concrete. From the pavilion there is a fine view of the city, described rather oddly by Geil in 1911 as 'a most eclectic omelette into which many eggs have been broken'. He appears to have been referring to the 'winding alleys' which had been 'modified by the foreign trader' and affected (physically less) by the 'cross-currents produced by the foreign missionary'. The pavilion now contains exhibits relating to Guangzhou's trading history. These include good tomb models from local tombs as well as items relating to foreign trade in the Sui and Tang and to the development of industry in the Ming and Qing when Guangzhou was a silk centre (thanks partly to the support of an Overseas Chinese, Chen Qiyuan, who introduced machine-reeling in 1872). There is an extensive display devoted to the history of foreign repression in the area.

The **Nanyue Tomb** is to the west of Yuexiu Park (leave by the exit on Jiefang bei lu). The tomb was unearthed in 1983 during building work and is now housed in an unmissable red modern building.

The Nanyue was a short-lived local kingdom, established at the end of the Qin in 206 BC by the general, Zhao Tuo, who had been sent by the emperor to control the area on behalf of the Qin. By acknowledging Han suzerainty, he managed to retain his local power. On his death in 137 BC, his grandson, Zhao Mo, succeeded him but the Han were gradually closing in.

The tomb is that of Zhao Mo, who had himself buried in one of the famous jade burial suits made of thousands of tiny square jade plaques (it was believed that jade prevented bodily decay and offered the potential for immortality). The museum at the site contains marvellous tomb furnishings and a video in English.

Guangzhou's temples

Just off the western part of Zhongshan lu, Section 7, is the **Chen Family Ancestral Temple** (Chenjiaci), which now houses an exhibition of local crafts (Guangdong minjian gongyiyuan) where the exhibits are changed quite often.

The ancestral temple, built in 1890–94 with funds collected from the members of the Chen clan from 72 counties in Guangdong province, is a marvellous example of the highly decorated architecture of the south. In plan it resembles the temples in Macau, with a long front hall and courtyards on several parallel axes behind, the whole forming a long, broad but rather shallow rectangle. Northern temple complexes tend to concentrate on an emphatic central axis and are deep rather than broad in plan. The facade and roof of the first building are lavishly decorated with cut brickwork and fantastic glazed tile figures: operatic scenes, masses of gods and goddesses crowded on roofs and in grey tile panels. Inside the same lavish decoration is found, combined attractively with sombre timberwork. The openness of the halls of the interior is also characteristically southern and practical for ventilation in the humid climate. There are some fine, massive pieces of temple furniture but the halls are mainly occupied by exhibits of locally produced Shiwan pottery (often figures with a dark body and somewhat curdled glaze), carved peach stones and mother-of-pearl.

2km due south of the Chenjiaci is the **Hualin** (Flourishing Grove) **Temple**, founded in 526 and visited by the famous Indian monk Bodhidharma, inspirer of the Chan (Zen) sect, soon after its foundation. The present buildings date from the Qing and the most notable feature is the group of 500 lohans in the main hall, which is said to include Marco Polo in a broad-brimmed hat, to the right of the altar at the far end.

Guangzhou: the Chen Family Ancestral Temple

To the west of the Hualin Temple is the **Huaisheng** (Cherish the Sage) **Temple**, which is Guangzhou's mosque (56 Guangta lu). It is said to have been founded by one of the Prophet's uncles during the Tang dynasty and thus to be the earliest Muslim foundation in

China. Its minaret, known as the 'Smooth Pagoda' (Guangta) for its difference from many pagodas and, indeed, from many Chinese minarets in that it has no marked eaves ends; in fact, it is smooth and Islamic in form (and now rather dependent upon concrete). Although the mosque contains many early stone stelae, it was burnt down in the Yuan and the buildings are recent.

Not far south of the mosque on Xiangyang si lu, off Huifu xi lu, is the **Wuxian guan** (Five Immortals Temple), dedicated to the mythical founders of the city.

There had been temples devoted to the famous Five from the Northern Song but it was not until the Ming that the temple was built on its present site. The main hall is one of the few surviving Ming timber constructions in Guangzhou (1377). Stelae dating from the Song to the Qing record the history of the building and rebuilding of the temple.

In front of the gate are two Ming stone *qilin* (Chinese unicorns with scales). To the left of the main hall is a great stone with a depression on the top known as the 'Mother of the Immortals'; it is supposed to have been washed into its present position during a flood of the Pearl River in the Yuan dynasty.

North of the mosque are the two major temples of Guangzhou, the Liurong Temple (and Huata Pagoda) at 87 Liurong lu and the Guangxiao si at 109 Guangxiao lu.

The **Liurong** (Six Banyan Trees) **Temple** was founded in 537 to house some of the ashes of the Buddha which had been brought back to China by a monk called Tanyu, uncle of one of the founders of the Liang dynasty (502–557). The ashes were placed in the **Huata** (Decorated Pagoda).

Originally contemporary with the temple, the pagoda was burnt down in the 10C and rebuilt in 1097. During repairs in 1980 bricks with Northern Song inscriptions were discovered. The octagonal nine storey pagoda is 57m high; the bronze finial dates from 1358. There are extra floors (17 in all) concealed within the pagoda, which has a bizarre staircase to the top involving an exit onto each eaves level.

Owing to its proximity to the Pearl River and the marshy ground, the foundations of the pagoda had to be built on nine linked stone ring-wells, a construction technique called 'plum blossom piles' because the linked wells looked like the petals of plum flowers. The temple had several changes of name throughout its history but in 1099 the famous poet, painter of bamboo, calligrapher and local government official, Su Dongpo, temporarily in political disgrace and exiled southwards, visited the temple and, being struck by the banyan trees, wrote the characters *liu rong* (six banyans). His calligraphy, carved in wood, now hangs over the gateway and has given the temple its name.

The major buildings include the Guanyin Hall and the Hall of the Sixth Patriarch (of the Chan or Zen school of Buddhism). In the hall of the Sixth Patriarch is a bronze figure of the patriarch himself, cast in 989, and three 6m Buddha figures cast in 1663. In the Guanyin Hall there is a 4m Guanyin figure, cast at the same time as the Buddhas.

The **Guangxiao** (Glorious Filiality) **Temple** is said to have been founded during the Han dynasty, although at the time it was the palace of the last southern (Nanyue) king.

Its gardens were developed during the Three Kingdoms period when the palace was owned by a high official whose family turned it into a temple on his death. Many Indian monks came here to preach before and during the Tang dynasty; the monk Huineng achieved sudden enlightenment here in 676 and later achieved considerable eminence as the Sixth Patriarch of the Chan school. This happened in what is now the Shuifo ge (Sleeping Buddha Hall) where, when the local priest was discussing the sutras, other monks felt something that they explained either as a gust of wind or a flapping of banners but Huineng knew that it was a movement of the heart.

Although the temple was once far larger, with 12 great halls and six minor halls, amongst other buildings, the grandeur of the original enclosure is still evident.

Most of the buildings date from the last major repair of 1832, although the huge main hall with its unusual tapering rhomboidal pillars is still very striking. Behind the main hall are three important pagodas: the small (6.7m) seven storey Jingfa Pagoda, built in 676 over a hair of Huineng, the Sixth Patriarch and the surviving storeys of the Dongtie (Eastern Iron) Pagoda (963) and the Xitie (Western Iron) Pagoda (967), both made of gilt iron with 900 niches for Buddha figures. During the Cultural Revolution, when the major Buddha figures were destroyed, they were found to contain within them smaller wooden figures dating from the Tang dynasty (now in the City Museum). Most Buddhist figures conceal relics, whether sutras or figures, but these were particularly important because of their early date.

North of these temples, on the other side of Jiefang bei lu from Yuexiu Park, is the **Orchid Garden** (Lan Yuan). It occupies part of the site of the old **Muslim burial ground**, which can be reached by walking round the outside of the park (turn right and right again) to the northwest. The graveyard contains a tomb said to be that of the Prophet's uncle, Abu Waqas, who is credited with bringing Islam to China (see the Huaisheng Mosque, p 366), although the dates are rather difficult to reconcile. His tomb is housed in a small stone building (usually locked) surrounded by other stone graves, all roughly oriented towards Mecca, and banyan trees.

The Orchid Garden contains more than 10,000 pots of orchids with varyingly ornate blooms and names like Silver-bordered Bodhisattva or Great Phoenix Tail. It is a quiet and pleasant garden full of pools and bamboos where you can also drink orchid tea.

Foshan

Foshan (Hill of the Buddhas), 20km southeast of Guangzhou, is a town which has been famous since the Song dynasty for its ceramic production (Shiwan ware), although excavations reveal that production flourished earlier, during the Han dynasty. The most characteristic wares are figurines in dark reddish clay covered in thick grey-blue glaze. It is possible to visit the ceramic factories by arrangement with the *China Travel Service*. The factories are divided: most of the kilns produce both utilitarian wares (drain-pipes, flowerpots) and figures.

The town is also known for its paper-cuts, which are made and sold in the

Foshan Folk Art Studio housed in a former Ming temple, Renshou (Benevolence and Longevity) Temple, on Zumiao lu.

The **Zuci miao** (Ancestral Temple) is in the south of the town. Founded in the Northern Song, it was extensively rebuilt in 1372 and many times in subsequent years.

> The temple is a Taoist foundation with no connection to the Confucian ancestral cult; it is called the Ancestral Temple because it is the oldest temple in Foshan. It is dedicated to the worship of the emperor of the north, Xuandi, Lord of the Black Pavilions of Heaven. Xuandi, a warrior king, was rewarded for his demon-slaying with honorific titles and positions and is often represented with a turtle and snake, symbols of the north for Taoists.

The surviving buildings, covering an area of 3000 square metres, date from the Ming and Qing and are most notable for the extraordinary elaboration of timber carving and roof decoration. Covered in Shiwan ceramic figures, illustrating famous scenes from history and folklore, the over-decorated roofs are characteristic of the southern provinces, a 'triumph of the artisan' according to the *Zhongguo mingsheng cidian* (*Dictionary of Famous Sites in China*). The Lingying *pailou* is another highly carved southern style construction.

Jinan

Jinan, capital city of Shandong province in east China, is a city with a long history, incorporating Neolithic sites and 19C German architecture. Its name means 'south of the river crossing' and it is c 5km south of the Yellow River.

The name dates from the 3C–4C AD when Jinan was part of a commandery of that name. At the time the Yellow River flowed north of the peninsula, much as it does now, but it has changed its course many times over the centuries as it overflowed from its silted bed. The silt that it carries down from the loess highlands gives it its name, Yellow River, and the disastrous changes of course caused by the silt have given rise to another name for the river, 'China's Sorrow'. The major changes of course took place in the Shandong area where it neared the sea; the last disastrous change was in 1851, when it shifted its mouth from south to north of the peninsula (a distance of some 350km), flooding everything in between.

Jinan has long been a major trading centre; its city walls (no longer extant) were built during the Ming and after the Germans obtained rights to build the Shandong railways in 1898 the city was opened to foreign trade (in 1906), for once without a treaty consequent upon some foreign incursion. It is famous for its natural springs, around which gardens have been constructed; it has a particularly interesting provincial museum and not far away is the earliest known pagoda in China.

Practical information

Getting there
By air

The airport is 40km to the east of the town. Shuttle buses drop visitors at the *CAAC* office at 348 Jinger wei lu. Taxis cost 150 yuan.

By train

Jinan is on the main route south from Peking to Shanghai and Nanjing; the railway station was of particular interest as it was a German construction more appropriate to Bavaria. Alas, it has been demolished.

Where to stay

Main hotels are the *Jinan Hotel* at 240 Jingsan lu, ☎ 793 8981, not far south of the railway station, the *Guidu Hotel* at 1 Shengping lu, ☎ 6900 888, fax 6900 099, in the same area and the *Nanjiao Guesthouse* at 2 Ma'anshan lu, ☎ 295 3931, fax 295 3957, in the southern suburbs, not too far from the Thousand Buddha Cliff but a long way from anywhere else.

The town itself is not picturesque in a Chinese way but contains a diminishing amount of German and Japanese architecture of the late 19C and early 20C, much of it solid administrative building, all in the European style favoured by the Japanese at the time. It is disappearing fast in favour of badly built 'international style' blocks. Sites to visit in Jinan are rather spread out and best visited by taxi.

History

German influence in Shandong province dates from the occupation of Qingdao in 1897. The harbour had long been coveted by Germany and it is said that the gunboat *Iltis*, which went down in a typhoon off the coast of Shandong on 23 July 1896, might have been making for Qingdao. Of the 89 crew members 77 went down with the ship, singing to the Kaiser and the flag as they sank; the accident was commemorated in a 'handsome monument on the Bund at Shanghai' which no longer stands.

As in so many other cases, the murder of two German missionaries (Fathers Nies and Henle) in Shandong gave the Germans the pretext they sought 'for violent action' and they used three warships under the command of Admiral Diederichs to take Qingdao on 14 November 1897. Prince Henry of Prussia was sent to take command after a farewell banquet in Kiel where the Kaiser made his notorious reference to the imposition of policy by means of 'mailed fist' (*'fahre darein mit gepanzerter Faust'*). Under such duress, the Chinese were compelled to sign a treaty, leasing c 50,000 hectares (about 193 square miles) of land around Qingdao and allowing a considerable 'sphere of influence' in the province. The Qingdao–Jinan railway was built by the Germans and completed in 1904.

Japan's interest in the area was no doubt as old as that of Germany, if not older, but her real chance came in 1914, when the First World War broke out. Acting under her treaty of alliance with Great Britain, **Japan** demanded that German warships at Qingdao be disarmed and eventually declared war, capturing Qingdao in November 1914. At the end of the war Japan's interests in the area, part of her 21 demands made to President Yuan Shikai in 1915, were recognised by Russia, Great Britain, France and Italy, and Japan took over the old German 'concessions'. Recognition was a complex affair: in return for a massive loan, Yuan Shikai conceded Japan's demand for control of Shandong, Manchuria (Dongbei), Inner Mongolia and the southeast coast and Yangtse valley, although he refused to agree to purchase 50 per cent of China's munitions from Japan or to employ Japanese 'advisers' throughout the Chinese administration. This had some influence on the western powers at Versailles, although the Chinese delegation there fiercely contested Japan's 'rights' in Shandong. Failure to resist the Japanese demands led to the wave of nationalist demonstrations known as the 'May Fourth Movement' (beginning with a demonstration by Peking students on 4 May 1919) which had a profound effect on subsequent Chinese cultural development. Nevertheless, the Japanese reigned in much of Shandong until the end of the Second World War, as their architectural remains demonstrate.

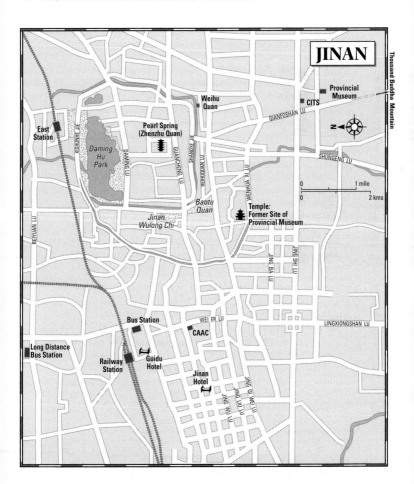

The site of the old **city walls** of Jinan, built in the Ming, can be traced in the course of the moat that still runs around the north of Daming hu Park and along Baotuquan lu (west) and Heihuquan lu (south). Two of the 72 springs said to rise in the area and that gave Jinan a reputation for cleanliness and healthfulness—mentioned in the *Japanese Railway Guide* of 1924, which also praised the 'generally salubrious' climate—can be found at the southwest and southeast corners of the old city wall. The **Baotu quan** (Fountain Spring), just outside the southeast corner of the old city, is the 'first' of the 72 springs and illustrates an interesting variation on northern garden design.

As greenery is lacking for much of the year in the cold north, the bubbling surface of the pool in which the spring rises is made the focus of the garden. Water surfaces are also important in southern gardens (where they should not be too much obscured by lily leaves to allow for the sight of clouds reflected and the play of wind on the surface) but in a northern garden on an overcast day when trees are bare, the constant bubbling of a spring and movement of water provide a major focus.

The focus of the park, which actually contains some 16 springs, lies in the three springs that rise in a squarish pool surrounded by stone railings. The spring was first mentioned in the *Spring and Autumn Annals* with reference to a meeting of nobles that took place here in 694 BC and in the notes to the *Classic of Water* the spring is described as 'bursting forth, bubbling as if turned by a wheel'. On the north side is a pavilion, the **Luoyuan tang** (Hall of the Source of the Luo), first built in the Song and rebuilt in the Qing; it is decorated with a couplet inscribed by the calligrapher and painter of the Yuan period, Zhao Mengfu (1254–1322), who is best known for his paintings of horses. The couplet reads: 'Clouds and mist in damp vapours, glory unfixed; the sound of the waves thunders in the Lake of Great Brightness'.

In the southwest corner is the **Guanlan ting** (Pavilion for Viewing the Waves) over a central stele which reads 'Baotu quan', with two other inscriptions, 'Wave Pavilion' and 'The First Spring'. The stone-carved inscriptions all date from the Ming and Qing. On the eastern side is a bridge with a tea house. The bridge is called 'Bridge of Arriving Cranes' and the teahouse 'Looking at Cranes'.

Li Qingzhao and Ci versification

Li Qingzhao (1084–1151) was born in Jinan and married the scholar and poet Zhao Mingcheng. She was herself an accomplished poet and painter and she helped her husband to compile the *Jin shi lu* (*Record of Bronze and Stone*), a compilation of inscriptions on the afore-mentioned bronze vessels and stone stelae. When her husband died in 1129, Li Qingzhao's most famous *ci* (poems) were composed; they broke new ground, for the *ci* form had more commonly been used to praise courtesans than to commemorate conjugality.

The *ci* is a verse form with different line lengths, its most important characteristic being that the poems were intended to be sung and were written to well-known tunes, the music dictating the rhythm.

In the east of the garden area, which contains a fine bonsai garden with many little old conifers grown in lovely blue and white pots, is the **Hall to Commemorate Li Qingzhao**. Built in 1956 and restored in 1980, the hall was constructed 'in the ancient style, but using steel frame and concrete'. In the halls surrounding the courtyard are portraits and extracts from literary accounts of the life and the works of one of China's most famous woman poets, Li Qingzhao. There are also poems and paintings by famous modern persons, including the polymath Guo Moruo (see Leshan, p 572) and Ye Shengtao, who died in 1988 at a very venerable age. Ye Shengtao was a short-story writer, educationalist and children's writer, associated with the vernacular fiction that developed after the May Fourth Movement of 1919.

Not far south of the Baotu quan, at 103 Wenhua xi lu, is a pleasant **old temple** which used to house the Shandong Provincial Museum, whose contents have now been moved to the outskirts of the city, near the Thousand Buddha Mountain. The museum in the temple was the first provincial museum to be opened after Liberation in 1956.

The **Heihu quan** (Black Tiger Spring) is on Heihuquan dong lu, at the southwest corner of the old city moat. It has been known by that name since before the Jin (1115–1234) and it rises in a cave from which it emerges through three stone tigerhead spouts. A Ming poem on the 72 springs of Jinan describes it: 'Twisted stones in the water mansion where all is green, green the depths are dark and murky like the lair of a tiger; at midnight when the cold wind blows, the stone splits, one resounding crack and the moon is dark'.

Nearby 14 more springs rise, forming a stream. These include the **Pipa Spring** which emerges from holes in grey rock and is said to sound like the stringed *pipa*—a sort of lute—at night, the **Jizhong Spring** ('Deep in a Gully' Spring) which rises to the surface in a square pool (it is also known as the Waterlily Spring) and the **Nine Women Spring** where nine fairy women were supposed to come at night to bathe and wash silk.

500m away is the **Five-Dragon Pool** (Wulong tan) formed by five springs where the king of a barbarian country was said to live in the Tang dynasty.

The northern wall of the old city enclosed the Daming hu (Lake of Great Brightness) Park, entered from Daminghu lu. The name was originally used in reference to another lake, further to the north, now covered by streets, so during the Jin (1115–1234) the name was transferred.

Describing the old city of Jinan in the Qing, Li Fenggao wrote: 'Waterlilies on four sides, willows on three, half the city is mountain, the other half lake'. The park incorporates several small gardens, including the **Xia yuan** (Distant Garden) built in 1909 in the south and the **Xiao canglang** (Small Blue Waves Garden) built in 1792 in the northwest, which offers a view of the distant Thousand-Buddha Mountain. This was described in the late Qing novel *The Travels of Lao Can* (or *Ts'an*) by Liu E as being 'like a screen painting ten miles long with a thousand Buddhas painted by a Song master'. The little pavilions are beautifully made, models of the sort of places in which scholars used to entertain their friends. One is carved with the words of Li Fenggao and there are other inscriptions carved in stone by Qing scholars, including Ruan Yuan and Liang Tongshu.

On the island is the **Lixia ting** (Historic Pavilion) where the Tang poet Du Fu is supposed to have met Li Yong, a calligrapher and local official, a meeting commemorated in a poem. The present pavilion, successor to Song, Yuan and Ming buildings, which were on a different site, dates from the Qing. On the gate are lines from Du Fu's poem, written by the Qing calligrapher He Shaoji: 'This pavilion stands to the right of the sea; there are many famous men in Jinan'. Inside the pavilion are portraits of Du Fu and Li Yong and behind the pavilion is a couplet by Guo Moruo (see above): 'Willows in the spring wind, music from all sides; lotus in the autumn moon, great brightness'. On the south side of the lake is the **Memorial Hall to Xin Qiji** (Xin Qiji ji nian ci).

Xin Qiji

Xin Qiji (1140–1207), a native of the nearby town of Licheng, was a famous *ci* poet of the Southern Song. He was also an official and an anti-Jin patriot, opposing the invasion of the north by the Jin and the failure of the Song to resist. He was banished for his memorials to the throne criticising its weakness in repelling the invaders.

The hall was built in 1961 and rebuilt in 1980, like the Li Qingzhao memorial hall, 'in the style of an ordinary house' with two courtyards and exhibition halls filled with commemorative calligraphy by famous contemporary figures. The main inscriptions are by Chen Yi (1901–72), an outstanding military commander, General of the New Fourth Army and later mayor of Shanghai, and Ye Shengtao (see above).

The pillars in the main hall are embellished with lines written by the omnipresent Guo Moruo; they refer to loyalty to the Song through a thicket of classical allusion: 'Iron columns and the bronze pipa continue the song of Su Dongpo to the east of the Great River; beautiful celery and tragic millet hope that the Southern Song can fly south with the wild goose.' Without following every reference in this over-crammed couplet, suffice to say that celery is first associated with beauty in the *Lu shi chun qiu* (*Spring and Autumn Annals*) of Master Lu, a late Zhou text (c 1066–221 BC).

The **Pearl Spring** (Zhenzhu quan) on the north side of Quancheng lu is said to bubble up like pearls in its square pool.

In his *Record of the Pearl Spring* Wang Chang said: 'The spring rises from sand, suddenly gathers, suddenly disperses, suddenly stops, suddenly continues, suddenly speeds, suddenly slows. In the sunlight the larger bubbles are like pearls, the smaller like seed pearls, rising from the depths.' The site of the spring used to be occupied by a government office and in the Chenghua reign of the Ming (1465–87) one of the members of the royal family built a residence by the spring. In 1666 it became a government office and later a military headquarters. In the *Gu ji ming sheng ce dian* (*Dictionary of Famous Sites*) a line from Liu E's late Qing novel *The Travels of Lao Can* is used in reference to this spring, which gathers with others to flow into the Daming Lake, and others in Jinan: 'A spring in every house, willows hanging over every home'.

The **Nanda si Mosque** is in Libai si jie. The name of the street can be translated either as 'week' or 'religious devotions' and is often used in reference to Muslims with their daily prayers at fixed hours. The mosque was founded in the Yuan and last restored during the Republican period (1911–49). The main hall, part of a large complex, is raised on a 4.2m high platform and composed of three linked parts. The roofs are black tiled and the windows in particular are highly decorated, incorporating Arabic inscriptions.

Shandong Provincial Museum

On the southern outskirts of the city, 2.5km from the centre, is the Thousand Buddha Mountain (Qianfo shan), not far from the Nanjiao Hotel (see below). At the approach to the mountain is the new Shandong Provincial Museum. The exhibitions undergo occasional rearrangement. The sculpture exhibit is particularly fine, with many very early Buddhist carvings, many originally free-standing shrine-like pieces with inscriptions on the back, as opposed to sculptures hacked out of cave temples. Many date back to just after the Han dynasty, revealing the speed with which Buddhism travelled to the eastern extremity of China. The sculptures vary from competent pieces in the Indian style to cruder, livelier pieces presumably by local sculptors, which often incorporate in the lower registers linked figures that recall the low-relief stone carvings in the well-known Han tombs of the area. When last seen, the exhibit was been arranged by type of sculpture rather than being part of the usual wide-ranging chronological display.

It is hardly surprising that a noted epigrapher, **Zhao Mingcheng** (husband of Li Qingzhao), should be associated with Jinan and Shandong, for the low reliefs of local Han tombs have long been admired. The tombs were lined with stone blocks, carved with mythological scenes of deities and dragons in the heavens, men banqueting or driving chariots in the earthly realm and strange fish- or serpent-tailed monsters in the lower depths. In content, whether mythological or baronial, these contrast strongly with the contemporary tomb bricks of clay made in Sichuan (best seen in the Chongqing Museum, also in the Sichuan Provincial Museum in Chengdu) which frequently depict scenes of daily life, including salt-mining, agriculture and hunting. The tombs were based on the same principle, underground and lined, but the stone slabs of Shandong provide a more frieze-like decoration than the squarer, more pictorial Sichuan bricks. Originals and rubbings from these Han tombs are to be found in the museum.

One of the most famous series of exhibits is that of the excavations at **Longshan** and **Dawenkou**, two Neolithic sites in the province. Longshan zhen (Dragon Mountain Village) in Shandong, where a Neolithic site was first discovered in 1928, has given its name to a group of later Neolithic sites, the 'Lungshanoid (or black pottery) cultures' and which have, incidentally, given rise to what archaeologists call 'the Lungshanoid problem'.

Longshan culture

Characterised by a strange, burnished black pottery, often fashioned into tripod shapes, the Longshan (or Lungshan in Wade-Giles romanisation) culture seems to anticipate the Bronze Age in vessel forms and use of scapulimancy (divination by means of the cracks appearing in a burning shoulder blade). The 'Lungshanoid problem' was that of the relation between what appeared to be two cultures in the Chinese Neolithic, the red pottery culture, sometimes called Yangshao, and the black pottery, or Longshan, culture. The fact that some sites have conveniently been sandwiched between a red pottery stratum and a later Bronze Age stratum has led some archaeologists obsessed with neatness to assume that this was the pattern of development everywhere in China. As more Neolithic sites are uncovered, the pattern has become less simple and there is now a greater stress on regional development rather than the simple relation between the two early sites.

The Longshan remains from Shandong have been dated to c 5000–2000 BC and comprise the famous thin, wheel-made, burnished black pottery wares, large numbers of stone and shell implements apparently designed for agriculture rather than hunting—in contrast with the mainly hunting tools of many Yangshao sites—and pig, dog, cattle and sheep bones, indicating widespread domestication and settled agriculture. Scapulimancy, jade-carving, class-distinctions manifested in different types of burial and some form of ancestor worship, apparently conducted by specialised persons, all indicate a fairly highly-developed, settled way of life anticipating many forms that persisted in the subsequent Bronze Age.

The Dawenkou remains, typographically associated with sites in northern Jiangsu, were unearthed in 1959. They probably date from between 4000 and 2000 BC and are of the 'Lungshanoid' type, although they show a development from red pottery to a wheel-made, black polished type.

Other important exhibits include the inscribed bamboo slips from a Han tomb at Yinque shan (Silver Sparrow Mountain). These include a full calendar for the year 134 BC, which thus provides a date for the entombment, the text of the *Sun Bin bing fa* (*Sun Bin's Art of War*), lost for some 1700 years, and other military and philosophical texts. Written with a brush and ink on thin strips of bamboo which were threaded together, these represent the earliest form of 'book' in China, antedating the use of paper which was known at the time but clearly not in common use. There is also a fine set of 406 wooden tomb figures, which have lost their paint, from the tomb of the tenth son of the founder of the Ming dynasty, enfeoffed as the King of Lu (Lu is the old name for Shandong). He died in 1389 at the age of 19 and his tomb, which was near Qu Fu, was excavated in 1970–71.

Thousand Buddha Mountain

Legend has it that the mythical Emperor Shun ploughed the soil here. Shun, successor to Yao, is supposed to have reigned from 2317–2208 BC and was held up as an example of filial piety, despite the fact that his father kept trying to kill him as he preferred his second son. He is supposed to have had double pupils to his eyes and to have invented the writing brush. Together with the Emperor Yao he is, in the words of Sellars and Yeatman, generally considered to be 'a Good Thing'.

A group of Sui carvings made between 581 and 600 are reached up 300 steps behind the **Xingguo si** (Temple of the Flourishing State), founded 627–649. The main carvings are on a cliff above the temple, although there are others in the Dragon Spring and other caves below.

In the eastern courtyard of the temple are sculptures of the Emperor Shun and his two wives (Yao's daughters). Nearby is a Ming pavilion, the **Lan ting** (Viewing Pavilion), which affords a view of the city, Daming Lake (like a mirror) and the Yellow River (like a belt), according to a Chinese guidebook.

Not far from Jinan, a few kilometres west–northwest, is the town of **Li cheng**. In the surrounding country are a number of Buddhist sites, some of whose carvings can be seen in the provincial museum in Jinan.

The Big Buddha Head (Dafotou zao xiang) is on **Fo hui shan** (Buddha Wisdom Mountain), 3.5km north of Jinan. The head, 7.8m high and 5.35m wide, was carved in 1035. There are Ming inscriptions on the west and two small pagodas carved on the east wall of the cave.

Carvings at the Dafo si (Big Buddha Temple) may be found on the southern slopes of the **Qing tong shan** (Bronze Mountain) in Li cheng county. The temple has disappeared but there is a Tang Buddha figure 9.05m high, with smaller attendants. On the platform in front of the Buddha are stone incense burners and an altar table, as well as three much-respected old cypress trees.

In the southeast of Li cheng county is the **Longdong shan** (Dragon Cave Mountain). It is said that the Great Yu ascended the mountain to request that the dragon help him control the waters and the cave has long been a place to which local farmers came to pray for rain. Inside the cave is a spring where the dragon is supposed to live; on either side of the entrance is the couplet: 'True spirit and the forest springs thickly up; spiritual achievements borrow from the primaeval chaos'. Below are the remains of the Sage Longevity Hall whose name and a record of imperial order for its construction was perhaps inscribed by the Song dynasty poet, bamboo painter, calligrapher and official Su Shi (Su Dongpo). Stone carvings on the mountain date from the mid 6C to the Tang; they are at first rather straight and narrow but grow increasingly sinuous in the Tang.

On **Qinglong shan** (Green Dragon Mountain), near Linbu cun in Li cheng county, is the earliest extant stone pagoda in China, the **Simen ta** (Four-Door Pagoda). Originally thought to have been constructed in 544 (according to an inscription inside), restoration of the top part in 1972 revealed a date of 611. 15m high, it is constructed from large slabs of stone and is a square building with arched doors in each side, hence the name. It has a decorative crown and a central stone pillar inside carved with Buddha figures.

Northwest of the Simen ta on **Baihu shan** (White Tiger Mountain) is the more decorative **Longhu ta** (Dragon Tiger Pagoda), possibly Song in date and associated with over 200 stone-carved figures from early Tang to Ming. They include emperors, officials, monks, three princesses, horses and figures of commoners apparently carved as part of a rain-seeking cult.

On **Lingjin shan** all that remains of the Nine-Pagoda Temple (Jiuta si) is the **Nine-pagoda Pagoda**, a 13m high Tang dynasty pagoda with nine little pagodas of great charm on the roof.

Tai shan

Tai shan (Honourable Mountain) in Shandong province has a religious significance that goes back beyond Confucianism and Taoism to the earliest cults. It is otherwise known as the Eastern Peak and is the most significant of the Five Holy Mountains loosely associated with the imperial cult and Taoism, not to be confused with the Four Buddhist Mountains. Tai'an town is at the foot of Tai shan.

Practical information

Getting there
By train
Tai'an is on the main line from Jinan to Nanjing and Shanghai and slower trains stop there (it is just over an hour by rail from Jinan).

By bus
Tai shan and the town at its foot, **Tai'an**, can be reached by bus or car from either Jinan or Qu Fu (it is about 70km from both).

Where to stay
The *Tai shan (Binguan) Guesthouse*, on Hongmen lu, ☎ 822 4678, fax 822 1432, is c 5km from the railway station, near the bottom of the central route up the mountain. On top of the mountain is the *Shenqi Binguan*, ☎ 822 3866.

The significance of the mountains

The Five Holy Mountains are: Tai shan, the eastern and most important for all life (like the sun) was thought to emanate from the east; Heng shan (southern) in Hunan; Hua shan (western) in Shaanxi; Heng shan (northern) in Shanxi; and Song shan (central) in Henan. They represent the five 'directions' sacred to the Chinese (north, south, east, west and centre) and this explains their imperial significance. The emperor came to be viewed as the son of heaven, a representative of heaven on earth and he lived at the centre of his realm. Every so often, he would 'beat the bounds' of his domain by visiting the mountains on the edge of it in order to commune with gods.

Mountains in general were seen as the abode of gods and spirits, particularly those associated with rain, whose timeliness and sufficiency was essential to the maintenance of the agricultural order upon which the livelihood of all (including the emperor who lived off agricultural taxes) was based. The association of mountains, whose summits are cloud-covered, with rain and rain-bearing dragons is logical. The size and weight of a mountain was also considered important in maintaining the stability of the earth and preventing earthquakes. The emperor's right to rule was conveyed by heaven and depended upon heaven's pleasure: if all was well, the people well-fed and content, then heaven allowed the emperor to continue. Manifestations of heaven's displeasure were earthquakes, disastrous floods and droughts, all of which could be seen to be connected with mountains. Thus the emperor would pay his respects to mountains and, since the Five Mountains in particular were considered to be gods in their own right, effectively attempt to rule together with the mountains.

History

According to **Sima Qian** (d. c 90 BC), the great historian of the Han period, as early as the Zhou the Five Mountains were regarded as the equals of the three dukes. In 725 AD the emperor granted Tai shan the title of King Equal to the Sky (*tian qi wang*). In 1101 the mountain was promoted to emperor.

There were numerous imperial visits to Tai shan throughout the centuries, although the great imperial ceremonies of *feng* (sacrifice to the earth, performed at the base of the mountain) and *shan* (sacrifice to the sky, performed at the summit) were last carried out in 1008. It is said that when the first emperor of the Qin came to sacrifice here in 219 BC, he had to shelter from a storm on the way down and was so grateful to the tree he had stood under that he made it an officer of the fifth rank.

Aside from the imperial cult celebrated in stelae, there were an enormous number of local and popular cults relating to Tai shan. Houses built in traditional Peking had the first stone in the foundations inscribed with the name of the mountain as a protection against the structure falling down and blind alleys in the capital often had a Tai shan stone set up in them to deter evil spirits. The easternness of the mountain, its source of life, meant that emperors prayed to Tai shan for sons and many childless women (some sadly elderly) still make pilgrimages to the mountain, offering incense and money at special shrines. One of the favoured deities of the mountain is the Princess of the Rosy Clouds (Bixia yuan jun), who became a sort of northern, roughly Taoist equivalent of the Bodhisattva Guan yin (the popular Buddhist 'goddess of mercy' who lived on the southern Buddhist mountain, Putuo shan). With the princess, two other females are often depicted, one holding an eye in her hand. She is the Eye Maiden (Yan jing niang niang) and is worshipped by those with eye problems. It was also believed that the souls of the dead gathered at the foot of Tai shan and that the mountain presided over their fate like the Buddhist Ksitigarbha at Jiuhua shan in Anhui. The cult of the eastern peak was such that most cities had a Dongyue miao (Eastern Peak Temple) with statues of judges and depictions of the torture of hell, where people would make offerings in the hope of avoiding them, in a Taoist borrowing from popular Buddhism.

Near the town of Tai'an, at the foot of the mountain in Dawenkou cun, the remains of an important late Neolithic site were discovered in 1959. The remains are sufficiently distinctive to be described as a 'culture' (the Dawenkou culture), although they are of the Longshanoid type (see Jinan, p 375).

The major building in Tai'an is the **Dai miao** (Tai shan Temple, using an old name for the mountain, *dai*), constructed for the use of emperors coming to make sacrifices and offerings to the mountain. There was apparently a temple on the site in the Han, rebuilt in the Tang and Song—in 1122 it was described as having 813 buildings and rooms—and in all succeeding dynasties. The temple is entered through a great *pailou*, **Dongyue fang** (Gate of the Eastern Peak), built in 1672 at the order of the Kangxi emperor. It is very much a conglomerate of beliefs, including many stelae commemorating imperial venerations as well as separate Taoist halls devoted to the 'wife of the mountain', a deity who 'appeared much later than her husband' which must have been inconvenient. She is commemorated in a hall at the rear of the temple.

In a side courtyard at the back is the **Temple of Yanxi**, a Taoist who lived on the mountain and who was linked to the cult of the mountain in the Tang dynasty. The great main hall, **Tianpei dian** (Hall of Heaven's Associate), is on the main axis, beyond a courtyard filled with stelae, which include one commemorating the mountain's elevation to emperorhood (1013). One of the most important stelae, carved in 209 BC and recording a visit of the second emperor of the Qin, is in the east courtyard, although only a minute fragment of the original seal-script inscription was discovered in 1815 to have survived the fires that destroyed its 'protecting' temple which originally stood on the summit. Two Ming bronze lions stand in front of the nine bay main hall, which was first built in

1009 and despite much restoration since is said to preserve the Song style. It stands on a carved white stone platform and the roof is covered with yellow glazed tiles. Inside is a wall painting, supposed to be Song in date, illustrating the mountain, its peaks, clouds, animals and spirits.

In the rear courtyard are two metal 'pagodas': the **Bronze Pavilion** and the **Iron Pagoda**. They originally stood elsewhere (the Bronze Pavilion on the summit of the mountain) but were moved here in the early 1970s, presumably for reasons of preservation. The Bronze Pavilion was cast in 1615 to house a figure of the Princess of the Rosy Clouds; the casting imitates wooden architectural construction perfectly. 4.4m high, 3.4m wide, it is one of several examples of cast bronze pavilions surviving in China. The Iron Pagoda was cast in 1533, a hexagonal, 13-storey tower, although only the three lower storeys survive today.

> The second courtyard of the temple was, apparently, once lined with cubicles serving as 'judgement seats', presumably used in ceremonies linked to significance of the mountain's judgement of souls, and the ancient trees in the side courtyards are said to have been planted by the Martial Emperor of the Han in 110 BC.

• **Climbing the mountain** The mountain, stepped like all holy mountains in China, is now provided with a cable car. In contemplating your ascent, which will take four to five hours for the middling fit, bear in mind that for larger western feet (even those of ladies), the 5500 narrow, unstable steps are more uncomfortable to descend. Ascent may leave you breathless but descent tends to paralyse the thigh muscles for days. If possible, I would use the cable car for the descent. The cable car to the summit starts about half-way up the mountain at the Zhongtian men (Gate of Middle Heaven), which can be reached by bus or taxi.

The mountain begins with a stone *pailou*, the **Daizong fang** (Gate of the Mountain Ancestor), built in the mid 16C and rebuilt in 1730, bearing the inscription 'Yi tian men' (First Gate to Heaven). Beyond, to the right is the Laojun tang (Hall of Prince Lao or Laozi).

Prince Laozi

One of the major writers of the early Daoist faith, Prince Laozi is depicted in the hall with two disciples, one of whom may be the mysterious disappearing frontier guard who prompted him to write the *Dao de jing* (*Classic of the Way and of Virtue*). He was said to have been tired of the world and had set off on an old buffalo to escape, when he met a guard at the frontier. After earnestly requesting him to return to philosophy, the guard disappeared. The fact that a recently excavated example has the two parts of the work in the reverse order means that we should now consider calling it the *De dao jing* (*Classic of Virtue and the Way*), which is a bit like having to reverse the order of the books in the Bible.

In the courtyard of the temple are two stelae under the same capital—the **Mandarin Ducks Stelae**, or Yuanyang bei—with poems and lists of names dating from 661 to 698.

Just beyond, to the right of the main path, is the Wangmu chi (Pool of the Heavenly Queen) in the forecourt of a small nunnery. The pool is one of the 'scenic spots' of the mountain and the founding date of the nunnery is uncertain—a poem of the Wei (3C AD) suggests that there was a house, rather than a temple, nearby. There is now a two-courtyard temple of Ming-Qing date. In the main hall is a statue of the **Xiwang mu** (Queen Mother of the West, the major female deity in Taoism); in the hall behind is a statue of the famous Daoist immortal Lu Dongbin.

> ### Lu Dongbin
> A real person, Lu Dongbin was born into an official family in 755. Legend recounts, however, that when he was 20 he went to Lu shan and met a dragon who gave him a magic sword which enabled him to fly. He devoted the rest of his life to various magical feats and practices around which countless legends have grown up.

The real starting point for the mountain is the **Hongmen guan** (Hall of the Red Gate) built in 1626, just northwest of the Pool of the Heavenly Queen (and it is here that you buy your ticket for the ascent). There was an earlier gate here but its dates are uncertain. The name is taken from the reddish stones nearby which appear to form a natural arched gate. The western hall is dedicated to the Princess of the Rosy Clouds, the eastern one used to be dedicated to Amitabha Buddha.

North is the **Wanxian lou** (Tower of the Myriad Spirits), built over the path in 1620 and restored in 1954. Stone-carved inscriptions are set into the walls, some mentioning the clumps of bamboo that surrounded the tower: 'Slow grow the ancient bamboos, rooted in Tai shan'. To the right, just below the tower is the **Tomb of the White Mule** (Bailuo zhong), said to be where the white mule that had carried the Tang emperor, Xuan zong, up and down the mountain in 726 dropped dead after finishing its task. The emperor posthumously gave it the title of general and had it buried here with pomp.

North of the Wanxian lou, on the west side of the path, is a two-character inscription with an incomprehensible first character followed by the character for the number two. The first character is made up of parts of the characters for moon and wind and refers to a four-character phrase, 'moon and wind without limit', which means that this spot is one of unrivalled scenery. The inscription was carved in 1899 by a scholar from Jinan, Liu Yangui.

Passing a memorial to the martyrs of the Liberation struggle, the next building is the **Doumu gong** (Temple of the Goddess of the Great Bear), lived in by Taoist nuns. Its date of founding is uncertain but it was rebuilt and given its present name in the Jiaqing reign of the Ming (1522–67). Outside the gate is a Ming dynasty locust tree (*Sophora japonica*) called the 'Sleeping Dragon Locust' because of the way it sprawls on the ground. The temple has three courts and three halls, the first court with trees and a pool. In the hall of the second court there used to be ceiling paintings of the 'mother star' and her 12 daughters. In the back courtyard, the Princess of the Rosy Clouds was worshipped.

1km north of the Doumu gong, off to the east of the main path, is a narrow gully, the **Stone Sutra Ravine** (Jingshi yu) where the text of the Buddhist *Diamond Sutra* has been carved on the rock face. This has been further carved by later calligraphers, including Guo Moruo (see Jinan, p 373, and Leshan in Sichuan, p 572), who wrote in 1961 'written by men of the Northern Ji'

(550–577). An anonymous Ming calligrapher also carved a passage from the Confucian *Da xue* (*Great Learning*) beneath the sutra.

Further up the main path is the **Hutian ge** (Pavilion of the Teapot Sky), apparently given this name in 1747 because the surrounding peaks create the impression of being in a teapot and looking up at the sky. Originally constructed in the Ming, the inscription on the gate reads 'When you have reached the Teapot Mountain, you are half-way to the summit, near the place of extreme and multiple good fortune.'

To the north of the Teapot Sky Pavilion, a stone gate marks the **Huima ling**, the 'mountain where the horses turn back', said to be the place where the Xuan zong emperor of the Tang (reigned 713–756; some say it was the Zhen zong emperor of the Song, reigned 998–1023) had to dismount and leave his horse for it could not negotiate the twists and turns above. Not far above is the **Zhongtian men** (Gate in the Middle of the Sky), also known as the Ertian men (Second Celestial Gate), marking the half-way point (and the cable car for those who are flagging). It is also the point where the main eastern path and the longer but infinitely less crowded western path start (almost temple-less and with good views). The stone gateway is a Qing construction; nearby is a large stone whose patterning is said to resemble that of a tiger. The Qing epigrapher Wu Dahui carved the seal-script character for 'tiger' on it and it is called the Reclining Tiger Stone.

If the weather is fine, the peak can be seen from here: if there is rain and mist, 'the yellow peak returns home to the clouds'. The path leading upwards towards the summit crosses the Yunbu qiao (Step Over the Clouds Bridge) which spans a stream flowing down from above.

In the words of a Ming poet, Chen Fengyu: 'The hundred foot cliff is locked into the kingfisher mist; the jade dragon hangs down in the emptiness. When the sun shines in the sixth month, there is often flying rain and when the wind is still there is the sound of stringed instruments.' Beside the bridge is a pavilion with the couplet: 'Lean on the stone railing and watch the flying spray; then cross the cloud bridge and greet the noble pine.'

Above is the **Wusong ting** (Five Pine Pavilion) where the first emperor of the Qin is said to have sheltered from a storm in 219 BC and gratefully ennobled the pine tree (as an official of the fifth grade; it is only since the Tang dynasty that this has been mistranslated as 'five pines'). The current three trees were planted in 1730. There is an old pine to the west of the five bay pavilion which is said to appear to be stretching out its hand in welcome, another candidate for the original title of 'the pine that welcomes guests', endlessly depicted in paintings in restaurants and waiting rooms. On the west of the path, a little above, is the **Chaoyang dong** (South-facing Cave), dedicated to the worship of the Princess of the Rosy Clouds and there are two poems by the Qianlong emperor inscribed in vast characters on a rock opposite.

At the Pine Tree Mountain (Duisong shan) the path turns sharply and the summit is visible. A stone gateway, **Shengxian fang** (Gateway to the Ascent to Immortality), leads to a steep stairway with the **Nan tian men** (Southern Heavenly Gate) at the top. First constructed in 1264, this was called the 'building where one can touch the void'; the stone-carved verses read: 'The gate opens up the nine clouds and leads to the famous places of the three heavens; ascending tens of thousands of steps we can see and are close to a thousand peaks.' To the west of the gate on a stone is a Yuan dynasty inscription, 'The Heaven's Gate

Inscription' composed by Du Renjie, written by Yan Zhongfan. It is apparently a protest against the evils of 14C society; it was buried during the Qianlong reign and rediscovered in 1956.

The summit is a mere 1km from the gate and the *Dictionary of Famous Sites in China*, noting this, immediately cites the words of the Tang poet Li Bai in his poem in praise of Tai shan: 'In a long breath at the heavenly gate, the fresh wind comes from a thousand miles away.'

The **Bixiayun jun ci** (Temple of the Princess of the Rosy Clouds), the focal point for pilgrims, is on the southern slopes of the summit.

From 1759 until the fall of the Qing, the emperor would send an official on the 18th day of the fourth lunar month each year to make an offering here. First built in 1008–16, it was enlarged in the Ming and Qing. In order to resist the winds and also the danger of fire from thunderstorms, it was roofed with iron tiles and has iron acroteria; there is also much brickwork. In the main hall, the figure of the princess is of bronze. There are even two bronze stelae, dating from 1615 and 1625. This use of metal in construction and decoration is unique in China.

There is a Temple to Confucius, founded very late, in the late 16C, just below the Bixiayun jun ci, the stone terrace of which was used as an observatory.

The summit of Tai shan is effectively enclosed in the **Yuhuang Temple** (Jade Emperor Temple); the peak itself, carved with the two characters for supreme summit, surrounded by a balustrade in a courtyard of the temple, is called **Tianzhu feng** (Pillar of Heaven Peak). In Chinese popular religion, which is a mixture of Taoism, Confucianism and much earlier beliefs, the Jade Emperor is the supreme ruler of heaven and is depicted as an emperor in an imperial hat with bead curtains hanging down by his face.

Outside the temple is the **Stele with No Words**, traditionally supposed to have been put in place by the first emperor of the Qin in 219 and the text weathered away by the winds and rains of the summit; historians consider it more likely that it was erected by either the Wu or the Zhang emperor of the early Han. On the **Daguan feng** (Peak of the Great View) is the stone-carved inscription (whose characters, cut into the rock, have been gilded) ordered by the Tang Xuanzong emperor in 726 when he ennobled the mountain. In it, the emperor describes his difficulties in ruling and how his officials persuaded him to carry out the two major sacrifices at the foot and summit of Tai shan and 'all was as it should be'.

Southeast of the Jade Emperor Temple is the **Riguan feng** (Peak for Watching the Sunrise) where thousands of visitors, who have stayed overnight in the rather rough hotel or the newer guesthouse and hired padded coats, watch the sunrise through the clouds, one of the sights of Tai shan. It was here that the Song emperor Zhenzong performed the *feng* ceremony in 1008. In 1747 two jade boxes were unearthed beneath the platform, containing slips of jade inscribed with texts of prayers to the mountain. South of the Riguan feng is the **Zhanlu tai** (Platform for Surveying Lu) from where the state of Lu (southern Shandong) could be viewed, clouds permitting.

Those who wish to walk down the mountain could take the longer but emptier (of buildings and people) western path from the cable car station, past the Heilong tan (Black Dragon Pool) and the Puzhao si (Temple of Universal Clarity) near the bottom, built against the mountain and famous for its Six Dynasties (222–589) pines.

The temple (a Buddhist centre) was said to have been founded during the Six Dynasties, expanded during the Tang and rebuilt in the Ming. In the main hall is a bronze figure of Sakyamuni, the historic Buddha, and behind is the main Six Dynasties pine. In the three-bay hall beside the pavilion at the back of the temple, Feng Yuxiang, the 'Christian Warlord', used to stay between 1932 and 1935.

> ### The Christian Warlord
> Feng Yuxiang (1882–1948) was one of the warlords who had command of a northern army but who more or less allied himself with the Nationalist cause as long as it was led by Sun Yatsen. He was given a post in the Nationalist (KMT) cabinet, although he retained his own power-base as a 'new national warlord' and challenged Chiang Kai-shek in 1929, allying himself with Wang Jingwei in a rival KMT government. He was called the 'Christian Marshall' not, as S.J. Perelman (who had trouble with Chinese names) suggested, in order to distinguish him from Feng the 'Jewish Marshall' but because he was a Christian convert and he used to baptise his troops with a hosepipe. His tomb is on the western slopes of Tai shan for, although he was a native of Anhui, his power-base was in the north.

The tomb is near the **Dachong Bridge**, which he built in the early 1930s when staying here. There is a bronze statue of Feng in front of the tomb and an inscription by Guo Moruo reading 'Mr Feng Yuxiang's tomb' as well as the single character wo ('me') in the general's own hand.

7.5km east of Tai'an are the remains of a **Ming Tang** (Bright or Sacred Hall) recorded in the Han histories as having been built by the Wudi (Martial) Emperor of the Han (reigned 140–86 BC) after a trip to Tai shan. The Ming Tang was a sacrificial building specific to the Han dynasty: a hall that had to be surrounded by water and an enclosure that reflected both the circle and the square and which was used for all sorts of sacrifices and acts of worship. As the Ming Tang remains a slightly mysterious edifice, the circular mound and quantities of Han tiles and pots unearthed here are of great interest to Han historians.

Qu Fu

Qu Fu, one of the most charming country towns in China, had a traditional importance quite out of proportion to its size for it was the birth place of **Confucius**, the First Sage Under Heaven. Slightly difficult to get to as the descendants of Confucius managed to protect the *feng shui* of their ancestral graveyard and force the railway into a detour away from Qu Fu, the small walled town lies on the Shandong plain some 100km south of Jinan, the foothills of mountains just visible in the distance. The tiny town is entirely dominated by the enormous Temple to Confucius and the Mansion of his descendants which occupy its centre.

Completely surrounded by walls until very recently, parts of the wall were knocked down when the essential Confucius theme park was constructed. I refuse to visit it as the town itself is the real thing but sometimes Chinese theme parks can offer some amusement (usually at an inflated price). Celebrations are held in Qu Fu on 28 September, which is Confucius's birthday.

Practical information

Getting there
By train

Qu Fu is c 13km west of Yanzhou, which is on the main line from Beijing to Nanjing (via Jinan). There are few taxis (about 50 yuan) at the station but hordes of minibuses which will take you to Qu Fu in 20 to 30 minutes for 7 yuan. It is also possible to drive from Jinan.

Getting away from Qu Fu can be a bit difficult as train tickets are sold at Yanzhou Station no more than eight hours before the train departs, so unless you want to spend much of your time going backwards and forwards to Yanzhou, it is easiest to ask the hotel to book a ticket for you for a small surcharge. As Yanzhou is an intermediate station, it is not usually possible to buy anything other than a hard seat ticket; if you want a sleeper, you will have to negotiate once you get on board the train.

Where to stay

The most romantic place to stay is inside the Mansion itself: the ***Kong fu Hotel*** run by Luxingshe, 9 Datong lu, ☎ 441 2686, fax 441 3786. There is also a luxury hotel, which is not much more expensive, the ***Queli Hotel***, 1 Queli jie, ☎ 441 1956, fax 441 2022, just opposite the Mansion. This is worth visiting as it is rather beautifully designed, a most unusual feature of contemporary hotel building in China. It combines fairly modern lines with the low roof line and grey colours of the houses around it.

Confucius

Confucius, said to have lived from 551 to 479 BC, was a teacher who was ignored in his own time but who has had the most profound effect on Chinese culture over the last 2000 years. His father died when Confucius was young and he was brought up by his mother. He is thought to have held various positions in the government (Keeper of Granaries, Director of Public Pastures) but he failed in his ambition to achieve the high status which would have made him more successful in his ambition to restore the old moral codes of the State of Zhou in his home state of Lu in Shandong. So he moved from state to state, attempting to influence rulers towards a higher moral standard. His teachings and some small details about his life and character are known through the *Lun yu* (*Analects*), a collection of anecdotes and quotations apparently compiled long after his death by the disciples of his disciples. From the *Analects* he emerges as a man of finicky habits (unable to sleep if his mat was not straight) but great determination ('He's the one who knows it's no good but keeps on trying').

His mission in life was 'to restore the old order' (a slogan used to attack Defence Minister Lin Biao in the early 1970s), to re-establish the virtuous ways of the State of Zhou, which he felt were being ignored. He was not an innovator, for he set forth ideas which were current but in his view ignored. In the hagiography that has grown up around him, however, all these ideas have become his own.

Fundamental to his theories were views on government, gentlemen and learning. Looking back to a past golden age when everything was perfect, he stressed the need for moral government in which the people could have confidence. The concept of heavenly approval was important: a ruler was sanctioned by heaven and if he ruled badly heaven's mandate could be withdrawn. Symptoms of the withdrawal of the heavenly mandate were natural disasters and such is the pervasive nature of Confucianism that the earthquake of 1976 which immediately preceded the death of Mao was viewed by many peasants as a heavenly portent. One story from the *Analects* tells of Confucius meeting a woman weeping by the road side. He leaned out of his carriage and asked her what was the matter. She told him that her son, husband, father and uncle had all been killed by a tiger. Confucius questioned the wisdom of her staying in such a dangerous place but she replied that the government was good. Confucius turned to his disciples and said: 'Bad government is worse than a tiger'. His views on what constituted good government included 'humaneness', the importance of ritual as a reinforcing agent and the importance of people knowing their position and behaving appropriately. 'Let the ruler be a ruler, the son a son ...' is one of his famous *dicta* and it illustrates his stress on social stability right through from the ruler to conduct within the family. If people failed to behave appropriately— and here ritual was an important underpinning—chaos would ensue.

He has been much criticised in recent decades for his conservatism, which incorporated views current at the time. The position of women both within society and within the home was subordinate. A woman should obey her father, her husband and her son; this was all part of knowing her place. He stressed the importance of proper behaviour: a man should not touch his sister-in-law, to the point that it was inappropriate for him to save her from drowning if that meant hand to hand contact (I suppose a bargepole might not have offended such propriety).

The ruler should be a 'gentleman', well educated in the classic texts, which in time became known as the *Confucian Classics*. He should also be humane, 'love others' and behave with 'courtesy, diligence, good faith and kindness'. If you behave with courtesy then you will not be insulted; if you are generous then you will win the multitude; if you are of good faith then other men will put their trust in you; if you are diligent then you will have success; and if you are kind then you will be able to command others.

Confucius' stress on education was to form the basis of the civil service exams in the Han dynasty, for which gentlemen had to learn (effectively by heart) the *Classics*, a syllabus which remained relatively unchanged until the first years of the 20C. Music and ritual were the outward signs of appropriate behaviour, means of showing respect to the living and the dead. The service of ancestral spirits was practised at the time and was part of

Confucius' view of the world. He also stressed the importance of filial devotion: 'When the father is alive, you see only the son's intentions. When he is dead, you see the son's actions. If for three years he makes no change from the ways of his father, then he may be called filial.' This three year period became institutionalised as the appropriate length of time to mourn a parent.

Confucianism as the state cult was adopted during the Han and persisted until the 20C. Its adoption meant that the descendants of the Sage became the 'First Family Under Heaven', of almost greater status than the imperial family; dynasties came and went, while the Kongs endured and, indeed, still exist.

The name 'Confucius' is a late 16C latinisation of Kong Fuzi (Master Kong) invented by Jesuit missionaries who were enormously impressed by the benevolent despotism of Confucian rule, seeing China as ruled by a class of philosophers schooled in ancient texts. Such were their enthusiastic reports that Confucius has been described as 'the patron saint of the Enlightenment', although Protestant missionaries were less impressed. James Legge (1814–97), who translated the *Confucian Classics*, said: 'He gave no impulse to religion. He had no sympathy with progress.'

Although the ideas he expressed may simply have been those of any 6C BC conservative, the longevity of the legacy of Confucianism is quite extraordinary. Even today his stress on filial piety is felt: it is against the law to neglect elderly parents, for example, and old people's homes are for those with no surviving relatives, while in education rote learning still plays an important part. It is interesting that the Teachers' Training College was established in Qu Fu rather than in the provincial capital, Jinan, early this century: although Confucius' influence was finally waning, it was as if the air of Qu Fu was specially conducive to education. And during the 1930s both Chiang Kai-shek and the invading Japanese sought to get the Kong family on their side in order to help legitimise their regimes. The story of the family and, in particular, the last of the Yansheng Dukes to live in the Mansion is told by Kong Demao in *The House of Confucius* (Hodder and Stoughton, 1988). Kong Demao was a 77th generation descendant, whose brother, the last of the Yansheng Dukes, now lives in Taiwan. It is a charming account of a strangely privileged yet isolated childhood amongst the dust and ghosts of 76 generations: a rather tragic tale of the intrusion of the 20C (in the form of vacuum flasks, wellington boots and political intrigue) on the backward stronghold of the 'First Family Under Heaven'.

History

Qu Fu—the name means 'winding hill' and was first glossed in the *Li Ji* (or *Book of Rites*) c 2C BC—was the capital of the state of Lu from c 1060 to 249 BC, although earlier settlements have been revealed by archaeological excavation of sites of the Dawen kou and Longshan Neolithic cultures (c 4000 BC). Although Qu Fu continued as the seat of local government, the present major buildings, including the Temple, Mansion and Drum Tower, mostly date from the Qing; the present layout, however, existed during the Ming.

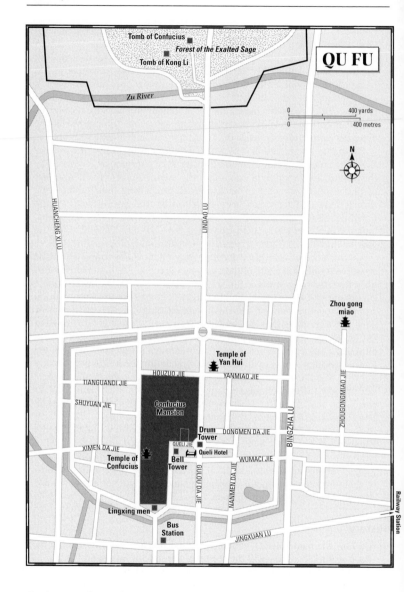

On the central axis of the small walled town is the Temple to Confucius, with the Mansion to the northeast (adjoining the rear part of the temple enclosure). The Drum Tower is at the southeast extremity of the Mansion's wall; north of it are the Yan Hui Temple on the right and outside the town to the north the 'Forest of the Exalted Sage', or graveyard of the Kong family. Much of the centre of the town around the Drum Tower has been extensively renovated. The two-storey grey brick buildings with their gaily painted timber fronts concealing banks and restaurants are recent constructions, modelled on Qing shopfronts, like those that have been reconstructed on Liulichang in Peking and at Wutai shan in Shanxi. The reconstruction is, however, quite tasteful and appropriately northern in architectural style.

Temple of Confucius

The Temple to Confucius (Kong miao) has been described as 'one of the three great classical architectural complexes in China', along with the Forbidden City in Peking and the Imperial Summer Resort at Chengde. Architecturally, it is related to the imperial complexes for it is very much of the north. The buildings are solid with sedate roof lines (not the tight, upward sweep of the south) and colour is important: roofs are imperial yellow or green, columns are painted red. It is a long, rectangular enclosure, over 1km long from north to south, the first part consisting mainly of a series of narrow courtyards dominated by a series of gates. A central courtyard houses the 13 stele pavilions, crowding the narrow space, and beyond are three parallel series of courtyards, long rather than narrow.

The first temple was built in 478 BC on the site near the Sage's family home, where his disciples commemorated Confucius. It is said that it was originally merely a three room building where Confucius' possessions—clothes, cap, musical instruments, carriage and books—were kept, until in AD 539 an emperor of the Eastern Wei dynasty renovated the building and set up a statue of Confucius for worship. From then on rulers made it their business to maintain and improve the temple in order to help legitimise their right to rule: 15 major reconstructions, 31 minor reconstructions and several hundred minor renovations have been recorded in the last 2000 years.

The **main south gate** in the town wall of Qu Fu was the first approach to the temple. It is known, hyperbolically, as the 'ten-thousand *ren* palace wall' (a *ren* being an ancient measure equivalent to 2.5 metres), a reference to one of Confucius' disciples Zi Gong, who said: 'If one compares a man's learning to a palace wall, then Confucius' palace wall must be a good many *ren* high.' The four-character inscription over the gate was set up by the Qianlong emperor in the mid 18C.

Not far north of the town wall is the **first gateway** (or *pailou*) **of the temple** (Jinsheng yuzhen fang). Of carved stone, it has four stone drums bearing octagonal pillars with one-horned beasts sitting on lotus thrones. The gateway is known as Striking of Gongs and Sounding of Musical Stones, a reference to the major musical instruments of Confucius' time, when L-shaped stones of varying sizes, hung on a great wooden frame, were struck like a giant musical chime.

Beyond is the **Lingxing Gate** (the Ling star is the 'star of literature' in the Great Bear and Confucius is also traditionally viewed as a 'literary star'). The gate, built in 1754 to replace a timber construction, has four stone pillars, iron crossbeams, red walls and a yellow tiled roof. The side gates—named (left) The Way that Has Predominated through Ancient and Modern Times and (right) Virtue Equal to Heaven and Earth—to this first courtyard have some rather impressive, early-looking stone lions. Two free-standing gates follow, the **Gateway of the Original Ether of Supreme Harmony** (Taihe yuanqi fang) and the **Archway of the Temple of the Exalted Sage** (Zhisheng maio fang).

Behind them is a true gate set in a wall, cutting off the first grassy courtyard. This is the **Gate of the Timeliness of the Sage** (Shengshi men) and it leads into a paved courtyard filled with cypresses, which has a stream, the Bi River, running through it, crossed by three stone bridges. On the left is a modern pavilion covering two stone figures dating from the Eastern Han (AD 25–220). These formed part of the approach to the tomb of the Prince of Western Lu, situated c 4km southeast of Qufu, and were moved here after 1949 for safekeeping.

Beyond the Bi River bridges is the **Gate of Augmenting the Truth** (Xuandao men), which leads to a narrow courtyard beyond.

The gate was first constructed in 1018 at the order of the Song Tianxi emperor and enlarged in 1504 during the reign of the Hongzhi emperor of the Ming. The name of the gate is taken from a line in the Analects: 'man can augment the truth'.

Inside the gate are two Yuan dynasty (1271–1368) **stelae**: the four-sided one on the right is inscribed with the 'Chronicles of Qu Fu County', that on the left is the 'Epitaph of a Gentleman Recluse' and was moved to the temple for safekeeping when the Cultural Revolution broke out in 1966.

Next comes the **Gate of the Great Mean** (Dazhong men; meaning 'the middle way', or avoidance of extremes, a cornerstone of Confucius' views on belief and behaviour). In the Song dynasty this was the main gate to the temple, although the present structure is Qing in date. Its previous function as the main entrance may be gathered from the two L-shaped, green tiled corner towers, first built in 1331, that stand on either side of the wall, while outside to the right is the Bell Tower of Qu Fu.

In the next courtyard is a central gate, the Gate of the Unity of the Written Language, with two side pavilions and behind is the 'lofty' **Kuiwen Pavilion** (Worship of Literature Pavilion).

First constructed in 1018, the pavilion was then called the 'Pavilion of Libraries'. It was reconstructed in 1191 on the order of the Jin dynasty emperor Zhangzong and given its present name. It has a triple roof, is three storeys high and, last rebuilt in 1504, has survived remarkably well. When much of Qu Fu was destroyed by an earthquake in the reign of the Kangxi emperor (1654–1722), the pavilion was quite undamaged, as is recorded in a stele on the terrace. There are two Ming stelae pavilions in front of the Kuiwen Pavilion and four huge Ming imperial stelae.

The small courtyards to each side of the main courtyard are called 'abstention lodges' where visiting emperors would retire to fast and bathe before participating in ceremonies of sacrifice to Confucius.

In the next courtyard are the **13 stelae pavilions**, reminiscent of the stelae pavilions in the Temple of Confucius in Peking. They were constructed to hold a total of 53 imperial stelae recording imperial visits, imperially sponsored repairs and gifts of lands or titles to members of the Sage's family. The earliest are Tang in date and the latest of the Republican period (1914–19). In the same courtyard, along the northern wall and in the southern corners, are stelae recording sponsorship of repairs and gifts made by the nobility and gentry.

Side gates—on the east the Gate of the Search for Purity, on the west the Gate of the Spectacle of the Virtues—lead to the town. In the north wall of the courtyard are five gates, four side gates subordinate to the central **Gate of Great**

Achievements. The gate on the far west is the **Gate of He Who Heralds the Sage** and on the far east, the **Gate of Succession of the Sage**.

'Great achievements' was Mencius' pronouncement on Confucius. **Mencius** (c 372–288 BC) was perhaps the most famous of Confucius' pre-Han followers whose assertion that human nature was essentially good became a prime tenet of later Confucianism.

The row of five gates marks a division within the temple, from the series of wide but narrow entrance courtyards to the three parallel courtyards beyond.

The Gate of Succession of the Sage leads to the eastern courtyards where sacrifices were offered to five generations of Confucius' ancestors (just as the eastern wing of the Forbidden City in Peking contains the ancestral hall), while the Gate of He Who Heralds the Sage leads to courtyards where Confucius' father and mother were worshipped. The central axis comprises halls where Confucius himself was worshipped.

Immediately behind the Gate of Great Achievements is a long courtyard full of cypresses and various types of pine (some with twisted bark that spirals up the trunk, some with stippled bark); it contains a tall vermilion pavilion called the **Apricot Altar** (Xingtan), by tradition the place where Confucius instructed his disciples.

The actual site of the original Apricot Altar is unknown but in 1018 the 45th generation descendant, Kong Daofu, renovated the temple and rebuilt the Great Hall to the north of its original site. The latter was covered with an altar, apricot trees were planted around it and it was named the 'apricot altar'. A pavilion was constructed over the altar during the Jin (1115–1234) and a stone tablet set up with calligraphy by a Jin scholar, Dang Huaiying. The present building dates from 1596 and survived a great fire in 1724.

Behind the Apricot Altar is the main hall of the temple, the **Hall of Great Achievements** (Dacheng dian). Built on the grand scale, its most notable feature is the series of 28 stone columns carved with dragons which support the lower roof of the double-roofed hall. Each 6m column is carved from a single block of stone and stands on a base of double lotus flowers. These were carved in 1500. The back and sides of the hall's lower roof are supported on 18 octagonal columns decorated with polished low relief carvings of dragons amongst clouds. The ten columns in the front of the hall are sculpted in low relief with pairs of dragons surrounded by clouds and pearls and are unique, although they recall the wooden columns with twisted dragons on the Shengmu dian in the Jin ci near Taiyuan in Shanxi province. When emperors came to the temple, these columns were concealed behind yellow cloths to prevent imperial jealousy, for there are no such carved stone columns in the Forbidden City. The original statues of Confucius, his four companions (Yan Hui, Zheng Shen, Kong Ji and Mencius) and 12 disciples were destroyed during the Cultural Revolution and replaced in 1984.

The main hall has yellow tiles on its roof but the sides of the courtyard are lined with green tiled, red columned side wings where Confucius' disciples were once worshipped. These now contain a display of some of the 2000 stone stelae, the earliest dating from the Western Han, preserved in the temple.

Worship of the disciples dates back to AD 72 when the Yongping emperor of the Han came to Qu Fu to venerate Confucius. He also made sacrifices to 72 disciples. In 647 the Zhenguan emperor of the Tang decreed that 22 more disciples should be included in venerations and succeeding rulers have 'expanded and re-shuffled' the disciples so that they are numbered as 172.

Just inside the Gate of Great Achievements on the right is a cypress surrounded by a fence. This is supposed to be the 'Cypress Planted by the Hand of the First Teacher' and its flourishing or withering was supposed to reflect the fortunes of the Kong family and the imperial house.

Behind the main hall is the **Inner Hall** for the worship of Confucius' wife, Qi Guan, its columns and ceilings painted with phoenixes (symbolic of the female, as the dragon is for the male). Qi Guan, mother of Confucius' son, Kong Li, was first worshipped separately in 1018.

Behind is the **Hall of the Relics of the Sage** containing 120 carved stone plaques depicting events in the life of Confucius, from his mother praying for a son on Nishan Hill to his disciples at his grave. The carvings were made in the late 16C from Song paintings. There are also stone-carved copies of Gu Kaizhi's 4C painting of Confucius as the travelling teacher, a portrait of Confucius by the Tang painter Wu Daozi and a seal-script inscription by the great Song painter Mi Fu.

The eastern axis, entered from the Gate of the Succession of the Sage, contains the **Hall of Poetry and Rites** (Shili tang), said to have been where Confucius instructed his son Kong Li in the study of poetry through the *Book of Songs*—'If one has not studied poetry, one cannot express oneself'—and ritual—'if one does not study the rites, one cannot strengthen one's character'. The present hall was built in 1504 and the courtyard contains a Tang dynasty cypress and two Song dynasty gingko trees. Each year the female tree still produces the nuts which formed the vital ingredient in 'Poetry and Rites Gingko', a dish served at banquets in the Kong family Mansion next door.

Nearby is a gate which leads east to the Mansion and behind the Hall of Poetry and Rites is a well said to have been used by Confucius.

East of the well is a small wall, the **Wall of Lu**, said to have been where the ninth generation descendant of Confucius concealed copies of the *Confucian Classics* during the 'Burning of the Books'.

The first emperor of the Qin, Shi huang di (c 259–210 BC) was extremely anti-Confucian, preferring the more brutally practical philosophy of Legalism. He took his persecution of Confucius and all things Confucian to a degree seen later in the literary inquisition of Qianlong (late 18C) and the Cultural Revolution. He is supposed to have insisted on the burning of all books and the burial alive of all scholars associated with Confucianism and thus unknowingly created a scholarly controversy that raged during the Han based on 'reconstructed' versus 'survived' texts of Confucian works. After the books were concealed in the Lu Wall to escape burning, they were forgotten until 154 BC when Liu Yu, son of the Jingdi emperor, enfeoffed as Prince Gong of Lu, decided to make extensions to his palace, which involved the demolition of part of Confucius' original home. During demolition, 'the rustling of silks and the clinking of bamboo slats' was heard inside a wall and the hidden documents discovered. The present Lu Wall was built later to commemorate the event.

Behind the Lu Wall are three small gates set in a wall enclosing the courtyard of the **Temple for Adoring the Sage** (Jia miao). This stands on a high platform and was built in 1723 by the Yongzheng emperor for the worship of five generations of Confucius' ancestors who had posthumously been granted high rank.

The rear western wing of the temple is the place where Confucius' parents were venerated and where musicians prepared for the major rituals. Entered through the Gate of He Who Heralds the Sage (on the western side of the north wall of the courtyard of the 13 stele pavilions), the first hall on a high brick terrace is the **Hall of Silks and Metals** (Jinsi tang; meaning string and percussion instruments). The front of the building was where the musical instruments used in ritual in the temple were stored; some of them can now be seen in the museum at the rear of the Mansion. Musicians and dancers used to practise on the terrace in front of the hall.

Behind are three gates leading to the **Hall of He Who Heralds the Sage** (Qinsheng dian). The five-bay hall has a green glazed tile roof and stone pillars carved with pairs of dragons chasing pearls. The original hall was a Song construction but the current building dates from 1724.

> The hall was built in honour of Confucius' father, Shu Lianghe, a minor official who was elevated to the nobility in retrospect because of the achievements of his son. In 1008 he was named Duke of Lu and in 1330 he was granted the additional title of 'He Who Heralds the Sage'.

On the same terrace to the rear is the smaller, three-bay Hall of the Wife of the King Who Heralds the Sage (meaning Confucius' mother, Yan Zhengzai, who died when her son was 24). She was ennobled with her husband: in 1008 entitled 'First Lady of the Sage of Lu' and in 1330 'Exalted Wife of the King Who Heralds the Sage'. The hall was first constructed in 1330.

The Confucian Mansion

The Kong Fu, or Confucian Mansion (open daily 08.00–16.30), is just to the northeast of the Temple approached by Queli jie, the narrow street lined with souvenir stalls that runs along the eastern wall of the temple. Descendants of the Sage are said to have lived here for over 2500 years (77 generations), although the first 'mansion' was further south on Queli jie.

Along Queli jie at the southern end is the **Queli Gate**, most recently renovated during the Republican era, although there was formerly a Han dynasty timber construction carved with flowers. There are the words *que li* on a horizontal board in the centre: *que* means 'stone tower' (and, indeed, two stone towers used to stand at the southern end of the road) and *li* is an old word for 'street'.

Further north up Queli jie, the **Bell Tower** straddles the road. It was first constructed in 1302 in the style of a city gate with the green tiled tower rising above a stone arch. The huge bronze bell inside (1.5m high) was rung to mark ceremonies in the adjoining temple and at dawn every day to mark the rising of the sun, except in the 12th lunar month when it was rung both at sunrise and sunset.

Beyond the Bell Tower is the gate of **Confucius' former dwelling**, with grey roof tiles and a lintel decorated with animals. Such gates were only permitted by sumptuary law to the highest ranks of the nobility and place the Kong family on a par with the imperial family. Inside the gate is a stele inscribed 'In Praise of the Gate of the Former Dwelling' in the handwriting of the Qianlong emperor.

The **present Mansion**, north of the site of the 'former mansion', was constructed here during the reign of the first Ming emperor (1368–98) and was extensively renovated and enlarged during the Qing.

The Yansheng Duke

The major inhabitant of the Mansion was always the Yansheng ('Extending the Line of the Sage') Duke, the oldest direct male descendant of Confucius. The title 'Yansheng Duke' was conferred in 1055 and remained unchanged until 1935 when Chiang Kai-shek changed it to 'State Master of Sacrifices to the Exalted Sage and First Teacher'. The status of the Yansheng Duke rose throughout imperial history from the rank of a fifth grade official in the 10C to a first grade official under the Ming (1368–1644), second only to the Prime Minister. During the Qing, further privileges, such as being allowed to ride a horse inside the Forbidden City when all others were called upon to dismount at the gates of all Qing imperial buildings, exemption from taxes and corvée labour and the power to preside over its own court of law, raised the position of the Yansheng Duke until he was effectively on a par with the emperor. This is illustrated by the marriage of a daughter of the Qianlong emperor to the Yansheng Duke in 1772. The princess was born with a mole on her face which, fortune-tellers predicted, would bring misfortune unless she was married into 'a family more illustrious than either the nobility or the highest of officials'. The Qianlong emperor had to marry her to the Yansheng Duke, the only other person in China allowed to walk with the emperor along the 'imperial way'.

There was a complication for Manchus (such as the imperial family) were not allowed to marry Chinese (such as the Kongs), so she first had to be given in adoption to an official's family. Her dowry included 20 villages and the taxes collected therefrom, several thousand trunks of clothing and jewellery, jasper *ruyi* (s-shaped carved objects, sometimes unhelpfully called 'sceptres', which were used as presents: *ru yi* means 'fulfilment of wishes', so they serve both as symbols of good wishes and approval), 27 metres of satin and many pelts. The Qianlong emperor was most amused by one gift amongst the thousands of wedding presents, a small gold axe sent by a magistrate 'for future imperial grandchildren to crack walnuts' (the 18C present for someone who has everything).

The Mansion is divided into three major parts: the front, or formal and administrative section, the rear part where the family lived and beyond that the garden. There are also the normal three parallel axes running through the front and rear: the western wing included the reception rooms for important guests, studies and rooms where the rites were learnt, while the eastern wing included the family temple and ancestral hall (just as in the Forbidden City) and apartments for various dependant relatives.

The main gates are painted black with red borders (a colour scheme more common around Xi'an) and have fine brass knockers as well as the inevitable pair of calligraphic inscriptions reading 'Sharing happiness with the whole nation, the peaceful, prosperous, respected, glorious Mansion of the Duke' and 'As long-lived as the heavens, the house of the learned Sage of moral excellence'. The two small gates beside it are supposed to mark the entrance to the original Mansion, which in the early 20C was a place where a small girl of the 77th generation used to play amongst relics supposed to have belonged to the Sage himself, a dilapidated (it would be after 2500 years) carriage and a zither.

Inside the gate to the main Mansion is a wide courtyard: the narrow building to the west was the **Hall for Sending Memorials to the Emperor** (Laizou ting). On the east was the carriage house which dealt with rather more mundane communications. Beyond is the second gate inscribed 'Gate of the Sage' and beyond that a screen gate with four black pillars standing on eight stone drums and carved beams terminating in flower buds, a form of decoration often found on internal gates which were known as 'hanging flower gates'. This screen gate was kept closed except when emperors visited and then it would be opened with a 13-gun salute. Above the gate is an inscription by the Ming Jiajing emperor (1507–66) which reads 'Bestowing double glory'. The same courtyard is lined with buildings housing six administrative departments modelled on the **six ministries of the imperial government**.

The **Department of Rites** was in charge of ancestral worship, the **Department of Seals of jurisdiction and edicts**, the **Department of the Hundred Households** was responsible for security and the administration of the burial ground; the others were the **Departments of Music, Letters and Archives, Rent Collection and Sacrificial Fields**. These departments, or minor ministries, were housed in the side wings of the courtyards of the Great Hall and the second and third halls, the Department of Letters and Archives (which has since the Cultural Revolution begun publishing an immense series of archives), for example, to the west of the second hall.

In the Great Hall (Da tang), behind the Gate of Double Glory, the Yansheng Duke, sitting on a wooden chair covered by a tiger skin, proclaimed edicts and administered the affairs of the family.

The Kongs owned vast tracts of land in different parts of China and received the taxes due on the land: 650 hectares were personally owned and some 24,000 further hectares were set aside for the peasants of Qu Fu to work. There was a Department of Punishments in the Mansion and a goose-winged pitchfork, a gold-tipped jade baton and a tiger-tail baton that had been presented by emperors to help inflict punishments for unpaid taxes or misdemeanours that fell within the family's jurisdiction. On the table in front of his seat were brushes and writing materials and the seal of authority. Ranged around are banners and signs used in public processions which say 'Silence' and 'Make Way'.

Behind the Great Hall is the **Second Hall** (Er tang) where the Duke gave audience to officials of the fourth rank and higher and where children were examined in rites and music under horizontal boards inscribed 'Respectfully inherit the cause of the Sage' and 'Poetry, literature, music and the rites'. Vertical tablets in the hall include one reading 'Happiness and Longevity' written by the Daoguang emperor (reigned 1797–1821) and one with the character for 'longevity' written by the Dowager Empress Cixi (there are similar inscriptions by her in the Summer Palace outside Peking).

Linked to the Great Hall by a covered way, there is a red-lacquered bench in the corridor, known as Yan Song's Bench.

Yan Song was a Prime Minister of the Jiajing reign period of the Ming and his daughter married a 64th generation descendant of Confucius. Owing to trouble at court, Yan Song was to be tried and he came to Qu Fu to beg his son-in-law to intercede. As the Yansheng Duke did not want to interfere, Yan Song sat interminably on the bench waiting for an audience.

In the **Third Hall** (San tang), behind, the Yansheng Duke attended to less important family matters and those involving the vast retinue of servants. When the
last generation inhabited the Mansion (and there were only four family members), there were 500 hereditary servants. The central room now contains sedan
chairs used by the family: the red one used by the Yansheng Duke within the
Mansion, the green one used for trips outside.

Behind the Third Hall is the **Gate to the Inner Apartments** (Neizhai men),
marking the division between the public areas and the private, which could
almost be described as the masculine and the feminine areas.

> Visitors came to the front halls; administrative work and official family cults
> (such as ancestral venerations, which were carried out in the two halls on the
> eastern axis of the front part of the Mansion, the Hall for Cherishing
> Ancestral Kindness and the Hall to Requite Ancestral Kindness) all took place
> in the front of the Mansion but only family members and trusted (mainly
> female) servants were allowed to pass into the rear part of the Mansion. Even
> the water-carrier had to pour his sweet well water into a trough that ran
> through the wall, just west of the gate.
>
> This strict seclusion could cause problems, as Kong Demao of the 77th gen-
> eration recalled: when a fire broke out only 12 of the 500 hereditary servants
> were allowed into the rear apartments to try and put it out with the result
> that it burnt for three days, destroying seven buildings (shades of the impro-
> priety of rescuing your sister-in-law from drowning persisting into the 20C).

The first hall in the Inner Mansion is the **Front Reception Hall** (Qianshang
fang), where relatives were received and wedding and funeral ceremonies conducted. The eastern room contains a set of furniture of dark tree-roots presented
by the Qianlong emperor and a dinner service (for banquets were held in this hall).

> 196 different dishes might be served at a single banquet including 'gold and
> silver fish' served on a special plate shaped like two fish and coloured white
> and yellow, 'lilac beancurd' (beancurd carved and arranged with a
> beansprout said to resemble a lilac blossom) sea-cucumber, shark's fin and
> duck (known as the 'big three') and glutinous rice.

The room on the far western end of the Front Reception Hall was used as a study
by the 76th Yansheng Duke (d. 1919).

To the east of the Hall, reached by a very narrow passageway, is the **Tower of
Refuge** (Binan lou), a tall, narrow, windowless tower built to preserve the
Yansheng Dukes from attack. It has never been used apparently, except by an owl
who lived there when Kong Demao was a child, like the hordes of crows that
roosted, and still do, together with the big blue-backed magpies, in the trees of
the Mansion and temple courtyards.

Behind the Front Reception Hall is a small gate which leads to the two-storeyed
Front Main Building (Qiantang lou) where the women of the 76th and 77th
generations lived, while the 77th Yansheng Duke, who was born after his father
died, lived in the hall behind, the Rear Main Building (Houtang lou).

The eastern central room of the Front Main Building was the bedroom of
Madame Tao, wife of the 76th Yansheng Duke, a terrifying figure to the small
Kong Demao and her sister, who together with their brother, the heir, were the
children of Concubine Wang, a secondary wife, taken because Madame Tao had

borne no children that survived. The two small girls had their bedroom in the easternmost room and until her death, their mother's room was the inner western room, where her photograph hangs on the wall.

Palace intrigue

Madame Tao appears to have poisoned Concubine Wang just 17 days after she gave birth to the posthumous heir to the Dukedom in 1919. Concubine Wang had originally come to the Mansion as her servant and, despite her position as mother of the Duke's children, whenever the Duke was away Madame Tao would whip her with a special whip she kept for the purpose.

Ostensibly an ardent Buddhist, officially in charge during the infancy of the 77th Duke, Madame Tao was Qu Fu's equivalent to the intriguing and all-powerful Dowager Empress Cixi. A secondary concubine of the Duke, Madame Feng, lived in the western inner room, almost a prisoner until she died in 1928, a year before her persecutor, Madame Tao. The building where the women lived is decorated with a motley collection of ancient and modern gifts and decorative objects, as is the Rear Main Building where Kong Decheng, the 77th Yansheng Duke (who is still alive in Taiwan), lived.

A sad picture of Kong Decheng's childhood is painted by his elder sister, Kong Demao; she, her elder sister and the young Duke rattling around in the dusty Mansion. The little boy's solitude increased unbearably as his sisters were married off and went to live in Peking. Kong Deqi, the eldest sister, died at the age of 25 after a terribly unhappy marriage to a useless, debt-ridden and unfaithful husband, who lost all his teeth the day he bought a car, immediately crashing it into a telegraph pole as he hadn't the faintest idea how to drive. He had been carefully selected for her by Madame Tao.

The Rear Building has been left as it was in 1940 when the Yansheng Duke departed for Chongqing (and later Taiwan) during the Japanese invasion, decorated in a 'mixture of Chinese and western styles' with rounded 1930s sofas mixed with congratulatory pieces of calligraphy sent for Kong Decheng's wedding in 1936. A picture of plum blossoms on the wall was painted and presented by the famous Peking opera singer Mei Lanfang (1894–1961), one of the greatest 20C male singers of female roles, who did much to promote Peking opera after Liberation.

Kong Decheng's wedding

The wedding of the Duke, reflected in the furnishings and presents, was a mixed Chinese-western affair, the bride in a white wedding gown and high heels, the groom in a long gown and mandarin jacket. Five orchestras led the marriage procession and three Chinese operas were performed in the town. The courtyard in front of the Front Reception Hall was filled with tables spread with auspicious foods—pine kernels and longans (symbolising the early birth of sons and daughters)—as well as with branches of pine and cypress (symbolising eternal youth) and 'happiness salt'. As the bride dismounted from the red bridal sedan chair, hordes of reporters in western suits rushed forward, flash-bulbs popping. She then made her way to the Rear Building to change into a Chinese bridal dress, a red *cheongsam* with red satin shoes, and sat cross-legged on the bridal bed waiting for her husband, who still had to sit through several hours of ceremonies in the Front Reception Hall.

West of the Rear Main Building is a Buddhist chapel and just south of it, on the western axis, is the family school where the Yansheng Dukes were trained in their duties, in calligraphy and couplet-writing as well as in standard school subjects, which in the 1920s included English.

Behind the Rear Building is the garden known as the **Iron Hill Garden** (Tieshan yuan), first constructed in 1503 and reconstructed when the Qianlong emperor's daughter married the 72nd generation Duke. Fairly typical of northern gardens, with water, artificial stone mountains, free-standing twisted rock formations on raised stone bases, bridges and pavilions, there is a 400-year-old cypress with five trunks and a juniper growing in the centre.

There is also a small **museum** (open 08.00–16.00) displaying items from the Mansion, which is extremely interesting. There are ritual bronzes in specially made silken boxes and a wealth of clothing, from children's garments to those of older women, all showing the bold mixing of colours that characterises Chinese costume and jewellery.

The Forest of the Exalted Sage, the Confucian family burial ground

A short walk north of the town is the **Forest of the Exalted Sage** (Kong lin or Zhisheng lin), the Confucian family burial ground. Walled, grassy and full of the indistinct hillocks that are the grave mounds of thousands of long-forgotten Kongs, it is a marvellous (and, on a cold November day, empty) place to wander in.

Turn left out of the Mansion and walk along the road until you reach the **Drum Tower**. This, like its pair, the **Bell Tower**, was constructed in the Ming on a solid brick base. The timber pavilion on top housed the drum, which was struck to mark the sunset and also used when important ceremonies were carried out in the Confucian Temple.

At the Drum Tower turn left (north) and the road will take you straight out of the northern city wall towards the burial ground. It is about a 20 minute walk through fields and a village. Pedicab drivers will harass you to be bicycled, although it is hardly worth it if you enjoy walking along relatively traffic-free roads. You will soon see the stone **Gateway of Eternal Spring** (Wangu changchun fang) which straddles the road. Built in 1594, the six stone columns are topped back and front by 12 stone lions, the lintels and columns carved with dragons, phoenixes, *qilin* (Chinese unicorns), horses, deer, flowers and clouds. Over the central gate are two dragons playing with a pearl, while carvings of phoenixes flying towards the sun can be seen over the side gateways.

Just before you reach the gateway, two square pavilions with green tiled roofs are set on either side of the road, each containing a stele. The eastern one was put in place in 1594 and is inscribed 'The divine road of Confucius, first teacher of sagely accomplishments' and that on the west is dated 1595 and commemorates the renovation of the forest and temple.

The **'forest'** is surrounded by a 7km wall (3m high and 5m thick) enclosing an area of two square kilometres, filled with graves since it has been used since the Han dynasty. There are over 100,000 trees of all sorts, for apparently Confucius' disciples collected exotic trees to plant here. These include cypress, japonica, oak, elm, pistachio, blackberry, maple, poplar, willow, cherry and scholar trees.

At the end of the 'divine road' is a decorative archway in front of the main gate. The archway, or **pailou** (Zhisheng lin), is a timber construction painted in red, blue and gold, with a green tiled roof. The inscription reads 'Forest of the Supreme Sage'. The *pailou* was first erected in 1424 and rebuilt during the Qing. Behind is the Gate Tower, the red railings protecting a collection of stone tablets recording renovations and restoration work at the forest and ceremonies held in commemoration. Inside the gate a long stone-flagged path leads to a watchtower built in 1732, with guardian stone lions. You can climb this for a view over the flat fields to Qu Fu and the grassy 'forest' below.

Running west from the gate is the **imperial carriageway** (previously used exclusively by emperors coming to offer sacrifices); 200m along the carriageway on the north side is a stone gateway inscribed in red characters 'Zhu River Bridge'. Beyond is an arched stone bridge over the river. This leads to the area where Confucius and his son are buried.

Apparently (or according to legend) Confucius chose this place for his burial, stating that the *feng shui* was good. His disciples objected because there was no flowing water: according to *feng shui* beliefs tombs should have a hill behind to the north and a river or stream flowing in front, just like any other building, but Confucius said that sooner or later someone would make good this deficiency. Legend continues to relate that during his intensive persecution of Confucianism by burning books and scholars, the First Emperor, Qin Shi Huangdi, attempted to decrease the influence of Confucianism by trying to destroy the *feng shui* of Confucius' tomb. He ordered that a river be dug through the burial ground, thus inadvertently improving the *feng shui* he was trying to destroy.

Just northeast of the bridge is a small courtyard and the **Hall of Deliberation** (Si tang), behind which is another small courtyard where visitors assumed ritual clothing before sacrifices to Confucius. In a third courtyard was the 'divine kitchen' where sacrificial animals were slaughtered.

Due north of the Zhu River Bridge is the **Hall of Sacrifices** (Xiang dian), approached by an avenue of carved stone columns, tigers, griffins and guardian figures (one pair dates from the Song, the other from the Qing). Behind the hall is the tumulus that now marks what is supposed to be the **Tomb of Confucius**. In front is a large stone tablet of 1443 reading 'Tomb of the Prince of Literary Excellence and Sagely Achievements' with a smaller Song stele behind.

Nearby, to the east, is the Tomb of Kong Li, Confucius' son, who 'died before his father, without making any noteworthy achievements'. South of Confucius' tomb is that of his grandson, Kong Ji, who was said to have been an active promoter of his grandfather's cause. West of Confucius' tomb is a three-bay building said to mark the site of the little hut that **Zi Gong**, one of his disciples, built to watch over the grave. Most of his disciples were said to have observed the current custom of watching over the grave for three years, the pious Zi Gong stayed on for another three.

> The graveyard is still used by direct descendants; when I last visited it, a Mrs Kong had been buried only a day before, the brilliant pink, white and silver paper flowers of her burial wreath the only colours to be seen.

As the graveyard has been in use for over 2000 years, many of the graves are unmarked and unknown but some groups may be distinguished.

Taking the main road that crosses the westernmost bridge over the Zhu River, to the left when facing Confucius' tomb, on the extreme west is a group of **Ming tombs**. Continuing round, almost due north of Confucius' tomb is the memorial archway and group of stone animals marking the **Tomb of Madame Yu**, daughter of the Qianlong emperor (reigned 1736–96), who married the 72nd generation Yansheng Duke. Her only child, a daughter, was buried outside the forest, for female descendants were not allowed inside the forest, only wives. Nearby is a huge stone stele marking the **Tomb of Kong Shangren** (1648–1718), a 64th generation descendant and author of the drama *Taohua shan* (*The Peach-blossom Fan*), an opera based on events in Nanjing in 1644–45, as the Qing took over, ranked as one of the greatest dramas in the Chinese language.

Kong Shangren

Kong Shangren served as an official but was dismissed from office in 1699 and spent much of his time in his 'Lonely Cloud Villa' northeast of Qu Fu, where he wrote and instructed some 700 descendants of the Sage in rites and music. He also wrote literary essays commemorating his official service on Yellow River conservancy work and a statistical work on the number of people in 16 provinces who were aged 70 or more in 1688.

Near Kong Shangren's tomb, on the eastern side of the graveyard, is the Tomb of the 76th Duke **Kong Lingyi** and the awful **Madame Tao**. The grave also includes Madame Wang, mother of the 77th generation, who was reburied there, against the strict rules that concubines could not be included in clan graves, to the joy of her small son.

The **Temple of Yan Hui** (Yan Hui miao) is just inside the northern city wall, on the east side of the road leading to the Confucian burial ground.

> Yan Hui was Confucius' favourite disciple and was therefore worshipped by emperors visiting Qu Fu along with his master. The founder of the Han dynasty (reigned 206–194 BC) is said to have founded the temple, which was

extensively restored in 1326 and then in the Ming and Qing. In 1330 Yan Hui was posthumously awarded the title of 'Fusheng Duke of the State of Yan' and the temple is sometimes known as the Fusheng (Return of the Sage) miao.

Said to have been built on the site of Yan Hui's house in Humble Alley, the temple covers 56 hectares with wide courtyards full of old conifers; the main buildings are arranged on the central one of the three axes, culminating in the Hall of the Sage Returned and the Hall of Yan Hui's Wife behind (echoing the arrangement in the Temple of Confucius). Notable features of this grand, empty enclosure are the well in the first courtyard, said to have been used by Yan Hui, now covered by a pavilion housing a stele inscribed 'Well of Humble Alley' by the Kangxi emperor of the Qing. Inside the gate to the second courtyard, which once contained side buildings for storing sacrificial implements, are two stele pavilions with stelae commemorating renovations in 1441 and 1509.

The Main Hall is, like the hall in the Temple of Confucius, supported by stone columns carved with dragons.

The side halls of the courtyard were once used for the worship of Yan Hui's descendants, who included Yan Zitui (c AD 531–590), a 34th generation descendant who wrote the *Moral Instructions for the Yan Family*, a remarkably Confucian document on family conduct. Similar works were written by many Confucians, although this is the earliest surviving example. A Ming work on the same subject contains a map of a house with separate paths marked for men and women of the family so that they should not meet by chance.

Other descendants of Yan Hui include Yan Shigu (581–645), who was famous for his annotations to the history of the Han dynasty, and Yan Zhenqing (709–785), a famous calligrapher who raised an army with his brother to help suppress the An Lushan rebellion of 755.

The eastern building now contains a display of locally excavated neolithic and early Zhou ceramics, illustrating the local development of the Longshan type of neolithic culture. From the second courtyard, an eastern gate, the Gate of Watching Advancement, leads to the eastern axis where, in the Hall for Withdrawal and Introspection, there is a Ming stele with an image of Yan Hui seated. The parallel western axis contains halls devoted to the worship of Yan Hui's father and, behind, his mother.

Outside the city wall, to the northeast, is the **Zhou gong miao** (Temple to the Duke of Zhou), a smaller temple than that of Yan Hui but equally tranquil and filled with fine cypress, juniper and pistachio trees.

The Duke of Zhou is a semi-historical figure. Fourth son of King Wen of the Zhou who assisted his brother, King Wu, in the suppression of the Shang dynasty (late 11C BC) and the establishment of the Zhou. He is credited with the formulation of the regulations by which the Zhou ruled and is therefore described in Chinese textbooks as 'the most famous politician of China's ancient slave-owning society' (as close to a 'Good Thing' as a slave-owner could get). In AD 1008 he was granted the title of 'King of Cultural Regulations' by the Song emperor and his temple was built on the site of an earlier temple erected by his son in the 11C BC and much restored in succeeding dynasties.

The main gate is a decorative wooden structure with a grey tiled roof. On top of the tall wooden columns are glazed figures of heavenly warriors seated on drums and over the western gate is an inscription 'Regulating the rites and creating music', while that over the eastern doorway is translated as 'Ability to make the warp and woof of the universe'. The main building, the Hall of the First Sage, has inscriptions by the Qianlong emperor.

The huge horizontal tablet reads 'Diligently practising illustrious virtue' and the seal reads 'Imperial calligraphy of the Qianlong emperor', who is also responsible for the antithetical couplets on the pillars praising 'The eternal influence on governmental and social regulations established by the Duke of Zhou and the illustrious spiritual model he provided for Confucius', who sought to bring contemporary rulers back to those golden days of regulations.

Set into the northwest wall of the building is a Han dynasty depiction of the Duke, described in a Chinese guidebook as 'the only extant portrait of the Duke of Zhou in China' but omitting to mention that it was made nearly a millennium after his death. The figures are replicas of those destroyed in the Cultural Revolution and comprise the Duke of Zhou in the centre, with Bo Qin, his filial son, to the east and Bo Qin's servant to the west. The servant has a board on his back with a few maxims from the Duke for his son.

> The Duke of Zhou was supposed to have feared that Bo Qin might occasionally show a lack of prudence in directing the affairs of the State of Lu so he had a trusted servant carry the inscribed board on his back and turn round whenever his young master needed an exhortation.

Sacrifices used to be offered on the broad terrace in front of the hall, which is now surrounded by inscriptions from 1008 onwards written in praise of the Duke of Zhou.

On the west of the road out to the Confucian burial ground (northwest of the Temple of the Duke of Zhou) is a high mound called the **Terrace for Gazing towards Father** where Bo Qin would sit and look westwards thinking of his father.

Another somewhat legendary site, 4km east of Qu Fu, in the northeast corner of Jiuxian village, is the **Tomb of Emperor Shaohao**, said to have been the son of the Yellow Emperor and a first ancestor of all the Chinese people.

> His divine status meant that the 'tomb' was improved throughout the centuries, most notably by the Huizong emperor of the Song, who had it bricked over like a pyramid in AD 1111 and by the Qianlong emperor, who ordered 421 cypresses and four junipers to be planted there in 1748 after a personal visit.

A carved stone *pailou* of 1739 leads to the Hall of Sacrifices with an inscription by the Qianlong emperor and the flattened pyramid of the tomb. Just to the south are two massive stone tablets lying face down, the only remains of the palace built in 1012 to commemorate Shaohao's father, the Yellow Emperor. The tablets were intended to be carved on site but the Song dynasty was driven from north China before this could happen.

Some 30km southeast of Qu Fu is **Nishan Hill** where Confucius' mother prayed for a second son, as her first had been too sickly to participate in the essential task of a son, the maintenance of the ancestral sacrifices.

Her wish was granted but Confucius was said to have been so hideous at birth that his father abandoned him on Nishan Hill where he was reared by a tigress and kept cool by an eagle that fanned him with her wings. These phenomena convincing his father that the child was exceptional, the child was allowed back home.

There is now a temple on the hill and the place is also famous for its ink-stones which were obviously appropriate souvenirs for Chinese visitors to the home of the effective founder of the Chinese bureaucracy.

Zibo

Zibo, 160km west of Jinan, is a very ancient city, incorporating the site of the capital of the state of Qi in the Spring and Autumn and Warring States periods (722–221 BC). Part of the Qi city wall can still be seen as well as a number of tumuli, thought to be the tombs of notables of the state of Qi. Zibo is today best known for its ceramic and glass production and some specialist groups with a particular interest in either glass or ceramics visit the town for this reason.

The **Glass Factory** produces objects of all sizes from snuff bottles to giant vases and its special characteristic is coloured glass. Most of the vessels are made from layers of different coloured glass, cut through so that red or blue or green silhouettes stand out against a white ground or vice versa.

The **Ceramics Factory** produces a variety of wares, specialising in darkish earthenwares, particularly 'oil spot' glazes. The dark brown or black glaze, whose colour is based on iron oxide, is spotted with tiny, regular silvery spots caused by concentrations of the oxide which appear on the surface during firing.

Satisfactory production of a good base colour and even spotting is extremely difficult, a trade secret passed from one craftsman to another. This sometimes leaves the factory administration at the mercy of their potters. They are anxious to increase oil-spot production as it is extremely popular in Japan: Deng Xiaoping had taken a tea-service from Zibo as a gift on an official visit to Japan and it is equally attractive to western visitors.

In the outskirts of Zibo (Zichuan qu), easily reached by taxi, is **Pu Songling's House** (Pu Songling gu ju). Pu Songling (1640–1715) is best known for his collection of short stories, *Liao zhai zhi yi* translated long ago by Herbert Giles as *Strange Stories from a Chinese Studio*, 1908, and recently partially translated and introduced by Jonathan Spence in *The Death of Woman Wang*, Penguin, 1979.

Although much restored, Pu Songling's old home is a good example of popular architecture of the Shandong region in the early Qing. It is a simple courtyard dwelling of grey brick and tile with courtyard gardens; the furniture is said to be that used by Pu Songling himself. There is an exhibition of translations of his works, manuscript and illustrated woodblock editions as well as many calligraphic inscriptions in his praise by famous people.

> ### Pu Songling
> Little known in his own time as a writer, Pu Songling passed the *juren* (first level) examinations with the highest marks but spent the rest of his life trying to pass the next stage (*xiu cai*) without success. He served as secretary to a local magistrate and as secretary to a friend, a retired magistrate, managed the affairs of his family and wrote stories and poems. The *Liao zhai zhi yi* is a collection of stories and legends, most with some basis in fact, although fox fairies mingle with the real-life characters.

Qingdao

Qingdao, one of China's major seaports, is on the south side of the Shandong peninsula at the mouth of a natural inlet. Until 1914 it was the 'seat of government of German China'.

History

It had been used as a winter anchorage for the Russian fleet in 1895, a considerable provocation to the Germans. Kaiser Willhelm II warned the Tsar that if Russia claimed territory in China, then Germany would have to demand a 'coal depot' at least in order to safeguard her own trading interests. Baron von Richthoven, the geographer who in 1877 had coined the phrase 'Seidenstrasse', or Silk Road, together with Admiral von Tirpitz, suggested that Shandong province would be a useful base area for Germany to balance the Russian fleet at Dairen (Port Arthur) and the British at Weihaiwei. On the pretext of avenging the deaths of two German missionaries in Shandong, Qingdao was taken on 14 November 1897 and, by a treaty imposed on the Chinese, land was leased around the port.

The Germans laid out a new foreign quarter 'under strict regulations as to sanitation and appearances, with every discouragement to the mere speculator', installed electric lighting and stationed 2000 men in the garrison. The city still (just) retains a German flavour to its architecture. In 1914 the Japanese, also anxious to acquire a foothold in China, took advantage of being allied with the British and demanded that Germany hand over Qingdao. When the demand was ignored, Japan declared war on 23 August 1914 and with the British bombarded Qingdao. Despite the German batteries on Mount Bismarck, Qingdao was taken on 7 November and 5000 luckless prisoners were taken to Japan.

At the end of the First World War, ignoring Chinese protests, Japan was granted authority over all the ex-German territories in China. The *Japanese Railway Guide* of 1924 naturally devotes much space to 'one of the most fashionable watering-places of the Orient', although it admits that 'being a newly opened district, historic places are scarce and the parks and other places created by the Germans are still too new to interest visitors'. It recommends trips to nearby (25km east) Lao shan, a mountain inhabited by Taoist priests, whose springs produce the best-known mineral water in China, *Laoshan kuangquanshui*, to Victoria Bay (the easternmost bathing beach beyond the piers) and to the Governor's Residence on the slopes of Mount Diederich (now Zhongshan gongyuan or park).

Practical information

Getting there
Qingdao can be reached by bus (quicker) or train from Jinan. Shanghai and Peking also have rail connections with Qingdao.

Where to stay
The *Xinhao shan yingbin-guan* (closed in winter Oct–May) is an old German mansion at 26 Longshan lu, ☎ 286 6209, fax 286 1985. The *Haitian Dajiudian*, at 48 Xianggang lu, offers ocean views, ☎ 287 1888, fax 387 1777.

The most interesting part of Qingdao, where the railway station on Taian lu, an impressive Teutonic construction celebrating the arrival of the railway from Jinan in 1904, and most of the hotels are found, is the old German Concession area towards the end of the peninsula. Like the beaches, it is an area simply for wandering in. The Public Security Office (29 Hubei lu) is a fine old German building with a clock tower; the Catholic church with its twin spires is to the east of Zhongshan lu, the railway station to the west and the beach area is lined with fine (crumbling) villas and guesthouses.

The **museum** (Qingdao shi bowuguan) on Daxue lu is housed in a Buddhist Welfare Institute built in 1931 for the Red Swastika Association and comprises a collection of Yuan to Qing paintings and an archaeological section which is best known for its large stone Buddha figures produced between 500 and 527 when Shandong was a major centre of Buddhist carving. The most impressive figure weighs 30 tons and is nearly 6m high; it is accompanied by 3m Bodhisattvas. The heads of the Bodhisattvas were cut off in 1928 by the Japanese who took them to the railway station for transportation but the move was foiled and the sculptures restored.

In **Lu Xun park**, on the tip of the promontory, immediately west of Beach No. 1 (the beaches of Qingdao are numbered 1–6 from west to east) are the **Aquarium** and **Museum of Sea Products** (Haichan bowuguan). The latter was founded in 1932, at least part of it set up by the Academia Sinica, and amalgamated with the Qingdao Museums Authority in 1955. The collection is intended both for research and 'to introduce the environment of the oceans, their origins and to popularise the sciences of the sea'. Next door is the **Naval Museum** (Haijun bowuguan).

In the industrial part of the town, east of the main harbour, is the **Qingdao Brewery**, which can be visited by arrangement with the *China Travel Service* (the main office is behind the Huiquan Dynasty Hotel at 9 Nanhai lu, ☎ 287 0876) or other tourist agencies. The brewery was established by the Germans before the First World War and hops were planted to supply it. It produces beer called 'Tsingtao', an earlier spelling of Qingdao, which is considered to be the best in China and is now widely exported. The beer is light and clear, although a dark brown stout is also produced (which I have not seen outside the brewery).

Yantai

Yantai, known to westerners of the late 19C and early 20C as Chefoo, was a fishing town on the northern tip of the Shandong peninsula.

Best reached by minibus from Qingdao (3hrs), the bus station is opposite the railway station.

History

It was opened to foreign trade in 1858 by the Tientsin Treaty, although it seemed at the time to be lacking various essential amenities, as the *Encyclopaedia Sinica* reports: 'The port lacks a harbour and a breakwater but we hope that the want will soon be supplied ... It also needs and hopes for railway communication with the interior ....' This last want has been supplied, for Yantai is on the railway line from Jinan via Weifang, a centre for kite-making with an annual kite-flying festival in March and other handicraft production, notably of 'New Year' prints, or *nianhua*, and yellow striped tiger toys. In the early days of the 20C the chief trade of Yantai was in beancake, hairnets, lace and fruits and the shipment of '100,000 coolies a year to Siberia'. There was also a pioneering winery set up by a Singaporean Chinese in 1893.

For the children of western missionaries in China, Yantai was home for much of the year for it was here that the famous Chefoo schools were set up, Yantai's climate being considered healthy and bracing. The remains of the school buildings can still be seen and the town is often visited by ex-alumni associations. There were separate boys' and girls' schools and the pupils whose parents were working in mission stations in the distant interior of China often only saw their parents briefly in the summer holidays after long trips by Japanese steamer down to Shanghai and thence up the Yangtse.

Apart from the beaches and harbour, there is also an impressive **Fujian Guild Hall** (Fujian hui guan) in the centre of the town. Begun in 1884, it took 22 years to complete. It was financed by Fujianese merchants, who used it as a lodging, and was built in the south in the decorative southern style, the pieces being shipped to Yantai for assembly. Its courtyards include a stage (the perfomance of plays was an important part of trade guild festivals, as in medieval Europe), a main hall and side wings and the **Yantai Museum** is now housed there. The timber parts are highly carved and painted.

In the museum there are relics of the old fishing industry: beautiful aprons with tiny appliqué decorations worn by fisherwomen, dishes with simple fish designs and boat models.

Weihaiwei

Weihaiwei, on the peninsula 65km east of Yantai (and best reached by bus), was an excellent port, seized by the Japanese during the Sino-Japanese War of 1894–95. In 1898 the port was ceded to the British for 'as long as Port Arthur is occupied by the Russians'. It was returned to China in 1930. Like Hong Kong, it was not a treaty port but British territory, ruled by a Commissioner who lived in relative isolation in a seven-room 'Government House'. Arriving from Hong Kong in 1902, the most famous Commissioner was J.H. Stewart Lockhart who ran Weihaiwei, assisted by a secretary (who also served as magistrate in the Port Edward district), a medical officer, a resident chaplain and a district officer and magistrate for the interior district, who was Reginald Johnston, later to act as tutor to the last emperor Puyi. Johnston spent much of his time travelling to court hearings within his jurisdiction and he wrote an account of his time in Weihaiwei, *Lion and Dragon in Northern China* (London, 1910). Some remnants of the British residence can still be found in Weihaiwei, which had been a popular summer resort for foreign residents with 'neat little bungalows', two golf courses and good shooting of snipe, duck, geese and quails. British sailors stationed there might 'grumble at the absence of facilities' found elsewhere in the East but 'from the point of view of healthfulness, Weihaiwei in the summer is not to be equalled'.

Xi'an

Xi'an ('Western Peace') is the modern capital of Shaanxi province and a major industrial centre. It does, however, preserve the Ming city walls in their entirety and is one of the most famous tourist centres in China, particularly since the discovery of the spectacular 'Buried Army' of terracotta warriors.

It served as the capital of China for most of the Han, Sui and Tang dynasties, when it was known as Chang'an ('Eternal Peace'). Particularly during the Han, it was used as a major capital in conjunction with Luoyang ('Eastern Capital'), whence the court retreated if Chang'an was menaced by barbarians from the West. Excavations have revealed the huge spread of the Tang city, far beyond the limits of today's Xi'an, and the surrounding countryside is dotted with the tumuli of emperors, empresses and courtiers of the Han and Tang.

Practical information

Getting there
By air
The airport is near the neighbouring town of Xianyang and the airport shuttle bus takes about an hour to reach the centre of Xi'an, dropping off at the **China Northwest Airlines** office on Laodang lu (20 yuan). Taxis cost c 130 yuan and firmness will be necessary.

By train

The station is in the north of the town just outside the walls. It is on the main east–west line from Peking or Shanghai to Urumqi and it is possible to get to Xi'an by rail from Nanjing, Qingdao, Zhengzhou, Chongqing, Chengdu, Lanzhou and Taiyuan.

 Where to stay

Many of the new hotels are situated in rather dismal and distant suburbs. The best-situated hotels include the *Renmin Dasha* (Remin or People's Hotel), 319 Dongxin jie, ☎ 742 8946, fax 742 2617, just west of the main square. This is a wondrous example of the huge old hotels built sometimes by, but invariably for, the Russian advisers of the 1950s. Before modernisation, when students were crammed into dormitory rooms for improving summer trips, we used to call it the People's Large Prawn (*daxia*, fourth tone, means 'prawn', *sha*, alternative pronunciation of *xia*, fourth tone, means 'mansion') and it was an unlovely place. It has since been modernised and is well-situated for walks to the city centre. The *Zhonglou Fandian* (Bell Tower Hotel), just southwest of the Bell Tower, is in the very centre of town and since 1987 has been under Holiday Inn management, ☎ 727 9200, fax 721 8970. There is a smaller, cheaper hotel well-situated at 351 Dong da jie, the *Wuyi Fandian* (1 May Hotel), ☎ 721 0255, fax 721 3824.

The most expensive hotel in Xi'an is the *Hyatt Regency* (Kaiyue Fandian) on Heping lu, ☎ 723 1234, fax 721 6799. The first 'luxury' foreign-managed hotel (a Swedish hotel chain) to be opened in Xi'an was the *Golden Flower* on Changle lu, which is, unfortunately, a stiff ten minute walk from the eastern city wall past a sugarbeet factory and its associated housing blocks. It is worth visiting the Golden Flower, if time hangs heavy (which is not often in Xi'an where visitors are rushed through and away to allow the next batch in), to see its extraordinary layout. The ground floor is cut in half by a deep channel filled with rushing water. This is quite attractive but it also cuts the dining area in half so that waiters have to walk a long way to the diners. To diminish the communication problem the channel is partially boarded over for breakfast and tables loaded with self-service foods placed above the gully. You did have to be rather careful not to step back from the table and so breakfast was a nerve-racking affair as incautious guests windmilled backwards, arms flailing, over the great divide. At night, a pianist and grand piano were placed over the stream.

A development that was first seen in Xi'an hotels and restaurants serving tourists was the use of self-service catering. A great variety of somewhat indifferent dishes were kept warm on heated tables and visitors helped themselves, ladling their chosen foods into plastic trays. In a country that prides itself on the freshness of its food and that is oversupplied with people to serve it, this was a great pity and represents one of the threats that tourism brings, reducing Chinese cuisine to a lowest common denominator of what prejudiced packaged travellers will accept or are thought to be able to accept.

History

Xi'an's historic importance lies mainly in its use as a capital by the Han and Tang, although there were earlier settlements in and near Xi'an. The city's significance in the early part of the 20C derived from its nearness to the Communist Party's 1937–45 headquarters at Yan'an. Travellers, such as the

American journalist Edgar Snow, were smuggled out of Xi'an to Yan'an in the late 1930s and the city is also famous for the Xi'an incident of 1936 when Chiang Kai-shek was captured by his own allies in a vain attempt to make him behave sensibly about the Japanese invasion.

Evidence of Early Man in the Xi'an area is provided by the discovery in 1963–64 of a skull, jaw and other bones of **Lantian Man** some 38km southeast of Xi'an. Lantian Man (who was actually almost certainly several Lantian women) exhibited characteristics slightly more 'primitive' than the famous Peking Man (or person), such as a thicker skull and smaller cranial capacity, and is thought to lie developmentally somewhere between *Pithecanthropus robustus* and *Pithecanthropus erectus* (Peking Man is assigned to the latter group). The jawbone of Lantian Woman lacked the third molar and this is supposed to be the first known example of this dental phenomenon, although apparently it is not uncommon amongst present-day Asian peoples. Lantian Woman appears to have lived about 800,000 BC during a warm interval, for the bones were associated with south Chinese Pleistocene faunal species and broadleaf trees. Some stone implements have been found near Lantian but so far there is no definite connection between the human fossil remains and stone implements.

A recent find is that of a considerably later human fossil skull in Dali county, near the Shaanxi–Shanxi border. **Dali Man** is thought to belong to an early subspecies of *Homo sapiens* of about 300,000 to 200,000 BC.

One of the major sites in the vicinity of Xi'an is the Neolithic village of **Banpo**, discovered in 1953 during excavation for the foundations of a factory. It is known that the fertile valleys of the Wei and Middle Yellow River were the sites of some of the earliest agricultural settlements of the Neolithic; Banpo is generally dated to an early stage of the Yangshao (or 'painted pottery' culture) and is thought to have been occupied from c 5000–4000 BC. The village remains are remarkably complete and about 4000 square metres have been roofed over as a site museum.

The Zhou people, who overthrew the Bronze Age Shang dynasty c 1027 BC, had their origins in western Shaanxi. Two sites near Xi'an have been tentatively identified as capitals: **Fengjing** on the west bank of the Feng River and **Haojing** on the opposite side. Haojing is supposed to have been the Western Zhou capital from its conquest of the Shang until 771 BC when nomadic tribes forced a move of the capital eastwards to Luoyang. This move from the Xi'an area east to Luoyang was to be repeated in the Han and Tang when Luoyang was the 'eastern' and secondary capital to Xi'an's 'western' capital. Artefacts unearthed during excavations of the two sites can now be seen in the Xianyang and Shaanxi Provincial Museums.

Similarly, the first emperor of the Qin, **Qin Shi huangdi**, established his imperial capital at Xianyang, some 15km northwest of Xi'an. *Qin* was the name of the state in which he rose to power and was used for the dynasty he established after conquering all the other states in 221 BC; *huangdi* means 'emperor'. As is well known, he was buried in a tumulus in Lintong county, 18km northeast of Xi'an, near the many subsidiary pits of his grave, which contained, amongst other treasures, the Buried Army.

Remains of the Han dynasty capital of **Chang'an** (Xi'an's ancient name), including parts of the city wall, are plentiful and the most spectacular are some of the Han tombs in the surrounding countryside: Mao ling, the tomb of the Wudi (Martial) emperor of the Han and the tomb of a famous general, Huo Qubing. None of the nine Han imperial tombs has yet been excavated.

The Tang capital of Chang'an was, in its time, probably the site of the most advanced culture of the contemporary world, full of traders from all over Central Asia and craftsmen producing wondrous silver and gold vessels for the imperial court, some of whose treasures (gold, silver, jade, silken textiles and ceramics) have been found in hoards, buried at the time of the An Lushan rebellion in the mid 8C, or in nearby temples that were granted imperial patronage. The Tang tombs of members of the imperial family and their courtiers surround the city with their sculpted 'spirit ways'.

The surviving city walls, bell and drum towers, all date from the Ming when Xi'an was a far smaller centre than it had been in its imperial heyday. Although the first Ming emperor appointed his second son to rule Xi'an, the palace that was built for him no longer survives and there was considerable destruction of the Manchu quarter of the city (a walled section of the north-east part of the town) in 1911 when the Qing dynasty was overthrown. In the subsequent Republican era Xi'an was a key communications centre, particularly for those wishing to reach the Communist headquarters at Yan'an.

Xi'an today sprawls out beyond the Ming city walls with cotton mills, electrical-equipment factories, fertiliser factories and many others surrounding the old walled city. It has seen the relocation of various industries from the overcrowded eastern seaboard, with whole factories including workers moved in to promote the development of the relatively backward northeast.

In the early days of visiting the Buried Army (late 1970s), before hotels and restaurants were built in the area to supply the needs of tourists, visitors were often given lunch in a neighbouring sewing-machine factory whose canteen ran a profitable sideline in tourist lunches. The visit was rather uncanny since the factory and its workers had all come from Shanghai (where there were two sewing-machine factories) to Xi'an (where there were none) and in the middle of rough rural Shaanxi all you could hear was the rather feminine Shanghai dialect. In the last couple of decades, particularly since the discovery of the Buried Army, Xi'an's major industry is that of tourism, with ever-expanding numbers of Chinese and foreign visitors being rushed through the major sites.

For most tourists travelling in groups, Xi'an is a 'two-day' stop. One day is spent visiting the Buried Army and Huaqing Hot Springs, usually with a brief stop at the neolithic village of Banpo en route. On the second day, the city walls, the Shaanxi Provincial Museum in the old Confucian temple, the famous mosque and nearby Bell Tower and some rather unlikely 'handicraft factories' are visited. As hotel facilities expand, visitors may be able to stay longer and this is to be recommended for the Han and Tang tombs, in particular, are enormously interesting.

With the exception of the Lintong County Museum, a standard itinerary of one day comprises the Buried Army, Huaqing Hot Springs, Lintong County Museum and Banpo with lunch usually provided, either at the Hot Springs or a nearby hotel or restaurant. Individual travellers can sign up for such a day excursion through the *China Travel Service* (*CITS*) or other tourist organisations contactable through your hotel.

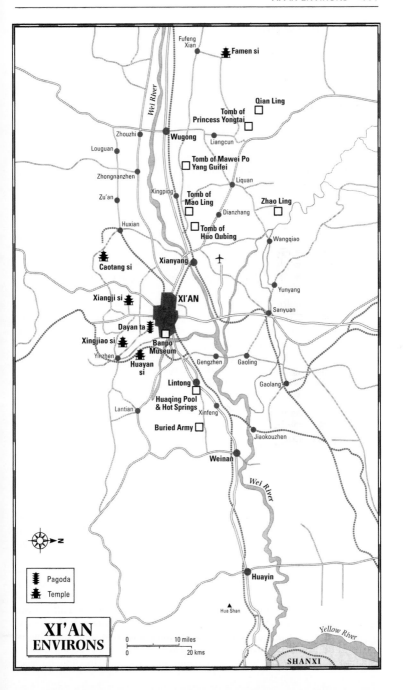

Fufeng Xian

Famen si

Qian Ling

Tomb of Princess Yongtai

Zhouzhi

Wugong

Liangcun

Louguan

Tomb of Mawei Po Yang Guifei

Zhongnanzhen

Liquan

Xingping

Zu'an

Tomb of Mao Ling

Zhao Ling

Dianzhang

Huxian

Tomb of Huo Qubing

Wangqiao

Caotang si

Xianyang

Yunyang

Xiangji si

Sanyuan

Dayan ta

Xingjiao si

Banpo Museum

Yinzhen

Gengzhen

Gaoling

Huayan si

Gaolang

Lintong

Huaqing Pool & Hot Springs

Xinfeng

Lantian

Buried Army

Jiaokouzhen

Weinan

Wei River

Huayin

Hua Shan

Yellow River

SHANXI

🛕 Pagoda
🛕 Temple

XI'AN ENVIRONS

0 — 10 miles
0 — 20 kms

The Buried Army

The Buried Army is just under 30km east of Xi'an and forms only a part of the huge grave of the first Qin emperor (reigned 221–209 BC).

Although only 13 when he ascended the throne of the state of Qin in 246, the first emperor managed to achieve the subjugation of all the other six states in 221 BC—'as a silkworm devours leaves', as Sima Qian put it—thus unifying China into one empire for the first time. Naturally a leader capable of such a feat is not generally characterised by historians as a gentle and humane character and Qin Shi huangdi is one of the tyrants of Chinese history, vilified in particular by Confucians throughout the ages for his support of Legalism, a philosophy which assumed that human nature was basically anarchic and evil and required firm government by rule of law rather than the moral precepts and examples of Confucianism. The first emperor is most famous for his 'burning of the books' in 213 BC, an event which also included burning (burying alive to be precise) quite a few of their authors. This was an attempt to wipe out all subversive writing and all works inimical to the ruling Legalist philosophy, including poetry and philosophy, historical chronicles and practically everything except manuals on farming and the law. Few works survived.

The Qin empire barely survived the death of its initiator, for his equally ruthless advisers eliminated his heir in favour of a more pliable second son, but they were finally overthrown in a series of revolts against their tyranny and the Han dynasty replaced the Qin in 206 BC. As part of their attempts to retain power, the first emperor's ministers are said to have tried to conceal the death of their patron as long as possible, driving his corpse around in an imperial carriage followed by a cart full of rotting fish (to conceal the odour of the decaying corpse). The first emperor was, however, finally laid to rest in the tumulus he had constructed for himself, beginning in the first year of his reign.

The Buried Army is part of a massive complex of burial pits which surround the tumulus in which the emperor is buried. The tomb itself, a grassy mound of considerable size some 1.5km west of the Buried Army, can be climbed by visitors. It has a stepped path to the top, running through stalls where peasants sell anything from appallingly fragile miniature clay warriors to apples and 'ancient coins'. It has not yet been scientifically excavated.

The contents of the mound, or its supposed contents, are well known from the account left by Sima Qian, the Grand Historian, in his *Shi ji* (*Historical Records*, 1C BC). He describes how 700,000 workmen laboured on the site, where a representation of the rivers of China in mercury was made to flow by machinery; the heavens were depicted and the whole was protected by automatic crossbows and arrows designed to fire if the tomb was entered. It is assumed that fantastic grave goods were also included, although it is most probable that, like almost all others, the tomb was robbed soon after it was closed and so precious metals and jewels were probably removed. The description of the contents of the tomb is so extraordinary that some said Chinese archaeologists were afraid to open it up in case the marvels crumbled before their eyes on exposure to the air. A month-long excavation in 1986, however, revealed extensive damage, probably by Tang and Song robbers, and archaeologists are now concentrating on subsidiary sites in the area.

The Buried Army, just further on, is in fact only one of three similar pits, each containing a buried army, and the scale of these subsidiary pits has only served to enhance expectations of the contents of the tomb itself. A huge vault has been built over Pit No. I so that the pit is viewed as it was when finished, with many of the terracotta figures restored and replaced in their original battle formation and the rear section of the pit left as it was when first discovered, with heads of warriors and horses emerging from the yellow earth. Side buildings contain displays of the contents of the three pits and there is an illuminated map of the entire grave area showing the numerous smaller burial pits that have been located.

It is known that the first emperor's paranoia extended beyond the grave. He is said to have ordered that all those who knew of the location and contents of his grave were to follow him into it and a number of pits containing human remains have been uncovered and are presumed to be the tombs of the unfortunate grave-diggers.

Pit No. 1 was discovered in 1974 when local peasants decided to build a well during a drought. They found a vast vault of some 12,000 square metres about 5m underground and constructed with 11 parallel pits running east to west containing an estimated 8000 terracotta figures. These were drawn up in battle formation with three rows, each of 70 archers as the vanguard, a single column of spearmen facing outwards and a central group of 38 columns of infantry and chariots. The wooden chariots have all but disappeared, except for the terracotta horses which drew them and their metal fittings. The soldiers were provided with real bronze arms: swords, daggers, spears, halberds, axes, crossbows (of wood and of which only the bronze fittings have survived) and arrowheads. Some of the alloys used were quite complex, with over ten elements included, and the weapons were sharp and untarnished on discovery.

The figures were about 1.8m tall on average and must have been considerably larger than life-size when they were made. The upper part of the body is solid clay, the lower part and legs hollow and, while there is a degree of mass-production about the bodies, the faces in particular were individually modelled, exhibiting a considerable range of facial expressions, hairstyles and head-dresses. It is almost certain that the figures were made in parts—the bodies as one, the legs, hands and head separately—and the different parts were luted together afterwards, thus enabling variety in the positioning of the hands (which held reins, swords, spears or other weapons in different grasps) and the great variety of facial modelling. All the figures have long hair, dressed in a variety of cloth-wrapped buns on top of the head, the form of masculine hairstyle in China from the Qin until the imposition of the queue by the Manchus in AD 1644. Those on the outside of the formation wear armour, possibly of lacquered leather in small squares, while those on the inside appear to be unprotected. The figures were all originally painted but few traces of the colours now remain. The vaults within the pit appear to have been covered with timbers in some form of roof, which was burnt in 206 BC when, it is said, General Xiang Yu (one of the warriors who struggled unsuccessfully for power at the end of the Qin) opened the vault after plundering the main mausoleum. The wooden timbers fell in on the contents, preserving them underground for 2000 years.

Pit No. 2, discovered northeast of the first pit in 1976, was an L-shaped vault with some 1000 terracotta figures including four chariots, cavalrymen leading horses, foot soldiers and crossbow men. One taller figure (1.95m) is assumed to be a general.

Pit No. 3 lay beside no. 2 and contained one chariot with some 70 soldiers. Some of the figures were removed from the smaller pits for use in the associated museum displays.

The bronze chariots

Aside from the major displays relating to the contents of the Buried Army pits (which allow a closer and usually less-crowded view of the figures), there is a small hall to the right of Pit No. 1 where two marvellous bronze chariots are displayed. These two, about half to a quarter life-size, were found near the tumulus, one in remarkably good condition. They have been restored (with colour photographs of the restoration work displayed on the walls of the hall) and are quite extraordinary, with all the parts made to move, from the lattice windows to the horse fittings. The four horses that draw each chariot were painted white and have accurately-depicted harness inlaid with gold and silver and decorated with plumes. In one chariot a single figure sits at the front, holding the reins and behind him is a covered vehicle with a sort of parasol-like roof or awning, little open-work windows that can be opened or closed and a body decorated with swirling cloud-patterns (characteristic of Han lacquer or bronze decoration). The other chariot attendant stands some 91cm high. Both are dressed as ninth grade officials. An exact replica of one of the chariots was presented to Queen Elizabeth when she visited Xi'an in the autumn of 1987.

Outside the enclosure is a vast open **market**, for the peasants of the area have realised the economic potential of tourism. They offer brilliant red embroidered clothes based on traditional children's garments.

The tiger shoes and hats they sell were worn by children as protection against evil spirits; I am not quite so sure about the function of the charming little black pig slippers (perhaps evil spirits were meant to think that the child was a pig and not bother to steal it away). The little parti-coloured padded waistcoats were often decorated (and still are) with the 'five poisonous creatures' (centipede, lizard, scorpion, toad and snake) in the hope that this would prevent them harming the child. Children's pillows of red cotton with two protective tiger-heads at either end were traditionally given when a new baby achieved its first 'hundred days' and stuffed cotton toys were often made in the shape of tigers.

Fengxiang, a town not far from Xi'an, is famous for its painted clay toys made of soft terracotta with a white slip covered in bright pink and green floral designs. These are often lion-dogs or tigers and usually have a little clay pellet inside to rattle. These traditional toys and garments (the latter all too often now made in giant adult sizes rather than for small children) are characteristic of the area and appropriate purchases but you will have to bargain with the peasant sellers.

The Huaqing Hot Springs

The Huaqing Hot Springs are c 30km from Xi'an, on the road to the Buried Army. The springs are set beneath the Li Mountain, on which there are still Buddhist and Taoist temples of no great significance, although the Taoist temples of Laomu (the mother goddess) and Li Er are charming little buildings with the sharply angled roofs characteristic of the area. Only individual travellers will have time to climb up to them.

The natural springs have attracted Chinese rulers since the Western Zhou, when the first palace or villa was built. The first emperor had a residence here and so did the Wudi emperor of the Han but the major associations of the Huaqing Hot Springs are with the Tang Xuanzong emperor and (rather an incongruous juxtaposition) Chiang Kai-shek.

The first Tang emperor, Taizong (his posthumous name, *Taizong*, means 'supreme ancestor'), had his palace architect Yan Lide build a palace at the hot springs in 644 and the palace was greatly enlarged by the Xuanzong (Profound Ancestor) emperor (reigned 713–756). He spent the winters here with his fat concubine Yang Guifei, whose affections were divided between the emperor and her adopted son, a non-Chinese general called An Lushan who led a nearly disastrous rebellion against the emperor in 755. The adopted son (who was killed by his own son) caused the death of Yang Guifei: popularly held responsible for the uprising, as she and the emperor fled west to Sichuan the imperial guard insisted that she be killed. This and the emperor's subsequent decline and death form one of the great subjects of Chinese romantic poetry and painting.

The **Tang baths** at Huaqing have been excavated and reconstructed in the 'Tang style' by a team from Nanjing Architectural College (1991).

As you enter the Huaqing Hot Springs Garden, straight through the main gates is the major public bath area (to which we will return). To the right is a large hall, the **Hall of Flying Clouds** (Feixia ge), one of several rebuilt in 1956 with the original names used in the Tang. On the far side of the hall is a large pool with a **marble boat** to the right. Given the opprobrium expressed over the Dowager Empress Cixi's construction of a (rather more vulgar) marble boat at the Summer Palace in Peking, squandering money meant for the Navy in 1888, it is interesting to note that this marble boat was built in 1956. On the far side of the pool is the **Longyin xie** (Pavilion of the Dragon's Song) and behind that, reached by a road that rises slightly up the mountainside, is the *Huaqing Guesthouse*, the most luxurious of the bathing places available (no need to book in advance).

There are some other sites to see before bathing. Crossing from the Pavilion of the Dragon's Song, along the top of the pool, you reach the major spring area, which is now being excavated and 'reconstructed'.

Above the springs is a small, five-bay building containing the bedroom where Chiang Kai-shek stayed in 1936. Just in front of this, in another building, is a small, elegantly shaped marble bath in the form of an elongated plum blossom. Before excavations began it was always said to have been the bath used by the fat concubine Yang Guifei; it must now be described as just another bath. Crossing the **Flying Rainbow Bridge**, you can follow the path up the mountainside to the kiosk marking the spot where Chiang Kai-shek was captured in 1936, according to the popular version, without his false teeth and wearing only a short nightshirt.

One guidebook states that the kiosk was originally erected by the Nationalists to commemorate Chiang's escape and named the Pavilion of National Regeneration. I cannot confirm this, although the classical stone pavilion looks more like a pre- than post-Liberation construction in style.

Chiang Kai-shek had gone to Xi'an to direct an offensive against the Communist forces, despite the threat of a full-scale Japanese invasion which had already led some of his allies to call for negotiations with the Communists to form an anti-Japanese united front. Chiang was chased up the mountain from his bedroom and seized by troops of Zhang Xueliang (the 'Young Marshall'), a warlord allied with the KMT. Zhou Enlai came to Xi'an to mediate, extracting from Chiang the (empty) promise of national unity against Japan. The Young Marshall was in turn taken prisoner by Chiang and held for decades.

The natural springs at Huaqing contain minerals said to be beneficial. The water bubbles up at a comfortable temperature of 43° Celsius. There are various grades of bath: communal and cheap, individual (just below the Tang bath site) and luxurious (with a bedroom and bathroom en suite) in the Huaqing Guesthouse; charges vary accordingly. Towels are provided for the top two grades and the large baths, more like small swimming pools, square and lined with tiles, are very pleasant.

On the mountain behind the springs, the Xixiu Peak, to the west is a restored **beacon tower** said to date from the Western Zhou. It is a tapering square brick tower with a wooden pavilion on top, fired apparently with wolf dung and the site of a legend similar to the western one of the 'boy who cried wolf'.

The Western Zhou king had a favourite concubine, Bao Si, who never smiled until a court officer suggested the king take her to the beacon tower and summon all his dukes by lighting the fire. They all rushed up when the flames were kindled and Bao Si smiled. One year later, however, a real invasion occurred and the beacon fire was kindled but none of the dukes turned up, thinking the king was only trying to amuse Bao Si.

This tower and the Laomu and Li Er Temples can be reached by climbing the mountain path that leads west around and behind the springs.

Lintong County Museum

Lintong County Museum (open 08.00–17.30) is just up the road (turning right out of the Huaqing Garden), a small but quite interesting museum. On the way you pass a small fairground on your right and beside it is a good example of local domestic architecture: a courtyard house with two side wings with single-pitched roofs angled sharply down into the courtyard. The local yellow bricks, black-painted woodwork with a thin red line outlining doors and windows and, above all, the sharp angle of the single pitched roofs are characteristic of the Xi'an area, a variation on the ubiquitous courtyard house.

The major display in the museum is of the Buddhist relics unearthed in the vicinity of the Qinshan Temple on the northeast of Li Mountain. In 1985 a group of Buddhist coffins and a reliquary of 741 were found there and are now displayed in the museum. The reliquary is of stone, just over a metre high, in the form of a stupa pagoda and decorated with scenes of Buddhist deities, lotus panels and *apsareses* with flowing garments in low relief. The reliquary contained two miniature coffins, a silver outer coffin and a gold inner coffin, decorated with gold figures of monks and ropes of baroque pearls and turquoises. The two tiny coffins with their high, boat-like prows are made in the form of the standard wooden coffin still in use.

Other items in the museum include stone pillar bases and carvings from nearby temples and tombs (there is a nice sheep in the courtyard), Tang ceramics and a strange copper ewer decorated with human heads, all locally excavated.

Banpo

The Neolithic village of Banpo is on the eastern outskirts of Xi'an. The site was discovered in 1953. Covering some 50,000 square metres, the village site included a dwelling area delineated by a surrounding trench, a ceramic centre and a graveyard (the latter both situated beyond the trench). Forty-five dwellings, six pottery kilns and 250 graves, including 73 ceramic urns containing the remains of small children, have been found, together with ceramics, tools, animal bones and the remains of fruit stones, millet and other edibles. Scattered throughout the dwelling area were pocket-shaped pits 1–2m deep, generally called storage pits.

The dwellings of the Banpo people were discovered in more than one stratified layer: it appears from pollen samples, showing wild species reappearing after periods of domesticated crop pollens, that the settlement was used for several occupations, not occupied continuously, and the dwellings demonstrate an apparent progression from circular, semi-subterranean to rectangular, ground-level constructions with a carefully prepared floor surface. Structurally, the houses were similar, with timber columns of varying heights supporting the roof, which seems to have been thatched. The small post-holes of short, closely-placed roof supports mark the outer edge of the roof and some of the better-made houses also have larger, central post-holes. The openings to the houses were almost invariably oriented towards the south and inside the entry was a slightly sunken hearth. One much larger floor has been found in a relatively central position (from a late stage of occupation) and this is usually interpreted as some kind of communal building or meeting place. It appears to have been sacred in some way, for the remains of a dog and some ceramics were found beneath the floor. Fox-tail millet (*Setaria indica*), cabbage, mustard and hemp (for clothing) were cultivated, pigs and dogs were domesticated and, since the settlement was situated near a river, fish caught with fine bone hooks formed part of the diet. The dead were buried with ceramic bowls and sometimes a few items of adornment, stretched out on their backs and, like their houses, oriented towards the south. Small children, buried in lidded ceramic jars, were interred within the settlement area, otherwise, the cemetery was beyond the ditch, as was the pottery-making area.

Chinese archaeologists have argued that Banpo represents a communal

society of a primitive sort and ascribe it to a matriarchal state of development. There does not seem to be any material evidence for either communality or matriarchy. The latter theory is derived from Engels' writings on the
development of society and Engels himself was deriving theories from a 19C
American anthropologist who drew upon native American legends of a
matriarchal golden age. The existence of an apparent central building, with
its foundation sacrifices, does not necessarily imply communality in terms of
shared storage pits, although it points to a central belief celebrated communally or to a seat of government.

The ceramics of Banpo are very fine examples of the Yangshao or 'painted pottery' type. Made by hand from fine red clay, the rims perhaps finished on a
turntable of some sort, those that were used in burial were often decorated with
black, white and red designs. Ceramics for everyday use—bowls, dishes and fine
amphorae with two lug handles—were usually of plain red clay, sometimes decorated with cord, mat or basketwork patterns. The painted pottery shows a clear
progression of design from representations of mainly fish, human faces and
small deer to an elegant geometric patterning derived from the fish forms.

In the two museum wings at the front of the Banpo enclosure the daily life of the
matriarchy is illustrated in oil paintings, together with illustrations of the development of ceramic designs and the use of fish-hooks, net weights and spindles.

Of the 50,000 square metres of settlement, some 4000 square metres is now
covered over and the outlines of houses, storage pits, part of the surrounding
ditch and the occasional ceramic jar burial of a child near a house can all be
seen, with diagrams and reconstructions to make the material evidence more
comprehensible.

There is now a Banpo theme park just beside the site, notable for the massive
reclining naked matriarch and a generally Flintstones atmosphere. This was one
of the first theme parks constructed in China (in the early 1990s) but will not be
the last. It is difficult to know what lies behind the development, possibly the
growth in local tourism and a demand for associated shopping opportunities.

The city of Xi'an

A normal tourist itinerary for a second day in Xi'an takes in the walls, provincial
museum, the forest of stelae, mosque and the bell and drum towers and usually
includes some handicraft establishments where items are finished or half prepared (there seemed to be nowhere to fire the cloisonné, for example) for the benefit of tourists. Depending on where you are staying, the same sort of itinerary
can be organised, to be followed mostly on foot, by individual tourists.

Shaanxi Provincial Museum

The old Shaanxi Provincial Museum (open 08.30–17.30), where the forest of
stelae is housed, is in the south of the city near the city wall and so provides a
suitable opportunity for climbing up onto the wall as well, although the major
barbican gates south, east and west are more impressive. The wall dates from the
early years of the Ming when the second son of the emperor was appointed to
rule the area from his palace in Xi'an. The mass of the wall consists of rammed
yellow earth (loess) on a base of rammed earth, lime and glutinous rice, now

mostly faced with grey brick. The east wall is 2590m, the west wall 2631m, the north wall 3244m and the south wall 3441.6m. It is 12m high, 12–14m wide at the top, 15–18m broad at the base and unadorned on the inside but battlemented on the moat side. There are four corner towers and a tree-lined moat surrounding the whole. There are four major barbican or double gates in the centre of each side: the eastern Gate of Extended Joy, the western Gate of Settled Peace (where there is a museum of the city's history), the southern Gate of Eternal Tranquillity and the northern Gate of Distant Peace. These are huge barbicans with inner and outer walls and a considerable area within.

Although the wall now looks fine, as it and the moat have been cleaned and tidied up and made into a park-like area, in 1990 there was a story in the Chinese press about someone demolishing a part of the wall that irritated him; conservation is not uppermost in the local consciousness. The **Forest of Stelae** (Bei lin), one of the oldest 'museums' in China, is situated in the old Confucian temple, just inside the gate immediately east of the south gate.

Founded in 1090 to protect the stelae of the 13 Confucian Classics which had been carved in stone in 837 during the Tang dynasty, the Forest of Stelae now has six halls in which over 1000 stelae and tomb inscriptions are displayed, covering the period from the Han to the Qing. Some of the stelae, including those of the 13 Classics, are set in the walls of the halls; others similar to those found in temples, usually standing on the backs of stone tortoises and topped with interknitted dragons, are free-standing in rows. All have blackened, shiny surfaces where their inscriptions have been rubbed and, if you are lucky, you may see someone taking a rubbing. The stone surface is gently inked with a soft, ink-laden pad, then the fine paper is pasted over the inked stelae and buffed with a pad or a soft brush.

Although the original intention in establishing the museum was to preserve ancient texts (for a text carved in stone is eternal and free from copyists' errors), the Forest of Stelae is today considered as the major museum of Chinese calligraphy for the writing of ancient calligraphers survives only in stone-cut versions. A few of the (mostly later) stelae have line-cut drawings of mountain scenery or the famous monkey figure made out of characters.

Visiting a carved stone stele, from Hong xue yin yuan *by Linqing, 1879*

One of the stelae of most interest to westerners (in the past at least) is the **'Nestorian Stele'** (Da qin jing jiao liu xing zhong guo bei, or the Jingjiao bei). This is to be found immediately on the left of the entrance in Room 2. It records the arrival of a Nestorian priest in Chang'an and the 781 foundation of a Nestorian chapel. There is a long text on the front of the stele describing the Creation and giving an outline of Christian doctrine followed by a shorter inscription in Syriac (characters written vertically). The edges of the stone are covered with Syriac names with Chinese equivalents. Although it is now well-known that Nestorianism was known in Chang'an during the Tang, the stelae, which was unearthed in 1625 apparently near Zhouzhi outside the western gate of Xi'an, provoked great excitement amongst 17C Jesuit missionaries in China and they used its discovery to prove the early 'conversion to Christianity' of the Chinese during the Rites Controversy. (For Nestorianism, see Quanzhou, p 645.)

The Nestorian church was based on the rather modern-sounding heresy of Nestorius, who postulated the dual nature of Christ (human and divine) and refused the title of Holy Mother to the Virgin. Nestorius was condemned at the Council of Ephesus in 431 but his followers survived, especially in eastern Turkey and further east, converting Khubilai Khan's mother amongst others. I note that the French *Guide Bleu* states that Nestorianism is today only 'almost extinct'. As Christian missionaries were all terribly interested in the antiquity of their profession in China (and prepared to overlook the Council of Ephesus' ruling) there are many copies of the Nestorian stele in Europe brought back by missionaries.

There is a small exhibition devoted to the Silk Road (which terminated in Xi'an in the Han and the Tang) but the old contents of the museum (a treasury and a chronological arrangement of excavated artefacts) have now been moved to a grand new site (Xiaozhai dong lu, Cuihua lu) considerably south of the city wall, between the two Goose Pagodas (see pp 423–424).

Just east of the museum, visible from the city wall and standing just south of Shuyuanmen da jie, is a small pagoda known locally as the **Huata si** (Coloured Pagoda Temple), although its full name was the Baoqing si and it is said to have been founded in 705. Nothing now remains of the temple except the little pagoda.

The **Bell Tower** (Zhong lou) in the centre of Xi'an is not far north of the Confucian temple. Either make your way west through the narrow streets to Nan da jie and then turn right (north) until you reach the Bell Tower in the centre of the street or turn left into Duanlumen jie, which runs north–south just outside the Confucian temple, and continue north until you reach Dong dajie where you will see the Bell Tower over to the west.

The Bell Tower originally stood (1384) some two blocks west of its present site. There it was at the centre of the old Tang city but it was moved to its present site in 1582 and restored in 1739. Its bell, which used to be rung at dawn, no longer exists. The triple-eaved, two-storey wooden structure (over 27m high) stands on a square brick platform 8.5m high.

Great Mosque

The **Drum Tower** (Gu lou), pair to the Bell Tower, is just northwest of the latter, straddling the second turning on the right (north) along Xi da jie. It stands overlooking the old Muslim quarter of Xi'an with the **Great Mosque** (Qingzhen si) at its centre on Huajue xiang. To reach the mosque follow the paved street lined with souvenir shops leading left just beyond the Drum Tower.

The mosque (popularly known as the Dong da si or Great Eastern Temple) is one of the most active in metropolitan China for there are said to be some 30,000 practising Muslims in Xi'an. According to a stele, the mosque was founded in 742, during the Tang, when Xi'an was full of foreign Muslims. Although most guidebooks now note that the architectural style and present layout is Ming, with restoration work in 1527, 1606 and 1768, the building presents a problem as it has been gradually restored from pillar-bases upwards over the last decade. This restoration was thorough in the extreme, although the new materials were being carved to the earlier forms. Thus the mosque can be said to be Ming in layout and inspiration but every bit of timber is of the late 20C.

The layout is interesting for it is built on an east–west axis, fitting to a mosque with the great prayer hall at the western extremity; it had some particularly fine woodcarving in the coffered ceiling and the front panels of the hall. Walking back from the prayer hall, you will see two stone fountains in the courtyard beneath the terrace on which the prayer hall stands. The courtyard terminates in the Phoenix Pavilion. The next courtyard contains the minaret, an octagonal pagoda with a turquoise tiled roof, and rooms surrounding the courtyard. These include the imam's living quarters and some exhibits, including a Qing illuminated Qu'ran (Koran) and a Qing Chinese Muslim map of the world with the black square of the Kaaba in Mecca at the centre. The entrance to this courtyard is a stelae hall with Ming and Qing stelae in Chinese, Arabic and Persian.

The second courtyard (where visitors enter) contains two free-standing stelae and a stone arch. The stelae are inscribed by two of the most famous calligraphers of China: Mi Fei (or Fu) of the Song, one of the great painting innovators, and Dong Qichang of the Ming. The first courtyard contains an elaborate wooden *pailou*, completely restored during the last decade.

The street that runs under the Drum Tower has some interesting wooden shopfronts with carved fascia (walk north beyond the tower to see these).

A number of temples in the city of Xi'an can be reached on foot, although most are now converted to other uses and may be difficult of access.

The **Chenghuang miao** (Temple of the City God) is just north of Xi da jie (which runs west from the Bell Tower). It is reached by turning north by no. 257 Xi da jie and following the little lane through the Muslim quarter past a mosque (left). Turn right at the T-junction and right again and the temple gate should be visible on the cobbled lane. The temple was founded in 1433 (it now houses a school and stores) and few of its buildings survive except a main hall built in 1723 with fine bracketing, carved doors and a blue tiled roof. The two Ming bronze lions of the Jiaqing period (1522–67), which used to stand in the temple, are now placed outside the main gate of the Provincial Museum.

The **Dongyue miao** (Temple of the Eastern Peak) is just to the northwest inside the eastern gate and now in the grounds of a primary school. It was dedicated to the worship of Tai shan (in Shandong), a major cult in Chinese Taoism, represented by temples in many towns. This one was founded in 1116, restored in the Ming and in 1895. Frescoes still remain on the eastern and western walls of the main hall (an imposing building), depicting female spirits and pavilions in the Yuan and Ming style. There are also stelae recording the restoration of the temple in the Ming and Qing.

The **Guangren si** (Temple of Extensive Humanity), sometimes also called the Lama si or Lama Temple, is in the northwest corner of the city wall. Founded in 1705, it is the only example of a Lamaist temple of the Yellow Hat faith in the Xi'an area. In front of the temple is a hexagonal stelae pavilion housing an imperial stele. Inside the temple there are three main halls—the great hall, the sutra hall and the hall where sutras are commented on—and side wings for the kitchen and other offices. The temple is particularly busy every year on the 14th and 15th of the tenth month of the lunar calendar when many Tibetan monks join the crowds that come to celebrate the enlightenment of Tsongkapa, founder of the Yellow Hat sect of Lamaist Buddhism.

Also near the Forest of Stelae is the **Wolong si** (Temple of the Recumbent Dragon), reached along a lane between Nos 25 and 27 Baishulin jie. Once one of the richest and best-known temples in Xi'an, founded under the Sui, last restored in 1952, its library of sutras (including a Southern Song example) is now in the Provincial Library. Only part of one hall remains, although it used to contain a stone engraving of Guanyin by Wu Daozi.

Big Goose Pagoda and Temple of Great Goodwill

The best known temples in Xi'an are the Little Goose and Big Goose pagodas and their associated temples. Once well inside the Tang city walls, they now stand outside the Ming walls, to the south.

The **Big Goose Pagoda** (Dayan ta) and the Temple of Great Goodwill (Da cien si) are some 4km south of the city wall.

> The pagoda was known as the Jing ta or Sutra Pagoda during the Tang and the source of its contemporary name (together with that of the Small Goose) is somewhat mysterious. Xuanzang's biography states that as a flock of wild geese flew over a monastery in an Indian kingdom, one bird fell dead to the ground; the monks decided that it was a saint and built a pagoda for its body. If that is the explanation of the name of the earlier Great Goose Pagoda, then the Small Goose Pagoda, which resembles it in form but was built later, presumably acquired its name through association.

The **Temple of Great Goodwill** was built in 647 by a Tang prince (later the Gaozong emperor, reigned 650–684) in honour of his mother. It was originally far bigger than it is now (with 13 courtyards and 300 monks). The temple was destroyed in 907 and the present buildings are Qing or later; complete restoration from ground level upwards has taken place in recent years. The main hall has a fine series of Qing lohans around the outer walls.

> The pagoda was first built in 652 on the recommendation of Xuan zang, the most prominent monk and translator of the sutras. He had returned to Chang'an and his temple after more than 15 years travelling through the Gobi Desert (via Dunhuang, Gaochang and other ruined cities of the desert) to India and Pakistan where he collected Sanskrit sutras, despite an imperial prohibition on foreign travel. On his return he set up a great translation bureau in the temple and recommended the construction of a fireproof store for his precious sutras. A square, five-storey building of rammed earth was constructed but it collapsed and a seven-storey brick structure was built (701–704). A further three storeys were added in 766–779 but they were destroyed. The surviving construction was faced with brick in the Ming to strengthen it.

The pagoda is square in plan, tapering towards the top with brick eaves marking each storey of the simple but elegant tower. Arched windows in each floor provide a view over the steadily encroaching city (it was set amongst cabbage fields in 1971 when I first saw it). There are important examples of stone carving and calligraphy in the temple. Tang carvings of Buddhist scenes are barely visible on the lintels; that above the west door is clearest, showing the Buddha preaching in a fine open hall. Two stone tablets set into the wall on each side of the south door were engraved by a Tang calligrapher, Chu Suiliang. They are of texts by two Tang emperors, Gaozong and Taizong, describing Xuan zang's epic journey to the west (fictionalised in *Monkey*) and his equally epic translation work.

Inside the pagoda is a small exhibition of photographs of Chinese pagodas of all sorts; below, outside and to the left, is a group of stupas housing the remains of the temple's monks (of the Qing dynasty) but not Xuan zang, whose remains are in the Xingjiao si, outside Xi'an.

Small Goose Pagoda and Daxingshan si

Slightly nearer town is the **Xiaoyan ta** (Small Goose Pagoda) in the Jian fu si (Commending Happiness Temple). Previously known as the Xiafu (Presenting Happiness) Temple, this was founded in 684, also by the Gaozong emperor of the Tang. The temple still contains a large bronze bell cast in 1192 (standing in a courtyard), a number of stelae and a small exhibition of Tang Buddhist artefacts, Song and Ming editions of the sutras and a history of the pagoda.

> The Small Goose Pagoda was also constructed as a fireproof sutra store in 707. It was built to house the sutras brought back from India by the monk Yi jing who was the first Chinese monk to make the journey by sea, rather than overland across the Gobi (the commoner route). Yi jing left for India in 671 and later spent some time on Sumatra before returning in 695 with some 400 sutras. He lived and translated in various monasteries before settling in the Jianfu temple, where he died in 713.

The pagoda is built of brick on a square plan and was originally 15 storeys high; earthquake damage has left only 13 storeys and a rather jagged top. It is 45m high, smaller than the nearly 60m of the Big Goose Pagoda. Although similar in plan and construction, with the same simple brick eaves marking the storeys, it is more elegantly tapered, in a gentle curve, closer in style to the Tang pagodas in Dali and Kunming than the resolutely angular Big Goose. It has arched doorways on the north and south sides of each storey with fine *intaglio* carvings of celestials and floral designs over the doorways.

Just south of the Little Goose Pagoda, on Xingshan si jie, in the Xinfeng Park, is the **Daxingshan si** (Temple of Great and Flourishing Goodness) founded in the 4C.

> During the Sui dynasty a large number of Indian monks came here to teach esotericism and between 716–720 yet more Indian monks came to translate esoteric texts, making the temple one of the three great translation centres of the time. Many Japanese monks also came to the temple to study. The temple was also famous for one monk, Yi xing, who made it a centre for the study of astronomy and mathematics (and who calculated the length of the meridian). The temple was destroyed in the late Tang persecution of Buddhism, leaving only some Tang dynasty carved waterspouts and pillar bases; the buildings are all of Ming–Qing date.

Shaanxi Provincial Museum

Within walking distance of the Daxingshan si and the Big Goose Pagoda is the new Shaanxi Provincial Museum, open daily from 09.00–17.30, no bags or cameras. Designed by an architectural team, whose previous major work had been the National Library of China (Peking) in the early 1990s, it is one of the handsomest modern buildings in China. It was inspired by Tang architecture, hence the heavy tiled roof and elegant black and white lines. It houses exhibits that were once displayed in the old Confucian temple complex (Forest of Stelae) but which are now set out in much better conditions.

On the **ground floor** is a chronological display of artefacts from the earliest periods of the Shang and Zhou, together with themed displays of funerary pieces: bronzes and ceramics (Zhou to Tang) and Tang gold and silver. This includes the most spectacular display of **bronzes** of any Chinese museum. All locally unearthed, it is not simply the quality of the Western Zhou bronzes but the quantity and the way they are arranged. Set out in tiers, matching sets of different implements united by surface decoration, they give a far better idea of the real contents of tombs than the isolated examples seen in other museums. Most bronzes were cast as 'altar sets', groups of utensils for the warming and serving of food to the gods, and this can best be seen here (unless the arrangement is dramatically altered). Exhibits include: the famous bronze *ding* (tripod) weighing 87.5kg and with two inscriptions, one Shang and one Zhou; the buffalo-shaped *zun* (wine vessel) from the 9C BC and the rhinoceros *zun* of the Warring States period, which is associated with a number of bronze fittings apparently used architecturally in palaces, perhaps in the legendary Afang Palace built by the first emperor of the Qin, and a marvellous bronze horse found near the Mao ling, tomb of the Wudi emperor of the Han (140–81 BC). The **silver and gold vessels** are extremely rare. Most museum exhibits of the period are grave goods and sumptuary regulations prohibited the burial of gold and silver. Even if such vessels were included in tombs, they would have been stolen by grave robbers, who seem to have entered most tombs of note soon after they were completed. These vessels were unearthed from Tang hoards—buried at the An Lushan uprising as their owners fled the city, intending to return when peace had been re-established—and include a wonderful little incense-burner with gimbals (to keep the incense upright) in a silver filigree ball and the agate rhyton with a gold nose, excavated during the Cultural Revolution, that was probably imported from Persia.

Upstairs are two further sections, one with mainly Han exhibits, including extraordinary goose- and human-shaped lamps and a representative selection of Han ceramic burial goods with representations of farmyards, pigpens, houses, stoves and other everyday paraphernalia.

The final chronological sequence has exhibits from the Sui and Tang and also some Song, Ming and Qing items. Tang ceramic tomb models, painted, unpainted, glazed and unglazed (in a far greater variety of treatments than seen in the exhibits in western museums) are a long way from their Han predecessors in subject matter. They depict warriors, guardians, horses and camels laden with goods from the west and, above all, courtly life—beautiful women, orchestras and dancers. There are copies of some of the murals from the Tang tombs that surround Xi'an—beautiful women in gardens or gentlemen playing polo.

Some exhibits from the **Famen si** (Temple of the Gate of the Law) are of particular interest. When much of the brick pagoda collapsed after heavy rains in 1981, a crypt was discovered which contained China's holiest Buddhist relic, a **finger of the Buddha** (often described as 'four finger' bones). The importance of this relic had attracted imperial attention during the Tang and the temple saw many imperial visits and donations. The gold, silver and jewelled reliquary which housed the relic was made in the form of a small coffin (like the reliquary in the Lintong Museum) and was associated with a great pile of coins (some 27,000) and other gold and silver items including a small spoon. Traces of the patterns of the silks in which the relic was wrapped were preserved and one of the most exciting finds was a piece of fine green-grey ceramic, the mise or 'secret colour' ware, previously only known through literary reference.

The museum's **sculpture collection** comprises some huge and wonderful pieces, mainly from tombs of the Han to Tang dynasties. There are sinuous, leopard-like *bixie* from a Western Han tomb; a copy of a horse from the Huo Qubing

(Han) tomb, which has some of the most powerful animal statuary anywhere; a wonderful, worn horse from northern Shaanxi (AD 424) and rhinoceroses and ostriches from Tang tombs (known as exotic gifts from foreign ambassadors to Tang emperors). There are also four of the six famous high-relief carvings of horses from Zhao ling, the **Tomb of Li Shimin**. Founder of the Tang dynasty, he loved horses, especially his favourite charger Quanmo, who was one of the six horses portrayed in the stone panels. Unfortunately two of the panels (including Quanmo) were taken to the University of Philadelphia Museum in 1914 and some of the other panels were broken into four pieces, presumably to facilitate their removal. This (and casts of the two missing panels) can be seen in the museum.

There is also a charming little stone building, complete in every detail. It is a Sui coffin, made for a small girl, the only daughter of a descendant of the Zhou imperial family who had thrown in his lot with the Sui emperor (unwisely, it turned out, for he was condemned to death by his new master as a result of court intrigue and his wife was poisoned soon after). The child died just before her parents, in 608, at the age of eight and her coffin, with a rich collection of funerary objects inside (now in Peking), was unearthed in 1957. The stone coffin is a lovely architectural piece with its curled ridge and details of tiles. There are also a large number of Buddhist stelae, carved with many scenes of deities or events in the life of the Buddha under the elegant, leaf-shaped top.

Along Xianning lu, east of the museum and southeast of the corner of the city wall, is the tree-filled **Xingqing Park**, once the site of the palace where the Xuanzong emperor lived as a child in the late 7C. The park was once famous for its peonies. Since huge efforts were made in the Great Leap Forward (1958), the park has a number of Tang style pavilions and an ornamental lake. There is a white marble stele erected to commemorate Abe no Nakamaro (701–770), a famous Japanese scholar who visited Chang'an before becoming Collator of Texts in the Japanese Imperial Library.

Temples in the vicinity of Xi'an

Major temples in the vicinity of Xi'an include the Xingjiao si, Xiangji si, Caotang si, Huayan si and Famen si. The Xingjiao si and Huayan si are both to the south of the city.

Xingjiao si

Xingjiao si (Temple of Flourishing Teaching) is c 22km southeast of Xi'an, beautifully situated on a hillside overlooking the Fan River valley. It was founded in 669 as one of the eight great temples of Fanchuan (the Fan River) in order to provide a home for the ashes of the great travelling and translating monk Xuan zang (602–664). His remains were originally buried at Bailuyuan (Plain of the White Deer), c 10km southeast of Xi'an, where the Ba ling, tomb of the Han Wendi (Cultural) emperor and his wife, is also to be found. They were moved to the present site in 669 when the temple was built by the Gaozong emperor.

Three little square stupas contain the remains of Xuan zang (the tallest one) and two of his disciples. The name of the temple was taken from an inscription written on the stupa by the Suzong emperor of the Tang, the two characters for 'flourishing teaching'. **Xuan zang's stupa** is square in plan and stepped, not unlike the Great Goose Pagoda but with brickwork closely imitating wooden construction. In its present form it is probably 9C. The two smaller three-storey pagodas contain the remains of Kuiji (632–82), a translation assistant of Xuan zang's of noble birth (his uncle was a famous general), and to the east the remains of a Korean follower of Xuan zang, Yuance. The latter stupa was built later (1115). Beside Xuan zang's stupa is a small pavilion with the famous stone carving of Xuan zang bringing back the sutras from India on a sort of backpack frame, carrying a flywhisk and other bits and pieces. The stone carving, which is a charming picture of a loaded traveller, is quite late, probably Qing, although it is remarkably similar to a Tang sketch of a pilgrim monk found at Dunhuang (now in the British Museum).

The stupas were fortunate to survive the constant accidents that destroyed the temple many times over. Apparently first abandoned after the suppression of Buddhism in 839, it was reoccupied and redestroyed many times and restored in 1922 and 1939. It is now a fairly busy temple with some 30 monks (and some quite interesting sutras in the library). Despite the newness of the buildings, the Great Hall contains a bronze Buddha of the Ming dynasty and, behind, in the Preaching Hall, there is a Ming bronze Amitabha and a Sakyamuni Buddha of 1922.

On the lower floor of the library building (the sutras are upstairs) is a fairly modern white jade Buddha, a present from Burma.

Huayan si

Huayan si is about 15km outside Xi'an on the way to the Xingjiao si. It is another of the eight great temples of Fanchuan, also very beautifully situated, although very little remains of the temple beyond two brick pagodas. It was, however, the birthplace of the popular Huayan sect of Buddhism.

Founded by the monk Du shun (557–640), Huayan followed the Tiantai sect's attempt to classify all the confusingly different sutras by ascribing different doctrines to different periods in the life of the Buddha. Huayan added the (then) new school of Chan (Zen) and also viewed the universe as ordered, the world of principle and phenomena being fused, with everything leading to the centre, the Buddha. The temple was destroyed by an earthquake in the 18C.

The two surviving pagodas include one to the east containing the remains of the Huayan founder. This is a square, seven-storey construction, 13m high, with the characters *Yanzhu* ('Master of Yan') carved on a stone at the top and six characters reading 'the pure, clean and bright precious pagoda' on the third storey. The remains of the fourth patriarch of the Huayan sect are inside the other pagoda, which is hexagonal, five-storeyed and 7m high with an inscription reading 'the miraculous pagoda of the great master of the Tang'. There are brick niches in the lower parts of both pagodas with incised figures and records of late Qing reconstruction. A stele dated 852, recording the life of the first patriarch, has been moved to the Forest of Stelae in Xi'an.

Caotang si

Caotang si (Straw-Hat Temple) is 55km southwest of Xi'an, in Hu xian (and c 20km southeast of the county town of Hu xian). It is very small and the buildings are comparatively recent, except for the stupa containing the remains of Kumarajiva (384–417).

Kumarajiva was a non-Chinese Buddhist (half-Kuchean, half-Brahmin) who set up a translation bureau of over 1000 monks. His translations are still used today, although he himself said that reading a translation was like eating rice that someone else had chewed. His stupa is small (2.33m high), with 12 storeys on an octagonal plan, and made from 'eight precious jade stones' of different colours, on a Sumeru (Buddhist holy mountain) base and carved with flowers and Buddhas. The stupa is judged to be Tang on the basis of the figure style and lotus carvings.

In the county town of **Hu xian** an exhibition hall displays paintings by the peasant painters of Hu xian county.

These bright, naive paintings of agricultural scenes with flocks of chickens, rows of pigsties and trees full of shiny red apples were immensely popular in China in the 1970s and during the last years of the Cultural Revolution were quite often exhibited abroad. Their popularity at the time was due to the political innocence of the content—themes of bumper harvests and hard work—but the brilliant colours and naive pattern-like effect were also extremely attractive. The painters apparently began painting in 1958 to record the construction of a local reservoir but their wide reknown came nearly 20 years later and promoted a general trend towards peasant painting in the late 1970s and early 1980s. Some of the artists, like the apple grower Wang Jinlong, are now very popular and their works are sold in places like the Alvin Gallery in Hong Kong, so the prices are at international heights.

Xiangji si

Xiangji si (Temple of Amassed Perfume) is due south of Xi'an, 20km by road, in Xiangji cun (Village of Amassed Perfume), which lies near the meeting of two rivers. The temple was originally built by his followers to commemorate Shan dao, the second patriarch of the Pure Land sect, perhaps the most lastingly popular of all Buddhist sects in China. Pure Land preaches salvation through faith rather than esoteric meditation and offers a haven in the Pure Land of Amitabha Buddha for good practitioners. All that remains of the temple today is a Qing dynasty great hall and the 33m Tang brick stupa (imitating timber construction) which is in poor repair. To the east is a far smaller stupa said to contain the remains of Shan dao.

The past glories of the temple were commemorated by the Tang poet Wang Wei who wrote *Passing the Temple of Amassed Fragrance*: 'Hard to find the Temple of Amassed Fragrance, many miles deep in clouds and peaks, ancient trees that no man has touched. Deep in the mountains, the sound of a bell.'

Famen si

Famen si (Temple of the Gate of the Law) is further away: over 100km west of Xi'an, the temple itself is 10km north of the country town of Fufeng xian. Some extraordinary archaeological discoveries were made at the temple in 1987; they are exhibited in the museum (open 08.00–17.00).

The major feature of the temple is the pagoda which contains a holy relic, one of the fingers of the historic Buddha, placed there by the Huizong emperor of the Tang (reigned 806–21). The existing pagoda is a Ming construction of 1579, an imposing 45m in height, octagonal in plan with 13 storeys. The pagoda tapers gradually towards the top and the brickwork imitates timber construction.

Since the partial collapse of the pagoda in 1981, excavations revealed a wealth of treasures bestowed on the temple by the Tang imperial house, which accorded it considerable patronage; partly because of the finger, it was the most famous temple of the later Tang. Silk garments of all sorts have been found, reliquaries of precious metals, the previously unseen mise 'secret colour' ceramic ware and also early tea-drinking implements (spoons, caddies), which are of particular interest because the beginnings of tea-drinking in China were previously only known through literary accounts. The museum's displays also include Roman and Persian glass (indicators of Xi'an's history of contact with the Silk Road), coins of all sorts, silks used to wrap the precious relics and reliquaries in silver, sandalwood, crystal and gold.

The Imperial Tombs

Some of the most splendid sites around Xi'an are the **Imperial Tombs of the Han and Tang**. There was also a considerable chariot burial of the Western Zhou unearthed to the west of the city, complete with horses and full chariots, not far from the Tomb of Yang Guifei at Mawei. With the exception of Yang Guifei's tomb, the Tang tombs are grouped c 80–l00km northwest of Xi'an, in the mountains surrounding the plain, while the Han tombs are nearly due west and only 30–40km away.

There are nine Han tombs in the vicinity of Xi'an but none of the imperial tombs has yet been excavated. Two are quite close together: **Mao ling**, tomb of the Wudi (Martial) emperor of the Han (157–87 BC), and the tomb of Huo Qubing (140–117 BC), one of Han Wudi's generals.

The name of Han Wudi's tomb is composed of a place name, *Mao*, taken from Maoxiang, the name of the area in which it was situated, and *ling*, which means 'tomb'. It is a trapezoid mound, 46.5m high, covering 54,054m. The surrounding wall has all but disappeared.

The emperor ordered the construction of his tomb as early as the second year of his reign, as was the custom. Literary records describe the contents: the corpse was dressed in a jade suit made of small pieces joined by gold wire (examples of such suits have been excavated: one can be seen in the museum in Nanjing), with a jade cicada in the mouth. Jade boxes were buried with the emperor and many animals were sacrificed to provide food for his spirit. It is also said that his favourite books were buried with him (and many important texts have been uncovered from Han tombs such as that of Mawangdui near Changsha).

Nearby is the **Tomb of Huo Qubing** with a fine series of stone-carved animals that once stood lining the approach to the tomb (they are now under cover) and a museum displaying relics of the Han tombs that have been found in the vicinity. Huo Qubing died young (of disease) but he had already led troops against 'Hun slave-owner intruders' and the emperor ordered that his tomb be constructed 1km away from Mao ling, amidst many other satellite tombs. There is a small brick kiosk on the top of the burial mound but the most remarkable feature was the series of huge stone-carved animals that lay before it. Anticipating the later 'spirit roads' which reached their zenith in the approach to the Ming tombs outside Nanjing and Peking. Huo Qubing's sculptures are not completely in the round as later examples are; the huge horses, tigers, bears and elephants appear to be struggling out of the stone. They are immensely lively, in contrast with the static majesty of later funerary carving, and full of movement: galloping horses, horses trampling 'Huns' and men wrestling with bears. Other items on display include a series of decorated bricks that lined Han tombs, hollow bricks decorated with dragons and tigers, tortoises and snakes (the latter symbols of the north), elegant bronze vessels used for serving wine and food in offerings to the gods and a range of the rather homely ceramic models found in Han tombs: ducks, sheep, farmyards and houses.

Beyond the Han tombs at **Mawei po** (Mawei Slope) is the tomb of the ill-fated fat concubine **Yang Guifei**, killed by members of the imperial guard as she and the emperor fled the capital during the An Lushan rebellion.

As An Lushan was a general she had adopted and whose career she had fostered, it was ironic that his ambition should cause her death. In the following year the emperor ordered that she should be buried here, under a round mound covering 3000 square metres. The simple stone with the inscription 'Yang Guffei's Tomb' has been joined by many others commemorating visits by historical personages, including the 19C opium commissioner Lin Zexu (see Fuzhou, p 630). The death of Yang Guifei at Mawei po was one of the great romantic milestones of Chinese history, endlessly commemorated by poets and painters.

On the way to the Tang tombs is the **Shanglin Park**. The site of the huge hunting park-cum-garden of the Qin and Han emperors no longer reflects its former glory: it was once filled with exotic animals and flora from each province of the empire but all that remains is a pair of large stone Han figures west of the lake. Said to represent two heavenly lovers, the herd boy and the spinning maid (he a mortal, she the daughter of a heavenly king living in the sky on either side of the Milky Way), they look more like Gog and Magog.

The tomb of the Empress Wu, outside Xi'an

Wu Zetian ~ the murderous empress

Although he was the ninth son of the second Tang emperor, Gaozong was chosen to succeed his father in 650 and he died at Luoyang in 683. His wife, Wu Zetian, had been a concubine selected by his father; on the death of the second emperor she became a Buddhist nun and retired to a temple. She was, however, sought out by the Gaozong emperor in 654 and in 655 he forced his empress Wang to abdicate, although some say she was murdered by Wu Zetian. Empress Wu's power at court grew: following the death of the Gaozong emperor and after a few years of controlling a couple of her hapless sons as 'emperor', she assumed power in 690. She changed the name of the dynasty to Zhou and ruled for 21 years with the help of a pair of corrupt courtiers, the Zhang brothers. She is supposed to have murdered her way to power and, once enthroned, the killing continued.

In 701 her granddaughter Princess Yongtai died at the age of 17, officially in childbirth. Yongtai's half-brother Yide died equally mysteriously (but certainly not in childbirth) at the same time. It seems probable that Wu Zetian had them put to death for criticising her favourites. Her second son was ordered by his mother to commit suicide, another was exiled and one was fortunate enough to succeed his mother when she was forced into retirement by a palace coup in which the Zhang brothers were killed. She died in Luoyang in 705, less than a year after the coup.

She was, in fact, an effective ruler: Korea was successfully conquered during her reign and the Turkic attacks from the west finally suppressed so that the great prosperity and cultural flowering of the Tang was made possible. Because of her ruthless elimination of rivals and family members at court, however, she has become one of the villains of Chinese history, along with the Dowager Empress Cixi of the Qing and Mao Zedong's wife, all of whom are vilified as negative examples of womanhood. Legends about her abound. She is supposed to have executed an enormous number of peonies because they refused to flower at her command (the Tang saw a peony-mania similar to the European tulipomania nearly 1000 years later). She was a great Buddhist enthusiast and promoted the growth of temples and monasteries.The Gaozong emperor was buried in the Qian ling in 684 and the tomb reopened at enormous expense to receive the body of the empress in 705.

The most impressive group of Tang tombs includes the triple-hilled **Qian ling** and the smaller tombs of the Prince Yide, Prince Zhanghuai and Princess Yongtai. The Qian ling is 85km northwest of Xi'an and was built for Li Zhi, the Gaozong (Exalted Ancestor) emperor of the Tang and his empress Wu Zetian.

The Qian ling has not been excavated but, externally at least, it is the grandest of all the Tang tombs. The tomb itself lies in a natural hill approached by a long spirit way (of some 3km) which passes between two artificial mounds, so that the whole appears to consist of three hills. The remains of two towers mark the beginning of the spirit way, which passes between the two mounds with tall towers on top. Two obelisks precede the procession of stone animals, beginning with a pair of sturdy winged horses of great elegance. Then follow a pair of ostrich-like birds ('scarlet birds', symbolic of the south), then five pairs of horses, ten pairs of large human figures and two stelae. That on the left has a eulogy of the reign of the Gaozong emperor, composed by Wu Zetian and written by the son who succeeded him but who was deposed by his mother. That on the right was known as the Stele with No Inscription (it awaited an eulogy of the Empress Wu); it has, in fact, much later inscriptions of the Song and Jin, the latter written in the language of the Nu zhen (founders of the Jin), with a Chinese translation.

Beyond are two towers and large groups of (headless) statues representing the foreign envoys and ambassadors who attended the funeral of the Gaozong emperor. It would be hard to tell that they were foreigners, were it not for the inscriptions on their backs. Beyond are two colossal stone lions and the remains of the Hall of Offerings with a stele erected by the Qianlong emperor. The whole vast enclosure used to be surrounded by a double wall.

When I first saw the spirit way in 1976 many of the statues had fallen over but they have now been righted and restored. The heads, alas, were probably stolen to order and sold abroad in the early years of the 20C. The sculptures are most impressive, far more expressive and alive than those of the Ming spirit ways (Nanjing and Peking).

Just beside the winged horses are some of the famous troglodyte dwellings of the loess area. You can stand above the courtyard, which is cut down into the yellow earth with tunnel-like chambers on three sides, fronted with wooden-framed windows pasted with paper. The wooden frames are painted black with the thin red outline which is so characteristic of domestic architecture of the Xi'an area.

Since 1960 five of the 17 satellite tombs have been excavated, including those of three victims of the Empress Wu: Princess Yongtai, Prince Yide and Prince Zhanghuai. All had been robbed but only of precious stones and metals; the ceramics and wall-paintings were left undisturbed.

The **Tomb of Princess Yongtai** can be entered to provide a view of the underground chambers of Tang tombs. Yongtai was probably murdered by the Empress Wu (or on her orders) in 701 and she was not buried in the Qian ling complex until 706, after her grandmother's death. When the tomb was opened the skeleton of a man was found inside; it is thought to be the body of a Tang tomb robber, murdered by his accomplices. The tomb is entered down a long sloping corridor with small stepped niches in the walls filled with rows of pottery tomb figures. It is most interesting to see them arranged in this way instead of standing as individual works of art in museums. The walls themselves are covered with paintings of women, court attendants and servants (some with the double-bun hairstyle of servants). They carry offerings and candles and flowers.

Their costume, with quite tight bodices to the high-waisted gowns and narrow sleeves and flowing scarves, is characteristic of the early 8C, before the influence of the fat concubine, Yang Guifei. Her bulk altered the idea of female beauty (in the eyes of the emperor at least) and determined new fashions in women's clothing. She introduced the Central Asian style of very loose, baggy, figure-concealing gowns. Funerary figures of the mid 8C often depict women with very fat faces, vast rolled, turban-like snoods and loose gowns, in contrast with the slim elegance of these early 8C figures.

The dark stone sarcophagus in the tomb chamber (whose ceiling is painted with stars) at the bottom of the long tunnel is carved with figures, birds and flowers.

The **Tomb of Prince Yide** was also constructed in 706, after the death of the empress, although he died with his sister in 701. It can also be entered and the tunnel, like that of his sister's tomb, is lined with niches and painted with court ladies and eunuchs, palace guards and mounted attendants with a large mural of a procession of guards beneath watch towers. The ceiling of the tomb chamber is painted with stars.

The **Tomb of Prince Zhanghuai** (second son of the Gaozong emperor, forced to commit suicide by his mother, who then buried him with the pomp due to his rank) has a famous wall painting of polo-playing. In this, as in the other tombs, the original wall paintings have been removed for safer storage (a closed tomb is one thing, crowds of heavily breathing visitors another) and replaced by exact copies. Two columns and two statues of rams guard the entrance to the tomb, whose ramp is set with niches filled with the *mingqi* ('spirit goods'), ceramic figures that accompanied the souls of the dead to the other world.

Polo ~ the wall painting

The painting of polo (a game introduced during the Tang from Persia) is immensely vivid. Large, rather stout horses (the cousins of those represented in the ceramic burial figures), their tails tied in neat knots, are depicted at full gallop, ridden by gentlemen wielding sticks that are more like hockey sticks than today's polo mallets. The figures are outlined in black, with colour wash; the painting is sure and swift. On the other wall is a hunting scene with yet another foreign import, falconry. Beyond are a group of officials together with foreign envoys and a palace guard. Two of the animals of the four directions—the green dragon of the east and the white tiger of the west—line the corridor where it joins the tomb chamber and they are followed by groups of servants bearing offerings: a cockerel, a *pen cai* (bonsai). Once again the ceiling is decorated with stars.

There is a small **museum** associated with these satellite tombs displaying Tang funerary ceramics, those of the mid 7C especially, decorated with the three colour glaze (yellow, green and brown), casually splashed over human figures, horses and vessels.

Zhao ling, the Tomb of Taizong, the second emperor of the Tang (reigned 626–649), is to the east of the Qian ling complex. As a group, the Zhao ling and its satellite tombs cover an even greater area than the Qian ling and comprise 177 subsidiary tombs spread across 20,000 hectares. The Zhao ling has not been excavated, so the mound may be seen and nearby there is a museum

'Striking the ball', a form of polo

of stelae and excavated ceramics. Taizong was the horse-lover whose tomb contained the beautiful low-relief panels of horses now in the Provincial Museum (and Philadelphia). The stelae are from the surrounding tombs, as are the ceramics. There is a grand series of 163 from a single tomb (that of a high official of Taizong's time), including dancers, officials, entertainers and warriors. There is also a series of copies of wall paintings from tombs, one of which, unusually, depicts a peasant in a kitchen garden, a more homely picture than most of the more elevated, courtly scenes usually found in Tang tombs.

En route for the Tang or Han tombs, if time allows, the museum in the county town of **Xiangyang** is filled with mainly Han funerary pieces of considerable interest. The museum is in the old Confucian temple. The greatest collection of funerary ceramics is the **army of 2548 pieces** from a tomb situated between that of the Gaozu emperor (reigned 206–195 BC) and the Jindi emperor (reigned 157–140). Just like the Qin emperor's Buried Army, these figures were found in trenches that mimicked the characteristic formation of the Han battlelines. The group also includes entertainers and officials. All the figures are between 48–53cm high (entertainers and officials) and 67–70cm (warriors). There is also a considerable display of jade pieces, which were included in large numbers in Han burials because of the strong belief that jade protected the corpse from decay and therefore enhanced the possibilities of longevity of the soul.

Yan'an

Rarely visited these days, Yan'an in Shaanxi province used to be the major revolutionary tourist centre, closely followed by Shaoshan in Hunan, Mao Zedong's birthplace. Buried deep in the yellow hills, on the bank of the Yan River, Yan'an was the headquarters of the Communist Party during the Anti-Japanese War. Driven out of their previous stronghold in the southern province of Jiangxi, Communist Party members set out on the Long March in 1934, arriving in Yan'an in October 1935, one year later.

Practical information

Getting there
By air
Yan'an is linked to Xi'an by air and there are also flights from Taiyuan and Beijing. These used to be in tiny aeroplanes (the one in which I travelled filled with white clouds at altitude).
By train

Yan'an may be reached by a slow train from Xi'an on a ten hour journey, to be recommended, if time allows, for the views of the yellow loess hills.
By bus

It is also possible to take an eight hour bus ride from the South Gate in Xi'an, stopping halfway at the Huang ling, the 'tomb' of the legendary Yellow Emperor. Traditional founder of the Han race, he is supposed to have ruled from 2698 to 2598 BC and to have invented the wheel, armour, ships and pottery.

Where to stay
The *Yan'an Hotel* on Yan'an lu, ☎ 211 3122, was built to cater for the hordes of revolutionary visitors.

History

Set in the dry yellow loess hills of north Shaanxi, amongst terraced slopes and troglodyte villages, Yan'an is sparely impressive. As Edgar Snow noted on his arrival in 1937, Yan'an is '... ideally suited for defence. Cradled in a bowl of high, rock-ribbed hills, its stout walls crawl up to the very tops and corners in newly-made fortifications, where machine-guns bristled ...' (*Red Star over China*, first published by the Left Book Club, 1937, but now a classic, currently reprinted by Random House). The pagoda on a hill-top by the river, the major landmark, has become the symbol of Yan'an, which is itself a major symbol of the Chinese Communist Party.

It was in Yan'an that **Mao Zedong** wrote many of his most important speeches, delivering them from an earthen platform in the Date Garden. During the Anti-Japanese War (1937–45) the Communist Party began to assume its Chinese (as opposed to Russian) characteristics in Yan'an. As there were no industrialised cities and therefore no proletarians in the vicinity, the party organised the local peasantry to seize land, collectivise production and, at the same time, assist in guerrilla warfare against the Japanese. Yan'an was visited by a number of distinguished foreign journalists: Agnes Smedley danced with General Zhu De (whose biography she later wrote) in the Date Garden and Edgar Snow described life in Yan'an, as well as giving the world the first biographical details of Mao Zedong and other Chinese leaders in *Red Star Over China*. Mao's account of his childhood and youth, as told to Snow, revealed his struggles with his autocratic father over his desire for education and his refusal to accept an arranged marriage and the hysterical scenes that ensued with Mao Senior threatening his son with beatings, Mao Junior standing by the village pond threatening to throw himself in and his mother in tears. His determination to educate himself led him away from home to the Hunan First Normal School (or Teacher Training College) in Changsha where, once again, his strength of will was revealed in his refusal to co-operate in courses that he thought worthless. As he told Snow:

Most of all I hated a compulsory course in still-life drawing. I thought it extremely stupid. I used to think of the simplest subjects possible to draw, finish up quickly and leave the class. I remember once drawing a picture of the 'half sun, half-rock' (a reference to a line in one of Li Bai's poems) which I represented by a straight line with a semicircle over it. Another time during an examination in drawing I contented myself with making an oval. I called it an egg. I ... failed.

During this most productive and positive period of his life, when he was writing his most important political essays and planning the way forward for the Chinese Communist Party, Mao was able to reveal himself to Snow as a humorous and fascinating character.

The Communist Party arrived in Yan'an in October 1935, at the end of the Long March, a 9600km journey on which some 100,000 had set out but only 8000 made it to Yan'an. There it joined forces with the Shaanxi Soviet. The new arrivals settled in the cave dwellings of the area, Mao Zedong, with his usual impatience, moving house several times during the decade of occupation.

Apart from the grim concrete blocks of the town centre, the traditional domestic architecture of Yan'an, characteristic of much of the loess area of Shaanxi and Shanxi, is fascinating and on that basis alone Yan'an is worth visiting. Although today's peasants build themselves 'modern villas' with little trace of traditional styles, the cave houses once occupied by the revolutionary leaders have been preserved. Yan'an cave houses are usually carved into cliffs, in contrast with the underground houses that can be seen near Xi'an which are dug down from the ground surface. Long caves with rounded roofs were dug into the cliffs in series, each one usually furnished with a *kang* (brick platform bed) built against the facade with a brick stove beside it. The flue from the stove led under the bed and out through the apron wall of the facade. Above the apron wall, a simple wooden lattice window, covered with white paper, lets light into the cave. The lattice designs are particularly interesting in Yan'an, for in many of the caves inhabited by military and political leaders the five pointed star of the Red Army uniform has been incorporated.

The **Revolutionary Museum** (open 07.30–18.00) contains an enormous display of relics of the period: photographs, items of clothing, utensils of all sorts, including looms on which the cloth for army uniforms was woven and the white horse (stuffed) that Mao Zedong rode on the Long March. The museum is subject to frequent closures and rearrangements.

Similar problems exist in the Revolutionary Museum in Jinggang shan on the Hunan border (the base from which the Long March began). I first visited this in 1971, just before the mysterious flight, disgrace and death of Lin Biao. In 1971 Lin Biao's carrying pole was proudly displayed as evidence of his willingness to do hard work. By 1976 it had been re-labelled as Zhu De's carrying pole and, when questioned, the curator explained that it was, indeed, Zhu De's carrying pole and always had been but that Lin Biao had stolen it. Similar problems dog the Yan'an Museum.

Inside the North Gate of Yan'an, at the foot of the **Fenghuang** (Phoenix) **Hill**, is the first site used by the Party as a headquarters after the Long March in 1937–38. Mao and Zhu De lived here briefly and Mao wrote many of his major political essays here as well as entertaining visitors, such as the Canadian doctor who died in the service of the Red Army, Dr Norman Bethune.

The **Yan'an Pagoda**, which stands above the river, existed from the Song dynasty, although the present construction is Ming in date. It is an octagonal brick pagoda, nine storeys and 44m high.

Northwest of Yan'an town is another 'revolutionary site', **Wangjiaping**, from 1937–47 headquarters of the Military Commission of the Central Committee of the Communist Party and of the Eighth Route Army. Mao Zedong lived here for a time, as did Peng Dehuai, Zhu De and Ye Jianying, one of the longest-lived Party leaders, his survival through major campaigns suggesting a certain deviousness, which was inherited by relatives who achieved high office through nepotism; one nephew was executed for corruption.

Date Garden
The Date Garden (Zao yuan) is 10km northwest of Yan'an and best reached by taxi.

From 1940 to 1942 and 1944 to 1947 it was the Secretariat of the Central Committee of the Communist Party. Behind the meeting hall and office buildings were the homes of Peng Dehuai (later Minister of Defence, 1954–59, an opponent of the Great Leap Forward, which lead to his disgrace and replacement by Lin Biao in 1959) and Liu Shaoqi (Chairman of the People's Republic from 1959 to 1969; the major target of the Cultural Revolution during which time he died in prison, having been refused medical treatment). The great survivors, Mao Zedong (1893–1976), Zhou Enlai (1898–1976) and Zhu De (1886–1976), a key military leader, lived on top of the hill.

A Russian doctor lived here, too, and it was here that some of the jollier events of the Yan'an period took place. Agnes Smedley recalled dances held here in the open air as did members of the ill-fated Dixie Mission of 1944. This was a US Army Observer Group sent to study the military potential of the Communists as part of the Second World War effort to combat Japan. Members of the mission, which was intellectually very high-powered, were impressed with the organisation and spirit they found in Yan'an, in marked contrast to the corruption of Chiang Kai-shek's government, but they later fell foul of Senator Macarthy precisely because they had reported favourably. The Dixie Mission and, indeed, America's presence in China during the Second World War have been admirably described by Barbara Tuchman in her *Sand against the Wind: Stilwell and the American Experience in China 1911–45* (London, 1981).

The garden, apart from its flowering trees, also boasts a huge plantation of Indian hemp.

Luoyang

Luoyang, in northwest Henan province, was the capital of nine dynasties from the Eastern Zhou to the Tang, although today's city is industrial and little of its past remains above ground. The nearby site of the Longmen Buddhist cave temples provides the major reason for visiting the city today, although during the Cultural Revolution it was famous for its pioneer tractor factory.

Practical information

Getting there
The airport is small and does not have very many connections but Luoyang is on the Long-hai railway which runs west to west from Xuzhou in Jiangsu to Lanzhou in Gansu, passing through Zhengzhou (better airport) and Xi'an.

Where to stay
Hotels include the *Peony*, 15 Zhongzhou zhong lu, ☎ 485 6699, fax 485 6699, and the *Youyi*

Binguan (Friendship Hotel), ☎ 491 2780, fax 491 3808, further west at 6 Xiyuan lu in the newer part of the city. This was one of the hotels built to house Soviet experts who came in the 1950s to help set up the tractor factory and others. It used to offer Chinese versions of Russian cakes, including poppy-seed roll with plum paste instead of poppy seeds. The attractive *Luoyang Binguan*, a traditional courtyard construction, has been demolished in favour of a high-rise version at 6 Renmin xi lu, ☎ 393 5414.

History

Luoyang's ancient glory is disproportionate to its present appearance, especially when viewed from the modern city. It was a major capital of the **Zhou**, becoming the main capital in 770 BC when a walled city was constructed, the remains of which have been found in the area now covered by the Wangcheng (Royal City) Park. According to legend, Confucius came here to study music and Laozi was in charge of the archives. During the first part of the Han, Luoyang was the second capital (secondary to Chang'an, modern Xi'an) but it was made the primary capital of the Eastern Han (AD 25–220). The **Han** city was to the east of the present city, east of the White Horse Temple. The ramparts can still be seen, running some 4000m north to south and over 2500m west to east, with the Luo River flowing through the middle of the enclosure. The Han imperial college was to the south of the walls and had over 30,000 students. Here lived Ban Gu (d. AD 92), the second great historian of the Han, and Cai Lun, the eunuch who first mentioned paper in a report to the emperor in AD 105. Paper was used some 200 years earlier, however, for examples have been found preserved in the dry atmosphere of Xinjiang and Gansu. Cai Lun's contribution was a report on improvements in manufacture and materials. He swallowed poison in AD114 when his patron, the Dowager Empress, died, after having 'formally bathed' and solemnly adjusted his robes and hat (H.A. Giles, *A Chinese Biographical Dictionary*, 1898). There were two palace complexes within the walls, north and south, linked by a raised and covered avenue with a central path reserved for the emperor. Many of the imperial altars lay outside the city walls.

The same city was occupied by the Wei (220–265) and Jin (265–316). The famous **Seven Sages of the Bamboo Grove** lived here in the Jin, reclusive scholars who despised politics and devoted themselves to 'pure discussions' (non-political and Taoist in inspiration), when they were not getting drunk, writing poetry or playing music. One was supposed to have been permanently accompanied by a servant carrying wine for his master's thirst and a spade to bury him should he suddenly drop dead. Another famous resident was Ma Jun, who constructed a 'south-pointing chariot' (or perambulating compass), models of which can be seen in the museum and at the Historical Museum in Peking. It had a wooden figure with an arm which always pointed south, owing to a system of cog-wheels, no matter in what direction the chariot was driven.

The **Northern Wei**, who had previously established their capital at Datong in the north, moved their centre of administration to Luoyang (494–534) and, continuing the work they had sponsored at Yungang, began the Buddhist cave temples at Longmen nearby. Yang Xuanxhi compiled a *Record of the Monasteries of Luoyang* in 547, which is a lengthy description of the city of half a million inhabitants during one of its periods of glory. It is an extraordinary tale, for the city, full of monumental architecture, was built rising above ruins in 493, only to be completely abandoned at three days' notice in 534. The Wei capital occupied the site of the Han city but the palace was moved to the centre and the rest of the city divided by walls into separate wards, with markets outside the walls, as in the Han. As the Wei were fervent Buddhists there were 1367 Buddhist temples in the city for a population of 109,000 families.

When the Wei fell to the **Sui**, their city was destroyed and although the Sui emperor chose to site his capital in Luoyang, he built it to the west, on a site now comprising the later walled town, which is far smaller. His grand capital, the walls of which were some 20km in circumference, covering both banks of the Luo River, was laid out as a checkerboard of streets running north to south and west to east. In the Sui the inhabitants probably numbered about one million (counted as over 200,000 families). Although the first Sui emperor is generally better known for his brutality, he was also said to love literature and music, bringing thousands of musicians to live in Luoyang, filling his park outside the city with exotic plants and animals and gathering a substantial library of nearly 400,000 volumes. As part of his canal building projects, the parts of the Grand Canal linking Luoyang with Hangzhou and Peking were constructed. Grain carried on the canal was stored in granaries, the foundations of which still survive.

With the fall of the Sui, Luoyang became once more a secondary capital for the **Tang**; as during the Han, it was secondary to Chang'an (Xi'an). It was mainly in the last years of the Tang that Luoyang became the favoured capital, for it was closer to the main supplies of grain. It was said to be the preferred capital of the Tang empress Wu, who built herself a palace outside the old Sui city, which continued to serve as the administrative centre. She is supposed to have brought the then-fashionable peonies there. After the Tang, Luoyang was sporadically used as a capital during the Five Dynasties period but it never regained its former splendour. The current town walls in the east of the city are those of the Song-Qing town, smaller than previous settlements.

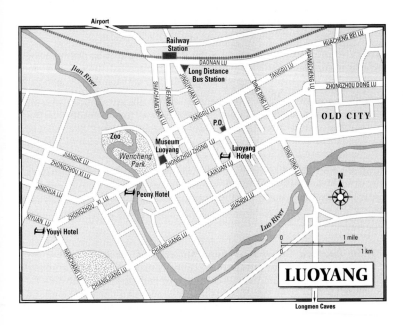

LUOYANG

Along Yan'an lu, the continuation of Zhongzhou zhong lu (named Dongfan-ghong lu/ East is Red Road in the Cultural Revolution), the **Wangcheng Park** is on the north side of the road. As with all of Luoyang's parks, it is filled with tree peonies which flower in April and May. It stands on the site of the old Zhou town of Wangcheng.

Just east of the park is the **Luoyang Museum** (open Tues–Sun 08.00–12.00, 14.00–17.30), which contains relics excavated in the city and provides a chronological history of the area, beginning with the late Neolithic Yangshao and Longshan cultures (no English). Notable are some oracle bones of the Shang and other articles excavated at **Erlitou** (a major Shang site about 30km east of Luoyang).

Erlitou was occupied c 2000–1500 BC, according to radiocarbon dates, and although not definitely identified as a capital, it represents a major site. It contained a palace, or ceremonial building, constructed on a platform c 100m by 100m, jade, bone and pottery artefacts as well as primitive bronzes, all produced in separate workshops. There is some suggestion that this may be a pre-Shang capital, perhaps associated with the preceding Xia dynasty, so far known only from textual reference; investigations continue. The Han pottery models of farmhouses, cooking stoves, grain-pounders and other scenes from daily life are very numerous, as are those representing jugglers, acrobats and musicians. A collection of Han bronze mirrors with finely decorated backs anticipates some fine Tang mirrors also in bronze. The Tang funerary ceramics, like those of the Han, are fine and numerous; the contrasts in colour and technique, and above all content, are interesting. The Han concentrated on scenes from agricultural life, while the Tang figures are courtly or exotic (camels and foreign attendants from along the Silk Roads).

The museum also contains a model of the Sui dynasty grain silos discovered outside the town; 400 constructed to hold the grain transported via the Grand Canal from Suzhou and other parts of the Yangtse delta to the capital.

Discovered north of the town (where the site can still be visited), the silos were underground, some 5–10m deep. The floors were hardened by fire, the walls of brick, some inscribed with records of the number of the pit, its content and the date of filling, as well as the names of the officials in charge. The wide mouths were 6–18m in circumference. Built during the Sui, between 606 and 618, they continued in use throughout the Tang. To prevent loss, the whole area was originally walled.

The old town, especially south of Zhongzhou dong lu, is a pleasant place to wander in and is in marked contrast to the brick blocks of the newer settlements to the west.

The **Luoyang Gumu Bowuguan/Museum of Ancient Tombs** (open 08.30–19.00; on the airport road) contains underground tombs formerly exhibited in the Wangcheng Park. The most impressive is the Western Han Tomb (206 BC–AD 8). Viewed with the later Eastern Han Tomb, it demonstrates the development in the Han from the use of hollow slab bricks, often with impressed and painted designs, towards the use of smaller, solid bricks. The central chamber, where the coffin was placed, is constructed from the large hollow slab bricks and has a pitched roof supported by columns bearing triangular lintels with painted decorations. The smaller side chambers, originally filled with pottery models and offerings, are constructed from the smaller solid bricks and the roof is vaulted. Later Han tombs were mostly made thus, from solid bricks with vaulted ceilings. The paintings on the lintels depict an exorcist with a bear's head and his assistants (back wall) and immortals riding on dragons on either side of two doors (central). The second, later Eastern Han Tomb (AD 25–220) has sculpted doors and abundant pottery furnishings.

In the suburbs of Luoyang on the **Xiangshan** (Fragrant Hill), alternatively known as the Dongshan (East Hill), is the **Kanjing si** (Temple for Reading the Sutras), built in the last years of the 7C when the empress Wu ruled; it is said that it was built at the order of her consort, Gaoxong, whom she dominated. The cave roof is carved with a lotus and with flying apsareses (Buddhist 'angels') of great lightness. Below are 29 lohans, again carved with considerable skill.

In the same area is the **Tomb of Bai Juyi** (722–846), the great Tang poet (translated by Arthur Waley in *Chinese Poems*, Allen and Unwin, 1946, and *The Life and Times of Po Chu I*, 1949). He served as an official at Hangzhou, where he is commemorated in his dyke on the lake. In Luoyang, he wrote of his official work:

At the western window I paused from writing rescripts
The pines and bamboos were all buried in stillness

and similarly in Chang'an:

At Chang'an a full foot of snow;
A levée at dawn to bestow congratulations on the Emperor ...
Suddenly I thought of Xianyu valley,
And secretly envied Chen Jushi,
In warm bed-socks dozing beneath rugs,
And not getting up till the sun has climbed the sky.

After the death of his small daughter, called 'Golden Bell', about whom he wrote two poems, although she died very young:

And I remember how, just at the time she died,
She lisped strange sounds, beginning to learn to talk ...

he retired to the hill and gained the name of the 'Scholar who lives on the Fragrant Hill'. There are a grove of cypresses and a stele with the inscription 'Tomb of Master Bao of the Tang'.

Longmen Caves

The major excursion out of Luoyang is to the Longmen Caves, via the Guanlin and Guandi Temple. They can be reached by public bus no. 81 (terminus at the north end of Jinguyuan lu) or no. 60 from outside the Friendship Hotel. Tourist buses run trips from the railway station or you could negotiate a day's excursion by taxi.

7km south of Luoyang, on the road to Longmen, are the **Guanlin** (Grove of Guan) and the **Guandi Temple**, said to be the site of the **Tomb of Guan Yu**, the Shu (Sichuan) general of the Three Kingdoms period (AD 220–280), an historical figure who was popularly canonised as Guan Di, the God of War.

> The grave mound is surrounded by a cypress grove with a Qing dynasty stele stating that this is the grave of Guan Yu but as it was erected some 1500 after the event it cannot be taken as gospel. The temple was a Ming construction with a gate, bell and drum towers and main hall.

As is often the case with Ming temples, the stone carving of the balustrades (which is original, while the timberwork cannot be reliably dated to the period of foundation) is very fine. A wing of the temple houses an exhibition of fine funerary sculpture in stone: horses and attendants that lined the spirit ways of tombs from the Han to the Qing, sarcophagi and carvings from Longmen. There is also a collection of inscribed stelae.

The **Longmen Caves** (open 08.00–18.00), with their Buddhist carvings, are amongst the finest in China. Carved into a cave beside the Yi River (a tributary of the Luo which gives Luoyang its name), the first caves were carved out during the reign of the first Wei emperor to settle in Luoyang in 493; carving continued to flourish under the Sui and especially the Tang. Although two-thirds of the caves are Tang in date, there a few from the Song and some as late as Ming and Qing. In all there are 1352 caves, some 750 smaller niches, containing in all 97,306 statues, 3608 inscriptions and 39 pagodas carved into the rock.

> The site is very different from the slightly earlier site at Yungang, which is in the yellow earth area of the north. There the stone is softer and more weathered; the river drier, allowing visitors to view the caves from a distance. At Longmen the stone is darker and harder, allowing for greater detail, but the cliff is close to the river so it is not so easy to see the cliff as a whole.

The most notable carvings are to be found in the following caves, from west to east:

Ludong Cave was carved between 534 and 550. The cave also includes inscriptions dated to 539, 549, 550 and 572. With a flame ceiling, there are notable low reliefs of a *jataka* story (the life of Sakyamuni, the 'historic' Buddha') on one wall and, opposite, a very architectural composition of Buddhas sitting in open halls approached by steps, with detailed roof carvings. The curved figures bearing offerings of long-stemmed flowers are simple but elegant.

Shiku (Stone Room) Temple Cave was carved in 516–528, with the best adoration scenes remaining in Longmen (after the removal of sections of the Pingyang Cave to the USA in 1935). Processions of figures carved in low relief, Bodhisattvas, elegant court ladies carrying single lotus blossoms with attendants bearing large long-handled fans and canopy-like parasols (or parasol-like canopies) are watched by groups of lohans and Bodhisattvas, their hands clasped together in greeting as they stand among stylised trees. Small servants hold up the trailing hems of the loosely draped, cross-over gowns of the nobles who wear high hats. All, lohans and mortals alike, have the elongated earlobes (weighed down by heavy earrings) that are one of the iconographic features of the Buddha image.

Huoshao (Burnt) Cave was in built 516–528; its name may come from the flame-decorated ceiling or from the cave's having been struck by lightning. The cave contains low relief carvings of Buddhas in architectural settings, in the Wei style found in the preceding cave and the Guyang Cave.

Guyang Cave has been identified as being carved out between 488 and 528 and is thus one of the earliest carvings in Longmen. The side walls are covered

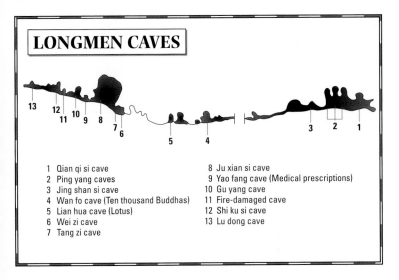

LONGMEN CAVES

1 Qian qi si cave
2 Ping yang caves
3 Jing shan si cave
4 Wan fo cave (Ten thousand Buddhas)
5 Lian hua cave (Lotus)
6 Wei zi cave
7 Tang zi cave
8 Ju xian si cave
9 Yao fang cave (Medical prescriptions)
10 Gu yang cave
11 Fire-damaged cave
12 Shi ku si cave
13 Lu dong cave

with carvings: major figures of Maitreya—(the Future Buddha) with crossed legs reaching the ground, sometimes attended by a pair of lithe, snarling lions—and Sakyamuni (legs crossed in the lotus position) in larger niches with silken swags above them and either smaller figures in niches or small inscriptions between them. Occasionally the niches are topped with an architectural roof rather than the silken swags, while lithe *apsareses* (Buddhist 'angels') fly above them. The major figure at the back of the cave is that of the 'historic' Buddha Sakyamuni and the upper parts of the walls are covered with tiny Buddha figures which almost fly up to the ceiling. The figures are characteristic of the Northern Wei: long-necked with rather square heads (where they have not been knocked off), scissor-like legs covered with drapery indicated by neat parallel lines, the relative rigidity of the Buddhas offset by the lithe, sinuous apsareses and lions. Restoration of the head of the major Buddha during the Qing produced a resemblance to the popular conception of the Taoist Laozi so that the cave is sometimes known as the Laojun Cave.

Liushi (Six Lions) Cave was carved in the Wei (516–528); the cave is noted for its lions carved in low relief with flat, bushy tails and snarling faces, defenders of the Buddhist law.

Yaofang (Medical Prescription) Cave was first carved under the Wei, during the Northern Qi; 120 remedies for skin diseases, diabetes, heart disease, madness and other ailments were carved around the entrance to the cave (550–577). The major Buddha figure with two disciples is carved in a fuller, more rounded style than the skinny Wei figures and is considered to represent the transition from the Wei to Tang style. Its stiffness is ascribed to iconographic uncertainty in the period of transition.

Juxian (Honour to Forebears) Cave was carved under the Tang in 675; this is the largest 'cave' carved at Longmen and, as can be gathered from the square holes in the walls into which supporting beams were inserted, was once covered by a large wooden structure. The figures were supposed to have been paid for by the Tang empress Wu Zetian, a great patroness of Buddhism (she is said to have taken an amorous interest in monks), who used over 2000 strings of cash from her cosmetics budget. The central Buddha figure is just over 17m high (his ears alone are 1m long), seated in the lotus position on a lotus throne supported by small figures. The drapery of the robes is schematic but the face is solid and imposing, with sensuous lips in the Indian manner. Immediately to the left and right of the Buddha are smaller figures of the favourite disciples, Ananda and Kasyapa (the latter almost completely destroyed), flanked by Bodhisattvas with elegant head-dresses, ropes of pearls and silken cords decorating their more lavish robes and heavy earrings pulling at their lobes. Smaller figures in niches fill the wall. Two of the most impressive figures are the huge guardians to the right of the Buddha figure. One of the four Celestial Guardians (Maharaja-devas) stands, hand on hip, one foot crushing a devil-like figure, his other hand holding a relic-stupa (or miniature pagoda). The sinuousness of the stance and the detail of the carving of his armour is in marked contrast to the stillness of the main icon but is echoed in the protective warrior who stands beside him, again in a naturalistic, challenging position with his muscular body modelled realistically. These figures represent the best of the Tang carving: lively, naturalistic and extremely decorative, in distinct contrast to the static icons of the Wei.

Weizi (Wei Inscriptions) Cave was carved in 516–528; the cave gains its name from the Wei inscriptions. It is also notable for some very successful, but damaged, Wei figures where the modelling of the drapery is particularly elegant; some of the figures stand in a more natural pose than is commonly found in the Wei. There are also some smaller low relief depictions of *jataka* stories.

Lianhua (Lotus Flower) Cave was carved under the Wei in 516–528; the cave's name is derived from the huge, daisy-like lotus flower on the ceiling, the petals flattened to reveal the seed-pod in the centre. It is surrounded by flying *aspareses*, while below is a standing Buddha figure minus the head and arms (removed presumably for sale to collectors in the late 19C and early 20C). The Buddha has a lotus halo and a flame mandorla (the larger 'halo' surrounding the whole body) and there are tiny carvings all over the walls of the cave, which is one of the most impressive for its all over detail. On the right is an impressive (headless) figure of the disciple Kasyapa bearing a stave, the drapery of whose robe with its frills and folds is richly detailed when compared, for example, with the treatment of the Buddha's robe. Notice, too, the cap-shaped carving above the entrance with its flame whorls.

Wanshou (Ten Thousand Buddha) Cave was completed in 680 under the Tang. It provides a good contrast in style with the Lianhua (Lotus Flower) Cave, both richly carved in styles separated by nearly 150 years. The cave's name is derived from the tiny multiple carvings on the side walls. There is also a lotus flower on the ceiling with petals carved more realistically than that in the Lotus Flower Cave. The major figures present the same grouping as in the largest (Juxian) Cave: a central Buddha, seated cross-legged on a lotus throne, flanked by two disciples, shaven-headed in monks' robes, and two Bodhisattvas with tiny attendants between them. Although the figures are Tang, they are not as naturalistic nor as sinuous as those in the major cave but the carving of the lotus throne is particularly fine, with small figures supporting the weight on their shoulders and grimacing with the effort. Underneath the Ten Thousand Buddha panels are some elegant musicians, casually seated on cushions with swirling silk behind them, and a dancer with arms raised and waist bent as her silken draperies fly.

Outside the cave is an equally elegant figure of the Bodhisattva Avalokitesvara (Guanyin in Chinese) holding a fly whisk (an essential Buddhist attribute for sweeping away flies to save their lives) and a water bottle containing the saving 'sweet dew' that Guanyin sprinkes. 85cm high, this figure was carved in 681 by Zhen hui, a monk from Xuzhou. With the head slightly held to one side and the gentle curve to the body emphasised by the silk drapery and knotted silk girdle threaded with a jade disc, the figure is quintessentially Tang, elegant yet fleshy.

Jingshan si (Veneration of Goodness Temple) Cave was carved during the Tang from 650 to 683; this cave has suffered greatly from the depredations of 'head collectors' but there are two low relief guardians of the faith, clad in armour and brandishing swords, and a seated figure, smoothed by the elements, that looks rather like a Maitreya Buddha (with feet reaching the ground) but is described as Udayana, King of Kusambi, a contemporary of the 'historic' Buddha, Sakyamuni, who made the first statue of the Buddha.

Nan Pingyang (Southern Sun-facing) Cave was begun during the Wei; the cave was finished under the Sui (595–616) and the central Buddha figure is, like some others, 'transitional' in style. The drapery of the robe is elegant and realistic and the figure is well fleshed-out, anticipating the Tang style, but the head (although with full lips) is rather block-like and elongated in form, reminiscent of the Wei. The ceiling lotus is carved with lotus-shaped petals, unlike the early Wei 'daisy' lotus of the Lotus Flower Cave.

Pingyang zhong (Middle Sun-facing) Cave was, like the Guyang Cave, one of the first to be carved at Longmen (c 494–515). An inscription states that the cave took over 20 years to complete and required the labour of over 800,000 workers. It contains 11 large Buddha figures. The figures are set against the low relief carvings of their flaming mandorla haloes and tiny Buddha figures on the walls. The major one is part of a group: the seated Buddha flanked by small disciples, slightly larger Bodhisattvas and two lions. All the figures are solid, with the characteristic thick neck and solid, rather block-like heads of the Wei. Details of the clothing, although chunkily carved, are revealing: skirts gathered at the waist and held by a knotted silk tie, overjackets with wide sleeves worn over diaphanous undershirts. Mandorla flames and the flowing robes of *apsareses* meet in the lotus ceiling.

Pingyang bei (Northern Sun-facing) Cave was begun under the Wei; the cave was finished during the Tang (627–649) and the figures, roughened by weathering, also date from the Tang. There is a Buddha seated in the lotus position, his feet clearly visible and his upper torso more bare than in many other figures, so that he looks more like the solitary meditating monk of legend. He is attended by disciples and Bodhisattvas with guardians at the entrance.

Qingqi si (Qingqi Temple) Cave was carved in the Tang (618–683); as late as 1913 the cave was still protected by a wooden temple inhabited by monks. The cave contains a seated Buddha figure, the drapery carved in elegant folds; the attendant Bodhisattva figures are particularly refined and more particularly female than elsewhere, contrary to Indian tradition where Bodhisattvas are strictly male.

Nearby is a small four-storey pagoda, nearly 3m high, built in the early Tang, one of many in the complex.

The **Baima si** (White Horse Temple) is 10km east of Luoyang. The temple is mainly Ming but was heavily restored in the 1950s and 1970s.

> Founded in AD 68, this is the oldest Buddhist foundation in China. According to legend, after the Han emperor Mingdi dreamed of a golden figure, which was explained to him as being the Buddha, Caiyin and Caijing went off to the west in search of Buddhist sutras and returned to Luoyang on white horses, bringing with them two Indian monks. A temple was built in the year after their return and it took its name from their horses.

Before the gate stand two statues of horses, possibly Song in date. Immediately inside the gate, at the eastern and western corners of the surrounding wall, are two tombs, said to be those of the Indian monks of the Han. On the main axis is the Hall of Celestial Guardians where the figure of Weituo (at the rear, facing the main hall) is said to be Ming. The Great Hall, which contains the main Buddha figures, was built in the Ming, apparently using many of the original Han bricks. The main figure is the 'historic' Buddha, flanked by the Bodisattvas Manjusri and Samantabhadra. In the hall behind are 18 lohans said to date from the Yuan dynasty. Steps behind lead up to the Cool Terrace, supposedly dating from the Han and built for the two foreign monks to translate the sutras. On the right side of the main axis is the Hall of Ancestors containing figures of the first six Chan (Zen) masters; the figures are Qing in date. Behind this is the Meditation Hall of the temple; as much as any temple in China can be said to belong to a school of Buddhism, this is a Chan or Zen temple.

East of the temple is a square brick pagoda built in 1175, 24m high, called the **Qiyun** (Level with the Clouds) **Pagoda**. The spread of dates associated with the temple is considerable. During the Tang, at the height of its power, it had over 1000 monks; these are now reduced to a handful who live at the back of the enclosure and grow their own vegetables.

Zhengzhou

Zhengzhou, capital city of Henan province, lies just south of the Yellow River in an area rich in Neolithic and Bronze Age remains. The city was one of the capitals of the Shang dynasty (c 1700–c 1100 BC) and other major Shang city excavations may be visited nearby. Its importance waned after the Shang, not to revive until the early 20C, when it regained prosperity after the construction of the Peking–Hankou railway line (1898–1906). Today it is a modern city, a major cotton textile centre, as well as still being a major railway terminus.

Practical information

Getting there
By air

There are flights to and from Peking, Xi'an, Changsha, Guangzhou, Hefei, Ji'nan, Nanjing, Nanyang, Qingdao, Shanghai, Shijiazhuang, Wuhan, Hong Kong and Yichang. An airport shuttle bus runs to the *CAAC* offices on Jinshui lu. A taxi from the airport costs c 100 yuan.

By train

The station is in the southwest of the town. As it stands at the nexus of China's railway system and on the new direct Peking–Hong Kong line, Zhengzhou can be reached from almost all points by train.

Where to stay

The major hotels are on Jinshui lu, in the northeast of the town; they include the *Holiday Inn* (Huangguan Jiari Binguan), 114 Jinshui lu, ☎ 595 0055, fax 599 0770, and the *Novotel International* (Yagao Guoji Fandian), 115 Jinshui lu, ☎ 595 6600, fax 599 7818.

History

The earliest site yet unearthed in the Zhengzhou area is that of **Dahe cun**, a Neolithic village of c 3760–3610 BC whose remains are classified as belonging to the Yangshao or 'painted pottery' culture. The term 'Yangshao' derives from Neolithic remains discovered in 1920 in Yangshao village in northwest Henan (c 75km west of Luoyang). The Swedish engineer, J. Gunnar Andersson, was amongst the first to describe the finds in his early classic work on Chinese archaeology, *Children of the Yellow Earth* (1934). A late Neolithic culture characterised by fine red pottery vessels decorated (or 'painted') with designs in black of animal forms gradually developing into geometric derivations, whose remains are widely spread throughout the Yellow River (Huang he) basin, it is still often named the Yangshao Culture, although the original site's stratigraphy is unclear and it may well post-date the Neolithic. Perhaps the most famous Yangshao site is that of Banpo, on the outskirts of Xi'an, but many later excavations, such as that at Dahe cun, are very rich.

Remains of the painted pottery culture at Dahe cun were overlaid by black pottery kilns of the Longshan Culture, a late neolithic culture characterised by burnished black ceramics. The eponymous Longshan site is in Shandong and while the red, painted pottery culture tends to be found to the west, with the generally later black pottery culture further east, in parts of Henan, such as Dahe cun, the stratigraphic sequence is clear. In 'ideal' sites, which fit a desired pattern of gradual progression, Yangshao is overlaid by Longshan, a culture which includes ceramic forms anticipating bronze shapes and the use of scapulimancy, another Bronze Age tradition; this, in turn, is overlaid by Bronze Age remains. If the Zhengzhou area is taken as a whole, this progression can be seen.

Zhengzhou appears to have been the site of one of the **Shang** (c 16C BC– c 1066 BC) capitals. The Shang kings moved their capital many times before finally settling in Anyang and the Zhengzhou city wall of the Shang, just to the west of Chengdong lu, may well have been Ao, one of the earlier capitals. Although an earlier capital has been unearthed at Erlitou near Luoyang, that at Zhengzhou represents a considerable expansion, with a city wall of over 7000m, enclosing an area of over three square kilometres. Bronze foundries and bone-carving workshops have been found on Huayuan lu, north of the city wall, and pottery kilns to the west on Minggong lu. Radiocarbon dates suggest that the site was occupied between 2000 and 1500 BC.

The importance of the city at the time may be judged from estimates of the amount of time put into the building of the **city wall**. It was constructed of tamped earth, or *pisé*, a method still used widely in northern China in domestic architecture where wooden plank frames are set up and earth pounded down inside the frames, which are subsequently removed, leaving a hard, firm wall. It was estimated that the wall averaged 10m in height and 20m in width and that if 10,000 workers put in 330 days a year, it would have taken 18 years to build. Although the remains of small, presumably domestic, dwellings have been found outside the wall, those within its perimeter are on the grand scale; thus it is assumed that the wall enclosed the administrative centre as well as aristocratic or palatial dwellings with many ordinary people living outside, near the foundries, potteries and workshops. In the northeast section of the city within the wall more than 100 human skulls, sawn across the middle, were unearthed and it is suggested that these may have provided the raw material for the bone-carving workshops. A tamped earth platform, perhaps an altar, was unearthed in the northwest corner of the city and many finely carved jade hairpins have been found within the walls—with rare examples unearthed outside, reinforcing the hypothesis that the inner city area was for the rich.

Zhengzhou's importance declined when the capital was moved to nearby Anyang, although the area continued to be occupied. A Han city wall, enclosing a far smaller area than that of the Shang city, has been unearthed and Han dynasty tombs and an ironworks have been found in Zhengzhou; a Tang tomb has also been found. Nevertheless, Zhengzhou was outshone—particularly in the Han, Wei, Sui and Tang—by Luoyang, which served as the second capital. In the 17C, Zhengzhou was again walled and the wall, like that of the Han, enclosed an area far smaller than that of the Shang capital.

When the **Peking–Hankou railway** was built (1898–1906), with later extensions to Guangzhou, as well as the Shanghai–Urumqi line, which passes through Zhengzhou from west to east, the city became a major terminus. 3000 years after its earlier prominence, it regained a position of importance as a manufacturing centre, particularly of cotton textiles, based on the railway and locally grown raw materials.

Its revolutionary history started early with the famous strike of workers on the Peking–Hankou line which began on 7 February 1923. The railway workers on the line had had 16 local trades unions which they planned to merge but the founding meeting of the 'Unified Syndicate of Railway Workers of the Peking–Hankou Line' was banned by the local warlord, Wu Peifu (1873–1939). His soldiers shot 35 strikers and wounded many more; the strike is now remembered as one of the first struggles of the workers' movement in China. Another tragedy in the vicinity occurred when Chiang Kaishek had the dykes holding back the Yellow River breached in 1938. This was done at Huayankou, 30km north of the city, in order to slow down the advance of Japanese troops. Its major effect was to drown at least one million

Chinese, render 12 million homeless and landless and inundate hundreds of square kilometres.

Railways were of particular importance to the warlords, who used them for troop movements: between 200,000 and 300,000 troops were moved annually in the early 1920s on the Peking–Hankou line alone, to the detriment of other traffic. Led by the newly formed Communist Party, the 7 February strike was one of the first events of the 'workers' movement' in China and railway workers in a modern industry, compared with the more traditional industries such as textiles, were politically further advanced than many others. There are displays of photographs and documents relating to the strike in the city centre's tall **Monument to the 7 February Strike**. Locally known as the Erqi ta (7 February Pagoda), it is a massive white tower set on a roundabout where Jiefang lu, Erqi lu and Dong da jie meet.

Taking Xi da jie east from the Monument to the 7 February Strike, you will find the **Chenghuang miao** (Temple to the City God) on the north side of the street. This is a Ming foundation, restored in 1502, with side wings added later in the Ming and Qing.

In the past every city had such a temple to the deity, alternatively called the God of Ramparts and Moats or Protector of the City (or town). Worship of the Chenghuang is said to date back to the reign of the legendary Emperor Yao (2357–2255 BC, according to legend) who instituted a sacrifice in honour of eight spirits, the seventh of which symbolised the city moat and ramparts. Later the deity took the form of a magistrate, a human 'defender of the people'. It was not uncommon for a notable local figure to be deified as the local Chenghuang and he is usually represented as a magistrate with his black official hat with two ear-flaps, attended by two secretaries, two constables (one with an ox's head, one with a horse's head), two further attendants, one white-faced, one black-faced and more servants, all of whose duty is to assist him by informing him of what is going on in his area of jurisdiction. Perhaps confounding the Chenghuang's duties as a judge with those of the judges who preside over the Chinese Buddhist hells where souls are judged, there are often representations of the ten Buddhist hells in City God temples.

The Zhengzhou temple is a complex oriented north–south, with a number of buildings, including a gateway, main hall and eastern tower, all with glazed tile roofs and striking eaves decorations comprising dragons, phoenix, lions among lotuses and peonies. The main hall's roof ridge has two animals 'swallowing' its extremities, phoenix and peonies and the hall bears the inscriptions 'Eight immortals crossing the sea' and 'Yang Xiang beats the tiger'. A great number of inscribed stone stelae are kept in the temple.

At the far end of the road is the T-junction with Erligang lu where you will find the ruins of the **Shang city wall**, described above. Much of the eastern wall has been unearthed, running parallel to Erligang lu and the east parts of the northern and southern walls. Turning left into Erligang lu and walking north, you will eventually cross the Jinshui River and then come to the T-junction with Jinshui lu.

The old **Henan Provincial Museum** (open 08.30–17.30) was on Jinshui lu where a forlorn statue of Chairman Mao now stands, peering at the new shiny hotels through a flyover. The new museum, a massive pyramid-style construction is at the northern end of Jingqi lu. As the provincial museum for one of the provinces richest in archaeological sites, the collection is stunning; and there are captions in English, There are rooms devoted to the Neolithic, with many of the finds from Dahe cun, the Neolithic village on the outskirts of the city where a number of house-floors were excavated, allowing for reconstruction of Neolithic buildings. The collection of bronzes is most notable and the funerary building models of the Han are striking, particularly the huge and unique example which has naked hermaphrodite caryatids instead of columns. Apart from the strength of its early collections, there are also exhibits from the Tang to the Song, including a fine Ming house-model.

There was an exhibition hall devoted to the Yellow River, just to the east of the old museum on Jinshui lu (closed at the time of writing). The exhibits depicted the river itself and its history as well as the engineering efforts devoted to maintaining the dykes and reducing the flow of silt which makes the river particularly difficult to control. So much silt is brought down the river (the yellow earth it carries giving it its name) that in many places the river flows within its dykes up to 10m above the surrounding countryside.

Around Zhengzhou

The **Yellow River Park** (28km north of Zhengzhou) can be reached by a public bus no. 16 from Minggong lu outside the station, for a view of the vast muddy river.

'The Yellow River', from Hong xue yin yuan *by Linqing, 1879*

The Neolithic village of **Dahe cun**, 12km north of the centre of town, was discovered in 1964. The excavations cover an area of 30 hectares. Twenty-eight house floors unearthed from different periods of habitation reveal varying structural methods. Some are surrounded by a metre high wall, which is unusual in Neolithic sites so far discovered. The fine red clay ceramics are decorated, mainly in white or black. Patterns have been identified as representing the sun, moon and stars.

Huayankou, the point where Chiang Kai-shek breached the Yellow River dykes, is c 30km north of Zhengzhou.

Dengfeng is either visited from Zhengzhou or from Luoyang (or en route between the two). It is 80km southwest of Zhengzhou and c 70km southeast of Luoyang. The road from Zhengzhou, however, has extra attractions in the form of Han tombs and a Yuan observatory (see below).

These sites can be reached on a day trip by tour buses leaving from the railway stations at either Luoyang or Zhengzhou (prices between 30 and 40 yuan).

The Han Tombs

The Han tombs at **Dahu ting** in Mixian, 60km from Zhengzhou, are those of a local official, Zhang Boyan and his wife. Tomb 1 (that of the official) is made of stone, while Tomb 2 is of brick. Both contain main chambers which contained the tombs and side chambers for offerings. The tombs are notable for their decoration in carved stone and wall paintings. In Tomb 1, in particular, they illustrate the preparation of food for the table. Of particular interest to Chinese archaeologists is the apparent depiction of the preparation of bean-curd (*doufu* or *tofu*). Literary evidence had suggested that this important protein source had been known from the Han but the evidence was scanty; Henan archaeologists regard the depiction in the late Han tomb at Mixian as confirming the literary account. The left-hand side chamber has depictions of chariots, horses and grain stores, with the official receiving grain, while a banquet scene is shown in the right hand chamber. Tomb 2 has a grand banquet scene with entertainers (acrobats, conjurors and fat wrestlers) painted on brick. There are also scenes from Taoist legends.

The Observatory at Gaocheng zhen

Inside the Zhougong miao (Duke of Zhou's Temple), at Gaocheng zhen, near Dengfeng, is a strange brick tower, rather like a pyramid. Built in the Yuan by Gao Shoujing (1231–1314), who was also responsible for the water supply of Peking, it was repaired in 1542 and is China's oldest surviving observatory. The 10m tower is ascended by two flights of stairs on either side while the north side has a runnel down it and a wall at the bottom. These were originally fitted with bronze markers and enabled the calculation of the winter and summer solstices.

Song shan

Dengfeng lies near the foot of the **Song shan** (Song Mountain; 1440m), one of the Five Sacred Mountains (see Tai shan). 2km north of the town is the **Songyang Academy**, one of the four 'great academies'; this one was founded in the early Song and housed in a temple founded in 484. It is notable today for its two old pines, survivors of three said to have been seen by the Wudi emperor of the Han in 110 BC when he came to worship at Song shan. He gave them titles as three generals. The second general is 15m high, the first 6m.

4km east of Dengfeng are two stone pillars, all that remains of the **Han temple** built in 118 at the foot of Song shan. Built of stone in imitation of wooden architecture, they are important architectural relics and also noted for their inscriptions in Han calligraphy (which is comparatively rare).

Song Shan itself has a number of temples dotted about its peaks. There are four Buddhist holy mountains but these five antedate them and are associated with the imperial cult and Taoism. Mountains have always had a special place in Chinese belief, their height suggesting proximity to the gods. The five represent the directions with Song shan in the centre. The emperors of the past used to make ceremonial visits to ascend each in turn, both 'beating the bounds' of his territory and sacrificing to the gods. There are many significant temples in the Song shan region and the practice of imperial ascent gave the name to the county town for *deng* means 'to ascend' and *feng* 'to bestow honours'.

Zhongyue miao (Temple of the Central Peak)

At the foot of the famous mountain, ascended by the Han emperor Wudi in 110 and by the Empress Wu (684–704), is the largest temple in Henan province, dating to the period of the Qing Qianlong emperor (late 18C), although there were earlier buildings on the site, the first constructed under the Qin (221–207 BC). There are over 30 white pines said to date from the Tang and Song. To the north-east of the Chongsheng gate are four 3m high iron guardian figures cast in 1064, with dates and inscriptions cast on their backs and very fierce faces. They are accurate representations of 11C soldiers and, being cast in iron rather than bronze, link with many other fine iron castings found in northern Henan and southern Shanxi (like the giant Tang Buddha head in Lin Fen). The gate-building with its fantastically decorated roof stands beside a smaller pavilion with temple guardians dating from the Northern Song. On the right in the main courtyard is a stele with carvings of the five peaks. This is in front of the main hall, which stands on a high stone platform with two Ming lions in iron. Inside is a central statue of the god of the mountain.

Songyue Pagoda

7km northwest of Dengfeng is the 6C Songyue (Song Peak) Pagoda, a solitary survivor of the numerous religious buildings constructed at Song shan in the Northern Wei, when the area was a particular centre of devotion, perhaps because of its closeness to the capital at Luoyang. It is one of the earliest surviving large brick pagodas in China. It stands amongst the remains of the Songyue Temple, also constructed in the Northern Wei, first as an imperial residence, later as a temple. It retained its popularity in the Sui and Tang when the Empress Wu frequently stayed in the temple. The remaining temple structures are Qing in date, although there are stone lions and stelae from the Tang. The pagoda is 40m high, hollow and gently curved. It has a substantial base with four arched, lotus-carved openings in the upper part topped by a series of narrower upper storeys separated by layers of corbelled brickwork. There are openings in each of the upper storeys into the rectangular interior whose walls are covered with polychrome Buddha images. Traces of paint indicate that the pagoda was originally whitewashed.

Shaolin Monastery

One of the most famous religious establishments in China, which has given its name to a form of the martial arts, the Shaolin Monastery, is c 15km northwest of Dengfeng (and open 07.00–18.00). It was founded in the Northern Wei in 495.

The Indian monk, Bodhidharma, founder of the Chan (or Zen) school of Buddhism, is supposed to have come to the Shaolin temple in 527, after seeing the emperor of the Liang in Nanjing. Disappointed over his failure to persuade the emperor that all his good works of Buddhist patronage amounted to nothing without an understanding of the nothingness of everything, Bodhidharma crossed the Yellow River on a single reed (thus he is often depicted, with a black curly beard, standing on a slim leaf on the waves) and arrived at the Shaolin Monastery where he sat for nine years facing a wall. Accounts of his subsequent career are equally mystic: dying in the monastery, he was buried there but subsequently returned to India wearing only one sandal; the other remained in his grave. He is known as the first patriarch of the Chan school, which preaches the rejection of doctrine (especially textual study) in favour of meditation alone. The martial art of wrestling ('Shaolin fists'), also known as kung fu, which was practised by the monks supposedly to help their concentration when meditating, is immensely popular now and many films have been made, both in Hong Kong and China, about the magical powers of the martial monks. Hundreds of people now come to visit Shaolin and study martial arts in the dozens of private academies which fill the town. The main streets are lined with souvenir shops selling martial arts clothing and equipment.

The temple and its subsidiary buildings were destroyed during a persecution of Buddhism (561–77) and restored in 579–80. The foundation flourished during the Tang, supporting a community of more than 2000 monks. It declined during the late Tang and Five Dynasties. A major renovation took place in 1735 but in 1928 the warlord Shi Yousan set it ablaze and it burned for over five weeks.

The monastery is still noted for its **frescoes**: that in the Thousand Buddha Hall,

Martial arts being practised at a monastery, from Hong xue yin yuan *by Linqing, 1879*

said to be Ming, depicts 500 lohan paying homage to Vairocana (the first of the five celestial Buddhas, the essence of wisdom and absolute purity, whose name means 'shining everywhere'); that in the White Drapery Hall shows the rescue of a Tang emperor by 13 martial monks.

Approximately 200m west of the monastery is the **Forest of Stupas**, the monastery's graveyard where over 220 brick stupas, in varying styles dating from the Tang to the Qing, contain the remains of notable monks. Such large graveyards are rare now, although there is one below the Tanzhe Temple outside Peking and a smaller one below the Big Goose Pagoda outside Xi'an. Behind the graveyard is the cave in which Bodhidharma was supposed to have sat for nine years and the Chuzu miao (Temple of the First Patriarch). In the main hall, constructed in 1125, stone pillars are carved with temple guardians (perhaps an earlier practice, antedating the custom of placing them in a gate-hall), dragons, flying phoenix and other figures. Southeast of the hall is a pine tree, said to have been planted by the sixth patriarch, Huineng, in the early Tang.

In the main temple, stone lions guard the gateway which leads to perhaps the most striking part of the monastery (also unaffected by the warlord's fire), the forest of stelae, which includes stones inscribed in 683 and others carved with the calligraphy of the Song artist Mi Fei, the Yuan artist Zhao Mengfu (also noted for his horse paintings) and the Ming calligrapher Dong Qichang. Passing through buildings, the halls at the back of the enclosure, the seven-bay Thousand-Buddha Hall and the White Drapery Hall to its right, contain the well-known frescoes.

The temple is still enormously popular amongst Chinese and foreign tourists and the area is now crammed with souvenir shops selling martial arts clothing and equipment but the cemetery, the forest of stelae with its old trees and the surrounding mountains still retain a certain grandeur.

Gong xian

On the main railway line between Luoyang and Zhengzhou, Gong xian is an important site for ceramic historians since a major **Tang dynasty kiln site** was discovered near the railway bridge. There is one main hotel, the *Gongyishi Binguan*, on the main street.

8km north of Gong xian are a group of five Northern Wei Buddhist caves, the

Shikusi. Carved between 517 and 534, the caves have the characteristic central pillar seen at Dunhuang, which pilgrims circumnambulated in a clockwise direction, saying their beads and prayers. There are three massive Boddhisattvas carved on the outside of the cliff and over 200 small niches. Cave 1 has an impressive scene of the adoration of the Buddha with an extraordinarily varied crowd of worshippers. In Cave 3 there is a frieze of musicians carved along the lower part of the walls and there are Buddhist 'angels' or *apsareses* on the ceiling of Cave 5.

The Northern Song Imperial Tombs

The Northern Song imperial tombs lie in an area 15km by 10km southwest of the town and are best visited by taxi. The first seven of the nine Northern Song emperors, the father of the first Song emperor, 21 empresses and over 200 minor members of the imperial family were interred here. All the graves were set on a northern axis, pointing towards the highest peak of the Song shan mountains. Unlike most of the other imperial tombs, which were built by their intended inhabitants during their lifetimes, all these tombs were constructed according to a strict reading of a passage in the *Zhou Li*, or *Book of Rites* (completed c 200 BC), which stated that the emperor should be placed in his coffin on the seventh day after death and buried seven months after death. Thus the emperor's successor had the tomb constructed in seven months, which means that the tombs were considerably smaller and less magnificent than most other imperial examples.

The tombs were sacked both by the invading Jin in 1125 and by the Mongols in the 14C but much of the structure above ground still stands. The spirit roads are generally much shorter than those of the Tang but the figures are generally taller. Engraved columns, horses with embroidered saddle-cloths, stirrups, bridles and attendants, lions and auspicious birds, tigers, symbolising martial strength, and kneeling sheep, symbolising filial piety, officials and elephants stand between guards to the north and eunuchs to the south and a group of foreign envoys demonstrating the centrality of the Chinese empire in East Asia. Korean envoys wear pill-box hats and have their robes fastened in a bow at the neck, Khotanese envoys have tall, pointed felt hats and long, loose hair, while those from Southeast Asia look rather like Buddha figures with shaved heads and bare feet. Arabs have turbans and luxuriant beards. These foreign visitors and a strange quadruped with wings and a single horn, the *jiaoduan*, which could travel thousands of miles in a day and understood all the languages of the world, thus serving as all-purpose interpreter and reporter for the emperor, are not found in any other imperial spirit way.

The military guards hold swords, the attendant officials hold tongue-shaped tablets, symbolising their office. These tablets were carried by officials to the daily imperial audiences; some say they were merely symbolic, others that they were used for notes.

Kaifeng

Kaifeng, east of Zhengzhou, was the capital of China during the Northern Song from 960 to 1127 when the court was forced to flee south in the face of the invasion of much of north China. Like Zhengzhou, it has suffered from its proximity to the Yellow River, for the dykes were deliberately breached in 1642 and the city was inundated again in 1855 when the river changed course because its bed had filled with silt. Little remains, therefore, of its former grandeur. Kaifeng is also famous for its historic Jewish community, which had all but died out by the mid-19C, although recent interest, particularly amongst Americans, has led to the identification of the old synagogue site, although the few Chinese-Jewish Americans who have arranged Barmitzvahs in Kaifeng have had to hold the ceremonies in the city's hotels. A giant theme park is planned, to recreate the city as it was during the Northern Song.

Practical information

Getting there
By train
Kaifeng is on the Shanghai–Urumqi line and is most easily reached from Nanjing or Zhengzhou, the latter being only an hour or so away. The station is in the south of the city. There is no airport nearer than Zhengzhou.

Where to stay
The main hotel, well situated in the centre of the old town, is the **Kaifeng Binguan** at 66 Ziyou lu, ☎ 595 5589, fax 595 3086, not far from the Xiangguo temple.

History

Kaifeng's history as a capital began in the Warring States period (403–221 BC) when it was the capital of the Kingdom of Wei. Wei was absorbed by Zhou which, in turn, was absorbed by the Qin empire (221 BC). A major statesmen of Wei was Shang Yang, author of the *Shang shu* (*Book of Lord Shang*), one of the most important Legalist texts. Shang Yang (c 390–338 BC) went to work in Qin well before it conquered all the other states, where he put his Legalist policies into practice, contributing to Qin's success and to the detriment of Wei. Kaifeng became a capital once again in the Five Dynasties period (AD 907–960) but its greatest period of pre-flood glory came when it was the capital of the Song from 960–1127. Little remains of its former glory because of later flooding.

Although Geil in his *Eighteen Capitals of China* (1911) states categorically 'Kaifeng is a has-been', the last part of his subsequent description still stands, for Kaifeng is a pleasant, rather sleepy little place. Geil continues:

It produces a worse impression than the wretched quarters of Constantinople. It has no streets, only broad straight stretches which, on rainy days, are seas of mud, on dry days, clouds of dust. 'It has no trade,' said a disappointed commercial traveller; no manufactures, no imports of any consequence; a local market-town it may be, but it seems to have the value of a big, casual village.

Yet during the **Song**, the imperial way was 300m wide. On each side there were covered arcades where merchants traded. Barriers painted black and a double barrier painted red partitioned the route from north to south, leaving a central passage which was reserved for the emperor and prohibited to people and horses. Traffic was confined to the arcades beyond the barriers. Two narrow canals ran alongside the arcades. They had lotuses in them and were planted with flowering trees (plum, peach and apricot) so that in spring one got the impression of a brilliantly coloured embroidery. Meng Yuanlao's flowery account of the eastern capital is quoted in Gernet, *Daily Life in China on the Eve of the Mongol Invasion*.

The literary account of Kaifeng's splendour is borne out by a wonderful genre painting by Zhang Zeduan of the Northern **Song, Going up the River at the Qing Ming Festival**, now in the Palace Museum collection in Peking. As it unrolls, Zhang's scroll takes the viewer up river, through the suburbs where wide barges with unfurled concertina-like sails and huge steering oars make their slow progress upstream; with its arched stone bridges and streets lined with tiled-roofed houses (most with a small upper storey), shops open to the street, tea-houses and grand city gates, Kaifeng itself is thronged with people, pedlars with their wares slung on shoulder-poles, donkeys, camel caravans, carts being pushed over the hump-backed bridge, sedan chairs with ladies peeping from behind patterned curtains, officials on horseback followed by servants on foot and somnolent customers in the tea-houses watching the world go by. Much of this disappeared when the Jurched (ancestors of the Manchus) overran northern China and captured Kaifeng, taking the emperor and many courtiers prisoner and driving the remnants of the imperial household south to Hangzhou. The Jurched established the **Jin dynasty**, renaming Kaifeng *Nanjing* or 'Southern Capital' in deference to their northern roots. The confusing profusion of names continued, for Kaifeng was known briefly as *Beijing* ('Northern Capital') under the Ming. The Jurched were themselves overthrown by the Mongols in 1232, despite their defence of Kaifeng by grenades (an event of significance in the history of weaponry).

In 1642, when the peasant army led by **Li Zicheng** threatened Kaifeng, the Yellow River dykes were breached, according to official sources by the rebel-leader but more probably by the officials defending Kaifeng in an attempt to halt Li Zichzeng's advance. As with Chiang Kai-shek's action near Zhengzhou, vainly attempting to halt the Japanese advance, all that happened was that a quarter of a million innocent people were drowned and Li Zicheng's uprising ran out of steam as the Manchus swept down to found the Qing dynasty. This and the 1855 flood when the Yellow River changed course of its own volition, having deposited so much silt that its bed was higher than the dykes, left Kaifeng bereft of many ancient relics.

An aspect of Kaifeng's history which has long fascinated Europeans is its **Jewish community**. Jewish relics in China begin with a paper document referring to the sale of sheep dating from 718. The document was found near the Buddhist caves at Dunhuang in 1901 and is now in the British Library. There are records of Jews in Canton in 877 and later small communities were recorded in Peking, Quanzhou, Luoyang, Ningbo, Hangzhou, Nanjing and Yangzhou. More is known about the Kaifeng community than others for several stelae that once stood outside the synagogue there record their history.

Although the stelae state that they arrived as early as the Zhou (c 10C BC), it is now thought that this is a *post facto* justification characteristic of the Chinese fascination with antiquity and that they did not appear until perhaps the Song. It is thought that, like the Muslim Chinese, their ancestors came to China from Central Asia and, like the Muslim Chinese in China proper as distinct from the Uighurs and Kazakhs of Chinese Central Asia, they are somatically Han Chinese.

This probable origin is borne out by their divisions of the *Pentateuch* into 53 instead of 54 chapters and their use of 27 letters of the Hebrew alphabet instead of 22, characteristics which they share with Persian Jews. The Jesuit missionary Matteo Ricci (1553–1610) was the first foreigner to note the existence of the Kaifeng Jews and he sent two Chinese Christian converts to Kaifeng in 1607 where they saw the synagogue and met the Rabbi. Later Jesuit visitors included Fathers Jean Domenge (1722) and Gaubil (1723). Domenge sketched the synagogue, providing the only illustration of the whole building that exists. In 1850 the Bishop of Hong Kong, together with missionaries from the London Society for Promoting Christianity among the Jews, visited Kaifeng and obtained a *Torah* in Chinese (now in the British Library). They found the community in dire straits after the great flood following the Yellow River change of course, reduced to selling the fabric of the synagogue as building material.

Bishop White of the Canadian Church of England, as Bishop of Kaifeng and a considerable sinological scholar, took a great interest in the survivors of the community and wrote about it, although his fundamental intention, like that of the London Society, was to teach them 'that Jesus Christ was a Jew and that he came to save the world' as he stated in 1912. Contemporary attempts were made by the sizeable European and Middle Eastern Jewish community of Shanghai to help the community through the *Society for the Rescue of the Chinese Jews* founded in 1900. In the relaxation following the death of Mao, articles have begun to appear in Chinese journals which reveal that there are still some 200 Jews in Kaifeng, with a smaller community in Yangzhou. Like Chinese Muslims, with whom they have frequently been confused, they do not eat pork but, unlike the Muslims, they trace their descent through the matrilineal line. The site of the synagogue, off Di Jie in the centre of the walled town, is now a hospital garage, although such is the interest of American Jews in particular that I would not be surprised if the synagogue were rebuilt as a tourist attraction. The three surviving stelae are now in the Kaifeng Museum (see 'Monographs of the Jewish Historical Society of Hong Kong', vol. 2, Hong Kong Jewish Chronicle, 1986).

Within the walls

Starting from the **Kaifeng Binguan**, turn right into **Ziyou lu**, past a turning on the right (Madao jie) and you will see the **Xiangguo si**. The name, given in the early 8C by a Tang emperor, commemorates one of his pre-imperial titles. One of China's best-known Buddhist temples, it was founded in 555 on the site of the palace of a Wei ruler of the Warring States period. The first temple was destroyed by fire during fighting in the pre-Tang period and was totally destroyed in the

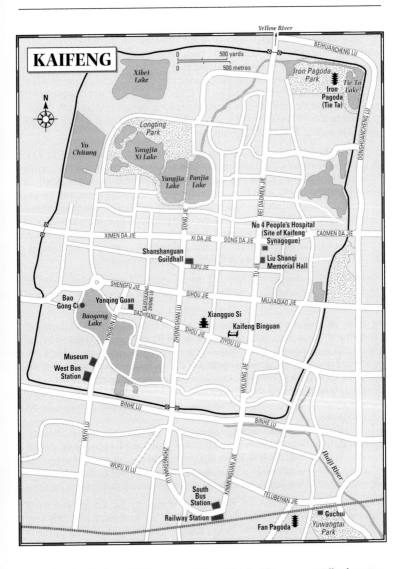

1642 flood. Rebuilt in 1766, the surviving Qing buildings, especially the sutra library (at the far end) and the main hall, are noted for their multiple eaves bracketing and yellow and green tiled roofs.

Entered through a stone *pailou* gateway, in the Bell Tower on your right is a Qing bronze bell 4m high and weighing 10,000kg; it is one of the 'Eight Sights of Kaifeng'. It is called the 'Frost Bell of the Xiangguo Temple'. In the main hall there is a small exhibition, including a fine bronze *arhat* (Northern Song), many Ming and Qing porcelains, jades, embroideries and a parasol once belonging to the Dowager Empress Cixi. Behind is the octagonal pavilion with uptilted eaves, housing a gilded, four-sided Guanyin of the 1000 arms and 1000 eyes (all seeing and compassionate). It is said to have been carved from a single piece of gingko wood. Behind it is the two-storey sutra library.

Turn right out of the temple into Ziyou lu and continue until you reach the main north–south road, Zhongshan lu. Cross straight over and continue to the end of the smaller road where it meets Baofukang zhong lu. Diagonally opposite (slightly to the right) is a small road which leads to the Taoist temple **Yanqing guan** (Temple of Extended Celebration).

Originally founded in the early Yuan, it was given its present name in 1373. All that remains is the Pavilion of the Jade Emperor, 13m high. The pavilion survived the floods of the 17C and 19C but its base was covered by nearly 2m of earth, for in 1973 the base was excavated to reveal the bottom of the iron-work windows (made in 1549, according to inscriptions). The base is square, the middle and upper parts octagonal with turquoise tiles above carved bricks imitating wooden construction. The temple was inhabited by a Taoist master, founder of the Quanzhen school which sought to synthesize the theories of *Laozi*, the Confucian classic of filial piety, and Buddhist belief.

Return to Zhongshan lu and turn left. At the second crossroads, turn right into Xufu jie, where you will find the **Shanshaangan huiguan** (Fellow Provincials' Association).

Now open to the public, although it was occupied by a school during the Cultural Revolution, this was originally a 17C guildhall established by merchants from Shanxi and Shaanxi provinces. These guildhalls, which functioned primarily as hotels for natives of particular provinces, were once scattered throughout China's cities and were useful for travellers of all sorts, if they could prove that they came from the relevant province. Scholars taking official exams in the capital would stay in the appropriate guildhall for very little money.

In the late Guangxu period (1875–1908) this hall was also joined by merchants from Gansu province. All the buildings in the enclosure, from the spirit wall at the front, the bell and drum towers and the ornamental arch to the main halls and side halls, are highly decorated with tiled roofs with elaborate ridge decorations and richly carved wooden panels, all dating from the Qing.

Returning to Zhongshan lu, turn right, Shuarong jie, brings you to the **museum**, on Yingbin lu near the Baogong lake, a run-down institution which suffers like so many others from lack of funding and does no justice to the history of the city.

Northwest of the museum on the far side of Baogong hu (lake) is the modern Bao gong ci memorial hall, built in 'Song style' to commemorate the life of a local governor of the Northern Song.

Continuing along Shuarong jie, the second crossroads is with the main road Tu Jie; the site of the synagogue in Jiaojing hutong, now a hospital, was formerly reached from Di Jie. Turn right into Di Jie and the next crossroads is with Dongda jie on the right and Caizhengting dong jie on the left. I have not been there but according to the map there is a hospital just off Tu Jie, immediately south of

Caizhengting dong jie, which should be possible to find.

Returning to Di Jie, continue south. The third crossroads is where Ziyou lu meets Di Jie. Turn right into Ziyou lu and you will find the Kaifeng Binguan.

In the old Agricultural Bank building on Bei tu jie is the memorial hall to Liu Shaoqi (1898–1969), once a close colleague of Mao Zedong, who died in prison in Kaifeng. He and his fifth wife were viciously attacked throughout the Cultural Revolution as rightist traitors.

Longting (Dragon Pavilion) **Park**, in the northwest corner of the walled city, was originally part of the imperial park of the Northern Song. The park was later used under the Ming and the high part on which the **Dragon Pavilion** stands was the only part not to be submerged in the floods of 1642. In 1692 a 'Longevity Pavilion' was built on top of the prominence and local officials used to come here and offer their respects on the emperors' birthdays. In 1696 it was named, somewhat inappropriately, Dragon Pavilion; the current building on the site, a Qing dynasty hall with a double-eaved roof, is a majestic structure closer to a corner tower on a city wall than a pavilion. There are two Song dynasty stone lions in front of the hall and below it, near the entrance to the park, a bronze statue of Sun Yatsen erected in 1929.

Although there were rumours in the 1980s of plans to 'rebuild' the old imperial way running along today's Zhongshan lu south of the Dragon Pavilion, a smaller reconstruction has taken place on Shudian jie which runs parallel to Zhongshan lu from the Xi dajie/Dong dajie crossroads to Gulou jie. This is part of the tourist thrust which has led to the reconstruction of the Confucian temple area in Nanjing and Liulichang in Peking as 'old-style' quarters. Shudian jie is lined with two-storey 'Qing' style buildings with elaborate balconies and carved stone pillar bases.

In the northeast corner of the city, the **Iron Pagoda** (Tie ta), open 08.00–18.00, stands in the Iron Pagoda Park. Kaifeng's major landmark, the pagoda was built in 1049 during the Northern Song as part of the Youguo (Protect the Country) Temple, which no longer survives. It is said that the pagoda houses relics of the Buddha. It is octagonal, 13 storeys high and almost 55m tall. Its popular name derives from the iron-like colour of the glazed tiles which cover the exterior. Like other early surviving buildings in Kaifeng, its base is buried under a couple of metres of silt deposited during floods. The brick and tile construction imitates timber and the tiles are further decorated with *apsareses* (Buddhist 'angels'), dragons, *qilin* (Chinese unicorns), lions and lotuses. It is possible to climb the pagoda. In a small octagonal pavilion just to the south of the pagoda is a Song dynasty bronze Buddha, 5.14m high and weighing 11.7 tons.

Outside the walls

Two kilometres southeast of the city, outside the walls, is the **Guchui** or Yu wang Platform in the Yuwang tai park (gongyuan). (It is best reached by taxi.) This elevation is said to have been created by the Great Yu, the legendary tamer of floods, hence the name Yu wang, or 'King Yu's Platform'. It is also said to have been a place where rulers of the Warring States period came to enjoy music, hence the name Guchui: *gu* means 'ancient' and *chui* means 'to play wind instruments'.

The park contains buildings with stelae commemorating the feats of the Great Yu and halls commemorating Tang poets, such as Li Bai and Du Fu, who are said to have given recitations and drunk wine on the platform.

Just outside the park to the west is a more interesting building, the **Fan ta Pagoda**. It was built in 977 and is the oldest standing building in Kaifeng. Built of brick, it is hexagonal in plan and now 31.67m high. As it has been deeply buried in silt it must originally have been considerably higher. It was described in the Ming as being nine storeys high but only three remain. Inside are many Buddhist sutras inscribed on stone; outside the carved brickwork is very fine.

Outside the city, 2km to the northeast, and also best reached by taxi, is the **Iron Rhinoceros**, housed in a Long miao (Dragon Temple). It was cast in 1446 to try and ward off floods but it and its temple were submerged in 1642. In 1691 the rhinoceros was dug up and a new temple constructed round it. It is about 2m high with an inscription on its back which reads:

One hundred smeltings of dark gold, liquidified and transformed into a magical rhino, majestic and brilliant. Set up as a protection against water, stable as Mount Tai, firm as a block of stone ... Rain falls and wind blows, men plough and women spin, the four seasons follow each other in order and the one hundred spirits do their tasks appropriately.

It is possible to see the **Yellow River** outside the town to the north at Liuyankou Ferry, where there is a tourist lookout point. Behind its dykes the river flows at a higher level than the flat surrounding countryside and is a rather frightening sight, inexorably bearing the tons of grey yellow silt which endlessly raise its bed.

Anyang

Anyang, a small town in the north of Henan on the Zhengzhou–Peking railway, was the site of the last Shang capital in the 12C–11C BC.

Practical information

Getting there
By train

The station is to the west of the old walled town off the west end of Jiefong lu.

Where to stay

The *Anyang Binguan* is at no. 1 Youyi lu, ☎ 592 2219, fax 592 2244, north of the small city wall, and the *Fenghuang Hotel* is on Jiefang lu.

History

Written records list seven **Shang capitals** and the ruins at Zhengzhou have been tentatively described as those of the capital of Ao, although this is uncertain and the other earlier capitals, assumed to be in Northern Henan, have yet to be found. The ruins of the capital of Yin, however, are known to lie on the banks of the Huan River, northwest of today's Anyang. In the *Shi ji* (*Records of the Grand Historian*) by Sima Qian (d. c 90 BC) these were described as 'the wastes of Yin' but they were not definitely recognised until the beginning of this century. In 1899 peasants began digging up and selling 'dragon bones', inscribed oracle bones of the late Shang which were ground up and sold as 'dragon bone medicine'. Wan Yirong (1845–1900), an epigrapher and archaeologist, noticed writing on some ground-up bones that he had bought as medicine and investigated their origins. Between 1928 and 1937 many seasons of excavation were undertaken in the area; these have been recorded by one of the leading archaeologists involved: Li Chi, *Anyang*, University of Washington Press, Seattle, 1976. Since 1950 excavations have continued.

The most dramatic finds include palace floors, the remains of large houses, a ceremonial altar and 11 massive royal tombs. In both the major building foundations (perhaps temples) and the royal tombs, human sacrifices have been found. The graves are cross-shaped underground pits up to 19m by 14m, with ramps leading down to the tomb chamber where human sacrifices, articles of jade, bronze, bone, shell and pottery were laid out around the coffin. It has been estimated that each one might have required 7000 working days to dig out. A recent discovery was that of the **Tomb of Fuhao**, consort of one of the late Shang kings, Wuding. Her tomb was smaller than those of the kings but it is significant for the perfection of its content, including lavishly decorated ritual bronzes with inscriptions and many tiny carved jades. Chariot burials of the Shang (with chariots complete with horses and grooms) have been found in Shandong but not yet in the Anyang area. The buildings, with their carefully prepared floors, seem to have relied greatly on *pisé* (tamped earth) construction, just as at Zhengzhou. As yet no wall has been found surrounding the Yin ruins; perhaps there wasn't one, although the discovery at Zhengzhou and the persistence of the practice of walling cities in later dynasties makes this a surprising omission.

The larger houses and palaces were built above ground with hard floors and stone pillar bases (as in later buildings right up to the Qing); smaller houses, assumed to be those of artisans rather than aristocrats, were often semi-subterranean, a form that was not uncommon in the late Neolithic. Bronze foundry sites, pottery kilns and bone workshops have also been found and under some of the larger floors are complex drainage channels. The Shang capital was burnt by the invading Zhou c 1066 BC, when the last king (whose burial has not been found) was also burnt to death.

Recent DNA analyses of Anyang burials have revealed, worryingly for Chinese archaeologists, that the DNA pattern is closest to today's Europeans.

The site of **Yin** can be visited by bus (a no. 1 passes the junction of Angang lu and Yinxu lu). Cross the railway line and follow the path which runs beside a bend in the river. Archaeological sites are not wildly exciting to non-archaeologists, as they require imagination to recreate from the patches of earth, but the walk is pleasant. The building on the site housing a study collection (the majority of the grand finds are to be seen either in the Provincial Museum in Zhengzhou or in the Historical Museum in Peking) is not open to the general public but is often opened to visiting groups.

The old city walls and surrounding moat of the small town still stand and the old town with its narrow streets and walled courtyards lies within. In the northwest of the walled town is the **Tianning si ta** (Pagoda of the Heaven's Will Temple). Originally associated with a temple founded in the Sui, its first pagoda, according to literary sources, dated from 952. Popular belief says there was a pagoda in the Sui. The current pagoda is Ming in date. Octagonal in plan, five storeys high and built of brick in imitation of wooden construction with imitation brackets under each of the eaves, the first storey is unusually tall. There are windows for light and ventilation in the upper storeys and the pagoda is decorated in the Ming style with stucco Buddhas, Bodhisattvas and scenes from the life of the Buddha. The pagoda is unusual in that it does not taper towards the top, which is adorned with a 10m Tibetan-style stupa. It is possible to climb to the top for a view over the old town.

The **Tomb of Yuan Shikai** is outside the town, only about 5km away on the north side of the Huan River.

Yuan Shikai

Yuan Shikai (1859–1916), a general of the late Qing and self-proclaimed emperor (1915), was a native of Xiangcheng in eastern Henan. He led one of the new regional armies founded towards the end of the Qing, which were to become the basis of local warlord power in the early 20C, and first sided with the Reformist Movement of 1898, only to betray the reformers (and the powerless emperor) to the Dowager Empress, probably out of pure self-interest for he could see she held ultimate power. Changing sides again, he joined the Movement for Constitutional Reform in the last years of the Qing and, when the dynasty fell, was declared Premier in 1911. He took over from Sun Yatsen as President of the Republic of China in April 1911 and was sufficiently confident of his personal power to declare himself Hongxi emperor in 1915, only to die in 1916, when China fell into division as local warlords struggled for power.

The tomb is a mixture of the traditional Chinese form and western influence, not uncharacteristic of the Republican era.

Recently the main road leading south out of Anyang has been taken over by the recreational branch of the People's Liberation Army, which established China's first sauna and massage parlour, amongst other attractions.

Datong

Datong, the largest town in northern Shanxi province, lies on the railway line from Peking to Mongolia and is today best known for its coal mine and what was China's last steam-engine factory, now given over to the production of diesel engines. Situated between two sections of the Great Wall, Datong was a frontier town for many hundreds of years and as capital of the Northern Wei (386–494) and the Liao (907–1125), two alien dynasties, preserves Buddhist cave temples and two early temple buildings.

Its closeness to Mongolia meant that Datong has long served as a centre of trade with Mongolia. On the edge of the traditional Chinese border (before the full 'incorporation' by China of Inner Mongolia in 1947), it was frequently overrun by alien groups and was twice made capital, under the Northern Wei and later under the Liao.

Practical infomation

Getting there
By train

Although there is a small airport, Datong is usually reached by rail from Peking in c seven hours; it lies on the main Trans-Siberian line to Mongolia and Russia and the northern line to Urumqi. Some visitors, arriving on the Trans-Siberian from Mongolia (24 hours from Ulan Bator), may choose Datong as their first stop in China. There is also a line to Taiyuan (seven hours).

The railway station is in the north of the town. Immediately outside the station there are usually many small stalls and street traders, including fortune tellers and performing monkeys.

Where to stay

The *Datong Binguan* is in the south of the town at 8 Yingbin xi lu, ☎ 0352 203 2476; the *Yungang Binguan* is at 20 Yingbin dong lu, ☎ 0352 502 1601.

History

The **Northern Wei**, a group of probably Turkic origin, otherwise known as the Tab gatch (sinicised to Tuoba or Toba), established themselves in Datong (then known as Pingcheng) in 368, in a period of Chinese disunion. In 494 they moved their capital south to Luoyang. Fervent Buddhists, the Wei rulers began the great task of carving out cave temples at Yungang just west of the town. They continued this devotional work after the move to Luoyang by financing the cave temples at Longmen.

Datong's second period of greatness came with the arrival of the **Khitan**, a Mongol group who had become semi-sedentary and who took advantage of a later period of Chinese disunion to establish the Liao dynasty with its capital in Datong (907–1125). The Liao made constant attempts to overthrow the Northern Song but were themselves eventually swallowed up by the Jin, ancestors of the Manchus. The major monuments remaining from the Liao are the halls, statues and Buddhist library of the Huayan Temple. During later periods, when Datong was on the frontiers of Chinese control, it was surrounded by military colonies whose inhabitants, charged not only with the defence of the frontier but also with the maintenance of agricultural supplies on the borders, enjoyed special privileges and status. The town's walls, most of which still stand, were built during the early Ming in 1372. Made of tamped yellow earth (*pisé*), they are some 7.5km in circumference.

Within the town

Huayan Temple

It is possible to walk to the temples from the Datong or Yungang hotels or else get a bus to the major intersection of the town. Take the first major turning (Nanguan nanjie) and head north. Walk up this road until you come to a major crossroads (about 1km) where you will see a busy market and the huge roofs of the Huayan Temple beyond.

During the Liao and Jin this was the most important centre of the Huayan (Kegon in Japanese) School of Buddhism, based on the *Avatamsakasutra* (or *Garland Sutra*). Huayan taught the essential sameness of things, an idea close to the Taoist notion of an underlying principle to be sought in all things.

The original temple was destroyed by fire in 1122. The layout today, of an upper and lower temple, dates from the Ming and most of the structures are Qing, although the main hall is Jin. The upper temple is unusual in that it faces east instead of south and not for reasons of topography; it is said that, as well as being Buddhists, the Khitan were also sun-worshippers and this is the reason for the orientation of the building.

The **Daxiongbao dian** (Mahavira or Powerful Treasure Hall) of the Upper Temple, said to date from 1140 (the only old building left in the ensemble where most are Qing in date), is a rare example of 12C northern building. Set on a high platform (over 4m high), it is a mighty nine-bay hall covering 1560 square metres. The scale of the whole is massive: the walls are well over 1m thick, hinting at freezing winters, and the ridge acroteria at either end are 4.5m high. The form of the acroteria, an incurved beak (its name in Chinese is 'owl's beak'), is strikingly different from the Ming and Qing acroteria seen on, for example, the roofs of the Forbidden City, where a realistically carved dragon-like head engulfs each end of the roof ridge. The owl's beak form is seen in Tang paintings (and as early as the Northern Wei in reliefs in the Yungang and Longmen caves) and persists in Shanxi (in the Guangsheng Temple at Lin fen) into the Yuan and very early Ming. The ridge decoration on the northern end of the roof is an original from the Jin dynasty.

The interior of the hall is similarly massive and constructed on the 'reduced column' principle (with 12 fewer columns than might be expected), allowing for some equally massive Buddha figures. The five Buddhas (of the five directions, including the centre) are Ming, seated on elaborate high thrones, and there are 20 attendants whose figures are elegantly inclined. The three central Buddhas are carved from wood and were made in Peking in 1427, the rest (and the attendants) are of stucco. They are in the Sino-Tibetan style popular in Buddhist images of the 14C–15C. The walls are painted with rather gaudy, very late Qing frescoes illustrating scenes from the life of the Buddha. They were painted by a local artist, Dong An, between 1875 and 1908. When I first visited Datong in

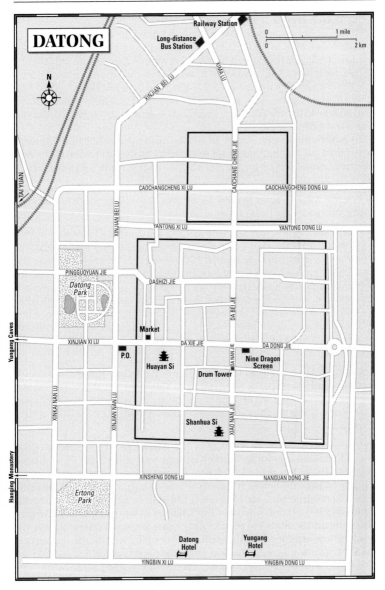

1976, the driver, who had previously taken us to the Yungang caves, which are impressively dusty yellow and monochrome, exclaimed with pleasure at the brightness of the wall paintings, which are more to the popular taste. The coffered ceiling is decorated with dragons, phoenix, flowers and Sanskrit letters. There is also a 2.5m high wooden tower in the hall, a model of one of the corner towers of the city wall, made in the Qing by Li Yangui.

The **Lower Temple** is southeast of the Upper Temple; the library (Bojiajiao cang dian or Bhagavan Hall), the second hall beyond the entrance, is a survivor from the Liao, built in 1038. It is a five-bay hall, four bays deep, with strong brackets holding up the eaves. It is a rare Liao construction and the architectural style is closer to the solid, simple Tang and Jin style than the more heavily decorated later styles. The interior ceiling is also Liao. On a platform stand 31 Liao stucco figures of great elegance. There are three central Buddhas (past, present and future) and the attendants are in different poses with flowingly modelled garments and inclined bodies.

The walls are lined with wooden bookcases, made to house Buddhist sutras and constructed like tiny buildings with a wonderful 'suspended palace' at the rear. The architectural detail is minute and accurate and the construction is unique.

Returning to the road and turning right (east), beyond the crossroads, on the right is the **Nine Dragon Screen**. If you look down to the south at the crossroads, you can see the Drum Tower.

The Nine Dragon Screen was built in 1392 and stood as a 'spirit wall' in front of the palace of the Ming founder's 13th son, who was viceroy of Shanxi. The palace was burnt down in the mid 17C, leaving only the ceramic screen. It is 45.5m long, 8m high and just over 2m thick and covered with glazed tiles in five colours. Just above the base are figures of lions, tigers, elephants, unicorns and other small animals and above these are nine dragons in high relief, rising from waves. The top is modelled on a roof, with tiles and ridge acroteria. Although it stands near its original position, the screen was in fact moved some 10m in 1954. A comparable, although later, screen can be see in the Forbidden City.

Returning to the crossroads, turn left, towards the **Drum Tower** (Gu lou) and continue until you reach the crossroads with Yingbin lu. The Drum Tower, a rare survival of those that used to stand in all city centres where the great drum beat out the time (using the Chinese traditional 'two-hour' hours), is said to be a Ming construction.

In the south suburbs of Datong is the **Shanhua si** (Temple of Good Transformations) founded during the Kaiyuan period of the Tang (713–742) but largely destroyed by fire in 1122. It is on Da nan jie just inside the old city wall, halfway between the hotels on Yingbin xi lu and Yingbin dong lu and the Drum Tower. Reconstruction took 15 years (1128–43). It was improved during the Ming and given its present name in 1445. Besides its function as a Buddhist temple, it was used by officials to practise and prepare for important ceremonies. The buildings are on the main north–south axis, beginning with the gate, which contains the guardian figures. This was originally constructed in 1123–48, in the 'Song style' with moon-shaped (lightly curved) beams. The guardians are Ming stucco figures. Behind is a Hall of the Three Sages (San sheng dian) built at the same time as the gateway but in the Liao-Jin style.

The interior makes use of the 'reduced column' method. The figures, of the Buddha and the Bodhisattvas Manjusri and Samantabhadra are Jin in origin but were repainted and restored in the Qing. A stele records the restoration of the temple in 1176. The main hall, seven bays wide and five bays deep, which contains Liao sculpture (a central Buddha and 29 other figures, including a six-armed Guanyin), is said to have been restored in 1123–48. The wall paintings are Qing but in the 'Yuan style'. One of the side buildings, to the west, a double-roofed pavilion of apparently two but actually three storeys, said to be Tang style, contains an inscription recording its construction in 1154. It is noted that this is only 100 years later than the Yingxian Pagoda, which also has concealed interior storeys (see below).

The Yungang Caves

The Yungang Caves, 16km west of Datong, can be reached by taxi or by tour bus. Tickets can be bought from the *CITS* offices: there is one in the railway station and one in the Yungang Hotel.

The caves were hollowed out in a south-facing sandstone cliff formed by the Wuzhou River beginning in 453 and probably ending around 525, after the move to Luoyang, although one cave in particular (No. 3) is thought perhaps to be Sui in date. Although some of the caves at Dunhuang are slightly earlier, the Yungang caves are the earliest stone-carved caves in China (those in Dunhuang were decorated with stucco figures and wall paintings). The format came from Indian Buddhism. According to the *Wei Shu* (*History of the Wei*), five Indian monks, who were also accomplished sculptors, arrived in Datong in 455, although the part they played in the carving is not known. There is much Indian influence in the carving and that itself is heavily influenced by the Graeco-Buddhist style, evidenced in the tridents and acanthus leaves. Other influences came from Iranian and Byzantine sources—lions, weapons, bearded figures—but there is also much that is Chinese in the buildings depicted, the heavily decorated aureoles and the use of Chinese images, such as dragons, tigers and phoenix.

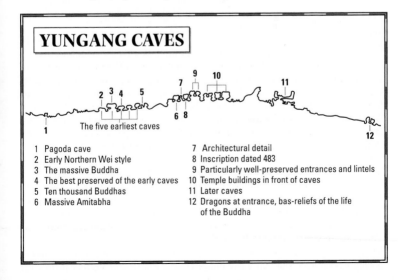

YUNGANG CAVES

The five earliest caves

1 Pagoda cave
2 Early Northern Wei style
3 The massive Buddha
4 The best preserved of the early caves
5 Ten thousand Buddhas
6 Massive Amitabha

7 Architectural detail
8 Inscription dated 483
9 Particularly well-preserved entrances and lintels
10 Temple buildings in front of caves
11 Later caves
12 Dragons at entrance, bas-reliefs of the life of the Buddha

The caves stretch for about a kilometre and are grouped into three main sections: east, central and west. There are four caves in the east section (Nos 1–4), nine in the central section (5–13) and 40 in the west (14–53). Nos 16–20, the 'Five Tan Caves' are the earliest (453–462) and most impressive and were carved under the supervision of a monk called Tan Hao. Most of those in the central section were carved between 462 and 495. The majority of the eastern and western caves date from c 495–524; quite a number in the western section were completed after the removal of the Wei capital to Luoyang.

Beginning with the earliest group, **Cave 20** has the largest figure, a seated Buddha with one surviving standing disciple on the right. The front of the cave has collapsed (there are square holes in the back wall indicating that the cave may have had a wooden facade), leaving the huge figure, nearly 14m high, exposed. The mandorla on the wall behind is composed of alternate rows of flames and small figures in low relief, Buddhas and musicians and attendants. The immobility of the figure is characteristic of the early Northern Wei style and the pattern-like effect of the folds, rendered almost like flames across the upper arm, is also characteristic of the early Wei.

The other early caves are all on the same pattern of an enlarged oval niche with a major, central Buddha figure. **Cave 19** is in three parts with a central Buddha over 16m high and two attendant Bodhisattvas with rather Grecian pleats to their robes, particularly that on the left. **Cave 18** is considered to be one of the finest at Yungang; the central Buddha, in the same rigid style, has rows of tiny Bodhisattvas on the folds of his robe and the crowned Bodhisattvas and almost caricatured disciples are extremely lively despite the rigidity of the style. An inscription outside **Cave 17** dates its carving to 480. Apart from the central figure with its standing and sitting attendants, there are bas-relief carvings all over the walls, including Indian *apsareses* (Buddhist angels) in transparent robes with silken scarves swirling around them. The standing Buddha in **Cave 16** has thick, almost chunkily folded robes and a face which is strongly reminiscent of Northern Wei sculpture at Luoyang, long and block-like, yet the hands are delicately moulded with distinct fingernails.

To take the rest of the caves in numerical order: **Cave 1** is most noted for its bas-reliefs of the life of the Buddha, with funny little Chinese buildings (whose roof acroteria resemble those of the Huayan temples in Datong) and scenes of hunting and horsemanship. In the centre of Cave 2 is a pagoda-like pillar with interesting architectural detail: the brackets (like Ws) are interspersed with inverted V-shaped props, a form found in buildings from the Tang to the Yuan but which then disappeared. **Cave 3** is the largest of all and was probably once covered with a wooden temple. The figures are fleshier and more plastic than many others and it is thought that they may be as late as the Sui, for in their sensuous fleshiness they approach the Tang style.

Caves 5, 6 and 7 lie behind the wooden temple and complex of galleries built against the cliff in 1652 and visited by the Kangxi emperor in 1697. He wrote the characters 'the unity of all doctrines' which can be seen at the entrance to Cave 6. The caves behind the wooden temple, protected from the elements, are in very good condition. Inside **Cave 5** is the largest **Buddha figure** at Yungang, nearly 17m high. It is said to have been carved at the order of the Xiaowen emperor of the Wei (471–500) in honour of his father and it marks a progression from the stiff early images towards a serene, fleshier form with

Yungang Caves near Datong

more naturalistically modelled garments. The walls are covered with tiny Buddhas in niches and the lively flames of the aureole dart upwards to the ceiling. Serene Boddhisattvas with gently inclined heads stand in attendance.

Cave 6 is equally well-preserved but very different in appearance, with its **highly carved central tower** (a form inherited from Indian cave carvings and ideal for the clockwise perambulating meditation that Buddhists perform), medium-sized Buddha figures in niches and outstanding low relief depictions of scenes from the life of the Buddha, which include Chinese figures in Chinese dress riding on Indian elephants. Scenes quite easy to identify are those of the historic Buddha going out on horseback, leaving a minute Chinese building, the hooves of the horse supported by kneeling figures while an *apsaras* holds an Indian style canopy over his head. In a similar scene on the eastern wall, the Buddha, again on horseback, meets a crippled old man with two sticks; this is one of the revelations of the existence of human suffering to the previously innocent and over-protected prince. The Buddha's entry into the state of Nirvana is also depicted: he lies with his head propped on one arm while a female orchestra plays below. In the central column, Buddhas and Bodhisattvas sit in deep niches with architectural roofs, surrounded by flying *apsareses* with floral garlands and orchestras. This cave, with its incredible variety of lively scenes, is said to have been commissioned by the Xiaowen emperor in honour of his mother, while Cave 5 was for his father.

In **Cave 7** the **ceiling** is particularly fine: a tangle of *apsareses* surround daisy-like lotus plaques and the female attendants depicted on the rear wall have charming, self-satisfied smiles. The whole reveals a mastery of forms and icons, in marked contrast with the solid rigidity of the early caves.

The entrance to **Cave 8** has extraordinary **multi-headed figures**, some derived from Hindu mythology: on the left, a five-headed Shiva with six arms clutching a bow and a bird, amongst other things, sitting on a huge bird; on the right a three-headed Vishnu holding a bunch of grapes (an Iranian motif) sits on a bull. These figures are regarded as successful fusions of Indian icons with Chinese art forms (the bird, in particular) and the confident carving of these and other figures suggests that sculptors were no longer wrestling with unfamiliar iconography but were enjoying the mastery of their craft.

Caves 9 and 10 are entered through columns and lintels in the style of the Indian caves and are noted for the charming orchestra in niches with Chinese style wooden balustrades in front. In Cave 10 a particularly fine and elaborate entrance leads to an inner niche; the flat floral scrolls recall near eastern metalwork and anticipate Chinese porcelain decoration of later periods.

Cave 11 has an inscription dating its carving to 483 and recording the participation of over 50 donors, who dedicated the cave to the emperor and his family. According to the inscription, they paid for 95 major figures.

The tapering columns at the entrance to **Cave 12** have lush acanthus leaf bases and multiple Buddha figures in tiny niches all over them. The interior of the cave is architecturally divided, providing information on the construction and bracketing of contemporary timber building (none of which survives). Under the beams, above the Buddhas, are complex nets of pearl ropes.

Inside the entrance to **Cave 13** are two wonderful Bodhisattvas, rather flatly carved, the folds of their light silk robes indicated with simple lines.

There is evidence of landscape depiction in the wavelike peaks beside them, which recalls the Tang landscape painting at Dunhuang. A huge figure of Amitabha Buddha has its raised arm supported by a small, four-armed figure standing on the knee of the Buddha. Traces of paint on the walls in this and Caves 9–12 are the remains of paintings paid for by a local landowner during the Qing, as described in a stele erected by his son. Caves 14 and 15 have been rather badly eroded by the wind owing to the collapse of the fronts.

Cave 21 is considered to be later than many others and may date from the late Northern Wei. It has a central pagoda.

Less attention is generally paid to the remaining caves, many of which are small. **Cave 50**, however, has the most extraordinary ceiling with casually arranged *apsareses* superimposed on a sketchily coffered ceiling, their trailing silk scarves curling amongst flying elephants and birds. There is another flying elephant on the east wall of **Cave 48**, approaching a reclining figure. This is Maya, mother of Sakyamuni, who dreamt that a white elephant entered her right side and subsequently the Buddha was born painlessly from the same spot.

On the road to the Yungang caves is the **Buddhist Guanyin tang** (Guanyin Hall), c 8km outside Datong, near Fozi wan. It was founded in 1038, under the Liao, when devout local people paid for a golden Guanyin figure and four attendant Bodhisattvas with ten guardian figures, apparently after the Bodhisattva Guanyin had appeared in the neighbourhood. It was rebuilt after a fire in 1651. A three-dragon screen of glazed tiles dating from the Ming (and similar to the nine-dragon screen in Datong) stands in front of the temple. The stone figures in the main hall are thought to be the Liao originals; they include Bodhisattvas, celestial guardians and Guanyin figure over 5m high.

Around Datong

More than 60km south of Datong is the **Yingxian Pagoda**, the earliest wooden pagoda still standing in China. The trip can be made by tourist bus or taxi. Built in 1056, on the main axis of the Fogong si (Temple of the Buddha's Palace), the pagoda is octagonal in plan and is just over 67m high. Its position on the main axis of the temple is reminiscent of the layout of the Great Goose Pagoda Temple in Xi'an. The first storey of the pagoda is more substantial than the rest: a mud and earth wall stand back from a columned gallery surmounted by a double eaved roof. The upper part of the pagoda is constructed entirely of timber and consists of four galleries with roofs in between.

The actual structure is more complex than it appears as there are four invisible (from the exterior) storeys, making an actual total of nine storeys. The pagoda is topped by an iron spire. 60 different types of bracket have been used in the construction, which has been intently studied by the doyen of Chinese architectural historians, Chen Mingda, who has linked the construction method to the description of pagoda construction in the 12C architectural manual *Ying zao fa shi.*

Although there were originally more figures, there remains an 11m high **Liao Buddha** inside the pagoda and, in recent repairs, a cache of holy relics was found, including manuscript and woodblock printed Buddhist sutras and coloured Buddhist images printed on silk. Such finds are of particular interest as they are presumably contemporary with the construction (this is reinforced by internal dates), which is early for colour printing.

A spectacular monastery, c 75km southeast of Datong (reached in c two hours by either taxi or a *CITS* tourist bus) is the **Xuankong si** (Temple Suspended in the Void) perched on a cliff in the Heng Mountains. The temple complex was founded in the 6C during the late Northern Wei and consists of 40 'rooms', caves in the cliff fronted with timber facades perched perilously on timbers jutting out from the cliff. Over 80 Buddhist figures—in iron, bronze, stucco and stone—are contained in the chambers.

The temple can be visited by *CITS* tourist excursion most days and the **Railway Engine Factory**, c 2.5km southwest of Datong, can also be visited but only by appointment through *CITS* (cost c 150 yuan per person), which has an office in the railway station, or through the hotels. The last steam engine was made in 1985 and the factory has made diesel engines since 1989 but there are some old steam engines on display and the factory operates short steam engine journeys for railway enthusiasts.

Taiyuan

Taiyuan is the capital of Shanxi province and lies in the Taiyuan basin where some of the world's richest deposits of coal and iron are to be found. It is today a major steel centre, twinned with Newcastle-upon-Tyne, but near the city are some important temples and it is the best starting point for the northern Buddhist mountain, Wutai shan.

Shanxi ('West of the Mountains') province, like Shaanxi (capital Xi'an) and Gansu (capital Lanzhou) provinces, is largely covered by a thick deposit of fine wind-laid yellow earth, known as loess. The loess deposit, up to 100m thick, creates the characteristic landscape of the area, with rolling yellow hills traversed by deep gullies in which rivers and streams run. These are the characteristic 'vertical' cleavages created by the surface 'cement' which binds the loose grains. In the loess highlands, whole villages are created by tunnelling into the perpendicular loess cliffs, each house tunnel is faced with an arched entrance of timber lattice stuck with window paper. Above, on the hillside, are the village fields, sometimes dotted with chimneys 'so that one sees the curious phenomenon of smoke issuing at numerous points in the midst of a field of grain' (George Babcock Cressey, *China's Geographic Foundations*, New York, McGraw Hill, 1934). Loess is very fertile soil but the vertical cleavages make agriculture difficult, except on the highlands which are often difficult of access.

Practical information

Getting there
By air

14km south of the town centre, there are daily flights to and from Peking and Xi'an, Guangzhou and Shanghai, with less frequent flights to most major destinations.

By train

Taiyuan lies on a main line from Peking to Xi'an and is also linked by rail to Datong in the north of the province. The station is on Jianshe bei lu in the east of the town centre.

Where to stay

The *Yingze Binguan*, ☎ 404 3211, fax 404 3784, (perhaps one of the 'two semi-foreign hotels' referred to in the 1924 *Japanese Railway Guide*) is on Yingze lu, a ten minute walk due west from the railway station. The joint-venture *Shanxi da jiudian/Shanxi Grand Hotel*, ☎ 404 3901, fax 404 3252, is on Xinjian lu, further out to the west.

History

Neolithic remains in the Taiyuan area are mainly of the Yangshao or 'painted pottery' culture, including the late settlement at Dongtaibao zhuang where horse and pig skeletons as well as bone artefacts have been found. When the Zhou dynasty was founded (c 1066 BC) the Fen River valley surrounding today's Taiyuan was made a fiefdom, eventually called Jin, a name that is commemorated in the Jin ci (Jin Temple) outside the city founded in honour of the first Jin ruler. Remains of the city wall of the Jin city built in 497 BC can be seen from the road to the Jin ci.

Situated in the far north, the Taiyuan area was vulnerable to attack from outsiders: the Huns attacked in 200 BC and the Tobas (who founded the Wei dynasty with their first capital in Datong just to the north of Taiyuan) in AD 396. During the Tang dynasty the Taiyuan area was an important part of the frontier defences. In the Five Dynasties period, after the fall of the Tang, the area was repeatedly invaded and the then major city of Jinyang was completely destroyed in 979 after several attempts to retake it by the founder of the **Song dynasty**. Not only was the town razed to the ground but the waters of the Fen River and its tributaries were diverted to sweep away the remains. The surviving inhabitants settled in what was to become Taiyuan, where the emperor apparently ordered that instead of the usual regular grid of streets there should be numerous T-junctions, which look like the character for 'nail' in Chinese, symbolising the 'nailing down' of Jinyang. Several of these junctions can still be seen.

In the **early Ming** the founding emperor appointed one of his sons as viceroy to the province with his headquarters in Taiyuan. This did not prevent the local people (who had suffered under subsequent viceroys) from welcoming the local peasant leader **Li Zicheng** when he tried to overthrow the Ming in 1644. Members of the Ming royal family were killed, although one escaped and his descendants still live nearby, but when Li Zicheng was defeated, the Manchu Qing dynasty captured the city after two assaults. It is said that a local feast day continued to commemorate Li Zicheng until the 20C. Confusingly, the day (18th of the sixth month in the lunar calendar) was called 'Resist Li Zicheng', apparently to mislead the Qing authorities, but it had become a token of anti-Manchu feeling, for all hairdressers, compelled by the Manchus to dress all Chinese men's hair in the pigtail or queue as a sign of submission, took the day off.

In 1900 Shanxi province, and Taiyuan in particular, became a major centre for anti-missionary activity. The **Boxer Movement** had started in Shandong province and, although originally anti-Manchu, it also focussed its attention on foreigners with isolated missionaries as vulnerable victims. In Taiyuan a mob set fire to the British mission, killing one woman. The killing led to a massacre when the provincial governor (a Boxer supporter who had been moved to Taiyuan from the Boxer birthplace in Shandong) assembled all the missionaries on the pretext of protecting them and had them publicly killed on 30 June. 44 foreigners, including women and children, were killed together with 17 Chinese converts. This represented the majority of the provincial total of missionary deaths (47 in all in 1901 with another 142 killed elsewhere in China in that year). In a book written by a survivor, Archibald Glover of the China Inland Mission, *A Thousand Miles of Miracle in China* (London, 1904), the foreigners' import of opium is held almost equally to blame along with the anti-foreign Boxer movement, although he also takes an almighty and most unecumenical swipe at the Roman Catholic missionaries in Shanxi province.

Anti-missionary campaigns did not rid the province of foreigners. The railway was half-financed by Russian money and built by French engineers, mines were owned by the British and the post office was partly French run. The university was largely directed by Timothy Richard, an English Baptist missionary who managed to get some of the Chinese government's reparation for the Boxer damage (the portion of the 'Boxer Indemnity' paid by Shanxi province) to found the Shanxi University 'on western lines' in Taiyuan in 1902.

From 1912 to just before 1949 Taiyuan was the headquarters of one of the most famous of China's 'warlords', **Yan Xishan** (1883–1960). A loyal supporter of Chiang Kai-shek, when not pursuing military campaigns under the direction of the Generalissimo, he promoted 'the moral and social welfare of his people' and was known by supporters as 'the Model Governor' (for he was Governor of Shanxi province).

Mining, metal-working and coal-mining have a long history in the area, with bronze working dating from the Warring States and the coal mines mentioned in Tang and Song literary accounts. Iron figures have been cast in the area since the Tang and glazed tile works seem to have operated since then if not before, the last two techniques being evident in many temple furnishings and roofing.

Provincial Museum

The holdings of the Provincial Museum are distributed amongst two temples in the city centre, thereby combining architecture and temple visiting with viewing the museum collections.

The nearest part to the Yingze Binguan is the **Chunyang gong Temple**: turn left out of the hotel along Yingze lu. At Wuyi Square (left) turn left along the side of the square. The Chunyang gong is on the right-hand side of the major turning to the left. Founded during the Ming (in the Wanli reign, 1573–1619), with the three-storey hall added during the Qianlong reign (1736–96), the temple, whose name means Purity of Yang (with *yang* meaning the masculine, light, positive principle) was a Taoist foundation, as its name of *gong* or 'hall' rather than the normal Buddhist *si* or 'temple' suggests.

A member of the Ming ruling family, Zhu Qiugui, wrote a poem, said to be in praise of the beauty of the temple (although the reference to monkeys is obscure):

> The clamour of the world does not reach here
> Clouds gather within the blue arch,
> White geese gather by the water and green monkeys sleep
>   alone on the sand
> Old pines block the moonlight,
> Bamboos are blown by the wind and it is said that nothing is
>   worth more than purity and tranquillity.

Within the temple are four courtyards. The major, three-bay hall is the Lu Hall, dedicated to Lu Dongbin, an historical figure who has been immortalised (in more ways than one) as one of the eight Taoist immortals.

Lu Dongbin

Lu Dongbin is thought to have been born in Yongle county in Shanxi province (not far from Taiyuan) into an official family and was presented with a magic sword by a fire dragon when he was 20 years old (still unmarried and on a trip to Lu Shan in Jiangxi province). He spent the rest of his life slaying demons with his magic sword, is worshipped as the God of Inkmakers and usually represented with his sword and a horsetail fly-whisk, also known as a 'cloud-sweeper' and a symbol of his ability to fly through the air and walk on clouds.

Behind the hall are multi-storeyed buildings 'strewn at random, winding and circling in most unusual forms' as the *Dictionary of Famous Sites* has it; ramshackle and charming country style temple architecture. The Towering Tower (Weige) of

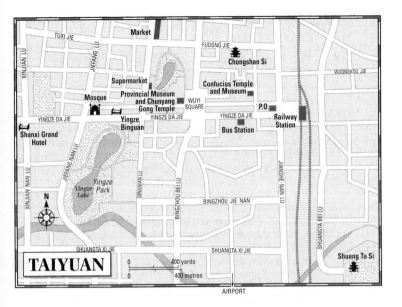

the back courtyard is the tallest building and affords a view of the city. Another building of note in the first courtyard is the octagonal pavilion on a square base. Exhibits scattered in the 'random' buildings include ceramics, bronzes, ivory, bamboo and wood carving, lacquer, paintings, stone-rubbings, embroidery and enamels, with some marvellous sculpture: stone figures from the Sui and later, bronzes and iron figures mainly from the Ming.

The other part of the museum is to be found just beyond the far (eastern) side of Wuyi Square. Cross the square to the far side and take the main road leading east. Just before reaching Jianshe lu (on which the station lies) turn left. The **Confucian Temple** (Wen miao), containing the main part of the Provincial Museum, is on your left. The temple, originally built during the Jin (1115–1234), was expanded in the Ming when it was situated in the west of the town. It was moved to this site in 1881 as the previous location was low-lying and damp.

The main structures from the spirit wall at the southern extremity of the considerable enclosure are: Six-sided Well Pavilion, Lattice Star Gate, Gate of Completeness, Hall of Completeness and the Hall of the Worship of the Sage. The courtyards are broad and filled with trees and the building style is lively. Exhibits include Shanxi's revolutionary history, Shang bronzes, weaponry, calligraphy attributed to Gu Kaizhi of the Eastern Jin, 317–420.

Just north of the museum is the **Chongshan si** (Temple of the Veneration of Goodness), founded under the Tang and previously known as the White Horse Temple; the temple gained its current name in the Ming.

Like the Confucian Temple, this was originally situated outside the old town but when the city moat was enlarged in the mid 14C the temple had to be moved. In 1381 Zhu Gang (third son of the founder of the Ming, Zhu

Yuanzhang) enlarged the temple and dedicated it to the memory of his mother. The main hall was nine bays wide and over 30m high. Much of the temple was destroyed by fire in 1864, leaving only the gate, bell tower, side wings and the seven-bay Dabei dian (Hall of Great Compassion) with its double-eaved, green and yellow tiled roof supported by brackets and its decorated ceiling inside. Within the hall is a thousand-eyed, thousand-armed Guanyin some 8.5m high, flanked by the other Bodhisattvas, Samantabhadra and Manjusri. The figures and the hall itself are all early Ming.

The temple contains an exhibition of Buddhist sutras printed in the Song, Yuan and Ming dynasties; most are dated. They include some leaves of a later printing (1108) from the blocks cut in Chengdu for the first printing of the Buddhist canon. Returning to the square, the hotel is easily regained.

Other sites in the city that can be visited by taxi include the mosque and the Twin Pagoda Temple.

The **mosque** is on the east side of Jiefang lu, northwest of the Yingze Binguan. A stele preserved in the mosque states that it was founded in the Zhenyuan reign period of the Tang (785–805) and rebuilt in the Song during the years 1034–38. The surviving buildings include a Ming great hall of timber and brick construction with timber columns sunk in the wall, interior columns decorated with gold and Arab style decoration. Arabic inscriptions from the Koran are found on the walls. The minaret in the courtyard is Ming with 'flying eaves' and there is a pair of stele pavilions with a 'grass style' inscription by Huang Tingjian and colophons by Zhao Ziang of the Yuan and Fu Qing of the early Qing.

The **Shuang ta** (Twin Pagoda) Temple is in the southeast suburbs in **Haozhuang** (Hao Village). The pair of pagodas which give the temple its popular name (it is actually called the Yongzuo or Eternal Good Fortune Temple) were built in the Wanli period of the Ming (1573–1619) by a monk called Fodeng, who later left for Wutai shan. They are of brick construction, nearly 55m high, with multiple brick eaves with brick brackets underneath and glazed tiles on top. They can be climbed as both have steps inside. The rebel leader Li Zicheng (who succeeded in overthrowing the Ming, only to be overthrown himself by the Qing) wrote a poem in praise of the twin pagodas which includes the line: 'The two pagodas of Haozhuang pierce the sky'.

Beneath the pagodas is the temple, with a main hall and two side wings, all made entirely of brick with brick-vaulted ceilings, the bricks used to imitate wooden construction with columns and brackets. The 'beamless brick hall' of Nanjing is the most famous (and southernmost) example of the type; examples such as this and that on Wutai shan are less well known. These brick-vaulted constructions mostly date from the Ming by which time much of China's forest cover had been destroyed by the expansion of agriculture. The use of brick was a response to the scarcity of timber for building. Peonies planted in the temple are said to date back to the Ming.

Temples in the vicinity of Taiyuan

Getting there

All of the sites mentioned in this section are best reached by taxi or tourist bus from outside the railway station in Taiyuan. You can book through *CITS* at 8 Xingjian nan lu, one block south of the Shanxi Grand Hotel or enquire at your hotel.

Tianlong shan

Outside Taiyuan, the major site is that of the Jin ci (Jin Temple), 25km southwest of the town (see below), but other sites, including the Buddhist cave carvings of Tianlong shan (Heavenly Dragon Mountain), 40km southeast of the town, are also worth visiting (and are rarely seen). Where the mountains rise from the flat plain, pines and other conifers are thick on the slopes and a number of springs rise in the area. There are eight caves on the eastern peak, 13 on the west, carved at different periods from the Eastern Wei (534–550) to the Tang, with the majority (15) dating from the Tang. The great Buddha of Cave 9 (Tang in date) is now exposed and many of the caves are in rather poor condition, although the traces reveal a high standard of carving. A temple originally stood in front of the caves and the ancient pines were remarked on by a Ming writer.

Dafo si

The Dafo si (Great Buddha Temple) is 20km northwest of Taiyuan in **Tutang cun** (Earth Hall Village), surrounded by a thicket of fine old pines which provide a major reason for the inhabitants of Taiyuan to visit it. A stele records a local legend that the ground here split during the Han dynasty, revealing a great Buddha figure; a temple was consequently built on the spot. The temple was first constructed in the 6C but the surviving buildings are Ming and Qing, with two stone lions (late 12C or early 13C) as the only survivors of earlier works. The storeyed buildings on the east and west sides of the temple are dated to 1541 and they contains groups of clay figures of the Buddha with disciples (the Buddha some 9m high) which also date from the Ming.

Jin ci

The Jin ci (Jin Temple) is today a considerable ensemble of buildings from very different dates in a large enclosure crossed by a stream and set against a hill.

> The founding date of the temple is uncertain but it is mentioned in a literary account of the Northern Wei (386–534): 'The ... temple is surrounded by mountains and rivers. An outdoor pavilion stands by the spring, with its beams reaching out over the water.' The temple, which must therefore have been founded some 1500 years ago, was built to commemorate the founder of the state of Jin, who lived c 1000 BC.

The earliest parts of the temple still standing are found at the back of the enclosure, farthest from the entrance. Because of the local topography, the halls, set against the hill, are east-facing rather than south-facing and the stream, led through the enclosure, flows in front of them. Inside the gate (the original entrance, the Jingqing men or Gate of Pure Landscape, is further to your left), there is a wide open space with an old stage, the Shuijing tai (Water Mirror Platform), in the centre, probably dating from the Ming. A stage for the performance of

Guardian figure at the Jin ci, outside Taiyuan

dramas, often financed by trade guilds, was commonly found in village squares or temples, and was used particularly by guilds (of carpenters, metal workers, etc) for performances to celebrate their annual festivals. Stages in village squares were also used by itinerant opera troupes.

Behind the stage is a bridge over the stream, the Huixian qiao (Bridge of the Gathered Immortals), and behind that is the **Metal Men Platform** (Jinren tai). The iron figures of warriors in armour, slightly larger than life-size, were first cast in the Song but, owing to wear and tear, are somewhat composite by now. That in the southwest has an inscription on its chest which dates its casting to 1097, that in the northwest was cast in the following year, although its head was apparently recast in the Ming in 1423. The figure in the southeast has an inscription dating its casting to 1089, although its head was remade in 1926, and that in the northeast was entirely recast in 1913. According to the the *Taiyuan Gazetteer* (*Tai yuan xian zhi*), the figures were placed here to guard the source of the Jin River.

Behind is the **Xian dian** (Hall of Offerings) where offerings to the Holy Mother were laid out.

The Holy Mother was the mother of Prince Shuyu, the founder of Jin, and her cult gradually eclipsed that of her son. She was believed to be possessed of magic powers able to bring rain and good fortune and is a good example of the mythicisation of history, not an uncommon feature of Chinese popular religion where historical figures gradually accrued magic powers. The Hall of Offerings was built in 1168, when the cult of the Holy Mother, 'illuminating and helpful', was beginning to overtake that of her son. It was restored in 1594 and 'rebuilt in the original style' in 1955, although it is not stated which of the two original styles was chosen.

The three-bay hall is two bays deep, its roof ridge decorated with glazed tiles (Shanxi province specialised in fine glazed tiles). The strong, simple brackets supporting the deeply projecting eaves are characteristic of pre-Qing architecture.

Beyond the Hall, in front of the Hall of the Holy Mother (Shengmu dian) is the **'Flying Bridge'** (Fei liang) over one of the three springs in the temple.

Although a bridge over the spring was mentioned in Li Daoyuan's *Shui jing zhu* (*Annotations to the Water Classic*) of the Northern Wei, the bridge was first built in its cross-shaped form in the Northern Song, when the Hall of the Holy Mother was constructed, and it was restored in 1955. Thirty-four small octagonal pillars with lotus bases stand in the pool as supports for the timber construction of brackets and beams. The crossbeams, known in Chinese as *fei liang* or 'flying beams' give the bridge its name. Although such cross-shaped 'architectural' bridges were known from literature, this is a rare surviving example.

On the far side of the bridge is the **Hall of the Holy Mother**, one of the earliest timber halls in China. First built in 1023–32 during the Northern Song, it was restored in 1102 and in the Yuan and Ming but restoration in each case did not affect the style or construction of the original. The east facing hall is seven bays wide, six bays deep with a double-eaved roof with decorative glazed tiles especially on the ridge.

The eight wooden columns at the front of the hall with writhing dragons twisted around them are the earliest surviving examples of a highly decorative form illustrated in the early 12C architectural manual *Ying zao fa shi* (*Building Methods and Styles*). In order to increase the internal space, fewer columns are used in the interior of the hall where the roof structure is clearly visible. There are 16 fewer columns than you would expect and the method is called (with little imagination), the 'reduced column style'. Outside, the brackets supporting the eaves (whose projection beyond the columns is considerable) are large and simple, characteristic of earlier timber construction. The eaves are lifted at the extremities, lightening the heavy roof of a most impressive building.

The contents of the building are also extremely important. There is a central image of the Holy Mother surrounded by 42 smaller female figures, most of which are Song in date. The life-size figures are of a clay and straw mixture built up on a wooden frame, with a top layer of finer clay which is brightly painted. Four of the women wear officials' headdresses and costumes, the others, more naturalistically depicted, appear to be attendants. The large pair of temple guardians outside the hall were originally Song in date, although that on the right-hand side is a 1950s' replacement.

Other buildings within the enclosure include a **Temple to Taitai**, legendary controller of the Fen River and patron of local agriculture, (immediately left of the Hall of the Holy Mother) and the **Mother of Water Tower** (Shuimu lou), a tall structure (a Ming construction of 1545 rebuilt in 1844).

The 'mother of water' legend concerns a young peasant girl whose tyrannical mother-in-law made her spend her whole time fetching water from a distant well. The generous girl nevertheless gave water to an old man who then presented her with a magic horsewhip which she could wave over the water pots and they were magically filled. One day the wicked mother-in-law found the whip and waved it in the house, whereupon water gushed from a pot, threatening a flood. The girl averted disaster by sitting on the water pot. A local saying commemorates the deed: 'The girl of the Liu family sits on the water pot, flourishing a whip she waters the horses.'

In front of the temple is an octagonal pavilion built over the Ever Young (Nanlao) Spring which bubbles with water at 17° Celsius throughout the year. Water from this and the other springs in the Jin ci irrigates the surrounding countryside and helps provide electricity for Taiyuan. In a poem in praise of the Jin Temple, the Tang poet Li Bai wrote the lines: 'Water like green jade flows in the Jin Temple, the waves are like dragons' scales and the banks are green.'

Below the octagonal pavilion, beside the spring, is a small stone boat-shaped pavilion, the **Unmoored Boat** (Buji zhou), near a small stupa-shaped pillar in the water. This is said to mark the grave of Zhang Lang who, according to legend, divided the Jin River.

The river splits near its source and local peasants used to quarrel about shar-ing the water. In order to solve local disputes, officials put a vat of boiling oil containing ten strings of copper money near the source of the river and chal-lenged people to remove the money: according to the amount removed, the water would be diverted. Zhang Lang managed to remove seven strings of money before succumbing to his burns; thereafter seven-tenths of the water has flowed north.

On the north side of the temple complex, just north of the Hall of Offerings, is a **Tang Stele Pavilion** (Tangbei ting), containing a stele dated to 647 and inscribed with a text by the second emperor of the Tang dynasty, who visited the temple in that year, praising the virtues of the founder of the Jin and asking his protection. The second stele is a copy of the first made in 1773. Further north is a late building (1771), the **Tang Shuyu ci** (Temple to Prince Shuyu), which includes stone-carved inscriptions of poems by Mao Zedong and Zhu De (Commander of the Red Army).

At the back of the enclosure, north of the Hall of the Holy Mother, are several natural caves in the hillside, some decorated with figures of local deities, in one of which lived Fu Shan (1608–84), a calligrapher, painter, poet, philosopher and Ming loyalist, who also wrote a treatise on gynaecology. He became a Taoist when the Ming fell and, despite personal entreaties from the Kangxi emperor, refused to accept official posts and imperial audiences. The cave in which he lived is called **Yun tao** (Staying in the Clouds). There is a small exhibition on the life and work of Fu Shan in a building on the right just inside the entrance (across the stream), in the northeast corner of the enclosure.

Pingyao

An exceptionally well-preserved town with Ming dynasty walls enclosing timber-frame houses, built by rich bankers in the 17C, Pingyao lies about 100km south of Taiyuan and is on the railway line between Taiyuan and Xi'an.

Getting there

Pingyao can be seen on a day trip from Taiyuan by taxi or minibus (1½ hours) or by train which is slightly quicker. Public minibuses depart from Taiyuan long-distance bus station about every half hour (on Yingze da lu, not far from the railway station).

Where to stay

Zhongdu Binguan, opposite the railways station in Pingyao, ☎ 05265318, or in

a restored bankers' house the
Yunjincheng Binguan, 62 Nan da jie,
☎ 0354 562 1830.

The town, which is easy to explore on foot, was featured in Zhang Yimou's film
Raise the Red Lantern. The narrow, car-free streets are lined with shops with
ornately carved wooden facades and complex lattice windows. The **walls** of the
city, some 6.4km in circumference and built in 1370, and are said to be the only
intact example left in China: Xi'an's walls, for which the same claim was made,
were seriously damaged a decade ago and restored. You can walk round the walls.

Inside the walls, at the centre of the town is a **Bell Tower** (Zhong lou) with
fine eaves decorations and a good view over the grey tiled roofs of the town. Just
south of the Bell Tower on Nan da jie is the *Yunjincheng Binguan*, a fine merchant or banker's house which also has a restaurant as well as accommodation.
Almost opposite is the **Tianjixuang Museum** (open daily 09.00–17.00), with a
small collection of artefacts relating to local history but worth visiting for more
exposure to fine Ming/Qing northern style domestic architecture.

On Dong da jie (northeast of the Bell Tower) is the **Rishengchang Museum**
(open daily 09.00–17.00). Once the home of Li Daquan, a successful late 18C
dye merchant whose outlets were eventually so flar-flung that, rather than collect cash (heavy and vulnerable to theft) he used a system of paper chitties and
established a bank in 1824. The bank itself prospered, with branches all over
China, until the Japanese invasion. The house/bank has over 100 rooms.

Around Pingyao

Around Pingyao (which is where a hired taxi might be ideal) are the Qiao family
mansion (Qiao jia dayuan), 40km from Taiyuan on the Pingyao road, and the
Shuanglin si, which is 7km southwest of Pingyao.

The **Qiao family mansion** was where all the concubines in Zhang Yimou's
film had their apartments in the courtyard complex. A Qing complex, originally
built by a local tea and bean-curd seller of the Qiao family, it is a stunning example of local domestic architecture with its courtyards divided by narrow alleys
and the fine brickwork and carved wood of the facades. The 300 or more rooms
of the complex now house Qing furniture and furnishings.

The **Shuanglin si** is surrounded by high walls of tamped earth. Founded in
571, it was extensively restored in the Ming. The main axis of the temple has
Buddhist halls: after the gatehouse of the Heavenly Kings or guardians comes the
Amitabha Hall, with the bell and drum towers on either side, then the Mahavira
Hall and, finally, the Hall of Buddha's Mother. In the first courtyard are side halls,
one with lohans, the other dedicated to Ksitigarbha, who presides over the underworld; but just before them are shrines to Guanyu, the God of War (hardly an
orthodox Buddhist theme), and the 'Earth God' or deity of locality. The convenient
mixing of local and popular beliefs in a predominantly Buddhist temple is characteristic of Chinese popular religion. In the side wings flanking the Mahavira Hall
are a 'Thousand Buddha' group and Bodhisattva Hall. There are said to have been
a total of 2052 Ming dynasty stucco figures in the temple, of varying sizes,
although only 1562 now survive. It is an important northern group.

15km north of Pingyao is the **Zhenguo si**, which has some fine trees in the courtyards, including two Dragon claw cassias. The temple was founded in 963 and after considerable damage during the Ming was largely rebuilt in 1815. In the first courtyard the main hall is a **Thousand Buddha hall**, said to be a surviving Five dynasties construction with contemporary statues; and there are steles recording the temple history on either side of the courtyard. The Thousand Buddha hall is almost square in plan, with considerable eaves projection and massive brackets. It is a rare survival. In the second courtyard, to the rear, the eastern wing is dedicated to Guanyin; although the statues have gone the western wing is dedicated to Ksitigarbha, Buddha of the underworld. The main hall houses figures of the Three Buddas (past, present and future), with Ming wall paintings on the walls.

Wutai shan

The Wutai Mountain, whose name means 'Five Platforms', rises some 3000m above sea-level roughly between Taiyuan and Datong in Shanxi province, not far from the border with Hebei province. It is the northern Buddhist holy mountain, supposedly once inhabited by the Bodhisattva Manjusri, the god of wisdom. Manjusri is usually represented with a sword (to cleave ignorance) and a flat oblong object, representing a palm-leaf manuscript of the text of the Perfection of Wisdom. He often rides on a lion. Although the centre was huge in the Tang dynasty, when it was at the height of its popularity, today its major temples are concentrated in a depression surrounded by mountains.

The 'platforms' are five peaks, north, south, east, west and central, rising in and around a depression in a now rather bare but imposing mountainous area.

Practical information

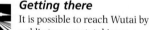

Getting there
It is possible to reach Wutai by public transport, taking a train from Taiyuan or Datong to Xin xian (on the Taiyuan–Datong line) and then a public bus to Tai huai (taking care not to descend at Wutai xian for this is the county town and not the centre of Buddhist temples). If you were to do so, it would be virtually impossible to see the two earliest standing temples in China, which are of great intrinsic beauty, and dramatically sited, as they are isolated and well off the main road. As they are so lovely, it is best to go to

Wutai from Taiyuan by a tourist bus, checking that it does, indeed, stop at Nanchan si and Foguang si, or else by car. In either case, Taiyuan is the best point of departure, although it is possible to travel from Datong. A taxi can be booked for three or four days through your hotel in Taiyuan and the price fixed in advance. Remember that you will have to pay for the driver's accommodation and food en route and in Wutai, so he counts as an extra person. If the taxi-driver does not speak English, it is probably wise to pre-book a local tourist guide. The trip from Taiyuan, including stops at the Nanchan and Foguang temples, covers some 240km and takes about eight hours.

Where to stay

Before 1986 all visitors stayed in one of three hostels; *No. 3 Hotel* (highly recommended) was attached to the Tayuan (Pagoda) Temple in the main village. Visitors were given rooms (with baths and rather leaky central heating in winter) in a series of courtyards and ate in a communal dining room across a lane. Any other facilities (shops, post office) were available in the village,

The *Wutaishan Binguan* is in the centre of Tai huan on Shijuliang cheng gong lu, ☎ 654 2342. The luxury hotel *Qixiange Binguan*, ☎ 654 2400, fax 654 2183, is south of the town but well-situated for walks.

History

Neolithic implements have been found in the vicinity but its Buddhist history seems to have begun after the Han with the first record of a temple being restored in the area in the Northern Wei (late 5C). By the Northern Qi there were over 200 temples in the mountain area. The Bodhisattva Manjusri was said to have appeared on Wutai, hence its consecration, and it became a centre for the study of the *Avatamsaka*, the principle sutra of the Huayan syncretist school (Kegon in Japanese), which viewed the universe as ordered, the world of principle and phenomena being fused, with everything leading to the centre, the Buddha. The growth of Wutai as a **Buddhist centre** before and during the **Tang period** and its subsequent relative retrenchment as a result of the late Tang persecution of Buddhism is still evident in the fact that the two earliest surviving buildings, the Nanchan si (782) and Foguang si (857) are today well outside the central circle of peaks where they were once part of a centre.

The Japanese monk Ennin made a pilgrimage to China, ancestral home of Japanese Buddhism, from 838–847 and left a diary which includes many references to Wutai. He described the five peaks or platforms as looking like 'upturned bowls' and perhaps fancifully described how he was frequently menaced by a lion (associated with the Bodhisattva Manjusri) as he made trips to the peaks. As lions are not native to China, the apparition was viewed as miraculous. He was impressed by the brocade-like covering of alpine flowers on the high peaks which are still to be seen, as well as by the cold of the mountainous area where he claimed there were glaciers, apparently still unmelted since the Ice Age but they have certainly melted since Ennin's visit. Some of the treasured relics he viewed in the temples there included part of the upper skull of a minor Buddha brought from India in the early 7C. Looking like a 'pumice stone', it had 'white hair ... about five inches long, apparently grown out since it had been shaved'.

Ennin left very detailed descriptions of relics and icons at Wutai: the portrait of 'Priest Big Shoes' who had been given a pair of miraculous shoes by Manjusri which rather mysteriously enabled him to make 15,000 robes and 75,000 meals for his fellow monks; the revolving sutra library in the Tayuan si (still in existence), the miraculous Manjusri image in the same temple whose lion breathed vapours, emitted light and manifested auspicious signs, all of which were reported to the throne. In the Jinge si (Temple of the Golden Tower) just 8km from Tai Huai, near the Southern Platform, there used to be a relic of a Japanese monk, Reisen, which was of particular interest to Ennin.

This was a piece of the skin of his arm, on which Reisen had drawn a picture of the Buddha, in a Buddhist mortification of the flesh that was abhorrent to Confucian or traditionalist Chinese who believed firmly that one did not have the right to destroy or damage one's body, which was a parental gift, and that mutilation would cause problems for the soul after death.

The importance of Wutai in the Tang was demonstrated by imperial favour: annually the court sent incense, pearl-covered banners, jade, golden incense-burners, flowered carpets, silk floss, scarves and 450kg (1000lb) of tea, as well as providing annual feasts for thousands of monks.

Despite the late Tang suppression of Buddhism, there was an upsurge of imperial interest in Wutai during the **Ming**, when impressive additions were made to many of the temples. By then the mountain had become a special place of pilgrimage for Mongolian Lamaist Buddhists, partly because the mountain is not that far from Mongolia but fundamentally because the Bodhisattva Manjusri had special significance in Lamaism. It became the favoured place for burial amongst those Mongolians who could afford to make the pilgrimage bearing the body of a parent. In the summer months of June and July Mongolians and Tibetans still come to Wutai, partly for religious reasons, partly for the animal markets that are held there then, a mixture of trade and faith which was characteristic of medieval religious centres throughout the world but of which we in the west have rather lost track.

Landscape with barrel-vaulted mud-brick houses and brick kiln near Wutai shan

Temples en route between Taiyuan and Wutai shan

On the road to Wutai from Taiyun, the following temples may be visited: Nanchan si, Yanqing si, Guangji si, Foguang si and Jinge si. If time is short, do not miss the Nanchan si and the Foguang si (you could do the others on the return trip).

Nanchan si

The Nanchan si (Southern Meditation Temple) is the first temple you reach, before arriving at Wutaixian cheng. It is in Lijiazhuang, near Dongzhizhen, in Wutai xian; a turning off the main road to the left. Although there are buildings from various periods in the temple today, the most important is the small main hall, built in 782 and containing a group of figures from the same period. It is thought that it survived the late Tang persecution of Buddhism, which involved the dissolution and destruction of many temples, because of its isolated position away from the centre of Wutai. Although much restored, it retains its original proportions and structural features and is the earliest surviving timber-frame building in China. Restoration is evident from comparison with photographs from the early 1950s where the roof is similar but the two façade windows are circular in form; today they are rectangular with a simple lattice of uprights. A lovely little hall of perfect proportions, it is the ideal starting point for anyone interested in Chinese architecture (and I feel that it is always helpful to start with something small; in Suzhou, the gardens make more sense if you start with the tiny Master of Nets Garden).

Standing on a high stone platform, the three-bay hall has an impressive roof with a considerable eaves projection supported on simple but massive under-eave brackets and a ridge decorated with the incurving 'owls' tails' at either end characteristic of pre-Ming buildings. An unusual and pleasing feature is the variation in the size of the bays, with the central bay somewhat wider than the two on either side. The variation conveys an impression of grandeur even in a small hall. Bracketing is restricted to simple, W-shaped brackets on top of the columns with none of the inter-columnar bracketing that came later. Two elegant bronze urns stand beside the steps, their colour harmonising with the plain dark wood of the façade. The 17 statues inside the hall, set on a platform, comprise a central Buddha on a throne with a mandorla, or aureole, simply decorated with flowers in relief, and attendants, guardians and Bodhisattvas (including Manjusri on his lion to the Buddha's right) in natural poses, slightly inclined towards the Buddha, forming a composition of great elegance. There is no ceiling inside the hall so the solid timber construction of the roof can be clearly seen.

Yanqing si

Beyond the Nanchan si is the Yanqing si (Extended Celebration Temple) in Puwen cun, whose main hall dates from the Jin (1115–1234). The hall is similar to that of the Nanchan si but the three bays are of even span and intercolumnar brackets are used. The two central columns are topped with horned beasts' heads, an unusual form found also in the Guangji si. In front of the hall is a Northern Song stone sutra pillar (sometimes called a *dharani* column) dated 1035. Standing on a lotus base, the 7m sutra pillar is a sort of elongated form of the Tang style stupa or reliquary, with a stupa-shaped top.

Guangji si

The Guangji si (Temple of Extensive Succour) is on Xi jie, inside the western city gate of the county town of Wutai xian. It was founded in the Yuan, in the Zhizheng reign period (1341–70), but extensively rebuilt during the Qing although the figures inside the hall are thought to be original, and the structure owes more to the Yuan than the Qing, with simple bracketing (columnar and inter-columnar brackets). The columns are all topped with the same horned beast-heads seen in the hall of the Yanqing si, a rather barbaric northern form. There is a fine, if stumpy, sutra pillar just below the hall with Buddhist scriptures carved on the stem and little figures set under the canopy just below the lotus top.

Foguang si

The Foguang si (Temple of Buddha's Glory) is well off the main road to Tai huai, north of the county town of Wutai, in Foguang xin cun, northeast of Doucun xiang, set against terraced slopes. It contains a number of early buildings but the Eastern Great Hall dates from 857 and, until the discovery of the small Nanchan si in the early 1950s, was regarded as the earliest surviving timber building in China. It was discovered in 1937 by China's foremost architectural historian, Liang Sicheng (1901–72), a son of the late Qing reformer, Liang Qichao, who found the date of construction recorded in an inscription on an interior beam. The hall is at the back of the temple which, probably because of the mountainous terrain, faces west (rather than the more usual south) along a valley.

The temple was founded in 471–499 but largely destroyed in the great Buddhist persecution of 845. The Eastern Great Hall (a comparatively modest building) was built in 857, in a period of relaxation of repression, to replace the grander buildings. Towards the front of the temple, the Manjusri Hall (on the left) is a Jin (1115–1234) construction, while the rest of the buildings are Ming or Qing.

You enter the temple through a steeply-stepped, tunnel-like gate which leads to the first courtyard, with tall stone sutra pillars and the Manjusri Hall on the left. The hall dates to 1137 and is seven bays wide, still preserving the relatively strong and simple bracketing system. The roof was restored in the Yuan, which accounts for the later style of the ridge acroteria in contrast with the older, incurving owls' tails on the Eastern Hall. The figures within the temple were entirely remade by a most effective local craftsman in 1985. The Eastern Hall stands above the Manjusri Hall and is also a seven bay, single-storey hall with the most magnificent eaves projection supported on four tiers of cantilevers, clearly seen under the eaves. Although the Nanchan si is perhaps more pleasing and unusual in its general proportions, the structure of the roof and eaves of this hall, with its huge brackets, is incredibly impressive. The roof ridge is finished with a pair of glazed owls' tails and a central pagoda in glazed tile, all of which I suspect are fairly recent but the owls' tails at least are in keeping with the original. In contrast with the chunky structure of the exterior eaves, the interior beams spanning from front to back are lightly curved 'moon beams'. Note, too, that the ridge purlin supporting the rafters has no king post (as would be found in Ming and Qing buildings) but is instead supported on a truss in the form of an inverted V. The statues in the hall are also late Tang in date, with the exception of the 500 lohans to left and right, which are Ming. There are Tang dynasty wall paintings of devils and guardians, as well as Song wall paintings, mainly in the form of circular cartouches containing Buddhist groups, interspersed with prayers and inscriptions in square cartouches.

Behind the hall, to the right, is the **Zushi** (Founding Teacher's Stupa), a Northern Wei funerary stupa containing the remains of the Meditation Master who founded the temple. It is of whitewashed brick, some 8m high, square in base plan and topped with a six-sided pagoda-shaped lotus crown. The interior was hollow, to receive the ashes of the founder. Beside it stands a Tang sutra pillar with a rather bulbous top (a form not uncommon in Japan). Other burial stupas near the temple include some from the Tang and a rather unusual Jin stupa in brick, with a hexagonal base decorated with architectural forms (eaves bracketing) and a complex crown which looks rather like a cabbage stalk with the leaves torn off.

Jinge si

The Jinge Temple (Golden Tower Temple) is just over the peak that you pass on the road, part of the encircling ring of mountains around Tai huai, and is about 15km south of the village. Founded in 770, the Daizong emperor of the Tang ordered that the roof of the Buddha Hall be covered with gilded bronze tiles, hence the name. Inside the two-storey Main Hall is a giant gilded stucco figure of the Bodhisattva Guanyin with 1000 arms, apparently with a bronze figure inside, under the later layers of stucco. Attendants surround the figure. Behind the hall are others, containing up to 1000 figures, with the great hall at the rear containing figures of the past, present and future Buddhas and 18 lohans. Evidence of Tang construction is found in some surviving stone pillar bases, carved with lotus petals, which are originals.

The reconstruction work in 1985 was sensitive, with window lattices being composed of original parts (carved floral motifs) worked in with modern copies. In richer parts of China like Fujian, where pious Overseas Chinese pay huge sums for the restoration of a temple, they are often recreated from the ground up. The Wutai shan restoration retains a closeness to earlier forms.

Within **Tai huai** village it is sometimes difficult to tell where one temple begins and another ends, for they virtually run together and, apart from the main street with its shops, most of the village consists of temples.

Tayuan si

The lower part of the village is dominated by the Tayuan Temple (Pagoda Temple) with its huge, 50m high white-washed *sarira* (reliquary) pagoda in the Tibetan style, which stands between the Great Hall and the Library. Originally part of the Xiantong Temple (see below), when the *sarira* pagoda was restored in the Wanli reign period of the Ming (1573–1620), this part of the temple was reconstituted as an independent entity. Approached through a gate with substantial walls pierced with two arched windows and a central arched door (a form often found in the Qing temples at Chengde; very much of the north), the Daxiong bao dian Buddha Hall is the main building in the first courtyard, a good, solid five-bay hall of late date, in which services are held quite frequently (often in the late afternoon at 16.00–17.00, if getting up before dawn does not appeal). The pagoda, behind the hall, is set on a high angular base, its upper part in the characteristic bottle-shape seen in Tibetan Lamaist stupas with a bronze 'umbrella' finial.

The fact that this form is not uncommon in Wutai is probably due to two factors: its importance as a centre for Tibetan and, especially, Mongolian Lamaists for whom this reliquary was important and also the fact that this smaller centre at Wutai concentrated around Tai huai was much patronised by the imperial house, amongst others, in the Ming and Qing when Tibetan styles were popular, almost fashionable, as can be seen in Peking and Chengde. The stupa, constructed of brick and lime and white-washed, is hung with 252 small bronze wind-bells which tinkle in the breeze.

Sutra Libary

Behind the stupa is one of the most famous buildings in Wutai, the Sutra Library. A two-storey timber-frame building (presumably of Ming foundation but subsequently restored), it was built to house the revolving sutra library case mentioned by Ennin in the 9C. This extraordinary 20-storey wooden structure, hexagonal in plan, narrow at the base and flaring at the top, rises through a hexagonal opening in the coffered ceiling of the library to the upper storey where it is finished with a conical pavilion. It revolves on a wooden lotus base, although being top-heavy due to its narrow base and wider upper part it must have been rather difficult to move when full of books.

There are few volumes now in the pigeon-holes (three to each of the six sides on each storey), as valuable volumes have been moved away for safer storage. There were once Mongolian and Tibetan editions of the *Tripitaka*, as well as Chinese and many smaller editions, such as a Ming copy of the *Avatamsaka* written in blood and a Qing scroll of the same sutra written out in the form of a seven-storey pagoda, Ming paintings of Buddhist notables on pipa leaves and a manuscript written in gold by the Qing Kangxi emperor.

Xiantong si

Behind the Tayuan Temple is the Xiantong Temple (Manifest Penetration Temple), said to be an Eastern Han foundation, dating from 58–75 but, like the Tayuan Temple, rebuilt in the early years of the Ming. The many halls and wings that survive are mostly of the Ming or Qing and the temple is noted for its bronzes and brick-vaulted halls. Built against a hill, the temple rises ever higher, with a central terrace with two elaborate Ming bronze pagodas on either side. Based on the Tibetan stupa, these have octagonal bases with tapering storeyed tops and are about 8m high. Beautifully cast, covered in images of Buddhas, fat guardian figures holding them up, tiny deities riding on fish or horses amongst waves, pagodas and haloed Bodhisattvas, they are exceptional examples of Ming bronze work. Behind them are a pair of two-storey, three-doored brick-vaulted Ming halls, smaller and more elegant than that at Nanjing or similar constructions in Taiyuan. Another grand example, the Hall of Immeasurable Splendour, with seven arched entrances and brick imitations of wooden brackets under the eaves, has fascinating 'bracketed' vaults filled with brightly painted wooden caisson

ceilings. Some of the treasures of the Wutai temples are exhibited in the Xiantong Temple.

Between the two small brick-vaulted halls is the **Bronze Pavilion**, the best example of this rare form. Cast in the Ming, it is a perfect imitation of timber construction and decoration. The interior is covered with thousands of tiny Buddha figures and lists of donors and the structure of the roof, apparently timber encased in

Miniature bronze pavilion, Wutai shan

bronze, is clear. Outside, the lattice windows and lower panels of the walls, as well as the little balcony surrounding the upper storey, are all cast in perfect imitation of fine timber work. The 'window lattices' include a variety of floral motifs in geometric forms and the panels below depict a wide variety of animals from carp and peacocks to deer in elegant cartouches. The central doors open to reveal the interior.

The **Pusa Ding** (Bodhisattva Peak) is behind the Xiantong Temple, up 108 steps which take you to the top of the hill dominating Tai Huai and offering a wonderful view over the temples spread out below.

Founded in the Northern Wei, when Wutai became a great pilgrimage centre for Tibetan and Mongolian Lamaists (especially those of the Yellow Hat sect), from the Yongle reign period of the Ming (1403–25) Lamaist dignitaries used to stay here, as it was said to be where Manjusri stayed on the mountain. The Qing Kangxi and Qianlong emperors also stayed here when they came to pay their respects. Remaining buildings date from the Qing and the stone-carving (of pillar bases and terrace walls) is considered to be of imperial quality. Owing to the number of important visitors there are many memorial stelae inscribed in Chinese, Manchu, Mongolian and Tibetan.

Luohou si

Down below, to the east of the Tayuan Temple, is the Luohou Temple (Rahu Temple). Rahu is the demon who seizes the sun and moon to cause eclipses and who is reborn as the eldest son of every Buddha. This is described as a 'Lama Temple', although there are clear Lamaist elements found throughout Wutai, in the Tibetan style white stupas and the immensely tall pine trunks with bronze tops set up outside many halls.

Founded in the Tang, it was rebuilt in 1492 and is the temple which is best preserved in its entirety. On the birthday of Manjusri, the fourteenth day of the sixth month of the lunar calendar (thus usually in August, although the exact day changes from year to year), the monks of the temple perform a devil dance of the sort also seen in Tibet and Mongolia for the Buddha's birthday and New Year. Apart from its full range of buildings—including meditation hall, hall of guardians and library—the hall at the back of the temple contains the famous circular altar with 18 lohans crossing the sea beneath a great red-petalled lotus flower which contains four Buddha images (Buddhas of the Four Directions) which are revealed when the huge petals, moved by means of an underground mechanism, are lowered. This is another temple in which regular services are held.

Yuanzhao si

Behind the Luohou Temple is the Yuanzhao Temple (Universally Illuminating Temple), founded in the Ming when an Indian monk came to the area. He died in the meditation position (called 'transformation while sitting' in Chinese) and was cremated according to the Buddhist tradition. His ashes were housed in a small white Tibetan style stupa in the centre of the temple, which was built in 1434.

It was in this temple that the founder of the Yellow Hat sect in Tibet, Tsongkhapa, stayed and preached in the early years of the Yongle period (early 15C), bringing the new discipline of Yellow Hat Lamaism to the area. The Yellow Hat sect of Tibetan Buddhism was founded in the early 15C and stressed the need for monastic discipline; its forebears wore red hats. Today's Dalai Lama is the head of the Yellow Hats, while the Panchen Lama who lives in Peking with his Tibetan headquarters in Shigatse, is the leader of the older, Red Hats.

The sculptures of the Buddhas—past, present and future, with their attendants—in the main hall of the Yuanzhao Temple are considered to be amongst the finest on Wutai. The courtyard in which the white stupa stands (with its holy relic inside) is surrounded by a covered walk and is a favourite place for circumnambulation (or walking around sacred buildings or figures), a practice known in Chinese Buddhism but apparently more popular amongst Lamaists; yellow-robed monks can frequently be seen walking clockwise around halls and stupas in the Wutai area.

Guangzong si
Behind the Yuanzhao Temple is the Guangzong Temple, one of the smallest (one description is 'squashed in') of those in the Tai huai area. Founded in the first years of the 16C, in its centre is the three-bay bronze tiled hall (today covered with glazed turquoise tiles said to resemble patinated bronze) with three Buddha figures of wood and 18 iron lohans.

Wanfo ge
South of the Luohou Temple is the Wanfo ge (Ten-thousand Buddha Hall), formerly part of the Tayuan or Pagoda Temple, founded in the Ming and rebuilt under the Qing. The main hall is in the east of the temple, a three-bay, two-storey, triple-eaved timber construction containing a considerable number of Buddhist figures, hence the name. In front of the hall hangs a 3500kg Ming bronze bell. In the southeast part of the temple there are two stone Tibetan style stupas of carved marble, 4m high.

The temple, unusually in this rather strict Lamaist Buddbist stronghold, contains a finely-carved **Dragon King Hall** (at the back of the enclosure).

The Dragon King is not a Buddhist deity: he belongs with Taoism and popular religion as a controller of waters and rain, but it was said that the local Dragon King was very fierce and threatened the stability of the temples, so a shrine was built to him here. Opposite is a stage for religious dramas, a centre of attraction in the major celebrations of the sixth lunar month.

Shuxiang si
South of the Wanfo Temple is the Shuxiang Temple, (Statue of Manjusri Temple) on Yanglin jie. Founded in the Tang, it was restored in the Yuan and subsequently burnt down, to be rebuilt in 1487. It contains a gate-hall, hall of guardians, verandahed courtyards with meditation hall, Manjusri Hall, kitchens and living quarters, as well as bell and drum towers. Inside the Manjusri Hall is a 9m Ming (1496) figure of Manjusri riding on a lion. Behind are three Buddhas, the Buddha of Medicine (extremely important as a Lamaist icon, frequently seen in

Tibet), the historic Buddha, Sakyamuni, and Amitabha Buddha, who presides over the Western Paradise, with 500 lohans on either side.

Outer temples that are best visited by car (the driver can have a day off when you walk around Tai huai) include the Longquan, Zhenhai, Nan shan, Puhua and Bishan Temples and the Guanyin Cave.

Bishan si

The Bishan Temple (Azure Mountain Temple) is just 2km north of Tai huai on the slopes of the northern platform, set in a forested area well supplied with water. It is thought to have been founded in the Northern Wei when the famous teacher Fa cong preached there. It was rebuilt in the Chenghua reign period of the Ming (1465–87) and restored in the Qing. On the central axis of the large temple are the hall of guardians, bell and drum towers, Thunder Sound Hall, hall of the ordination altar and side wings, with a hanging flower gate marking the back part of the main axis where the library is situated. Most of the buildings in the front part are single storeyed, while those behind are multi-storeyed and multi-eaved. All the sculptures are Qing, including a 1.5m white jade Buddha presented by Burmese Buddhists set in front of the historic Buddha figure in the Vairocana Hall. Out in the wooden surroundings are a number of white stupas containing the ashes of notable monks.

Nanshan si

On the far side of the river that runs just east of Tai huai is the Nanshan Temple (Southern Mountain Temple) which is made up of three temples: **Youguo Temple** (Protect the Nation), **Jile Temple** (Extreme Joy) and **Shande Temple** (Goodness and Virtue) which were joined together early last century. The complex was founded in 1296, rebuilt in 1541 and restored in the Qing. Built against the mountain, the temple is reached, like the Pusa ding, by 108 steps; the significance of 108 being that it is the number of beads on the Buddhist rosary (also the 108 passions or delusions, the 108 karmic bonds and the 108 tolls of temple bells at dawn and dusk) so that the rosary can be said en route. A fine brick spirit wall marks the entrance to the temple, which is full of further steps and decoratively carved stone railings, and there is much decorative cut-brick work and stone-carving depicting spirits, scenes from drama and history as well as Buddhist scenes. In the **main hall** the 18 lohan figures which date from the Ming are thought to be the best lohans on Wutai. Each very different, with separate attributes, they are not as caricatured as many of the Qing assemblages (which enjoy greater popularity) but, set under their carved wooden canopy, retain a certain dignity. Behind them are wall paintings of scenes from the life of the Buddha, who is depicted as a Chinese gentleman; these also date from the Ming.

Beyond is the **Guanyin Cave** where a six-armed Guanyin figure of no great note is set in a cave behind a main hall, reached up a stepped path.

Puhua si

The Puhua Temple (Universal Transformation Temple) is of uncertain founding date; it was rebuilt during the Ming. It lies beyond the Nanshan Temple and Guanyin Cave. Many of the halls and canopies over the figures are decorated with elaborate carvings, brightly painted and there is a lot of decorative cut-brick work.

Zhenhai si

The Zhenhai Temple (Calm Sea Temple) is 5km south of Tai huai, beautifully set beside a spring, called the Spring from the Bottom of the Sea, surrounded by pines and poplars. The temple as it stands today was founded in 1711. It has a fine stupa in the centre, built in 1786 and carved with scenes from the Buddha's life, above which are four Buddhas. Around the courtyard are covered walks with paintings of Bodhisattvas. The temple, which is still very active (although the monks, many of whom are from Mongolia, were very elderly when I last visited), was the home of a famous 'living Buddha' of the Qing and is an important pilgrimage site for Mongolian and Tibetan Buddhists.

Pailou on Wutai shan

Longquan si

The Longquan Temple (Dragon Spring Temple), southwest of Tai huai, is an extraordinary mixture of styles. It was founded in the Song, rebuilt in the Ming and most notably in the late Qing and early Republican period. Reached by the inevitable 108 steps, the first edifice is a stone *pailou* (arch) dating from the early Republican period, lavishly carved, partly in imitation of timber construction but covered with dragons and foliage. The temple buildings appear greatly restrained beside the stone carving, not only on the *pailou* but also on the two carved stone stupas, especially the Puji Pagoda (Universal Succour Pagoda), with fat, smiling Maitreya (Future) Buddhas on four sides, beneath an elaborate mock-timber pagoda top, above a series of fat, supporting guardian figures, the whole set behind an elaborately carved railing. In the west of the temple is a 10m three-storey, hexagonal pagoda said to contain the relics of a Song notable.

In the outer temples, but also from a lot of the temples in Tai huai which is small and quiet, many birds can be seen. The most numerous in early winter are red-legged choughs who tumble above. They have a nerve-wracking habit of 'free-falling', apparently hurling to a certain death before they flap upwards at the last moment.

The Yongle gong

The Yongle gong (Palace of Eternal Joy) is a major Taoist temple near Rui cheng in the southwest corner of Shanxi province. It lies in an area that is rich in well-preserved architectural remains which can be reached from the town of Lin Fen, on the railway line south of Taiyuan.

Lin Fen

Lin Fen is a small, rather bleak town, interesting in that, despite its bleak northernness, it was chosen as an area for resettlement of a large number of Indonesian Chinese who fled Indonesia during anti-Chinese riots there in 1960, when Zhou Enlai sent boats to rescue them, and again when Sukarno took over in 1965 and there was considerable persecution of Overseas Chinese.

Its major monument is a pagoda built in 1715, originally part of the Dayun si (Great Cloud Monastery) founded in the Tang. The pagoda, built to replace one destroyed by an earthquake in 1695, has a square base and six square storeys above, topped with an octagonal storey and decorated with poorly preserved glazed tiles, characteristic of Shanxi buildings, made by craftsmen in Yangcheng xian, depicting Buddhist figures. It was built over a magnificent iron Buddha head which fills the base. The head, which has a large hole in the back, was cast in parts, in sand which ran out of the hole, and is very thick at the base. It is 5m high and very imposing, sitting on its chin in the pagoda. The drum tower, said to be the largest of its kind in China (at 43.5m high) and to be over 1000 years old, was opened to visitors in November 1987.

Jiezhou

In Yuncheng xian, about 100km south of Lin Fen, is Jiezhou which has a fine Qing **temple** dedicated to Guan di (Guandi miao), the god of war. The temple was founded in 589, rebuilt in 1017, destroyed by an earthquake in 1555 and rebuilt, only to be destroyed by fire in 1702. Over the subsequent ten years it was rebuilt, apparently with faithful attention to its previous form.

Although there are many temples and shrines to the god of war throughout China, this one is the most important (apart from being a very fine piece of Qing building) because Jiezhou was the birthplace of **Guan Yu** who was deified by the Wanli emperor of the Ming, after many previous posthumous honours. He was a great hero of the Three Kingdoms period (220–280), a follower of Liu Bei who became first emperor of the Minor Han or Shu dynasty (221–263) and one of the great folk-heroes of China, celebrated in the *San guo zhi* (*Romance of the Three Kingdoms*) which reached its final form as a novel by Luo Guanzhong in the 14C. Plays celebrating the life and legendary accomplishments of Guan yu (or Guan di) were performed inside the first main gate at festivals.

The temple, which is built to the same plan as most temples in China, has a main axis with subsidiary buildings to the east and west. It is most noted for its fine glazed tile work—all locally produced and characteristic of southern Shanxi—seen on the roofs, on the dragon screen at the front of the temple and on the wooden *pailou*. The stone carving is also very fine: the carved pillar bases are fine examples of Qing stone carving, which is not to be dismissed lightly as 'late'; the stone-carved *pailou* is also extremely interesting.

Hongdong and Guangsheng si

Some 25km north of Lin Fen is **Hongdong** and 17km northeast of the town is the **Guangsheng si** (Temple of Widespread Victory). This has a famous glazed tile pagoda with a very strange staircase inside and some extremely early buildings, as well as an unusual wall painting depicting a temple play. The temple is divided into three parts: upper, lower and the Yongshen miao, which contains the wall painting. The temple was founded in AD 147 and rebuilt in 769. In 1303 it was destroyed by a major earthquake and rebuilt soon after; sections that date to this last rebuilding—in the last years of the Yuan or the first years of the Ming—are quite rare early survivals. The upper temple has three main halls and the spectacular **Feihong ta** (Soaring Rainbow Pagoda).

The halls, built soon after the 1303 earthquake, preserve the Yuan style of building, solid and massive, closer to the earlier Tang examples on Wutai shan than the more decorative and lighter examples of Ming and Qing building in, for instance, the Forbidden City. There are fewer brackets under the eaves, those that there are usually sit on top of the columns, rather than forming, in effect, a decorative frieze as in the Forbidden City. The ridge acroteria consist of simple inturned 'owls' tails' rather than the highly elaborate later versions. The halls and their sculptures are all fine surviving examples of early building: the figures of Amitabha and his attendants in the Front Hall being Yuan, while this and the other halls and sculptures are early Ming.

One of the early printed versions of the Buddhist *Tripitaka*, or canon, was still in this part of the temple in 1942 and narrowly escaped being taken to Japan; soldiers of the Chinese Eighth Route Army rescued the volumes from the occupying Japanese. Most of the canon is now in the **National Library** in Peking (4330 scrolls were sent by the Eighth Route Army and further finds brought the total to 4541) with 152 scrolls in the Shanxi Provincial Museum.

This edition of the *Tripitaka* was published during the Jin dynasty (1115–1234) in nearby Jiezhou. It is known as the *Zhaocheng Tripitaka*. The woodblocks for printing it were cut between 1148 and 1173. This length of time is not surprising when you consider that the full set consisted of about 7000 scrolls, each of which would have been printed on mulberry paper from a considerable number of blocks and mounted on red rods. A set was stored in the temple and re-discovered in 1934. The scrolls have handsome frontispieces and the printing is unusual in that it relied for finance upon donations from local Buddhists, whereas printing the entire Buddhist canon of well over 1000 titles was usually dependent upon imperial finance as it was so expensive; this happened with the first printing (in Sichuan, 972–983) and most subsequent reprintings. In the early Yuan the blocks were removed to Peking for storage where they were used as a model for the Yuan dynasty edition of the *Tripitaka*.

The pagoda is on the central axis of the temple, a feature common to early Chinese temple layouts; it may be compared with the two Goose Pagodas and their associated temples in Xi'an. Thirteen storeys high, octagonal in plan and covered with lively glazed tile decorations, the pagoda was built in 1527 and the verandah on the ground level was added in 1622. It is 47.3m high, built of 'green brick' with tiled eaves imitating timber bracketed construction at each storey and decorative tilework depicting Buddhist figures, plants and animals in between. The finial is very fine, with a central stupa-shaped 'diamond finial' and four tiny pagodas surrounding it so that it forms a five-stupa group which is said to have Lamaist connections. The interior is hollow and has the most extraordinary steps which can only be climbed with great difficulty. Leaving aside the height of the steps, the opening gets narrower and narrower as you ascend and there is a total lack of illumination; the steps mount in a gradual zig-zag with a yawning gap in between so that you have to keep climbing over a black hole below you. I climbed some of the way up behind a wonderful but stout expert in architectural history from Taiyuan who was too tubby to get terribly far up (she said that in her youth she had managed it) and in descending in total darkness tended to land heavily on the fingers of those behind her. The glazed tilework, which is in very good condition, is a local speciality.

The lower temple is built on a single axis; the rear hall, built in 1309, is particularly fine, as are the three Buddhas and Manjusri and Samantabhadra figures in the upper part. The Yuan dynasty wall paintings in the temple were removed in 1928 and are now in the Nelson Atkins Museum in Kansas City.

Beside the lower temple is the **Shuishen miao** (Temple of the Water God), said to be the site of worship of the god of the Huo spring. In the Hall there are wall paintings, the most famous of which depicts Yuan dynasty drama (on the eastern part of the south wall). The painting was made in 1324 and depicts a troupe in performance, showing the scenery, orchestra, props and actors on a brick-paved stage of the sort that might have been found in temples. The 11 actors are shown in the ritualised roles of *sheng* (older male), *dan* (female), *jing* (painted face) and *mo* (young male) with the appropriate make-up, embroidered costumes and beards. The musical instruments include bamboo flute, drum and clapper for keeping time. It is an extremely rare illustration from the golden age of the Chinese drama.

In the town of Hongdong there is a **Ming prison** (the earliest to survive in China) with high surrounding walls and two gates with cave-type cells inside. There is a tiger-headed stele in the back courtyard with a list of the criminals held.

Ruicheng and the Yongle gong

Some 240km south of Lin Fen in the southwest tip of Shanxi province is Ruicheng; 3km north of Ruicheng is the present site of the Yongle gong (Palace of Eternal Joy), one of the major centres of northern Taoism.

Its name sounds appropriate but it derives from the fact that the temple (or palace) was originally located in Yongle village. First built as a memorial temple, later a monastery, the temple commemorated one of the Eight Taoist

Immortals, **Lu Dongbin**, who was a native of the village. Lu Dongbin was born in 755 and came from a family of officials. He is a fine example of the historicisation of myth and/or the mythicisation of history. As E.T. Chalmers Werner has it, Lu 'was five feet two inches in height and at 20 he was still unmarried' but he met a dragon on Lu shan who gave him a magic sword with which he could hide himself and also fly. He met a general in Chang'an who had discovered the secret of immortality, which all Taoists sought, and had successfully survived from the Zhou until the Tang, a period of some 2000 years. He passed the secret on to Lu Dongbin who was then subjected to ten temptations but survived to do good deeds through magic for the next 400 years. This is but one version of the many legends about him and the temple which was built on the site of his house, according to a stele of 1262 in the Yongle gong, and called the Temple of Mr. Lu.

The temple today is most famous for its wall paintings and for the fact that in 1959–60 it was transported with the help of Eastern European experts from its original site in Yongle on the banks of the Yellow River to just north of Ruicheng when the Sanmen gorge dam of the Yellow River was built and Yongle submerged. The buildings were moved stone by stone (with each brick and roof-tile numbered for reinstatement) and the frescoes were cut up into blocks and remounted. An exhibition at the rear of the temple describes the work.

The layout of the temple is interesting for it reflects a peculiarity of the period in which it was originally constructed (1232–1358). The main buildings are aligned on a single north–south axis, standing high off the ground on a series of terraces linked by walkways. The Chinese would describe the layout of the buildings linked by raised walkways as resembling the character *gong* (work) which consists of two horizontal strokes joined by one vertical stroke. This form of layout has also been found in excavations of Yuan dynasty domestic architecture. It can also be seen in palace architecture of the Ming and Qing in the Forbidden City.

The first building on the central axis is the **Wuji men** (Gate of the Unfathomable) with wall paintings of door gods and celestial generals and armies, characteristically protective in this first building in the temple. Behind is the **Sanqing dian** (Hall of the Three Pure Ones) with its huge murals of the Three Pure Ones or major Taoist deities surrounded by all the other Taoist deities—the complete pantheon. In this representation of the entire pantheon and the paintings of door gods in the gatehouse the Taoists are borrowing from the Buddhist tradition. The figures are immensely tall and portrayed in rows four deep, with strong outlining and rich colours of bronze, red, brown, pink, light blues and greens. In the third building, the **Chunyang dian** (Hall of Essential Yang—as in *yin* and *yang*—one of Lu Dongbin's Taoist names), 52 extraordinary episodes from his long life are depicted in misty, mountainous landscape settings which serve to frame and separate the episodes (like the frames in a comic strip). Behind is the Zhongyang dian (Hall of Zhongyang), dedicated to Wang Zhongyang, c 1120–1170, founder of a Taoist sect called the Teaching of True Integrity (Quanzhen jiao), which was particularly strong during the Yuan.

The life of Wang and his seven disciples is depicted in the frescoes of the hall which are not considered to be quite up to the standard of those in the Chunyang dian. All the frescoes were painted between 1325 and 1368 with the Zhongyang dian frescoes finished last, in 1368.

The Silk Road

The Silk Road or Roads is the name given to tourist itineraries that take you out into Gansu and Xinjiang provinces to many of the oasis towns that stand on what was the ancient silk route, a trading route across the Gobi Desert to Central Asia and thence to the western world. Although the route is named after its most famous commodity, the Silk Road, and indeed the whole of Central Asia, have been vital meeting points of west and east, a place of changing governments and peoples (particularly in the first millennium AD when kingdoms rose in importance in different parts of the area, only to be supplanted by the rise of another group) and, despite the physical barriers, a corridor, not only for trade but also for the movement of ideas. Religions such as Nestorian Christianity, Manichaeism and, above all, Buddhism and Islam travelled across the deserts permanently to influence the Far East and far western China respectively.

History

The Chinese silk, which gave the trade route its name, was carried by camel trains across the deserts and transported to ancient Rome, although not by Chinese merchants for the loads changed hands in the Pamirs and Persian traders took the cargo onward. Just as porcelain was to puzzle the world less than a thousand years later, silk was a fabulous mystery in the western world where people struggled to reproduce the raw material. Traditionally the Chinese were supposed to have guarded the secret of the manufacture of silk and, later, porcelain; folklore relates how a Chinese princess, sent to marry the King of Khotan in the 5C and forewarned that there was no silk in Khotan, smuggled silk-moth eggs in her piled-up hair and established the silk industry on the far side of the Gobi. The story continues with the smuggling of eggs to Constantinople in 552 by two Persian monks who travelled to China as Christian missionaries. Whether or not this is true, the manufacture of these luxury products was concealed from most travellers for they were made in the hinterland, far from visitors' eyes and, above all, far from the west. Fantastically light and delicate (sometimes considered a bit too light and flimsy for decency; the Roman emperor Tiberius banned men from wearing silk in AD 14), silk was a mystery to its enthusiastic wearers. Pliny described how silk grew, as 'wool' in the 'forests' and Virgil described the harvest, 'the Chinese comb off leaves their delicate down'; not much wider of the mark than a 16C English entrepreneur and would-be silk producer who started a moth farm but was cultivating the wrong moth.

The **Silk Road** started from the Han and Tang capital of Xi'an (known as Chang'an in those times) and led almost due west to Lanzhou and Dunhuang where it divided just beyond Dunhuang at the Yumen guan or 'Jade Gate'. A northern loop took in the fertile oasis towns of Turfan and Hami; the central, and most direct, route passed through Loulan, then on through Kucha and Aksu to Kashgar, while a southern route, following the southern rather than the northern edge of the Taklamakan Desert (or Tarim Basin), passed through Miran, Niya, Khotan and Yarkand before reaching Kashgar. From Kashgar, too, although here we are outside Chinese territory, there were northern and southern routes, through Samarkand and Bokhara or alternatively through Balkh.

For many centuries much of the Silk Road was also a pilgrimage route to India, home of the Buddhist faith. Monks would turn southwards from Yarkand, down through Leh and Srinagar into India in search of sacred texts and images which they carried back to China. Their route, like that of the merchant caravan trains, skirted the edge of the Taklamakan for it was an 'abomination of desolation', believed to be full of demons that led men and animals astray, quite apart from the wind-blown and shifting sands which made it almost impossible to find the way through. The routes were also bounded by high, freezing mountain ranges, the Pamirs to the west, the Tian shan or Heavenly Mountains to the north, and the Kunlun range to the south of the Taklamakan.

The **trade route** was first opened up during the reign of the Han Emperor Wudi (the Martial Emperor). He sent Zhang Qian, an official at his court, on an expedition in 138 BC to seek an alliance with the peoples of Yuezhi (sometimes identified as Indo-Scythians, they later migrated to northwest India and founded the Kushan Kingdom) against the Xiongnu of the steppe who presented a real threat to the westwards expansion of the Han empire.

The Xiongnu are often tentatively identified as Huns; their language was part of the Turkish group. It took Zhang Qian 13 years (which included being taken prisoner twice by the Xiongnu) to get back to the Chinese capital with a wealth of information about the kingdoms of Central Asia. One of his greatest finds were the 'heavenly' horses of Ferghana (just north of Kashgar), larger, faster and stronger than the small native horses the Chinese knew (Prjevalsky's horse, now only to be seen in zoos, I believe), ideal for pursuing Huns. The Han emperor expended many men on expeditions along the Silk Road to acquire these large beasts.

Han Wudi reinforced Chinese control over the Silk Road by extending the Great Wall westward and establishing a series of beacons and garrisons out into the Gobi (where the beacon towers made of tamped earth can still be seen outside Dunhuang) protecting, as far as was possible, the chain of oasis towns where travellers could rest and change their animals before continuing westwards. Chinese control over the area continued during the Tang dynasty when China was at its most cosmopolitan, open to the luxuries of the West (grapes, silver vessels, glass, ivory, coral and amber, saffron, fragrant timbers, parrots, peacocks, leopards and carpets) and relatively liberal about western ideas which came with them, such as the Buddhist, Manichean and Nestorian faiths, all of which were celebrated in Xi'an and other parts of China (the latter on a small scale). Large numbers of non-Chinese traders and craftsmen came to live in Xi'an and many influential citizens had non-Chinese blood, like the General An Lushan and perhaps even the poet Li Bai, who was born in Central Asia.

The end of the Silk Road as a major route of transportation came gradually over the centuries. The decline of the Tang (which collapsed in 907) meant the end of cosmopolitan openness in China, for succeeding dynasties were inward-looking and generally suspicious of the outside world and most of its goods. Yet this was only one factor. The desert moved inexorably and now and then would claim an oasis, such as the settlement at Niya which was explored

(I hesitate to say excavated) by Sir Marc Aurel Stein in 1901, revealing numbers of wooden tablets with clay seals inscribed in Prakrit in *Kharosthi* script and some fine pieces of carved wooden furniture now in the British Museum. Niya had been suddenly abandoned in the 3C AD when the water supply failed. Another factor in the decline of free travel along the Silk Road was the rise of Islam which gradually spread to influence the entire Taklamakan area. In the 9C, too, marauding Tibetans threatened the small pockets of Chinese settlers and it is believed to be in response to this last threat that the library of the great cave-temple complex at Dunhuang was walled up for safety, remaining sealed for some 900 years.

The Silk Road area today remains largely Islamic in faith, inhabited by some of China's 'national minorities', mainly the Uighurs and Kazakhs. The importance of the Uighurs, particularly to the Chinese of the metropolitan area, has been crucial at many times. Inhabiting border areas, they have held the key to national defence but have often been somewhat unamenable to control from distant Peking. The Song and Ming dynasties were too concerned with threats from the north and northeast to try and regain control of the Gobi region but the Qing emperors devoted much of their time, money and military resources to the area. Threatened by the Russian empire, which was interested in territorial expansion, by Uighur uprisings and by the Mongols who were eager to win control of Tibet (with which their shared Lamaist Buddhist faith made a strong link), the Qing were hard pressed to control the area and by the end of the 19C had almost lost it.

The **Kangxi emperor** was keen to take Mongolia into the Chinese empire, a task in which he was helped by dissention between the Eastern and Western Mongols in particular. When, in 1688, an Eleuth or Western Mongol leader sought to conquer the Eastern Mongols in Outer Mongolia, the latter appealed to the Qing court for assistance, which was readily granted. By 1696 the Qing army, personally led by the Kangxi emperor, had beaten the Eleuths and incorporated Outer Mongolia into the empire. The struggle was not over for it was only in 1720 that the Chinese succeeded in eliminating and replacing Eleuth influence in Tibet. The Kangxi emperor's grand son, the Qianlong emperor, had to wage a second war against the Eleuths in 1755–57, his success resulting in the extension of Qing control into northwest Xinjiang. In 1758, the area controlled reached the Pamirs, as it had done nearly 2000 years previously, after the conquest of the Uighurs of Eastern Turkestan.

Later, in 1862, came one of many uprisings against the Qing, that of the Muslims of Gansu and northern Shaanxi, followed by that of Kashgaria and Dzungaria (areas to the south and north of the Tian shan) under **Yakub Beg**, who also moved north towards Urumqi (where his progress was blocked by invading Russians). His rebellion and conquests were only really ended by his death in 1877 and were complicated by the fact that the Russians and the British both supported him against the Qing (Xinjiang being an area involved in the Great Game where both hoped to set up puppet, buffer states against the other). The Chinese managed to take Xinjiang again in 1878 but, as central power declined, so did control over the border regions of Xinjiang and Tibet.

More recent history. In the early years of the 20C and for several decades afterwards, although most of Xinjiang was nominally under Chinese rule, as contemporary travellers', spies' and archaeologists' accounts relate, there were many other contenders for power, as Peter Hopkirk describes in the prologue to his *Setting the East Ablaze: Lenin's Dream of an Empire in Asia* (Oxford University Press, 1986). He starts with Lenin and his ambitions for British India (reached across the Taklamakan Desert) but notes that:

... three other would-be Genghis Khans were to arise in Central Asia, the battlefield of the new Great Game. The most notorious by far was a psychopathic White Russian general named Ungern-Sternberg, 'the Mad Baron', whose dreadful atrocities are still remembered with a shudder in Mongolia ... The next to try his luck was Enver Pasha, Turkey's flamboyant but defeated wartime leader, then in exile in Central Asia ... The last of these dreamers was a young but charismatic warlord called Ma Chung-yin, sometimes known as 'Big Horse'. A Chinese Moslem visionary barely out of his teens, he was to leave a trail of blood across the Gobi desert before fleeing west along the Silk Road in a stolen lorry, pursued by Soviet bombers.

While all this was going on, a minor archaeological 'great game' was being played out in the same area, graphically described by Peter Hopkirk in his first book on the area, *Foreign Devils on the Silk Road: the Search for Lost Cities and Treasures of Chinese Central Asia* (John Murray, London, 1980). In the 'Great Manuscript Race', as he describes it, the Swede Hedin, Sir Marc Aurel Stein, a Hungarian working for the British Government, the Japanese Baron Otani, Paul Pelliot of the Ecole Française d'Extrême-Orient, Von le Coq of the Indian section of the Ethnological Museum in Berlin and (later) Langdon Warner seeking exhibits for the Fogg Museum at Harvard, raced across the desert in search of manuscripts and other buried treasure.

At the same time, two lady missionaries, Mildred Cable and Francesca French, were plodding steadily across the desert, distributing Bibles and taking notes on the warlord General Ma amongst others for their book, *The Gobi Desert* (Hodder and Stoughton, London, 1942), while Peter Fleming and Ella Maillart, a British journalist and a Swiss ski champion, were compelled for reasons of convenience to travel across the Gobi together, a trip recorded separately in *News from Tartary* by Fleming (London 1936) and *Forbidden Journey* by Maillart (London 1937), the title of the latter hinting at one of the fundamental difficulties they encountered.

Even in recent years, the Chinese have found Xinjiang difficult to control. Most of the nationality peoples have cousins across the border which, even if the Russians and Chinese officially close it, does not preclude contact. In the late 1950s, when conditions in China became too hard, some thousands of Kazakhs simply crossed into the Soviet Union, and the problems of racial and religious tension never entirely disappear. Although the Chinese have populated the area, both by means of great state farms (there is a huge sugar-beet state farm and factory out beyond Urumqi, peopled and worked entirely by Shanghainese) and individual settlement (like a Sichuanese taxi-driver in Turfan who had lived there since the 1950s but still did not know enough Uighur to make a satisfactory purchase in a local store), the Uighurs are still numerically superior, if administratively and politically inferior.

Tension occasionally reaches boiling point and incidents involving the military are not unknown. In the years of greater relaxation since the Cultural Revolution the Uighurs are now abandoning the romanised alphabet the

Chinese helpfully insisted upon during the 1960s and 1970s in favour of a return to the old Arabic script which is familiar to the old and to the post-Cultural Revolution young but something of a problem for those educated in the period 1966–76. The Islamic faith is still extremely strong, perhaps partly as a rallying point against the Chinese, as Lamaist Buddhism serves in Tibet, and the Chinese authorities are torn between a desire to control it and the knowledge that they are powerless to do so if they wish to avoid more confrontation in the border areas. They are quite reasonably worried by the rise in Islamic fundamentalism in Iran and Afghanistan, which in Central Asian terms are not far away.

Owing to the occasional trouble in the area, the Silk Road is one part of China, like Tibet, that is occasionally closed to tourists.

Tourist itineraries in the Silk Road area are now expanding. Some take in Lanzhou, Dunhuang, Turfan and Urumqi, all on the northern silk route, while others continue as far as Kashgar, often taking in part of the southern silk route via Hetian (Khotan). It is possible to continue from Kashgar over the Pamirs into Pakistan (by bus), or to cross by rail or air from the some of the major cities like Alma Ata in Kazakhstan.

The railway line from Turfan to Korla has been extended to Kashgar but most travel beyond Urumqi is still by bus. Tourist buses are reasonably comfortable, public buses are extremely uncomfortable (unpadded and overcrowded seats) and distances are enormous so travellers should be prepared for discomfort and very long hours spent bouncing over rough roads, with stops in somewhat primitive oasis hotels.

Lanzhou

Lanzhou, capital city of Gansu province, lies on the upper reaches of the Yellow River (Huang he). Now a major transport and industrial centre, Lanzhou was once a stopping place on the old Silk Road, near the end of the Great Wall proper, whose major westernmost fort is that at Jiayuguan, some 450km northwest of Lanzhou.

Practical information

Getting there
By air
The airport is c 72km outside town (the trip can take up to 90 minutes by car or bus). The airport buses stop on Dongang xi lu, near the Lanzhou Fandian. There are daily flights to Peking, Xi'an and Jiayuguan, fairly frequent departures for Dunhuang, Guangzhou and Shanghai and departures twice or three times a week to Chengdu, Guilin, Taiyuan, Urumqi and Xining.

By train
Lanzhou is on the Xi'an–Urumqi line and it is not uncommon for tour groups travelling out on the Silk Road to stop in Lanzhou.

Where to stay
One of the solid old hotels, the *Lanzhou Fandian*, ☎ 0931 841 6321, is on Donggang xi lu lu in the centre of town. Just up the road is the luxury *Jincheng Hotel*, ☎ 0931

841 6638; right out in the west of town is another big, old Russian-style hotel, the *Youyi Binguan* (Friendship Hotel) on Xinji xi lu, ☎ 0931 233 051.

The discovery of oil in the desert has brought petrochemical industries to Lanzhou which is now a major industrial centre with two pleasant parks set on hillsides and the Yellow River flowing between. It also has a very good Provincial Museum. A possible day excursion from Lanzhou is to the Buddhist Caves at Bingling si (see p 508).

Wuquan shan

In the south of the city, on the far side of the railway line, is Wuquan shan (Five Springs Mountain), some of whose springs descend the mountain in waterfalls. The steep slopes with rocks and buildings are quite impressive, containing all the required elements of a Chinese garden (water, rocks, pavilions, plants) but in an unusually dramatic setting.

> The mountain, with its abundant water supply, is said to have been where the Han dynasty general Huo Qubing (whose tomb can be visited at Xi'an) encamped with his cavalry in 120 BC on his way out to the west. Folklore credits him with the discovery of the springs, dashing his sword against the rocks until water poured out to water his troops and horses.

The major buildings on the mountain include the **Chongqing si** (Temple of Lofty Celebrations), founded in 1372, while the Qianfo ge (Tower of the Thousand Buddhas), Mani si (Mani Temple), Dizang si (Ksitigarbha Temple) and the Sanjiao dong (Cave of the Three Teachings) are all later, and much restored after 1868.

In the Chongqing si is preserved an iron bell, cast in 1202. It is 3m high, with a diameter of 2m and weighs nearly 10,000 *jin* (a *jin* is half a kilogram) with a longish inscription cast on it, beginning: 'When the immortals hear it they rejoice, when ghosts hear it, they cease their wickedness. It strikes at the gates of hell and saves from a myriad sufferings ....'

Five Springs Mountain was opened in 1955. It is one of the most interesting modern parks in China because of the rather imaginative use of concrete in both traditional and modernistic garden forms. Decorative gates, a major design feature of traditional gardens, are made in brick and concrete, some pure moon gates, others more fanciful: quatrefoil (or plum blossom) moon gates, moon gates with concrete lotuses set in a vase neck above the circular opening (so that the whole looks like a vase with two ring handles on the neck, filled with lotus flowers), a strange opening in a wall framed with entwined blossoming cherry trees in concrete, and so on.

On the north bank of the Yellow River, opposite the Iron Bridge, is the **Baita shan** (White Pagoda Mountain). The bridge (Tie qiao) which leads to it is said to be situated at the oldest bridging point on the Yellow River for it was first built during the Ming in 1368–98.

At a crucial point on the Silk Route, the Yellow River had to be crossed. According to the *Lan zhou fu zhi* (*Gazetteer of Lanzhou*) of the late 19C, in the past this was done from the late Ming by making a floating bridge of 24 boats chained together across the river, a method which was set up every spring and abandoned every winter. In winter, when the ice was thick enough the 'ice bridge' method was used (people simply crossed the frozen river), and it was the latter method that the Han armies had used to get across to the Gobi Desert and Central Asia. In 1907 the floating bridge was replaced by a proper iron bridge with concrete supports (based on 'foreign construction methods') which lasted for 30 years. The bridge was restored and improved in 1954.

The White Pagoda Mountain takes its name from the White Pagoda (of the Lamaist stupa type) on top of the mountain. This was constructed as part of a Buddhist temple during the Yuan, restored between 1450 and 1456 and again in 1980. It is some 17m high and stands amongst many other temple halls built against the mountain on terraces. The whole area is now a park.

The **Gansu Provincial Museum** (Gansu sheng bowuguan) is in the west of the town on Xixin xi lu, opposite the Youyi fandian (Friendship Hotel). Its major collections include a tremendous display of the Yangshao or red pottery of the late Neolithic period, of which many sites have been excavated in Gansu.

One of the pioneers of Neolithic archaeology in China was a Swedish engineer called J.G. Andersson, a mining consultant employed by the Chinese government in the early years of the Republic who also discovered painted pottery in Henan province. In 1923–24 he found a cemetery area in the Banshan Hills in eastern Gansu where the dead were buried with great red

THE SILK ROAD

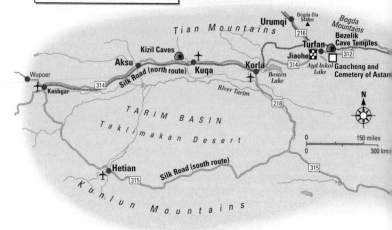

pottery urns decorated mainly in black, with some white, in swirling bands of geometric patterns along the broadest part of the body up to the neck. He later excavated similar vessels in the vicinity of Lanzhou.

The Gansu painted pottery culture is thought to date from c 3000–1850 BC; it is later than the metropolitan painted pottery culture (which begins c 5000 BC) and is presumed to have been brought from eastern China by settlers. The museum contains the finest group of these late Neolithic pots in China. There is also a major display of Silk Road artefacts, including the wood slips used for documentation and records by the soldiers of the Han garrisons and beacons along the Silk Road.

Tombs in Gansu of different periods have yielded various interesting finds: Western Zhou bronze harness pieces and fine Han bronzes. There is a cortège of 14 chariots, 17 horses and 45 attendants from the Eastern Han (AD 25–220) Tomb of General Zhang in Wuwei which was also the site of the Eastern Han tomb which contained the famous 'flying horse' of Gansu.

Slightly later tombs in the Jiayuguan area (c 220–316) were lined with fine painted bricks with scenes from daily life including much butchery of oxen and pigs, chicken plucking, as well as agricultural scenes. One of the similar tombs discovered near Jiuquan (not far from Jiayuguan) has been reassembled in the museum's garden.

The Red Army's Long March (which did not involve Lanzhou) is commemorated in a large exhibit and there is also a mammoth skeleton, found in the Yellow River basin in 1973.

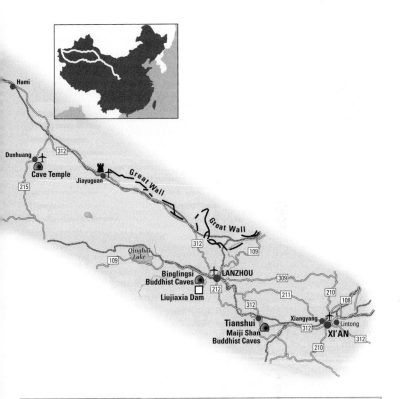

The Flying Horse of Gansu

A small bronze horse at full gallop, one hoof delicately mounted on a swallow's back; the piece was exhibited in the great travelling exhibition of Chinese archaeology seen in London, Paris and New York in the early 1970s (London in 1973; see William Watson, 'The Genius of China', London, *Times Newspapers*, 1973). It is interesting to note that the title chosen in London caused absolute fury at the time in China because 'genius' was considered to be a class-ridden concept in the Cultural Revolution period when egalitarianism ruled.

The 'flying horse' is one of the many major archaeological discoveries whose actual whereabouts is the subject of much discussion: like the Mawangdui banner of Changsha, the original may be in the museum vaults or perhaps in Peking—the exhibit is almost certainly an exact replica.

Bingling si

A rather long day's excursion from Lanzhou is to the Buddhist caves at Bingling si c 100km from the city. The journey includes some two hours by bus and nearly two hours by boat. If you go with a tourist group, whether a foreign one or a tour group arranged from Lanzhou by the *China Travel Service* (*CITS*), you will almost certainly stop at the **Liujiaxia Dam** en route where, as long as the water level allows (and this is most certain in autumn), you embark in a boat for the caves.

Liujiaxia Dam

The Liujia Gorge Dam is one of five dams planned with the help of Soviet advisors in the mid 1950s. It is one of the biggest hydroelectric power stations in China and was completed in 1974. It has five turbo-generators, the first of which began operation in 1969, the last in 1974 and the generating equipment (as may be gathered from the operating dates) is not Russian but Chinese. The barrage itself (147m high, 840m long) was finished much earlier, within the period of Sino-Soviet co-operation which ended in 1960. The output is now 5.7 billion kilowatt hours, more than the entire national electrical output before 1949 and power is transmitted to Lanzhou and Tianshui, to Xining (capital of Qinghai province upstream) and to the Wei River area in neighbouring Shaanxi province.

A major problem in the construction of all the Soviet dams on the Yellow River is silting, the yellow earth (loess) it carries giving it its name and the subsequent flooding its other name, 'China's Sorrow'. The river brings more silt with it than any other in the world (its silt concentration being, for example, 34 times higher than that of the Nile) and this problem has dogged the dam builders anxious both to exploit and control its flow. The nearby Sanmenxia Dam's reservoir was almost completely clogged by the time the barrage was finished and the dam had to be rebuilt.

The **Bingling si** (Temple of the Bright Spirit) **Caves** spread along 2km of the stone cliff on the north bank of the Yellow River, some 50km west of the dam and accessible only by water. There are 34 caves and 149 niches containing (for those numerically inclined) 679 stone-carved Buddha figures, 82 of clay and 900 square metres of wall painting. The largest Buddha figure is 27m high and there are also four clay pagodas and one in stone.

The earliest caves were carved in the Northern Wei (368–534) and work continued through to the Ming and Qing, with the greatest period of activity being the Tang dynasty and the Tang cave carving, probably of Cave 169, being recorded in the *Notes to the Water Classic* (*Shui jing zhu*), where the cave's dimensions tally with those described. The style of carving resembles that of contemporary carvings at Yumgang and Longmen.

Much of the wall painting dates from the Northern Song and Ming and it is most impressive in Caves 3 (where the figures are Tang in date), 4, 10 and 11, where a landscape with palm trees is depicted, Caves 70, 82 (Song paintings) and 114 (immediately to the left of the largest Buddha figure), where the somewhat crude paintings date from the Tang. The largest Buddha is a Maitreya figure rather similar to that at Leshan in Sichuan and probably Tang in date. Maitreya, the Buddha of the Future, is usually depicted seated with feet on the ground, as here.

Jiayuguan

Jiayuguan, the site of the **fort** that marks the western extremity of the Great Wall proper, is *c* 600km northwest of Lanzhou at the far end of the Gansu corridor (the province of Gansu is squashed between mountains which force it into a narrow pass). It is on the main railway line from Xi'an through Lanzhou westwards to Urumqi.

Where to stay
In the centre of town is the *Jiayaguan Binguan*, ☎ 622 6983, fax 622 7174.

The fort was constructed from tamped earth in 1372 under the Ming. Whether seen simply from the train across the flat desert or close to, it is a spectacular construction, the same colour as the surrounding land but with long lines of battlements from which elegant, tiled roofed and red pillared gate towers rise. The circumference of the fortress' walls is 733m, enclosing 33,500 square metres; the walls are some 10m high. The fort has been substantially reconstructed (1988) with the gate towers being substantially renewed: they are very much in the same style as the surviving gates in Peking like the Desheng Gate, Qian men and the Drum Tower.

Today, with its elegant and brightly painted gate-towers and the proliferation of tourist 'attractions' (dressing up clothes and horses to be photographed in and on), the fort has lost some of its historical significance. Traditionally, it was the last place in China and exiles, soldiers off to guard the frontiers, pilgrims and merchants felt, as they past it, that they had left China and entered unsafe, unknown barbarian territory.

20km northwest of Jiayuguan, and best reached by taxi, are the stone-carvings of **Hei shan** (Black Mountain). Over about 1km, figures have been carved into the side of the mountam, about 3m above ground level. The figures are depicted dancing, riding horses, shooting with bows and arrows, hunting and at military drill. There are no scenes of agriculture and on the basis of this, together with the stress on hunting and the absence of knives and spears in the hunting and military scenes, they are thought to be carvings of some of the local nomadic peoples, perhaps the Qiang, a minority group of herdsmen found in the northwest. First mentioned in oracle bone inscriptions, they flourished in Gansu, Qinghai and Sichuan from the Han to the Song after which they seem to have disappeared through intermarriage with Chinese. They were charitably known by the Chinese as one of the Five Barbarians and may have been connected with the (later) Tanguts. Other possible groups are the Xiongnu (Huns) or the Dayuezhi, another minority group that flourished in the Han period around the Dunhuang area. Whoever painted them, the rock paintings must presumably date from about the Han period or between the Han and Tang.

The painted bricks (of which there are many examples in the Lanzhou Museum) that lined local tombs of the Western Jin (AD 265–316) were mainly unearthed *c* 20km northeast of Jiayuguan town. In 1972 a group of eight tombs was excavated, six of which had wall paintings of agricultural, herding, hunting, building, cooking, banqueting and musical scenes. One feature is the depiction of mulberry trees and sericulture which proves that mulberries and silk production had 'moved west of the river' (i.e. beyond the Yellow River into the far west) by this period. There are also depictions of ploughs with two yoked oxen. Tomb One was that of a local notable of the Yin family which, according to the *Jin shu* (*History of the Jin*) was famous in the west.

Maiji shan

Maiji shan (Corn Rick Mountain) is the site of a major Buddhist cave carving group in Tianshui xian, c 30km southeast of Tianshui, a town on the major Xi'an–Urumqi railway c 300km southeast of Lanzhou.

The mountain is an amazing tump, reminiscent of a haystack, hence its name. Of all the Buddhist sites and holy mountains in China it most resembles Sumeru, the mythical mountain of the Buddhists which rises from the seven seas as a single peak.

Getting there

The caves are best reached by bus from Tianshui. All arrangements to visit the caves must be made in advance and a picnic taken as there is nothing provided at the caves. The basic admission charge does not cover some of the 'special caves' for which an extra charge per cave of 300 to 400 yuan is levied; otherwise the caves which have locked doors will not be opened for you. The climbs are somewhat dizzying and precarious and many have to be viewed through iron grilles. A good torch is essential.

Where to stay

There is no accommodation at Maiji shan so travellers must stay in Tianshui where there are several adequate three-star (Chinese stars) hotels, including the **Tianshai Binguan**, 5 Yingbin lu, ☎ 821 4242.

History

The earliest inscription on Maiji shan is dated AD 502 but, according to literary records, the first caves were carved out during the Later Qin (384–417), a short-lived dynasty, one of the Sixteen Kingdoms (304–439), founded in the northwest by the Qiang minority. Carving of caves and images continued during the Wei, when some of the balustrades were repaired, and the Northern Zhou (557–581), when the local military commander Li Chongxin had seven caves carved out in memory of his father. A contemporary poet described the mountain where: 'The walls are covered with inscriptions from holy texts, multiple images of Buddha fill the niches....' The caves were carved some 30–80m above the foot of the mountain and reached by a series of wooden steps and ladders. The cliff face was split in two (east and west) by an earthquake in 734.

There are now 54 surviving caves on the east cliff, 140 on the west, dating from the Northern Wei (386–584) to the Qing dynasty; over 7000 Buddha figures either in clay or stone and 1300 square metres of wall painting. Surprisingly, there was little activity during the Tang, although the poet Du Fu passed by in 759 and wrote a poem on mountain temples: 'High narrow paths, Musk deer sleeping amongst bamboo and cockatoos amongst golden peaches ... Cells ranged across the hanging cliffs, Tiered chambers to the very peak....'

The largest figure is a 16m high Amitabha Buddha which now stands exposed to the air in the middle of the series of galleries high up on the side of the mountain. It stands in a major triad with Avalokitesvara (Guanyin) on the right and Mahasthamapraptna on the left.

The **Western Cliff Caves** have apparently been left untouched since the Tang and Song and date mainly from the Northern Wei–Northern Zhou (4C–6C AD). When the famous painter Zhang Daqian visited Maiji shan in 1943 he could only see the eastern caves because he would have had to pay for the construction of ladders and galleries to reach the western caves. In **Cave 100** the direct influence of the Hellenistic West is apparent in the features, shoulders and general bearing of the Northern Wei figures; much of the early Buddhist iconography in China is Hellenistic, influenced by Gandharan sculptures by way of Central Asia. The light treatment of drapery and slender bodies of the figures are Chinese rather than Hellenistic features.

Cave 133 is recognised as Maiji shan's finest, containing sculptures and 18 engraved stones, the latter in a hard stone which must have been brought to the mountain from elsewhere. The stone engravings date from the Western Wei and Northern Zhou. One is particularly graceful, a depiction of a Buddha flanked by two others with hands raised and sleeves and garments falling in elegant folds. In the centre of the cave are two standing Buddha figures of the Tang dynasty. **Cave 121** has two clay Buddhas apparently Western Wei (534–550) in date and **Cave 165** is a Song work (960–1279) with very realistically depicted figures.

The **eastern side** of the mountain has always been easier of access and the caves are in poorer condition, with more restoration. **Cave 4** has apparently escaped restoration, although it is so tiny that the fine wall paintings are difficult to see properly. They are probably late Tang or early Song in date with some fine Bodhisattvas and pavilions against an ornamental ground. **Cave 7,** known as Niu er tang (Calf Cave or Cave of the Son of the Cow), contains a well-observed statue of a calf.

Notable caves include **13** with the colossi, probably dating from the Sui and repaired in the Ming, surrounded by a great number of square holes in the cliff face for galleries and protective buildings which have since disappeared. **Cave 4** has a magnificent Song guardian figure to the west: **Cave 72a** has wall paintings from the 5C and **Cave 93** has a mysterious grouping of the historic Buddha with Maitreya (with pendant legs), mysterious since they are never normally associated. It may be that the sculptor has exercised license in borrowing the common Wei grouping of Sakyamuni with Prabhutaratna and this is not uncharacteristic of the rather free treatment of iconography often found in China.

Cave 102 has a very fine Wei seated Buddha with the characteristic Wei long head, small features and beautifully draped gown. In the open niche of **Cave 169** there is a pretty Sui Maitreya and there are elegant figures of very young worshippers on the left and right walls of **Cave 123** (6C). In **Cave 127** the halo of the seated Buddha is most unusual—a lotus halo with floral scrolling (reminiscent of Tang silver decoration) is surrounded by a halo of elegant little *apsareses* (Buddhist angels). **Cave 133** is full of stelae; no-one knows quite why they have been gathered into the one cave but it is a fine collection of 6C carvings. The Bodhisattvas outside **Cave 191** are remarkably elegant (and of uncertain date).

Although there are fewer of them, and they are less well-preserved and less well-known, the cave paintings at Maiji shan have been compared usefully with those at Dunhuang, which is generally held to be a more important site.

By contrast, the clay carvings are generally more lively than those at Dunhuang. Maijishan is set in some delightful scenery, with trails through the woods, and with its rickety ladders and balconies has a dramatic charm of its own.

Dunhuang

Dunhuang, a small oasis town in Gansu province, is the most important site on the Silk Road itinerary. Its name, 'Blazing Beacon', is old, dating back to the Han dynasty when it was sited at the virtual end of the line of communication beacons and fortifications of the Great Wall that stretched west from the last major fort on the wall (at Jiayuguan, near Lanzhou).

Dunhuang's importance lies in the cave-temple complex outside the town which contains the greatest grouping of early Chinese Buddhist painting to survive. Once the last stop in China for the great pilgrim monks of the Tang on their way to India in search of sutras and sculptures, the cave-temple, carved into a cliff with a small stream running in front of it, served as a lodging for them but was also a major Buddhist centre and a storehouse of local documents and papers.

Practical information

Getting there
Dunhuang is about two hours by tourist bus (over three hours in a public bus) from the nearest station, Liuyuan, on the Lanzhou–Urumqi line. For the **cave-temple complex**, tourist buses leave daily at 08.00 from the *Dunhuang Binguan* (see Where to stay).

By air

There are daily flights to and from Jiayuguan and Lanzhou and three flights a week from Urumqi and Xi'an. The airport closes during the fairly frequent sand storms.

By bus

The tougher individual traveller may well use buses in the Gobi: 12 hours to Golmud (in Qinghai) or nine hours to Jiayuguan.

Where to stay
When I first visited Dunhuang, it was very much a one-street town, although in the 1930s it had boasted the sobriquet of 'little Peking' and had been one of the most sophisticated and lively towns on the trade route. In the late 1970s, there was an impressive array of traffic signs hung over the main cross-roads, forbidding hand-tractors, horse-carts, hooting and U-turns but there was practically no traffic to obey or contravene these regulations. Bustle has returned to Dunhuang and there are a number of hotels and a night market on Dong da jie which is lined with souvenir shops and restaurants with names like 'Manhattan' and 'Shirley's Cafe'. There are several hotels, including the *Dunhuang Binguan*, on Yangguan dong lu, ☎ 882 2415, fax 882 2309, the *Dunhuang International Hotel* on Mingshan lu, ☎ 0937 882 8638, and the *Silk Road Dunhuang Hotel* on Dunyue lu, ☎ 883 2088, fax 888 2086. There is also a two-star hotel at the caves themselves, the *Mogao Hotel*, which would facilitate early and late viewing.

Equipment

Everywhere in China a torch is a very useful thing but it is essential to take a very good one when visiting caves filled with paintings and not otherwise illuminated.

Charges

Unless you are part of a specialist group which has made particular arrangements, the 'special caves' will not be opened unless an extra charge of 800 yuan per person is paid.

DUNHUANG

N

0   200 yards
0   200 metres

SHAZHOU BEI LU

P.O.

Dunhuang
Museum

CAAC
Office

Dunhuang
Hotel

YANGGUAN DONG LU

YANGGUAN XI LU

YANGGUAN ZHONG LU

Night
Market

Buses for
Mogao Caves

Airport & Mogao Caves

WENMIAO XIANG

MINGSHAN LU

SHAZHOU NAN LU

HUANGCHENG DONG LU

HESHUI LU

XINJIAN LU

Buses to Liuyuan

XIYU JIE

Long Distance
Bus Station

HUANGCHENG NAN LU

Dang River

CITS
Office

International
Hotel

History

Dunhuang was made a prefecture in 117 BC under Han Wudi and was then on the very edge of 'China' or the territory roughly controlled by China. Some of the beacons made of tamped yellow earth can be seen on the road between Dunhuang and the railway station at Liuyuan: these were part of the Han extension of the Great Wall (whose westernmost fort is at Jiayuguan), used for signalling between garrisons.

Buddhism entered China sometime around the beginning of the Christian era, making its way along the Silk Route which passed through the Dunhuang oasis. In AD 366 the **first caves** were carved by Buddhist monks in a long cliff some 25km outside the oasis town. The caves are known to the Chinese as Mogao ku (the 'Mogao Caves', *mogao* being an old name for the administrative district during the Tang) or Qianfo dong, 'Thousand Buddha Caves'. The conglomerate cliff into which the caves were cut was an oasis in itself for the River Da, fed from glaciers in the distant mountains, runs along in front of the cliff, in the past enabling a sizable community of monks and pilgrims to live in the caves.

As the caves were carved out, between 366 and the last years of the 10C, they were fitted with **wall paintings** and **stucco figures**, all of which were extremely well-preserved, partly because they were left virtually forgotten and undisturbed for nearly 1000 years and partly because of the dry climate of the desert. The painters who worked in the caves ranged from well-known figures who travelled out to the oasis to local jobbing-painters. Their rates of pay and supply of materials have been described in some of the manuscripts found in the caves: famous painters were often paid 'by the painting' while others were on daily (or weekly or monthly) rates and some of the more expensive pigments used were measured out carefully and their distribution recorded.

'Mass-production' techniques were used, especially in some of the Thousand Buddha friezes. Figures were drawn on paper and the outlines pricked out. The paper pounces were then placed on the wall and red chalk blown or rubbed through the holes to produce a dotted outline which could be reproduced *ad infinitum*; some of these pattern pounces survive in the Stein collections in the British Museum and British Library and in the Pelliot Collection in Paris (Bibliothèque Nationale de France and Musée Guimet). A later step was the production of small stamps (presumably of clay, perhaps metal) of Buddha figures which could similarly be repeated endlessly. This repetition of figures probably had quite a lot to do with the beginnings of printing and most of the earliest surviving Chinese examples of printing come from Dunhuang.

Despite its distance from metropolitan China, it is clear that famous painters were happy to come and work in the caves during their period of pre-eminence in the Tang. For much of the 1000 years after the fall of the Tang, however, Dunhuang was known by the name of Shazhou, 'Sand City', a more appropriate description of the oasis that had slipped from prominence into desert oblivion. As manuscripts discovered in the caves testify, Dunhuang was an extremely important centre, from the 4C to the 10C. Although distant, it was by no means cut off from metropolitan China for the monks had a ready supply of good paper (still probably quite rare and expensive in the 4C and 5C) made in central China on which devoutly to copy sutras. Fragments of calendars printed in the capital Chang'an and in Sichuan have also been found in the library.

Dunhuang's importance as a **Buddhist centre** survived the 8C Tang persecution of Buddhism, perhaps because of its distance from Chang'an, but it did not survive for long. As the Tang declined, it was isolated and threatened by invading Tibetans, by the spread of Islam in Chinese Central Asia and by the Tanguts, or Xi Xia, a people of the Tibetan language group, who used a form of script based on Chinese characters and who founded the Xi Xia Kingdom in northwest China (Gansu province and neighbouring areas), 1038–1368. It was probably in response to the last threat that, before they themselves dispersed, the remaining monks at the Dunhuang Cave temples closed up one cave which they had filled with documents from the temples that were not to be rediscovered until the last years of the 19C. The documents, virtually all written on paper, consist mainly of Buddhist sutras copied out as an act of devotion by monks and include a dated sutra copied on paper in AD 406 (some 800 years before paper was widely known in Europe). The last date on a document is 1004.

Although the Buddhist sutras often provide dates and form the majority of the manuscripts from Dunhuang, there are also a very large number of secular documents including census returns, tax documents and bills of sale (including some relating to slaves). These may have been placed in the temple for safe-keeping, rather as one might deposit important papers in a bank today. Although the majority are manuscripts on paper, the cave library has also thrown up the world's earliest printed 'book', a paper scroll some 8m long, printed with the text of the *Diamond Sutra* and with a colophon giving a date of AD 868. Slightly earlier examples of printing have survived in Japan (and possibly Korea) but they are simple, stamped incantations, whereas the *Diamond Sutra* from Dunhuang is a long, complete text, with beautifully carved characters and a complex frontispiece.

The technique used was woodblock printing, with one block for the frontispiece and all the other sheets of paper printed from blocks carved with text. A scribe first wrote out the text on thin paper which was laid face down on a block of (probably) pearwood and the text cut out. Produced some 500 years before the first printing in Europe, the *Diamond Sutra* is clearly not the first printed book made in China for the elegance of the frontispiece and calligraphy demonstrates that it must have been the product of a long period of development; it is a lucky survivor of the dry, dark walled up cave. The *Diamond Sutra* was purchased by Sir Marc Aurel Stein and is now in the British Library in London.

The contents of the **cave library** are now scattered about the world, the majority of the manuscripts being in the British Library, the Pelliot Collection in the Bibliothèque Nationale in Paris, the Academy of Sciences in St Petersburg, and in the **National Library of China** in Peking, with some ex-Otani examples now in Scandinavia. Many of the banner paintings on silk and canvas are now in the British Museum and the Musée Guimet in Paris.

Stein was the first westerner to reach the caves (in 1907) followed by Pelliot and Otani. Stein found that the caves were being looked after by a self-appointed curator, a Taoist priest called Wang Yuanlu, who had discovered the hidden library and who spent his time collecting money to restore the caves' sculptures. After much bargaining Stein persuaded the priest to let him buy silken painted banners (now in the British Museum, London) and manuscripts with money that Wang was to use for his restoration work. Stein was in a hurry and, knowing no Chinese, although he had a Chinese helper with him, bought in bulk. The collection he brought back to England, consisting of some 7000 virtually complete scrolls and a similar number of fragments, consisted mainly of copies of major sutras, of little interest in terms of content, although the paper, ink and calligraphy, especially of the dated items, has been invaluable in establishing a chronology and revealing the history of writing, paper-making and the book. But his bulk buy happened to include the *Diamond Sutra*, other printed items including very rare calendars (some of which were privately printed in the early 10C in defiance of a law prohibiting the private publication of calendars and almanacs) and a number of secular texts which are still providing scholars with research material. Paul Pelliot, a sinologist, made a more careful selection so that the Paris collection is full of precious items.

Because of these western intrusions there are few documents to be seen at Dunhuang, although some copies are displayed in the local museum, but the caves still contain a wealth of statuary and painting, mainly from the Wei to the end of the Tang (with some later over-painting and additions by such as Wang Yuanlu). The paintings are on the walls and ceilings of caves carved out of the conglomerate cliff. The surfaces were plastered with mud, then successive layers of plaster, dung and animal hair or straw. The surface was then smoothed and dressed with white kaolin (china clay) to provide a smooth surface for painting. Pigments were mixed with water and painted onto the dry plaster surface; the major pigment colours were malachite green, azurite blue, orpiment yellow, iron oxide or earth red, cinnabar vermillion, red ochre, kaolin white, white lead, lampblack (using soot from oil lamps) as well as powdered and leaf gold and silver. These same pigments were used to paint the statues in the caves. Chemical changes have occurred, especially in the earlier caves of the Wei and Sui periods: pink flesh tones have oxidised to dark grey and brown, and the dark, Rouault-like outlines to some of the figures were originally pale, perhaps invisible. The figures in the caves were made in different ways: smaller, free-standing figures were probably made on a wooden frame, wrapped in straw and plastered, while the figures on the walls and pillars were roughly rock-cut and then plastered.

The caves were excavated from AD 366 by monks who carved themselves plain caves to live in at the northern (right-hand) end of the cliff. Most of them are square and some of the earlier caves still have a square stone pillar in the centre, which is carved with figures and provides a focus for perambulating, clockwise meditation (as do central sculptures). They either have a door to the outside or a passage to an antechapel leading to the cliff face. The whole of the interior, every bit of wall and ceiling, was painted with icons, scenes from the life of the Buddha, paradise paintings and donor portraits in a palette dominated by green, blue, black and white with some reds (although more reds appear on silken banners), almost blinding to the viewer. There are various forms to the ceilings of the cave, some are 'tent-shaped' (in an inverted V), although most are lantern-shaped or coffered, with a series of smaller squares, one on top of the other, each set at an angle to the last.

The cliff face was limited in size; by the end of the Tang there was no space left to carve new caves so 'later' caves are reworkings of earlier ones, raising a dating problem that is eternal to China. A cave may be described as 'Wei' but have a large number of much later figures in it and it is difficult to know how far the earlier date remains valid. Of the surviving caves, 23 are described as Wei (Northern Wei 386–534, Western Wei 535–557), 95 as Sui (581–618), 213 as Tang (618–907), 33 from the Five Dynasties (907–960), 98 as Song (960–1279), three are Tangut or Xi Xia and nine date from the Yuan.

The caves

Access to the upper caves may have been easier in the past for wind and sand erosion have affected much of the façade but wooden ladders and balconies must have existed from very early on. These have now been largely replaced by pebble-dash and concrete (safer), although there is still a nine-storey wooden pagoda-like building rising in the centre of the cliff in front of Cave 96 which houses a 33m high Buddha.

- Although there are hundreds of caves, only some 40 are generally open to the public. Those in the centre of the cliff are amongst the earliest, while those to each end are roughly the latest. Scholars and specialists may be able to have access to others granted through contacts with the Bureau of Cultural Relics or the local Research Centre; any group of people hoping to see specific caves other than those listed should apply well in advance through their host organisation; for a greater chance of success apply to a relevant specialist organisation, although the considerable charges mentioned above may still be levied. It should be remembered that long-term conservation of the caves becomes more and more difficult as more visitors come and breathe in them, brush against the walls and allow light and sand in. Closure of the caves is in the interest of their preservation. In recent years, the Getty Conservation Institute has been working with the local curators on the conservation of the wall-paintings.

The caves are closed for lunch and quite early in the afternoon (opening hours being c 08.30–11.30 and 14.00–16.00). Many groups return to Dunhuang for lunch but it is possible to eat just outside the cave complex entrance where you will also find a good *Research and Exhibition Centre* (open daily 09.00–17.00, separate entrance fee). There, the most impressive exhibits are the seven replica caves (3, 217, 220, 249, 275, 285 and 419) which allow you to see the colours of the paintings in bright illumination and understand the construction more easily. The reproductions are of a high standard and there are English language captions.

Abbot Wang's old house is currently being restored and will contain an exhibition about his life.

Caves known to have been open recently are listed below in rough chronological order from the Northern Wei to the Xi Xia or Tangut period, 1036–1227.

Chinese art historians divide the Tang period caves into the following divisions: Early Tang 618–712; High Tang 712–781; Middle Tang 781–848; Late Tang 848–907.

Northern Wei

Cave 246 This cave is Northern Wei in form only; the wall paintings and figures are of the Xi Xia or Tangut period (early 11C). The cave is square with the central pillar and has an inverted V ceiling with lotus flowers.

Cave 257 Another Northern Wei cave with pillar (with a Buddha in the niche with a very elaborately painted halo), this is famous for the unrestored wall-paintings depicting the *jataka* (or 'birth story'—stories about the previous life of the historical Buddha) of the Deer King.

The story, which is depicted at the back of the cave on the west wall, rather confusingly starts at both ends, as it were, and finishes in the middle, its episodes divided by saw-toothed mountains (one of the earliest landscape depictions surviving in China). An interesting feature is the deep red used as a background colour which occurs in the *jataka*, for the treacherous man explains that the deer is to be found 'within yonder clump of flowering sal and mango, where the ground is as red as cochineal' and apparently the earth around Benares is a deep red colour. The artist was presumably working with the text in mind.

The Deer King

The nine-coloured Deer King rescued a man (shown wearing an Indian *dhoti*) from drowning in a river but made the man promise to tell no-one. The Queen of Benares wanted the skin of a nine-coloured deer; the man told the King of Benares where to find the deer but it was alerted to the danger by a swallow and explained the treachery to the King of Benares. The Deer King (representing Buddha) stands quite unafraid. The man who betrayed him falls ill and is depicted covered in spots before he dies.

Other wall paintings include Northern Wei Buddhist angels (*apsareses*) vigorous, blackened figures with looped drapery and haloes, flying amongst bands of flame. There is also a fine depiction of a garden and garden buildings (used by architectural historians). Figures sit on cross-legged stools in an open-fronted hall in a walled garden fitted with clumps of flowers. Beside the hall is a four-storey tower of a slightly impossible type; the artist has not quite mastered the intricacies of structure, although the style is credible. Each storey has a roof (like that of the pavilion) with curled acroteria at the end of the ridge, between which the next storey rises, although the combination of ridge acroteria and upper storey is unlikely. In other construction details the tower is exactly like the ceramic burial models of towers found widely during the Han and suggests the continuity of the form, as well as putting it in a context.

Amongst the **sculpture**, a meditating Bodhisattva with one leg crossed over the other and one hand held pensively to the chin shows strong Indian influence in the bodily form and especially the face. The narrow, almost hooked nose and chiselled, curved lips are in the Indian tradition, while more characteristic Northern Wei figures have slightly block-shaped heads, high, thin arched eyebrows and rather tiny smiling lips and eyes.

Cave 259   A Buddha figure in this cave is very characteristic of the Wei. Seated with three folds of its lower garment concealing the lower part of the body, the figure is slightly stiff and upright with a block-shaped head, curving linear eyebrows and small, slightly self-satisfied features. One of the earliest caves, this does show strong Indian influence in the form of the niches with their elegant, wide and lightly pointed arches and Buddhas with very Indian features.

The major figures are a pair (reminiscent of the common pairing of small Northern Wei Buddhist bronzes), the historic Buddha and Prabhubaratna, the 'ancient' Buddha who had been in Nirvana for long but who reappeared to hear the historic Buddha, Sakyamuni, preach the Lotus sutra. His presence revealed that Nirvana did not mean annihilation and also affirmed that the Lotus doctrine was the Buddha-gospel. The cave's ceiling resembles a tiled ceiling with beams.

Western Wei (535–556)
Cave 249   The major Buddha figure of Maitreya (the Buddha of the future) shown, as almost always, sitting with both feet firmly on the ground, has been altered, the head and hands replaced during the late Qing, but the paintings are original. The **coffered ceiling** has fine pictures including a four-armed, four-eyed figure supporting the sun and moon; he stands with his feet in a river from

which a red deer drinks. On the north ceiling face is a **hunting scene** which includes a beautifully drawn outline (unfinished) of a wild ox and a leaping wild cat amongst the saw-toothed mountains, trees and clouds.

This landscape style with the real (ox, hunting scene, trees and mountains) mixed with the heavenly (dragons, flying angels, human-headed birds) is reminiscent of Han painting and decoration in content and, to some extent, in style. Han incense burners in the form of mountains have the same grouping of animals and mountains and clouds and the swirling linear style is like that found on lacquer wares. On the east wall are musicians and a tumbler.

Northern Zhou (557–581)

Cave 428 The cave is of the central pillar type with an inverted V-shaped roof. The niches around the pillar have the same wide, lightly-pointed arches as in Cave 259. Under the figures in the niches (repaired in the late Qing) runs a row of donor figures, men and women in elegant stances, the women in long dark outer robes with paler underdresses, the men in knee-length gowns.

Paying for holy paintings was a devout act, which would help the donor to pass quickly through courts of judgement into Amitabha's paradise and small figures of the donors were frequently included in wall paintings and silken banners from Dunhuang. The largest group of donors (4200) are found in this cave, a crowded group to be seen under a triple-row version of the *Mahasattva jataka* (a story from the former life of the historic Buddha) at the northern end of the eastern wall.

This is a fascinating painting, with its fan-shaped trees and frequent depiction of open-fronted halls with roof-ridges terminating in curled owls' tail acroteria (which are of great interest to architectural historians since no actual timber buildings survive from the period). The scenes are broken up by saw-toothed mountains and the open-fronted halls and there are small cartouches for entitling the scenes so that the whole is a sort of cartoon-strip version of the tale in which three brothers go hunting. Before they leave they do some target practice (top row). When hunting, they find a starving tigress and her cubs and one brother stays and lies down in front of the tiger so that she may eat him and feed her cubs. She doesn't so he climbs a cliff and drops dead in front of her to save her the effort. When his brothers return, they build a stupa for him to commemorate his unselfishness (bottom right) and he is later reborn as the Buddha (bottom left). Notice the lotus ceiling, whose design is also strongly reminiscent of floor tiles.

Sui Dynasty (581–618)

Cave 244 This includes some later painting: Five Dynasties painting on the west wall and some Xi Xia overpainting of the Five Dynasties paintings in the passage and on the west wall, otherwise the Buddha figures—past on the south wall, historic on the west wall and future (Maitreya) on the north wall—Bodhisattvas and flying angels are of the Sui.

Cave 410 The niche with five figures is original; behind is a tunnel-like passage.

Cave 420 A Sui cave, this has one of the **most original compositions amongst the ceilings** at Dunhuang, a huge grouping of buildings. Encircled by zigzag walls which are topped with rooflike tiling, a variety of halls are depicted— simple open halls with gable half-hip roofs or double-roofed halls. There are taller, pagoda structures and rather fine gates with double roofs. Bracketing is indicated by a zigzag line under the eaves and the whole busy temple complex—perhaps based on a major centre like Wutai shan which is and was filled with temples—is a fascinating survival from a period from which no timber building still stands. The **sculptures** are also rather fine, with a quite Indian cast to the features, especially of the attendant Bodhisattvas, but a greater confidence in modelling which anticipates the plastic freedom of the Tang.

Cave 427 This has a Song antechamber with two guardian figures repainted in the Qing. Song dynasty donors paid for the roofbeams of the antechamber which bear dates. The inner cave is Sui with the same grouping of Buddhas as in Cave 410, although the garments of the Bodhisattvas and attendant figures show strong Persian influence in their decoration. It is said that the gold leaf on the ceiling was stolen by Russian soldiers in 1920.

Early Tang (618–712)

Cave 202 The sculptures are of the Qing period, the wall paintings original. On the east wall is the Buddha teaching, on the north wall Buddhas of the ten directions and on the south wall is Maitreya and a very agricultural painting of a paradise of plenty (with two harvests from one sowing). Heavenly kings guard the four corners and the farmers' clothes have been hung in the trees while they work.

Cave 209 Here again the figures were replaced or restored in the Qing and only the paintings are original. The coffered ceiling is decorated with grapes and pomegranates, the former, in particular, often found on Tang silverware and ceramic decoration. The cave contains some of the **best Tang landscapes**. Some of the distant mountains are reminiscent of the patterned saw-toothed Wei mountains in form but they rise from clouds, are mountain-coloured and generally more in a landscape tradition. Foreground mountains are outlined by different sorts of trees treated in a variety of ways, with little curlicued clouds floating above. A group of women with piled-up hair listens to a preaching Buddha.

Cave 323 This contains **paintings** that are very highly regarded and considered to be by the hand of a great master. The landscapes include a scene of a boat containing Buddhist figures being rowed through a landscape of small mountain peaks. It may represent the arrival in Guangzhou of a famous sandalwood statue sent to an emperor of the Liang dynasty by an Indian king in the 6C. The mountains are not inappropriate to the Guangzhou area. The detail of the painting is charming: a man carrying a lotus rides on an ox with a small boy mounted behind him and tiny attendant figures are amongst those shown welcoming the arrival of the boat.

Cave 329 This has a painting of Amitabha Buddha and the western paradise over which he presides on the west wall; paradise scenes such as this were immensely popular in Dunhuang and a large number have been found painted on silken banners (of which there are many examples in the British Museum).

Although the landscape scenes found at Dunhuang have excited more interest—for their social and architectural content and their links with the enormously important tradition of landscape painting on silk and paper—the **paradise paintings** are complex and beautiful. Amitabha's western paradise was not the only one depicted, although it is probably the most popular, but other Buddhas presided over other paradises which were also painted. Amitabha's paradise usually has a lotus pond in the foreground, with ducks and small babies sitting on lotus leaves, while beside the Buddha is a crowd of saints and Bodhisattvas; above are land-scape scenes with temples amongst clouds.

Cave 332 The most dramatic painting in this cave is the cavalry charge on the south wall.

Cave 387 A niche-type cave with the major figures grouped in a niche, rather than around a central pillar as in the earlier caves; the central figures are probably Qing.

High Tang (712–781)

Cave 96 This cave, with its **giant 33m Buddha**, lies behind the nine storey pagoda-like structure which rises the full height of the cliff.

> ### The view from the clifftop
> Climbing to the top of the cliff, above the pagoda, onto the sands above, is highly recommended. It allows a view over the valley with the poplars and the river close against the cliff, the wide expanse in front dotted with the small stupa-graves of monks and dark mountains in the distance. The rolling sand dunes behind contrast with the stark mountains in front; thus the Gobi, not one desert but many with extraordinarily varied topography and geology.

The giant Buddha is Maitreya, the Buddha of the future, seated with his feet on the ground; the figure has a rock core covered with clay and the tunnel behind is hollowed out of the rock. Although originally Tang, the figure was much restored under the Republic and the left hand was last restored in 1987.

Cave 130 This contains the **second largest Buddha at Dunhuang**, 26m high, which can be seen at three viewing levels. The head is 7m high with 2m ears. The elegant left hand over the left knee is the original Tang hand; the right hand is a Song replacement. Behind the Buddha are an elegant ceiling and halo, painted in black, red and green in brocade patterns. 15m high Bodhisattvas stand beside the Buddha and there are beautifully painted Bodhisattvas in the passageway.

Cave 148 The cave was carved in AD 775 and contains a **17m Sleeping Buddha** (the Buddha on his deathbed about to enter Nirvana) whose robes were overpainted in the Qing. Lines of disciples stand behind the figure and on the east wall is a painting of Amitabha and the western paradise. The date of the cave is recorded on a stele in the antechamber in which stand large guardian figures. Paintings echo the sculpture with five scenes showing Sakyamuni entering Nirvana.

Cave 172 The cave is dated AD 781 and the paintings are of the Tang, although the figures are Qing in date. On the north and south walls are **Amitabha and the western paradise**, including some startling architectural detail in the upper register, an open-fronted hall with incredibly complex and deeply projecting bracketing (similar to that on the 9C Foguang si on Wutai shan and presumably not uncommon on contemporary buildings). There is also the most marvellous canopy over the head of the Buddha.

Details in the painting include a tiny landscape of Queen Vaidehi sitting on a mat beside a fast-flowing stream. She sits with a silver censer in her hand, meditating on the rising sun, which has been, like her face, blackened by chemical action. Queen Vaidehi was imprisoned by her son but sustained by Amitabha Buddha who appeared to her in prison and recommended 16 subjects for meditation. The way she sits on the mat is interesting, not only because mats are still used for meditation, especially in Japan, but the painting antedates the common use of chairs in China ('chairman', as in Chairman Mao, translates as 'chief mat' in Chinese). The leafless trees on the riverbank, with hints of blossom in the distance and the cold blue of the rippling water, all convey the chill of an early spring dawn. The 1000-armed Guanyin figure in the antechamber is of Xi xia (11C) date.

Cave 320 The Tang figures in the cave were originally covered in gold and one (Ananda) is missing, taken by Langdon Warner in 1924, together with 12 paintings from the walls and now in the Fogg Museum. The **Amitabha's paradise** painting has children emerging from lotus leaves in the pool beneath the pantheon. There are, as always, intriguing vignettes beside the more systematised central depiction. Here one is of monks meditating before the setting sun. They sit on mats, some in front of small pools lined with bright tiles of blue, green, red and brown, some under pine trees or bushes, against a rocky cliff with the red setting sun slowly sinking behind distant blue mountains.

Cave 328 This cave was also visited by Langdon Warner and one figure is missing; the statues are Tang, the wall and ceiling paintings are Song.

Middle Tang (781–848)

Cave 321 The **paintings** are Tang in date, the **statues** are Qing and, in the passageway, Song paintings cover the Tang originals. A heavenly palace depicted in one painting is a broad expanse, in effect on three axes, with gardens on either side and several courtyards within a walled enclosure. Octagonal garden pavilions stand amid flowering trees and the bracketing of the open-fronted halls is very impressive.

Cave 237 Again, Qing **statues**—of Sakyamuni together with Samantabhadra on his white elephant and Manjusri on his lion—accompany Tang paintings of the western paradise (south wall), the Buddha with orchestra and dancers (north wall) and the Buddha teaching (east wall). In the centre of the painted coffered ceiling is a triangle enclosing three rabbits. Some of the painting, the quick, fluent outlining of feet and the silken folds of garments, is very attractive in its liveliness, with portraits of Buddhist notables set in frames of brightly coloured lozenges.

Cave 365 The cave has a barrel-shaped roof and a row of seven Buddhas along the west wall. Of the **1000 Buddhas on the walls**, many have had their faces scraped off by Muslim iconoclasts objecting, according to Koranic proscriptions, to the depiction of human form which was prohibited because no one could equal the work of God.

There was relatively little destruction at Dunhuang, especially when compared to the fate of some of the caves nearer to Uighur settlements like Bezeklik (rather than mainly Chinese settlements) but the occasional Muslim and then a group of White Russians interned in Dunhuang after escaping into China from Russia in 1922 ruined some of the paintings. It was the Russian desecration that persuaded Langdon Warner that he was quite justified in removing figures and paintings from Dunhuang, although the desecration is hardly as widespread as he suggests and removal, in consequence, hardly as easily justified.

Late Tang (848–907)

Caves 16 and 17 Cave 16 is a large cave with a sizeable platform on which stand nine Qing figures. One of the most interesting features is that the **floor of patterned tiles** still survives (a rare example of the type of flooring seen in the frontispiece to the printed *Diamond Sutra* of AD 868). The long entrance passage to Cave 16 is painted with Song Bodhisattvas and the tiny Cave 17 is off the passageway. It was in **Cave 17** that Wang Yuanlu discovered the **hidden library** of the temple, whose contents have now been scattered over the world.

The cave has an interesting assemblage of **wall paintings of trees** covered with creepers from whose branches a satchel and water-bottle have been suspended and by which an attendant, holding a crook, waits patiently. An attractive **sculpture of the monk Hong Bian** seated in the meditation position, his limbs invisible, wrapped in the patchwork robe of a monk, is inside the small cave. Today's monks' robes are made of several squares of cloth joined together, imitating the patchwork of poverty; in Dunhuang, in both drawings and sculpture like this one, the patchwork is suggested by a black criss-cross line so that Hong Bian rather looks as if he has been trussed up. The sculpture is an impressive combination of icon (upright, with slightly Indian or classically Buddhist features) and portrait (lines at the corners of the eyes, the angle of the neck).

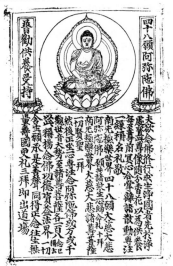

A prayer sheet with an illustration of Amitabha Buddha, from the hidden library at Dunhuang

Five Dynasties (907–960)

Cave 16 On a platform in the cave there was once a huge figure of the Bodhisattva Manjusri seated upon his lion but all that remains is the tail of the lion at the back of the platform. Behind the platform, the entire west wall is covered by a **painted map of Wutai shan** in Shanxi province, the Buddhist holy mountain sacred to the worship of Manjusri.

It is possible that the painting was based on a sort of pictorial pilgrim's map (of the kind still sold) for a monk from Dunhuang is known to have made the pilgrimage to Wutai shan at about the time the painting was made. According to the inscription the cave was built and decorated by the third daughter of the King of Xinjiang and there is a fine series of donor paintings on the east wall, a whole family richly dressed. In the Wutai painting the temples and the surrounding mountains are laid out and labelled and dark-plumed birds fly over the mountains, just as red-legged choughs do today.

Cave 98 This cave contains some of the **best 10C painting at Dunhuang**, including very varied forms: a fine, rather formal, portrait series of the King of Khotan and his family with the King wearing a very complicated hat with the imperial rows of beads hanging down on either side; a lively hunting scene amongst mountains and a richly painted, jewel-like assemblage of an all girl orchestra and dancer.

Cave 146 The statues are Qing in date. The **ceiling** is covered with paintings, including a fine central design and some lively but slightly crude guardian figures in the four corners and the 1000 Buddhas on the walls with large donor paintings (the donors do appear to get proportionally bigger as time passes in Dunhuang).

Cave 385 A niche-type cave, this has some beautjful Bodhisattvas in it.

Northern Song (960–1127)

Cave 55 The statues and paintings are all original. The major figures are of the past, present and future Buddhas with the statue of a king on the south side; there are four guardians in the corners. There is a dragon in the centre of the coffered ceiling.

The **paintings**, particularly the screen-like scenes on the lower register of the walls, are interesting as they are close in style, although slightly superior in technique, to a small illustrated booklet of part of the *Lotus Sutra* now in the British Library (originally from Cave 17). The scenes include one which is usually interpreted as Prince Siddharta (the Buddha) riding out on a white horse, leaving the haven of his father's palace for the first time, before his first view of the old, poor, sick and dying citizens of his father's kingdom, a sight which was to shock him profoundly. The horses with their neatly tied tails are well painted, as is the solid fortress with its imposing entrance gate. Other parts of the painting include agricultural scenes of ploughing and animal husbandry and of a boat with a beehive-shaped canopy being beset by crocodiles and demons as those on board call upon the Bodhisattva Guanyin for protection (as instructed in the *Lotus Sutra*).

Cave 152 The long passageway into the cave has Song floor tiles still in place and Song paintings on the ceiling, although the wall paintings are Xi Xia.

Cave 256 The cave's ceiling paintings have fallen down so that the chisel marks of the monks who hollowed out the cave can now be seen; the statues are Qing. Paintings include donors who are non-Chinese minority peoples on the east walls and some highly decorative Bodhisattvas under jewelled and silken canopies.

The **Bodhisattvas** are interesting for they are moustached: Bodhisattvas in Indian Buddhism are invariably masculine but in China, Guanyin (Avalokitesvara), in particular, assumed a somewhat ambivalent but increasingly female form as 'he' was associated with the 'female' qualities of mercy, provision of children for the childless and the rescue of those in distress. Some of the earlier Indian-influenced figures are also slightly female in form but here (as in some of the silken banners from Dunhuang in the British Museum), although the jewelled robes could be somewhat female, the thin, curly moustache is unambiguous.

Cave 454 The cave has served as a **sort of 'Lady Chapel'** for women came in to pray to the Qing Guanyin figure, apparently perambulating around the figures in one direction if a boy was required, the other for a girl (a highly unlikely thing to wish for in traditional China). The floor tiles and four heavenly kings in the corners are original, as are the Song paintings on the walls, some of which have been blackened by fires lit by the White Russian soldiers so abhorred by Langdon Warner. There is a particularly fine procession of non-Chinese notables in striped under robes and gowns richly patterned with flowers.

Although the figures (including Guanyin) are Qing in date, they are said to have been made before Wang Yuanlu arrived; perhaps this was the only cave that was still in use by those wishing to pray to Guanyin for the boy-girl perambulation sounds characteristic of late traditional popular religion.

Xi Xia (1036–1227)
Caves 354 and 367 Later caves apparently show a greater Tantric influence, not surprising given the Tibetan influence over the area. Mandalas (mystic meditational diagrams) have been found amongst the paper documents in the caves, probably dating from the 10C and it is said that some of the Yuan caves, such as no. 465, include tantric paintings of sex.

- The above (with the exception of no. 465) are caves that are or have been generally open to the public, under supervision. Virtually every cave has something to offer and once the eye is in, it is not too difficult to distinguish roughly between the narrow iconic figures of the Northern Wei with their wedge-shaped heads, the increasing confidence of the Sui figures and the supreme confidence of the Tang; to enjoy the glimpses of the landscape revealed in paintings and appreciate the genre figures.

Other caves that might be requested could include (Early Tang) **Cave 431** which has a scene of finely drawn horses, some with long natural tails, others with their tails tied up decoratively and a small groom, or *ma fu*, (the 'mafoo' of expatriates and expatriate novels set in the 1920s and '30s) resting with his head on his knees. High Tang caves include **23** and **148** with genre scenes of ploughing in the rain and a flock of oxen, simply, almost crudely drawn. **Cave 45** has illustrations of Chapter 25 of the *Lotus Sutra* describing how those in various sorts of distress should call upon the Bodhisattva Guanyin for salvation. A wonderful **boat with striped sails** is beset by demons and some travellers meet with thieves in a landscape, all very beautifully drawn. **Cave 217** has some marvellous **Bodhisattvas in outline** (unfinished) and drawings and paintings signed by various artists. **Cave 39**, as well as many others, has some wonderfully confident **apsareses** in swirls of cloud and trailing silks, the 'flying angels' sometimes used as a sort of logo for Dunhuang.

Mid Tang caves include a herd of softly painted oxen in **Cave 238**. Late Tang caves of interest include **156** with a huge cavalry force drawn up with banners and armour and **Cave 85** where a series of scenes from the life of the Buddha in a Chinese setting includes genre scenes of a butcher at work and a couple playing the *qin* under a tree.

Outside the caves, far across the river are scattered stupas, burial places for the ashes of some of the monks who lived at Dunhuang. Near the road back to the oasis is the **Stupa of Wang Yuanlu**, a rather tall and ornate structure with a long inscription.

Behind the cliff face and caves are extensive sand dunes and in the dunes some 7km south of Dunhuang town is the **Crescent Lake**, a small, new-moon shaped pool fed by a spring, which used to have temples and resthouses for pilgrims on its south side (of which some ruined walls remain). Now there is a gate with camels and drivers ready to take tourists around the dune to the lake. You can climb to the top of the dunes (on the previously inhabited side of the lake, I believe) and slide down on your bottom in an attempt to make the sands 'sing' or roar like thunder (I have never succeeded). Trees growing beside the lake include tamarisk and saksaul (*Anabasis ammondendron*); coots swim and dive on it and the intrepid missionaries Cable and French reported in the 1940s that they found the sweet-scented sand jujube (*Eloeagnus latifolia*), a silver-leafed plant with small fragrant flowers, growing by the lake in early summer.

Near the caves opposite the car park is the **Dunhuang Research and Exhibition Centre** (open daily 09.00–17.00) which includes replicas of several caves and some manuscripts and paintings found at the site.

Turfan

Turfan or Turpan (a Uighur word for 'lowland'), an oasis town on the northern silk route between Hami and Korla, lies in the Turfan depression which reaches 154m below sea level at its lowest point at Lake Ayd Ingkol. Unlike Dunhuang, which is in appearance and population a 'Chinese' oasis, Turfan is very much Uighur and Islamic today. It is, however, surrounded by ruins of previous oasis cities which, although Uighur rather than Chinese, date from before the Islamic influence on the area and include many Buddhist sites.

Turfan itself is a pleasant, small market town with many of its streets like green tunnels covered with shady vine trellises. It does not have a very long history, although the Imin Mosque dates back to 1777, but it is close to the ancient capital of the Uighurs and some early cave-temples.

North are the Flaming Mountains and the water which flows from the melting snows there is supplied to Turfan by man-made underground channels, or *karez*, which prevent the water from evaporating in the summer desert heat before it reaches the town. The *karez* system is thought to have been introduced from Persia some 2000 years ago; there are said to be 1600km of underground channels in Turfan county. The gradient down from the mountains enables the water to flow naturally throughout the system. Every so often there is a well cut from the surface down into the *karez* to allow ventilation and access in order to keep the channels clear. The water is used to irrigate grapevines, a feature of the oasis.

In Turfan the day tends to start some two hours later than in eastern China. It is a good idea to return to the hotel during the intense heat between 14.00 and 16.00 and keep the curtains drawn on south-facing windows.

Practical information

Getting there
By train

The nearest station is Daheyuan on the Lanzhou–Urumqi line, 32km north of the town. There is now a railway line to Kuqa and Kashgar.

By bus

Tourist groups are often brought by bus from Urumqi (the journey takes three hours) and less often from Dunhuang (ten hours so this sector is more often made by rail); long distance public buses ply the same routes.

Where to stay

The *Turfan Binguan*, 21 Qingnian lu, ☎ 0995 852 2301, fax 0995 852 3262, is a very pleasant old hotel, once a caravanserai with vine trellises in the garden; it is a short walk (or donkey ride) from the museum and the market. As there are performances of Uighur singing and dancing nightly, it may be pretty noisy in some parts. But then the same is also true of the *Silk Road Turpan Oasis*

Hotel (Luzhou Binguan), 42 Qingnian lu, ☎ 0995 852 2491, www.the-silk-road.com; it houses the mian *CITS* branch. The Oasis is newer than the Turfan Binguan but it still has a vine-covered courtyard.

History

The Uighurs, still numerically dominant in the area, are descended from nomadic Turkic tribes from the Lake Baikal/Lake Balkash area in Siberia, who grouped themselves together as a political unit in the 7C AD after defeating the Xiongnu. They speak a Turkic language, some of which is intelligible to speakers of modern Turkish, many words being identical. Between the 9C and 12C the Uighurs settled and began to farm, establishing themselves from 840 to 1209 in the area with their capital at what is now called Gaochang (c 45km southeast of Turfan near the village of Karakhoja) but which was known in Turkish as Kocho (Chotscho to German archaeologists like Von Le Coq who excavated in the area in the 1920s), also as Idikut Shahri.

The Uighurs were converted to Islam from the 9C as the faith was carried into Central Asia, just as Buddhism in Chinese territories was anyway beginning to lose its sway in the face of imperial prohibitions and persecution. Islam has had its effect on the Uighur way of life: the women wear chiffon headscarves and trousers under dresses (which are sometimes made of *ikat* weave silk with its different coloured stripes fading into each other) and men wear small squared skull-caps of black cotton with white embroidery in the sort of curled leaf-shape found on paisley shawls.

The town today is very different in appearance from Dunhuang and other Chinese oases. The streets are lined with poplars and the distinctive mud-brick houses of the Uighurs. These are square, often with dark, cool semi-subterranean rooms and a yard in which there is usually a high round bread oven built of clay, the yard itself covered with timbers over which vines are grown to provide both grapes and shade from the sun. The windows of the houses are very small and some use is made of open-work brick windows for ventilation. Cable and French describe how the inhabitants of Turfan in the 1930s slept on high beds because of the:

...large and virulent scorpions which creep under sleeping mats, drop onto the unconscious sleeper from the beams or hide themselves in his shoes. One jumping spider with long legs and a hairy body as large as a pigeon's egg leaps on its prey and makes crunching noises with its jaws. Turfan cockroaches are over 2 inches in length with long feelers and red eyes which make them a repulsive sight.

Many of the houses have open-brick towers attached, for drying grapes to produce raisins of many grades and shades. The gateways to the mosques are brightly painted with little minarets and some of the modern municipal buildings have very distinctive façades of an architectural type I can only describe as Communist Central Asian. The market stalls show the difference of culture: they are piled high with dried raisins and sultanas; food-stalls sell large flat loaves of unleavened bread, mutton kebabs, mutton pasties and pilau made from rice, mutton, carrots and sultanas. Cable and French described the dried-fruit market in Turfan as:

...one of the most varied and certainly the cheapest in the world. The vendor sits amid piles of sultanas of varying quality—the dark, the pale, the golden and the jade green ... dried black plums and apricots ... there are also piles of apricot kernels so sweet as to be almost indistinguishable from the almond; it is used in making an emulsion which is served as a drink at feasts ... there are also dried peaches, nectarines and mulberries, piles of shelled walnuts and dried jujube fruit ... Sellers of cotton goods are numerous ... some of this material is very cleverly dyed, for the women know how to knot little bunches in the length of stuff before it goes to the dyer, so that when it comes back they open it out and find a pattern of flowers or butterflies scattered at regular intervals over the material ... The silk merchants exhibit skeins of floss silk dyed in every colour and Turfan silk is highly prized by the women of Turkestan for embroidering caps. Each city has its own characteristic skull-cap and men from any locality can be recognised by their head-dress. For example, the Aqsu men wear a handsome cap of black velvet heavily embroidered with gold and silver thread, the Hami and Turfan men wear variegated silk embroideries, but the pattern and design is different in each...

They also mention carpet weaving, the leather merchant and the leather boots he sold, melon sellers (from Hami), herbalists and the food-sellers with their kebabs and pilau.

Outside the town, on the road out to Gaochang, you pass the cemetery with its distinctive graves, the finer ones like small domed houses in whitewashed brick.

Sites to visit in Turfan itself include the market, the museum, grape farms and the *karez* system and the Imin (or Emin) Minaret.

The **museum** on Gaochang lu (open 09.00–20.00) is easily reached from the old guesthouse on foot, as is the market. Turn right out of the guesthouse and walk up the road to the first main crossroads where the museum is diagonally opposite on the northwest corner, approached through a poplar-filled garden. It contains exhibits excavated from some of the Tang tombs in the Astana Desert, which include some fine examples of Tang silks and a single (apparently fossilised) stuffed dumpling, or *jiaozi*.

This is insufficiently publicised for it should put paid to the argument about whether Marco Polo found spaghetti and ravioli (or *jiaozi*) in China or introduced them from Italy. This dumpling antedates Marco Polo, whether or not he went to China, and such foodstuffs are thought to have originated in Persia, anyway.

There are also exhibits from the old Uighur capital at Gaochang, including documents relating to land tenure in the early 7C.

Turn right out of the museum, go straight over the next major intersection, on whose corners are the main department store and a Minorities Store where you may find some of the traditional items like leather boots, skull-caps and *ikat* cloth and take the next turning on the left for the centre of the **market** (see p 527). It is open every day but, as elsewhere in Xinjiang, Sunday is the busiest day.

The **Imin Minaret** is also walkable (about half an hour) from the old guesthouse, or you could travel on one of the tiny donkey carts controlled by small boys who hang around outside the guesthouse if the weather is terribly hot.

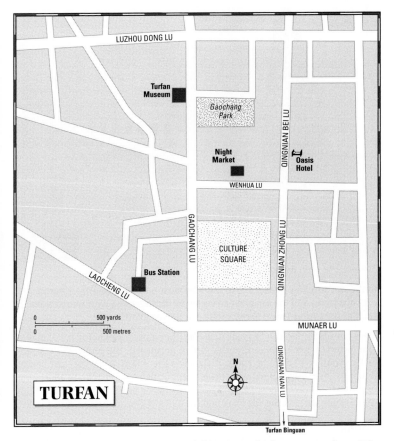

Turn left out of the guesthouse, turn left again at the first crossroads and the road takes you to the fine brick minaret.

> The minaret is the most striking building of the mosque. Designed by a Uighur architect, it was built in 1778 by the then local ruler (as a Chinese work on architectural history has it), Prince Sulaiman of Turfan, in honour of his father Prince Emin, a Hajji. Most European guidebooks call it the Imin Minaret; the name of the man to whom it was dedicated is rendered in Chinese as Emin and the local Chinese name for the minaret is Sugong ta (Prince Su's Pagoda).

The minaret is constructed entirely of brick, in the style of the pre-Safavid architecture of Iran and is a lovely example of decorated brickwork. 44m or 36m high, depending on whether you follow the *Zhongguo mingsheng cidian* or Qinghua University's *Historic Chinese Architecture* (1985), the minaret is broad at the base and tapers markedly. Broad bands of bricks set in different patterns—of the sort that Robert Byron in *The Road to Oxiana* (1937) described as 'tweed' or zig-zags, here herringbone, lozenges, crosses and daisies— give a wonderful texture

Turfan: the Imin Mosque

to the warm yellow bricks. The mosque beside it has been recently restored.

Grape farms and the *karez* can be visited by arrangement with tourist agencies such as the **China Travel Service** (office in the old guesthouse).

Trips outside Turfan can be made to Jiaohe (the ruins of Yarkhoto), c 9.5km west and to the cave temples of Bezeklik (48km northeast), the cemetery at Astana (40km southeast) and the ruins of Gaochang (c 45km southeast, just beyond Astana). These huge ruined settlements are difficult for the layman to understand or reconstruct, except in scale: their size and number, however, convey something of the importance of the Silk Road and the oases of Central Asia in earlier times.

Jiaohe

Jiaohe (Meeting of Rivers), the Chinese name for Yarkhoto, which in Turkish means the same thing, is thought to have been a Han foundation as a Chinese garrison town, taken over in the 6C by the Uighurs. The ruins of Jiaohe are clearer and slightly easier to comprehend than those at Gaochang which was the more important town. Jiaohe was a rectangular, unwalled settlement about 1000m north–south, 300m east–west, with a strongly marked central avenue running from north to south. Different quarters have been distinguished within the town on the basis of excavated artefacts and architectural remains: the northwest corner was mainly full of Buddhist temples with Buddhist figures, stupas and pagodas, while the northeast corner was filled with courtyard dwellings. The grander architectural remains with multi-courtyard buildings of the southeast corner suggest that this was the governmental centre of the town. There was also a grand Buddhist temple at the northern end of the central avenue, built, like everything else, in brick with Tang period tile ends decorated with lotuses.

Much pottery was found in Jiaohe, mainly unglazed with stamped and impressed decoration or crude, red-bodied glazed wares. A Tang dynasty copy of the *Lotus Sutra* copied in 722 was unearthed here in 1901. The settlement was abandoned in the Yuan period, for reasons which are not yet clear: some suggest that Muslim fanatics destroyed it for its Buddhist remains, others assume that the water supply failed.

Bezeklik

Some 48km northeast of Turfan are the **Cave Temples of Bezeklik** where 57 caves were carved on a river terrace high above the Sengim River in a striking setting, approached across the desert and up a barren gorge. The monastery existed from the 6C to the early 14C, abandoned, as were so many of the settlements in the area at the beginning of the Yuan period. In Eastern Turkish, *bezeklik* means 'place of paintings and ornaments'.

The caves, which were originally protected by wooden constructions in front, were badly damaged by centuries of use as shelters by goatherds (who blackened many of the walls with their fires) and there are few wall paintings remaining for many were removed by a series of German archaeological expeditions (1902–03, 1904–05, 1905–07, 1913–14) led by Albert Grunwedel (1856–1935) and Albert von le Coq (1860–1930), whose finds were brought back to the Museum fur Indische Kunst, Staatliche Museen Preussischer Kulturbesitz, Berlin.

It is ironic that Grunwedel's intention, to save the wall paintings from the Muslim population of local villages, which had 'got into the habit of breaking off pieces thereof to fertilise their fields', was thwarted by Allied bomber raids on Berlin between November 1943 and January 1945 which destroyed 28 of the largest wall paintings, almost all from Bezeklik, and damaged many others brought back from Central Asia on the four expeditions. The remains are on display in Berlin, many in pocket-handkerchief-sized fragments.

In contrast with the Chinese style of the Dunhuang cave paintings, those at Bezeklik show distinct western influences mixed with Chinese and are often described as being in an Indo-Iranian style, still apparent in the faces and figures of Caves 37, which includes pictures of Mongolians and an Indo-Iranian Bodhisattva, and 39 where many local rulers are depicted making offerings. The mixed influences are also apparent in the inscriptions which are frequently bilingual (in Chinese and Uighur) and are written in the Central Asian *Brahmi* script.

Gaochang

Gaochang and the Cemetery of Astana are some 45km and 40km southeast of Turfan respectively.

History

Like Jiaohe, Gaochang was founded by the Han Chinese in the 1C BC as a garrison town and as a base for grain production to supply the frontier troops. By the 4C AD, during the Eastern Jin, it had become the capital of the 'Western Territories' and the centre of Gaochang prefecture. As the Chinese lost control of the 'Western Territories', it became the capital of various local kingdoms until 640 when the Chinese regained control of the area and reinstated Gaochang as capital of the western territories. The great pilgrim **Xuan zang** came through Gaochang in 630 on his way to India in search of Buddhist sutras and the local king, having heard him preach, wanted to keep this savant permanently in Gaochang. After Xuan zang resorted to a hunger strike he was allowed to go with a promise to return, which he did not but since it was 16 years before he returned on the southern silk route, Gaochang was by then in Chinese hands again. In this second period of Chinese rule, Gaochang was a true local economic, religious and cultural centre, with a population of 37,000. The German archaeologist Von le Coq found substantial Manichean and Nestorian remains, as well as Buddhist relics.

The **Nestorian remains** (chiefly wall paintings) found in a three-room temple north east of the city walls, excited the eurocentric archaeologists of 100 years ago for the Nestorian Heresy was part of the history of Christianity based on the views of Nestorius, Patriarch of Constantinople, who was deposed by the Council of Ephesus in 431 and whose ideas were transmitted to Persia by 485 and thence to Central Asia and China. Sacred writings of the **Manicheans**, thought to have been lost in the savage persecutions of the religion in the Middle East and the Balkans, were found in some numbers, although Von le Coq was appalled to hear that five years before the first expedition a local peasant had thrown 'five cart-loads' of writings in 'small characters' into the river as he was 'fearful of the sinister nature of the writings'. Nevertheless, the expedition recovered texts in 24 scripts in 17 different languages, including Manichean texts.

From 840 to 1209 Gaochang became the Uighur capital; it was eventually abandoned or destroyed in the 14C at the beginning of the Ming. At its height, it was a roughly rectangular double-walled city covering two million square metres, the outer wall being some 5km in circumference.

The remains are less clearly defined than those at Jiaohe. In the southwest area, just outside the wall, the remains of a **Buddhist Temple** were quite well-preserved (and have been reconstructed recently). The temple covered c 10,000 square metres, with a gate, courtyard, hall and pagoda. Inside the town walls the only clear surviving remains are those of a high platform and wall, built of sun-baked bricks and pisé (and where Xuan zang is said to have preached in public).

Astana

Astana (which means 'Capital City' in Kazakh) is the site of a major **cemetery** whose contents can be dated on the basis of inscriptions and artefacts to between 272 and 778. Family graves in the cemetery were divided by stones and mostly consisted of earthen chambers surmounted by earth mounds.

The graveyard, as the *Zhongguo mingsheng cidian* states, was visited in the late 19C and early 20C by predatory archaeologists from Russia, England, Japan and Germany and 'elsewhere'. Official Chinese excavations began only in 1959, revealing well-preserved bodies (preserved by the dryness of the atmosphere) wrapped in silks and provided with grave goods of wood and pottery, documents, coins and paintings (many of which can be seen in the Provincial Museum in Urumqi, some in the Turfan Museum). The documents which relate to all aspects of life—military, political and private—have been extensively studied and published in China. Three of the caves can be visited, two containing Tang paintings and the other two effectively mummified bodies (with, when I last saw them, the extra protection of mothballs stuffed into various orifices).

As Cable and French reported, destruction of the remains was considerable in the 1930s, when the area was simply known to cart-drivers and camel caravanners as *er pu*, or 'second stage', in their assessment of mileage. Local farmers used the earth to fertilise fields and ploughed within the city walls, their irrigation channels causing further havoc, although their ploughshares constantly turned up little treasures:

> ... we came away with a seal, an old metal horse, a fragment of an Uighur manuscript and other small relics. Many beads are collected by children as they play among the ruins and any old pots which are unearthed are taken into immediate use by the women, to save the expense of buying others.

Other sites in the Turfan area listed in the *Zhongguo mingsheng cidian* are: the **Shengjinhou Buddhist Caves** (Shengjinhou qian fo dong), 40km northeast of Turfan, a collection of ten caves dating from the 7C to the 14C which sound similar to those at Bezeklik in style, with wall paintings which include Chinese and Uighur inscriptions; the **Yaerhu qian fo dong** (Thousand Buddha Caves of Yaerhu), c 10km northwest of Turfan, said to date from the Tang and Song periods. There are seven caves, six of which are said to be 'mausoleum caves' or 'relic caves', the seventh a monk's cave. There are wall paintings to be seen and an inscription in Turkish in Cave 5 on the west wall.

Urumqi

Urumqi is the capital of Xinjiang province and the Uighur Autonomous Region. It is situated on the northern part of the old Silk Route at the north end of a corridor between the east and west Tianshan mountains which separate the Dzungarian basin (north) from the Tarim basin (south). Just east of Urumqi is one of the highest peaks in the Tianshan range, the 5000m **Bodgo Ola** and the snow-capped Tianshan are one of the most attractive things about Urumqi.

The major site in the city is the **Provincial Museum**; outside, tourists are often taken to spend a night in a damp *yurt* in a Kazakh tourist settlement (hot-water bottle recommended) at Heaven Lake. Carpet-weaving factories and the inevitable shopping opportunities are also often included on tourist itineraries.

Practical information

Getting there
By air
The airport is 15km outside Urumqi. There are flights to and from most major Chinese cities and Xinjiang destinations as well as international flights to Almaty, Islamabad, Moscow, Tashkent and Istanbul. Airport shuttle buses leave from the *Xinjiang airlines* ticket office (c 50 minutes, 10 yuan); taxis cost about 60 yuan.

By train
The station is in the southeast of the city;

Urumqi is the terminus for the main line from Peking. Long-distance travel to Peking (three days) or Xi'an (two days) gives an impressive view of the ever-changing Gobi and the loess areas nearer Xi'an. There is a line beyond Urumqi to Almaty which many travellers use; and there is now a daily service to Kashgar which passes through Turfan, Korla, Kuqa and Asku. Although there is a *Kazakh Consulate* in Urumqi, western tourists should sort out their visas in their own country before departure.

By bus

The bus station for buses to every city in Xinjiang is on Heilongjiang lu, north of the railway station, although buses often stop outside their respective regional offices, which are all in the vicinity.

Where to stay

Hotels include the *Holiday Inn,* Xinhua bei lu, ☎ 0991 281 8788, fax 281 7422, email: holiday@ mail.wl.xj.cn, and the *Overseas Chinese Hotel* at the other end of the street, Xinhua nan lu, ☎ 0991 286 0793.

Urumqi

Urumqi, whose name is said to mean 'beautiful pastures' in Mongolian, is not a city with a very long history of significance. During the Tang dynasty it was merely an *en route* stop to the administrative centre of the region of Jimusaer (to the northeast of Urumqi). In 1760, the Qianlong emperor defeated the Mongols and regained Chinese sovreignty over the northwest and gave Xinjiang ('new dominions') its name. In 1884, Urumqi became the capital of the new province. Muslim rebellions against Chinese rule were common and in 1911, after the overthrow of the Qing, Xinjiang was ruled by a series of warlords.

From 1911 to 1928, 'Marshall' Yang Zhengxin controlled the area, despite border problems with the Soviet Union during which time he allowed a number of White Russians to settle in Urumqi. His ferocity made him unpopular and his habit of inviting his enemies to banquets and beheading them caught up with him when he was shot at a banquet in 1928. His successor did not last long for his policy of seizing land that belonged to local Muslims and giving it to Chinese settlers led to a revolt in 1931. This was led by the young Muslim Ma Chongying who managed to take much of Xinjiang. In 1934 he and his 'Tungan' troops (see p 535) were beaten back from Urumqi for a third time by Soviet Russian troops summoned by the desperate provincial Governor, Sheng Shicai. Mysteriously, ironically perhaps, Ma Chongying took refuge in the Soviet Union where he eventually disappeared, presumed killed on Stalin's orders.

The influence of the Soviet Union on Urumqi had grown considerably since the opening of a consulate there (together with others in Kashgar and other parts of Xinjiang) in 1922. Although Sheng Shicai was to ally himself with the KMT government in the 1940s, the distance and isolation of Urumqi from metropolitan China meant that allegiance with and assistance from the neighbouring Soviet Union was much easier to obtain. The varied foreign residents of the town in the 1930s were divided between the walled Chinese town and separate Russian and Uighur or Muslim quarters and the most often cited description of the town by Cable and French was unpromising: 'The town has no beauty, no style, no dignity and no architectural interest. The climate is violent, exaggerated and at no season pleasant.'

Architecturally, Urumqi remains somewhat unprepossessing and its situation is similar, in a rare part of Xinjiang that looks like a large slag heap. What charm it has derives from an attractive population of cheerful Uighurs and their bustling street markets. The residents are divided between Chinese settlers (50 per cent, the vast majority post 1949 arrivals) and 50 per cent 'minority' peoples of whom the Uighurs are the most numerous but which also include Hui, Kazakh, Tatar, Uzbek, Khalka, Mongolian, Tahur, Tajik, Manchu and Sibo (descendants of Manchu soliders) and Russians.

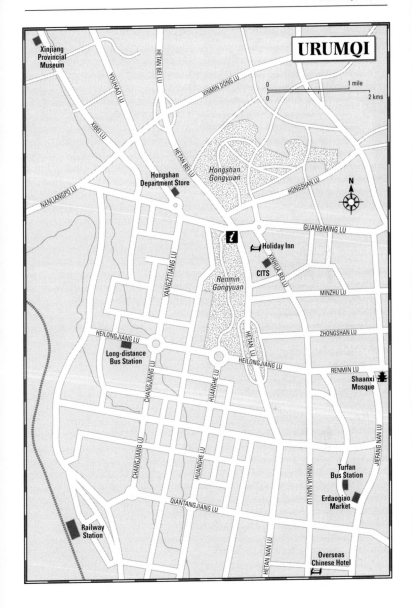

URUMQI

Xinjiang Provincial Museum

YOUHAO LU

XIBEI LU

HETAN BEI LU

XINMIN DONG LU

NANLIANGPO LU

Hongshan Department Store

Hongshan Gongyuan

HONGSHAN LU

GUANGMING LU

Holiday Inn

CITS

XINHUA BEI LU

MINZHU LU

YANGZITIANG LU

Renmin Gongyuan

HETAN LU

ZHONGSHAN LU

HEILONGJIANG LU

Long-distance Bus Station

HEILONGJIANG LU

RENMIN LU

Shaanxi Mosque

CHANGJIANG LU

HUANGHE LU

JIEFANG NAN LU

XINHUA NAN LU

Turfan Bus Station

Erdaogiao Market

QIANTANGJIANG LU

Railway Station

HETAN NAN LU

Overseas Chinese Hotel

N

0   1 mile
0   2 kms

The peoples of Urumqi

The **Hui**, formerly often referred to as Tungans, are Chinese-speaking Muslims of mixed origin who live mainly by sheep-farming in Gansu, Ningxia and Qinghai provinces, although there are quite a number in China proper, especially the northwest provinces. The term *hui*, which is applied to all Chinese Muslims, means 'to return' and one explanation of the term is that when these Muslim Chinese first appeared in China proper they were unwanted and so promised to return from whence they came. Uighurs, Kazakhs, Uzbekis and Tatars all speak Turkic languages and are found on both sides of the Sino-Kazakh and Sino-Kyrgyz borders.

Manchus and **Sibos** both originated in the northeast while **Mongols** and **Tahurs** originated in Mongolia. The **Khalka** (or Kalmuck or Torgot) are a Mongolian tribe who left Mongolia early in the 17C to settle on the Volga in Russia. In 1770, because they wished to practise their Buddhist religion in freedom, they made a mass exodus back to the newly-reclaimed northwest territories of China where they were welcomed by the Qianlong emperor and settled west of Urumqi at Karashahr and in Mongolia.

Distances in Urumqi, particularly from the hotels, are considerable and most visits will be best made by taxi.

Xinjiang Provincial Museum

The Xinjiang Provincial Museum (Xinjiangsheng bowuguan) is on Xibei lu (open Mon–Fri 09.30–19.00, Sat–Sun 10.30–17.00). It consists of two parts, one displaying archaeological and historical relics unearthed in the province, notably in the Turfan region, including some of the sand-preserved bodies from the Astana graveyard and charming little multi-coloured clay tomb figurines. There are also numerous examples of silk textiles mostly excavated in the area, including Tang silk paintings from Turfan. From the Astana and other graves, marvellous padded silk shoes, brocade slippers and robes, as well as fragments of silk with figured designs, woven designs and patterns reflecting western influences all testify to the wealth of the area at the time. A torch will help.

There is a new interest in some of the **sand-preserved bodies**, especially those from Loulan and Cherchen, sites far to the southwest along the southern edge of the Tarim Basin. Some of these, up to 4000 years old, have the most extraordinarily well-preserved clothing. A Cherchen baby was wrapped in a plum-coloured cloth tied with a vivid red and blue braid. The same startlingly bright colours were used for the baby's hat and the bodies of adults were often buried wearing tall witch-like hats or little pointed hats with large jaunty feathers stuck in them. Although burial must have affected them in some ways, many experts detect a 'Western' look about the faces and much effort has been spent trying to link these strangers with the West. Claims that Chinese archaeologists dispute this theory on the basis of Han chauvinism are exaggerated: the first Chinese explorations of the area were not made until the Han, well after these brightly-dressed persons had been buried (see Elizabeth Wayland Barber, *The Mummies of Urumqi*, New York, 1999).

The other part of the museum is devoted to the local minorities and includes a Uighur house, Kazakh, Mongol and Kirghiz *yurts* of felt, Mongolian riding boots and decorated saddles, heavy silver jewellery and the bizarre hats of the Daur made from animal heads. The shop has quite a good selection of books.

The finest surviving Qing building in Urumqi is the **Shaanxi Mosque** on Yonghezheng xiang, off Heping nan lu. Built with money from Muslims in

Shaanxi province, the main hall is constructed in two parts: the front a simple pitched roof structure; behind, a pavilion style building with a complex roof.

The **Yanghang** or **Tatar Mosque** at the southern end of Jiefang lu was built with contributions from the local Tatar families in 1897. The timber and brick construction and decoration of the dome is in the Tatar style.

In the south of the city in Yanerwo gongyuan (Yanerwo Park), is the **Martyrs' Memorial Hall**. It stands beside the tomb of the local Communist martyrs, who included Mao Zemin, younger brother of Mao Zedong, executed in 1942 by Sheng Shicai, the provincial Governor. In 1942, Sheng Shicai abandoned the Communists and made an alliance with the KMT government in Nanjing for he claimed he had just uncovered a plot by his erstwhile supporter Stalin to take over Xinjiang. In front of the tomb is a stele inscribed in Chinese, Uighur, Mongolian and Kazakh.

Hongshan gongyuan (Hongshan park) is in the centre of the city, at the northern end of Xinhua bei lu; it is the place where the Qing army's cavalry were stationed and there was once a large temple to the Jade Emperor, which burnt down in 1929–30 and now only a small nine-storey brick pagoda, the **Zhenlong ta** (Pagoda of the Tranquil Dragon), remains. It is said to have been built in a place where dragons endlessly appeared and needed calming. Its date is uncertain but it can be no earlier than the 18C and it is a *feng shui* pagoda, not associated with a Buddhist temple but built to improve the local *feng shui*. It is solid and has shallow eaves marking each storey.

Outside the park, just west of the entrance, is the main department store of Urumqi, the **Hongshan Department Store**, with a major market area in front of it.

South, down Xinhua bei lu, the fifth major turning on the left will bring you to another important market, the **Erdaoqiao Market**, filled with silks, *ikat* cottons, carpets and food of all sorts.

A frequent excursion from Urumqi is to **Tian chi** (Heavenly Lake), some 112km across the desert to the east of the city. Situated at 1800m in the Tianshan (Heavenly Mountains), the 3.2km long lake lies in scenery reminiscent of the Swiss Alps with steep green pastures, conifer forests and snowy mountain peaks. Nearby are Kazakh yurt settlements, now set up for tourists.

Hetian

On the southern Silk Road, south of the Taklamakan Desert, is Hetian (the modern Chinese name for Khotan). South are the foothills of the Kunlun mountains where two rivers rise to flow past Hetian and join the Tarim River. They are the Black Jade River (Karakash) to the west and the White Jade River (Yurungtash) to the east and they bring boulders of jade down from the mountains.

Getting there
By air

The airport 10km west is reached by taxi or airport shuttle bus.

By train

Trains to Aksu, Kashgar, Urumqi pass through Kuga Station, 7km southeast of the new town.

By bus

The bus station is in the north of the town. The *CITS* office is in the *Hetian shi Binguan* at the junction between Nuerwake lu and Tanai lu, ☎ 0903 204 6101.

History

Khotan was the source of **Chinese jade (nephrite)** probably since Neolithic times. Nephrite is only one of a group of hardstones that the Chinese carved and polished. The group includes chalcedony, saussurite, soapstone, serpentine, bowenite, jadeite and others and is collectively known as *yu* (usually translated as 'jade') with only nephrite singled out as *zhen yu* (or 'true jade'). The recovery of jade boulders from the rivers and their subsequent trade was noted by Zhang Qian on his mission of exploration for the Han emperor in 125 BC and Chinese tradition had it that jade was best found by women, who had an affinity for the stone. Technological works such as the *Tiangong kaiwu* (*Creations of Nature and Man* by Song Yingxing, late 16C) contain illustrations of ladies diving for jade in the rivers of Khotan, although the material was being more systematically mined in the Kunlun mountains by that time.

Khotan was the capital of the Kingdom of Yutian and traditionally maintained trading links with China, although at times, especially during the Han and Tang dynasties, it was incorporated into the Chinese empire. Like many of the other oasis kingdoms of the Talklamakan, it was a Buddhist centre, following the Hinayana tradition, rather than the later Mahayana which was followed in China proper. The pilgrim monk Xuan zang visited Khotan in about 645 on his way back to China from India and noted the jades of light and dark colours in the market and also the fine, locally-produced silks. Legend had it that local **silk production** only began when a Chinese princess arrived in AD 440 with silk-moth eggs smuggled in her hair. The silks were, and still are, woven into the distinctive *ikat* weave with wave-like stripes produced by tie-dying the warp threads so that the pattern is in the warp. Xuanzang was greeted by the King of Khotan and escorted in a procession with musicians, flowers and incense to a nearby monastery where he stayed for several months. Marco Polo also claimed to have passed through Khotan and, with his usual unerring ability to miss the point, failed to notice either jade or silk.

It was from Khotan that the first rumours of **buried cities and lost civilisations** reached western archaeologists in the late 19C, as a result of preliminary moves in the Great Game. The Great Game (English name; the Russians called it 'The Tournament of Shadows') described the rivalry between Britain (with its Indian empire) and Russia which in the late 19C was expanding southwards through Samarkand and Bokhara, threatening British India. The British in India were keen to map and survey the Taklamakan and the eastern fringes of the Pamirs. In the 1860s the head of the Survey of India had the idea of sending Indians out secretly to survey the area, posing as simple travellers through Yarkand to Ladakh. They were to count their paces, sometimes using Buddhist beads and use false 'prayer wheels' to map and measure distances. The first Indian surveyor died before he reached home but his notes were retrieved by an English surveyor, William Johnson, who was, to his surprise, invited to visit Khotan by the Khan who had heard of his surveying trips and apparently wished to try and hold him hostage to force the British to arm Khotan against the Russians. While in Khotan, Johnson heard of the sale of excavated tea-bricks dug up from the desert and managed to acquire one. Frugal local people, whose supply of tea from China had dried up, were using the old bricks of pressed tea dust that they found in ruins in the desert, just as in Gaochang where Cable and French saw excavated pots used in local households to save the expense of buying new ones. Johnson managed to get away and was followed by Sir Douglas Forsyth in 1870. He went to Yarkand (between Khotan and Kashgar) to try and forge an anti-Russian alliance with a local ruler, Yakub Beg, who had seized much of Chinese Turkestan. Forsyth, whose missions to Yakub Beg met with mixed success, later read a paper at the Royal Geographic Society in London entitled 'On the buried cities in the shifting sands of the great desert of the Gobi' and which, with its mention of Bactrian gold coins and Buddha figures, started the great archaeological race which first centred on Khotan.

A sidelight on the effect of the sudden arrival of numerous competing archaeologists in a small oasis town on the fringes of the Taklamakan is the story of **Islam Akhun** and the **lost languages of Central Asia**. Birchbark manuscripts that had filtered back to Calcutta from Kucha in the 1890s were deciphered by Dr Augustus Rudolph Hoernle. He was so excited by their antiquity that he had all sorts of people looking out for manuscripts, including the British Consul at Kashgar, George Macartney, who purchased a number from Islam Akhun in Khotan. These caused Hoernle considerable headaches as he attempted to decipher the 'lost languages' until Sir Marc Aurel Stein managed to catch Islam Akhun in 1901 and prove what he had begun to suspect, that he had been making his own 'ancient' manuscripts in gobbledegook scribbles (many of which are now in the British Library).

In Hetian, the remains of the yellow earth wall surrounding the Chinese or 'new' city can still be seen in places. The **Hetian Museum** (open daily 09.00–14.00, 16.00–19.00) includes the recently excavated bodies of two mummified Buddhist monks (c 5C–6C), in their dowelled coffins, many carved timber fragments from Niya and fragments of silk and carpets. There are also some very fine small gold and silver items including very charming long filigree hairpins. The Hetian Sunday market is as lively as the better-known one in Kashgar.

Sites in the vicinity of Khotan include **Yotkan** (Yuetegan), c 10km west of the town. The remains, which include potsherds, are said to be those of an important town of the Yutian Kingdom, occupied from the 3C–8C AD.

The remains of an ancient city, variously known as **Malikewate** or **Shensibier** to the Chinese, lie c 25km south of Hetian and include architectural remains such as pillar bases, platforms and a Han dynasty pottery kiln (excavated in 1978). Parts of the site have been tentatively identified as a royal residence. 10km south are the remains of a stone stupa, some 60m in circumference and only 6m high (now), associated with small pottery fragments including Buddha heads.

Further away (east 300km) is the site of **Niya**, excavated by Stein in 1901 and 1906. The site is considerable, some 10km north–south and 2km east–west but the shifting sands mean that the site is barely recognisable when compared with the photographs taken by Stein at the time. The houses Stein found were large, made mainly of wood and plaster. A number of beams carved in the Gandharan style were found by Stein, together with bits of furniture, also of carved wood (these can be seen in the British Museum). The most significant finds were of wooden tablets inscribed in Prakrit with much Sanskrit mixed in, in the *Kharosthi* script. Both script and language are thought to have originated in the extreme northwest of the Punjab. These gave some credence to the local belief that the area was colonised by Indians from Taxila in the 1C and 2C AD. Chinese wooden documents dated to AD 269 confirm that the area was under Chinese control in the late 3C. The site of Niya was apparently abandoned in the late 3C, perhaps because the Chinese withdrew, perhaps because of a shortage of water.

Kuqa

Kuqa, known to early western travellers as Kucha and to Chinese today as Kuche, is the second largest town in southern Xinjiang, a major oasis on a tributary of the Tarim River.

Practical information

Getting there

Kuqa may be reached by bus from Urumqi or Turfan or by rail from Turfan. It takes about 12 hours from Turfan, allowing for stops en route at places like Korla. It is on the new railway line to Kashgar. Flights from Kashgar are also a possibility.

Where to stay

The *Kuqa Hotel* is on Jiefang lu, ☎ 0997 712 0285. The *Qiuci Hotel* is on Tianshui lu, ☎ 0997 712 2005, fax 0997 712 2524.

History

Once the capital of the independent Kingdom of Qiuci that flourished until the mid 8C when its ruler accepted Chinese rule, Kuqa was a town with many contacts with India and the West. It also had a long history of communication and co-operation with China from the Han when a Chinese garrison was stationed in the town to help protect the trade route and when a Prince of Qiuci married into the Han imperial family in 69 BC. After 658 it became one of the four garrisons of the Chinese western territories. It had long been a Buddhist centre and was the birthplace of one of the greatest translators of Sanskrit Buddhist works into Chinese, **Kumarajiva** (344–*c* 431). Son of a Princess of Kuqa and a Brahmin father, Kumarajiva eventually settled in China as a Buddhist monk and headed a translation bureau of some 1000 monks. He was admired for the faithfulness of his translations, which were yet extremely elegant in style. Despite his industry, he was said to have believed that no translation could capture the flavour of the original Sanskrit and that reading translations was like eating rice that someone else had already chewed.

Xuanzang passed through after visiting Karashahr and noted that the air here was 'soft'. He found the population clothed in ornamental silks and the children with their heads flattened 'by the pressure of a wooden board'. Recent excavations at the old site of Subashi (the capital of the local kingdom until about the 12C, some 20km north of Kuqa) included a corpse with a remarkably square skull, presumably as a result of this treatment in childhood.

The inhabitants of Kuqa were then Hinayana Buddhists, in a tradition perhaps closer to the original canon, offering salvation only to an elevated few, less philosophically developed than the later Mahayana, which offered the possibility of salvation for all. Xuanzang followed the Mahayana tradition and refused to eat the meat offered to him. He also claimed that he thoroughly defeated the King in a philosophical debate. Evidence of the Buddhist faith at Kuqa and its neighbourhood can be seen in nearby caves, most notably at Kizil.

Kuqa is a largely Uighur town with earthen walls and narrow lanes in contrast with the 'new' settlement of the Chinese who are the 'national minority' here. In the Uighur or 'old town' there is a bustling Friday market that brings buyers and sellers of foodstuffs, cloth, saddles, animals, medicine and trinkets from the surrounding areas.

Korla is 480km southwest of Urumqi, just beyond the site of Karashahr (modern Yanchi), one of the Han garrison towns later visited by Xuanzang on his way to India in 630.

After being robbed by bandits, Xuanzang was happy to reach the peaceful haven of Karashahs where the 'air is soft and agreeable' and the soil suitable for 'red millet, winter wheat, scented dates, grapes, pears and plums'. Karashahr was excavated by the German archaeologists Von le Coq and Grunwedel, who brought back a number of ceramic Buddha figures with very round faces and unmodelled backs (for they were made to fit into niches), and by Sir Aurel Stein.

160 kilometres west of Korla is **Bugur**, an oasis town believed by Stein to be the site of ancient Luntai, seat of the Chinese Protector General of the Tarim basin in the Han dynasty, although he could find no trace of it. West of Bugur many of the old Han watchtowers or beacon towers that were built along the northern Silk Route can still be seen, their tamped earth (*pisé*) construction resistant in the dry atmosphere and only weathered by wind. Around such watchtowers, which were garrisoned during the Han, Stein found masses of the woodslips which served as writing material for army documents and letters and which have provided a surprisingly vivid picture of the life of the army garrisons.

Written up by Michael Loewe in his *Records of the Han Administration* (Cambridge University Press, 1967) and listed by the French scholar Henri Chavannes, *Les documents chinois decouverts par Aurel Stein dans les sables du Turkestan oriental* (Oxford, 1913) and *Les documents de la troisième expedition de Sir Aurel Stein en Asie centrale* (London, 1953—catalogues of the woodslips in the British Library collections), they are mostly routine accounts of military life c 100 BC–AD 100 spent counting and tidying the piles of brushwood for the beacons or rounding up the local civilians and stray dogs but there are some poems, letters, calendars and doodles that enliven the overall picture.

Kizil

Kizil was excavated by Von le Coq and the French sinologist Paul Pelliot. Apart from the removal of a depressingly large number of frescoes to Berlin, they uncovered manuscripts on palm leaves, birch bark, paper and wood, including many items written in Kuchean or Tocharian, an entirely independent branch of the Indo-European family, lost for 1000 years until these manuscripts were found and deciphered by Sylvain Levi in Paris at the turn of the century. Some have tentatively described the Urumqi mummies (see p 536) as Tocharians.

The **caves** at Kizil are a 90 minute drive from Kuqa and are situated in cliffs along the banks of the Muzart River which is lined with mulberries, poplar and tamarisk trees. The caves can be visited by taxi from Kuqa by arrangement with *CITS* (in the Qiuci Hotel).

• Tourist facilities are limited (better to stay in Kuqa) and it is common to open only half a dozen caves. There are extra charges of c 100 yuan for 'special' caves at Kizil and visitors are warned that access is sometimes quite dangerous, with unguarded walkways.

The caves date from 500–700, their gradual abandonment reflecting the arrival of Islam in the area in the 14C. They are strongly in the Indo-Iranian style with no trace of Chinese influence, which was non-existent in the region during the time that the cave paintings were being made. The Indian element of the style is found in the basic iconography and depiction of the Buddha and the choice of subjects from the Buddhist canon. The Iranian element is identified in decorative details, such as borders, or on dress and furniture depicted in the murals. Scrolls and friezes of circular medallions with elegant stylised birds, ribbons and flower-strewn grounds are derived from similar patterns on Sassanian silks, metalwork and painting.

The caves are now numbered but were originally named by Grunwedel and Von le Coq after the subject matter of the wall-paintings: the Musicians Cave, Stairs Cave, Prayer-wheel Cave, Foot-washing Cave and so on. Earthquake damage to the caves has been frequent but the worst problem for the visitor is that the best frescoes (or the wartime survivors thereof) are all in Berlin. Those interested are referred either to the Berlin museums or to the catalogue of a travelling exhibition, *Along the Ancient Silk Routes: Central Asian Art from the West Berlin State Museums*, New York, 1982.

There are 236 caves at Kizil of which only 74 still have reasonably well-preserved wall-paintings. Chinese art historians, stressing the non-religious aspect (in an atheist state) single out the musicians of Cave 38 and the scenes of ploughing and pottery-making in Cave 175.

There is a similar group of caves at **Kizil Kara** (usually locked unless special arrangements have been made in advance), closer to Kuqa (only 17km north-west). Very little remains of the frescoes of the 47 caves (contemporary with Kizil) except for the *apsareses* playing musical instruments in Cave 30 and some small repeated Buddha figures. There is a tamped earth beacon tower (late Han).

Kashgar

Kashgar (Kashi in modern standard Chinese) in the far west of Xinjiang provinces, is situated at an altitude of some 1200m above sea level, in the foothills of a ring of mountains that surround the Taklamakan Desert with the Tianshan (Heavenly Mountains) to the northeast and the Pamirs to the south-west. It was the point at which the southern and northern silk routes joined and the 'gateway to the west' for the mountain passes through the Pamirs and Karakorum mountains, leading to Pakistan, Afghanistan, India and Russia, lie just south of Kashgar. Although remote, Kashgar's strategic position has given it an importance throughout history and it remains a major transport centre, especially since the construction during the Cultural Revolution of the Karakorum Highway linking China and Pakistan.

Practical information

Getting there
By air
The airport is 12km to the north of the town. Four shuttle buses leave from the *Xinjiang Airlines* ticket office on Jiefang nan lu (2½hrs prior to departure). There are twice-daily flights to Urumqi and other destinations in Xinjiang and international flights to Almaty have been announced.

By rail
The new railway station is on Renmin dong lu, about 15km east of the city centre. The *CITS* office is beside the Chini bagh Hotel (Friendship Hotel) on Seman lu.

By bus
There are two major bus stations: the Chini bagh hotel (ex British Consulate) is the starting point for buses to and from Pakistan via Tashkurgan; Xinjiang buses terminate on Tiannan lu, south of Renmin dong lu.

Where to stay
As in the past, the competition must be between the Chini bagh, which was once the British Consulate (traces can still be found in the old wing but the famous garden has gone; see p 544), and the marginally more luxurious *Seman Hotel*, formerly the Russian Consulate. The Chini bagh Hotel (Qiniwake) is now known as the *Friendship Hotel* (Yonyi Binguan), 148 Seman lu, ☎ 823 5949. The *Seman Hotel* is at 170 Seman lu, ☎ 255 2129.

History

In AD 78 the Chinese set up a garrison in Kashgar to guard the western frontier but the area was overrun by the Western Turks until the Chinese once more assumed control in the early Tang dynasty, although this sovereignty was soon challenged by the rise of Islam. In 747 a Chinese army was sent out across the Hindu Kush to repel the Arab threat. The army was eventually defeated in 751 at the **Battle of Talas River** (northeast of Tashkent) and Central Asia was gradually opened to Islam. The Battle of Talas River is also supposed to have marked the beginning of paper-making in the west with the capture of Chinese paper-makers. The paper-makers are supposed to have been moved to Samarkand to start a paper industry there, although paper fragments dating back to some 900 years earlier have been found at Silk Road sites and the spread of material and techniques was probably more gradual.

Kashgar had become a Muslim centre by the 10C and did not come under Chinese control again until the 18C. In the interim it may have been visited by Marco Polo whose account contains a description of vineyards, cotton, hemp and flax fields and 'close-fisted' inhabitants, as well as the importance of the town as 'the starting point from which many merchants have set out to market their wares all over the world'.

Chinese control from the 18C was constantly threatened both by the local inhabitants and by outside powers. In 1865 **Yakub Beg** (c 1820–77), a

Muslim apparently from Russian Central Asia, proclaimed himself Khan of East Turkestan and by 1873 was 'master of the entire Tarim region ... attracting the attention of Delhi, London, St. Petersburg and Constantinople' with both Russia and Britain signing treaties of friendship with him. Yakub Beg apparently committed suicide in 1877 when Turfan fell to the Chinese but outside interest in the area continued for this was the beginning of the **Great Game**: the Russian occupied Western Turkestan in 1860 and were viewed as a threat to British India, hence the interest of Delhi and London. Kashgar was a major centre of information gathering: in 1882 the Russians opened a Consulate in Kashgar (their consulate is now the Seman Hotel), ostensibly to 'control trade' and in 1890, the British opened a 'listening post' which was elevated to consular level in 1909 and which controlled Indian (British) representatives in every oasis of the Silk Road.

The extraordinary comings and goings on both sides of the Pamirs have been described by Peter Hopkirk in *Setting the East Ablaze: Lenin's Dream of an Empire in Asia* (Oxford, 1986) in which he relies in part on the many memoirs of British Consuls in Kashgar. Lady Macartney, wife of the first British Consul, Sir George Halliday Macartney, who was there from 1909–18, has left a charming account of the early days in her *An English Lady in Chinese Turkestan* (1931; reprint, Hong Kong, 1984). George Macartney was not related to Lord Macartney, who led the first British Embassy to China in 1792–94 (see Chengde, p 234), but was the son of Sir Halliday Macartney who had assisted General Gordon in the suppression of the Taiping uprising of 1850–64. After the Taiping 'Wangs' or 'Kings' had been executed, Halliday Macartney married the daughter of one of them. Although his Chinese was excellent as a result, George Macartney apparently never referred to his Chinese mother.

Lady Macartney described the Consulate, Chini bagh (the name means 'Chinese garden'). It had originally been a flat-roofed courtyard house when her husband and Colonel Young of the Indian Army (and the Lhasa Expedition of 1904) first arrived in 1890 but was rebuilt in 1913 as an 'imposing European house'.

Some idea of intra-consular relations may be gathered from the problem of glazing the windows, for glass was almost unknown in Kashgar. The Russian Consul, Monsieur Petrovsky, 'had, as a great mark of friendship, lent my husband a large pane of glass in a frame for one window, but unfortunately before long they had a quarrel and the precious piece of glass had to be returned'. The garden at Chini bagh was famous for its fruit trees grown from cuttings from England and the family house (with a pet gander who lived in the drawing room) was a haven for travellers such as Peter Fleming and Ella Maillart who arrived in the summer of 1935 to enjoy baths after five and a half months crossing the deserts.

Peter Fleming's chapter on Kashgar in *News from Tartary* (1935) is even entitled, 'Kashgar-les-Bains'. He described Chini bagh as 'a pleasant house with a lovely garden, standing on a little bluff outside the city' and Kashgar itself as 'very prone to spy fever', although he went swimming in the pool at the Russian Consulate and played 'tennis with the Russians'. For his travelling companion, Ella Maillart, Chini bagh was also a source of sybaritic memories: 'Hot water in the bath up to one's neck ... the gleam of crystal and silver and flowers on the mahogany table ... The luxurious sense of black coffee ... Morning slices of bread drowned under butter and honey' and 'playing football with the Hunza Guards of the British Consulate'. (*Forbidden Journey*, London, 1937). There are contradictions between their accounts (they were unwilling travelling companions for both would have preferred to explore the Gobi alone but the complications and dangers were too great) for while Fleming mentions tennis with the Russians, Ella Maillart stated that neither she nor Fleming could play tennis, hence her indulgence in football.

Since 1949, when the Chinese reassumed full control, Kashgar has altered somewhat, with Chinese settlers bringing a statue of Chairman Mao (still standing in Renmin Square), wide streets and department stores, although much of the town remains Uighur. Uighurs are in a majority here, although the population also includes Kyrgyz, Uzbeks and Tajiks as well as many cross-border traders from Kazakhstan and Pakistan.

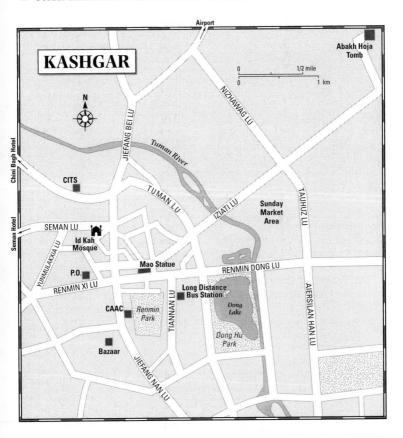

KASHGAR

The **market** on Sunday in Kashgar is one of the biggest in the area and is a chaotic mix of horses, sheep, donkeys, melons, grapes, hats of all sorts from furry to felted, furniture, musical instruments and knives. The Sunday market is held on open ground just east of the river in the east of town. At other times, the main bazaar area is just to the east of Jiefang bei lu (the main north–south street), due east of the Id Kah mosque. Boots, hats of all kinds, saddles and fast food of all muttony sorts can be found there.

The **Id Kah Mosque** (Aitika qingzhen si in Chinese) in Id Kah Square (Aitika guangchang) is the largest mosque in Xinjiang. It is said to have been founded in 1738 and repaired and altered throughout the succeding century, achieving its present form in 1838. Two minarets over 10m high stand beside the imposing main gate built in yellow brick with white tiled patterns. Inside the gate is an octagonal gate pavilion and there is a pool in the courtyard. The main hall is 160m by 16m and there is room for some 6000–7000 worshippers; 140 carved green pillars support the white roof of the hall.

In the south of the town is the **old mosque**, reached by a lane which leads south off Renmin lu, almost opposite, slightly to the east of the Mao statue. The old mosque, about which there is little historical information, is a mud-brick construction with traces of coloured tilework remaining.

On the outskirts of the town are the Abakh Hoja Tomb, the San xian Buddhist caves and the ruins of Aisikeshaer, all best visited by taxi.

The **Abakh Hoja Tomb** (Abahejia mazha mu in Chinese) is in the suburbs of the town, to the east. Abakh Hoja was a man of great saintliness and reknown, who ruled over Kucha, Hetian, Korla and Kashgar, as well as being a major spiritual leader. Said to have been constructed in the 17C, the tomb is surrounded by plane trees and covered with tiles. The dominant tile colour of the dome, for example, is green and the framing of the façade panels is also mainly green but the charming minarets are gaily striped in green and yellow bands with Gaudi-like patchwork patterns and bands of carved blue glazed tiles which are used to frame the main entrance. The tombs, which have been damaged, contain the remains of Abakh Hoja and five generations of his family, 72 people in all. The tomb was renovated and enlarged in 1807 but was apparently vandalised before 1949 when the gold leaf on the ceiling was stolen, together with a board

The Fragrant Concubine

The story goes that a Muslim princess was captured in the mid 18C and taken to Peking as an imperial concubine, where she was known as 'fragrant' because she naturally emanated perfume. She pined for the desert and refused to let the emperor near her; despite this the Qianlong emperor (for it was he) was supposed to have built her Turkish baths and a tower in the imperial garden in Peking so that she could at least look towards her home. In the end, the emperor's mother, who feared that the concubine would kill her son, is said to have forced her to commit suicide by 'self-strangulation' (which I always thought was impossible). Two oil portraits by Castiglione of a woman in armour (in the Palace Museum Collection) are supposed to be the 'fragrant concubine'. Hummel's *Dictionary of Eminent Chinese of the Qing Period* says '...while there is little doubt that such a person actually lived, many of the stories about her are probably legendary'.

personally inscribed by the Qianlong emperor. Only 58 tombs remain, covered with bright saddle cloth.

The tomb gains extra visitors for it is also said to contain the body of the Qianlong emperor's legendary 'fragrant concubine', said by some to have been a grand-daughter of Abakh Hoja.

The **San xian dong** (Buddhist Caves of the Three Immortals) are c 10km north of Kashgar. Their origin is somewhat doubtful: some say they are amongst the earliest Buddhist cave carvings in China, dating back to the 2C–3C but restoration during the Qing appears to have effaced virtually all that remained of the frescoes and figures. Seventy tiny Buddha figures remain in one cave with traces of a lotus ceiling. Access requires negotiation with *CITS* (office in Kashgar) and, these days, the Fire Brigade, which possesses the only acceptable ladders.

In **Wupoer**, 28km to the west of Kashgar, is a newly rebuilt tomb and museum commemorating the life and work of **Muhammed Kashgeri**, an 11C philologist and scholar, best known for a Turkic dictionary in Arabic.

There is apparently the tomb of a noted Uighur poet inside Kashgar's no. 12 Primary School. Information (gathered from Chinese sources) is not terribly illuminating. His name in Chinese is Yusipu Hasi Hajimazha. He was a scholar, poet and writer whose most famous work was an epic poem called (in Chinese) *Fule zhi hui* which means something like 'wisdom through joy'. He was apparently first buried elsewhere but river damage to his tomb necessitated its removal to its present site.

Chengdu

Chengdu, capital of Sichuan province, is a city which managed to preserve some of its traditional flavour for a considerable time despite recent improvements (the old Ming viceroy's palace was only knocked down to make way for the major department store during the Cultural Revolution, 1966–76). The great expansion of wealth in the late 1980s and 1990s has, however, largely completed the destruction. The history of the city dates back to the Spring and Autumn period (220–475 BC), although its greatest glory came when it was capital of the state of Shu during the Three Kingdoms (AD 221–263). From the Han it was known for its production of silk brocade (its major river is still known as the Jin jiang or Brocade River), lacquer and salt.

Sichuan province in southwest China has the highest population of any province (over 100 million) and although one of the largest provinces, it contains much mountainous, sparsely populated terrain. In the eastern part of the province is the **Sichuan Basin** (at about 1000m), of which the most fertile and highly populated part is the Chengdu Plain, irrigated by the Min River, which has been artificially controlled since the 3C BC to improve the agricultural water supply. Sichuan is ringed by mountains, with the Yangtse passing through the narrow gorges to the east and the western part of the province (amalgamated into the present province in 1955) rising sharply to meet the Himalayan massif.

The Sichuan Basin is very beautiful in an intensely cultivated way: hillsides carved and sculpted with terraced fields, softened by feathery giant bamboo, much silvery water, citrus groves and a remarkable natural flora which, together with that of neighbouring Yunnan, attracted the 19C and early 20C plant hunters from the West. Apart from the primulas, buddleias, rhododendrons and azaleas of the Himalayan slopes, the province is also the home of the **giant panda**, now protected in a few reserves, most notably Wolong in western Sichuan (which can be visited) and its faster moving relative the lesser, or red, panda. As well as the panda reserve at **Wolong**, which is not far from Chengdu, there is **Jiuzhaiyou**, close to the border with Gansu province, some 200km northwest of Chengdu. At Jiuzhaiyou, the main attraction is dramatic scenery, including waterfalls, the Pearl Rapids, lakes and the slopes of Mount Zanglong.

The weather varies according to area and altitude: the basin has mild winters and hot summers with most of the plentiful rain falling in July and August. The sky is frequently, almost permanently, overcast and it is said locally that the dogs bark when the sun comes out (as it is such an unusual event). The damp and warm conditions are ideal for agriculture, with all year cultivation of a variety of vegetables and fruit as well as two grain crops, but it can be a bit uncomfortable for the visitor, who is recommended to bring (or acquire) a light mackintosh, waterproof footwear and fast film.

Practical information

Getting there
By air

Chengdu's airport is 18km from the centre of town to the south-west and there are twice daily (or more frequent) flights from Peking, Lhasa, Chongqing, Shanghai, Kunming, Guangzhou and Xi'an and slightly less frequent arrivals and departures from Changsha, Guilin, Guiyang, Hefei, Lanzhou, Nanjing, Shenyang, Taiyuan, Urumqi, Wuhan and Xichang. There are daily flights to Bangkok and Hong Kong. Direct flights to Europe and Japan are planned for 2001. An airport shuttle bus (30mins) leaves from the *China Southwest Airlines* office, Renmin nan lu.

By train

The railway station in the north of the city connects with Kunming, Chongqing and Guiyang, also with Xi'an and Lanzhou.

Where to stay

The most conveniently situated hotel is the *Holiday Inn-Crowne Plaza* (Zongfu huangguan jiari-jiudian) (Zong fu lu ☎ 678 6666, fax 678 6599). One of the oldest hotels in Chengdu is the *Jinjiang Hotel*, 180 Renmin lu, ☎ 558 2222 beside the river. It was refurbished with overseas help (American Standard bath fittings) and although large, it is no longer invariably used for tour groups. It is well situated, with the old quarters of town reached in a short walk up Renmin lu (turn left out of the hotel and take side-streets on either side of Renmin lu). Opposite is the 21 storey *Minshan Hotel* ☎ 558 3333, fax 558 2154 where many groups now stay.

Food

For those who like spiced food, Sichuan cuisine is the best in China. It is usually described as 'hot', meaning peppery, but this is not entirely accurate. There is much use of chilli, although it is rarely as palate burning as in some Indian dishes, but the great local spice is Sichuan pepper which imparts a lemony pepper flavour. Hotels tend to underplay flavouring for foreign visitors and the food may be blandly acceptable but unexciting. When I was in Chengdu with three friends (forming a 'cultural delegation'), our most important morning task was to order three good local dishes rather than the usual hotel fare provided for lunch and supper: *Hui guo rou*, a stewed pork dish with pepper, coriander and lemon balm, *Ma po doufu*, chilli hot, spiced beancurd and *Dandan mian*, dumplings or noodles in spicy soup with a plate of fresh green vegetables, was a favourite menu.

History

Because of its mountainous isolation, Sichuan has been a semi-independent province at many periods of Chinese history. It was first incorporated into the empire in the 4C BC; before that, its connections with the separate cultural area of Yunnan and the fringes of Southeast Asia appear to have been stronger. A report in the summer of 1987 described the discovery of an extraordinary hoard of about 1000 bronze figures, some nearly 3m high and weighing about 300kg, with strange, barbaric, mask-like faces. Found at Sanxingdui, north of Chengdu, these early figures, quite distinct from contemporary bronzes of metropolitan China, emphasise the difference of Sichuan at the time, as well as its advanced technology.

In the period after the Han, the state of Shu in Sichuan produced semi-legendary heroes like Zhuge Liang, Liu Bei and Wang Jian, whose historical exploits have been embroidered into myth. The independence and initiative of the Sichuanese has persisted to the present day. **Deng Xiaoping** was a native of the province and most of those associated with Deng and the immediate post-Mao economic reforms were from Sichuan (to the point that after the 'Gang of Four', there was talk of the 'Sichuan Gang').

The city of Chengdu was first walled in 311 BC and was made the state capital of Shu some 500 years later. In the 1920s its heart was the square walled and moated enclosure of the old palace. Hemmed in by two rivers, the Nanhe and the Fuhe, a street map still shows how the irregular rectangle of the outer city was contained by the two, with the small rectangle of the palace quarter (correctly oriented north–south) in the centre. There are varying accounts of Chengdu in the 1920s and 1930s. The 1924 *Japanese Railway Guide* states: 'The only buildings of any consequence in the old palace quarter are the bazaar and the examination hall ... to the west ... is a separate quarter, surrounded by walls, which is occupied by Manchu bannermen and their families. The busiest quarter is inside the East Gate where a street, 50 feet wide, is lined with rows of silk shops, whose signboards with their gilt inscriptions will at once attract the eyes of a stranger.' In the 1933 *Handbook for China* by Carl Crow the 14.5km outer city wall is described and the well-paved broad streets are also remarked upon, while the palace quarters in the centre are described as being occupied by a teacher training college.

The city has long been an important trade centre. During the late Tang and Song it was a **major printing centre**, with the entire Buddhist canon printed from 130,000 woodblocks in Chengdu between 971 and 983, while in an amalgamation of the business and printing enterprises, printed paper money first appeared in Chengdu in the early 11C.

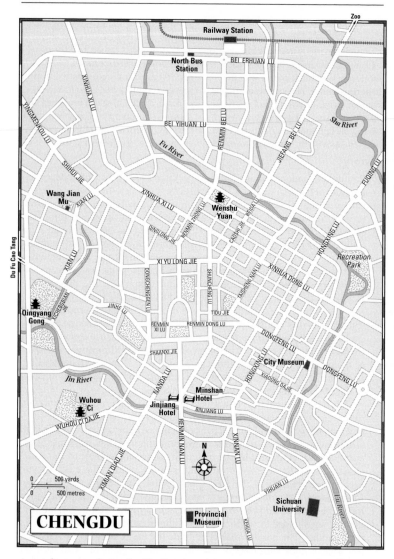

Apart from wandering beside the river (recent reports suggest that this is no longer wise in the evening as pickpockets etc. are about) or hoping to find a surviving wooden-fronted shop in the narrow streets on either side of Renmin lu (near the huge statue of Mao in front of the vast exhibition hall), distances between cultural sites in Chengdu are considerable so they are best visited in groups by taxi or bus.

Sichuan Provincial Museum

The Sichuan Provincial Museum (open Tues–Fri, 09.00–12.00, 14.00–17.00) is on Renmin nan lu, south of the Jinjiang Hotel.

It contains a rich collection of artefacts unearthed in Sichuan and is very strong in graphic arts of the Han dynasty. There are a number of pottery models of houses, models of entertainers of all sorts and an array of the local incised ceramic bricks used to line Han tombs (including copies of some in the Chongqing Museum) depicting buildings, chariots, archery and hunting, salt mining and banquet scenes. There is a fine bronze 'money tree' (another example is in the Nanjing Museum), with coins amongst the branches, a concept which has given rise to a popular opera about a celestial maidservant whose passion for the good things in life on earth was so troublesome she had to be recalled to heaven. Many of the Han tomb figures in greyish clay are larger than the green glazed figures from metropolitan China; characteristic of Sichuan are large females with flowers in their hair and rather daft smiles. The museum also holds some fine Eastern Han Buddhist reliefs and a large Ming funerary cortège in clay. Later exhibits of articles unearthed in Sichuan from the Ming and Qing reveal the widespread use of porcelain from Jingdezhen in Jiangxi. There is also a Qing brocade loom of great complexity.

Whuhou ci

In the southwest of the city is the Wuhou ci (Temple of the Military Marquis), founded in the early 5C in honour of Zhuge Liang.

Zhuge Liang

Zhuge Liang (181–234) was a military genius; a native of Shandong, he assisted Liu Bei (161–223), who proclaimed himself emperor of Shu (based in Chengdu) when the Han fell in AD 220. Zhuge Liang is a good example of a man becoming a myth; a wealth of folklore has grown up around him and he is credited with the invention of various odd military machines as well as military strategies. One story tells of how he promised to acquire 100,000 arrows in four days for a battle against Cao Cao (155–220), founder of the state of Wei, arch enemy of the state of Shu and therefore of Zhuge Liang and Liu Bei. For three days Zhuge Liang did nothing, on the fourth he filled ships with bales of straw and sent them out towards Cao Cao's fleet in the foggy night. Safely concealed below deck, soldiers made a great noise and Cao Cao's fleet let loose with their arrows. The ships returned home, the straw bales filled with reusable arrows, 'borrowed' from Cao Cao, against whom they were to be turned.

The temple was originally linked with one commemorating Liu Bei which stood beside it. Both were destroyed by fire and the existing complex was substantially rebuilt in 1672. The Tang poet Du Fu described the temple in the Tang: 'Where is the temple of the famous minister to be found? In a pine forest outside Brocade City (Chengdu). Spring grass covers the steps and birds sing in the trees. He answered the third call to affairs of state and gave his all to two generations. Before he could achieve conquest, he died and since then, heroes have wet their sleeves with tears.'

The temple is still quite green and full of trees. It has red surrounding walls

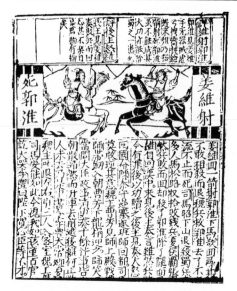

Scene from The Romance of the Three Kingdoms (San guo zhi zhuan), *which featured Liu Bei, Cao Cao of Wei and Zhuge Liang. This edition of 1592 was illustrated by Yu Xiangwu*

topped with green tiles. It encloses a hall dedicated to Liu Bei, with some famous pieces of congratulatory calligraphy, statues of Liu Bei and (east and west) red-faced Guan Yu (the God of War, one of those who helped Liu Bei to establish Shu, subsequently elevated to the status of God of War and Justice), Zhang Fei, another noted general, and others.

Galleries contain brightly painted stucco figures of military heroes of the Three Kingdoms period. In the **Zhuge Liang Hall** (inside the second gate, beyond a courtyard filled with stone stelae) there is a gilded figure of Zhuge Liang with, on one side, an inscription of Zhuge Liang's memorial on setting out on a campaign by Yue Fei (the famous Song general whose own temple is in Hangzhou) and, on the other, a carving recording a meeting with Liu Bei in his retreat. In front of the figure (encased in glass) are three bronze drums in a form that recalls the bronze casting of Yunnan, said to have been cast during Zhuge Liang's lifetime.

On either side of the Zhuge Liang Hall are smaller halls containing statues of the red-faced Guan Yu and Zhang Fei. In covered galleries there are statues of noted officials and military figures, each with a small stone stele recording his life and deeds.

To the west of the enclosure is a walled area surrounding the high, grassy mound said to be Liu Bei's Tomb, which has yet to be excavated. At the rear of the temple is a fine *pen cai* (bonsai) garden.

Just north of the Wuhou ci, in the western suburbs, just to the west of Xi cheng bian jie, is the **Qingyang gong** (Green Sheep Hall) in a park of the same name. Founded in the Tang, the surviving buildings of this Taoist temple date from the Qing. In the main hall (Sanqing dian or Hall of the Three Pure Ones—the Jade Emperor, ruler of heaven, the 'Mystic Jewel', a god who lives beyond the North Pole, and Lao zi are gilded figures of the trinity as well as other gods. In front of the altar table are two bronze sheep. The one-horned sheep has an inscription dating it to 1723 and stating that it was brought from the capital to Chengdu to add to the relics of Lao zi. It is said to incorporate the attributes of all the 12 animals of the Chinese zodiac—rat ears, ox nose, tiger claws, rabbit back, dragon horn, snake tail, horse lips, sheep whiskers, monkey neck, chicken eyes, dog belly and pig buttocks. The two-horned sheep was cast in 1829.

A flower festival is held in the park every year in the second month of the lunar calendar (late February–March).

Du Fu cao tang

Further west of the Green Sheep Hall, outside the main ring road, is the Du Fu cao tang (Thatched Cottage of Du Fu), a bamboo-filled park built on the supposed site of a small rustic retreat inhabited by the poet Du Fu (712–770) in the mid 8C after the rebellion of An Lushan (756) had disrupted life in the capital.

Du Fu

Many of Du Fu's poems refer to the 'Brocade City' of Chengdu and the 'Brocade River' beside which he lived, as well as to the local heroes Liu Bei and Zhuge Liang and their associates. His stay outside Chengdu seems to have been one of peaceful respite in a life of considerable difficulty. Du Fu constantly failed the civil service exams, partly because of general corruption and his own lack of patronage, partly because his extraordinary literary skills may have seemed threatening to the examiners. His personal difficulties were compounded by the disaster of the An Lushan rebellion (766) which laid waste to the capital. Du Fu's family frequently faced starvation (one of his children effectively starved to death) and this, combined with his great sensitivity to the suffering of others and a keen sense of social injustice, has made him a favoured poet of contemporary China where correct social content is an important aspect of literary evaluation.

The tranquil poems written in his 'thatched cottage' refer to natural images far from the war-torn capital, willows carpeting the path with white fluff (a common sight in spring when the seeds with their fluffy coating are released in white clouds), pheasants among the thick bamboo stems, ducklings sleeping pressed against their mothers on the riverbank, peach and plum petals falling on dark pools and swallows nest-building and midge hunting over the water.

Du Fu's poems have been widely translated but the best versions are to be found in Arthur Cooper's *Li Po and Tu Fu* (Harmondsworth, Penguin Books, 1973/1986) and David Hawkes' *Little Primer of Tu Fu* (Oxford University Press, 1967).

Whatever it was that Du Fu actually lived in on the banks of the Washing Flowers Stream, the site was venerated and replicas of various sorts of thatched cottages have been built there since the early 11C. Today there is a sizeable park with various buildings apart from the thatched garden-house. There are exhibition halls with displays relating to Du Fu's life, paintings illustrating scenes from the poems and examples of the multiple editions of his works, including translations. The park itself is well planted, with huge bamboos in thick groves, trees including peach and cedar and small garden areas with flowering plants, *pen cai* (bonsai) and *pen jing* ('pot scenes' with rocks, water and flowers).

Outside the gate, there is a Gaudi-like inscription, 'Thatched Cottage of Du Fu', made from bits of broken decorated porcelain.

Just northeast of the Thatched Cottage is **Wang Jian mu** (Wang Jian's Tomb), inside the ring-road at Santong qiao. Excavated in 1942, the tomb contained the remains of Wang Jian (847–918), ruler of the semi-independent kingdom of the Former Shu during the Tang dynasty. The earth mound is 15m high and more than 80m in diameter. A brick-vaulted construction with three chambers, there are fragmentary wall paintings in the first chamber, a stone-carved portrait of Wang Jian in the back hall and and a great stone-carved platform, on which the coffin rested, in the middle chamber.

Artefacts in the tomb included a jade belt and silver and iron items, including an iron cow. Many of these are displayed in two exhibition halls in front of the tomb. The carved figures around the stone platform are the most interesting items. Warriors hold up the platform, their faces distorted by the effort (like some of the figures at Dazu, they are depicted from the waist up) and a female orchestra is also depicted. The small figures, in varying life-like postures with elegant, wind-tossed robes, play drums, cymbals, various sorts of wind instruments and the *pipa* (lute), accompanying elegant dancing figures (on the front of the platform). The small group illustrates the lively style of Sichuan sculpture in the late Tang and Song (as seen also at Dazu).

Sichuan University

In the east of the city, on Dongfeng lu (not far from the Chengdu Fandian) is the **Daci si** (Temple of Great Benevolence). This now houses the **City Museum** in late Qing buildings, which are all that remain of a Tang temple once famous for its wall paintings. These were praised by Su Shi and Li Zhicun who said: 'The best and most numerous Tang wall paintings in the world are in Chengdu and those in the Daci Temple are the most numerous.'

Southeast of the Daci si is the large compound of **Sichuan University** (once the missionary West China Union University) and the Wang jiang lou (River-viewing Pavilion) both open 08.30–16.30. The university houses one of the most remarkable small **museums** in China, strongest in archaeology and local crafts but also very interesting for its cheerful display. The museum's history goes back to missionary days, for it was founded by the American anthropologist, Daniel Sheets Dye, who also wrote an interesting book on windows called *A Grammar of Chinese Lattice*. It was created to display the finds of archaeological expeditions and local artefacts collected by the anthropology department.

There is a lively display of folk crafts, costumes and handicrafts of all sorts and, remarkably (for the art of display is still in its infancy in China), an imaginative presentation of the collections. Sculptures have been placed in 'niches' as if in a cave-temple, peasant *lan bu* (blue and white indigo-dyed cotton with wax resist patterns) has been used as a background to the anthropological displays. There is a shadow-puppet theatre which is still used. The museum was recreated by the remarkable archaeologist and ex-science fiction writer, Tong Enzheng, a great defender of Sichuan's archaeological independence and difference. Sadly, he died recently in America.

The **River-viewing Pavilion** (Wangjianglou) is on the banks of the Brocade River in the southeast corner of the university campus. The building that stands today is a late Qing pagoda-like tower with sharply upturned eaves, 30m high, square at the base, octagonal in plan on the two upper storeys. It is associated with one of the few famous women poets of China, Xue Tao (d. c 834).

> ### Xue Tao
> A native of Chang'an (present day Xi'an), Xue Tao came to Chengdu with her family and after her father's death she lived in poverty. She is said to have written her poems on red-dyed paper and a well in the park is traditionally supposed to have been where she washed her poem-paper after dyeing it. The area is now a popular children's park.

Wenshu yuan and Chengdu Zoo
In the north of the city are the Wenshu yuan (Manjusri Temple), the Tomb of Meng Zhixiang and the Zoo.

The **Wenshu yuan** (or Manjusri Temple) is just east of Renmin bei lu, on Wenshu yuan jie. It is a thriving religious centre; the path leading to the temple is lined with stalls selling a mixture of religious necessities: fire crackers (for scaring evil spirits), candles, incense, holy pictures and rosaries, mixed in with spiced noodles and cotton knickers. This sort of approach to a temple by means of a street of stalls is reminiscent of the surroundings of cathedrals and shrines in medieval Europe.

The temple is the headquarters of the *Sichuan (and Chengdu) Buddhist Association* and bursts with old ladies lighting incense sticks in bronze burners. The temple dates back to the Nan chao (Southern Kingdoms period, 420–589) but was destroyed in military action during the Ming. It was rebuilt in 1691 and renamed Manjusri Temple. It encloses five linked halls and contains over 100 bronze Buddha figures of different sizes, many cast by famous craftsmen of the Qing. In the Hall of the Law (towards the rear) are ten iron figures of the Song period. The stone used for pillar bases and platforms is local.

The **Chengdu Zoo**, best reached by taxi, is in the north of the city and is naturally best known for a large number of pandas, both giant and lesser. The giant pandas, at feeding time, do seem to be less lethargic and bored in their home province than elsewhere. When they hear the keeper coming, they occasionally push, shove and fight, growling and honking in a very un-panda-like way. There are fairly frequent births, so quite a number of young pandas can often be seen. Beside the giant panda enclosure is that of the lesser (red) pandas, who are always lively and jolly.

Seven kilometres north of the city at **Moban shan** is the **Tomb of Meng Zhixiang** (893–934), excavated in 1971, which yielded a similar array of artefacts as that of Wang Jian (jade belts and tablets and decorative items) but it is otherwise noted for the wall paintings of figures and carvings of dragons.

Around Chengdu ~ Guan xian

Outside Chengdu are two major sites, the **Baoguang si** (Divine Light Monastery) to the northwest in Xindu xian county town and the **Dujiangyan Irrigation Scheme** and **Qingcheng Mountain** in Guan xian to the west.

Guan xian is c 60km from Chengdu. It used to be reached by a road of considerable interest, which ran through green paddy fields, past half-timbered farm houses hidden in damp, dark groves of bamboos towering over the thatched roofs. Some of the villages on the road were very picturesque, the main street lined with wooden fronted shops open to the street to display their brightly coloured wares.

Hardware stores sold choppers, wooden buckets, birdcages, basketwork fish-traps, baskets and scoops; teahouses (very popular in Sichuan), with their low bamboo chairs spilling out onto the roadside, were full of tradesmen, their loads piled outside, and street traders included butchers and toffee toy-makers with special tables. Small children paid a few cents to spin a pointer on a board surrounded by paintings of animals and then the toffee was dribbled onto a marble slab in the form of a dragon, goldfish or monkey, according to the animal that the pointer indicated. Traffic on the road included huge pigs, immobilised by being tied with a plank along the spine, being taken to market on the back of a bicycle. The road has since been straightened and widened but if you have a chance to make detours through villages, they are well worth it.

In the county town of Guan xian, a road to the left leads to **Qingcheng shan** (Green City Mountain), one of the lesser Taoist mountains; climbable in a day. During the Han the 'Heavenly Master' Zhang Daoling ascended the mountain and built a thatched hut for himself; since then the mountain has been a Taoist centre. You can see old Taoists, dressed in short black robes, their legs bound in cloth leggings, their hair in a small bun (in the Ming men's hairstyle which antedates the Qing imposition of the queue or 'pigtail') in the Guan xian market or on the mountain.

The highest temple is the **Shangqing gong** (Hall of Supreme Purity) at 1600m above sea level. Although most of the temples are Tang (or earlier) foundations, the damp, dank atmosphere is not conducive to timber preservation and those now standing are mostly late Qing (or far more recent). The mountain contrasts with Buddhist holy mountains in its stress on nature and natural appearance. The small thatched shelters at resting points on the steps are unpainted, built of timber and thatch, blending with the trees that tower over them. In some, twisted, curling branches have been attached just under the eaves, in imitation of the complex brackets found on grander buildings.

As one of the Taoists greatest tenets was reverence for nature and a refusal to interfere with natural processes, the mountain, with its rustic shelters almost indistinguishable from their surroundings, is a fine illustration of this and remarkable in contrast with Emei where the Buddhist temple buildings stand out from their setting.

About half way up the mountain is the **Tianshi dong** (Cave of the Heavenly Master), headquarters of the Taoist Association, the site where Zhang Daoling used to deliver his sermons. There is a stone-carved portrait of the master on the rock and statues of three emperors of the Tang dynasty in the main hall (which is late Qing in date). The buildings, rickety wooden halls perched on the rocks with windows framing misty views and verandah seats, have a dark charm. There is a huge gingko, said to have been planted by Zhang Daoling in the Han dynasty (described in a local guidebook as 'doddering, whirling and imposing'), a palm said to date from the Tang, nine Song dynasty pines and a 'fairy pine' of the Ming. Small stone carvings on the balustrades depict small boys in unusual, faintly improper, postures.

Outside the gate of the Shangqing gong (near the summit) are two gingkos, believed to be several hundred years old, and on either side of the hall are two springwater wells, one square, one round, known as the 'Mandarin Duck Wells' (meaning that they are a male and female pair).

The **Dujiangyan Irrigation Scheme** on the outskirts of Guan xian is one of China's earliest irrigation schemes, begun in about 250 BC when the local prefect Li Bing and his son diverted the waters of the Min River to irrigate the plain.

Guan xian stands at the point where the Chengdu plain meets the mountains of west Sichuan and the Min River reaches the plain. The river was divided into two channels (the 'inner' and 'outer' river) by means of a 'fishmouth' dyke, constructed from stones held in bamboo nets, with a further movable dyke to divert the water in case of flood and to prevent excessive silting. The 'outer' river is the natural course of the Min. The scheme brought water to some 1300 square km (an area expanded to 5300 square km after 1949 with the aid of some slightly more modern methods).

The scheme is best viewed from the **Fulong** (Subdued Dragon) **Temple**; first built in the Song to commemorate Li Bing and his son, it stands on a promontory where the river divides. Approached through a park, the Qing dynasty temple buildings, dark-roofed with upturned eaves, now contain relics relating to Li Bing and his son. The highest part, overlooking the division of the river waters, is the Guanlan ting (Looking out over the Waves Pavilion). In the main hall is a large stone statue of Li Bing (nearly 3m, weighing 4.5 tons) carved in AD 168. This was excavated from the river in 1974 and is thought to have been cast into the river in a superstitious gesture to ensure the maintenance of successful irrigation.

As the *Mingsheng cidian* records, the posterior hall contains an electric, movable model of the dam for the edification of visitors; these days there is also a video.

Some distance from the Fulong Temple, on the east bank of the Min River, above the division, is the **Erwang miao** (Two Kings Temple), dedicated to Li Bing and his son. This is usually approached from the road above, leading up through the mountains from Guan xian. Seen from above, the Two Kings Temple is wonderfully sited: grey tiled roofs with extravagantly upturned eaves and tiled decoration sit amongst a sea of green trees on the high bank above the racing river and the chain bridge below.

The temple was founded in the Nanchao period (420–589), although the surviving buildings are Qing. As you descend the steep steps to the temple, notice the roofs with their tiled figures: elephants, cats, dragons, horses and phoenix. Inside the temple halls are modern stucco figures of the two kings as healthy heroes (despite or because of the filmstar looks of the younger Li in particular, old ladies still burn incense in the temple). There are many stone-carved inscriptions in the temple, including Li Bing's famous dictum 'Dig canals deep, make embankments low' which was later half-hijacked by Mao Zedong in regard to planting rice.

Although lavish in its roof decoration, as you reach the lower parts of the temple, the use of whitewash and dark wood in the 'half-timbered' Sichuan style is

Erwang miao (Two King's Temple), Guan xian

restrained and attractive. Note, as you descend, a sort of cage with sculpture in it, including some fine iron pieces.

Below the temple is the **Anlan** (Pacifying the Waves) **Bridge**. This is an iron chain version of a common form of low slung bridge (originally on bamboo ropes) common in the southwest of China.

> The first bridge was built here before the Song but it was destroyed by fire in the Ming and rebuilt in the Qing. A local story says that a local tutor's wife proposed the rebuilding of the bridge and gave some money but because of the corruption of the local officials, who took the money, nothing happened. The tutor exposed the corruption and was killed for his pains so local people, enraged by this, helped his wife to continue with the bridge building.

You can cross the 500m bridge, although a major tourist pastime seems to be to jump up and down on it, which makes it feel very unlike a 'wave-pacifying' bridge.

Divine Light Monastery

The Divine Light Monastery is c 19km northwest of Chengdu in a small market town. It is best reached by taxi.

> The monastery is said to have been founded in the Eastern Han. In 881, when the Yellow Turbans uprising laid waste to the Tang capital, the emperor fled to Sichuan (as his ancestor had done during the An Lushan rebellion over 100 years earlier) and stayed in this temple. At his orders the temple was restored and renamed the Divine Light Temple. It flourished during the Ming and the Qing (with a major restoration in 1670).

Today it comprises a (leaning) pagoda, five halls and 16 courtyards (and a figure of over 400 stone columns involved in the buildings is given). The pagoda appears to be Tang in date (while the rest of the temple is Qing), with close-packed eaves in 13 storeys above a square base. The slightly upturned eaves are probably a later addition; Tang pagodas of this type do not tend to have upturned eaves. An early feature of the pagoda is its position in the heart of the temple, common in Tang layouts. It has a pronounced list.

In the large and flourishing temple, the most popular attractions are trying to touch the centre of the spirit wall outside the main gate, with your eyes shut for luck, and a gaudy collection of 500 lohans of the Qing period.

> If you notice people wandering past the lohans and laughing uproariously, it is probably because they have been practising another local custom, which is to walk past the lohans, counting the years of your age. The lohan they reach at the appropriate moment is a form of fortune-telling. As they all have 3m eyebrows or other grotesque attributes, this gives rise to hilarity.

In the small courtyards at the back of the temple, where tea is offered, there are some charming 'sunken' gardens. The buildings are raised above the open courtyards (because of the heavy rainfall in Sichuan) and these lowered stone courts are filled with marvellous pot plants. There are also some interesting and rather baffling old photographs of famous monks of the temple, who were known for their meditational acrobatics (balancing on one finger on a tiny teacup, levitation, etc.).

Zigong

Getting there
Zigong is best reached by long-distance bus from Chengdu, Chongqing or Leshan. The long-distance bus station is in the south of the town.

Where to stay
The *Shawan Bingnan* is on Binjiang lu (☎ 0813 220 8888, fax 0813 220 1168).

A town rarely visited is Zigong, some 200km southeast of Chengdu (or 200km west of Chongqing), famous since the Han for its salt production. The rock salt is found in wells, deep beneath the earth, drawn up by water buffaloes. There is a **Museum of Salt Production** set up at Deng Xiaoping's suggestion in 1959, housed in the lavish Xiqin Guild. This was the salt producers' guildhall, sometimes known as the 'Shaanxi Temple' and built in 1736 for the salt merchants who came to trade in Zigong. Built in the traditional courtyard style, the guildhall is particularly extravagant in construction, from the incredibly complex gate through to the rear. It was said of it: 'Every five paces a tower, every ten paces a pavilion, with covered walks all round, eaves projecting like teeth and brackets and corners', suggesting palatial construction. The columns, whether of wood or stone, are mostly carved and there is hardly a surface left uncarved or umembellished. It is one of the most extraordinary buildings in China and a fine example of merchant ostentation.

On the Dashanpu road to the north you can visit the **Xinhai Well**, a working salt mine until 1966. Beyond the mine is the **Zigong Dinosaur Museum** (open 08.30–17.00, closed Mon). Sichuan and the Gobi desert have produced most of China's dinosaurs. The exhibits here include the local velociraptor, Yangchuanosaurus.

Dazu

The small town of Dazu is just north of the Chengdu–Chongqing railway line, roughly equidistant between the two. Set in beautiful, lush countryside, it is famous for its stone carvings which date from the last years of the Tang to the Qing, with the majority carved during the Southern Song. The carvings are largely Buddhist in theme but combine elements of Confucianism and Taoism, as well as being fairly eclectic within the Buddhist tradition.

Practical information

Getting there
By train

The nearest station to Dazu is Youtingpu (five hours from Chongqing, seven hours from Chengdu). From Youtingpu, public buses take about one hour to get to Dazu.

By bus or car

Dazu is 160km northwest of Chongqing and the easiest way to get to it is by car or bus from Chongqing. This now takes less than three hours on the new Chengdu–Chongqing highway. The old road involved a journey of c five hours through green hilly country, carved out with paddy fields. There is a regular bus service from Chongqing's northwest bus station (on the far side of the Jialing River bridge), with buses usually leaving from 08.00 to 16.00.

Where to stay
There are two hotels in Dazu, the *Dazu Binguan* and the *Beishan Binguan*, near Beishan, ☎ 437 22888.

History

The stone carvings of Dazu represent the last great group of stone carvings in China but, in contrast with Yungang and Luoyang, they also represent a strong local tradition with no imperial connections. Sculpture in Sichuan is everywhere remarkably plastic and lively, nowhere more so than in Dazu, where strict iconography is subservient to movement and story telling. There are **two major groups of sculpture** around Dazu, the **Bei shan** (North Hill) and **Baoding shan** (Precious Summit), with other smaller groups scattered in the hills.

The sculptures were begun in 892, just before an independent kingdom was set up in Sichuan (Earlier Shu, 907–971), presaging the general breakup at the end of the Tang. The North Hill group was started in 892 by Wei Junjing, the local Commander-in-Chief and Governor of Changzhou, representative of the imperial Tang government in the area. He presided over the early Buddhist carvings, which were continued through the collection of donations by local gentry, Buddhist monks and nuns over the succeeding 250 years, resulting in some 10,000 carved figures.

The Baoding group centred on a monastery 15km northeast of the town. A local monk, Zhao Zhifeng, who returned to Dazu after years of study of Tantric Buddhism, worked for 70 years (1179–1249) to collect money to finance the carving of a similar number of figures to those on North Hill. He became known as the 'Sixth Patriarch of Tantric Buddhism'. Another name for Tantric

Buddhism is Esoteric Buddhism; it relied on incantations and meditational techniques (including meditation on mandalas or diagrams of the disposition of deities) to achieve union with the Buddha. This is another method of 'simplifying' or shortening the process of enlightenment, an important aspect of Buddhism in China with its frequent anti-monastic movements.

North Hill

North Hill is just 2km north of Dazu, with 290 caves carved into a 500m cliff. The first figure (**Cave 2**) is a statue of the founder, Wei Junjing, with an inscription dated to 895 recording the making of the sculptures as well as a contemporary peasant uprising. The earliest caves (of the Wei Junjing period) are **Cave 3** (containing a Vajra Bodhisattva), **Cave 5** (a Vaisravana Devaraja), **Cave 9** (Thousand-armed Guanyin), and **Cave 10** (Sakyamuni, the historic Buddha) and the solid, smooth-faced figures are more simply disposed than some of the later figures. In **Cave 245** there is a sort of mandala or meditational diagram in low relief, based on the Pure Land Sutra which relates to the Pure Land or Paradise of Amitabha.

In an assemblage of over 650 figures, there are three levels: at the top, in a mixture of palace buildings and ribbon clouds is the Western Paradise or 'World of Extreme Joy', the Chinese Buddhists' heaven; in the centre are the three deities of the Western Paradise, with Amitabha Buddha in the centre, Guanyin on the left and Mahasthamaprapta on the right; the last is a Bodhisattva who represents the Buddha wisdom of Amitabha and this grouping is characteristic of all representations of the Western Paradise. At the bottom is a section of the sutra where rulers request the Buddha's help, a request which resulted in an apparition of the paradise and also the 16 paths to be cultivated. As with almost all the sculpture at Dazu, this is elegantly designed and positioned, framed by a stepped series of square-framed Buddha images. The architectonic base adds strength and grandeur to the more fluid crowd and cloud-filled upper section, where straight lines give way to swirls and circles.

Cave 273 has a rather stubby Thousand-armed Guanyin with almost caricatured attendants.

Cave 101 has a fine example of Song calligraphy by Cai jing.

Cave 279 has another beautifully designed, asymmetrical niche with the Buddha of Medicine, Bhaisajyaguru, as its centre. To the left is a pagoda, to the right are shelf-like niches of Bodhisattvas with (headless) attendants; above are a row of Buddhas sitting on lotuses; below are the 12 protectors of Bhaisajyaguru above a row of naturalistic lotus buds and leaves. The somewhat stolid carving of the main figures and the Viennese whorl clouds below the protectors do not detract from the balanced design of the whole.

Caves 125 and 113 The different representations of the Bodhisattva Guanyin in Caves 125 and 113 (sometimes said to be the work of one sculptor) reveal a more confident phase. Here the figures themselves are elegantly designed, rather than being like some of the others mentioned, stumpy icons in elegant frames. In Cave 125 the Guanyin with a rosary is an elegant woman with swirling sleeves and scarves standing on a lotus against a plain oval halo. In Cave 113 the Bodhisattva is depicted in the pose called 'royal ease', one knee drawn up, the other dangling carelessly, ribbon drapery flowing around the casually disposed limbs, pearls and silks decorating the impressive head-dress and loose robes.

Cave 136 The largest cave on the North Hill is Cave 136, carved between 1142 and 1146. In the centre is an octagonal 'Cart of Mental Divinity' resting on a huge dragon. There is a Buddha figure and several representations of Guanyin: seated in the lotus position with meticulously carved draped robes; with four arms; with two arms in a *mudra*; with two holding up discs representing the sun and moon. Beside is a standing Guanyin casually holding a rosary and wearing an extraordinary crown with two crossed ribbons floating ceilingwards; another standing figure has a flame-halo and is holding a sprig of willow and the bottle of sweet dew which is one of Guanyin's more common attributes. Another seated Guanyin in the cave, with crisp robes and a beautifully detailed head-dress, holds up a jade seal; a standing Guanyin, with a veil partially covering the head-dress, holds a strange, ethereal version of a *ruyi* 'sceptre' in the form of a ball from which a ribbon swirls up and over the deity's shoulder. A very female-looking Bodhisattva Samantabhadra with a flaring head-dress, sitting on an elephant whose trunk is missing, is matched by Manjusri, in a petalled head-dress, sitting on a lotus throne on a lion's back.

Cave 130 In this cave a slender, rather threatening figure brandishing swords and spears in her eight arms, is the 'bright-eyed daughter', or Prabhacaksadevi, a former incarnation of Ksitigarbha, the Bodhisattva who presides over the underworld. She is surrounded by monster-headed protectors.

Cave 155 In the Thousand Buddha Cave (155) where the walls are lined with tiny Buddha figures, there is a four-armed Buddha figure on the back of a giant peacock, a representation of the 'Peacock King', a former incarnation of Sakyamuni who, as a peacock, sucked water with healing power from a rock. Like the 'Cart of Mental Divinity', this central figure provides a focus for perambulating meditation.

Cave 177 The rather squat figure of Ksitigarbha (dressed as a lama) seated on a square plinth in Cave 177 was carved by the same man who made the Peacock King, You Yuanjun, not perhaps the most skilled of the Dazu sculptors. The grotesque attendants to Ksitigarbha in Cave 177 are more skilfully carved, dismally representing the terrors of judgement, and the figures on the walls in lama robes, looking variously serene and disturbed, are metamorphoses of Kistigarbha.

Cave 180 In Cave 180 there are 13 representations of Guanyin, elongated and serene, with filigree head-dresses, very characteristic of Song art at its most elegant.

The **Many Treasure Pagoda** (Duobao ta), 114–54, an octagonal, multi-eaved pagoda, 31m high, stands over the cliff above some large Buddha figures carved against the rock.

The Baoding carvings

The Baoding carvings, (15km northeast of Dazu), reached by a road that runs up through neat terraced slopes towards misty mountains, are more exposed, carved in a horseshoe-shaped gully. To reach the carvings walk to Beishan. Between Beishan and Baoding white minibuses shuttle back and forth.

Above the gully are some temple buildings, totally rebuilt in the 1980s, and steps leading down to the sculptures below. These were almost all carved between 1179 and 1249. At the bottom of the steps, turn right towards the huge 'Sleeping' Buddha (**Niche 11**); on your right are 'a fierce tiger coming down the mountain' (**Niche 1**), a series of guardians (**Niche 2**) and a great 'wheel of the law' (**Niche 3**).

> In the centre is the monk, Zhao Zhifeng, who founded the site, above him is a pavilion representing the Western Paradise. The two outer rings contain the animals of the cycles of rebirths and the deeds that lead either to paradise or hell or rebirth as a lower animal. The wheel is gripped in the teeth of a monster and supported below by more human attendants; ribbons of Buddha figures emanate from the centre.

A little further along are three large (7m) figures flanked by pagodas and with 1000 small Buddha images carved into the rock behind (**Niche 5**). These are the Three Saints of Huayan or Avatamsaka Buddhism (which viewed the universe as ordered and classifiable with everything leading to the centre, the Buddha): Vairocana Buddha in the centre, flanked by Manjusri and Samantabhadra, all bearing pagodas (Vairocana Buddha's has disappeared).

Cave 8 Further on, Cave 8, which is fronted by a timber facade set further into the cliff than most of the Baoding sculptures, contains China's largest **Thousand-armed Guanyin figure**. The central figure is about 3m high but the assemblage of 1007 hands, each with an eye in the palm (the Bodhisattva is 'all-seeing' as well as 'all-succouring'), covers 88 square metres. The popularity of Guanyin as a saviour is evident from the number of scarves and offerings draped over the hands.

The **'Reclining' Buddha**, actually entering Nirvana, filling the east cliff and measuring 31m from head to knees, forms a backdrop for an extraordinary sculptural ensemble. The Buddha, who rather than dying is entering a state of non-being (Nirvana, not to be confused with Heaven), is surrounded by smaller figures that emerge, waist-high, from the rock. They include Bodhisattvas bearing the symbols of their attributes; at the central altar, topped with more Bodhisattvas, three officials in official hats preside over the offerings. The grouping of these figures, some with their backs firmly turned, others facing this way and that, is remarkably naturalistic.

Niche 12 At the far end of the Nirvana scene, Niche 12 contains a fountain dripping from the mouth of one of nine dragons into a pool below where the baby Buddha is being bathed.

Niche 13 contains another Peacock King cave, with inscriptions from the *Mayurasanasutra*.

Niche 14, where Vairocana Buddha is depicted preaching, is the centre of tantric, or esoteric, worship in Dazu. Disciples are depicted listening to the Buddha and the elegance of the carving is considerable.

Niche 15, which depicts parental care and the consequent debt owed by all to their parents, is an interesting mixture of the Confucian stress on filial piety (which is a fundamental tenet of Chinese society) and its takeover by Chinese Buddhism. Non-canonical Buddhist texts presented virtually the same contents as the Confucian texts on filial piety. In Dazu the representation of childbirth, suckling and childcare is in the form of a three dimensional comic-strip, with text included. From the top are scenes of praying for a son, pregnancy, childbirth (the mother, standing, is about to give birth, the kneeling midwife rolls up her sleeves), suckling, washing babyclothes, lying with the child, the concern of the father about to depart on a journey, arranging a marriage for a child, killing a pig to celebrate it and 100-year-old parents still worrying about their 80-year-old offspring.

Niche 16 In this niche are the deities of wind (holding an inflated bladder), rain (riding on a dragon, for dragons are associated with water, both in rivers and clouds), lightning (holding two mirrors) and thunder (a pig-headed figure banging a drum).

Niche 17 returns to the theme of filial piety, essentially Confucian, here showing how Sakyamuni, the historic Buddha, repaid the kindness of his parents, a distinctly Chinese embroidery on the few facts. Beside a large figure of the Buddha, the stories are told, as in Niche 15, in a three dimensional comic-strip, with blocks of text from the apocryphal sutra on Mahopaya Buddha requiting the kindness of his parents set between the scenes.

The Buddha offers his own flesh to nourish his parents (a story duplicated in the Confucian *Twenty-four Examples of Filial Piety* when, during a famine, a daughter-in-law thoughtfully cuts off her finger to feed her elderly parents-in-law); the Buddha's parents bend over a skeleton, that of their child devoured by a tiger, but the infant miraculously reappears; below, brahmins accuse the Buddha of being unfilial; to the right of the major statue, Sakyamuni helps carry his father's coffin and, further on, when a doctor prescribes a human eye as the only remedy for his father's blindness, the Buddha offers his own.

Niche 18 In Niche 18 the Western Paradise theme is illustrated, the presiding Buddha and attendant Bodhisattvas apparently looking down over the scene, with tiny pavilions representing heaven between them. Below, meritorious believers who will enter heaven stand before the judges who preside over heaven and hell and small boys emerging from lotuses (symbols of purity) tumble over the balustrade.

Niche 21 By contrast with the relative calm of Niche 18, Niche 21 has a three-tier representation of judgement resulting in relegation to hell. Above is the Bodhisattva Ksitigarbha, who sits in judgement over the souls of the dead; in the centre are the judges and below are the tortures of hell. As in other sections at Dazu, isolated figures set between the major scenes tell stories by themselves. scenes of husbands and wives or brothers and sisters unable to recognise each other because they are drunk foretell inevitable consignment to hell; even the charming 'hen-wife', a gently smiling woman tending her chickens, is doomed, presumably because she has reared the chickens to be killed and eaten, contravening the Buddhist law against taking life.

Niches 24 and 25 Crossing the bridge, or returning to the bottom of the steps, a number of late Taoist images from the late Ming and Qing can be seen and a lion guards the entrance to **Cave 29**, the Cave of Perfect Enlightenment, deeply carved into the rock and filled with a pantheon of the three Buddhas (past, present and future) with attendant Bodhisattvas. Typically, there is a sculpted kneeling figure, with his back to the visitor, recalling the interesting placing of the attendant figures to the Reclining Buddha and illustrating the difference of Dazu where straightforward icons are rare.

Niche 30 Finally, beside the steps in Niche 30, cowherds are shown tending their oxen, taking them out to pasture (where the cowherd can rest or play the flute).

The Buddhist significance of cowherding relates to the 'taming' of one's nature. There is a charming Chinese Buddhist work with illustrations that depict the ox turning from black, through half-black, half-white, to white as the cowherd manages to tame it. At first it must be led by means of the ring through its nose; when it knows what it is meant to do, the cowherd need no longer lead it, it follows him docilely; thus should Buddhists tame their passions.

Emei shan

Emei shan (Lofty Eyebrow Mountain), 3099m above sea level, is the western Buddhist holy mountain, the abode of Samantabhadra, the Bodhisattva of Pervading Goodness, patron of followers of the *Lotus Sutra*, who is usually depicted on a white elephant. The mountain, rising on the southwest of the Sichuan basin, is thickly wooded almost all the way to the Thousand Buddha and Golden Summit and frequently covered with cloud, often at several levels. It is said locally to be 'beautiful, like moth's eyebrows, long and fine', perhaps because the soft outline of the summit can occasionally be seen above the thick cloud. It was not the only moths' eyebrows to be admired: beautiful women were also said to have moths' eyebrows. It is c 50km from the foot to the summit. A Ming poet exaggerated slightly when he said: 'Emei is lofty, piercing heaven; a hundred miles of mist, built in the void where birds whirl and turn; lotuses open amongst the strange peaks.' The earliest temples were built here during the Eastern Han (AD 25–220), although those that stand today have all been very recently restored.

Practical information

Getting there
By train

The Emei station on the Chengdu–Kunming line is some distance (c 4km) from Emei town and the mountain itself is 7km southwest of Emei town. As buses from the station are rare, it is best to take a taxi (c 20 yuan) to the Baoguo si and the foot of the mountain. The train journey from Chengdu takes two to three hours.

Where to stay

There are frequent local buses from the station to the Baoguo (Protect the Nation) temple which is close to the major hotel, the *Hongzhushan Hotel*. Though travellers in 1924 were advised to bring cooking stoves, pots, pans, charcoal, chickens, vegetables and sugar (*Japanese Railway Guide*) there are now hotels at the base of the mountain. The *Qinggong Binguan*, ☎ 559 0921, is near the Baoguo si.

Climbing the Mountain

Emei is the most arduous of the Buddhist mountains; those with heart conditions should remember that it is over 3000m high and consult a doctor (it might be wiser to stay lower down), although it only takes a couple of days to ascend or descend and there are minibuses which run from the **Baoguo**

Temple to the **Jieyin dian** (Welcoming Hall) at 2540m, near the summit. There a cable car takes you to the **Golden Summit/Jinding** (3077m above sea level) and a monorail leads to the **Wanfoding Ten Thousand Buddha summit** (3099m). In bad weather, or for those not accustomed to climbing slippery steps, one day could be spent taking the bus to the Jieyin dian (individual travellers may find that the fare involves considerable bargaining) and walking to the summit from there, or taking the cable car before returning to take the bus back to the Baoguo Temple.

On the second day take the bus to the **Wannian** (Ten Thousand Years) **Temple**, about halfway up the mountain, and either explore at this level (and get the bus back) or descend to the Baoguo Temple on foot. The third day can be spent in the temples around the foot of the mountain. Obviously the plan can be reversed, although waiting for clear weather for the peak is not a very profitable planning method as it so rarely comes. Better climbers may prefer to take a bus to the Jieyin dian and then walk the whole way down the mountain, staying overnight in a temple.

Those wishing to see the famous **monkeys** in their natural surroundings should descend via the **Xianfeng** (Fairy Peak) **Temple** and remember not to tease the monkeys, which are said to have rushed the odd visitor off a cliff before now.

Because of rain and cloud, the mountain is very damp: a light waterproof cape with a hood is useful and a stick is helpful on the slippery stepped paths (these can usually be bought from persistent sales persons dotted about the mountain). If you are to stay overnight in temples, you may have to hire extra bedding or a thick padded coat as it is very cold and damp at high altitudes. It is best to organise accommodation in monasteries as early as possible as these dormitories become full quite early.

There are porters on the higher slopes of the mountain above the Jieyin Hall. They carry everything up the mountain: all the equipment for the cable car from the Jieyin Hall was carried by teams of porters. Although very small (as are most people in Sichuan) they are used to their job. They have a wooden contraption on their backs with a sort of shelf and carry T-shaped sticks. When resting, they place the stick under the load, to take the weight. They are quite keen to carry visitors, for about 10 yuan, although they very much object to being photographed doing so.

From the Jieyin Hall, follow the stepped path to the **Golden Summit** (Jin shanding; 3077m). The climb is steep, with occasional flat parts for relief, the steps rising through thick forests of conifer and rhododendron, mist and cloud. When you emerge from the forest, the summit lies along a steep cliff. Some stay overnight at the summit to see the dawn, others wait for the 'Buddha Light' (15.00–16.00, Oct–Nov, weather permitting, which it rarely does) when rainbows appear above the cloud below the cliff and, if the sun is in the right place, giant shadows may be cast on the cloud. Railings were set on the cliff edge as early as the Song dynasty, for ecstatic believers cast themselves into the cloud at the sight of the miraculous light. The temple has been completely rebuilt and has a yellow glazed tile (golden) roof.

The original temple at the Golden Summit was constructed in the Eastern Han and was the most important of the 100 or so that flourished from the 6C on the mountain. Apparently the summit was often struck by thunderstorms and buildings were frequently destroyed by lightning. There was a temple, much decorated in gold (hence its name of Golden Temple), housing a bronze Buddha and a Ming bronze stelae of the Chenghua reign period (1465–87) which recorded one reconstruction and was written in the calligraphic style of Wang Xizhi. The stelae was said to be housed in the Woyun (Sleeping Clouds) Hermitage (with the corrugated iron roof just below the site of the Golden Temple) but it may reappear in the Golden Temple.

For those making the full descent, retrace your steps to the Jieyin Hall and continue down the stepped path until you reach the **Xixiang chi** (Elephant Bathing Pool) at 2100m above sea level, said to be where the Bodhisattva Samantabhadra's elephant bathed. Beside the pool is a small hermitage, founded in the Ming and enlarged in the Qing (1699). In the hall are figures of Guanyin, Ksitigarbha and Mahasthama. The rare sight of the

Mountain peaks, from Hong xue yin yuan *by Linqing, 1879*

'nightmoon in the elephant's pool', as the Tang poet Li Bai put it, is one of the famous views of Emei. It is round about the Elephant Bathing Pool that you may first see the troupes of 'wild' monkeys that live on the mountain (and off tourists), begging for food. They can be very persistent and quite dangerous if teased.

The next major building below the Elephant Bathing Pool, at 1752m, is the **Xianfeng** (Fairy Peak) **Temple**, built by a Ming dynasty monk in 1612. The original buildings were said to have been constructed with lead planks and iron tiles. On the hillsides nearby grow dove trees (*Davidia involucrata*) and more monkeys.

Descending to 1120m, the **Hongchun** (Tall Tree of Heaven) **Temple** was also founded by a Ming monk (a Chan, or Zen, follower) but rebuilt in 1790 by another Chan monk. The temple takes its name from the 'trees of heaven' in front of it. Inside the hall is a late Qing Thousand Buddha lotus lamp carved with seven dragons and 100 Buddha figures.

At 710m is the **Qingyin** (Clear Sound) **Pavilion**, about 10km from the foot of the mountain; those descending from the summit may wish to stay overnight here, or in the Hongchun Temple. The White Dragon and Black Dragon Streams meet just below the pavilion, where a large black shiny rock projects; this is known as the Oxheart Rock, from its shape. Nearby is the Flying Rainbow Bridge spanning the two streams. The local gazetteer describes the scene: 'Clear sounds are heard near the lofty pavilion, as if Buddhist spirits were playing musical instruments; incline your ear near the double bridge where the water strikes the ox's heart.'

Those who have made the descent from the summit may then climb up to the **Wannian** (Ten Thousand Year) **Temple** at 1020m, slightly to the west of the Qingyin Pavilion. Those who returned to the foot of the mountain should take a bus up to near the Wannian Temple, which is not quite half way up the mountain. This is the major surviving temple on the mountain. The many subsidiary buildings have been quite recently reconstructed; when I first visited the mountain in 1981 there was virtually nothing except the square brick building enclosing the Bodhisattva riding on his elephant.

The temple was founded during the Jin (3C–4C AD) and greatly expanded in the Wanli reign period of the Ming (1573–1620) when there were seven great halls. With the exception of the brick building (also Ming in date), these were destroyed by fire in 1946.

The brick building, with a beamless vaulted ceiling, is 16m high and each side is 15.7m long. Inside is a Northern Song figure (cast in 980) of the presiding Bodhisattva on his white six-tusked elephant. Cast from bronze, the whole is 7.3m high and weighs over 60 tons. As the figure has been plastered with stucco and painted, no traces of the casting technology are visible; it must have been a complex task. Around the central figure there are 24 niches on the lower part of the walls, containing small iron Buddha figures; above are six rows of niches containing 307 small bronze Buddha figures.

In pools on the mountain nearby and in front of the hall lives another animal speciality of the mountain, the '**lute frog**' whose croaking on summer nights is said to sound like lute music.

Just below the Wannian Temple is the Cave (or Temple) of the White Dragon, **Bai long dong**. This is locally said to be the place where the legend of the White Snake took place, although the story is also associated with Hangzhou's Leifeng Pagoda.

A white snake which had turned itself into a beautiful girl married a young man. He was eventually persuaded by a Buddhist monk that she was fundamentally evil and she was incarcerated alive, either here or in the Leifeng Pagoda. Around the temple building are many huge old *nanmu* cedars, said to have been planted by a Ming monk. He planted them while reciting the Lotus Sutra, planting a tree for every character he uttered. Although he is said to have planted 69,777 trees, only a few stand today.

Following the path downwards, you reach the Qingyin Pavilion (see above). From there, head south along the ridge towards the **Chunyang** (Pure Brightness) **Hall** (920m), first built in 1585 and restored in 1633. This was originally a Taoist temple, transformed into a Buddhist temple in the early Qing. In front of the hall is a stone, said to be the place where Samatabhadra rested when he arrived on the mountain.

Either retrace your steps to the bus near the Wannian Temple or continue down the mountain past the **Leiyin** (Thunder-sound) **Temple**, founded in the Ming. In the Qing it was known as the 'casting off' hermitage for it was said that pilgrims to the mountain cast off the dust of the world here.

Below is the **Fuhu** (Crouching Tiger) **Temple**, which can also be visited, for those based at the foot of the mountain, by climbing up from the hotel. It was founded in the Tang and gained its name either from the hills behind looking like a crouching tiger or because the monks here in the Song suffered from the depredations of tigers and prayed in the temple for protection. The temple was rebuilt in 1651. Surrounded by *nanmu* cedars, the temple was described by the Qianlong emperor as 'the garden far from impurity'; the inscription can still be seen.

The lowest temple on the mountain is the **Baoguo** (Protect the Nation) **Temple**, just north of the hotel. Founded in the Ming, it was restored in the Qing and the inscription over the gate (with the three characters of the name of the temple) is in the Qianlong emperor's handwriting. The main halls rise one above the other and comprise a Maitreya Hall, Main Hall, Seven Buddha Hall and Sutra Library. The greatest treasure of the temple is a **Ming ceramic Buddha** (1415), 2.4m high, and the **Huayan** (Garland) **Pagoda**, a 7m, 14 storey, dark bronze pagoda, also dating from the Ming. This has the complete text of the *Garland Sutra* (*Avatamsakasutra*) cast on it, as well as 4700 tiny Buddhas.

In the side wing before the main hall there is an exhibition of the stuffed animal life of Emei—including bearded frogs, lesser pandas and small deer—its geology and history.

Leshan

Leshan, 167km south of Chengdu, is famous for its giant Buddha, carved out of a cliff in the Tang dynasty. Since the destruction of the Bamiyan Buddhas in Afghanistan, this is the tallest surviving Buddha figure, despite its seated position.

Practical information

Getting there
By bus
Leshan is now probably best reached by bus from Emei (1hr), Chengdu (c 3hrs) or Chongqing (5hrs) on the newly constructed motorways.

The Buddha is best reached either by road (by taxi) or by a ferry that crosses from Binjiang lu to Lingyun hill.

By train
Leshan is some distance from the railway, the most convenient station is Emei, near Emei shan (Mount Emei), where buses run to Leshan (about 90 minutes).

Where to stay
The *Jiayhou Binguan* on Baita lu, ☎ 213 9888, fax 213 3233, may be singled out as one of the rare hotels in China which is wonderfully situated. It stands high above the confluence of two rivers, the Dadu and the Qingyi, offering a fine view of river life and, in the misty distance, the giant Buddha.

Three rivers converge at Leshan—the Dadu, Qingyi and Min—and the Buddha sits against a cliff on the bank of the Min. The town has grown, sprawling downhill away from the rivers, and while the Jiayou Hotel used to be surrounded by old

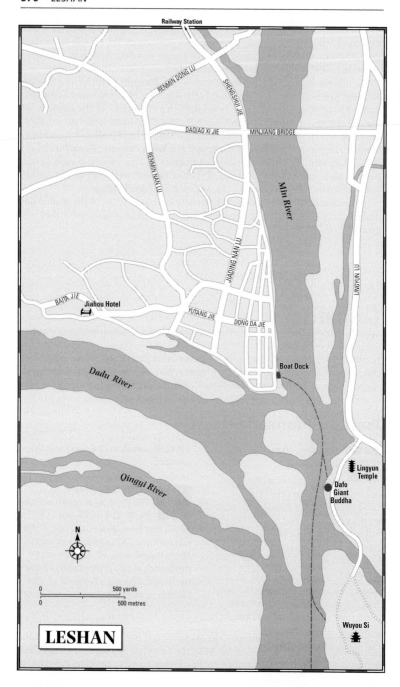

Railway Station

RENMIN DONG LU

SHENGSHUI JIE

DAQIAO XI JIE

MINJIANG BRIDGE

RENMIN NAN LU

Min River

JIADING NAN LU

BAITA JIE

Jiahou Hotel

YUTANG JIE

DONG DA JIE

LINGYUN LU

Dadu River

Boat Dock

Qingyi River

Lingyun Temple

Dafo Giant Buddha

N

0   500 yards

0   500 metres

Wuyou Si

LESHAN

streets, pleasant to wander in, with its open-fronted timber frame shops and restaurants, the area is now new and modern.

The **Giant Buddha**, carved between 713 and 803, the largest of its kind in China, is 71m high. The head alone is 14.7m high and 10m broad with 7m-long ears (all Buddha figures have long ears, the lobes dragged down by earrings). It is said to have been built with funds raised by a monk who gouged out one of his own eyes to impress potential donors. One of his motives was to subdue the river floods, hence the position of the figure, dominating the rivers.

According to Chinese sources, it is the largest stone-carved Buddha in the world and a local saying states: 'The mountain is a Buddha, the Buddha is a mountain'. Impressive rather than beautiful, it is a figure of the Buddha of the Future, Maitreya, sitting as if on a chair, with hands on knees. A local guide says that it is 'deeply impressive not only because of its perfect proportion, but also the advanced scientific principles it embodies. For example, it has a complete hidden drainage system ... to prevent its surface from weathering'.

To the right of the Buddha a narrow series of steps with nine turnings has been cut into the rock to enable visitors to descend to the feet and the riverside (100 people are supposed to be able to sit on one foot). As the steps are very narrow and have to accommodate those ascending and those descending, it is something of a struggle but the feet are worth it.

Above the Buddha are temple buildings and the **Lingyun** (Spirit Cloud) **Pagoda**, first built in the Song and restored in the Ming and Qing. It is built on a square base, with 13 close-eaved storeys built in brick.

If you walk past the Buddha along the river away from the town, you will see in the distance a low-slung suspension bridge and you will pass a number of tombs built in natural caves along the cliff. Low down, near the river, is one dating from AD 159 with a roughly carved Buddha figure in the lintel. This is a very early example of a Buddha figure, dating from the first years of the introduction of Buddhism to China.

Further along is the **Wuyou Temple**, founded in the Tang, with a Guardian King Hall, Maitreya Hall, Tathagata Hall and Mahavira Hall, all of the Ming and Qing. The last houses 3m figures of Sakyamuni, Manjusri and Samantabhadra carved from camphor wood. In the temple is the *Er ya* platform, supposed to be the place where the text of the *Er ya*, a 3C BC 'dictionary' of glosses on early texts, the forerunner of the tradition of dictionary-making and literary exegesis, was first expounded. The original text by Guo Sheren was lost but much survived in Guo Pu's work of some 500 years later. The name of the temple was originally Dajue si (Temple of the Great Awakening) but it is now known by the name of a nearby mountain, Wuyou (Black Splendour).

Another Guo, whose family home is c 35km east in **Shawan** (best visited by taxi), is Guo Moruo (see box on p 572). The house is a fine example of local domestic architecture. Three courtyards and a garden formed the home of one of the most extraordinary figures of 20C China.

Those who have reached Leshan from Chengdu by coach or car may stop at the **San Su ci** (Memorial Temple to the Three Sus), pretty well halfway between the two. Set in a huge park, which is itself of passing interest as it contains in one section some concrete walls, quite effectively modelled on the pierced walls of Suzhou gardens (here openings filled with bamboo to enhance the view beyond are all in concrete, rather than tile) and is an interesting development. The park and halls commemorate three generations of poets.

Guo Moruo

Guo Moruo (1892–1978) studied medicine in Japan but never practised. He became a prominent member of the political and literary establishment from his discovery of Marxism in the 1920s. He was also a major historian, literary critic, scholar of early texts, translator, poet and playwright. His political position meant that his literary talents have not really been critically assessed but his tendency to flaunt his wide reading, dotting his works with foreign names and terms, which had to be written sideways to fit in with Chinese typography, has provided amusement for students of Chinese. An unforgettable line of his reads: '*Wo tebie xihuan Spinosa, yinwei wo ai tade pantheism*' (I especially like Spinosa because I love his pantheism).

Su Shi

The most famous poet in the Su family was Su Shi or Su Dongbo (Su Tung-po, 1037–1101), whose family lived in this part of Sichuan. His father and younger brother were also well-known poets. Su Shi passed the civil service exams in 1057 but his career as a bureaucrat was blighted by his opposition to the reigning reformer, Wang Anshi. He was endlessly exiled, as far away as Hainan Island on one occasion. Also a noted painter of bamboo (the all-round cultivated scholar of the Chinese ideal), he is said to have been able to turn the lyric form to an incredible variety of themes.

Chongqing

Wartime capital of Nationalist China, Chongqing is dramatically situated at the meeting place of the Yangtse and the Jialing rivers in Sichuan province. The city, Sichuan's largest (although it is now separated from the provincial administration, having, like Peking, Tianjin and Shanghai, 'metropolitan status') is situated on the southeast edge of the Red Basin of Sichuan, which is surrounded by high mountains. The rivers that meet at Chongqing are fed by the snows of the Qinghai plateau and swell dramatically in the spring, rushing through deep gorges that cut the city into three.

Until the bridges were built after liberation in 1949, the separate parts of the city were accessible only by ferry. Ferries can still be seen, viewed best from the Chaotianmen Point where, when the river is high and fast, they are pulled at top speed downstream before struggling back against the flood to reach the jetties. Mainly used as a starting point for a boat trip through the Yangtse gorges, Chongqing has a good museum, some picturesque stepped streets lined with rickety, dark tiled houses on stilts and sinister wartime relics.

Practical information

Getting there
By air

Services operate several times daily from Peking, Shanghai and Guangzhou; there is a daily flight from Hong Kong and less regular flights from Kunming, Shanghai, Changsha, Guiyang and Wuhan. The new Jianbei airport is 25km north of the city and has transformed access to Chongqing. The city is famous for its damp and fogs. It is known in Chinese as 'foggy Chongqing'; flights to and from the old airport were frequently delayed, although Sir Archibald Clark Kerr, British Ambassador during the Second World War, described the climate with some enthusiasm as being like that of Scotland.

By train

The station is in the southwest of the town, near the north bank of the Yangtse and connects Chongqing with Chengdu (an overnight trip) and also with Guiyang and Wuhan.

By boat

For the Yangtse gorges (and beyond, Wuhan and Shanghai) boats leave from Chaotianmen Point. The booking office is just nearby, at the end of Shaanxi lu.

Where to stay

The major hotel is the *Yangtse Holiday Inn*, Yangzijiang jiari jiudian. ☎ 638 03380, but the *Renmin dalitang*, 173 Renmin lu, ☎ 638 51421, fax 638 52076, set back from Renmin lu in the west of the town, is unmissable for its Temple of Heaven design.

History

The old part of town is situated on a spur of land, or high rocky bluff, above the fast running rivers below, giving it another of its epithets, 'mountain city'. It was a centre of trade, standing at the head of the Yangtse gorges, through which the Yangtse flows down to the ports of Wuhan and Shanghai, and much of Sichuan's trade with the rest of China passed through the town, for the Red Basin is surrounded by mountains which made overland trade difficult. Its present name—'Repeated Celebrations', a name which derives from the Song emperor's subjugation of the area, an event quickly followed by his ascent to the throne—dates from the Song dynasty; it was declared a 'city' as late as 1927.

Chongqing had attracted the interest of **western entrepreneurs** anxious to reach the markets of the hinterland of Sichuan somewhat earlier and Archibald Little's steamer *Leechuan* was the first to make the upriver trip to Chungking (as the city's name used to be romanised) in the low water season of 1898. This was after the town had been opened to foreign trade by an Additional Article of 1890 to the Chefoo Agreement of 1876. The Chefoo Agreement followed the murder of the British Consul, Augustus Raymond Margary (1846–75) in Yunnan where he had gone to meet Colonel Browne's mission from Burma. The intention of the agreement on the British side was to open trade routes between Yunnan—and eventually Sichuan, too—and British-ruled India.

The difficulties of Yangtse navigation were, and still are, complicated by the annual rise of the river—between 21m and 33m—the height and volume of water being most marked in late summer and early autumn after summer rains and melting snow.

After the opening of the city and the start of regular steamer trade the foreign population grew rapidly, with some 180 residents in 1920 (British, American, French and Japanese all with their own consulates) and all the major firms: Butterfield & Swire, Jardine & Matheson, Asiatic Petroleum, the British-American Tobacco Company, Standard Oil and the India and Eastern French Trading Company, dealing in yellow silk, goatskin hides, bristles, musk, rhubarb, insect wax and wool (from Tibet).

Chongqing's greatest period of population expansion came in October 1938 when **Chiang Kai-shek's Nationalist Government** moved here from Nanjing, which was captured by the Japanese on 13 December 1938. Over 2000km inland, protected by the gorges and mountain ranges, Chongqing was quickly filled, as government officials and refugees of all sorts flooded into the walled city. The population spilled out to fill the other small walled city on the north bank of the Jialing River, described in 1920 as 'occupying a space less than one mile square ... built on solid rock with no possible chance for drainage and consequently reeks with odours even more pronounced than in most Chinese cities'.

Grander houses were perched on top of the city, while poorer houses were clustered on stilts along the stepped lanes. When the American General Stilwell arrived in 1942 to try and clarify his position in relation to Chiang Kai-shek and the command of the Chinese armies in Burma, he had to climb 365 stone steps up to his western style house near the Chaotianmen promontory. Transport within the city was mainly by sedan chair, for the lanes were impassable to motor vehicles; even today Chongqing is virtually empty of bicycles because of the steep inclines.

During the brief and rather unsuccessful **United Front** (of Nationalists and Communists against the Japanese invaders) in 1937–41, the overcrowded city was home to leaders of both parties and, as a consequence, simply bursting with secret agents and spies. Soaring inflation and corruption meant that coolies carried $50 notes, according to General Stillwell, and it was generally agreed by foreign correspondents that government salaries were so low and infrequently paid that there were no fat Chinese under the rank of Minister of Finance. The miseries of overcrowding were complicated by Japanese bombing raids which devastated the unprotected city whenever the fogs lifted. Bombshelters were carved out of the rocks wherever possible but the flimsy wooden houses of the city were flattened in their thousands.

It was described in the 1890s by the *Times* correspondent, Morrison, as a city full of temples and pagodas and spacious public buildings, whose grandeur was said to be due to opium revenues. These have all disappeared, together with the city walls. Today the city has been much rebuilt in concrete and only those sections which escaped the Japanese raids still reveal what it was like in the 1930s.

To see the town at its most dramatic, at the point where the two rivers meet, go to **Chaotianmen Point** at the easternmost end of the city. This can be reached by taxi or by a No. 12 bus from outside the Renmin hotel, which takes you to the junction of Minzu lu and Xinhua lu. From the terminus, walk towards the point (northeast along Xinhua lu). From the point where once you could see the gunboats of foreign nations at anchor ready to protect trade and the interests of foreign nationals, as well as more junks than anywhere else on the upper Yangtse,

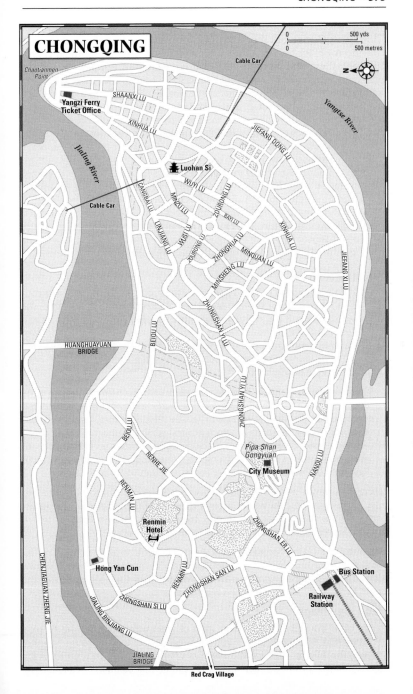

CHONGQING

Chaotianmen Point

SHAANXI LU

Yangzi Ferry Ticket Office

XINHUA LU

Cable Car

0   500 yds
0   500 metres

N

Yangtse River

JIEFANG DONG LU

Jialing River

Cable Car

Luohan Si

CANGBAI LU

WUYI LU

MINZU LU

ZOURONG LU

LINJIANG LU

WUSI LU

ZOURONG LU

BAYI LU

ZHONGHUA LU

MINQUAN LU

XINHUA LU

ZHONGSHAN YI LU

MINSHENG LU

JIEFANG XI LU

BEIQU LU

HUANGHUAYUAN BRIDGE

BEIQU LU

RENHE JIE

RENMIN LU

ZHONGSHAN YI LU

Pipa Shan Gongyuan

City Museum

NANQU LU

Renmin Hotel

ZHONGSHAN ER LU

CHENJIAGUAN ZHENG JIE

RENMIN LU

Hong Yan Cun

ZHONGSHAN SAN LU

Bus Station

ZHONGSHAN SI LU

JIALING BINJIANG LU

Railway Station

JIALING BRIDGE

Red Crag Village

you can watch the cablecar crossing the Jialing River (to the left) and the many ferries struggling against the currents.

Returning to the bus terminus area, just off Minzu lu on the south side, opposite where the road is joined by Cangbai lu, is the **Luohan Temple**, virtually the only surviving temple in Chongqing. Founded in the Song, it was heavily restored in 1752, only to be burnt down during the Japanese bombing raids and restored in 1945. In front of the gate is a stele dated 1623, bearing, rather mysteriously, the inscription 'Ancient traces of the West Lake'. Inside, on either side, are Buddhist carvings in the rock of Buddhas and lohans, rather weather worn. The 500 stucco lohans that once stood in the main hall and gave the temple its name have been destroyed.

South of Zhongshan yi lu is the **Loquat Park** (Pipa shan gongyuan), named after the loquat trees that grow there. Before 1949 it was the site of the private residence of a family named Wang and was therefore called the Wang Garden.

Take Zaozi gangya south of the Renmin hotel until you reach the junction with Zhongshan er lu; turn right for the entrance to the park which stands (as you will already be aware) at Chongqing's highest point, offering a view of the city, fog permitting. The tea houses of the park are popular with the elderly.

City Museum

The City Museum (open 08.30–17.00) is on the south side of the park and contains most notably one of the best collections of **carved tomb bricks** from the Han dynasty, a small but rare **ethnographic exhibit**, including puppets and woodblock prints and paintings mainly by the local painter Zhang Daqian, born in 1898, who spent his later life in Brazil and Taiwan. The Han tomb bricks are displayed with photographs of *que* pillars (also of the Han), which have been quite widely found in Sichuan.

> Erected in front of major buildings, these usually have timber architectural details reproduced in brick or stone. The tomb bricks, made of incised and stamped earthenware, were used to line the interior of local tombs and bear a variety of designs, many of which illustrate daily life under the Han: chariots and horses, courtyard houses, acrobats and tumblers performing at banquets and hunting scenes, fulfilling the same function as wall paintings in Egyptian tombs. These bricks were peculiar to Han tombs in Sichuan.

There is a separate wing to the museum (separate entrance charge) which, when they are not travelling the world, displays some of Sichuan's **dinosaur remains**, including the skeleton of the world's largest beast, *Mamenchisaurus* and a smaller, fiercer *Yangchuanosuarus* and nests of dinosaur eggs.

A number of sites in Chongqing recall the days of the anti-Japanese war and the United Front, mostly those sanctified by the presence of well-known Communists. The best known is **Hongyan cun** (Red Crag Village), near the south bank of the Jialing River, best reached by taxi.

Red Crag Village

> In 1938 the Eighth Route Army (part of what was to become the People's Liberation Army) set up its southern headquarters in Chongqing, together with the office of the *Xinhua Ribao* (*New China Daily News*, forerunner of the *People's Daily*). Zhou Enlai was in charge of this southern headquarters,

assisted by such notables as Dong Biwu, Deng Yingchao (Zhou Enlai's wife) and Ye Jianying. Their first office was destroyed by Japanese bombs, so this three storey building was built by the officers of the southern headquarters themselves. Together with the nearby Gui yuan (on Zhongshan si lu) and the New China Daily Office at 208 Minsheng lu, the whole grouping is known as 'Red Crag Village'. The new headquarters building backs onto the river and, to the left, the KMT established their police headquarters (non-secret variety), while the headquarters of Dai Li, head of the secret police, were moved to the right.

Dai Li—described by Barbara Tuchman as 'China's combination of Himmler and J. Edgar Hoover' and his 'organisation' by General Stilwell as a 'gestapo'—can hardly have been a reassuring neighbour for the Communists. Not a very confidence-inspiring landlord, either: it was he who supplied General Stilwell with lodgings on Chaotianmen Point, a building which was presumably bugged by whatever means, electronic or human, he had at his disposal. As well as being surrounded by buildings full of police and spies, it appears that every street hawker and tea stall proprietor in the road outside was suspect. The red building, with its wooden walls and verandahs, seems curiously flimsy and unsafe even today and it is easy to imagine the enemy outside.

Mao Zedong stayed here when he arrived in August 1945 to negotiate with Chiang Kai-shek after the Japanese had been defeated. The Chongqing negotiations, a vain attempt to stave off the inevitable civil war, which involved substantial concessions from the Communists—withdrawal from their southern 'liberated' zones and a huge reduction of their armed forces in return for greater democracy in the Nationalist Government—did not long survive. In 1947, under threat, the Communists left the Red Crag Village for Yan'an.

Returning to Zhongshan si lu, turn right along it until you reach the Gui yuan (Cassia Garden) on your right, just before the roundabout. The small two storey western style house was the **home of Zhang Zhizhong**, who had served as director of the Huangpu (Whampoa) Military Academy in Guangzhou and was an important Nationalist general.

Zhang Zhizhong

Zhang Zhizhong (1890–1969) was a KMT delegate at the Chongqing negotiations and later led the KMT delegation which made peace with the Communists in 1949 (in Chiang Kai-shek's absence). After 1949 he remained in China, serving as a Deputy Chairman of the National People's Congress and on defence committees. He let Mao Zedong use the house during the negotiations, moving to another residence with his family. On 10 October 1945 the Chongqing negotiations were concluded in the house and the next day Zhou Enlai wrote a poem for Zhang Zhizhong: 'We are hoping for brightness, ten thousand miles ahead; the new China will belong to our young people.'

From the roundabout, the turning on the right leads to one of the two bridges of Chongqing, the **Jialing Bridge**, high above the river, constructed in 1963–66. The road opposite, Renmin lu, leads back to the hotel.

Outside Chongqing

Sites to be seen outside Chongqing (check with your hotel for details of tourist bus trips) include two hot springs and the **US-KMT joint prison** (SACO, or the Sino American Cooperation Organisation) site at Gele shan. The latter is in the northwest suburbs and consists of an exhibition hall displaying photographs and manacles. The prison, established by the KMT in 1943, was where a number of Communists and KMT opponents were killed, particularly on the eve of the liberation of the city on 27 November 1949, when over 300 inmates were put to death.

The **Northern Hot Springs** are in **Beipei**, a suburb in the northwest of the city, an area of pretty mountain and river scenery, including a temple with a main Buddha hall built in 1432. Spring water baths may be taken, where the water arrives naturally warmed to 32–37°C. They can be reached by bus no. 306.

The **Southern Hot Springs** are some 20km from the city on the south bank of the Yangtse, again set in a pretty, cliffside garden.

The Yangtse River

The upper reaches of the Yangtse River (Chiang Jiang in Chinese) have been navigated for thousands of years despite difficulties. Rising on the high Qinghai plateau, on the border with Tibet, the river flows fast down through Sichuan province, swelled in the late summer by melting snow from the highlands and the summer rains. Near the border of Sichuan and Hubei provinces, the Yangtse flows through a series of narrow gorges where the river level falls 150m. Now valued for their attraction to tourists, until 1898, the gorges were navigable only by small boats.

As is widely known, a new dam is being constructed at **Gezhou**, near Yichang; expected to be completed in about 10 years' time, it will raise the level of the water in the gorges considerably. Since the construction of the first dam (1970–81), many of the trackers trails and dangerous rocks have disappeared under water and the new dam will make the whole experience even less interesting. The local human cost is enormous: hundreds of thousands of peasants have had to leave their homes and ancestral graves and the ecological effects hardly bear thinking about. I leave the following account in for those who still take the boats, perhaps as a break, but would not recommend it as highly as in the past.

Practical information

Getting around

Travellers today generally embark at Chongqing and disembark after two days at Wuhan. Although it is possible to continue to Shanghai or Nanjing, beyond Yichang the river is flat and immensely broad and not terribly exciting. It is also possible to see the gorges by going upriver from Wuhan to Chongqing, which is cheaper, but it takes four days against the current.

There are luxury-class liners which offer first class (single or twin) cabins. More commonly used are the boats of the Dongfang hong (East is Red) line which offer second, third, fourth and fifth class accommodation. Second class means a neat two berth cabin with its own wash-basin (hot and cold water), desk and chair. Second class passengers may use the lounge at the front of the boat (where they sometimes fight in an ugly manner for the best photographic vantage points). Third class passengers are accommodated in rooms with ten berths (two-tiered bunks); Fourth class is similarly arranged with space for 12 or more and fifth class is a vast area of three-tiered bunks. There is a dining room, available to all, at the back of the upper deck at the opposite end to the lounge.

History

Determined to gain better access to the riches of Sichuan province (silks, goatskins, hides, bristle, minerals, timber) and those of Tibet, distributed via Sichuan (musk, rhubarb, medicines and wool), Archibald Little (1838–1908) first got a steamer up the Yangtse through the gorges to Chongqing. Downstream navigation involved riding the treacherous rapids, which were particularly dangerous since there were numerous obstacles hidden at high water, but it was upstream navigation that was hardest and slowest. It was particularly difficult during the high water season as the water flow was so rapid. Boats had to be dragged by trackers, usually teams of 80 to 100 men hauling on a 400m rope of twisted bamboo. In the gorges they frequently used narrow trackers' paths cut into the rock many metres above the water level, which made their task all the more difficult and dangerous. These paths can still sometimes be seen, although the generally higher level of the water has covered many parts. In the late 19C these were described thus:

Narrow, steep flights of steps are in many places cut into the rock to facilitate tracking, as well as rock paths a foot or so wide, some only fifteen or twenty feet above the river, others at a giddy height on which the trackers looked no bigger than flies. On all of these and indeed for much of the upward journey, the life of the tracker is in continual peril from losing his foothold owing to the slipperiness of the rock after rain and from being dragged over and drowned by the backward tendencies of a heavy junk tugging at the end of 1200 feet of a heavy bamboo hawser as thick as an arm.

Travellers described how the trackers, the rope on their calloused shoulder, were bent double with effort, their fingers touching the ground. Apparently even Archibald Little's steamer required trackers to guide it through the gorges. His boat was only 16.5m long and he travelled at low water when many dangerous rocks were at least visible.

In her book, The *Yangtse Valley and Beyond* (1899), Isabella Bird describes the organisation of the tracking team, their work directed by a rapid beating of gongs and drums on board ship when they were required to pull hard, their pace slowed by a slower drumbeat. There was also a flag-signalling system operated from boat to shore with the trackers' foreman communicating the message to his men. The need for these subtleties of direction was due to the complex water-flow through rapids with whirlpools and eddies that threatened to take a boat off-course. The many semi-submerged rocks in the rapids added to the dangers; some of these can still be seen at low water, although since the construction of the first Gezhou Dam just above Ichang, the water above Ichang is never as low as it was in Mrs Bird's day.

A British naval commander who served on the Upper Yangtse in 1926–28 and 1932–34 wrote a book called *Excelsior: being an inadequate description of the Upper Yangtse Compiled by 'Charon'* (Shanghai, 1934), describing the late summer high water:

Vast volumes of water come pouring down from Tibet in the form of 'freshets', rais-
ing the level of the river by leaps and bounds. In their struggle to fight their way
through the 'bottleneck' formed by the Gorges in the last hundred miles above
Yichang, they turn these hitherto peaceful reaches into boiling, seething infernos of
tumbling, tossing water, whirlpools, eddies, backwaters and sudden vertical 'boils'.

Mrs Bird watched a junk falling foul of such conditions:

A great cargo junk was being hauled up with two hawsers, over 200 trackers and
the usual enormous din, the beating of drums and gongs, the clashing of cymbals
and the incessant letting off of crackers to intimidate the spirit of the rapid, when
both ropes snapped, the trackers fell on their faces and four hours' labour was lost
for in a flash the junk was at the foot of the rapid and the last sight I had of her was
far below twirling round in a whirlpool with a red lifeboat in attendance ...

Apparently one junk in ten was stranded and one in 20 lost annually. Mrs Bird noted that all this:

... climbing over the huge angular boulders of the river banks, sliding on their backs
down spurs of smooth rock, climbing cliff walls on each other's shoulders or hold-
ing on with fingers and toes, sometimes on hands and knees, sometimes on shelving
precipices where only their grass sandals save them from slipping into the foaming
race below ... on a narrow track cut into the rock ... on which narrow and broken
ledge a man unencumbered and with a strong head would need to do his best to keep
his feet ... was accomplished on a diet mainly of rice.

Chongqing Departure from Chongqing is in itself impressive: the confluence of the two rivers, Yangtse and Jialing, adds to the volume of water swirling east-wards; the many ferries swing out in wide circles as they cross from bank to bank and the city stands high above. As you leave the city, most of the boats that you pass are either steamers loaded with passengers or small sailing vessels on short-haul, often loaded with rock, presumably for building.

If possible, it is interesting to get onto the deck at the prow; on the boats I have travelled on this was officially reserved for the crew but our crews did not seem to mind. From there you can look back, up to where the captain or pilot directs the course and communicates with other vessels. Although the river level is higher than it was, his activities still indicate the dangers that lurk. He is constantly scan-ning the river and the course may appear peculiar for he has to navigate past many hidden shoals and rocks which may not be visible at high water. The towns and villages that you pass also indicate the perils of river life. They are perched high, 'scattered on carefully terraced heights' reached by steep flights of hun-dreds of slippery steps, for the river may rise as much as 40m in the summer.

Shibao zhai The first major sight on the river, c 280km from Chongqing, is Shibao zhai (Stone Treasure Storehouse), a 30m high rock which is said to look like a stone seal (inscribed stone, rather than animal).

This is the first of thousands of stones said to look like other things that you encounter on the Yangtse. Combined with folk legends attached to peaks and caves, these can seriously interrupt study of the scenery; this form of narrative is, however, the way the Chinese see the gorges and hence the way the scenery is presented or explained.

A temple was built at the top of the Stone Treasure Storehouse during the Qianlong emperor's reign (1736–96) and the pagoda-like structure of 11 storeys, which conceals a spiral staircase leading to the temple, was built during the reign of Jiaqing (1797–1821). This tapering multi-eaved structure with its upturned eaves and porthole windows is most impressive.

Wan xian 50km beyond is Wan xian, where most boats used to moor for the night. If the current was particularly strong, this was an impressive moment. Often the anchor had to be laid near the far bank and the anchor chain fed through the boat to enable it to resist the pull of the water and moor in Wan xian (rather than miles downstream). Wan xian, a county seat, was perched high above the river and was reached by a broad sweep of steep stone steps, beneath which a multitude of boats were moored. The rise in the height of the river resulting from the construction of the new Three Gorges Dam (partially completed) has changed this approach. Passengers can usually disembark and fight their way up to the town, whose streets are lined with stalls selling lidded baskets (a Sichuan speciality; most have black and red patterns), which you can fill with other local products, tangerines and pomeloes. Sometimes groups of tourists are taken to factories where silk is spun and woven.

Historically, Wan xian was known as the 'Gateway to East Sichuan'. Situated between the two river ports of Chongqing in Sichuan and Yichang in Hubei where the river broadens for easier navigation, it was an important centre of riverine commerce and still is. Indeed, it became a foreign treaty port in 1902 for just that reason. Mrs Bird was suitably impressed by it:

Graceful pagodas and three-storeyed pavilions guard the approaches. The Feng Shui of Wan xian is considered perfect. Rich temples on heights above the river ... retain their hold on the people. The wealth of vegetation is wonderful ...

While for Charon, the stalls in the markets were of interest:

All sorts of quaint objects of local manufacture can be bought ... Such weird items as flea-traps for carrying in the sleeves of gowns (these one must buy in the spring), prayer mats (a joy to upper deck sleepers), cow-horn opium boxes, bamboo baskets ...

He noted that:

The foreign community, except for missionary bodies, is practically non-existent. A Danish chemical expert and his wife live at the Standard Oil installation ... In years gone by there was quite a large community, mostly engaged in the 'wood-oil' trade ...

He does not, however, mention the 'Wan-hsien incident' when two British gunboats opened fire on the city in 1926 because the local warlord had taken to seizing foreign ships to load his own goods. This led to a lengthy boycott of British goods and a refusal to load or unload British ships.

The next day is that on which the boat passes through the famous gorges. I have

YANGTSE RIVER

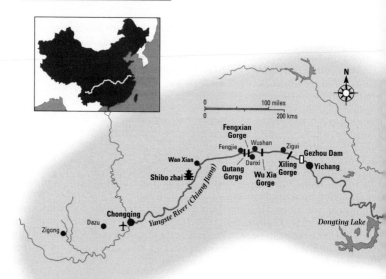

to admit to a slight disappointment, due to the relative height of the river since the construction of the first dam downstream, but on one trip when the weather was particularly cloudy the steep cliffs of the gorges were impressively cloaked in mist and looked very much like a Chinese painting.

Qutang Gorge After passing the town of **Fengjie** (119km downstream from Wan xian), the first gorge appears. This is Qutang Gorge, known to earlier western travellers as 'Windbox Gorge'. Charon waxes lyrical: 'Try and picture a mountain 3000 feet high split down the centre by a titanic axe ...'. The gorge is 8km long and is entered through the **Chijia** (Red Shoulder) **Mountain** to the north and the **Baiyan** (White Salt) **Mountain** to the south.

At low water it was sometimes possible to see great 2m high iron pillars in the water on either side, formerly used to attach chains which traversed the river. During the Tang, these were defensive barriers but by the Qing they were used to stop vessels in order to collect taxes, most notably the *likin*, an inland tax on the transport of goods, in the mid 19C supposedly fixed at one-tenth of one per cent their value but often as much as 20 per cent in certain areas.

On the side of the **White Salt Mountain**, a zig-zag series of square holes cut into the cliff is known as Meng Jiang's Ladder.

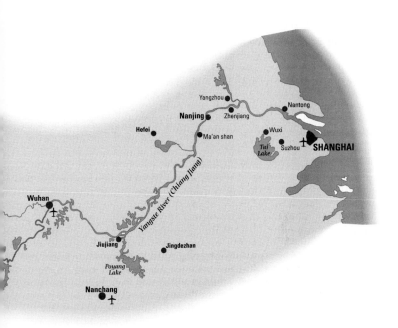

A Song dynasty general, Yang Jiye, was said to have been buried high up on the cliff, far from his home. One of his comrades, Meng Jiang, decided to collect Yang's bones and take them home for reburial in his native place. He was hewing steps out of the cliff when a monk discovered him and began to crow like a cockerel at dawn. Fearing discovery by daylight, Meng Jiang gave up but he later discovered the monk's ploy and hanged him from a rock further up the cliff, known as the Monk Hanging by his Feet; and, indeed, it is said to look like a monk hanging by his feet.

Meng Jiang's stairway is probably the remains of a form of access to a city of the 6C AD, the remains of whose walls have been found on top of the White Salt Mountain. Right at the top of the cliff, above the suspended monk rock, is the Kuangjia (Armour) Cave, so-called because a Tang dynasty woman general was supposed to have used it as an armoury. Thirty years ago archaeologists discovered three wooden coffins in the cave; their siting and dating to c 1000 BC are similar to the boat burials high up in the Wuyi mountains in Fujian province.

For those who are good at the Chinese game of seeing things in rocks, there is a 20m stalactite visible on the White Salt Mountain called the Drinking Phoenix since it is said to resemble a phoenix drinking from a spring. Nearby is the Fengbi tang (Chalk Wall Hall); it is easier to spot, with inscriptions by Song dynasty calligraphers carved on the rock face, which was smoothed and enhanced as a writing surface by the application of chalk or whitewash.

Fengxiang Gorge On **Red Shoulder Mountain** (opposite) is the Fengxiang (Windbox or Bellows) Gorge, named after some more square indentations on the rock supposed to have been used as a bellows by Lu Ban, the great inventor, magical carpenter and patron saint of all woodworkers and masons. These were recently (1971) discovered to contain more wooden coffins like those found opposite. High up along the north face of the cliff above the gorge is the old towpath. On both sides of the gorge there are deep holes (visible only at low water and now presumably lost forever) used when boatmen used to pole or punt their boats up the river.

Just beyond the Armour Cave, on the south side, a huge stone on top of a black rock is known as the Rhinoceros Looking at the Moon since that is what it is supposed to look like.

Daixi The end of the first gorge is marked by the appearance of the town of Daixi on the south bank of the river. Two dark peaks can be seen on the south bank; they are said to be the remains of two dragons that used to block the river.

The dragons had been playfully whipping up tornadoes and hurricanes and wreaking destruction when Yao Ji, youngest daughter of Xi wang mu (Queen Mother of the West) caused a thunderbolt to stop them in their tracks. As they were then blocking the river, the Great Yu, legendary founder of the Xia dynasty (21C–16C BC), 'tamer of the floods', came rushing to unblock the waters. A muddle ensued since the goddess and the 'flood-tamer' moved the dragon-rocks the wrong way at first, thus the two peaks are known as Cuokai (Wrongly Opened) Gorge.

Wushan Some 20km downstream, the town of Wushan is on the north bank; behind lie mountains where there are many tong trees from whose fruit is derived the wood-oil mentioned in connection with foreign trade at Wan xian. Tong oil has been widely used in China for treating timber (caulking boats, bringing out the grain in fine hardwood furniture, etc.) and it was traditionally incorporated in the mixture of pig's blood, clay and straw that was painted onto wooden columns in palaces and temples to protect the timber from the elements. Some stop here for an excursion up the Daning River to see the three 'mini gorges'.

Wux xia Not far beyond Wushan is the second gorge, Wu xia (Wu Gorge). This is 44km long and lined with 12 peaks, six on either side of the river. Here, Charon felt 'the littleness of Man and the wonder of Nature. One felt as if one had been caught "blowing a bine" in Westminster Abbey'. Just at the beginning of the gorge on the south side is a small valley called the **Valley of the Golden Helmet and Shining Armour**, apparently so-called because the walls of the valley are lined with a grey folded limestone formation which looks like ancient armour. The rounded mountain top is coloured yellow-brown by iron in the local water and is thus said to resemble a golden helmet above the armour. On the north bank of the gorge are: Goddess Peak, Dragon Peak, Holy Spring Peak, Facing the Clouds Peak, Pine Ridge Peak and Gathered Immortals Peak. On the south side are: Gathered Cranes Peak, Cloudy Screen Peak and Flying Phoenix Peak with Pure Altar Peak, Rising Cloud Peak and Soaring Peak behind.

The accompanying legend states (in one version authorised by the Yangtse Branch of the China International Travel Service) that the Goddess Peak represents Yao Ji, youngest daughter of the Queen Mother of the West (who made the mistake over the Wrongly Opened Gorge). Bored with life in heaven, she secretly descended to earth with her 11 sisters. At Wushan she met Yu the Great, tamer of the floods, who was fighting 12 dragons who had caused a flood. The 12 maidens killed the 12 dragons and then helped Yu to organise China's waterways. They failed to remove all the obstacles to river transport in the Wu Gorge and so stayed there (as the 12 peaks) to assist sailors 'and to help the peasants bring in bumper harvests'.

Two lines in Mao Zedong's poem 'Swimming' refer to Yao Ji: 'The mountain goddess, if she is still there, will be startled to find her world so changed.'

The Gathered Immortals Peak appears almost in the middle of the river at one bend. On its side is a pale rock, the Kong Ming Rock, with an inscription which reads: 'Wuxia Gorge has peaks rising higher and higher.'

The inscription is supposed to have been written by Kong Ming, better known as Zhuge Liang, Prime Minister of the state of Shu during the Three Kingdoms period (see Chengdu, p 551). Further inscriptions recorded Zhuge Liang's masterly handling of the alliance between the states of Shu and Wu against Wei. It is said that during a later battle between Shu and Wu (Zhuge Liang's alliance proving short lived), the Wu general was in hot pursuit of the army of Shu when he passed the rock. Moved by the inscription and its exhortation to unity, he abandoned the chase. It is thought that all the inscriptions are Ming or later in date.

Beishi 5km further along the south bank is the small town of Beishi where, as the poet, historian, epigrapher, playwright, politician and native of Sichuan (see Leshan, p 572) Guo Moruo (1872–1978) said: 'When the bow of my boat enters Hubei province, the stern is still in Sichuan.'

A few kilometres beyond, on the north bank, is the **Iron Coffin Peak**, said to be shaped like a man kneeling by a coffin, a symbol of filial piety. The gods were so moved by the son's devotion to his mother that he was turned to stone.

Zigui Some 45km beyond, on the north bank, is the town of Zigui, famous as the home town of Qu Yuan (c 3C BC), the loyal but falsely betrayed minister of the state of Chu.

Qu Yuan had always advocated resistance to the advance of the state of Qin but his advice was unheeded and he was banished. His despair at his treatment and at the seizure of Chu by Qin in 278 BC was such that he drowned himself. It is said that the local people venerated him so much that they did not want the fish to eat his body but wanted to preserve it whole for burial, so they threw food into the river to feed the fish and this is the origin of the lotus-wrapped sticky rice bundles that people eat on the fifth day of the fifth month of the lunar calendar. The festival is known as the Dragon Boat Festival, when gloriously decorated boats with dragon prows are raced, apparently to commemorate the search for Qu Yuan's body by boat.

Just beyond Zigui, on the north side of the river, where the next gorge begins, is a small stream, the **Fragrant Stream**.

Although many will be weary of the interminable folktales associated with every pebble and the attributes of form mysteriously assigned to every boulder, they may not be surprised to know that a romantic tale is associated with the Fragrant Stream. It flows by the birthplace of Wang Zhaojun, one of the concubines of the Yuandi emperor of the Han dynasty (reigned 48–32 BC). It is said that once the concubine washed her face in the stream and dropped a pearl from her head-dress; ever since the water has been fragrant.

Every year small fish appear in the stream at peach-blossom time and they are called Peach-blossom Fish. They recall the time when Wang Zhaojun was sent off to the north to marry a barbarian chieftain. She sailed down the stream singing so plaintively that even the peach trees were moved to shed their blossoms. The petals dropped into the water and turned into little fish, which swam alongside Wang Zhaojun's boat.

Xiling Gorge Immediately beyond is the last of the three gorges, Xiling Gorge, 75km long and full of folklore. It comprises four smaller gorges: the Gorge of the Sword and the Book on the Art of War, the Gorge of the Ox's Liver and Horse's Lung, the Kongling Gorge and the Gorge of Shadowplay.

The Sword and the Book on the Art of War Gorge is said to be the place where Zhuge Liang stored grain for his troops in a cave and where he also placed his book on military strategy for safe-keeping. There is a small cave on the north bank, near a stratified layer of rock, which is supposed to look like a stack of paper; beside it is a narrow rock 'resembling a sword thrust into the river'. An alternative story is that the book and the sword belonged to Zhang Liang, a follower of Liu Bang (founder and first emperor of the Han dynasty), whose book and sword were stored here after his death.

Between this and the next gorge is the **Blue** (or New) **Shoal**, formed by the collapse of a cliff.

Invisible at high water, the rocks are still something of a hazard at low water, despite dredging and cleaning. In the past such was the danger that ship's passengers would disembark here and walk. It was after numerous accidents at this spot in particular that the red lifeboats described by Mrs Bird were established here in 1854 by public subscription amongst local merchants who were losing cargoes.

Ox's Liver and Horse's Blood Gorge is named after stones that look like an ox liver (north bank) with a lung-shaped rock above. According to the official guide, imperialist warships invaded the gorge in 1900 and destroyed half the Horse's Lung Gorge with their bombardment.

Kongling Gorge and Kongling Shoal is beyond the Ox's Liver and Horses's Blood Gorge, with a hidden rock 220m long, which divides the bed into two channels. There are other boulders of danger here, such as the 'big pearl' and its three smaller pearls, a hazard which is clearly illustrated in the woodblock pilot's guides published in Chinese. Charon describes the boulders as being the target of blasting in 1933 by the Chinese Maritime Customs.

Yellow Ox Gorge is a small gorge named after a low rock on the south shore said to look like a person leading an ox, leads to the **Huangling Temple**, dating from the Ming, although originally supposed to have been a Spring and Autumn period (770–476 BC) foundation dedicated to the Great Yu and his yellow ox which cut channels for water with its horns.

Shadowplay Gorge   The Shadowplay, or Bright Moon, Gorge, follows: its double name refers to the way the rocks shine in the moonlight and also to the appearance of four rocks on the right which, viewed preferably from Yichang (that is, from downstream), against the setting sun, look like the silhouettes of the four major characters in the Ming novel *Journey to the West* by Wu Cheng'en (c 1500–80), translated by Arthur Waley as Monkey. The monkey king stands at the front as a lookout; behind is the pig leading a horse. The monk-pilgrim Xuan zang sits up straight, while his assistant Sha carries the Buddhist sutras on a shoulder-pole.

Beyond is another small gorge, the Yellow Cat Gorge, named after a yellow rock that looks like a cat.

Gezhou Dam   Then the river widens and the next event is the lock on the Gezhou Dam. 70m high, with three shiplocks, the dam cuts the Yangtse in two, which is good for electricity but not for ecology, nor for some rare species, such as the freshwater dolphin, now in even greater danger since its construction. It was built in two parts, the first (1970–81) was the major construction across the river, the second, completed in 1986, is said to provide an annual production of 14 billion kilowatt hours. It was a fascinating sight to watch, particularly at night, when the site was illuminated by pink and pale blue acetylene flares. The dam's locks are also impressively high and all ships must pass through them before reaching Yichang.

Yichang was an important entrepôt on the Yangtse and was therefore made a treaty port by the Cheefoo Convention of 1876.

The Cheefoo (proper name Yantai) Agreement, or Convention, followed the murder of Margary in Yunnan in 1875, while he was attempting to meet Captain Browne's mission from Burma. Wuhu, Yichang and Wenzhou, on the coast, were opened to foreign trade. In 1917 Yichang was described as having a population of 40,000 with 187 foreigners supervising the transit of beans, grain, sesame seed, vegetable tallow and wood (or tong) oil. It was also noted that in 1910 work had begun on a railway between Yichang and Wan xian which, as it does not exist, must have been abandoned.

The riverfront still has a number of European buildings and three more can be seen in the grounds of the ***Taohualing Hotel***, 29 Yunji lu, ☎ 643 6666, fax 623 8888. Otherwise, the city is a neatly laid out modern one with quite pleasant blocks of flats lining straight streets, the most recent development being due to the construction of the dam and its hydroelectric power station.

Wuhan

Wuhan, capital of Hubei province, is a modern city, with a major iron and steel industry. The city is made up of three older cities lying on two sides of the Yangtse where the Han River joins it. Wuchang lies on the south bank of the Yangtse, while Hanyang and the later settlement of Hankou (a treaty port) are on the other side of the river, divided by the Han. Wuhan is a mainly modern city with some rather fine treaty port architecture and a famous university; it is a centre of communication but it also has a very important collection of recently unearthed bronzes in the Provincial Museum.

Hubei province is a Qing creation, established in the early 18C when the previous province of Huguang was divided. It was the site of one of the most distinctive of the Warring States (403–221 BC), the kingdom of Chu, whose wood carvings (composite animal forms with deer antlers and long tongues) and bronzes covered in lost-wax tangles, more like worms than dragons, can be seen in the Provincial Museum. When central control disintegrated at the end of the Han, another independent kingdom, the kingdom of Wu, was established in the area and the province saw some of the epic battles described in the *San guo yan yi* (*Romance of the Three Kingdoms*).

Industrial development of the Wuhan complex began in the late 19C and Wuhan is noted by historians of the Communist Movement for its proletarian uprisings.

The province, named 'North of the (Dongting) Lake', has a population of 49,310,000.

Practical information

Getting there
By air

The central position of Wuhan is evident from the number of flights from Peking, Changsha, Chengdu, Chongqing, Fuzhou, Guangzhou, Guilin, Hangzhou, Hefei, Nanchang, Nanjing, Shanghai, Shashi, Shenyang, Xi'an, Yichang and Zhengzhou.

The airport is 19km from Wuhan city centre. Shuttle buses to the airport (40mins) leave from the *China Southern Airlines* office on Hangkong lu; a taxi will be quicker.

By train

There are two stations, one in Wuchang (for Guilin, Guangzhou, Chongqing, Xi'an and Zhenjiang) and one in Hankou for Anyang, Peking, etc., although the situation is not as clear-cut as it sounds, since many trains cross from one station to the other on the Yangtse Bridge.

By boat

Many passengers on Yangtse Gorge steamers disembark or embark at Wuhan. It is possible to reach other destinations on the Yangtse by boat and some places, such as Nanjing and Shanghai, are more easily accessible by water than by rail, since the train goes north to Zhengzhou before heading east. The jetty and ticket office are on the waterfront in Hankou.

Where to stay

The nicest hotels are old foundations in Hankou: the *Xuangong*, 57 Jianghan yi lu, ☎ 8281 0365, fax 8281 6941, in the old British concession, dates from the 1930s and is in the centre of the commercial district; and the *Jianghan*, 245 Shengli lu, ☎ 8281 1600, fax 8281 4342, in the old French concession near Hankou rail-way station; built in 1914 by the French, it is a fine surviving treaty port building.

History

Wuhan's legendary history begins with the Great Yu, tamer of the floods, who is supposed to have done some work in the Hanyang area vulnerable to floods. There was a Shang dynasty settlement to the northeast of Wuhan, **Panlong cheng**, excavated in 1950–60 and 1974, where a palace and a city surrounded by a wall and moat were uncovered. A middle Shang site, it also comprises tombs, including one with human sacrifices, and evidence of local bronze production. The latter finds are of interest since Panlong cheng was some distance from the metropolitan Shang centre; other non-metropolitan Shang finds often include bronzes thought to have been imported but here they were produced locally.

Settlement continued in the area and **Wuchang** was briefly used as a capital by the state of Wu during the Three Kingdoms (222–280) before power was transferred to Nanjing in 229. It later served as a provincial capital under the Yuan and Ming, although the provincial boundaries were different from those of today: in the Yuan the area was larger, incorporating Hubei, Hunan, Guangdong and Guangxi, while in the Ming only Hubei and Hunan were included. As late as 1924, as the *Japanese Railway Guide* demonstrates, both Wuchang and Hanyang were surrounded by walls, Wuchang's being far more extensive than those of the smaller settlement at Hanyang.

The town of **Hanyang** on the other side of the river was founded under the Sui (581–618) and saw great expansion in the 19C when the Hanyang arsenal was founded and **Zhang Zhidong** (1837–1909), an official and reformer, promoted the development of the iron and steel works, cotton mills, silk factories and tanneries amongst other industrial enterprises. In 1889, after his energetic promotion of the construction of the Peking–Hankou railway line (completed in 1906), Zhang Zhidong was appointed governor general of Hubei and Hunan (still administratively regarded as one in the Qing), with his headquarters in Wuchang. Hummel's *Eminent Chinese of the Ch'ing Period* (US Government Printing Office, 1943–44) notes that many of his projects in Hanyang were 'riddled with graft and conducted at a loss, but it is largely to his great initiative that the Wu-Han cities owe their subsequent position as the "Chicago" of China'.

The third of the three cities, **Hankou**, developed as a treaty port, with the British arriving in 1861, the French, Russians and Japanese in 1896. With river transport plus the railway from 1906, Hankou 'boomed' as a trading town with sesame and goat skins from Hunan, beans, silk, cotton, hides and gypsum from the Hubei plains and nutgalls, varnish, wood oil and vegetable tallow from the western mountain regions (according to the *Encyclopaedia Sinica*, 1917). Its factories, second in importance only to those of Shanghai, processed some of these raw materials, while the 'Chicago' reputation was based on the arsenal, the mint in Wuchang, the Hanyang iron and steel works, the railway and electric light works.

Wuhan's revolutionary history is perhaps due in part to the arrival of the railway, for railway workers were amongst the earliest of China's small number of proletarians to become politicised. The **1911 Revolution** which overthrew the Qing started in Wuhan, gathering strength as it spread to other cities until it succeeded. Much of Hankou was destroyed in the weeks of fighting between revolutionaries and imperial troops but it was rebuilt under the Republic. From 1926–27 Wuhan was the headquarters of part of the KMT, the faction which opposed Chiang Kai-shek. Wang Jingwei, who later associated himself with the Japanese and finally set up a puppet government in Najing in 1940, was one of the leaders of the 'Left KMT' which maintained an alliance with the Communist Party after April 1927 and claimed to adhere more closely to Sun Yatsen's principles than his successor, Chiang Kai-shek. Sun's widow, Song Qingling, was associated with the Wuhan Left KMT government, as were Russian advisers like Mikhail Borodin, described rather threateningly by a recent American biographer as 'Stalin's man in China'. The Wuhan government's alliance with the Communist Party did not survive long; in July 1927 Wang Jingwei turned on his former allies just as Chiang Kai-shek had done, killing some 100,000 Communist supporters in Wuhan and the surrounding countryside. Song Qingling just managed to escape with her life.

In 1957, the bridge across the Yangtse was built, effectively joining the two halves of China (north and south) in the centre and improving rail links dramatically.

Hanyang

The major sites in Hanyang are Gui shan (see below), north of the old (originally) walled city and just south of the Hanyang iron and steel works, the old arsenal to the left of the iron and steel works and the **Guiyuan si** (Temple of the Return to the Fundamental Principle) at the western end of Cuihui jie in the west of Hanyang.

The temple was founded in the first reign of the Qing (1644–62) by a monk, Bai guang, on the site of a Ming garden. Owing to 'economic and military vicissitudes' (Zhongguo mingsheng cidian), the present buildings date from the late Qing (1864–95) and the Republican period. Although a Buddhist temple, it has preserved something of the garden layout but its 500 lohan figures are the most famous part of the temple, sculpted in 1822–31. It contains a few earlier relics, such as a Northern Wei Buddha (4C–5C) with strong Indian influence in the stance of the figure and the delineation of its robes. Some Ming bronzes are also on display and there is a group of 17C stucco figures on wooden frames.

Gui shan, Turtle Mountain, where Yu tamed the local floods, was named after a magic turtle that emerged to help the deity by imposing its body between the waters of the Han and the settlement at Hanyang. It was covered with pavilions and temples, which had virtually all disappeared by 1949. Reconstructions include the Guqin tai (Guqin Terrace) at the western end of the mountain near Yue hu (Moon Lake), where the most famous musician of antiquity, the legendary Bo Ya, used to play his zither-like instrument. When his favourite listener, Zhong Ziqi, died Bo Ya broke his *guqin* and never played again. The terrace was said to have existed during the Northern Song and to have been restored in the Qing and again after 1949.

On the east end of the mountain is the **Yugong ji** (Breakwater Built by Yu). A couple of tombs survive on the mountain: that of **Lu Su** (172–217) was once at the southern foot of the mountain and moved higher up the southern slope in 1955 in the course of water works. Lu Su was a general of the state of Wu, of which Wuchang was briefly the capital during the Three Kingdoms period. The tomb of He Jingyu (1895–1928), one of the earliest women leaders of the Communist Movement, killed when Wang Jingwei turned on the Wuhan Communists, is at the western end of the mountain.

There used to be a Qingchuan lou (Pavilion of the Clear Sky and the River) on Gui shan, a pair to the tower on She shan (Serpent Mountain) in Wuchang on the opposite side of the Yangtse. Built by Fan Zizhen, a prefect of Hanyang during the Ming, the two towers were named after references in a Tang poem by Cui Hao (early 8C): '... climbing the yellow crane tower ...' and '... the clear sky and the river are eternal and the trees of Hanyang ...'. The poem is said to have left Li Bai, one of the greatest of the Tang poets, silent in admiration. The tower was repaired many times during the Qing and the last repair was made by Zhang Zidong, who wrote a pair of couplets to commemorate the act, but it did not survive the fighting during the 1911 Revolution. It has recently been rebuilt in the Qing style.

Wuchang

Over the river in the old Wuchang, the She shan (Snake Mountain), Hong shan (Vast Mountain) and Dong hu (East Lake) area, which includes the Provincial Museum, are all quite close together. If you are pressed for time make straight for the museum, which is quite small but closes at lunchtime, when some rather nice mice emerge in the quiet rooms.

She shan (Snake Mountain) is on the riverbank, once used as a stronghold by local rulers such as Huang Wu of Wu, who built a castle on it in AD 223. It was, however, much praised for its beauty by innumerable poets: 'In winter, blossom dances over the stones, thick forests and a line of tall pavilions', 'Thick with peach blossoms, soft clouds floating, when the leaves are red, a green pavilion towers over them'. The **Huang he lou** (Yellow Crane Pavilion) is said to have first been built in the 3C AD and much restored in the Qing, most recently after a fire in 1884. Images of earlier towers have survived in Song and Yuan paintings, in Qing silks and late Qing photographs.

The name, commemorated in the Tang poem, is supposed to have derived from a stopover made on the mountain by the Taoist Wang Zian, who was riding on a yellow crane. Another version of the name is that a family called Xin used to sell wine here; a Taoist priest often came to drink it and they didn't like to ask him for money. The Taoist used a piece of orange peel to draw a picture on the wall of a yellow crane with the inscription: 'The guest comes to drink wine and make obeisance; the yellow crane comes down to dance' and the Xin family grew rich. The Tang poem by Cui Hao, also supposed to have been the source of the name, describes how: '... in ancient times a man flew in on a yellow crane to the place that was bare of buildings apart from the Yellow Crane Pavilion, the yellow crane flew off, never to return, white clouds float for ever and ever. The clear sky and the river are eternal and the trees of Hanyang ...'. The pavilion was also central to a poem by Cui Hao bidding farewell to his friend, Meng Haoran, another poet: 'You leave me in the west at the Yellow

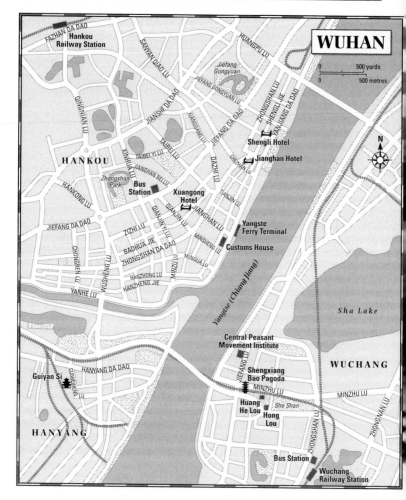

Crane Pavilion, amongst the cloudy flowers of April you sail to Yangzhou; the single sail, a distant form, disappears in the blue of the horizon and I can see nothing but the Great River as it flows towards the sky.'

The last pavilion was burnt down in 1884, although its foundations remain and a new one is being built.

On the west end of Snake Mountain is the **Shengxiang bao ta**, a 'bottle-shaped' or Lamaist stupa style pagoda, moved to this site in 1957 because of work on the bridge over the Yangtse. Built in 1343 and restored in 1394, the pagoda is over 9m high and rather wonderfully carved.

There is also a tomb on the southern slopes, that of **Chen Youjing** (1320–63), who had declared an independent kingdom in the area in the confusion of the late Mongol period, only to be conquered and killed by Zhu Yuanzhang, future

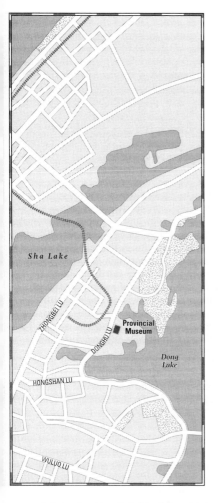

founder of the Ming dynasty. Showing a magnanimity that was apparent in his early years and lacking in his later life when paranoia appears to have set in, Zhu Yuanzhang himself wrote the four characters for the tomb stele: 'Man builds but Heaven determines'. The stele actually in front of the tomb reads 'Tomb of the king of Han, Chen Youjing'.

Also on Snake Hill is the late Qing **Baobing tang** (Hall to Cherish the Ice), built in 1907 and restored in 1953; it was apparently first erected in memory of Zhang Zhidong.

At the northern corner of Yuema chang Square, on Minzhu lu, near the foot of the mountain, is the red-brick building, the **Hong lou** (Red Building), with a statue of Sun Yatsen outside it. This was the headquarters of the 1911 Revolution and now contains an exhibition relating to it. The square was originally used by the Qing troops to exercise their horses, hence the name, which means drilling-horses square. On the banks of the river not far from the square is a tall square tower, the **Nine Women's Grave** (Jiu nu dun) which commemorates nine women who participated in the Boxer uprising.

Beyond Snake Hill, before you reach Dong hu (East Lake) and the university and museum area, is **Hong shan** (Vast Hill) with the Lingji (Universal Spirit) Pagoda behind the **Baotong zhan si** (Temple of Precious Communication). The temple, whose surviving buildings date from 1865 and 1879, although it was founded under the Southern Song, is built against the mountain. The pagoda was first built in 1307 and rebuilt in 1865; it is an octagonal, seven storey pagoda and is 43m high. The exterior is brick modelled on timber construction.

Another smaller pagoda can be found on the southwest slopes (it was moved in 1963 from the eastern slope of the hill). This is the **Xingfu si Pagoda** (Pagoda of the Temple of Flourishing Good Fortune). It is just over 11m high and was built in 1270, again in brick imitating timber construction with lively carving around the mock doors.

Also in Wuchang, in Huang xiang, is the site of the **Central Peasant Movement Institute** (Zhongyang nongmin yundong jiangxi suo), founded in January 1927 and housed in what had formerly been part of a school founded by Zhang Zhidong, later the Hubei Province No. 1 Commercial School. Over 800 students came here in the brief period that it was open (by the end of the year Wang Jingwei had turned on the Communists who were running the Institute) and Mao Zedong taught here. There is now an exhibit relating to the Institute and its teachers and pupils.

The most important site in Wuchang is the **Provincial Museum** on the shore of Dong hu (East Lake) in a pleasantly wooded area which also contains the university (part of which is apparently modelled on the Temple of Heaven) and many of Wuhan's institutes of higher education.

The museum is almost entirely devoted to the display of articles discovered in a local tomb unearthed at **Sui xian**, which contained lacquer vessels and a complete set of musical instruments of the day and a quite extraordinary collection of bronzes. The tomb was that of a Prince Yi of the state of Zeng, who was buried in 433 BC. Pride of the collection is the set of 64 graded bronze bells, displayed on a three-tiered rack supported by six bronze figures carrying swords. The decoration on the rack, more startlingly obvious on the complex ritual vessels also found in the tomb, is of extraordinarily intricate lost-wax spaghetti. Even the dragons that crawl over the spaghetti-covered vessels have interlaced bodies and curling limbs. The bells were struck from outside (they don't have internal clappers) and there is also a set of 16 musical stones which were similarly hung on a frame and struck to sound.

Other buildings around the lake include the **Xingling ge**, a hall built to commemorate Qu Yuan, the great poet of the 3C BC, author of the Li sao and the Chu ci (Songs of the South), who drowned himself in despair when his warnings to his ruler were disregarded and in whose honour the dragon boat festival was created.

Hankou

Hankou, the old treaty port section of Wuhan, was bounded on the north by the railway line. Between the railway and the river it was divided between the British, whose concession lay between Jianghan da dao and the railway station, the French, whose concession was separated from the British by a couple of Russian streets, the Germans, whose concession began at roughly Sanyang da dao and ran for some six streets northeast and the Japanese, whose concession lay beyond that of the Germans.

Along the waterfront just north of the Han river (heading down river) were the Customs House, Butterfield and Swire, Nippon Yusen Kaisha, Yokohama Specie Bank, Hongkong and Shanghai Bank, British Consulate, Nishin Kisen Kwaisha, Litvinoff and Co. (of the Shun-fung brick tea manufactory), Russian Consulate, American Consulate, Terminus Hotel, German Consulate, Melcher's Wharf, Arnhold Karberg and Co. Wharf, Swedish Consulate, British-American Tobacco Company, Italian Consulate, Mitsubishi Co., Japanese Consulate and Hsieh-chang Match Factory.

In the 1924 *Japanese Railway Guide* the visitor to Hankou is recommended to visit various 'manufactories—Brick-tea factory, Match factory, Albumen factory (*Societé Anonyme Belge pour l'Industrie des Oeufs*)' on the first day, the Hankow Iron and Steel Works, Hanyang Government Arsenal and Powder Factory on the second day and rounding off the third with the Cotton Spinning and Weaving Factories and a hemp factory.

In the old days visitors to Wuhan found themselves disembarking 'at the hulk' and could always find rickshaws, although they had to telegraph ahead for motor vehicles in order to visit the tree-lined Bund with its 'handsome modern buildings, automobile boulevards and beautiful residences policed by turbaned Sikhs'. The beautiful residences were provided with a 'thorough system of sewerage', although in 1924 Hankou was not considered a 'healthy place to live in'.

It is difficult to track down specific buildings, particularly as few locals seem to remember what was what, but the **Customs House** on the Hankou waterfront is quite a good place to start simply looking for treaty port architecture by wandering.

On Poyang jie (in Hankou) is the site of the 'Eight-Seven Meeting' (Ba qi huiyi hui zhi) of 7 August 1927, at which Mao Zedong and others, including Qu Qiubai and Li Weihan, argued that 'political power grew out of the barrel of a gun' and that the Communist Party should arm itself. The meeting, however, 'succumbed to the right-opportunist line of Chen Duxiu' and continued to support Stalin's line of unity with the KMT against the northern warlords, a mistaken choice as the KMT turned on its Communist allies and killed them.

Also in Hankou on Changchun jie is the site of the Eighth Route Army Headquarters in 1937 (before the army moved to Nanjing) where, amongst others, Zhou Enlai worked briefly.

Lu shan and Guling

Lu shan is c 30km from Jiujiang, a sizeable town on the south bank of the Yangtse River (see below, p 597). Lu shan is a mountain without particular religious associations; it has always been appreciated simply for its beauty: its sheer cliffs and twisted pines, its mists and peaks. There are return day-trips from Jiujiang which can be booked through *CITS*.

It was a favourite, perhaps the favourite, hill resort for the foreign community in China at the turn of the 20C (opened as a resort in 1895) and later; the town of Guling is almost entirely composed of foreign architecture: villas, guesthouses and sanatoria. Chiang Kai-shek also had a villa on Lu shan and a training centre for KMT officials but its fame in recent years is due to the Lu shan plenums of 1959 and 1970; two extremely bitter conferences of the Central Committee of the Communist Party which were held in these charming surroundings. At the first, in 1959, Defence Minister Peng Dehuai (1898–1974) strongly criticised the Great Leap Forward of 1958.

The **Great Leap** had been an attempt rapidly to increase production, notably of coal and steel. Production quotas were raised everywhere and 'backyard furnaces' (inefficient and dangerous) sprang up throughout the country. In agriculture the same increase in production was required at the same time as the implementation of the commune policy, increasing the size of the agricultural production units.

It is now recognised that the policy was not successful, partly because it was implemented in far too much of a hurry, partly because figures were falsified by local officials trying to curry favour with the central government, thus giving rise to ridiculous expectations. Peng Dehuai's criticism was prescient (the ensuing years of natural disasters compounded the problems already existing in the new communes) but at the time it led to his dismissal and disgrace. He has only been rehabilitated since the death of Mao in 1976.

Similarly, the second plenum of 1970 developed into a bitter and eventually fatal struggle, in this case between Mao and Lin Biao (also Defence Minister at the time). Ostensibly it was over the vacant post of State Chairman, which Lin coveted. Chen Boda (1904–1989), Mao's secretary and speech-writer, strongly associated with Cultural Revolution policies, was the sacrificial victim of the second plenum but in the following year Lin Biao, apparently having plotted to kill Mao, died in a plane shot down over Mongolia, assumed to be heading for sanctuary in the USSR.

There are famous photographs of Mao at Lu shan, relaxing in a wicker chair on a grassy peak. They were taken by his wife, Jiang Qing, who amused herself with photography on the mountain, dropping glycerine dewdrops on roses for greater effect.

Guling

The bus to Lu shan from Jiujiang takes about two hours and stops at Guling. The site was developed at the very end of the 19C, well after the Taiping rebellion (1850–64), by the ex-missionary E.S. Little, as a summer resort where missionaries could recoup their strength.

The name is now a mess: Little decided on the Chinese-sounding 'Kuling' (pronounced 'cooling') to encourage those who lived and worked on the sweltering plains to take their summer holidays in the cooling mountain resort. The name worked in the old Wade-Giles romanisation but the modern pinyin system insists that *ku* be rendered *gu*, so the cooling effect of Kuling has been lost.

In the past, missionaries and their families, coming up for the fresh mountain air, would be carried on sedan chairs with all their luggage. In 1917 there were 320 houses and a foreign population of 1731.

The streets of Guling are interesting for their foreign resort architecture and occasional transformations (church into cinema). The **Lu shan Museum**, next to the theatre where the plenums were held, is housed in Chiang Kai-shek's library and some of the villas inhabited by celebrities are now open to the public.

Lu shan

There are major 'scenic spots' on the mountain—**Dragon Head Peak**, **Floral Path** (wild azalea and peach blossom in April and May), **Fairy Cave**, **Three Waterfalls** and **Five Immortals Peak** (near the Rujin Lake, or Three Ancient Trees), **Black** and **Yellow Dragon Pools** (near the Lulin Lake)—but as these are almost invariably dramatically overcrowded, wandering on smaller paths is recommended. As there are few temples and religious sites remaining after the devastation by the Taiping rebels, the scenery can be enjoyed in tranquillity.

One temple at the foot of the mountain is of note, the **Donglin si** (Temple of the Eastern Grove).

> It was the home of the founder of the Pure Land sect, Hui Yuan, built for him as a school in 381. Pure Land Buddhism, with its stress on the possibility of salvation in the 'pure land' of Amitabha Buddha, was to have a profound effect on popular Buddhism in China, for it offered a view of a 'life' or state after death for the faithful. Such was the popularity of Hui Yuan and the Pure Land that many visitors came from China and abroad and during the Tang there were 'halls, courtyards and pagodas numbering over 310'. The monk Jian Zhen passed by on his way to Japan from Yangzhou and took two monks with him, taking the Pure Land to Japan, where Hui Yuan is also revered as the founder of the sect.

In front of the temple is the **Tiger Pool** where Hui Yuan would bid farewell to guests. He practised his devotions nearby when, it is said, he had no shadow, 'it did not cleave to his body'.

> Here he discussed Buddhist doctrine with such visitors as the poet Tao Yuanming. Hui Yuan was supposed never actually to cross the bridge over the pool. Once, when seeing Tao Yuanming and the Buddhist Lu Xiujing off, he inadvertently crossed the bridge, at which point the tiger spirit in the water began howling ceaselessly and the three men laughed, giving rise to the saying: 'three (men) laughing on the tiger pool'.

The temple buildings were frequently destroyed, most recently by the Taipings, so they are all now late Qing in date. The site was visited by a great number of famous people, including Li Bai, Lu You and Bai Juyi (Tang poets), Wang Yangming (the Ming Buddhist) and others, their visits commemorated by stelae.

The poet and chrysan-themum grower Tao Yuanming (365–427 AD)

Jiujiang

Starting point for a visit to Lu shan, Jiujiang was opened to foreign trade in 1861, when the previously flourishing town had been devastated by the Taiping uprising, like so many others in the area, and much of the land within its walls reduced to weed-covered rubble. It became a major centre for the foreign tea trade, with Russian factories producing tea bricks for the home market (powdered tea compressed into solid bricks) before 1917. Tea still produced on the slopes of Lu shan and other hills is known as Yunwu ('Misty Clouds') and is a green tea. Known to westerners as Kiukiang, Jiujiang (which in Chinese means 'Nine Rivers') was the major port for shipment of the porcelain of Jingdezhen. Jiujiang's previous prominence as a Buddhist centre is marked by the **Ningren Temple** (founded in 502–49) but the surviving buildings are all post-Taiping (late l9C).

Jiuhua shan and Wuhu

The southernmost of the four Buddhist holy mountains, Jiuhua shan (Nine Glories or Nine Flower Mountain), is over 100km southwest of Wuhu on the Yangtse River, upstream from Nanjing.

Dedicated to the Bodhisattva Ksitigarbha, who rules over the underworld and delivers souls from hell, the mountain has long been the prime place of pilgrimage for the recently bereaved who came (and still come) to pay for a series of masses to be held for the soul of the departed. At the eastern end of a ridge of mountains, with the more picturesque and therefore more popular Huang shan (Yellow Mountain) to the east, Jiuhua shan is, nevertheless, quite pretty and, at 1342m above sea-level, is easily climbed in a day.

Practical information

Getting there
By train and bus

Jiuhua shan is easily reached from Nanjing, either by rail and bus or by boat and bus. The former method is quicker but less picturesque. A branch line runs from Nanjing Station to Tongling on the Yangtse, 12 stops in all and the slow-moving train stops at all of them. There is only one class (hard seats, very crowded) and the journey takes five to six hours. There are buses from Huang shan, Nanjing (4hrs) and Wuhu (3hrs).

By boat

A pleasant way to reach the mountain is to take a small boat upriver on the Yangtse from Nanjing to Wuhu. The river port of Nanjing is in the northwest of the town, at the river end of Zhongshan bei lu, within sight of the extraordinary Yangtse River Bridge, its piers topped with red concrete revolutionary 'flames'. The bridge was built between 1960 and 1968, begun with Russian assistance and blueprints, both of which were almost immediately withdrawn with the Sino-Soviet split of August 1960. It is a matter of national pride that the inexperienced Chinese managed to finish the bridge themselves and decorate it with revolutionary flames and street-lamps in the form of magnolia buds.

The boat from Nanjing to Wuhu takes

the greater part of a day; such small boats stop at all the river ports—in this case only Ma'an shan, where China's greatest poet, Li Bai, died after falling overboard when drunk, and Wuhu— loading and unloading passengers and cargo. The boat I travelled on, the *Red Flag No. Seven*, was British built (pre-1949), with much decorative marquetry in the saloon reserved for cabin-class passengers, where a Sheffield-plate cocktail shaker in the form of a penguin and glasses with elaborately folded napkins in the shape of birds and flowers stood in a glass-fronted cabinet. The small, two-berth cabins with fitted sink, tiny cupboard and well-polished elderly fittings made it the sort of boat that Evelyn Waugh's Gilbert Pinfold might have had his ordeal on.

Where to stay

On arrival at Wuhu (literally 'weed-filled lake'), turn right out of the ferry terminal for the *Ganlong Binguan*, ☎ 383 1319, on the left hand side of the main street. Before settling in, buy tickets for the bus to Jiuhua shan for the following day in the bus station, as the bus departs early and fills up quickly.

History

It is said that in the 3C–5C AD there were Taoist and Buddhist temples on the mountain. In the 5C a Buddhist monk called Huai Du (a name which means 'embrace the crossing of the ocean') came to live on the mountain in a thatched hut where he read the sutras. In 643 a member of the royal family of Korea, Jin Qiaojue, crossed the sea (an event prophesied in the religious name of the earlier monk) and came to Jiuhua shan. For 75 years he led a life of asceticism and mortification of the flesh, dying while meditating at the age of 99. His body was miraculously preserved and closely resembled the icons of the Bodhisattva Ksitigarbha, to the point that he was acknowledged as a reincarnation. Thus Jiuhua shan is the only one of the Buddhist holy mountains (Putuo, Emei and Wutai are the others) which has an historical figure as its incarnation; on the other mountains, visions of the presiding deity sufficed to sanctify the area.

Imperial favours to the mountain were evident in the gold seals and calligraphic inscriptions of the Tang, Song, Yuan, Ming and Qing emperors once preserved on the mountain. The Ming Wanli emperor visited the mountain in 1586 and 1599; the last emperor of the Ming wrote the inscription 'the incarnate Bodhisattva' for the Bai sui gong (Hundred Year Hall); the Qing Kangxi emperor visited in 1705 and later sent a carved inscription in his own hand, 'the magical scenery of Jiuhua', for the Huacheng Temple, which was also graced with calligraphy by the after his 1766 visit. Owing to lavish gifts (including two of over 40,000 taels (a Chinese ounce) of silver from the Kangxi emperor), the monastic population of monks and nuns grew to more than 5000 in over 300 temples during the Qing.

Wuhu

If stuck in Wuhu, there are a number of sites to visit and some quaint thatched cottages to be found even along the main streets, with round thatched roofs and thick mud walls pierced with tiny windows, rather like the toadstool houses of pixies in children's books. Wuhu is also the home of a particular form of Chinese handicraft, the 'iron picture', where thin strips of iron are twisted to make silhouettes, mainly of landscape scenes.

The **Guangji si** (Temple of Universal Rescue) is on the southwest slopes of Zhe shan (Red Mountain) and, as a traditional stopping place for pilgrims on their way to Jiuhua shan, is sometimes known as 'Little Jiuhua'. Built against the mountain, with anterior halls 10m above those in front, the temple was founded in 894–97, destroyed by fire in the Xianfeng reign period (1850–61), presumably by the Taiping rebels, and rebuilt in the Guangxu era (1875–1908).

The **Zhe Pagoda** behind is one of the 'Eight Sights of Wuhu' (I have been unable to find a list of the other seven). There are a number of 'mountains' in the town: Zhe shan, 86m high, of reddish earth, where a pavilion built in 1522–66 stands on top, affording a view of the town, the river and Shen shan (Spirit Mountain); here, according to the local gazetteer, swords were forged by Gan Jiang the magical sword-maker of Chu (one of the Warring States, 8C–4C BC).

On **Shen shan** are the Tomb of Gan Jiang, the Sword-honing Stone and the Forging Pool as well as the remains of a Luohan Temple. In the centre of the town is the Jinghu, or Mirror Lake, whose clear waters bear little relation to the weed-filled lake from which the town takes its name.

Jiuhua shan

As the bus approaches the mountain from the plains you can see the start of the stepped pilgrim path which leads from the Yitian men (First Heavenly Gate) past the Ganlu si (Sweet Dew Temple), named for the ambrosial nectar of immortality dispensed by the gods, and the Ertian men (Second Heavenly Gate).

> The Ganlu si, founded in 1667 in an area where 'sweet dew' was said to drip from the bamboos and pines, was rebuilt in the Tongzhi reign period of the Qing (1862–75) after destruction by the Taiping rebels. The golden-tiled buildings are constructed high against the mountain slopes.

The bus stops below the **Huacheng Temple**, beside which there is a new guesthouse. Ideally, walk on and around a bend to a long whitewashed building, the **Zhantanlin si** (Temple of the Sandalwood Grove), and try to get a bed there.

> Behind the main temple hall are other halls, above which, reached by steep, ladder-like steps (which are agonising to ascend after a day on the stepped mountain path) are dormitory rooms for pilgrims, simply furnished with mosquito-netted beds and basins. Cold water may be drawn from the well, hot water is available in vacuum flasks and vegetarian meals are served communally for pilgrims, visitors and monks in the main courtyard.

The mountain area, which covers some 100 square km, was originally known as the Jiuzi shan (Nine Mountains) after the nine peaks behind the village. These are also sometimes known as the 'brush-rest' peaks as they resemble the zigzag of brush rests used by calligraphers and painters. A rather banal explanation for the Nine Mountain name is given in the local gazetteer (compiled in the Tang dynasty): 'These mountains are strange and beautiful, with peaks reaching the clouds, rising and falling. There are nine in number, therefore they are called the Nine Mountains.'

The great poet Li Bai visited the area in the Tianbao reign period of the Tang and he regarded the nine peaks as resembling lotus flowers, describing them in a poem: 'Once I stood by the nine rivers and gazed at the nine splendid peaks in the distance; nine lotus flowers rising from the blue waters of the Milky Way ...' and henceforth they were known as the Nine Splendid Peaks (Jiuhua shan). Famous visitors after Li Bai include the Tang poet, Du Mu, the Song poet, Su Dongpo, the great tax reformer of the Song, Wang Anshi, the philosopher, Wang Yangming, and the painter and art theorist, Dong Qichang of the Ming. Poems that they wrote to commemorate their visits tended to follow the lotus flower image of Li Bai.

Very little survives of the mountain's former grandeur, for the area was devastated by the Taiping uprising in 1850–64, which centred on Nanjing, and all existing temples have been rebuilt since. Rebuilding probably started quite early, for a Buddhist Association was established on the mountain in 1914 to organise work there, set up educational institutes and arrange lectures and visits by famous monks from within China and abroad (a level of organisation not seen on other holy mountains at the time). For those interested in Republican period ceramics, a number of unusual blue and white porcelain incense burners with Republican inscriptions can be found in temples and halls.

The religious life of the mountain is still intense, more than on any of the other Buddhist holy mountains. A substantial number of monks are congregated in the major temples and the tiny halls dotting the mountain itself and the village are all inhabited by elderly monks and nuns who provide locally grown tea for visitors (and should be rewarded with a small donation). Services are held most evenings in the main hall of the Zhantanlin Temple and the Huacheng Temple.

In general the bereaved pay for two ceremonies, held on consecutive evenings. The first, longer ceremony fundamentally takes the soul of the departed through the ten Buddhist hells. The abbot of the temple, wearing the red crown-like hat of Ksitgarbha, takes the soul through the ten hells, interceding on its behalf. The abbot scatters grains of rice and flicks water (sweet dew), expressing the benevolence of the Bodhisattva, and the assembled monks mumble their way through prayers for some hours. The members of the family of the dead person stand at the threshold of the hall, kneeling and kowtowing as instructed by a monk.

The second ceremony on the second evening is much shorter and is intended to welcome the soul into the western paradise of Amitabha Buddha. Having passed through the ordeals of the hells (each intended for specific crimes such as meat-eating or unfiliality), the soul is given a cheerful send-off as those present join in a conga-like file weaving through the temple hall, chanting 'O-mi-tuo-fo' (Amitabha Buddha). In the ceremonies that I watched, the widow in question, who had travelled nearly 2000km in the company of a young monk from Guangdong province, was solemn and serious on the first evening, cheerful on the second and positively radiant at breakfast next morning, having ensured her husband a safe trip to paradise.

Such ceremonies are not connected with burial or cremation but, according to the Buddhist belief that the soul is present on earth for 49 days after death, should be carried out within the 49 days after a death. Grander ceremonies can be held, very much depending on the means of the bereaved family. It is clear that holding such ceremonies on the mountain where the Bodhisattva who presides over the underworld was incarnated is seen to provide a particularly powerful guarantee of salvation.

The major temples in the village below the mountain are the **Huacheng si** (Illusion City Temple), a reference to a state of temporary or incomplete Nirvana referred to in the Lotus Sutra, and the Roushen si (Temple of the Physical Body).

The Huacheng Temple, just north of the Zhantanhn Temple, is built against the mountain and comprises four courtyards, rising with the terrain.

One of the most impressive of all the temples on the mountains, it is said that it was built in 757 as a residence for the Korean prince. In 781 it began to be used for funeral rituals and was therefore given the name 'Illusion City' by the emperor. It was visited by the Ming emperors Xuande and Wanli and both Kangxi and Qianlong of the Qing, most of whom left gold-carved inscriptions in commemoration.

Many times destroyed by fire, only the Sutra Tower (or Library) is considered to be of early 15C date. The temple is famous for its great bell, which is also a recent replica, made in the last years of the 19C to replace an earlier one. The names of the dead are often written on paper and placed under the bell, which is rung during religious ceremonies.

The **Roushen si**, also known as the Roushen bao dian (Precious Hall of the Physical Body), stands on the far side of the village, reached by a steep flight of 81 steps. The temple hall contains a 17m high wooden pagoda, reconstructed in 1862–78 after the Taiping rebellion, with eight niches on each storey holding tiny golden Ksitigarbha figures. On either side of the pagoda are figures of the ten kings of hell (each presiding over one hell). Behind the hall is a semicircular stone platform with a great iron incense burner.

Climbing the mountain

The first temple at the base of the eastern ridge is the **Qiyuan si** (Temple of the Garden of Veneration), east of the Huacheng si. Founded in the Ming (1522–66) but rebuilt several times since, it is the biggest of Jiuhua's temples. It has a tall main hall, covered with yellow tiles, the roof combining upturned eaves and stepped gables. In common with much of the local architecture, the edges of the stepped tops of the gable-end walls are painted in white and decorated with cartouches enclosing landscape and other scenes in black on white. Figures in the main hall include the trinity of Amitabha, Avalokitesvara and Mahasthamaprapta, who receive souls into the Western Paradise.

Above, on the ridge, is the **Baisui gong**, or Hundred Year Hall, a deceptively small building; because of the topography, it comprises five storeyed towers and numerous 'heaven well' courtyards and, according to one source, can hold 5000 people. In front of the whitewashed hall is an inscribed stele recording the arrival here from Wutai shan in the north, during the Wanli reign period of the Ming (1573–1620), of a monk called Hai Yu (Sea Jade). When he died at the age of 100, his body was found to stay in a state of perfect preservation and his remains can still be seen. The precious 'Hundred Year' relic that gives the hall its name is a small seated figure, the size of a small monkey and much lacquered. There are also three 'blood sutras' preserved in the hall (sutras written in human blood by Buddhist devotees).

In 1983 the middle-aged Shanghainese monk who looked after the hall described to a small group (including two disapproving members of the People's Liberation Army) how on hearing of the Cultural Revolution on their transistor radios the monks buried the precious relics and retired to the top of the mountain, expecting the arrival of Red Guards. They never came and ten years later the monks descended, disinterred their relics and recommenced their religious life. A brief guide to Jiuhua shan published in 1980 states that there was some destruction during the Cultural Revolution and Colin Thubron, who visited the mountain and described his visit in *Beyond the Wall*, also heard long stories of Red Guard atrocities; so either the Shanghainese monk's earlier version may not be accurate or the later revision may be equally unfounded. The number of Republican period relics, however, suggests that Cultural Revolution destruction was considerably less thorough than that of the Taipings, a hundred years earlier.

At the southern end of the ridge on which the Baisui gong stands is a tiny **Bell Tower**. This used to be inhabited by an elderly monk who came down to the Zhantanlin Temple early in the morning carrying a Buddhist pilgrim staff (with a leaf-shaped bronze head and a couple of loose, clinking bronze rings) and a basket for his provisions. He sat in the tiny tower surrounded by his meagre possessions (a stove, condiments, wellington boots, warm padded winter coat and alarm clock), holding a string that he pulled to activate the wooden clapper of the huge bell, when the mood took him, sending a sonorous boom out across the valley below.

Descending the ridge's eastern slope, the 'brush-rest' mountains and the peak usually climbed, the **Tiantai** (Heavenly Platform) **Peak**, are ahead. The path leads beside, and occasionally through, small temples and tiny halls inhabited by little old ladies or gentlemen, who sleep beside the images they care for, burn incense and provide tea (often with sugar added, as you near the top, for extra energy).

The climb is not too strenuous, although the steps are uncomfortable, being too narrow for large western feet; the scenery provides views of twisted pines and handsome rocks, with dog-roses scenting the air in spring. There is now a cable car up the peak.

Hefei

Hefei, capital city of the province of Anhui, which straddles the Yangtse, is in the northern part of the province and has few partisans, except those who live there. If you pass through, however, it does have a fine museum (the Anhui Provincial Museum) with one of the rare Han dynasty jade body suits (another is to be found in the Nanjing Museum).

Getting there

Hefei can be reached by train or bus (from Nanjing 2½hrs).

Where to stay

Hotels include the *Anhui Fandian*, 18 Meishan lu, ☎ 281 1818, fax 281 7583, and the *Holiday Inn*, Gujingjiari Jiudian, ☎ 429 1188, fax 429 1166.

Anhui province is crossed by both the Huai and Yangtse Rivers and has a population of some 51,560,000. It is a fairly recent creation (1662), made by the Qing, who subdivided the Jiangnan ('South of the Yangtse') region. Although a relatively fertile area, with irrigation making rice cultivation possible in what was previously a wheat area, and famous during the Ming for its rich salt merchants whose elegant houses can still be seen in She xian, it is currently regarded as a backward area, the 'Appalachians' of China, with all that this implies.

Currently known for its production of domestic servants for Peking, where recent economic and political changes have made it possible for the urban rich to employ domestics, it was previously known for the Red Turban uprising (1344) lead by a charismatic bandit, who claimed to be the Buddha of the Future, Maitreya, and as the birthplace of the first Ming emperor, Zhu Yuanzhang (1328–98), an equally charismatic character, who rose through the White Lotus rebel band to overthrow the Mongol Yuan dynasty. It was originally his intention to establish the capital of China in his birthplace in Anhui (Fengyang) but some years into construction he was persuaded that Nanjing was a more logical choice.

Hefei is a possible starting point for long car journeys to the two major sites in northern Anhui, the Tomb of Li Bai, China's foremost poet, near Ma'an shan on the south bank of the Yangtse, and the first of the Ming imperial capitals near Fengyang, c 100km northeast of Hefei.

The **Tomb of Li Bai** (also accessible by car from Ma'an shan or Wuhu on the Yangtse, although both of these are, as yet, less well-organised for tourists and car hire may be problematic), is c 7km from Ma'an shan, near Caishiji (Coloured Stone Boulder), the place where the poet is said to have drowned while drunkenly trying to catch the moon reflected in the river below.

Li Bai

Li Bai (701–762), together with his near-contemporary, Du Fu, (see Chengdu, p 553) is perhaps China's major poet. He was born in distant Central Asia, in Sujab, near Lake Balkash, but when he was five his family moved to Sichuan province. Despite his origins, he came to be viewed as the master of the brief lyric, his most famous example being that in which he invites the moon and his own shadow to drink with him. He was a famous drunk, unlike the sober and socially concerned Du Fu, and has therefore sometimes been regarded with less favour during more puritannical episodes in China's recent past. It is said that when he fell into the river, all that fishermen could retrieve were his gown and cap, which were buried at Caishi village and later reinterred in the present tomb.

Although there have been memorial halls on the site since the early 9C, the present buildings date from the reign of the Guangzu emperor of the Qing (1875–1908), reflecting a last major destruction during the Taiping uprising.

The base of the tomb is of azurite, topped by the grassy mound, and the inscription on the stele, which would normally just record the name of the deceased, reads 'Robes and cap of the great Tang poet Li Bai'.

More impressive are the sculptures from the imperial **Mausoleum of Zhongdu** (Middle Capital), virtually all that remains of the first great capital built at the order of Zhu Yuanzhang, the first ruler of the Ming, in 1369–75. These are to be found near **Fengyang** in northern Anhui and can be reached from Hefei, or perhaps from Fengbu, which is on the railway line north of Hefei and consequently closer, although transport other than public buses will be harder to find.

All that remains of the vast construction of Zhongdu—the palace and city walls built for the first emperor—are some foundation floors, bases of walls, stone balustrades and remnants of stone carvings, northwest of Fengyang. Construction had begun here at imperial orders because this was the home base of the emperor, who came from a poor local family; he was later convinced that Nanjing was a more appropriate seat for the imperial capital, although the Ming finally shifted its capital yet again to Peking in the early 15C.

The spirit way, marking the approach to the tomb of his parents, which was intended originally to serve as an imperial mausoleum for the entire dynasty, is 5km southwest.

It is said that when Zhu Yuanzhang's parents died in poverty, they were buried here on a small plot provided by a kind neighbour. When their son eventually became emperor, he was loath to move the bodies for fear of disturbing their spirits, so he began the construction of the imperial mausoleum around his parents' grave. The vast enclosure was attacked and virtually destroyed at the fall of the Ming; all that survives is the avenue of stone animals and figures, more numerous than in any other surviving spirit way in China and rare examples of the period (1369–80).

Huang shan

Huang shan (Yellow Mountain), in Anhui province, is famous for its spectacular scenery and is therefore spectacularly crowded. It is part of the range that includes the southern Buddhist mountain Jiuhua shan (see p 598), which is infinitely more peaceful, although its peaks and pines are less spectacular.

Practical information

Getting there
By air

The Huangshan airport is 10km west of Tunxi and an airport

shuttle bus runs back and forth to the CAAC office on Huang shan lu.
By bus or train

Huang shan may be reached by bus

from Hefei (7hrs), Jingdezhen (6hrs), Nanjing, Hangzhou (c 9hrs) or Wuhu (c 5hrs) or Tunxi on the railway line from Nanjing (90mins).

Where to stay
There is the *Taoyuan Binguan*, ☎ 556 2666, fax 556 2888, at the foot of the mountain and the *Beihai Guesthouse*, ☎ 556 2552, fax 556 2996 (full to bursting in the season from May to late October) at the summit.

Huang shan is considered to be the most beautiful mountain in China, ascended by emperors in sedan chairs, by poets and by Chinese travellers. Li Bai wrote: 'Huang shan is 9666 metres high, with 32 lotus peaks. Rock pillars press against red cliffs, luxuriant golden lilies; Ancients ascending the matchless peak looked down on the sky and the pines.' The height of Huang shan was somewhat exaggerated, the highest peak being less than 1900m, but Li Bai used poetic licence; he actually said it was 4000 *ren*, a *ren* being an ancient measure equivalent to six or seven *chi*, a *chi* being about a third of a metre.

Paths of steep stone steps up the mountain are easily followed; it is recommended that you take the eastern path upwards and the steeper western path down. As on all of China's famous mountains, there is now a cable car. Near the top of the eastern path is a view of the 'brush-rest' peaks, a number of pointed peaks rising from the mist. Just off the western path, about half way down, near the **Yuping lou** (Jade Peak Tower) is the **Huang ke song** (Welcoming Pine), which is reproduced on hundreds of thousands of paintings in restaurants and hotels to 'welcome guests'.

74km south of Huang shan is **She Xian**, best reached by taxi or minibus from Tunxi. Here the best preserved group of Ming dynasty houses, once the home of the Huizhou salt merchants, can be seen. Massive, whitewashed, closed to the exterior, they have richly carved interior timbers and internal courtyards of the closed 'heaven well' type characteristic of the warm south. The narrow opening in the roof (the 'heaven well') allows some ventilation while preventing the sunshine from heating the cool, dark interior. The whitewashed exterior walls, with their elegant, stepped gable-ends, are decorated with grey 'cut brick' work, like that of Suzhou, which is also to be seen, although in less lavish forms, in Peking.

Nanchang

Nanchang, capital city of Jiangxi province, is a city that has existed (under different names) since the Han. In the last years of the 16C the pioneering Jesuit missionary Matteo Ricci (1553–1610) came to stay in the flourishing city full of merchants and alchemists. For Chinese Communists the city is famous for the Nanchang uprising of 1 August 1927, a date which has provided Army Day (1 August). In that difficult year when the Nationalists, under their new leader

Chiang Kai-shek, turned bloodily on their former allies, the Communists, Zhou Enlai, Zhu De, He Long, Liu Bocheng and others led a peasant army to seize the city. The seizure was part of a protest against Chiang's attack on the Shanghai Communists in April. The city was held for three days before the Nationalist Army retook it and what was to become the Red Army fled to the provincial borders and the mountains of Jinggang shan. The formation of the Red Army was one result of the abortive uprising; another was the beginning of Mao Zedong's firm conviction that the Soviet line (armed insurrections, work in cities) was wrong for China.

Practical information

Getting there
By air
There are flights to Ganzhou, Fuzhou, Guangzhou, Wuhan, Shanghai, Peking, Hefei, Xiamen and Jingdezhen. The airport is 28km north of the city and shuttle buses (40mins) travel from the *CAAC* office at 37 Beijing xi lu.
By train
The station is in the east of the city. Nanchang is on a branch line to Jiujiang, off the Shanghai–Yunnan/ Guangzhou line, but a number of Shanghai–Guangzhou express trains make the detour to Nanchang.

Where to stay

The major hotel for foreigners is the *Jiangxi Binguan* at 368 Bayi da dao (☎ 622 1131, fax 622 4388); it is on the corner of Bayi da dao (the main north–south thoroughfare) and Changzheng lu.

There are a surprising number of things to see in Nanchang, a city whose centre has been extensively modernised. Most people simply pass through on the way to Jingdezhen or Jiujiang, in which case, the major things to see are the Provincial Museum and Ba da shan ren (Zhu Da's Residence) and, for those interested in revolutionary history and revolutionary interior design, the Revolutionary Memorial Hall.

The two museums are easily reached on foot from the Jiangxi Binguan. The newly restored **Provincial Museum** (Jiangxi sheng bowuguan) is on the south of Bayi gongchang (1 August Square): turn left down Bayi da dao, past Renmin gongchang (People's Square). In the middle of 1 August Square is a tower commemorating the uprising.

The museum contains funerary remains of local cultures during the Spring and Autumn Period, a considerable display of Jingdezhen ceramics from the 4C to the end of the Qing and a good collection of Ming funerary wares: jade belts, filigree jewellery and funerary figures from the tomb of the 16th (or 17th; there is some confusion) son of the Ming founder and his son, enfeoffed in Nanchang.

The **Revolutionary Museum** (Nanchang bayi qiyi jinianguan; open 08.00–17.30, closed Mondays) is on Zhongshan lu, which runs along the east side of 1 August Square. Turn right out of the museum and left at the far side of the square and continue up Zhongshan lu. The five storey grey building used to be a hotel (with 96 rooms). It was used as a headquarters by the leaders of the uprising, who held meetings in the main hall. In 1957 it was made into a memorial museum; the museum's name is inscribed in the calligraphy of another

NANCHANG

major military figure, Chen Yi, and the displays consist of old furniture, in recreations of rooms used by notables (Zhou Enlai, Liu Bocheng) as dressing stations, and photographs.

To return to the Jiangxi Binguan, turn right out of the museum up Zhongshan lu. The next major crossroads is with Changzheng lu; turn left and cross Bayi da dao to the hotel.

If time allows, the **Bayi Park** contains much water and relics both ancient and modern. It was the site of the provincial examination halls and also encloses a small square garden known as Old Man Su's Vegetable Plot, for it was originally cultivated by Su Yunliu of the Song dynasty.

The **Residence of Zhou Enlai and Zhu De** during the 1927 uprising was close by at 2 Huayuan jiao, while opposite the North Gate (29 Huanhu lu) is the **Youmin** (Assist the People) **Temple**, founded in 502–519. One of the most famous temples in the province, it has a sizeable bronze Buddha in the rear hall, a bronze bell of the Wanli reign period of the Ming and, most notably, a bronze bell cast in 967 at the order of a general of the Southern Tang.

Other temples include the **Daan** (Great Peace) **Temple** (just inside the Desheng Gate in Yuzhang hou jie), built on the site of the headquarters of a local general in 398 and possessing an iron incense burner said to have been cast during the Three Dynasties (220–280) and the **Wanshou** (Ten Thousand Year)

Temple in Cuihua jie, with its iron pillar said to have been cast by the Taoist Xu Sun of the Qingyun pu.

Another revolutionary site is the former **Residence of Ye Ting**, another of the famous generals of the 1927 uprising, in the No. 2 Middle School beside the Huazhou dong hu.

Almost nothing now remains of the old **Headquarters of Zhu Quan** (the 16th or 17th son of the founder of the Ming dynasty, enfeoffed here), except some carved stones on Xinghuo lu, but there is still a fine **Drum Tower** on the west bank of the East Lake (south of the Guangji Bridge) and the fine **Shengjin** (Gold Restraining) **Pagoda** near Zhishi jie, first built in the 10C but entirely rebuilt in 1708–88. Part of the temple which lies beneath it, this particular pagoda also has an association with geomancy, the belief that disasters could be averted by the construction of a pagoda, for it was reconstructed after having collapsed because of a series of disastrous fires in the locality. A golden tripod vessel was placed at the top of the pagoda to try and avoid more fires. The pagoda is 59m high, octagonal and seven-storeyed, of brick construction imitating timber, with upturned eaves on each storey.

Qingyun pu

The Qingyun pu (Blue Cloud Text) is a country retreat where the wandering painter **Zhu Da**, or Ba da shan ren—the 'Man of Eight Great Mountains' (1626–1705), one of the most innovative of Chinese painters—lived for a while. Near Dingshan qiao in the southern suburbs, about 10km from the city centre, it can be reached by a suburban bus from the bus station on Bayi da dao or by taxi.

Set beside a pool, the Qingyun pu was first built in 321 as a country retreat-cum-Taoist retreat by the Taoist adept, Xu Sun, also known as Xu Zhenchun and the 'True Prince of Miracles'. It was then known (perhaps because of the pool) as the True Mirror of Brilliance and later named the View of Heavenly Peace. After Zhu Da had stayed here it was renamed Qingyun *pu*, or Garden of Blue Clouds, and for some reason in the Kangxi era the last character pu (meaning 'garden') was changed to pu (meaning 'text').

Zhu Da was a ninth generation descendant of a member of the Ming royal house (surnamed Zhu). At the fall of the Ming he went into hiding, partly for fear of persecution by the Qing, partly because he was reclusive anyway. He lived in various (mainly Buddhist) monasteries and stayed here in the Taoist retreat from 1661 to 1687 with disciples, including Qiu Yue (whose studio name was 'The Wisdom of the Stone Ox').

Zhu Da's paintings, of which there is a fine collection in the Shanghai Museum, here only displayed in reproduction, are strikingly modern. Painted in the Chan (or Zen) style, with a few, immensely strong strokes, they frequently depict, in a Chinese minimalist way, fish beneath rocks, birds on rocks, or just rocks. Like their creator, the birds, in particular, often look wild and hunted, on the brink of a nervous breakdown. Zhu Da's influence on 20C Chinese painters such as Pan Tianshou has been enormous, for he anticipated 20C western modernism.

The complex retains its part-religious, part-secular feeling: the rooms used by Zhu Da have been preserved, while reproductions of his works and those of his followers have been added to the display; there are also figures of popular deities, including the Jade Emperor, Xu Sun and the God of War, with Ming bronze altarpieces (vases, incense burners and bells) and in the 'heaven well' courtyard at the rear is a cassia tree and four other trees said to have been planted in the Tang dynasty. There are a number of tombs in the vicinity.

Jingdezhen

Jingdezhen, in Jiangxi province, has long been the **ceramic centre** of China. There have been ceramic kilns in operation here since before the Tang, although it was with the development of porcelain, manufactured from locally produced clays based on feldspathic rocks, that the town came to occupy its dominant position from the Five Dynasties (907–979). It is still one of the major porcelain centres of China.

A visit to Jingdezhen is best organised through the *China Travel Service*, at 21 Lianshebei lu, or, for those professionally interested, through ceramic connections. It is possible to visit the Taoci guan (Ceramic Exhibition Hall) without an introduction but factories and old kiln-sites are out of bounds. A factory visit is extremely interesting as are the great mounds of thousand-year-old mistakes (waste sites associated with ancient kilns).

Practical information

Getting there
By air
There are flights to Shanghai, Beijing and Guangzhu. The aircraft used in the 1980s on the 50 minute journey from Nanchang were tiny, twin-winged propellor planes with room for about six passengers tightly squeezed in, straight out of the old Howard Hawks film *Only Angels Have Wings*. The pilot stood up at the front in a leather flying cap and the plane was steered by wires through the cabin. We flew very low over the Poyang Lake and landed in Jingdezhen, scattering chickens. It was very exciting, although flights were often cancelled if there was any cloud at all. According to the CAAC timetable, the plane used was a Yun 5.

By train
Jingdezhen is on a branch line from Guixi in Jiangxi to Tongling in Anhui, best joined from Shanghai or Nanchang at Guixi. The station is in the east of the town.

By bus
There are minibuses from Jiujiang and Nanchang as well as long distance bus services to more distant destinations.

By car
Jingdezhen is about 300km from Nanchang; it is possible to make the journey by taxi quite comfortably.

Where to stay
The *Jingdezhen Binguan*, 60 Fengjin lu, ☎ 822 5010, fax 822 6416, is in the north of the town in forested hills beyond a small lake and is an easy walk from the town centre.

A history of porcelain production in Jingdezhen

Textual evidence suggests that there were kilns operating in Jingdezhen during the Eastern Han. During the 4C the local court at Nanjing ordered various pottery items for use in palace building, a practice which continued under the Sui. The kiln sites that survive in and around Jingdezhen mostly contain shards from the Five Dynasties onwards. The Five Dynasties shards are mostly of white-bodied wares with the characteristic glassy Qingbai glaze, transparent with a blue colour where it collects thickly. Those of the Yuan dynasty and the Ming are predominantly underglaze blue, for which Jingdezhen is renowned, and it was blue and white from the many kilns here which made its way by river to the coast and was eventually exported to Southeast Asia, Japan and, increasingly, to Europe from the 17C onwards.

One of the most famous accounts of Jingdezhen and its porcelain manufacture was that of the Jesuit Père D'Entrecolles in 1712, published among the *Lettres edifiantes et curieuses de Chine par des missionaires jesuites 1712–1776* (Garnier-Flammarion, 1979). His description of the town, a veritable inferno at times when all the kilns were firing, is still applicable, since the methods are still very much labour intensive and unmechanised:

Jingdezhen stands on the banks of a beautiful river (the Nan jiang) … and contains a prodigious multitude of workers; it is said that there are more than a million souls and they eat daily more than 10,000 catties of rice and more than 1000 pigs … There are now over 3000 kilns and it is not surprising that fires are frequent; for this reason there are several temples to the god of fire.

He also mentions the number of ships on the river, tied up three-deep at the quays and:

… the whirlwinds of smoke and flame that rise from different parts, illustrating the size and spread of the town; at dusk these create the impression of a large town fully ablaze or a huge furnace with many vents. Surprisingly, this populous place is not walled and is the province of a single mandarin … but policing is admirable.

D'Entrecolles continues with a description of the raw materials of porcelain, which has confused experts for centuries, since he distinguishes between two forms of local clay, suggesting that they are chemically distinct (kaolin and petuntse), although it is now thought they are different forms of the same material: 'The clay is first refined and broken up and then formed; larger pieces being made in one or more parts and then luted together.' He stresses the number of hands through which each piece passes, which is most remarkable when the pieces are painted before glazing. 'One simply traces the lines at the rim; another outlines flowers which are painted in by a third. This one does mountains and water, that birds and other animals.' He mentions the variety of colours, although at the time: 'In Europe, we only see blue on a white ground, although I believe our merchants have brought other sorts. Some have mirrored grounds, some are red all over … and there are porcelains where the painted scenes are a mixture of all possible colours, enlivened by gilding.' He describes a particularly successful type of vessel: 'I saw a cat, painted quite naturally. A tiny lamp was placed inside it, the light shining out of the eyes and I was assured that it frightens rats at night.' A couple of such pieces, small nightlights in the form of a crouching cat decorated in blue and white, were found in the 1752 wreck of an East Indiaman, the *Geldermaasen*, whose contents were sold in Amsterdam in 1985 (one is now in the British Museum).

From the Song onwards, the court took a great interest in the production of Jingdezhen. The town takes its name from a reign period of the Song, Jingde (1004–07), when pieces destined for the court were marked 'made in the Jingde reign period'. Imperial kilns were established at the beginning of the Ming and continued through the Qing, with occasional special orders, as when the Kangxi emperor ordered paintings by Jiao Bingzhen to be copied onto porcelain and Yongzheng and Qianlong later took an especial interest in the production of fine tiny pieces of overglaze enamelled wares called Guyue xuan (Pavilion of the Ancient Moon) production, which came to an end with the death in 1753 of Tang Yin, the last of the great superintendents of the imperial kilns.

In the past, as today, high-class or imperial production went side by side with the production of lesser pieces in smaller, private kilns. The kilns in the south of China, including Jingdezhen, were 'dragon kilns', multi-chambered constructions, usually built up hills and fired with wood. Around the hotel, you can see great stacks of timber for the kilns and it is still fascinating to watch a wood-firing. The kiln supervisor keeps his eyes fixed on a vent, in which two balls of clay (between golf-ball and tennis-ball in size) are placed and with minimal hand gestures controls a team of young men, stripped to the waist in the heat, who toss logs into the kiln. Elsewhere in the factory, workers still paint by hand and pass pots from one to the next, although the cheaper wares are often stencil-decorated.

The **Taoci guan** (Ceramic Exhibition Hall) is on Lianshe bei lu: pass the two lakes in front of the hotel and turn right. It includes a small historical exhibition of production at Jingdezhen as well as a display of currently produced ceramics, many of which are based firmly on past production.

If you turn left out of the Jingdezhen Binguan and take the curving Fengjing lu, which leads to Zhonghua bei lu, one of the town's pleasant main streets, you pass small factories and can often find white porcelain golf-ball-like testers in the gutters. When you reach Zhushan dong lu, turn left and you will reach the centre of the town. Alternatively, turn right and you will reach the river which, if not quite as busy as in the days of Père D'Entrecolles, still bustles.

Surrounding the town, and inaccessibly underneath it, are many kiln sites. These consist of huge hills, now apparently natural and rounded in contour but actually artificial, made from hundreds of thousands of kiln wasters (broken or faulty pots) thrown out from the kilns. If you get permission to visit them, by all means pick up pieces to look at them but try to replace them where you find them (and resist the temptation to take them home), for you are standing on an archaeological site.

One of the most fascinating places in Jingdezhen is the **Taoci lishi bowuguan**, which has been sited in one of several rare surviving Ming houses in Jingdezhen. Entered from the side, past a whitewashed, grey tiled, stepped gable, characteristic of southern building, the tall hall with its small, almost enclosed courtyard (the small opening in the roof is called a 'heaven well') in dark, carved wood with elegantly curved beams, reveals the wealth of local merchants in the Ming. Exhibits in the hall include reconstructed vessels from some of the imperial kilns now

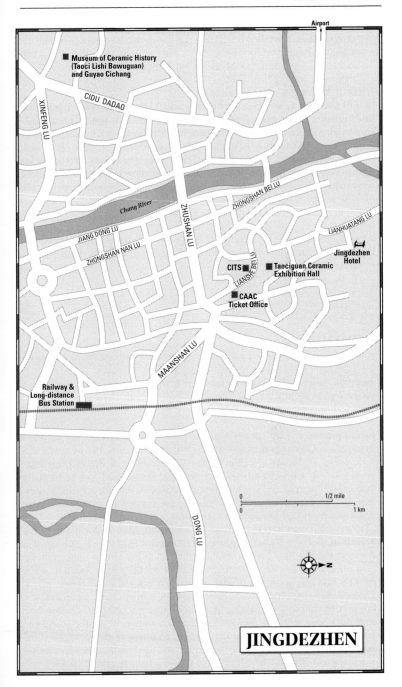

Airport

Museum of Ceramic History
(Taoci Lishi Bowuguan)
and Guyao Cichang

CIDU DADAO

XINFENG LU

ZHUSHAN LU

Chang River

ZHONGSHAN BEI LU

JIANG DONG LU

ZHONGSHAN NAN LU

LIANHUATANG LU

LIANSHE BEI LU

CITS

Taociguan Ceramic
Exhibition Hall

Jingdezhen
Hotel

CAAC
Ticket Office

MAANSHAN LU

Railway &
Long-distance
Bus Station

0   1/2 mile
0   1 km

DONG LU

N

JINGDEZHEN

buried under modern housing estates and photographs of the excavations.

A 'Qing' ceramic workshop has been set up for tourists next door to show them how firing was done: it is much better if you can manage to see this in a real kiln. The Taoci lishi bowuguan and Guyao chicang are open 08.00–17.00.

Ancient kiln sites

Ancient kiln sites to be seen out of town include the **Baihu wan** (White Tiger Bend) remains, 9km east of Jingdezhen, off the Jingwu road. This includes remains from the Five Dynasties, Northern and Southern Song. Further out is the **Liujia wan** (Willow Family Bend) kiln site, 22km from Jingdezhen, 10m high, covering over 10,000 square metres. Finds here are mostly middle to late Northern Song *qingbai* (blue-white) or *yingqing* (shadow blue) white wares with incised decoration under the blue-tinged glassy glaze. Nearby is the Nanshijie site.

Just over 7km east of the town, on a hill behind the Huangnitou primary school, is a site covering 5000 square metres. To the west are Five Dynasties shards (grey-bodied, white-glazed and white-bodied, white-glazed wares) and to the east, *yingqing* of the Northern Song. The **Hutian kiln site**, east of Jingdezhen in Hutian village, covers the broadest time span, from the Five Dynasties to the mid Ming.

Changsha

Changsha, capital of Hunan province, is a city of enormous historical and archaeological significance but little of its past remains to be seen outside the Provincial Museum.

Hunan province, 'South of the Dongting Lake', is one of China's major tea-producing areas. Created at the same time as Hubei, in the early 18C by the division of Huguang, its history is similar for the Chu kingdom of the Warring States period (403–221 BC) also occupied present-day Hunan and had its capital at Changsha. Long regarded as a border region (the Chu did not, apparently, speak Chinese), Hunan was nevertheless linked to the north through the network of canals and rivers that allowed rice to be transported north.

The revolutionary history of Hunan is important. **Mao Zedong** was born in **Shaoshan**, just over 100km southwest of Changsha. Shaoshan is a small village which, at the height of the personality cult during the 1960s, apparently saw some 8000 pilgrims a day. Now relatively deserted, the village—with its ancestral hall and the pond where Mao threatened suicide when faced with an arranged marriage—has considerable charm and is worth a visit for anyone with time on their hands in Changsha. The natal house is a substantial yellow brick farmhouse beyond a lotus pool entered through a room where the family altar stands with ancestral tablets. In the kitchen, an image of the stove god stands above the stove and the rooms arranged around the interior courtyard include Mao's bedroom, those of his parents and younger brother, and the stables.

Practical information

Getting there
By air

The airport is south of the city. There are flights to and from Peking, Guangzhou, Chengdu, Wuhan, Shenyang, Xi'an, Zhengzhou, and departures for Nanjing, Shanghai, Shijiazhuang and Yichang. Shuttle buses to the airport (c 2hrs before flights) leave from the *CAAC* office 5 Wuyi dong lu.

By train

The station is in the east of the city.

Changsha is something of a major intersection, with lines to Shanghai and Beijing and south to Guangzhou as well as west to Yunnan, Guizhou and Sichuan.

Where to stay

The *Xiang jiang Binguan*, 36 Zhongshan lu, ☎ 440 8888, fax 444 828, in the centre of the city and the *Huatian Dajiudian*, 380 Jiefang dong lu, ☎ 444 2888, fax 444 2270.

History

During the Eastern Zhou (771–256 BC) the **state of Chu** on the Yangtse, with Changsha (then known as Qingyang) at its centre, was one of the strongest of the Warring States and one of the major texts of the period, the *Zhan guo ce* (*Intrigues of the Warring States*), a 'work of fiction in a magnificent prose style') is greatly taken up with the battles for supremacy between Qin (the eventual victor) and Chu. As well as battling against its neighbours, taking over the southern state of Yue in the 4C BC, the state of Chu developed a system of administration by which ministers' offices were regularly changed to prevent the growth of corruption, hereditary offices were decreased and officials were fairly strictly controlled.

The separateness of Chu is evident in its artefacts: the bronzes of Chu, in the Huai style, were decorated with knobbly, high-relief coiled dragons; the use of lacquered wood in sculpture (including funerary sculpture) was distinctive, and a rare literary survival, the *Chu ci* (*Songs of Chu*) describes the beliefs and feelings of the Chu people who lived at that time on the frontiers of China and were regarded as hardly Chinese by the northerners. Shamanistic beliefs and descriptions of the haunted horrors of the underworld, echoed in somewhat mysterious paintings and jade monsters, are described.

Even after its subjugation to the Qin and the establishment of the first empire, Chu, with its capital at Changsha, remained to some extent detached from the centre, a principality under the Han and part of the southern border regions that to those from the north and centre of China were fetid realms of exile. Until 187 BC, when a series of rebellions compelled the emperor to revise policy, Chu was ruled by nobles who were not members of the imperial clan—one of the famous Mawangdui tombs is that of a marquis and his wife who were not related to the imperial Li family. The town's population more than quadrupled between AD 2 and 140 (years of census) because of a population influx from the troubled north; the population was over a million at the second census. A second Chu state was declared from 906–923, before the empire was reunited, and Changsha grew steadily throughout the succeeding centuries.

Its second period of glory (in retrospect) was when **Mao Zedong** studied at the Teacher Training College here between 1912 and 1918, a period of great importance to him as he developed his interest in social matters. The first meeting of the provincial Communist Party Committee was held in Changsha in 1921. After considerable destruction during the Sino-Japanese War (1937–45), Changsha was rebuilt after Liberation and is today a modern city with few traces of its past visible outside the museum, which is full of evidence of fascinating excavations relating in particular to the state of Chu and the city during the Han period.

The city lies mainly on the east bank of the Xiang River with a narrow island (Juzi zhoutou or Orange Island) in the centre. The island was where foreign residents chose to live when Changsha became a '**treaty port**' in 1903. Some of their residences survive there; they are described in one of the novels by Alice Tisdale Hobart, wife of the Standard Oil Company representative, *City of the Long Sands*. In 1908, the British Consul (whose three predecessors had respectively died of TB, suffered from nervous prostration and temporary insanity) arrived to find his living rooms, 'a nightmare ... damp streamed down them'. The upper floors were rickety, rats flourished everywhere and 'it was no rare thing to find frogs in the dining room'. As if this were not enough, the local inhabitants were very anti-foreign and 'easily roused'. The traveller and writer Peter Fleming found Changsha a paradise after adventuring in the 1930s, for the Commissioner of Customs (a fat American) enabled him to fill his stomach and get 'very nearly clean'. In 1938 there was still a 'big weekly do' at the club when you could dance to the gramophone and eat a buffet supper. Heads would be cleared the next morning with 'morning gin on any British gunboat that happened to be in' and there was a weekly musical evening at the British Consulate when local businessmen scraped away at their violins. Such jollity ended abruptly on 12 November 1938 when Changsha was set ablaze to prevent anything of value falling into Japanese hands.

On the west bank of the river is **Hunan University**, built on part of Yuelu Mountain, which is a favourite 'scenic spot'. The mountain, which is only 297m high, was nevertheless considered as one of the 72 peaks of the old southern state of Yue and described as such in the *Account of Southern Yue* in the Nan bei chao period (420–581).

The area has a history: the university includes the site of the Yuelu Academy of the 10C, one of the four major scholastic establishments of the Song. Major figures, including the philosopher **Zhu Xi** (1130–1200) taught here. Zhu Xi was a statesman and historian whose commentaries on the Confucian Classics became the set texts for the imperial examinations for the succeeding centuries. He is very much associated with the revival of interest in Confucianism (Neo-Confucianism) of the Song period, which was later to become something of a philosophical and educational straitjacket. In 1903 the academy was transformed into a teacher training college and in 1918 the Hunan Provincial Technical College also moved to the site so that in 1925 these diverse academies were joined to form the Hunan Provincial University.

The earliest surviving buildings on the site date from the Qing, although there is a stele left of the academy carved in 730 with a description of the Lushan Temple written by the famous calligrapher Li Yong. The stele was later further embellished by other calligraphers, including Mi Fei of the Song in 1080.

Just behind the University is the two storey **Aiwan ting** (Love of the Evening Pavilion) with its exaggeratedly upswept eaves. It is also known as the Red Leaf Pavilion and the Love of Maples Pavilion, the latter name taken not only from the trees that surround it but also from a line in a poem by the Tang poet Du Fu: 'In the evening I stop and sit in the grove of the love of maples; the frost reddens the leaves and in the second month they flower.'

The name of the pavilion was written out by Mao Zedong after restoration in 1952 and on the columns are couplets reflecting its importance in poetry written by students of the nearby academies in the late Qing period. They read: 'Staying at night in the red house on the side of the mountain, surrounded by 500 newly planted peach trees. The clouds wreathing the peaks are deep and the greenery drips and I bring two tame cranes in a basket.'

On the summit of the mountain, north of the University, is the **Yunlu gong** (Misty Hill Hall), now just a pavilion built in 1863 to replace an 18C original destroyed during the Taiping rebellion in 1852. Below, half-way up the mountain, is the **Lushan si**, or temple, over whose gate are the words: 'First famous in the Han and Wei, the first in Hunan'. It was indeed the first Buddhist temple in Changsha, founded in 268. The main hall was destroyed in 1944 and only the gate and library now remain.

There are two graves on the mountain, those of Huang Xing (1874–1916), a leader of the 1911 revolution, and Cai E (1882–1916), a military leader who led an unsuccessful rising in Hankou in 1900. Huang Xing's grave is just above the road, a three-stepped structure (wide, stepped graves are characteristic of the south) and Cai E's, also stepped, is above the White Crane Spring on the mountain.

The south of the city

Three sites in the south of the city may be visited together, either by taxi or on foot. These are the Tianxin Park, the Hunan No. One Teacher Training College and the headquarters of the local Communist Party, *Zhonggong xiangqu weiyuan-hui jiuzhi* (also known as Clearwater Pool or Qing shui tang), which is virtually opposite the hotel (just to the east) at no. 22 Qing shui tang.

This was where the first meeting of the Provincial Party Committee, with Mao as Party Secretary, was held in July 1921 and where Mao and his first wife, Yang Kaihui, the daughter of one of Mao's former teachers in Changsha (they married in 1920 and had three sons; she was executed by the KMT in 1930), lived from 1921 to 1923. The room in which they lived has been reconstructed and forms part of the exhibition on Mao's life and achievements.

Heading west along Zhongshan lu, turn left (south) down Jiangxiang lu and after a major crossroads with Wuyi lu you will find a park on your right, the **Tianxin gongyuan** (Park of the Heart of Heaven). This used to mark the southeast angle of the city wall, just inside which were the Tianxin ge (Pavilion of the Heart of Heaven) and the Wenchang ge (Pavilion of the Flourishing of Literature).

During the Taiping uprising the park was occupied by a local Taiping leader, the Western Heavenly King, who executed a large number of Qing imperial troops here. In 1930, when the Red Army attacked Changsha, Peng Dehuai held a meeting here.

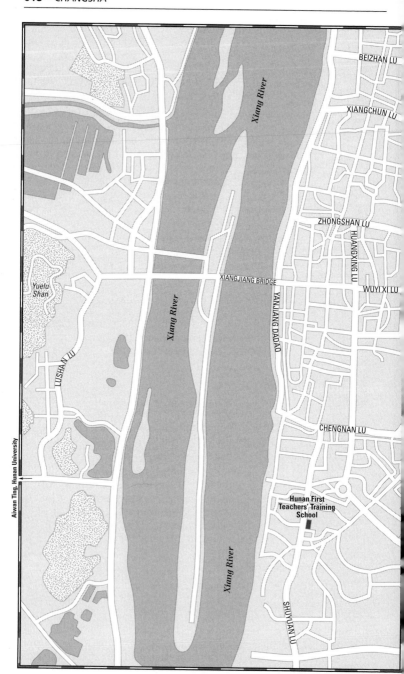

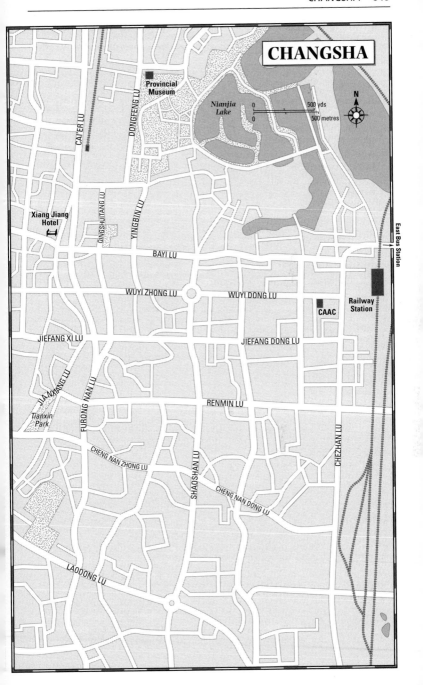

CHANGSHA

Provincial Museum

Nianjia Lake

0   500 yds
0   500 metres

N

East Bus Station

CAIER LU

DONGFENG LU

QINGSHUITANG LU

YINGBIN LU

Xiang Jiang Hotel

BAYI LU

WUYI ZHONG LU

WUYI DONG LU

CAAC

Railway Station

JIEFANG XI LU

JIEFANG DONG LU

JIANXIANG LU

FURONG NAN LU

Tianxin Park

RENMIN LU

CHENG NAN ZHONG LU

SHAOSHAN LU

CHENG NAN DONG LU

CHEZHAN LU

LAODONG LU

The **Hunan No. One Teacher Training College** (or Normal School) is on Shuyuan lu. Leaving the park, turn right along Chengnan lu, which marks the southern line of the old city wall, and take the second major turning on the left, Shuyuan lu. The old college is not far down the road on your right.

Mao studied here from 1913 (when he was 19 years old) to 1918, impressing his student colleagues and teachers, including his future father-in-law, by his activity: organising student societies and a night-school and becoming 'Student of the Year' in 1917, despite his varied application. It was here that he failed his art exam (by drawing a circle and calling it 'an egg') and he also consistently got practically no marks for mathematics and none at all for English, which he must have seen as being as useless as art to a man who wanted to change society.

You could return to the Xiang jiang hotel by retracing your steps to Chengnan lu and turning left. The road, which changes its name to Yanjiang da dao, runs along the riverside. The first major turning on the right, after Wuyi lu, is Zhongshan lu, which crosses the bridge over to Orange Island. Turn right into it to find the hotel.

Not far northwest of the hotel is the **Kaifu si** (Opening to Luck Temple) on Xiangchun jie. Leaving the hotel, turn right into Zhongshan lu, cross Jianxiang lu and take the next major turning on the right, Dazhai lu. The second major turning on the left is Xiangchun jie, which runs west–east from the river.

Founded in the Five Kingdoms period (907–960) by Ma Yin, then king of Chu, the temple was added to by his son and extensively rebuilt in succeeding dynasties, the main hall most recently in 1923. Its great stone *pailou*, with highly decorated roof tiles, stands in front of a temple whose roofs are decorated in the lavish southern style.

Provincial Museum

The greatest glories of today's Changsha are to be found in the **Provincial Museum** (open 08.00–12.00, 14.30–17.00), just north of the hotel in the northwest corner of the Martyrs' Park (Hunan lieshi gongyuan). It can be reached by taking the first street heading north towards Jingdu lu, which runs along the southern edge of the park.

The museum contains an important collection of red-painted Neolithic pottery and bronzes from the Shang and Zhou, as well as a chronological display of artefacts from the Han to the Qing unearthed in Hunan. The major display is that referring to the three tombs at Mawangdui in the east suburbs of the town, accessible by taxi, (where Tomb 3 can still be seen).

Tomb 1, excavated in 1973, is that of a woman, the wife of the marquis of Dai. Tombs 2 and 3, discovered in the following year, contain the bodies of her husband and son. The marquis of Dai, Li Cang, was appointed prime minister to the king of Changsha in 193 BC and died in 186 BC. The third tomb, containing the body of a younger son of the marquis, is dated by an inscription to 168 BC.

Tomb 1 was constructed later than the other two, slightly damaging them during construction. Li Cang appears to have been the last prime minister appointed by the king of Changsha; his successor was appointed by the central Han government.

All the tombs were vertical shafts cut into the ground and surmounted by a cone-shaped mound. This southern form contrasts with the hollow brick chambers of the north, the brick chamber serving as a sort of outer coffin. The Mawangdui tombs contained a nest of four inner coffins within a wooden outer coffin. The outer coffin was surrounded by a layer of charcoal and a layer of white clay, which preserved the contents admirably. The inner coffins were: a black-painted coffin containing a black-lacquered coffin painted with mythological animals and figures, containing a red-lacquered coffin decorated with auspicious emblems, which in turn contained the inner coffin housing the dead body.

The bodies were dressed in up to 20 thin silk garments. The body of the woman in Tomb No. I was remarkably well-preserved, her flesh still reasonably elastic to the touch (as can be seen in a rather gruesome film of the excavation and subsequent autopsy). She appears to have died from some sort of seizure shortly after eating melon (pips and all) and had TB, a slipped disc, intestinal worms, marked arthritis and arteriosclerosis, although she was only about 50.

The **coffins**, some of which are on display, are beautifully painted with swirling clouds in which tiny animals sit on the black-lacquered versions, the whole outlined with almost art nouveau interlocked cloud swirls, while on the end of the red-lacquered coffin a pair of prancing deer, heraldic in appearance, are surrounded by swirling cloud scrolls and bordered by a geometric interlocking pattern with fleur-de-lys. The same sort of swirling linear designs are seen on the huge quantity of grave goods, some life-size and everyday, such as the double-lugged lacquer cups and bowls, compartmented toilet boxes and combs and food containers, the others miniaturised and symbolic like the small painted wooden statuettes of servants.

The dual nature of the funerary furnishings have been interpreted as intended to serve the two souls that the Han believed in, the hun and the po (there were thought to be three *hun* and seven *po*). On death, the *hun* soul leaves the body and makes its way to heaven and the place of the spirits, while the *po* souls stay around in the tomb (hence the food and drink provided) before descending to the Yellow Springs in the centre of the earth. It was, and still is, considered important to keep the *po* souls happy and well fed lest they leave the tomb early and come to create havoc for the deceased's descendants. Foods provided in the 48 bamboo food baskets and 51 ceramic food containers in Tomb I alone included wheat, barley, rice, soya, kidney beans, lotus roots, melon, chives, lentils, ginger, pears, plums, peaches, oranges, persimmons, waterchestnuts, beef, mutton, pork, dog, chicken, pheasant, duck, quail, sparrow, bream, perch, carp, salt, sugar, honey, vinegar, cinnamon, alcohols and fruit juices. Many of the foods provided were salted, smoked or pickled in vinegar.

There were musical instruments in the tombs and fabrics of silk, notably a fine gauze, figured and embroidered silks and there was a variety of colours used in dying and painting the fabrics. Designs on the textiles echo those on the lacquered and painted coffins and lacquered utensils.

For the Chinese, some of the most important finds in the tombs were those of **books and documents**. These included a text of the *Zhan guo ce* (*Intrigues of the*

Warring States), the *Yi jing* (*Book of Changes*), the Taoist classic *Dao de jing* (with its sections reversed to read *De dao jing*), and texts on punishments, astronomy, meteorology, divination, horse physiognomy, maps of the Changsha area and an exercise chart. The last is very charming, showing various figures bending and stretching and touching their toes. The texts appeared either on narrow wooden strips or painted on silk in the case of the illustrated works, such as maps and charts.

Apart from the still fascinating bodies in the tombs, one of the most significant pieces to emerge was the **T-shaped silk banner from Tomb 1**, which serves as a graphic illustration of Han beliefs about the world.

At the base is the subterranean world, the realm of water and darkness represented by two fish. From there two dragons ascend, their bodies interlocked in a jade *bi* disc; the disc, with a hole in the centre, is decorated with characteristic raised circles and has a silken thread knotted through it. Below the *bi* disc hangs another decorative jade, the *heng* (an inverted V form, part of a characteristic series of jade pieces threaded with silken cords and hung from the belt in the Han), and below that is a picture of the sorts of food vessels containing offerings which were left in the tomb. The dragons were believed to assist the *hun* soul on its journey to heaven, so it must be assumed to be rising with them from the depths. Above the *bi* is a platform with figures, that of a woman assumed to be the marquess of Dai, in whose tomb the hanging was found. An owl flies above, supporting a canopy upon which stand two birds. These have been interpreted as phoenixes, birds of good omen who escort the *hun* soul to the heavens, just as the nice spotted leopards beneath the figures are thought to be protective of the soul on its journey upwards.

Above the canopy is an opening into the heavens presided over by two gentlemen, seen by some as representatives of the celestial king come to greet the hun soul. Beside them are two more protecting leopards and above them hangs a bronze bell. At the top (left) is the moon with the toad and the hare who live there and to the right are the red disc of the sun and the black crow, symbolic of the sun. At the top, in the centre, is a female figure enlaced in a snake that grows, mermaid-like, from her own body. She is thought to be Nu wa, ancestress of mankind, here representing the celestial gods ready to welcome the soul to this upper realm.

This physical depiction of the realms of the spiritual world (otherwise known only from literary accounts, which are necessarily less graphic and difficult to interpret) is one of the great treasures from Mawangdui and you can amuse yourself not only in trying to penetrate the Han mind but also in trying to decide whether that which is displayed in Changsha's museum is the original banner, or has Peking won and the example in the Historical Museum there is in fact the real thing? Or is the real thing locked away for preservation in rather better storage conditions?

Shaoshan

Shaoshan, birthplace of **Chairman Mao** is some 90km southwest of Changsha. For those interested in iconography and the Communist process of canonisation it is well worth a day trip from Changsha.

Getting there

Daily tour buses leave from outside Changsha railway station from 06.00; alternatively you could take the daily train (3 hours) at 06.30. Minibuses wait at Shaoshan station to take pilgrims up to the village 6km away.

The first stop is **Mao's family home**. This is a yellow-earth open courtyard building with dark tiled roofs and outhouses beside a lotus pond. Mao Zedong, the eldest of four children, was born here on 26 December 1893. The house, substantial in Shaoshan terms, indicates the relative prosperity of Mao's father who supplemented his farming income by grain dealing. Mao was frequently at odds with his father and the lotus pond was the scene of a threatened suicide. Mao's father was supposed to have followed local tradition and arranged a marriage for his son when he was only about 13. Mao Zedong stood by the lotus pool threatening to drown himself until his soft-hearted mother forced the father to abandon the project.

The house is (unsurprisingly) a well-preserved example of local domestic architecture and contains some simple furniture.

In the main square of the village is the **Mao Zedong Exhibition Hall** (open 08.30–17.00), like so many others, subject to constant political revision. Beside it is the **Mao Clan Ancestral Hall**, another fine example of village architecture. The village, as elsewhere in China, consists mainly of Maos, most restaurant owners and souvenir sellers now claiming close familial ties with the Great Helmsman. The souvenirs, out-Lourdesing Lourdes, are truly amazing and 'improve' with every new technological advance. Where once they were mainly the equivalent of St Christopher medallions to dangle from the rear mirror of every taxi, there are now luminous, electrical and computer-generated icons.

Fuzhou

Fuzhou is the capital of Fujian province (Fukien in the old Postal Service romanisation, Fu-chien in Wade-Giles), which is on China's southeast coast, the southern part of the province facing the island of Taiwan.

Fujian is a very beautiful province, in general, fitting the Chinese term for landscape, which is shan shui, meaning 'mountains and water'. They say that there are more mountains and water in Fujian than almost anywhere else, therefore more 'landscape'. The province has a semi-tropical, or tropical, climate with average winter temperatures in Fuzhou of nearly 11°C and July averages of nearly 29°C. The mountainous areas inland are rather cooler and there is considerable rainfall (1500mm to 2000mm a year), with typhoons on the coast in the summer months. The mountains have made communications difficult inland, although two railways lines connecting Fuzhou and Xiamen with the interior were built in 1955. Much transport goes by road or by sea along the coast, for Fujian has a long maritime tradition.

As a provincial capital, Fuzhou houses the Fujian University and industries including chemicals, machine-building, paper-making, timber and foodstuffs, such as jasmine tea, with handicrafts in lacquer, wood and stone, notably a local stone related to pyrophyllite, and ivory carving.

The proximity of Taiwan has meant that for many decades Fujian has been a military centre. It was only opened to foreign tourism in 1979; the coast is generally open, but parts of the interior are still closed, for military reasons. It seems likely, as tourism continues to develop, that many significant sites currently in military zones may yet be opened. Recently, the word has seemed to be that 'in a couple of years' various sites that were still closed would finally be opened. Tourist maps are somewhat misleading as they indicate sites (such as a cave in Xiamen in which Zhu Xi may have taught) that lie smack in the middle of barracks or military zones and are therefore inaccessible. The major list of sites of cultural interest, *Zhong guo ming sheng ci dian* (*Dictionary of Famous Sites*), produced by the Bureau of Cultural Relics, which supervises their preservation, also lists a number of protected sites (such as the tombs of Lin Zexu and Yan Fu outside Fuzhou) that are still out of bounds to foreigners. I will list them, with a caution, in the hope that they will eventually be accessible. The military presence in Fujian is not obvious but it is obtrusive when you search for out-of-the-way tombs and taxi-drivers who seem to have been instructed not to tell the simple truth, always so much more acceptable, appear both stupid and obstructive at times as a result.

Practical information

Getting there
By air

The airport is to the south of the city—about an hour by bus from the hotel area at the northern end of Wusi lu. Airport buses depart from the *Fujian Civil Aviation hotel* next door to the *CAAC* office, 185 Wuyi zhong lu. There are flights to Beijing, Nanchang, Wuhan, Shanghai, Guangzhou, Hefei, Hangzhou, Hong Kong and Nanjing.

By train

The station is in the north of the city and is only about ten minutes by bus from the major hotel area. The line to Fuzhou, one of only two in Fujian, breaks off from major east–west and north–south lines at Yingtan in Jiangxi province. Within Fujian the line branches again at Waiyang, splitting into a Xiamen and Fuzhou branch. It is therefore possible to reach the interior of China from Fuzhou or Xiamen by rail, whereas travel within Fujian by rail is impractical, since Fuzhou–Xiamen by road is some 250km but almost twice as far by rail.

By bus

The most comfortable buses can be booked and boarded from major hotels and these represent the best way for individuals to travel down the Fujian coast. It takes just over two hours to get to Quanzhou and about seven hours to get to Xiamen.

By boat

Shanghai and Xiamen can be reached rather slowly by boat; the passenger terminals are near the Jiefang bridge.

Where to stay

The *Success Link International Hotel* (Chenglong guoji dajiudian), 252 Wusi lu, ☎ 782 2888, fax 782 1888, and *Wenquan da Fandian* (Hot Springs

Hotel), 218 Wusi lu, ☎ 785 1818, fax
783 5150.

History

Fuzhou lies on the Min River, some 40km from the coast. The wide river, protected from coastal typhoons, has provided a safe anchorage for over 1000
years and Fuzhou has long been a major port. It was given its name in 725 during the Tang dynasty, when the state of Min came under central Chinese control and Minzhou (Min City) became Fuzhou (Happy City). The *fu* comes from
the Fu mountains to the northwest. The city is beautifully situated, the Min
River passing through dark mountains, the plain lush and green with subtropical foliage, including *banyans* (Fuzhou is sometimes called Banyan City).

Before the Tang, Fujian lay outside the Chinese empire, part of the kingdom
of Min-Yue and, despite loose integration under the Jin (AD 265–420), it was
not really settled by the Chinese until the Tang dynasty.

As Fuzhou lay outside China proper before the Tang, little is known about
it. When the Min kingdom was absorbed the safe, inland port of Fuzhou on
the Min River quickly became prosperous. It was described in Marco Polo's
late 13C *Description of the World*. Polo says that the city is full of idolators,
ready to rise against the Mongol rulers, and they therefore garrisoned a large
number of imperial troops there (just as large numbers are still stationed in
Fujian owing to the proximity of Taiwan): 'Through the midst of the city
flows a great river ... It is crossed by a very fine bridge resting on huge pon-
toons ....' This last is an accurate description of the city divided by the Min,
with a small island in the centre dividing the bridge in two. Polo also mentioned the quantities of sugar cane, still to be seen in the area, and the trade
of the city in pearls and precious stones by 'merchants who traffic in the
Indies'. A long passage, with no apparent basis in fact, describes the lions said
to infest the neighbourhood, which were lured into pits by means of howling
white dogs.

From the early days, the province's prosperity grew on the basis of **maritime trade**. Local products, fine teas from the north of the province and
cane sugar from the south, were exported to north China and as early as the
1C AD, ships came from Southeast Asia seeking Chinese produce. The protected harbours of Fuzhou, Quanzhou and Xiamen (essentially protected
against typhoons by being situated up-river from the sea or sheltered by off-
shore islands) were major trading centres with Japan, Southeast Asia and
beyond, shipping Fujian lead and tin, Fujian lacquer (highly polished lacquer
vessels made on a hemp base formed over a wooden mould), cotton, tea,
ceramics from neighbouring Jiangxi and silks from Zhe jiang; and returning
with luxury goods, such as ivory, amber, spices and rare timbers. In the 13C
Quanzhou was known as Zaytun, the name eventually applied to satin which
was shipped to Manila and thence to Mexico in the 16C. In the 13C Fuzhou
presented the scene of 'large numbers of ships, loaded with goods' mentioned
in Marco Polo's dubious *Description of the World*. The famous eunuch, Zheng
He, who led the grand series of maritime expeditions in the early Ming
(1405–33), set off from Zhejiang but stopped in Fuzhou to replenish provisions and recruit sailors.

As one of China's major ports, Fuzhou was also attractive to western traders and was one of the first ports to be opened to **foreign trade and residence** by the earliest of the 'unequal treaties' signed in Nanjing in 1842 after the Opium War. The new foreign residents settled on the south bank of the Min, building their fine houses and offices on the sloping land facing the old walled Chinese city on the north bank. By the time they arrived, the river was crossed by a stone bridge (now called Jiefang or Liberation Bridge) in two parts, built originally in 1297.

Due to their favourable trading conditions and pleasant climate (except for the hot, humid summers), the ports of Xiamen (Amoy) and Fuzhou were favourite places of residence for traders and missionaries. The name for tea, one of the early trade items, derives from the pronunciation of the character in the Xiamen or Amoy dialect: *te*. In modern standard Chinese, however, it is pronounced *cha*. In the middle of the 19C each vessel to leave for North America carried an average of 1000 tons of tea, although as late as 1910 the trans-shipment of opium through Xiamen was still a major aspect of trade. The writer who noted the movement of opium in 1910 was the Reverend Philip Wilson Pitcher in *In and Around Amoy, Shanghai and Foochow* (1910/1912); he also noted that 'the great export from this port is labour. Many thousands go abroad every year to Singapore, Java, Borneo and Manila'.

One of the distinguishing attributes of Fujian is its enormous contribution to the Chinese diaspora: **Overseas Chinese communities** in Singapore, Malaysia and Manila, in particular, virtually all originate in Fujian (including the ancestors of Cory Aquino). They are linked by language, the communities overseas still speaking the distinctive local dialects, a link emphasised by Reverend Pitcher's praise for the English Presbyterian missionary Carstairs Douglas' 'inestimable *Dictionary of the Vernacular or Spoken Language of Amoy*—the joy and delight of everyone living in this region, across the Channel [i.e. on Taiwan], or in the Straits Settlements, fortunate enough to possess a copy'. Some 45 per cent of the Chinese on Taiwan are said to have originated in the town of Quanzhou. Probably the oldest Overseas Chinese settlement was in the Philippines in the 16C, when successful Chinese traders from Fujian made their money in silver, which originated in the New World mines of the Spanish *conquistadores*. Silver from the Philippines was remitted to China in considerable quantities, where it was used as currency in the Ming.

The impact of the Overseas Chinese on Fujian is considerable. Money is remitted to relatives and, since the relaxation following the death of Mao in 1976, Overseas Chinese have been returning for visits in greater numbers than ever. Many Buddhist temples in Fujian have been rebuilt with money from Overseas Chinese and their incredibly lavish decoration, together with a considerable structural use of concrete, sets them apart from the more sober buildings of the north. In late 1987 the first Taiwanese visitors since 1949 were finally permitted to return (through the Chinese Red Cross) by the Taiwanese authorities, who had held out against it. People had been returning during the 1950s, particularly following anti-Chinese government regulations and bloody riots in places such as Indonesia. Many were settled in 'Overseas Chinese farms' in Fujian, although some younger people have now left the farms and found employment elsewhere in China.

One of the earliest Overseas Chinese to pour money back into his home town was Chen Jiageng (1874–1961), whose name in Amoy dialect is rendered Tan Kah-kee, which underlines the extremely different pronunciation of this dialect. From the Xiamen area, he spent much of his life in Singapore, where he made his money in rubber. Between 1913 and 1920 he established primary and middle schools, a teacher-training college, business, agricultural, marine-engineering and fishery colleges in Jimei on the outskirts of Xiamen. The architecture of Jimei, a startling combination of western and Chinese in the early 20C style, still survives, as do the institutions he founded. He died in Beijing, having returned to China where he held many important posts, including membership of the Committee for Overseas Chinese Affairs.

The **Ming city walls** have disappeared (they were still present in 1924, with their six gates, two sluice gates and frequent gun-towers), although their position can be traced along Huancheng lu (west), Wushan lu and Gutian lu (south), Dongshui lu and the Puan River (east), cutting across to Hualin lu (north) with the West Lake lying just outside the ramparts. The city has filled out: in the mid 19C there were many open spaces, those within the east wall were the result of devastating fires to the southwest, the Wushan area, currently the seat of local government, and a parkland full of temples where 'houses cease to appear and the domain of temples begins. The silence deepens'. Elsewhere, the common noise and bustle of a Chinese city was apparent to an American missionary in the 1850s:

> ... blacksmith shops, brasier shops and a variety of other noisy trades each congregated in its own locality ... the dwellings have one room open to the street and two or three back of it ... with dirt floors and pigs and chickens common tenants with the inhabitants. Handicrafts of various descriptions are prosecuted by the inmates.

Lake Xi hu and the Provincial Museum

It is possible to walk to the lake from Wusi lu, cutting through to Guping lu, turning north to the next major crossroads and turning west into Hubin lu where the entrance to the park is on the north side of the road. Cross the lake Xi hu by the bridge and cross the central island. On the far side of the lake is the Fujian Provincial Museum, divided into two parts, one of revolutionary, one of pre-revolutionary history.

Provincial Museum

In the pre-revolutionary archaeological exhibition, one of the most striking exhibits is that of the **boat coffin** from Wuyi shan, excavated (if removing a wooden coffin from a cave high up on a cliff can be called excavation) in 1978. The full-sized covered boat with raised prow and stern was made from nanmu cedar and the Carbon-14 date ascribes it to 3445 years ago. Iron tools and implements, including cog-wheels and crossbow fittings, were found in a Western Han city in Fujian and there is a large collection of locally produced green wares of the Tang, including some small tiger-headed, almost gargoyle-like pots, described as having a 'hygienic function'. They are not dissimilar to (although much smaller than) the flattish, wide-spouted ceramic chamberpots still sold today.

Another good collection is that from the Five Dynasties when the kingdom of Min controlled the area. A stone- and brick-lined tomb of the period produced a

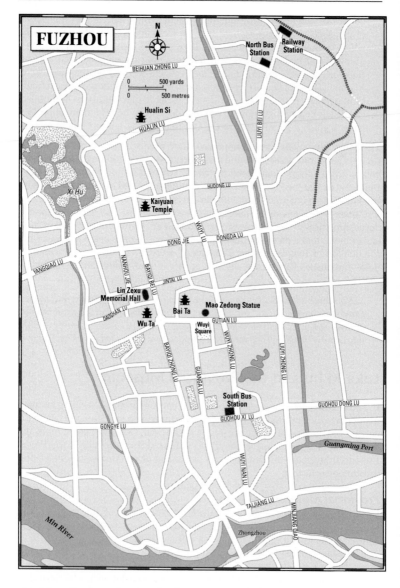

sizeable collection of **ceramic figures**, some half life-size, others smaller, grouped in a central case. There is an interesting group of Song bronzes and some charming iron cattle and pig sculptures, as well as many funerary jars with tall, elaborately decorated covers. These were used for secondary burials, when the bones were dug up some two years after burial, cleaned and broken to fit into the jars, which were then placed in final resting places. There are a number of stone-carved Nestorian crosses from Quanzhou (see Quanzhou, p 645). A variety of locally produced Song ceramics shows the well-known Fujian black wares (known in Japanese as *temmoku*) with hare's fur iron patterning in the glaze. Many kilns, such as that as Dakou, produced both black and white wares. Evidence of Song overseas trade is clear in the boat excavations, mainly from around Quanzhou. There are good Yuan celadons and blue and white export wares from the Anxi and Dehua kilns, the latter most famous for its white Buddhist figurines and altarpieces from the Ming.

There is an interesting collection of metal filigree wares from the **tomb of Zhang Hai**, a contemporary of Qi Jiguang (1528–88), a major military strategist of the Ming, who for many years was responsible for local coastal defences.

Fujian's revolutionary history was one of struggle, with a failure of the Chinese Soviet government to carry through an alliance with a KMT rebellion against Chiang Kai-shek (over his failure to resist Japan), which was led by the commander of the KMT's Nineteenth Route Army, Cai Tingkai. The rebellion was suppressed brutally by Chiang Kai-shek in 1933.

The exhibition of **revolutionary relics** in the museum has a certain charm, for it comprises all sorts of objects used by famous Communists when passing through the area and other items produced by local guerillas for their own use. There are Qing dynasty handcuffs and false-bottomed buckets used for carrying messages past enemies, He Shuheng's and Mao Zedong's hurricane lamps and Qu Qiubai's binoculars.

Qu Qiubai (1899–1935) served briefly as CCP General Secretary in 1927–28 and was a prominent writer and translator associated with the League of Left Wing Writers, translating Gorky and Tolstoy as well as Marxist works until his execution by the KMT when he was already half dead of TB.

Articles used and produced by guerrilla groups in Fujian, which was close to the Jiangxi Soviet, include conch shells used as bugles, printing plates and locally made banknotes with Marx and Lenin on them, straw and bamboo sandals and cloth bags for carrying grain rations. The most charming item of all, next to a group of crankshafts, is a small bamboo cup with a handle, carved with a simple figure of a horse, used by guerrillas in northern Fujian.

The lake itself is artificial, dug in 282 to collect water from the nearby hills in order to irrigate local fields. Since the period of the state of Min in the Five Dynasties it has been a local park, embellished by buildings. By the early 19C the lake was in a poor state when one of the best known Qing officials, Lin Zexu (see boxes on p 630 and 634), returned to Fuzhou to observe the Confucian ritual of mourning for his father.

One of the first buildings to be restored was the old **Memorial Hall to Li Gang** of the Tang behind the Lotus Pavilion, where there were two cassia trees; after his death the Gui zhai (Cassia Study) was constructed there in his memory. In 1929 it was designated the **Lin Zexu Memorial Hall** but it gradually crumbled and was rebuilt in 1985 to commemorate the 200th anniversary of his birth. It is a pretty site with open courts, moon gates and cool dark halls in the southern style.

Lin Zexu

Born just outside Fuzhou, Lin Zexu (1785–1850) was best known for his moral stand against the opium trade, for which he was made Imperial Commissioner with plenipotentiary power to investigate the opium question in Canton (1839–40). Despite his failure to withstand the massed might of the West placed behind the opium traders, he remains an heroic figure in Chinese history for his principled letter to Queen Victoria requesting the end of the opium trade and for his destruction of the over 20,000 chests of opium confiscated at Canton, which sparked off the first Opium War. On his filial return to Fuzhou in 1827, when he was Financial Commissioner in Nanjing, Lin noted the disrepair of the lake and local officials, prompted by his observations, spent a year clearing and restoring it.

Leaving the West Lake, take the road straight ahead (leading south), Tonghu lu; turn left into the first main road, Guxi lu. Continue east, traversing five small crossroads until you come to a big main road with bus routes, which at this crossroads is called Guping lu to the north and Bayiqi bei lu to the south. Cross straight over and take the third turning on your left to find the Kaiyuan Temple (Kaiyuan si). Straight ahead of you is a primary school (Kaizhi xuexiao): turn right past it, following the narrow lane (when you pass by some sort of noisy metalworking factory) and, as the road turns again, the **Kaiyuan Temple** is ahead of you. This consists of two main halls, the second way above the first.

It is said to be a Liang (early 6C) foundation and according to the old monk who lives there, the major Buddha figure is Tang dynasty in date, made of iron and weighing about 40 tons. Over 5m high, seated on a lotus throne, the figure was thought to have been one of the late Tang bronze Buddhas cast on the order of the king of Min but when the temple was restored in the early Qing (1659) it was discovered that the figure was made of iron and a small silver pagoda was found under the Buddha with an inscription dating it to 1083 in the Northern Song. It is now gilded.

On the platform in front of the hall behind are two wonderful Song stone troughs with lotuses growing in them (Buddhist emblems of purity).

Retrace your steps to the main road, turn left and then, when you reach the main road at the end, turn right. Very soon on your left you will see a narrow lane (Qingcheng si lu) where you will see a highly decorated temple (Qingcheng si) front on the left.

Restored in late 1987, the temple, with its elaborately carved facade and roofline, was dedicated to the ruler of the Min state (862–925). At the end of the Tang an independent kingdom of Min was proclaimed in Fujian and the ruler is said to have promoted culture and the economy so successfully that he was called the 'king who developed Min' (Kaimin wang). The temple is built on the site of his palace, which in 946 was turned into a commemorative hall. From the Song to the Qing it was here that the local officials came at the Spring Festival to initiate ceremonially the spring ploughing by making little mud figures of the 'spring oxen' which pull the ploughs. In the temple there is a great stele almost 5m high, carved in 906 and describing the achievements of the king of Min and his family and the successes of the early years of his reign in local economy, culture, military affairs and foreign trade.

If you walk along Qingcheng si lu to the east end, you are on Wuyi lu. Turn left and you will soon see the ***Overseas Chinese Hotel*** on your left and the ***Foreign Trade Hotel*** further up on your right.

Yu shan, the City Museum and the White and Black Pagodas

It is also possible to walk from the Wusi lu area to the White Pagoda on Yu shan, the Black Pagoda, the mosque and Li Zexu's Memorial Hall.

To reach the White Pagoda, head south down Wuyi lu. Cross straight over the major crossroads with Dong da jie and continue, passing a small, tree-draped stream visible on the right hand (west) side of the road. Soon after this, there is a shop on the same side of the road, selling seals, brushes and white plaster busts of Marcus Aurelius and others. Next to the shop a lane leads to steps winding up and over **Yu shan** (Yu Mountain), a rocky, tree-covered eminence. As you climb the steps you pass the abandoned Wangtian Temple and reach the summit of the hill where the White Pagoda is visible ahead, like a lighthouse.

The west side of the mountain boasts over 100 stone-carved inscriptions dating from the Song to the present day and several temples.

It has traditionally been a favourite place for local inhabitants to climb during the mid autumn festival, which falls on the 15th of the eighth lunar month, usually some time in late September. Described in the 1920s, the festival involves admiring the full moon and 'it is believed that if a mountain is not ascended, evil spirits will visit the home and consequently the whole family packs off to the nearest mountain, making the event a sort of picnic'.

As you descend from the summit, on your right, a solid red wall with steps beside it leads up to the site of the **Dashi Hall** (or Guanyin Hall) and the Huguo Temple, built side by side up the slope. The Huguo Temple housed an exhibition on relations between Fuzhou and Japan. The Dashi Hall was a Song foundation, rebuilt in 1713 as the Ten Thousand Year Pavilion where all the officials in the city (the 'hundred officials') prayed for good fortune. In 1737 it was renamed the Dashi Hall (Hall of Great Men).

During the 1911 Revolution which established the Republic, the Dashi Hall was the headquarters of the uprising. On 9 November 1911 a beacon was fired here by the revolutionary forces to launch the attack on government forces and captives were executed near a well west of the hall.

Today the building houses the **City Museum** of Fuzhou (open 08.00–17.00, closed Mondays), with a special exhibition in the left wing of a Southern Song tomb excavated in 1986 in the suburbs of Fuzhou at Chayuan shan.

The tomb, underground and lined with stone slabs, contained the bodies of a man and a woman, both of which can be seen in formaldehyde baths in the exhibition. The grave goods included a number of miniature silver foliate dishes and bowls, such as a doll's tea set, silver chopsticks and serving tongs, legal documents and a quantity of well-preserved silk garments, which are of considerable interest since they demonstrate clearly the distinction between clothing of the Song and later dynasties.

The bodies were wrapped in silken shrouds, which were neatly knotted around them, and silk shoes and purses were found on them. There are silk

> wrap-around 'apron' skirts, one with 'Fortuny' pleats, cross-over under and outer jackets, some with bands of embroidery at the edges or edged with darker silk. Robes have a distinct waist, where the panelled skirt is joined to the cross-over top, and either wide, square sleeves or bulging, gourd-shaped sleeves. Both corpses had good sets of teeth with the front teeth filed down, which is assumed in the commentary to have been a contemporary burial practice.

In the main hall is an exhibit of articles excavated in the Fuzhou area, from the Neolithic to the Qing. This mainly consists of ceramics, from Sui and Tang Yue wares (greenish southern stonewares), Southern Song, Yuan Yue and brown wares and many examples of the white porcelain of Dehua (some 70km northwest of Quanzhou) from the Ming. There is a particularly interesting floor tile of the Five Dynasties with quite high relief decoration strikingly similar to the frontispiece of the 868 printed edition of the *Diamond Sutra* (British Library) and presumably representative of contemporary temple and palace floors (impossible to dust and not very hard-wearing). The Qing items are a rather motley gathering of ceramics with a fine wooden document box and there is a *guqin* (zither-like instrument) with instruction manuals donated by a local inhabitant. On the far right is a display of ceramics unearthed on the sea bed at the mouth of the Min River, downstream from Fuzhou, an example of the sea trade with Southeast Asia, Japan and Korea by which China shipped silks and ceramics to these eager markets.

Behind the main halls, up the hill, is a courtyard with a central pool surrounding a mock mountain sprouting a creeper-draped tree. Behind is an almost smooth stele of 1779 with a nearly invisible depiction of a rather masculine Bodhisattva Guanyin. The stele apparently describes the story of Guanyin 'turning from a man into a woman'.

> Scripturally inaccurate (for in Indian Buddhism it was naturally assumed that all Bodhisattvas and any figures of importance were masculine), this change is typical of Chinese Buddhism, which in its popular aspects paid little attention to doctrinal niceties. In early Buddhist iconography, the Bodhisattvas were depicted according to Indian concepts of beauty as sinuous, fleshy, soft figures and this, combined with the 'female' attributes of Guanyin as the succourer, bringer of children and deity of mercy, caused the gradual but incomplete change of sex in Chinese Buddhism. That it was not a complete change is evident in the natural, unbound form of the bare feet that are often evident, particularly in the Ming and Qing *blanc de Chine* porcelain figures from Dehua.

Descending the west side of the hill to the base of the pagoda, you pass a small stone Tang pagoda. On the east side of this is the **Qi Gong Memorial Hall**, dedicated to Qi Jiguang (1528–87), a major military strategist of the Ming.

> A native of Penglai (Shandong), Qi led an army in support of the Fujian garrison when menaced by the Japanese in 1562 and inflicted three major defeats. Some say he was a hen-pecked husband and that it was his formidable wife who defended the coast. When Qi Jiguang was about to return to Zhejiang, a banquet was held in his honour on the Pingyuan platform on Yu shan where a hall in his honour was later built.
>
> The present structure dates from 1918, built beside five green pines, with the Pingyuan platform in front of it. Beside the hall is a rockery with a great

stone inscribed with two characters which mean 'drunken stone', supposedly where Qi slept when drunk after the banquet.

Below is the pagoda. Its proper name is **Dingguang** (Certain Brightness) but for obvious reasons it is popularly known as the **White Pagoda**. The present structure is a seven storey brick octagon, 41m high, with an internal wooden structure. First constructed in 904, it owed its name to a brilliant pearl concealed in the foundations.

The pagoda was originally built the other way round, with a brick core and wooden exterior, but it was destroyed by lightning in 1534 and reconstructed with a brick exterior in 1548. The temple building below was constructed in 905 but the present structures, used as a children's library and meeting rooms, are Qing. They have characteristically decorated columns of local stone, carved with high-relief dragons curling some two-thirds of the way up. The facility with which the local stone can be carved into such high-relief designs adds to the generally highly decorated appearance of much architecture of Fujian.

Leaving Yu shan by the exit on Gutian lu, turn right and take the first major turning on the right, Bayiqi bei lu, for those who recognise Chinese numerals, Eight One Seven Road North, which I think refers to the Nanchang uprising of 1 August 1927. Although not successful, this marked the beginning of the Communist Party's independent leadership of the revolutionary war and is usually referred to as the 'First of the Eighth', without the seven. Cross the road; not far up on the west side is a narrow lane with a wirework archway over it. Take this lane and soon, on your right, you will see a turning, again with the entrance marked by a green concrete deer and crane archway, with the **Black Pagoda** (Wu ta) visible beyond. This smaller stone pagoda, with fine carvings of protective guardians on the lower register, was built in 799 and was originally part of a temple which has since disappeared.

The mosque is a little further north, up Bayiqi bei lu, reached by a lane near no. 247 on the west side of the road.

A stele records its foundation as being in 628, although the area was subsequently occupied by the palace of the king of Min in the Five Dynasties and in 936 the buildings were apparently taken over by Buddhists and called the Ten Thousand Year Temple. It reverted to Islam in the mid 13C. It was commonly known as the 'Weekly Worship Temple', a name often given to Islamic temples because of the weekly service on Fridays. Chinese religions did not have a weekly service, or a special day. Services, whether Buddhist or Taoist, were held daily and people attended when they could. Temples also set great store by special festivals. The buildings were destroyed by fire in 1541 and subsequently rebuilt.

The main hall was large and square and built in the Chinese style (as opposed to the Islamic style of the old Quanzhou mosque). It had a five-edged roof, was five bays deep and five bays wide in the characteristic Chinese mosque style. Unlike Chinese temple buildings, whose 'great hall' was usually built on a larger scale than the others, with a higher roof, taller columns and wider bays, the main hall in mosques built in the Chinese architectural style (with the exception of the Xi'an mosque) is often low-roofed but deep and wide. This main hall, however, was rebuilt in 1955 and transformed in shape. Steles include an imperial edict of Yongle (early 16C) and one recording the rebuilding in the mid 16C.

Continue north a little way up the main road and take the first main turning on the left, Jibi lu, which runs beside a small stream. At the other end of Jibi lu is Xiamen lu; turn left into it. Not far down on the west side of the road is the **Lin Zexu Memorial Hall**, threatened with demolition in the early 1990s because of the real-estate value of the site. Said to have been built on the site of Lin's house, the recently rebuilt, traditional-style complex in a series of courtyards surrounded by white-walled and dark wood halls is now a sort of domestic museum to the 'upright official' of the Qing.

Lin Zexu and the Opium Trade

Lin Zexu (1785–1850) served as Secretary to the Governor of Fujian after passing his *zhuren* exams in 1810. In 1811 he passed the higher examinations in the capital and was selected as a member of the Hanlin Academy. In 1819 he was chief examiner for Yunnan province, later serving as a local official in Zhejiang, Jiangsu and Shanxi and as Financial Commissioner in Nanjing, Hubei and Henan. In 1832 he became Governor of Jiangsu, later Governor General of Hunan and Hubei. In 1838 he reported to the throne on the measures he was taking to eradicate the opium habit by confiscating smokers' equipment, providing prescriptions for cures and requiring them to be followed within a time limit and by drastically punishing smugglers and dealers. Such was his success in Hunan and Hubei that in 1838 he was appointed Imperial Commissioner to try and stamp out the problem at its root, with the European importers of illegal opium in Canton.

Although its import was officially prohibited, with the ending of the East India Company's trade monopoly in 1834 the trade had grown to vast proportions and made enormous profits both for the foreign importers and Chinese dealers, none of whom was prepared for the drastic action undertaken by Lin Zexu. He deprived the Hong merchants (those licensed to trade with foreigners) of their buttons of rank, ordered all Chinese servants and traders out of the 'factories' (or foreign warehouses and residences) in Canton and demanded the surrender of all opium. The British Superintendent of Trade, Captain Elliot, refused to sign a paper promising non-importation of opium in future, although nearly 2½ million *catties* were handed over and destroyed. The Opium War of 1840 grew out of this and further complicating events.

In July a Chinese was killed in a brawl involving British and American sailors in Kowloon. Captain Elliot refused Lin's demand to hand the culprit over to the Chinese for punishment. Unable to determine a single offender, Elliot held a trial of those most likely to be involved and sentenced them to imprisonment in England. Lin then expelled the British from Macau (whence they went to Hong Kong, which was no great hardship), although he compounded this by refusing to allow the British to buy food in Kowloon. Skirmishes were followed by an imperial edict prohibiting all trade with Britain on 13 December 1839.

When the Opium War broke out Lin Zexu was dismissed from office and eventually banished to Chinese Turkestan, where he distinguished himself (as he had done previously in his official career) particularly by opening the area to agriculture. Recalled to Peking in 1845, he served with particular success in Yunnan, where he managed to lessen considerably the tension between local resident Chinese and Muslims. Although he had been appointed Imperial Commissioner to suppress the Taiping rebels in 1850, he died before he could take up the task.

The epitome of the 'upright' official, one of Lin's most interesting contributions is his letter to Queen Victoria of August 1839, apparently never received, certainly never acknowledged, a letter couched in the standard language of the Chinese official edict:

We find that your country is 20,000 miles from China. Yet there are barbarian ships that strive to come here for trade for the purpose of making a great profit. The wealth of China is used to profit the barbarians ... By what right do they in return use a poisonous drug to injure the Chinese people? ... Let us ask where is your conscience? I have heard that the smoking of opium is very strictly forbidden by your country; that is because the harm that is caused by opium is clearly understood. Since it is not permitted to do harm to your own country, then even less should you let it be passed on to the harm of other countries—how much less to China! Of all that China exports to foreign countries there is not a single thing which is not beneficial to people: they are of benefit when eaten, or of benefit when used, or of benefit when they are resold: all are beneficial ... Suppose there were people from another country who carried opium for sale to England and seduced your people into buying and smoking it; certainly your honourable ruler would deeply hate it and be bitterly aroused ...

Lin also raised the vexed question of legal process in his letter:

Suppose a man of another country comes to England to trade, he still has to obey the English laws; how much more should he obey in China the laws of the Celestial dynasty? Now we have set up regulations governing the Chinese people. He who sells opium shall receive the death penalty and he who smokes it also the death penalty. Now consider this: if the barbarians do not bring opium then how can the Chinese people resell it and how can they smoke it? The fact is that the wicked barbarians beguile the Chinese people into a death trap. How then can we grant life only to those barbarians? He who takes the life of even one person still has to atone for it with his own life; yet is the harm done by opium limited to the taking of one life only? Therefore in the new regulations, in regard to those barbarians who bring opium to China, the penalty is fixed at decapitation or strangulation. This is what is called getting rid of a harmful thing on behalf of mankind ...
(Based on Fairbank and Teng, *China's Response to the West, 1839–1923*)

Lin Zexu's lack of success is not reflected in the heroic paintings in the Lin Zexu Hall, which also displays photographs relating to other famous sons of Fuzhou (such as a photograph of Yan Fu's tomb). Inside the gate a small series of Qing funerary statues of animals (tiger, horse, sheep) and military and civil officials in the local green stone line the path. These are not from Lin's grand tomb.

To return to the Wusi lu area, retrace your steps up Xiamen lu until you reach Jibi lu (running alongside the stream). This can be followed across Bayiqi bei lu as far as Wuyi lu, where the hotels are to the north (turn left across the bridge).

The narrow street is lined with houses on the right and on the left, the stream is overhung with trees growing out of cracks in the stone-lined banks with wooden houses perched above.

A pleasant area to wander in is the river bank, across the stone bridge with its central island to the old **Foreign Concession area** on the south bank.

One of the most distinguished inhabitants was the poet and writer Paul Claudel, who served as French Vice Consul here (1896–1904) and subsequently in Tianjin (1906–07). He noted that, as the area allocated for foreign residence had previously been used for tombs, it was very difficult to keep servants, since they feared the ghosts. Although better known for his imaginative writing, Claudel wrote consular papers with such diverse titles as 'The olive oil business at Fuzhou' (1896) and 'The packaging of biscuits for export' (1901) and became involved with an unsuccesful French entrepreneur, Monsieur Vetch, with whose wife Claudel fell in love.

Claudel supported Vetch in ventures such as the supply of Fuzhou coolies to Madagascar and Réunion (most of them died) and the promotion of Monkey Island as a coaling station for French ships. In 1905 Claudel broke off relations with Madame Vetch (who was to serve as the model for Ysé in *Partage de Midi*), reassumed relations with God and married before taking up his post in Tianjin.

The Foreign Concession area is beyond the bridge, which is divided by a small island, **Zhong zhou**. On the south bank were the major foreign banks, businesses, consulates and residences. If you turn left along Guanjing lu, the Hong Kong and Shanghai Bank was near the corner with Liuyi nan lu.

Continuing up Liuyi nan lu, take the fourth on the right, which wiggles until it joins Gongyuan lu; here, turning left and continuing south a little way, you will find the Sports Ground, built on the old racecourse of the foreigners. Retracing your steps back down Gongyuan lu towards the river, you will pass the old Trinity College on your right and on the slopes on your left, above the park, were the Foochow Club and the British and American Consulates, with the Japanese and French Consulates higher up the hill behind. The majority of the domestic buildings reflect the colonial style (out of Renaissance Italy by way of Portuguese Macau): solid, square, houses with a verandah and windows on all four sides so that cooling breezes could be created during the worst of the summer heat, when missionaries slept on Chinese mats rather than hot stuffed mattresses and 'the lives of hundreds of natives [were] sacrificed daily through the ravages of bubonic plague and cholera'.

The Hualin Temple Hall and the Xichan Temple

The **Hualin Temple Hall** is inconveniently situated just inside the Provincial Government compound on Hualin lu, at the northeast corner of the Xihu Park.

Founded as a Buddhist temple in 964, the description in the *Zhong guo ming sheng ci dian*, compiled in 1981, states that the great hall, the only surviving building of the temple, preserved the architectural style of the Tang and Song and that it was three bays wide, four bays deep, with brackets and beams in a very early style. In late 1987 it was rebuilt from the foundations upwards and, unlike some of the restoration work on Wutai shan or in the mosque at Xi'an, for example, there did not appear to be a single old timber incorporated; this was rebuilding rather than restoration. In Fuzhou and Quanzhou rebuilding appears to be more common than restoration, which is to be regretted.

The **Xichan** (Western Zen) **Temple** is best reached by taxi. Just south of Fujian University campus, in a district called Yi shan (Yi Mountain), the Xichan Temple has unfortunately also suffered from an excess of complete rebuilding and is now mainly interesting as an example of contemporary architectural taste and the effect of funds supplied by devout Overseas Chinese on ancient buildings.

The temple site was first (in the early 6C) that of the palace of a local ruler but was later abandoned. In 867 Buddhists came to live on the site in a settlement first called 'Pure Meditation', later 'Extended Longevity'. In 933 the temple was renamed Changqing (Lengthy Celebration), which remains its official name, although it is popularly known as Xichan Temple. It covers a considerable area (100 Chinese *mou*, or over 260 hectares) and comprised over 40 buildings. There is a grove of over 100 old lychee trees beside the temple and the monks are said to hold 'lychee meetings' annually, when poems are recited and paintings painted—'eating Yi mountain lychees' means participating in a cultural event.

The recent history of the temple has been one of close connections with Overseas Chinese. Most of the buildings surviving in 1981 were of the Guangxu period of the Qing (1875–1908) when a monk named Wei miao (Subtle Wonder) went abroad to collect money from Overseas Chinese originally from Fuzhou to pay for restoration. Although it is unlikely that any monks have been abroad in the last five years with begging bowls, the temple had been almost entirely rebuilt by 1987, presumably with much Overseas Chinese help, so that virtually nothing remains even of the late Qing construction.

Gu shan

Gu shan (Drum Mountain), about 9km east of the city centre, on the north bank of the Min, rises nearly 1000m above sea level and is perhaps the most famous site in the Fuzhou area. The mountain is covered with stone-carved inscriptions from various periods. The Buddhist inscriptions are most numerous to the east of the **Yongquan** (Gushing Spring) **Temple** in the Lingquan (Spirit Spring) Cave. The temple is one of the most famous in Fujian, partly because of its site, half way up the pine-covered mountain.

Gu shan is served by minibuses, which depart from Wuyi Square, and tourist buses, which leave from the Chating bus sation on Guangda lu in the south of the city.

Founded in 908, the buildings have been constantly repaired, restored and rebuilt and there is a distressing amount of painted concrete on the mountain. The temple was favoured in the past with imperial patronage and there is a fine collection of early Qing sutras presented by the Kangxi and Qianlong emperors.

In front of the first major hall (of three), the Hall of the Heavenly Kings, is a pair of Northern Song ceramic pagodas, dated by inscription to 1082, of nine storeys, almost 7m high, with ceramic bells dangling from the eaves and 1078 Buddha figures decorating each. They were apparently made and fired in separate storeys and finally joined together. They originally stood in the Longrui temple in Fuzhou itself and were moved here in 1972.

2500 stone steps above the temple (just over 1km) is the summit of the 'drum-shaped' mountain, a recommended point for viewing the sunrise.

The tombs of Lin Zexu and Yan Fu

Two tombs outside the city, but still in forbidden military zones, may be opened to visitors in the future. Judging by photographs, they are well worth visiting.

Compared with the simple earth mounds of the north, southern tombs are lavish. Built against hillsides, they are often called 'horseshoe-shaped' tombs, as the central chamber is surrounded on either side by walls that curve around but do not completely enclose a flat area in front of the tomb itself.

The **Tomb of Lin Zexu**, the Opium Commissioner (see box on p 634), is stepped on four levels (still in the shape of a horseshoe) and has a pair of lions before it. It was originally built by Lin for his father and has six chambers which contain the remains of Lin Zexu and his wife, his brother and his wife as well as his parents. The tomb is in the northern suburbs of Fuzhou on the slopes of Jinshi (Golden Monkey) Mountain, opposite Wufeng (Five Phoenix) Mountain near Maan cun (Horsewhip Village).

The **Tomb of Yan Fu** (1853–1921) is in the suburbs of Fuzhou at Yangqi cun. Yan Fu was born in Houguan, now part of Fuzhou city, and studied at the Fuzhou Shipbuilding School which, together with the Fuzhou Arsenal, was one of the first 'modern' (western-style) institutions set up in the wake of the Taiping uprising and the Opium War in order to try and bring China's defences up-to-date.

The Fuzhou arsenal was founded by Monsieur Giquel in 1866, three years after the first modern arsenal was established in Nanjing by Sir Halliday Macartney, who was serving under Li Hongzhang against the Taiping rebels and was 'painfully making better shells, powder and guns than the Chinese could produce alone'. In pursuit of modern technology, Yan Fu was sent to England to study (1877–79), first in Portsmouth and later at the Greenwich Naval Academy where, although his class performance was good, he was far more interested in the theoretical basis of western wealth and power and the British political and legal systems. He used to discuss these late into the night with China's first ambassador to the UK, Guo Songtao, who informed Peking that Yan Fu was better qualified than himself for his job; a message regarded as absurd by his superiors. Yan Fu returned to China to run the Tianjin Marine Academy and from 1911 until 1916 he was head of Peking University.

He is, however, best known for his translations from the English of John Stuart Mill, Adam Smith's *The Wealth of Nations*, T.H. Huxley's *Evolution and Ethics*, Darwin's *The Origin of Species* and Herbert Spencer's *The Study of Sociology*. He had his own tomb built in 1910, from stone with a stone-carved inscription: 'This is the longevity domain of Mr Yan Jidao of Houguan of the Qing period.'

The Wuyi shan Natural Reserve

The Wuyi Mountain Natural Reserve, covering some 60 square km, is inland, to the north of Fujian near the border with Jiangxi province.

Getting there

There is an airport at Wuyi shan (actually 10km north at Chishi) where minibus transport is available to Wuyi gong. Trains from Fuzhou, Quanzhou and Xiamen stop at Wuyi shan shi, 15km from the mountains: minibus transport is available.

The major aspects of the local scenery are described as the **Three Times Three Crooked Stream** (Jiuqu xi or Nine Bend Mountain Stream) and the **Six Times Six Surrounding Mountain Peaks** (or the Thirty-six Peaks). The scenery is spectacular and best viewed first from a bamboo raft, down-river from Xingcun or up-river from Wuyigong. Peak-like mountains rise individually from the riverside, some draped with spectacular waterfalls, peaks and slopes softened by bamboo clumps.

Many of the peaks can be climbed, notably the **Dawang feng** (Great King Peak) at the mouth of the stream, of which it is said: 'if you haven't climbed the Great King Peak, you have not undertaken a trip to the Wuyi Mountains' and from where you can see virtually the whole area. Another is the **Tianyou feng** (Travelling in the Heavens Peak), near the fifth bend in the river, praised by the great Chinese tourist and geographer of the Ming Xu Xiake (1586–1641) as 'the first peak in the area, affording a view of the glories of the nine bends in the river'. 840 stone steps from the bottom, you reach the Tianyou guan, a two-storeyed building with upturned eaves, surrounded by 'red bean trees' (*Ormosia*). Higher up, on the top of the peak, are smaller buildings, including a small temple.

Although it tends to dry up in winter, the **Shuilian** (Water Curtain) **Waterfall** in the northeast is the most dramatic in the area, falling in a sheet down a cliff and viewed from a small tea house set against the rock behind the water curtain. The whole area is covered in the low, rounded bushes of tea plantations and Wuyi tea (a 'black' tea, one of the Wulong or Oolong types) is well-known.

Wulong tea

A locally produced (and locally translated) description says that it has a strong taste, which is famous worldwide: 'Since Song dynasty it has been appreciated by culturists. In Yuan dynasty, Wuyi tea was used to entertain the emperor. Wuyi tea is a general term for Wulong tea from Chongan county. The tea leaves turned golden with red edges. After drinking Wulong tea people feel moist in throat and sweet between teeth. It will help people's moral, digestion and avoid sickness of heat and intoxication.'

Your morals improved by tea, turn next across the nearby bridge to the Eagle Beak Rock, named for the shape of the summit.

One of the most interesting features of the area is the presence of '**boat-shaped' coffins** pushed into depressions in the cliffs high above the river. Remains can be seen best above the fourth bend but they have been found all along the river.

The wooden coffins, nearly 5m long, carved out of a solid log of *nanmu* cedar (perhaps imported from Yunnan province), with a wooden cover, were placed some 50m above the ground in the cliffs. They contained individual burials, the bodies wrapped in cloth made from hemp, silk and cotton, similar to those of the Warring States period found in river cliffs in north-central Sichuan province. There is an excavated example of a Wuyi boat burial in the Provincial Museum in Fuzhou.

These burials appear to antedate those of Sichuan, although there is some controversy over the date. Carbon-14 dating suggests that they may be over 3000 years old, yet comparison with the later bronze age examples from Sichuan and the possibility that iron tools were used in their construction has led some to suggest they may be slightly later. Owing to their odd position, local people have called them 'hanging' or 'suspended' coffins and 'immortal' coffins. How the coffins were raised into their cliff homes remains something of a mystery. The great Song dynasty philosopher, Zhu Xi, thought that the area might have been flooded at the time and the coffins simply rowed into place but archaeologists discount this early hypothesis. The local annals record grave robbers of 500 years ago lowering themselves by winches from the top of the cliffs to get at the coffins. Remains of planking along the sides of the cliffs suggest that there were wooden walkways built there in the past, which may have been used to move the coffins.

Fuzhou to Quanzhou

The road from Fuzhou to Quanzhou offers two very different types of scenery with very differing domestic architecture. Near Fuzhou the countryside is lush and green, dark mountains tower in the background and water is plentiful. The old houses have highly elaborate gable-end walls and highly decorated roof ridges. The gable-end walls are stepped and curved at once and are vaguely reminiscent of, although unconnected with, tent profiles. Nearer Quanzhou the mountains recede but the earth itself is rocky and far less verdant. Rock seems close to the surface, with little top soil, and houses and even fences are built of stone slabs. The scarcity of top soil in the Quanzhou area helps to explain the incredible migration from the area. It seems apparent, even to the naked eye, that the land can only support a limited population and this may have driven surplus people to seek their fortunes overseas from as early as the Song period.

A roadside custom described by a friend is that of hanging dead cats on fences. I wondered whether this is to encourage mice or to discourage cats but Wolfram Eberhard states that cats must never be buried as they turn into demons, so these cats may have just passed away naturally (*A Dictionary of Chinese Symbols*, London, 1986).

Quanzhou

Quanzhou was the foremost port in China during the Song and Yuan. With its cosmopolitan population, at that time it was almost a later equivalent of the Tang capital Chang'an. It has perhaps the most interesting mosque in China and relics of Nestorian Christianity, as well as China's only museum dedicated to the overseas trade that made Quanzhou so important. Today the city, with perhaps a quarter of a million inhabitants, is hardly any bigger than it was in the Qing.

Practical information

Getting there
It is only possible to get to Quanzhou by car or bus. The long-distance bus station is on Quanxiu lu.

Getting around
Within the town itself, taxis refuse to take tourists to many destinations, as the streets are mainly stone-paved lanes too narrow for cars. If possible, hire a bicycle from the lobby of the taller block of the Overseas Chinese Home and be prepared to spend time in a bicycle repair shop; the nearest is on

Houcheng gu jie xiang (turn right out of the hotel and first right) and there is another just beyond the mosque.

Where to stay
Despite the sentimental name, the *Overseas Chinese Home* (Hua qiao zhi jia), 149 Wenling lu, ☎ 228 3559, a few minutes north of the bus station, or the *Overseas Chinese Hotel* (Hua qiao Dasha) on Nanjun nan lu, ☎ 228 2192, fax 228 4612, which is conveniently near the mosque and other sites.

History

Known as a settlement of some size since the Tang, it was in the Song and Yuan and early Ming that Quanzhou was at its peak. Like Fuzhou, the port is situated up the Jin River some way from the coast and this afforded protection from the coastal typhoons. Quanzhou was known to Arab geographers as Zayton (or Zaiton) from which our word 'satin' derives. The origin of Zayton is somewhat mysterious: some suggest it may derive from the citong tree (a prickly tree that grows in the area) or from Ruitong, an early name for Quanzhou. The account in Marco Polo's *Description of the World* gives an idea of its contemporary importance:

... the splendid city of Zaiton ... is the port for all the ships that arrive from India laden with costly wares and precious stones of great price and big pearls of fine quality. It is also a port for all the merchants of ... all the surrounding territory, so that the total amount of traffic in gems and other merchandise entering and leaving this port is a marvel to behold ... And I assure you that for one spice ship that goes to Alexandria or elsewhere to pick up pepper for export to Christendom, Zaiton is visited by a hundred. For you must know that it is one of the two ports in the world with the biggest flow of merchandise.

Apart from the emphasis on pepper, this is not an inaccurate description of medieval Quanzhou, borne out by Chinese records detailing the work of the local customs inspectors during the Song (960–1279).

Trade brought foreign residents in the Song and Yuan, whose origins are still evident in the large number of Muslim gravestones in Arabic script and the Nestorian Christian crosses carved in stone to be found in the Museum. A recent book by David Selbourne, *City of Light*, purporting to be the extensive diary of an Italian Jewish trader who, he claimed, visited Quanzhou just before Marco Polo, is a fiction but it contains most of the references to the city and area in the late 13C. *City of Light* has been demonstrated by Hebrew scholars, Arabists, Sinologists and Italian historians to be utterly improbable on a wide variety of grounds (reference to the reigning emperor by his posthumous name, to Arab taxes not yet invented at the time and similarly to place names not yet invented, etc.) but it has been greeted with excitement by Quanzhou citizens as it appears to place their home town on a larger map.

Quanzhou remained an important port in the early Ming, partly through its contacts with the Philippines, although ports further up the coast were used for Zheng He's voyages of exploration. It was threatened in the mid 15C by Japanese pirates, who made sea travel dangerous and even occupied Quanzhou as a base for attacks on local shipping.

Quanzhou is still a town of narrow winding streets, paved with the stone that is everywhere; fences of stone are to be found in the town as well as outside.

Opposite the hotel in the small park is a single hall of the **Tong fo si** (Bronze Buddha Temple); despite its small size, it is quite an active shrine about which no details appear to be available.

Turning right out of the hotel and taking the second turning on the left (Tumen jie), you can reach the mosque in a few moments (on your left). Called the **Qingzheng Temple** (Pure Truth Temple), another name often given to Islam in China, it was built in 1009 and restored in 1309, according to an Arabic inscription inside the mosque. It was further repaired or restored in 1350 and 1609, according to a Chinese stele. The surviving buildings include the great gate, which is strongly reminiscent of Islamic architecture, with a pointed arch and scooped-out vaulting. In its solid stone construction and vaulting as well as the form of the entrance, it owes nothing to Chinese architecture. In this it is quite unique, for other mosques in metropolitan China are fundamentally Chinese buildings (with pagoda-shaped minarets) adapted for the purpose. Particularly in Fujian, where architecture is highly decorated, the mosque is extremely restful in its restrained elegance.

For the moment, the rest of the building is roofless, a wooden roof presumably having disappeared. Inside there is a small museum display explaining Quanzhou's importance as a centre of foreign trade and the non-Chinese writers who mention it, including an Iranian, Khajha Rashid E-din (1247–1317), a Syrian, Abul Fedha (1273–1331), and the Moroccan traveller, Ibn Battuta (1304–97).

During the Song and Yuan there were apparently tens of thousands of foreigners, the majority of whom were Muslims. An honorary title was bestowed on a Muslim merchant who brought vast quantities of frankincense to Quanzhou and another was made Superintendent of Customs; they helped to finance the building of the city wall during the Southern Song. The name of the major Chinese Muslim clan in the city was Ding and a notable, Ding Gongchen of the Qing, is mentioned as having written a book, *Gunnery*

QUANZHOU

through Diagrams. All the medieval settlers took sinicised surnames: Pu, Ge, Shang, Mi, Zhang, Guo, Yang, Huang, Lin and Li. There were ten communal burial grounds north of the city, which contain the remains of thousands of Muslims who died here, the earliest dated tombstone being of someone called Hussain, who died in 1171.

Kaiyuan si and the Museum of Overseas Trade

Walking back from the mosque, continue past the hotel road going west until you reach the main north–south artery of Quanzhou, Zhongshan lu. Turn right up Zhongshan lu, with its arcaded shops, for some five to ten minutes, until you come to the major crossroads with Xi lu and Dong lu. Turn left into Xi lu and soon you will see the tree-lined enclosure of the major temple in Quanzhou, the **Kaiyuan Temple** (open daily 07.30–18.00).

It is said that this was a mulberry grove during the early Tang. When white lotuses miraculously appeared on the mulberry trees (since the lotus grows in beauty out of mud, it represents purity in the midst of the mire, to which we should all aspire) the landlord gave the land for a temple, which was first called the White Lotus Temple. In 738, during the Kaiyuan reign period, it was renamed.

The temple covers an area of 50 *mou*. The **Great Hall** is in the Ming style with a double-eaved roof. Standing 20m high, it is nine bays wide and six bays deep. The central columns are stone-carved in high relief with dragons. The floor is covered in red terracotta tiles. The interior beams are carved with birds. There is a five Buddha group with 18 lohans behind assembled around a Guanyin figure. At the back of the main hall, two columns in the local green stone are carved with acrobats, multi-armed wrestlers, elephants and phoenixes. Topiary is found on either side of the main hall: a hedge pierced with 'windows' like a decorative garden wall and two lions behind. To the west of the Great Hall is a mulberry, said to be the Tang tree that sprouted lotuses. Behind the Great Hall is a second, the **Sweet Dew Vinaya Hall**, originally a Song construction (1018) but much restored since. Set amongst huge poinsettia trees, this has a complex ceiling with a square topping the rectangle and a figure of the Bodhisattva Ksitigarbha (who presides over the world of death) sitting high on a throne. The third hall behind is inhabited by monks and nuns, judging by the washing.

To the right and left of the main axis with its huge, wide halls, stand **two pagodas**, 200m apart. That on the east side was built in wood in 865, rebuilt in brick in the Southern Song (1225–28) and finally rebuilt in stone as an octagonal, five-storeyed structure imitating wooden construction between 1238 and 1250. It is just over 48m high. Near the base, scenes from the life of the historic Buddha are carved. The western pagoda was also first built in wood in 916 and rebuilt in stone between 1228 and 1237. It is 44m high and very similar to the eastern pagoda. Both are considered to be monuments of considerable national importance owing to the skill of the carving and construction.

Also within the temple enclosure, on the east side, are two museum halls. The main one, a new building, houses the **Museum of Overseas Trade** (open daily 07.30–18.00), built around the preserved hull of a **Song boat**.

During the Song ships left Quanzhou exporting all the way to the Arabian Gulf, along the coast of Africa, to India, Southeast Asia, Korea and Japan. They carried porcelain, silks, lacquerware, medicines, handicrafts, cloth, wine, silver, gold and iron ore; and imported spices, medicinal herbs, semiprecious stones (like amethysts), rhinoceros horns, ivory, glass, precious woods and dyestuffs. Pagodas were used not as lighthouses but as coastal and upriver landmarks, as can also be seen near Fuzhou. The Song ship was discovered during dredging in 1973. It is 24m long and 9m wide and was originally higher, although some parts have been destroyed, probably by shipworm. It dates from about 1274, the hull planking is of cedar and is constructed in a mixture of carvel and clinker with separate bulkheads (an early Chinese safety invention). It had sails of woven bamboo and hempen cords. Near Fuzhou in 1982 a similar boat was found with a sail of woven bamboo. There are various shipboard items displayed, a squashed straw hat, a bucket and a game of Chinese chess. Illustrations from the Song painting *Qing ming shan he tu* (*Going Upriver on the Eve of the Qingming Festival*) by Zhang Zeduan (late 11C–early 12C), depicting river boats at Kaifeng, have been used to reconstruct the ship. Unfortunately for ceramic historians, who have been most interested in the dating of Chinese ceramics from underwater excavations and in the spread of Chinese export wares, this particular ship was on its way home, carrying tortoise-shell, frankincense, mercury, rare woods and various desiccated herbs, many of which are displayed.

The other part of the museum contains stone carvings which illustrate the cosmopolitanism of the area, particularly of religious belief, during the Song. There are a number of Muslim inscriptions, including many of the tombstones mentioned in the mosque, all inscribed in Arabic script. There are also **stone carvings** related to Manichean beliefs and Nestorian Christianity. A Manichean temple has been found not far from Quanzhou, a rare survival of the 'religion of light' close to Persian Zoroastrianism, and there are a number of Nestorian crosses.

Nestorian Christianity

The Nestorian schism is named after Nestorius (d. c 451), a Syrian ecclesiastic born in Antioch, who was Patriarch of Constantinople (428–431) until he clashed with Cyril, Patriarch of Alexandria. Cyril got the Roman Pope to condemn Nestorius (in his absence) at the Council of Ephesus in 431 and he was subsequently exiled by the emperor Theodosius II. He represented the Antiochene school of historical exegesis, whose best exponent was said to be Theodore of Mopsuestia (350–428); this school opposed the allegorical and speculative school of Alexandria. Nestorius denied the validity of the title 'Bearer of God' to the Virgin Mary and also held that Jesus possessed a genuine human nature, connected with his equally genuine divine nature by means of free human will. Cyril denied this, saying that it made Jesus into two people. The rather modern-sounding heresy survived in Syria, Persia and China until the Mongol period and the Nestorian crosses with funny little angels are evidence of its survival in Quanzhou. There are also 14C Franciscan fragments; it is said that there were three Franciscan bishops in Quanzhou following the embassy of John of Montecorvino, who died in Peking in 1328.

To the river past the Tian fei gong and the House of Li He

Turn right out of the Overseas Chinese Home and right into the first turning (Houcheng gu jie). Walk west until you reach the main road, Zhongshan lu. Turn left into it and continue south for about ten minutes until you come to a wide stretch, where Zhongshan lu virtually ends. Turn left into Tudi lu and almost immediately on your left you will find the **Tian fei gong** (Palace of the Heavenly Concubine) built in memory of a filial daughter of the Lin family in 1196, a girl who became a sort of 'sea spirit' and saviour of sailors. It has the same green stone-carved pillars as other Quanzhou temples.

It was said that this was a 'gathering place of boats', for it is close to the shore, and the temple was restored in 1415 at the express wish of the sea-going eunuch admiral, Zheng He. During the Ming, whenever ships left for the Ryukyu islands or more distant parts, the sailors would all come here first to offer sacrifices for a safe journey. It is now a wireless factory and institute and not open to visitors.

Turning back to the end of Zhongshan lu, immediately opposite it leading south is a small road, Wanshou lu (Street of Ten Thousand Longevities). At no. 159 is the **House of Li He** (1527–1602), a philosopher of the late Ming, one of the leaders of the 'feudal enlightenment'. The house is now said to be late Qing in style but Li He lived on the same spot as a child and youth.

If you continue down Wanshou lu as it curves round to the west (notice on the curve, a small Buddhist altar on your right), turn left and then first right into Zhushu gang, you will eventually reach the river; note that the last building on the right before the quayside road is a combination temple hall and old persons' club with tea, chess, music and occasional storytellers. The quayside is no longer the bustling place it must have been some 600 years ago but boats are loaded with gravel and other heavy cargoes for shipment.

Chengtian si and the House of Shi Lang

The Chengtian Temple is northeast of the hotel: turn left and walk up Baiyuan lu to the intersection with Dingxi lu (left) and Jiuyi lu (right). Continue north up Nanjun lu (the continuation of Baiyuan lu) and the entrance to the temple is not far up on your right.

The site was originally a garden belonging to a local official in the Wudai period. Between 957 and 958 a temple was constructed there and named the Nan chan (Southern Meditation) Temple, although the name was changed to Chengtian (Carrying Heaven). The large complex, not much smaller than the Kaiyuan Temple enclosure, was frequently restored and rebuilt through the centuries.

The most important stone carvings, including the stone-carved 'Ten Scenes', have been moved to the Stone Carving Museum housed in the Kaiyuan Temple.

In 1938 the Central Fujian Red Army stayed in the temple enclosure for 'training and consolidation' preparatory to moving north to participate in the Anti-Japanese War. The army was surrounded by KMT troops and five Red Army soldiers were killed in the 'Quanzhou Incident'.

As with so many other temples in Fujian, the Chengtian Temple was rebuilt from the ground up in 1987, including completely new stone foundations; the implication is that the temple buildings will not even be the same size as their ancestors, for if the same pillar bases are not used proportions are liable to change. The fine trees of the enclosure were, however, carefully preserved. Much of the extremely heavy sawing and timber work was being carried out by slim girls from Huian, less than 25km northeast of Quanzhou.

In Huian a slender waist is considered very beautiful and it is emphasised by the local costume. Women wear short, bright blue tops whose hems dip in the centre and rise at the sides. Their wide black trousers are cut tight at the hips and bound tightly with brightly coloured braid and silver belts. As the girls work their slim waists are clearly visible. They also wear light, flowery headscarves tied over a frame that holds them out from the head and has red braided and embroidered decorations.

From the Chengtian Temple, turn back to Nanjun lu and head north. Take the first turning on the left (Guitan xiang) and then the second on the left, Dongbian xiang. Not far along on your right, you will see a large gateway, which is the entrance to the local Agricultural College. Inside, not really officially open, is the **House of Shi Lang** (1621–96), a general who supported the Qing.

Shi led attacks on the Ming loyalists of Taiwan in 1683, apparently also to establish a Qing military presence on the island to fend off the westerners who were beginning to threaten invasion. His house, across the top of the playing field and obviously an old building amongst the new dormitory blocks, is a charming example of Fujian domestic architecture. Built with much of the local red brick streaked with black, creating a sort of herringbone effect, and characteristically upswept eave lines, it consists of buildings grouped around a low stone courtyard.

As in the major temples, like the Kaiyuan Temple, the floor of the splendid, open-fronted main hall, which stands above the others, is of red terracotta tiles, although, according to the current inhabitant, these were deliberately smashed by Red Guards during the Cultural Revolution. Picking around outside Shi Lang's house were splendid white chickens with thickly feathered legs and bright blue skin around the eyes, apparently an expensive type of chicken favoured in the past by emperors.

Excursions outside Quanzhou

There are a number of other sites around Quanzhou that are preserved but not really open to the public, although from the outside, at least, they give a good impression of the fine domestic architecture of the town in the past. One is the **Ancestral Temple** and **Home of the Hong Clan**, not far from Shi Lang's Residence and, like the latter, a low red and black striped brick building with elaborately curved and decorated roofs, enclosing a large courtyard. Turning left into Dongbian xiang, take the first left (Feng chi), which leads to the main road on the east of the town, Dong da lu. Turn left into Dong da lu and cross over the road. Not far north of the junction with Feng chi is a narrow lane on your right where you will find the Hong clan Hall on your right (with a block of flats on your left).

A slightly longer trip, north up Zhongshan bei lu, which runs through the centre of the town, will take you (c 45 minutes on foot) to **Qingyuan shan**, a hill which overlooks the town and where the only surviving relic of a Taoist temple built here in the Song is a giant statue of the bearded sage, Lao zi, one of the founders of Taoism. Carved from a single rock, it is 7m broad at the base and just over 5m tall. It is a rare example of Song stone carving in Fujian.

There is a famous '**holy tomb**' said to be that of two sages who visited China in the Tang (618–626), a site of pilgrimage, which was visited by Zheng He, who erected a stele there in 1417. All these tombs are situated on Ling shan, a hill to the east of the town.

Xiamen

Xiamen, known in the 19C West as Amoy, is an island off the Fujian coast; in 1956 it was linked to the mainland by a road and rail causeway 5km long. The town dates from the Ming dynasty and has been of significance in coastal trade—whether piratical, imperialist or local—ever since. Opened to foreign trade by the Treaty of Nanking in 1842, it had a substantial foreign population until the Japanese invasion, mostly concentrated on the small island of Gulangyu.

Practical information

Getting there
By air

Situated to the east, the airport is about 30 minutes by taxi from the city centre. There are flights to and from Peking, Guangzhou, Guilin, Hangzhou, Nanchang, Nanjing, Shanghai and Xi'an. There are weekly *CAAC* flights to and from Manila and daily scheduled flights from Hong Kong.

Shuttle buses leave for the airport from the waterfront area. Bus no. 27 calls at the airport, railway station and ferry terminal.

By train

The station is in the east of the town; Xiamen is the terminus of the short Longyan–Xiamen line, which joins the line to Fuzhou well inland.

By bus

There are minibuses and air-conditioned buses to and from Quanzhou and 20 hour buses to Guangzhou; enquire at your hotel desk. The long distance bus station is in the north of the city on Hubin nan lu.

By boat

There are twice weekly boats to Shanghai and Hong Kong, as well as shorter trips to nearby Shantou, whence you can get an overnight boat to Guangzhou.

Where to stay

The *Xiamen Binguan* at 16 Huyuan lu, near the Botanic Gardens, east of the town, is pleasant and quiet. The cheaper *Huaqiao Dasha* (Overseas Chinese Hotel) is in the centre of town, just east of the junction of Zhongshan lu and Siming lu. There is also a rambling and sleepy *Guesthouse* with billiard tables and 1920s' dark wood panelling on the west side of Gulangyu Island at 25 Huangyan lu (☎ 22052). This is perhaps the most atmospheric but it is hopelessly inconvenient if you have much luggage, as it is only accessible by foot; and it is on the far side of the island from the ferry pier. Other hotels are the *Lujiang Dasha*, on the waterfront opposite the Gulangyu ferry terminal, ☎ 202 2922, fax 202 4644, and the *Holiday Inn* (Jiari Huargguan Haijing dajiudian), 12 Zhenhai lu, ☎ 202 3333, fax 203 6666.

History

The city was founded during the Ming at the end of the 14C and at the end of the Ming it was a stronghold of Zheng Chenggong (1624–62), who is often referred to as Koxinga. This is a Dutch version of Guo xing ye (Lord of the Imperial Surname), a title granted to Zheng by one of the surviving members of the Ming royal family, which he supported loyally after the Manchu invasion of 1644 proclaimed the Qing dynasty. Zheng and his family were fierce supporters of the Ming and he led an attack (it failed) on Nanjing in 1659, retreating in 1661 to the island of Taiwan off the coast near Xiamen. There he finally forced the Dutch, who had settled on Taiwan in 1624, to withdraw to Batavia. The Qing government, in an effort to cut him off, ordered all the coastal inhabitants of Fujian and much of Guangdong province to withdraw at least 16km inland but they only managed to gain control of Taiwan after Zheng committed suicide in 1662.

Xiamen's troubles were not simply due to the Ming loyalist, for in the mid 16C the area was occupied by Japanese pirates who ravaged the eastern seas as far as the Philippines and Borneo. When western traders arrived after 1842, they settled mainly on the tiny island of Gulangyu, a few minutes by boat from Xiamen proper. Gulangyu became the 'International Concession', although there was also a British Concession in the town of Xiamen, just north of the Lujiang Hotel, along the quayside where the Customs Building and several major banks were situated. During the **Taiping rebellion** (1850–64) Xiamen was occupied by the rebels in 1853 and held for a year, despite attacks by government troops and a naval battle offshore. In 1864, nearly ten years after they had been driven out, the Taipings reappeared and were soon joined by the American General Burgevine, who had previously commanded the joint foreign-imperial 'Ever Victorious Army', subsequently led by General Gordon. Burgevine apparently wished to go over to the rebels and made his way to Xiamen, then to Taiwan, then back to the mainland. At some point on his way north he appears to have been betrayed by his black servant and subsequently drowned.

As in so many other cities in Fujian, a vast number of people left to work either on plantations in Southeast Asia, in tin mines or on the American railways. Xiamen, in particular, has been a favourite place to return to and is full of rather grand mansions built by **Overseas Chinese** for their retirement. The most notable local is **Tan Kah-kee** (1874–1961); Chen Jiageng in *putonghua*, the Amoy dialect version of his name revealing how wildly different Amoy dialect is from the Northern standard. His home town of Jimei, some 10km east of Xiamen, near the new causeway, is full of grand buildings in a mixture of western and Chinese architectural styles built to house the educational institutes that he endowed.

The industrial area to the east of Xiamen has been declared a 'special economic zone', open to foreign investment to attract more patriotic Overseas Chinese funds; the grand exhibition halls and tall office buildings can be seen on the way to the airport.

Gulangyu

With their usual care for health, the foreign inhabitants of Gulangyu (Drum Wave Island), installed sewerage works and, as a Japanese guide of the 1920s noted: 'The authorities carefully inspect all foodstuffs for sale, including milk. In the native town, however, conditions are very different—dirty water lies about and rubbish, piled up in the streets, gives out most offensive odours; cholera and plague often break out.' The island officially became an International Concession in 1903 and 'buildings in foreign style, consulates of various nations, schools, churches, a hotel, hospitals and residences are situated amid luxuriant groves and strangely shaped rocks'.

Reached by a ferry, which takes about ten minutes and runs from 05.00 to 24.00 (for which a single fare is paid for a two-way journey), the island is entirely traffic-free and also bicycle-free, so it is extremely pleasant to wander in. The residences are large and spacious, for in 1912 there were only 250 foreign residents. The major business houses and banks were located on the Amoy side of the island and, running south from the ferry jetty, were the British Consulate, German Consulate, King George Hotel and the Amoy Telephone Company.

Follow Zhangzhou lu to the south along the waterfront. The road then turns north and eventually arrives at the Sports Ground. Immediately behind the Sports Ground, on Huangyan lu, is the Gulangyu Hotel and if you continue on Huangyan lu past the hotel you reach the 1962 building, clearly architecturally inspired by some of the grander surrounding mansions, which houses the **Zheng Chenggong Memorial Museum**. The museum offers a marvellous view of surrounding houses, many of which closely resemble those found in Macau (where they are described as typical old Portuguese houses): square, brick buildings with verandahs all round and large rooms with windows on either side, presumably to allow a through draught in the hot, humid summers. That immediately below the museum closely resembles the Amoy Club, which was situated nearby.

Zheng Chenggong

Zheng Chenggong was born of a Chinese father and a Japanese mother in Japan. At the age of seven he returned to China with his parents. He early gained favour with the last of the Ming emperors and, although his father openly accepted the new Qing regime, he initiated a long campaign along the Fujian coast from his base on Gulangyu. He was said to have had a fleet of 8000 war junks, 240,000 fighting men, 8000 Ironsides and 'with all the pirates that infested the coast of Southern China under his command he claimed to have a combined force of 800,000 men'. His personal bodyguards were selected by a test of strength: anyone who could lift a stone lion weighing 270kg (600lb) was selected for his 'Tiger Guards'. Another name for them was the 'Ironsides'; they wore iron masks and protective iron aprons and carried red and green striped bows and arrows and long-handled swords for killing horses.

In 1661 he drove the Dutch from Taiwan and from this new base attempted to induce the Spanish in Manila to accept his suzerainty. He had endless trouble with his family. His father went over to the Qing early on but was subject to ceaseless pressure to bring his son to his senses and was eventually executed by the Qing; in 1650 he killed his cousin and took over his troops and in 1651 he killed his uncle whom he had left in charge of Xiamen but who had been overcome by the Qing troops. His death in 1662 on Taiwan was believed to be suicide when enraged by a series of set backs: the execution of his father and brothers in 1661 by the Qing court, the failure of his mission to Manila and a massacre of the Chinese there and the refusal of his own generals to execute his son 'who had illegally consorted with a nurse'.

The memorial museum contains paintings and impressions of scenes from his life and a number of gunpowder bottles and double-dragon cannon weighing over 82kg, as well as items depicting the ancient history of Taiwan.

Behind the garden and the museum is the main bathing **beach**, a clean, sandy shore with a view of further offshore islands, most obviously **Jinmen** (Quemoy), which is still occupied by Nationalist forces. The more expensive ferry to

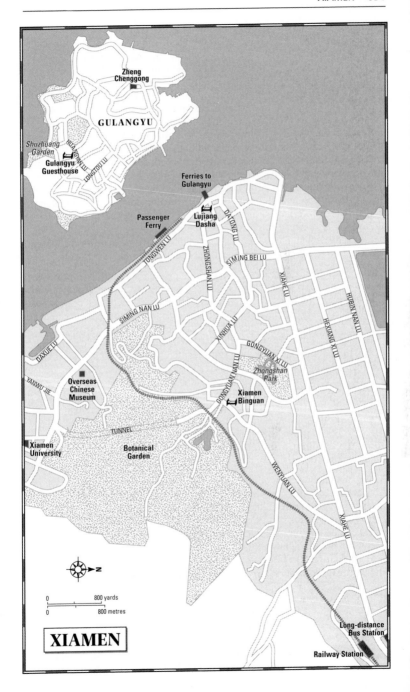

Zheng
Chenggong

GULANGYU

*Shuzhuang
Garden*

Gulangyu
Guesthouse

HUANGYAN LU

LONGTOU LU

Ferries to
Gulangyu

Passenger
Ferry

Lujiang
Dasha

DATONG LU

TONGWEN LU

ZHONGSHAN LU

SIMING BEI LU

XIAHE LU

HUBIN NAN LU

SIMING NAN LU

XINHUA LU

GONGYUAN XI LU

HEXIANG XI LU

DAXUE LU

GONGYUAN NAN LU

Zhongshan
Park

YANWU JIE

Overseas
Chinese
Museum

Xiamen
Binguan

TUNNEL

Xiamen
University

Botanical
Garden

WENYUAN LU

XIAHE LU

N

0   800 yards

0   800 metres

XIAMEN

Long-distance
Bus Station

Railway Station

Gulangyu from the mainland first takes visitors on a circuit of Gulangyu and provides binoculars for hire (as well as cups of coffee) so that the Nationalist occupied islands between Gulangyu and Taiwan can be observed at leisure. Around the corner from the beach, near the southern tip of the island, are a small pencai (bonsai) garden and a small enclosure with a pool and a few pavilions, the **Shuzhuang Garden** built in 1913 by a rich merchant from Taiwan, Lin Erjia. He had fled Taiwan when it was occupied by the Japanese in 1895.

Walk north from the museum along Yongchun lu, take the second on the left and just beside the next crossroads at 71 Anhai lu is the **Sanyi Protestant Church**, a large, plain hall, probably that of the London Missionary Society; in 1912 it was said to seat 1000, although the current guide suggested several hundreds. It was built in 1904 to replace several smaller chapels on the mainland.

If you continue down Anhai lu towards the Xiamen side of the island, turn right into Gushan lu and then take the first turning on the left from where you can see the **Xiamen Museum** (in the Bagua lou) on top of a hill, a substantial domed building near the site of the old Anglo-Chinese college, which was a square, arcaded building. The museum, said to be a general historical museum serving the area, is closed for renovation.

Turn back into the centre of the town, taking Guxin lu and its continuation, Longtou lu; as in all other parts of Gulangyu, there are fine residences amongst the banyans, poinsettia, bougainvillea and bauhinia. Fine stucco doorways have blank ovals where enamelled coats of arms have been removed. 27 Guxin lu has a gate with Corinthian columns, which are echoed in the massive two storey porch, but modernism is more evident at 18 Guxin lu where the gateway, built in 1935, recalls militaristic modernism in contemporary Germany. Nos 261 and 227 Longtou lu provide the same contrasts between old style curlicues and eagle-topped modernism, while 151 Longtou lu is in the Chinese baroque style with lions, grapes, swathes and swags in stucco and curly balconies. Faded lettering announces the *Hok Heng Hoat*, Chinese and foreign restaurant, tea and bathrooms (and it is still a restaurant).

Following Longtou lu round, near the junction with Huangyan lu is the **Roman Catholic Church**, said to be about 100 years old and built in the charming, whitewashed wedding-cake style often found in Chinese churches.

The roads on Gulangyu wind impossibly, so that it is difficult to follow street names and house numbers but the traffic-free whole (with a single, immobilised pre-war American car, a Plymouth, found round one corner) is a delightful place simply to wander in and the fresh prawns and other seafood served in tiny roadside cafés are also highly recommended.

Botanic Garden

Returning to Xiamen, in the east of the city, at the top of Huyuan lu is a very fine Botanic Garden, which also contains, on the far side of the lake, the site where Zheng Chenggong killed his cousin. A huge grey stone, apparently pocked with machine gun bullets, marks the spot. The garden is rich in southern Chinese and Southeast Asian plants and trees with a number of the eucalypt variants (all natives of Australasia), which are planted quite widely in Fujian, including ghostly white-barked examples planted in a slightly sinister clump and others with bark like elephant skin. There is a huge bamboo plantation (with over 100 varieties), a grove of palms (*Arenga pinata*) at the head of the lake and plenty of bauhinia, native to China, with their sweet-scented flowers and half-split leaves, delonix, native to Southeast Asia but seen widely in Fujian, *Malvaviscus pendulifloris*, *Ficus microcarpa*, with its thread-like roots trailing from branches, also seen in the Hong Kong Botanic Gardens, and thunbergias. Just inside the gate, on the right, is a grassy slope with small trees set in paved plots, including a small cassia and a *Cinnanmomum gladuliferum* (a native of Yunnan) planted by Deng Xiaoping in 1982. In late winter paper narcissus bulbs are on sale at the gate; these are very popular native bulbs grown in beautiful bowls filled with colourful pebbles and water, used to flower and scent rooms in winter.

Woodblock print of a pine, a favourite subject for painters

Within easy reach of the Botanic Garden and the Xiamen Binguan is the **White Tiger Cave**, said to have been a place where Zhu Xi (1130–1200), a native of Fujian, expounded on the Confucian Classics.

> Zhu Xi was the foremost exponent of Neo-Confucianism, a Song re-examination and re-interpretation of the Confucian Classics, a sort of revival of State orthodoxy through Confucianism. His commentaries became the standard for exams until this century.

The White Tiger Cave was called a 'university' but it is now unfortunately in the middle of a military camp and is thus described unseen. To reach it, take the road opposite the entrance to the Xiamen Binguan, Bai lu lu, and follow it upwards until you reach a gateway with army buildings beyond (identifiable from the khaki washing on the balconies). Ahead, there is a basketball pitch, occasionally used for high speed, baked earth croquet by old ladies. Beyond, in the wooded hill, is the White Tiger Cave.

It is easy to retrace your steps or return to the Botanic Garden. In the latter case, instead of taking the right fork, where Bai lu lu turns towards the main road, take the left fork (Huyuan lu), which leads to the entrance to the Botanic Garden. Immediately beside the entrance to the Botanic Garden (north) is the tall column of the memorial to the revolutionary martyrs on a stepped approach.

Overeas China Museum

The Overseas Chinese Museum, Nan putuo Temple and Xiamen University are easily reached by taxi from the city centre.

The Huaqiao, or Overseas Chinese Museum, is open 09.00–16.30, closed on Mondays. Built with Overseas Chinese money, it contains three floors of exhibits: the first (or ground floor) exhibit is devoted to the history of the Overseas Chinese, with many reproductions of newspaper photographs and artists' impressions; the second (western first) floor has the most extraordinary collection of (mostly late) Chinese bronzes and a less extraordinary collection of ceramics; the third floor has an exhibition of paintings.

> The exhibit on the Overseas Chinese runs through the early Chinese settlements in Japanese cities for trade and the trade routes to Europe and

Southeast Asia and beyond. Oil paintings depict coolie labourers on ships, opium dens and slave-drivers beating slaves with whips on plantations. Perhaps owing to the concentration on the Overseas Chinese in Southeast Asia, less attention is paid to the coolies sent to Europe to work behind the lines in the First World War, many of whose graves can still be seen in war cemeteries in northern France. There are sections depicting with illustrations the transmission of Chinese words into Indonesian and other Southeast Asian languages and items used by the Overseas Chinese: puppets, shadow puppets, straw shoes, pewter teacups and other handicrafts. Famous Overseas Chinese, including the first Chinese astronaut, are illustrated from newspaper articles and there is a bust of Mr Tan Kah-kee, benefactor of Xiamen University and the Jimei township.

The **bronzes** are the most interesting group on the next floor, although some of the altar groups in ceramic are also unusual. The bronzes are interesting in that they must have come from private collections (presumably of Overseas Chinese) and they cover an unusually broad time-span, from the Shang, over 3000 years ago, to the Republican period (1911). It is the latter period that is of especial interest, as it is relatively unknown in the West. The substantial deer settling itself (Song) and the vast Song vessels, the huge (1m) Ming vessels covered with rings, the inlaid and gilt Republican bronzes, all these are rare in the West and little studied as yet.

The **Nanputuo Temple** is just beyond the museum. It is set against a mountain in pretty surroundings. To the east side of the temple are rocks carved with calligraphic inscriptions (the largest reading *yuan tong* or 'perfect communication'), concrete lions and the tombs of two eminent monks, both erected in 1982, in the characteristic stupa style; that on the left contains the remains of a late Qing monk from Anhui and that on the right the remains of a monk from the Ming dynasty.

The temple itself, as with virtually all in Fujian, has been extensively rebuilt: two highly decorated bell towers stand in the first courtyard and in front of the Three Buddha Hall is an iron incense burner dated 1982, made in the Suzhou Min feng iron works and donated by pious Buddhists whose names are cast on the vessel. Inside the hall, which is filled with sculpture, including 18 rather horrible lohans, there are many items of dark wood furniture and an important looking grandfather clock. There is a small octagonal hall with a thousand-armed Guanyin.

Behind are more buildings, including a two storey, triple-roofed Fa dian (Hall of the Law).

Just beyond the bus station to the east of the temple is the entrance to **Xiamen University** (founded by Tan Kah-kee over 80 years ago). Turning right inside the entrance, heading towards the sea, there is a small exhibition commemorating the short stay of Lu Xun (1881–1936), the most prominent writer of the early 20C. He taught in the university in 1926–27 before going on to Zhongshan University in Guangzhou.

Set up in the building he lived in at the time, the first two rooms contain material, including photographs relating to Lu Xun's life, among them pictures of him and colleagues from the university relaxing in the hills behind the

Nanputuo Temple. The third room is arranged ostensibly as it was when he lived and taught in the university. This contains a mosquito-netted bed, tables, chairs and a desk with an Yixing (dark red terracotta ware) teapot and four cups, as well as a number of cases and wicker baskets. There are also some faded cloth banners carried at his funeral.

On the shore road, near the southeast corner of the University, is the **Huli Cannon**, set there in 1891. Of German manufacture, nearly 14m long and weighing nearly 49,000kg, it is set up in a favourite spot for hiring binoculars to peer at the off-shore islands.

Guilin

Guilin, or Cassia Forest, in Guangxi province, is surrounded by the best known scenery in China, the narrow mountains that rise, one by one, from the flat banks of the Li jiang (Li River). The scenery remains magnificent and the trip along the Li jiang to Yangshuo does offer the most wonderful peaceful views of the river, 'a belt of fine green silk', and the mountains, 'like kingfisher jade hairpins', as the poet and essayist Han Yu (768–824) described them. It is generally agreed, however, that Guilin has been pretty well ruined by tourism. Hordes of hawkers and touts surround visitors and planes and buses are overloaded so that frequent delays ensue; prepared for the worst, it is possible that the scenery can still be enjoyed.

Practical information

Getting there
By air

The airport is 30km west of the city of Guilin. There are over 50 flights a week from Guangzhou alone, twice daily from Peking and Shanghai and slightly less frequent services from Chengdu, Chongqing, Guiyang, Hangzhou, Kunming, Lanzhou, Nanjing, Nanning, Xiamen and Xi'an, not to mention the innumerable flights from Hong Kong. These may give you some idea of the volume of tourist trade. A shuttle bus runs from the *CAAC* office on Sanghai lu.

By train

The station is in the southwest of the city. Guilin is on the line that runs from southeast China (Shanghai, Hangzhou) to the southwest (Nanning, Kunming).

By boat

It is possible to take a boat from Guangzhou to Wuzhou, then a bus to Yangshuo, which is just south of Guilin on the Li River. From Yangshuo, which individual travellers recommend as less rapacious and overrun than Guilin, you could take the Li jiang boat trip to Guilin (or a bus, c one hour).

Where to stay
Well situated hotels are the
Sheraton Guilin Hotel (Guilin
Dazi Fandian), Binjiang lu, ☎ 282

5588, fax 282 5598; the *Ronghu
Fandian*, 17 Ronghu lu, ☎ 282 3811;
and the *Holiday Inn Guilin* (Guilin
Binguan), 14 Ronghu lu, ☎ 282 3950.

History

The name Guilin dates back only to the Ming; before that it was called Shian and then Guizhou. The town was established as a commandery under the first emperor of the Qin when he made his southern expedition to Guangzhou in 214 BC. At the same time the Lingqu canal was begun, linking the river networks of the Pearl and the Yangtse and Guilin's importance as a regional trading centre grew. From the Ming until 1914 it was the capital of Guangxi province; in 1914 Nanning replaced it. In the early Ming it was made the capital of a principality ruled by Zhu Shouqian, a nephew of the founding emperor of the Ming, who established himself there in 1369, building a residence, which he had walled in 1393. The walled enclosure was converted into the provincial examination hall during the Qing and now encloses the provincial teacher training college.

At the end of the Ming, Zhu Youlang, who had been holding Guangzhou against the Qing, was forced to leave Guangzhou and he set up his capital in Guilin in 1647–60, before the Qing troops drove him onwards to Yunnan.

During the Sino-Japanese War the population of Guilin was enormously increased by refugees from the north, who also moved to Kunming in large numbers, where one of the major university centres was temporarily established, and the city was bombarded by the Japanese. This destruction is part of the reason for the enormous amount of new building since 1949.

The landscape

Guilin's famous scenery, the 'best under heaven', was well known from the Tang, as Han Yu's poem illustrates. The peaks are part of the karst topography of much of Guangxi and the Stone Forest in neighbouring Yunnan: limestone formations of peaks and pot-holes, underground waterways and caverns filled with stalactites and stalagmites. The formation dates from about 200 million years BC, when the land began to push up from under the sea that had previously covered it and the gradual erosion of the limestone began, leaving the needle-like points of harder rock sticking up out of the plain. Numbers of painters and poets came to the city and some of them have left inscriptions carved onto the rock-faces of the famous mountains; the long held Chinese view that nature is greatly improved if you carve an inscription on it is evident in the 'more than 2000 stone-carved inscriptions' mentioned in the *Zhongguo mingsheng cidian*.

The highlight of a stay in Guilin is a **boat trip** on the Li River. The trip takes about six hours to cover the 85km stretch between Guilin and Yangshuo. Some 60 boats depart at about 08.00 from the boat dock on Binjiang lu, just south of Jiefang qiao (Liberation Bridge). Most tourist groups then return by bus; to avoid overcrowding, some are first taken to Yangshuo and make the trip upriver instead. The scenery along the river is at its most spectacular with the breadloaf peaks rising from the flat green paddy fields; fishermen, some with cormorants,

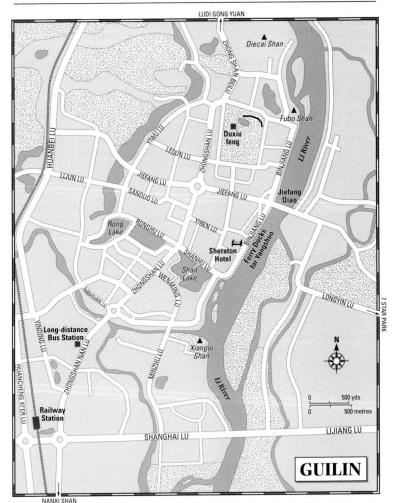

Map labels: LUDI GONG YUAN · Diecai Shan · ZHONG SHAN BEILU · Duxiu feng · Fubo Shan · HUANBEI LU · YIWU LU · LEQUN LU · ZHONGSHAN LU · BINJIANG LU · Li River · LIJUN LU · JIEFANG LU · JIEFANG LU · Jiefang Qiao · SANDUO LU · YIREN LU · BINJIANG LU · Rong Lake · RONGHU LU · SHANHU LU · Sheraton Hotel · Ferry Docks for Yangshuo · Shan Lake · NANHUAN LU · ZHONGSHAN LU · WENMING LU · LONGYIN LU · 7 STAR PARK · YINDING LU · Long-distance Bus Station · ZHONGSHAN NAN LU · MINZHU LU · Xiangui Shan · N · HUANCHENG XI'ER LU · Railway Station · Li River · 0 500 yds · 0 500 metres · SHANGHAI LU · LIJIANG LU · **GUILIN** · NANXI SHAN

fishing from flat boats of bamboo stems lashed together, water buffaloes and workers in the paddy fields are amongst the other rural sights.

In and near Guilin are many groups of mountains that can be visited. In the centre of the town is the **Duxiu feng**, or Peak of Solitary Splendour, also known as the Pillar under the Southern Sky. The Duxiu feng is just east of the northern part of Zhongshan lu, inside the old Ming palace. It was described by the poet Yan Yanzhi of the Song dynasty of the Nan bei chao (420–479) as 'unrivalled in its solitary beauty; towering, it floats in the middle of the town'. It can be climbed (306 steps) and it has many cliffs and caves, bridges, small pavilions and stone inscriptions, including that written by Huang Guocai of the Qing, 'a pillar of the southern sky', and Zheng Shuji of the Tang, 'record of the reopening of the stone chamber of solitary splendour'.

The **Ming Palace** (Wang cheng or King's Palace) is in the very centre of town, with Zhongshan lu running along its west side. It was constructed on the site of a Song temple, the Tieniu si or Temple of the Iron Cow. Nothing now remains of the buildings constructed by the 'king' of Guilin, nephew of the first Ming emperor in 1369, but one of the gates and some of the floors of the halls.

Fubo shan

Just northeast of the palace is Fubo shan (Sleeping Wave Hill), beside the river with a small garden planted with bamboos, palms and flowers on its south side. The Song dynasty pavilions built on its south side were burnt down and all constructions are now post 1949. On the eastern side, at the base, is the famous **Huanzhu dong** (Cave of the Returned Pearl), which can be entered by boat from the Li River. It has a 3m stalactite inside said to resemble something hacked away by a sword; the Han dynasty general, Fu Bo, is supposed to have sharpened his on it. It is also described as 'hanging in the void, looking like a floating pillar'. The cave is supposed to have been the home of a dragon which, like those in paintings and on ceramics, used to play with a pearl. The pearl was stolen by a fisherman but he returned it almost at once.

On the **Thousand Buddha Cliff** (Qianfoyan) nearby are more than 200 Buddha figures carved in 853 during the Tang. Inside the cave are some of the best of the numerous stone carvings in Guilin, the earliest dating from 863 with colophons by local officials. They include a self-portrait by the famous Song painter Mi Fei.

Further north, at 98 Zhongshan lu, is the reconstructed **Headquarters of the Eighth Route Army** (Balujun Guilin banshiqu), part of the Red Army commanded by Zhu De and Peng Dehuai. The brick and timber two storey building was destroyed in 1944 and has been reconstructed as a museum. It served as the office in Guilin from 1938 and was three times visited by Zhou Enlai before operations were moved back to Yan'an in 1941. Despite being a reconstruction, it is worth visiting for its urban architecture.

Diecai shan

Just north is Diecai shan (Pleated Silk Mountain) with numerous small peaks. All the present pavilions and walkways are post 1949 constructions, replacing earlier ones; the cassia planting is also post 1949, although the old path up to the peak on the south still remains. The Feng dong (Wind Cave) is open at both ends and cool and breezy throughout the year. The view from the top is spectacular, 'the place where mountains and water meet', and has been celebrated since the Five Dynasties (10C AD) when the king of Chu built a pavilion here.

There are many stone carvings on the mountain, of which the most notable are the *Record of the Pleated Silk Mountain* and *Record of the Four View Mountain* by Yuan Hui of the Tang, the poems *Visiting the Pleated Silk Mountain* by Zhu Xiyan of the Song, *Pleated Silk Mountain* by Liu Tai of the Ming, *Enjoying the Wind Cave* and *Climbing up to Watch the Magical Birds amongst the Gathered Peaks by the Light of the Bright Moon* by Yuan Mei of the Qing, a well known exquisite, poet, essayist and gourmet, whose life has been written up in English by Arthur Waley. There are also stone-carved pictures, such as Li Bingshou's orchids and bamboo, and Tang and Song Buddhist figures carved into cliffs.

Just northeast of the Pleated Silk Mountain, by the river, is the **Mulong dong ta** (Pagoda of the Wooden Dragon Cave), a tripartite pagoda with separate base, body and top, made of stone. The Sumeru base is carved with lotuses and supports a rounded, bottle-shaped body with Buddha figures in niches to the east and west and Bodhisattvas to the north and south; the top of the pagoda has a gourd-shaped finial. It is said to be Tang in date; the date of 1885 carved on the south side relates to waterworks on the river rather than to the pagoda.

Baoji shan

Almost due west of the pagoda, on Zhongshan bei lu, is Baoji shan (Precious Pile Mountain); it is said that during the Northern Song the city wall stretched between this and the Pleated Silk Mountain. South of the mountain is the **Kongming tai** (Platform of Emptiness and Brightness) and on the north side of the mountain, behind the Tiefo si (Temple of the Iron Buddha), is the **Huajing dong** (Cave of the Beautiful View); this leads, twisting and turning, through to the platform on the other side. Stone carvings include some by Li Shizhong, Lu Yuanzhong and Zhang Ziming of the Song. In 1979 two fossilised human teeth, together with stone tools and animal fossils, were found in the mountain.

Yu shan

Further north, on the banks of the Li, just past a small island, on the east side of Beiji lu, is Yu shan (Yu Mountain), also known as Shun shan. This is a 'solitary' mountain but the Tang and Song buildings on it were destroyed by Japanese bombardment.

> According to legend, the good emperor Shun, chosen by Yao as his successor in the second millennium BC and canonised as one of the 24 examples of filial piety, possessor of double pupils in both eyes, often visited this mountain on his travels in the south and because he was of the Yu clan (his full name being Yu Shun), the mountain was named after him and a temple was constructed here in his honour.

There is a stele, 'Stele of Shun's Temple', the three simple characters *shun miao bei* apparently the joint work of three notables of the Tang dynasty: Han Yunliu selected the characters, Han Xiushi wrote them and Li Yangbing wrote the seal.

On the west is the **Shaoyin dong** (Cave of the Beautiful Sound), so-called because the wind in the trees and the noise of the nearby water was supposed to sound like a performance of music for the emperor Shun. Inside the cave are the three characters, *shao yin dong*, written by a Song calligrapher, the *Record of the Shaoyin Cave* by Zhang Shi and orchid and bamboo paintings by Li Bingshou; other examples can be seen on the Pleated Silk Mountain (Diecai shan).

Southern Guilin ~ Sheli ta and Xiangbi shan

In the south of the town are the small lakes, Rong hu (Banyan Lake) and Shan hu (Fir Lake) that Zhongshan lu crosses on the Green Belt Bridge; once part of the city moat, they are now part of a small park and are surrounded by bamboos, willows, kumquat and peach trees.

Further south is a bridge that crosses the **Taohua jiang** (Peach River) coming in from the west to join the Li River in the south of the town; just southwest of that is the **Sheli ta** (Relic Pagoda). The 'relic' was a stone box, encased in the brick pagoda, which is part of the Wanshou si (Ten Thousand Year Temple), the earliest Buddhist foundation in Guilin, although the present temple buildings are Ming, Qing and later.

> The temple existed in the Sui, when it was called the Greening Temple (Luhua si); its subsequent names were Flourishing Goodness, Longevity and Eternal Longevity. The present name dates from the Ming. The pagoda was first built in the Tang, when it was said to be a seven storey brick construction. This gradually decayed and was rebuilt in its present form in 1385.

It is a Lamaist stupa (bottle-shaped) pagoda set on a high square base or platform. The base has four doors and over the main entrance are the four characters *she li bao ta* (precious relic pagoda). Above, the base of the pagoda itself is octagonal with Buddha figures in the eight openings and the top part of pagoda is in the characteristic bottle-shaped form.

On the east side of the road, right against the Li River, where the Taohua joins it, is another single mountain peak, the **Xiangbi shan** (Elephant's Trunk Mountain), said to look like an elephant bending to drink the river water through its trunk. The peak can be climbed by a path that starts on the west side and leads up to the flat summit. There is a Ming pagoda on the north side, the **Puxian ta** (Samantabhadra Pagoda), said to look like a precious flask from a distance. I don't know if the name is coincidental or whether it refers to the fact that the Bodhisattva Samantabhadra is usually depicted on the back of a white elephant. The **Moon and Water Cave**, at the base of the mountain on the riverside, can be entered in a small boat.

> The Song poet Jibei chushi is supposed to have written his *In Praise of Moonlit Nights* about the cave and mountain: 'The bright moon is far below the water's surface; the bright moon floats on the water's surface. The water flows where the moon cannot go; when the moon goes, the water cannot flow.'
>
> The cave is full of stone-carved inscriptions including the Added preface to the poem on the pavilion facing the sun by the Song poet Zhang Xiaoxiang, Fan Chengda's 'On the inscriptions in the moon and water cave' and the Tang poet Lu You's Poetic notes.

Much further south, best reached by bicycle or taxi, is the **Nanxi shan**. It can be reached by continuing south along Zhongshan nan lu until you reach the bridge over the Nan xi (Southern Stream), another tributary of the Li River. On your left, on the south bank of the Nan xi, is the Nanxi Peak. This is actually a double-peaked mountain, whose stone is a greyish colour said to shine after rain. The caves on the mountain are considered to have particularly fine baroque stalactites and stalagmites and the multiple caves have almost 200 stone-carved inscriptions in their praise.

Western Guilin

Out to the west of the town are the Hudi shan (Reed Flute Mountain), Xi shan (West Mountain) and Yin shan. The last two are not far apart, reached by following Lujun lu west from the centre of town. Just after crossing the railway, **Yin shan** can be seen on your right. Once entirely surrounded by water but now by fields, this mountain—whose name is the *yin* of *yin* and *yang*, meaning dark, shady, the female principle—is particularly famous for its numerous caves and grottoes, many filled with water. It also includes a stone-carved drawing of the Bodhisattva Guanyin by the famous Tang painter, Wu Daozi, and, most notably, carvings of the 16 worthies originally made in the 10C by a monk of the Five Dynasties, Shi Xiu, and recut during the Qianlong period by Li Yimin. Shi Xiu was noted for his Buddhist figure depiction and the carving in the Huagai an (Parasol Hut) is very highly prized.

Beyond, further west, is **Xi shan** (Western Hills), a collection of peaks where a number of temples were built during the Tang and Song; they have since disappeared. The hills, however, are scattered with niches containing Buddhist figures, over 200 in all, mostly dating from the Tang. In their lightness and vivacity they are considered by some to be amongst the best **Tang carvings** in China and are of some importance in the study of Buddhist iconography in south China, for most of the major sites are elsewhere. They range in height from 20cm to 2m.

Following the road round as it turns north just beyond the Xi shan, you come to a bridge on your left (west) that crosses the Taohua River. Turn left (west) here and the road takes you to Hudi yan (Reed Flute Cliff) on **Guangming shan** (Brightness Hill). The cliff takes its name from the reeds growing nearby, which are used in the making of musical instruments. The vast cave in the cliff can be visited on a guided tour, which takes you past peculiar limestone formations, all with names.

Eastern Guilin

Concentrated in the east of Guilin, across the Li River, are a number of mountain peaks in a large park, perhaps the best site to visit if your walking time is limited. Take Jiefang dong lu heading east across the Li River. The first, modern bridge is Jiefang qiao but the second, roofed bridge that crosses the Xiao dong jiang (Little Eastern River) is the Hua qiao, or Flowery Bridge, first built in the Song dynasty.

It was washed away by floods during the Mongol Yuan dynasty and a wooden bridge built on the site in 1456. In 1540 a stone bridge with four arches replaced the wooden one and the bridge was extended by seven extra arches. It is now 125.2m long and 7.2m broad. The extra seven 'dry' arches are useful at times of flood, when they help to disperse water, which might otherwise affect the main structure.

Immediately ahead is the great **Putuo shan** (named for the abode of the Bodhisattva Guanyin, like the Buddhist holy mountain off the coast south of Shanghai); it is part of the Qixing Park (Seven Star Park) where the rocks are said to be laid out in the form of the Seven Star or Great Bear Constellation. This also has a cave on its west slope called the **Yuan feng dong** (First Windy Cave), open at both ends, described in a poem by the Ming poet, Yu Anqi: 'The deep cave is truly dark and shady; Cool winds blow unceasingly. Water falls endlessly on the stone and in the hot months, breath turns to snow.'

In 1974 a pavilion was built beside the cave to house the three characters in calligraphy by Yan Zhenqing of the Tang, which read *Xiao yao lou* (Carefree Tower), as well as the *Account of the Tower South of the River* by Li Yanbi of the Song and the *Account of the Repair of the Stele* by Bao Gu of the Ming, amongst others. The inscription on the cliff, *bixu yan*, meaning 'cliff of the azure void', was written by a Ming Taoist, Pan Changjing; *Cliff of the Azure Void* was the old name for the Seven Star Cliff.

The Putuo 'stone forest' of strangely shaped rocks lies below, where a Tang building was supposed to have stood, called 'View of the Celebration of the Forest'; the three characters (*qing lin guan*) are supposed to have been written in the hand of the founding emperor of the Tang, Li Shimin.

The **Seven Star Cliff** (Qixingyan) is to the left of the Putuo hill and contains caves of considerable size, the largest being 43m wide and 27m high. This large cave used to contain an underground river and is full of strange rock formations, including the elephant with the rolled trunk, the lion playing with a ball, the gate of heaven and the magpie bridge, a reference to a famous folk story about a lovers' separation, the herd boy and the spinning girl.

> Fated to be separated on earth, they flew to heaven, where they became the stars Altair and Vega, separated by the Milky Way, except for one day a year, when a flock of magpies forms a bridge across the Milky Way.

The cave has been a tourist site since the Sui dynasty and the earliest stone-carved inscription in it dates from 590.

South of Putuo shan in the park is the **Luotuo shan** (Camel Mountain), so called because it is said to resemble a crouching camel. It is also said to resemble an ancient wine pot and is sometimes called 'pot mountain' (Hu shan) and the two characters for pot mountain are carved on its south side.

Close to the Xiao dong jiang (Small Eastern River), south of Putuo shan, is the **Yueya shan** (Crescent Moon Hill), made up of the three remaining peaks of the Seven Star Constellation. Seen from the Hua qiao (Flowery Bridge), a cliff on the mountain is said to resemble a crescent moon. The **Longyin dong** (Dragon Darkness Cave) is near the foot of the Crescent Moon Hill, opening onto the river.

> The roof of the cavern is said to look as if the imprint of a dragon's body had been left after it flew away and an inscription reads: 'It broke down the wall and flew off'. Fang Yanru of the Song said: 'There are living dragon scales in the rock and its eyes suddenly open' and Zhou Jinlong of the Ming described it as 'Having flown off many thousands of years ago, the dragon's scales remain to this day'. There are stone-carved inscriptions from the Tang and Song.

Kunming

Kunming, capital city of Yunnan province, is situated in the centre of the eastern Yunnan plateau on a large plain. South of the city is the largest lake in the province, Lake Dian, Dian chi in Chinese, Dian being an alternative name for Yunnan province.

Yunnan province is situated on the southwestern tableland, a spur of the Tibetan plateau. Much of the province is high, with an average altitude of 1800m above sea level. The plateau is divided by deep river valleys and high mountains, all of which make large scale agriculture and communications difficult.

Owing to its height, the climate of what would otherwise be a semi-tropical region is tempered; even in winter frosts are rarely heavy. Kunming is known as the 'Spring City' for the temperature remains pleasant virtually throughout the year.

The area is rich in minerals, tin and copper in particular. During the Qing (1644–1911) much of China's copper cash was made from Yunnanese ore, although the difficulties of transport meant that a considerable proportion was exported through Burma rather than directly overland to the capital in Peking. Much of the province is too mountainous to allow cultivation. Such soil as there is is a rich red laterite and major crops include rice (only one harvest per year), wheat, oil seeds of various sorts, tobacco, tea, hemp, a variety of vegetables throughout the year and fruits including peaches, pears, apricots, persimmons, oranges, lemons, walnuts and chestnuts. Recent agricultural innovations are leading to over-cultivation and soil erosion is likely to become a serious problem, as peasants are currently growing crops on plots that stretch down the hillsides rather than the erosion-preventing but labour-intensive and time-consuming terraces built along the contours of the slopes.

History of Yunnan province

The name of the province means 'South of the Clouds', referring to the mist and cloud that constantly cover the neighbouring province of Sichuan to the north. Although now part of China proper, Yunnan was only brought into the Chinese empire during the Mongol Yuan dynasty (1279–1368). Before that it had been ruled by independent kings. One of the most interesting kingdoms in Yunnan was that of the **Dian**. The Dian (see also p 666) ruled during the 2C and 1C BC and in 109 BC the Dian ruler submitted to Han Chinese suzerainty, the gesture made concrete in a fine golden seal, which used to be on display in the Yunnan Provincial Museum in Kunming. Dian tombs excavated south of Kunming in the late 1950s have revealed a complex bronze-working culture whose artefacts are quite different from those of contemporary China. Most impressive are the bronze drums that stand 55cm or 85cm high and have scenes of daily life, animal herding, battle and human sacrifice on their tops. The fine horned cattle represented are unlike any cattle found in China today and it may well be that the cultural contacts of the Dian were stronger with other Southeast Asian peoples than with the Chinese. Despite the treaty of sovereignty, Chinese control of Yunnan remained tenuous for the next 1000 years.

During the Tang dynasty (618–907) a new kingdom rose to power in Yunnan. This was the Nan chao kingdom with its centre in the town of Dali, some 200km west of the present provincial capital, Kunming. The Nan chao rulers are thought to have been Thai, although they followed the Chinese pattern of government. The Nan chao kingdom successfully defeated a Chinese army near Dali in 751, one of the first presages of the mid Tang collapse.

It was not until the Mongols invaded China to establish the Yuan dynasty (1279–1368) that the Nan chao were subjugated (in 1253) and Yunnan finally brought under Chinese control. During the **Ming dynasty** (1368–1644) the Chinese began seriously to colonise the province by voluntary and forced settlement. Many of the Han Chinese living in Yunnan today can trace their origins back to the Ming, when their families arrived from other provinces in China proper. In the final defeat of the Ming ruling house by the invading Manchus, who took the dynastic name Qing (meaning 'bright' or 'pure'), one of the last of the Ming princes fled to Yunnan, pursued by a Chinese general, Wu Sangui, who had him strangled in 1662. Although most histories record the strangling as having taken place on the Burmese border, a stele erected in the first year of the Republic (1912) records his death within the city of Kunming.

During the **Qing** (1644–1911) revolts against the ruling house persisted, the most long-lived and disastrous being the **Muslim uprising** of 1857–72, connected with the Taiping uprising. The uprising decimated the considerable Muslim population of the province and some of the surviving Yunnanese Muslims still refer to it with bitterness. The self-proclaimed Sultan of Yunnan, Tu Wenxiu, who had led the uprising, is said to have offered his sultanate to Queen Victoria when he despaired of maintaining resistance to Peking but the offer was declined, apparently. The uprising was only quelled when the imperial house persuaded the French in neighbouring Indochina to send an expeditionary force.

Because of their colonial interest in the area, the French were the first to bring a railway to Yunnan, breaking its physical isolation. A narrow gauge railway was constructed in 1904–10, running between Kunming and Haiphong via Hanoi. The route is still in use and trains can be seen from the road from Kunming to the Stone Forest. Travellers by rail from Peking to Hanoi have to change at Kunming because of the different gauge. During the Cultural Revolution Red Guards made specific attacks on some of the surviving Muslim communities.

Ethnic minorities in Yunnan province

One of the most striking aspects of Yunnan is its population. Half of the fifty-odd minority races of China live in this province, making one-third of the total population; the remaining two-thirds are Han Chinese. The minorities include Tibetans and Miao, who cross the provincial borders and the national border, as do the **Yi**, who also live in Sichuan. The Yi are the main 'minority' group, followed by the **Tai**, **Bai** and **Na Xi** in the region of Dali and the **Li Su**, **Wa** and **Jing po** in the Burmese frontier area. In the past these separate cultural and racial groups survived because of the relative isolation of Yunnan and even within the province the difficulty of transport made contact rare. Today official Chinese policy is to promote the cultural and linguistic heritage of the different groups. Many are exempt from the strict population control methods to which the Chinese are subject, because their numbers are low. Those groups that have a script have books translated and published in that script at the Yunnan Provincial Publishing House. Tourism has had its effect in promoting the interests of minority groups, who are encouraged to perform traditional dances for visitors and sell their handicrafts to them.

Yunnan flora

Visitors to Yunnan in the late 19C were drawn by the incredible variety of plant life. Some 80 per cent of European and North American garden flowers were originally native to China; Yunnan and the highlands of neighbouring Sichuan were perhaps the most fertile provinces for plant hunters. One of the most beautiful of Yunnan's native plants is the **camellia** and *Camellia* *japonica* was one of the first Chinese plants to be introduced into Europe by the East India Company in the 17C. In Chinese the camellia is called *cha hua* or 'tea flower' and although Linnaeus originally separated camellia and tea (he named the tea plant *Thea sinensis*), it has now been renamed *Camellia sinensis*. Another major species from Yunnan and Sichuan is the **rhododendron**; more than half of the nearly 400 species of rhododendron originate there and plant hunting in China was once described as a 'hectic hunt for rhododendrons'. Chinese rhododendrons are all of the azalea group and, as with tea and camellia, the Chinese simply have one name for both rhododendron and azalea.

Plant hunters had to face difficulties in transportation—azaleas couldn't stand sea water and perished en route, until John Dampier Parks suggested transporting them under glass bell jars—as well as the dangers of the frontiers—Soulié, who introduced *Rhododendron souliei*, *Primula souliei* and *Buddleia variabilis*, was murdered by Tibetan monks in 1905, as was Dubernard of the *Primula dubernardiana*, although Forrest, who introduced 22 rhododendrons and nine primulas, managed to escape. Despite such obstacles, *Rosa banksiae* and others, *Lilium regale*, *henrya* and *sargentiae*, viburnum, mallow, hibiscus and hollyhock all made their way from Yunnan and Sichuan to the gardens of the world.

Industry in Yunnan

In the past gold and silver were mined around the lake and today there is a major smelting industry and ironworks, as well as textile, electrical, chemical and food-processing industries.

Practical information

Getting there
By air

Kunming airport is to the south of the town, a taxi ride to the centre taking approximately 20 minutes. Apart from frequent domestic flights, there is a daily service to Hong Kong and a daily Thai flight to Bangkok, which connects with their European, American and Australian services.

Airport shuttle buses depart from the *CAAC/Yunnan Airlines* office on Tuodong lu.

By train

The station is to the south of the city, at the south end of Beijing lu. One of the most **beautiful railway trips** in China is that between Chengdu (Sichuan) and Kunming. The line was built during the Cultural Revolution (1966–76), following first the Dadu and then the Anding River valleys through the Xueshan (or Snow Mountain) range.

The line traverses the home of the Lolo national minority, once fierce warriors jealous of their territory, who terrified missionaries and other would-be travellers. The Lolo have their own script, which can be seen used in conjunction with Chinese for station names, and they are a handsome people with high-bridged noses, large silver and coral earrings and dark fringed capes.

The only problem with the scenic beauty of the line is that, owing to the terrain, it is 50 per cent tunnel. If you take the early morning departure from Chengdu (c 09.00), by about 13.00 the train has reached the Lolo area, which is not only distinctive for the people and script at the stations but also for the way they cut their rice straw higher and nearer the ear than the Chinese and then stack it in long narrow piles raised above the ground, in contrast with the circular Chinese haystack, which is usually built around a wooden pole.

The old Kunming–Hanoi railway line has a narrower gauge than that used elsewhere in China. The line skirts the Stone Forest (see p 675). The first stop in Vietnam at Laocai is often the start of a Vietnam tour, since it is the stop for the former French hill station at Sapa.

Where to stay

The *Kunming Hotel*, 145 Dongfeng dong lu, ☎ 316 2036, fax 316 3784/313 8220, is in the town centre; diagonally opposite is the *Holiday Inn* (Yinghua jiari Fandian), ☎ 316 5888, fax 313 5189. The *Cuihu Guesthouse*, ☎ 515 8888, fax 515 3286, is at 6 Cuihu nan lu in the northwest, opposite a pleasant park with a lake (*cui* means green, *hu* means lake) near the Yuantong Temple; behind it is an interesting group of narrow lanes lined with small shops.

Food

Rice is the Yunnanese staple and perhaps the most sought-after local product for visiting Chinese is

Yunnan ham, which is rather like prosciutto. Cheese made from buffalo milk, which is rather rubbery, resembling something between gouda and mozzarella, is eaten as a side dish, often with a hot pepper sauce. The use of cheese is unusual for most Chinese abhor it and it is generally associated only with Mongolians and Tibetans. Its occurrence in Yunnan may owe something to the Tibetan inhabitants of northwest Yunnan or possibly to the old French influence.

The two most famous dishes from Yunnan are stewed chicken (*qiguoji*), which is boiled with medicinal roots in a special ceramic pot, producing wonderfully soft meat and delicately flavoured soup, and 'crossing the bridge noodles' (*quoqiao mian*), a southern version of the Mongolian hot-pot, where side dishes of vegetables, meat and noodles are provided to be cooked in the boiling pot of chicken stock set in the centre of the table. The dish is said to date from antiquity when a young scholar retired to an island to concentrate on his studies, hoping to pass the civil service examinations. His young wife felt that he should be nourished during his ordeal but found that food cooled when she took it across the bridge to him. Finally she discovered that a good chicken stock kept warm enough and she would take it, together with raw noodles and other delicacies, across the bridge.

History of Kunming

The present name of Kunming ('Generations of Brilliance') is only one of many that were used in the past. The earliest town on the site was founded by the Dian in the 1C BC and called Yizhou jun. Remains of the Dian civilisation have been unearthed in the hills around Lake Dian on Mount Shizhai and Mount Lijia and the best of these are on display in the Yunnan Provincial Museum in Kunming. The Dian established a slave-owning society based on agriculture and produced marvellous **bronzes** with the lost-wax method, which in the earliest phase (4C BC) sets them apart from the bronzes of China proper. The latter were mainly cast in ceramic moulds, although lost-wax was beginning to gain favour. The forms of the Dian bronzes—great drums and drum-shaped cowrie containers with fine, thin walls and three dimensional scenes of hunts, warfare and human sacrifice or groups of long-horned cattle, a type no longer seen in the area—are also very different from those of contemporary China. There is virtually no physical evidence in Kunming of the Nan chao rulers who established their second capital there in 809, although it is possible that the two pagodas of the East and West Temples were Nan chao foundations, for they are very similar in form to the largest of the three pagodas at Dali.

After the Mongols seized Kunming and made it the headquarters of the Zhongqing district in 1253, a description in Marco Polo's *Travels* mentions the sizeable Muslim population, the cultivation and consumption of rice and, surprisingly, the persistence of the cowrie shell as an object of value.

In 1382 the Ming armies conquered Kunming and, as in so many other towns, built an enclosing wall and gave the town the name of **Yunnan fu**, a name still current in the 1920s, as can be seen from Gabrielle Vassall's *In and Around Yunnan fou* (Heinemann, 1922). When the Qing dynasty of Manchu origin invaded China, Yunnan fu was one of the last towns to submit, retaining allegiance to the Ming until almost 40 years after the Qing established themselves at Peking. Nothing now remains of the walls that surrounded the city as late as 1922, although the few surviving small narrow streets in the northwest, behind the Cuihu Guesthouse, convey something of what the city must have been in the Ming and Qing.

There was considerable damage during the long Muslim revolt (1857–72), which had begun with disputes in the silver mines and was continued by arms supplies from Burma until the French helped to put it down bloodily. There used to be quite a few buildings in the centre and near the Cuihu and Dian Lakes that showed influence of the French colonial style with mansard roofs and green or grey tiling, for the French, who established themselves in the late 19C in neighbouring Indochina, had a strong presence in Kunming before the Second World War. I could only see one, the last time I visited, near the central square.

During the **Anti-Japanese WarAnti-Japanese War** (1937–45) Kunming was one of the major places of exile, most notably for the two major universities of Peking, Peking University and Qinghua University; together with Nankai University from Tianjin, they established a campus in 1938 in Kunming called the Southwest Associated University. The campus they occupied is now that of Kunming Teachers' College on Huancheng bei lu, literally the North Circular Road. Students had to move from a temporary refuge in Changsha (Hunan province), the men on foot, the women by rail, first to Haiphong and then back into Kunming. The male students, accompanied by, amongst other distinguished academics, the poet Wen Yiduo, covered some 1900km (1200 miles) in 68 days, a sort of mini Long March. Although most of the teachers from Peking came to Kunming, Wen Yiduo is remembered for his increasing participation in the Democratic League, which advocated civil liberties, avoidance of civil war, nationalisation of the Chinese armed forces and convocation of an elected national congress; his participation led to his assassination in 1946 by agents of Chiang Kai-shek's Guomindang. Wen was killed immediately after a memorial meeting commemorating the assassination of one of his closest friends in the Democratic League. His writings and activities reflected the increasing politicisation of intellectuals appalled at the state of the Guomindang army, with soldiers starving to death before their eyes, as well as Guomindang attacks on patriotic students.

Kunming was affected not only by the arrival of thousands of refugees flee-ing the Japanese but also by the American presence. In order to supply the Anti-Japanese War, General Stilwell, who was in charge of the China-Burma-India theatre, oversaw the building of the Burma Road from Yunnan across the border. When the Japanese closed the road, Kunming's airport became a major factor in the replacement flights across 'the hump'.

With the construction of the French railway linking Kunming and Haiphong in Vietnam and the Burma Road during the Second World War, Kunming developed as a supply centre, a role which continued during the Vietnam War, when railway links were maintained, despite the growing bor-der conflict between China and Vietnam.

Kunming today, with its high-rise centre, is not very different from any other modern Chinese city centre; only the back streets and the mixed population with the colourful clothes of the national minorities single it out.

The Pagodas of the East and West Temples

The trip can be made on foot or by taxi, although many taxi drivers are not very familiar with cultural sites. Maps, whether in Chinese or English, showing the points of interest, including the two pagodas, can be used easily.

The **East Temple** (Dong si), near no. 64 Shulin jie, no longer stands; all that remains is the pagoda. This, like many other late Tang pagodas, has a square base, while the top is stepped, rising to a slightly rounded top, like a head of lilac.

According to the *Zhongguo mingsheng cidian* (*Dictionary of Famous Sites*), the pagoda originally stood in the Changle Temple (Temple of Constant Joy), which was also known as the East Temple. It was thought to have been built during the Nan chao period and is thus related to the Dali pagodas and dates from the 8C. It was badly damaged by an earthquake in 1833 and rebuilt, preserving the 8C form, in 1882. No reference books refer to the four extra-ordinary bronze birds that are perched on the top. They look rather like turkeys and resemble bird forms on Ming ceramics and fabrics. It is possible that they are original, although they may have been added later. There is a tiny park and tea house around the base of the pagoda.

The site of the **West Temple** (Xi si) on Xisi jie is now, unfortunately, within an army barracks. The sentries will not allow photographs and are unsympathetic to lovers of architecture. There is quite a good view of the pagoda from a lane fur-ther up the street to the north.

The West Temple, which no longer stands, was originally called the Huiguang Temple (Temple of Brilliant Wisdom) and was built between 824 and 859. There is no record of its having suffered earthquake damage, like the East Temple, but it probably did. Almost identical in form to the East Temple Pagoda, this one is 36m high and has Buddhist texts in Chinese and Sanskrit carved on the bricks. It has the same four bronze birds and finial as the East Temple Pagoda.

Local people say that the East Temple is intimately connected with the fate of the inhabitants of Kunming and that they protected it during the Cultural Revolution from Red Guards who wished to destroy it. They believe that

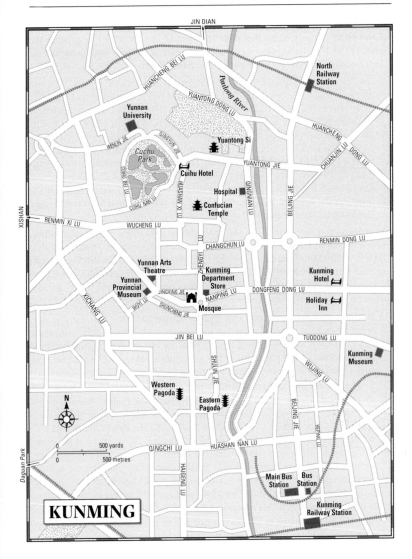

Kunming itself would be destroyed by an earthquake if anyone toppled the East Temple Pagoda.

The Confucian temple, Stele of the Ming Emperor, and the Yuantong Temple

From the Cuihu Guesthouse near Cuihu Park, turn right out of the guesthouse and take the first right off Cuihu nan lu and the first right again, which is Huashan xi lu. Not far to the right of the back entrance of the guesthouse, near no. 156 Huashan xi lu, is a **concrete stele** erected in memory of the last prince of the Ming dynasty, strangled near the spot at the order of the general Wu Sangui (1612–78) who, after a complicated series of shifts in loyalty, backed the Manchu invaders who set up the Qing dynasty (1644).

Invested with the title of the 'Generalissimo who pacifies the West', Wu was given civil and military control of Yunnan in 1657. Zhu Yulang (1623–62), grandson of the Ming Wanli emperor, led the remnants of the Ming forces to Yunnan, where they were defeated by Wu Sangui at Dali in 1669. Zhu Yulang fled to Burma, pursued by Wu Sangui; he and his young son (born 1648) were taken back to Yunnan fu (Kunming) and put to death by strangulation with a bowstring on 2 March 1662. The stele commemorating this simply gives Zhu's name and titles and the date of erection (1912). This is interesting in itself, for during the Qing it would have been virtually treasonable to mention the deposed Ming dynasty but once the Qing had been overthrown the Ming became respectable again.

Continue down Huashan xi lu; the road changes its name at the point where Huashan nan lu leads off to the left and becomes Minquan jie. At the bottom of the hill, where Minsheng jie crosses the road, there is the old **Confucian temple** set back from the road on the left. Little remains of the temple buildings but there is a garden in the enclosure with a small pool and a tea house; a cup of tea is included in the small entrance fee.

In the past, every town and city had its temple to Confucius, the presiding spirit behind the imperial ideal, but the Republic, founded in 1911, discarded the Confucian ideology. There is little information on the original buildings but Gabrielle Vassall's account of her visit, published in 1922, provides a picture of what was already a temple in decay:

… we made our way to the central building. It was dark and cool inside but we were disappointed to find it nearly empty. There was one single Buddha behind a piece of wire netting in a corner but the whole place had evidently been neglected for a long time. Our Chinese guide … informed us that during the Revolution in 1911 the temple had been pillaged and all the Buddhas beheaded. The ancient cult was apparently unpractised and all that remained of former glories were one or two bronze incense burners, which had evidently resisted destruction and been too heavy to carry away. The carved columns and the ceiling with its highly coloured and ornamented beams were all that had been left intact … In the middle of the garden was a small pond with a round Chinese bridge stretching across it.

Mrs Vassall mentions in her account of trying to find the Confucian temple how the cats belonging to shopkeepers along Huashan xi lu wore 'collars and were chained up like dogs'; they can still be seen, crouched on stools in the sun but firmly attached. She received the explanation that cats were valued for they brought good luck to merchants. This may still be the case but there is an added incentive to keeping a cat in Kunming today: apparently after the destruction of dogs and cats before and during the Cultural Revolution the rat problem became uncontrollable and now people are paid a small subsidy for keeping a cat. Pet dogs are now more popular with the inhabitants of Kunming: pretty little Pekingese-like animals can be seen trotting along behind their owners in the warm evenings, when many people come out for a Spanish style stroll.

The street that stretches downwards from the Confucian temple is where all the sign-painters and letter-writers still live, appropriately since Confucius was, in effect, the god of literature and written culture.

Retrace your steps up Minquan jie and turn right at the first major turning (Huashan nan lu). To your left (north) are myriad charming little lanes with courtyard houses, potted plants, caged birds and other domestic scenes. They are all cut off to the north by a group of government buildings and bear no names in romanisation, but they are interesting to wander in before you return to Huashan nan lu.

At the end of Huashan nan lu turn left into Huashan dong lu, which climbs a steep hill. About halfway up on the right (opposite no. 40 Huashan dong lu) there is a painting of a pair of pagodas, the twin pagodas of the **Da de Temple** (Temple of Great Virtue). Miniature versions of the East and West Temple pagodas, presumably originally of Tang date, given their form, they have been rather brutally restored in concrete and are hidden within the housing estate associated with a pharmaceutical enterprise. You can, however, get in to see them.

Continuing up Huashan dong lu, which at the next crossroads changes its name to Pingzheng jie, you eventually reach Yuantong jie. Turn left into it at the T-junction and soon, on your right, you will see the entrance to the **Yuantong Temple** (Temple of Universal Penetration); my translation is based on the Buddhist significance of the characters, while on the tourist map of Kunming it is called the Full and Smooth Temple. It is the headquarters of the Provincial Buddhist Association.

Founded in the Tang and restored during the Yuan, Ming and Qing, apart from its impressive gateway, the most charming part of this temple is the back courtyard, built against a rock-face, with an octagonal pavilion set in a pool crossed by four bridges, the whole surrounded by cool walkways with whitewashed walls cut by fancifully shaped openings with bamboos planted behind. It is one of the finest temple gardens in China. In the first hall behind the entrance gateway is a white jade Buddha, presented in 1985 by Thai Buddhists, emphasising both the outside support that Chinese Buddhists receive from Buddhist countries and Yunnan's special Southeast Asian connections.

When you leave the temple turn right and Yuantong lu will bring you down to the Cuihu lake. Turn left at the lake to return to the hotel.

Yunnan Provincial Museum

The Yunnan Provincial Museum (open Tues–Thurs 09.00–17.00, Fri 09.00–14.00) is in the centre of town, on the corner of Wuyi lu and Dongfeng xi lu. It is possibly the most depressing museum in China now. It was built in 1951 and used to be one of the best organised museums. The two major exhibits were the excavated finds of the Dian kingdom, excavated between 1956 and 1960 south of the city, and an exhibition of the national minorities of the province. The Dian exhibit contained bronze drums and cowrie containers (cowries had value as currency as late as the Qing dynasty) with scenes representing warfare, agriculture and sacrifice on their tops.

The famous gold seal of 109 BC, which cemented the suzerainty of the Han Chinese over the Dian, is no longer on display, or at least the original is no longer there. It is rumoured that a theft took place in the museum sometime in the late 1970s and the gold objects of the Dian culture were stolen. In the National Minorities exhibit, clothing, photographs and cultural artefacts depict the life of the minorities.

The museum is now virtually dead, with nothing much left except a few bronze drums and some dusty bits of minority costume, barely labelled, even in Chinese. It would appear that the local government had diverted all its 'cultural' funds to the construction of the vast Kunming Expo site out near the Jin Dian (opened in 1999). At weekends, the forecourt of the Provincial Museum is filled with big black cars being prepared for weddings. Elaborate decorations made from real flowers are carefully stuck on with sellotape.

The **bird and flower** (and 'antiques') **market** is quite close to the museum and is worth seeing. It is on Tongdao jie, north of the Kunming Department Store. From the museum, turn left up Wuyi lu and take the first major turning on your right (Guanghua jie); the market is in the lanes around the second turning on your right.

Daguan Park, Xi shan and the Qiongzhu Temple

Some of Kunming's most famous sites lie outside the town. These are best visited by taxi and may be grouped as follows: to the west, Daguan Park, Xi shan (Western Hills) and the Qiongzhu (Bamboo) Temple; to the north, best visited separately, is the Jin dian or Golden Temple.

Daguan Park can also be reached by public bus; it is at the end of the no. 4 route. The park lies beside the huge Lake Dian, 2km west of the city.

There has been a park here since the Ming dynasty. After the construction of a Guanyin temple on the site (1682), it became an increasingly popular beauty spot and in 1690 the park was enlarged by the construction of the Daguan lou (Tower of the Magnificent View) and many other small pavilions. In 1828 a third storey was added to the tower. It was burnt down in the Muslim uprising (1857) and the existing structure was built in 1869. It became a public park in 1913.

The tower, with its whitewashed walls and curving eaves, is best known in China for the pair of carved inscriptions on its main pillars. All gardens and places of interest in China have been decorated for centuries with carved inscriptions extolling their significance but this pair of couplets is known as the 'finest long pair of inscriptions in China'. The couplets were originally carved in 'grass' or running hand but were destroyed with the original tower and those you see now were inscribed in regular hand by Zhao Fan at the order of the Provincial Governor in 1888 and carved in gold on blue. Roughly translated, the first reads:

The 500 li Lake Dian stretches before my eyes, spread out like a garment, The banks its head-dress, a vast expanse. To the east gallops a spirit horse, magic birds fly west, a snake-like wriggle to the north and gossamer hovers in the south. Who could prevent us approaching the crab peninsula and snail island, wind in the hair, spray on the temples; reeds cover the ground, spotted wings amongst red sunset clouds. I am not alone surrounded by green rice fields, a vast expanse of clean sand, nine summers of lotuses and three springs of willow.

While the second reads:

Several thousand years of history in my heart, wine cools in the pot. Heaving sighs for absent heroes, I think: the Han built tall ships, the Tang set up iron pillars, the Song wielded jade axes, the Yuan rode with leather saddle-bags. The exploits of their heroes were glorious, inspired by the spirit to move mountains, they respected the pearl curtains and painted ridgepole [i.e. the emperor and the state], through endless evening rains and morning clouds. But the stelae recording their exploits are cracked and broken, gone to ashes, scattered; all they achieved, a double line of autumn geese, a frosted pillow.

Sun Ran, the poet (late 17C–early 18C) who wrote these lines, was a reclusive scholar from Kunming who often met with other poets at the Daguan lou. Although some 26 of his poems are included in a Qing collection of Kunming poetry, he lived in great poverty, surviving by casting Yijing predictions in the Yuan tong temple. He is said to have been a Ming loyalist who refused to seek office under the invading Manchu Qing dynasty.

The couplets are by no means untypical of one strand in Chinese poetry, whereby the poet points to the glories of the past to highlight present decay. The Tang poet Bai Juyi (Po Chu-i) wrote many poems in this vein; in one he complains that the present emperor is not up to the last one and this is evident because tbe elephants in the imperial zoo are dying, something which never happened under the previous glorious administration. Sun Ran uses the locality—the lake—to set the mood of nostalgia for past glories.

The Western Hills (Xi shan) overlooking the lake are 15km southwest of the city. The best view of the huge lake is obtained from the Longmen (Dragon Gate) near the top of the hill. The lake itself is the sixth largest in China and an impressive sight, for it covers some 297sq km. Although there is anxiety about recent pollution, it still looks clear and blue and is crossed by a variety of small boats and junks.

The **Dragon Gate** (Long men)is approached up stone steps starting from the San qing ge (Pavilion of Three Purities), first built as a summer resort for the king of Liang in the Yuan dynasty and then converted into a Taoist temple in the Ming. The present buildings are an amalgam of Yuan, Ming and Qing. Beyond, the path leads up through caves and steps carved out of the rock; the walls of the caves are also carved, often with Buddhist figures. The carvings were made between 1751 and 1853. At the top, beyond the Dragon Gate, is a tiny Moon Viewing Platform with stone railings looking out over the lake.

Below the Sanqing ge is the **Taihua Temple**, named after the Taihua Hill, one of the Western Hills, on which it stands. Originally a Yuan foundation, it was rebuilt in the Qing (1688) and much restored after 1949. It is most notable for the carved Dali marble balustrades and for the trees and plants in its courtyards, particularly an ancient magnolia; the camellias are also fine.

The Bamboo Temple (Qiungzhu si) is c 10km northwest of the city and also has some magnificent trees in its courtyards, as well as an inscription in the main hall dated 1316, written in both Chinese characters and Mongolian, asking that officials, soldiers and the local population protect the temple and the copy of the *Tripitaka* it houses. The temple was believed to be the first place where Chan (Zen) Buddhism was brought to Yunnan from central China.

According to a legend, during the Northern Song period (960–1126) two of the princes of the kingdom of Dali were hunting and they followed a horned bull as far as the Yu'an hill on which the Bamboo Temple stands, where it disappeared. Through the cloud they saw a monk. Soon afterwards the staff of bamboo the monk had been holding grew into a clump of bamboo, which gave the temple its name. The only concrete evidence for the date of construction remains, however, the inscription.

The temple is now best known for the painted clay figures of the 500 lohans and guardian kings. These were made between 1883 and 1890 by Li Guangxiu, a Buddhist lay brother from Sichuan, and his five assistants. The figures, about 1m tall, are almost caricatured in their greatly admired variety, as is common in these multi lohan assemblages.

The Jin dian (Golden Temple) is 7km northeast of Kunming, also in wooded hills. Its most distinctive feature is a small bronze hall, which stands at the back of the main temple enclosure. There is also an exhibit featuring the bronze temple bell, cast in 1423, in a hall to the left before you reach the bronze hall. The bronze hall stands in a courtyard surrounded by a crenellated wall of grey bricks, like a toy fort protecting the bronze pavilion within.

Bronze pavilions are not uncommon in China; the original one in this temple was said to have been based on one in Wudang shan in Hubei, a slightly smaller example than this, built in 1416. Another can be seen on Wutai shan (Shanxi), also of Ming date, inscribed inside with long lists of donors' names arranged by province, and in the Summer Palace in Peking. There used to be a Qing example at Chengde (Hebei) but it was apparently melted down by the Japanese in the 1930s.

The Jin dian bronze hall is like others in that it faithfully reproduces timber architecture in cast bronze. A small square pavilion, 6m wide and 6.7m high, it has a double roof, lightly curved eaves and is a standard timber style construction, with columns consisting of bronze wrapped around real timbers, presumably to support the weight of the roof, while elsewhere little timber appears to be used. The walls consist of panels carved below and with open-work lattice windows above. It is a perfect miniature of a highly carved timber construction. The original bronze temple here was made in 1602 but was apparently moved to Bingquam (c 200km northwest of Kunming) in 1637. The present bronze hall was donated in 1671 by Wu Sangui, who had driven the last of the Ming from the province.

Other surviving bronze halls are not surrounded by castle walls but they seem appropriate here in view of the military donor. As in many other Kunming temples, the trees are important; they include two camellias said to date from the Ming.

The Kunming Expo site is near the Jin dian (opened 1999). This was a vast international garden expo, its theme 'Man and Nature'. In a huge area, whose empty surfaces are completely filled with blinding beds of shocking pink busy lizzies and cerise petunias, there are separate small gardens, designed and built by each of China's provinces and by various other countries. There is a Japanese garden quite near the entrance and, further up, near the exhibition hall, a Swiss garden with a grubby white concrete mountain, an English garden designed by specialists from the Edinburgh Botanical Gardens, a Finnish garden (concrete with a bright blue bus shelter) and many others. There are further variations on the theme inside the exhibition hall. The entrance fee is very high (90 yuan). The expo has left its mark on Kunming, too, which filled up with giant floral sculptures of elephants and giraffes made of chrysanthemums.

The Yunnan minzucun (Minorities Village) is another giant theme park and is on the northeast side of Lake Dian at the point nearest the city. The drive out is quite interesting, for the broad new road is lined with bizarrely decorated restaurants, nightclubs and several massive new municipal buildings of varying architectural merit. They include the local government administration, law courts, concert hall and city museum. Some are absolutely extraordinary. The **Kunming Bowuguan** (open daily 10.00–17.00, closed Mondays) includes displays of local dinosaurs (*Yunnanosaurus robustus*), many bronze drums of the Dian culture and a major assemblage of Song Buddhist stone carving from a local temple.

The Minorities Village is also very expensive (48 yuan) and fundamentally offers a myriad of shopping opportunities amongst the separate 'villages', which are occupied during opening hours by gaily dressed 'minority people' who sing and dance. It has an anthropological interest, not through observation of the 'happy' natives but in the bare-faced exploitation of their colourful costumes and dances.

Stone forest

The Stone Forest (Shi lin) is a limestone karst formation of extraordinarily tightly packed pillars of grey stone weathered into fantastic shapes; it lies 126km southeast of Kunming and can be reached by bus or taxi in about three hours.

Along the road the distinctive local houses are made with timber frames, often with a narrow, open upper storey for storing hay. Their brick walls are of sun-baked red clay and enclose a small courtyard in front of the house. Near a large lake, about one hour out of Kunming, the narrow gauge railway track to Vietnam can be seen and slightly further along the road appears a new form of local transport, horse buses. These are open or canopied carts, where some ten passengers sit facing each other, drawn by minute horses or donkeys. As you approach the Stone Forest you can see the beginnings of pointed limestone rocks protruding from the soil on either side of the road. The sharp karst peaks were apparently formed under the sea some 270 million years ago. The softer earth between the peaks has been gradually eroded since the sea retreated, leaving the limestone.

To visit the Stone Forest from the Stone Forest Hotel (Shi lin Binguan), turn left out of the guesthouse and along the road until you pass a small pool on the left (Lion Pond). Turn left after the pond, up to the Lion Pavilion, from which the forest can be seen.

For the Chinese much of the interest of the Stone Forest lies in finding pictures or similarities in the rock formations: submerged rocks that look like baby water buffalo, strangely placed stones atop columns that look either like two birds feeding each other or two birds kissing (depending upon the prurience of your guide), a stone that looks like a profile of Napoleon and so on. Thus maps and points of identity rest upon these anthropomorphic interpretations.

From the Lion Pavilion, follow the path until you reach the stone screen. This serves as the main 'gate' into the Stone Forest and the name of the site has been carved upon it. This is another aspect of the Chinese attitude to nature; as in gardens, where poetic names for pavilions and calligraphic inscriptions are seen as integral to the garden, in places such as the Stone Forest the carving of inscriptions on the rock enhances the beauty and significance of the area. Take the right hand path towards Sword Peak Pond, where the rocks have begun to close in and tower over you, occasionally with a jagged boulder apparently poised on the edges of two knives above your head. The pond, like others, deep between grey walls, is supposed to have been formed by the sweep of a giant sword. From this point you can take whichever path you like, the shorter cut leading directly to the pavilion 'commanding a view of the whole' then back towards the Lion Pond or further round on the southern route.

The Minor Stone Forest, immediately east of the guesthouse, is often quieter than the main one and has some very fine giant bamboos.

The local people are called Sani or Hani and are a branch of the main Yi minority. The women wear colourful dresses over trousers, with aprons all embroidered and sewn with ribbon. They also wear flat headbands or scarves.

The advent of tourism has transformed the local economy; you are likely to be followed round the forest by a horde of very high-pressure salesmen masquerading as women and children. If you want to buy things, like embroidered aprons or the typical canvas cross-stitched bags appliquéd with bright cotton, a certain amount of bargaining is possible, particularly if you buy several items, but prices seem to have been mutually agreed and are fairly immoveable. The guesthouse has been expanded recently to accommodate the numbers of tourists (this is a very popular place with the Japanese and for weekenders from Hong Kong). In the evening a Sani entertainment is offered with local people singing and dancing. This is surprisingly good fun as it remains spontaneous and reasonably authentic and the Sani, apart from blowing on leaves to produce a comb-and-paper effect, have a remarkable, if high-pitched, way of singing.

Yunnan to Dali

Dali, once the capital of the Nan chao rulers of Yunnan (c 740–1253), is a pretty little town set beside another of Yunnan's large lakes, the Er hai (Ear-shaped Sea) and beneath a long high mountain, Cang shan (the Green Mountain), which has snow on its peaks as late as June, for they are as high as 4000m above sea level. The lake itself and the town of Dali are at almost 2000m above sea level. Quiet, pretty, offering marvellous walks from the picturesque town through rice fields to the incredibly blue lake, Dali is a charming place to wander in and well worth visiting, although it is sometimes very crowded.

Practical information

Getting there
By air
There is a new airport at Xia guan (see below, p 678) and flights from Kunming take about 45 minutes.

By road
There is also a new highway from Kunming, which reduces the time taken by following the Burma Road, although this has its own, rather exhausting, interest.

Where to stay
Jinhua Dajiudian on Huguo lu, ☎ 267 3343, fax 267 0573, or *Sijikezhan* (previously the Dali Four Seasons Inn) on Boai lu, ☎ 267 0382, in an old school.

The Burma Road

Dali is on the Burma Road, built as a vital supply route for the India-Burma-China theatre in the Second World War. The road departs from Yunnan and Dali lies c 250km as the crow flies west of Kunming. As it passes over many hills and down into valleys, the road is full of hairpin bends, not wide enough for the current volume of traffic and the journey, with a break for lunch, takes about 11 hours. For almost all of its length the road is lined with eucalyptus trees, presumably imported during the period of French influence, for they are common in Sichuan province, too, but are not native to China. Tall and ragged, frequently suffering from stripping of the lower branches, they give a rather French air to parts of the road. The area between Kunming and Dali is clearly one of substantial tobacco production for tall ragged tobacco plants can be seen in the fields and almost every house has a high, windowless tower, which looks almost military but is used for drying and curing the tobacco leaves.

The first part of the road (c 100km) follows the route of the Kunming–Chengdu railway, which was built in the late 1960s and early 1970s (dates of their construction can be seen on the tunnels). The road then descends towards **Chu xiong**, where most buses (tourist or public) stop for lunch. For tourist buses, there is a good meal arranged in the *Chu xiong Hotel*. Once a walled town, Chu xiong is now resolutely modern, the administrative capital of an autonomous county (autonomous regions are national minority areas, Chu xiong county is an Yi county). Notices, shop and hotel names are often written in a combination of Yi and Chinese. Although the town centre is quite new and furnished with a fine white concrete municipal statue of an Yi maiden in the middle of the main roundabout, the street markets down both the first and second turnings on the left out of the hotel are pleasant to walk in.

A visitor in the 1930s gives a very different account of arriving in the town:

It is a walled town. The gates are so narrow that the car could barely squeeze through ... It is quite likely that a private car had never been seen before in the shopping street of Chu-Hsiung. Several hundred gaping people began to pack themselves into a tube behind and in front of us. A single policeman tried to control their helpless movements. Our ephebe lost his head and ran backwards into a wall. Subsequent manoeuvres showed that he had not yet learnt how to reverse the car. Local feeling began to surge against him as a possible child murderer. (Gerald Reitlinger, *South of the Clouds*, Faber & Faber, 1939).

Beyond Chu xiong the road follows the bed of the Longquan jiang (Dragon Spring River) before crossing a broad plain, a high pass and descending towards Xia guan.

Xia guan is c 10km south of Dali, at the southern tip of the lake. The town, with its airport and the standard tourist hotel where many visitors to Dali stay, is more of an administrative and commercial centre than Dali and not terribly prepossessing. Even in the 1930s Reitlinger described it as 'a long gloomy street like a Welsh mining village', although it does have a good market beside the river and, over the bridge on the slope of a hill, a narrow street lined with traditional shops leads up to an imposing bell tower.

The relationship between Xia guan and Dali seems to have been problematic in the early part of the century:

When the Government carried the new road through to Tali, the inhabitants of Hsia Kuan, a mushroom town with no history, feared that Tali, the old western capital, would recover the trade monopoly which had once been wrested from it. So they claimed that the stone bridge in the middle of the town, crossing the torrential Hsia Kuan river, was unfit for heavy traffic ... the lorries therefore stop short of the bridge.

The same resentment felt by Reitlinger, who had to break his journey to Dali at Xia guan, is felt by many of today's visitors, anxious to stroll to the lake from the attractive town of Dali, not to be marooned in Xia guan.

It is, however, worth walking from the hotel, which backs onto the river, into the centre of the town to inspect the offending bridge and markets alongside it and walking up to the bell tower on the other side of the bridge. Start by turning right out of the hotel; turn left off this street down to the river and follow it upstream until you reach the bridge. If you are with a tour group your bus will take you to Dali; if not, there are very frequent buses between the two towns.

Dali

Dali is approached from Xia guan by a road that arrives at the South Gate, one of two gates; the North Gate is at the end of the main street, Fuxing lu. These are the major remnants of the old city wall. The buildings as they stand are in the Qing style, brightly painted towers surmounting a battlemented gateway—like miniature versions of the surviving gates (the Desheng Gate, for example) that can still be seen in Peking—but they have been heavily restored in the last decade. Further along the main street lies the central bell tower, the **Tower of the Five Glories** (Wuhua lou), apparently once the south gate of the town before its enlargement some time in the past. The main street has small shops open to it, many selling bits of Dali marble, which is quarried in the hills to the northwest of the town (scars of quarries can be seen high up on the slopes).

A turning off Fuxing lu to the right, Yuer lu, just past the Bank of China (also on the right), leads down to the lake, as do all the right turns. This one goes past a marble cutting factory (right) where thin slabs of marble are sliced and polished in the open yard. Two of Dali's best restaurants, the *Happy* and the *Garden*, are further down the road on the right.

Dali marble

The marble has long been popular in China. During the Qing, in particular, the 'landscape' effect of the dark corrugated veins against the white was used to create landscape pictures, slabs of marble mounted in mahogany frames resembling a painted landscape of mountain peaks rising above mist. Slabs of landscape marble were also set into dark wood furniture, chair-backs, tabletops and tablescreens; examples can be seen in the mosque at Xi'an, many of the Suzhou garden buildings and the Summer Palace in Peking. Local stone is also used to make distinctive gravestones, visible in undertakers' shops, often adorned with a photograph of the deceased, possibly through French influence.

The major sites lie just out of town. The most famous, the **Three Pagodas** (Santa si), is north of Dali. The pagodas once stood inside a temple which was destroyed under the Qing. The tallest is the earliest, built under the Nan chao (824–839). It stands over 69m tall, with 16 storeys, each embellished with small

Buddha figures of Dali marble and openings on each side. In form it resembles the East and West Temple Pagodas of Kunming. The smaller pair are probably slightly later, although still of the Nan chao; they are more than 42m tall, ten-storeyed and more elegantly proportioned than the bulbous earlier form, closer to the classic pagoda with its evenly tapered line. They are beautifully carved with Buddhas, lotuses and cloud scrolls. Unlike the larger pagoda, which is hollow, they are solid. On top they have bronze finials added in the Five Dynasties period (907–979).

Bai people

Local traders also sell embroidered clothes and bags made by the Bai people who live in and around Dali. The Bai, a branch of the Yi, have a distinctive language, whose affinities are still problematic; one of the major authorities on the Bai, Fitzgerald, writing in 1941, saw it as quite unique, unrelated to any of the neighbouring languages or dialects, although apparently Japanese anthropologists now claim that it and the Bai culture have distinct similarities to Japanese. The Bai culture is in some ways very different from that of the Chinese, perhaps most notably in that they stress affinity on the basis of friendship, rather than kinship, which is still the most important affinity for the Chinese. Many Bai women, in bright tunics, head-dresses with embroidered ribbons and black cloth shoes with red trimmings, often carry-ing a baby strapped to their backs, can be found in the street markets and at tourist sites, selling vegetables, garlic and spices, embroidered bags, marble pestles and mortars and household goods like little earthenware stoves.

Butterfly Spring (Hu die quan) and Zhou cheng

The Butterfly Spring (Hu die quan), 20km north of Dali, has been mentioned in Chinese guidebooks since the Ming. It is a pool enclosed by a railing of Dali mar-ble, overhung by a large old tree said to flower in the fourth month of the lunar calendar, when its flowers look like butterflies. To make up for the absence of but-terflies or butterfly flowers at other times of the year, a small museum displaying moths and butterflies, as well as handicrafts made from butterfly wings, has been built beside the spring.

One is also told that this is a favourite meeting place of the Bai youth and that young women come here to choose their mates. Bai women are supposed to take the lead in choosing a marriage partner, although Fitzgerald's account of marriage practices in the 1930s sounds exactly like those of the Chinese, with parents and go-betweens deciding everything and women, in particular, lacking any rights. Women certainly still do much of the heavy work, carrying huge loads strapped to their backs, the weight supported on the forehead by a woven band which passes over the forehead and around the load on the back.

Although the Butterfly Spring has very fine trees and, once you have escaped the ladies selling embroidered bags at the gate, is quite peaceful, its main attraction is that reaching it involves getting out into the countryside; you can also achieve this, however, by walking from the centre of Dali down to the lake.

Going back towards Dali, the first small village you pass after the Butterfly Spring is **Zhou cheng**, with a few shops on the main road and a fine market square just off it. Turn up the road away from the lake and towards the mountains at the north end of the village and you will reach the square, shaded by a huge old tree under which the market traders sit with meat, spices, garlic and fruit spread out before them. At the east end of the square is a fine old stage, probably Qing in date, on which travelling operatic troupes would perform and where performances would have been held at special festivals.

> Fitzgerald describes one Bai festival usually held in late May or early June, roughly between the wheat harvest and rice planting, when young men from Bai villages travelled around performing special dances in a series of villages, ending up at the lake shore with a special dance in honour of the local village god. Such performances must have taken place on the stage; indeed, open air stages in village squares used to be a major feature of village life in China but are now very difficult to find.
>
> In autumn it is interesting to note the way the Bai thresh their rice in the fields. Apparently a new type of rice, called 'dropping rice' was introduced, perhaps in the early 1930s, and this had to be threshed in the fields when cut because the grain fell very readily when ripe. Thus Fitzgerald described it in 1941 and the same type of rice must still be used, for in the fields you can see huge baskets with inverted rims, like vast inverted sun-hats, into which the Bai thresh the rice by hand as they harvest it.

Villages by the lake live by both agriculture and fishing. Fishing with tame cormorants is still practised, although much fishing is now done with nets and some villages have invested in processing plants where fish can be canned for export. Where cormorants are used, they have rings around their necks to prevent them actually swallowing fish; they get their food from their master. Fish caught this way are necessarily smaller than those caught in nets and may be damaged, thereby lowering their market price.

Lijiang

Many people take a five hour bus ride to Lijiang, north of Dali, near Tibet. Lijiang, in effect, consists of two towns. There is the new Chinese town full of dusty blocks, which proved horribly vulnerable during the disastrous earthquake of 1996, but to the southeast is the old town with its charming timber houses, narrow cobbled streets and bubbling water channels. This suffered much less during the earthquake. The inhabitants are Naxi, one of Yunnan's many minority people, and the older women still wear the traditional dress of bright blue cotton with ribbons and apron. Like many places in southwest China (Yunnan, Guizhou and Guangxi provinces), Lijiang's great attraction is its inhabitants and their vanishing way of life.

> Lijiang was the base for many of the great plant hunters. Joseph Rock, born in Vienna c 1879, spent over 25 years in Yunnan and on the Tibetan borders and wrote, apart from his plant books, *The Ancient Nakhi Kingdom of Southwest China*. Despite the length of his stay and the detail in which he explored his chosen area, plant historians note that he was following in the footsteps of George Forrest (1873–1932) and Frank Kingdon Ward and his actual discoveries were not many.

Hong Kong

Hong Kong, until 1997 a British colony and one of the great maritime entrepôts of the Far East, lies at the mouth of the Pearl River delta, just north of Macau. It consists of Hong Kong island, an archipelago of some 230 smaller islands, mostly uninhabited, a stretch of the Chinese mainland called Kowloon ('on the shore') and the New Territories. The island was ceded to Britain in 1842 under the Treaty of Nanking; the stretch of the Kowloon shoreline was ceded in 1860 as part of the Treaty of Peking and the New Territories were leased to Britain until 1997 under the second Treaty of Peking in 1898. Before the arrival of the British, Hong Kong and the New Territories area came under the jurisdiction of the Chinese Governor of Guangdong province. On 31 July 1997 Hong Kong was handed back to China in a grand ceremony in the pouring rain.

The total land area is some 1064 square km with a population of over six million living in extremely cramped conditions, possibly the densest urban concentration in the world, for much of the land is very hilly and both uninhabitable and unfarmable. Its free port status means that Hong Kong for the tourist is usually a shopping stop but in recent years a greater interest in culture and local history has led to the opening of a number of museums, although the interest has, alas, come too late to save many buildings.

Practical information

Visas

Apart from UK citizens, visitors to Hong Kong from most western countries do not need visas; those who come to Hong Kong or Macau from China and wish to return to China will need double-entry visas for China.

Getting there

By air

The new airport, **Chek Lap Kok**, on Lantau island, opened in 1997. Designed by the British architect Norman Foster (who was also responsible for the Hong Kong and Shanghai Bank headquarters building in the 1980s), it is elegant in appearance but somewhat difficult to use (with many confusing levels) and the catering is pretty awful.

The old airport was Kai Tak in Kowloon on the mainland. Surrounded by crowded public housing bristling with washing, the runway was built out into the bay by French engineers in 1959 so that the descent, at first apparently into the sea then with the aeroplane wings practically brushing the washing, is spectacular. The view before you reach the airport of the hundreds of tiny islands dotting the sea like green mushrooms is lovely.

Apart from international departures, there are direct flights to Hong Kong from all major cities in China, although fares are much lower from Shenzhen and Guangzhou airports. Most visitors take the rail express into town but there are also a number of buses that drop off at the main hotels. If you take a taxi, bear in mind that the tunnel is a toll tunnel (HK $20) and so the toll fee there and back will be charged to you.

Although the new airport is not far from Hong Kong island, taking about half an hour by car if traffic allows, the traffic is often very bad, especially in heavy rain or when the horse races are on in Kowloon, so check with your hotel before deciding when to leave for the airport.

By train

The railway station for China and the New Territories is also in Kowloon, not far from the airport, so the same traffic considerations apply.

By bus

City Bus, 33 Canton Road, ☎ 2736 3888, runs a bus service to Shenzhen (1½ hrs) and Guangzhou (3½ hrs), but add 1hr minimum for delays crossing the border.

Getting around
By underground

This is a very easy method of getting around Hong Kong island and the New Territories on the mainland. The simplest form of ticket to buy is a fixed value ticket, which operates like a phone card, deducting the price of each journey on exit. Single tickets come in a confusing variety of types.

By tram

Trams, operating in Hong Kong since 1904, follow a limited route along what used to be, before land reclamation, the northern edge of the island from Kennedy Town, through Central, Admiralty, Wan chai and Causeway Bay.

Information

The **Hong Kong Tourist Association** main office (open 08.00–18.00) is in The Center, 99 Queen's Road Central (ground floor); other branches are in the Star Ferry Concourse (open 08.00–18.00) and in the transit area (Butter Halls A&B) of the new airport (open 24hrs). Email: info@hkta.org, website: www.hkta.org.

Where to stay
Hotels on Kowloon

The Peninsula, Salisbury Road, Tsimshatsui, ☎ 2366 6251, fax 2722 4170, is one of the most long-established and luxurious.
Salisbury YMCA, 41 Salisbury Road, Tsimshatsui, ☎ 2369 2211, fax 2739 9315, is next door to the peninsula.

Hotel on Hong Kong island

The Furama, 1 Connaught Road, ☎ 2525 5111, fax 2845 9339, is very central.
The Grand Hyatt, 1 Harbour View, Wanchai, ☎ 2588 1234, fax 2802 0677.

History

The **New Territories** were inhabited by various groups, mainly of rice farmers or fishermen, Cantonese, Holkos, the Hakka—or 'Guest People', who seem to have originated in Sichuan and migrated to Guangdong and Fujian and whose women still wear flat straw hats with curtains of black cotton—and the Tankas or 'Egg People'. The last are supposed to have been called thus because the awnings of the boats on which they live are supposed to be egg-shaped. Couling, in his *Encyclopaedia Sinica* (1917) says this view is mistaken, although he offers no other explanation save to say that these are the traditional 'boat people' of Canton, forbidden to marry Chinese or to take the civil service exams but allowed since 1730 to live in seashore villages, although many still prefer to live on their boats. Apart from the Tankas, the inhabitants of the New Territories lived mainly in fortified 'walled towns', some of which can still be visited (Shan La Wai near Shatin, the Luk Keng-Fanling area, Kat Hing Wai, Wing Lung Wai and Shui Tau Tsuen in Kam Tin), because of the pirate raids which devastated the area. Indeed, it was not for nothing that the

Portuguese called the islands of the area, including pre-British Hong Kong, the *Ladrones* (meaning thieves).

In 1277 the last emperor of the Song dynasty, a small boy of nine, spent a year in the area, driven south with the remnants of an army and court by the Mongols. As the Mongols approached, his Chief Minister is said to have taken the child in his arms and jumped into the sea with him. His death is commemorated by a rock inscribed *Song huang tai* (Song Emperor's Terrace) in a garden beside Kai Tak Airport. Government impinged in the area hundreds of years later when, at the beginning of the Qing dynasty, the Manchus ordered a scorched-earth evacuation of the entire area (moving some 16,000 people) to prevent any foothold being gained by the anti-Manchu loyalists on Taiwan. There were defences built, mostly against pirates, but in general the clans in their walled villages were left largely alone to farm and fish by the provincial government as long as taxes were collected regularly.

While Hong Kong was a relative backwater, the great port of Guangzhou, up the Pearl River, was beseiged by foreign traders from the late 17C. Forced by Chinese government regulations to move backwards and forwards between Portuguese Macau and Canton, the **British** were looking for a **territorial base**. Before any treaty had been drawn up following the first Opium War of 1840, a British naval party landed and raised the Union Jack on Hong Kong island on 26 January 1841. Charles Elliot, the Chief Superintendent of Trade, was impressed by the deep-water harbour in the Kowloon Strait but Lord Palmerston in London felt that Elliot could have done better and sent him off to Texas to be the British *chargé d'affaires*.

In the **Treaty of Nanking** Palmerston's grander designs of access to Chinese ports were recognised but Hong Kong, 'deep water and a free port for ever', was also ceded 'in perpetuity'. It was to become, as its first Governor, Sir Henry Pottinger (1789–1856) proclaimed, 'a vast emporium of commerce and wealth'. The territory was expanded to take in the *de facto* cricket ground on the tip of the Kowloon peninsula (1860) and the New Territories (1898), securing the harbour's sea approaches.

The treaty that gave Hong Kong to the British also served to diminish its importance for some 100 years, for as Shanghai developed, Hong Kong remained in its shadow. As Jan Morris has pointed out in *Hong Kong* (1988), it was the Chinese Revolution of 1949 and the effective closure of China (including Shanghai) that promoted the incredible growth in prosperity of Hong Kong.

There was one anomaly in the treaties: the 'walled city of Kowloon' just north of Kai Tak Airport, bounded by Tung Tau Tsuen Road. Built in 1847 as a defence against the British on Hong Kong island, the Chinese officials who lived there, protected by 5m thick walls and a garrison of 500 soldiers, were ejected by the British after the acquisition of the New Territories but they never actually managed to control the area within the walls. It became a 'no-go' area with its very narrow lanes, tightly packed buildings and reputation as a Triad stronghold. Its walls disappeared during the Second World War, when the Japanese occupation force used the stones to extend Kai Tak's runway, and now the whole area is gradually being razed to the ground, its population rehoused and the site transferred into a public park. There is therefore no need to reiterate the warning given to tourists to stay away.

The **Japanese** invaded Hong Kong in the Second World War and the tiny garrison of British, Indian and Canadian troops and local volunteers surrendered on Christmas Day 1941, not before losing some 2000 men (and 4000 civilians). Civilians were imprisoned in an internment camp at Stanley on Hong Kong island, soldiers in prisoner-of-war camps in Kowloon, while the Japanese administration set up office in the Hong Kong and Shanghai Bank building. They rebuilt the Governor's residence to the designs of a 26-year-old engineer, set up torture cages on the balconies of the Supreme Court building on Statue Square and the barber of the Hong Kong Hotel turned out to have been a Japanese Naval Commander undercover. Hong Kong was liberated in August 1945.

1949 and the preceding years of civil war brought a huge influx of **refugees** into Hong Kong, their numbers swelled by Shanghainese factory-owners and entrepreneurs, some of whom brought their entire factories with them. By 1956, when there was a further wave of immigration from China, the population was 2½ million; now over 6 million. The latter figure comprises 98 per cent Chinese, of whom the vast majority are refugees themselves or the children of refugees. Crises of fire and flood in squatter camps, like that on Christmas Day 1953 which left 53,000 homeless, promoted the government's housing programme, first of crowded blocks of flats in Kowloon, more recently seen in the construction of elegant clusters of tower blocks, which are still crammed with tiny flats, in the new towns of the New Territories built in the late 1970s and 1980s. It is estimated that by the end of the 1980s half the population will be accommodated in public housing.

A further major wave of refugees arrived in 1962 as a result of the famines in China following the Great Leap Forward of 1958 and a series of natural disasters. This group was virtually encouraged to leave by the Chinese authorities (for they left fewer mouths to feed) but the Hong Kong border patrols tried to send them back. Later the police began to operate a 'touch base' policy, allowing refugees who managed to reach the urban areas and find relatives there to remain. This policy was discontinued in 1980 not long after the beginning of the last major wave of refugees, the second group of 'boat people', ethnic Chinese fleeing Vietnam.

During the Vietnam War Hong Kong became a major holiday place for GIs on leave (some 3000 a month) but the relative peace of the rest of the colony was interrupted by the Cultural Revolution in China. **Riots** broke out in Hong Kong **in 1967** in support of the sacking and burning of the British Embassy in Peking and the arrests of Hong Kong rioters led to the imprisonment of the Reuters' correspondent in Peking, Antony Grey. In the previous year Hong Kong had been shocked by the disappearance of the Chief Superintendant of the Police Force Special Branch, John Tsang, who had been one of the highest ranking Chinese policemen in Hong Kong, while also being a spy. He re-emerged as Chief of Security for Guangdong Province, just across the border from his old beat.

The 1970s saw the opening of the first Cross Harbour Tunnel (1972) and the beginnings of the famous *ICAC* (Independent Commission Against Corruption), which sought to root out corruption, particularly in the police force. At its lower levels this was said to be infiltrated by Triads, while to those at higher levels it offered handsome opportunities: one policeman who was granted immunity after testifying against his superior boasted of having made US $1 million during his short career as a (not very well paid) officer in the Hong Kong Police.

Confidence in the future of Hong Kong fluctuated throughout the 1970s and early 1980s, with uncertainty over the appropriate length of property leases and the amount of time required to repay an investment. Those uncertainties were resolved when in 1982 China and Great Britain finally began negotiations for the return of Hong Kong to Chinese rule. A Draft Agreement was signed on 26 September 1984 despite considerable opposition by the British Prime Minister Margaret Thatcher to the cession of Hong Kong island, which according to the Treaty of Nanking was British 'in perpetuity'. The Chinese government refused to recognise this and other 'unequal treaties' forced upon China but it took the Prime Minister a while to see that Hong Kong on its own (with a very limited water supply and no agriculture) was hardly a viable colony.

Expressions of confidence in the future were seen in the new buildings—the Hong Kong and Shanghai Bank by Norman Foster was completed in 1986; I.M. Pei, whose father was the bank's first manager in the 1930s, designed the new Bank of China—and in the changing pattern of investment, with China taking a small interest (now a majority stake) in Cathay Pacific Airlines, in garages, in shoring up rocky banks and sharing with the Hong Kong based China Light and Power Company in the joint Daya Bay nuclear project which supplies electricity to both Hong Kong and Guangdong province. Expressions of doubt were seen in the removal of the headquarters of Jardine Matheson (the oldest European trading company) to Bermuda and the enormous number of people applying to leave for Canada, the USA and Australia, or anywhere that will take them.

As negotiations continued, rival interest groups arose: there were those who believed that nothing should rock the boat and there were those, led by the lawyer Martin Lee, who believed that it was essential to establish some constitutional rights before the Chinese took over as there was far less likelihood of achieving them thereafter. In the end, such small advances as were made in the extension of a franchise, were abandoned after 1997.

Immediate changes made when China took Hong Kong back included painting all the red pillar boxes green (the Chinese postal colour), removing the flags from the cenotaph and the Royal coat of arms from the Post Office. It was reported in late 1998 that the Prince of Wales' feathers were still attached to the wall of the People's Liberation Army barracks (ex-Royal Navy) because they were so firmly embedded that the whole wall would have to be demolished.

Nevertheless, people in Hong Kong still drive on the left (as opposed to the right in the rest of China), Hong Kong keeps a separate currency as well as most of its old imperialist street names, uses English as its business language and maintains a very strongly guarded border with China.

Hong Kong island today presents a very different appearance from the barren rock that was first taken by the British in 1841. **Victoria Peak**, the top of the island, has been covered with trees, including some dozens of varieties of Australian eucalyptus. The Peak remains less thickly inhabited than the lower levels, partly because of its topography but also because it is frequently veiled in cloud in the rainy season of the summer when everything smells of mildew. Below the Peak, on the north side of the island are the **'Mid-levels'** where tall blocks of grand flats house the expatriate workers in considerable luxury (with a tiny hut for the maid on the balcony). Below the Mid-levels is the **Central District** where most of the major institutional buildings are to be found.

Walking is not very easy in Hong Kong, except in the small streets above Queens Road Central; even there you are endangered by fast moving buses and vans. On more major streets, particularly those which lead to the few monuments of interest, there appear to be virtually no concessions made to pedestrians, except in the downtown shopping area where you can cross above street level from one vast business/shopping centre to another.

Hong Kong shoreline

Central Hong Kong

Flagstaff House (open daily 10.00–17.00; closed on Wednesdays) is on the east side of Cotton Tree Drive, just beside the Hilton Hotel. Cotton Tree Drive is, unfortunately, a major motorway with, at this point, very little in the way of pedestrian facilities. Flagstaff House contains a **Museum of Tea Drinking**. One of the finest surviving colonial buildings in Hong Kong, with a colonnade, cool verandah and shuttered windows, it was built in 1845 as the residence of the general in charge of the Hong Kong garrison. Nearby, where the huge new **Bank of China** building rises on the far side of the road—I.M. Pei's new bank is 70 storeys high, higher than anything else in Hong Kong as yet—there was once an associated group of colonial buildings, Murray Barracks. It was demolished to make way for the bank and earlier plans to reconstruct it somewhere appear to have been abandoned.

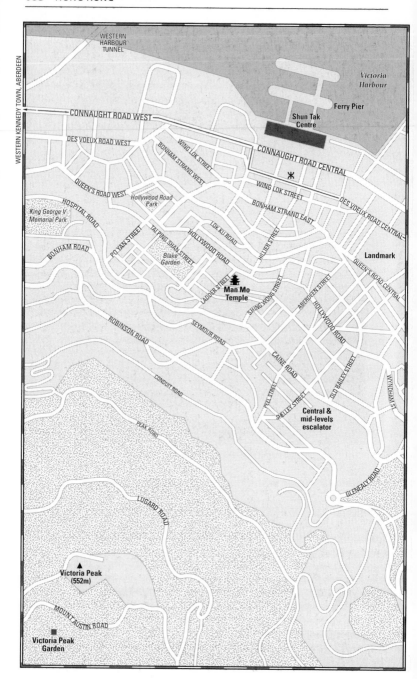

WESTERN KENNEDY TOWN, ABERDEEN

WESTERN HARBOUR TUNNEL

Victoria Harbour

Ferry Pier

Shun Tak Centre

CONNAUGHT ROAD WEST

CONNAUGHT ROAD CENTRAL

DES VOEUX ROAD WEST

WING LOK STREET

BONHAM STRAND WEST

WING LOK STREET

DES VOEUX ROAD CENTRAL

BONHAM STRAND EAST

QUEEN'S ROAD WEST

Hollywood Road Park

HOSPITAL ROAD

King George V Memorial Park

LOK KU ROAD

HILLIER STREET

Landmark

BONHAM ROAD

PO YAN STREET

TAI PING SHAN STREET

Blake Garden

HOLLYWOOD ROAD

LADDER STREET

Man Mo Temple

SHING WONG STREET

ABERDEEN STREET

HOLLYWOOD ROAD

QUEEN'S ROAD CENTRAL

ROBINSON ROAD

SEYMOUR ROAD

CAINE ROAD

OLD BAILEY STREET

WYNDHAM ST.

CONDUIT ROAD

PEEL STREET

SHELLEY STREET

Central & mid-levels escalator

PEAK ROAD

GLENEALY ROAD

LUGARD ROAD

Victoria Peak (552m)

MOUNT AUSTIN ROAD

Victoria Peak Garden

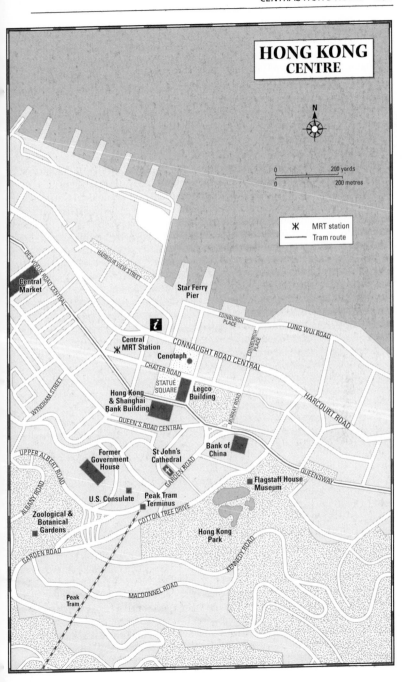

HONG KONG
CENTRE

N

| 0 | | 200 yards |
| 0 | | 200 metres |

✳ MRT station
— Tram route

DES VŒUX ROAD CENTRAL

HARBOUR VIEW STREET

Central Market

Star Ferry Pier

ℹ️

EDINBURGH PLACE

LUNG WUI ROAD

Central MRT Station

CONNAUGHT ROAD CENTRAL

EDINBURGH PLACE

Cenotaph

CHATER ROAD

HARCOURT ROAD

STATUE SQUARE

Legco Building

WYNDHAM STREET

Hong Kong & Shanghai Bank Building

MURRAY ROAD

QUEEN'S ROAD CENTRAL

UPPER ALBERT ROAD

Former Government House

St John's Cathedral

Bank of China

QUEENSWAY

GARDEN ROAD

Flagstaff House Museum

ALBANY ROAD

U.S. Consulate

Peak Tram Terminus

COTTON TREE DRIVE

Zoological & Botanical Gardens

Hong Kong Park

KENNEDY ROAD

GARDEN ROAD

Peak Tram

MACDONNEL ROAD

The displays in the Flagstaff House Museum change from time to time but are usually associated with tea and its accoutrements. There is a very fine collection of the (usually) brick-red Yixing ware, favoured by connoisseurs of tea. Yixing teapots are small and often quite amusing; they are produced in a variety of forms: cloth-wrapped bundles, peaches complete with stone, lotus buds and sometimes speckled with gold dust, rimmed with metal or polished. According to the portrayal of gangsters in Chinese films, tea was drunk by gangsters straight from the spout, with no time for cups. There is a pictorial display on the history of tea and the tea trade. The house is surrounded by a splendid garden.

Head up Cotton Tree Drive towards the Peak and away from the Harbour. On your right is the **Peak Tram Terminus**. Cross the road with care. Before taking the tram to the Peak, you could look at the **Botanical and Zoological Gardens** which lie ahead of you on Garden Road, a dark green haven between the motorways. St Joseph's Roman Catholic Church, built for the English speaking Catholic community in 1876, replacing a building that had been destroyed in the typhoon of 1874, is on your left along Garden Road.

Botanical specimens in the gardens include those native to Hong Kong and China as well as many tropical varieties that have been established for over 100 years. The gardens have a considerable history, featured in the 1893 *Hong Kong Guide* (when they were merely botanical, not yet zoological), where it was recommended that 'many a spare hour may be profitably spent'. They remain a quiet retreat on the noisy, overcrowded island.

The Peak

Returning to the Peak Tram Terminus beside the US Consulate, you can take the tram (actually a funicular railway) up to the Peak (a 9-minute journey) at any time between 07.00 and 24.00 for a few dollars. The funicular was built in 1888 by a Scottish railway engineer and its green cars with mahogany-slatted seats have been climbing the 45 per cent incline ever since without a single accident.

There are four intermediate stations: Kennedy Road, near the masonic temple, MacDonnell Road, May Road and Barker Road, all pleasant little Victorian halts, before you reach the Upper Peak Terminus. Alternatively, you could take the local bus up to the Peak and use the tram to descend; this way you get a greater variety of views.

On the Peak, cloud permitting, various walks are possible. The normal 3.2km 'circuit' is Lugard Road-Harlech Road past the spacious mansions which still exist, for the Peak was the 'hill station' of this Victorian colony.

In 1847 the Colonial Surgeon recommended residence on the Peak for reasons of health. At that time, before the funicular, everything had to be carried up to the fine residences on the backs of coolies, some of whom were mere children, hauling loads of coal up the incline for some ten hours a day, seven days a week. The inhabitants themselves had to be carried up in palanquins. Today the early morning trams are often filled with uniformed schoolchildren and dark-suited businessmen.

If it isn't too hot and the hill isn't too much, Mount Austin Road, which also starts from the Upper Peak Terminus, leads up to the Peak itself (554m above sea level) through the gardens of what was once the Governor's Summer Residence, **Mountain Lodge** (destroyed by the Japanese during their occupation). The view of the island below, with its crammed skyscrapers and yellow beaches, the shipping out on the blue, island-dotted sea, is spectacular. At quiet times, there is still some remaining wildlife on the Peak. I'm not sure whether I believe that there are still barking deer lurking amongst the rhododendrons, tallow trees and jasmine but kites and blue magpies abound.

Returning by tram to the Lower Terminus, walk up to Upper Albert Road for a peer through the gates of **Government House**, the now abandoned residence of the Governor of Hong Kong.

The building used to stand in splendid isolation on the hillside beside the Botanic Gardens, a white neo-classical building, colonnaded and surrounded by a sloping garden and five tennis courts. It was extended by the Japanese during the Occupation when the tower was added. Its view of Central District is gradually being eroded as buildings rise around it.

Government House in Hong Kong

If you walk back around the grounds, with the US Consulate on your right, the road twists around until it joins Wyndham Street. At the bottom of Wyndham Street, turn left into Hollywood Road, which takes you through some of the older residential and commercial areas of Hong Kong above Queens Road Central. This sort of mix of buildings antedates the post Second World War International style of high-rise buildings in reinforced concrete that has come to dominate the central area, partly because of the lack of space for building. The verandahs, balconies and shuttered windows of the older mixed areas reflect considerable

Portuguese influence (from Macau) but the interiors are usually Chinese. Some of the more interesting older buildings lie beyond the end of Hollywood Road and the Man Mo Temple; you may care to leave these for another outing.

Man Mo Temple and Lo Pun Temple

The **Man Mo Temple** at the west end of Hollywood Road is a Taoist temple, built in two sections with a 'smoke hole' for incense in between. A bell in the temple records a date of 1847, which is generally assumed to be the year of its foundation. The buildings were enlarged in 1850.

> The temple is dedicated to the twin deities of Literature and Martial Matters. The God of War is the deified general of the Three Kingdoms, Guan yu, while the God of Literature (or Civil Matters) was supposed to have lived in the 3C AD and to have had jurisdiction over the lives of government officials. It was not uncommon to find shrines to these two on either side of a temple dedicated to Confucius (a feature of most Chinese towns) and this temple is in effect the 'city temple' of Hong Kong.

Huge coils of incense suspended at the Man Mo Temple, Hollywood Road, Hong Kong

There is lavish use of Shekwan (or Suiwan) ceramic tiles on the roof and stucco relief work and the gables are arched in the curved 'cat's back' shape characteristic of the decorated roofs of the south. The two stone lions in the forecourt were presented to the temple by the Pork Butchers' Guild in 1851. In the first hall there are some gilded, highly carved sedan chairs, dating from 1885 and 1862, used to carry the deities in religious processions. On the right are the bell and drum used in temple ceremonies and in the centre is the open 'smoke hole' courtyard with large censers for incense. Beyond is the main hall. The major figures of the Gods of War and Literature are straight ahead, while to the right is the shrine of the locality deity, the Earth God.

Not far away is the **Lo Pun Temple** on Ching Liu Terrace, dedicated to the God of Carpenters (Lu Ban in putonghua). It has fine stepped gables and black and white painting around the eaves in an architectural style found in south central China.

Just south of Hollywood Road, centred on Taiping shan Street (one down), the whole Taiping shan area was demolished and replanned after the plague of 1894, which killed 2500, including the Governor's wife, although most victims were the tenement-dwelling Chinese. Despite this, the incessant rebuilding that goes on everywhere else in Hong Kong means that the area still includes some of the earliest surviving tenement buildings in Hong Kong.

> The following have all been demolished and replaced by high-rise buildings: nos 103–107 Hollywood Road, for example, was a narrow, balconied tenement with a rare Chinese tiled roof; and just round the corner from the Man Mo Temple to the left is Ladder Street where nos 2–6 had shuttered, full-length windows.

The area below Hollywood Road is worth exploring for the occasional older buildings and Chinese shops; the roads down to Queens Road Central are often stepped 'ladder streets' lined with small stalls.

Soho and the Mid-levels

The extreme western end of the built-up area, **Kennedy Town**, is where the first British landfall was made, where the old waterfall, which ships used for fresh water and which figures so prominently in early photographs and engravings of the island, reached the sea. The street names, including Possession Street, record the early landing, as does Belcher Street, named after the Captain of HMS *Sulphur*, whose crew was the first to step ashore.

Some quite interesting older buildings are to be found on Caine Road, which turns into Bonham Road at its western extremity; at no. 2 Bonham Road is the **Hop Ya Church** with red-brick decoration and Robinson Road above it. They are best reached from Aberdeen Street, which runs upwards from Hollywood Road. On Caine Road, the **Cathedral of the Immaculate Conception** is at no. 16; built during the 1880s and described in 1893 as a 'handsome modern cruciform construction in the gothic style'.

> The following have all gone: nos 66–69 had enclosed verandahs above shops; no. 99, with its cupolas and plaster ornamentation, cast-iron panel balustrades and grand Chinese style windows, was Buxey Lodge, built in the 1870s for the prominent Parsee merchant Hormusjee Mody (of Mody Road); no. 115 Caine Road had a rusticated ground floor with an arched door and keystones above the windows repeated on the third floor and Doric columns; the Police Quarters at no. 150–156 Caine Road, built in the 1920s, has gone too. There is, however, an ex-police station at no. 10 Hollywood Road which bears the insignia 'G.R. 1919'.

On Bonham Road, no. 44–46 was the 'Euston' Mansion with a grand iron gateway, built in 1931; no. 63a, with its 1930s' curved frontage, was built in the garden of Ball's Court, which was the residence of Judge Ball in the 1860s; it was once used as a home for St Stephen's Boys School. No. 90 once belonged to the Church Mission Society but was integrated into the University of Hong Kong in 1918. It boasts classical features assembled in a non-classical fashion with fluted Corinthian columns.

Backtracking to Caine Road, at the junction with Peel Street, you can climb upwards towards Robinson Road, passing the Old Mosque on the way. The **Ohel Leah Synagogue** (1901) on Robinson Road is a late foundation, despite the early arrival of prominent Jewish citizens, such as the Sassoon family in 1857. They later founded the synagogue, Jacob Elias Sassoon paying for the construction, his brothers for the land. The architects were Leigh and Orange, the firm which established itself in Hong Kong in 1874 and also built the Mandarin Hotel in 1963; they chose an Hispanic style with red brick and whitewashed walls. The synagogue was dedicated to Leah Gubbay Sassoon, mother of the brothers who provided the funds.

Also on Robinson Road, no. 62 was an eclectic building with Baroque, Classical and Renaissance motifs and an interior court; no. 68 was a grand residence with ceramic bamboo decoration and baroque iron grill balconies. There was a Chinese gateway to no. 88B; all gone in 1999.

The **University of Hong Kong**, founded in 1911 but incorporating a number of older buildings, such as no. 90 Bonham Road, stands above the Western District. The Vice-Chancellor's Residence at No. 8 University Path was built of brick and stone in 1911.

There is an art gallery in the University, which may be visited by the public: the **Fung Ping Shan Museum**, no. 94 Bonham Street (open daily 10.00–18.00, except Thursdays, Sundays 14.00–18.00).

> This is the oldest museum in Hong Kong, founded in 1953. It contains a good chronological display of Chinese art, including archaic bronzes, ceramics of all periods and some Ming and Qing paintings. It is a fine collection, established to assist in the teaching of Chinese art to the students and its most unusual feature is the largest collection of Chinese Nestorian Christian crosses in the world: 966 of them, dating from the Yuan dynasty.

Returning to the eastern part of Central District, **St John's Cathedral** stands below Government House on the west side of Garden Road. It was built in the Gothic style between 1847 and 1849 to replace a temporary church.

> It has seen many services, including some strange ones, such as that of the thanksgiving after the bread poisoning incident of 1857. The major supplier of bread to the British, Cheong Ah Lum, decided to free Hong Kong of the colonial yoke by poisoning all his customers with arsenic in the bread. He put in far too much so that they vomited before ingesting a lethal dose. Acquitted for lack of evidence, Cheong Ah Lum was deported to China and the Governor of Hong Kong, Sir John Bowring, himself composed a hymn of thanksgiving for the cathedral service.

Hong Kong and Shanghai Bank

The unmissable grey building at no. 1 Queens Road Central is the new headquarters of the **Hong Kong and Shanghai Bank**, completed in 1986 to designs by the British architect, Sir Norman Foster. Hung between a criss-cross exterior scaffolding of dull grey steel girders, it contrasts with the other glassy skyscrapers and towers over the old Bank of China, a 1930s building next door. The ground floor is open to the street, with crossing escalators taking clients up to the airy halls above. In front stand the two old bronze lions named Stephen and Stitt after two bank officials of the 1930s (when the previous building was erected). One bears the marks of Japanese bullets.

> The first bank building was designed in 1886 by the local architects Palmer and Turner, who built the next in 1935, a skyscraper—the tallest building between Cairo and San Francisco—equipped with squash courts and heli-

pads and with a fine mosaic ceiling by a Russian artist from Shanghai. This was taken down to make way for Foster's new building.

Not to be outdone, the **Bank of China** has moved to new headquarters just diagonally across the road beside the Hilton, designed by I.M. Pei (see p 686).

In front of the two banks is **Statue Square**, now rather devoid of statues, since the massed royal group with Queen Victoria and her family was taken down by the Japanese during the Occupation. The **cenotaph**, erected after the First World War, still stands but the only remaining statue (in bronze) is that of Thomas Jackson, manager of the Hong Kong and Shanghai Bank at the end of the 19C.

The Gothic **Hong Kong Club**, which used to stand on the eastern side of the square, was demolished in 1981. It was replaced with a small white skyscraper (of which the Club occupies four floors) that stands next to what was until 1997 the Legco Building. The latter, with its dome and Ionic columns, was designed for the Supreme Court in 1900 by Sir Aston Webb, the architect of the Victoria and Albert Museum. It was previously separated from the Club by a cricket pitch.

Kowloon

Immediately south of Statue Square, on the waterfront, is the **Star Ferry Terminus** for Kowloon. The Star Ferry (04.30–23.30) is the best way to reach Kowloon from the Central District in a few minutes, with a fine view of the harbour. The old open green and white double-ended diesel ferries, all with stars in their names, have been in operation since 1868. Founded by an Indian, the ferry

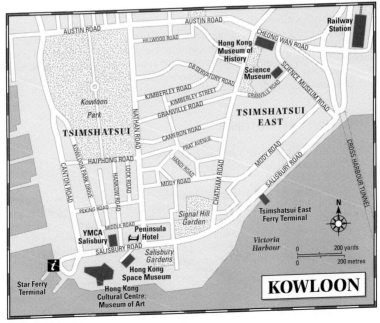

company belonged to the shipping magnate from Ningbo, Sir Y.K. Pao (d. 1991), who also owned Lane Crawford's department store.

Walk down Salisbury Road along the waterfront in Kowloon, past the old YMCA and the *Peninsula Hotel* to Nathan Road, which runs inland along the far side of the Peninsula. The Peninsula Hotel, built in the early years of the 20C, remains perhaps the grandest hotel in Hong Kong, with its fleet of eight green Rolls Royces and its famous tea lounge and restaurants. It is certainly the oldest hotel building since the lamented demolition of the Repulse Bay Hotel in the early 1980s.

Nathan Road is the major shopping street of Kowloon and stretches for miles past Boundary Road, which marks the boundary between Kowloon and the New Territories. Some three blocks up, on the far side of Haiphong Road, on the left-hand side of the street, is **Kowloon Park**. The old colonial building there used to house the Hong Kong Museum of History; this has now been moved to Chatham Road.

There is now a **Museum of Space** (open Mon, Wed, Thurs, Fri, 13.00–21.00, Sat & Sun 10.00–21.00) in the domed planetarium (which blocks the harbour view from the Peninsula) on Salisbury Road. Its exhibitions change fairly regularly, so check newspaper listings. Also on Salisbury Road, nearer the Clock Tower and the Star Ferry Terminal is the modern **Hong Kong Cultural Centre** built on the site of the old Kowloon railway station. This houses concert halls and auditoria and, to one side, the **Museum of Art** (open Mon, Tues, Wed, Fri & Sat 10.00–18.00, Sun 13.00–18.00) with a wide-ranging series of exhibits on traditional Chinese art and archaeology.

The **Hong Kong Museum of History**, is on Chatham Road (closed Fridays, open daily 10.00–18.00, Sundays and public holidays 13.00–18.00). It has a fairly permanent exhibition on Hong Kong before 1841, with fine models of sea-going junks and a good use of photographs and other illustrative material. Its other exhibitions change from time to time but are usually concerned with aspects of the traditional culture of south China: weddings, puppet theatres, etc. They are well researched and beautifully presented. There are occasional visiting exhibitions (check newspaper listings).

The New Territories

You can take the new Mass Transit Railway (opened in 1979 but still expanding) either from Hong Kong island or from Tsin Sha Tsui on the tip of Kowloon to Sham Shui Po.

The **Lei Cheung Uk Museum** in Sham Shui Po (open Mon, Tues, Wed, Fri, Sat 10.00–13.00 and 14.00–18.00, Sundays and public holidays, 13.00–18.00, closed Thursdays) is based around a Han dynasty tomb, discovered when the vast area of squatter housing was cleared following a devastating fire in 1954. It is in the middle of the oldest group of public housing blocks in Hong Kong, Shek Kip Mei, at no. 41 Tonkin Street.

The Han tomb is dated to AD 100–200 and comprises three chambers with shards; a separate exhibition hall has drawings and contemporary rubbings illustrating life in the Han, rubbings from the carved bricks of the tomb and bronze and ceramic artefacts unearthed in it. It is interesting for it illustrates Chinese control of the area as early as the Han, contrary to the assertion of early British settlers: 'the Colony has grown to its present position and importance within the last half century, as a result of the necessities of English trade with China' (1893).

Staying on the MTR, changing at Prince Edward Station, you could travel on to Wong Tai Sin where there is a recent (1973) 'multi-faith' temple just beside the station, with shrines to the Buddha and a central hall devoted to the Taoist deity, Wong Tai Sin, who heals the sick. The tap water in the temple is believed to be efficacious. You could then take the MTR to Yaumatei (a Cantonese transliteration of Waterloo). The Yaumatei/Mongkok area is a good place to shop for prices are lower than in the shops near the Star Ferry Terminus. Credit cards are accepted and shop staff speak English.

The area was built in 1915 after a terrible typhoon and is now virtually self-sufficient, with shop *sampans*, medical and educational facilities. Some of the larger junks are lovely; all serve as home for the Tanka, who wear flat-brimmed straw hats, and Hoklo (possibly from Fujian province), who have hats that look like huge solar topees with angled brims. There is often a tiny shrine to Tin Hau, empress of heaven, roughly the same deity as A-Ma of Macau.

Although some guidebooks describe **Tin Hau** as a Taoist deity, I think it likely that she is a version of the Buddhist Avalokitesvara or Guanyin, thoroughly female, unlike the Buddhist original, and specifically associated in this area with the protection of boats and sailors at sea as one aspect of her compassion. There are, of course, Taoist aspects to the deity and her worship, just one being her sex.

If time allows, more far-flung trips into the New Territories are interesting. They are easily made by tourist bus, arranged through your hotel or any travel agent, although tourist buses are expensive and necessarily involve tourist stops, such as the amazingly kitsch Sung Dynasty Village (certainly an experience). Some of the walled villages (see p 684) are also fascinating, although they are full of old ladies demanding money for photographs.

For those interested in botany, the **Kadoorie Experimental and Extension Farm**, in Lam Tsuen Valley, has fine botanical gardens attached; a group of columns on a hill are all that remain of the fine central Post Office that used to stand on Statue Square (see p 686). Another enterprise of the Kadoorie family is the **Taipo Carpet Factory** in Taipo, which can be visited by arrangement. There you can see the mechanised weaving of carpets, the designs of which are based on traditional Chinese carpets. The weavers use what look like power drills and the designs are finally cut and carved with electric clippers (rather than scissors) in the traditional manner.

A trip that can be made by public transport is to the Museum of the Chinese University and the Temple of Man Fat in Shatin. Take a train to Shatin from the Kowloon Station.

The **Temple of Ten Thousand Buddhas** and the **Man Fat Temple** are reached by climbing 431 steps up from the railway station and then a further 69 steps to the Man Fat Temple. The former temple was founded in 1950 and boasts a pink pagoda, 12,800 Buddha figures and a small fairground for children. The

Man Fat Temple contains the preserved body of the Reverend Yuet Kai, buried in a sitting position—Buddhist adepts attempt to emulate the sages who died sitting in the meditation position—at the age of 87 in 1965. Eight months after his death his body was discovered still to be in perfect condition and was covered in gold leaf, leaving his hair and beard still visible. The body and its treatment are reminiscent of that on Jiu hua shan in Anhui.

On the next hill, Tao Fong Shan, is the **Lutheran Chinese Mission to Buddhists**, founded by Karl Reichelt, a Scandinavian missionary who arrived in the area in 1929 after teaching Christianity to Buddhists in China and becoming an expert on the religion, writing a number of useful books about it. He employed a Chinese Buddhist architect to design the mission, the foundations of which were laid in 1931. It now has a guesthouse and a pottery workshop in which converted Buddhist monks do overglaze enamel painting on porcelain.

The **Chinese University** is a bus or taxi ride from Shatin Station, magnificently sited on hills above the sea. It was founded in the 1960s with Chinese as its main, although not exclusive, teaching language and the campus incorporates some earlier colleges. Its museum was founded to assist in the teaching of Chinese art history but its collections are sometimes displayed and it often houses loan exhibitions of interest, especially since its relations with the art historians and museums of China are very good. The museum is open 10.00–16.30 on weekdays and you can find listings of its exhibitions in newspapers.

You can catch buses back to the railway station or to Kowloon from just outside the university gates (be careful that the bus does go to Tsimshatsui) or you may find a passing taxi if you are lucky.

Hong Kong Island

Apart from extended walks in the old Chinese areas of Western and Kennedy Town, there are some places of interest to the east of Central, although this eastern district is in general newer than Western and Kennedy Town. Much use has been made of reclaimed land to build apartment blocks on the extended waterfront in Causeway Bay and North Point.

Wanchai, famous as the red light district in the 1950s and through the Vietnam War period, is not quite the single-minded bar district of fiction (*The World of Suzie Wong*) and its Post Office has just been singled out for preservation.

Take the Mass Transit Railway to Wanchai and go up O'Brien Road, across Johnston Road and straight ahead for Queens Road East. Before land reclamation, this was the harbour front. The Post Office stands next to the Wu Chung Building (Hopewell Holdings).

> A white, Dutch influenced building, its gables, shuttered windows and brick-arched doorway are perfect examples of turn-of-the-century architecture in Hong Kong. It was built between 1912 and 1913 and became a post office in 1915, so it may not have been originally designed as such.

Further west of the Hopewell Centre (64 storeys high) is a temple, variously known as the **Hung Shing** or the Pak Tai Temple, a single storey temple to the god of seafarers with a fine line of Shekwan ceramics along the roof added at the turn of the century. The temple was built in 1860, although the shrine inside is dated 1847–48 and the copper image is said to date to 1604.

On the other side of the Hopewell Centre is the narrow Tik Loong Lane leading up steps to a row of 19C houses and the **Sui Pak** or Chai Kung Woot Fat (Living Buddha) Temple (c 1870), whose deities have proved efficacious in the control of disease as the many inscribed mirrors, presented by those whose prayers were answered, testify.

The side streets off Queens Road East contain many shops selling traditional goods: paper offerings to be burnt at funerals (including paper aeroplanes), cars, houses, birds and birdcages and crickets. **Wanchai Market** (open daily), which runs from Queens Road East to Wanchai Road, is quite interesting.

Walk east along Queens Road East. Just beyond the point where Stubbs Road—named after the Governor from 1919 to 1925, Sir Reginald Stubbs, who attended Council meetings on Thursday mornings and afternoons and said he might as well have tripe for lunch on Thursdays, too—leads upwards towards the Peak, are the European cemeteries. On the corner is the **New China News Agency Building**. Until the signing of the Joint Declaration and open discussion on Hong Kong directly with Peking, it was viewed as a sort of unofficial Chinese embassy in Hong Kong. It is interestingly situated, for its proximity to the cemeteries would make it a rather unattractive piece of real estate to any Chinese but the atheist Communists. There is also a Sikh temple near the corner.

The cemeteries include the **Muslim Cemetery** with a mosque, then the **Catholic Cemetery** (1847) and beyond that the Colonial Cemetery (1845); beyond that is the **Parsee Cemetery** (1852).

There was a small but influential Parsee community in Hong Kong, one of the most famous members being Sir Hormusjee Naoro Mody, born in Bombay in 1838, who spent fifty years in Hong Kong and founded the university before dying and being buried here in 1911.

Way up Shan Kwong Road, on the other side of the road from the Hong Kong Jockey Club, is the **Jewish Cemetery**, consecrated in 1855; its earliest headstone is dated 1859.

The Colonial Cemetery is not as fascinating as the Protestant Cemetery in Macau, nor is it as old, but it contains the remains of all sorts of people from Lord Napier, who died in Macau in 1834 after presiding over the opening of trade that followed the ending of the East India Company's monopoly in the same year that he died of fever, to Karl Friedrich August Gutzlaff (d. 1851), a Pomerarian missionary who travelled the China coast by junk, writing religious tracts in Chinese and deploring the idolatry of Putuo shan and other Buddhist centres. He worked as an interpreter during the negotiation of the Treaty of Nanking and became Chinese Secretary to the Hong Kong Government from 1834 to 1851. He was apparently 'very greatly deceived by his native helpers but his zeal never failed'. The Chinese *comprador*, Sir Robert Hotung, who rose from humble beginnings to enormous wealth and philanthropy, is also buried here with his English wife. The first husband of the American evangelist, Aimee Semple MacPherson, Robert Semple, died at the age of 29 and was buried here.

The cemetery, which covers a large sloping area, is also very peaceful and full of well-tended plants and birds. It can be entered from Queens Road East or you could climb up Stubbs Road and descend through the quiet cemetery.

Further along the shore, in **Causeway Bay**, just south of Causeway Bay MTR station, is the place on Gloucester Road (in front of the Excelsior Hotel) where the noon-day gun used to be fired every day at noon and again at midnight on New Year's Eve, an event commemorated by Noel Coward in *Mad Dogs and Englishmen*. And, if you care to take the MTR to Tin Hau, walk up Tung Lo Wan Road, continue southwards along Wun Sha Street to the end and wiggle round behind the True Light Middle School, you will find the **Tiger Balm Gardens** (otherwise known as the Aw Boon Haw Gardens; open daily 09.30–16.00), built in the 1930s by the eponymous millionaire who made his fortune out of Tiger Balm, the eucalyptus-scented 'cooling' balm sold in tiny red tins with tigers on them. It is nicely crazy with its great plaster animals wearing clothes and exaggerated rockeries.

Stanley, Repulse Bay and Aberdeen

On the far side of the island, reached by bus or taxi from Central, are Stanley, Repulse Bay and Aberdeen.

Stanley Beach and village lie on the southeast tip of the island, near Stanley Prison (all named after Lord Stanley, Secretary of State for the Colonies at the time of Hong Kong's annexation). Stanley is most famous for its street market which, although open every day, is most crowded on Sundays. The street is lined with shops and stalls selling rattan, porcelain and, above all, cheap casual clothing, much of it 'designer label'.

There is a temple dedicated to **Tin Hau**, the heavenly empress, sometimes identified as a Taoist deity but who appears also to be one of the incarnations of Avalokitesvara, the Bodhisattva of Mercy, in his sinified and feminised incarnation as Guan Yin. Tin Hau is the same as A-Ma of Macau and the Tian Hou of the temple in Tianjin, a young female deity, protector of seafarers. The temple lies at the end of Stanley Main Street: turn right at the bottom of the market and continue along a narrow lane at the end of the main street.

The temple is thought to have been founded by the pirate Chang Po Chai some 200 years ago, making it the oldest temple on the island. Chang Po Chai captured the island of Hong Kong in 1770 and set up his headquarters in Stanley, when he wasn't forced to retreat to a cave on Cheung Chau (see p 702). A drum and bell that he is supposed to have used to signal to his ships are now in the temple; the bell with an inscription dating it to 1767, the drum with a maker's inscription from Guangzhou. An interesting collection of little wooden, gilded deities is ranged on a ledge that runs round the inner wall of the temple. The deities include the City God, the God of War, the barefoot Emperor of the North, the Dragon Mother (who hatched a dragon from an egg) and Guan yin. The front doors of the temple are painted with door gods, whose paper images are pasted on household doors throughout China at the lunar New Year, and a tiger skin labelled as having been shot outside Stanley Police Station 'by an Indian policeman Mr Rur Singh' in 1942.

The next bay is **Repulse Bay**, named after HMS *Repulse* which attempted to keep pirates down in the 19C. Its most famous landmark, the *Repulse Bay Hotel*, with a long verandah and glass fan-shaped porch, was built in 1918 and demolished in 1980 (just before the bottom dropped out of land prices, so it was really a mistake to demolish it anyway). Apparently a *Repulse Bay Restaurant* has been built there now in an attempt to recreate the gracious dining room on the verandah.

Deep Water Bay, filled with mansions and a golf course, lies next to **Aberdeen** (named after Lord Aberdeen, Foreign Secretary in the mid 19C at the time of Hong Kong's annexation) which, unlike the constructed Yaumatei Typhoon Shelter, has been a natural typhoon shelter and home to some 20,000 of Hong Kong's original boat people, as opposed to the more recent sea-going arrivals from Vietnam. Life on board the boats that cram the harbour is the main attraction for visitors.

You can also go by ferry or by road to the nearby island of **Apleichau**, the main boat building centre of the island where junks are made beside luxury cruisers.

There is a **Tin Hau Temple** in Aberdeen—naturally, for the goddess protects fishermen—built in 1851 and one of the most crowded during the Tin Hau festival in April.

Lamma, Lantau and Cheung Chau

The other islands of the archipelago can be visited by ferry from the Outlying Districts Ferry Pier on Connaught Road, Central, just along from the Star Ferry Pier. The three major islands are Lamma, Lantau and Cheung Chau; others can be explored at will.

Lamma
Lamma is sparsely inhabited and lovely to walk in; it only takes a couple of hours to get from one end to the other, although it is the third largest of the islands. Depending on where you land, visit the **Tin Hau Temple** in Sok Kwu Wan.

Lantau
Lantau is the largest of the outlying islands, about twice as big as Hong Kong. Its very size has protected it from the incursion of the new airport on the northern shore. Most ferries land at Silvermine Bay, where buses take tourists to the **Po Lin Monastery**, a rather theatrically bright red and gold building (1970) on a hillside north of the reservoir.

The temple was founded in 1927. The images in the main hall are of Sakyamuni, the Buddha of Medicine (left) and Amitabha (right). In the hall above are figures of Guan yin, Bodhisattva of Mercy, Manjusri on his lion, symbol of wisdom, and Samantabhadra on a white elephant, the patron saint of Mount Emei in Sichuan. On a hilltop near the monastery is the only cremation tower in Hong Kong, where the bodies of Buddhists, monks, nuns and lay-believers are cremated in the open air. There is now a new Buddha, the 'largest seated bronze outdoor Buddha' in the world, until the next one.

You could walk on west to the **Yin Hing Monastery**, closer to the sea, or visit the **Lantau Tea Gardens**, opened in 1959 to recultivate disused tea terraces, just by the Po Lin Monastery. On the north side of the island is the **Tung Chang Fort**, built in 1817 against pirates, with solid ramparts and six cannon.

On the east side of the island is the **Trappist Monastery** of Our Lady of Joy where the monks, who have taken a vow of silence, serve simple meals and run a guesthouse as well as caring for a fine herd of dairy cattle that supply milk to the top hotels in Hong Kong. You can reach the monastery on foot from

Silvermine Bay, heading northeast around the bay; alternatively, some of the ferries stop at Peng Chau island just opposite whence a sampan will take you across the narrow stretch of water between Lantau and Peng Chau.

Cheung Chau

Cheung Chau is an island with far more houses on it; more town than boat, the main urban area is concentrated on a narrow strip linking two rounded and wooded hills. There is, however, no traffic so that wandering in the narrow streets of the little town is still restful. The oldest temple on Cheung Chau, the **Pak Tai Temple**, is on the waterfront, just left of the ferry pier. It was founded in 1783 and contains a Song sword found in the sea nearby.

Pak Tai is the local God of the Sea, also known as the Emperor of the North. He is supposed to have been a scholar, immortalised for his courage and brilliance. Appointed to stop a demon king from threatening the earth, he defeated the demon and the tortoise and snake (symbols of the north) summoned by the demon, hence his title of Emperor of the North. He is depicted in the temple in his usual form, barefooted and with flowing black hair. Before his altar are two figures of assistant generals, Thousand Li Eye and Favourable Wind Ear.

The temple is the centre of the famous **Cheung Chau Bun Festival**, held annually between the last ten days of the third lunar month and the first ten days of the fourth, usually in late April or early May.

The festival originated after the discovery of skeletons, probably pirates' victims, which precipitated a series of natural disasters on the island. A Taoist priest recommended that the hungry spirits of the dead be placated by offerings of food. During the festival, huge bamboo towers, 20m high, are completely covered with about 5000 buns, which are eventually donated to the thousands of visitors, after the spirits have partaken of their essence during the days of the festival, in order to bring them good luck. They are said to cure disease so that bits of dried bun are used throughout the year, boiled with water and drunk in search of a cure for headaches, backaches and other ailments. There used to be rather dangerous fights amongst the young men who clambered up the towers to reach the top buns (the luckiest) and one tower collapsed so that now the buns are more sedately distributed by Taoist priests.

Cantonese operas are performed in the streets on temporary stages and a strange procession includes tiny children dressed up in all sorts of things from mermaid costumes to dinner jackets and bow ties. They are tied into metal frames so that they appear to float on air, unsupported, as they are carried through the streets atop wooden poles.

On the southwest tip of the island is the **Cheung Po Tsai Cave**, supposedly the hideout of the most famous local pirate of the 18C, who is also supposed to have founded the Tin Hau Temple at Stanley. He is said to have had an English mistress with whom he hid in the cave.

The **Tin Hau Temple** on **Tap Mun** is perhaps the most important of all Tin Han temples as it is the last temple before junks reach the open sea with all its dangers. The 100 year old temple is thus visited by fishermen to pray for a safe return and successful voyage before they leave the archipelago.

Macau

The former Portuguese colony of Macau, on a peninsula linked by a narrow isthmus to Guangdong province on the Chinese mainland, lies just south of Hong Kong island, an hour away by hydrofoil. Filled with Hong Kong visitors who come to gamble in the casinos (forbidden in Hong Kong) at holidays and weekends, it is on weekdays a comparatively quiet place filled with pretty colonial buildings in flower-filled gardens and baroque churches.

Practical information

 Visas
For a three-day stay visas are no longer required for nationals of the USA, Philippines, Japan, Australia, Canada, New Zealand, Malaysia, Thailand, Brazil, Austria, Belgium, France, Denmark, Spain, Greece, Italy, Norway, the Netherlands, Sweden, UK, Germany and Hong Kong.

 Getting there
By air
There is a new airport on **Taipa island** for flights from Peking, Shanghai and many other Chinese cities, as well as Taipei and Southeast Asian countries.

There are shuttle buses from the Macau ferry terminal to the airport, and from the airport to major hotels and the jetfoil pier.

By bus

There are now fast buses from Guangzhou, which take about three hours, including the time taken at the border.

By boat

Jetfoils (55 minutes) and Hydrofoils (75 minutes) depart at half hourly intervals (c 07.00–18.00 daily) from the modern Macau Ferry Pier on Connaught Road, Hong Kong, which is beyond all the other ferry jetties for the outlying islands. It is also possible to take overnight ferries from Guangzhou.

 Getting around
In Macau it is best to travel by foot and taxi.

 Information
There is an official Macau Government **Tourist Information Office** at the Macau Ferry Terminal, and the main office is at 9 Largo de Senado (open 09.00–18.00), www.macautourism.gov.mo. At the offices you can buy maps and a variety of fascinating publications about Macau's history, almost all of them by the indefatigable Father Teixeira. It is quite possible to see most of Macau in reasonable comfort in a day. You can buy quite useful 1:6000 maps of Macau with street names in Chinese and 'English'; these are to be recommended, for if you speak neither Cantonese nor Portuguese, communication, especially with taxi-drivers, can be a bit difficult.

 Currency
The Macau *pataca* is worth about the same as the Hong Kong dollar. It is not necessary to change money before a trip as Hong Kong notes and coins are accepted in Macau, although *pataca* are only accepted in banks or moneychangers' establishments in Hong Kong.

Where to stay

There are a number of luxury hotels in Macau, most clustered near the Hong Kong Ferry Pier because of their casino facilities. One of the most charming of the luxury class is the *Pousado de Sãotiago*, 170 Avenida da República, ☎ 378 111, fax 567 193, in what was once the 17C Barra Fort, Fortaleza da Barra, in Avenida Republica. It stands high on the shore overlooking the sea and has been tastefully converted; it also has a fine restaurant serving Macanese food. The *Mandarin Oriental* is centrally situated on Avenida da Amizade, ☎ 567 888, fax 594 589.

History

The name of Macau, first mentioned in 1555, is derived from *Ma-kan-ngao* (or Ma-ngao), meaning 'port or bay of Ma' in Fujian dialect. The local waters were said to be sacred to Ma (known to the Cantonese as Tin Hua), merciful goddess of the sea, and since the peninsula was frequently used by fishermen from Fujian province, further up the Chinese coast, the use of Fujian dialect is not surprising. Macau, in fact, consists of the peninsula and Taipa and Coloane islands, linked by bridges, although the major historical sites are on the peninsula.

Before the arrival of the Portuguese, there was a small village on the peninsula and the temple dedicated to A-Ma, goddess of the sea, was founded during the reign of the Ming Wanli emperor (1573–1621). The first **Portuguese** to approach Macau were traders based in Malacca in the early 15C. Their numbers grew when in 1542 they discovered Japan. Owing to Japanese pirate activities, the Chinese emperor had forbidden direct trade between China and Japan and the Portuguese were able to act as middlemen. Given the distance and the dangers of the seas during the typhoon season, the Portuguese were anxious to establish a secure foothold in China. They set up a number of somewhat insecure trading posts in the coastal provinces of Guangdong, Zhejiang and Fujian. Relations with Chinese officials remained extremely difficult until in 1556 a Portuguese fleet under Leonel de Souza forced an agreement out of the Admiral of Guangzhou that gave the Portuguese the right to trade at various places in the vicinity of Guangzhou. The Portuguese settlement in Macau is generally thought to have begun in 1557, against payment of a lease.

By the end of the 16C there were 900 Portuguese based in Macau, with their retinues of servants and Bantu slaves, who were to play a considerable part in the repulsion of a Dutch attack in 1622, and the small number of Chinese inhabitants was swelled by the arrival of pedlars, traders, shopkeepers and craftsmen, despite an imperial prohibition on their residence in Macau. In 1573 the Chinese built the first wall across the isthmus. Attacks by the Dutch led to the appointment of a Captain General or Governor in 1623. Previously Macau's administration had been entrusted to an annually appointed Captain-Major, in actual fact the commander of the Japan trading fleet, although his existence did not end the attacks, which continued throughout the 17C.

Macau's importance declined with the decline of the Portuguese empire, complicated by local problems, such as the loss of Malacca to the Dutch and the rebellions in Timor, which put an end to the lucrative sandalwood trade in which Macau had participated. There were moments of glory, however, as in the 1760s during the early European passion for tea. The Kangxi emperor, perturbed by the demands of foreign traders and missionaries, reversed previous prohibitions and ordered that henceforth the Chinese should trade only with the Japanese. This had the effect of re-routing Dutch tea through Macau to the latter's profit. By the beginning of the 19C, however, the bulk of foreign trade was conducted through Guangzhou (Canton). As the Chinese refused the traders permission to reside there permanently and embargoed all family members, Macau eventually became the residence of the families of the Canton traders and, for the same reason, missionaries and their families. This was only after Portuguese restrictions on the residence of foreigners had been relaxed in 1757.

After the **Opium Wars** and the forced opening of the Chinese hinterland to trade and religion and the rise of Hong Kong, Macau's importance decined once again to the point that it was described in 1917 as 'a quiet retreat and a sanatorium'. It had, nevertheless, seen a small revolution in the early 19C, reflecting events in Portugal itself. Conflicts between the Portuguese appointed Governor and the locally elected Senate led to the formation of a **Liberal Party** in Macau which drafted a petition to the Portuguese King in 1822, even though the King had seen his absolute power curtailed, demanding the restitution of the Senate's privileges, the reservation of senior posts for Macanese and a suspension of subsidies to other distant colonies. The Governor, Jose Ozono de Cabral, refused any compromise and was asked to resign when the Liberals won the elections. He refused and was deposed but he led several attempts to regain power.

The Liberals were eventually deposed by the arrival of a gunboat sent from Goa in 1823, driving the editor of the *Abelha da China* ('China Bee'), the first printed newspaper in the Far East and a mouthpiece of the Liberals, into exile and unfortunately re-establishing the rather sinister **Judge Miguel de Arriaga**. Arriaga only survived a year after his reinstatement, leaving a huge pile of debts and willing his opium connections to his son-in-law. Arriaga had been in illegal partnership with **Thomas Beale**, for many years Macau's foremost opium trader, whose dealings in the illicit drug were concealed behind his 'general agency'. Beale was one of the notables of early 19C Macau, living in a fine old Portuguese house with a marvellous garden and an aviary of rare birds, collected for him by his agents throughout East Asia. When the Governor of Guangdong imprisoned Chinese opium dealers and searched ships, Beale was caught with several hundred chests of unsaleable opium, for which he owed the British East India Company thousands of pounds. His partner, Arriaga, who as a judge was not supposed to trade at all, offered Beale little assistance and, after many years in hiding, Beale committed suicide on Cacilhas Bay in 1841, 17 years after the hypocritical Arriaga had died in his bed.

Despite the machinations of politics and opium dealers and the expulsion of the religious orders in 1834, Macau has a long **religious history** and some of its greatest monuments are associated with religion. It began with St Francis Xavier's dream of the conversion of China. **Francis Xavier** (1506–52) was a founding member of the Jesuit order. Sent to Goa, he made thousands of converts before travelling to Japan in 1549. His main ambition was to enter China and in 1552 he travelled to Sheungchuen island, just southwest of Macau, where he died as he prepared for the great trip. His body was later transferred to a temporary resting place in the nave of the now-ruined church of São Paulo before being sent to its final grave in Goa. His proximity to Macau at the time of his death lent credence to the view that the Portuguese occupation of Macau was a miracle willed by the saint.

The **'Rites Controversy'** that divided the Catholic Church in the late 17C also divided Macau. A sort of religious power struggle, it centred on the appropriate approach to traditional Chinese practices of ancestor worship and the state cult of Confucius. The Jesuits held that these were not idolatrous but the Franciscans and Dominicans, partly out of jealousy over the Jesuits' success in penetrating the Chinese court, disagreed and 'reported' the Jesuits to the Pope. The dispute began in the mid 17C and was revived under Pope Clement XI in the early 18C, when he sent an envoy, Père Tournon, to the Chinese court to investigate the problem. Tournon, in his turn, gained temporary favour with the Kangxi emperor but was eventually ordered out of the country; he had already instructed missionaries to reject the Chinese rites. When he arrived in Macau, Tournon was imprisoned in the Santo Agostinho monastery, for the Bishop of Macau disagreed with his view. Moreover, Portugal was concerned that the Pope was ignoring the padroado (Portuguese prerogative regarding the China missions). Tournon died in Macau in 1710 but not before the Pope had made him a cardinal.

The churches of Macau were immensely impressive, as mid 17C chroniclers record: Father Alexander of Rhodes felt that São Paolo was equal to all the best churches in Italy, with the sole exception of St Peter's, and the surviving examples, including the façade of São Paolo and the church of São José, illustrate the Macanese taste for the Baroque and Rococo. The survival of 17C churches and a number of 18C and 19C villas and gardens is in marked contrast to the fate of Hong Kong's older buildings, which have almost all vanished. There, even skyscrapers are razed to build bigger and higher and little attention is paid to conservation, while the 'quiet retreat' of Macau still preserves much of its 18C and 19C charm, despite an ever-increasing traffic problem.

During the Cultural Revolution (1966–1976) following the liberation of Portugal from the dictator Salazar, the new government of Portugal offered to return Macau to Chinese rule. The offer was not accepted at the time but as the Hong Kong handover negotiations proceeded, the rendition of Macau was announced and it returned to Chinese rule in December 1999.

Unless you are a racing car enthusiast, a time to avoid Macau, if possible, is the second or third weekend in November when the **Macau Grand Prix**, which races through the streets, cuts the peninsula in half, making transport difficult. Part of the circuit runs behind the Lisboa Hotel, between the centre and the ferry piers, completely cutting road access from the piers to the centre. Taxis can only take you as far as the Lisboa Hotel, when you have to get out and walk on flimsy bamboo walkways over the roads. As half the taxis are marooned on one side of the island, they become extremely scarce on the other side.

Although the peninsula only covers 520 hectares, the monuments are rather scattered and are perhaps best visited by a combination of taxi and walks. Use a taxi to take you to the outer monuments: the A-Ma Temple on the southernmost point, the Porta do Cerco and Lin-Fong Temple at the northernmost point, near the isthmus and the Chinese border, Sun Yatsen's House and the Kun Ian Temple northeast of the centre of the peninsula. If the taxi then drops you at the Camões Museum in the centre, you can walk to most of the other central monuments.

A-Ma Temple

The A-Ma Temple (Ma kok miu), is just beyond the Barra Fort, now the *Posada de Sãotiago Hotel* (see p 704), on the western side of the southern tip of the peninsula, at the entrance to the inner harbour.

A-Ma, who has given her name to the peninsula of Macau, appears to be one of the manifestations of the Bodhisattva of Mercy, Guanyin (Avalokitesvara in Sanskrit, Kun Yam in Cantonese). The temple devoted to her is said to date from the Ming and the present buildings are of Wanli foundation (1573–1621), with major restorations, commemorated in an inscription over the gateway to the first pavilion, in the Daoguang period (1824–56). This last major restoration was funded by merchants from Fujian province and Macau and an Association of Piety and Benevolence, apparently founded during the Ming to upkeep the temple, support one priest to conduct services and maintain a school for the poor, which still exists, all within the context of the desire to 'worship the Buddha, spread good doctrine, practise charity and keep a school for the poor' as set out in the aims of the Association.

The major legend relating to the foundation of the temple recounts how a young woman begged a lift on a fleet of junks about to set off from Fujian province for Macau. The richer junks were all fully laden but the captain of the poorest junk allowed her on board. In a terrible storm, all but the poorest junk were sunk and the young woman steered the latter safely to port, whereupon she climbed up a hill and disappeared. When the junk passengers searched for her, all they found was the image of a goddess. A temple was built on the site and a junk carved in the rockface, which can still be seen.

The feast day of A-Ma is the 23rd day of the third lunar month (effectively late April, early May) and celebrations in the A-Ma Temple are followed by a noisy celebration the next day with firecrackers set off on junks moored outside the temple on the Macanese island of Coloane.

The temple is built against a rocky slope with steps carved out of the rock leading from one hall to the next. Topography dictated this

The a-Ma Temple, Macau

piled and stepped plan, different from the usual layout of local temples, but the halls themselves have the typical exaggerated southern upturn to the eaves. The lower three are dedicated to Tian Hou (Tin Hau in Cantonese), the heavenly

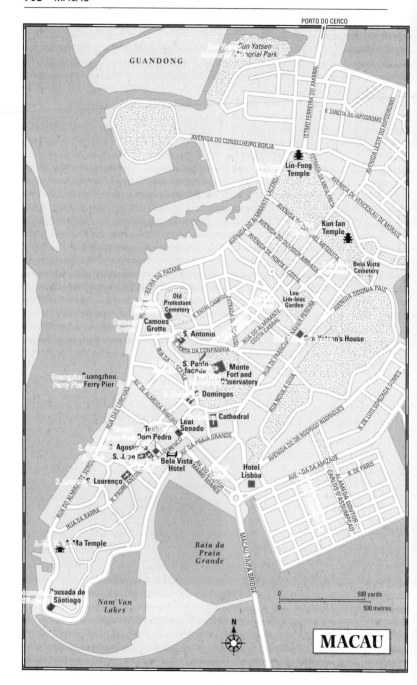

PORTO DO CERCO

GUANDONG

San Yatsen
National Memorial Park

ISTMO FERREIRA DO AMARAL

R. DIREITA DO HIPODROMO

AVENIDA LESTE DU HIPODROMO

AVENIDA DO CONSELHEIRO BORJA

ESTRADA DA AREIA PRETA

Lin-Fong
Temple

AVENIDA DE VENCESLAU DE MORAIS

AVENIDA DO CORONEL MESQUITA

AVENIDA DO ALMIRANTE LACERDA

Kun Iam
Temple

AVENIDA DO OUVIDOR ARRIAGA

AVENIDA DE HORTA E COSTA

Bela Vista
Cemetery

RUA TOMAS DA BEIRA DO PATANE

AVENIDA SIDONIA PAIS

Lou
Lim-Ieoc
Garden

R. ENTRE CAMPOS

ESTRADA D. TOMASO

Old
Protestant
Cemetery

Camoes
Grotto

Camoes
Grotto

RUA DO ALMIRANTE COSTA CABRAL

S. Antonio

RUA DE FRANCISCO XAVIER PEREIRA

Sun Yatsen's House

R. DA HORTA DA CONPANHIA

RUA DA TERCENA

S. Paulo
façade

Monte
Fort and
Observatory

RUA NOVA DA GUIA

RUA DA BEIRA DO PATANE

Guangzhou
Ferry Pier

Guangzhou
Ferry Pier

AV. DE ALMEIDA RIBEIRO

RUA DAS LORCHAS

S. Domingos

Cathedral

R. DE LUIS GONZAGA GOMES

AVENIDA DO DR RODRIGO RODRIGUES

Teatro
Dom Pedro

Leal
Senado

R. DE PARIS

S. Agostinho

AV. DA PRAIA GRANDE

AVENIDA DA AMIZADE

S. José

Bela Vista
Hotel

Hotel
Lisboa

ALMEIDA DOUTOR CARLOS D'ASSUMPCAO

RUA DO ALMIRANTE SERGIO

S. Lourenço

R. PADRE ANTON

RUA DA BARRA

AV. DO DUTOR MARIO SOARES

A-Ma Temple

Baia da
Praia
Grande

MACAU-TAIPA BRIDGE

0   500 yards

0   500 metres

Pousada de
Sãotiago

Nam Van
Lakes

N

MACAU

empress, and the highest to Guanyin (Kun Yam or Avalokitesvara), thus effectively separating deities who are fused in folklore; such is the complexity of popular religion. The gate is guarded by two stone lions whose teeth are in very poor condition, apparently because they used to escape at night and eat the tender rice sprouts in the paddy-fields of Lapa island until the peasants broke their teeth.

Inside the gate on the right is a courtyard between the two lower temples; the courtyard is surrounded by a wall with stone carvings. It contains banyan trees (a major feature of temples of the far south of China), two small 'ovens' (one of brick, one of iron) for burning paper offerings and painted carvings of junks on two large rocks. The small flag on the stem of the junk reads 'crossed the great river in safety', for these are pictures of the junk rescued by A-Ma. Beside the steps to the left of the junk-carved rocks is a niche dedicated to the earth spirit (Tu di) who guards the place. Two stone archways are carved with inscriptions reading: first arch at top: 'Temple of the Heavenly Goddess'; right side: 'Virtue changes the whole universe'; left: 'Benevolence nourishes the living'; behind: 'Her mercy is as boundless as Heaven'; second arch: 'Calm sea of the south'; behind: 'Pavilion for contemplating sadness' and 'Swallows and herons offer congratulations'.

Behind is the first hall, called **Tian hou miao** (Temple of the Heavenly Empress), with inscriptions on the lintel recording the foundation and repairs to the temple. On the altar, the figure of the goddess is dressed as a bride, in red, her attendants carved on the walls. Apart from the usual altar table with incense burners and candlesticks, there is a smaller table with cylindrical bamboo tubes filled with bamboo sticks by which fortunes can be told.

Worshippers light three incense sticks, 'kowtow' three times (kneel with head on the ground) and then shake the bamboo tube until a stick falls out. This is exchanged for a slip of yellow paper inscribed with characters revealing the fate which will be interpreted by the temple attendant. Another form of fortune-telling, a major feature of temples in Fujian (whose connection with Macau through sea junk trade is clear), is the *pan* (*pooi* in Cantonese), pairs of small pieces of wood or bamboo. These are thrown to the ground in pairs (the musical clatter can constantly be heard in Fujian temples) and the temple assistants interpret the future from the way they have fallen.

The **second temple**, devoted to the same goddess, has been painted by many foreign artists, including Chinnery (see p 715), John Webber (Captain Cook's draughtsman) and Auguste Borget (1808–77). Higher, with a fine view of the sea and the hills of Lappa, it also has an image of the goddess as a Chinese bride and is covered with inscriptions relating to her mastery of the sea: 'Can use her intelligence to control the rough sea with her bare hands', 'Under her protection when I go sailing in springtime, the sun rises and sets appropriately and the sea is calm', 'Under her protection my ship can sail safely on the enormous sea', etc. A side altar on the right is dedicated to Dizang wang (Ksitigarbha), ruler of the underworld, and on the left Weituo, the ubiquitous guardian of the Buddhist law and Buddhist temples, usually found in Chinese temples facing towards the main hall.

Weituo is a somewhat mysterious Chinese invention, although the characters in his name are also used for Vitasoka or Vigatasoka, younger brother of King Asoka, who did so much to promote Buddhism in the 2C BC.

In the left corner of the circular window, near a dried swordfish, is a junk model, claimed to be 400 years old and to replicate that which brought the goddess from Fujian. On the left wall of the hall is a drum, on the right wall, a drum and bell with the inscription 'favourable wind and seasonable rain', referring to agriculture. It is at this level that the entrance to the Buddhist Association's school for children is to be found, as well as a winding stepped path, 'the path of enlightenment', through a moon gate, inscribed 'touching the clouds', which leads to a tiny chapel called the Hall for Increasing Virtue, dedicated to the same goddess. Up a path is the fourth hall, the **Guanyin ge** (Tower of Guanyin), with a major image, crowned with pearls, flowers and a veil, seated on a throne behind two smaller images that are used in processions. A small altar on the left is dedicated to Wei tuo, protector of the faith; on the left wall is a painting of Guan gong (or Guan Yu), the God of War, dated to 1887.

Guan Yu is part of Chinese popular religion and his presence is yet another example of its eclecticism, which has here elevated a manifestation of Guanyin at the same time as celebrating Guanyin unmanifested.

Just beside the temple is the **Maritime Museum** with exhibits relating to local shipping traditions.

At the northern extremity of the peninsula is the **Porta do Cerco**, the battlemented border gate, built in 1870 on the site of previous barriers, the first of which was put up by the Chinese in 1573 to control the flow of goods into Macau (it was at first opened only twice a month) and to remind the settlers of the temporary and uncertain nature of their sojourn.

It was the scene in 1849 of the murder of the Governor, João Ferreira do Amaral. His instructions from Lisbon were to make Macau a free port and consolidate Portuguese control of the island. This he did by expelling the Chinese customs officials (the Hoppo) and destroying their residences and offices on the Rua de Nossa Senhora do Amparo. His schemes upset more than the Chinese authorities for he cleared graveyards near the Porta to build a road, thereby upsetting local inhabitants and he managed to upset the distant Lord Palmerston by imprisoning James Summers, an English chaplain who had come for the Macau regatta but refused to remove his hat during a Corpus Christi procession. A British mission was sent to rescue Summers and one man was killed before Foreign Secretary Palmerston intervened. It was the Guangdong authorities who were most upset and posters were stuck up in Guangzhou offering a price for Amaral's head. Seven assassins disguised as beggars attacked him near the Porta and took his head and left hand across the border for their reward. It seems that he had already lost his right hand.

Lin Fong Temple

Not far south of the Porta do Cerca, at the junction of the Avenida do Almirante Lacerda and the Estrada do Arco, is the Buddhist Lin Fong (Lotus) Temple, founded in 1592. It used to serve as a guesthouse for officials travelling between Macau and Guangzhou.

It is a typical Guangdong temple (similar to the Chen family temple in Guangzhou, for example), quite different from the northern temples with their long, deep north–south axis. These southern temples have broad east–west buildings, arranged in rows so that there are three parallel north–south axes (much shorter than those of the north) but the effect is of three long, broad east–west buildings with open courtyard gardens between. The same variation is also seen in Guangdong, where houses are ranged in terraces with a communal courtyard in a long strip running between the terraces.

The façade of the Lin Fong Temple is grand and lavishly decorated with glazed tiles. There are many halls in the three east–west rows, with A-Ma (known in Hong Kong as Tin Hau) presiding over the main hall.

At the back, on the right-hand side, is a temple garden with some squiggly bonsai and near the vegetarian temple kitchen is an altar for family use. These altars, decorated with paper flowers and photographs of the recently deceased, are set up for 49 days after death (regardless of date of burial) for the spirit of the dead needs feeding and placating in that period according to the popular version of Buddhism.

The temple's collection of bronze bells includes examples dating back to the early years of the 17C; they were donated by grateful inhabitants of the Pearl River delta to the boat-builders of Macau.

Kum Iam Temple

The Kum Iam (Guan yin) Temple is on the Avenida do Coronel Mesquita, southeast of the Lin Fong Temple. It is a smaller, plainer temple, built to the same east–west plan as the Lin Fong Temple, but its façade is decorated with more sober but quite fine grey cut-brick work, rather than lavish glazed tile decoration.

The temple was the scene of the signing of the first treaty between America and China on 3 July 1844 at a stone table in the temple. Caleb Cushing, the American Minister to China, was sent to try and negotiate the same terms ('extra-territorial rights' and the right to trade and send missionaries) for America as Great Britain had recently obtained through the Opium War.

Cushing was prevented from travelling to Peking but placated somewhat by the news that Qi Ying (sometimes romanised as Kiying), the Manchu official who had ratified the British Treaty of Nanking, had been appointed Governor of Guangdong and would come to negotiate a treaty with him in the south. Qi Ying (died 1858) was an imperial clansman, probably descended from the Qing founder Nurhaci and while in Macau he stayed in the Kum Iam Temple. On a circular stone table in the forecourt of the temple, the Treaty of Wanghia (Wangxia in pinyin, Mong Ha in Cantonese pronunciation) was signed. The treaty was named after the district of Macau in which the temple stands. Its name, Wangxia, means 'looking towards Xiamen', thus reflecting the Fujianese origins of many Macanese.

Extra-territoriality arose from the incompatibility of laws and the question of whether a traveller 'carried his own law with him', a problem that dates back to Roman times and the extension of Roman dominions. The first Europeans to arrive in the Far East were subject to *lex loci* ('local laws') but conflict soon arose over the executions of Europeans and Americans for causing the death of Chinese in the foreign settlements. The principle, that the law of the defendant's nationality should apply in trial and administration of justice, had been accepted in the earliest treaties made by the Russians with the Chinese (Nerchinsk, 1689, and Kiakhta, 1727) but was not extended to other powers until one by one they forced it upon the Chinese during the mid 19C.

In the main hall of the temple are fine figures and banners used in A-Ma processions in front of the carved and gilded altar to A-Ma (or Tian Hou or Tin Hao). The temple is two 'terraces' deep with a lotus pool at the back.

At the back left-hand side is the Hall of the Golden Flower Mother, who appears to give protection from smallpox and other diseases. There are some strange figures in the temple, including an official with two pairs of eyes, as well as some fine stone carving.

South of the Kum Iam Temple, on the corner of the Estrada Adolfo Loureiro (an engineer who first drew up the plans for the Inner Harbour in 1884) and the Avenida do Conselheiro Ferreira de Almeida, is the **Lou Lim-leoc Garden**. Described as the 'grandest example' of the late neo-classical phase in Macau, it is a Chinese garden with a pavilion supported on Corinthian columns and it belonged to a family of officials from Guangzhou, the Lous. Dating back to the 19C, it takes its name from Lou Lim-yeoc (or leoc), a merchant and diplomat of Macau who was awarded the Order of Christ by the Portuguese Government in 1925. The garden was restored and made public after his death.

Just a few hundred metres east of the garden is the house in which **Sun Yatsen** lived while working at the Kiang Vu Hospital on the Estrado do Repouso during one of his many periods of exile from China before 1911. There is a small exhibition devoted to his life in the house, which is an imposing yellow Victorian villa. There is some doubt as to whether this is the actual house or a more recent construction.

Camões Grotto and Gardens

The Camões Grotto and Gardens with the adjoining Protestant Cemetery are on the west side of the peninsula, off the Rua Palmeira, high above the harbour.

Luiz Vaz de Camões (1524–78), one of Portugal's great poets, was supposed to have spent some time in Macau in the year of its foundation (1557), when he wrote his most famous work, the epic poem *Os Lusiades* on Vasco da Gama's voyage, a poem that is seen as a commemoration of the golden age of discovery. The tradition that he visited Macau and even held an official post as Trustee for the Dead and Absent, is an old one, dating back to the early 17C, and is a little difficult but not impossible to square with what is known of his extraordinary life.

Exiled from Lisbon for his political lampoons, he lost an eye in the Portuguese campaigns in North Africa and, on his return to Lisbon, was banished to Goa for duelling over a lady. His political views got him exiled (with the suggestion that he had better go as far away as possible, perhaps to Japan or China) from Goa. He travelled widely, gaining inspiration for his exotic poem, but died in great poverty in Lisbon some six years after its publication.

The Camões Grotto, where he is supposed to have taken the evening air after a hard day acting for the dead and absent, now stands in the Camões Garden, formerly known as the Casa Garden, which houses the **Casa Villa** (now housing the Fundacio Oriente), a fine colonial house, containing a museum, which used to belong to the British East India Company and where Lord Macartney stayed in 1794 on his return from Peking.

The house has seen many changes since the middle of the 18C, when it was first built as a country villa by the Jesuits, just north of the walls of the 'Christian city'. The first Portuguese settlers lived at the foot of São Paolo do Monte, with the Monte Fort built by Jesuit priests high above them to defend them from land or sea attacks with its cannon. The Chinese city, Mong Ha (Looking towards Xiamen), lay to the north and the Casa Villa was off to the west. In the 1780s it was rented by an East India Company supercargo called William Fitzhugh and later by another British East India Company merchant, James Drummond. It was during his tenancy that Macartney came and his botanist, James Stromach, examined the plants in the garden.

In 1796 it became the property of the Leal Senado ('Loyal Senate'), Macau's governing body, and in 1815 Senator Manuel Pereira bought it. He rented it for some time to the Dents, owners of a major opium firm, before giving it to his daughter as part of her wedding present. Pereira's daughter married Lourenco Marques, who installed the classical canopy over the rocks of Camões and had a bust of the poet (a much-prettied portrait of the one-eyed satirist) installed in the 'grotto'.

The Casa Villa has been altered considerably throughout its history, although its basic plan remains the same, like that of other mansions in Macau, 'large, roomy, two-storeyed structures composed of piano nobile and basement'. A classical balustrade with urns was added in the early 20C but has almost disappeared. The neo-classical interior hints at what the building might have been like in the 18C and the cool, breezy interior is typical.

The **Luis de Camões Museum** inside contains some especially interesting

Ming bronzes and a collection of Chinese furniture (ornate beds, tallboys and chests) not very often seen outside the Victoria and Albert Museum in London.

Old Protestant Cemetery

Opening off the front garden to the Casa Villa is the old Protestant Cemetery, on two terraces below the villa, a calm and pleasant garden area with some very interesting gravestones. There is a new Protestant cemetery, on the Rampa dos Cavaleiros, just off the Avenida do Coronel Mesquita to the east of the Kun Ian Temple. It is called the Bela Vista Cemetery because it is south of the Estrada de Bela Vista but is not to be confused with the Bela Vista Hotel, which is near the southern tip of the Peninsula.

The earliest graves in the cemetery date to the 1770s but the cemetery was not formally opened until some time later. Some of the earliest stones in this cemetery were in fact moved here from Meesenberg Hill (named after William Meesenburg of the Dutch East India Company, first to be buried there) under the supervision of Sir Lindsay Ride (1898–1977), Professor of Physiology and Vice-Chancellor of the University of Hong Kong, who was passionately interested in the Protestant Mission to the Far East and also in the history of Macau. His ashes are now in the cemetery.

The formal opening date of the Protestant Cemetery remains a mystery and this is not helped by the inscription above the gate, which reads 'Protestant Church and Old Cemetery (East India Company 1814)', the date most likely referring to the year of the new charter of operation of the EIC. The most probable date is 1821, the year in which the wife of Robert Morrison died.

From the beginning, none but Catholics were permitted by the ecclesiastical authorities to be buried in Macau, for it was Catholic soil; non-Catholics had to be buried in the area between the walls of the 'Christian city' and the Porta do Cerco. A complication to non-Catholic funerals was the resistance of the Chinese to foreign burials, which sometimes required armed guards for burials of foreigners amongst Chinese graves; and from the fate of Amaral it is known that there were Chinese burial grounds in the area.

Robert Morrison (1782–1834), first Protestant missionary in China and translator of the Bible into Chinese, was appalled at the prospect of a hasty burial for his wife and her unborn child ('Mary died! and our little baby alas found a grave in her mother's womb') in front of hostile crowds and pushed the Committee of the English Factory into buying a piece of land 'to lay the remains of my beloved wife in a place appropriated to the sepulture of Protestant Christians, denied a place of interment by the Romanists'. He had already tried to reach the grave of his firstborn son on a nearby hilltop, so that he could bury his wife with him, but had been driven away by Chinese squatters there. He was eventually able to move the remains of 'James Morrison Born and Died March 5th 1811' to a place beside his mother in the cemetery.

Beside the cemetery entrance is a small chapel (often closed; I've never seen inside), built by the British East India Company in 1831 and reconstructed and reconsecrated in 1921. There is a memorial to Endicott, a missionary buried at Happy Valley in Hong Kong, two of whose children are 'sleeping here' (Fidelia and Rosalie in grave nos 33 and 34). The graves on the **upper terrace** include that of **George Chinnery**, the painter who was born in 1774 at Gough Square in London (where Dr Johnson lived) and who died in Macau in 1852, after working there for 27 years.

Chinnery was a competent jobbing painter, who had worked for 23 years in India before arriving in Macau in 1825 (owing £40,000 in Calcutta), declaring that he had come to escape from his wife, 'the ugliest woman I ever saw'. At one point a rumour arose that Mrs Chinnery was on her way to Macau from Calcutta and Chinnery decamped to the safety of Canton, where one of the Chinese government's regulations regarding foreign residents ran: 'Neither women, guns, spears nor arms of any kind can be brought in to the factories'. Chinnery made his living by painting the notables of the area (including Morrison) in great numbers, travelling to other parts of the Far East to paint, but he also left a number of lively sketches of Macau, showing the city and its people as they were in the early 19C. Although Macau's fortunes were beginning to wane as Hong Kong developed in the early 19C, Chinnery never moved from peaceful Macau, only ever visiting Hong Kong once.

Also on the upper terrace is the tomb of **Lieutenant Joseph H. Adams** of the US Navy (died 1853), a grandson of President John Adams and nephew of President John Quincy Adams, and that of the American who 'assisted in setting up the first magnetic telegraph in Japan in 1854', John P. Williams.

Most of the memorials on the upper terrace are simple headstones commemorating American, French, German and Danish missionaries and seamen who died in the area. In the era of sail, several seamen died from falls from the rigging, like John P. Griffin, 'seaman born in New York and died on board the US ship *Plymouth*, Macao Roads, by a fall from aloft, June 10, 1849' and the unfortunate apprentice boy, Thomas Pennington, 'through the effects of a fall into the hold' and the US frigate *Brandywine* lost its musician in October 1844, Charles F. Ganger, 'May he rest in piece' (sic).

On the **lower terrace**, no. 60 is the grave of **Anders Ljungstedt**, Knight of Wasa, Scholar and Philanthropist, his tomb erected by 'A Mournful Friend'.

Ljungstedt wrote the first history of Macau, published in 1834, on the basis of a series of articles he had written in the *Canton Miscellany* magazine, although Father Manuel Teixeira S.J., who is the oldest Portuguese in Macau (having arrived in 1924) and its most prolific historian, does not appear to approve Ljungstedt's early effort.

Also on the lower terrace are the three monuments to infant Colledges, the increasing despair of their parents evident in the increasingly grim epitaphs chosen for the babies' graves, and the memorial to Edmund Roberts, who died in Macau in 1836 on his way to Japan where he was to sign a treaty for the US Government. The stone records how 'He devised and executed to their end under instructions from his government treaties of amity and commerce between the United States and the courts of Muscat and of Siam'.

Winston Churchill's great-great-uncle, Henry Spencer Churchill, fourth son of the fifth Duke of Marlborough, was 'Captain of Her Britannic Majesty's Ship *Druid* and Senior Officer in the China Seas' when he died off Macau in 1840 and his successor, Sir Humphrey Lee Fleming Senhouse, died on board HMS *Blenheim* (curiously named after the seat of the Dukes of Marlborough) 'at Hong Kong on the 13th June 1841 aged 60 years from the effects of fever contracted during the zealous performance of his arduous duties at the capture of the heights of Canton in May 1841'.

Thus naval involvement in the first Opium War is commemorated in the graveyard, as are the vexations of free trade in the drug which seems to have dogged the career of James Innes (1787–1841)—*Haud procul ab esto, mari terraque, litibus multo vexatus* ('vexed by much discord by land and by sea')—who had declared himself an independent trader in opium in defiance of the East India Company's monopoly. Morrison's grave, together with those of his wife and sons, dominate the lower terrace but there are numerous other graves of interest.

The Church of **São Antonio** lies just below the Camões Gardens and if you walk round the church on the Largo da Companhia, you will soon find on your right the Calcada de São Paolo, which leads to the symbol of Macau, the wonderful baroque façade of **São Paolo**, all that survives of the old Jesuit college and church of Madre de Deus, standing above a flight of 70 steps.

The facade of São Paolo, Macau

Peter Mundy, who visited Macau in 1637, saw São Paolo just two years after the carved stone façade had been put up with the help of Japanese Jesuit converts. He remarked particularly on the rest of the church (which burned to the ground in 1835): '... of excellent workmanship, carved in wood, curiously gilt and painted with exquisite colours ...' and for Mundy's contemporary, Father Alexandre de Rhodes, it was more beautiful than any Italian Church except St Peter's. It is believed that the architect of this, the second Jesuit Church to be built in Macau, was an Italian Jesuit, Carlos Spinola, and that the work took place between 1602 and 1638.

The façade of local granite is European in design, its inspiration taken either from late 16C churches in Genoa and Milan or from Spanish retable-façades (according to your source) but it incorporates Chinese decoration amongst the European Christian imagery. The design is separated into three major horizontal planes, the major figure of the Virgin in a niche in the centre, surrounded by angels. Binoculars are required to make out the lines of Chinese characters running beside the columns. Other details include a figure of the Virgin stamping on a chimera, a Portuguese carrack (very similar to the carved Chinese junk in the A-Ma Temple, which makes one wonder if the latter were not a Portuguese carving or directly inspired by Portuguese boat carvings?), a ladder, crown of thorns and a supine skeleton, a memento mori beside the fat scaly chimera and a line of Chinese characters.

The wooden part of the building suffered a series of fires but the last, in 1835, left only the façade standing. It occurred the year after the dissolution of the religious orders in Macau when the buildings were used as a barracks by Portuguese soldiers and is said to have started in their kitchen.

Overlooking the façade of São Paolo, to the east, is the old **Monte Fortress and Observatory**. Bronze cannon, some dating back to the early 17C when Manuel Bocarro's foundry supplied the best weapons in Asia, still stand in position.

Monte Fort was half built when the Dutch launched a major attack in 1622 with three warships in the front line and a following fleet of 13 with over 1000 men. They would have had two more boats and an ally, had the British not pulled out of the engagement through a disagreement about the proposed invasion and looting of Macau. Jesuits manned the Monte Fort and one of their cannon shots blew up a barrel of the Dutch gunpowder, forcing a retreat during which the fleeing Dutch were attacked by the African slaves of the Portuguese, whose assistance led to their freedom from slavery.

In the following year Francisco Mascarenhas was appointed Captain-Major (effectively military governor) of Macau and his first task was to complete the construction of Monte Fort and other defences. One of his successors, Governor Diego de Pinho Teixiera, had a violent disagreement with the Leal Senado in 1710 and turned the cannon of Monte Fort on his opponents, who had decamped to the College of São Paolo below, but the Bishop's intervention prevented major bloodshed. The same thing happened during the revolution of 1622 when the guns, used by the Liberals this time, failed to prevent the arrival of a fleet come to overthrow them.

Returning to the façade of São Paolo, take the Rua São Paolo, which leads due south from the church, until it joins the Rua Palha. Continue south and a narrow street with a market on the left leads to **São Domingos Church and Monastery** (founded in 1588) with a fine yellow and white baroque façade (but which is often shut). Its silver and mother-of-pearl tabernacle with Solomonic columns, made in 1683, is one of the finest surviving examples of the rich church furnishings of the 17C when Portuguese colonies and overseas trade flourished.

The church of São Domingos, Macau

Largo do Senado

Returning to the Rua Palha, take the second turning on the left beyond the church and you are in the Largo do Senado with the building of the Leal Senado in front of you. The Largo do Senado, broad with central gardens, is lined with arcaded commercial buildings, mostly dating from the 19C and early 20C. Despite their recent construction, the style is characteristic of the colonised cities throughout southern China, where buildings with cool verandahs are built out over the streets so that their upper storeys, supported on columns, shade the street and the shops below and the whole, from a distance, is elegantly arcaded. The design harks back to Italian city planning of the Renaissance.

The **Leal Senado** itself is part of the design of the triangular 'square' of the Largo do Senado, which was originally laid out in the 1580s. The building as it stands today was dedicated in 1784, although the facade was not completed until 1876 (and much restoration was undertaken in 1939). Today the building has been half-converted to house art exhibitions.

Behind the elegant classical façade is a charming garden with blue and white tile plaques set into the walls. There is some fine carved woodwork in the library and council chamber and before the entrance is a stone tablet inscribed 'City of the Name of God, There is None More Loyal', dating from 1654, placed there by the Governor, Joao de Souza Periera, at the order of the King of Spain, to commemorate Macau's loyalty to Portugal during the Spanish Hapsburg rule of the home country. The title of 'Leal' ('Loyal') was also granted in recognition of the same fealty, much later, in 1809.

The new **cathedral** is just northeast of the Senate, reached by taking the turning on the east of the square (on the right if the Senate is behind you). This leads round to the Largo da Se and the cathedral, which no longer bears any resemblance to the 17C Santa Casa da Misericordia. If you return to the Largo do Senado, on the right is a highly decorated building with an internal courtyard, the Chinese 'Holy House of Mercy', a privately endowed clinic and pharmacy with much green painted wrought-iron.

From the Largo do Senado, turn east along the major road that runs in front of the Senate (Avenida Almeida Ribeiro) and take the first major turning on the left, Rua Central. This takes you along past the bottom of a raised square in which the pretty **Dom Pedro V Theatre** stands. Built in 1858, during the reign of King Pedro V of Portugal, the designer was the Macanese Pedro Marques. The present façade was built some 20 years later and the tiny theatre is now restored to its former elegance, after being occupied until 1985 by the 'Crazy Paris' strip show, which is now in the Hotel Lisboa.

Behind the theatre is the **Sir Robert Ho-tung Cultural Centre**, once the summer residence of the Hong Kong philanthropist, after whom it was named, for he donated it to the Portuguese government. With its light, airy rooms and pleasant garden it is a fine example of late 19C–early 20C regional domestic architecture. The arcaded lower floor is open so that you can see through to the green of the garden behind.

To the right behind the theatre is the church of **Santo Agostinho**, founded in 1586, another yellow and white Baroque façade whose interior with rosettes on the blue wooden ceiling and suffering Christ is faintly reminiscent of Mexico.

The monks of Santo Agostinho were partisans of the Papal envoy Tournon in the first decade of the 18C (when he ignored the advice of the Jesuits and instructed missionaries to reject the Chinese rites under pain of excommunication) and Tournon was held under 'church arrest' in the church at the order of the Viceroy of Goa after his expulsion from China. The Viceroy also ordered that the monks of Santo Agostinho be deported to Goa for a decade, for he believed that the Pope was flouting the agreement that the Portuguese and not the Vatican were responsible for the China mission.

To the left, on the slope of the hill, is **São José Church and Seminary**, founded by the Jesuits in the early 18C.

> Built on land donated by the Senate to the Jesuits, its foundations were laid in 1730 and the church was finished in 1758; its domes are unique in Macau. It now looks rather modern and concrete with a Chinese tiled roof. The seminary was built expressly to train missionaries for China, so its classrooms are rather empty now, although it is the home of Father Manuel Teixeira, the great historian of Macau. The church is only used once a year on New Year's Eve.
>
> It used to house St Francis Xavier's humerus (now in the Chapel of St Francis on Coloane island), together with relics of the 'Japanese Martyrs' killed in the anti-Christian persecution of the Shogun Hideyoshi in the last years of the 16C, instigated mainly because Hideyoshi feared that religious faith might be put to political use. It still, however, houses many of the fine polychrome wooden figures, probably locally made in the 17C, which were rescued from the destructive fire of São Paolo.

Beyond the theatre, where the Rua Central changes its name to the Rua de S. Lourenco, and past the Imprenca Nacional or Government Printing Press on the corner of the Rua Prata and Rua de S. Lourenco, is the church of **São Lourenco** (St Lawrence), whose construction, funded by the Jesuits, began between 1550 and 1570. The painter Chinnery lived behind São Lourenco, on the Rua of the same name, for most of his stay in Macau. São Lourenco's last major reconstruction was in 1897–98 to designs by the architect Augusto Cesar d'Abreu Nunes in the late neo-classical Macanese style, although the pair of towers to the east and the single nave were earlier features that can be distinguished in some Chinnery drawings.

I have not seen the interior except through the doorway, which offered a view of grand Corinthian columns and chandeliers in contrast with the Doric exterior.

If time allows, you could continue west towards the **Penha Church** and **Bishop's Residence** (not open to the public) on the Colina da Penha ahead of you and the Hotel Bela Vista, otherwise you could turn down towards the bay along the Travessa Padre Narciso (left, just behind the church) and then back eastwards along the Praia Grande towards the Lisboa Hotel and the Macau–Taipa Bridge.

For the **Hotel Bela Vista** (now the official residence of the Chinese governor; not open to the public), continue west along the Rua São Lourenco, which changes its name to the Rua Padre Antonio. The second major turning on the left is the Rua Penha, which then joins the Rua Boa Vista. As the Rua Boa Vista approaches the bay, the Hotel Bela Vista is on your left.

> It was founded in the late 19C by an English couple, a sea captain William Edward Clarke and his wife, who named it the Boa Vista ('Good View'). When Clarke wished to sell it in the early years of the 20C, interest was expressed in making it a sanatorium and hospital for French soldiers (mostly recuperating victims of marsh fever caught in the French Indo-Chinese colonies). This plan was vetoed by the British, who were extremely concerned about the growth of French influence in the Far East and the threat this posed to British interests, and they managed to persuade the Portuguese administration to expropriate the whole area, including the hotel. The matter had, apparently, reached the

British Houses of Parliament where, according to Father Teixeira's entertaining history of the Bela Vista, the matter served to 'substantiate the fear that it was part of a deep-laid plot of the French to exchange Macao for some part of the Congo'.

The history of the hotel in the subsequent decades was complex, although it remained a hotel until 1917, when it became a secondary school, the Liceu Central. In 1923 the Government took it over, only to sell it to a Chinese lady in 1932 but her debts to the Caixa Economica Postal de Macau were such that it became the property of the Caixa. It was rented as a language school for the study of Cantonese by recruits to the Hong Kong Civil Service and after the Japanese invasion of China it was filled with refugees from north China and Shanghai. When the Japanese occupied Hong Kong, Portuguese residents forced to flee the British colony occupied it. From 1946 to 1950 it was rented to the Hong Kong government as a NAAFI (canteen) for British servicemen stationed in Hong Kong.

In 1948 the Caixa sold the hotel to three ladies, 'Mesdames Kwok Chi Chan, Chan Sok Fong (represented by Ho Yin) and Ng Tong Ying (now the widow of Chong Chi Kong)', as Father Teixeira puts it. Under their ownership, the Bela Vista—which acquired its new name of Bela or 'Beautiful' Vista around the same time—once again opened as a hotel, only to close in the 1990s. It is a fine colonial building with the characteristic arcaded verandahs offering breezy and shaded views over the Baia da Praia Grande, or 'a surprising look over the harbour' as the historian has it. It is now the new Chinese governor's official residence.

Traffic on the **Praia Grande**, the 'Bund' of Macau, is unfortunately rather noisy but at siesta time it is a pleasant, tree-shaded street which leads back towards the Lisboa Hotel, the Macau–Taipa Bridge and, beyond, the hydrofoil piers for the return trip to Hong Kong. The Praia Grande is lined with grand villas on its western end, including the pink **Portuguese Governor's Residence**, formerly marked by the Portuguese flag flying over it and a tennis court in front. Nearer the point where it leaves the bay and runs into the town, the buildings are similarly grand, tall arcaded structures with classical columns and urns decorating the façades, but these apparently conceal a Chinese heart behind the classical western exterior. Hidden inner courtyards are surrounded by symmetrical dwellings arranged according to traditional principles.

At the angle of the Praia Grande and the Avenida Amizade (which leads to the Lisboa Hotel and Taipa Bridge) was the stone **Jorge Alvares Monument**, commemorating the first European to reach China in 1513; the place he landed is usually thought to be Tuen Mun in Hong Kong. Just in front of the Taipa Bridge was the Ferreira do Amaral Monument, an equestrian statue in bronze in which the one-handed Governor appeared to be flogging his horse without mercy.

This is the Amaral who was murdered at the Porta do Cerco in 1849; the statue was erected in 1940. I am told that it was considered 'too colonial', dismantled and returned to Lusitania. A better reason would have been that he was not a worthy person to be commemorated in public.

Taipa and Cloane

These islands can now be reached by taxi or bus.

Taipa, where the new Macau airport has been built, is linked to the peninsula by an impressive arching bridge to the west, which you can walk over, allthough it is very long. There is another bridge for motor vehicles only near the jetfoil terminal to the east of the island. It boasts a very popular restaurant, which serves Macanese food (wonderful salt cod, or bacalhau, and spiced African chicken) in an open courtyard roofed by trees: *Pinocchio*, No. 4 Rua do Sol. There is a **museum** on Taipa's own Praia, in one of the fine 19C houses that line the street. This is filled with furniture and fittings of the period, revealing both the strength of the Catholic tradition and the adoption of some Chinese furnishings (Casa Museu). The museum is closed on Mondays and at midday (13.00–15.00); entry is free.

Coloane is accessible via the Taipa–Coloane causeway. In Coloane village is the Chapel of St Francis Xavier where the precious relic of the saint (his humerus) and those of the Japanese martyrs once housed in the São José Seminary are now preserved.

Chrysanthemum

Glossary

Amitabha Buddha, 'luminous and of infinite life', who rules over the Western Paradise, an important concept in late popular Buddhism as it offers the consolation of an 'afterlife' in heaven.

Apsara, Buddhist 'goddess'; they appear in Buddhist paintings as flying women.

Bodhisattva, technically a future Buddha, in popular Chinese belief a being who has attained enlightenment and could enter nirvana, a state of non-being, but has chosen to stay in the world of men in order to alleviate suffering.

Buddha, the founder of Buddhism, Sakyamuni, was an Indian prince whose sheltered upbringing meant that the sufferings of ordinary people came as a painful revelation. His meditations on suffering and eventual attainment of 'enlightenment' (overcoming human failings, most notably desire) and nirvana formed the basis of later belief and practice. Buddhism entered China during the early Han dynasty (206 BC–AD 220) and was of the Mahayana school which stressed the attainment of Bodhisattva-hood (qv), although it was eventually much changed to encompass Chinese ideals of family worship and duties. Sakyamuni, the 'historic Buddha', is widely represented in Chinese temples, usually seated with crossed legs in the position of meditation and wearing a simple cloth thrown over one shoulder. His various manifestations are also represented: the most popular form in China is Maitreya, the Buddha of the Future, is usually represented seated with his feet flat on the ground and also appears as the fat, jolly, welcoming Buddha beyond the four guardian figures at the entrance to Buddhist temples.

Caisson, or coffer: ceiling composed of inset decorated wooden panels.

Catties (jin) and **Taels** (liang), are traditional Chinese measures. There are 16 taels in a catty but as the *Encyclopaedia Sinica* notes, in 1889 'the catty ranges between 4 ounces avoirdupois for tea in Peking and 40.4 ounces avoirdupois for coal in Honan. The other weights and measures show similar variations. It does not seem to be of much use therefore to give a Table of Weights and Measures.'

Chan Buddhism, the Chinese term for zen (Japanese), a form of Buddhism developed in China. The stress on 'sudden enlightenment' through meditation, rather than a lifetime of monastic textual study, meant that lay persons, who remained in the home and carried out their filial duty to parents and ancestors could achieve enlightenment.

Chi, 'hornless dragon' design found in architectural decoration.

Chi wen, 'gaping dragon' an auspicious design found on the end of roof ridges in temple and palace buildings. Dragons, associated with water, were believed to protect timber frame buildings from fire.

Cloisonné, enamelling technique used mainly from the Ming. Copper vessels were covered with little copper wire shapes (or cloisons) to separate enamel colours.

Comprador, a term deriving from Portuguese (*comprar*, to buy) used by Treaty Port and earlier western traders to designate the Chinese agents used by foreign merchants to do their buying and selling.

Corvée workforce, from the Qin, a form of government service, like a tax, required annually from all able-bodied men. Roads, irrigation schemes and projects like the Great Wall were constructed by the corvee workforce.

Dagoba, see Pagoda.

Daoism, see Taoism (the former pinyin, the latter Wade-Giles romanisation).

Dharani, Buddhist spell, formula or incantation.

Dougeng, characteristic bracketing structure used to support the weight of projecting eaves.

Fascicle, 'booklet'. Chinese books were published as a series of small, thread-bound booklets encased in a cloth-covered protective wrapping (*tao*). Sometimes the fascicle coincided with a chapter or section of a work but not necessarily.

Feng shui or **Geomancy**: a view of natural forces developed in early times, first recorded in Han dynasty texts with eccentric names like the 'Mysteries of the Blue Bag' (i.e. the universe). The Chinese term is composed of the words for wind and water. Geomantic texts held that natural forces in all areas could be harnessed for good or evil and that building, whether of tombs or dwellings, should attempt to harmonise with natural forces. Thus pagodas were often constructed on hilltops after natural disasters, such as floods, in order to placate and divert the local forces and the sites for tombs were selected by geomantic specialists (often Taoist priests) using a special compass marked with 'good' and 'bad' directions. Tomb-building was a complex matter, particularly in the south where geomantic beliefs were strongest. There, secondary burial was practised. Bodies were first buried in temporary tombs, then exhumed by relatives after a couple of years, the bones scraped and broken, and rehoused in ceramic funerary urns (tall, lidded jars). The final burial place, often a family tomb housing many urns, was the one that required careful siting in order to preserve the prosperity of the family.

The geomantic rules concerning building and planning were based on practicalities. Southwards orientation and siting near water, as well as axial balance, all antedate geomantic texts and are clearly practical. Later refinements included the erection of a spirit gate inside or outside the main entrance to prevent the entrance of evil spirits, who could only fly in straight lines, and a height limit on the spires of missionary churches to prevent interference with good spirits, which fly at approximately 30m above ground.

Gablet, half gable, seen on major hall roofs such as the Hall of Preserving Harmony (Bao he dian) in the Forbidden City, Peking.

Guan, hall or otherwise used as a suffix denoting an institution, as in *tushuguan* ('charts and books institution' or 'library'), *meishuguan* ('arts institution' or 'gallery'), *jinianguan* ('memorial hall' or 'museum') and *bowuguan* ('myriad things institution' or 'museum').

Guanyin, the Bodhisattva (qv) who hears the cries of the world, the Chinese translation of Avalokitesvara, a Bodhisattva who became associated with mercy and the succour of those in distress, a bringer of sons. Through these attributes the Bodhisattva came to assume in China a semi-female form and is one of the popular images in temples; patron of Putuo shan.

Guomindang, Wade-Giles **Kuomintang** (KMT): National People's Party, founded by Sun Yatsen in 1900, although it did not acquire the name until 1911. On Sun's death in 1926, Chiang Kai-shek assumed leadership of what is often referred to as the Nationalist or Republican Party.

Hutong, a Peking word for small lanes (the literal meaning is 'together with barbarians').

Jie, avenue; see Lu.

Ksitigarbha (Dizang wang), the Bodhisattva who judges souls after death and determines their fate, depicted wearing a sort of crown of lotus petal shaped lappets; patron of Jiuhua shan.

Lu, street, sometimes divided into *bei* (north), *zhong* (middle), *nan* (south), *xi* (west), *dong* (east); sometimes into numbered sections: *yi* (one), *er* (two), *san* (three); sometimes preceded by terms such as *huan* (circular), as in Bei huan lu or 'North Circular Road'; see also Jie.

Lohan, or **Arhat** (Buddhist). An elightened being who achieved the state of nirvana, escaping the cycle of re-births. In Chinese Buddhist iconography, often a group of 12, 16 or 500 or more meditating figures, sometimes with specific attributes or exaggerated features.

Mandorla, halo around Buddhist deities.

Manjusri (Wenshu), the Bodhisattva of wisdom, usually depicted with a lion; patron of Wutai shan.

Miao, see Temple.

Pagoda, probably derived from an Indian name for a temple complex, used for the tall tower-like buildings, usually associated with Buddhist temples but also constructed free-standing on hills outside towns. The Chinese word is *ta*, possibly derived from a Sanskrit term.

The original Indian form was known as a stupa in Sanskrit, a domed reliquary building. An elongated version of the squat original form is preserved in the Lamaist stupas (*dagoba*) found in Peking temples and on Wutai shan. Chinese pagodas were first found in Buddhist temples of the Han dynasty, either on the central axis as storehouses of precious relics (such as the ashes of abbots or religious texts) or paired on either side of the main axis, more reminiscent of the tapering towers (*gopura*) that encircled later Indian temples, such as the 17C Madurai Temple. The use of elegant single pagodas, tapering structures, usually of wood but sometimes of brick, on hills outside towns was related not to Buddhism but to the pseudo-science of feng shui (qv) which held that the natural good fortune of an area could be adjusted by such construction. Thus they were often built after, for example, disastrous floods.

Pailou, 'triumphal arch', free-standing wooden, sometimes stone, gateway, set on the approach to temples, palace gardens and tombs. These were also traditionally erected in honour of 'virtuous widows', women who had committed suicide rather than survive their husbands.

Pinyin, see Language and Script, p 88.

Qilin, auspicious mythological beast with scales, hoofs and a single horn.

Samantabhhadra (Puxian), the Bodhisattva of pervading goodness, usually depicted riding a white elephant; patron of Emei shan.

Scapulimancy, divination by means of the cracks appearing in a burning shoulder blade.

Shan, mountain or hill.

Sheng, province.

Shi, city.

Si, see **Temple**.

Stele, upright stone carved with inscription.

Stupa (Buddhist), originally a funeral or memorial mound, containing bones, ashes or relics.

Sutra, Buddhist text containing the discourses of the Buddha.

Ta, see **Pagoda**.

Taels, see **Catties**.

Tangkas, Buddhist paintings of Lamist deities.

Taoism, a Chinese system of belief based on the ideal of man's attunement with nature. The antithesis of Confucianism, which stressed organisation and the supremacy of human order, Taoism stressed non–action, the contemplation of nature and acceptance of the flow of natural events. The major texts of Taoism are the writings of Zhuang zi (late 4C BC), charming fables, and the more esoteric Lao zi (3C BC), the Dao de jing (Classic of the Dao, 'the Way' and Power). Recent archaeological discoveries suggest that the order of the books should be reversed and it should be known as the De dao jing.

Temple, Buddhist temples are called si, Lamaist temples gong, Taoist temples guan and those dedicated to Confucius or other official cults, miao. The layout of all is similar. Outside the gate is a spirit wall and there may be a pailou. In the first hall, the gate hall, are guardian figures (in Buddhist temples they are the four celestial guardians of the four directions) then (in a Buddhist temple), facing the visitor, comes the fat, smiling figure of one of the manifestations of Maitreya, the Buddha of the Future, behind whom is the serious, military figure of Weituo, a guardian of the faith. In the first courtyard of a temple of any denomination are usually drum (left) and bell (right) towers, echoing their presence within city walls. Halls and courtyards succeed one another, dedicated to different deities, and the living quarters are almost invariably to the rear.

Thuja, *Thuja orientalis*, a native conifer.

Tungus/Tungusic, the forested Manchu homeland, east of the Mongolian plain, home of the Jurched or Qitan and the Manchus. Tungusic languages are of the Altaic group.

Xian, county, a lower administrative level than province.

Yingqing, 'shadowy blue' or qingbai 'blueish-white', a white glazed porcelain of the Song and later, from southern Chinese kilns. The glassy glaze has a blue-ish tinge where it collects in drops.

Sweet chestnut

Index